CRIMINAL EVIDENCE

12th Edition

Jefferson L. Ingram

University of Dayton

John C. Klotter Justice Administration Legal Series

Routledge
Taylor & Francis Group
LONDON AND NEW YORK

First published 2015 by Anderson Publishing

Published 2015 by Routledge
2 Park Square, Milton Park, Abingdon, Oxon OX14 4RN

and by Routledge
711 Third Avenue, New York, NY 10017, USA

Routledge is an imprint of the Taylor & Francis Group, an informa business

Acquiring Editor: Shirley Decker-Lucke
Editorial Project Manager: Ellen S. Boyne
Project Manager: Mohana Natarajan
Designer: Russell Purdy

Library of Congress Cataloging-in-Publication Data
Application Submitted

British Library Cataloguing-in-Publication Data
A catalogue record for this book is available from the British Library

ISBN 978-0-323-29458-4 (pbk)

Printed and bound in the United States of America by Sheridan Books, Inc. (a Sheridan Group Company).

CRIMINAL EVIDENCE

12th Edition

Acknowledgments

The author would like to thank Ellen Boyne, editor, for all of her diligent and careful work and assistance in producing the Twelfth Edition of *Criminal Evidence.* Special thanks are also extended to Dean Paul E. McGreal of the University of Dayton School of Law for his invaluable assistance in facilitating my research. Special thanks go to Jason Pierce, Chairman of the University of Dayton Department of Political Science, for his support and understanding in a variety of areas that fostered the research and completion of this edition.

Preface

In revising *Criminal Evidence*, Twelfth Edition, the author continues to honor John Klotter's extensive work on criminal evidence by following the excellent approach he initiated by updating evidentiary themes, trends, and cases, while remaining generally true to the original organization and presentation. As with prior editions, this book remains primarily a textbook with illustrated cases for those involved in the study of criminal evidence and in the administration of justice. The cases in Part II are designed to demonstrate many of the more salient principles of evidence that appear in the text portion. With the exception of the Chapter 1, the organization of the book closely follows the Federal Rules of Evidence, although a student or professor could easily choose to follow a different order when learning or teaching the laws of evidence. Many stylistic changes in the Federal Rules of Evidence became effective on 1 December 2011, and the text has been updated to reflect these and subsequent changes. Chapter 1 offers the reader an overview of the significant legal systems that predate our present American system and demonstrates that all effective legal systems must have a mechanism that logically decides which evidence should be considered as important and which evidence should be excluded based on logic or for policy reasons. Prior legal systems, such as the Chinese and Egyptian systems, attempted to discern truth and justice from a perspective that was different from our modern point of view. All legal systems evolve as time passes, as our system continues to evolve as well, with newer interpretations replacing older rules as time and events present novel challenges.

This book is adaptable to most levels of the educational spectrum, and it may be used as an entry-level evidence text or as the lead evidence text to deliver a moderately advanced evidence course. Ancillary materials should appropriately serve the needs of both instructors and students. *Criminal Evidence* should prove valuable for students learning the basic foundations to prepare for careers in criminal justice or law, or for an attorney needing a source to consult when clarifying a point of law.

This book has been prepared as a textbook for individuals teaching or learning about the evidentiary framework in the administration of criminal justice. The materials presented cover general evidence law and illustrate, by example and case reference, the law of evidence as it is practiced in criminal courts. When civil use of evidence impacts criminal justice or where a civil evidence example is especially relevant, the book references civil cases as appropriate. Where appropriate to the text, selected sections of the current version of Federal Rules of Evidence are isolated within callout boxes for easy identification. Similar callout boxes identify many references to important concepts and are also incorporated within the glossary located with the back matter of this book. State rules of evidence exhibit significant uniformity because many states have adopted versions of the Federal Rules of Evidence or the Uniform Rules of Evidence. While many differences exist in the way a rule of evidence is administered and interpreted in the various American jurisdictions, significant similarities exist, with states often looking to interpretations of the Federal Rules of Evidence for guidance. Where differences exist, effort has been made to identify the areas where legal interpretations have diverged and the law remains unsettled or state courts follow it differently than the federal courts do. Although the states that have adopted a version of the federal evidence rules tend follow, and look to, the federal courts for interpretations of those rules, this practice has not been uniform, and different judges have taken slightly different routes in various state and local jurisdictions.

For the reader or instructor, this book retains its familiar organization, with related ancillary materials, including the glossary, an up to date version of the Federal Rules of Evidence, and the table of contents of the Uniform Rules of Evidence. In Part II, where cases demonstrate some of the evidentiary principles, the author has added some newer legal cases that illustrate current legal principles and explain the evolving principles of evidence in a contemporary case context. Several landmark cases are presented in Part II, and this version of the book retains some older cases in which the judicial writers offered particularly excellent explanations of legal principles. Also in Part II, the glossary permits the reader to find the typical legal definitions, and for many entries, it goes further and explains some of the concepts in greater detail. Although the text portion of this book does not deal with every section of the Federal Rules of Evidence, Appendix I permits the reader to consult the sections that have not received complete mention in the text portion of this work.

Constitutional reinterpretations by the Supreme Court of the United States often change the admissibility of evidence. Several terms ago, the Supreme Court of the United States reinterpreted the Sixth Amendment right of confrontation in a way that affected the admissibility of hearsay evidence by requiring more in court testimony, but the Court has backtracked somewhat from what was thought to be required from an initial reading of some of the cases. Four years ago, the Supreme Court revised the admissibility of evidence seized from automobiles under the search incident to arrest theory. In 2010, the Supreme Court relaxed the rigidity of reading *Miranda* warnings and permitted less than clear warnings to suffice, a fact that may mean the admissibility of more evidence that police obtain from arrestees. Congressional legislation under the Patriot Act has the potential to affect the admissibility of some evidence, and the direction Congress will take in reforming this legislation remains unclear, although significant agitation has occurred within some quarters of the legislature related to the Patriot Act and the need to restrict some data collection that is being conducted by various federal agencies. Much of the intelligence that is collected has not been offered for admission in criminal courts, so those Fourth Amendment issues and their effects on the admission of evidence remains to be determined. How these evidentiary issues will be resolved remains an open question, given the fact that politics are involved. Recognizing that the law of evidence evolves, the author makes every effort to recognize changes in evidence law and to incorporate the new material into the text discussion of the principles.

The study of criminal evidence involves some understanding of collateral legal subjects, such as constitutional law, criminal procedure, and criminal law. In this book, evidentiary principles are illustrated by references to actual criminal legal cases, and the legal cases in Part II should assist in understanding specific evidentiary principles that are fairly universal to all American courts. By using examples from actual criminal prosecutions, this book presents the traditional rules of evidence that most often create problems and issues in criminal cases that lawyers, police, and criminal justice professionals will encounter and will have to resolve.

To assist professors, an Instructor's Guide, which includes a test bank and a complete 16-chapter PowerPoint presentation illuminating the text section of this book, is available from the publisher to authorized adopting professors.

Jefferson Ingram,
University of Dayton, April 2014.

Table of Contents

Chapter 11
Opinions and Expert Testimony 415

Chapter 12
Hearsay Rule and Exceptions 479

Chapter 13
Documentary Evidence 535

Part I
History and Approach to Study

History and Development of Rules of Evidence

1

The fundamental basis upon which all rules of evidence must rest—if they are to rest upon reason—is their adaptation to the successful development of the truth.

Funk v. United States, 290 U.S. 371 (1933)

Chapter Contents

KEY TERMS AND CONCEPTS

- Due Process
- Evidence
- Federal Rules of Evidence
- Objection
- Privileged Communications
- Relevant Evidence
- Uniform Rules of Evidence

§ 1.1 Introduction

To the lay observer of any criminal trial, the activities of the attorneys and the judge often confound obvious logic, creating confusion about the procedures surrounding the admission and exclusion of **evidence.** The form of the **objections** offered, the arguments presented by the attorneys, and the judge's reactions only add to the confusion. Logically assuming that the purpose of a trial is to seek the truth, the lay observer is likely to be challenged by objections to the introduction of apparently **relevant evidence.** Observers may conclude that evidence that could have a direct bearing on the case is, in fact, excluded from use at the trial. To understand why certain evidence is admitted and other evidence is excluded, it is helpful to study the history and evolution of the rules of evidence in several cultures and nations across history.

Evidence Proof, either written or unwritten, of allegations at issue between parties.

Objection A resistance or protest on legal grounds to the admissibility of evidence or to the entry of an order or judgment.

Relevant evidence Evidence having any tendency to make the existence of any fact that is of consequence to the determination of the action more probable or less probable than it would be without the evidence. Fed. R. Evid. 401.

§ 1.2 Early Attempts to Determine Guilt or Innocence

Through the ages, humankind has sought fair methods of reaching the truth in criminal cases. Each culture arrived at a method that was consistent with that culture. Some of these systems of determining guilt or innocence were ridiculous and often barbaric. However, history has helped succeeding generations to develop systems that are more workable.

Every tribe and every people devised a system for protecting the lives and property of its citizens. Authorities noted, however, that there were only a few cultures that developed a well-defined, organized, continuous body of legal ideas and methods that could be called a legal system. According to Wigmore, 16 legal systems developed to a stage at which they could be recognized as a legal system: Egyptian, Mesopotamian, Chinese, Hindu, Hebrew, Greek, Maritime, Roman, Celtic, Germanic, Church, Japanese, Mohammedan, Slavic, Romanesque, and Anglican.[1] Although all of these systems had some effect on modern evidence rules, only a few of the older systems have been selected for discussion because they represent systems that were adopted in part by other cultures and eventually led to our judge–jury system, which in turn was responsible for our rules of evidence. Some of the procedures that developed under these systems are gone, while some remain.

A. Egyptian Legal System

In the Egyptian system (the oldest of the systems just listed), the court was made up of 30 judges chosen from the states that constituted Egypt. The defendant was advised in writing of the charges against him or her, and he or she was authorized to answer each charge in writing by: (1) asserting that he or she did not do it; (2) stating that if he or she did it, it was not wrongful; or (3) if it was wrongful, it should bear a lesser penalty than that advocated by his or her accusers. It is interesting to note that at this time (beginning at approximately 4000 B.C.E.) all formal proceedings of the court were conducted without speeches from advocates. It was believed that speeches of advocates would cloud the legal issues, and those speeches, combined with the cleverness of the speakers, the spell of their delivery, and the tears of the accused, would influence many persons to ignore the strict rules of law and the standards of truth.[2]

The Greek historian Diodorus describes the procedure developed by the Egyptians as follows:

> After the parties had thus twice presented their case in writing, then it was the task of the thirty judges to discuss among themselves their judgment and of the chief justice to hand the image of truth to one or the other of the parties.[3]

B. Mesopotamian Legal System

Under the early Mesopotamian system, the king was the fountain of justice, receiving the law from divine guidance. But under King Hammurabi, approximately 1795 to 1750 B.C.E.,[4] the system envisioned the king as the source of law, granting the king

---

1 For a complete, interesting, and informative study of the world's legal systems, see WIGMORE, A PANORAMA OF THE WORLD'S LEGAL SYSTEMS (1928).

2 WIGMORE, A PANORAMA OF THE WORLD'S LEGAL SYSTEMS (1928).

3 KOCOUREK & WIGMORE, SOURCES OF ANCIENT AND PRIMITIVE LAW, EVOLUTION OF LAW SERIES (1915).

4 Charles F. Horne, *The Code of Hammurabi: Introduction*, Ancient History Sourcebook: Code of Hammurabi, c. 1780 BCE, Fordham University, Feb. 11, 2014, http://www.fordham.edu/halsall/ancient/hamcode.asp.

the ability to personally administer justice or to allow local governors or courts of law to handle the matters.[5] The Mesopotamian system did not operate with police or a prosecutor, but the judges, who were originally royal priests, found the facts from the evidence and applied the law.[6] A record of the trials of this period indicates that the judges called upon the accusers to "produce witnesses or instruments to show guilt." The judges then examined the facts and reached a conclusion as to guilt or innocence. Once matters had been proven, Hammurabi's Code had harsh aspects, because it noted, "[i]f a man destroy the eye of another man, they shall destroy his eye."[7] This body of law was perhaps the origin of the modern use of testimony and real evidence.[8]

C. Hebrew Legal System

In the early period of the Hebrew legal system, rabbis developed the law. The law was tied closely to religion, and the judges were considered to act with divine authority. The Pentateuch, which consists of the five books collectively known as the Torah, served as the central foundation of the Hebrew legal system from approximately 1200 B.C.E. to 300 B.C.E.[9] When the Jewish people came under the control of the Persian, Greek, and Roman rulers, they continued to have their own court system. Individual jurists made the decisions because there appears to be no record of the use of a jury or of counsel to represent the defendant.[10]

D. Chinese Legal System

One of the earliest recorded legal systems in the world is the Chinese legal system, beginning before 2500 B.C.E. It is unique in that it is the only system that survived for approximately 4,500 years, until the country was taken over by the communists during the twentieth century. Under the ancient Chinese system, there was little difference between civil law and criminal law, because the Chinese believed in the existence of the natural order of things, or the law of nature, and considered the written law good only if it was a correct translation of the law of nature. One person—from emperor down to magistrate—made the decision concerning guilt or innocence. Under the Chinese system, there was little distinction between morality and law when determining guilt or innocence. The Chinese legal system employed no lawyers as we know

---

5 99 MIL. L. REV 1 (1983).

6 *Id.*

7 Dyer v. Calderon, 151 F.3d 970, 1999 U.S. App. LEXIS 18171 (9th Cir. 1998) (O'Scannlain dissenting).

8 WIGMORE, *supra* n.2.

9 Summum v. City of Ogden, 152 F Supp. 2d 1286, 2001 U.S. Dist. Lexis 12760, n.10 (2001). *See* Wigmore's THE PANORAMA OF THE WORLD'S LEGAL SYSTEMS at 104 and 107.

10 WIGMORE, *supra* n.2.

them now. There were notaries and brokers, but no licensed professional class. Only judges made the decisions, but higher courts were permitted to review these decisions.[11]

E. Greek Legal System

Unlike the systems previously discussed, under the early Greek legal system, a jury determined whether a person charged with a crime was guilty. According to the records, in Athens in approximately 500 B.C.E., a jury list of about 6,000 names was drawn up. Ordinarily, a panel of 201 names was drawn by lot, but for special cases a panel might consist of as many as 1,000 or 1,500 people. At the trial of Socrates in approximately 400 B.C.E., 501 jurors voted and found a verdict of guilty by a majority of only 60. In one period in Greek history, the decision of guilt or innocence was entirely in the hands of nonprofessionals. The presiding magistrate was selected by lot, and the jurors were drafted from the whole citizen body. Under this system, the defendant conducted his or her own defense and presented his or her own evidence. There was no presiding judge to declare the law, and there was no appeal.[12]

F. Roman Legal System

The Roman instinct for constitutional and legal ideas produced the best and most well-developed system of law. Because this system had the greatest influence on modern evidence law, it is discussed in greater detail.

The Roman legal system can be divided into three periods: the Period of the Republic, the Period of the Early Empire, and the Period of the Later Empire. During the Period of the Republic, the Romans began a code that was chiefly procedural. Even this early period, approximately 400 B.C.E., has influenced the law of the present day. During this period, the lay courts were made up of judges of both law and fact, there was little judicial discretion, and there was no appeal. Under this early system, the decision of the tribunal that first tried the case was final.

During the Early Empire Period, professional judges and jurors came to the forefront, while the culmination of Roman judicial science was reached in the second and third centuries A.D. By this time, the Roman legal system had developed far beyond that of any earlier civilization. The administration of justice was separated from general political administration, and schools of law were started for the training of lawyers. Also during this period, records of cases were kept and, according to Wigmore, these court records were of a type strikingly similar to those later kept in England.

During the Period of the Later Empire (approximately 550 A.D.), Justinian undertook to reduce the enormous bulk of laws to a manageable form. The results were the famous *Pandects* (or *Digest*), the *Code*, the *Institute,*[13] and the *Novels. Black's Law*

---

[11] *Id.*

[12] *Id.*

[13] *Id.*

Dictionary defines the *Pandects* as "[t]he 50 books constituting Justinian's *Digest* (one of the four works making up the *Corpus Juris Civilis*) first published in A.D. 533."[14] The *Code* collected the laws and constitutions of the Emperor Justinian and contained 12 books. The Code is another of the four works that are part of the *Corpus Juris Civilis.*[15]The *Institute* was an "elementary treatise on Roman law in four books."[16] The Institute was also one of the four component parts of the *Corpus Juris Civilis.* The *Novels* are a collection of 168 of the constitutions issued by Emperor Justinian and subsequent emperors that collectively make up the final component of the *Corpus Juris Civilis.*[17]

Jurisprudence had been one of the most advanced Roman sciences, and it perished with the fall of the Roman government. As other civilizations appeared and evolved, the legal concepts developed by the Romans, including the use and admissibility of evidence, strongly influenced later legal procedures. As a matter of fact, Quintilian's teachings, recorded about A.D. 68 to 88, contained legal precepts that are pertinent today and reveal how little the nature of legal practice has changed in 2,000 years. Some of the evidence rules, such as those relating to the testimony of witnesses and preparation of real and documentary evidence, are still valid today.

Thus we have examples of ancient systems in which guilt or innocence was determined by professional judges without the assistance of a jury, and examples of procedures in which the determination was made entirely by laypersons who were not instructed in the law. In some civilizations, the legal systems were well developed, while in others the administration of justice was a farce, with the person or group in power making decisions concerning life and liberty without guidelines or precedent.

Not only have the experiences of other cultures affected our own evidence rules today, but they have also served as guides for other modern systems and surely will be considered during future attempts to reach just and fair methods of administering justice.

§ 1.3 Modern Legal Systems—Romanesque System

From the world's 16 systems, as described by Wigmore, 3 primary world systems exist today. These systems have spread beyond the country and people of their origin. These are the Romanesque, the Anglican, and the Mohammedan. The two that are most dominant in modern times and of most importance in Western civilization are the Romanesque and Anglican.

Approximately five centuries after the Roman Empire fell, the law texts that were prepared by Roman scholars were resurrected and became the basis of the legal system

---

14 *See* BLACK'S LAW DICTIONARY 1219 (9th ed. 2009).

15 *Id.*

16 *Id.*

17 *Id.*

in Italy, then in many other countries in Europe, and finally far beyond Europe. In Italy, the city of Bologna became the center of the study of the Roman law, and legal scholars arrived from all over Europe. During the 1200s, 1300s, and 1400s, thousands of foreign students carried the new advanced ideas of the Roman law to the countries of Europe. Faculties of law sprang up in Spain, France, Germany, and the Netherlands. Roman law, or a modification of it, was codified and nationalized.

In the early 1800s, after three centuries of effort, France completed civil, criminal, and commercial codes and developed rules of civil and criminal procedure. Freedom of contract, recognition of private property, and family solidarity were the three ideological pillars of the *Code Napoleon.*[18] Napoleon himself presided at many of the debates, and his wishes shaped the code.[19] This so-called Code Napoleon was soon translated into almost every language, and set the fashion in the other European countries. The Code Napoleon of 1804 served as the basis for Louisiana law[20] and remains a strong influence both in principles and in legal terminology.[21] It was adopted in Austria in 1811, the Netherlands in 1838, Italy in 1865, Spain in 1888, Germany in 1898, and Switzerland in 1907. The Code had taken eight centuries from the resurrection of the Roman law in the 1100s to the final formation of the Romanesque law in the 1800s.

When the Romanesque system was first developed, the judges established the rules for gathering and admitting evidence and were the finders of fact as well as the law. At first there were few rules of evidence, but eventually, a complex set of rules for obtaining and weighing evidence evolved. As often happens, these rules became merely restrictive—that is, they were not guides, but self-sufficient formulas.

The restrictive rules of evidence became so overdeveloped that they were abolished as being a mere hindrance. To replace this system, the continental nations of France, Germany, and Italy adopted a system that allowed a judge to hear and weigh any evidence, without limitations. Although certain rules have developed in recent times to limit the type and amount of evidence to be considered in this judge-directed system, there are no elaborate controlling rules, such as have been developed in the Anglo-American system. A main reason for this is that the judge's discretion, even when a jury is used, largely determines what evidence will be admitted.

The Romanesque system is now used in many areas of the world, including Quebec, Cairo, Budapest, and Buenos Aires. Millions of people now live under this system, and of the three world systems today, the Romanesque system is the most extensive. In 1928, it governed almost one-sixth of the world's inhabitants.[22]

---

18 Gallo v. Gallo, 861 So. 2d 168, 173, 2003 La. Lexis 3448, n.6 (2003).

19 WIGMORE, A PANORAMA OF THE WORLD'S LEGAL SYSTEMS (1928), at 1031.

20 Madisonville Boatyard, Ltd. v. Poole, 2001 U.S. Dist. Lexis 20589 (E.D. La. 2001). *See also* Pepper v. Triplet, 864 So. 2d 181, 189, 2004 La. Lexis 151 (2004).

21 *See* Forterra Capital, L.L.C. v. Mamal, Inc. 2011 La. App. Lexis 29 (2011), where the Code Napoleon figures prominently in a creditor/debtor action.

22 WIGMORE at Chapter XV.

§ 1.4 —Anglican System

Unlike the other countries of Europe, England rejected the Romanesque legal system. As with other systems, the Anglican legal system developed in several phases. The first of these was the Period of Building a Common Law; the second was the Period of Rejection of the Romanesque Law; the third was the Period of Cosmopolitanization and Expansion.

The early methods of determining guilt or innocence in England were crude by our modern standards. For example, one kind of trial known as "trial by battle" was brought to the British Isles by William the Conqueror in 1066. Instead of a formal trial before a judge, the accused was required to fight his or her victim or the victim's representative. This method of trial continued until the 1800s, when Parliament finally passed an act abolishing it.[23]

The case that finally brought trial by battle to the attention of Parliament involved a man who was accused of murdering his sweetheart. He claimed the right of trial by battle. The judges, after considering the law in the matter, agreed that this type of trial had never been abolished. They therefore allowed the accused to select this type of trial. The brother of the deceased refused to fight the accused, and the accused went free.

Following the Norman Conquest, the Norman judges organized the jury to assist in their investigation. However, jurors were not selected as unbiased triers of fact, as is the practice today, but were selected because they had knowledge of the case. An ordinance of Henry II in the twelfth century provided that a certain number of jurors should be selected in criminal cases, and it specified that jurors be knights.[24] In contrast to modern procedure, the prospective juror was excused if he was ignorant of the facts of the case. The jurors were first left to their own discretion in the use of evidence and were allowed to go among the people in the community and ask for information outside of court. During this period, the jurors were forbidden to call in outside witnesses. However, starting in approximately 1500, witnesses were used more frequently, and gradually the requirement that the triers of the facts possess knowledge of the crime came to be less important. By the end of the 1600s, the jury was allowed to receive no information except that which was offered in court. Initially, the jury served as a substitute for trial by battle, compurgation, and ordeal,[25] but during this period, it evolved into a body that listened to evidence and used logic to render a verdict. Thus, in a period of three or four hundred years, there was a complete reversal of the juror's role.

Given the development of the jury system and the English tradition of protecting the rights of the individual, the need for guidance was obvious. Both the judges and the

---

23 TRACY, HANDBOOK OF THE LAW OF EVIDENCE (1952).

24 *Id.*

25 Crist v. Bretz, 437 U.S. 28, 36, 1978 U.S. Lexis 107, n.12 (1978). "Trial juries were at first merely a substitute for other inscrutable methods of decisionmaking, such as trial by battle, compurgation, and ordeal." BLACK'S LAW DICTIONARY 327 (9th ed. 2009) refers to compurgation as a trial where a defendant could bring friends, frequently numbering 11, to state that they believed the defendant was telling the truth. If a defendant gathered sufficient compurgators and their oaths, he could win the case.

laymen who participated in the trial recognized that the jurors must have guidance to prevent them from being misled by false testimony or by evidence that was not relevant to the issue. Accordingly, in the 1600s and 1700s, numerous exclusionary rules were developed to keep certain kinds of evidence from the jurors unless the evidence met various tests, as determined by the judge. These rules of admissibility were based upon long judicial experience with parties, witnesses, and jurors. The purpose of these rules was to allow the jury to consider only evidence that was as free as possible from the risks of irrelevancy, confusion, and fraud.[26]

The Anglican system is now followed in England, Scotland, and Ireland; Sri Lanka, Hong Kong, and some other countries in Asia; to a great extent in India and some African countries; Canada; and, of course, the United States. From the very beginning, the American colonies followed English law. For example, part of Virginia's plan of governance in 1606 was that "the disposing of all causes happening within the colonies should be done as near to the common law of England and the equity thereof as may be."[27]

§ 1.5 Development of the Rules of Evidence in the United States

During the past two centuries, a system of rules for the presentation of evidence has been established in the United States. In some instances, the rules are the result of centuries of deep thought and experience. In other instances, the rules have been established in a haphazard manner without much thought. Although the United States inherited the English system, rules concerning the admissibility of evidence have taken separate developmental paths and are not the same in the two countries. Federal evidence rules are not necessarily the same in the various states within the United States, and even states that have adopted a version of the Federal Rules of Evidence have some different interpretations. Due to legislation and court decisions, some of which interpret constitutional provisions, the rules for obtaining and weighing evidence are now more restrictive in the United States than in England.

Certainly, the rules are not perfect and are always subject to change—either by the courts or by statute. As stated in *Funk v. United States*:

> The fundamental basis upon which all rules of evidence must rest if they are to rest upon reason is their adaptation to the successful development of the truth. And, since experience is of all teachers the most dependable, and since experience also is a continuous process, it follows that a rule of evidence at one time thought necessary to the ascertainment of the truth should yield to the experience of a succeeding generation whenever that experience has clearly demonstrated the fallacy or unwisdom of the old rule.[28]

---

[26] WIGMORE ON EVIDENCE 5 (1935).

[27] *Id.*

[28] 290 U.S. 371 (1933). *See* case in Part II.

The rules of evidence are changed not only by court decisions, but also by congressional or legislative enactments. For example, in 1878, Congress changed federal law to allow a defendant in a federal criminal case to be a witness at his own request, but included a provision that, when a defendant did not desire to testify, no negative presumption could be drawn.[29] In addition, Congress has prohibited the admission into evidence, in any court, of any wire or oral communication that has been obtained in violation of the Federal Wiretap Act, even if it would be considered relevant and truthful evidence.[30] In Illinois, the legislature provided that, under the Sexually Dangerous Persons Act, evidence of a defendant's prior crimes and punishments, if any, may be admitted against a defendant[31] in contrast with the usual rule that prevents admitting a defendant's past criminal acts in subsequent proceedings.

A. *Adoption of the Federal Rules of Evidence*

In an effort to obtain more uniformity in court procedures, the United States Supreme Court in 1972 adopted the Rules of Evidence for United States Courts and Magistrates. Congress initially blocked their effective use until it was satisfied with the wording of the rules. Subsequently, in 1987, the scope of these rules was extended to include proceedings before United States bankruptcy judges.[32]

A study of the development and application of this set of rules demonstrates how rules of evidence are changed by legislative action. The Supreme Court order of November 20, 1972, directed the federal district courts and United States magistrates to follow these rules after July 1, 1973. However, in accordance with federal laws, the proposed rules were required to be transmitted to Congress for approval. The House Judiciary Committee wrestled with the provisions for nearly a year, and finally approved a modified version in early 1974 by a vote of 377 to 130. Before approving the Supreme Court draft of the rules of evidence, the House Judiciary Committee changed provisions concerning **privileged communications.** The current enhancement of the Federal Rules of Evidence became effective in December 2010.

Privileged communications Statements made by one person to another when there is a necessary relation of trust and confidence between them, such as the statements made by a husband to his wife, or a client to his or her attorney. The person receiving the statements cannot be legally compelled to disclose them.

---

29 *See* Reagan v. United States, 157 U.S. 301, 305 (1878). "By the Act of March 16, 1878, c. 37, 20 Stat. 30, a defendant in a criminal case may, 'at his own request but not otherwise, be a competent witness.'" The modern version can be found at 18 U.S.C. § 3481 (2011). Competency of accused, "In trial of all persons charged with the commission of offenses against the United States . . . the person charged shall, at his own request, be a competent witness."

30 *See* 18 U.S.C. § 2515 (2011).

31 *See* 725 ILCS 205/5 (2011).

32 Federal Rules of Evidence, Title 28 United States Code (1972). These rules, updated through December 2010 by Congress, are included as Appendix I and are referred to throughout this text.

In explaining the purpose and construction of the Federal Rules of Evidence, the drafters included this comment:

> These rules shall be construed to secure fairness in administration, elimination of unjustifiable expense and delay, and promotion of growth and development of a law of evidence to the end that the truth may be ascertained and proceedings justly determined.[33]

The adoption of the Federal Rules of Evidence has contributed to establishing a uniform body of law. However, there is some doubt that the adoption of the rules has achieved the goal of simplicity that its drafters envisioned.[34]

B. *Uniform Rules of Evidence*

As Congress worked toward adoption of the Federal Rules of Evidence, the National Conference of Commissioners on Uniform State Laws prepared new **Uniform Rules of Evidence** patterned after the Federal Rules. In 2005, the Commissioners approved an updated draft of the Uniform Rules of Evidence that reflected the then current amendments to the Federal Rules. This codification of evidence laws was designed and suggested for adoption by the state legislatures and has been periodically revised to keep it in fair conformity with the Federal Rules,[35] which federal courts have followed since 1975.

To avoid confusion and encourage uniformity, the numbering systems for the two sets of rules are consistent. As the Federal Rules have been changed by Congress, the Commissioners on Uniform State Laws have made an effort to bring the Uniform Rules into conformity.

As the evidence rules followed in the federal and state courts of the United States today are products of a combination of legislative acts (as discussed in previous paragraphs) and court decisions, a study of evidence requires an examination of federal and state legislation and the cases interpreting the rules.

§ 1.6 Application of the Rules of Evidence in State and Federal Courts

The history of the United States and the separation of powers concept have influenced the legislative bodies and courts in establishing evidence rules. As a general rule, the laws of the forum govern questions of evidence; that is, the state rules of evidence apply in state courts, and the federal rules apply in federal courts. If the state has jurisdiction over the parties and the cause of action, the rules of evidence and the laws of that state generally will apply.

---

33 FED. R. EVID. 102.

34 WIGMORE ON EVIDENCE § 6.5 (1988).

35 Uniform Rules of Evidence (2005). National Conference of Commissioners on Uniform State Laws. The Table of Contents for the Uniform Rules of Evidence is included in Appendix II.

The United States Constitution gives Congress the power to make regulations guiding the Supreme Court and to create tribunals inferior to the Supreme Court. The rules of evidence established by Congress are to be followed in federal courts. However, no codification of rules can be applied without court interpretation. Therefore, one must carefully examine federal cases, especially United States Supreme Court cases, in applying the law governing the admissibility of evidence in federal courts.

While the legislation of each jurisdiction is supreme, and state rules of evidence provide general guides in state courts, legislation is subject to such limitations as may be prescribed in federal constitutional provisions applicable to the states. For example, the United States Supreme Court has determined that a state rule that requires a willing criminal defendant to testify prior to the admission of any other defense testimony violates the Fifth Amendment to the Constitution, as well as the **due process** clause of the Fourteenth Amendment.[36] Also, where constitutional authority exists, Congress may establish rules relating to the admissibility of evidence in state courts. Demonstrative of such principle is the Omnibus Crime Control and Safe Streets Act of 1968—Title 18 of the United States Code—which provides that evidence relating to a wire or oral communication that has been intercepted in violation of that section shall not be used "in or before any court, grand jury, department . . . or other authority of the United States, state or political subdivision thereof."[37]

> **Due process** (1) A flexible term for the compliance with the fundamental rules for fair and orderly legal proceedings; for example, the right to be informed of the nature and cause of the accusation, to be confronted with the witnesses against you, to have compulsory process for obtaining witnesses in your favor, to have the assistance of counsel for your defense, and to have a fair and impartial jury. (2) Legal proceedings that observe the rules designed for the protection and enforcement of individual rights and liberties.

Even though the adoption of the Federal Rules of Evidence and the Uniform Rules of Evidence has not achieved the goal of simplicity that the drafters envisioned, these rules have produced more uniformity and consistency. Because the Federal Rules of Evidence regulate evidentiary matters in all federal courts of the United States, including bankruptcy courts and proceedings held before United States magistrate judges, uniformity has been accomplished to a substantial degree in the federal system. Given that our nation is based on a federalist system, there naturally is far less uniformity among the states. At one point, only 36 jurisdictions had adopted evidence codes that followed the model of the Federal Rules and/or the Uniform Rules patterned after the Federal Rules.[38] Currently, 42 states as well as Guam, Puerto Rico, the Virgin Islands, and the United States military have adopted evidence codes based partially or

---

36 Brooks v. Tennessee, 406 U.S. 605 (1972).

37 For a more thorough discussion of the powers of the federal and state governments, see KANOVITZ, CONSTITUTIONAL LAW (12th ed. 2010).

38 Charles W. Gamble, *Drafting, Adopting and Interpreting the New Alabama Rules of Evidence: A Reporter's Perspective*, 47 ALA. L. REV. 1, *n.55 (1995)*.

completely on the Federal Rules of Evidence.[39] California, Georgia, Illinois, Kansas, Massachusetts, Missouri, New York, and Virginia have not adopted a version of the Federal Rules.[40] The District of Columbia has not adopted the Federal Rules of Evidence for the District's courts, but the Federal Rules, of course, apply in federal courts sitting within the District of Columbia.[41]

Because the Federal Rules of Evidence have had a major impact on state laws and evidence rules, and because the states have increasingly looked to federal decisions for interpretations, provisions of the Federal Rules of Evidence and federal cases interpreting the Federal Rules are cited throughout this text.[42]

The Federal Rules and the Uniform Rules have generated a reform of the evidence rules. However, the states have not given up their independence on evidence issues. State courts are free to interpret evidentiary rules in a manner different from federal courts and interpretations offered by the courts of sister states. To develop a more comprehensive understanding of the rules, state cases as well as federal cases are cited and examined. Nevertheless, because some state evidence rules differ from both the Federal Rules and the Uniform Rules, it is necessary to consult the laws and decisions of the state that has jurisdiction over the parties.[43]

§ 1.7 Future Development of the Rules of Evidence

In studying rules of criminal evidence, it must be recognized that our rules are a product of progressive growth and adaptation to new circumstances. The rules of evidence will continue to change and, in fact, probably will change more rapidly in the next several years as judicial officials and members of legislatures attempt to fashion a more effective system to meet the needs of an evolving society. Evidence rule changes may reflect some new pressing social needs such as allowing admission into evidence of prior sexual offenses by a defendant when other offenses might not be admissible and limiting the admissibility of the past sexual history of the victim.[44] Alterations to the Dead Man's statutes[45] indicate that the old fears of fraud by witnesses against the dead have been overblown, and the usual avenues of **cross-examination** may work

---

39 *See* 6-T WEINSTEIN'S FEDERAL EVIDENCE, "Table State Adaptations of Federal Rules of Evidence." (2010). Appendix II contains a list of states that have adopted the same system of uniform rules of evidence with the effective dates and the respective statutory citations.

40 *Id.*

41 *Id.*

42 The Federal Rules of Evidence, as amended through December 1, 2010, are included in Appendix I.

43 For comprehensive coverage of the differences in state rules and interpretations, see Joseph & Saltzburg, Evidence in America, The Federal Rules in the States (1994).

44 29 HAMLINE L. REV. 177 (2006).

45 In civil cases, an interested party may be prohibited from testifying about communication that the witness had with the deceased person when the testimony is against the interests of a deceased person or his or her estate. The rule that prohibited such testimony was designed to prevent or reduce fraudulent claims against the estate of a deceased individual by closing the mouth of the claimant who could not testify against a person who could never offer an answer.

perfectly well.[46] Changes have come to other areas of evidence law. For example, older evidence interpretations allowed the past sexual history of complaining witnesses to be introduced in sex crime prosecutions. However, modern evidence codes generally limit the prior sexual history of the victim of a sex crime, even though it could be argued that such history might have some minimal relevancy. The changes to the Dead Man's statutes and limiting prior sexual activity may stand the test of time, remaining long enough to have lasting influence on the law of evidence.

Demonstrative of evolutionary development of the rules and interpretations of the rules of evidence is the change made to the marital testimonial privilege recognized by federal courts. Prior to *Trammel v. United States,*[47] both husband and wife were considered holders of the testimonial privilege and could prevent the other from testifying against a defendant spouse. The original theory involved the protection and promotion of marital harmony. The Supreme Court reasoned that if "one spouse is willing to testify against the other in a criminal proceeding—whatever the motivation—their relationship is almost certainly in disrepair; there is probably little in the way of marital harmony for the privilege to preserve."[48] In such a situation in federal courts, the old rule had to give way to the modern interpretation of the marital testimonial privilege favoring admissibility of the testimony offered by a willing witness spouse.

The application of the rules of evidence to the administration of the law is and should be within the sound discretion of the judiciary. However, contrary to statements made in some cases, recent decisions of reviewing courts appear to require more strict application of the rules of evidence, thus leaving lower courts with less discretion concerning the administration of the business of the court and the admissibility of evidence.

Acts of Congress have effects on the admission of evidence, and executive branch orders may have some similar effects in other types of proceedings. Following the attacks of September 11, 2001, Congress passed the USA PATRIOT Act, which changed some of the ways in which the federal government is permitted to collect and use evidence.[49] Although the USA PATRIOT Act was designed to make the nation safer from terrorist activity, some civil libertarians became concerned that the new powers granted to federal law enforcement could have the effect of curtailing some civil rights. Among other things that affect the use or admission of evidence in some cases, the President of the United States issued an Executive Order that limited some indictments, jury trials, and other civil liberties of some noncitizen individuals accused of terrorist activities.[50] The same Executive Order directed that the defense secretary issue orders that purported to limit admission of evidence in special tribunals in cases of trials of international terrorists.[51] However, the Foreign Intelligence Surveillance Act of 1978 authorized some evidentiary searches prior to obtaining a warrant, but the statute anticipated

---

46 53 CLEV. ST. L. REV. 75 (2005).

47 444 U.S. 40, 1980 U.S. Lexis 84 (1980).

48 *Id.* at 52.

49 PUB. L. NO. 107-56, 115 STAT. 272 (2001).

50 51 AM. U.L. REV. 1081 (2002).

51 *Id.*

that a warrant would be forthcoming in most cases. The Act excluded the use of any evidence unlawfully obtained through illegal electronic searches and surveillance.[52]

In an earlier effort at influencing the admission of evidence in courts, Congress passed the Omnibus Crime Control and Safe Streets Act of 1968, which included a Title III section that regulated the manner in which wiretap evidence could be admitted in court. As part of Title III, the Congress provided that evidence seized illegally in violation of the statute would not be admissible in courts or other venues.[53] In another adjustment of search and seizure law, the Congress amended the Foreign Intelligence Surveillance Act by passing relevant provisions of the Patriot Act that had the effect of limiting the use of the Foreign Intelligence Surveillance Act for domestic law enforcement purposes.[54] In summary, the Congress has adjusted the admission of seized evidence through statutory enactments that mirrored public policy initiatives of interest groups and to accommodate the needs of the executive branch. The general thrust has been to allow more evidence to be admitted into court when the legal proceeding involves terrorism or related criminal matters.

Have the restrictive rules of evidence become overdeveloped? Perhaps our society has reached the point where some of the rationales for exclusionary rules are no longer valid, and the rules no longer provide appropriate results. However, it would prove unwise to abolish our system entirely, as was done in France in the 1700s. Appropriate changes should be made by the courts and legislatures after careful study and with regard to the objectives to be achieved. Therefore, not only is it necessary that all who are involved in the criminal justice system be aware of the rules of evidence as they exist today, but everyone must also be familiar with the history of the rules, keep up with changes as they occur, and take an active part in recommending improvements when time and events have dictated that changes need to be made to some of the current rules of evidence.

§ 1.8 Summary

In every society, efforts have been made to determine the guilt or innocence of a person charged with violating the rules of that society. Some of the world's legal systems were built on sound foundations and have continued for many centuries. However, other legal systems disappeared when the governments responsible for developing them were overthrown, or when governments developed other methods for determining guilt or innocence. The experience of history has proven to be a strong teacher that has preserved evidence of prior legal systems, so that nations today can harness the knowledge of the past to help the law of evidence evolve in a productive path toward the future.

[52] 82 B.U.L. REV. 555 (2002).

[53] *Id.*

[54] 28 HARV. J.L. & PUB. POL'Y 319 (2005).

In England, after centuries of experimentation, a system for determining guilt or innocence developed by utilizing parts of earlier systems. With the development of the jury system, a complex set of rules for determining the admissibility of evidence gradually developed. Although a jury system patterned after that of England was adopted by the United States, the rules for admitting the evidence have been changed by our courts and legislative bodies. Today, the rules of exclusion are stricter in the United States than in England.

The rules for determining the admissibility of evidence have changed and will continue to evolve. In this country, judges, legislators, and other criminal justice personnel must work together to seek better methods for determining guilt and protecting society, while at the same time protecting the rights of the individual.

CHAPTER ONE: QUESTIONS AND REVIEW EXERCISES

1. Was the Egyptian legal system likely to produce accurate and fair criminal justice?
2. With respect to reaching a fair verdict, would the use of several hundred jurors in the Greek legal system promote equity and due process?
3. How did the Romanesque system of the Code of Napoleon develop such a great influence on western civilization?
4. Under the Anglican system of law, how was the jury system different from what is typically seen in the modern American jury system?
5. In what ways has the American Congress influenced the development of the rules of evidence and changed the admission of evidence?

Approach to the Study of Criminal Evidence

2

The word "evidence" is applied to that which renders evident; and is defined to be any matter of fact the effect, tendency, or design of which is to produce in the mind a persuasion, affirmative or disaffirmative, of the existence of some other matter of fact.

State v. Ward, 61 Vt. 153, 17 A. 483 (1889)

Chapter Contents

KEY TERMS AND CONCEPTS	
Beyond a Reasonable Doubt	Hearsay Evidence
Circumstantial Evidence	Legal Evidence
Competent Evidence	Material Evidence
Corroborative Evidence	Prima Facie Evidence
Cumulative Evidence	Proof
Direct Evidence	Real Evidence
Documentary Evidence	Relevant Evidence
Evidence	Testimony

§ 2.1 Introduction

The general concepts and definitions in the law of evidence provide a valuable foundation for the study of cases and statutes involving guidelines on specific evidentiary issues, such as the admissibility of hearsay evidence, the exclusionary effect of evidentiary privileges, or how constitutional provision affects evidence. Rational thought and history have shaped the rules regulating the admissibility of evidence, while similar reasoning and fairness have provided the justifications for excluding pertinent evidence. The overall goal of the rules of evidence is to produce the truth, while reducing the chance for falsehood. A knowledge of these rules and the rationale used by the courts in framing the rules that exclude some evidence assists immeasurably in understanding the specific rules of evidence. Under the Anglican system (with the jury deciding the facts), evidence is not admitted when it would be unfairly prejudicial to the accused.

Although the rules of evidence generally apply in both civil and criminal cases, there are some important differences that are of special interest to those involved in criminal justice. These differences are discussed in this chapter. In addition, this chapter considers the flow and use of evidence from the time it is located, processed, and analyzed by the investigator to the time it is considered by the parole board. In Chapter 4 the use of evidence at the trial is more particularly considered.

§ 2.2 Definitions

In order to fully understand the discussion of the rules of evidence, it is necessary to define some of the words and phrases used. Other words or phrases are defined in future chapters as they are discussed.

A. *Evidence*

Evidence has been defined as *the means employed for the purpose of proving an unknown or disputed fact*, and it is either judicial or extrajudicial. Every determination of the judgment, whatever its subject may be, is the result of evidence.[1] Evidence is any information upon which a person can base a decision. For example, before a used car is purchased, the car dealer is questioned as to the condition of the car, and, in some instances, the car is taken to a mechanic for an inspection. All of this information, or evidence, is then considered before a decision is reached as to whether the purchase will be made.

B. *Legal Evidence*

Legal evidence is defined in *Black's Law Dictionary* as "[a]ll admissible evidence, both oral and documentary, of such a character that it reasonably and substantially proves the point rather than merely raising suspicion or conjecture."[2] Legal evidence is evidence that is used or is intended to be used at the trial or at inquiries before courts, judges, commissioners, referees, and so forth. To state this more succinctly, evidence as used in law means "that which demonstrates or makes clear or ascertains the truth of the very fact or point in issue, either on the one side or the other."[3]

> **Legal evidence** General term meaning all admissible evidence, both oral and documentary, that is of such a character that tends reasonably and substantially to prove the point, not to raise a mere suspicion or conjecture.

C. *Direct Evidence*

Direct evidence is "[e]vidence that is based on personal knowledge or observation and that, if true, proves a fact without **inference** or **presumption**."[4] Direct evidence has been defined as evidence that proves the existence of a fact at issue without the use of an inference or presumption.[5] "Historically, direct evidence has been viewed as evidence that is within a

> **Inference** A rational conclusion of the existence of a different fact deduced from facts originally proved.

> **Presumption** A conclusion or inference drawn from the proven existence of some basic fact or group of facts.

---

1 RICE, LAW OF EVIDENCE (1893).

2 BLACK'S LAW DICTIONARY 638 (9th ed. 2009).

3 Leonard v. State, 100 Ohio St. 456, 127 N.E. 464 (1919), quoting Blackstone (3 BLACKSTONE'S COMMENTARIES 367).

4 BLACK'S LAW DICTIONARY 636 (9th ed. 2009).

5 People v. Jovan, 2013 Ill. App 103835 (¶ 64), 2013 Ill. App. LEXIS 643 (2013).

witness's personal knowledge and does not require drawing an inference to support the proposition for which it is offered."[6] For example, a witness testifies that he saw the acts that constituted the precise fact to be proved. If, in a homicide case, the witness testifies that he saw the accused stab the victim, this would be direct evidence.

D. Circumstantial Evidence

Circumstantial evidence, sometimes called indirect evidence, is so called because the truth is inferred from probabilities arising from an association of facts. An Indiana jury instruction defines circumstantial evidence for a jury as "evidence that proves a fact from which you may conclude the existence of other facts."[7] It has been defined as "[e]vidence based on inference and not on personal knowledge or observation."[8] One court observed that circumstantial evidence was testimony not based on actual individual knowledge or observation of the historical facts of the case, but knowledge of other facts from which deductions can be drawn, showing indirectly the facts that are sought to be proved.[9] An example of circumstantial evidence is the testimony of a police officer that he apprehended a subject who had a bag of money covered in red dye from an exploding dye pack. It should be noted that circumstantial evidence has the same value, force, and weight as direct evidence because the law makes no distinction between the weight to be given to either direct or circumstantial evidence.[10]

> **Circumstantial evidence** Evidence of one fact from which a second fact is reasonably inferred, although not directly proven.

E. Testimony

Testimony is evidence that comes to the court through witnesses speaking under **oath** or affirmation. In some instances, the word *testimony* is used synonymously with the word *evidence*. It is obvious when considering the two words, however, that testimony is exclusively oral, while evidence includes writings, physical objects, and other forms. Evidence is the broader term and includes testimony, which is only one type of evidence.[11]

> **Oath** Various solemn affirmations, declarations, or promises, made by a declarant or a witness, under a sense of responsibility to God, for the truth of what is stated or the faithful performance of what is undertaken.

---

6 Compton v. Lowe's Cos., 2011 U.S. Dist. Lexis 12207 (S.D. Ill. 2011).

7 Hamilton v. State, 2010 Ind. App. Unpub. Lexis 1237 (2010).

8 BLACK'S LAW DICTIONARY 638 (9th ed. 2009).

9 State v. Chandler, 2011 Ohio 590, 2011 Ohio App. Lexis 576 (2011).

10 *See* United States v. Thomas, 627 F.3d 146, 2010 U.S. App. Lexis 24176 (5th Cir. 2010).

11 31 C.J.S. *Evidence* § 3 (1964).

F. *Documentary Evidence*

Documentary evidence consists of objects that have tangible existence and have the capacity to convey a fact or to establish the truth or untruth of a proposition at issue. Documentary evidence possess a rather broad meaning and includes all types of traditional documents, records, photographs, pictures, X-ray images, drawings, analogue and digital audio and video recordings, as well as cursive and printed writings. Modern methods of storing information have expanded the concept of documentary evidence to include e-mail and text messages as well as data on CD and DVD disks, memory sticks, flash drives, hard drives, optically stored information. Cloud storage of data has become one of the newer places to store significant amounts of data that will be considered documentary evidence. With documentary evidence, it is the object or thing that speaks to offer evidence: "Evidence supplied by a writing or other document, which must be authenticated before the evidence is admissible."[12] A ransom note in a kidnapping case and a photo printout from a Web site in a child pornography prosecution are examples of documentary evidence.

> **Documentary evidence** Evidence that is furnished by written documents, records, cell phone text messages, e-mail, computer-generated reports, and any other method of storing data.

G. *Real Evidence*

Real evidence, or "physical" evidence, has been defined as *a fact, the existence of which is perceptible to the senses.* As compared to an intangible concept, real evidence possesses a physical essence and existence that can be observed, touched, and handled. A clearer definition is "physical evidence (such as a knife wound) that itself plays a direct part in the incident in question."[13] When a party wants to introduce real evidence, that party must demonstrate that the actual object involved in the crime is being introduced and that it has not been subject to tampering.[14] Real evidence also includes weapons or implements used in the commission of a crime, as well as evidence of the physical appearance of a place (as obtained by a jury when the members are taken to view a crime scene).

> **Real evidence** Evidence that has physical essence; evidence provided by producing the physical items themselves in court, as opposed to descriptions of the evidence.

---

12 BLACK'S LAW DICTIONARY 637 (9th ed. 2009).

13 *Id.*

14 See People v. Ortiz, 2011 NY Slip Op 240 (2011), where the prosecutor introduced the actual underwear worn by the victim in a sexual assault case.

H. Prima Facie Evidence

Prima facie evidence is the body of evidence that, if unexplained, uncontradicted, or not called into question, is sufficient to carry a case to the jury and to sustain a verdict in favor of the issue that it supports. Current Montana law describes prima facie evidence as "that which proves a particular fact until contradicted and overcome by other evidence."[15] Prima facie evidence has also been described by Texas courts as the minimum quantum of evidence required to support a rational inference that a particular allegation is true.[16] The phrase *prima facie* means "at first sight" or "on the first appearance" or "on the face of it." Prima facie evidence is "evidence that will establish a fact or sustain a judgment unless contradictory evidence is produced."[17] For example, willfully concealing merchandise on the defendant's person while inside a retail store created a prima facie case of an intent to steal where there was no contradictory evidence.[18] Such prima facie evidence exists unless or until the opposing side introduces contradictory evidence that is sufficient to meet any **burden of proof**.

> **Prima facie evidence** Proof of a fact or collection of facts that creates a presumption of the existence of other facts, or from which some conclusion may be legally drawn, but which presumption or conclusion may be discredited or overcome by other relevant proof.

> **Burden of proof** The duty of proving facts disputed on the trial of a case by the proper weight of the evidence.

I. Proof

Proof is the effect of evidence; that is, it is "*[t]he establishment or refutation of an alleged fact by evidence*"[19] Even though the terms *proof* and *evidence* are sometimes used synonymously, they are different. Properly speaking, evidence is only the medium of proof; proof is the effect of evidence. Proof implies persuasion, and proof has been defined as "as evidence necessary to convince a trier of fact beyond a reasonable doubt of the existence of every element of the offense."[20] The Kansas Rules of Evidence define proof as "all of the

> **Proof** (1) Establishing the truth of an allegation by evidence. (2) The evidence itself. The person claiming the affirmative of an allegation ordinarily has the necessity of proving it. (3) The affidavits made to support a claim or statement of fact, which is doubted or disputed, or of which a person acting in a representative capacity requires evidence under oath.

---

15 MONT. CODE ANN. § 26-1-102 (6) (2013).

16 *See* Rehak Creative Services v. Witt, 404 S.W.3d 716, 2013 Tex. App. LEXIS 6196 (2013).

17 BLACK'S LAW DICTIONARY 638 (9th ed. 2009).

18 Talley v. Commonwealth, 2010 Va. App. Lexis 441 (2010).

19 BLACK'S LAW DICTIONARY 1334 (9th ed. 2009).

20 *See* People v. Lamont, 977 N.Y.S.2d 540, 2014 N.Y. App. Div. LEXIS 28 (2014).

evidence before the trier of the fact relevant to a fact in issue which tends to prove the existence or non-existence of such fact."[21]

J. Cumulative Evidence

Cumulative evidence helps to prove what has already been established by other evidence. Montana offers this definition: "'Cumulative evidence' is additional evidence of the same character to the same point."[22] In legal phraseology, it means evidence from the same or a new witness that simply repeats, in substance and effect, or adds to, what has already been offered in court. For example, where ten people witnessed a defendant assault a person on a public street, to have all these witnesses come to court and render virtually the exact same story identifying the defendant could be considered cumulative evidence. Having two or three witnesses explain what was observed would generally be appropriate and not be considered cumulative evidence.

> **Cumulative evidence** Testimony that is offered to prove what has already been proven by other evidence.

K. Corroborative Evidence

Corroborative evidence is evidence that is supplementary or complementary to evidence already presented in court. It tends to strengthen or confirm previously admitted evidence. Montana defines corroborative evidence as "additional evidence of the same character to the same point."[23] It is additional evidence of a different character, but it seeks to prove the same point as the earlier evidence. (For example, historically, a conviction cannot stand based solely upon a defendant's confession without corroborating evidence.) Such corroborating evidence may be the testimony of a witness who saw the accused at the scene of the crime. Similarly, evidence from a conspirator made during the existence of the conspiracy may provide corroborating evidence of the crime that will permit the use of the confession.

> **Corroborative evidence** Additional testimony to reinforce a point that was previously the subject of proof; additional proof that confirms evidence previously admitted on a particular point.

L. Relevant Evidence

According to the federal rules, evidence is relevant when it has any tendency to make the existence of any fact that is of consequence to the determination of the action more probable or less probable than would have been the case without the evidence.[24] The Kansas Rules of Evidence define "relevant evidence" as "evidence having any

---

21 *See* KANS. STAT. § 60–401(b) Definitions. (2012).

22 MONT. CODE ANNO. 26-1-102 (4) (2013).

23 *Id.* (3).

24 FED. R. EVID. 401. For further discussion concerning relevant evidence, see Chapter 7.

tendency in reason to prove any material fact."[25] To be considered relevant, the evidence must help one party either support or disprove a fact while not being unfairly prejudicial to the opposing party's case. Evidence of a past conviction to help prove guilt might help the prosecution gain a conviction, but the admission of the evidence of the prior conviction might result in a conviction because the jury thought the defendant was a bad person.

M. Material Evidence

Material evidence pertains to the substantial matters in dispute or has a legitimate and effective influence or bearing on the decision of the case. Material evidence has been defined as "[e]vidence having some logical connection with the facts of consequence or the issues."[26] Material evidence could be considered evidence that was both logically relevant and legally relevant and therefore admissible as a general rule. A Tennessee court noted that "substantial and material evidence has been defined as such relevant evidence as a reasonable mind might accept to support a rational conclusion and such as to furnish a reasonably sound basis for the action under consideration."[27]

N. Competent Evidence

Although the terms **relevancy, competency**, and **materiality** are frequently used conjunctively, a matter may be relevant and material to an issue but still be incompetent, and therefore inadmissible under the established rules of evidence. **Competent evidence** is *evidence that, in legal proceedings, is admissible for the purpose of proving a relevant fact.* Evidence that is considered competent evidence must be such that a reasonable mind might accept

Material evidence Evidence that goes to the substantial matters in dispute or has a legitimate and effective influence or bearing on the decision of the case; evidence that may tend to prove or disprove a fact that is at issue in a case.

Relevancy The connection between a fact tendered in evidence and the issue to be proved.

Competency The legal fitness or capacity of a witness to testify on the trial of a case that requires an oath, original perception, recollection, and an ability to communicate.

Materiality Importance; relevance; capable of properly influencing the result of a lawsuit.

Competent evidence The quality of evidence offered that makes it proper to be received.

---

25 KANS. STAT. § 60–401(b) (2012).

26 BLACK'S LAW DICTIONARY 638 (9th ed. 2009).

27 City of Memphis v. Payton, 2012 Tenn. App. LEXIS 768 (2012), citing Macon v. Shelby County, 309 S.W.3d 504,509 (2009). Internal quotation marks omitted.

it as adequate to support a particular position or finding.[28] Evidence may be made competent (or incompetent) by legislation or judicial construction.[29]

O. Hearsay Evidence

Hearsay evidence involves an out-of-court statement offered inside a courtroom for proof of the truth it purports to contain. "'Hearsay' means a statement that: (1) the declarant does not make while testifying at the current trial or hearing; and (2) a party offers in evidence to prove the truth of the matter asserted in the statement."[30] A witness's statement made in court but based upon what someone else has told him or her outside of court, and not from personal observation or knowledge of the original facts, constitutes **hearsay evidence**. In Virginia, hearsay has been defined as oral testimony or written evidence of a statement presented in court but made out of court, where the statement is being presented to show the truth of the matter being asserted and resting its value on the credibility of the out-of-court declarant.[31] As a general rule, hearsay evidence is not admissible unless it meets an exception to the rule that excludes such evidence. When an eyewitness has explained to a police officer that the witness observed the defendant breaking into a store, the officer is not generally permitted to tell the court what the witness told the officer, because such testimony constitutes hearsay evidence if offered by the police officer for proof of its truth; the eyewitness would have to testify to what the witness observed.

> **Hearsay evidence** Statements offered by a witness, based upon what someone else has told him or her, and not upon personal knowledge or observation.

§ 2.3 Reasons for the Rules of Evidence

By the seventeenth century, the evolution of the jury function was well advanced, and the jury depended on the testimony of witnesses for facts on which to base a verdict. Members of juries were generally ordinary laypeople, impressionable and unacquainted with the law. It was therefore recognized that specific rules for filtering the evidence were necessary. To protect the accused, rules were gradually developed to help assure that evidence was dependable, credible, and trustworthy before it could be considered. Evidentiary rules developed, in part, to keep out untrustworthy evidence or unfairly prejudicial evidence even if it contained the truth. To achieve order and

---

28 Blackburn v. Duke Univ., 2010 N.C. App. Lexis 897 (2010).

29 Funk v. United States, 290 U.S. 371, 64 S. Ct. 212, 78 L. Ed. 2d 369 (1933).

30 Fed. R. Evid. 801(c). For further definitions of hearsay and terms related to hearsay evidence, *see* Chapter 12.

31 Baker v. Commonwealth, 2009 Va. App. Lexis 75 (2009). Unpublished opinion.

decorum, it was necessary for courts to establish rules to carry out the proceedings in an efficient manner. To meet these objectives, courts and legislatures have formulated our present-day evidentiary rules.

Efforts have been made to state in more specific terms the reasons for the rules of evidence and to account for the many varied rules that must be interpreted by the courts. As these rules have been developed by gradual evolution and in fact are still developing, it is difficult to categorize them and to explain why each rule exists. Although it appears that, in some instances, there is an effort to rationalize or justify an outmoded or outdated rule, there is logic to the explanations supporting most of the specific rules of evidence.

§ 2.4 Reasons for Excluding Evidence

Much evidence is excluded even though it would help the jury or the court in determining the true facts concerning the matters at issue. The reasons for excluding various items of evidence are numerous, and they are phrased in many diverse ways. An effort is made here to categorize these reasons in order to make them more meaningful and understandable. The general reasons for excluding otherwise pertinent evidence are listed as follows.

A. Protect Interests and Relationships

There are times where protecting particular relationships carries a higher value than determining the truth of some matters. For that reason, courts weigh the value of having all the facts admitted in court against the protection of certain interests and relationships, and it may decide to exclude relevant evidence when the protection of interests is more important than the truth. Such interests and relationships are regarded, rightly or wrongly, as having sufficient social importance to justify some incidental sacrifice of sources of fact needed in the administration of justice.[32] Protecting interests and relationships by the exclusion of otherwise relevant evidence may also harm the search for the truth. Examples of evidence excluded on the basis of this public policy of protection of relationships are:

- Evidence protected by the husband and wife confidential communication privilege
- Evidence protected by the husband and wife testimonial privilege
- Evidence protected by the attorney–client privilege
- Evidence protected by the penitent–confessor privilege[33]

---

32 McCormick, Evidence § 72 (4th ed. 1992).

33 Testimonial privileges are discussed in Chapter 10.

B. *Avoid Undue Prejudice to the Accused*

Some evidence that would be relevant to the issue is not admitted because of the risk that it might create undue or **unfair prejudice** to the defendant's case. Evidence that might help demonstrate guilt in the present case is appropriate for admission, but to allow evidence of prior crimes might cause the jury to convict based on the evidence of the prior crimes and not on evidence concerning the case presently in court. In some situations, evidence might have such a low level of relevance that to allow its admission would create undue prejudice by changing the outcome in a defendant's case.[34] In some cases, gruesome photographs of deceased victims may be excluded from evidence, even though relevant, because admitting them might inflame the jury with unfair prejudice against the accused.

> **Unfair prejudice** A prejudgment, or bias, that interferes with a person's impartiality and sense of justice.

C. *Prohibit Consideration of Unreliable Evidence*

Evidence considered to be unreliable is generally excluded from admission in court, even though it might have a bearing on the case. This category of evidence includes hearsay evidence and some **lay witness** opinion evidence.[35] To illustrate, the testimony of a police officer that a bystander told him or her that the accused was driving the car that had been involved in a bank robbery is not admissible. Such evidence is considered hearsay and, although it possesses some relevance, is not considered sufficiently reliable for use in court.

> **Lay witness** Any witness that is not an expert.

D. *Reduce Violations of Constitutional Safeguards*

In order to ensure respect for constitutional provisions regulating search and seizure, as well as to ensure respect for other constitutional rights, the Supreme Court of the United States, in the latter half of the twentieth century, developed rules of exclusion to be applied when evidence has been illegally seized. Until the beginning of the previous century, it was almost universally accepted that evidence was admissible even though it was obtained illegally.[36] However, because of later interpretations of the federal and state constitutions, the courts now reason that such evidence secured by an illegal search and seizure, evidence obtained in violation of the **self-incrimination** provisions, or evidence taken in violation of

> **Self-incrimination** An act or declaration either as testimony at trial or prior to trial by which one implicates oneself in a crime.

---

34 *See* State v. Anthony, 218 Ariz. 439, 2008 Ariz Lexis 123 (Ariz. 2008). *See* case in Part II.

35 These rules are discussed in Chapters 11 and 12.

36 *See* Weeks v. United States, 232 U.S. 383, 34 S.Ct. 341, 58 L.Ed. 652, 1914 U.S. LEXIS 1368 (1914).

the right-to-counsel provisions, should generally be excluded, even though relevant to the case. In fact, such evidence might provide the only basis for a conviction.[37] The rationale for excluding such evidence has not been consistent, but generally, exclusion has been justified on the grounds that, by rejecting such evidence, there will be little incentive for law enforcement officials to violate the Constitution in an effort to obtain incriminating evidence.

E. Conserve Time

Cumulative evidence is evidence that is unnecessary and repetitive, and thus may be excluded upon proper **objection** by one of the parties or upon the court's own motion. The admission of cumulative evidence would otherwise constitute a waste of the court's time as well as the time of the individuals involved. Rejection of cumulative evidence is consistent with and follows the principle of judicial economy.

> **Objection** A resistance or protest on legal grounds, regarding such topics as the admissibility of evidence or the entry of an order or judgment.

There have been arguments that some of the historical reasons for excluding relevant evidence have long since disappeared, leaving the technical rules without a logical basis. In some instances, so many exceptions have developed that the rules are no longer meaningful. However, most of the justification for the rules is still valid and should be carefully considered, because understanding the reasons behind the rules can help one to understand their application.

§ 2.5 Rules of Evidence in Criminal Cases Compared to Rules of Evidence in Civil Cases

Consistent with much modern law, an early English court noted that no distinction exists between the rules of evidence in criminal and civil cases. The court stated:

> What may be received in the one case, may be received in the other; and what is rejected in the one ought to be rejected in the other. A fact must be established by the same evidence, whether it is to be followed by a criminal or civil consequence.[38]

In some states, case law or statutes have made civil rules of evidence more applicable in criminal cases, unless otherwise provided by statutory enactment.[39]

---

37 Constitutional rationales for excluding evidence are discussed more thoroughly in Chapter 16.

38 Rex v. Watson, 2 Stark. 116 (1817), Lord Melville's Case, 29 How. St. Tr. 763 (1806).

39 MCLS. § 768.22 (1) Rules of evidence; applicability of criminal and quasi criminal proceedings; evidence of prior conviction. (Mich. 2013). "The rules of evidence in civil actions, insofar as the same are applicable, shall govern in all criminal and quasi criminal proceedings except as otherwise provided by law."

For example, a Washington statute provides that "[t]he rules of evidence in civil actions, so far as practicable, shall be applied to criminal prosecutions."[40] The Federal Rules of Evidence "apply to proceedings in the United States courts"[41] subject to limited exceptions. There are, however, some differences in the current rules and in the application of the rules of evidence that arise solely, or more frequently, in criminal cases. Constitutional law cases that regulate how and when a suspect or arrestee may be questioned have produced rules relating to admission or exclusion of evidence in criminal cases that have no comparable place in civil cases.[42] In addition, evidence produced by searches and seizures[43] or from a coerced confession[44] may be excluded on federal or state constitutional grounds where police conduct failed to meet constitutional standards.

Beyond a reasonable doubt Fully satisfied, entirely convinced, satisfied to a moral certainty.

Preponderance of the evidence The greater weight of the evidence, in merit and in worth.

The burden of proof in civil cases, while on the plaintiff, does not create any presumption in favor of either of the contending parties and the civil litigants negotiate through the legal process with positions of rough equality. However, in criminal cases, the law seeks to protect the person accused of a crime, and a presumption accompanies him or her from the time of apprehension to the moment of conviction: the presumption that he or she is innocent until proven guilty. Throughout the trial, the burden of proof remains on the prosecution, and the government must prove guilt **beyond a reasonable doubt**, rather than by a **preponderance of the evidence**.[45]

In addition to requiring the government to meet a higher (or greater) standard of proof in a criminal prosecution, the rules differ in a few other instances. For example, when a victim in a homicide case makes a statement concerning the manner in which death-threatening injuries were received and who caused the injuries, older rules indicate that the **dying declarations** are available only in prosecutions for the homicide. However, many revised state evidence

Dying declarations Hearsay evidence of what a person said when he or she was aware that his or her death was imminent that must relate to the way the declarant received final injuries.

---

40 REV. CODE WASH. (ARCW) § 10.58.010, Rules – Generally. (2013).

41 FED. R. EVID. 101(a).

42 *See* Miranda v. Arizona, 384 U.S. 436, 1966 U.S. Lexis 2817 (1966) and Melendez-Diaz v. Massachusetts, 557 U.S. 305, 129 S. Ct. 2527, 174 L. Ed. 2d 314, 2009 U.S. Lexis 4734 (2009).

43 *See* Mapp v. Ohio, 367 U.S. 643, 1961 U.S. Lexis 812 (1961).

44 *See* Arizona v. Fulminante, 499 U.S. 279, 111 S. Ct. 1246, 113 L. Ed. 2d 302, 1991 U.S. Lexis 1854 (1991).

45 Apprendi v. New Jersey, 530 U.S. 466 at 483, 120 S. Ct. 2348, 2359, 147 L. Ed. 2d 435, 450, 2000 U.S. Lexis 4304 (2000).

codes, especially those based on the Federal Rules of Evidence, generally do not require that the victim actually die before the evidence is admissible, and many states allow the declaration to be admitted in civil cases. Consistent with this view, one state provides that "[i[n a prosecution for homicide or in a civil action or proceeding, a statement made by a declarant, while believing that his or her death was imminent, concerning the cause or circumstances of what the declarant believed to be his or her impending death" may be admitted into evidence.[46] The doctor–patient privilege operates differently in many jurisdictions depending on whether the case is civil or criminal and, to some degree, whether the need for the evidence is great.[47]

Although many state civil juries operate with fewer than 12 jurors, most state criminal cases involve the use of 12 jurors and require unanimous verdicts. Although the degree of proof is higher in criminal cases, except for some **affirmative defenses,**[48] the accused must generally be found guilty by all 12 members of the jury. In civil cases, however, a unanimous decision may not be required. Logic suggests that it should be easier to obtain a money judgment against a defendant in a civil case than to send a defendant to jail or prison in a criminal case. For example, a defendant who has been acquitted in a criminal assault prosecution may be found liable for a monetary judgment in a subsequent civil case brought by the original victim based on the conduct that was the subject of the criminal case.

Affirmative defenses A defendant's response to a criminal charge that would relieve the defendant of guilt for the charged offense by proving a legally sufficient reason for having done the charged act or by proving a legally sufficient reason for doing the act.

The distinction between criminal evidence and civil evidence may be slight when defining the rules, but from a practical standpoint, there is a great deal of difference. While a jury may accept weak evidence in determining the rights of parties in a civil case, the members of the jury are less likely to accept such evidence when life or liberty is at issue. To the prosecutor, this means that evidence must be presented that will be given great weight by the jury, and sufficient evidence must be presented in court to overcome any **reasonable doubt** on the part of the jury or judge. In a criminal case, the judge has a duty to protect the rights of the defendant. Circumstances or conduct

Reasonable doubt A reasonable doubt is an actual and substantial doubt arising from the evidence.

46 OHIO EVID. R. 804(B)(2) Hearsay exceptions; Declarant unavailable. (2013).

47 *See* OHIO REV. CODE ANN. § 2317.02 (2013). *See also* WYO. STAT. § 1-12-101 (2013).

48 *See* Johnson v. Louisiana, 406 U.S. 356 (1972), which upheld a conviction in a criminal case in which the state statute provided that 9 of 12 jurors may find the defendant guilty. *But see* Burch v. Louisiana, 441 U.S. 130 (1979), which held that a state defendant who has been placed on trial for a nonpetty offense and is subsequently convicted by a nonunanimous six-person jury has been denied his right to a trial by jury.

that may call a judge's impartiality into question may result in an appellate court reversing a conviction.[49]

§ 2.6 Pretrial Flow of Evidence

Although laypersons unconnected to the criminal justice process often provide valuable evidence in court, police officers and investigators are more frequently responsible for discovering, evaluating, protecting, analyzing, and presenting evidence. If the officer does not present the evidence him- or herself, that officer is still primarily responsible for guiding the flow of evidence, at least until the indictment or information stage.

The officer must develop and preserve the evidence in such a way as to maximize the chances that the evidence will be admitted in court. For example, if an officer does not record the names and addresses of witnesses to a crime at the beginning of an investigation, this information may be lost forever. The techniques of sound criminal investigation are outside the scope of this text, but it bears repeating that the failure to properly gather, store, and preserve the available evidence affects all subsequent proceedings.

The Federal Rules of Criminal Procedure and the rules of criminal procedure of all states require an officer making a warrantless arrest to take the arrestee before the nearest available judicial official without unnecessary delay.[50] In presenting evidence at the first appearance of an arrestee, the prosecutor and police are not required to present sufficient evidence to convict, but must produce sufficient evidence for the judge or magistrate to determine whether there is probable cause[51] to believe that an offense has been committed, as well as probable cause that the accused committed the offense.[52]

Following a review of the evidence, if the judicial official determines that there is probable cause to hold the arrestee for further proceedings or to have the case presented to a grand jury in a felony case, law enforcement officials must make available all of the evidence that they have collected, together with names and pertinent information, to the prosecutor. Although the prosecutor may and should enter into the case at an earlier time, this is usually the step where the prosecutor takes charge and makes a decision concerning how to proceed.

---

49 State v. Tody, 2009 Wisc. Lexis 21 (2009). Appellate court reversed a conviction when the judge's mother sat as a juror in the judge's court.

50 *See* County of Riverside v. McLaughlin, 500 U.S. 44 (1991); *see also* FED. R. CRIM. P.5.

51 Probable cause has been shown "[i]f the facts and circumstances before the officer are such as to warrant a man of prudence and caution in believing that the offense has been committed, it is sufficient." Carroll v. United States, 267 U.S. 132, 161, 1925 U.S. Lexis 361 (1925).

52 *See* Chapter 16 for a discussion of evidence needed to determine probable cause for the issuance of a search warrant.

In many jurisdictions, in order to move a serious case toward trial, the prosecutor must present the evidence to a grand jury in order to procure an indictment. In the federal arena and in states that require the use of a grand jury, with the consent of the arrested defendant, the prosecution may be initiated with the use of an information. In many states, prosecutors do not have to obtain a grand jury indictment, but may file an information against the defendant. The prosecution must have sufficient evidence to demonstrate probable cause for a grand jury, and in the case of using an information, the prosecutor must believe that the evidence indicates the existence of probable cause. One might argue—and with justification—that the process of determining probable cause before a judge or magistrate and then presenting the evidence to a grand jury for a probable cause determination seems redundant. Following a law enforcement determination of probable cause, a judicial determination is required to hold a suspect further. In such an instance, at a minimum, a hearing is required, during which the judge makes the initial judicial determination of probable cause. At this point, a grand jury indictment should be procured or, in states using an information process, the case may proceed toward trial based on the prosecutor's filing of the information.

The prosecutor controls the flow of evidence that is presented to the grand jury by calling police officers and investigators as witnesses and any eyewitnesses to offer testimony before the grand jury. Sufficient evidence must be presented to a grand jury that will allow it to conclude that probable cause exists to believe a particular person has committed a particular crime, but in virtually all United States jurisdictions, the formal evidence rules are not followed when presenting evidence to the grand jury.[53] However, sufficient admissible evidence must be presented to convince the grand jury (usually 12 to 23 persons by a simple majority vote) that an offense against the state or the federal government has been committed by the person accused.

In some states, where neither the state constitution nor state law requires a grand jury indictment, process by way of information can substitute for the grand jury hearing. The prosecutor, using the evidence presented by officers and other witnesses, evaluates the evidence to determine whether probable cause exists. Where probable cause appears and where the prosecutor concludes that a prosecutable case exists, the prosecutor makes the decision to prepare the information, files it with the proper court, and serves notice to the accused of the specific charge.

Following the return of the indictment or the preparation of the information, the defendant appears personally before the judge. In federal courts, the rules of evidence are not applied at "a preliminary examination in a criminal case"[54] except for the rules involving privileges. Here, the defendant is arraigned (informed of the charges against him or her), defense counsel may be appointed, and the defendant may enter a plea. Because probable cause is not an issue to be proved at arraignment following a grand jury indictment, there is no need for the judge to admit or evaluate evidence except when the case originated with the filing of an information. However, at the conclusion

---

[53] *See* FED. R. EVID. 1101(d).

[54] *Id.*

of the arraignment, the judge may suggest a time for a preliminary hearing or set a date to hear pretrial motions.

At the pretrial hearing, the defense and the prosecution may present some evidence concerning pretrial motions. Where admission of evidence at trial depends on the manner in which the evidence was seized, both sides will normally present evidence to support their respective positions. Police officers and the defendant may offer evidence of the facts surrounding the search and seizure of evidence, so that the judge can determine the legality of the procedure and rule on the trial admissibility of the evidence. Often, the outcome of the suppression hearing determines the fate of both the accused and of the prosecution's case. If, for example, the judge determines that the police obtained a confession illegally or that they unconstitutionally seized illegal drugs in the possession of the arrestee, the prosecutor may decide to drop the charge when the judge suppresses the evidence. Conversely, if the judge rules against the defendant at the suppression hearing, the defendant's attorney may advise him or her to consider a negotiated plea or enter a guilty plea. If there are no more pretrial motions or legal issues to be resolved, the case is ready for trial.

§ 2.7 Use of Evidence at the Trial

Even before the trial, the evidence acquired by the police officer, the prosecutor, or by other means has been evaluated several times: when determining to make an arrest, deciding to take the case by the prosecutor, and presenting the evidence to a grand jury or a judge. Assuming that there has been sufficient evidence to indict the defendant, the case eventually comes before the court and the jury at the trial. By this time, there is a good possibility that the court has found some evidence to be inadmissible. If so, the prosecutor must determine whether there is still enough admissible, relevant evidence to meet the burden of proof beyond a reasonable doubt.

In addition to the parties on each side, the court is made up of the judge, jury, witnesses, prosecutor, and defense attorney.[55] In early English proceedings, the jurors were the only witnesses and were called upon by the judge to give information concerning the case because they had knowledge of the facts. However, the modern juror ideally should have no or limited knowledge of the case, and certainly, the juror should not have sufficient evidence to be called as a witness. The jury determines what facts have been proved after it has heard the evidence presented by the witnesses, evaluated the facts judicially noticed by the judge, and considered the inferences and presumptions, as instructed by the court.

The trial judge has the duty, upon proper objection, to determine whether a particular item of evidence is relevant, material, and competent, and whether the item should be admitted or excluded from jury consideration. Generally, a judge may ask

---

[55] State v. Perkins, 130 W. Va. 708, 45 S.E.2d 17 (1947). In Chapter 4, the procedure for introducing and considering evidence at trial is presented in more detail.

questions of a witness, but the judge must be careful not to appear to favor one party over the other.[56] At the close of the case, when all the evidence has been heard, the trial judge's duty is to instruct the jury concerning the law applicable to the case. In a bench trial (without a jury), the judge continues to make evidentiary rulings and takes on the additional role of the trier of fact in determining guilt or innocence.

The prosecutor has the responsibility to evaluate all evidence presented to him or her, to determine the legality of the evidence, to arrange the evidence in sequence so that it is best suited to achieve the objective, to identify the witnesses for the prosecution, to examine the witnesses, and to cross-examine defense witnesses.

Finally, the defense attorney is responsible for seeking evidence with which to present a defense for the accused. The defense attorney also arranges the evidence in the sequence most likely (in his or her opinion) to convey the defendant's legal position in a positive light to the finders of fact. Defense counsel has the opportunity to introduce, examine, and cross-examine witnesses and to introduce evidence through the defense witnesses. Even in a case that from the beginning appears to be hopeless, the defendant has the right to "put the prosecution to its proof" by pleading not guilty and going to trial.

With respect to the sentencing phase of a criminal trial, the rules of evidence generally have no application, except those rules dealing with privileges,[57] so that other evidence may be introduced by either the defense or by the prosecution that could not have been used at a trial.

§ 2.8 Consideration of Evidence on Appeal

If the jury or the judge acquits the defendant at the trial, the state has no right to appeal the acquittal in a way that would affect any rights of the defendant.[58] The prohibition against double jeopardy mandates this result. If, however, the defendant is convicted, he or she may appeal the conviction, and the appellate court may examine what occurred in the trial court and may reverse the conviction, with or without granting the state the opportunity to retry the defendant. As a general rule, the presumption on appeal is in favor of the decision,[59] and, therefore, an appellate court will uphold the guilty verdict unless there were clear legal errors that could have affected substantial rights of the defendant or the evidence was insufficient to meet the government's burden of proof. However, if evidence has been wrongly admitted or improperly excluded in a manner that may have affected the outcome of the trial, an appellate court will often reverse the conviction with directions to retry the case. When a defendant succeeds in

---

56 *See* Craft v. State, 274 Ga. App. 410, 2005 Ga. App. Lexis 778 (2005). *See* case in Part II.

57 State v. Dunlap, 313 P.3d 1, 31, 2013 Ida. LEXIS 262 (2013).

58 *See* Benton v. Maryland, 395 U.S. 784, 1969 U.S. Lexis 1167 (1969).

59 People v. Davis, 184 Cal. App. 4th 305, 311, 108 Cal. Rptr. 3d 536, 541, 2010 Cal. App. Lexis 603 (2010).

having a conviction overturned on appeal, the state may appeal to a higher appellate court in an effort to overturn the lower appellate court and have the trial verdict reinstated. Changes in the application of the rules of evidence happen gradually and may result in different outcomes, as newer cases reach appellate courts. For example, in *Trammel v. United States*, the Supreme Court approved a change in the old rule that a spouse could not testify against another spouse without that spouse's consent.[60] When the Court revisited the logic behind the rule that a defendant spouse could prevent the other's adverse testimony, it approved the new interpretation offered by the trial court.

§ 2.9 Use of Evidence at the Probation Hearing

Following a verdict of guilt by the trier of fact, the judge may make additional use of evidence in determining whether the defendant will be placed on probation or incarcerated or whether some other disposition is appropriate. In many jurisdictions, a probation/parole officer will conduct an investigation and prepare a presentence report for the judge's use. The rules of evidence that exclude the use of some evidence at the trial do not apply to the use of the presentence reports by the judges and, in federal courts, do not apply to the "granting or revoking probation or supervised release."[61] Although this presentence report should be factual, evidence such as hearsay evidence is not excluded from the report. However, it is obvious that this evidence is available only for determining the disposition of the person who has been convicted of a crime and that it cannot be used in determining guilt or innocence. Where a person has been granted probation that may have to be revoked, similar evidentiary policies control the use of evidence at a revocation hearing. When revoking federal probation, the rules of evidence, except those governing privileges, have no application.[62]

While in most states the probation report or presentence investigation report is confidential and available only to the judge, some jurisdictions require that the presentence report be made available for inspection by the offender or by the defense attorney.[63]

§ 2.10 Use of Evidence When Considering Parole

State parole boards consider evidence when determining whether a person who has served time in an institution merits conditional release under the supervision of a parole officer. After making a complete investigation in the field, a parole officer prepares a

---

60 Trammel v. United States, 445 U.S. 40, 1980 U.S. Lexis 84 (1980). *See* case in Part II.

61 *See* FED. R. EVID. 1101(d).

62 United States v. Aspinall, 389 F.3d 332, 344, 2004 U.S. App. Lexis 23954 (2d Cir. 2004), and FED. R. EVID. 1101(d)(3).

63 *See* CARLSON, CRIMINAL JUSTICE PROCEDURE (8th ed. 2013).

report that covers the personal position of the convict and his or her history while in custody, among other factors. Once a person has been granted parole, the individual must meet the conditions of release. When the parolee fails to adhere to the required conditions, the conditional freedom may be revoked. In one case, a parolee committed a new crime of attempted rape, violating a condition of parole that he avoid committing any new crimes, and his parole was revoked, returning him to custody.[64] The court rejected his **due process** argument that the people testifying against him at his revocation hearing did not have first-hand knowledge of his new criminal activity. Given that parole revocation hearings are not considered criminal prosecutions, the rules of evidence do not apply at those types of hearings[65] or reports,[66] and the information compiled serves as important evidence that assists a parole board.

> **Due process** A flexible term for the compliance with the fundamental rules for fair and orderly legal proceedings.

§ 2.11 Summary

In putting together a prosecutable criminal case, the prosecution needs to evaluate all the evidence in the case, whether it is favorable or unfavorable, and conclude whether a prosecutable case exists. In many cases there will be direct evidence that requires no inference or presumption, and there will be circumstantial evidence that requires a trier of fact to make deductions or inferences from that evidence. Other subcategories of evidence, such as real, corroborative, or documentary evidence may help the prosecutor devise a strategy to produce a winning case. Not all evidence that might help procure a guilty verdict will be admitted because it may not have relevance; indeed, even clearly relevant evidence may be excluded from trial evidence. The rules for excluding evidence are generally justified on the grounds that they prevent waste of time and confusion, protect certain interests and relationships, avoid undue and unfair prejudice to the accused, prevent the jury from considering unreliable evidence, and enforce constitutional rights of defendants.

Generally, there is little distinction between the rules of criminal evidence and rules of civil evidence. However, because the prosecution must prove the accused guilty beyond a reasonable doubt and because the jury verdict usually must be unanimous, a higher degree of evidence is required for proof of guilt in a criminal case.

The importance of recognizing, protecting, preserving, and evaluating evidence begins at the time that the crime is committed. Even prior to trial, the evidence plays a very important part in determining whether sufficient grounds exist for the judicial

---

64 Curtis v. Chester, 626 F.3d 540, 544, 2010 U.S. App. Lexis 24172 (10th Cir. 2010).

65 State v. Abd-Rahmaan, 154 Wash. 2d 280, 111 P.3d 1157, 2005 Wash. Lexis 461 (2005). *See* this case in Part II. *See also* Peters v. State, 984 So. 2d 1227, 2008 Fla. Lexis 757 (Fla. 2008).

66 Simpson v. Florida Parole Commission, 2006 U.S. Dist. Lexis 18068 (2006).

official to bind the defendant over to the grand jury and for the grand jury to determine whether sufficient evidence exists for an indictment. In some jurisdictions, where the filing of an information may be substituted for an indictment, the prosecutor must evaluate the evidence to determine whether a prosecutable case exists.

The evidence has been filtered, challenged, and evaluated prior to the time that the trial begins, but it is at the trial that evidence is of greatest importance. In a criminal case, the prosecution must introduce sufficient evidence that, taken together with facts judicially noticed, and legal presumptions and inferences, will justify the fact finders in declaring the defendant guilty beyond a reasonable doubt. At the trial, the judge, jury, witnesses, prosecutor, and defense attorney are all concerned with the admissibility and weight of evidence.

Upon appeal, the reviewing courts consider whether the evidence that was admitted proved sufficient for a conviction. Appellate courts do not reweigh the evidence, but generally confine reviews to matters of law. During the appellate process, all the presumptions are in favor of upholding the verdict because the presumption of innocence no longer exists. If evidence has been admitted or excluded in a way that affects the substantial rights of the defendant, the reviewing court will order a new trial. The prosecution may appeal an intermediate court decision to a higher court with hopes of having the original verdict reinstated.

Following a conviction, evidence that was inadmissible at trial, as well as legally acquired evidence, may be considered by the judge to determine whether a convicted defendant should be placed on probation. This evidence may also influence the judge in determining the conditions on which probation might be granted. In gathering information for a court hearing concerning the granting of probation, the probation officer may present the court with evidence that could not have been admitted at a trial because the rules of evidence do not strictly apply when considering the possibility of granting probation. If probation, once granted, must later be revoked, the rules of evidence do not limit the evidence that the judge may consider because traditional rules of evidence are not applied at these hearings.

Finally, in jurisdictions that still allow early release on parole, evidence is again considered by the parole board in making a determination concerning whether the person who has served time in institutional custody should be granted early release. Once again, the evidence considered by the board need not meet the rules of evidence followed by a court in a trial on the merits. According to the Supreme Court of the United States, the federal exclusionary rule, which helps enforce the Fourth Amendment, does not prohibit a state parole board's use of evidence seized in violation of a parolee's rights.[67]

In the chapters that follow, the many general admissibility tests and special tests for the use of evidence are discussed more comprehensively.

---

[67] Pennsylvania Board of Probation and Parole v. Scott, 524 U.S. 357, 1998 U.S. Lexis 4037 (1998). *And see* O'Neal v. Renico, 2005 U.S. Dist. Lexis 31045 (E.D. Mich. 2005).

CHAPTER TWO: QUESTIONS AND REVIEW EXERCISES

1. Define direct evidence and circumstantial evidence. Give an example of each type of evidence.
2. What is documentary evidence? What are three examples of modern methods of storing documentary evidence?
3. Prima facie evidence may allow a conviction, if no contrary evidence is produced by the defendant. Construct a fact pattern of evidence that could be called prima facie evidence.
4. Cumulative evidence has been defined as the kind of evidence that proves what has already been established, and may not be admissible in some situations. Offer a fact situation that demonstrates cumulative evidence that should be excluded from admission.
5. Closely related to cumulative evidence is evidence that is described as corroborative evidence. What is corroborative evidence? Too much corroborative evidence might be called cumulative evidence. Construct a fact pattern that begins as demonstrative corroborative evidence and, arguably, becomes cumulative evidence.
6. Hearsay evidence is a statement, other than one made by the declarant/witness while testifying at the trial or hearing, offered in evidence to prove the truth of the matter asserted and generally is not admissible. Give one example of evidence that is clearly hearsay in nature.
7. What are some of the reasons why rules of evidence are necessary? Do they always help in the search for the truth? Why or why not?
8. When courts exclude evidence, they may do so for broad constitutional reasons, for interests of fairness, to avoid needless waste of time, and to protect some relationships, among other reasons. Do these exclusions assist in finding the truth or do they have the effect of hiding the true facts? Explain.
9. Evidence plays a role during the pretrial stage. For what purposes may evidence be used during the pretrial stage of a criminal prosecution? At what times and under what circumstances would a court consider pretrial evidence?
10. What is the role of the trial judge with respect to evidence during the trial?
11. How may a judge use evidence that may have been excluded at trial in determining sentencing?

Proof by Evidence and Substitutes

Burden of Proof

3

The term "burden of proof" imports the duty of ultimately establishing any given proposition. This phrase marks the peculiar duty of him who has the risk of any given proposition on which the parties are at issue, who will lose the case if he does not make this proposition out, when all has been said and done.

Thayer, Evidence (1898)

Chapter Contents

KEY TERMS AND CONCEPTS

Affirmative Defense
Alibi
Beyond a Reasonable Doubt
Burden of Going Forward
Burden of Persuasion
Burden of Proof
Clear and Convincing Evidence
Insanity Defense
Preponderance of the Evidence
Self-defense
Sufficiency of the Evidence

§ 3.1 Introduction

In approaching the study of evidence logically and progressively, one might start by considering the task of producing evidence with which to prove the truth of a given proposition. No attorney takes a civil or criminal case to court unless there is a good chance that the level of proof is sufficient to establish the ultimate proposition. In a criminal case, the state has the burden of proving the guilt of the accused beyond a reasonable doubt. Therefore, the "burden of proof" is on the prosecution throughout the trial, and this burden never shifts. The term denotes the duty to establish the truth of the charge against the accused. Ascertaining the truth then becomes an important, if not the most important, objective of the court and jury.

In the criminal justice process, it is necessary that those involved understand the considerations and obligations of the parties in presenting sufficient evidence, as well as the consequences of failing to do so. Failure on the part of the prosecution to introduce sufficient evidence or failure to properly explain the evidence will make it impossible for the jury (or judge, when the case is tried without a jury) to determine the truth and thus will result in a miscarriage of justice. Therefore, a thorough knowledge of the concept of burden of proof is an essential starting point on which to build an understanding of the rules of evidence.

In a civil case, the party who has the burden of establishing the truth of a given proposition is a private individual, corporation, or, in some instances, a governmental unit. In a criminal case, however, the prosecution has the responsibility of establishing the truth of the charges stated in the indictment or information. The rule that assigns to the states the burden of proving the guilt of the accused beyond a reasonable doubt in criminal cases does not apply in civil actions. Therefore, the burden of proof becomes even more important when considering criminal cases than when considering civil cases.

In a criminal case, the investigator must compile evidence sufficient to convince the jury that the accused is guilty not only by a "preponderance of the evidence," but also "beyond a reasonable doubt"—that is, the prosecution or the state has the burden of proving the existence of every element of the crime charged.

Recognizing this requirement, the defense will likely deliver an attack against the weak links in the chain because the defense knows that, if even one of the elements is not proved beyond a reasonable doubt, there can be no conviction on that specific charge.

Because there has been some confusion concerning the term burden of proof, the pertinent terms are comprehensively defined and explained in the following sections of this chapter. Other sections of the chapter discuss the obligation of the prosecution to prove guilt and the obligation of the accused to produce evidence in a criminal trial.

In Chapters 4–6, rules relating to the process for establishing or ascertaining truth at the trial are defined, explained, and considered.

§ 3.2 Definitions and Distinctions

A statement of what the burden of proof is not makes it easier to frame a positive definition. First, the burden of proof does not relate to the number of witnesses, but rather to the merit and weight of the evidence produced—whether by one or many witnesses. Second, the fact that evidence is admissible in conformity with the general principles regarding admissibility, **relevancy,** materiality, and **competency** does not necessarily mean that it will be given enough weight to sustain the burden of proof. The testimony of one well-prepared, reliable witness or evidence of a documentary or real nature may result in better proof than testimony from a large number of witnesses whose credibility is suspect.

Generally, the phrase *burden of proof* denotes the duty of establishing the truth of a given proposition or issue. Because the term has been used somewhat loosely by some courts, the definition of burden of proof as used in law requires further explanation. To avoid confusion, the phrases **burden of going forward** and **burden of persuasion** are also defined.

Relevancy The connection between a fact tendered in evidence and the issue to be proved.

Competency The legal fitness or capacity of a witness to testify in the trial of a case that requires an oath, original perception, recollection, and an ability to communicate.

Burden of going forward The obligation resting upon a party to produce *prima facie* evidence on a particular issue.

Burden of persuasion The burden of persuading the factfinder of the truth of the evidence produced by one side or the other.

A. Burden of Proof

This term is defined as "[a] party's duty to prove a disputed assertion or charge."[1] The burden of proof may also be defined as the duty upon one party to establish the truth of an issue that is important to the case by the quantum of evidence demanded by law. *Black's Law Dictionary* notes that "[t]he burden of proof includes both the burden of persuasion and the burden of production."[2] The burden of persuasion means that one party must convince the judge or jury to see the facts in a manner that favors the party who introduced the evidence, while the burden of production means that the party has a duty to introduce evidence intended to prove a particular point or issue. In a criminal case, the burden of proof means that the prosecution has the duty of proving the guilt of the accused beyond a reasonable doubt. This duty or burden never shifts during the course of the trial, but remains with the prosecution throughout the trial. The emphasis is on the ultimate result rather than on individual issues or questions within the case.

B. Burden of Going Forward

At the start of a criminal trial, the prosecution has the obligation to introduce evidence that will move toward meeting the burden of proof. The burden of going forward has been defined as "[a] party's duty to introduce enough evidence on an issue to have the issue decided by the fact finder, rather than decided against the party. . .."[3] This is a way of saying that the government possesses the initial burden of going forward by initiating its presentation of evidence. In a sense, at the beginning of the legal contest, the government begins the case and must start by introducing evidence that will build toward and eventually reach the level of proof beyond a reasonable doubt. If the prosecution meets the burden of going forward with the evidence and survives a defendant's request for a directed verdict, the burden of going forward with the evidence shifts to the defense, which must begin building its case.

Demonstrative of the principle that the burden of going forward was met is a case in which the defendant had been accused of the rape of a child. The prosecution, during its **case-in-chief**, had introduced evidence that the defendant had blood on his clothes, the child had blood in her diaper, the victim had torn flesh in the private area, and technicians found the defendant's **DNA** profile

Case-in-chief Proof that a party primarily relies upon in order to support his claim or defense; the major presentation of evidence for either the defense or the prosecution.

DNA Deoxyribonucleic acid. A long, threadlike chain of molecules found in the nucleus of virtually every cell of the body.

---

[1] BLACK'S LAW DICTIONARY 223 (9th ed. 2009).

[2] *Id.*

[3] BLACK'S LAW DICTIONARY 223 (9th ed. 2009).

on a diaper. At the close of the prosecution's case, the defendant requested a directed verdict of acquittal on the theory that the prosecution had failed to meet its burden of going forward with the evidence. The reviewing court upheld the trial court's denial of the motion because the evidence, both circumstantial and direct, was sufficient for the conviction of child rape if a jury would choose to believe the evidence.[4] If the defendant, in meeting the burden of going forward with the evidence, succeeds in creating a reasonable doubt in the prosecution's case, the burden of going forward will shift to the prosecution at the close of the defendant's case-in-chief. In the case of a defendant who pleads an affirmative defense such as **alibi**, **self-defense**, mistake of fact, insanity, or another legal theory, the burden of going forward with the evidence supporting the defense initially rests on the defendant.

Alibi A defense strategy where the party accused, in order to prove that he or she could not have committed the crime with which he or she is charged, offers evidence that he or she was in a different place at the time the offense was committed and otherwise had nothing to do with the crime.

Self-defense The protection of one's person and property from injury.

Similarly, in a case involving a felon in possession of a firearm,[5] the defendant had the burden of going forward with evidence that he had been pardoned or had otherwise had his right to bear firearms restored. If the defendant succeeds in going forward with evidence sufficient to meet any burden of proof for that affirmative defense, the burden of going forward shifts to the prosecution to negate the defendant's proof of the defense. This is often expressed by the term burden of evidence.[6]

C. Burden of Persuasion

The burden of persuasion refers only to the burden of convincing the factfinder of the collective truth of evidence produced by one side or the other. When the burden of persuasion has been met, the attorney will be able to refer to the evidence during closing arguments to assist the jury in understanding why his or her party should prevail and to demonstrate that his or her client's version is the truth.

When the term burden of proof is used in the following sections, the definition as stated in subsection A, *supra*, is applied.

In meeting the burden of proof, the amount of evidence varies depending on whether the case is criminal or civil and whether the case involves an affirmative defense. Generally, in a civil case, the party who initiated the lawsuit possesses the duty of establishing the truth of specific propositions and must do so by a preponderance of

---

4 Terry v. State, 2006 Ark. Lexis 326 (Ark. 2006).

5 State v. Kelly, 210 Ariz. 460, 112 P.3d 682, 2005 Ariz. App. Lexis 70 (Ariz. 2005).

6 *Id.* at 464 and 686.

the evidence. However, there are some issues in civil cases that must be proved by higher degrees of proof—clear and convincing or beyond a reasonable doubt.

For example, in a civil case in which a state wants to keep a mentally ill person in custody following the end of a criminal sentence, the burden of proof required in order to meet minimal due process requirements must be greater than a preponderance of the evidence that an offender remains a dangerous person.[7] Minnesota permits sexually dangerous predators to be committed to civil custody beyond a prison term when there was **clear and convincing evidence** that the subject had demonstrated a "habitual course of misconduct in sexual matters and an utter lack of power to control sexual impulses."[8] Viewing matters a bit differently, Kansas chose to use the criminal burden of proof in civil cases in which it desired to commit dangerous pedophiles to civil custody beyond their criminal sentences.[9] The Kansas statute committing sexually violent predators uses the same burden of proof that the prosecution has in proving guilt in criminal cases—beyond a reasonable doubt.[10] These three degrees of proof are discussed and distinguished in the following sections.

> **Clear and convincing evidence** A flexible term concerning the degree of proof required for certain issues in some civil cases. It is less than the degree required in criminal cases, but more than required in the ordinary civil action.

§ 3.3 Preponderance of the Evidence

The plaintiff in a civil case possesses the burden of proof, which requires that the truth of the plaintiff's claim be established by a fair preponderance of the credible evidence when considered with the defendant's evidence. The preponderance standard means by the greater weight of evidence and has been stated to be anything more than 50 percent of the believable evidence, although a mathematical model often does not provide a precise analogy. The concept of preponderance of the evidence does not mean the greater number of witnesses or the greater length of time taken by either side. The phrase preponderance of the evidence refers to the quality of the evidence; that is, its ability to convince and the weight and the effect it has on the jurors' minds.

In order for the civil plaintiff to prevail, the evidence that supports the claim must appear to the jury at least slightly more believable than the evidence presented by the opposing party. If the evidence presented by the plaintiff fails to be more believable than the defendant's evidence, or if the evidence from both sides weighs so evenly that the jurors are unable to say that there is a preponderance on the plaintiff's side, the jury

7 Addington v. Texas, 411 U.S., 418, 432, 1979 U.S. Lexis 93 (1979).

8 In re Civil Commitment of Barber, 2005 Minn. Lexis 355 (Minn. 2005).

9 In re Care and Treatment of Ward, 131 P.3d 540, 547, 2006 Kan. App. Lexis 296 (Kan. 2006).

10 Kohlsaat v. Parkersburg & Marietta Sand Co., 266 F. 283 (4th Cir. 1920) and In re Winship, 397 U.S. 358 (1970) for proof beyond a reasonable doubt as a federal constitutional requirement.

must resolve the question in favor of the defendant. Because the plaintiff has the burden of proof by a preponderance of evidence in civil cases, a failure to meet the burden means that the opposing party prevails due to a failure of proof.

Some civil cases that use the preponderance standard may seem more like criminal cases in some contexts. For example, in California, when an individual is declared to be a sexually violent predator and, as a result, held civilly after the completion of his or her prison term, the state allows that person to petition for unconditional release. The burden of proof by a preponderance of evidence has been placed on the civil detainee to prove that he or she is no longer dangerous and is entitled to release from postconviction civil confinement.[11] The appellate court found no violation of any constitutional right in requiring an alleged sexually violent petitioner to bear the burden of demonstrating his fitness for release.

Although the preponderance of the evidence standard finds primary application in civil cases, some criminal cases use the standard for different purposes. In a California case in which the defendant pled legal insanity, the burden of persuasion for the defendant to prove insanity was only proof by a preponderance of the evidence, because insanity was not considered an element of the crime. According to the California reviewing court, the civil burden was appropriate even though the defendant argued that the prosecution should have to prove his sanity beyond a reasonable doubt.[12] In Arizona, when a defendant has introduced some evidence supporting a statute of limitations defense, the prosecution shoulders the burden of disproving the validity of the statute of limitations defense by the standard of a preponderance of the evidence that the prosecution is not time barred.[13] In the death penalty phase of a capital case, North Carolina permitted the defendant to bring for jury consideration any evidence of mitigation that had been proved by the defendant by a preponderance of the evidence. This creates a reduced standard that a convicted defendant might more easily meet in avoiding the death penalty.[14] Similarly, in Ohio, to prevail using the defense of insanity or any other affirmative defense, a defendant has the "burden of going forward with the evidence of an affirmative defense, and the burden of proof, by a preponderance of the evidence."[15] In approving the use of the preponderance standard for a defendant's burden in an insanity defense, the Supreme Court in Patterson v. New York noted that:

> [O]nce the facts constituting a crime are established beyond a reasonable doubt, based on all the evidence, including the evidence of the defendant's mental state, the State may refuse to sustain the affirmative defense of insanity unless demonstrated by a preponderance of the evidence.[16]

---

11 *See* People v. Force, 170 Cal. App. 4th 797, 2009 Cal. App. Lexis 85 (Cal. 2009).

12 People v. Farris, 130 Cal. App. 4th 773, 780 30 Cal. Rptr. 3d 426, 430, 2005 Cal. App. Lexis 1017 (2005).

13 *See* State v. Aguilar, 218 Ariz. 25, 178 P.3d 497, 2008 Ariz. App. Lexis 44 (Ariz. 2008).

14 State v. McNeill, 360 N.C. 231, 249, 624 S.E.2d 329, 341, 2006 N.C. Lexis 1 (2006).

15 OHIO REV. CODE ANN. § 2901.05 (2013). *See* State v. Hancock, 108 Ohio St. 3d 57, 62, 2006 Ohio 160, 840 N.E.2d 1032, 1043, 2006 Ohio Lexis 215 (2006).

16 Patterson v. New York, 432 U.S. 197, 206 (1977).

In essence, civil cases primarily use the preponderance of the evidence standard for decision-making purposes, but in a variety of contexts, the civil standard has application in criminal cases, especially concerning affirmative defenses.

§ 3.4 Clear and Convincing Evidence

While the level of proof required for civil cases has been described as proof by a preponderance (greater weight) of the evidence, some aspects of civil litigation dictate a greater level of proof known as clear and convincing evidence. As one court noted, "to be clear and convincing, is somewhere between the rule in ordinary civil cases and the requirement of criminal procedure—that is, it must be more than a mere preponderance but not beyond a reasonable doubt."[17]

Clear and convincing evidence is the degree of proof that "will produce in the mind of the trier of facts a firm belief or conviction as to the allegations sought to be established. It is intermediate, being more than a mere preponderance, but not to the extent of such certainty as is required beyond a reasonable doubt as in criminal cases."[18] Another way of describing the clear and convincing standard suggests that the level of proof should be evidence that:

> [W]hen weighed against evidence in opposition, will produce in the mind of the trier of fact a firm conviction as to each essential element of the claim and a high probability as to the correctness of the conclusion. Proof by clear and convincing evidence requires a level of proof greater than a preponderance of the evidence or the substantial weight of the evidence, but less than beyond a reasonable doubt.[19]

In determining that the clear and convincing standard of proof defies precise definition, a Tennessee court noted that

> While it is more exacting than the preponderance of the evidence standard, it does not require such certainty as the beyond a reasonable doubt standard. Clear and convincing evidence eliminates any serious or substantial doubt concerning the correctness of the conclusions to be drawn from the evidence. It should produce in the fact-finder's mind a firm belief or conviction with regard to the truth of the allegations sought to be established.[20]

The use of the clear and convincing standard of proof was first applied to actions for fraud or deceit.[21] The rationale for employing a higher standard of proof in civil

---

17 In the Interest of B.D.-Y., a Child under the Age of 18, 286 Kan. 686, 693, 187 P.3d 594, 599, 2008 Kan. Lexis 343 (2008).

18 State v. West, 2008 Ohio 1391, 2008 Ohio App. Lexis 1210 (2008), quoting Cross v. Ledford, 161 Ohio St. 469, 120 N.E.2d 118 (1954).

19 CODE OF ALA. § 6-11-20(b)(2)(4) (2013).

20 Department of Children's Services v. K.B., 2008 Tenn. App. Lexis 122 (2008), quoting O'Daniel v. Messier 905 S.W.2d 182, 1995 Tenn. App. Lexis (1995).

21 Appellate Review in the Federal Courts of Findings Requiring More Than a Preponderance of the Evidence, 60 HARV. L. REV. 119 (1946).

cases in which fraud or criminal conduct has been alleged implicates other concerns. Alleged civil fraud or other wrongdoing suggests that more than money may be involved in a civil case where a defendant's reputation or freedom may be at risk. New Jersey and some other states use the clear and convincing standard to commit sexual offenders to civil custody when those offenders are determined to remain dangerous after their criminal sentence has been served.[22] Jurisdictions mandating that convicted sexual offenders register usually require that the state prove that the individual is subject to classification on a three-tier system by clear and convincing evidence.[23] In addition, state statutes permitting commitment of dangerous sexual predators to mental facilities following completed prison terms typically require the civil proceeding to use a heightened level of proof, such as clear and convincing evidence.[24]

In distinguishing the levels of proof, the Supreme Court of New Jersey noted that the state's rules of evidence set forth at least "three standards of proof: a preponderance of the evidence, clear and convincing evidence, and proof beyond a reasonable doubt."[25] The court mentioned that, as a general rule, the preponderance standard applies in civil cases in which the litigant must show that the desired inference is more likely than not to be true.[26] According to the court, the second standard, clear and convincing, denotes a higher standard than proof by a preponderance and less than proof beyond a reasonable doubt.[27] This second tier standard should produce in the mind of the finder of fact a firm belief concerning the facts sought to be proven.

Lawsuits involving significant interests beyond money, such as a suit to correct a mistake in a deed or other writing, disputes involving an oral contract to make a will or to establish the terms of a lost will, and disputes regarding the specific performance of an oral contract, frequently dictate that sufficient proof requires clear and convincing evidence. In some states, the termination of parental rights generally requires proof by clear and convincing evidence.[28] Some jurisdictions recognize that a person's reputation might be at risk in a defamation case or in a case terminating parental rights to a child and require the higher burden of proof of clear and convincing evidence in such cases.[29]

---

22 In the Matter of the Civil Commitment of W.X.C., 204 N.J. 179, 208, 8 A.3d 174, 191, 2010 N.J. Lexis 1213 (2010).

23 State v. Gross, 2010 Ohio 3727, 2010 Ohio App. Lexis 3173 (2010).

24 *See* In the Matter of John W. Morgan v. State, 2009 Mo. App. Lexis 8 (2009).

25 Liberty Mutual v. Land, 186 N.J. 163, 168, 892 A.2d 1240, 1243, 2006 N.J. Lexis 375 (2006).

26 *Id.*

27 *Id.*

28 State v. Sonya, 270 Neb. 870, 880, 708 N.W.2d 786, 795, 2006 Neb. Lexis 5 (2006). A higher standard of proof beyond a reasonable doubt is required for termination of parental rights for Indian children. *See* R.R.S. Neb. § 43-279.01 (2013).

29 *See* In the Matter of S.H., 2008 Tenn. App. Lexis 262 (2008). *See also* ALASKA STAT. § 47.10.088, Involuntary termination of parental rights and responsibilities (2013).

Following an assassination attempt on President Reagan in 1984, Congress strengthened the federal insanity defense by requiring federal criminal defendants to prove the affirmative defense of insanity by clear and convincing evidence.[30]

§ 3.5 Beyond a Reasonable Doubt

In criminal cases, where freedom or life itself may hang in the balance, the federal constitution has been interpreted to require the highest level of proof, known as proof beyond a reasonable doubt.[31] This demanding level of certainty requires that the prosecution prove that the accused is guilty by introducing strong and overwhelming evidence of guilt beyond a reasonable doubt. The proof presented by the prosecution must have sufficient believability and substance to rebut the strong constitutional presumption of innocence. In legal theory this means that each and every element of the offense charged in the indictment, as well as any aggravating circumstances that affect a sentence, must be proved beyond a reasonable doubt.[32] Otherwise, the accused generally must be acquitted of the charge.[33] The reality is that a jury considers all the evidence together and reaches a verdict without close judicial scrutiny concerning what the jury found on each and every element.

In 1970, the United States Supreme Court traced the history of the "beyond a reasonable doubt" requirement and concluded that this standard of proof is indispensable to command the respect and confidence of the community in applications of criminal law. In recognizing this constitutional requirement, the Court emphasized:

> Lest there remain any doubt about the constitutional stature of the reasonable-doubt standard, we explicitly hold that the Due Process Clause protects the accused against conviction except upon proof beyond a reasonable doubt of every fact necessary to constitute the crime with which he is charged.[34]

In some states, statute dictates the exact wording of the charge to the jury, requiring it to explain the criminal standard of proof. In other states, there is no requirement to

---

30 18 U.S.C. §§ 17, 4241–4247, and *see* § 3.11.

31 Clark v. Arizona, 548 U.S. 735, 2006 U.S. Lexis 5184 (2006), quoting In re Winship, 397 U.S. 358, 1970 U.S. Lexis 56 (1970).

32 *See* Ring v. Arizona, 536 U.S. 584, 2002 U.S. Lexis 4651 (2002) (Scalia, J., concurring).

33 An acquittal is not always required in federal courts where the error was harmless beyond a reasonable doubt. In Neder v. United States, 527 U.S. 1, 1999 U.S. Lexis 4007 (1999), the Court held that failure to include an element of the crime in the charge to the jury did not necessarily result in an unfair trial.

34 In re Winship, 397 U.S. 358, 90 S. Ct. 1068, 25 L. Ed. 2d 368, 1970 U.S. Lexis 56 (1970). *See* case in Part II. See also Clark v. Arizona, 548 U.S. 735, 2006 U.S. Lexis 5 (2006) in which the Court notes that all elements of criminal cases and juvenile adjudications that involve acts that would be crimes if committed by adults must be proved beyond a reasonable doubt.

explain the concept of proof beyond a reasonable doubt,[35] and some do not allow any instruction on reasonable doubt. However, where a state statute contains an appropriate jury instruction, and the court reads it to a jury, the instruction should be presented exactly as it appears in the statute. For example, the California Penal Code offers this definition of the concept of reasonable doubt:

> It is not a mere possible doubt; because everything relating to human affairs, and depending on moral evidence, is open to some possible or imaginary doubt. It is that state of the case, which, after the entire comparison and consideration of all the evidence, leaves the minds of jurors in that condition that they cannot say they feel an abiding conviction, to a moral certainty, of the truth of the charge.[36]

In conveying the reasonable doubt concept to a jury, the Michigan Supreme Court voiced approval for an instruction that phrased the criminal burden of proof as:

> A reasonable doubt is exactly what it infers. A reasonable doubt is a fair, honest doubt growing out of the evidence or lack of evidence in this case; or growing out of any reasonable or legitimate inferences drawn from the evidence or lack of evidence. It is not merely an imaginary doubt or a flimsy, fanciful doubt. But, rather, it is a fair, honest doubt based upon reason and common sense.[37]

However, other courts hold that not only is there no error in refusing to give an instruction explaining reasonable doubt, but it also constitutes reversible error to instruct the jury on the meaning of reasonable doubt. In a Wyoming arson case, the defendant attempted to have his conviction reversed because the prosecutor mentioned the concept during closing arguments, when court interpretations prohibited any jury instruction covering reasonable doubt. The Supreme Court of Wyoming upheld the conviction on the theory that the prosecutor was not instructing the jury, but was merely saying that there was no precise formula for reasonable doubt.[38]

In a case in which the trial judge failed to offer a jury instruction covering the concept of reasonable doubt, the defendant was convicted on lesser homicide offenses. The circuit court eventually vacated his conviction on the ground that the original trial contained "structural error" and was a nullity because the trial court failed to give the reasonable doubt instruction. The reviewing court affirmed the circuit court decision, sending the case back for a new trial.[39] The Michigan, Wyoming, and Alabama views on reasonable doubt show that state courts are nowhere near a consensus on the correct way to deal with the concept of reasonable doubt in jury instructions.

---

[35] *See* Padilla v. State, 254 S.W.3d 585, 2008 Tex. App. Lexis 2719 (2008). *See also* Ex parte Gillentine, 2006 Ala. Crim. App. Lexis 107 (2006), in which the court held that a trial judge must give an instruction on reasonable doubt and failure to do so constitutes reversible error.

[36] CAL. PEN. CODE § 1096 Presumption of innocence. (2013).

[37] Michigan v. Allen, 466 Mich. 86, 87, n.1, 643 N.W.2d 227, 229, n.1 (2002).

[38] Callen v. State, 2008 WY 107, 146, 192 P.3d 137, 2008 Wyo. Lexis 111 (Wyo. 2008).

[39] Ex parte Gillentine, 2006 Ala. Crim. App. Lexis 107 (2006).

Where a court offers a reasonable doubt jury instruction, whether it is required to do so by a state law or rule, the court must give the jury an instruction that meets minimum federal constitutional standards. In *Sullivan v. Louisiana*, the United States Supreme Court decided that giving a constitutionally flawed reasonable doubt instruction is not subject to a harmless-error standard of review and requires a reversal.[40] In this first-degree murder case, the prosecution agreed that the instruction did not comply with the requisite instruction mandated by a previous case,[41] but argued that the error was harmless.

The Supreme Court first reaffirmed that:

> What the factfinder must determine to return a verdict of guilty is prescribed by the Due Process Clause. The prosecution bears the burden of proving all elements of the offense charged,... and must persuade the factfinder "beyond a reasonable doubt" of the facts necessary to establish each of these elements. This beyond-a-reasonable-doubt requirement, which was adhered to by virtually all common law jurisdictions, applies in state, as well as federal, proceedings.
>
> It is self evident, we think, that the Fifth Amendment requirement of proof beyond a reasonable doubt and the Sixth Amendment requirement of a jury verdict are interrelated. It would not satisfy the Sixth Amendment to have a jury determine that the defendant is probably guilty, and then leave it to the judge to determine whether he is guilty beyond a reasonable doubt. In other words, the jury verdict required by the Sixth Amendment is a jury verdict of guilty beyond a reasonable doubt.[42]

Rejecting the prosecution's argument that the reasonable doubt instruction error was harmless, the Supreme Court reversed the judgment of the Louisiana court and remanded the case. If a federal constitutional error is to be held harmless, the reviewing court must be able to declare its conviction that the error was harmless beyond a reasonable doubt. Where a court has not been convinced beyond a reasonable doubt, the conviction under review must be reversed.

In 1994, in *Victor v. Nebraska*, the United States Supreme Court referred to the landmark case of *In re Winship*, reiterating that the government must prove beyond a reasonable doubt every element of a charged offense and acknowledging that the proof beyond a reasonable doubt requirement of our criminal justice system defies any easy explanation. The *Victor* Court noted that both cases, *In re Winship* and *Cage v. Louisiana*, involved appeals arising from two attempts to define the concept of reasonable doubt.[43] The United States Supreme Court first restated that the "beyond a reasonable doubt" standard is a requirement of due process, but the Constitution neither prohibits trial courts from defining a reasonable doubt, nor requires them to do so as a

---

40 Sullivan v. Louisiana, 508 U.S. 275, 113 S. Ct. 2078, 124 L. Ed. 2d 182 (1993).

41 Cage v. Louisiana, 498 U.S. 39, 111 S. Ct. 328, 112 L. Ed. 2d 339 (1990).

42 *Sullivan* at 227, 228.

43 Victor v. Nebraska, 511 U.S. 1, 114 S. Ct. 1239, 127 L. Ed. 2d 583 (1994). *See case* in Part II.

matter of course.[44] The Constitution does not require any particular form or words to be used in advising the jury of the government's burden of proof. However, when a court gives a jury instruction, it must correctly convey the concept of reasonable doubt to the jury. In addition, a jury instruction must not have the effect of shifting the burden of proof to the defendant because such an instruction relieves the prosecution of proving the case beyond a reasonable doubt.[45]

In *Victor v. Nebraska*, the instruction included, "[y]ou may find the accused guilty upon the strong probabilities of the case, provided such probabilities are strong enough to exclude any doubt of his guilt that is reasonable." The instruction also included, "A reasonable doubt is an actual and substantial doubt arising from the evidence." In evaluating the merits of the defendant's objection to the jury instruction, the Court noted:

> So long as the court instructs the jury on the necessity that the defendant's guilt be proved beyond a reasonable doubt, the Constitution does not require that any particular form of words be used in advising the jury of the government's burden of proof. Rather, "taken as a whole, the instructions [must] correctly convey the concept of reasonable doubt to the jury."[46]

A state or federal prosecutor is not required to prove the defendant guilty beyond all possible doubt, and the Constitution of the United States does not require that any particular form or words be used in advising the jury of the government's burden of proof or to advise the jury at all concerning the reasonable doubt standard. However, if the jury is erroneously instructed in such a manner that effectively relieves the prosecution of its burden to establish every element of guilt, automatic reversal is often required, "because it is constitutionally mandated that the prosecution prove guilt beyond a reasonable doubt, an erroneous jury instruction on reasonable doubt is never harmless."[47] In a Maryland case, the reviewing court reversed the defendant's conviction of first-degree murder because his trial attorney failed to object to an erroneous jury instruction. The way the judge phrased the jury instruction on reasonable doubt, it could have permitted the jury to convict the defendant by a preponderance of the evidence standard or some standard lower than proof beyond a reasonable doubt.[48]

From the time a law enforcement official begins investigating and preparing a criminal case, the focus is directed toward gathering sufficient evidence to meet the trial evidentiary standard of proof beyond a reasonable doubt. The standard not only applies at the trial, but also influences appellate courts reviewing a case, because they may reverse a conviction if a review of the trial court indicates an absence of proof beyond a reasonable doubt. The high level of proof necessary in criminal cases constitutes one of the fundamental differences between criminal and civil cases.[49]

---

44 *Id.* The syllabus of this case is included in Part II. The instructions to the jurors are included in the case.

45 Sandstrom v. Montana, 442 U.S. 510, 523 (1979).

46 *Victor*, at 5.

47 State v. McClellan, 2006 Md. App. Lexis 103 (2006).

48 *Id.*

49 Jackson v. Virginia, 443 U.S. 307, 99 S. Ct. 2781, 61 L. Ed. 2d 560 (1979).

§ 3.6 Burden on the Prosecution

From the initiation of the prosecution and throughout the trial, the government has the burden of proof and the obligation to convince the jury or the court of the guilt of a defendant beyond a reasonable doubt. Because the due process clause of the Fifth and the Fourteenth Amendments requires the prosecution to introduce evidence that proves a defendant's guilt beyond a reasonable doubt, trial judges must be vigilant in offering jury instructions concerning proof beyond a reasonable doubt, lest the instructions contain defects that might allow a jury to convict on a lower standard of proof. Although not all jurisdictions require that a trial judge give a detailed definition of proof beyond a reasonable doubt, where a judge is required or decides to offer such an instruction, it must properly explain the concept of reasonable doubt. The explanation of the standard must be offered to the jury in a way that ensures that a jury does not convict a defendant where the prosecution has introduced insufficient proof.[50] Where the crime requires proof of criminal intent, or *mens rea*, the responsibility rests with the prosecution to introduce evidence to prove intent. No defendant has any burden to prove innocence, and a prosecutor must not imply that the defendant has any duty to disprove the case. For example, in a New York prosecution for driving while impaired, the prosecutor asked the defendant whether he asked to take a breath test in order to prove his innocence. The trial court judge overruled the defendant's objection to the question. The reviewing court reversed the conviction because the prosecutor's question improperly implied that the defendant had a burden to prove his innocence.[51] The prosecutor has a duty that prevents the government from effectively reducing its burden of proof. With the exceptions of affirmative defenses, no defendant possesses any burden of proof in a criminal trial and no defendant ever has a duty to prove that he or she did not commit the crime. Defendants do have some responsibilities during criminal trials—these will be discussed in future sections.

If the defendant pleads not guilty to a criminal charge, the defendant's plea necessarily imposes upon the government the burden of introducing proof of all the elements of the crime beyond a reasonable doubt, and meeting the burden of proof can involve the use of presumptions.[52] The due process clause of the federal Constitution requires that the prosecution bear the burden of proving all the elements of each offense charged.[53] In addition to the elements, the prosecutor must prove that the court has jurisdiction of the case and that the case is being tried in the proper venue.[54] Additionally, there must be

---

50 Arizona v. Fulminante, 499 U.S. 279, 291 (1991).

51 People v. Handwerker, 2006 N.Y. Slip Op. 26119, 12 Misc. 3d 19, 816 N.Y.S.2d 824, 2006 N.Y. Misc. Lexis 662 (2006).

52 In re Winship, 397 U.S. 358 (1970). *See also* UNIF. R. EVID. 303(b) (2005).

53 Sullivan v. Louisiana, 508 U.S. 275, 113 S. Ct. 2078, 124 L. Ed. 2d 182 (1993). *See also* Perkins v. State, 441 S.E.2d 511 (Ga. 1994).

54 State v. Miller, 2003 Utah App. 76, 2003 Utah App. Lexis 247 (2003).

proof that the alleged crime violated the law of the particular jurisdiction and the defendant was the person who committed the crime.[55]

The burdens on the prosecution become most clear when an appeal alleges that the government failed to prove all the elements of a crime. In an Ohio case where the defendant had been convicted of trademark counterfeiting, she successfully contended that the prosecution's expert failed to compare the appearance of the allegedly infringing product with how a genuine article appeared. Because proof of an element of the crime was missing, the case had to be reversed.[56] Generally, an appellate court will uphold a conviction where a rational finder of fact could have determined that the state proved all the essential elements of the crime.[57]

§ 3.7 Burden to Prove All Elements of the Crime

"As a matter of due process the prosecution must prove beyond a reasonable doubt every fact necessary to constitute the crime with which the defendant is charged."[58] To win a conviction, the prosecutor must introduce sufficient believable evidence that proves all the elements of the charged crime beyond a reasonable doubt. For example, in the common law crime of burglary, there are seven elements: (1) trespass, (2) breaking, (3) entering, (4) the dwelling house, (5) of another, (6) at night, and (7) with intent to commit a felony. Meeting the duty of the prosecutor involves introducing proof of each of these elements of common law burglary with sufficient evidentiary weight that meet the burden of proof. Evidence that the defendant interfered in the property rights of another would meet the "trespass" standard, as proof that the defendant used force to make entry shows a "breaking." But where the evidence also demonstrated that the defendant had permission to stay the night at the bed and breakfast inn, the element of "trespass" would be negated, and no conviction for common law burglary would be proper.

Both state and federal courts have consistently reversed convictions after determining that the prosecution did not prove one of the elements of the crime charged. For example, in a New York case, *People v. Sandoval*, the reviewing court reversed the defendant's conviction for burglary because an erroneous jury instruction had the effect of relieving the prosecution of the duty to prove that the defendant had unlawfully entered the apartment building, a crucial element in a burglary prosecution.[59]

An appellate court reversed a defendant's conviction of endangering a child where the defendant had been charged with willfully allowing a minor child to enter or remain

---

55 *See* People v. Moreland, 226 Ill. Dec. 814, 686 N.E.2d 597 (1997).

56 State v. Troisi, 2008 Ohio 6062, 2008 Ohio App. Lexis (2008).

57 State v. Butler, 2008 La. App. Lexis 1388 (2008). *See also* United States v. Lopez, 443 F.3d 1026, 1030, 2006 U.S. App. Lexis 9560 (8th Cir. 2006).

58 29 AM. JUR. 2D *Evidence* § 168.

59 People v. Sandoval, 56 A.D.3d 253, 866 N.Y.S.2d 656, 2008 N.Y. App. Div. Lexis 8238 (2008).

in a building where the defendant knew that methamphetamine was stored. Under appellate review, the court determined that the defendant was entitled to a jury instruction that covered all the elements of the crime. In this particular case, the trial judge, in failing to instruct the jury that it must find that the defendant willfully permitted the child to enter the drug storage building, committed reversible error because the jury may have convicted the defendant without making a determination that the defendant knowingly allowed the child to enter the drug house.[60] Where one of the elements of a crime was not proved beyond a reasonable doubt, a reviewing court must reverse the conviction.

Many jurisdictions will reverse a conviction where one element has not been proved, where the existence of the element was in dispute, and a trial court omitted a jury instruction requiring proof of the element. In a Connecticut case, a defendant had been charged with possession of cocaine in his automobile and in a jacket alleged to belong to the defendant. The defendant disputed the allegation that the cocaine was in his possession, and the trial court failed to instruct the jury on the element that the defendant had to have knowledge that the substance was cocaine. The reviewing court reversed the trial court and held that harmless error could not be found because the issue of knowledge was in dispute.[61] On different facts, a Kentucky appellate court upheld a conviction for robbery in the first degree that required a threat while armed with a deadly weapon. The judge failed to instruct the jury that it first had to find that the defendant's gun was a deadly weapon before it could convict him of first-degree robbery. Over the defendant's objection that his case was not proved beyond a reasonable doubt because one element was missing, the Supreme Court of Kentucky held that the jury would most certainly have found that the gun was a deadly weapon, and it applied the harmless error standard of review to uphold the conviction.[62]

In contrast to state practices, federal courts treat a neglected element somewhat differently. In one case in which the trial court failed to instruct the jury that the element, materiality, in a mail and wire fraud case was an element of both crimes, the Supreme Court allowed the conviction to stand. According to the Court, a jury instruction that omits an element of the crime does not necessarily result in a fundamentally unfair trial and should be judged on the harmless error standard. Even though the jury did not consider all the elements in the case, the Court upheld the convictions that resulted.[63] Normally, factors that must be found for sentence enhancements must be determined by the jury and are treated like elements of the crime. In federal prosecutions, where the government must prove sentencing factors beyond a reasonable doubt and fails to do so, these factors can be treated just like elements of the crime that were not proven and can be measured by the harmless error standard. In a case in which the jury in a domestic assault case found that the defendant had assaulted his wife with a

---

60 Granzer v. State, 2008 WY 118, 193 P.2d 266, 2008 Wyo. Lexis 124 (2008).

61 State v. Gooden, 89 Conn. App. 307, 319, 873 A.2d 243, 251, 2005 Conn. App. Lexis 202 (2005).

62 Thacker v. Commonwealth, 194 S.W.3d 287, 2006 Ky. Lexis 174 (2006).

63 Neder v. United States, 527 U.S. 1 (1999).

deadly weapon, the trial court enhanced the sentence because the proof in the case showed that the deadly weapon was a firearm, even though the jury verdict form only mentioned a "deadly weapon." The Supreme Court believed that, even though the jury had not specifically found that a firearm was used, and the verdict was for a "deadly weapon," the harmless error standard should be applied and the defendant should have been sentenced as if the jury had found that he used a firearm.[64]

If the prosecution fails to prove one element of the crime beyond a reasonable doubt, the accused may sometimes be found guilty of a lesser degree of that crime or a lesser included offense. For example, under some statutes, a person may be found guilty of burglary in the second degree if the prosecution failed to prove that the breaking and entering occurred at night. In such instances, of course, the penalty is less severe. Similarly, if a sentencing factor is not proved in a state case, the sentence enhancement should not be imposed.

§ 3.8 Burden on the Accused

As a strong general rule, no defendant has any duty to present any evidence, to introduce any witnesses, or to testify personally because a defendant has no burden to prove or disprove anything.[65] A defendant need not prove anything in order to prevail in a criminal trial. In fact, a strong general rule exists that "[i]t is improper for a prosecutor to suggest that a defendant shoulders the burden of proof in a criminal trial."[66] This concept is such a universal principle of American criminal justice that, if a prosecutor were to hint or inadvertently imply during opening or closing statements that any burden rests on the defense, that suggestion could result in a reversal of a conviction on appeal. In a Florida case involving a defendant's arrest for leaving her baggage unattended at an airport, she testified that the deputies who arrested her were unreasonably rough during the booking process and left bruises on her arm. The defendant allegedly battered a police officer, which brought additional charges that she denied. During cross-examination at the battery trial, the prosecutor asked the defendant whether she had any photographs of her injuries. The prosecutor emphasized the lack of photographs during cross-examination and while making closing arguments. According to the reviewing court, this emphasis on the defendant's lack of evidence amounted to an improper shifting the burden of proof to the accused and required a reversal of her conviction.[67] The court upheld the principle that a defendant does not have to prove anything and that this particular defendant did not have to introduce other evidence of her

---

64 Washington v. Fecuenco, 548 U.S. 212, 2006 U.S. Lexis 5164 (2006).

65 Generally, a defendant has no burden of proof unless the defendant has pled an affirmative defense.

66 Stephenson v. State, 742 N.E.2d 463 (Ind. 2001).

67 Ramirez v. State, 2009 Fla. App. Lexis 739 (2009). *See also* People v. Johnson, 218 Ill. 2d 125, 140, 842 N.E.2d 714, 723, 2005 Ill. Lexis 2072 (2005).

oral theory of the incident. Therefore, the prosecution committed reversible error in implying that the defendant had any burden of proof.

In constructing a defense, an accused may make some issues logically and legally relevant by pleading an affirmative defense where the burden of proof at some level may rest on the defendant. In the case of an insanity defense, the defendant may have the burden of proof by a preponderance or by clear and convincing evidence, or the defendant may merely have to raise the issue of insanity and introduce some slight evidence of insanity to meet the required affirmative burden. Once the defendant has met whatever burden was required in the jurisdiction, the burden of going forward with the evidence will fall on the prosecution to negate insanity or to introduce evidence to contradict the defendant's claim.

When pleading an affirmative defense, such as coercion, self-defense, entrapment, statute of limitations, or mistake, all of which would absolve a defendant of liability, the defendant generally has the responsibility of "going forward with the evidence." Because the allocation of the burden of persuasion varies in many jurisdictions, the burden of proving affirmative defenses may fall on either the government or the defendant, as determined by state or federal statute or court decision. For example, in New York[68] and Ohio,[69] defendants must prove affirmative defenses by a preponderance of the evidence. Once the prosecution has proved the elements of the crime, the defendant must prove the existence of the affirmative defense in order to prevail. Where the burden of proof has been allocated to the defendant who has asserted an affirmative defense, the reality is that, in order to win the case, the defendant need only introduce sufficient believable evidence to create a reasonable doubt. To warrant submission of the particular defense to the jury, the defendant must produce substantial evidence to support the particular defense theory sufficient to create a reasonable doubt.[70]

The Supreme Court of California explained that, where a defendant presented sufficient evidence that, if believed by the jury, could support an affirmative defense, the trial court must offer the jury an instruction explaining the concept of affirmative defenses and how they operate. The court reversed a conviction for selling unregistered securities because one defendant offered a sufficient evidentiary foundation that he personally did not know that the securities he was selling must be registered prior to sale. Because the defendant made a proper showing of evidence in support of an affirmative defense, the trial court committed reversible error in not giving the jury an instruction on affirmative defenses.[71] If the defense introduces a sufficient foundation showing an affirmative defense, the defendant is entitled to an appropriate jury instruction on the affirmative defense.

---

68 *See* N.Y. C.L.S. PENAL § 25.00 Defenses; burden of proof (2013).

69 OHIO REV. CODE ANN. § 2901.05(A) (2013). "The burden of going forward with the evidence of an affirmative defense, and the burden of proof, by a preponderance of the evidence, for an affirmative defense, is upon the accused."

70 State v. Babers, 514 N.W.2d 79 (Iowa 1994).

71 People v. Salas, 37 Cal. 4th 967; 127 P.3d 40, 38 Cal. Rptr. 3d 624, 2006 Cal. Lexis 1900 (2006).

Because the prosecution possesses the burden of proof for each element of the crime, there is no lawful way to shift that burden to a defendant through a jury instruction or a prosecutor's final argument. For example, in a Montana drunk driving case, a judge gave the jury an instruction that indicated a defendant's refusal to submit to a test to detect alcohol or other drugs could be a factor that the jury might consider in determining whether the defendant was under the influence at the time of his arrest. The Supreme Court of Montana rejected the defendant's contention that the jury instruction and a prosecutor's mention of the refusal constituted a reversal of the burden of proof.[72] The court noted that the government, and not the defendant, had the burden of proof on all the elements of impaired driving.

Statutory wording or the effect of jury instructions in allegedly altering or shifting the burden of proof has been attacked in a variety of cases. The Supreme Court accepted a case, *Sandstrom v. Montana*, which involved a jury instruction claimed to be an inference that allegedly shifted the burden of proof from the prosecution to the defendant.[73] In this case, the state charged the defendant with deliberate homicide, and the question of the defendant's intent was crucial to both the defense and the prosecution. At the trial, the defendant's attorney informed the jury that, although his client admitted to killing the victim, he did not do so "purposely or knowingly," and he was therefore not guilty of a deliberate crime but rather of a lesser crime. The defendant's counsel objected to the instruction that "the law presumes that a person intends the ordinary consequences of his voluntary act." He argued that this instruction had the effect of shifting the burden of proof on the issue of purpose or knowledge to the defendant, and it was therefore impermissible, because it was in violation of the constitutional guarantee of due process of law. The Supreme Court, in reversing the decision, reasoned that:

> [A] reasonable jury could have interpreted the presumptions as "conclusive," i.e., not technically as a presumption at all, but rather an irrebuttable direction by the court to find intent once convinced of the facts triggering the assumption. Alternatively, the jury may have interpreted the instruction as a direction to find intent upon proof of the defendant's voluntary actions, unless the defendant proved the contrary.[74]

Under either interpretation, according to the Court, the burden of persuasion on the element of intent effectively shifted to the defendant. The Court then stated:

> We conclude that under either of the two possible interpretations of the instruction set out above, precisely that effect (relieving the state of the burden of proof) would result, and that the instruction therefore represents constitutional error.[75]

---

72 State v. Slade, 2008 MT 341, 346 Mont. 271, 194 P.3d 677, 2008 Mont. Lexis 574 (Mont. 2008).

73 Sandstrom v. Montana, 442 U.S. 510, 1979 U.S. Lexis 113 (1979).

74 *Id.* at 517.

75 *Id.* at 521.

To summarize, the defendant has the burden of going forward with the evidence to show an affirmative defense such as alibi or insanity; however, an instruction that tends to require the defendant to prove his or her innocence, or any instruction that relieves the prosecution of proving an element of the crime, violates the due process requirement that the prosecution must prove every element of the offense beyond a reasonable doubt.

§ 3.9 Burden of Proving Affirmative Defenses—General

Once the prosecution has introduced sufficient evidence that, if believed, would permit a finding of guilt beyond a reasonable doubt on every element of the charge, the accused may avoid conviction by providing evidence that raises or permits a reasonable doubt that he or she is guilty as charged.[76] In most instances, the defense has only to introduce sufficient evidence to raise a reasonable doubt in the minds of the jury.

Some states follow a slightly different path and allocate a higher burden to the prosecution where a defendant introduced evidence in support of an affirmative defense. Demonstrative of this theory, when a defendant has made a prima facie showing of an affirmative defense, the government has the burden of proving beyond a reasonable doubt that the affirmative defense does not exist.[77] States following this theory hold that the prosecution bears the burden of proving the defendant's guilt beyond a reasonable doubt, as it relates to the issue raised by affirmative defense evidence. Other jurisdictions place the burden of proof firmly on the defendant to prove the affirmative defense by a preponderance of the evidence and place no burden on the prosecution.[78] In a federal prosecution for illegally purchasing firearms, the defendant contended that her affirmative evidence of duress should force the prosecution to disprove duress beyond a reasonable doubt. The Supreme Court rejected her position because a majority of the Court presumed that the Congress intended a defendant accused of firearms offenses to bear the burden of proving duress by a preponderance of the evidence.[79] In a prosecution for illegally purchasing firearms, this was especially the case because the elements of the crime, if proved, show guilt, while duress constitutes an excuse for the crime, but does not negate an element of the crime.

Allocating the burden of proving an affirmative defense by statute does not violate due process, even where the burden is placed on the defendant to prove insanity beyond a reasonable doubt.[80] Using a lower standard, Congress reformed the federal insanity defense, requiring a defendant to prove insanity by clear and convincing evidence.[81]

---

76 People v. Gonzalez, 275 Cal. Rptr. 729, 800 P.2d 1159 (1990).

77 *See* Fields v. State, 998 So. 2d 1185, 2008 Fla. App. Lexis 11871 (2008).

78 State v. Ray, 290 Conn. 24, 37, 961 A.2d 947, 2009 Conn. Lexis 5 (2009).

79 Dixon v. United States, 548 U.S. 1, 2006 U.S. Lexis 4894 (2006).

80 Leland v. Oregon, 343 U.S. 790, 1952 U.S. Lexis 1955 (1952).

81 United States v. Freeman, 804 F.2d 1574 (11th Cir. 1986). *See also* People v. Spry, 68 Cal. Rptr. 2d 691 (1997). As of mid 2011, the Supreme Court has never accepted a case to review the constitutionality of the federal insanity defense statute.

In the sections that follow, some of the more common affirmative defenses are discussed, including alibi, self-defense, justification, excuse, and other affirmative defenses, with special emphasis on the question of burden of proof.

§ 3.10 —Alibi

In the alibi defense, the defendant admits that the crime occurred, but alleges that he or she was not present to commit the crime because he or she was at a different location and otherwise had no connection to the alleged crime, whether in planning or in execution. Some jurisdictions hold that the presentation of an alibi constitutes an affirmative defense, and when it is asserted, the defendant has the burden of proof by a preponderance of the evidence.[82] Georgia law takes an opposite view, and in an armed robbery case where the defendant disputed the allegation that he was the robber, the burden of proof remained on the prosecution to prove the defendant's presence beyond a reasonable doubt.[83] A third view, represented by Delaware, holds that an alibi defense is not an affirmative defense, and the defendant holds no burden of proof. Under the Delaware theory, an alibi instruction informs the jury that, if the defendant's alibi evidence creates a reasonable doubt, the jury must acquit the defendant.[84] Because the defense of alibi denies any connection with the crime, a successful alibi defense requires that the defendant be acquitted.

In order to prevent unfair prejudice to the case of the prosecution, most jurisdictions require by rule or statute that the defense give the prosecution pretrial notice of an intention to present an alibi defense. For example, within 20 days of arraignment, New York permits the prosecution to request notice of whether the defendant intends to assert an alibi defense. The defendant must respond within eight days and allege the place where the defendant claimed to have been located at the time of the crime and offer the names and addresses of each alibi witness upon whom the defendant intends to rely.[85] In New Jersey, the defendant must furnish a signed alibi statement stating the specific places the defendant claims to have been to establish the alibi, and if the defendant fails to furnish the details to the prosecution within 10 days, the court may refuse to allow the witnesses to offer evidence of the defendant's alibi.[86] Connecticut follows a similar rule and excludes evidence of alibi when the notice

---

82 State v. Stump, 254 Iowa 1181, 119 N.W.2d 210 (1963).

83 Hill v. State, 290 Ga. App. 140, 658 S.E.2d 863, 241, 2008 Ga. App. Lexis 272 (2008).

84 *See* Brown v. State, 958 A.2d 833, 2008 Del. Lexis 468 (2008).

85 NY CLS CPL § 250.20 Notice of Alibi (2013). *See also* CONN. PRACTICE BOOK § 40–21. Defense of Alibi; Notice by Defendant (2013). The Connecticut rule requires that the defendant give notice to the prosecutor within 20 days following the prosecutor's written demand. The defendant must state the specific places at which he claims to have been at the relevant time and give the names and addresses of the witnesses who are expected to be called to establish the alibi.

86 *See* N.J. CT. R. 3:12–2(a) and (b) (2013). *See also* FLA. R. CRIM. P. 3.200 Notice of Alibi (2013). *See also* McEwing v. State, 2006 Ark. Lexis 332 (2006).

requirement has been violated. The reasons for this exclusion, according to a Connecticut case, is that exclusion is a sanction for failure to obey the notice rules; that otherwise, the state could suffer surprise at trial because it would not have time to investigate the witnesses; and that it was proper for the trial court to view late identification of alibi witnesses with suspicion.[87]

If a defendant fails to file and serve a copy of the alibi notice as generally required, a trial court may exclude defense witness evidence offered for the purpose of providing an alibi, with the exception that the defendant may give personal alibi testimony whether or not notice was given.[88] Consistent with this principle, the Supreme Court of New Jersey in *State v. Bradshaw* upheld the reversal of the defendant's conviction, because the trial court had abused its discretion in not allowing the defendant to testify concerning his alibi, even though he had not complied with the notice of alibi requirement.[89]

In explaining the burden of proof requirement in alibi cases tried in a state that does not view such a defense as an affirmative defense, the Supreme Court of Delaware indicated that the defendant does not have the burden of proving his alibi. All that is demanded of the defendant who presents an alibi defense is that he or she introduce evidence that raises a reasonable doubt concerning presence of the accused at the time and place where the crime was committed.[90]

In *Dat Pham v. Beaver*, a New York court charged the jury that the government had to prove that the defendant was the individual who committed the crime and that the government had to disprove the defendant's alibi beyond a reasonable doubt. The appeals court approved the jury charge and refused to disturb the defendant's conviction,[91] because the charge correctly explained New York law, which required the prosecution to rebut evidence of alibi by proof beyond a reasonable doubt.

A court is generally required to instruct the jury on the alibi if the defendant requests the instruction and has presented some credible evidence to support the alibi.[92] However, an alibi instruction is appropriate only when the defense evidence demonstrates the defendant's presence elsewhere for the entire period during which the government's evidence shows he or she was involved in criminal activity.[93]

---

87 *See* State v. Salters, 89 Conn. App. 221; 872 A.2d 933; 2005 Conn. App. Lexis 200 (2005). *See also* State v. Lewis, 391 N.W.2d 726 (Iowa 1986), which held that a trial court's exclusion of the defendant's alibi witness was an abuse of discretion when the defense counsel filed a notice of alibi one day after he heard of the existence of witnesses, witnesses were made available for all informal interviews or depositions before the trial, and the state had one week before the trial to investigate the alibi defense, but chose to do nothing, even declining interviews with witnesses.

88 McKenny v. State, 967 So. 2d 951, 2007 Fla. App. Lexis 15581 (2007). *See also* FLA. R. CRIM. P. 3.200 Notice of Alibi (2013) *and* Sanchez-Andujar v. State, 60 So.3d 480, 483, 2011 Fla. App. LEXIS 5421 (2011), where the state cannot exclude alibi witnesses when it made no demand for the list under the Florida statute.

89 State v. Bradshaw, 195 N.J. 493; 950 A.2d 889; 2008 N.J. Lexis 873 (2008).

90 Brown v. State, 958 A.2d 833, 839, 2008 Del. Lexis 468 (Del. 2008).

91 2006 U.S. Dist. Lexis 46109 (W.D.N.Y. 2006).

92 Brown v. State, 958, A.2d 833, 838, 2008 Del. Lexis 468 (2008).

93 Bright v. United States, 698 A.2d 450 (D.C. App. 1997).

§ 3.11 —Insanity

The competency of a defendant to stand trial is related to, but separate from the issue of legal insanity. Every defendant comes to court with a presumption that he or she is competent to stand trial, to enter a plea, and to receive a sentence. Where a question of competency to stand trial arises, as a general rule the burden of proof is on the defendant to prove by a preponderance of the evidence that he or she is not competent.[94] In determining a defendant's competence, a court considers whether a defendant can consult with his or her lawyer with a reasonable degree of rationality and whether the defendant has an understanding of the nature of the criminal proceedings and is able to assist in his or her defense. This type of mental difficulty affecting competency is different from legal insanity, and a person may be competent but still legally insane.

A defendant comes to court with not only a presumption of competency, but also with a presumption of sanity. Unless the defendant takes steps to make sanity an issue in the case, the prosecutor has no special duty to prove sanity. Although the prosecution has the ultimate burden of proof on sanity if it does not become an issue, the prosecutor has to offer no evidence proving insanity. To raise the issue of sanity, the defendant has the burden of introducing evidence sufficient to evoke the possibility that, as a result of mental disease or defect, he or she lacked a substantial capacity to appreciate the wrongfulness of his or her conduct or to conform his or her conduct to the requirements of the law. If the defendant places sanity at issue, there are several ways that different jurisdictions handle the issue. One group of states requires the defendant to raise the issue and offer some proof of insanity, and then the burden of proof shifts to the prosecution to prove sanity either by a preponderance or, in some cases, beyond a reasonable doubt. Other jurisdictions require the defendant to raise the issue and to affirmatively prove insanity by providing clear and convincing evidence or proof beyond a reasonable doubt.

The rule followed by most state courts (and federal courts until 1984) requires that, when the defendant introduces substantial evidence of his or her insanity, the issue of his or her capacity to commit the offense becomes a question of proof, and the prosecution's burden of going forward with the evidence requires it to introduce sufficient evidence on the issue of sanity to preclude a verdict of acquittal for the defendant.[95] However, the defendant must introduce sufficient evidence to meet the burden of proof required in that particular jurisdiction to prove insanity. In a prosecution in which the defendant alleged legal insanity as a defense and offered proof, the judge rejected the defense because, as a matter of law, the evidence directed toward proving insanity failed to meet the clear and convincing level of proof. According to the reviewing court, "[t]he clear and convincing standard requires a

---

94 State v. Were, 118 Ohio St. 3d 448, 2008 Ohio 2762, 890 N.E.2d, 2008 Ohio Lexis 1615 (2008).

95 United States v. Westerhausen, 283 F.2d 844 (7th Cir. 1960).

quantum of proof greater than a preponderance of the evidence, but less than proof beyond a reasonable doubt"[96] and requiring clear and convincing proof did not violate standards of due process.

The legislatures of a large number of states have taken a somewhat different approach to the insanity defense, as demonstrated by Washington, which provides that "[i]nsanity is a defense which the defendant must establish by a preponderance of the evidence."[97] The statutes in these states allocate the burden of proof for legal insanity to the party asserting insanity[98] by a preponderance of the evidence.[99] For example, in California, when a defendant pleads not guilty by reason of insanity, the defendant has the burden of proof by a preponderance of the evidence to prove that he or she was insane at the time he or she committed the act.[100] In several instances, the United States Supreme Court has determined that placing this burden on the defendant does not violate the Constitution of the United States,[101] even where the burden is on the defendant to prove insanity beyond a reasonable doubt.[102]

In 1984, as part of the Comprehensive Crime Control Act, Congress enacted legislation titled "Insanity Defense Reform Act of 1984." Section 17 of Title 18 of the United States Code defines the scope of the insanity defense for federal offenses and shifts the burden of proof to the defendant. This section provides:

> (a) Affirmative Defense. It is an affirmative defense to a prosecution under any Federal statute that, at the time of the commission of the acts constituting the offense, the defendant, as a result of a severe mental disease or defect, was unable to appreciate the nature and quality or the wrongfulness of his acts. Mental disease or defect does not otherwise constitute a defense.
>
> (b) Burden of Proof. The defendant has the burden of proving the defense of insanity by clear and convincing evidence.[103]

The clear and convincing evidence standard is a higher standard than a mere preponderance of the evidence and remains lower than Oregon's current standard for its insanity defense, which requires proof beyond a reasonable doubt.[104] The revised federal insanity defense was designed to eliminate the confusion that might result from

---

96 People v. Clay, 361 Ill. App. 3d 310, 332, 836 N.E.2d 872, 882, 2005 Ill. App. Lexis 994 (2005).

97 ANN. REV. CODE WASH. § 10.77.030(2) (2013).

98 *Id.* § 10.77.030(2). See also Turner v. Arkansas, 2005 Ark. App. Lexis 237 (2005).

99 ARK. CODE ANN. § 5-1-111 (d)(1) (2013).

100 People v. Farris, 130 Cal. App. 4th 773, 30 Cal. Rptr. 3d 426, 2005 Cal. App. Lexis 1017 (2005).

101 Patterson v. New York, 432 U.S. 197, 97 S. Ct. 2319, 53 L. Ed. 2d 281 (1977). Leland v. Oregon, 343 U.S. 790, 72 S. Ct. 1002, 96 L. Ed. 1302 (1952). *See also* Fleenor v. State, 622 N.E.2d 140 (Ind. 1993), in which the court held that instructing the jury that a capital murder defendant was required to prove insanity at the time of the offense by a preponderance of the evidence, if the state proved that the defendant knowingly killed the victim, was proper.

102 *See* Leland v. Oregon, 343 U.S. 790 (1952).

103 18 U.S.C. § 17.

104 People v. Clay, 361 Ill. App. 3d 310, 325, 836 N.E.2d 872, 885, 2005 Ill. App. Lexis 994 (2005).

Expert witnesses A person who has acquired by special study, practice, and experience, peculiar skill and knowledge in relation to some particular science, art, or trade.

expert witnesses testifying to directly contradictory conclusions regarding the ultimate legal issue to be found by the trier of fact. Under the revised insanity defense, expert psychiatric testimony is limited to presenting and explaining the diagnosis completed by the psychiatrist. In federal criminal trials, expert witnesses may not "state an opinion as to whether the defendant did or did not have the mental conditions constituting an element of the crime charged or of a defense. Those matters for the trier of fact alone."[105]

Another provision of the Crime Control Act relates to the disposition of a person found not guilty by reason of insanity.[106] This section of the Act provides:

> If a person is found not guilty only by reason of insanity at the time of the offense charged, he shall be committed to a suitable facility until such time as he is eligible for release pursuant to subsection (e).

Subsection (d) of the Act relates to burden of proof. It provides that:

> In a hearing pursuant to subsection (c) of this section, a person found not guilty only by reason of insanity of an offense involving bodily injury to, or serious damage to property of, another person, or involving a substantial risk of such injury or damage, has the burden of proving by clear and convincing evidence that his release would not create a substantial risk of bodily injury to another person or serious damage of property of another due to present mental disease or defect. With respect to any other offense, the person has the burden of proof by the preponderance of the evidence.

Following the enactment of the Insanity Defense Reform Act, defendants attacked its constitutionality and claimed that placing the burden of this affirmative defense on a defendant by clear and convincing evidence violated due process. The Supreme Court had noted that placing the burden of persuasion on a defendant to prove insanity, whether by a preponderance of the evidence, or to some more convincing degree, does not violate the Constitution.[107] Many states have adopted the federal burden of proof when modernizing their individual insanity defense statutes. Demonstrative of following the federal standard is the state of Illinois, which holds that "the burden of proof is on the defendant to prove by clear and convincing evidence that the defendant is not guilty by reason of insanity."[108] Louisiana follows a lower standard and provides that "[t]he defendant has the burden of establishing the defense of insanity at the time of the

---

105 FED. R. EVID. § 704(b).

106 18 U.S.C. § 4243.

107 *See* Clark v. Arizona, 548 U.S. 735, 2006 U.S. Lexis 5184 (2006).

108 *See* § 720 ILCS 5/6-2. Insanity (2013). *See also* People v. Houseworth, 2008 Ill. App. Lexis 1290 (2008).

offense by a preponderance of the evidence,"[109] on the theory that most people are sane. However, the burden of proof remains on the prosecution to prove every element beyond a reasonable doubt.

In summary, the United States Congress established that the burden of proof of insanity in federal courts would rest upon the defendant and require him or her to prove the insanity defense by clear and convincing evidence. In some states, where the defendant has raised a mental defense, the issue of whether a defendant possessed the proper mental capacity to be convicted of a crime requires the prosecution to introduce sufficient evidence to avoid a verdict of acquittal in the defendant's favor. In other states, the defendant must not only go forward with the evidence, but has the ultimate burden to prove insanity by a preponderance of the evidence. A third group of states places the burden of proof on the defendant, using the standard of clear and convincing evidence. In any situation, to have any chance of prevailing on an insanity defense, the defendant who claims insanity has at least a minimal burden to go forward with evidence to overcome the presumption of sanity and constitutionally may have the burden completely placed on him- or herself by proof beyond a reasonable doubt.

§ 3.12 —Self-Defense

In criminal prosecutions involving violence to the alleged victim, justifiable self-defense may be set up as a complete defense to, or exoneration from, liability for the act charged. Preservation from harm, whether the danger rises to the level of defense of life or of defense from lesser physical harms, is generally recognized as proper conduct if the defender is not committing any wrong.[110] As a general rule, during the presentation of a homicide case, the prosecution has the burden of establishing the death of a human caused by the defendant under circumstances in which the defendant did not appear to have acted in self-defense. If the defendant alleged self-defense in this hypothetical homicide case, the burden of proving this affirmative defense requires the defendant to go forward with proof of facts that indicate that the defendant had a right of self-defense and used no more force than was appropriate under the circumstances.

Several states place the ultimate burden of proof for affirmative defenses squarely on the defendant. For example, the Ohio Revised Code provides that "[t]he burden of going forward with the evidence of an affirmative defense, and the burden of proof, by a preponderance of the evidence, for an affirmative defense, is upon the accused."[111] Demonstrative of this principle, a woman, who was allegedly under the influence of alcohol, had been convicted of misdemeanor assault in Ohio for striking hospital personnel, while an intoxicated friend was being treated for injuries and wanted to leave

---

[109] La. C. Cr. P. Art. 652 Burden of proof. (2013). *See also* State v. Coleman, 976 So. 2d 268, 2008 La. App. Lexis 142 (2008).

[110] *See* People v. Lee, 131 Cal. App. 4th 1413, 32 Cal. Rptr. 3d 745, 2005 Cal. App. Lexis 1278 (2005), where victim fired gun at two menacing dogs.

[111] OHIO REV. CODE ANN. § 2901.05 (2013).

the hospital.[112] The defendant's involvement occurred when she attempted to assist her friend in leaving the hospital by intervening in an existing fight. In alleging and proving self-defense, the defendant had the burden of proof to demonstrate lack of fault, had reasonable and honest belief that force was necessary, and that the force was not likely to cause death or serious bodily injury. She was unable to affirmatively prove that her intervention was on behalf of a person who also had a right of self-defense, and therefore, she failed to carry her burden of proving either self-defense or reasonable defense of another person. In an older case that is also demonstrative of the principle that a defendant may be required to prove an affirmative defense, an Ohio woman was convicted of killing her husband with a firearm, even though she offered evidence of self-defense. In her appeal she argued that the Ohio procedure that required her to prove her affirmative defense by a preponderance violated the due process clause of the Fourteenth Amendment because it required her to prove her innocence. The Supreme Court of the United States rejected her contention and held that the allocation of the burden of proof to a defendant did not require her to prove her innocence. Ohio's definition of aggravated murder required the prosecution to prove that she had both purposely and with prior calculation and design caused her husband's death. According to the Supreme Court of the United States, the fact that evidence offered to support self-defense might negate a purposeful killing by prior calculation and design does not mean that elements of the crime and self-defense impermissibly overlap. Evidence that could create a reasonable doubt about one element of the crime necessary for a finding of guilt could easily fall far short of proving self-defense by a preponderance of the evidence.[113] Where a reasonable doubt appears in the state's proof or results because of the defendant's presentation of an affirmative defense, the defendant would have to be acquitted. The United States Supreme Court agreed that neither Ohio law nor the instructions concerning self-defense violated the due process clause of the Fourteenth Amendment by shifting to the petitioner the state's burden of proving the elements of the crime. The Court went on to note that the "mere fact that all but two States have abandoned the common-law rule that affirmative defenses, including self-defense, must be proved by the defendant does not render the rule unconstitutional."

Within the past several years, several states enacted affirmative presumptions that presume a defendant was acting in self-defense in particular situations. Instead of placing the burden on a defendant to prove self-defense, these jurisdictions have helped prospective defendants present self-defense claims by giving a defender a positive presumption of self-defense without requiring the introduction of any evidence other than proof of the fact situation. Ohio has determined that a person is presumed to have acted in self-defense or in defense of another person when a different person has unlawfully invaded the home or motor vehicle of the person using defending force.[114]

---

112 *See* State v. Belcher, 2013-Ohio-1234, 2013 Ohio App. LEXIS 1133 (2013).

113 Martin v. Ohio, 480 U.S. 228, 107 Sup. Ct. 1098, 94 L. Ed. 2d 267 (1987). *See* case in Part II.

114 OHIO REV. CODE ANN. § 2901.05(B) Burden and degree of proof; presumption concerning self-defense or defense of another; jury instructions concerning reasonable doubt. (2013).

The presumption in favor of self-defense is rebuttabled by the opposing party. In a similar fashion, Florida statutes indicate that a person is presumed to have a reasonable fear of imminent peril of death or great injury to himself or others when he uses defensive force that is calculated to cause death or serious bodily injury to the wrongdoer when [t]he person against whom the defensive force was used was in the process of unlawfully and forcefully entering, or had unlawfully and forcibly entered, a dwelling, residence, or occupied vehicle.[115] Florida does not require that the defendant prove that retreat was not a reasonable option in order to make use of the statutory presumption on self-defense under the "stand your ground" statute.[116]

While a state statute requiring the defendant to prove self-defense does not have an unconstitutional burden-shifting result, some states require only that the defendant raise some evidence tending to prove self-defense. For example, in Texas criminal prosecutions where a defendant pleads self-defense, the defendant has the duty to introduce some evidence to support the alleged claim of self-defense. The state then has the burden of disproving self-defense beyond a reasonable doubt.[117]

An Alaska decision followed prior case law in applying the rule that, when a defendant has presented some evidence of self-defense, it becomes the prosecution's duty to disprove the defendant's evidence of self-defense beyond a reasonable doubt.[118] In this case, the prosecution's evidence showed that the defendant had hit the victim in the forehead with his hand, punched her in the face, dragged her to the floor, and choked her. The defendant's evidence was that the woman was the aggressor and that he held her on the floor to prevent her from harming him. The self-defense claim failed, but the defendant's evidence was sufficient to force the prosecution to disprove self-defense beyond a reasonable doubt and to obtain a jury instruction on self-defense.

To summarize, in some states when the accused offers the affirmative defense of self-defense and produces some evidence in support of the self-defense theory, the burden rests on the prosecutor to prove beyond a reasonable doubt that the accused did not act in self-defense. Procedurally, the defendant must raise the issue and offer some evidence that shifts the burden of proof to the prosecution. In other states, the accused not only has the initial burden of going forward with evidence of self-defense, but also carries the ultimate burden of proof by a preponderance of the evidence that he or she acted in self-defense. While imposing any burden of proof on a defendant might appear to raise constitutional issues, state statutes allocating the ultimate burden of proof to the defense have been determined not to run afoul of the requirements of the Constitution.

---

115 FLA. STAT. § 776.013 (2013).

116 *See* Floyd v. State, 2014 Fla. App. LEXIS 99 (2014).

117 London v. State, 2008 Tex. App. Lexis 9039 (Tex. 2008).

118 Ross v. State, 2006 Alaska App. Lexis 41 (2006).

§ 3.13 Sufficiency of Evidence

Once a court or jury has rendered a decision, there is a strong presumption of regularity and that the case was properly determined. When a defendant appeals a conviction, he or she must contend that serious defects exist in the case sufficient to warrant a reversal of the judgment. A Texas reviewing court noted that, in considering the **sufficiency of the evidence** to support a criminal conviction, "we view the evidence in the light most favorable to the verdict and examine whether a rational fact-finder could have found the essential elements of the crime beyond a reasonable doubt."[119] A reviewing court, on appeal or in a habeas corpus action, may determine that the evidence was insufficient to support the finding of guilt, even though, technically, an appellate court does not reweigh the evidence or reconsider the credibility of the witnesses.[120] In *Jackson v. Virginia*, the United States Supreme Court, in confirming the authority of a federal court to review a state court decision on the sufficiency of the evidence, made this comment:

> **Sufficiency of the evidence** In a criminal case, whether the evidence is such that a jury could logically have found that a defendant was guilty beyond a reasonable doubt or that an affirmative defense was properly proven.

> Yet a properly instructed jury may occasionally convict even when it can be said that no rational trier of fact could find guilt beyond a reasonable doubt, and the same may be said of a trial judge sitting as a jury.[121]

Once it is recognized that a reviewing court can look behind the decision of the jury to determine whether there was sufficient evidence to justify a finding of guilt beyond a reasonable doubt, the question then becomes: What is the test of sufficiency?

In *Jackson*, the United States Court of Appeals for the Fourth Circuit determined that an appellate court should uphold a state court decision so long as there was any evidence in the record to support it. Following this theory, if there is absolutely no evidence to justify the jury in finding guilt, then the court will reverse the conviction as a violation of due process. But if there is any evidence to support the conviction, as there was in *Jackson*, the case will be affirmed.

The defendant in *Jackson* appealed to the United States Supreme Court, claiming that the "any evidence rule" was inadequate to protect against misapplication of the constitutional standards of reasonable doubt. The United States Supreme Court agreed, stating that the rule that should have been applied was not the "any evidence rule," but rather the rule that was stated in *In re Winship*,[122] which held that a federal habeas corpus court must consider not whether there was any evidence to support a

---

119 Everson v. State, 2008 Tex. App. Lexis 4834 (2008).

120 United States v. Zavala, 2006 U.S. App. Lexis 15848 (3d Cir. 2006).

121 443 U.S. 307, 317, 1979 U.S. Lexis 10 (1979).

122 In re Winship, 397 U.S. 358, 90 Sup. Ct. 1068, 25 L. Ed. 2d 368 (1970). *See* case in Part II.

state conviction, but whether there was sufficient evidence to justify a rational trier of fact to find guilt beyond a reasonable doubt. The Supreme Court in *Jackson* first held that the "any evidence rule" is simply inadequate to protect against misapplications of the constitutional standard of proof beyond a reasonable doubt. That Court then insisted:

> Instead the relevant question is whether after reviewing the evidence in the light most favorable to the prosecution, any rational trier of fact could have found the essential elements of the crime beyond a reasonable doubt.

In affirming that a federal court can and will apply the *Winship* sufficiency rule, the Court in *Jackson* made this conclusion as to the rules to be followed:

> We hold that in a challenge to a state criminal conviction the appellant is entitled to habeas corpus relief if it is found that upon the record evidence adduced at the trial no rational trier of fact could have found proof of guilt beyond a reasonable doubt.

After a review on the new standard, the Court found on the merits that Jackson's case would not be reversed. The Court said that, from the evidence in the record, it was clear that the judge could reasonably have found beyond a reasonable doubt that Jackson did possess the necessary intent at or before the time of the killing to justify the first-degree murder conviction.

To summarize the sufficiency-of-the-evidence rule, in a criminal case the prosecutor must introduce relevant and otherwise admissible evidence sufficient for the trier of fact to find the defendant guilty beyond a reasonable doubt. Although an appellate court does not reweigh the evidence, the reviewing court may set aside a conviction if that reviewing court finds that no rational trier of fact could logically have found the defendant guilty beyond a reasonable doubt.

§ 3.14 Summary

In every criminal case, the ultimate burden of proof rests with the prosecution to prove every element of a charged crime beyond a reasonable doubt. This burden of proof or burden of persuasion rests on the prosecution from the start of a trial to the end, and it never shifts to the defendant. By asserting an affirmative defense, a defendant may, depending on the jurisdiction, have an ultimate burden of proof concerning the defense. The burden of going forward with the evidence initially rests on the prosecution, but may shift to the defense if the prosecution succeeds in introducing evidence that, if believed by the jury or judge, would result in a conviction. To avoid an adverse result, the defendant must meet the burden of going forward with the evidence and introduce evidence that either creates reasonable doubt or establishes an affirmative defense. Constitutional interpretations dictate that proof beyond a reasonable doubt must be used in criminal cases while civil plaintiffs only need to meet the burden of proving their case by a preponderance of the evidence.

Depending upon the nature of the case, there are three degrees of proof required. These are a preponderance of the evidence, clear and convincing evidence, and beyond a reasonable doubt. In a civil case, the plaintiff is usually only required to establish his or her claim by a preponderance of the evidence. Some civil cases go beyond this standard and require proof by clear and convincing evidence because other important interests, such as reputation, may be at stake. The use of the higher standard of beyond a reasonable doubt in criminal cases has been justified because life, freedom, and liberty may be at risk—not merely money. In a criminal case, however, there is no doubt that the accused retains the presumption of innocence until his or her guilt is established beyond a reasonable doubt.

The burden is on the prosecution in a criminal case to show affirmatively the existence of every material fact, including each element of the crime, the identity of the person who committed the crime, and that the crime was perpetrated in violation of the penal laws of the place where it took place.

Even though the burden of proving the elements in a criminal case rests solely with the prosecution, the accused must be allocated a burden of proof when the accused gives notice of asserting an affirmative defense. For example, when a defendant alleges an affirmative defense such as coercion, self-defense, entrapment, or mistake, the burden of proof may rest with the defendant to prove the defense, usually by a preponderance of the evidence. Some jurisdictions require that a defendant raise the issue of an affirmative defense and present some evidence in order to require the prosecution to disprove the affirmative defense beyond a reasonable doubt. In some jurisdictions, an affirmative defense may not be proven, but the evidence may create a reasonable doubt, which has the same effect as a successful affirmative defense.

Even though alibi, strictly speaking, is not an affirmative defense, because the defense merely offers evidence that the defendant had no involvement in the crime, the defendant must affirmatively introduce evidence to substantiate this alibi claim. If the defense is insanity, the law in some jurisdictions requires that the defendant prove his or her legal insanity by a preponderance of the evidence or by clear and convincing evidence, and even proof beyond a reasonable doubt has been approved. When evidence is introduced to show self-defense to justify an otherwise criminal act, the defendant may be required to offer proof by a preponderance of the evidence that he or she acted in self-defense.

All criminal justice personnel need to recognize the additional evidentiary burden placed on the prosecution in criminal cases and must be aware that sufficient evidence should be gathered to convince the jury or the judge not only that the accused is probably guilty of the offense charged, but also that guilt has been proved beyond a reasonable doubt. Those involved in the criminal justice process should also recognize that the defense will make every effort to create reasonable doubt in the minds of the jury and need only create a reasonable doubt concerning one element for the defense to prevail.

A study of the burden of proof accentuates the need to become familiar with other evidence rules that bear upon the admissibility of evidence. Much of the remainder of the book is devoted to a discussion of these rules.

CHAPTER THREE: QUESTIONS AND REVIEW EXERCISES

1. What is the difference between the burden of proof and the burden of going forward with the evidence?
2. Theoretically, three different levels of proof may exist in a criminal case. Explain the distinctions that exist among proof by the preponderance of the evidence, proof by clear and convincing evidence, and proof beyond a reasonable doubt.
3. The burden of proof has been placed on the prosecution to prove the case beyond a reasonable doubt. What is the result when the prosecution fails to convince the jury beyond a reasonable doubt concerning one element of the charged crime? What happens when an appellate court finds that a single element of the charged crime has not been proved beyond a reasonable doubt?
4. Depending on claims by a defendant, there may be occasions during some criminal cases where the defendant may have a burden of proof. Develop and explain three fact situations where a defendant would have a burden of proof in a criminal case.
5. In the case of an alibi defense, some jurisdictions hold that the burden of proof can be placed on the defendant, while some jurisdictions hold that the burden of proof is placed on the prosecution to demonstrate that the defendant was the perpetrator. From what you have learned in this chapter, make the argument that, for the alibi defense, burden of proof should be placed on the defendant.
6. Explain the various views that different jurisdictions possess concerning where to place the burden of proof for insanity defenses. Concerning the placement of the burden of proof for the insanity defense, which view best serves justice and is fair to a defendant? Why?
7. Upon which party does the federal insanity defense place its burden of proof? What level of proof is required for a federal defendant to win a case involving the insanity defense?
8. Although a plea of self-defense generally concedes that the alleged criminal activity occurred, what kind of proof or evidence must a typical defendant introduce to gain a not-guilty verdict? Do some states place the burden of proof squarely on the defendant? Give an example.
9. Once a court or jury renders a conviction, there is a presumption of correctness of the verdict on appeal, and a reviewing court will consider the appeal in the light most favorable to the prosecution. Why should this presumption of correctness exist?

Proof via Evidence

4

At the trial of a person charged with murder, the fact of death is provable by circumstantial evidence, notwithstanding that neither the body nor any trace of the body has been found and that the accused has made no confession of any participation in the crime. Before he can be convicted, the fact of death should be proved by such circumstances as render the commission of the crime morally certain and leave no ground for possible doubt; the circumstantial evidence should be so cogent and compelling as to convince a jury that upon no rational hypothesis other than murder can the facts be accounted for.

Rex v. Horry, 1952 N.Z.L.R. 111

Chapter Contents

Section

KEY TERMS AND CONCEPTS

Case-in-Chief	Proof
Circumstantial Evidence	Rebuttal
Direct Evidence	Role of Judge
Objections	Rejoinder
Pretrial Motion	Weight of Circumstantial Evidence

§ 4.1 Introduction

The previous chapter cites and discusses cases that clearly indicate that the prosecution possesses the burden of proving guilt in criminal cases. The prosecutor must introduce evidence or use evidentiary tools that produce substitutes for evidence in order to meet the standard of proof beyond a reasonable doubt.

To prove a criminal case, it is not absolutely essential for the prosecution to actually present the jury or judge with each fact or bit of knowledge in the form of direct evidence. To save time and to avoid placing an unnecessary burden on the parties, the judge may take judicial notice of certain facts and may advise the jury that they may make certain presumptions and inferences. The factfinders may also consider facts stipulated by the parties. Therefore, the jury or other factfinders may make a decision from: (1) facts presented in the form of evidence; (2) information noticed by the judge; (3) legal presumptions; (4) judicially approved inferences; and (5) accepted stipulations. This chapter presents the method of proving facts by the introduction of evidence in the courtroom.

After considering the procedure related to pretrial motions to exclude evidence, this chapter discusses general admissibility tests. The following section describes the order of presenting evidence at the trial. The chapter also explains the roles of the judge, jury, witness, prosecuting attorney, and legal counsel for the defense in relation to the introduction and evaluation of evidence. Finally, the text comprehensively considers the rules governing the admissibility and weight of direct and circumstantial evidence.

In Chapters 5 and 6, "substitutes for evidence"—judicial notice, presumptions, inferences, and stipulations—are defined and examples of each are offered.

§ 4.2 Pretrial Motions Pertaining to Evidence

Rule 104

PRELIMINARY QUESTIONS

(a) **In General**. The court must decide any preliminary question about whether a witness is qualified, a privilege exists, or evidence is admissible. In so deciding, the court is not bound by evidence rules, except those on privilege.

(b) **Relevance**. That Depends on a Fact. When the relevance of evidence depends on whether a fact exists, sufficient proof must be introduced to support a finding that the fact does exist. The court may admit the proposed evidence on the condition that the proof be introduced later.

During the pretrial stage of a criminal prosecution, either party may file motions challenging the admissibility of evidence that an opposing party is expected to introduce at the trial. As a general rule, pretrial motions should address any procedural defense or evidentiary objection that can be determined without a trial of the general issues. The rationale behind determining some procedural or evidentiary issues during the pretrial stage is that the resolution could make a trial unnecessary, but, in any event, it resolves issues that would otherwise disrupt the smooth flow of the trial. These pretrial motions include challenges to the court's jurisdiction, competence or fairness of the tribunal, the statement of the charges, the competency of the defendant to stand trial, the legality of the way in which police gathered evidence, flaws in a grand jury indictment, and constitutional challenges, such as double jeopardy, speedy trial, and search and seizure issues.

As a general rule, the motion to suppress evidence must be made within a reasonable time before the scheduled trial, but a failure to challenge the evidence in a timely manner may be excused by the court for good cause. If the defense offers a motion to suppress some of the prosecution's evidence, a hearing will be scheduled within a reasonable time so that the attorneys for each party might present evidence and argue the merits of their respective positions. Police officers and the defendant may be called as witnesses in support of each party's legal theory. If the judge agrees with the defendant's legal position, the evidence, even if relevant to the issues, will not be admitted at the trial.

One of the most common pretrial motions to exclude evidence challenges the use of evidence illegally seized in violation of either the Fourth Amendment to the United States Constitution or the comparable search and seizure provisions of state constitutions. For example, if the defendant alleges that law enforcement officials obtained evidence by conducting a warrantless search and seizure of the defendant's home in violation of the defendant's Fourth Amendment rights, the defense attorney will file a pretrial motion to suppress the evidence. At the hearing, the defendant will have to introduce some evidence that his or her rights have been violated by law enforcement officials' conduct, and then the prosecutor will have the burden of proving that the warrantless search was lawful. The defense counsel will present evidence to support the seizures as unlawful. If the accused can demonstrate that the evidence was obtained by an unlawful search and seizure, and such evidence does not come within an exception to the rule that excludes illegally seized evidence, the judge will order that the evidence will be suppressed from introduction at the trial.[1] But if the prosecutor can show that the evidence was obtained without violating the defendant's rights under the Constitution, that the search was within one of the recognized exceptions to the exclusionary rule,[2] or that the social costs of applying the rule outweigh the benefits,[3] the motion to suppress will be denied, and the evidence will be admitted, absent exclusion for some other evidentiary reason.

Evidence may also be challenged as having been secured in violation of other constitutional provisions. For example, evidence may be inadmissible if the self-incrimination provisions of the Fifth Amendment, the right-to-counsel provisions of the Sixth Amendment, the due process clause of the Fifth or Fourteenth Amendments, or the principles of the *Miranda* warnings have been violated by law enforcement personnel.[4]

§ 4.3 General Approach to Admissibility

As a general proposition, all evidence is admissible unless a particular rule of evidence requires its exclusion. Therefore, all evidence offered in a criminal case carries with it a presumption of admissibility, unless there is a timely and specific objection by the opposing party. Following an appropriate objection, the trial judge will be required to entertain the basis for the objection and make a ruling concerning the admissibility of the questioned evidence. When one party asks a question of a witness and the opposing party offers an objection to it, the objection will normally be based on either the form or phrasing of the question that was asked or on the substance of the expected answer. A helpful way to approach the rules of evidence is to keep these simple tests concerning form and substance in mind as each rule of evidence is discussed.

A. *Objections as to Form*

In order to avoid confusing the witness, the court will require that a question be clear and intelligent. Judges will not permit questions to be asked of witnesses where those questions are confusing, compound, improperly phrased, misleading, or intended

---

1 Mapp v. Ohio, 367 U.S. 643 (1961), Wong Sun v. United States, 371 U.S. 471, 1963 U.S. Lexis 2431 (1963). *See also* Weeks v. United States, 232 U.S. 383 (1914).

2 *See* Massachusetts v. Sheppard, 468 U.S. 981, 1984 U.S. Lexis 154 (1984), and Dickerson v. United States, 530 U.S. 428, 2000 U.S. Lexis 4305 (2000).

3 Hudson v. Michigan, 2006 U.S. Lexis 4677, 74 U.S.L.W. 4311 (2006).

4 *See* Chapter 16, Part I, for more comprehensive coverage of the exclusion of illegally obtained evidence based on federal constitutional issues.

as arguments directed toward an objection raised by opposing counsel. In fact, the judge will often ask that such questions be rephrased. Questions with phrasing that prevents any definite answer will, of course, mislead the witness as well as the jury.

Compound questions, which have two parts, are generally objectionable as to form, because the witness may not be able to answer both parts with one answer; if one answer is given, there is no way to know to which question the answer responded. Other questions that are sometimes objectionable as to form, especially during direct examination, are classified as leading questions.[5] Such questions generally suggest the desired answer by the manner in which they are phrased.

B. Objections as to Substance

No party raises an objection as to form, or if an objection is made and settled, the court then applies the test of substance. One easy way to understand the test of substance is to imagine three hurdles erected between the evidence and the court. Before the evidence can be admitted into court, all three hurdles must be cleared. They are relevancy, materiality, and competency.

The concept of relevancy concerns whether the information has a tendency to prove or disprove one or more of the facts at issue in the case. To be relevant, the information must have a tendency to establish or disprove matters at issue in the case.[6]

In other words, will the matter at issue be more or less likely to be believed or disbelieved if the jury hears the evidence, than if it does not hear the evidence? If the evidence affects the probabilities of belief, it will be considered relevant evidence. Materiality involves the relative importance of evidence. Evidence is material only when it affects a fact or issue of the case in a significant way. The definition of competency is more elusive. Competent evidence is that which is legally adequate and sufficient. The competency test is a catch-all for the exclusionary rules. For example, evidence obtained by an illegal search in violation of the Constitution is inadmissible not because it is immaterial or irrelevant, but because of its legal inadequacy or incompetency.

If the proposed evidence meets the tests of form and substance, it is admitted into court. The weight or the importance to be given to the evidence by the jury or the judge depends on many other factors.

§ 4.4 Order of Presenting Evidence at the Trial[7]

The judge has a great deal of discretion in establishing court procedures, and local court rules play a role, but he or she generally follows the procedures that have been

---

5 Leading questions are discussed in Chapter 9.

6 The relevancy and materiality rules and examples are comprehensively discussed in Chapter 7.

7 For a more comprehensive explanation of criminal procedure from arrest to final release, *see* CARLSON, CRIMINAL JUSTICE PROCEDURE (8th ed. 2013).

developed over a period of years and have become standard. The usual order of procedure in presenting the case is as follows:[8]

1. Prosecution's case-in-chief
2. Defendant's case-in-chief
3. Prosecution's case in rebuttal
4. Defense's case in rejoinder

Each of these steps is discussed in some depth to point out its scope and limitations.

A. *Prosecution's Case-in-Chief*

At the beginning of the trial after preliminary matters have been concluded and when opening statements of the parties have concluded the prosecution begins to introduce testimonial and physical evidence. The prosecution introduces evidence in the early stages of the trial because it possesses the burden of going forward with the evidence and has the ultimate burden of proof. The prosecutor may call as many witnesses as necessary and may introduce exhibits, photographs, documents, or other types of evidence that may help the jury determine the guilt or innocence of the accused—provided that the evidence meets appropriate admissibility tests. During this phase of the procedure, the prosecutor is "carrying the ball," "calling the plays," and going forward with the presentation of evidence. The lead prosecutor determines which of the potential witnesses for the government will actually testify, decides the order in which the witnesses are presented to the court, and guides the flow of evidence. The prosecutor also questions each prosecution witness before the defense attorney has the opportunity to cross-examine that witness.[9] At this stage, the defense cannot introduce its own witnesses, and, according to the majority view, must limit cross-examination to subject matters mentioned by prosecution witnesses during the direct examination.

The prosecuting attorney concludes the presentation of the case-in-chief, when he or she feels satisfied about having met the burden for going forward with the evidence, or that sufficient evidence has been presented to make a case against the defendant by proof beyond a reasonable doubt. He or she then signifies the completion of the case-in-chief by stating, "The prosecution rests," or other words to that effect.

B. *Defendant's Case-in-Chief*

If the defense believes that the prosecution evidence failed to meet the government's burden of proof, the defendant's counsel may ask the judge for a "directed verdict" of acquittal after the prosecution has concluded its case-in-chief. If the judge believes that no rational jury could convict on the basis of the evidence presented, the judge will order an acquittal. In this situation, the case ends, and no retrial is

---

8 MCCORMICK, EVIDENCE 7.

9 The procedure to be followed in the examination of witnesses is discussed in Chapter 9, *infra*.

possible because the judge's decision operates as a verdict on the merits of the case. For example, in a Medicaid fraud case where the state alleged that the defendant had lied on an important matter on her application, but the prosecution failed to prove the lie or any deception, the judge should have directed a verdict of acquittal, upon the defendant's motion, because the prosecution failed to meet its burden of proof as a matter of law.[10] If this motion by the defense attorney fails, the defense has the opportunity to present its evidence or case-in-chief. However, the defendant is not required to put on a defense, because the burden of proof remains with the prosecution. The defendant may present evidence in denial of the prosecution's claim; he or she may introduce evidence designed to destroy the prosecutor's proof of one or more of the elements of the offense; the defendant may attempt to establish an alibi or a different affirmative defense through the use of witnesses. In all cases, the defendant has a Fifth Amendment privilege not to become a witness in his or her own behalf, but all defendants have an opportunity to personally become a witness. If the defendant chooses to testify, he or she is usually the first witness to take the stand at this stage of the proceedings.[11] As with the prosecution, the defense counsel conducts direct examination of each defense witness, and then immediately following the direct examination of each witness, the prosecution has an opportunity to cross-examine each defense witness. When the defense counsel has completed the presentation of the evidence, the defendant's attorney states, "The defense rests."

C. State's Case in Rebuttal

The prosecution now has the opportunity to rebut or refute the evidence, or important portions of it, presented by the defense. At this stage, the prosecution may not present witnesses who merely support the allegations of the indictment. All of that type of evidence should have introduced when the prosecution presented its case-in-chief, as the prosecution attempts to build the strongest case during that stage. As a result, during rebuttal, the prosecution is limited to the introduction of testimony or other evidence that is directed toward refuting the evidence that has been offered by the defense. New witnesses may be called at this time, but only if they can rebut, contradict, or cast doubt upon the evidence presented by the defendant, and the witness's testimony must not exceed the scope of the defense case. For example, if the defense raised the question of insanity, the prosecution may offer evidence to show that the defendant was not insane as defined by law. In this stage, as in other stages, the witness may not only be examined directly, but may also be cross-examined by opposing counsel.

---

[10] Folds v. State, 2013 Ala. Crim. App. LEXIS 115 (2013).

[11] In 1972, the United States Supreme Court held that requiring the defendant to testify before other defense witnesses violates the self-incrimination provisions of the Constitution. Brooks v. Tennessee, 406 U.S. 605, 92 S. Ct. 1891, 32 L. Ed. 2d 358 (1972), State v. Glover, 636 So. 2d 976 (La. 1994).

D. Defense's Case in Rejoinder

The defense also has the opportunity to introduce evidence contrary to that introduced by the prosecution during its case in rebuttal. This phase of the trial is called the defense case in rejoinder. With a view to narrowing the subject matter, the evidence is limited to refuting or discrediting the evidence presented by the prosecution during the state's case in rebuttal. Returning to the previous example, where the state has offered evidence to demonstrate that the defendant may not have been legally insane, the defendant has the opportunity to offer testimony to correct the evidence offered by the prosecution by showing that the defendant was insane, according to the legal definition. If the prosecution managed to introduce new evidence that "opened the door" to new material, the defense is also permitted to rebut the new material with relevant evidence during this stage of the case.

There are instances when the case may continue with the prosecution and the defense each having the opportunity to refute the evidence presented by the other. However, the subsequent rebuttals obviously become more and more limited, and in the usual case, both parties will have presented all the evidence that they intend to present by the end of the defendant's case in rejoinder.

When both parties have announced that they have rested their cases, the hearing on the facts comes to an end, and the trial proceeds with the closing arguments of counsel and the court's instructions to the jury.

§ 4.5 Procedure for Offering and Challenging Evidence

Rule 103

RULINGS ON EVIDENCE

(a) **Preserving a claim of error**. A party may claim error in a ruling to admit or exclude evidence only if the error affects a substantial right of the party and
(1) if the ruling admits evidence, a party, on the record:
(A) timely objects or moves to strike; and
(B) states the specific ground, unless it was apparent from the context; or
(2) if the ruling excludes evidence, a party informs the court of its substance by an offer of proof, unless the substance was apparent from the context.
(b) **Not needing to renew an objection or offer of proof**. Once the court rules definitively on the record—either before or at trial—a party need not renew an objection or offer of proof to preserve a claim of error for appeal. [12]

---

12 FED. R. EVID. 103. The Federal Rules of Evidence, effective 1975 (Pub. L. No. 93-595), apply to United States federal courts, judge magistrate proceedings, and bankruptcy courts. Portions of these rules, as well as the committee comments thereto, are inserted when relevant to the text discussion. The complete rules as approved through 2013 appear in the Appendix I, *infra*.

As a general proposition, neither side will have all of its desired evidence admitted by the court and will of necessity structure individual cases with this consideration in mind. Constitutional and statutory considerations and the rules of evidence will operate to exclude evidence. Unique situational reasons may require that judicial decision-making evaluate the relevancy of evidence in determining admissibility. State and federal courts follow a complex set of rules in determining what evidence should be admitted and what evidence should be excluded. A significant portion of the remainder of this book is devoted to the rules that have been developed for judicial application in determining the admissibility of evidence. Most of these rules are rules of exclusion, and the parties often argue that exceptions to these rules are applicable in particular situations, depending on which side desires the admission of the evidence.

The usual way of offering and eliciting oral testimony involves placing the witness on the stand and asking the witness a question or series of questions. If an opposing counsel believes a question is improper, that counsel makes an objection with an accompanying rationale, and then the judge rules concerning whether the answer should be allowed. A specific objection is required, unless the context of the testimony and the objection makes the reason obvious. The counsel asking the question may offer the judge the legal rationale concerning why the objection should be overruled and the evidence admitted. If the judge sustains an objection that keeps evidence from being presented, the attorney for the party wishing to present the evidence should make an offer of proof (a proffer) of what the evidence, if it had been allowed, would have shown. The Supreme Court of New Hampshire suggested that an offer of proof must set forth the specific basis for the admissibility of the proffered evidence and must describe the evidence and what it tends to show.[13] The offer of proof allows the trial court to properly consider the arguments for admissibility, while preserving the record for appeal. In a child pornography case, a judge sustained a prosecutor's objection, preventing the defendant from offering testimony concerning the version of incriminating statements the defendant initially made to law enforcement officials.[14] Since the defendant's attorney failed to make an offer of proof concerning what the defendant would have said, the reviewing court properly refused to consider whether the trial judge was correct in the initial ruling. Adverse appellate consequences follow from a failure to make an offer of proof once a judge rules to exclude evidence.

If the judge makes what one party considers to be an erroneous ruling, the party can challenge the ruling on appeal, provided that the opposing counsel made a proper and timely objection, including an offer of proof. In order to prevail on appeal, the trial judge's error in excluding evidence must rise to the level that the error affected the outcome of the trial; any lesser error is considered "harmless error" and will not support a reversal of the verdict.

To avoid an unnecessary expenditure of trial time, the rules in virtually all states provide that the use of the archaic formal exception procedure is unnecessary, but the

---

13 State v. Noucas, 165 N.H. 146, 158, 70 A.3d 476, 486, 2013 N.H.LEXIS 83 (2013).

14 United States v. Larman, 2013 U.S. App. LEXIS 22936 (5th Cir. 2013).

objecting attorney must have made an appropriate and timely request, objection, or motion, stating "the grounds for the ruling that the complaining party sought from the trial court with sufficient specificity to make the trial court aware of the complaint, unless the specific grounds were apparent from the context."[15] Consistent with this concept, the rules of evidence for federal courts provide that "[o]nce the court rules definitively on the record—either before or at a trial—a party need not renew an objection or offer of proof to preserve a claim of error for appeal."[16]

In a North Carolina case involving a state version of Rule 103, the court concluded that, in order to preserve the admission or exclusion of evidence for appellate review, the significance of the admitted or excluded evidence must appear in the record, and a specific offer of proof must have been made to the court unless its significance was obvious or apparent from the record. If a defendant alleges error in the exclusion of testimony, but has failed to offer proof for the record, there is no issue on which an appellate court may rule.[17] However, an appellate court may use the concept of "plain error" as the standard for review as a way to allow an appeal where a party failed to make an appropriate Rule 103 objection.[18]

In the case of introducing real evidence, such as bullets, guns, and articles of clothing, the offering party has the evidence identified or authenticated by a witness and then submits it to the opposing counsel for inspection. When this has been done, it is presented to the judge, and depending upon the type of evidence, it may be presented to each juror individually or to the jury as a whole.

The requirement that the objecting party offer specific grounds for an objection permits the judge to understand the objection, its purpose, and the legal basis. It allows the opposing counsel to properly meet the objection and address it. A precise objection permits opposing counsel to understand the objection, while it allows the judge to correct any errors by making an informed and appropriate decision at the time of the trial, and the objection also has the effect of preserving the record for appeal.[19]

§ 4.6 Role of the Trial Judge in Evidence Matters

In the English and American systems, the trial judge is responsible for controlling order, decorum, and court procedure in the courtroom, while ensuring that the trial is administered fairly and that the cases progress efficiently and smoothly. When a defendant has requested a jury trial, the jury evaluates the evidence and determines which

---

15 *See* TEX. R. APP. P.33(c)(1) (2014).

16 FED. R. EVID. 103(b).

17 State v. Cousar, 660 S.E.2d 902, 905, 2008 N.C. App. Lexis 1076 (2008).

18 FED. R. EVID. 103(d). According to the Tenth Circuit, "To establish plain error, a defendant must show that: (1) an error; (2) that is plain and obvious, (3) that affects substantial rights, and (4) seriously affects the fairness or public reputation of the judicial proceeding." United States v. Vazquez, 2009 U.S. App. Lexis 2473 (10th Cir. 2009).

19 75 AM. JUR. 2D *Trial* § 312 (2013). *See also* Gbur, Executrix v. Golio, 2009 Pa. Lexis 177 (2009).

facts it collectively believes have been established beyond a reasonable doubt; however, the judge still plays an important role in relation to the admission and exclusion of evidence. Some of these duties are enumerated and explained as follows. The judge:

- *During pretrial hearings, determines whether some of the evidence will be admissible at the trial*—In the first instance, after listening to arguments from both sides, the judge determines what evidence will be admitted during the trial and what evidence will be suppressed. If a motion to suppress is made before the trial starts, the judge's decision generally stands for the duration of the trial. In most situations, the judge's pretrial evidence rulings will stand, although the prosecution may appeal a ruling suppressing evidence where the matter is crucial to the prosecutor's case. Where the pretrial ruling effectively ends the prosecution's case, the prosecutor must decide to either drop the case or pursue an immediate pretrial appeal.
- *Acts on motions and objections regarding evidence during the trial*—If a party challenges the admission of evidence as being irrelevant, immaterial, incompetent, or otherwise excludable under the rules of evidence, the judge determines whether the evidence will be admitted or excluded and announces that ruling in court.

As a general rule, trial judges have the inherent power to admit or exclude evidence at trial and appellate courts "review the admission of evidence for abuse of discretion."[20] Putting this in somewhat different terms, a federal appeals court observed that a trial judge has broad discretion in ruling on the admissibility of evidence, and an appellate court will not reverse a trial judge's decision unless a clear abuse of discretion was demonstrated.[21]

- *Makes decisions concerning the constitutionality of law enforcement activities*—A motion to exclude evidence obtained in violation of the Constitution must generally be made at a pretrial hearing on a motion to suppress, or such a motion may be made during the trial if the issue first surfaces at that point. To decide this challenge properly, the judge must be familiar with the decisions regarding such matters as search and seizure, confessions, right to counsel, self-incrimination, and due process. If a motion is made to exclude evidence because these provisions were violated, and the judge nonetheless admits the evidence that has been obtained in violation of the Constitution, the reviewing court on appeal can and probably will reverse the decision, unless the error is harmless.
- *Protects the witnesses from overzealous examination and cross-examination by counsel*—Overzealous counsel sometimes browbeat witnesses by continuing to ask questions that have been answered or by harshly or unnecessarily cross-examining a witness. Because the judge has the duty to control the courtroom and the manner in which witnesses are questioned, the judge may intervene on his or her own motion or from objections made by counsel for the parties.

---

20 State v. Payne, 306 P.3d 17, 32, ¶ 56, 2013 Ariz. LEXIS 166 (2013). *See also* Grace v. City of Cheyenne, 2006 U.S. App. Lexis 15182 (10th Cir. 2006).

21 United States v. Fuller, 2006 U.S. App. Lexis 14852 (5th Cir. 2006).

- *Takes judicial notice*—The judge plays a very important role by taking judicial notice of the commonly-known facts that may be considered by the jury in making their decision.[22] Many scientific, historical, and geographic facts are so well known that requiring these facts to be proved via witnesses would constitute a waste of a trial court's time. For example, that water boils at 100 degrees Centigrade is a universally known scientific fact. Having a physicist or other expert prove the boiling point of water would certainly waste the court's resources. The judge may accept without proof that water boils at 100 degrees, and both parties would generally have no legal objection.
- *Determines competency of the witness to testify*—The judge determines whether the witness meets the requirements of competency.[23] "[I]t is a general principle of law that everyone is presumed to be competent"[24] as a witness, unless the opposing party can demonstrate otherwise. For example, where the witness possessed sufficient memory of the facts and would tell the truth, an appellate court held that the trial court did not abuse its discretion in holding that the challenged witness was competent to testify.[25] Judicial determinations of competency are reviewable on appeal, based on an abuse of discretion standard.
- *Rules on issues of law*—In addition, the judge instructs the jury concerning the law to be applied to the facts that the jury determined, advises the jury as to what facts may be considered, and provides alternatives with respect to lesser included offenses in returning its verdict.
- *Acts as a finder of fact in some cases*—Finally, when a trial takes place without a jury, such as when the defendant waives the Sixth Amendment right to jury, the judge has the role as the factfinder. In this instance, the judge performs a dual role: the judge acts in his or her normal capacity, managing the case and ruling on evidentiary matters, and the judge performs the function of the jury in deciding which facts have been properly proven.

A criminal trial judge is not an advocate for either party, but serves as a neutral referee placed between the parties and their attorneys and commits error if he or she acts as an advocate for either party.[26] Generally, a trial judge has discretion to comment on the evidence presented at trial and to make other comments during the course of a trial,[27] but some jurisdictions do not permit the judge to comment on the evidence.[28] When a judge determines to offer comments to the jury concerning the

---

22 Judicial notice is discussed in Chapter 5.

23 Competency of witnesses is discussed in Chapter 9, *and see* Commonwealth v. Alicea, 464 Mass. 837, 846, 985 N.E.2d 1197, 2013 Mass. LEXIS 172 (2013).

24 Walker v. State, 986 N.E.2d 328, 333, 2013 Ind. App. LEXIS 177 (2013). *See also* ARK. R. EVID. 601 (2008).

25 People v. Watson, 245 Mich. App. 572 at 583, 629 N.W.2d 411 at 420 (2001).

26 Commonwealth v. Baumhammers, 960 A.2d 59, 2008 Pa. Lexis 2078 (Pa. 2008).

27 United States v. Zidar, 2006 U.S. App. Lexis 11858 (9th Cir. 2006).

28 State v. Francisco, 148 Wash. App. 168, 179, 2009 Wash App. Lexis 22 (Wash. 2009).

evidence, the judge must take great care to assure that the comments do not create unfair prejudice to either party.[29]

While a trial judge must avoid any actual or apparent partisanship to, for, or against a party, the judge must be actively engaged in overseeing the trial. In *Brown v. State*, the trial judge denied a defense request for a mistrial, because the prosecution had not notified the defense of some evidence that the prosecution had an obligation to disclose.[30] The judge properly recognized that the state was not being unfair, because the prosecution notified the defense as soon as it became aware of the evidence. The judge remained impartial in ruling on the case. In a different case, a judge abandoned this impartial role, making jokes and light-hearted comments and generally displaying an irreverent attitude during a murder trial. He joked about not wanting to be there and told lawyer jokes during the trial. The appellate court, in reversing the murder conviction that resulted, noted that:

> The trial judge has primary responsibility for maintaining order and decorum in the courtroom and must control criminal proceedings so as to insure that justice is done. We recognize that the trial judge's intent in the instant case may have been to create a casual atmosphere to put jurors at ease and make them feel welcome; however, the trial judge not only failed to maintain order and decorum but also actively contributed to creating an aura of jocularity inappropriate to the gravity of the proceedings.[31]

When a jury appears to be confused about a legal issue and needs additional guidance during deliberations, and when a resolution of the question is not apparent from earlier instructions, a trial judge has a responsibility to give the jury additional guidance by a clear statement of relevant legal criteria.[32] As a general rule, after a jury has retired to deliberate and desires to be informed on a point of law, the judge may consult with both parties and then offer additional instructions to the jury.[33]

§ 4.7 Function of the Jury

In a criminal trial, the jury has the duty to decide what facts were proved by the evidence, resolve conflicts in the evidence, and apply the law to the facts based on the facts as determined. As one law encyclopedia stated, "[T]the province of the jury to decide or determine the facts of the case from the evidence adduced and to render a verdict in accordance with instructions given by the court."[34] A jury faces a host of challenges when evaluating the evidence and rendering a decision, because almost every case presents contradictory and sometimes confusing testimony and physical

29 United States v. Frederick, 406 F.3d 754, 2005 U.S. App. Lexis 7770 (6th Cir. 2005).
30 Brown v. State, 897 A.2d 748, 2006 Del. Lexis 163 (Del. 2006). *See* case in Part II.
31 State v. Langley, 896 So. 2d 200, 207, 2004 La. App. Lexis 3177 (2004).
32 United States v. Evans, 431 F.3d 343, 347, 2005 U.S. App. Lexis 27403 (8th Cir. 2005).
33 Howard v. State, 2008 Miss. App. Lexis 478 (2008).
34 47 Am Jur 2d Jury §15 (2013).

evidence. The criminal justice system has given the jurors the challenge of determining the credibility of witnesses and which evidence should be given the most weight. In a jury trial, the ultimate goal is to determine whether the prosecution has proven the defendant is guilty beyond a reasonable doubt. Following the presentation of all the evidence by the prosecution and the defense, and after the attorneys have presented closing arguments, the jury retires to deliberate. No judge, attorney, or other court employee meets with the jury; the case decision rests entirely with the jury.

The jury has no role in resolving difficult questions of law, because the judge is responsible for making legal decisions and resolving legal disputes during the trial. Immediately prior to the jury retiring to deliberate, the judge instructs the jurors concerning the law to be applied, giving the jury what amounts to a lesson in law that covers the case the jury has just heard. The charge by the judge, called the jury instruction, attempts to educate the jury concerning the law, and the jury instruction needs to have sufficient particularity that the jury can understand and apply the law. In a nutshell, the trial judge is required to explain the law correctly to the jury, so that it may apply the law to the facts and determine a defendant's guilt with respect to every element of the crime.[35] In jury trials, the jurors have the exclusive responsibility to find the facts, and the trial court may not interfere with this function.

In determining what actually happened, the jurors must have the opportunity to see and hear the prosecution and defense witnesses and some jurisdictions permit jurors to ask questions of the witnesses,[36] including the defendant when on the stand. Based on the questions asked by counsel, the answers given by the witnesses, the documentary and real evidence, the demeanor of the witnesses, and their own knowledge of people, the jurors must reach a decision based on the evidence and substitutes for evidence that have been made available at the trial. Jurors must make decisions only on the evidence obtained by virtue of courtroom presentations, and a juror's private investigation beyond the courtroom can be grounds for a reversal.[37]

In one case, a defendant argued that his conviction for homicide should be reversed because of alleged juror misconduct, as jurors possessed information that had not been introduced at court. In determining the defendant's intent, there was some evidence that the defendant had fired a gun at one of the victims, but two of the jurors noted that, when a gun is fired, it moves upward and to the left, evidence that had never been introduced at trial. The reviewing court held that the jurors had not conducted themselves improperly; they were just relying on their knowledge and common sense in evaluating the evidence.[38] A reversal is not appropriate if the juror's conduct constituted nothing more than applying everyday perceptions and common sense to evaluating the issues presented at trial. In an Arizona case involving an allegation of jury misconduct, the

---

35 *Id. See also* People v. Miller, 164 Cal. App. 4th 653, 662, 2008 Cal. App. Lexis 971 (2008).

36 Amos v. State, 896 N.E.2d 1163, 1170, 2008 Ind. App. Lexis 2544 (Ind. 2008). *See also* Ex parte Malone, 2008 Ala. Lexis 271 (2008).

37 State v. Cook, 2006 Kan. Lexis 361 (2006).

38 Robinson v. Woodford, 2006 U.S. App. Lexis 6009 (9th Cir. 2006).

court noted that a reversal warrants a new trial only if the defendant can demonstrate both juror misconduct and actual prejudice or prejudice that could be assumed from the facts. For example, a homicide conviction was not reversed where jurors observed a witness hug a homicide victim's relative and a newspaper that did not address the case was found in the jury room.[39]

§ 4.8 Role of Witnesses

In presenting evidence in a criminal trial, witness testimony proves to be an absolute necessity, because no actual evidence can be introduced without a witness.[40] Witnesses may be classified as either lay or expert, with lay witnesses generally answering "who," "what," "where," and "when" types of questions, while expert witnesses are permitted to offer opinions. Criminal cases usually involve criminal justice officials, such as police officers, parole and probation officers, and correctional officers, who offer testimony based on their respective first-hand knowledge of the facts of a particular case. These and other witnesses offer the court and jury important facts and assist in introducing narrative evidence of what they observed at the crime scene or other relevant location. Witnesses serve as the essential link in bringing physical and documentary evidence to the court for jury consideration. When properly presented, the witnesses' testimony "paints" a picture of the operative facts of the prosecution or the defense case. The jury must evaluate the testimony of the witnesses for truthfulness, and therefore, it is important to recognize that the jury must consider not only the content of a witness's testimony, but also the witness's demeanor and delivery. For this reason, a trial witness must have some concern about his or her demeanor, the method of presenting the facts, voice, and even his or her dress. Although the direction of witness interrogation falls to the attorneys, it is important that all witnesses give answers that are responsive to the questions actually asked, explaining fully each piece of evidence in context, so that the jury can understand its significance.[41]

The courts have long recognized the importance of witnesses in the judicial process. Under constitutional and statutory provisions, including the Sixth Amendment to the federal constitution, persons accused of crime have the right to compel the courtroom attendance of witnesses on their behalf. The defendant, with a few exceptions,[42]

---

[39] State v. Cruz, 218 Ariz. 149, 2008 Ariz. Lexis 49 (2008), *cert. denied*, Cruz v. Arizona, 2009 U.S. Lexis 428 (2009).

[40] A court may take judicial notice of facts or accept party stipulations as substitutes for evidence. *See* Chapter 5, Judicial Notice.

[41] *See* Chapter 9 for a discussion of the examination of witnesses.

[42] *See State v. Pesqueira*, 2 CA-CR 2011-0198, 2013 Ariz. App. Unpub. LEXIS 947 (Ct. Appls. 2013). Confrontation did not happen because witness asserted a Fifth Amendment privilege. *And see* People v. Bunyard, 2009 Cal. Lexis 1102 (2009). Confrontation right could not be enforced where witness disappeared, state made good faith effort to find witness, and defendant previously had opportunity to confront and cross-examine.

has the Sixth Amendment right to confront and cross-examine adverse witnesses.[43] In a New Jersey case, a defendant had properly requested that an incarcerated witness testify for the defense, but the authorities did not produce the witness. The Supreme Court of New Jersey reversed the lower court and remanded the case to determine whether the proposed witness's testimony would have been favorable to the defendant, because the defendant had the right to have the government's assistance in using compulsory process to produce the witness.[44] "The rights to confront and cross-examine witnesses and to call witnesses in one's own behalf have long been recognized as essential to due process."[45]

§ 4.9 Prosecuting Attorney's Responsibilities

In legal theory, prosecutors have a first duty to seek justice and must not seek a conviction at any cost. As representatives of the executive branch, prosecutors are tasked with administering justice, but also serve as advocates for the government's position. Prosecutors are charged with seeing that defendants receive fair trials and are not convicted unless competent and admissible evidence has been introduced.[46] In a federal prosecution, a court of appeals noted that the courts have no authority to interfere with a prosecutor's decision to prosecute and that a prosecutor can choose to add charges to a prosecution by the use of a superseding indictment without any judicial intervention.[47] In a landmark case, the Supreme Court of the United States held that a prosecutor could actually procure an additional indictment under the habitual offender statute where the defendant refused to accept a plea bargain.[48] An Illinois court noted that a prosecutor has broad discretion in what crimes to charge, and generally prosecutors are permitted to file additional and harsher charges against any defendant,[49] provided the evidence supports it.

In a criminal case, a prosecuting attorney represents a state government or the government of the United States and has the duty to bring criminal cases for which sufficient evidence exists and to decline to prosecute cases for which evidence is insufficient.[50] "[I]f a prosecutor has possible cause to believe that the accused committed an offense defined by statute, the decision of whether to prosecute, whom to prosecute, and what charge to file or bring before a grand jury rests entirely in his or her discretion."[51] In addition, the prosecutor generally has the power to dismiss cases when

---

43 Marshall v. State, 2009 Ala. Crim. App. Lexis 16 (2009).

44 State v. Garcia, 195 N.J. 192, 201, 2008 N.J. Lexis 771 (2008).

45 AM JUR 2D § 1072 (2013).

46 People v. Williams, 170 Cal. App. 4th 587, 2009 Cal. App. Lexis 78 (2009).

47 United States v. Banner, 442 F.3d 1310, 1315, 2006 U.S. App. Lexis 5967 (11th Cir. 2006).

48 *See* Bordenkircher v. Hayes 434 U.S. 357, 1978 U.S. Lexis 56 (1978).

49 People v. Smith, 2013 Il App 120677-U, ¶ 67, 2013 Ill. App. Unpub. LEXIS 2115 (2013).

50 63C AM. JUR. 2D § 20 (2013).

51 *Id.*

the interests of justice require it. Above all, the prosecutor has the duty to see that justice is done, not that the government merely secures convictions. To carry out these responsibilities, the prosecutor's duties include the collection of physical evidence, interviewing witnesses, and preparing the case for trial.

With respect to evidence, the prosecutor must decide not only what evidence is to be introduced, but how that evidence is to be produced, taking into consideration the appropriate time during the trial when each item should be presented. Legal cases that support admission should be available to present to the court in the event that opposing counsel challenges an item of evidence as violating one of the many rules of exclusion.

The prosecutor guides the case for the state by putting prosecution witnesses on the stand and proving the state's case-in-chief. After asking questions, the prosecutor must be so familiar with the evidence that appropriate follow-up questions may be directed to the witness during redirect examination to clear up any possible misconceptions. It is not enough for prosecutors to be familiar with the state's case—the prosecutor should be aware of the accused's defense and have questions prepared for cross-examination of the defendant's witnesses.

In presenting the case, part of the prosecutor's duties involves making opening and closing statements or arguments. During the opening statement, the prosecutor explains what the state intends to prove and how the state will present its evidence. Ideally, the opening statement provides a "road map" for the jury that predicts the manner in which the prosecution's case will be presented. In the closing statement or argument, the prosecutor summarizes the evidence that has been presented in such a way as to cast it in the light most favorable to the prosecution. The prosecutor must anticipate the defense's closing argument because, following the closing argument of the defense, the prosecution has a final opportunity to counter it during the prosecution's closing rebuttal.

Constitutionally, the prosecutor has some responsibilities to the defense, and to a possibly innocent defendant, and, as a result, the prosecutor is required to make exculpatory evidence available upon request. In the interests of justice, there is a general duty to disclose evidence that might be exculpatory to the defendant and would include any evidence that might help impeach a prosecution witness. It is reversible error for the prosecutor to use evidence that he or she knows—or should know—is untrue, to use evidence that was acquired in violation of the law, or to withhold evidence favorable to the defense.[52] In the 1963 case of *Brady v. Maryland*, the United States Supreme Court held that suppression by the prosecution of evidence favorable to the accused upon request violates due process where the evidence is material either to guilt or to punishment. Such withholding constitutes a violation irrespective of good faith or bad faith on the part of the prosecution. In interpreting the *Brady*

---

52 Maddox v. Montgomery, 718 F.2d 1033 (11th Cir. 1983). *See* case in Part II. Brady v. Maryland, 373 U.S. 83, 83 S. Ct. 1194, 10 L. Ed. 2d 215 (1963).

decision in a 1999 case that remains good law, the United States Supreme Court noted that:

> There are three components of a true *Brady* violation: The evidence at issue must be favorable to the accused, either because it is exculpatory, or because it is impeaching; that evidence must have been suppressed by the State, either willfully or inadvertently; and prejudice must have ensued.[53]

The Court pointed out that in order to prevail on a claim under *Brady*, it must be shown that the prosecution violated its duty to disclose information favorable to the defendant, which affected the outcome of the trial. A "*Brady* violation does not exist unless the nondisclosure was so serious that there [was] a reasonable probability that the suppressed evidence would have produced a different verdict."[54]

The duty to disclose exculpatory evidence becomes demonstrably critical, both for the defendant and for the nondisclosing attorney. In a New Orleans murder case, a man and his date were leaving a restaurant in the French Quarter when one of three subjects shot the man in the face, resulting in his death. When police questioned his date, she indicated that she had not been wearing her contacts or her glasses and as a result she did not get a good look at the killer and could only see patterns and shapes. However, three weeks later, she made a positive identification of the eventual defendant by picking him from a police lineup. The prosecutor shared the woman's story about not seeing the perpetrator well on the night of the murder, and the defense had one police report that the witness needed corrective lenses to see properly, but a second police report three days later that expanded on her need for corrective lenses was never shared with the defense. The defendant's conviction and death sentence were reversed, and the prosecutor received sanctions from the Louisiana bar for violating the Rules of Professional Conduct because he had failed to share exculpatory impeachment evidence with the defense, possibly causing the wrong person to be convicted of murder.[55] Finding that the prosecutor had improperly withheld exculpatory evidence from the defendant, and that there existed a reasonable probability that the conviction might not have resulted but for the prosecutor's wrongdoing, the Supreme Court of Louisiana sanctioned the prosecuting attorney. The Court noted that:

> By withholding material exculpatory evidence from a criminal defendant, respondent violated a duty owed to the public. As a prosecutor, respondent is charged with a high ethical standard and may not carelessly skirt his obligation. [Citation omitted.] Although neither *Brady* [*v. Maryland*] or Rule 3.8 [of Professional Responsibility] incorporates a mental element, Rule XIX, § 10(C) does. Based on the testimony of respondent and the character evidence discussed below, we find that respondent knowingly withheld *Brady* evidence. As to the element regarding actual injury, this Court reversed [the defendant's] conviction on other grounds and granted him a new trial. However, this Court's actions in reversing the conviction does not vitiate

---

53 Strickler v. Greene, 527 U.S. 263, 281-282 (1999).

54 *Id.* at 282.

55 In re Roger W. Jordan, 913 So.2d 775, 2005 La. Lexis 2104 (2005).

> the potential injury to the criminal justice system, or to [the defendant], caused by respondent's actions, and warrants serious consideration and discipline by this Court.[56]

Although the defendant's conviction had been reversed prior to the sanction applied to the prosecutor by the Supreme Court of Louisiana, the Court noted that a prosecutor's duty "to disclose is imbedded in the principle that a criminal defendant is deprived of a fair trial when the state withholds exculpatory evidence that is material to guilt or punishment."[57]

Thus, where a state prosecutor failed to offer the defendant information that was important to either his guilt or innocence, a violation of the due process clause of the Fourteenth Amendment occurs, and a reversal of any resulting conviction should result where the error is outcome-determinative. A prosecutor's duties do not end with the trial, but also exist after the trial if the prosecutor becomes aware of exculpatory information that existed, but was not disclosed to the defendant prior to or during the trial.[58]

§ 4.10 Defense Attorney's Responsibilities

When the Bill of Rights was adopted as part of our Constitution in 1791, the right to counsel was included as part of the Sixth Amendment. The Amendment reads in part:

> In all criminal prosecutions the accused shall enjoy the right . . . to have the assistance of counsel for his defense.

In addition to the federal Constitution, all the state constitutions require that the accused shall have the right to appear in person and be represented by counsel.

The right to counsel entitles criminal defendants to have effective assistance of counsel, a standard that contemplates the services of an attorney with the customary skills and diligence that a reasonably competent attorney would perform under similar circumstances.[59] According to the Supreme Court, "In assessing attorney performance, all the Federal Courts of Appeals and all but a few state courts have now adopted the 'reasonably effective assistance of counsel' standard in one formulation or another."[60] In a landmark case, *Strickland v. Washington*, Justice O'Connor wrote, "The benchmark for judging any claim of ineffectiveness must be whether counsel's conduct so undermined the proper functioning of the adversarial process that the trial cannot be relied on as having produced a just result."[61] *Strickland* required a complaining defendant to demonstrate that (1) the defense counsel's performance was deficient and

---

56 *Id.*

57 *Id.*

58 Aaron v. Scutt, 2013 U.S. Dist. LEXIS 167485 (E.D. Mich. 2013).

59 United States v. Boone, 437 F.3d 829, 839, 2006 U.S. App. Lexis 3531 (8th Cir. 2006).

60 Strickland v. Washington, 466 U.S. 668 at 683, 1984 U.S. Lexis 79 (1984).

61 *Id.* at 686.

(2) that the deficient performance prejudiced the defense in a way that adversely affected the outcome of the trial.[62] As a general rule, reviewing courts must imply a strong presumption that counsel's conduct falls within the wide range of reasonable professional assistance. The primary function of a defendant's trial attorney is to force the prosecution to introduce sufficient evidence of the alleged offenses and to assure that the defendant's legal and constitutional rights have not been violated. Pretrial preparation is essential and includes consulting with the prosecutor and preparing the case for trial. Pretrial preparation includes researching and filing pretrial motions and, where necessary, pretrial conferences with the defendant and interviews with all defense witnesses.

In preparing the case, the defense attorney has the duty to prepare the defendant for the trial by explaining the procedures that the court will follow and what the prosecutor's role will be. A good defense attorney will not tell the defendant what to say, but will advise the defendant on courtroom demeanor and cover the topics for which the defendant might have a constitutional right not to answer. Proper preparation of the defendant as a witness, including previewing expected questions and answers, is an essential defense counsel task. The defense attorney will have investigated the case, will have prepared questions for the defendant and other witnesses, and will be ready to introduce the witnesses in such a manner that the evidence has its maximum force and impact for the defense. He or she has a responsibility to cross-examine the prosecution's witnesses, to introduce evidence to rebut the testimony of such witnesses, and where possible, to impeach their credibility.

A violation of the Sixth Amendment right to effective counsel can result in a new trial, where the error may have had an effect on the outcome. In an Illinois case,[63] the defendant was a houseguest in another person's apartment. Police requested consent from the apartment holder to conduct a search of the apartment for illegal drugs. Without a warrant, police conducted a search of the apartment, including a separate bedroom that the defendant occupied, and discovered controlled substances within the guest's bedroom. The guest never gave any permission to search the bedroom she occupied. Her defense counsel did not effectively pursue a motion to suppress evidence, even in the face of a fairly clear constitutional error by the police in warrantlessly searching the bedroom and in seizing the controlled substance. Her appeal contended that she received ineffective assistance of counsel. In order to prevail on this legal theory, the defendant must generally demonstrate that her counsel's performance was objectively unreasonable, and the attorney failed to meet the prevailing professional norms. If the defendant can also demonstrate that the outcome would likely have been different had the counsel met proper legal standards, the conviction should be reversed. According to the reviewing court, there was a great probability that, had a motion to suppress been filed, it would have been granted, and in that event, there would have been no controlled substance evidence with which to proceed to a trial. Accordingly, the appellate

---

[62] *Id.* at 687.

[63] People v. Givens, 384 Ill. App. 3d 101, 2008 Ill. App. Lexis 684 (2008).

court reversed the conviction and remanded the case based on incompetency of legal counsel.[64]

In determining standards for evaluating the Sixth Amendment right to counsel, the Rhode Island Supreme Court stated that it would reject an allegation of ineffective assistance of counsel, unless "the attorney's representation was so lacking that the trial has become a farce and a mockery of justice."[65] A New Jersey appellate court noted that "[t]he benchmark for judging ineffective assistance of counsel claims is whether the defense attorney's professional errors 'materially contributed' to the defendant's conviction."[66] A different court held that in order to "warrant a reversal of a conviction, a convicted defendant must show (1) his counsel's performance was deficient and (2) the deficient performance prejudiced his defense."[67] Another way to measure an ineffective assistance of counsel claim requires that the defendant "show that there is a reasonable probability that, but for counsel's unprofessional errors, the result of the proceeding would have been different. A reasonable probability is a probability sufficient to undermine confidence in the outcome."[68] A defense attorney's appointment a few weeks prior to trial does not demonstrate ineffective assistance of counsel.[69] Ineffective assistance of counsel was not demonstrated in a multiple murder case in which the evidence clearly established that defendants were busy stealing cattle from a farm at the time the defendants killed the farmer and his wife. Yet, counsel's failure to request that some information about a prior conviction be removed from a police report before it was introduced as evidence did not qualify as ineffective assistance of counsel.[70] In other words, if a case was not tried with adequate representation, and the outcome of the case would have been different, the error was not harmless, and a new trial should be ordered. However, where there would have been no change in outcome with different counsel, the harmless error rule should be applied and the conviction sustained.

In an overall sense, the Sixth Amendment demands that defense counsel effectively represent the defendant in a criminal case by taking advantage of the available legal tools, including pleading affirmative defenses. In an Alabama case,[71] a defendant had been charged with murder related to a fight among several people, and there was evidence that the defendant had stabbed the deceased. Prior to the start of the murder trial, his defense attorney suggested that the defendant perjure himself and tell the jury that he did not stab the deceased. This defense plan of perjury had the effect of giving up a viable self-defense argument, because at the moment the victim was stabbed, the defendant was trying to get away from the fray. At a hearing for a new trial, the original

---

64 *Id.* at 115.

65 Moniz v. State, 933 A.2d 691, 696, 2007 R.I. Lexis 100 (2007).

66 New Jersey v. Velez, 329 N.J. Super. 128 at 134, 746 A.2d 1073 at 1077 (2000).

67 *See* United States v. Keller, 2013 U.S. Dist. LEXIS 172789 (E.D. Pa. 2013).

68 Strickland v. Washington, 466 U.S. 668, 694, 104 S.Ct. 2052, 2068, 80 L. Ed. 2d 674, 698, 1984 U.S. LEXIS 79 (1984).

69 *Id.*

70 Rousan v. Roper, 436 F.3d 951, 959, 2006 U.S. App. Lexis 3003 (8th Cir. 2006).

71 McCombs v. State, 2008 Ala. Crim. App. Lexis 139 (2008).

defense counsel admitted getting the defendant to commit perjury concerning the stabbing. Giving up a viable claim of self-defense suggested by the defense attorney constituted ineffective assistance of counsel, because a proper assertion might have resulted in an acquittal based on self-defense. The appellate court reversed the conviction and granted a new trial.

Finally, the defense attorney has the responsibility to make opening statements following the prosecution's opening statements. The defense counsel may defer an opening statement until the start of the defense case-in-chief so that the preview of the defense theory or "road map" of the case will be presented to the jury at a more appropriate time. The defense attorney also has the right to give a closing statement immediately prior to the final statement given by the prosecutor. In the closing statement, the defense attorney reviews and summarizes the evidence presented by defense witnesses, emphasizes inconsistencies in the prosecution's case, focuses on credibility issues of the prosecution's witnesses, and explains the evidence in such a way as to be most favorable to the defendant.

§ 4.11 Admissibility and Weight of Direct and Circumstantial Evidence

In a criminal case, the prosecutor has the responsibility to prove beyond a reasonable doubt that the defendant committed all of the elements of the crimes charged, and that the defendant's acts violated the law. On the opposite side, creating a reasonable doubt is the goal of the defense attorney, a task that can be accomplished by the introduction of evidence calling into question the facts presented by the prosecutor, by casting doubt on the credibility of the prosecution witnesses, or by the presentation of an affirmative defense. Direct evidence proves a point without any other evaluation by a juror, so long as a juror believes the witness, while circumstantial evidence proves a point but that a juror must make deductions or inferences to conclude that a separate fact is true or should be believed to exist.

In the process of introducing sufficient proof of guilt, both parties may rely on direct and circumstantial evidence. Although some jurors may not place circumstantial evidence on equal footing with direct evidence, the law makes no distinction between circumstantial and direct evidence, and circumstantial evidence alone can be sufficient to sustain a conviction.[72] Demonstrative of this equality is the fact that, in considering a defendant's motion for acquittal following the prosecution's case-in-chief, courts give equal weight to direct and circumstantial evidence.[73] A Minnesota reviewing court upheld a conviction for being a felon in possession of a firearm when the gun was found inside a box in a closet of the bedroom where the defendant regularly slept. Inside the

---

72 *See* Green v. State, 2013 Ark. App. 63, 2013 Ark. App. LEXIS 79 (2013).

73 United States v. Bailey, 169 Fed. Appx. 815, 821, 2006 U.S. App. Lexis 3402 (5th Cir. 2006).

box containing the firearm was a letter from the county sheriff addressed to the defendant. This circumstantial evidence was sufficient to prove that the defendant possessed the gun.[74] Rape convictions have also been upheld, despite the victim being unconscious at the time of the crime, due to the presence of the defendant's DNA on the victim.[75]

While some academic doubt may exist in the minds of legal scholars as to the admissibility, weight, and sufficiency of circumstantial evidence, many cases have reached a judgment of guilt in the absence of direct evidence. The basic difference between direct and circumstantial evidence is that, in the case of direct evidence, the witness testifies concerning his or her own personal knowledge of the facts. In the case of circumstantial evidence, the witness gives evidence to establish one fact, and the use of logic allows the jury to decide whether a second fact naturally follows from proof of the first fact. As categories of evidence, both direct and circumstantial evidence carry equal weight and the elements of a crime may be established by either direct or circumstantial evidence.[76]

There is a classic story that helps explain the difference. In a case, a witness testified that he observed a fight where one man was accused of "biting off" the other fighter's ear. When he testified that the one man "bit off" the other man's ear, the testimony was that he was present when it happened, and he saw the fight. On cross-examination, the witness was asked whether he actually observed the one bite the other's ear. He stated that he did not actually see it being bitten, but that he saw the defendant spit out the ear. Although he did not see the biting event, circumstantial evidence told him and the court that the defendant must have bitten the ear during the fight, because there is no other logical explanation concerning how it got in the one man's mouth. In this context, it is difficult to argue that circumstantial evidence would not have the full force and effect of direct evidence.

The mere fact that evidence is characterized as either direct or circumstantial may indicate that one type may be superior to the other with respect to reliability. As part of California's jury instructions, the following wording might suggest to jurors that circumstantial evidence might be worth less than direct evidence. The jury instructions state that:

> A finding of guilt as to any crime may not be based on circumstantial evidence unless the proved circumstances are not only (1) consistent with the theory that the defendant is guilty of the crime, but (2) cannot be reconciled with any other rational conclusion.[77]

California also notes that, prior to using circumstantial evidence to establish guilt, each fact or circumstance on which the inference rests must be proved beyond a reasonable doubt.[78]

---

[74] State v. Smith, A13-0003, 2013 Minn. App. Unpub. LEXIS 1149 (Ct. Appls. 2013).

[75] Bartman v. State, 2009 Alaska Lexis 17 (2009).

[76] 29A AM. JUR. 2D § 1391 (2008).

[77] *See* CAL. JURY INSTRUCTIONS – CRIM. 2.01 (2005).

[78] *Id.*

Taking a position slightly different from California, Ohio rejected any distinction between the two types of evidence. An Ohio court of appeals approved of using a jury instruction that told the jury,

> Direct evidence and circumstantial evidence are of equal weight. The law makes no distinction between direct and circumstantial evidence as to the degree of proof required. And facts may be proven by either type of evidence or a combination of both. Each type is accepted as a reasonable method of proof.[79]

Although it is true that, all things being equal, direct evidence probably carries more weight with juries, circumstantial evidence has a definite place in the trial of criminal cases because the case law is replete with examples of convictions based exclusively on circumstantial evidence and many others in which direct evidence proved insufficient for a conviction.

The need for circumstantial evidence appears obvious, because criminals generally prefer cover and often do not commit their activities in plain view. For this reason, the use of some circumstantial evidence is usually a necessity, especially in stealth-type crimes, such as burglary, larceny, and embezzlement. In a variety of criminal cases, without the use of circumstantial evidence, a prosecutor would have a difficult task in obtaining convictions.

There is often the mistaken belief that circumstantial evidence fails to carry sufficient weight to result in a criminal conviction, or at least a belief calling into question a conviction based wholly or primarily on circumstantial evidence. For example, a capital murder case involved the death of a child whose body was covered in cuts, bruises, and puncture wounds, all in different states of healing. The appellate court upheld the conviction based on circumstantial evidence.[80] No one observed the child receiving injuries, although the defendant claimed the child had fallen in a bathtub and fallen down a stairway. On appeal, the defendant contended that because no one had seen her injure the child and because she was not the only person with access at the time of the injury, the circumstantial evidence was insufficient to sustain a conviction for capital murder. The Texas Court of Appeals noted that circumstantial evidence can be used to prove a culpable mental state, as well as to prove the other elements of capital murder beyond a reasonable doubt.

Before continuing with the discussion of admissibility, weight, and sufficiency of direct and circumstantial evidence, some definitions and explanations are in order.[81]

A. Direct Evidence

"'Direct evidence' is that which proves a fact without an inference or presumption and which in itself, if true, establishes that fact."[82] It is evidence that is applied immediately and directly to the fact to be proved, without the aid of any intervening fact or

---

79 State v. Barnes, 2014 Ohio 47, 2014 Ohio App. LEXIS 45 (2014).

80 Williams v. State, 2009 Tex. App. Lexis 1045 (2009).

81 *Id.*

82 MONT. CODE ANN. 26-1-102(5) (2013).

reasoning process. For example, in a trial for murder, a witness positively testifies that he saw the accused inflict the fatal wound. Evidence is declared to be direct and positive when persons who have actual, factual knowledge of the disputed event testify as to those facts. When direct evidence is introduced, it is not necessary that the factfinders make any inferences or deductions of fact, or that there be any presumptions flowing from the evidence to connect it with the crime. Where the witness is believable, the factfinder will find that the existence of the fact has been established, unless and until other contrary evidence of equal credibility is introduced.

B. *Circumstantial Evidence*

The Montana evidence code notes that "'Circumstantial evidence' is that which tends to establish a fact by proving another and which, though true, does not of itself conclusively establish that fact but affords an inference or presumption of its existence." [83]"Circumstantial evidence is evidence that, if found to be true, proves a fact from which an inference of the existence of another fact may be drawn."[84] California's definition of circumstantial evidence is "evidence that, without going directly to prove the existence of a fact, gives rise to a logical inference that such fact does exist."[85] While circumstantial evidence may not always be given the recognition by a jury that it deserves in all situations, Justice Kennedy noted that, "[c]ircumstantial evidence may be as probative as testimonial evidence."[86] The Supreme Court of Virginia noted that "circumstantial evidence is competent and is entitled to as much weight as direct evidence[,] provided that the circumstantial evidence is sufficiently convincing to exclude every reasonable hypothesis except that of guilt."[87]

After observing the differences between direct evidence and circumstantial evidence, the reader must remember that the jury is only required to weigh all the evidence—direct and circumstantial—against a standard of reasonable doubt. This was made clear in an Ohio case in which the defendant contended that the evidence presented by the state was insufficient because it was based on circumstantial evidence of intent. The appellate court noted:

> The elements of an offense may be established by direct evidence, circumstantial evidence, or both. Circumstantial and direct evidence are of equal probative value. When reviewing the value of circumstantial evidence, we note that the weight accorded an inference is fact-dependent and can be disregarded as speculative only if reasonable minds can come to the conclusion that the inference is not supported by the evidence.[88]

---

83 *Id.*

84 CAL. JURY INSTRUCTIONS – CRIM. 2.00 (2005).

85 Bland v. Fox, 172 Neb. 662, 111 N.W.2d 537 (1961) (quoting C.J.S. § 2).

86 Siegert v. Gilley, 500 U.S. 226, 236 (1991) (Justice Kennedy concurring).

87 Finney v. Commonwealth, 277 Va. 83, 89, 2009 Va. Lexis 12 (2009) (quoting Dowden v. Commonwealth, 260 Va. 459, 468, 536 S.E.2d 437, 441 (2000)).

88 Ohio v. Thomas, 2002 Ohio 7333, 2002 Ohio App. Lexis 7226 (2002).

When evaluating whether the weight and sufficiency of circumstantial evidence should justify a determination of guilt, the United States Supreme Court, in the landmark case of *Holland v. United States*,[89] clearly stated that circumstantial evidence alone will support a conviction. In unambiguous language, the *Holland* Court did more than reject the jury instruction that, in circumstantial evidence cases, the evidence must be such as to exclude every reasonable hypothesis other than that of guilt; it clearly stated that, "where the jury is properly instructed on the standards for reasonable doubt, such an additional instruction on circumstantial evidence is confusing and incorrect."[90] In a recent case that followed the rationale indicated in the *Holland* case, a federal district court in a habeas corpus case refused to disturb a conviction for attempted aggravated kidnapping. The defendant alleged that the prosecution failed to prove its case because the evidence was circumstantial, showing only the defendant chased two children and attempted to grab one child's leg. The court noted that, "[c]ircumstantial evidence alone, however, may be sufficient to support a criminal conviction."[91]

The federal courts have consistently held that the proof of guilt by the use of circumstantial evidence alone "may be sufficient to support a conviction, and it is not necessary that the evidence preclude every reasonable hypothesis except that of guilt"[92]that some state courts require. Consistent with this view, the Tenth Circuit Court of Appeals recently reiterated that circumstantial evidence should be given the same weight as direct evidence and noted that "[t]o sustain a criminal conviction [based on circumstantial evidence], the Government's evidence must be 'substantial' or raise more than a 'mere suspicion of guilt,' but it need not disprove every other reasonable theory of the case."[93]

Although most states follow the federal courts' reasoning that circumstantial evidence is of equal weight to direct evidence, some states still hold that the jury instruction must contain the language "it must exclude every other reasonable hypothesis consistent with innocence," only if the case rests wholly on circumstantial evidence. In *Terry v. State*, an Arkansas case involving the rape of a child, the father appealed his conviction on the ground that the trial court erred when it refused to grant his motion for a directed verdict based on a failure of proof. The father had been left alone with his infant daughter, who was in good health. When the child's mother returned after a short absence, the father was standing over the infant with blood on his chest and on the victim's clothing. He stated that he had cut his cuticle, but the baby had a significant amount of red blood in her private area when her mother checked. A medical exam indicated tears in her private area, and the doctor suspected sexual abuse. Two semen stains on the baby's diaper matched the defendant's DNA profile. Following his conviction and life sentence, he appealed, contending that circumstantial evidence used to

---

89 Hudson v. United States, 348 U.S. 121, 140 (1954).

90 *Id.*, 139.

91 Sparrow v. Lindamood, 2006 U.S. Dist. Lexis 9640 (M.D. Tenn. 2006).

92 United States v. Hardman, 2005 U.S. Dist. Lexis 28923 (M.D. Tenn. 2005), and United States v. Barnett, 398 F.3d 516, 522, 2005 U.S. App. Lexis 2644 (6th Cir. 2005).

93 United States v. Winder, 2009 U.S. App. Lexis, 3647 (10th Cir. 2009).

convict must exclude every other reasonable hypothesis consistent with innocence and that only conjecture by the jury that he was the perpetrator supported the conviction. According to the Supreme Court of Arkansas:

> Circumstantial evidence may constitute substantial evidence to support a conviction. The longstanding rule in the use of circumstantial evidence is that, to be substantial, the evidence must exclude every other reasonable hypothesis than that of the guilt of the accused. The question of whether the circumstantial evidence excludes every other reasonable hypothesis consistent with innocence is for the jury to decide. Upon review, this court must determine whether the jury resorted to speculation and conjecture in reaching its verdict. [Internal citations omitted.][94]

The Supreme Court of Arkansas affirmed his conviction over his contention that there was no direct proof of what caused the baby's trauma. The reviewing court noted that the jury could have found the circumstantial evidence to be substantial, and there was DNA evidence that the defendant was the guilty party.[95]

Some states follow a slightly different view of the manner in which circumstantial evidence should be evaluated. Florida holds that a judgment of acquittal should be granted in situations where the only proof of guilt is based completely on circumstantial evidence, unless the evidence is inconsistent with any reasonable theory of innocence. In one murder case, the defendant was the last person to see the deceased and was familiar with the layout of her home. He also knew that victim was by herself and that she had a 2-carat diamond ring. The defendant was seen in his own home shortly after the murder, washing out blood from his clothing. He gave his girlfriend a 2-carat diamond ring that evening, his story concerning his absence from his place of employment did not square with known facts, and his cell phone was used three times near the murder scene at the relevant time. The defendant made a cash deposit that was not consistent with his usual practice, and he retrieved the diamond ring from his girlfriend and took it to the beach after which time it was never seen again. Some of the victim's jewelry was found in the shed at a house to which the defendant had access. In addition to other circumstantial evidence of guilt, there was no evidence that supported any other hypothesis other than guilt. The Supreme Court of Florida held that the defendant was not entitled to a directed verdict of acquittal under the circumstances of this case and that the trial court had acted properly in denying an acquittal.[96]

Notwithstanding some disagreement concerning the "hypothesis of innocence" instruction, courts all hold that a conviction may be based solely on circumstantial evidence. Whether a prosecutor introduced sufficient evidence to meet the constitutional standard for "the sufficiency of the evidence is whether, upon viewing the evidence in the light most favorable to the prosecution, any rational trier of fact could conclude that the state proved the essential elements of the crime beyond a reasonable doubt."[97]

---

94 Terry v. State, 2006 Ark. Lexis 326 (2006).

95 *Id.*

96 Gosciminski v. State, 2013 Fla. LEXIS 1988 (2013).

97 State v. Singleton, 922 So. 2d 647, 650, 2006 La. App. Lexis 115 (La. 2006).

This measure of evidence sufficiency applies in cases involving both direct and circumstantial evidence.

§ 4.12 Summary

The prosecutor in a criminal case has the responsibility of introducing evidence sufficient to prove guilt beyond a reasonable doubt. The defense attorney has the responsibility to introduce evidence that challenges the sufficiency of the state's evidence, while offering evidence to substantiate the defendant's theory of the case, including presenting evidence of affirmative defenses where applicable. Over the years, courts and legislatures have established rules for the admissibility of evidence and for the procedure to be followed in presenting evidence in court.

To promote a smooth and orderly flow of evidence at trial, pretrial evidentiary motions to exclude or suppress certain types of evidence may be made and resolved prior to trial. When a motion to suppress is presented, the burden is on the party making the motion to show that there is a legal reason that the evidence should not be admitted.[98]

For all practical purposes, the rules of evidence are rules of exclusion. All evidence is admissible as a general rule, unless it is excluded based on an objection or upon the court's own motion. Objections may be based on the form of the question, constitutional issues, or the substantive rules of evidence. For example, if the attorney's questions are confusing, improperly phrased, misleading, argumentative, or compound, the opposing party may object based on the form. Objections may also be made based upon the substance of the question asked by the opposing counsel. If the objection is made because the evidence is irrelevant, immaterial, or incompetent, the complaining party should offer a legal theory to support the objection.

The usual order for presenting evidence is for the state to present its case-in-chief, followed by the defendant's case-in-chief. The prosecution then has the opportunity to introduce evidence to rebut the evidence presented by the defense. The defense may, if it deems necessary, follow up with evidence contrary to that introduced by the prosecution during the rebuttal. When both parties have rested their cases, the hearing on the facts comes to an end, and the trial proceeds with the closing arguments and the court's instructions to the jury.

The customary method of offering evidence involves having the party place its witness on the stand and conducting direct examination by asking a series of nonleading questions. The opposing party, through counsel, may challenge any question before an answer is given by making a specific objection. The attorneys must be ready to offer grounds for their respective positions. The court considers the contentions of both parties and then determines whether the answer should be allowed into evidence.

---

98 Where a defendant files a motion to suppress evidence and no arrest or search warrant was used, the burden of proving a valid search or arrest is placed on the prosecution.

In order to preserve an objection to admission or exclusion of evidence for appeal, the objection or motion must have been timely and made with sufficient specificity that the trial judge was aware of the complaint, and the court must have actually made a ruling on the objection or motion. In some cases, the attorney who lost the objection or motion may make an offer of proof to preserve the record for appeal.

In English and American courts, the trial judge, jury, witnesses, prosecuting attorney, and defense attorney all have specific functions. The judge determines whether evidence is admissible and gives instructions to the jury. The jury determines the facts from the evidence and applies the law to the facts, using the instructions given by the judge. The witnesses are the eyes and ears of the court. The prosecuting attorney guides the case for the state by producing witnesses on behalf of the state, and the defense attorney represents the accused by challenging prosecution witnesses and by presenting evidence designed to counter the prosecutor's case.

Although a few American jurisdictions question the weight and sufficiency of circumstantial evidence as compared to direct evidence, most jurisdictions hold that circumstantial evidence has equal weight when compared to direct evidence. A case built entirely upon circumstantial evidence may meet the prosecutor's burden of proof beyond a reasonable doubt. Juries may give circumstantial evidence somewhat less weight than direct evidence, but as long as the jury is satisfied that the total weight of all the evidence demonstrates the defendant's guilt beyond a reasonable doubt, a conviction is appropriate.

All who are involved in the criminal justice process, whether they are directly or indirectly involved in collecting, preserving, presenting, or evaluating the evidence, should be aware of the process by which evidence is introduced, challenged, and evaluated during the trial.

CHAPTER FOUR: QUESTIONS AND REVIEW EXERCISES

1. In approving a criminal case for active prosecution, the prosecutor must present facts for consideration by the jury or the judge in a bench trial. What are the five sources of information upon which a judge or jury may rely in coming to a decision concerning guilt or innocence?
2. Defense attorneys often develop objections to the introduction of evidence against their clients. What are some of the constitutional bases for pretrial motions to suppress evidence from being introduced at trial?
3. Both the prosecutor and the defense attorney have the opportunity to make objections concerning the form of the question used by the opposing attorney. What are some of the objections concerning the form of a question or the way that a question has been phrased that an opposing attorney might make?

4. Evidence that is presented at trial must be offered in a rational and orderly manner. What occurs during the prosecution's case-in-chief? What occurs during the defense's case-in-chief? May each side cross-examine the witnesses offered by the other side? What are the subject or topic limitations during the prosecution case in rebuttal and in the defense case in rejoinder?
5. Assume that a defense attorney has offered testimony or evidence in court to which the prosecutor has objected. What is the process that the defendant's attorney must follow to preserve the record for a possible appeal?
6. If a defense attorney is aware of an error that the judge has made, is it appropriate for the attorney to let that error go unmentioned and hope that it will prove to be a successful ground for an appeal, in the event his or her client is found guilty?
7. In every criminal case, a judge will preside over the actual trial. Explain in significant detail the different duties that a judge possesses in ruling on evidence and managing the orderly trial procedure.
8. In many jurisdictions, judges are permitted to make comments on evidence, but this can prove to be a decision that might invite an appellate reversal of any eventual criminal conviction. What challenges exist to a judge when commenting on the significance of evidence or when asking a question of any testifying witness?
9. In its role as factfinder, a jury has many functions. May jurors be given the opportunity to ask questions of trial witnesses? What is the role of a jury in hearing, evaluating, and deciding a criminal case?
10. In presenting or defending a criminal case, witnesses are crucial to the presentation of the case, and without witnesses, no evidence or testimony could be introduced. What functions do witnesses serve in taking the witness stand in a criminal case?
11. Explain what the prosecuting and defense attorneys do in preparing a criminal case for court and explain what the attorneys do to manage their respective cases once the trial is under way.
12. Direct and circumstantial evidence generally are considered equal in force and effect and a criminal conviction may rest completely on circumstantial evidence. What is direct evidence? Give an example. What is circumstantial evidence? Please offer an example. If you were a juror, would you treat direct and circumstantial evidence as having equal weight in making a decision?

Judicial Notice

5

Judicial notice takes the place of proof, and is of equal force. As a means of establishing facts, it is therefore superior to evidence. In its appropriate field, it displaces evidence, since, as it stands for proof, it fulfills the object which evidence is designed to fulfill, and makes evidence unnecessary.

State v. Maine, 69 Conn. 123, 36 L.R.A. 623, 61 Am. St. Rep. 30, 37 A. 80 (1897)

Chapter Contents

KEY TERMS AND CONCEPTS

Adjudicative Facts
Judicial Notice
Judicial Notice of Geography
Judicial Notice of Historical Facts
Judicial Notice of Law
Judicial Notice of Scientific Facts
Legislative Facts

§ 5.1 Introduction

Near the close of a criminal trial, the judge has the duty to educate the jury concerning the law to be applied to the particular facts that will be determined by the jury. In this phase of the trial, it is said that the judge "instructs the jury," which means that the judge explains to the members of the jury that they are to determine the guilt or innocence of the accused using the facts presented at the trial, consistent with the explanations of the applicable law given by the judge. Generally, the prosecution and the defense have the burden of establishing facts by producing sworn witnesses, authenticated documents, or real evidence. However, the courts recognize that it would be unreasonable to require the opposing parties to introduce evidence for every fact considered by the jury or the judge in a bench trial, and, as a result, they have made some exceptions. Criminal trials can be lengthy affairs under our present system, and it would be unwise to require the parties to prove facts that are so well known that their truth is not in any dispute.

To save the court's time and for procedural convenience, legislative enactment and case law have established formal procedures that serve as substitutes for evidence. The first substitute for evidence is **judicial notice.** The principle of judicial notice authorizes the court to accept appropriate facts as true, without requiring one of the parties to offer formal proof and not permitting the other party to introduce evidence that would dispute the judicially noticed fact. For example, a court would judicially notice that excess alcohol consumption degrades human motor skills or that gravity causes an object to fall to earth, thus removing the requirement of formal proof for those facts.

Judicial notice The acceptance by the court of certain notorious facts without proof.

The second substitute for evidence is the category called presumptions and inferences. Court decisions and statutory enactments have established that, once a basic fact has been proved, parties can use this basic fact to deduce another fact, thereby relieving parties of the burden of presenting evidence to prove a particular fact. One way to consider the difference between a presumption and an inference is to consider that, in the case of a presumption, the deduction must follow the proof of the basic fact, while in the case of an inference, the trier of fact may make the deduction after the basic fact is proved but is not required to do so. In any event, a jury or judge in a criminal case is not required to make the deduction of fact from either a presumption or an inference and may choose to ignore it.

Stipulation An agreement, bargain, proviso, or condition, such as an agreement between opposing litigants that certain facts are true and are not in dispute.

Stipulations are the third substitute for evidence. The stipulation serves the goal of judicial economy by saving the court's time and by allowing the court to continue its business without requiring proof of a fact or issue over which the parties have no disagreement. The agreed stipulation renders proof unnecessary as to the matters stipulated. The remainder of this chapter is devoted to a discussion of specific examples of judicial notice of facts and judicial notice of laws. In the following chapter, the other substitutes for evidence—presumptions, inferences, and stipulations—are explained.

§ 5.2 Judicial Notice Defined

Judicial notice may be defined as the recognition and acceptance of certain facts that are reasonably undisputable. Under the rules of evidentiary procedure, a judge may properly take or act upon such facts without proof—either because the facts noticed are indisputable as a matter of notorious common knowledge or are capable of being immediately verified by consultation with standard reference works. "Judicial notice is a method of dispensing with the necessity for taking proof, and is intended to avoid the formal introduction of evidence in limited circumstances where the fact sought to be proved is so well known that evidence in support thereof is unnecessary."[1] Facts that are well known to the general population, to those within the relevant field of knowledge, or to those within the jurisdiction's geographic area may be the proper subject of judicial notice. When a court takes judicial notice of a fact, the court is dispensing with requiring proof of a fact where the fact is one of public knowledge or is of sufficient notoriety to be known by all well-informed persons within the court's jurisdiction.

Judicial notice involves the acceptance as true of certain facts and laws without the necessity of introducing evidence. Judges will not close their minds to obvious truths that other reasonable people see and understand, but a judge does not necessarily need

---

1 29 AM. JUR. 2D § 24.

to have personal knowledge of a fact judicially noticed.[2] When a court judicially notices a fact as true, the party requesting judicial notice need not introduce any evidence in support of the fact, and the opposing party is generally prevented from introducing evidence to contradict the judicially noticed fact.

In using judicial notice as a substitute for evidence, courts are generally permitted to take judicial notice at a pretrial hearing,[3] during a trial,[4] and at the appellate stage[5] of a criminal case. In federal courts, judicial notice may be taken at any time during any stage of a proceeding.[6] A limitation on matters that may be judicially noticed by any court is a requirement that the fact, concept, or principle must be relevant to the issues in the case, or judicial notice would be inappropriate.[7]

In taking judicial notice, what passes for common knowledge will vary with the geographic area where the court sits and does not necessarily depend upon the actual knowledge of the judge. A court may take judicial notice of a fact if that fact is not subject to reasonable dispute and it is "(1) generally known within the trial court's territorial jurisdiction, or (2) can be accurately and readily determined from sources whose accuracy cannot be reasonably questioned."[8] For instance, a judge might not understand the exact science involved in **deoxyribonucleic acid** (DNA) testing, but could still judicially notice the accuracy of the scientific principle where there was general acceptance of the principle by those with knowledge in the field. In other fields of knowledge, a judge may consult authoritative sources to verify the validity of taking judicial notice. For example, in making a decision, a court could properly take judicial notice of the English language and consult "[r]epresentative authoritative sources for verification [of facts that] include such materials as historical works, science and art books, language and medical journals and dictionaries, calendars, encyclopedias. . . ."[9]

Although the judge has discretion in taking judicial notice, the power of judicial notice must be exercised with caution. If there is any doubt whatsoever, either as to the fact itself or as to its being a matter of common knowledge, evidence should be required. Generally speaking, matters of judicial notice meet at least two basic requisites and one final consideration: (1) a matter must be of common and general knowledge to those in the relevant field of knowledge; and (2) it must be authoritatively settled, not subject to reasonable dispute, and not uncertain.[10] Finally, because judicial

---

2 A judge may not use his or her personal experience as a substitute for evidence that was not a proper subject for judicial notice. *See* State v. Sarnowski, 2005 Wis. App. 48, 280 Wis. 2d 243, 251, 694 N.W.2d 498, 502, 2005 Wis. App. LEXIS 150 (2005).

3 United States v. Haque, 2009 U.S. App. LEXIS 4231 (6th Cir. 2009).

4 United States v. Dedman, 527 F.3d 577, 583, 2008 U.S. App LEXIS 11407 (6th Cir. 2008).

5 *See* United States v. Elashyi, n.9, 554 F.3d 480, 2008 U.S. App LEXIS 27088 (5th Cir. 2008).

6 FED. R. EVID. 201(f).

7 29 AM. JUR. 2D *Evidence* § 25 Relevancy of information required.

8 FED. R. EVID. 201(b).

9 Stokes v. Commonwealth, 2008 Ky. LEXIS 321 Ky. 2008), quoting RICHARD H. UNDERWOOD & GLEN WEISSENBERGER, KENTUCKY EVIDENCE 2005–2006 COURTROOM MANUAL 44 (2005).

10 State v. Shanks, 640 A.2d 155 (Conn. 1994).

notice is a substitute for evidence, and only relevant evidence is admissible, a court will not take judicial notice of facts that are not relevant in the particular case.[11]

The judge may take judicial notice upon his or her own motion, even in the absence of a request, and must take judicial notice when a party requests it and the court has been supplied with the appropriate supporting information.[12] In deciding whether to judicially notice a fact, the judge may consult statutes and case law, as well as review legal encyclopedias, while seeking sources of information regarding the appropriateness of taking judicial notice. A judge may seek assistance in reaching the decision by consulting any authoritative source of information that serves the purpose. The judge may decline to take notice where the defendant has failed to provide information to support the request.[13] In a California homicide case, the defendant contended that a recent change in California law altered the death penalty so that almost anyone in a gang would be responsible for any murder done by the gang, and he argued that the change would have the effect of widening and not narrowing the class of people eligible for the death penalty. The appellate court noted that, because the defendant had failed to provide any sources from which the court could take judicial notice of the defendant's contention, the trial court properly declined to take judicial notice.[14]

With respect to the topics of proper judicial notice in criminal cases, one North Carolina court consulted a leading legal encyclopedia that suggested the existence of a wide range of miscellaneous facts that may be the subject of judicial notice, including:

> The laws of nature; human impulses, habits, functions and capabilities; the prevalence of a certain surname; established medical and scientific facts; well-known practices in farming, construction work, transportation, and other businesses and professions; the characteristics of familiar tools and appliances, weapons, intoxicants, and poisons; the use of highways; the normal incidence of the operation of trains, motor vehicles, and planes; prominent geographical features such as railroads, water courses, and cities and towns; population and area as shown by census reports; the days, weeks, and months of the calendar; the effect of natural conditions on the construction of public improvements; the facts of history; important current events; general economic and social conditions; matters affecting public health and safety; the meaning of words and abbreviations; and the results of mathematical computations.[15]

While these categories are not all-inclusive, and some courts might reject some of them, they represent many topics on which courts regularly take judicial notice. For

---

11 People v. Young, 34 Cal. 4th 1149, 1171, 105 P.3d 487, 499, 24 Cal. Rptr. 3d 112, 126, 2005 Cal. LEXIS 1017 (2005).

12 FED. R. EVID. 201(c).

13 People v. Herrera, 2007 Cal. App. Unpub. LEXIS 3965 (2007).

14 *Id.*

15 Simpson v. Simpson, 703 S.E.2d 890, 894, 2011 N.C. App. LEXIS 67 (2011), referencing Hinkle v. Hartsell, 131 N.C. App. 833, 836, 509 S.E.2d 455, 457–58 (1998) (quoting 1 Kenneth S. Broun, Brandis and Broun on North Carolina Evidence § 27, 104–09 (5th ed. 1998)).

convenience, the rules concerning judicial notice are often categorized as judicial notice of facts and judicial notice of laws. In the following sections, the two categories are discussed and distinguished.

§ 5.3 Judicial Notice of Facts

Rule 201

JUDICIAL NOTICE OF ADJUDICATIVE FACTS

(a) Scope of Rule. This rule governs judicial notice of an adjudicative fact only, not a legislative fact.
(b) Kinds of Facts that may be Judicially Noticed. The court may judicially notice a fact that is not subject to reasonable dispute because it:
  (1) is generally known within the trial court's territorial jurisdiction; or
  (2) can be accurately and readily determined from sources whose accuracy cannot reasonably be questioned.
(c) Taking Notice. The court:
  (1) may take judicial notice on its own; or
  (2) must take judicial notice if a party requests it and the court is supplied with the necessary information.
(d) Timing. The court may take judicial notice at any stage of the proceeding.
(e) Opportunity to be Heard. On timely request, a party is entitled to be heard on the propriety of taking judicial notice and the nature of the fact to be noticed. If the court takes judicial notice before notifying a party, the party, on request, is still entitled to be heard.
(f) Instructing the Jury. In a civil case, the court must instruct the jury to accept the noticed fact as conclusive. In a criminal case, the court must instruct the jury that it may or may not accept the noticed fact as conclusive.[16]

Adjudicative facts Facts that concern the immediate parties and are determinative of the outcome of the case.

Rule 201 of the Federal Rules of Evidence addresses only judicial notice of **adjudicative facts** and does not cover legislative facts. Adjudicative facts that are appropriate for judicial notice are the facts that are specific and unique to a particular case and will determine the result of the case. These facts can be established by judicial notice, but are usually proved by the introduction of actual evidence, as they will prove or disprove elements of the crime or defense. Adjudicative facts are facts that are specific to the individual case and are typically required to be proved by evidence and may be described as facts that are relevant to the determination of issues presented in an

---

[16] FED. R. EVID. 201.

individual case. When a judge takes judicial notice of adjudicative facts, the notice allows the finder of fact to accept these facts as true or as existing without the necessity of any formal proof.[17] In accordance with Subdivision (b) of Rule 201, a court may take judicial notice of the facts that are well known within the territorial jurisdiction of the trial court, or that the judge has determined by reference to an authoritative source not to be subject to reasonable dispute.

As indicated in Subdivision (c) of Rule 201, a court may take judicial notice without a formal request from either counsel. According to the general rule, a judge may take judicial notice at any time, whether during the trial or whether for the first time on appeal,[18] so long as judicial notice would have been appropriate at the trial. The judge is required to take judicial notice if asked by a party and supplied with the necessary information. In a North Carolina case, the appellant requested that the reviewing court take judicial notice of the existence of an arrest warrant for the first time during the appeal. Given that a warrant was a public record, and the court had been supplied with the necessary information, the court judicially noticed the warrant.[19]

As a general rule, courts may, but are not required to, initiate research to discover indisputable sources of information, and if the information supplied to a trial or appellate court is not sufficient, the court is entitled to refuse to take judicial notice of the matter requested. In a California capital case where the defendant alleged that a constitutional flaw existed in relevant legislation, the court refused to take judicial notice of the flaw, because the defendant failed to demonstrate on the record, or through sources of which the court could have taken judicial notice, that his claims were empirically accurate.[20] In dismissing a case as moot, one federal district court conducted its own research to locate two obituary notices that indicated the litigant had become deceased and dismissed the case on that basis.[21]

Judicial notice of facts is not dependent on the extrajudicial or the personal knowledge of the judge; what the judge knows and what facts the judge may judicially notice are not identical. Case interpretations in federal and state courts are quite clear that the private knowledge of the judge is not a sufficient basis for taking judicial notice of facts.[22] And, just because the judge has personal knowledge, this knowledge is not sufficient, by itself, to allow judicial notice to be taken. In most courts, a judge must take judicial notice of facts regardless of whether the judge is personally aware of the fact for which notice has been requested. In *State v. Vejvoda,*[23] the reviewing court, after explaining the limits on the use of judicial notice, decided that the trial court improperly took judicial notice of the fact that the defendant was driving in a city within the county of prosecution, as the arresting officer's testimony referred only to street names, but not

---

17 29 AM. JUR. 2D § 29 (2013).

18 Crooks v. Lynch, 2009 U.S. App. LEXIS 4020 (8th Cir. 2009).

19 State v. Tyson, 658 S.E.2d 285, 287, 2008 N.C. App. LEXIS 652 (2008).

20 People v. Michaels, 28 Cal. 4th 486, 541, 49 P.3d 1032, 122 Cal. Rptr. 2d 285 (2002).

21 Hatten v. Pennsylvania, 2013 U.S. Dist. LEXIS 170381 (W.D. Pa. 2013).

22 *See* 29 AM. JUR. 2D § 35 (2013).

23 *See also* State v. Vejvoda, 231 Neb. 668, 438 N.W.2d 461 (1989). See case in Part II.

their location. The fact that the judge was aware that the streets were probably in the county of prosecution did not cure the failure to introduce evidence. In a different case, the Ninth Circuit Court of Appeals held that a judge should not have relied upon his personal knowledge in commenting on the location of stop signs, the fact that the area at issue was extremely rural, and that there was not a lot of traffic on a particular road after 10:30 at night. The Court of Appeals noted that a judge is prohibited from taking judicial notice when he or she relies upon personal experience to support the taking of judicial notice.[24]

Courts do not always reach predictable results when asked to take judicial notice. California appellate courts do not generally take judicial notice of matters that were neither presented nor requested of a trial court[25] and do not take judicial notice of documents that were not presented to the trial court.[26] Other jurisdictions seem quite comfortable in taking judicial notice in post-conviction proceedings.[27] Even though courts are not in complete agreement as to what facts must be judicially noticed, when to take notice, and what facts may be judicially noticed on request, some matters have traditionally been considered proper topics for consideration. These are discussed in the sections that follow. However, the examples given are merely demonstrative of the general principles and are not meant to be exhaustive.

§ 5.4 —Matters of General Knowledge

While it is accepted practice to take judicial notice of facts of common knowledge, and such facts need not be proved by the opposing party, determining what facts can be classified as common knowledge may prove to be a challenge in some situations. A fact is said to be generally recognized or known when it is not open to reasonable dispute. A fact that possesses sufficient notoriety will be deemed to be a proper subject for judicial notice. In other words, in order to be considered for judicial notice, a matter must only be familiar to the majority of humankind or to those persons familiar with a particular matter in question. For example, the fact that whiskey and rum are intoxicating liquors is generally known, and their qualities are not subject to any reasonable dispute.[28] This does not mean that everyone must be aware of the fact, because scarcely any fact is known by everyone. When the matter depends upon uncertain testimony or rests on speculation, it becomes a disputable item in court, ceasing to fall under the heading of common knowledge, and this fact should not be judicially recognized. For example,

---

24 United States v. Berber-Tinoco, 510 F.3d 1083, 1091, 2007 U.S. App. LEXIS 29301 (9th Cir. 2007), *cert. denied*, 2008 U.S. LEXIS 7266 (2008).

25 Habib v. Seuhr, G038212, 2008 Cal. App. Unpub. LEXIS 2713 (Cal. Ct. Appl. 2008).

26 The Termo Company v. Luther, 169 Cal. App. 4th 394, 404, 2008 Cal. App. LEXIS 2430 (2008).

27 Trotter v. State, 392 So. 2d 1045, 1048, 2006 Fla. LEXIS 940 (2006).

28 *See* State v. Aiken, 121 Ohio Misc. 2d 7, 2002 Ohio 6436, 779 N.E.2d 1105, 2002 Ohio Misc. LEXIS 44 (2002).

in a criminal case that arose from an episode of domestic violence, that criminal judge took judicial notice that the judge in the related domestic violence case determined the defendant could not have arrived on the scene in time to have committed the violence. In the criminal case, it was reasonably disputed whether the defendant committed the violent acts, and the criminal court erred in taking judicial notice of the decision of the judge who refused to issue a domestic restraining order.[29]

In many instances, facts that may be properly judicially noticed involve matters of purely local knowledge that are open and notoriously known to people who live in a local geographical area. These facts might include where intersecting streets serve as an accepted center of a city, or they may indicate where a statue dedicated to a war hero is located, or the name of the major street that runs through a city. For example, in a federal civil rights case in Georgia, the judge took judicial notice of the identity of the new county sheriff, because the new sheriff's name had to be substituted for the name of the former sheriff.[30] In one suit, a federal district court took judicial notice of the fact that Operation Iraqi Freedom did not begin until March 19, 2003, as well as the fact that there was a long standoff that preceded military operations.[31] The date of the military operation was in the current memory of many people and was subject to easy verification and served as an appropriate fact for judicial notice.

Courts may take judicial notice of notorious nationally known facts that are not the subject of reasonable dispute. For example, one court took judicial notice that, because the eBay auction process had been in business longer than ten years, its methods of operation constituted a matter of common knowledge, concerning how bidding and selling operated.[32] Another court took judicial notice that, in litigation concerning the Star Wars series of movies, Luke Skywalker was nurtured by Obi-Wan Kenobi.[33] Because it is a well-known fact that tobacco products pose disease-related risks, including lung cancer, it is proper for a court to take notice of the harm of tobacco.[34] But a different court decided "that reasonable minds could differ as to whether public knowledge about the health risks of developing disease and nicotine addiction from smoking cigarettes was so certain and generally known" at a particular time in history, and in that situation, judicial notice was not appropriate.[35]

Concerning the proper subjects of judicial notice, courts have held that the judge may take judicial notice of mortality tables as proof of life expectancy.[36] Other

---

29 State v. Silva, 394 N.J. Super. 270, 2007 N.J. Super. LEXIS 200 (2007).

30 Young v. Graham, 2005 U.S. Dist. LEXIS 20882 (2005).

31 Lynch v. Robertson, 2007 U.S. Dist. LEXIS 60835 (W.D. Pa. 2007).

32 Choice Auto Brokers, Inc. v. Dawson, 274 S.W.3d 172, n.1, 2008 Tex. App. LEXIS 7236 (2008).

33 Twentieth Century Fox Film Corp. v. Marvel Enterprises, 155 F. Supp. 2d 1, 41, 2001 U.S. Dist. LEXIS 11568 (S. Dist. N.Y. 2001).

34 Spain v. Brown and Williamson Tobacco, 363 F.3d 1183, 1194, 2004 U.S. App. LEXIS 5792 (11th Cir. 2004).

35 Smith v. Brown & Williamson Tobacco Corp., 2007 Mo. App. LEXIS 1144 (2007).

36 Tobin v. Liberty Mutual, 2007 U.S. Dist. LEXIS 23680 (D. Mass. 2007), *aff'd,* 553 F.3d 121, 2009 U.S. App. LEXIS 1278 (1st Cir. 2009).

examples of instances in which courts have taken judicial notice of matters of general knowledge are these: firearms serve as the tools of the trade to substantial dealers in narcotics,[37] an attorney's state of admission to the bar,[38] farmers in South Dakota produce significant amounts of seed corn,[39] navigability of a river in Montana,[40] the capitol building in Utah is located on State Street,[41] Tiffany & Co. is a very well-known jewelry store,[42] and dates based on consulting a calendar for a particular month and year.[43]

In discussing judicial notice, a Georgia court explained that the courts will generally take judicial notice of a fact if the fact is of common knowledge, meaning all people of average intelligence are presumed to know and that is certain and indisputable.[44] A Maryland court noted that it was appropriate for a court to take judicial notice that most men do not carry purses.[45] A Florida court took judicial notice that a well-known local Christian school was a school for purposes of state law because the trial judge should not be compelled to force the school's principal to spend valuable time at the courthouse confirming a status that seemed to be common knowledge.[46] Although perhaps not well known by most people, one court took judicial notice in a fraud case "that when one consumes telephone service, one is consuming an applied form of electricity that uses an electric current to transmit the human voice—is a fact readily discernable from a variety of sources. . . ."[47]

On the other hand, the courts have held that certain facts are not presumed to be known by the court. Bringing case law to a court's attention has been held not to be a proper topic for judicial notice,[48] and in a criminal case, the specific findings of a domestic violence judge will not be considered a proper topic for judicial notice.[49] Courts have refused to take judicial notice of unauthenticated e-mail,[50] that all the detainees from Iraq and Afghanistan at Guantanamo Bay were "enemy combatants,"[51] and that Liechtenstein and the British Virgin Islands are regarded as tax havens.[52] A federal district court could not properly take judicial notice that seven victims of a defendant had suffered any number of losses as a result of a defendant's actions when

---

37 United States v. Riley, 452 F.3d 160, 165, 2006 U.S. App. LEXIS 15584 (2d Cir. 2006).

38 Geron v. Seyfarth Shaw L.L.P., 736 F.3d 213, 220, 2013 U.S. App. LEXIS 23123 (2nd Cir. 2013).

39 Braun v. E.I. du Pont de Nemours & Co., 2006 U.S. Dist. LEXIS 37431 (D. S.D. 2006).

40 *See* P.P.L. Mont. v. L.L.C. Montana, 132 S.Ct. 1215, 182 L.E.2d 77, 2012 U.S. LEXIS 1686 (2012).

41 Utah Gospel Mission v. Salt Lake City, 316 F. Supp. 2d 1201, 2004 U.S. Dist. LEXIS 12966 (2004).

42 Correa v. Comm'r of Corr., 101 Conn. App. 554, 557, 2007 Conn. App. LEXIS 225 (2007).

43 Givens v. Martel, 2012 U.S. Dist. LEXIS 34517 (N.D. Cal. 2012).

44 Weems v. State, 485 S.E.2d 767 (Ga. 1997).

45 Ransome v. State, 2003 Md. LEXIS 39 (Md. Ct. App. 2003).

46 Cox v. Florida, 764 So. 2d 711, 713, 2000 Fla. App. LEXIS 7516 (2000).

47 State v. Howard, 2008 Wis. App. LEXIS 807 (Wis. 2008).

48 Hyde v. Paskett, 383 F. Supp. 2d 1256, 2005 U.S. Dist. LEXIS 23165 (D. Idaho 2005).

49 State v. Brown, 394 N.J. Super. 492, 507, 2007 N.J. Super. LEXIS 247 (2007).

50 Becerra v. Radio Shack Corp., 2012 U.S. Dist. LEXIS 175522 (N.D. Cal. 2012).

51 Rasul v. Bush, 215 F. Supp. 2d 55, 67, 2002 U.S. Dist. LEXIS 14031 (D. D.C. 2002).

52 United States v. Cohen, 2012 U.S. Dist. LEXIS 18891 (C.D. Ill. 2012).

the notice was based on the judge's own professional experience.[53] A Florida court improperly took judicial notice of the value of a nonworking motor vehicle based on a reference value book, because the reference book considered only vehicles that were operable.[54] A court should not take judicial notice of the age of a juvenile, because that fact was an element of the charge of underage alcohol consumption.[55] As many people have knowledge of events around them that may affect everyday lives, judicial notice of contemporary happenings and events may be the subject of judicial notice. For instance, it is common knowledge that there has been an increase in the number of serious crimes committed by persons less than 18 years of age. The judge may take judicial notice of economic facts, such as the constant increase in the cost of living and the decrease in the purchasing power of the dollar. In such instances, the facts are noticed judicially without proof by either side.

§ 5.5 —History and Historical Facts

The historical facts that make up the history of the states and our nation are either well known to contemporary members of society or have been recorded in works of history. As such, these facts are either common knowledge or are subject to ready verification by consulting standard reference works. In taking judicial notice of historical facts or events, courts simply recognize the reasonably irrefutable facts of our history that, if proof was required by a court, would constitute a waste of time. Many Americans vividly remember the historic events involving airplane terrorists that occurred on September 11, 2001. In one case, a parole hearing was not held in a timely fashion on September 11, 2001, due to the terrorist attacks in Pennsylvania and the governor's response. Therefore, court took judicial notice of the events of that day, recognizing that a sufficient reason existed for the hearing to be rescheduled later than the time demanded by administrative regulations.[56] According to a case cited by the court, "matters of history, if sufficiently notorious to be subject to general knowledge, will be judicially noticed."[57] In an Alabama child custody case, where objections had to be filed within a set period of time, the court took judicial notice that the courthouse was open for business on the last day to timely file the objections to the decision.[58]

The financial history of the United States, including events such as the 1929 stock market collapse and the depression of the 1930s, are proper matters for judicial notice. In a bankruptcy matter, a court can take judicial notice of the average rate of a 30-year

---

53 United States v. Gregory, 2009 U.S. App. LEXIS 1970 (11th Cir. 2009).

54 Walentukonis v. Florida, 2006 Fla. App. LEXIS 9766 (2006).

55 State v. K.N., 124 Wash. App. 875, 103 P.3d 844, 2004 Wash. App. LEXIS 3135 (2004).

56 Wiley v. Commonwealth, 801 A.2d 644, 2002 Pa. Commw. LEXIS 510 (2002).

57 *See* Fatemi v. Fatemi, 371 Pa. Super. 101, 537 A.2d 840 (1988).

58 Ex parte L.S., 2013 Ala. Civ. App. LEXIS 190 (2013).

mortgage at a particular time by consulting the *Wall Street Journal*.[59] The price of listed stocks on recognized exchanges constitutes historical data that cannot be subject to any serious dispute and can be the subject of judicial notice.[60] The day of the week on which a particular date fell, the date on which war was declared or ended, the destructive character of a flood or other disaster—all can be matters of judicial notice. The court, in an action to declare life insurance policies in force, judicially noticed the flight of refugees from Castro's Cuba to Miami, Florida, and their acceptance, encouragement, and support by the United States.[61]

In criminal cases as well as civil cases, the court may take judicial notice of historical facts of a national character, such as the fact that 97 percent of the population of Iraq is Muslim,[62] that a political disturbance and civil war existed in Croatia after it declared independence in 1991,[63] and, in a modern environmental suit, that the decade following 1953 was one of heightened military concern in the United States.[64]

The judge does not have to be personally aware of historical facts to take judicial notice of them. It would be asking too much for the judge to be aware of all the details of history. He or she may refer to properly authenticated official public documents, encyclopedias, history books, periodicals, or even newspaper articles. However, in taking judicial notice, a judge is limited to what is appropriate in his or her judicial capacity and may not take notice of historical facts known only to the judge and not generally known by the public. Historical facts within historical documents that may themselves be subject to dispute as historical facts are not proper subjects for judicial notice.[65] Although a court may take judicial notice of historical facts, the court is not required to do so unless the party so requesting supplies the necessary information.[66]

§ 5.6 —Geography and Geographical Facts

Although the prosecutor must introduce evidence to show that the court has jurisdiction in the case during the initial stages, he or she does not have to introduce evidence to show, for example, that Chicago is in Cook County, Illinois, or that the Mississippi River flows generally from the north to the south. In Florida, courts are permitted to take judicial notice "of the prominent geographical and natural features

59 In re Chaing, 274 B.R. 295, 305, 2002 Bankr. LEXIS 170 (D. Mass. 2002).

60 Grimes v. Navigant Consulting, 185 F. Supp. 2d 906, 913, 2002 U.S. Dist. LEXIS 1708 (N.D. Ill. 2002).

61 Blanco v. Pan-American Life Ins. Co., 221 F. Supp. 219 (S.D. Fla. 1963); Perez v. Department of Revenue, 778 P.2d 326 (Colo. Ct. App. 1989).

62 Sulieman v. Roswell Park Cancer Inst., 2007 U.S. Dist. LEXIS 46599 (W.D. N.Y. 2007).

63 Abrambasic v. Ashcroft, 403 F. Supp. 2d 951, 958, 2005 U.S. Dist. LEXIS 31713 (D. S.D. 2005).

64 Gould Electronics v. United States, 2002 U.S. Dist. LEXIS 262 (E.D. Pa. 2002).

65 New York v. Shinnecock Indian Nation, 523 F. Supp. 2d 185, 262, 2007 U.S. Dist. LEXIS 80443 (E.D.N.Y. 2007).

66 State v. Hofland, 151 N.H. 322, 327, 857 A.2d 1271, 1276, 2004 N.H. LEXIS 146 (2004).

of the country, such as the large lakes and rivers; the division of the country into states; the existence, location, and population of political subdivisions; and distances between well-known points."[67] It is permissible for Florida courts to take judicial notice of the territorial limits of the United States[68] and of the prominent geographical and natural features of the country that are common knowledge, such as lakes and other bodies of water, and whether the body of water is tidal water or whether it can be navigated.[69] In a similar way, a federal district court sitting in the District of Columbia can take judicial notice that the geographic locations mentioned in the testimony are in the District of Columbia, as a way to find venue and jurisdiction.[70] In some jurisdictions, proof of the geography of venue cannot be made using judicial notice of the location of the crime, and appellate courts may not judicially notice venue by judicial notice on appeal.[71]

Using newer techniques to determine geographical distances, Illinois courts have permitted courts to take judicial notice of information on public web sites to determine distances between two points. In a murder case, one court measured the distance from where a defendant met the victim to the place where her body was discovered using Google Maps®, and the reviewing court generally approved of taking judicial notice of the reliability of Google Maps® and MapQuest® and using them to calculate distances.[72]

In a cocaine case involving possession too near a school, a Texas court noted that courts "may take judicial notice of the location of cities, counties, boundaries, dimensions, and distances, because geographical facts such as these are easily ascertainable and capable of verifiable certainty."[73] But a federal judge is prohibited from relying on his own experience to support the taking of judicial notice of the locations of stop signs or the narrow features of a road within his or her jurisdiction.[74]

Topography of the land and geographic features change very slowly, which makes judicial notice of these facts quite appropriate in many cases. Municipal boundaries may change more frequently due to annexation and consolidation, but the exact area and location of a municipal border can be discerned by reference to topographical maps, reference works, and common knowledge. "Trial courts are generally permitted to take judicial notice of any geographic facts that are common knowledge within its jurisdiction."[75] In one case involving well-known geography, the court took judicial notice that there was no city or town called Idaho within the jurisdiction of the state

---

67 23 FLA. JUR. § 40 (2008). *See also* TEX. WATER CODE § 49.066 (2013) where all courts must take judicial notice of the creation and boundaries of water districts.

68 *Id.*

69 *Id*, § 41.

70 Long v. United States, 940 A.2d 87, 99, 2007 D.C. App. LEXIS 667 (D.C. Cir. 2007).

71 Muldrow v. State, 322 Ga. App. 190, 192, 744 S.E.2d 413, 416, 2013 Ga. App. LEXIS 477 (2013).

72 *See* People v. Crawford, 2013 Il. App. 100310, 2013 Ill. App. LEXIS 871 (2013).

73 Lovelady v. State, 65 S.W.3d 810, 813, 2002 Tex. App. LEXIS 378 (2002) and New Process Steel, L.P. v. Sharp Freight System, n.5, 2006 Tex. App. LEXIS 2967 (2006).

74 United States v. Berber-Tinoco, 510 F.3d 1083, 1091, 2007 U.S. App. LEXIS 29301 (9th Cir. 2007).

75 State v. Davis, 2004 Ohio 5680, 2004 Ohio App. LEXIS 5144 (2004).

of California.[76] In these cases, the facts were notorious and well known within the judicial district or were subject to verification by unimpeachable sources. However, it would be improper for a judge to take judicial notice that a particular road had "a very tapered grass shoulder road [that went] into a heavy ditch in low lying swamp ground."[77] Such a description was subject to some reasonable dispute, and the court noted that "if there is even a mere possibility of dispute as to whether the fact asserted is accurate, or of common knowledge, judicial notice is inappropriate and evidence is required to establish the fact."[78]

A court may take judicial notice that a geographical area of a city is within a particular county or is within an Indian reservation. In a case involving an Indian who had to register under the federal version of Megan's Law for convicted sex offenders, the trial court properly took judicial notice that a city was completely surrounded by the territory of the Navajo Nation reservation, and that the reservation's boundaries were within the confines of a local county.[79] Other geographical facts that have been judicially noticed include the fact that a traffic stop occurred within the jurisdiction of the police officer,[80] and the question of whether an alleged crime occurred within "particular geographic boundaries is proper subject for judicial notice."[81]

§ 5.7 —Facts Relating to Nature and Science

Facts relating to nature and science can be the subject of judicial notice where the facts are reasonably undisputable. In a Florida murder case where it was important to determine when a defendant arrived at his campsite and there was testimony that he arrived at daybreak, a court properly took judicial notice that sunrise took place at 7:04 A.M. on that particular morning, so that proof of when the sun rose was not required.[82] According to a Maryland court, "A trial court may take judicial notice of the reliability of scientific techniques and methodologies that are widely accepted within the scientific community."[83] Even where general public knowledge does not exist concerning a fact about nature or a principle of science, courts may take judicial notice of the truth of facts that can readily be determined by references to accurate sources. In some cases where a scientific fact or principle proves complicated, courts may have to hear expert testimony before taking notice. In novel areas of scientific

---

[76] In re Suhey, 221 Cal. App. 4th 732, 735, 164 Cal. Rptr. 3d 772, 776, 2013 Cal. App. LEXIS 939 (2013).

[77] State v. Smith, 2006 Del. C.P. LEXIS 34 (Del. 2006). See case in Part II.

[78] *Id.*

[79] State v. John, 308 P.3d 1208, 1210, 2013 Ariz. App. LEXIS 202 ((2013).

[80] State v. Burkhalter, 2006 Ohio 1623, 2006 Ohio App. LEXIS 1520 (2006).

[81] United States v. Kelly, 535 F.3d 1229, 2008 U.S. App. LEXIS 16572 (10th Cir. 2008), *cert. denied,* 2009 U.S. LEXIS 1053 (2009).

[82] Swafford v. State, 125 So.3d 760, 2013 Fla. LEXIS 2421 (2013).

[83] Montgomery Mutual v. Chesson, 399 Md. 314, 327, 2007 Md. LEXIS 331 (2007).

inquiry, where there may initially be some dispute concerning a fact or principle that has yet to reach the level of near-universal acceptance, courts require expert testimony to establish the validity of the fact or principle before taking notice.. As a particular scientific fact or process gains general acceptance and becomes reasonably undisputed by those in the field, a court may judicially notice the fact and dispense with formal proof. In some cases, trial and appellate courts have taken judicial notice of scientific literature even when neither party presented any supporting information.[84] Such practice, however, may pose a danger if the court misapplies the principle or the scientific conclusion.

Consistent with the proper use of judicial notice, courts frequently take notice of the elementary principles of physics, such as the force of gravity or the laws of thermodynamics. Also, facts relating to the climate of the state and the climate elsewhere may be judicially noticed. Of special significance in criminal cases is the fact that the courts may take judicial notice of scientific facts that have a bearing on the case, and scientific facts that have been well established by authoritative scientists and are generally accepted as irrefutable. For example, the general reliability of expert medical testimony based on reasoning from epidemiological data is generally considered a proper subject for judicial notice.[85] With respect to judicial notice of weather, courts usually take judicial notice of historical weather conditions because past weather conditions are not subject to reasonable dispute.[86] In an unpublished opinion, a federal judge took judicial notice of the weather conditions on a prison yard in a suit brought by a dissatisfied prisoner.[87]

The scope of judicial notice in science and nature is not static and changes as new discoveries are made, expanding the human knowledge base. A number of these scientific areas are of special interest in the criminal justice process. For example, **ballistic identification** for firearms was once unacceptable because the scientific principle behind the process was not generally accepted, but presently, the validity of ballistic identification techniques is a proper subject for judicial notice. Likewise, courts were reluctant to admit DNA identification evidence because the science was not well known by scientists or understood by courts, but as the science became accepted in the relevant scientific community, courts recognized the principle that human DNA is unique to each person.[88] Over a defendant's objection concerning

Ballistic identification The use of machine markings, produced on gun projectiles fired from the weapon, to identify the source of the projectile or the particular gun that was used.

[84] Mata v. State, 46 S.W.3d 902, 910, 2001 Tex. Crim. App. LEXIS 45 (2001).

[85] Knight v. Kerby Inland Marine, Inc., 363 F. Supp. 2d 859, 2005 U.S. Dist. LEXIS 10615 (2005).

[86] Easy Sportswear, Inc. v. Am. Econ. Ins. Co., 2008 U.S. Dist. LEXIS 51402 (W.D. Pa. 2008) (Memorandum opinion).

[87] Conn v. Does, 2008 U.S. Dist. LEXIS 17733 (D. N.J. 2008).

[88] DNA profiles are unique except for identical twins.

DNA testing and its reliability, a Utah court took judicial notice of the scientific reliability of Y-STR (short tandem repeat process) DNA analysis and determined that the DNA testing had been properly conducted in the case.[89]

In a different situation, courts have "been known to take judicial notice that improperly performed DNA tests have resulted in wrongful convictions."[90] An Ohio reviewing court noted with approval that a trial court took judicial notice of the scientific accuracy and reliability of a laser speed-measuring device.[91] Judicial notice may be appropriate in recognizing the scientific validity of the principle underlying the horizontal gaze nystagmus (HGN) test, used as a diagnostic tool to identify alcohol-impaired drivers. In a Maine prosecution for driving while intoxicated, the state's top court approved the use of the HGN test as circumstantial evidence of impairment.[92] As a general rule, courts have been unwilling to take judicial notice of the scientific validity of the polygraph or to admit the results in criminal cases due to concerns about reliability or relevancy,[93] but some courts will take judicial notice of reliability of the polygraph due to the fact that it is used extensively by police agencies.[94]

Courts often take judicial notice of facts involving a mix of science and law. In one case, where a prisoner complained of inappropriate medical care, a federal district court took judicial notice that treating a specific ailment involved using an approved drug, doxycycline, was a medically acceptable course of treatment.[95] A Texas trial court judicially noticed "the Controlled Substances Act, which lists hydrocodone as a Schedule II drug, and took judicial notice of the fact that Vicodin and Lortab both contain hydrocodone."[96] An Arizona appellate court took judicial notice of the legislative determination and of the expert scientific opinion concerning the effects and harmfulness of marijuana.[97]

When considering nature and science as topics for judicial notice, it "is generally limited to matters of public record and to matters of common knowledge that cannot reasonably be disputed."[98] These subjects include notice of a date on a calendar, the

---

89 State v. Maestas, 2012 Ut 46, 299 P.3d 892, 906, 2012 Utah LEXIS 106 (2012).

90 Brown v. Farwell, 525 F.3d 787, 796–97 (9th Cir. 2008).

91 State v. Kim, 2008 Ohio 6928, 2008 Ohio App. LEXIS 5814 (Ohio 2008). *Contra*, State v. Miko, 2008 Ohio 1991, 2008 Ohio App. LEXIS 1703 (2008).

92 State v. Just, 2007 ME 91, 2007 Me. LEXIS 92 (2007). *But see* People v. McKown, 226 Ill.2d 245, 2007 Ill. LEXIS 1163 (2007), where the court rejected judicial notice for the principle behind the horizontal gaze nystagmus test.

93 United States v. Ramirez-Robles, 386 F.3d 1234, 1248, 2004 U.S. App. LEXIS 21847 (9th Cir. 2004). The Fourth Circuit Court of Appeals continues to enforce a per se ban on polygraph evidence. *See* United States v. Prince-Oyibo, 320 F.3d 494, 501, 2003 U.S. App. LEXIS 3568 (4th Cir. 2003).

94 State v. Domicz, 377 N.J. Super 515, 2005 N.J. Super. LEXIS 161 (2005).

95 Banks v. County of Allegheny, 2008 U.S. Dist. LEXIS 107544 (2008).

96 Smith v. State, 2008 Tex. App. LEXIS 4779 (2008).

97 State v. Hardesty, 2008 Ariz. App. LEXIS 121 (2008). *Review granted*, 2009 Ariz. LEXIS 22 (2009), *aff'd.* 222 Ariz. 363, 214 P.3d 1004, 2009 Ariz. LEXIS 255 (2009).

98 Timm v. Reitz, 39 P.3d 1252, 1258, 2001 Colo. App. LEXIS 2019 (2001).

principle of gravity, or an unquestioned law of mathematics.[99] Notice should be taken of scientific principles and authoritative treatises that are generally known and accepted or are readily verifiable from sources of indisputable accuracy. However, courts generally will not take judicial notice of scientific facts or principles that remain of questionable validity. For example, in an assault case, an Ohio appellate court refused to take judicial notice of a defendant's offering of a complicated scientific formula that he alleged computed the rate of the acceleration of falling objects, which the prosecution contended injured other people. The court believed that the formula did not represent a proven scientific principle that was so well understood as to be part of the common knowledge of every person.[100]

§ 5.8 —Language, Abbreviations, and Symbols

Judges may take judicial notice of commonly used words, phrases, symbols, and slang words having a clearly fixed meaning, where the language has a settled community meaning by the group that uses the terminology. The personal knowledge of judges does not qualify them to take judicial notice merely because they have an extensive knowledge of words and phrases; they may take judicial notice of usual words that are known by the community, even if not known personally by the judge. Where a word or phrase has a plain meaning to those in the relevant field, but is not understood by the judge, a judge may consult a generally accepted dictionary "to aid in the ascertaining of such meaning."[101] Judges may consult dictionaries directed to specific fields such as a medical dictionary in determining the meaning of a particular word.[102] In a case where the language or meaning of a statute is ambiguous, a court may take judicial notice of the legislative history in evaluating the meaning of a word or phrase.[103]

Ordinarily, the court may not take judicial notice of the meaning of obscure slang words or expressions common to a small group. However, if the word has come into such frequent use as to convey a particular meaning, and it no longer can be considered as simply a slang term understood only by a certain segment of the population, the court may take judicial notice of the word. For example, a federal court took judicial notice of the slang term "booty" and recognized that it served as a common term for human buttocks.[104] Idioms that have acquired a special meaning may be judicially noticed. The term "Democrat" may be judicially noticed as meaning the members and candidates of

---

99 Johnson v. Commonwealth, 12 S.W.3d 258, 267, 1999 Ky. LEXIS 159 (1999).

100 State v. Mendez, 2004 Ohio 3107, 2004 Ohio App. LEXIS 2755 (2004).

101 Service Corporation of Westover Hills v. Guzzetta, 2007 Del. Ch. LEXIS 84 (2007).

102 *See* Stokes v. Commonwealth, 2008 Ky. LEXIS 321 (2008).

103 *See* County of Orange v. Superior Court of Orange County, 155 Cal. App. 4th 1253, 2007 Cal. App. LEXIS 1649, n.1 (2007).

104 Requa v. Kent School District No. 415, 492 F. Supp. 1272, 2007 U.S. Dist. LEXIS 40920 (W.D. Wash. 2007).

the Democratic party, and the court may take judicial notice that "pig" has come to be used as a derogatory name for the police.[105]

The corporate and institutional use of graphics and symbols can be proper subjects for judicial notice. Trademarks, logos, and similar graphic representations convey identifying messages to interested persons. Corporations frequently use symbols to make a company image or product recognizable to the public. In one case, the court took judicial notice that Microsoft's trademarks were valid and properly registered.[106] The designs of badges assigned to police officers are generally unique to the particular department. In an unpublished opinion in a case alleging impersonation of an officer, one court took judicial notice of the design, writing, and symbols incorporated into a genuine badge carried by a bona fide police officer.[107]

The courts may take judicial notice of the meaning of abbreviations generally known and in common use, such as abbreviations for days and months. But judicial notice may not be taken of the meaning of abbreviations, symbols, or initials when the meaning is not generally known or when they have no meaning without explanation. A court, for example, may take judicial notice that the initials "M.D." refer to a physician,[108] and that "Chas." is an abbreviation for "Charles,"[109] or that the abbreviation "G.I." refers to a soldier.[110]

§ 5.9 Judicial Notice of Laws

While courts often take judicial notice of facts, judicial notice of law follows from the same basic premise of allowing for the notice of undisputable facts. Because the statutory law has been written by legislative bodies and is easily accessed and brought to the attention of a court or of opposing counsel, to require a party to produce evidence to prove that laws that are currently in force would be a waste of time. A court must take judicial notice of the statutory law applicable in its own individual jurisdiction as well as the laws of the state in which it sits. A federal appellate court recently quoted an old case, noting that "The law of any state of the Union, whether depending upon statutes or upon judicial opinions, is a matter of which the courts of the United States are bound to take judicial notice, without plea or proof."[111] Many states permit judicial notice of the laws of sister states and some will allow notice of foreign law on a proper occasion. To facilitate judicial notice of law, counsel usually brings the judge's attention to statutes or citations in references to decisions applicable to the case being tried. An Ohio court

---

105 St. Petersburg v. Waller, 261 So. 2d 151 (1972).

106 Microsoft v. Atek 3000 Computer, 2008 U.S. Dist. LEXIS 56689 (E.D.N.Y. 2008).

107 People v. Diaz, H026161, 2005 Cal. App. Unpub. LEXIS 3559 (Cal. Ct. Appls. 2005).

108 State v. Brady, 223 Or. 433, 354 P.2d 811 (1960).

109 Cumbol v. State, 205 Tenn. 260, 326 S.W.2d 454 (1959).

110 Still v. Secretary of the Commonwealth, 73 Pa. D. & C. 106, 1950 Pa. D. & C. LEXIS 247 (1950).

111 United States v. Dedman, 527 F.3d 577, 586, 2008 U.S. App. LEXIS 11407 (6th Cir. 2008), quoting Lamar v. Micou, 114 U.S. 218, 1885 U.S. LEXIS 274 (1885).

noted that it could take judicial notice of a sister state's public statutory or case law within the United States and "may inform itself in such manner as it deems proper."[112]

State trial courts judicially notice federal law, and a federal court will judicially notice the law of every state. In fact, when sitting in a diversity jurisdiction case, the federal court is acting as if it were a state court and will follow state law concerning judicial notice as precisely as possible. For example, as is the case in most states, the California Evidence Code requires that judicial notice be taken of the "decisional, constitutional, and public statutory law of this state and of the United States".[113] However, when the United States Supreme Court reviews the decision of a state court, it will not take judicial notice of the law of another state, unless the state court below could have done so.[114]

Sections 5.10 through 5.16 specifically discuss the extent to which courts take judicial notice of laws prevailing within the forum, the laws of other states, and foreign nations.

§ 5.10 —Law of the Forum

It goes without saying that all courts must take judicial notice of the law prevailing within the forum; that is, the law that exists within the state or that applies to the particular federal jurisdiction. One of the reasons for having state and federal laws is that they are to be used and adjudicated by the courts. It would be foolish to permit courts to take judicial notice of federal laws and laws of other states and countries without taking judicial notice of their own laws. A court sitting in a particular state must take judicial notice of the law of its own state, including both statutory and case law.[115] In addition to notice of laws, courts generally take judicial notice of their own court records, as well as court records generated by other courts in the state. For example, California courts may judicially notice the records of any court in the state.[116]

If prior case law has established a particular principle, a trial court may judicially notice the principle, and the trial court is not required to hold a pretrial hearing before taking judicial notice. For example, an Illinois appeals court determined that it was unnecessary to hold a pretrial hearing prior to admitting DNA identification testimony if case law had established the validity of the principle in a previous case.[117] The court

---

[112] Ohio v. Turner, 105 Ohio St. 3d 331, 341, 2005 Ohio 1938, 826 N.E.2d 266, 278, 2005 Ohio LEXIS 961 (2005).

[113] CAL. EVID. CODE § 451 (2014).

[114] Hanley v. Donoghue, 116 U.S. 1, 6 Sup. Ct. 242, 29 L. Ed. 535 (1885).

[115] Carmona v. Warden, 2007 Conn. Super. LEXIS 3425 (2007).

[116] *See* People v. Young, 34 Cal. 4th 1149; 105 P.3d 487; 24 Cal. Rptr. 3d 112; 2005 Cal. LEXIS 1017 (2005). (In n.3, the court noted its power to judicial notice of all state court records under the authority of CAL. EVID. CODE § 452(d).)

[117] People v. Johnson, 199 Ill. Dec. 931, 634 N.E.2d 1285 (1994). *See also* United States v. Martinez, 3 F. 3d 1191 (8th Cir. 1993).

Deoxyribonucleic acid (DNA) A long, threadlike chain of molecules found in the nucleus of virtually every cell of the body.

could take judicial notice of DNA identification as an accepted scientific procedure based on prior rulings. But a court could not judicially notice a denial of a motion to suppress that occurred in a case that was dismissed and later refiled. In a Wisconsin case, the judge improperly took notice that the defendant's motion to suppress had been denied in a prior proceeding, and when the case was refiled, the prior suppression decision was not a proper subject of judicial notice because the earlier proceeding had not concluded on the merits.[118]

§ 5.11 —Federal Law

Article VI of the United States Constitution provides that the "Constitution, and the laws of the United States which shall be made in Pursuance thereof, and all Treaties made, or which shall be made under the Authority of the United States, shall be the supreme Law of the Land; the Judges in every State shall be bound thereby. . .." Accordingly, all federal and state courts must take judicial notice of the provisions of the federal Constitution, its amendments, and the laws of the United States made pursuant to the Constitution. In regard to congressional enactments, judicial notice is not limited to their existence, wording, and interpretation, but extends to all matters connected therewith.[119] For example, a federal district court may properly take judicial notice that a drug was classified as a Schedule I drug.[120] In addition to traditional federal law, federal courts have found that records and reports of administrative bodies are proper subjects of judicial notice because administrative bodies create administrative law by promulgating rules and regulations.[121]

§ 5.12 —Law of Sister States

Many states have adopted a version of the Uniform Judicial Notice of Foreign Law Act. Wisconsin's version provides that "[e]very court of this state shall take judicial notice of the common law and statutes of every state, territory and other jurisdiction of the United States."[122] Under Wisconsin law, a court "may inform itself of such laws in such manner as it may deem proper, and the court may call upon counsel to aid it in obtaining such information."[123]

---

118 State v. Wasserman, 2008 Wis. App. 148, 2008 Wis. App. LEXIS 669 (2008).

119 Gardner v. Barney, 73 U.S. (6 Wall.) 499, 18 L. Ed. 890 (1868).

120 United States v. Arroyo, 2009 U.S. App. LEXIS 4165 (7th Cir. 2009).

121 United States v. 14.02 Acres of Land, 530 F.3d 883, 894, 2008 U.S. App. LEXIS 13309 (9th Cir. 2008).

122 WIS. STAT. § 902.02(1) (2013).

123 *Id.* § 902.02(2).

Typical of many states, Ohio law requires a party who plans to rely on the law of a sister American state to give notice in the pleadings or other reasonable written notice. The court may consider any reasonable source to determine the substance of foreign law.[124] The reasonable notice requirement is intended to assure fairness and to avoid undue surprise to the opponent when a party plans to rely on laws of other jurisdictions by using judicial notice. In an expansive view of notice of law, a Kansas statute requires that "[j]udicial notice shall be taken without request by a party, of common law, constitutions, and public statutes in force in every state, territory and jurisdiction of the United States. . . ."[125] Florida follows a similar plan, but mandates that a court take judicial notice of the laws of sister states where an adverse party has given a "written notice of the request, proof of which is filed with the court, to enable the adverse party to prepare to meet the request" and "[f]urnishes the court with sufficient information to enable it to take judicial notice of the matter."[126]

Public laws of general application are clearly included within the term "statutes." This term also fairly includes other states' constitutions and rules of procedure and evidence having force of law throughout each such state, even though some of the "law" consists of rules that were adopted by the highest court of the state. These materials are usually accessible through state codes and through verifiable Internet sites, and because they are in the general nature of public laws, these laws and rules should be judicially noticed. In a Texas case that concerned a breach of contract, the trial court took judicial notice of Illinois case law in resolving the controversy.[127] Although not a sister state, a federal court may take judicial notice of state law where appropriate. In fact, judicial notice may not even be required in the future because the Sixth Circuit has recently explained that "we used to allow judicial notice of state law, [but] now we consider that state law is simply a matter for the judge to determine."[128] In a federal drug prosecution in which the defendant was attempting to suppress evidence, a federal district court took notice of the Nebraska and California requirements for display of vehicle license plates, which helped determine whether a vehicle stop was legal.[129]

§ 5.13 —Law of Foreign Countries

As a practical matter, foreign civil and criminal law has an infrequent, but not necessarily unimportant, usage in criminal cases in either federal or state courts. United States federal courts may take judicial notice of the laws of foreign countries

---

124 State v. Turner, 105 Ohio St. 3d 331, 341, 2005 Ohio 1938, 826 N.E.2d 266, 2005 Ohio LEXIS 961 (2005).

125 K.S.A. 60–409(a) (2012).

126 *See* FLA. STAT. ANN. § 90.203(1), (2) (2013).

127 Orion Ref. Corp. v. UOP, 259 S.W.3d 749 (Tex. 2007).

128 United States v. Dedman, 527 F.3d 577, 587 (6th Cir. 2008).

129 United States v. Molson, 2006 U.S. Dist. LEXIS 2292 (D. Neb. 2006).

where a party has given written notice to raise the issue.[130] The Federal Rules of Criminal Procedure require that one party give notice to the other party that a matter of foreign law will be an issue at the trial.[131] The trial judge is then permitted to consider relevant material, whether offered by the prosecution or by the defense. In an immigration case having criminal overtones, a federal appellate noted that courts may take judicial notice of foreign law when the parties have given written notice of the intent to involve foreign law. Foreign law was sufficiently important in an immigration deportation case that the law of El Salvador needed to be referenced in support of the immigrant's legal position.[132] Because the El Salvadorian society recognized that drug cartels punish relatives of witnesses who have testified against their members, the concept was sufficiently recognized to have caused El Salvador to pass laws protecting such witnesses. It was relevant in the immigration context, because the existence of the specific El Salvadorian law helped prove a well-founded fear of harm if the person was deported to El Salvador where the witness was related to anti-drug cartel witnesses.

Following modern logic, federal courts will be required to take judicial notice where a federal law or a treaty specifically requires it.[133] In a child abduction case where the children had been taken from Mexico to the United States, federal courts took judicial notice of the signatory status of the United States and Mexico as parties to the Hague Convention on the Civil Aspects of International Child Abduction.[134] State courts often judicially recognize foreign law, and parties may introduce into evidence statutes or case law to support judicial notice.[135] Massachusetts also takes a progressive approach and requires its courts to take judicial notice of the "law . . . of a foreign country whenever the same shall be material."[136] Ohio law serves as a typical model, requiring a party who plans to rely on the law of a foreign country to give notice in the pleadings or other reasonable notice.[137] The court may consider any reasonable source to determine the substance of foreign law.[138] Some states allow their courts to judicially notice foreign law as a substitute for proof, while others are less accommodating. For example, a Wisconsin statute under the Uniform Judicial Notice of Foreign Law Act holds that the laws of foreign nations "shall be an issue for the court, but shall not be subject to . . . the provisions concerning judicial notice."[139]

---

130 Eshelman v. Orthoclear Holdings, 2009 U.S. Dist. LEXIS 19293 (N.D. Cal. 2009).

131 *See* FED. R. CRIM. P. 26.1.

132 Henriquez-Rivas v. Holder, 707 F3d, 1081, 1092 (9th Cir. 2013).

133 Baxter v. Baxter, 423 F.3d 363, 2005 U.S. App. LEXIS 19825, n.4. (3d Cir. 2005).

134 *See* Bernal v. Gonzalez, 923 F. Supp.2d 907 (W.D. Tex. 2012).

135 K&K Leasing v. Tech Logistice, 2008 Iowa App. LEXIS 1107 (2008).

136 ALM GL ch. 233, § 70 Judicial Notice of Laws of Other Jurisdictions (Mass. 2013).

137 *See* OHIO CIV. R. 44.1 (2013).

138 OHIO CIV. R. 44.1 is incorporated by OHIO CRIM. R. 27 (2013).

139 WIS. STAT. § 902.02 (2013).

§ 5.14 —Municipal Ordinances

State and local courts are often required to take judicial notice of local government ordinances passed by any subdivision of a state that has power to enact ordinances. For example, in Pennsylvania, all courts must take judicial notice of the ordinances of all the municipal corporations within the Commonwealth. A Pennsylvania court "may inform itself of such ordinances in such a manner as it may deem proper and the tribunal may call upon counsel to aid it in obtaining such information."[140] For example, a California appeals took judicial notice of the City of Monterey's municipal ordinances and approved the taking of judicial notice by a trial court of the City's ordinance that prohibited the operation of any medical marijuana dispensaries within the City of Monterey.[141] A medical marijuana dispensary had opened in contravention to the ordinance, and the City was attempting to close the shop. During court proceedings, the trial court had been asked to take notice of the City's anti-dispensary ordinance, pursuant to the evidence code of California, Section 452, Matters which may be judicially noticed. The state evidence statute allows courts to take notice of "[r]egulations and legislative enactments issued by or under the authority of the United States or any public entity in the United States."[142]

In many jurisdictions, reviewing courts may be required or permitted to exercise the same judicial notice over municipal ordinances as is allowed by the municipal trial courts themselves.[143] The court may obtain information sufficient to take judicial notice of ordinances in any manner it may deem appropriate and may consult with counsel for assistance in obtaining the information. As a general rule, when municipal courts are permitted to take judicial notice, they do so under the same rules that apply to courts of general jurisdiction and appellate courts.

Although many jurisdictions either allow or require their courts to take judicial notice of the municipal ordinances, some states require proof of the ordinance. Georgia retains the rule that municipal ordinances "must be alleged and proved by production of the original or of a properly certified copy."[144] In a case involving the City of Atlanta, a Georgia reviewing court noted that neither a trial court nor appellate court can take judicial notice of municipal ordinances.[145] Although not representative of the modern trend in judicial notice, in Georgia, when a prosecutor or defendant wants to rely on the provisions of a municipal ordinance, those provisions must be alleged and proved in the trial court, because the state has a well-established principle that judicial notice cannot be taken by superior and appellate courts.[146] Louisiana has a slightly different approach

---

[140] 42 PA. CONS. STAT. § 6107(b) (2013).

[141] City of Monterey v. Carrnshimba, 215 Cal. App. 4th 1068, 156 Cal. Rptr.3d 1, 2013 Cal. App. LEXIS 328 (2013).

[142] CAL. EVID. CODE § 452 (2013).

[143] *See* PA. R. EVID. 201 (2013).

[144] Bailey v. City of Atlanta, 2009 Ga. App. LEXIS 306 (2009).

[145] Latimore v. City of Atlanta, 289 Ga. App. 85, 86, 2008 Ga. App. LEXIS 2 (2008).

[146] Flippen Alliance v. Brannan, 267 Ga. App. 134, 136, 601 S.E.2d 106, 109, 2004 Ga. App. LEXIS 460 (2004).

from actually requiring proof and allows judicial notice to be taken of parish ordinances when a copy of the ordinance is filed with the court with a judicial notice request.[147]

Demonstrative of modern practice, Ohio rules require criminal courts to take judicial notice of the rules of the supreme court of the state and of the decisional, constitutional, and public statutory law of the state. If a party intends to rely upon a municipal ordinance, it must give the opposing party notice in the pleadings, in order to obtain judicial notice, and counsel for the moving party may be required to assist the court in obtaining the information.[148] The modern practice of allowing judicial notice of municipal ordinances and rules enhances the concept of judicial economy and appears to demonstrate a trend in this direction.

§ 5.15 —Administrative Regulations

Under Federal Rules of Evidence, administrative regulations, acts, orders, and records of federal agencies fall within the category of facts that "can be accurately and readily determined from sources whose accuracy cannot be reasonably questioned"[149] and for which judicial notice proves appropriate. Federal courts have held that records and reports of administrative bodies are proper subjects of judicial notice because administrative bodies create administrative law by promulgating rules and regulations.[150] Demonstrative of most states, Ohio, under Civil Rule of Procedure 44.1, permits its courts to take judicial notice of administrative regulations of its state agencies as does the state of Illinois.[151]

In addition, the Uniform Rules of Evidence provide that judicial notice may be taken of the published regulations of governmental subdivisions or agencies of the state. Administrative regulations published in the Federal Register must be judicially noticed by all federal courts, and many state courts also notice such regulations in the interest of judicial economy. In an unpublished opinion, the Tenth Circuit Court of Appeals observed that a federal court sitting under its diversity jurisdiction may judicially notice that state's administrative regulations.[152] Naturally, a federal court can take judicial notice of reports of the federal Department of Health and Human Services and of relevant Ohio Administrative Code provisions.[153]

---

147 Bayou Liberty Association v. St. Tammany Parish Council, 2006 La. App. LEXIS 1378 (2006).

148 *See* OHIO CIV. R. 44.1 (2013). *See also* OHIO CRIM. R. 27 (2013). Rule 27 notes that it incorporates Civil Rules 44 and 44.1 involving judicial notice and applies the rules to criminal cases.

149 FED. R. EVID. 201(B).

150 United States v. 14.02 Acres of Land, 530 F.3d 883, 894, 2008 U.S. App. LEXIS 13309 (9th Cir. 2008).

151 People v. Olsen, 388 Ill. App. 3d 704, 708, 903 N.E.2d 778, 781, 2009 Ill. App. LEXIS 45 (2009).

152 Samson Resources v. Wamsutter, 117 Fed. Appx. 641, 644, 2004 U.S. App. LEXIS 22795 (10th Cir. 2004).

153 Gamble v. Ohio Department of Job and Family Services, 2006 U.S. Dist. LEXIS 968 (S.D. Ohio 2006).

In a 2013 federal case involving an inmate's 42 U.S.C. § 1983 suit, a federal district court took judicial notice of the Commonwealth of Pennsylvania Department of Corrections administrative regulations, because the regulations were on the public web site and were capable of accurate and ready determination pursuant to the federal evidence rules.[154] In California, a trial court took judicial notice of regulations requiring death row prisoners to provide the state with blood and saliva samples containing DNA.[155] In a challenge to the proper promulgation of the Indiana Administrative Code in a driving under the influence case, the reviewing court upheld the manner in which the administrative rule had been established, holding that the trial court acted properly in taking judicial notice of the code's provisions.[156]

Where courts have taken judicial notice of state and federal administrative regulations and orders, logic dictates that such notice is appropriate because matters addressed under administrative law are capable of easy verification from official printed sources whose accuracy cannot reasonably be disputed.

§ 5.16 —Jurisdiction of Courts

As a general rule, courts have limited territorial jurisdiction and generally, but not always, have a limited subject matter jurisdiction. For a criminal conviction to withstand appellate challenge, the court trying a defendant must have possessed subject matter jurisdiction covering the alleged crime, and the operative facts of the crime must have occurred within the court's territorial jurisdiction. A criminal conviction must be reversed where the evidence or substitutes for proof failed to provide evidence that the offense was committed within the jurisdiction of the court. A court has power to take judicial notice that an alleged crime occurred within the territorial jurisdiction of the court.[157] In a delinquency case, the prosecution must prove that the offense was committed within the territorial jurisdiction of the court, and a failure to prove jurisdiction or to have judicial notice taken of jurisdiction may reverse the case.[158] However, a juvenile court cannot take judicial notice of its jurisdiction when part of the requirement of jurisdiction depends on the age of the juvenile; the juvenile's age must be proven in the case as part of jurisdiction.[159] A court may also take judicial notice of the fact that an alleged crime occurred within the court's territorial jurisdiction where there is no dispute on the matter, and it may take judicial notice that the venue within the jurisdiction is proper.[160] Some state courts are reluctant to allow judicial notice to establish venue

154 *See* Riley v. Grainey, 2013 U.S. Dist. LEXIS 183702 (M.D. Pa. 2013)

155 Alfaro v. Terhune, 98 Cal. App. 4th 492, 120 Cal. Rptr. 2d 197, 2002 Cal. App. LEXIS 4116 (2002).

156 Disabato et al. v. State, 840 N.E.2d 1, 4, 2005 Ind. App. LEXIS 2390 (2005).

157 *See* United States v. Pierre, 525 Fed. Appx. 237, 2013 U.S. App. LEXIS 10547 (4th Cir. 2013).

158 In the Interest of A. C., 263 Ga. App. 44, 45, 587 S.E.2d 210, 211, 2003 Ga. App. LEXIS 1087 (2003).

159 State v. K.N., 124 Wash. App. 875, 877, 103 P.3d 844, 845, 2004 Wash. App. LEXIS 3135 (2004).

160 See In re Aleman, V., 2012 Ariz. App. Unpub. LEXIS 1418 (Ariz. Ct. Appl. 2012).

or jurisdiction[161] and have been known to reverse cases where it was not properly proved, even though some states would allow it to be established by judicial notice.

The courts have been consistent in holding that a court may take judicial notice of its own jurisdiction. In one case, an officer observed a driver speeding on the opposite side of the road. When the officer stopped the speeder and initially observed him, the speeder was in a different city, because the city and court boundary ran down the middle of the road. The officer cited the driver for speeding, as well as driving while intoxicated, but the trial court took judicial notice that the defendant had not been driving within the city over which it had territorial jurisdiction. When the defendant requested that the judge take judicial notice that the defendant had committed no offense within the court's jurisdiction, the court agreed and dismissed the case due to the judicial notice it took concerning the limits of its jurisdiction.[162]

§ 5.17 Judicial Notice Process

Rule 201

JUDICIAL NOTICE OF ADJUDICATIVE FACTS

* * *

(c) Taking Notice. The court:
  (1) may take judicial notice on its own; or
  (2) must take judicial notice if a party requests it and the court is supplied with the necessary information.
(d) Timing. The court may take judicial notice at any stage of the proceeding.
(e) Opportunity to be Heard. On timely request, a party is entitled to be heard on the propriety of taking judicial notice and the nature of the fact to be noticed. If the court takes judicial notice before notifying a party, the party, on request, is still entitled to be heard.
(f) Instructing the Jury. In a civil case, the court must instruct the jury to accept the noticed fact as conclusive. In a criminal case, the court must instruct the jury that it may or may not accept the noticed fact as conclusive.[163]

In proving or disproving a criminal case, the attorneys for the parties introduce evidence of adjudicative facts that the fact finder must either believe or disbelieve. These types of facts normally concern questions involving what a defendant did, where the events occurred, what actually happened, and how the alleged crime was

161 State v. Prescott, 290 Ga. 528, 529, 2012 Ga. LEXIS 151 (2012).
162 City of North Ridgeville v. Stack, 2006 Ohio 1177, 2006 Ohio App. LEXIS 1063 (2006).
163 FED. R. EVID. 201.

accomplished. The evidence that supports or refutes these facts must be determined by the fact finder, and proof of some of the facts may come from the use of judicial notice.

When one of the parties wants a judge to take judicial notice of a particular point, principle, or fact, the attorney for that party makes a request and offers the reasons that support the taking of judicial notice. The request is sometimes made in open court, but is often made out of the hearing of the jury, in case the judge denies the request. Once a request has been made and prior to the judge's decision, the opposing party is entitled, on timely request, to have an opportunity to be heard—outside the hearing of the jury—on the propriety of taking judicial notice and on the nature of the matter proposed to be judicially noticed.

Because a jury in a criminal case serves as the ultimate finder of fact, it is free to adopt as true or reject as false any fact judicially noticed. In fact, Federal Rule of Evidence 201 provides that, in criminal cases, where a court has taken judicial notice of an adjudicative fact, it is required to instruct the jury that it has the sole discretion to accept the judicially noticed fact as true or false.[164] Under this doctrine and without hearing evidence, a jury could accept (or reject) as a fact that a particular drug was considered a Schedule I controlled substance.[165] In one case, the judge instructed the jury that, using judicial notice, the judge accepted as proved that a marriage between a grandfather and his adopted granddaughter is illegal under the law of the state.[166]

Under the process of taking judicial notice, how does a jury become aware that it may consider facts judicially noticed by the court when there has been no formal evidence introduced? When a party requests by motion or in open court that the judge take judicial notice of a particular matter and when the judge agrees that taking notice is proper, the judge will state in open court to the jury that such fact is noticed. In the alternative case, in the absence of any party's request and upon the court's own motion, the judge may determine that a particular fact will be judicially noticed and so advise the jury after hearing arguments of any party concerning the appropriateness of taking notice.

Once a matter is judicially noticed, a court will not admit evidence to dispute the fact noticed. One court noted that it would not "accept as true allegations that contradict matters properly subject to judicial notice."[167] To allow evidence to contradict judicially noticed facts would be contrary to the rationale on which judicial notice is based. However, a court commits error if it takes judicial notice of a fact where the fact is doubtful, uncertain, or subject to reasonable dispute. In a criminal case, with respect to facts judicially noticed, the jury is not required to accept any fact as conclusive. Demonstrative of this practice, the Ohio Rules of Evidence instruct that "the court shall instruct the jury that it may, but is not required to, accept as conclusive any fact judicially noticed."[168]

---

164 United States v. Davila-Nieves, 670 F.3d 1, 8, 2012 U.S. App. LEXIS 249 (1st Cir. 2012).

165 United States v. Arroyo, 2009 U.S. App. LEXIS 4165 (7th Cir. 2009).

166 United States v. Dedman, 527 F.3d 577, 584, 2008 U.S. App. LEXIS 11407 (6th Cir. 2008).

167 Brown v. Hawai'i, 2009 U.S. Dist. LEXIS 10546 (D. Hawai'i 2009).

168 OHIO R. EVID. 201(G) (2013).

In some states, the rules relating to the procedure followed in judicial notice are spelled out by rule or statute. For example, in California, there are matters that must be judicially noticed and are mentioned in the state's evidence code.[169] Matters that fall into this category include notice of laws of the state, federal law, rules of all courts, and the rules of pleading, practice, and procedure for federal and state courts. Permissive notice is regulated by § 452 and includes notice of foreign states' law, regulations, and legislative enactments issued under the authority of the United States, court records of California, and facts and propositions that are not subject to any reasonable dispute and which are capable of rapid and accurate determination. Permissive notice becomes mandatory under § 453 when the adverse party has been given proper notice, and the moving party supplies the court with sufficient information to enable the court to take notice of the matter. A court may judicially notice a fact, concept, or principle at any time during a case, even during the appellate stage.

§ 5.18 Judicial Notice in Criminal Cases

As a general rule, criminal trial courts may take judicial notice of court records of any state or federal jurisdiction,[170] the hour of sunrise on a particular day,[171] the scientific accuracy of **laser speed detection,**[172] the speed limit on a highway,[173] the fact that a defendant has prior convictions,[174] legislative history of state law,[175] and a variety of other verifiable facts. In a Texas case, the punishment was enhanced following the trial court's judicial notice of the defendant's prior felony conviction for aggravated robbery. On appeal, a defendant argued that the taking of judicial notice of his prior convictions and their finality for appellate purposes was improper. The reviewing court determined that taking notice of the prior conviction and its finality was not an abuse of the trial court's discretion, because a silent record allows a court to presume that a conviction is final.[176] However, some courts are more reluctant to

Laser speed detection Measures speed of objects by bouncing light energy off the object to be checked for speed and measures the time it takes for the light to leave and return to the laser detector; completing these measurements hundreds of time a second, the detector compares the length of time the light requires to return to the sensor, enabling a speed to be calculated.

---

169 CAL. EVID. CODE § 451 (2014).

170 Schwab v. State, 969 So. 2d 318, 2007 Fla. LEXIS 2011 (Fla. 2007). *See also* FLA.STAT. § 90.202(6) (2011).

171 Swafford v. Florida, 828 So. 2d 966 at 967, 2002 Fla. LEXIS 789 (2002).

172 State v. Williamson, 144 Idaho 597, 602, 2007 Idaho App. LEXIS 43 (2007).

173 Hicks v. Jones, 2008 U.S. Dist. LEXIS 104274, n.5 (N.D. Ok. 2008).

174 *See* People v. Schulte, A136105, 2013 Cal. App. Unpub. LEXIS 2650 (Cal. Ct. Appl. 2013).

175 People v. Acosta, 29 Cal. 4th 105 at 120, 52 P.3d 624 at 634, 124 Cal. Rptr. 2d 435 at 447 (2002).

176 Figueroa v. State, 250 S.W.3d 490, 504, 2008 Tex. App. LEXIS 2028 (2008).

permit the use of judicial notice in criminal cases than in civil cases, especially where it involves an element of the crime. In an underage sale of alcohol case, the conviction was reversed because the trial court had taken judicial notice that a Bud Lite® beer contained greater than ½ of one percent alcohol, and the judicial notice taken in the case involved an element of the crime.[177]

Judicially noticed facts are treated differently depending on whether the case is civil or criminal. Rule 201(g) of the Federal Rules of Evidence notes that a court shall instruct the jury to accept as conclusive any fact judicially noticed in civil cases, but in criminal cases, the rule requires that a court instruct the jury that it may, but is not required to, accept as conclusive any fact judicially noticed. Every defendant has the right to have the jury or the judge serve as fact finder, and taking judicial notice of a fact, a principle, or other matter has the effect of removing the issue from the jury's consideration. Therefore, in close cases where there might be an argument against judicial notice, judges are often reluctant to take judicial notice. It is better practice to prepare traditional evidence that would prove the fact or concept that might be the subject of judicial notice. This proof would assist a judge either in taking judicial notice or in cases where judicial notice was declined. The matter can then be introduced and proved in court.

§ 5.19 Summary

The usual procedure directs parties to introduce evidence to prove a fact in dispute. But, in some instances, such evidence is unnecessary, because the court will take judicial notice of certain facts. This procedure is necessary and reasonable in order to save the time of the court, the parties, and the attorneys.

Judicial notice involves the court recognizing the existence of certain facts and laws without requiring the parties to introduce proof. For convenience, the rules concerning judicial notice are often categorized as judicial notice of facts and judicial notice of laws. Rule 201 of the Federal Rules of Evidence only relates to the taking of judicial notice of adjudicative facts.

The general rule is that the trial judge may take judicial notice without motion of counsel or take judicial notice of fact following a formal request. The judge, in fact, is given a great deal of discretion concerning judicial notice, and an appellate court will not disturb the taking of judicial notice unless there is a clear abuse of discretion. Where a trial court could have taken judicial notice on its own motion, but did not, or where a trial court could have taken judicial notice, but declined, an appellate court may generally take judicial notice.[178] Yet, many appellate courts will not judicially notice a fact where a trial court could have done so, but declined for appropriate reasons, within the limits of a trial court's discretion.

In the interests of judicial economy, there are many facts that are commonly known and need not be proved in court. Examples of these facts include historical facts,

---

177 State v. Kareski, 137 Ohio St. 3d 92, 93, 2013 Ohio LEXIS 2133 (2013).
178 In re Solis, 2008 Tex. App. LEXIS 7529 (2008).

geographical facts, scientific facts, and other facts that are generally known to the ordinary person. A judge may take notice of facts that may be ascertained by consulting standard reference works. In addition to facts, the judge may take judicial notice of certain laws, such as the Constitution of the United States, administrative regulations, laws of the several states, and in some instances, municipal ordinances and foreign law.

While judicial discretion permits a judge to take notice of certain facts and certain laws, it is not a certainty that a judge will always view the suggestion in a manner favorable to the party requesting it. Judges in criminal cases often err on the side of caution when faced with a request for judicial notice. If there is any doubt concerning the appropriateness of the fact to be introduced or proved in court, traditional proof should be acquired and made ready for court presentation. The availability of traditional evidence to present to the judge may assist or prompt the judge to take judicial notice of certain facts.

CHAPTER FIVE: QUESTIONS AND REVIEW EXERCISES

1. As used in courts, what are three concepts that operate as substitutes for evidence?
2. Judicial notice has been defined in a variety of ways. Explain how the concept works and why the judge need not necessarily possess personal knowledge of what the judge judicially notices. Give five examples of broad categories overwhich a judge might properly take judicial notice.
3. Upon the court's own initiative or upon the request of a party, a judge may take judicial notice of matters that are common knowledge. Identify four facts, principles, or matters that should qualify for judicial notice.
4. One category of judicial notice includes well-known and generally undisputable matters of history and historical fact. Identify four undisputable matters of history or discrete historical facts that should qualify for judicial notice in a case where such facts were relevant. Assuming relevance to a criminal case, would it be appropriate for a judge to take judicial notice that World War II began for the United States on December 7, 1941? Concerning matters of history, should a judge take judicial notice that the District of Columbia has never been admitted to the Union as a state?
5. Geography and facts that relate to geography are generally considered proper subjects for judicial notice. Identify three geographic facts that should be the subject of judicial notice as a general rule. Identify one item of geography or geographic fact that might be unique to the jurisdiction or court district in which you are studying that might not be appropriate to a court in another state. Would it be appropriate for a judge in Missouri to take judicial notice that the Mississippi River generally flows

from the north to the south? Would it make any difference if the judge were sitting in a California court? Why or why not? Explain.

6. In the category of nature and of science, there may be topics that are appropriate for judicial notice. It would be appropriate for a court to recognize the principle that, except for identical twins, DNA is unique to each human being. Name two other scientific principles that should be appropriate for judicial notice and a proper case.
7. In our society and culture, we commonly use language and symbols that have set meanings. Abbreviations are used to indicate complete words. Slang in our language often indicates definitive concepts. Identify and suggest an abbreviation and a use of slang language that might be appropriate for judicial notice. Identify two symbols that are commonly used and have a set meaning that might be appropriate for judicial notice.
8. Courts may be required to take judicial notice of statutory laws and of principles contained within case law. Must a court take judicial notice of the laws in its own jurisdiction? Is a state court required to take judicial notice of federal law and our federal Constitution? Would a court sitting in Ohio be required to take judicial notice of a Nevada statute or would the Ohio court require that the Nevada statute and its contents be proved? Is it ever appropriate for a federal or a state court to take judicial notice of the laws of a foreign nation?
9. Concerning municipal ordinances, must a judge within the municipality where the court sits be required to take judicial notice? Is there a difference among the states, where some states might require that municipal ordinances be pled and proved, the same as other evidence?
10. The geographical area over which a court has legal jurisdiction may prove crucial to a criminal case. Is it proper for a court to take judicial notice of the limits of its territorial jurisdiction? Where a court's jurisdiction was dependent upon the age of the juvenile, as a general rule, could the court take judicial notice of the age of the child and, therefore, indirectly take judicial notice that the court had jurisdiction over a juvenile case?
11. The taking of judicial notice may fall into the category of mandatory judicial notice or discretionary judicial notice. When is a court required to take judicial notice, assuming the topic is an appropriate one for judicial notice? Once a court officially takes judicial notice over a fact or concept, would a judge allow evidence to be introduced that contests the existence of the fact or concept? If a court takes judicial notice and indicates this fact to the jury, is the jury bound to accept as a fact the factor that the court has used judicial notice to recognize?

Presumptions, Inferences, and Stipulations 6

The use of presumptions and inferences to prove an element of the crime is indeed treacherous, for it allows men to go to jail without any evidence on one essential ingredient of the offense. It thus implicates the integrity of the judicial system.

Barnes v. United States, 412 U.S. 837, 93 S. Ct. 2357 (1973)

(Douglas, J., dissenting)

Chapter Contents

KEY TERMS AND CONCEPTS

Conclusive Presumption
Constitutional Tests for Presumptions
Flight after Crime
Inference
Possession of Recently Stolen Property
Presumption
Presumption Against Suicide
Presumption of Facts
Presumption of Law
Presumption of Sanity
Presumed to Know the Law
Rebuttable Presumption
Stipulation

§ 6.1 Introduction

Chapter 4 describes the process of introducing evidence in criminal cases. To the extent that it has a burden of proof,[1] each party in a criminal case is obligated to introduce evidence to establish facts from which a judge or jury will make a decision. However, in some instances, the jury may consider facts other than those introduced by the prosecution and defense. One way of distinguishing this information source from actual evidence is to designate it as a substitute for evidence.

Judicial notice, which is discussed in Chapter 5, is one of several substitutes for evidence. That chapter includes a discussion of the legal reasoning that permits a trial or appellate judge to take notice of certain facts and laws. In addition, Chapter 5 introduces case decisions and statutes limiting the use of judicial notice. Chapter 6 considers three additional substitutes for evidence—the presumption, the inference, and the stipulation.

The use of inferences and presumptions in criminal trials, although based on logic and predictability, has the effect of relieving one party or the other from actually proving facts and elements of the crime. The use of an inference to help prove that a defendant possessed sufficient knowledge to commit the crime or that a defendant possessed a particular criminal intent may only be proved by the use of circumstantial evidence because no one can really know what another person was thinking. Whether a

1 Generally, a defendant has no burden of proof, and the burden of proof beyond a reasonable doubt rests with the prosecution. Where a defendant pleads self-defense, insanity, alibi, mistake of fact, or some other affirmative defense, there may be a burden of proof on a defendant to establish the defense by a preponderance of the evidence, by clear and convincing evidence, or beyond a reasonable doubt.

defendant knowingly possessed recently stolen property or whether a defendant possessed a specific intent to defraud in a forgery case can only be inferred by considering the surrounding facts and making a deduction based on those facts. Ultimately, the use of presumptions and inferences relieves a party of the burden of presenting evidence to prove a particular fact where the fact can be inferred or deduced from proof of other facts.

This chapter defines, distinguishes, and demonstrates how presumptions, inferences, and stipulations affect criminal trials. In addition, the chapter discusses the theoretical basis for allowing presumptions and inferences, as well as the types of presumptions recognized by the courts and legislatures. This chapter also gives detailed attention to specific examples of common presumptions and inferences, explaining how these possible substitutes for evidence play an important role in the trial process. Finally, the chapter explores the remaining substitute for evidence—the **stipulation**—and demonstrates some significant specific examples of how attorneys use stipulations.

> **Stipulation** An agreement; a bargain, proviso, or condition, such as an agreement between opposing litigants that certain facts are true and are not in dispute.

§ 6.2 Definitions and Distinctions

Rule 301

PRESUMPTIONS IN CIVIL CASES GENERALLY

In a civil case, unless a federal statute or these rules provide otherwise, the party against whom a presumption is directed has the burden of producing evidence to rebut the presumption. But this rule does not shift the burden of persuasion, which remains on the party who had it originally.[2]

A. Presumptions

When the Federal Rules of Evidence were being written, the committee considering Rule 301 intended to limit the scope of the rule to civil actions and proceedings and declined to have the rule cover federal criminal proceedings. The committee chose not to address the thorny questions of presumptions in criminal cases and therefore limited Rule 301 to civil actions. In criminal cases, the parties must look to state statutes and state court decisions, as well as federal court decisions, for answers to questions relating to presumptions. Because the federal Constitution has been interpreted to require

2 FED. R. EVID. 301.

proof beyond a reasonable doubt for criminal cases, presumptions cannot be designed to allow a conviction due to the use of a presumption that shifts the burden of proof. In order for a presumption to operate in a fair manner, the power to "establish them is reserved solely to the courts and the legislature, and the presumptions that are created either judicially or legislatively arise from considerations of fairness, public policy, and probability to allocate the burden of proof."[3]

Courts and legal writers have used the term *presumption* to describe several different consequences that flow from the introduction of evidence in a trial. Under the California Evidence Code, "[a] presumption is an assumption of fact that the law requires to be made from another fact or group of facts found or otherwise established in the action."[4] In Illinois, "[a] presumption is a legal device that permits or requires the fact finder to assume the existence of an ultimate fact, after certain predicate or basic facts have been established."[5] A presumption is a rule of law that allows a jury in a criminal case to infer or deduce the existence of a second fact from the proof of the first, or basic, fact. Demonstrative of this concept is a section of the penal code in California providing that, when one person is injured by another, but the first individual's "death occurs beyond three years and a day, there shall be a rebuttable presumption that the killing was not criminal."[6] In Texas, when there is independent proof of a burglary, unexplained possession of recently stolen goods connected to the burglary may provide sufficient evidence for a conviction.[7] However, "[m]ere possession of stolen property does not give rise to a presumption of guilt, but rather it will support an inference of guilt of the offense in which the property was stolen"[8] In other words, a presumption draws a particular conclusion as to the existence of one fact, not actually known, arising from its usual connection with another fact or facts that are known or proved.

Some courts and legislative enactments hold that a true legal presumption is in the nature of evidence and is to be weighed as such. Other jurisdictions hold that a presumption is not considered evidence but is a substitute for evidence,[9] and, as a result, the presumption may be treated as evidence to be accepted as fact or disregarded.

Mandatory presumptions in criminal cases are generally unconstitutional because they relieve the prosecution of having to prove all the elements beyond a reasonable

---

3 23 FLA. JUR. 2D *Evidence and Witnesses* § 101 (2013).

4 CAL. EVID. CODE § 600 (2014). According to the California statute, a presumption is not considered evidence.

5 People v. Cazacu, 373 Ill. App. 3d 465, 2007 Ill. App. LEXIS 484 (Ill. 2007) (citing People v. Woodrum, 223 Ill. 2d 286, 308, 2006 Ill. LEXIS 1633 (Ill. 2007)) *cert. denied*, Woodrum v. Illinois, 2007 U.S. LEXIS 4140 (2007).

6 CAL. PENAL CODE § 194 (2014).

7 *See* Richmond v. State, 2012 Tex. App. LEXIS 6631 (2012). To warrant an inference of guilt based solely on the possession of stolen property, it must be established that the possession was personal, recent, and unexplained.

8 *Id.*

9 *See* Ament v. Reassure America Life Insurance Co., 2009 Ohio 36, 2009 Ohio App. LEXIS 23 (Ohio 2009) and CAL. EVID. CODE § 600 (2008).

doubt, thus calling into question the presumption of innocence. If a renter did not provide the rented property to its rightful owner within five days of receiving a demand for its return, a statutory presumption might consider this action to be evidence that the renter had unlawfully converted the property to his own use. Yet, this presumption could not stand because of its mandatory nature.[10]

B. Inferences

One state defines an inference as "a deduction of fact that may logically and reasonably be drawn from another fact or group of facts established by the evidence."[11] Phrased in a slightly different manner, an inference has been defined as a deduction of fact that a criminal jury may make but cannot be required to make. "Whether the inferred fact is found to exist will be decided by the trier of fact."[12] In accepting the existence of one fact and making a deduction from that fact that another fact exists, the jurors are free to make the deduction or to not make the deduction and, thus, reject the inference.

Although the terms *presumption* and *inference* are sometimes used synonymously, the courts have attempted to distinguish between them as to both their origins and effects. According to some courts, an inference should be recorded as a permissible deduction drawn from the evidence before the court, which the jury may accept or reject. A presumption, on the other hand, is a rule of law, relatively fixed or relatively defined in scope and effect, which attaches to certain evidentiary facts and produces a specific procedural consequence. To state this more simply, a presumption is a mandatory deduction that the law expressly requires while an inference is no more than a permissible deduction that the trier of fact may adopt. Any criminal jury is free to disregard the finding of the deduced or inferred fact because the jury has the sole power to determine the facts in a criminal case. Concerning the historical facts of the case, it would almost be true to state that, in criminal cases, only inferences may exist because presumptions of fact cannot be enforced. In adopting this view of inferences and presumptions, the Supreme Court of Pennsylvania noted that:

> Inferences and presumptions are staples of our adversary system of factfinding. It is often necessary for the trier of fact to determine the existence of an element of the crime—that is, an "ultimate" or "elemental" fact—from the existence of one or more "evidentiary" or "basic" facts. Nevertheless, to the extent that these logical tools impede rather than assist in the jury's exercise of its fact-finding function, they cannot be employed to prove the elements of a crime. Hence, "virtually all so-called criminal presumptions are really no more than... inferences." Commonwealth v. DiFrancesco, 458 Pa. 188, 329 A.2d 204, 207 n.3 (Pa. 1974).[13]

10 Sherrod v. State, 280 Ga. 275, 275, 627 S.E.2d 36, 37, 2006 Ga. LEXIS 145 (2006).

11 Bowlin v. Chrones, Warden, 2008 U.S. Dist. LEXIS (E.D. Cal. 2008), citing CALJIC 2.00.

12 CHARLES W. EHRHARDT, FLORIDA EVIDENCE § 301.1 at 89-90 (2003 ed.), quoted in Palmas y Bambu v. E.I Dupont, 881 So. 2d 565, 2004 Fla. App. LEXIS 7372 (2004).

13 Commonwealth v. Salter, 2004 Pa. Super. 318, 858 A.2d 610, 615, 2004 Pa. Super. LEXIS 2687 (2004).

In a Georgia murder case,[14] the reviewing court noted with approval a jury charge that stated, "[y]ou may infer, if you wish to do so, that the acts of a person of sound mind and discretion are the product of that person's will. A person of sound mind and discretion intends the natural and probable consequences of those acts. That's the second thing that you can infer."[15] According to the appellate court, the wording of this jury instruction creates a lawful inference and fails to require a jury to draw any particular conclusion. Because the jury has free choice, no constitutional errors exist with this type of inference. In another case, the court made this distinction concerning the difference between an inference and a presumption:

> Presumptions are one thing; inferences another. Presumptions are assumptions of fact which the law requires to be made from another fact or group of facts; inferences are logical deductions or conclusions from an established fact. Presumptions deal with legal processes, whereas inferences deal with mental processes.[16]

In the court's view, an inference is simply a logical deduction or conclusion that the law allows, but does not require, following the establishment of the basic facts.

A jury or trial court may "draw inferences from circumstantial evidence so long as the inferences are rationally related to the proven fact."[17] That is, a rational connection must exist between the fact initially proven and the fact later inferred. According to the Supreme Court of the United States, a jury may properly infer from one fact the existence of another fact that is essential to guilt, if reason and experience support the inference.[18] However, finding an inferred fact from an earlier inferred fact has its limits because, at some point, inferences become so removed from the fact that supported the first inference that the final conclusion may not be accurate. A federal court of appeals cautioned that "reasonable inferences supported by other reasonable inferences which have an evidentiary basis may warrant a conviction. Nonetheless, where a conviction appears to be based on multiple and successive inferences, we must exercise caution"[19] to ensure that a conviction rests upon more than conjecture.

When a state revises its evidence code, a state legislature may create statutory inferences that follow logic, and the statute should withstand litigation, provided that there is a predictable relationship between the fact proved and the fact to be inferred, as well as no mandatory requirements. For example, Florida has a statute that provides that

---

14 Smith v. State, 284 Ga. 33, 2008 Ga. LEXIS 540 (2008).

15 *Id.*, 36.

16 *See* State v. Jackson, 112 Wash. 2d 867, 774 P.2d 1211 (1989). *See also* State v. Parks, 245 Neb. 205, 511 N.W.2d 774 (1994), in which the court held that a "presumption" is a fact inferred from another proved or established fact or facts, whereas an "inference" is a conclusion on the existence of a particular fact reached by considering other facts in the usual course of human reasoning, and thus an "inference" is a deduction that the fact finder may draw at his or her discretion but is not required to draw as a matter of law.

17 State v. Germany, 2006 Wash. App. LEXIS (2006).

18 Tot v. United States, 319 U.S. 463, 63 S. Ct. 1241, 87 L. Ed. 2d 1519 (1943).

19 United States v. Michel, 446 F.3d 1122, 1128, 2006 U.S. App. LEXIS 11665 (10th Cir. 2006).

"[p]roof of possession of property recently stolen, unless satisfactorily explained, gives rise to an inference that the person in possession of the property knew or should have known that the property had been stolen."[20] Applying this statutory inference, a Florida appellate court upheld a defendant's convictions where the evidence demonstrated that he attempted to sell the victim's recently stolen computers, and he was wearing the victim's watch taken during the burglary.[21] The reviewing court held that a jury could conclude the defendant illegally acquired the property.

While a court may give instructions regarding inferences that can be drawn from proven facts, an instruction that permits the jurors to infer an element of the crime charged is constitutional only if the presumed fact follows beyond a reasonable doubt from the proven fact. In the case of *State v. Jackson*, which involved a charge of attempted second degree burglary, the Supreme Court of Washington held that a trial court cannot instruct the jury that it may infer the defendant acted with intent to commit a crime within a building, based on evidence suggesting that the defendant may have attempted to enter the building. The court cannot provide such an instruction, because other equally reasonable conclusions might follow from the circumstances.[22] In this case, an officer saw the defendant kicking the front door of a shop. When the door was examined, it was found that about 10 inches of Plexiglas had been pushed inward and that part of the wood stock around the Plexiglas was broken out of its frame. The judge instructed the jury that it might infer that the defendant acted with intent to commit a crime within the building. In reversing the conviction, the court noted that an inference shall not exist when other reasonable conclusions could follow from the circumstances. Applying this reasoning, the court determined that the instruction was improper because the jury might have inferred that the defendant intended to commit a crime within the building when he might have had different plans.

A proper inference cannot be mandatory and still meet approval under the Constitution of the United States. Therefore, a jury instruction that permits a jury either to draw an inference of an element of a crime or to choose not to draw the inference will survive an attack based on constitutional grounds. In a Florida case, to prove enhancements to the charged crime, the prosecution established prior driving while intoxicated (DUI) convictions by admitting as evidence official Florida records.[23] The records were sufficient in themselves to prove a prior conviction for DUI, but the statute allowed that evidence to be contradicted or rebutted by other evidence that a defendant might want to introduce. According to the reviewing court:

> The statute authorizes the prosecution to offer into evidence the records of the Department of Highway Safety and Motor Vehicles showing that the defendant has been previously convicted of the offense of driving under the influence. If the State does so, the record evidence is "sufficient by itself" to establish the prior

---

20 FLA. STAT. § 812.022(2) (2013).

21 Yudin v. State, 117 So. 3d 457, 459, 460, 2013 Fla. App. LEXIS 11299 (2013).

22 State v. Jackson, *supra* note 16.

23 Ibarrondo v. State, 2008 Fla. App. LEXIS 20619 (2008).

convictions. The statute says only that the introduced records are prima facie evidence of that element of the offense.[24]

The court took the view that, because the statute permitted a defendant to rebut the inference that the prior record has been proved, the inference is permissive and not mandatory, thus creating only a rebuttable inference that the defendant has prior offenses.

In summary, when the finder of fact is free to ignore an inference or to accept it, regardless of whether or not the defendant introduces any evidence, the inference will be determined to be permissive and will not offend either the federal or the Florida constitution.

C. *Stipulations*

As another substitute for evidence, the stipulation is less difficult to define and understand than presumptions and inferences. When the parties stipulate to a fact, it simply means that they have agreed that proof of the matter is not be required. "A stipulation of fact relieves a party from the inconvenience of proving the facts in the stipulation."[25] A stipulation implies that both parties have conceded to the existence or nonexistence of a fact, the contents of a document, the testimony of a witness, or other matter that has an important connection to the case. When the parties have agreed to a stipulation, the effect is to remove the fact as an issue in the case, because the parties no longer have any dispute as to the fact, document, principle, or testimony. A stipulation may be in writing or offered orally, and normally, the trial judge will consent to entering the stipulation on the record.[26] Judges generally encourage the liberal use of stipulations so that parties have agreed to the admissibility of exhibits and stipulations of fact prior to trial. Once parties have agreed to stipulate to a particular fact, the stipulation remains binding on both parties. A stipulation authorizes the court to find the existence of such a fact and to consider that fact without any further proof. The triers of fact are not, however, bound to accept the fact as true and may find to the contrary, if persuaded by other evidence. In addition, a trial judge may not automatically accept a stipulation of fact between the parties, and sentencing courts are not bound by stipulations of fact in plea bargains.[27] Many courts refuse to accept polygraph evidence, even where both the prosecutor and defendant have stipulated prior to the examination to agree to the admissibility of the test results.[28]

---

24 *Id.*

25 Iowa Mortgage Center v. Baccam, 841 N.W.2d 107, 2013 Iowa Sup. LEXIS 129 (2013). Stipulations in criminal cases are not binding on a jury.

26 *See* Briceno v. Scribner, 555 F.3d 1069, 2009 U.S. App. LEXIS 3524 (9th Cir. 2009), in which an oral stipulation was read to the jury, and United States v. Miranda-Lopez, 532 F.3d 1034, 1036, 2008 U.S. App. LEXIS 15200 (9th Cir. 2008), in which a written stipulation was entered in the record.

27 United States v. Evans-Martinez, 530 F.3d 1164, 2008 U.S. App. LEXIS 13972 (9th Cir. 2008) and United States v. Toepfer, 317 Fed. Appx. 857, 2008 U.S. App. LEXIS 14811 (CA 11th July 9, 2008).

28 *See* People v. Muniz, 190 P.3d 774, 786, 2008 Colo. App. LEXIS 237 (2008).

When the parties have stipulated concerning a fact or facts, such agreement authorizes the court to find the existence of such a fact and to consider the fact proven beyond a reasonable doubt. In a murder case, the parties agreed to a stipulation of many facts, including the fact that the defendant admitted to committing the killings. The stipulations of fact indicated that the defendant and the prosecution were in agreement concerning the facts of the case, and no proof was necessary.[29] In a different case, the prosecution and the defense stipulated that a government **expert witness** would have testified to the presence of cocaine base in a sample that had been tested.[30] The stipulations in the two cases were proper because neither side had any disagreement with the other on the stipulated facts or issues.

Expert witness A person who has acquired by special study, practice, and experience peculiar skill and knowledge in relation to some particular science, art, or trade.

Although the general rule is that parties are bound by their stipulations, a trial court has the discretion to consider issues not actually covered in a pretrial stipulation. For good cause shown, a trial court may allow a party to withdraw a stipulation, but where the stipulation survives the trial, a reviewing court is usually bound by the stipulation.[31]

§ 6.3 Reasons for Presumptions and Inferences

The use of presumptions and inferences in criminal trials plays an important part in expediting the judicial process, even though many disagreements among judges, prosecutors, and defense attorneys exist concerning their application in a particular case. In many jurisdictions, inferences and presumptions serve as a substitute for evidence, taking the place of actual proof. In allowing the use of inferences and presumptions as circumstantial evidence, the courts hold that they possess the same theoretical evidentiary weight as direct evidence.[32] In jurisdictions that do not consider them to be substitutes for evidence, the operative effect is quite similar with respect to the importance and the effect of their use. In countless appellate court decisions, the rule that circumstantial evidence based on inferences or presumptions is sufficient by itself, in the absence of any direct evidence, to prove the most serious crime.[33] Naturally, in criminal cases, the finder of fact may choose to accept or to ignore any presumption

---

29 Johnson v. Wilson, 2006 U.S. App. LEXIS 15479 (6th Cir. 2006).

30 United States v. Anderson, 450 F.3d 294, 2006 U.S. App. LEXIS 14177 (7th Cir. 2006).

31 State v. Stegman, 2009 Kan. App. LEXIS 124 (2009).

32 State v. Nulf, 2008 Wash. App. LEXIS 2278 (2008). *See also* State v. Roberts, 2008 Ohio 5750, 2008 Ohio App. LEXIS 4821 (2008) (noting that "direct and circumstantial evidence carry equal weight.").

33 United States v. Stackhouse, 2009 U.S. App. LEXIS 2760 (8th Cir. 2009) (quoting United States v. Wesseh, 531 F.3d 633, 636 (8th Cir. 2008)).

or inference. In the final analysis, when presented with an inference or presumption, most jury members will probably make the deduction of fact suggested by proof of the basic fact, because a good deal of everyday reasoning and decisionmaking follows a similar path of logic.

A. Procedural Technique

Most presumptions serve as rules of evidence that provide for a particular result in a case, unless the opposing party introduces evidence that refutes the presumption. The evidentiary effect of proving the basic fact in a presumption is to shift the burden of going forward with the evidence to the opposing party, requiring that party to introduce evidence that displaces the circumstantial conclusion offered by the presumption.[34] These are not absolute rules, because a jury in a criminal case has no duty to follow the logic proposed by a presumption or inference. Without the use of presumptions, it would be difficult in some instances for the trial to go forward. One purpose of the presumption is to place the burden on the party who alone is in possession or control of the facts with respect thereto. To make it possible to go forward with the trial, the presumption assumes a certain condition to exist until the contrary is shown.

The use of a presumption as a substitute for evidence alters the burden of offering evidence. As noted, the effect of a presumption is that the existence of the presumption shifts the burden of going forward with the evidence to the opposing party.[35] Once the presumption exists, the presumed fact remains proved unless and until the opposing party introduces evidence that casts doubt on the truth of the presumed fact. When **rebuttal** evidence is introduced, the finder of fact must determine whether the rebuttal evidence is sufficiently strong as to negate the existence of the presumed fact, thus leading the fact finder to ignore the presumption or to decide whether the presumed fact remains.[36] As the Supreme Court of Indiana noted, "[w]hen the party against whom the presumption operates introduces evidence that disputes the presumed fact, the presumption ceases to operate, disappears from the case, and no longer remains to assist any party."[37] Therefore, whether a presumption remains operative in the face of contrary evidence or disappears altogether under the "bursting bubble theory," it has the operative effect of placing the burden of going forward with the evidence on the party best able to produce the evidence on that point.[38]

> **Rebuttal** Proof that is given by one party in a lawsuit to explain or disprove evidence produced by the other party.

[34] BLACK'S LAW DICTIONARY 1304 (9th ed. 2009).

[35] Gross v. FBL Financial Services, Inc., 526 F.3d 356, 359, 2008 U.S. App. LEXIS 10355 (8th Cir. 2008).

[36] Barnes v. Yoshikawa, 2002 Cal. App. Unpub. LEXIS 12095 (2002).

[37] Bonilla v. Commercial Services of Perry, Inc., 900 N.E.2d 22, 22 Ind. App LEXIS 112 (2009) (quoting Schultz v. Ford Motor Co., 857 N.E.2d 977, 982 (2006)).

[38] Green v. Ransor, Inc. 175 S.W.3d 513, 516, 2005 Tex. App. LEXIS 8125 (2005).

B. Public Policy

Courts and legislatures sanction some presumptions of law for public policy purposes. Because most children born to a married couple are the children of the husband, the Maryland family code states "[t]here is a rebuttable presumption that the child is the legitimate child of the man to whom its mother was married at the time of conception."[39] Public policy promotes a finding of legitimacy, and this presumption serves that purpose. Similarly, when a child is born or conceived during wedlock, the child is presumed to be legitimate, with the husband of the wife being the presumed father.[40]

An oft-stated example of a **presumption of law** is the general assumption that everyone knows the law,[41] and that presumption applies with equal force to trial judges.[42] Likewise, criminal defendants are presumed to be innocent until the contrary may be proved.[43] When a government agent has authority to exercise discretion, such as a federal prosecutor in bringing a criminal charge, the presumption is that the prosecutor acted in good faith in making a decision to prosecute.[44] Therefore, when a prosecutor exercises discretion in a criminal case or when a governmental agent makes a decision, a strong presumption exists that the official possesses legitimate grounds for the action taken and is acting with regularity.[45]

Presumption of law An inference or deduction that, in the absence of direct evidence on the subject, the law requires to be drawn from the existence of certain established facts in civil cases. This deduction cannot be enforced in criminal cases, however.

C. Allowance of Normal Governmental Activities

Presumptions such as honest and proper conduct by public officials allow normal governmental activities to be accepted at face value. Without this presumption, it would be burdensome, if not impossible, for prosecutors and defendants to prove affirmatively each and every routine record that is material to a case. Consequently, there is a general presumption: "that trial judges know the law and apply it properly is of long standing, and [the presumption] springs from multiple sources. One of these sources is the strong

---

39 MD. FAMILY LAW CODE ANN. § 5-1027 (2011).

40 Stubbs v. Colandrea et al., 154 Md. App. 673, 682, 841 A.2d 361, 366, 2004 Md. App. LEXIS 9 (Md. 2004).

41 State v. Blunt, 2008 N.D. 135, 2008 N.D. LEXIS 137 (N.D. 2008).

42 United States v. Saddler, 538 F.3d 879, 2008 U.S. App. 17211 (8th Cir. 2008).

43 Mejia v. Garcia, 534 F.3d 1036, 1042, 2008 U.S. App. LEXIS 15933 (9th Cir. 2008).

44 United States v. Abdelaziz et al., 2008 U.S. Dist. LEXIS 49076 (W.D. Tex. 2008).

45 Hartman et al. v. Moore, 126 S. Ct. 1695, 1705, 164 L. Ed. 2d 441, 456, 2006 U.S. LEXIS 3450 (2006).

presumption that judges, like other public officers, perform their duties properly."[46] It would be virtually impossible to prove a record when, for example, the clerk who made the entry has died, or when, due to the heavy caseload of the trial court, no one in the court or clerk's office can personally remember anything about the case in question. The presumption that the government acted in good faith and with proper conduct proves to be quite strong, and a person who wishes to prove differently must have sufficient evidence to actually prove bad faith.[47]

§ 6.4 Presumptions of Law

A presumption of law is "[a] legal assumption that a court is required to make if certain facts are established and no contradictory evidence is produced."[48] Presumptions of law may be rebutted by the introduction of evidence that contradicts the original presumption and effectively replaces that presumption with a different conclusion. Examples of presumptions of law are the presumption of innocence until proven guilty, the presumption in favor of sanity, and the presumption that people do not act with criminal intent. Naturally, every person is presumed to intend the natural and probable consequences of his or her acts, but such a presumption may be rebutted.

Generally, there is a presumption that regularly enacted laws are constitutional,[49] but this is a rebuttable presumption. Following a similar rationale, a judge's findings or rulings carry with them a presumption of correctness,[50] and a properly performed voir dire of a jury will assure the seating of a fair and impartial jury.[51] However, not all presumptions of law presume regularity. For example, the presumption of law is that prejudice to a defendant's case has resulted if the judge spoke with the jury without the defense counsel's knowledge.[52] With respect to Congress, there is a presumption of law that the plain language used by Congress in enacting a statute properly expresses congressional intent.[53]

A presumption of law is a rule of law that allows a judge or jury to assume that a fact is true until such time as the opposing party introduces other evidence that disproves or outweighs the presumed fact. When a presumption of law exists, such as the presumption of innocence in favor of the defendant, it has sufficient strength

---

46 White et al. v. The Pines Community Improvement Assn., 173 Md. App. 13, 2007 Md. App. LEXIS 23 (2007).

47 United States v. Case, 2008 U.S. Dist. LEXIS 33891 (S.D. Miss. 2008).

48 BLACK'S LAW DICTIONARY 1305 (9th ed. 2009).

49 Smith v. Doe, 538 U.S. 84, 110, 2003 U.S. LEXIS 1949 (2003).

50 Lacaze v. Leger, 2008 U.S. Dist. LEXIS 37107 (W.D. La. 2008).

51 Ross v. State, 954 So. 2d 968, 988, 2007 Miss. LEXIS 235 (2007).

52 Wells v. State, 2009 Ga. App. LEXIS 384 (2009).

53 United States v. Clintwood Elkhorn Mining Co., 128 S. Ct. 1511, 1518, 2008 U.S. LEXIS 3472 (2008).

Presumption of fact A deduction that is not the subject of a fixed rule, but merely of natural presumptions, such as those that appear from common experience. Presumptions of fact arise from the particular circumstances of any case.

and will support an acquittal unless the prosecutor overcomes the presumption to a reasonable and moral certainty.[54]

In distinguishing between a presumption of law and a **presumption of fact,** one reviewing court noted, "There can be presumptions of law or presumptions of fact. Presumptions can be artificial or logical. Artificial presumptions are those created because of considerations of public policy. Logical presumptions are those where there is a 'rational connection' on the basis of 'logical probability' between the elemental fact and the evidentiary fact."[55]

§ 6.5 Presumptions of Fact

One court defined a presumption of fact as being "an inference of the existence of one fact from the existence of some other fact, or an inference as to the existence of a fact not actually known, arising from its usual connection with another which is known."[56] When a particular fact has been established and a conclusion naturally follows from proof of that fact, it is permissible for a jury to infer or presume the truth of the deduced fact. The terms *presumption of fact* and *inference* seem to be used more frequently when the deduced fact is permissive in nature and rebuttable if contrary facts exist. A presumption of fact must generally be used only where the proof of the basic fact has been founded on direct evidence and not upon another inference or presumption.[57] This concept is intended to prevent inferences or presumptions from becoming too uncertain or being based on improper speculation or conjecture.[58] To say this differently, presumptions do not create their own foundations. Presumptions of fact are derived from circumstances in a particular case, by using ordinary logic and reasoning.

Presumptions of fact may be permissible "if there is a sound and rational connection between the proved and inferred facts and when proof of one fact renders the existence of another fact so probable that it is sensible and timesaving to assume the truth of the inferred fact until the adversary disproves it. . . ."[59] The presumption may be destroyed by refuting the basic fact upon which the presumption of fact rests or by demonstrating that the fact presumed is not true. For example, an inference of fact arises

---

54 Stoltie v. People, 501 F. Supp. 2d 1252, 2007 U.S. Dist. LEXIS 53333 (C.D. Cal. 2007).

55 Wasserman v. Parciasepe, 377 N.J. Super. 191, 198, 871 A.2d 781, 784, 2004 N.J. Super. LEXIS 4 (2004).

56 State v. Narron, 666 S.E.2d 860, 2008 N.C. App. LEXIS 1758 (2008) (quoting Bryant v. Burns-Hammond Const. Co., 197 N.C. 639, 1929 N.C. LEXIS 321 (1929)).

57 42 OH. JUR. *Evidence and Witnesses* § 110 (2013).

58 *Id.*

59 USX Corp. v. Barnhart, 395 F.3d 161, 171, 2004 U.S. App. LEXIS 26868 (3d Cir. 2004) (quoting Sec'y of Labor v. Keystone, 331 U.S. App. D.C. 422 (D.C. Cir. 1998)).

that a properly mailed letter arrived at its destination, when the sender demonstrated that she properly addressed, stamped, and mailed the letter.[60] This inference or presumption of fact could be rebutted where the recipient demonstrated that the letter never arrived.

§ 6.6 Classes of Presumptions

For purposes of discussion, presumptions are further divided into conclusive (irrebuttable) presumptions and rebuttable presumptions. A **conclusive presumption** (presumption *juris et de jure*) is a rule of substantive law rather than a rule of evidence. A disputable or rebuttable presumption is a species of evidence that may be accepted and on which reliance may be placed when there is no other evidence to refute the contention for which it stands.

A statute may make a presumption conclusive; in which case, the presumption cannot be destroyed or overcome by evidence. However, in criminal cases, conclusive presumptions have been held to violate the Constitution and no longer may be used in criminal cases. In *Sandstrom v. Montana*, the United States Supreme Court held that mandatory conclusive presumptions are unconstitutional because they conflict with the presumption of innocence.[61] In California, a conclusive presumption once existed where:

> Intent to commit theft by fraud is presumed if one who has leased or rented the personal property of another pursuant to a written contract fails to return the personal property to its owner within 20 days after the owner has made written demand by certified or registered mail following the expiration of the lease or rental agreement for return of the property so leased or rented. CAL. PENAL CODE ANN. § 484(b) (West 1988).

The Supreme Court of the United States reversed a California conviction of grand theft auto because the statute created an impermissible mandatory conclusive presumption in violation of the due process clause of the Fourteenth Amendment, as prohibited by *Sandstrom v. Montana*. When faced with the proof of the basic fact that a defendant had not returned personal property within the statutory time limit, a conclusive presumed fact arose that the defendant possessed an intent to commit theft by fraud.[62]

A traditional conclusive presumption held that a child born in wedlock was conclusively the legitimate child, but modern court decisions hold that the presumption is rebuttable. Even so, a Hawai'i court of appeals noted that the presumption of legitimacy for a child born to a married couple is "one of the strongest and most persuasive known

---

60 *See* Rothwell v. Yeager, 2008 Ark. App. LEXIS (2008).

61 Sandstrom v. Montana, 442 U.S. 510, 523, 99 S. Ct. 2450, 2458, 61 L. Ed. 2d 39, 50, 1979 U.S. LEXIS 113 (1979).

62 *See* Carella v. California, 491 U.S. 263, 109 S. Ct. 2419, 105 L. Ed. 2d 218, 1989 U.S. LEXIS 2973 (1989).

to the law."[63] In days before the availability of reliable blood and DNA testing, courts traditionally upheld the conclusive presumption of fatherhood and did not permit the husband or another man to introduce evidence to contest or to support the possibility of paternity. However, all modern evidence codes allow the admission of contrary evidence of paternity when certain conditions are present, making the presumption rebuttable. The advent of irrefutable genetic testing dictated that the conclusive presumption of paternity had to be reconsidered.[64] Demonstrative of this change is an Indiana case in which the court noted that:

> [a] child born during marriage is presumed legitimate. This presumption is not conclusive although it may be rebutted only by direct, clear, and convincing evidence.[65]

But definitive genetic testing has resulted in a new conclusive presumption in favor of paternity in some situations. Rhode Island law provides that, if the "results of the blood or tissue typing tests duly admitted into evidence establish a ninety-seven percent (97%) or greater probability of inclusion that a party is the biological father of the child, then that probability shall constitute a conclusive presumption of paternity."[66] If a jury chose to disregard this presumption in a criminal case, it would have the power to do so, despite the statutory language that the presumption is conclusive.

A rebuttable presumption (presumption *juris tantum*) requires the trier of fact to consider the deduction as true until disproved by contrary evidence. An example of a rebuttable presumption of law is the presumption stating that an accused person is presumed to be innocent, given that a prosecutor's presentation of evidence to a guilty verdict negates the presumption of innocence, as does a guilty plea.[67] In Georgia, proof that a defendant had control of his automobile gave rise to the presumption that he had possession and control of any contraband found in the vehicle. This presumption was rebuttable by proof that other persons had equal access to the contraband that would overcome the strength of the presumption.[68]

In some jurisdictions, presumptions are evidentiary devices that are categorized into two groups—mandatory and permissive. According to a federal district court, a mandatory presumption tells a jury that it must find that an element of the crime has been proved if the prosecution proves certain basic or predicate facts.[69] A federal court of appeals noted an improper use of a presumption where a jury was told that,

---

63 Inoue v. Inoue, 118 Haw. 86, 101, 2008 Haw. App. LEXIS 50 2008). *See also* G.M.H. v. J.L.H., 700 S.W.2d 506 (Mo. Ct. App. 1985), which reaffirmed that at common law the presumption that a child born in wedlock is conclusively presumed to be legitimate, but indicated that today the presumption is rebuttable, is an evidentiary presumption, and is overcome by a showing of substantial evidence to the contrary.

64 D.F. v. Department of Revenue, 823 So. 2d 97, 98, 2002 Fla. LEXIS 1162 (2002).

65 State v. Black, 877 N.E.2d 1239, 1242, 2007 Ind. App. LEXIS 2762 (2007).

66 R.I. GEN. LAWS § 15-8-11(e) (2013).

67 United States v. Madoff, 2009 U.S. App. LEXIS 5985 (2d Cir. 2009).

68 Hamilton v. State, 293 Ga. App. 297, 298, 2008 Ga. App. LEXIS 926 (2008).

69 Nicholson v. Kane, 2009 U.S. Dist. LEXIS 21889 (N.D. Ga. 2009).

because a dead body was found in a particular county, they "shall consider" the cause of death to have occurred in that county.[70] A mandatory presumption of this nature violates due process because it relieves the prosecution of the burden of persuasion on an element of an offense. However, a "permissive presumption" in a criminal case allows, but does not require, the trier of fact to infer an elemental fact from proof of a basic fact.

A "permissive inference" or presumption allows, but does not require, the finder of fact to infer the fact, while it places no burden on the defendant to rebut it. The judge or jury can accept the existence of the inferred fact or reject it. In a Florida burglary case in which the defendant was found in possession of property taken from the victim's residence, the judge charged the jury that "[p]roof of possession of recently stolen property, unless satisfactorily explained, gives rise to an inference that the person in possession of the property knew or should have known that the property had been stolen."[71] Despite the defendant's allegation, the standard jury instruction did not create a mandatory presumption by suggesting to the jury that it might infer that the defendant knew the property was stolen, but was free to decide otherwise.

Regardless of whether a presumption is categorized as conclusive, rebuttable, mandatory, or permissive, a presumption will generally be considered unconstitutional if it relieves the prosecution from having to prove every element of the crime.[72] For example, where a statute notes that a person who fails to return a rental car within five days after the lease expires, a presumption arises that the person embezzled the vehicle, but this mandatory presumption violates the due process clause of the Fourteenth Amendment, because it relieves the prosecution of proving part or all of the crime.[73] A mandatory presumption may not shift the burden of proof on any element of the offense, because doing so conflicts with the overriding presumption of innocence and invades the fact-finding function of the judge or jury.

§ 6.7 Specific Presumption Situations

A study of the most common presumptions used in criminal cases produces a clear understanding of their purposes and limitations. A strong general rule is that the finder of fact is never bound by a presumption in a criminal case and may choose to ignore a presumption completely. In studying presumptions, it is important to appreciate the legal reasoning that supports the concept of a presumption and to understand the statutory and constitutional limitations that apply to specific presumptions. State

---

70 Owens v. McLaughlin, 733 F.3d 320, 327, 2013 U.S. App. 21599 (11th Cir. 2013).

71 Walker v. State, 896 So. 2d 712, 714, 2005 Fla. LEXIS 361 (2005), quoting FLA. STD. JURY INSTR. (CRIM.) 14.1.

72 United States v. Haberek, 2006 U.S. Dist. LEXIS 44670 (N.D. Ill. 2006); United States v. Edelkind, 2006 U.S. Dist. LEXIS 41056 (W.D. La. 2006).

73 People v. Laughlin, 137 Cal. App. 4th 1020, 1024, 40 Cal. Rptr. 3d 737, 739, 2006 Cal. App. LEXIS 388 (2006).

legislatures have created some presumptions by statute, while others have developed as a result of state and federal court decisions. When legislatures create presumptions as examples of public policy, virtually all of these presumptions may be rebutted with the presentation of substantial evidence to the contrary. One clear limitation on a presumption is that it cannot have the effect of shifting the burden of proof to a criminal defendant.

One view of presumptions holds that a presumption is not evidence of anything and merely determines which party should go forward and produce evidence pertaining to the matters at issue. Along with this position is the collateral view that a presumption should not be treated as evidence and should not be placed on the scale of justice to be weighed with actual evidence when making a decision.[74] As a Pennsylvania court held, "[a]ffirmative evidence of a material element of the crime charged may never be displaced by a mere evidentiary presumption; nor may that presumption substitute for evidence."[75] The principle that a presumption is not evidence has not gained universal acceptance, because some jurisdictions hold that a presumption actually serves as a substitute for evidence. A North Dakota court noted that, where a presumption has been "established by credible evidence, the presumption serves as evidence until such time as it is rebutted."[76] Some courts have held that "a presumption has the effect of evidence"[77] and must be given the same force and effect unless rebutted or called into question.

Presumptions in criminal cases have limitations and are scrutinized very carefully by reviewing courts to determine whether they place an unconstitutional burden on the accused. Moreover, statutory presumptions must not have the effect of creating a mandatory presumption in a criminal case or have the effect of reversing the normal burden of proof of any element of a crime.[78]

The number of statutory presumptions and judicial presumptions is extensive, and most of these presumptions are used in civil cases. As such, those presumptions are not discussed in detail. Some examples of presumptions used in civil cases are (1) a private transaction has been fair and regular; (2) the ordinary course of business has been followed; (3) a promissory note or a bill of exchange was given or endorsed for a sufficient consideration; and (4) a writing is accurately dated.

Although presumptions possess a more limited usage in criminal cases, presumptions do still play an important role in such trials and are often litigated on appeal. The following sections discuss and demonstrate the most significant and important presumptions related to criminal cases.

---

74 Mullin v. Brown, 210 Ariz. 545, 548, 115 P.3d 139, 142, 2005 Ariz. App. LEXIS 83 (2005).

75 Commonwealth v. Salter, 2004 Pa. Super. 318, 858 A.2d 610, 614 2004 Pa. Super. LEXIS 2687 (2004).

76 Kortum v. Johnson, 2008 N.D. 154, 2008 N.D. LEXIS 161 (2008). *See also* N.D.R. Ev. Rule 301(a) Presumptions in general in civil actions and proceedings. (N.D. 2013).

77 People v. Niene, 8 Misc. 3d 649, 652, 798 N.Y.S.2d 891, 894, 2005 N.Y. Misc. LEXIS 981 (2005).

78 Gross v. Jackson, 2008 U.S. Dist. LEXIS 37095 (S.D. Ohio 2008). *See also* People v. Illinois, 2009 Ill. App. LEXIS 45 (2009).

§ 6.8 —Innocence

As a matter of well-settled law, the defendant in a criminal case is presumed innocent from the time the prosecution begins and retains this presumption forever or until a finder of fact returns a guilty verdict. This rebuttable presumption of innocence places upon the prosecution the burden of proving the defendant guilty beyond a reasonable doubt. This presumption exists until the time the finder of fact renders a guilty verdict.[79] Upon a conviction, a defendant's presumption of innocence ends because the evidence presented by the government has overcome it.[80]

The so-called presumption of innocence is not, strictly speaking, a presumption in the sense of a deduction from a given premise or basic fact. It does not involve the proof of a basic fact from which a deduction may be drawn. It is a fact that exists until sufficient proof to the contrary appears. More accurately, the "presumption of innocence serves as a procedural doctrine that allocates the burden of proof in criminal trials."[81]

A Maryland trial court explained that the presumption of innocence covers a defendant at the start and throughout the trial, whereby a:

> Defendant is presumed to be innocent of the charges—charges. This presumption remains with the defendant throughout every stage of the trial and is not overcome unless you are convinced beyond a reasonable doubt that the defendant is guilty. The State has the burden of proving the guilt of the defendant beyond a reasonable doubt. This burden remains on the State throughout the trial. The defendant is not required to prove his innocence. However, the State is not required to prove guilt beyond all possible doubt or to a mathematical certainty, nor is the State required to negate every conceivable circumstance of innocence. A reasonable doubt is a doubt founded upon reason. It is not a *fanciful doubt*, a *whimsical doubt*, or a *capricious doubt*. Proof beyond a reasonable doubt requires such proof as would convince you of the truth of a fact to the extent that you would be willing to act upon such belief without reservation in an important matter in your own business or personal affairs. However, if you are not satisfied of the defendant's guilt to that extent, then reasonable doubt exists and the defendant must be found not guilty.[82] [Emphasis added.]

The reviewing court rejected the defendant's contention that, by using the words *fanciful, whimsical*, and *capricious doubt*, the trial court probably prevented the jury from understanding the meaning of reasonable doubt, because those words were not included in the Maryland jury instructions. Where a judge deviates in some manner from approved jury instructions covering the presumption of innocence, the deviation does not necessarily indicate a reduction in the protections offered by the presumption of innocence principle.

---

79 State v. Halls, 2006 Utah App. 142, 549 Utah Adv. Rep. 21, 2006 Utah App. LEXIS 136 (2006).

80 United States v. Medina et al., 430 F.3d 869, 2005 U.S. App. LEXIS 26772 (2005).

81 United States v. Scott, 2006 U.S. App. LEXIS 14182 (9th Cir. 2006).

82 Turner v. State, 181 Md. App. 477, 481, 2008 Md. App. LEXIS 106 (2008).

In an appeal based partly on an alleged jury instruction error, the Third Circuit Court of Appeals, in *United States v. Dufresne*,[83] rejected the defendant's contention that the trial court improperly instructed the jury on the presumption of innocence. The judge's instructions told the jurors that if:

> After careful and impartial consideration of all of the evidence in the case, have a reasonable doubt that a defendant is guilty, you must find the defendant not guilty. If, members of the jury, you view the evidence in the case as reasonably permitting either of two conclusions, one of innocence, the other of guilt, then you *should* of course adopt the conclusion of innocence. [Emphasis added.][84]

According to the reviewing court, the use of the word "should" did not dilute the presumption of innocence. So long as the trial judge informed the jury about the concept of guilt beyond a reasonable doubt, while properly covering the presumption of innocence in the jury instruction, due process had been satisfied. The jury instruction additionally indicated that the presumption of innocence could be sufficiently strong that it would permit an acquittal where the prosecution's evidence failed to establish a prima facie case.[85]

Generally, judges offer a jury instruction that covers the presumption of innocence, and some earlier decisions suggested that failure to give a specific instruction on the presumption of innocence was reversible error. However, in a major case, *Kentucky v. Whorton*, the Supreme Court held that failure to give a requested instruction on the presumption of innocence did not, in and of itself, violate the Constitution.[86] In this case, the defendant was charged with committing several armed robberies in three separate indictments. At the conclusion of all the evidence, the defendant's counsel asked that the jury be instructed on the presumption of innocence. The instruction requested was:

> The law presumes an accused to be innocent of crime. He begins a trial with a clean slate, with no evidence against him. And the law permits nothing but legal evidence presented before the jury to be considered in support of any charge against the accused. So the presumption of innocence alone is sufficient to acquit an accused unless the jury members are satisfied beyond a reasonable doubt of the accused's guilt from all of the evidence in the case.[87]

The judge refused the defense counsel's request, but instead instructed the jurors that they could return a verdict of guilty only if they found beyond a reasonable doubt that the defendant had committed the acts charged in the indictment with the requisite criminal intent. The jury found the defendant guilty on numerous counts, and he

---

83 United States v. Dufresne, 58 Fed. Appx. 890, 2003 U.S. App. LEXIS 2126 (3d Cir. 2003), *cert. denied*, 538 U.S. 1064, 2003 U.S. LEXIS 4193 (2003).

84 *Id.*

85 *Id.*

86 Kentucky v. Whorton, 441 U.S. 786, 99 S. Ct. 2088, 60 L. Ed. 2d 640 (1979).

87 *Id.* at 788, n.1.

appealed. The Supreme Court of Kentucky held that the failure to give the instruction concerning the presumption of innocence was reversible error. The commonwealth attorney appealed to the Supreme Court of the United States.

In reversing the top Kentucky court and reinstating the convictions, the Supreme Court of the United States found that an instruction on the presumption of innocence is not required in all cases. Accordingly, the *Whorton* Court held that:

> In short, the failure to give a requested instruction on the presumption of innocence does not in and of itself violate the Constitution.[88]

The Court went on to explain that failure to give a specific instruction on innocence should be evaluated in light of the totality of the circumstances, including the jury instructions, arguments of the attorneys, the strength of the evidence, and any other relevant factor. In a later case, the Supreme Court noted that "[a] jury instruction on the presumption of innocence is not constitutionally required in every case to satisfy due process, because such an instruction merely offers an additional safeguard beyond that provided by the constitutionally required instruction on reasonable doubt."[89]

In a different case, a defendant objected to the trial judge's jury instruction concerning reasonable doubt and contended that the instruction diminished the presumption of innocence. Part of the jury instruction stated that "[t]he law presumes a defendant to be innocent of crime. Thus, the defendant, although accused, begins the trial with a clean slate with no evidence against him."[90] The defendant contended that the phrase "clean slate" implied that the prosecution and the defendant started the case on equal ground, thus making the presumption of innocence less forceful. The Tenth Circuit Court of Appeals rejected the argument, noting that similar language had previously been approved and did not have the effect of reducing the protections of the presumption of innocence.

The universal rule is that, in an appeal following a conviction, "the presumption of innocence no longer avails and [an appellate court views] the evidence in a light most favorable to the verdict."[91] When an appellate court reviews a case, it begins its work with the presumption that the trial court was correct in its verdict and that the defendant is guilty. In a Tennessee case, *State v. Lee*, the court explained the effect that a guilty verdict has on the presumption of innocence, noting, "[a] guilty verdict removes the presumption of innocence and replaces it with a presumption of guilt, and on appeal the defendant has the burden of illustrating why the evidence is insufficient to support the jury's verdict."[92]

---

88 *Id.* at 789.

89 Arizona v. Fulminante, 499 U.S. 279, 291, 1991 U.S. LEXIS 1854 (1991).

90 United States v. Smith, 531 F.3d 1261; 2008 U.S. App. LEXIS 14797 (10th Cir. 2008).

91 Parker v. State, 2009 Ga. App. LEXIS 319 (2009).

92 2009 Tenn. Crim. App. LEXIS 177 (2009).

§ 6.9 —Sanity

"The presumption of sanity is equally universal in some variety or other, being (at least) a presumption that a defendant has the capacity to form the *mens rea* necessary for a verdict of guilt and the consequent criminal responsibility," according to the Supreme Court of the United States.[93] Therefore, a prosecutor does not have to prove sanity as one of the elements in every crime. On the strength of this rebuttable presumption, a judge may offer a jury instruction that states that every person is presumed sane until the contrary is shown by the evidence. The presumption of sanity is a rule of law that stands in the place of evidence, unless evidence is introduced to rebut the presumption. In some states, the presumption is considered so strong that, even if there was a unanimous opinion by expert witnesses, the presumption still retains evidentiary value.[94]

The concept of competency to stand trial, while related to legal insanity, involves different considerations. The presumption of capacity to stand trial exists so long as a defendant understands the nature and importance attached to a trial and is able materially to assist in his or her defense. For example, in Illinois, to be mentally fit for trial, a defendant must have "sufficient present ability to consult with defense counsel with a reasonable degree of rational understanding and... has both a rational and factual understanding of the proceedings."[95] In Alabama, where the issue of lack of competency has been raised, the trial judge preliminarily reviews reports of medical personnel. The judge then schedules a hearing and notifies the parties if he or she believes that there is reasonable ground to doubt the particular defendant's competency.[96] Each party may present evidence at the hearing that relates to the defendant's ability or inability to assist in his or her defense. In Georgia, a finding of competency generally permits the state to move forward with prosecution of the appropriate crimes.[97]

Under the insanity defense provisions of the 1984 Comprehensive Crime Control Act, mental disease or defect constitutes a defense in federal criminal trials where the defendant proves "the defense of insanity by clear and convincing evidence"[98] and that, "at the time of the commission of the acts constituting the offense, the defendant, as a result of a severe mental disease or defect, was unable to appreciate the nature and quality or the wrongfulness of his acts."[99] If the defendant fails to meet the burden of proving insanity by clear and convincing proof, the presumption of sanity has not been rebutted, and the defendant fails to have the benefit of this affirmative defense.

---

93 Clark v. Arizona, 2006 U.S. LEXIS 5184 (2006).

94 Commonwealth v. Chiero, 24 Mass. L. Rep. 376, 2008 Mass. Super. LEXIS 245 (2008).

95 People v. Schoreck, 384 Ill. App. 3d 904, 916, 2008 Ill. App. LEXIS 829 (2008).

96 *See* ALA. R. CRIM. P. 11.6 (2014).

97 GA. CODE ANN. § 17-7-130 (g) (2013).

98 18 U.S.C. § 17(b).

99 *Id.* § 17(a).

Although some states have adopted a state version of the federal insanity defense, federal law concerning the insanity defense applies only in federal courts. The states are free to enact their respective insanity defenses and related presumptions without regard to federal law or to choose not to recognize any insanity defense.[100] In some states, after the defendant has presented some credible evidence that supports a defense of insanity, the burden of proof with the evidence shifts, and the prosecution is given "the burden of proving sanity beyond a reasonable doubt."[101] In those states, if the evidence is legally sufficient to raise the issue of insanity and rebut the presumption of sanity, and if the prosecution offers no evidence of sanity, there is no factual issue for the jury, and the defendant is entitled to a directed verdict of acquittal.

The nature and quantum of evidence that the prosecution must produce to meet the burden of proof of sanity, as determined by jury instruction, vary with both the jurisdiction and with the nature and quantum of evidence indicating mental illness. For example, in Pennsylvania, insanity is considered an affirmative defense that requires a defendant to both raise the issue and to prove insanity by a preponderance of the evidence.[102] In its penal code, California takes a similar position to Pennsylvania, stating that the insanity defense "shall be found by the trier of fact only when the accused person proves by a preponderance of the evidence that he or she was incapable of knowing or understanding the nature and quality of his or her act and of distinguishing right from wrong at the time of the commission of the offense."[103] A judge will offer a jury instruction concerning insanity where the defendant has presented evidence, that if believed, would establish the defendant's insanity. However, the judge is not obligated to give a jury instruction where a defendant has not raised legally sufficient evidence.

In support of an insanity defense, lay testimony may be sufficient to satisfy the defendant's burden of proving insanity according to the Supreme Court of New Hampshire.[104] New Hampshire provided that a defendant alleging an insanity defense "shall have the burden of proving the defense of insanity by clear and convincing evidence."[105] According to a Texas court, lay witness opinion may be admitted when an insanity defense has been pled, and such opinion "may be sufficient to raise the defense of insanity,"[106] even in the absence of expert testimony.

In 1984, Congress completed a comprehensive overhaul of the insanity defense as applied in the federal courts. Under the provisions of the Insanity Defense Reform Act, Congress gave defendants the burden of proving the defense of insanity by clear and convincing evidence.[107] Legal challenges attacked the revised federal insanity defense by alleging that the law violated the due process clauses of the Fifth and Fourteenth

---

100 Medina v. California, 505 U.S. 437, 449, 1992 U.S. LEXIS 3696 (1992).

101 People v. Grenier, 200 P.3d 1062, 2008 Colo. App. LEXIS 356 (Colo. 2008).

102 *See* 18 PA. C. S. § 315 (2013).

103 CAL. PENAL CODE § 25(b) (2014).

104 State v. Fichera, 2006 N.H. LEXIS 76 (2006).

105 N.H. REV. STAT. ANN. 628:2 (2013).

106 Johnson v. State, 2008 Tex. App. LEXIS 5476 (2008).

107 18 U.S.C. § 17(b) and § 4242(b).

Amendments.[108] In a case heard before the United States Court of Appeals for the Eleventh Circuit, the defendant alleged that placing the burden of proof of insanity by clear and convincing evidence on him violated his rights under the Fifth Amendment. The Eleventh Circuit noted that several states had constitutionally placed the burden of insanity defenses on defendants, without creating any due process violations. Two other federal circuits that had addressed due process claims involving similar state insanity statutes had also rejected the theory that placing a burden on a defendant to prove insanity violated the federal Constitution.[109] Similar to the federal insanity defense, Illinois presumes that sanity is a default mental state and requires that defendants who allege insanity introduce evidence to rebut the general presumption of sanity. When the defense of insanity has been alleged at trial, Illinois law provides that "the burden of proof is on the defendant to prove by clear and convincing evidence that the defendant is not guilty by reason of insanity."[110] Against a defendant's contention that the elevated burden of proof needed to rebut the presumption of sanity violated due process by being "irrational, unfair, and contrary to contemporary practice," an Illinois reviewing court affirmed his conviction. It held that the Illinois statute did not violate due process, even if only seven jurisdictions used such a high burden of proof in insanity cases.[111]

§ 6.10 —Suicide

The presumption against suicide stems from and is raised by our common knowledge and experience that most sane persons possess a natural love of life and an instinct for self-protection that effectively deters them from suicide or the self-infliction of serious bodily injury. In support of this concept, "[t]here is a rule of law that presumes that an unexplained death by violence requires the conclusion that death was not self-imposed until credible evidence of suicide is offered in rebuttal."[112] Most jurisdictions recognize the existence of an affirmative presumption of death by accidental means and recognize a presumption against suicide,[113] but the presumption is not universally recognized.[114]

---

108 *See* for example, United States v. Freeman, 804 F.2d 1574, 1986 U.S. App. LEXIS 34268 (11th Cir. 1986). As of 2011, the Supreme Court of the United States has not directly ruled on the constitutionality of the Insanity Defense Reform Act of 1984, 18 U.S.C. § 17.

109 United States v. Wattleton, 296 F.3d 1184, 2002 U.S. App. LEXIS 13686 (11th Cir. 2002); United States v. Amos, 803 F.2d 419 (8th Cir. 1986).

110 720 ILL. COMP. STAT. 5/6-2 (2013).

111 People v. Clay, 361 Ill. App. 3d 310, 836 N.E.2d 872, 2005 Ill. App. LEXIS 994 (Ill. 2005), *appeal denied*, 2006 Ill. LEXIS 164 (Ill. 2006).

112 23 FLA. JUR. 2D *Evidence and Witnesses* § 150 (2014).

113 Estate of Norman Holly v. American Family Life Assurance, 2005 Ohio 2281, 2005 Ohio App. LEXIS 2190 (2005).

114 New Mexico does not recognize a presumption against suicide. Solorzano v. Bristow, 136 N.M. 658, 662, 2004 NMCA 136; 103 P.3d 582, 586, 2004 N.M. App. LEXIS 121 (2004).

The presumption against suicide may be overcome by affirmative evidence of suicide, which effectively rebuts the presumption. When it was shown that a prisoner died two days after his arrival at a federal prison transfer center, the prison contended that he had committed suicide. The guards found the decedent's blood-soaked body hanging from torn bed sheets affixed to a ceiling vent in his cell. Oklahoma has a presumption against suicide, but it has been described as a procedural tool for ordering proof and is not considered affirmative evidence. In a suit between the federal government and the estate of the deceased, the government offered sufficient evidence to rebut the presumption against suicide by showing that the deceased had been locked alone in a cell, and his injuries appeared to be self-inflicted.[115]

The "presumption against suicide is not evidence and cannot be treated as evidence by the jury in reaching a verdict, and an instruction that such presumption has the effect of affirmative evidence is erroneous"[116] and should not be weighed as such. However, courts in several states follow the minority view that the presumption is itself evidence or has evidentiary weight.[117] Once a case gets to trial, this presumption against suicide and in favor of accident or natural cause operates procedurally. In one case in which the deceased had multiple serious medical problems and was taking a variety of very strong drugs, she died from multiple drug intoxication, which could indicate suicide.[118] In seeking a reversal of a medical examiner's determination, her administrator contended that the decedent had not committed suicide because she was a former nun who remained deeply religious and was enthusiastic about enjoying life with her two adopted children. Although the decedent had a history of depression, and her blood concentration indicated a high level of antidepressant drugs, the evidence indicated that she would never have wanted to expose her children to discovering her body or to leave them with a renewed legacy of abandonment. When the reviewing court determined that the trial court erred in dismissing the petition to change the cause of death, it reversed the lower court's determination. According to the court, even though the decedent died from drug intoxication, the evidence was insufficient to rebut the strong presumption against suicide.[119]

In the majority of cases, it proves to be a tall order to rebut the strong presumption against suicide, but where "death by external violence is shown by facts or circumstances, inconsistent with accident, the presumption against suicide is displaced, and no longer continues to operate in favor of the plaintiff."[120] In Texas, as in many other

---

115 Estate of Trentadue ex rel. Aguilar v. United States, 397 F.3d 840, 863, 2005 U.S. App. LEXIS 1811 (10th Cir. 2005).

116 City of Indianapolis v. Taylor, 707 N.E.2d 1047, 1051, 1999 Ind. App. LEXIS 456 (1999).

117 Under North Dakota law, the presumption that death was accidental has the weight of affirmative evidence. Dick v. New York Life Ins. Co., 359 U.S. 437, 79 S. Ct. 921, 3 L. Ed. 2d 935 (1959).

118 Matter of Infante v. Dignan, 865 N.Y.S.2d 167, 169 2008 N.Y. App. Div. LEXIS 7118 (2008).

119 *Id.*

120 Elrod et al. v. J.C. Penney Life Insurance Company, 2000 Tenn. App. LEXIS 407 (2000).

jurisdictions, the presumption against suicide must fall when contrary evidence proves otherwise, and the only reasonable inference is death by suicide.[121]

§ 6.11 —Possession of Fruits of Crime

When there is proof that the accused possessed recently stolen property, and no satisfactory explanation exists for this possession, an inference of guilt may arise, but this inference or presumption is not conclusive and may be rebutted by contrary evidence.[122] Generally, there must be actual proof that the property was recently stolen, or this inference should not be applied. In some jurisdictions, this inference may be sufficient for a conviction, but in others additional proof will be required. Upon proof of possession of recently stolen property, a jury may make this inference of guilt or of guilty knowledge, but when other evidence in a case has been considered, the jury may decline to make the inference.[123]

In *State v. Draine*, a case in which the defendant had been convicted of theft of a tractor and trailer, the defendant had been found in possession of the recently stolen property and had possession of the keys to operate the property.[124] The Court of Criminal Appeals mentioned that Tennessee recognizes that, when a person is found in possession of recently stolen property, the situation gives rise to an inference that the defendant has stolen the property or possesses knowledge that the property is stolen. In this case, the reviewing court emphasized that the "defendant was in possession of the recently stolen property, based upon his possession of the keys, the inference that he had stolen it or had knowledge that the property was stolen arose. The proof established that the theft occurred no more than three days prior to the time in which the defendant was in control of the tractor."[125] In addition, the defendant had no rational explanation for why he possessed the recently stolen property. The reviewing court upheld the conviction and found no legal or constitutional problem with the use of the inference.

The strength of such an inference or presumption, which the possession of stolen property raises, depends upon the circumstances surrounding the case. The defendant's possession must be exclusive, and it must have occurred within a relatively short time after commission of the crime. The longer the period from the crime to the point at which the defendant was found in possession of the stolen property, the weaker the presumption becomes.

Although some appellate defendants have occasionally been successful in getting convictions reversed on state or federal constitutional grounds, the doctrine of knowledge or guilt based on possession of recently stolen property remains strong in many

---

[121] 35 TEX. JUR. § 141, Evidence. (2013).

[122] *See* Bozeman v. State, 931 So.2d 1006, 2006 Fla. App. LEXIS 8986 (2006). *See* case in Part II.

[123] *See* 23 FLA. JUR. 2D *Evidence and Witnesses* § 134 (2014).

[124] 2008 Tenn. Crim. App. LEXIS 623 (2008).

[125] *Id.*

jurisdictions. In *Kerr v. State*, a Florida appellate court noted that two rebuttable presumptions may arise from proof of possession of stolen property, depending on the surrounding facts.[126] The first presumption is that the possessor of the stolen property is the guilty party, and the second is that the possessor knew that the property was recently stolen. In the *Kerr* case, the owner of a car had been working on it in front of his place of residence, but found it missing when he returned from inside his home. The next day, police encountered the defendant in possession of the car, while removing some parts from it. The defendant stated to the officer that he had purchased the BMW for $500, but had no paperwork concerning the sale, and he did not know the identity of the person from whom he had allegedly purchased the car. The reviewing court found the defendant's explanations incredible and not worthy of belief and noted that he lied to the police officer concerning his identity. The court upheld the conviction on the strength of the inferences and because of the defendant's lack of believable rebuttal, the prima facie proof of the charge remained.

In contrast to these cases, California considers the presumption or inference related to possession of recently stolen property to have a much weaker evidentiary effect. California courts instruct juries that mere possession, without some corroboration, is not sufficient to prove a defendant's guilt of the particular offense. The typical California jury instruction counsels jurors that:

> If you find that a defendant was in [conscious] possession of recently [stolen] [extorted] property, the fact of that possession is not by itself sufficient to permit an inference that the defendant is guilty of the crime of [which crime]. Before guilt may be inferred, there must be corroborating evidence tending to prove defendant's guilt. However, this corroborating evidence need only be slight, and need not by itself be sufficient to warrant an inference of guilt.[127]

In *People v. Parson*, a capital murder case in which the defendant was found in possession of a variety of property belonging to the victim, the Supreme Court of California rejected the defendant's contention that the preceding jury instruction was erroneous because it reduced the prosecution's burden of proof so that the prosecution no longer had to establish guilt beyond reasonable doubt.[128] The prosecution introduced proof that, following the victim's death, the defendant possessed and used the decedent's ATM card, following a burglary and a robbery. During the trial, the court informed the jury that it should consider additional attributes of possession, such as time, place, and manner, that might connect a defendant to a charged crime. The Supreme Court of California held that the jury instruction given did not create a presumption or inference in a way that violated due process. According to the court, commonsense reasoning justified the conclusion that, although the defendant's possession

---

126 954 So. 2d 692, 693, 2007 Fla. App. LEXIS 5617 (2007). This Florida court seems to use inference and presumption as rough synonyms probably because a jury is not bound to find the deduced fact from the first proven fact.

127 CAL. JURY INSTRUCTIONS-CRIM. 2.15 (2005).

128 44 Cal. 4th 332, 355, 2008 Cal. LEXIS 8243 (2008).

of the decedent's recently stolen ATM card was not sufficient evidence to permit an inference of guilt, other factors presently existed that tended to corroborate the stolen property and the defendant's guilt of robbery and burglary. In upholding the convictions, the Supreme Court of California noted that the jury instructions on recently stolen property were also accompanied by the other typical instructions covering reasonable doubt, the presumption of innocence, and the prosecutor's overall burden of proof.[129]

The net effect of the California jury instruction covering possession of recently stolen property weakened the traditional inference or presumption concerning knowledge that property was stolen, but still permits the jurors to use natural and logical reasoning.

In summary, where the presumption or inference concerning recently stolen property is applied, these conditions must be met: (a) the possession must be unexplained by any innocent origin; (b) the possession must be fairly recent; and (c) the possession must be exclusive,[130] as a general rule, although many jurisdictions will find that joint possession is sufficient. As noted earlier, some states require some corroboration with the inference in order to allow a conviction.

§ 6.12 —That a Person Intends the Ordinary Consequences of His or Her Voluntary Acts

In most situations, humans do particular acts and intend or expect fairly certain results. Where criminal activity is concerned, similar considerations and expectations occur, so that it would be fair to state that a person intends to have the usual and predicted result happen given the criminal act that the person performed. Recognizing this connection, state and federal courts have used various methods to convey to a jury the proposition that, from a legal perspective, "a person is presumed to intend the natural and probable consequences of one's actions."[131] The presumption mentioned, often delivered by a jury instruction or in closing argument, cannot be phrased in terms that appear mandatory or require that the presumption to be given complete effect. Otherwise, proof that a person did a physical act would effectively transfer the burden of proof to a defendant who must prove lack of guilt in order to prevail, a procedural effect that is unconstitutional.

The United States Supreme Court considered the effects of this type of jury instruction in the case of *Sandstrom v. Montana* in 1979,[132] and the Court recognized

---

129 *Id.* at 356.

130 Constructive possession is sufficient to allow the presumption. *See* Ahmed v. Yates, 2006 U.S. Dist. LEXIS 18549 (N.D. Cal. 2006), and Ferguson v. State, 920 So. 2d 838, 840, 2006 Fla. App. LEXIS 2283 (2006).

131 Boldin v. State, 373 Ark. 295, 300, 2008 Ark. LEXIS 277 (2008).

132 Sandstrom v. Montana, 442 U.S. 510, 99 S. Ct. 2450, 61 L. Ed. 2d 39 (1979).

the principle that a jury instruction that has the effect of shifting the burden of proof to a defendant on a required element of the crime violates due process. Sandstrom had been convicted of deliberate homicide, in that he purposely or knowingly caused the victim's death. At the trial, the defendant admitted killing the victim, but contended that he did not do so purposely or knowingly, and therefore, he was not guilty of deliberate homicide.

The trial court instructed the jury that "the law presumes that a person intends the ordinary consequences of his voluntary acts,"[133] but the court did not tell the jury that the presumption could be rebutted or that the jury did not have to accept the presumption. The defendant's attorney argued that the instruction had the effect of shifting the burden of proof on the issue of purpose or knowledge to the defense, and that the instruction was impermissible under the federal Constitution, as a violation of due process of law.

Following a guilty verdict, despite the defense's trial objections, Sandstrom appealed to the Supreme Court of Montana. That court upheld the conviction, conceding that cases cited by the defense prohibited shifting the burden of proof to the defendant by means of the presumption, but held that the cited cases permit placing some "burden of proof to the defendant under certain circumstances."[134] The court also found that, because the defendant had only the burden of producing some evidence that he did not intend the ordinary consequences of his voluntary act, but not to disprove that he acted purposely or knowingly, the burden of proof had not shifted.

The Supreme Court of the United States reasoned that it was possible for the jury to interpret this instruction as conclusive on the issue of intent. The Court agreed that the instruction violated the Fourteenth Amendment's requirement that the state prove every element of a criminal offense beyond a reasonable doubt. The Court therefore found that the instruction "that the law presumes a person intends the ordinary consequences of his voluntary acts"[135]—in this case, at least—was improper and unconstitutional.

In *Sandstrom v. Montana*, the United States Supreme Court held that the due process clause of the Fourteenth Amendment was violated by a jury instruction inferring that the law presumes that a person intends the ordinary consequences of his voluntary acts in the absence of an instruction noting that the presumption could be rebutted. The Court expressly left open the question of whether, if a jury is so instructed, the error can be held harmless.

Following *Sandstrom*, courts took different approaches to the harmless error problem, and the Supreme Court considered the matter again in 1983 in *Connecticut v. Johnson.*[136] In the *Johnson* case, the defendant was convicted of robbery and attempted murder, following a jury instruction that noted a person intended the ordinary consequences of his voluntary act. The jury was permitted to use a conclusive presumption,

---

133 *Id.* at 515.

134 Sandstrom v. State, 176 Mont. 492, 497, 580 P.2d 106, 109 (1978).

135 Sandstrom v. Montana, 442 U.S. 510, 525, 99 S. Ct. 2450, 61 L. Ed. 2d 39 (1979).

136 Connecticut v. Johnson, 460 U.S. 73, 1983 U.S. LEXIS 131 (1983).

without examining the element of intent necessary for the convictions. The trial court's charge to the jury, which was challenged, included instructions regarding the presumption of innocence and the state's burden of proving guilt beyond a reasonable doubt for all elements of the crime. The trial judge instructed the jury on the issue of intent and stated "a person's intention may be inferred from his conduct and every person is conclusively presumed to intend the natural and necessary consequences of his act."[137] With respect to attempted murder, the court again spoke of a conclusive presumption.

The respondent argued on appeal that the conclusive presumption language in the jury instructions on intent rendered the instructions unconstitutional under *Sandstrom.* Over the state's contention that any error was harmless, the Supreme Court of Connecticut affirmed some of the other convictions, but reversed the convictions for attempted murder and robbery on the grounds that the jury instructions included a conclusive presumption that shifted the burden of proof concerning intent. The court concluded that the "unconstitutional conclusive presumption language in the general instruction was not cured by the specific instructions on attempted murder and robbery."

When the defendant appealed to the United States Supreme Court, that Court agreed with the state supreme court that the proposition, "every person is conclusively presumed to intend the natural and necessary consequences of his act," constituted error violating the Fourteenth Amendment's due process clause. The Supreme Court further explained that "an erroneous presumption on a disputed element of the crime renders irrelevant the evidence on the issue because the jury may have relied upon presumptions rather than upon that evidence."[138] If the instruction is given on the presumption, especially the conclusive presumption, the concern is that the jury will look no further in determining the intent, which is an element of the crime.

In *Connecticut v. Johnson*, the Supreme Court indicated, "[t]here may be rare situations in which the reviewing court can be confident that a *Sandstrom* error did not play any part in the jury's verdict. For example, if the instruction had no bearing on the offense for which the defendant. . . was convicted, it would be appropriate to find the error harmless."[139] However, the Court explained that, in the *Johnson* case, the conclusive presumption instruction permitted the jury to convict the respondent using what amounted to a conclusive presumption. According to the Court, such an error deprived the respondent of "constitutional rights so basic to a fair trial that their infraction can never be treated as harmless error."[140]

In a California case, the defendant was convicted of killing his former wife's boyfriend, after pleas of not guilty and not guilty by reason of insanity. The Ninth Circuit Court of Appeals reversed the conviction, however.[141] The bifurcated, or two-stage, trial involved a guilt phase in which the jury had been informed, for the purposes of

---

137 *Id.* at 78.

138 *Id.* at 85, 86.

139 *Id.* at 87.

140 *Id.* at 88, citing Chapman v. California, 386 U.S. 18, 23, 1967 U.S. LEXIS 2198 (1967).

141 Stark v. Hickman, 455 F.3d 1070, 1077, 1078, 2006 U.S. App. LEXIS 19296 (9th Cir. 2006).

that phase, that the jury was to conclusively presume that the defendant was sane. At the second phase, the jury found the defendant sane as well. The reviewing court reversed the conviction on the basis that the trial judge had given a jury instruction containing a conclusive presumption that relieved the prosecution of proving the crucial element of mental state for guilt of murder. The Court of Appeals followed the *Sandstrom* rationale and concluded "[t]hat the jury instruction in this case violated the Due Process Clause of the Fourteenth Amendment and that the error was not harmless."[142]

Sandstrom and related cases held that the due process clause bars the state from using evidentiary presumptions that effectively relieve the state of its burden of persuasion beyond a reasonable doubt as to every essential element of the crime. A permissive presumption, which suggests a possible conclusion but does not require it to be drawn, does not shift the burden of proof and is permissible as long as the conclusion follows logically from the predicate. But a mandatory presumption, even a rebuttable one, is prohibited if it relieves the state of the burden of persuasion as to an element of the offense.

While United States Supreme Court decisions involving inferences or presumptions of ordinary consequences have not proved to be models of clarity, the decisions appear to indicate that, where jury instructions relating to intent create a mandatory presumption that unconstitutionally shifts the burden of persuasion on an important element of the crime to the defendant, the instruction violates due process. As a general rule, such decisions should not survive judicial scrutiny, but some state decisions may follow the principle in every case. However, where the inference is clearly rebuttable and does not change the ultimate burden of proof, a jury instruction may not always, in every case, be objectionable, and some state courts may not be following the *Sandstrom* case properly. As an Arkansas court observed, "[i]ntent or state of mind is seldom capable of proof by direct evidence and must usually be inferred from the circumstances of the crime."[143]

Accordingly, courts have generally allowed the prosecution to introduce indirect evidence to show intent. For example, an Arkansas appeals court held that "[d]ue to the difficulty in ascertaining a defendant's intent or state of mind, a presumption exists that a person intends the natural and probable consequences of his or her acts."[144] A Virginia court permitted the measuring of a defendant's intent by considering the natural and probable consequences of the defendant's acts.[145] The Georgia code provides that "[a] person of sound mind and discretion is presumed to intend the natural and probable consequences of his acts but the presumption may be rebutted."[146] However, in a Mississippi homicide case, the state's top court reversed a conviction where the jury instructions indicated that a "person is presumed to have intended the natural and

---

142 *Id.* at 1080.

143 Taylor v. State, 77 Ark. App. 144, 150, 72 S.W.3d 882, 885 (2002).

144 Jones v. State, 2009 Ark. App. LEXIS 109 (2009).

145 Thornburgh v. Commonwealth, 2006 Va. App. LEXIS 90 (2006).

146 GA. CODE ANN. § 16-2-5 (2013).

probable consequences of his voluntary and deliberate acts." The reviewing court felt that, under the circumstances, the instruction, combined with other jury instructions, created a presumption that shifted the burden of proof improperly, and the court reversed the murder conviction based on the presumption condemned by the United States Supreme Court in *Sandstrom v. Montana*.[147] In an assault case, a Maryland reviewing court also recently approved the use of the phrase "one intends the natural and probable consequences of his act."[148] From a review of these cases, it may become somewhat apparent that many courts regularly come dangerously close to violating the principles announced in *Sandstrom v. Montana*. However, because most cases are not litigated to the state supreme court level, and almost never reach the Supreme Court of the United States, some deviation from the black-letter case law occurs.

§ 6.13 —Knowledge of the Law

A society that operates on the rule of law requires that the individuals within the society make strong efforts to obey the law, whether civil or criminal. "The general rule that ignorance of the law or a mistake of law is no defense to criminal prosecution is deeply rooted in the American legal system."[149] Therefore, as a legal principle, all persons are presumed to know the general public laws of the nation, state, and locality where they reside and to know the legal effects of their acts. The maxim that "[a]ll persons are conclusively presumed to know the law"[150] is necessary for the functioning of an orderly society. For example, a federal court held that the defendant was presumed to know that an American Indian cannot kill a bald eagle without a federal permit,[151] and federal courts can include the phrase "ignorance of the law is no excuse" in jury instructions.[152] While a number of decisions have held that the presumption that one knows the law is a conclusive presumption, it is recognized that no single person knows all the law or even comes close to understanding all its meanings. One federal court of appeals noted that the concept that "everyone knows the law" is based on an "embarrassing tenacity of legal fictions."[153] If everyone really always knew the law, no court cases would ever be reversed, because the judges would know the law and would apply it properly, and no police officer would ever make an illegal arrest.

---

147 *See* Williams v. State, 111 So. 3d 620, 2013 Miss LEXIS 160 (2013). *See* this case in Part II, Chapter 6.

148 Jones v. State, 213 Md. App. 208, 218, 73 A.3d 1136, 2013 Md. App. LEXIS 98 (2013).

149 United States v. Hancock, 231 F.3d 557, 561, 2000 U.S. App. LEXIS 26827 (9th Cir. 2000), quoting Cheek v. United States, 498 U.S. 192, 199, 1991 U.S. LEXIS 348 (1991).

150 35 TEX. JUR. Evidence § 130 (2013).

151 United States v. Friday, 525 F.3d 938, 2008 U.S. App. LEXIS 9919 (10th Cir. 2008), *cert. denied*, 2009 U.S. LEXIS 1548 (2009).

152 United States v. Turcotte, 405 F.3d 515, 525, 2005 U.S. App. LEXIS 6710 (7th Cir. 2005).

153 Atwell v. Lisle Park District, 286 F.3d 987, 2002 U.S. App. LEXIS 6775 (8th Cir. 2002).

As a general rule, trial judges are presumed to know the law and to follow it properly when making sentencing decisions,[154] "police officers are charged with knowledge of the law"[155] and defendants are presumed to know the law they have been charged with breaking and to know the consequences.[156]

While the presumption extends to judicial decisions, police officers are not charged with knowing how a court will construe a law or when or if a court will declare a law to be in violation of a state or the federal Constitution. In one case, an Illinois police officer was permitted to follow and enforce an Illinois law that was later ruled unconstitutional. Even though a police officer is presumed to know the law, the officer cannot foresee how a court will construe the law in future litigation.[157] In fact, prisoners gain no exemption from the maxim "everyone is presumed to know the law" when they pursue postconviction relief in state and federal appellate courts. This presumption is so strong that governments need not assist a prisoner in negotiating the complex matrix of postconviction relief past the first appeal of right.[158] Consequently, when prisoners fail to file briefs or other responses in attempts to gain writs of habeas corpus or other remedies, these failures do not normally serve as an adequate excuse.[159]

A person is not presumed to know the laws of a sister state or foreign country, but he or she is presumed to know that laws are subject to change, and is presumed to know of the changes.[160]

§ 6.14 —Flight or Concealment

"Evidence that the accused fled after the offense, intentionally absented himself or herself from court to avoid trial, escaped, or concealed himself or herself, is admissible as an indication of guilt."[161] Even though law enforcement officers assume that flight after a crime tends to prove guilt, human conduct is often ambiguous. This evidence rule deserves careful attention because the factual situation of each crime might result in different conclusions being drawn from similar conduct. When a defendant departs the scene of a crime, it can be considered flight, if the facts indicate that the defendant left the crime scene with the design of avoiding capture or apprehension. Proof of flight alone is not sufficient for a conviction where no other evidence connects a defendant to the crime.[162] For flight to have evidentiary consequences, the defendant need not necessarily be in hiding or fleeing or attempting to flee from custody. A New Jersey court

---

154 United States v. McGlothen, 2009 U.S. App. LEXIS 3600 (10th Cir. 2009).

155 Sneed v. State, 876 So. 2d 1235, 1238, 2004 Fla. App. LEXIS 8390 (2004).

156 State v. Robbins, 986 So. 2d 828, 835, 2008 La. App. LEXIS 862 (La. 2008).

157 *See* Illinois v. Krull, 480 U.S. 340 (1987).

158 *See* Nehls v. Norris, 2008 U.S. Dist. LEXIS 101820 (E.D. Ark. 2008).

159 *See* Allen v. Houston, 2008 U.S. Dist. LEXIS 72474 (D. Neb. 2008), and Dean v. Houston, 2006 U.S. Dist. LEXIS 2544 (D. Neb. 2006).

160 *See* 31A C.J.S. *Evidence* § 147.

161 18 TEX. JUR. *Criminal Law: Offenses Against the Person* § 118 (2013).

162 McBride v. State, 7 So.3d 1146, 2009 Fla. App. LEXIS 2281 (2009). According to the court, mere presence, knowledge of the crime, and flight are insufficient to justify a conviction.

explained that, in order to judicially recognize conduct as flight, the circumstances must indicate leaving accompanied by no rational explanation. This gives rise to an inference that the defendant possessed a consciousness of guilt and desired to avoid capture or apprehension for the alleged crime.[163] Alternatively, a suspect's flight from a crime scene or from a police officer could indicate a consciousness of guilt of some completely different offense or of a desire not to be involved in a police investigation. Evidence of flight need not prove that a suspect fled immediately following the alleged crime, but it could also show that a person fled months later when the police efforts focused on the defendant. The strength of the evidence of flight depends upon all the facts and circumstances, because flight may show consciousness of guilt or may indicate nothing. The defendant may introduce evidence in an attempt to offer an innocent explanation concerning why flight or concealment occurred, but an innocent explanation does not negate a jury's ability to infer a consciousness of guilt.[164]

In a federal prosecution involving a felon in possession of a firearm and ammunition, state agents attempted to serve a search warrant, which the defendant initially resisted. The eventual search revealed a gun and ammunition and indicated that the defendant was the only resident. He admitted to owning the gun and the ammunition. The gun's presence resulted in a referral for federal prosecution, and after agreeing to surrender in Rhode Island, the defendant absconded and was not arrested for several years. The fact that the defendant had agreed to surrender and then fled permitted the trial judge to allow evidence of flight without unfairly prejudicing the defense. In approving the admission of flight evidence, the Court of Appeals noted:

> In the case at hand, the appellant's resistance to the execution of the search warrant, his admissions on that occasion, and the unfulfilled promise of self-surrender formed a sufficient factual predicate for the introduction of the flight evidence. This predicate substantially diminished the possibility that the jury might infer guilt solely on the basis of the appellant's flight. To cinch matters, the court's cautionary instructions, twice repeated, mitigated any risk that the jury might give the flight evidence undue weight.[165]

Here, the evidence of flight explained the long delay from the date of indictment to the trial date and added to the inference of consciousness of guilt.[166]

In a California case[167] in which the defendant contested a jury instruction concerning flight, he contended that, when he left the state and committed serious crimes in Arizona following an alleged multiple murder case in California, the act of leaving the state to travel to Arizona could not be construed as flight. He contended that giving

---

163 State v. Ingram, 196 N.J. 23, 951 A.2d 1000, 2008 N.J. LEXIS 879 (2008).

164 People v. Brown, 2009 Cal. App. Unpub. LEXIS 1600 (2009).

165 United States v. Benedetti, 433 F.3d 111, 116, 2005 U.S. App. LEXIS 28490 (1st Cir. 2005).

166 *Id.* at 118.

167 People v. Loker, 80 Cal. Rptr. 3d 630, 2008 Cal. LEXIS 9275 (2008).

the standard jury instruction allowed the jury to draw impermissible inferences concerning his thought processes. The trial court gave the usual jury instruction, which read:

> The [flight] [attempted flight] [escape] [attempted escape] [from custody] of a person [immediately] after the commission of a crime, or after [he] [she] is accused of a crime, is not sufficient in itself to establish [his] [her] guilt, but is a fact which, if proved, may be considered by you in the light of all other proved facts in deciding whether a defendant is guilty or not guilty. The weight to which this circumstance is entitled is a matter for you to decide.[168]

The California reviewing court noted that the facts and the jury instruction did not address the defendant's specific mental state at the time of the alleged crime or of his guilt of any crime, but did allow the jury to consider the circumstances suggesting the defendant's consciousness that he had committed some offense.

While California law requires a flight instruction in cases in which the defendant has removed him- or herself from the scene, judges in other states may have to evaluate the situation to determine whether a defendant's acts actually constitute flight due to a consciousness of guilt. One Florida reviewing court held that flight from a police officer did not have sufficient connection to any crime to make the flight instruction proper.[169] The defendant was near a shopping center during a hurricane when a police officer encountered him standing by a boarded up window that had a couple of boards missing.

Evidence of flight or concealment need not be extremely obvious or visible to everyone. In a District of Columbia case, the alleged perpetrator left the crime scene immediately, removing himself from the area rather quickly, even though his apartment was nearby. The suspect also changed the clothes he had been wearing at the crime scene. He had friends go to his apartment and retrieve his clothing and deliver it to him at his alternate location. The appellate court approved the use of a flight instruction to the jury and agreed that the judge had properly instructed the jurors that, if they found flight, they could give the evidence whatever weight they thought it deserved.[170]

In referring to flight instructions, a federal district court instructed the jury that it could consider a defendant's flight from police to infer consciousness of guilt.[171] Police noticed the defendant driving without a buckled safety belt and attempted a traffic stop. The defendant, who had prior felony convictions, sped away, but police eventually captured him, discovering a gun and drugs. As a general rule, a flight instruction may be given when the evidence warrants it. The trial court told the jury, "[y]ou may also

---

168 CAL. JURY INSTRUCTIONS – CRIM. 2.52 (2005).

169 Remor v. State, 991 So. 2d 957, 2008 Fla. App. LEXIS 14242 (2008).

170 *See* Graham v. United States, 12 A.3d 1159, 2011 D.C. App. LEXIS 30 (2011). *See* case in Part II.

171 United States v. Webster, 442 F.3d 1065, 1066, 2006 U.S. App. LEXIS 8061 (8th Cir. 2006).

consider any evidence of flight by the defendant, along with all of the evidence in the case, and you may consider whether this evidence shows a consciousness of guilt and determine the significance to be attached to any such conduct."[172] Because the jury instruction allowed an inference of guilt, but did not require such a deduction, the reviewing court held that the giving of the flight instruction was proper.

Flight need not come immediately following the crime or its discovery, but may occur months later. In an Indiana child molestation case, the defendant complained on appeal that the trial court erred in admitting evidence concerning his initial failure to appear for trial, the state's investigation to find the defendant, his use of an assumed identity, and evidence of his flight to Mississippi 18 months after being charged. He contended that flight had to occur immediately following the crime or its discovery.[173] The appellate court rejected his argument that his alleged "flight" was not a flight and stated "[t]he evidence of Bennett's flight and assumption of false identity are indicative of a guilty mind and were properly before the jury."[174]

If evidence of flight is used to infer consciousness of guilt, the court may give a flight instruction. Reciprocal fairness would seem to dictate that an instruction on lack of flight should be given, but case law does not require a lack of flight instruction.[175] Courts appear reluctant to offer an absence of flight instruction because the conduct of staying at the crime scene or area is ambiguous at best. In this situation, a suspect may not realize that he or she is soon to be a defendant, or the accused might believe that staying may be viewed as innocence or is actually indicative of innocence.[176]

The decision concerning whether to give a jury instruction on flight is generally left to the discretion of the trial judge. There should be unexplained actual flight, and the flight instructions should be given only where the evidence of flight has considerable **probative value.** Evidence of flight should neither be admitted nor a jury instruction given when there is an independent justification for flight for reasons that cannot be explained to the jury because of a separate prejudicial effect.[177] Typically, the trial judge will advise the jury that flight may be prompted by a variety of motives, and best practice suggests that the judge should instruct the jury to consider all evidence before making an inference of guilt from the fact of flight.

Probative value The tendency of an item of evidence to assist in proving what it was introduced to prove.

172 *Id.* at 1067.

173 Bennett v. State, 883 N.E.2d 888, 892, 2008 Ind. App. LEXIS 713 (2008).

174 *Id.*

175 State v. Williams, 2004 Tenn. Crim. App. LEXIS 191 (2004).

176 *See* Commonwealth v. Hanford, 2007 Pa. Super 345 (2007).

177 Walker v. State, 913 So. 2d 198, 232, 2005 Miss. LEXIS 216 (2005).

§ 6.15 —Unexplained Absence as Death

Pursuant to traditional common law rules and the statutes of many states, "[t]he unexplained absence of a person for seven successive years raises a presumption of death, unless there is proof that the person was alive within the seven year period."[178] Upon a petition by an interested party and upon proof of absence, a court will enter a degree finding a presumption of death if no person has seen the missing person, and there is no explanation other than death.[179] Absentee individuals who have been declared dead prior to the statutory period have often been involved in suicide, accidents, shipwrecks, aircraft accidents, or similar occurrences in which the body would not likely have been found and in which there was a high likelihood of death.

In one New York case, the trial court ruled that the missing person was deceased. The evidence showed that he had told his business partner and his wife that he was intent on ending his life. When he left the marital home, he did not take his driver's license, credit cards, or any personal effects. Medically, he had terminal heart disease, suffered from shortness of breath, and had been diagnosed as an alcoholic. The court took testimony that about 70 percent of individuals with his heart disease do not live five years. Significantly, the missing man's diagnosis was a late-term diagnosis of cardiomyopathy that indicated he needed a heart transplant. A search of all the usual databases, including Social Security, Board of Elections, and others disclosed no activity. The court concluded that the missing man was dead as of the date of his disappearance.[180]

Cases are not in agreement with respect to the presumed death of a fugitive from justice, because that person, if alive, has a good reason to be absent. A good reason or motive for a person's absence may provide sufficient evidence to determine that the individual is not deceased. Absence to avoid a criminal prosecution may constitute a sufficient reason to conclude that a person has not died, but is absent to avoid potential incarceration.[181] In one case, a surety on a defendant's bail bond attempted to avoid forfeiture of bail and introduced evidence that the defendant had disappeared after leaving his car at an airport, and that an intensive search failed to locate him. Other evidence indicated that the defendant had been indicted, was a member of a group on whom a murderous assault had been made, and had a good reason for flight. The court upheld the forfeiture on the grounds that, where there exists a **motive** for or the

> **Motive** The purpose underlying a defendant's conduct; the reason a person forms a criminal intent prior to engaging in a criminal act.

[178] 28 TEX. JUR. *Death* § 4 (2013).

[179] Cavanagh v. Lentz, 2005 Conn. Super. LEXIS 2731 (2005). Due to proof that a woman's husband was missing, had severe mental problems, and had tried to commit suicide at a prior time, the coroner was ordered to prepare a presumptive death certificate.

[180] Matter of Bennett, 2006 N.Y. Slip Op. 50889U (2006).

[181] Starr et al. v. Old Line Life Insurance Co., 104 Cal. App. 4th 487, 496, 128 Cal. Rptr. 2d 282, 288, 2002 Cal. App. LEXIS 5174 (2002).

absence or doubt about the reason for the absence, the presumption of continued life remains.[182]

If a court presumes that a person is dead when he has been missing at least seven years, and his location is unknown and undetermined, the presumption of death can have important consequences for those who would inherit by will or intestate distribution. In many states and in Indiana, the common law presumption of death requires a seven-year absence that is inexplicable.[183] This term has been interpreted by Indiana courts to mean missing from the usual place of residence and no intelligence concerning the missing person has been received by relatives or friends. Washington follows a similar presumption, but presumes that the missing person remains alive. Under the statute, the presumptive heirs and legatees may petition for a distribution of the presumed deceased person's estate. When the court is satisfied that the statutory requirements have been met, a final order distributing the property to the presumptive heirs, devisees, or legatees of the absent person will be entered.[184]

In many states the statutory period has been reduced to five years of absence or less. The rationale and logic for following a period shorter than the traditional seven years makes sense in the present environment given the access to large computer databases and the search abilities available on the Internet. Under present circumstances, disappearing is more difficult than ever, in the absence of actual death. Representative of many jurisdictions, California law provided that a

> person who has not been seen or heard from for a continuous period of five years by those who are likely to have seen or heard from that person, and whose absence is not satisfactorily explained after diligent search or inquiry, is presumed to be dead. The person's death is presumed to have occurred at the end of the period unless there is sufficient evidence to establish that death occurred earlier,[185]

New York has shortened the period for a presumption of death to a continuous absence of three years but allows proof of death in fewer than three years.[186]

§ 6.16 —Regularity of Official Acts

"The government is always presumed to act in good faith,"[187] and this presumption extends to its appointed and elected officials. This rebuttable presumption of regularity supports the official acts of public officials and police officers, and courts presume that

---

[182] People v. Niccoli, 102 Cal. App. 2d 814, 228 P.2d 827 (1951).

[183] Malone v. ReliaStar Life Ins. Co., 2009 U.S. App. LEXIS 5106 (7th Cir. 2009). For probate purposes, Indiana uses a five-year absence.

[184] WASH. REV. CODE § 11.80.100 (2013).

[185] *See* CAL. PROB. CODE § 12401 (2014).

[186] *See* NY CLS EPTL 2-1.7 Presumption of death from absence; effect of exposure to specific peril. (2013). *See also* Matter of Philip v. Lieberman, 851 N.Y.S.2d 141, 2008 N.Y. App. Div. LEXIS 57 (2008), declaring a woman dead after the World Trade Center bombing of 2001.

[187] Long Lane Limited Partnership v. Bibb, 159 Fed. App'x. 189, 2005 U.S. App. LEXIS 26912 (Fed. Cir. 2005).

public officials have properly discharged their official duties, in the absence of clear evidence to the contrary.[188] When a person wishes to prove that a public official has not performed his or her duties properly, that person must meet and overcome the strong presumption that administrators and other public officials have discharged their duties in good faith.[189] To rebut the presumption of proper conduct, the moving party will have to meet the burden by clear and convincing evidence to the contrary[190] or, as one court phrased it, "competent and substantial evidence."[191]

As a general rule, the presumption that governmental officials have acted properly extends to grand jury proceedings.[192] For example, in *United States v. Exson,*[193] the reviewing court refused to dismiss the indictment on the strength of the defense allegation that the prosecution misled the grand jury on material matters. According to the Court of Appeals, even if there were some irregularities in a grand jury proceeding, a dismissal would not be appropriate. The court noted that:

> The proceedings of a grand jury are afforded a strong presumption of regularity, and a defendant faces a heavy burden to overcome that presumption when seeking dismissal of an indictment. See *United States v. Hintzman*, 806 F.2d 840, 843 (8th Cir. 1986). Dismissal due to errors in grand jury proceedings is appropriate only if the defendant shows actual prejudice, see *United States v. Kouba*, 822 F.2d 768, 774 (8th Cir. 1987), and "the petit jury's guilty verdict rendered [any] errors harmless." *Id.*[194]

The presumption of regularity attending official acts applies to the acts of most public officials. One court may presume that another court properly performed its duties until the contrary has been shown and therefore a rebuttable presumption of regularity attaches to a defendant's prior convictions.[195] The Court of Appeals for the Seventh Circuit noted that there is a presumption that a federal trial court acted properly when it admitted evidence and there is a presumption that the evidence has been properly secured by police since its seizure.[196] Unless there has been some showing of fraud, deceit, or other misconduct by the affiant, the police, the prosecutor, or the judge, a presumption of regularity attaches to the obtaining of a warrant from a court.[197]

---

188 Butler v. Principi, 244 F.3d 1337, 201 U.S. App. LEXIS 5270 (Fed. Cir. 2001), United States v. Chemical Foundation, Inc., 272 U.S. 1, 47 S. Ct. 1, 71 L. Ed. 131 (1926), Charleston Television, Inc. v. South Carolina Budget and Control Bd., 373 S.E.2d 890 (1988).

189 Hill v. Geren, 2009 U.S. Dist. LEXIS 10237 (D.C.D.C. 2009).

190 Tecom, Inc. v. United States, 66 Fed. Cl. 736, 768, 2005 U.S. Claims LEXIS 195 (2005).

191 Harrell v. City of Gastonia, 2009 U.S. Dist. LEXIS 6542 (W.D.N.C. 2009).

192 United States v. Diaz, 2006 U.S. Dist. LEXIS 46315 (N.D. Ga. 2006), and United States v. Lucarelli, 2006 U.S. Dist. LEXIS 39664 (D. Conn. 2005).

193 United States v. Exson, 328 F.3d 456, 459, 2003 U.S. App. LEXIS 8836 (8th Cir. 2003).

194 *Id.* at 459.

195 Montana v. Kvislen, 2003 Mont. 27, 314 Mont. 176, 2003 Mont. LEXIS 26 (2003).

196 United States v. Prieto, 549 F.3d 513, 524, 2008 U.S. App. LEXIS 24323 (7th Cir. 2008).

197 In re Directives Pursuant to Section 105b of the Foreign Intelligence Surveillance Act, 2008 U.S. App. LEXIS 27417 (Fed. Cir. 2008).

Unless there is some particularized proof of misconduct, grand jury proceedings are given a presumption of regularity.[198] Trial jurors are considered public officials for purposes of this presumption and are presumed to have followed jury instructions properly and in good faith.[199] As an officer of the court, a prosecutor's decisions are granted a presumption of regularity unless a defendant can demonstrate that a prosecutor acted with an improper animus toward a defendant.[200]

§ 6.17 Constitutionality Tests for Presumptions and Inferences

Criminal cases require the prosecution to prove all the elements of any charged crime beyond a reasonable doubt, but when inferences and presumptions are presented in a case, the prosecution may be proving one fact and not actually proving the inferred fact. A legislature may create inferences and presumptions by providing that "certain facts shall be prima facie or presumptive evidence of other facts."[201] Even though a legislature may have created an inference or presumption, due process clauses in the Fifth and Fourteenth Amendments require that legislation meet a fundamental fairness standard in a criminal trial. If the legislation requires a jury to make a mandatory deduction from proof of a basic fact, this violates due process. A law or jury instruction that might allow a jury to interpret a presumption as conclusive or mandatory violates due process.[202] Even allowing or permitting the jury to make the deduction or inference constitutionally requires a close logical connection between the basic fact and the presumed fact.

Early decisions of the United States Supreme Court set forth a number of different standards to measure the validity of statutory presumptions. One test was whether there was a "rational connection" between the basic fact and the presumed fact. A second was whether the legislature might have made it a crime to do the thing from which the presumption authorized an inference. A third was whether it would be more convenient for the defendant or for the prosecution to adduce evidence of the presumed fact.

However, in *Tot v. United States,*[203] the Court singled out one of these tests as controlling, and the *Tot* rule has been followed in the two subsequent cases in which the issue has been presented. The *Tot* Court considered a federal statute that, as construed, made it a crime for a person previously convicted of a crime of violence to receive any firearm or ammunition that had been transported in interstate or foreign commerce.

---

198 United States v. Davis, 2009 U.S. Dist. LEXIS 19404 (S.D. N.Y. 2009). *See also* Culp v. State, 2005 Miss. LEXIS 828 (2005).

199 United States v. McCuiston, 2006 U.S. App. LEXIS 16292 (5th Cir. 2006).

200 United States v. Woods, 2009 U.S. App. LEXIS 93 (4th Cir. 2009). Unpublished opinion.

201 29 AM. JUR. 2D *Evidence* § 7 (1994).

202 *See* Sandstrom v. Montana, 442 U.S. 510, 1979 U.S. LEXIS 113 (1979).

203 Tot v. United States, 319 U.S. 463, 1943 U.S. LEXIS 531 (1943).

The statute further provided that "the possession of a firearm or ammunition by any such person shall be presumptive evidence that such firearm or ammunition was shipped or transported or received, as the case may be, by such person in violation of this Act."[204] Proof of possession and a prior violent crime equaled guilt with the presumption carrying half the burden of proof. The *Tot* Court noted that the "due process clauses of the Fifth and Fourteenth Amendments set limits upon the power of Congress or that of a state legislature to make the proof of one fact or group of facts evidence of the existence of the ultimate fact on which guilt is predicated."[205]

The Court held the presumption unconstitutional and decided that the controlling test for determining the validity of a statutory presumption was that there be a rational connection between the fact proved and the fact presumed. The Court stated:

> Under our decisions a statutory presumption cannot be sustained if there be no rational connection between the fact proved and the ultimate fact presumed, if the inference of the one from proof of the other is arbitrary because of lack of connection between the two in common experience. This is not to say that a valid presumption may not be created upon a view of relation broader than that a jury might take in a specific case. But where the inference is so strained as not to have a reasonable relation to the circumstances of life as we know them, it is not competent for the legislature to create it as a rule governing the procedure of courts.[206]

In two subsequent cases that remain good law, *United States v. Gainey*[207] and *United States v. Romano,*[208] the Supreme Court evaluated the constitutionality of criminal presumptions related to companion sections of the Internal Revenue Code dealing with illegal alcohol stills. The presumption in *Gainey* was that Jack Gainey's presence at an illegal distillery permitted, but did not require, a jury to infer that Gainey was "carrying on" the business of a distiller, unless the defendant explained being present at the still to the satisfaction of the jury. The trial judge told the jury that the presumption was permissive and did not require the jury to convict even if he was proved to be present at the still. The Supreme Court held that the *Gainey* presumption should be tested by the "rational connection" standard announced in the *Tot* case, and sustained the statutory presumption and the conviction. The presumption of "carrying on" the business carried weight because few illegal distillers would allow strangers to observe their illegal still. The *Gainey* Court recognized that, in enacting the statutory presumption, Congress allowed the unexplained evidence to have its natural probative value.

The presumption under attack in the *Romano* case was identical to that in *Gainey*, except that the *Romano* jury was authorized to conclude from the defendant's presence at an illegal still that he or she had possession, custody, or control of the still. In the *Romano* case, the trial judge explained to the jury that proof of the defendant's presence

---

204 15 U.S.C. 902 (f).

205 *Tot* at 467.

206 *Id.* at 467-468.

207 United States v. Gainey, 380 U.S. 63, 1965 U.S. LEXIS 1733 (1965).

208 United States v. Romano, 382 U.S. 136, 1965 U.S. LEXIS 207 (1965).

at the still would be sufficient evidence to support a conviction. The Court held this presumption invalid on the ground that "absent some showing of the defendant's function at the still, its connection with possession is too tenuous to permit a reasonable inference of guilt; the inference of the one from proof of the other is arbitrary"[209] and not based on good probabilities. In effect, presence did not indicate possession, although sometimes presence might indicate "carrying on" the business of distiller. Though quite similar to the *Gainey* presence at the still, the *Romano* case had a different outcome based on the manner in which the Supreme Court interpreted the two presumptions and the judges' jury instructions.

A "statutory presumption for criminal cases must be regarded as 'irrational' or 'arbitrary' and thus unconstitutional, unless it can at least be said with substantial assurance that the presumed fact is more likely than not to follow from the proof of the proved fact on which it is made to depend."[210] The Supreme Court applied this legal standard in *Leary v. United States*, when the Court overturned a federal statute that authorized juries to infer from the defendant's possession of marijuana that the defendant knew that the marijuana had been illegally imported into the United States. The presumption of knowing that marijuana was imported from proof of mere possession was invalid under the due process clause because there was no proof that typical marijuana possessors are generally aware that their marijuana was locally grown, that their marijuana was likely to have been imported, or that it actually was imported.[211]

In the year following the *Leary* decision, the Supreme Court considered the constitutionality of instructing a jury that it may infer from the defendant's possession of heroin and cocaine that the defendant knew that the drugs had been illegally imported.[212] The Court noted that there was a reason for the logic of the presumption of knowledge of importation from proof of possession.

> It may be that the ordinary jury would not always know that heroin illegally circulating in this country is not manufactured here. But Turner and others who sell or distribute heroin are in a class apart. Such people have regular contact with a drug which they know cannot be legally bought or sold; their livelihood depends on its availability; some of them have actually engaged in the smuggling process.[213]

The Court held that the inference with regard to heroin was valid, judged by either of the two tests stated in the *Tot* decision.

As a general rule, when dealing with statutory presumptions that declare that, on proof of one fact, another fact may be inferred or presumed, such a statute is probably constitutional, provided that there is a rational relationship between the basic fact proved and the fact presumed, that the presumed fact proved from the original fact cannot be arbitrary or unreasonable, and that the finder of fact may give the presumed fact

---

209 Tot v. United States, 319 U.S. 463, 467, 1943 U.S. LEXIS 531 (1943).

210 Leary v. United States, 395 U.S. 6, 36, 1969 U.S. LEXIS 3271 (1969).

211 *Id.*

212 Turner v. United States, 396 U.S. 398, 1970 U.S. LEXIS 3146 (1970).

213 *Id.* at 416.

the weight it believes to be appropriate.[214] In New Jersey, the state law governing presumptions holds that, any time a firearm or other weapon is found in a vehicle, the individual in the vehicle is presumed to be in possession of the firearm and that, where more than one person is in the vehicle, the presumption is that all persons possess the firearm, unless it is found on a particular person.[215] Any person who possesses a handgun is presumed to possess the firearm illegally, according to New Jersey law, because of the state's strong licensing requirements that most individuals cannot meet. The New Jersey statutes on presumptions involving firearms appear to be in compliance with the *Tot* standard on presumptions, in that it is more likely than not that a person possessing a gun in New Jersey does so illegally.

In a case involving similar reasoning concerning presumptions, police approached a vehicle that matched the description of a car occupied by individuals suspected of criminal activity. When the driver saw the officer approaching, he attempted to get into the car to leave. A struggle ensued, and the police prevailed. At that time, an officer discovered a handgun wedged between the driver's seat and the console. Under New York law, the presence of a firearm in an automobile serves as presumptive evidence of its illegal possession by all persons then occupying the vehicle. The officers testified that none of the defendants was ever actually seen handling the gun, but they observed the defendant as one of the occupants of the vehicle. The driver's testimony that he alone possessed the gun failed to rebut the presumption of New York law that implicated all the passengers in possession. The evidence showed that the occupants of the car had been traveling together for several weeks and must have known about the gun. The Appellate Division of the Supreme Court believed that the presumption of possession by all the vehicle occupants was entirely rational. Because it was more likely than not that all occupants possessed the gun, and the presumption had not been rebutted, the reviewing court upheld the conviction for criminal possession of a gun.[216] The result was consistent with the Tot rationale covering the constitutionality of presumptions, and the New York jury rationally could have determined that the passenger did not have possession of the firearm, if it believed that the evidence rebutted the presumption and that the defendant–passenger was not also in possession of the gun.

In an Illinois case involving a presumption that a driver had been proven to be under the influence of alcohol, the Supreme Court reversed a double homicide conviction. In accordance with then existing Illinois law, the trial court instructed the jury with language from 9-3(b) of the Illinois code and rephrased it into a jury instruction that stated: "If you find from your consideration of all the evidence that the defendant was under the influence of alcohol at the time of the alleged violation, such evidence shall be presumed to be evidence of a reckless act unless disproved by evidence to the

---

214 29 AM. JUR. 2D *Evidence* § 7 (1994).

215 N.J. STAT. 2C:39-2 (a) (2013).

216 People v. Tabb, 12 A.D.3d 951, 952, 785 N.Y.S.2d 193, 194, 2004 N.Y. App. Div. LEXIS 14284 (N.Y. 2004), *appeal denied*, 4 N.Y.3d 768, 2005 N.Y. LEXIS 419 (2005).

contrary."[217] Other jury instructions assisted the jury in finding that the defendant was under the influence of alcohol, when there had been proof that his blood-alcohol level was .08 or greater, but the instructions did not require such a finding. The court instructed the jury that:

> If you find beyond a reasonable doubt that at the time the defendant drove a vehicle that the amount of alcohol concentration in the defendant's blood or breath was 0.08 or more, you may presume that the defendant was under the influence of alcohol. You never are required to make this presumption. It is for the jury to determine whether the presumption should be drawn. You should consider all the evidence in determining whether the defendant was under the influence of alcohol. Illinois Pattern Jury Instructions, Criminal, No. 23.30 (4th ed. 2000).[218]

According to the Supreme Court of Illinois, because a reasonable juror could conclude that the jury instruction mandated a finding of recklessness without any factual connection between the intoxication and the reckless act, the statute had created a mandatory presumption. The effect of this mandatory presumption improperly and unconstitutionally shifted the burden of disproving recklessness to the defendant, which required a reversal of the homicide convictions.[219]

In a Virginia case, the law provided that a person who possessed rental property and failed to return the property within five days of the written date of return would be deemed guilty of larceny.[220] The statute appeared to create a mandatory presumption, but the defendant could introduce evidence that would rebut the *prima facie* case created by the failure to return. In one Virginia case, the woman rented a motor vehicle for one day, but extended the rental agreement verbally several times, at least through the middle of the rental month. The renter ignored two demand letters for the return of the vehicle, and a month later, she still had the car. Using the permissive inference, the reviewing court upheld the conviction of motor vehicle theft based on holding over the rental period, given that the defendant offered no reasonable explanation sufficient to rebut the prima facie inference of theft.[221]

One California case appeared to create a mandatory presumption that would be inconsistent with due process and the cases decided by the Supreme Court of the United States. A trial court convicted a California defendant of possessing hydriodic acid with intent to manufacture methamphetamine. State law provided that, when a person possessed sufficient amounts of red phosphorus and iodine, the person would be deemed to have possessed hydriodic acid, even if no acid had ever been synthesized. The defendant contended on appeal that the statute created a mandatory presumption that if one

217 People v. Pomykala, 2003 Ill. LEXIS 7 (2003).

218 *Id.*

219 *Id.*

220 VA. CODE ANN. § 18.2-117 (2014).

221 Reed v. Commonwealth, 62 Va. App. 270, 278 (2013). For a decision overturning a conviction based on a mandatory presumption, *see* Carella v. California, 491 U.S. 263, 109 S. Ct. 2419, 105 L. Ed. 2d 218 (1989).

possessed the two precursor chemicals then one was guilty of possessing hydriodic acid. The effect of the law permitted the government to convict for possession of hydriodic acid without any proof of possession of hydriodic acid. In a decision by the Supreme Court of California, the court held that there was no presumption at issue, but that the language that appeared to be a mandatory presumption was really a "valid exercise of the Legislature's power to create substantive law and define crimes."[222] The defendant's intent to manufacture methamphetamine required proof of possession of hydriodic acid, which she did not possess. The Supreme Court of California upheld the conviction,[223] and the Supreme Court of the United States refused to review the decision.[224]

To summarize, when determining the constitutionality of statutory presumptions, the court must find a rational connection between the basic fact and the presumed fact, and it must find that there is a reasonable possibility in the ordinary course of events that the conclusion required by the presumption is in accord with human experience. To meet constitutional standards, the presumed fact must more likely than not flow from the basic fact. Second, a presumption that has the effect of shifting the burden to the defense to disprove an element of the crime is unconstitutional.

§ 6.18 Stipulations

A stipulation "is an agreement, admission, or concession made in a judicial proceeding by the parties or their attorneys."[225] The stipulation serves as a substitute for evidence that has the effect of removing some issues from the lawsuit because the parties have clearly indicated that they have no disagreement or dispute concerning the subject or matter covered by the agreement. A stipulation amounts to a concession by both parties to the existence or nonexistence of a fact, an agreement concerning the contents of a document, or an agreement over what a witness would have said if the witness had actually testified. An Ohio court suggested that a stipulation is a substitute for evidence that does away with the need for evidence and is actually considered evidence.[226]

The parties may make stipulations orally or in writing, but the agreement must clearly be part of the court record. While stipulations may be encouraged, the opposing side is not obligated to stipulate, as stipulating would otherwise have the effect of preventing that party from presenting part of its case with actual evidence. In one case involving aggravated domestic violence, the defendant complained that the prosecution

---

222 People v. McCall, 32 Cal. 4th 175, 179, 82 P.3d 351, 354, 8 Cal. Rptr. 3d 337, 340, 2004 Cal. LEXIS 8 (2004).

223 *Id.*

224 McCall v. California, 542 U.S. 923, 2004 U.S. LEXIS 4451 (2004).

225 73 AM. JUR. 2D *Stipulations* § 1 (2014).

226 State v. Scott, 2008 Ohio 1862, 2008 Ohio App. LEXIS 1579 (2008).

should have accepted his offer to stipulate to prior domestic violence convictions. Because no party can be required to stipulate to any fact and because the prosecutor wanted the jury to hear some evidence concerning the prior crimes and not just the existing convictions, the prosecutor properly refused to stipulate.[227] If a defendant dissents from his counsel's offer to stipulate to a matter, the stipulation cannot be accepted.[228]

A stipulation authorizes the court or jury to find the existence of such a fact and to consider that fact without any further proof. A judge does not have to allow the stipulation when the stipulation would create a potential for unfair prejudice to one party or would be against public policy. The triers of fact in criminal cases are not, however, bound to accept the stipulated fact as true. In spite of this fact, California jury instructions indicate that stipulations between the parties are binding on the jury.[229] California juries are told that "if the attorneys have stipulated or agreed to a fact, you must regard that fact as proven,"[230] but juries hearing criminal cases may choose to disregard the stipulation and are permitted to find to the contrary if persuaded by other evidence or for any reason or for no reason.

In some situations, stipulated testimony merely amounts to a mutual agreement by both parties that, if a certain person were present, he or she would testify under oath to the facts contained within the agreed stipulation. As a general rule, once a stipulation is agreed upon, it may not be unilaterally withdrawn.[231] Following this principle, in a Washington case, a defendant was not permitted to withdraw his trial stipulation that he had been properly given his ***Miranda* warnings,** even after a police officer testified that the officer had not been the one who gave the warnings.[232] Similarly, in a Texas murder case, the defendant entered a written stipulation at his first trial that he had stabbed and killed his wife, among other facts. When the trial court declared a mistrial, an issue for the second murder trial involved whether the stipulation from the first trial should be binding on the defendant for the second trial on the same issues. The trial judge admitted the stipulation at the second trial, noting that it had originally been made for trial, and it would be admitted as a valid stipulation. On appeal, the reviewing court upheld the trial court decision that admitted the stipulation at the second trial,[233] noting that the defendant had placed no limitation on its use, and the stipulation had never been withdrawn.

> ***Miranda* warnings** Warnings that must be given to persons who are in custody (arrest) and who police wish to interrogate.

227 State v. Newman, 208 Ariz. 507, 95 P.3d 950, 2004 Ariz. App. LEXIS 118 (2004).

228 People v. Lee, 379 Ill. App. 3d 533, 538, 2008 Ill. App. LEXIS 117 (2008).

229 CAL. JURY INSTRUCTIONS – CRIM. 1.02 (2005).

230 *Id.*

231 State v. McCullough, 2008 Ohio 3055; 2008 Ohio App. LEXIS 2574 (2008).

232 State v. Howell, 2008 Wash. App. LEXIS 799 (April 8, 2008). Unreported opinion.

233 Carrasco v. State, 154 S.W.3d 127, 128, 2005 Tex. Crim. App. LEXIS 76 (2005).

While the courts have indicated that stipulations should be encouraged, a party is not required to accept the adversary's offer, and a trial court cannot require that one party stipulate to evidence when the other party wants to present evidence. In an Alabama murder case, the defendant contended that the trial court had committed error when it refused to require the prosecution to disclose any mitigating circumstances evidence and to stipulate for the jury that these mitigating circumstances were to be considered in determining whether to impose the death penalty. The appellate court rejected the defendant's contention and noted that, in Alabama, no party is required to accept the opponent's offer to stipulate and may insist that the opposing party introduce facts to prove the offered stipulation.[234] However, a court in a different jurisdiction held that a party may be required to stipulate. In a case involving a felon who possessed a gun under a disability and who was charged with aggravated assault, the defendant offered to stipulate that he was not permitted to possess firearms due to his prior felony conviction. The prosecution refused because it wanted to introduce evidence of his prior aggravated assault convictions, rather than allow the defendant merely to admit that he was a felon. The reviewing court reversed the conviction because the facts underlying the prior felony proved to be unduly prejudicial, considering the probative value was considered and the defendant's admission to being a felon.[235] The rule seems to be that, where an element of a crime requires proof of a prior felony and the defendant offers to stipulate to the felony, a prosecutor may be forced to agree to a stipulation of the felony where some prejudice to the defendant's case might otherwise result.

A stipulation is also used as a means of determining whether certain evidence will be admitted into court. In criminal cases in which the parties have stipulated to the admissibility of certain evidence, that evidence is admissible to corroborate other evidence of the defendant's participation in the crime charged. In the absence of any claim that the stipulation was entered into by mistake, inadvertence, fraud, or misrepresentation, counsel may stipulate regarding evidence that may be received. As a general rule, once a stipulation has been the subject of agreement and has been filed with the court, one of the parties may not withdraw from the stipulation without the consent of the other,[236] and usually consent of the court will also be required. Judges typically ask that the application for withdrawal be made in a timely manner, and an effort to withdraw a stipulation on appeal will not usually be considered timely.[237] In a death penalty case,[238] an Arizona trial court properly accepted a defendant's stipulation, which served as an aggravating circumstance, that he had been convicted of a crime where a sentence of life imprisonment was imposable. Because he made the stipulation

---

234 Lewis v. State, 2007 Ala. Crim. App. LEXIS 201 (2007).

235 Ferguson v. State, 2005 Ark. LEXIS 361 (2005).

236 73 AM. JUR. 2D *Stipulations* § 11 (2014).

237 Malutin v. State, 198 P.3d 1177, 2009 Alaska App. LEXIS 5 (2009).

238 State v. Tucker, 215 Ariz. 298, 308, 2007 Ariz. LEXIS 64 (Ariz. 2007), *cert. denied*, Tucker v. Arizona, 128 S. Ct. 296, 2007 U.S. LEXIS 10884 (2007).

and made no contemporaneous objection, the reviewing court found that there was no error regarding the stipulation.

There are limitations on the use of stipulations. It is clear that a stipulation amounting to a complete concession by the defense to the prosecutor's case would be inconsistent with a plea of not guilty and should not be permitted. A stipulation that is clearly erroneous should not be accepted, and its acceptance probably would be justification for reversal on constitutional grounds. Also, the court is not required to admit a stipulation as a substitute for evidence that may be detrimental to the defendant's case.[239]

As a rule, a stipulation may be withdrawn, but doing so generally requires the trial court's consent. Relief from a stipulation may be granted where the agreement was made as the result of inadvertence, mistake, or excusable neglect, as long as the opposing party has not been damaged by relying on the stipulation.[240] Once withdrawn, a stipulation ceases to be effective for any purpose. The withdrawal of a stipulation, however, would be a reasonable basis for a continuance to allow the opposing party time to prepare evidence concerning matters formerly embraced by the stipulation and to avoid undue surprise.

§ 6.19 —Polygraph Tests

As a general rule, the results of **polygraph examinations** are not admissible in criminal cases, although there are a few examples where the results will be admissible. For example, where the prosecutor, defense counsel, and the defendant all stipulate to the admissibility prior to the examination, Nevada will permit the admission of the test results.[241] Where all parties agree to the admissibility of the results, there seems to be no reason to exclude them, even though many courts believe that the polygraph produces unreliable evidence and may involve possible dangers of undue prejudice to one of the parties. Jurisdictions, represented by Nevada, have determined that the admissibility is appropriate when the parties agree. The changes brought to scientific evidence admissibility after the *Daubert v. Merrell Dow Pharmaceutical* case in 1993 have caused some federal courts to retreat from a general exclusion of polygraph evidence, and the old per se rule of exclusion has also retreated to some extent.[242]

Polygraph examinations An electromechanical instrument that simultaneously records certain physiological changes in the human body, which are believed to be involuntarily caused by an examinee's conscious attempts to deceive an interrogator while responding to a carefully prepared set of questions.

---

239 United States v. Grassi, 602 F.2d 1192 (5th Cir. 1979).

240 73 AM. JUR. 2D *Stipulations* § 13 (2014).

241 Houston v. Schomig, 533 F.3d 1076, 1086, 2008 U.S. App. LEXIS 16251 (9th Cir. 2008) citing Jackson v. State, 116 Nev. 334, 2000 Nev. LEXIS 35 (2000).

242 140 A.L.R. FED. 525 (2013).

Recognizing the changes in scientific evidence admission after *Daubert*, the Fifth Circuit Court of Appeals follows a three-step analysis to determine polygraph admissibility.[243] Courts must first determine whether the polygraph evidence possesses sufficient reliability to be admissible as scientific, technical, or other specialized knowledge, Next, the court must determine whether the offered evidence is relevant to any issue in the trial. Finally, the court must decide whether the polygraph evidence will have an unusually prejudicial effect when considered with its probative value (ability to make issues clearer). This does not mean that every polygraph exam result will be admitted, but it opens the door to the prospect that more test results could find admissibility. A majority of jurisdictions hold that polygraph evidence is generally inadmissible. Representative of the majority view, Louisiana holds that polygraph evidence is not admissible at a criminal trial for any reason, because it encourages jury speculation and usurps the jury's role.[244] An Illinois appellate court reversed a conviction for first-degree murder on the ground that prejudicial error occurred when the trial judge permitted the prosecution, during its case-in-chief, to mention that the defendant had been driven by police to take a polygraph examination. An officer testified that, during the drive to the testing station, she stated that she feared the test results would not help the defendant's case, and the officer noted that the defendant made some inculpatory statements to the officer. In reversing the conviction, the reviewing court noted, "[t]he State's suggestion of reliability of the defendant's statement based on her anticipated failure of the polygraph test is an improper purpose for the admission of polygraph evidence."[245] When witnesses inadvertently mention polygraph testing, the refusal, or offer, to take this test does not automatically result in a reversal of a resulting conviction, especially where a defense attorney improperly asked a polygraph-related question.[246]

Although 27 states have a complete ban on admitting results of polygraph testing,[247] a substantial minority of courts admits polygraph evidence upon stipulation of the parties.[248] New Jersey prohibits the admission of polygraph results in virtually all cases, but permitted it in one case in which the defendant told the jury in mid-trial from the witness stand that he would take a polygraph test. The test results were admitted, but upon very unusual facts.[249] Georgia generally prohibits the admission of polygraph evidence, but Georgia courts will admit the results where the parties have stipulated in favor of admission.[250] Some states have statutes that provide for the

---

243 Ulmer v. State Farm, 897 F. Supp. 299, 302, 1995 U.S. Dist. LEXIS 13295 (W.D. La. 1995).

244 State v. Franklin, 956 So. 2d 823, 2007 La. App. LEXIS 901 (La. 2007), *writ denied*, 2008 La. LEXIS 86 (2008). *See also* Cook v. State, 928 So. 2d 589; 2006 La. App. LEXIS 242 (2006).

245 People v. Washington, 363 Ill. App. 3d 13, 20, 842 N.E.2d 1193, 1199, 2006 Ill. App. LEXIS 24 (2006).

246 State v. Stewart, 265 S.W.3d 309, 316, 2008 Mo. App. LEXIS 1098 (2008).

247 *See* Lee v. Martinez, 136 N.M. 166, 2004 N.M. LEXIS 378 (2004), for a list of states that refuse to admit polygraph testing results.

248 *Id.* Case offers a list of states admitting polygraph results upon stipulation.

249 State v. A.O., 2009 N.J. LEXIS 51 (2009).

250 Hortman v. State, 293 Ga. App. 803, 807, 2008 Ga. App. LEXIS 1082 (2008).

admissibility of polygraph results by stipulation, while others accomplish this result by court decision.

The California Evidence Code provides that:

> Notwithstanding any other provision of law, the results of a polygraph examination, the opinion of a polygraph examiner, or any reference to an offer to take, failure to take, or taking of a polygraph examination, shall not be admitted into evidence in any criminal proceeding, including pretrial and post conviction motions and hearings, or in any trial or hearing of a juvenile for a criminal offense, whether heard in juvenile or adult court, unless all parties stipulate to the admission of such results.[251]

A California court held that the stipulation statute that withholds admission unless all parties agree does not violate the defendant's constitutional rights where the defendant wanted polygraph results admitted at his trial, but the prosecutor would not stipulate to admission.[252] The defendant in the mentioned case unsuccessfully alleged that the statute violated his due process right to introduce relevant evidence and that the statute was unconstitutional.

§ 6.20 Summary

Presumptions and inferences are utilized in order to save the time of the court and to achieve results that the courts and legislatures have determined are necessary in the administration of justice. The presumption takes the place of evidence in certain instances, and until facts that overcome the presumption are shown, the presumptive facts are accepted as true.

Presumptions are classified as rebuttable presumptions and conclusive presumptions. A rebuttable presumption may be overcome by evidence to the contrary; a conclusive presumption cannot be rebutted.

There are many specific examples of both rebuttable and conclusive presumptions. Presumptions are used sparingly in criminal cases and are looked at very carefully by reviewing courts to determine whether they place an unreasonable burden on the accused. Some of the specific presumptions that are prevalent in criminal cases are the presumption that a person is innocent until proven guilty beyond a reasonable doubt, the presumption that a person is sane, the presumption that a person in possession of recently stolen property knows that the property was stolen, and the presumption that all people know the general public laws of the state and country in which they reside.

Legislative bodies are not without controls when determining what presumptions are effective in law. The due process clauses of the Fifth and Fourteenth Amendments set limits upon legislatures when making proof that one fact or a group of facts serve as

---

251 CAL. EVID. CODE § 351.1 (2014).

252 People v. Richardson, 77 Cal. Rptr. 3d 163, 221, 2008 Cal. LEXIS 6208 (2008).

proof of a deduced or presumed fact. There is the danger that a presumption may subtly shift the burden of proof in an unconstitutional manner. Particularly in recent years, statutory presumptions have been subject to review on the grounds that they are unconstitutional. A presumption that was arbitrary, irrational, or shifted the burden of proof would violate the due process clauses of the Constitution.

Stipulation provides another means of relieving the parties of the necessity of introducing evidence. The stipulation, which should be used more often by the courts, indicates that the parties are willing to agree to the truth of certain allegations, leaving only the truly disputed facts to be determined by the jury or court.

It is a mistake for those involved in the criminal justice process to rely heavily on presumptions. Countervailing evidence may be offered when the presumption is in favor of the prosecution, and the prosecution must be prepared to reinforce the presumption. The prosecution must also be prepared to rebut presumptions that are favorable to the defense.

Although stipulations are excellent ways of assuring judicial economy, their improper use can lead to acquittal of guilty individuals and retrials for some. Many prosecutors have gone to trial unprepared because of misinterpretation of the effect of a stipulation. To avoid this pitfall, the investigator and prosecutor should be prepared with admissible evidence in the event that the opposing party disputes the fact that a stipulation was made, or if mistake or fraud is claimed.

CHAPTER SIX: QUESTIONS AND REVIEW EXERCISES

1. What is a presumption and how does this evidence theory operate? How is an inference different from a presumption? What is a stipulation?
2. In the case of a presumption, what is the procedural effect when one party introduces evidence that, if believed, would establish the basic fact of the presumption?
3. Offer two examples of presumptions of law.
4. Explain why a conclusive presumption of fact is probably not appropriate in a criminal case and would most likely violate due process.
5. How would a prosecutor rebut the presumption of innocence? As a practical matter, at what point has this presumption of law been rebutted?
6. It is often stated that everyone is presumed to be sane, so that generally, a prosecutor need not prove sanity. Where the defendant pleads the defense of insanity and introduces some evidence of lack of sanity, what are the various theories that the prosecutor must follow to rebut the evidence of insanity?
7. What is the logical basis for the presumption against suicide in a criminal case?

8. When a person has been found in possession of recently stolen property, should an inference that the person knew that the property was stolen arise? What could a defendant do that would explain the apparent possession of recently stolen property?
9. It has often been stated that a person intends the natural and probable consequences of his or her actions. In *Sandstrom v. Montana* (1979) the Supreme Court ruled that giving such a jury instruction that included the concept of "natural and probable consequences" language had the effect of shifting the burden of proof to the defendant. How can a court judge use this language and avoid the error noted in *Sandstrom v. Montana*?
10. When a person takes flight or conceals his or her whereabouts immediately following a criminal act, may such conduct by a suspect indicate a knowledge or consciousness of guilt? In the absence of an explanation, should this inference be used in criminal cases? Why or why not?
11. A "statutory presumption for criminal cases must be regarded as 'irrational' or 'arbitrary' and thus unconstitutional, unless it can at least be said with substantial assurance that the presumed fact is more likely than not to follow from the proof of the proved fact on which it is made to depend."[253] Why should a court take a different position with respect to possession of marijuana and possession of heroin, if possession of either one gave rise to a presumption or inference that a possessor knew that the marijuana or heroin was imported? Explain.
12. When is a stipulation appropriate? May a judge force a party to stipulate to facts that are not really in dispute? Explain. Could the parties stipulate to the results of a polygraph exam and make the exam admissible when the results normally would not be admitted by the judge?

---

253 Leary v. United States, 395 U.S. 6, 36, 1969 U.S. LEXIS 3271 (1969).

General Admissibility Tests

Relevancy and Materiality

7

There is a principle—not so much a rule of evidence as a presupposition involved in the very conception of a rational system, as contrasted with the old formal and mechanical systems—which forbids receiving anything irrelevant, not logically probative.... The two leading principles should be brought into conspicuous relief, (1) that nothing is to be received which is not logically probative of some matter requiring to be proved; and (2) that everything which is thus probative should come in, unless a clear ground of policy or law excludes it.

Thayer, Evidence (1898)

Chapter Contents

KEY TERMS AND CONCEPTS	
Exculpatory Circumstances	Relevancy of Defenses
Incriminating Circumstances	Relevancy of Character Evidence
Materiality	Probative Value
Motive	Unfair Prejudice
Relevancy	Unfair Surprise

§ 7.1 Introduction

This chapter and Chapter 8 focus on general admissibility tests (relevancy, materiality, and competency) for evidence that are applied by the courts when considering whether to admit or exclude evidence. This chapter concerns the concepts of general relevancy and materiality, as well as their effects on admission and exclusion of evidence, and Chapter 8 explains competency of evidence and witnesses.

Because the primary objective and purpose in a criminal trial are to determine the truth regarding the issues presented, the general rule considers all evidence admissible unless, upon proper objection, it is subject to exclusion under the established evidence rules. In times past, the opposing attorney raised a general objection, contending that the proposed evidence was irrelevant, immaterial, incompetent, or not relevant. The better and more common practice suggests that the objecting party offer a specific objection such as a hearsay objection, an objection to a compound question, or an objection that a question assumes facts not yet in evidence so the judge has a clear basis for making a ruling. Unless the reason for the objection is obvious from the context, the judge may ask the challenger to offer a reason that supports the claim that the evidence should be excluded from trial consideration.

For those involved in the criminal justice process, it is important to understand these relevancy and materiality rules. In many instances, evidence that has been laboriously obtained and prepared for introduction is excluded because it does not meet the relevancy and materiality tests.

§ 7.2 Relevancy Defined

Rule 401

TEST FOR RELEVANT EVIDENCE

Evidence is relevant if:

(a) it has any tendency to make a fact more or less probable than it would be without the evidence; and

(b) the fact is of consequence in determining the action.[1]

One way to analyze the concept of relevancy is to divide it into two separate concepts: logical relevancy and legal relevancy. One Missouri court noted that "[e]vidence must be both logically and legally relevant to be admissible."[2] An item of evidence may meet the logical relevancy test if it sways the trier of fact concerning the existence or nonexistence of any important fact. As one court noted, "[e]ach piece of logically relevant evidence need not be a slam-dunk; it must only be evidence which makes a fact of consequence more probable than not."[3] Even though a proposed item of evidence is logically relevant, that item of evidence may be excluded where it lacks legal relevancy. For example, a series of gruesome color photographs might be logically relevant because they prove death or some other issue. When the fact of death has not been disputed, it is possible to contend that the introduction of photographs of the deceased person should be excluded because they may have the tendency to cause the jury to render a decision based on emotion rather than logic. Although most photos in this category are admitted, some cases will exclude such images after a careful scrutiny by a trial judge. In this type of case, the photographs can be classified as logically relevant because they prove one or more issues in the case, but some of the photographs may be excluded as legally irrelevant because those photographs present the unfair danger of inflaming the jury.[4]

In an older case, a Connecticut court clearly explained the connection between logical and legal relevancy when it stated:

> It is not logical relevance alone, however, that secures the admission of evidence. Logically relevant evidence must also be legally relevant... that is, not subject to exclusion for any one of the following prejudicial effects: (1) where the facts offered may unduly arouse the jury's emotions, hostility or sympathy, (2) where the proof and

---

1 FED. R. EVID. 401.

2 Crow v. Crawford, 259 S.W.3d 10, 2008 Mo. App. LEXIS 666 (Mo. 2008) and Murrell v. State (In re Murrell), 215 S.W.3d 96, 2007 Mo. LEXIS 21 (2007).

3 State v. Miller, 208 S.W.3d 284, 2006 Mo. App. LEXIS 1737 (2006).

4 As a practical matter, gruesome photographs are often admitted. *See, e.g.*, State v. Bowman, 289 Conn. 809, 2008 Conn. LEXIS 565 (Conn. 2008). *See also* Franklin v. Bradshaw, 2009 U.S. Dist. LEXIS 23715 (W.D. Ohio 2009).

> answering evidence it provokes may create a side issue that will unduly distract the jury from the main issues, (3) where the evidence offered and the counterproof will consume an undue amount of time, and (4) where the defendant, having no reasonable ground to anticipate the evidence, is unfairly surprised and unprepared to meet it.[5]

As a general rule, logically relevant evidence may be excluded by a judge as legally irrelevant where the "probative value is substantially outweighed by a danger of one or more of the following: unfair prejudice, confusing the issues, misleading the jury, undue delay, wasting time, or needlessly presenting cumulative evidence."[6]

A. Relevant Evidence

Black's Law Dictionary defines relevant evidence as "[e]vidence tending to prove or disprove a matter in issue."[7]

Relevant evidence has also been described as "evidence that in some degree advances the inquiry, and thus has probative value and is prima facie admissible."[8]

In *Corpus Juris Secundum*, logical relevancy is defined as "the existence of such a relationship in logic between the fact of which evidence is offered and a fact in issue that the existence of the former renders probable or improbable the existence of the latter."[9]

A California case noted that the "[t]est of relevance is whether the evidence tends, logically, naturally, and by reasonable inference to establish material [important] facts such as identity, intent, or motive."[10]

Other definitions include:

> Evidence that is "relevant" will, by definition "prejudice" the other side.[11]

> Relevant evidence is evidence that has a logical tendency to aid the trier [of fact] in the determination of an issue.[12]

> The usual test for relevancy is whether the evidence offered renders a material fact... more probable than it would be without the evidence.[13]

> Relevant evidence is defined as "having any tendency in reason to prove or disprove any disputed fact that is of consequence to the determination of the action."[14]

---

5 Connecticut v. Crnkovic, 68 Conn. App. 757, 793 A.2d 1139, 2002 Conn. App. LEXIS 159 (2002) (quoting Connecticut v. Joly, 219 Conn. 234, 593 A.2d 96 (1991)).

6 FED. R. EVID. 403.

7 BLACK'S LAW DICTIONARY 639 (9th ed. 2009).

8 MCCORMICK, LAW OF EVIDENCE 319 (1954).

9 31A C.J.S. *Evidence* § 198 (1996).

10 People v. Wilson, 38 Cal. 4th 1237, 1245, 2006 Cal. LEXIS 8228 (2006).

11 United States v. Kapp, 2003 U.S. Dist. LEXIS 4178 (N.D. Ill. 2003).

12 State v. Mungroo, 104 Conn. App. LEXIS 668, 2007 Conn. App. LEXIS 436 (2007).

13 State v. Kelly, 2009 Conn. Super. LEXIS 172 (2009).

14 People v. Prothro, 2014 Cal. App. Unpub. LEXIS 671 (2014).

"Relevant evidence" means evidence having any tendency in reason to prove any material fact.[15]

In a evaluating the concept of relevancy, a Florida court did not abuse its discretion in excluding, as not relevant, evidence of the defendant's arrest and possession of a .22 caliber weapon eight months after the murder for which he was then on trial.[16] The crime scene evidence indicated that .25 and .380 caliber firearms were used in the murder, and the other caliber firearm had nothing whatsoever to do with the murder prosecution. Simply stated, there was no probative evidence that a .22 caliber weapon was involved in the murder, indicating that the .22 caliber gun had no probative value. In discussing the definition of relevancy in a different case, the Court of Appeals for the Ninth Circuit held that the trial court had allowed irrelevant evidence to be admitted against a defendant in a case in which the defendant had been charged with interstate travel to have sexual relations with a minor. A police detective had been chatting with the defendant in an Internet chat room, and the defendant agreed to meet the "police officer/child" in Las Vegas. The police arrested the defendant and discovered numerous stories of adults having sex with children, especially incest, on the defendant's PDA (personal digital assistant). The trial court admitted five of these stories against the defendant. On appeal, the Ninth Circuit held that the sex stories on the PDA were not relevant because the stories were not inextricably linked to the charged crimes and the stories were not part of the activity that led to the defendant's arrest.[17]

Judicial discretion determines the trial court's decision concerning the logical relevancy of evidence and, consequently, the admission or exclusion of that evidence based on legal relevancy. The decision to admit or exclude evidence will not be disturbed on appeal, absent proof of an abuse of the trial judge's discretion. In a Kentucky child sexual abuse case, the trial court properly admitted some evidence of the defendant's involvement with the minor children.[18] However, during the trial, witnesses for the prosecution were permitted to testify concerning the defendant's possession of marijuana and pornography, ownership of sex toys, and trips to strip clubs. In ordering a new trial, the reviewing court found that the evidence about the pornography and sex toys in the house, trips to the strip club, and marijuana use was not legally relevant to prove any issue in the case, determining that the evidence was improperly introduced for the purpose of showing bad character and failed to demonstrate any sexual intent toward the children. As a result, a new trial was warranted.

---

15 KAN. STAT. ANN. § 60–401(b) (2012).

16 Joyner v. State, 2009 Fla. App. LEXIS 1492 (2009).

17 United States v. Curtin, 443 F.3d 1084, 1093, 2006 U.S. App. LEXIS 8071 (9th Cir. 2006).

18 Jenkins v. Commonwealth, 275 S.W.3d 226, 229, 2008 Ky. App. LEXIS 377 (2008).

B. Material Evidence

Black's Law Dictionary defines material evidence as "[e]vidence having some logical connection with the facts of consequence or the issues"[19] in the case. Evidence that does not have a clear relationship to a matter at issue is immaterial.

Materiality concerns whether the evidence meets a minimum threshold of being able to prove or disprove a particular point or to affect the probabilities of proving a point or principle. Evidence is material only when it significantly affects the matter or issue in a case. As one court noted, "[t]he concept of materiality does not relate to the weight of evidence. Rather, it involves the relationship between the proposition that the evidence is offered to prove the issues in the case."[20] The concept boils down to this question: Would the evidence offer a substantially important fact in this case to prove or disprove a charge against the defendant without being unfairly prejudicial to the defendant?

In describing material evidence, courts have noted that:

> Material evidence is evidence, fact, statement, or information that, if believed, would tend to influence or affect the issue under determination.[21]
>
> "[M]aterial" evidence is evidence that is more than merely probative or relevant.[22]
>
> Material evidence is that which reasonably could be taken to put the whole case in such a different light as to undermine the confidence in the jury's verdict.[23]
>
> Material evidence may include evidence that is wholly impeaching if the result of the proceeding would have been different had the evidence been disclosed.[24]

Material evidence that would otherwise be considered relevant may lose its probative value when it becomes too far removed from the event in question. For example, the fact that a testifying defendant had a poor reputation for truthfulness 25 years ago may be excluded due to a lack of any current probative value concerning his present reputation for honesty. The decision to exclude evidence based on its remote character is a matter left to the sound discretion of the trial judge.[25]

C. Materiality and Relevancy Distinguished

In making any meaningful distinction between materiality and relevancy, it must be noted that the two concepts have clear similarities, with both concepts being used to regulate the admission or exclusion of evidence. Material evidence must have a

---

19 BLACK'S LAW DICTIONARY 638 (9th ed. 2009).

20 In re Estate of Bean, 2005 Tenn. App. LEXIS 754 (2005).

21 United States v. Bonsu, 291 Fed. App. 505, 2008 U.S. App. LEXIS 17998 (4th Cir. 2008).

22 People v. Valles, 2013 COA 85, ¶ 33, 2013 Colo. App. LEXIS 864 (2013).

23 State v. Monda, 198 P.3d 784, 2009 Kan. App. LEXIS 28 (2009).

24 State v. Macdonald, 122 Wash. App. 804, 810, 95 P.3d 1248, 1251, 2004 Wash. App. LEXIS 1859 (2004).

25 People v. Owens, 183 P.3d 568, 574, 2007 Colo. App. LEXIS 884 (2007).

sufficiently close relationship to issues that need to be proved in the case, and evidence that is described as material must help prove or disprove one of these issues. In a similar manner, relevant evidence also must possess a close connection to facts or principles that need to be proved or disproved by one party in the suit. Even though some fact or principle may need to be proved or disproved and meets the definition of relevancy, some evidence may be deemed too unfairly prejudicial to be admitted and will be excluded by the trial judge.

Although evidence may be relevant, it is not necessarily material.[26] For example, if a party wanted to impeach a defendant with proof of the defendant's poor reputation for truthfulness dating from 25 years ago when the defendant was attending college, the evidence might arguably meet a test for logical relevancy, but the defense could also argue that the defendant's college reputation was immaterial (legally irrelevant) because the evidence relating to truthfulness was so remote in time. If a proposition of fact need not be proved under applicable rules of substantive law governing a case, that evidence is not material (not logically relevant) under Rule 401 and should be excluded from admission. Evidence introduced solely to prove or disprove an inconsequential or collateral fact could be called immaterial and/or irrelevant and should be excluded.[27] Although evidence may be relevant because it relates to or has some bearing on the case, it may have such slight relevancy as to be labeled immaterial.

In making these fine distinctions between relevancy and materiality, it is important to note that, in actual practice, the distinction is not always clear, and in most cases, when the terms *material* or *immaterial* are used by attorneys and judges, the terms may be used interchangeably or linked with the terms *relevant* or *irrelevant.*[28]

§ 7.3 Admissibility of Relevant Evidence

Rule 402

GENERAL ADMISSIBILITY OF RELEVANT EVIDENCE

Relevant evidence is admissible unless any of the following provides otherwise:
- the United States Constitution;
- a federal statute;
- these rules; or
- other rules prescribed by the Supreme Court.

Irrelevant evidence is not admissible.[29]

---

26 Another way to say the same thing is to say that an item of evidence may be logically relevant but not legally relevant due to its risk of unfair prejudice to the opposing party.

27 *See* United States v. Goodson, 2009 U.S. App. LEXIS 6013 (4th Cir. 2009).

28 *See* United States v. Robinson, 2008 U.S. Dist. LEXIS 102689 (S.D. Fla. 2008) and State v. Stout, 2008 Mont. Dist. LEXIS 233 (2008).

29 FED. R. EVID. 402.

According to Federal Rule of Evidence 402, all relevant evidence is admissible, but this rule is subject to a variety of exceptions, and some evidence that has logical relevance may still be excluded from introduction in court. If an item of evidence tends to prove or disprove any fact or principle that is at issue in the case, it will be admissible unless one of the parties makes an objection. If the proposed item of evidence is only barely logically relevant, the trial judge might exclude it when other evidence also proves or disproves the point with equal or greater emphasis. If the item of evidence does not possess logical relevance and has little or no chance of assisting the jury or the judge in determining an important fact at issue, it will be excluded from evidence. Similarly, when the admission of the evidence would create a risk of confusion of the issues or has the effect of wasting time, the judge, upon appropriate objection, will refuse to admit the evidence from consideration, because it is deemed legally irrelevant.

All evidence that is logically and legally relevant is admissible, unless the constitution of the federal or state government, a statute, or a rule of law excludes evidence for a specific reason. As the California Evidence Code provides, "Except as otherwise provided by statute, all relevant evidence is admissible."[30] If an objection is made to the admissibility of arguably relevant evidence, the burden is on the party making the objection to show that unfair prejudice occurred as a result of the admission.

An appellate court will review the admission of evidence based on considerations of whether the trial judge abused his or her discretion in admitting the evidence.[31] In undertaking a review of a trial court's decision on admission or exclusion, one federal court of appeals noted that the trial courts generally have broad discretion in admitting or excluding evidence and that appellate courts should be mindful that a trial judge is in a much better position than an appellate court, regarding the evaluation of the probative value of evidence relative to potential unfair prejudice.[32] The reviewing court agreed that a trial court's decision concerning relevancy should stand unless a trial court's decision was arbitrary and irrational.

The Federal Rules of Evidence positively state that evidence should be admitted unless a specific rule or interpretation forbids the admission of the evidence. When formulating their own rules, many states have adopted variations of the federal evidence rules, but those states have adopted the federal rules with modifications that reflect state considerations. For example, in the Utah Rules of Evidence, Rule 402 provides that "[r]elevant evidence is admissible unless any of the following provides otherwise; –the United States Constitution; –the Utah Consititution; –a statute; or— rules applicable in courts of this state. Irrelevant evidence is not admissible."[33] State interpretations of evidence rules, including variants of Rule 402, may have some local interpretations that vary somewhat from the federal interpretation.

---

30 CAL EVID. CODE § 351 (2014).

31 State v. Baker, 287 Kan. 345, 363, 2008 Kan. LEXIS 694 (2008).

32 United States v. Washington, 100 Fed. App. 39, 2004 U.S. App. LEXIS 11453 (2d Cir. 2004).

33 UTAH R. EVID. 402 (2013).

When interpreting federal evidence provisions, recent decisions of federal courts have followed the reasoning that all evidence should be admissible unless it comes within one of the specific exceptions. In a prosecution for being a felon in possession of a firearm, a federal district court abused its discretion by finding an exception when it prevented the defendant, a member of a racial or ethnic minority group, from cross-examining a prosecution witness about the witness's swastika tattoos. The trial judge apparently considered the fact that the prosecution witness exhibited swastika tattoos as logically irrelevant on any matter before the court. The reviewing court viewed the situation differently and held that an inquiry into the tattoos was appropriate because it might indicate witness bias against the defendant that might affect the witness's credibility. Although the appellate court found that the exclusion of the evidence constituted harmless error, it held that the tattoo evidence should have been admissible under Rule 402.[34]

Although federal rules contemplate admitting most evidence, when the collection of the evidence transgresses federal law and federal constitutional interpretations, the evidence may be excluded, despite otherwise being legally and logically relevant. In a federal prosecution for armed bank robbery and other charges, United States marshals arrested a defendant, but failed to take him in front of a United States magistrate for almost 30 hours following his arrest, thus violating federal rules of criminal procedure.[35] During that 30-hour period, the defendant offered a confession that the trial court admitted into evidence against him on the theory that a different federal law permitted admission. The Supreme Court of the United States reversed the conviction and rejected the prosecution's argument that Rule 402 should make evidence admissible despite other statutory and court interpretations that might allow or require exclusion.[36]

Evidence that assists in proving or disproving an element of a case is generally considered relevant and should be admissible. In a Vermont case involving allegations of sexual assaults, the defendant wanted to offer evidence that the complaining witness used crack cocaine before and after she allegedly traded sex to the defendant in exchange for the drug. The trial court refused to allow the evidence of prior and subsequent use, because it considered such evidence irrelevant. The defendant's attorney contended there were witnesses who would testify that complainant used and sold crack cocaine within 30 days before and after the alleged assaults, and the complainant's crack-related activities were both relevant to his defense of consent and relevant to impeach the complainant, who in her deposition denied using crack before or after the incident. The Supreme Court of Vermont reversed the conviction on the theory that, as consent was the defense that the accused wanted to use, the exclusion of relevant evidence of other crack cocaine use prevented the defendant from presenting his defense that the complaining witness exchanged sex for crack cocaine.[37]

---

34 United States v. Figueroa, 548 F.3d 222, 229, 2008 U.S. App. LEXIS 23697 (2d Cir. 2008). (Affirmed as harmless error).

35 *See* FED. R. CRIM. P. 5.

36 Corley v. United States, 556 U.S. 303, 129 S. Ct. 1558, 173 L. Ed. 2d 443, 2009 U.S. LEXIS 2512 (2009).

37 State v. Jackson, 2011 Vt. 15, 2011 Vt. LEXIS 12 (2011). *See* case in Part II.

§ 7.4 Reasons for Exclusion of Relevant and Material Evidence

Rule 403

EXCLUDING RELEVANT EVIDENCE FOR PREJUDICE, CONFUSION, WASTE OF TIME, OR OTHER REASONS

The court may exclude relevant evidence if its probative value is substantially outweighed by a danger of one or more of the following: unfair prejudice, confusing the issues, misleading the jury, undue delay, wasting time, or needlessly presenting cumulative evidence.[38]

Although relevant evidence is generally admissible, there are some rules of exclusion. Evidence that may be described as logically relevant may be excluded as legally irrelevant when there is the danger of unfair prejudice, the admission of the evidence could confuse the issues being litigated, the jury could become confused by the evidence, or the presentation of the evidence would be unduly time-consuming. The Federal Rules of Evidence enumerate and codify some of these exclusions, but the practitioner must look to the cases for explanations that apply to specific fact situations. Some of the reasons for excluding relevant evidence are discussed here.

A. The Probative Value Is Substantially Outweighed by the Danger of Unfair Prejudice

Probative value concerns the tendency of an item of evidence to help prove or refute a fact or principle that is at issue in a criminal case. Where the probative value of relevant evidence is of marginal value, but is highly and unfairly prejudicial, the trial court should exclude the offered evidence so that the jury never hears it.[39] When a cause is tried before a judge, an objection to the admission of evidence must still be made, and the judge must make a ruling. But, even if aware of the evidence, the judge will likely not consider it, if that evidence has been ruled to be inadmissible due to the danger of unfair prejudice. Thus, an item of evidence may be excluded from admission, despite the fact that it is logically relevant and may help prove or disprove a fact at issue. When the probative value of offered evidence is outweighed by the danger of unfair prejudice, or when the offered evidence would tend to confuse the issues, mislead the jury, or unduly waste the time of the court by presentation of cumulative evidence, the evidence may be refused.[40] Evaluating prejudice involves determining "undue

---

38 FED. R. EVID. 403.

39 State v. Patel, 949 A.2d 401, 413 (R.I. 2008).

40 Culver v. State, 2008 Ala. Crim. App. LEXIS 107 (2008).

prejudice," because most relevant evidence offered by one party is designed to harm the merits of the opposing side's case. Under Rule 403, concern is directed only at prejudice that is unfair under the circumstances.[41] The concept of "undue prejudice" "applies to evidence which uniquely tends to evoke an emotional bias against the defendant as an individual and which has very little effect on the issues."[42]

In one Tennessee murder case, the trial court committed an error when it permitted gruesome photographs of the deceased to be admitted at the capital sentencing proceeding, for the purpose of demonstrating the presence of an aggravating factor. The reviewing court noted that the photographs were extremely unpleasant and gruesome to varying degrees, in that they depicted the victim's body in a state of decomposition. The court held that the prejudicial value of the photographs outweighed the probative effect, but it did not overturn the sentence. The reviewing court viewed the photographic evidence as harmless error that did not affect the judgment of the jury, because it did not sentence the defendant to death.[43] In another case involving prosecution for possession of sexually explicit photographs of minors, the trial court erred in admitting two sexually explicit violent narratives involving rape and torture found on the defendant's computer. The probative value of the explicit literary narratives was outweighed by prejudicial effect because the defendant had been charged with possession of child pornography found on his computer, and the pornographic pictures did not involve violence, but had illegal sexual content only.[44] In the Tennessee murder case and the child pornography case, the evidence was arguably logically relevant to each prosecution, but the unfair harm to each defendant's case outweighed the effect that the evidence could have presented.

In interpreting the unfair prejudice portion of Ohio Rule of Evidence 403, an Ohio court of appeals approved a trial judge's decision to admit a defendant's conviction for the rape and murder of his wife, at the defendant's trial for conspiracy to commit murder of his wife's sister. Normally, a defendant's prior criminal acts would not be logically relevant to proof of a new crime, or if the prior acts were considered logically relevant, the prejudicial value would exclude the evidence. Allegedly, the defendant, who was in prison, wanted his wife's sister murdered in the exact manner that he had killed his wife, so that it would look as though the defendant was not guilty of his wife's death. The trial judge admitted the prior crime evidence to show the defendant's **motive** and plan for engaging in the conspiracy to have the sister murdered. The reviewing court upheld allowing the prior crime evidence, holding that the probative value to help prove the conspiracy outweighed any unfair prejudicial effect on the defendant's case.[45]

Motive The purpose underlying a defendant's conduct; the reason a person forms a criminal intent prior to engaging in a criminal act.

---

41 United States v. Bennafield, 287 F.3d 320, 202 U.S. App. LEXIS 8009 (4th Cir. 2002), *cert. denied*, 537 U.S. 961, 2002 LEXIS 7487 (2002).

42 People v. Cotton, 2002 Cal. App. Unpub. LEXIS 421 (2002).

43 State v. Banks, 2004 Tenn. Crim. App. LEXIS 793 (2004).

44 United States v. Grimes, 244 F.3d 375 (5th Cir. 2001).

45 State v. Bloomfield, 2004 Ohio 749, 2004 Ohio App. LEXIS 692 (2004).

In a prosecution for aiding and abetting the distribution of crack cocaine, a judge admitted evidence of other related crimes, after conducting an on-the-record review of the case law, evaluating the probative value of the evidence, and weighing the potential prejudice to the defendant. In interpreting this provision, a second federal court explained that, in the context of the balancing test for exclusion of evidence whose probative value is outweighed by its prejudicial effect, "unfair prejudice" means the undue tendency to suggest a decision on an improper basis.[46]

Unfair prejudice, which may justify exclusion of otherwise probative evidence, speaks to the capacity of some concededly relevant evidence to lure the fact finder into declaring guilt on different grounds from proofs specific to the offense charged. The critical issue is the degree of unfairness of the prejudicial evidence and whether it tends to support a decision on an improper basis.[47] In the federal prosecution of a leader of the Outlaws motorcycle gang, the government managed, over the defendant's objection, to have portions of the gang's constitution shown to the jury. The Outlaws' constitution mentioned that membership was open only to white men, an irrelevant fact that the defendant believed would create an unfair prejudice against his case in the minds of the jury. The federal court of appeals held that the probative value of allowing the jury to see the racism of the gang's policies did not outweigh the clear danger of unfair prejudice. Despite the error, the conviction was not reversed, because under the circumstances of the case, the error was held to have been harmless.[48]

Although the trial judge has broad authority in weighing the testimony's probative value against the possible prejudicial effect, his or her determination is subject to review by an appeals court. For example, the Ninth Circuit Court of Appeals held that, where the evidence possesses very slight, if any, probative value, it is an abuse of discretion to admit it, even assuming a modest likelihood of unfair prejudice or small risk of misleading the jury.[49]

B. *Introduction of the Evidence Would Confuse the Issues*

The right of any party to introduce logically releveant evidence favorable to the position of that party has been clearly established, but the introduction of relevant evidence is not without limit and may be restricted or curtailed where the evidence could confuse the jury or might detract from the main issues of the case.[50] Because the introduction of confusing evidence may introduce unimportant side issues in a criminal case, a judge may exclude that evidence from a jury trial. However, an objection on the ground that evidence would be confusing would not normally be offered in a bench trial, because the implication would be that the attorney seeks to prevent the judge from

---

[46] United States v. Sills, 120 F.3d 917 (8th Cir. 1997).

[47] United States v. Payne, 119 F.3d 637 (8th Cir. 1997).

[48] United States v. Bowman, 302 F.2d 1228, 1239, 1240, 2002 U.S. App. LEXIS 17165 (2002).

[49] United States v. Hitt, 981 F.2d 422 (9th Cir. 1992).

[50] Clark v. Arizona, 548 U.S. 735, 2006 U.S. LEXIS 5184 (2006).

becoming confused, a suggestion that would not help the client's case.[51] Evidence of prior crimes by the accused is often inadmissible, even though material and logically relevant, because such evidence would tend to confuse the issues by bringing up previous wrongdoing by the same defendant. Similarly, when a defendant in a methamphetamine possession trial wanted to introduce evidence that another man had been convicted of similar crimes arising out of the same underlying conduct for which the defendant was on trial, the trial judge refused to admit the evidence of the other man's difficulties with the law. The judge's theory was that the other evidence was not relevant, and even if it had been somewhat relevant, the other case evidence posed a danger of confusing the jury.[52] Trial and appellate courts attempt to ensure that evidence introduced at trial does not distract the jury from the case being tried or encourage the jury to find guilt for the wrong reason. Consistent with Federal Rule 403 and similar state rules, evidence may have some logical relevance and still be excluded from a criminal trial.

When considering the "confusion of the issues" provision of Rule 403 in a burglary and aggravated assault case, a Texas court permitted a pretrial cellmate to testify that the defendant told him that the defendant would have been better off if he had just killed his ex-girlfriend, who was the victim in the case. The defendant admitted he illegally entered the apartment because he entered through a window without her consent. On appeal, the defense contended that the cellmate's testimony regarding the defendant's statements about killing his ex-girlfriend had the tendency to confuse or distract from the issues in the case, thus confusing the jury. In upholding the admission of the cellmate's testimony, the reviewing court noted that the evidence negated the defendant's contention of self-defense and shed light on his intent for being inside her home.[53] In a different case, a trial court improperly permitted the admission of evidence that the defendant, who was on trial for murder, had been convicted in a prior murder, even though the two cases had some connection.[54] A primary issue in the second trial involved whether the defendant had conspired with his half-brother to kill the victim in the second case. The appellate court expressed concern that the introduction of the evidence of the first murder case might cause the jury to blend the details of the first murder with the details in the second murder prosecution, thereby creating confusion.

C. *The Evidence Would Mislead the Jury*

Where evidence might have the tendency to lead the jury to an incorrect conclusion or decision, the trial judge should refuse to admit the evidence. For example, in an Arkansas prosecution for rape and sexual assault, the trial judge permitted the

---

51 People v. Rogelio, 2005 Cal. App. Unpub. LEXIS 3013 (2005), in which the court noted, "The trial court observed that in a bench trial, factors such as the inflammatory nature of the crime, confusion of the issues, and the consumption of time involved in addressing the prior offenses were less significant than they would have been in a jury trial."

52 United States v. Darling, 238 Fed. App. 258, 2007 U.S. App. LEXIS 15650 (9th Cir. 2007).

53 Padilla v. State, 254 S.W3d 585, 594, 2008 Tex. App. LEXIS 2719 (2008).

54 State v. Pona, 948 A.2d 941, 2008 R.I. LEXIS 69 (2008).

prosecution to introduce 1,022 pornographic images taken from the defendant's computer, with the images being placed on a compact disc for the jury to consider.[55] According to the appellate court, the trial court should have weighed the probative value against the possibility of unfair prejudice, and the trial court should have also considered whether the photographs could mislead the jury in making a wrong decision. According to the reviewing court, the images depicted a wide range of pornographic actions and situations beyond those directly related to the charged offenses, and the inflammatory nature of the images was readily apparent. While some of the images were relevant in corroborating the complaining witness's allegations, the overall effect was, among other things, to mislead the jury.[56] In determining whether evidence would mislead the jury, in a federal felon in possession of a firearm case, the trial court refused to exclude evidence that the defendant shot and killed an alleged aggressor with the firearm that he allegedly illegally possessed.[57] Over the defendant's contention that mention of the witness's death was irrelevant or might be confusing, the trial court determined that evidence of the deceased's death was probative because it offered a complete picture of the alleged offense and explained why the key witness was not testifying in the case.

However, in another case in which the possibility of the jury being misled by evidence seemed strong, the federal district judge properly prevented the prosecution from introducing prior acts of the defendant.[58] A defendant had been indicted for aggravated child sexual abuse, and the prosecution wanted to introduce into evidence prior uncharged instances of sexual assault by the defendant. The dates, times, and precise details of these uncharged offenses were lacking or were not sufficiently specific for the admission of the evidence. In one situation, the alleged prior victim never reported the crime until much later, and one woman reported the molestation of her sister. The third woman could not recall how many times the defendant molested her, and there were some differences between the new charges and the older allegations. Following the philosophy of Rule 403 of the Federal Rules, the trial court considered how forcefully the prior acts had been proved and how important the prior evidence would be to the prosecution. Additionally, in making such an evaluation, the trial judge should consider how seriously the prior evidence is disputed, how much the prior evidence would distract the jury, and how much time the prior act proof would consume. In this case, the trial judge determined that, although the evidence would be helpful, it should be excluded, given the risk that the jury might convict the defendant based on the evidence of the prior allegations and that the introduction of the evidence of prior molestations might create confusion. The reviewing court upheld the trial determination and noted that it would reverse only if the trial judge had abused his discretion, which the court did not find.

---

[55] Blanchard v. State, 104 Ark. 31, 35, 2008 Ark. App. LEXIS 775 (2008).

[56] *Id.*

[57] United States v. Williams, 2008 U.S. Dist. LEXIS 36623 (M.D. Fla. 2008).

[58] United States v. Begay, 2009 U.S. App. LEXIS 2577 (10th Cir. 2009).

D. The Evidence Would Unduly Delay the Trial of the Case, Waste Time, or Needlessly Present Cumulative Evidence

Evidence that might be relevant and could assist the jury in making a decision may still be excluded when a judge determines that admission of the evidence could cause a delay in the trial proceedings. At his or her discretion, the judge may exclude relevant evidence if its admission unnecessarily wastes time or could be considered cumulative.[59] For example, in a mail and computer fraud case, the prosecution alleged that the defendant had committed the crimes while working for the government as a civilian computer specialist. One of the defendant's supervisors testified about how the defendant's fraudulent schemes operated. In an effort to impeach the supervisor, the defendant wanted to cross-examine the supervisor concerning the supervisor's financial problems ten years earlier. At that time, the defendant had loaned money to the supervisor, violating government policy. In an unpublished opinion, the reviewing court held that the trial court properly excluded this line of cross-examination, because the evidence would have been a waste of time, even if it could have been somewhat relevant.[60] Against a defendant's argument, under Rule 403, that the trial court had allowed the government to introduce cumulative evidence against him, the appellate court upheld the ruling of the trial judge.

In a drug-selling prosecution, police had arrested a defendant after he threw a bag of cocaine out a window. Subsequently, police arrested him again for dropping a jar of rock cocaine out a window as police were entering the apartment. Later, the defendant was arrested a third time, after police observed a known drug seller enter an apartment occupied by the defendant. At his trial for possession with intent to distribute 50 grams or more of cocaine base, the defendant contended that bringing evidence of the first and third arrests for drug possession was improper because the government had more than sufficient evidence to prove the case, and, therefore, the proof of the other crimes was unfairly prejudicial. The Court of Appeals for the Eighth Circuit held that the evidence was not improperly cumulative, because the other crime evidence helped establish knowledge that he possessed cocaine base and that it tended to prove that he had the intent to distribute cocaine products.[61] In another criminal prosecution for, among other things, firearm and drug offenses, the court permitted the defendant to offer evidence of an alternative source for the firearm found where he was staying.[62] His theory was that another man was upset that the defendant was staying with a particular woman, and this other man's displeasure indicated that the firearm might have been accidentally left in the apartment or planted by the other man. The court prohibited the defendant from introducing evidence of the other man's prior arrests for firearm and crack possession. In upholding the trial court's limitation on introducing the other man's legal

---

[59] People v. Brooks, 2008 Mich. App. LEXIS 1581 (2008). Unpublished opinion.

[60] United States v. Benjamin, 125 Fed. Appx. 438, 440, 2005 U.S. App. LEXIS 3943 (2005).

[61] United States v. Gipson, 446 F.3d 828, 2006 U.S. App. LEXIS 11040 (2006).

[62] United States v. Lucas, 499 F.3d 769, 2007 U.S. App. LEXIS 20076 (8th Cir. 2007).

difficulties, the appellate court noted that cumulative, remote, or speculative evidence may be excluded by the trial court under Rule 403 to avoid confusing or misleading the jury.

Evidence is considered cumulative when it adds nothing to what the jury has already heard or adds to proof that does not need reproving. An Indiana appellate court noted that:

> Cumulative evidence is "[a]dditional evidence that supports a fact established by the existing evidence (especially that which does not need further support)." *Mundy ex rel. Mundy*, 820 N.E.2d 128, 135 (Ind. 2005) (quoting *Black's Law Dictionary* 596 (8th ed. 2004)).[63]

Evidence that is not needed, duplicates the existing evidence, delays the trial needlessly, or potentially confuses the jury may be excluded upon proper objection by the opposing counsel.

E. The Evidence Would Unfairly and Harmfully Surprise a Party Who Has Not Had Reasonable Opportunity to Anticipate That Such Evidence Would Be Offered

In the interests of fairness and due process, many courts will refuse to admit evidence where the opposing party failed in its duty to give prior notice of an intention to introduce unanticipated evidence, such as evidence of an affirmative defense.[64] Some courts advocate the exclusion of evidence if the opposing party is caught by unfair surprise. The reasoning for such an exclusion holds that, if the opponent has been unfairly surprised by unanticipated evidence, has received no warning, or could not have logically anticipated that such evidence would be offered, then the evidence should be excluded, regardless of relevance. Confusion surrounding this rule has generated concern by many writers who suggest that the situation should be addressed by jury instructions at the trial stage. In some jurisdictions, if an allegation of unfair surprise occurs, the complaining party must ask for a continuance or the objection concerning surprise is deemed to have been waived.[65]

For example, in a case where the defendant had been charged with operating a motor vehicle without a license plate, the trial evidence demonstrated that the defendant had been towing a trailer that had no license plate. According to the reviewing court, a reversal of the conviction was necessary. Nothing in the accusation indicated that the defendant would have to defend against towing a trailer without a tag, and by allowing the prosecution to introduce evidence to prove a crime that was allegedly committed in a completely different manner, the court would be subjecting the defendant to

---

63 Gaddie v. Manlief (In re H.R.M.), 864 N.E.2d 442, 2007 Ind. App. LEXIS 775 (2007).

64 *See* Payne v. Tennessee, 501 U.S. 808 (1991), and Ransom v. State, 919 So. 2d 887, 888, 2005 Miss. LEXIS 595 (Miss. 2005), *cert. denied*, 2006 U.S. LEXIS 4985 (2006).

65 Burns v. State, 2005 Tex. App. LEXIS 1772 (2005).

unfair surprise.[66] In a different case, no unfair surprise occurred when the state introduced a 911 call made by a defendant accused of murder. The government had taped the 911 call, and in the recording, the defendant stated that he had stabbed and killed the victim.[67] Despite the defendant's contention that he was unaware that 911 calls were routinely taped, the defendant had made the call and knew its content. So, admission of the 911 tape was within the sound discretion of the trial judge.

§ 7.5 Relevancy of Particular Matters

Previous sections of this chapter focus on the general concepts relating to relevancy and materiality, as well as how those concepts affect admission and exclusion of evidence. These rules apply in situations in which a party to a criminal action offers evidence for introduction. However, there are some particular instances in which not only the general rules apply, but also specific rules that relate to particular situations.

Evidence necessary to prove the essential elements of a case, as well as the preliminary facts, such as identity, jurisdiction of the court, and the mental condition of the accused, must generally be admitted under one legal theory or another. However, trial and appellate challenges to admissibility or exclusion frequently occur regarding character evidence, evidence of prior crimes, identification issues, scientific testing evidence, the use of real evidence (especially in criminal cases), and other particular matters. These rules of exclusion and admissability are discussed in detail in the sections that follow.

Logically relevant evidence is sometimes excluded by rape shield laws that are designed to protect complaining witnesses from having prior or subsequent sexual history divulged in court, so as to encourage the reporting of sexual crimes. Legislatures in many states have made legislative determinations that inquiries into a victim's prior sexual history might be somewhat logically relevant, but carry a significant danger of unfairly prejudicing and misleading a jury, and as a result, the victim's sexual history should be deemed legally irrelevant or immaterial. For example, the California Evidence Code generally prohibits admission of "opinion evidence, reputation evidence, and evidence of specific instances of the complaining witness' sexual conduct"[68] in a sex crime prosecution. This is not to say that the prior history of a sexual assault victim can never be determined to be legally relevant or material, but a defendant must make a strong showing of both logical and legal relevance to have such evidence admitted. In a teenage rape prosecution, the Supreme Court of New Mexico upheld a lower court reversal of the conviction, because the victim's prior sexual history gave a reason to

---

66 Younger v. State, 293 Ga. App. 20, 2008 Ga. App. LEXIS 898 (2009).

67 People v. Nickson, 2006 Mich. App. LEXIS 2911 (2006).

68 CAL. EVID. CODE § 1103(c)(1) (2014).

doubt her story.[69] The defendant alleged that the victim gave consent for sexual activities, while she told others a different story later. The alleged victim's rather religious parents had previously punished her for engaging in sexual activity with a different boy in the past. The defendant contended that she may have been lying to avoid punishment by her parents for a second episode of sexual activity, this time with the defendant. Her prior sexual history was deemed relevant to her bias and credibility, central issues in the case.

§ 7.6 —Identity of Persons

In order to ensure that the proper persons are tried and, if guilty, have appropriate sentences imposed, the court must positively identify those accused as the perpetrators. Therefore, courts allow a great deal of latitude in admitting evidence designed to prove identity, and appellate courts are reluctant to second-guess. A Georgia court rejected a complaint by armed robbery defendants that the alleged victim had misidentified them at an in-person showup at the original crime. The perpetrators were not masked, wore the same clothes, and matched the victim's original descriptions of the defendants. Given that the identification process was not unduly suggestive, it could not give rise to the possibility of irreparable misidentification, and as a result, the identification was properly admitted, according to the reviewing court.[70] In regards to a separate case, an Arkansas court noted that it would not reverse a trial court ruling on the admissibility "of an in-court identification, unless the ruling [was] clearly erroneous under the totality of the circumstances."[71]

When evaluating the admissibility of evidence to prove identity, the court must consider not only the relevancy test, but in some instances, constitutional grounds, such as due process violations, the lack of counsel at lineups, or other similar arguments. If the proposed evidence relates to the witness's actual observation of the accused or others, the evidence is generally admissible. For example, suppose the witness intends to testify that, "I know the accused from high school. I saw him enter the bank with nothing and exit rapidly with some bags that had the bank's logo on them." This testimony would be relevant, generally admissible evidence. Other challenges may be in order, such as the credibility of the witness, but the testimony would probably not be challenged on constitutional grounds.

Identification may become more complicated when the witness does know the person he or she saw at the crime scene, but indicates that he or she can identify that person in a lineup, a showup, a photographic array, or a PowerPoint presentation. Here, the evidence must meet the relevancy test, but it may be challenged if law enforcement agents performed the pretrial identification procedure in an unduly suggestive manner, thus contaminating

---

69 State v. Stephen F. 144 N.M. 360, 2008 N.M. LEXIS 391 (2008).

70 Singleton v. State, 324 Ga. App. 141. 143, 2013 Ga. App. LEXIS 812 (2013).

71 *See* Rodgers v. State, 2008 Ark. App. LEXIS 552 (2008).

the in-court identification of the witness.[72] The witness may be testifying from his or her memory of the identification procedure and not from the crime-scene observation.

In *Neil v. Biggers*, a landmark case concerning eyewitness identification, the Supreme Court of the United States offered a test to determine whether an identification has been made accurately. The *Neil* five-factor totality of the circumstances test considered "the opportunity of the witness to view the criminal at the time of the crime, the witness' degree of attention, the accuracy of the witness' prior description of the criminal, the level of certainty demonstrated by the witness at the confrontation, and the length of time between the crime and the confrontation."[73] In the *Neil* case, the rape victim had been in close proximity to her attacker for a considerable length of time, had paid attention to his appearance, had given police an accurate prior description, had not misidentified any other person, and was very certain of her identification. In addition, only about six months had elapsed since the crime. She made her identification at a one-person "walk by" in the police station, recognizing the defendant's voice. The *Neil* Court approved the identification process under the five-factor test, and held that the woman's identification of her attacker satisfied relevancy and due process standards when the totality of the circumstances test has been met.[74] In another case, a woman was properly permitted to identify her rapist following the rape, but the identification occurred on a public street immediately following the attack. When she ran for help following the rape, she encountered a man who helped find her clothing and called police. Subsequently, she observed her attacker leave the basement and enter another apartment. Her spontaneous identification was held to have been properly made, done without undue suggestiveness, and was accomplished without any police involvement.[75]

When a pretrial identification procedure has been unnecessarily suggestive due to "steering" by police or the presentation of the suspect in several successive lineups or photo arrays, the identification evidence is not challenged at trial with arguments concerning relevancy, but with the possible violation of due process.

Is evidence of a suspect's past activities admissible to show identity, even though this may include evidence of other crimes? Evidence of a defendant's prior crimes or crimes subsequent to the one for which he or she is currently on trial may never be used solely for the purpose of suggesting that a defendant has a criminal disposition. Under certain circumstances, however, such evidence may be offered to prove other facts of consequence such as identity. In a Hawai'i case involving an armed robbery with the use of a baseball bat by two assailants, the trial court permitted the prosecution to introduce evidence that a defendant had pleaded guilty to a subsequent armed robbery in

---

72 *See* Neil v. Biggers, 409 U.S. 188, 1972 U.S. LEXIS 6 (1972) for five factors used to evaluate the accuracy of eyewitness identification. *See also* WALKER AND HEMMENS, LEGAL GUIDE FOR POLICE: CONSTITUTIONAL ISSUES (9th ed. 2010), Chapter 8, for a comprehensive discussion of pretrial identification procedures.

73 *Id.* at 199–200.

74 *Id.*

75 State v. McElroy, 29 Kan. App. 2d 990, 992–993, 35 P.3d 283, 286–287 (2001).

which a baseball bat was used under similar circumstances.[76] One of the issues in the case concerned the identity of the defendant wielding the baseball bat. The Intermediate Court of Appeals of Hawai'i approved of the admission of the prior conviction, but only where it could be linked to motive or plan. Many jurisdictions would have permitted the introduction of the other criminal conviction to show identity because the two crimes are so clearly similar and would not have required any other purpose for the evidence.

The courts require more than a mere general similarity between factual situations being compared before admitting evidence of a separate crime to show identity under the similar crimes theory.[77] There must be identifiable points of significant similarity that pervade both factual situations, and the points of similarity must have some special character or be so unusual as to point to the defendant's identity. In an unreported California case,[78] the defendant and a male companion had robbed a Greyhound bus station attendant at gunpoint 20 years earlier. In the original robbery, one defendant ordered an employee into the back room, where a safe was located. According to the trial judge, the only difference in the current case was that the defendant now knew about the safe in the back room because he was one of the original robbers years earlier. Although the newest crime of robbery of the bus station attendants occurred more than two decades after the first one (the defendant definitely committed the earlier one because he pleaded no contest), the court permitted evidence of the earlier robbery case to be admitted for purposes of identification because it was almost identical to the one for which the defendant was currently on trial. The defendant had not been charged with robberies since the first one because he had spent 20 years in prison for the first robbery.

The results of scientific tests may be considered relevant in proving a defendant's identity. In an Alabama rape case, the victim had been asleep and was blindfolded by her attacker during the crime. She was unable to identify her attacker, but the perpetrator left two DNA samples that were collected by hospital emergency room employees.[79] Eventually, the unidentified DNA results were posted to the national Combined DNA Index System (CODIS), where a match of the unknown DNA with the defendant's DNA indicated that he was the perpetrator. In addition, a subsequent swab of his mouth produced DNA that matched the other two samples. In approving the use of DNA as the sole identifying characteristic, the reviewing court upheld the defendant's rape conviction, with no additional evidence. Naturally, DNA testing must be conducted by properly trained technicians, according to accepted standards, and introduced in court by a qualified witness. When done properly, DNA test results offer circumstantial evidence that the defendant's identity has been sufficiently established.[80]

---

76 *See* State v. Yamada, 116 Haw. 422, 2007 Haw. App. LEXIS 663 (2007).

77 Wimberley v. State, 2005 Ala. Crim. App. LEXIS 103 (2005).

78 People v. Hill, 2008 Cal. App. Unpub. LEXIS 3341 (2008).

79 Ex parte James Lee Ware, 2014 Ala. LEXIS 5 (2014).

80 Commonwealth v. Gaynor, 443 Mass. 245, 266, 820 N.E.2d 233, 251, 2005 Mass. LEXIS 7 (2005).

§ 7.7 —Identity of Things

Subject to some exceptions, a court generally declares evidence to be relevant, if that evidence helps prove the identity of things or objects connected to a crime. Items of personal property associated with a victim or a defendant may be relevant because they may have the effect of placing a particular person at a particular place or suggesting that property may have been used in a particular way. For example, in order to identify the accused as the perpetrator of a double homicide and to support intent, the prosecutor introduced evidence that the defendant possessed old coins that one of the deceased was known to collect and that other similar coins remained at the crime scene, thus demonstrating the defendant's motive and actions.[81] In an unpublished California case, the defendant denied participating in a robbery, despite having been found in possession of all the proceeds of the robbery, as well as the gun used to intimidate the robbery victims, while wearing the jacket and pants worn by the actual robber. The evidence of his possessions and clothing was sufficient to establish his identity as the perpetrator.[82]

Other examples of relevant, tangible evidence against a defendant are found in the following cases: In a North Carolina capital murder case, the reviewing court held that blood found on the pants that the defendant wore on the night of the homicide, which matched the blood type of the decedent, was properly admitted. In addition, the fact that evidence technicians recovered DNA evidence from the pants of the defendant that indicated that the decedent was the source of the DNA also helped tie the defendant to the crime scene, thus supporting the government's case.[83] In a Massachusetts homicide case, a forensic odontologist identified the body of the defendant's wife by examining the jaw and skull and comparing the results to known dental records of the deceased.[84] Comparisons of victim bite mark evidence to a defendant's teeth impressions, when offered by qualified experts,[85] has been admitted in many cases in which scientific, technical, or other specialized knowledge would assist the trier of fact. In a Texas murder case, where the deceased victim had five visible bite marks on her arm, the trial court permitted a forensic odontologist to compare the bite marks on the victim with impressions taken of the defendant's mouth. The forensic odontologist, who was qualified as an expert witness, offered the opinion within a reasonable medical certainty that the defendant made two of the five bite marks. Because the marks appeared

---

81 *See* People v. Zamudio, 43 Cal. 4th 327, 2008 Cal. LEXIS 4431 (2008).

82 People v. Wardell, 2005 Cal. Unpub. App. LEXIS 11539 (2005).

83 Daughtry v. Polk, 2006 U.S. App. LEXIS 17962 (4th Cir. 2006).

84 Commonwealth v. Roy, 464 Mass. 818, n. 5, 985 N.E.2d 1164; 2013 Mass. LEXIS 88 (2013).

85 Meadows v. Commonwealth, 178 S.W.3d 527, 536, 2005 Ky. App. LEXIS 131 (2005). "Forensic dentists are experts on identifying persons based on unique characteristics of their teeth, which may include determining the identity of an unknown deceased person based on dental records, determining the age of a person based on his or her teeth, and determining who made a bite based on an analysis of the bite mark and the suspect's teeth."

to have been made about the time of death, such evidence was relevant to prove that the defendant was in close proximity to the victim.[86]

In an Arizona misdemeanor marijuana prosecution, the basis for the initiating the case involved the identification of marijuana during a vehicle stop by a police officer. According to the reviewing court, the officer's recognition of the odor of marijuana and of the physical sample was properly based on his training and experience as an undercover narcotics officer.[87] In an Eighth Circuit case, the court approved the introduction of a prerecorded $20 "bait" bill found on a defendant following a drug transaction. The appellate court upheld the introduction into evidence of scales used to weigh drugs found in the defendant's trailer home that was used to prove the defendant's intention to distribute 50 or more grams of cocaine. Police found pre-bagged rock cocaine in the home, a factor that also helped establish the intent to distribute cocaine base.[88]

§ 7.8 —Circumstances Preceding the Crime

A defendant's preparation, planning, and calculation prior to the alleged criminal act may be relevant in establishing criminal intent or other elements of the crime. Following a crime, efforts to escape detection or apprehension, if planned prior to the crime, may also have the effect of providing circumstantial evidence of a defendant's proper *mens rea.* The purchase of items necessary for the commission of the crime and arranging to arrive at the appropriate place at the proper time will also be of interest to the prosecution. Similarly, any efforts to disguise the crime or the crime scene or to destroy evidence, as well as efforts involving escape or avoidance of detection, may assist a prosecutor in proving a defendant's knowledge as an element of a crime. Conduct that is inconsistent with innocence and affirmative actions that tend to demonstrate a consciousness of guilt will normally be relevant and admissible against the accused. Some witnesses may have observed the crime as it occurred, and other witnesses may have overheard threats directed toward a victim. Still other witnesses may have conveyed a firearm or sold the defendant items used in the commission of the crime. Evidence of circumstances preceding the crime may be derived from e-mail accounts, web sites, social networking sites, thumb drives, hard drives, cell phone data from cell carriers, and metadata from all these sources. Most of these types of evidence, whether they involve physical objects, human conduct, or oral evidence, should be considered relevant and generally admissible against an accused individual.

The best test of the relevance of testimony and evidence concerning antecedent circumstances is whether the evidence of prior planning or engaging in specific activities would help prove or disprove any element of the charged crime. If the evidence

---

86 Villa v. State, 2008 Tex. App. LEXIS 1025 (2008).

87 State v. Walker, 2013 Ariz. App. Unpub. LEXIS 263 (2013).

88 United States v. Johnson, 439 F.3d 947, 955, 2006 U.S. App. LEXIS 6040 (8th Cir. 2006), *motion to vacate denied,* Johnson v. United States, 2009 U.S. Dist. LEXIS 8363 (E.D. Mo. 2009).

affects the probabilities of conviction, a court will generally consider that proof to be relevant evidence. In an unpublished California case, circumstances indicated that the defendant's wife wanted him to move out of her residence because the marriage was in disarray. The defendant procured a sharp knife from the kitchen, unplugged all the telephones in the apartment, and entered her bedroom, locking the door behind him. The defendant's activities before he stabbed his sleeping wife with the kitchen knife tended to indicate that he possessed the *mens rea* for attempted murder.[89]

Evidence of prior planning also played a role in a Florida capital murder case involving an attempted robbery of men who ran a check-cashing business.[90] Prior to the shooting, the felons had stolen two sport-utility vehicles that were to be used to "box in" the victims' car, which carried the large amount of cash. The defendants had previously scouted the schedule of the business owner with respect to his bank visits. A firefight between the armed businessmen and the armed felons erupted when the masked felons stopped the money car using the vehicles. The felons killed one of the occupants of the money car. Proof of the planning was sufficient to prove the intent necessary for the attempted robbery conviction, which, in turn, supported the first-degree murder conviction under the felony-murder rule.

A short period of time might separate activities that precede the crime and the actual act, but such activities may still be considered relevant evidence of planning the crime. In an unpublished Michigan case, evidence that preceded the crime of murder helped prove both premeditation and malice on the part of the defendant. In rejecting the defendant's appeal that the jury should have been instructed on manslaughter, the court noted that the defendant had a chance to reflect or decide to control his passions after he obtained a kitchen knife during his walk to his girlfriend's bedroom. His acts of slashing her throat and windpipe demonstrated that he had the intent to kill her and had time during his walk to the bedroom to premeditate. His behavior helped prove two elements of the crime of first-degree murder.[91]

Evidence of prior difficulties between a defendant and the victim may be admissible in a murder case where it may help establish motive or one or more elements of the crime. Where the defendant had beaten his "off and on" girlfriend two weeks prior to her death, such circumstance could be admissible at his later murder trial.[92] A confrontation between the defendant and the victim a week prior to her death involved disagreements that led to the defendant jumping on the hood of the victim's car and refusing to leave. The defendant's prior behavior on the day of the murder (he procured a butcher knife from his sister's kitchen) was also antecedent conduct that was admissible at his murder trial for stabbing his girlfriend.

The defendant may also introduce evidence of events preceding the crime. For example, a defendant in a manslaughter case may introduce evidence that the deceased

---

89 *See* People v. Huerta, 2008 Cal. App. Unpub. LEXIS 2827 (2008).

90 *See* San Martin v. State, 995 So. 2d 247, 2008 Fla. LEXIS 1460 (2008).

91 People v. Benore, 2005 Mich. App. LEXIS 2718 (2005).

92 *See* State v. Johnson, 284 Kan. 18, 2007 Kan. LEXIS 328 (2007).

entered defendant's real property, appeared drunk, tossed the defendant around like a rag doll, and threw the defendant to the ground. In one case, the defendant was permitted to introduce evidence that he followed the alleged victim away from his property to tell him to wait for the police. Evidence demonstrated that the alleged victim choked the defendant almost to unconsciousness, after threatening to kill him, before the defendant stabbed the victim twice with a knife, with fatal results to the alleged victim.[93] Prior conduct of an alleged victim may be relevant to a defendant's plea of self-defense, as well as to the alleged victim's reputation for violence, if that evidence suggests that the alleged victim may have been the aggressor.

§ 7.9 —Subsequent Incriminating or Exculpatory Circumstances

Following suspicious activity, the actions or conduct of a suspect may assist in establishing a defense through proof of **exculpatory circumstances,** or those actions may provide the prosecution with evidence that helps prove guilt. As one Kentucky court noted, the "common-law rule is based on the inference that the guilty run away but the innocent remain."[94] For example, evidence of flight, resisting arrest, concealment, assuming a false name, and criminal conduct during flight for the purpose of financing and accomplishing further flight is admissible in a criminal prosecution. An Ohio court of appeals held that no error occurred when the trial court allowed the introduction of evidence of the defendant's use of a false name to law enforcement officers. Additionally, with approval, the court referenced an earlier case that noted, "[i]t is today universally conceded that the fact of an accused's flight, escape from custody, resistance to arrest, concealment, assumption of a false name, and related conduct, are admissible as evidence of consciousness of guilt, and thus of guilt itself."[95] While flight and other such conduct do not raise a legal presumption of guilt, the jury may consider these circumstances together with other facts in evidence and give the evidence the weight it thinks the evidence deserves, given the facts presented.[96]

> **Exculpatory circumstances** Exonerative facts; excusing evidence; facts tending to clear a defendant from a charge of fault or guilt.

According to the Supreme Court, when an individual sees police officers and flees immediately, such conduct may be relevant to criminality and deserves some

---

93 *See* Behanna v. State, 985 So. 2d 550, 2007 Fla. App. LEXIS 19318 (2007), *review denied,* 988 So. 2d 622, 2008 Fla. LEXIS 1338 (2008).

94 Rodriguez v. Commonwealth, 107 S.W.3d 215, 219, 2003 Ky. LEXIS 138 (2003).

95 State v. Stribling, 2009 Ohio 1444, 2009 Ohio App. LEXIS 1240, citing State v. Eaton, 19 Ohio St. 2d 145, 150, 2, 1969 Ohio LEXIS 348 (1969), citing 2 WIGMORE, EVIDENCE (3 Ed.) 111, § 276.

96 Connecticut v. Beverly, 72 Conn. App. 91, 104, 805 A.2d 95, 104 (2002).

investigation by police to determine whether the flight reflected a consciousness of guilt.[97] As then Chief Justice Rehnquist noted, "Headlong flight—wherever it occurs—is the consummate act of evasion: it is not necessarily indicative of wrongdoing, but it is certainly suggestive of such."[98] As a general rule, unexplained flight can be admissible as evidence to infer consciousness of guilt, according to a Connecticut court. For example, a defendant in a sexual abuse case fled to Puerto Rico within three or four days following the victim's allegations and before police could interview him, and as a result, evidence of flight was properly admitted. The defendant testified in his own defense, but he offered no rebuttal explanation of why he needed to go to Puerto Rico at that specific time and why he remained there for six years.[99]

There are limitations on the weight of such evidence. In a very old case, *Hickory v. United States,*[100] the United States Supreme Court set aside a conviction because the trial judge had charged the jury that flight created a presumption of guilt. The Court concluded that flight and concealment "are mere circumstances to be considered and weighed in connection with other proof with that caution and circumspection which their inconclusiveness when standing alone require."[101] Flight following a criminal act constitutes a type of circumstantial evidence of consciousness of guilt, but its probative value usually depends on all the surrounding facts and circumstances. The inference of consciousness of guilt upon flight has been subject to considerable judicial criticism on the grounds that common experience does not always support the assumption. In recognition of this concept and consistent with the earlier *Hickory* case, one court charged the jury that "the government bore the burden of showing that the appellant had intentionally fled and that flight does not create a presumption of guilt but, to the contrary, may be completely consistent with innocence."[102] Essentially, jury was responsible for determining what inference, if any, to draw from proof of flight.

The length of time between the crime and the flight may have a bearing on both the admissibility and the weight of the flight evidence. Where a defendant in a murder case fled from police at a traffic stop seven days after the crime, the court held that evidence of consciousness of guilt could still exist and was not too remote in time to be properly associated with the crimes of murder and kidnapping. The court held that the defendant's explanation of the flight seven days after the crime should go to the weight of flight evidence, rather than its admissibility.[103]

When evidence of flight has been introduced in a case, the judge normally will assist the jury in evaluating the importance of such evidence by offering a jury instruction. In California, in any case where there is evidence of flight, the judge must instruct the jury that flight following a crime is never sufficient to prove guilt, but is only a

97 Illinois v. Wardlow, 528 U.S. 119, 120 S. Ct. 673, 145 L. Ed. 2d 570, 2000 U.S. LEXIS 504 (2000).
98 *Id.* at 124.
99 State v. Gonzalez, 272 Conn. 515, 530, 864 A.2d 847, 857, 2005 Conn. LEXIS 20 (Conn. 2005).
100 160 U.S. 408, 16 S. Ct. 327, 40 L. Ed. 474 (1896).
101 *Id.* at 417.
102 United States v. Benedetti, 433 F.3d 111, 116, 2005 U.S. App. LEXIS 28490 (1st Cir. 2005).
103 United States v. Young, 2003 U.S. App. LEXIS 7432 (8th Cir. 2003).

factor the jury may consider in light of all the other evidence in a case. The judge also instructs the jury that the flight does not require a person to reach any particular place, but rather it must indicate that the defendant intends to avoid being seen or arrested. It is completely up to the jury to consider what weight to give flight evidence.[104]

In a federal prosecution for having a firearm under a disability, *United States v. Webster*, the trial court further amplified jury instructions regarding flight, permitting the prosecution to introduce evidence that, when the defendant was ordered to stop his car for a seatbelt violation, he sped away in an attempt to elude the officer. When the police viewed the interior of the car, they found a bag of marijuana and a semiautomatic pistol. The judge charged the jury that:

> You may also consider any evidence of flight by the defendant, along with all of the evidence in the case, and you may consider whether this evidence shows a consciousness of guilt and determine the significance to be attached to any such conduct.
>
> Whether or not evidence of flight shows a consciousness of guilt and the significance to be attached to any such evidence are matters exclusively within the province of the jury. In your consideration of the evidence of flight you should consider that there may be reasons for this which are fully consistent with innocence.[105]

The Eighth Circuit Court of Appeals approved the jury instruction because it allowed the jury to decide whether or not to infer that the defendant had a consciousness of guilt, after considering the defendant's offer of an innocent reason for flight.[106]

If flight may indicate an inference of guilt, engaging in a standoff with a SWAT team after being cornered and disposal of a murder weapon following flight may also indicate a desire not to face arrest and trial, due to a consciousness of guilt. Against an argument that the evidence should not have been admitted against the defendant, a California reviewing court concluded that "the [trial] court did not abuse its discretion in allowing the evidence of [the defendant's] SWAT standoff as probative of his consciousness of guilt."[107]

Just as evidence of escape may be admitted to allow a jury to consider whether an inference of consciousness of guilt should be drawn,[108] a suicide attempt may be a form of avoidance of responsibility and should be admissible for any weight a jury might want to give it. In a case involving an allegation of rape of a 15-year-old girl by the man she considered her father, the defendant apparently attempted to kill himself with an overdose of drugs on several occasions after his arrest on the charges.[109] The trial judge allowed the evidence of attempted suicide by drug overdose to be admitted so that

---

[104] Connecticut v. Crnkovic, 68 Conn. App. 757, 766-767, 793 A.2d 1139, 1147, 2002 Conn. App. LEXIS 159 (2002).

[105] United States v. Webster, 442 F.3d 1065, 1067, 2006 U.S. App. LEXIS 8061 (8th Cir. 2006).

[106] *Id.*

[107] People v. Garcia, 168 Cal. App. 4th 261, 292, 2008 Cal. App. LEXIS 2050 (Cal. 2008).

[108] Bigby v. Dretke, 402 F.3d 551, 557, 2005 U.S. App. LEXIS 3815 (5th Cir. 2005).

[109] Strong v. State, 372 Ark. 404, 416, 2008 Ark. LEXIS 112 (2008).

the jury might determine the value of the evidence. The Arkansas reviewing court upheld the admission of the overdose evidence with the comment, "we cannot say that the circuit court erred in permitting testimony regarding [the defendant's] overdose attempts. In light of the case law from other jurisdictions, as well as our holdings regarding flight, refusal to submit to testing, and escape from incarceration, we cannot say that the circuit court abused its discretion."[110] Attempts by a defendant to intimidate or threaten witnesses can be evidence of consciousness of guilt. In a New York robbery case, the trial court permitted police officers to testify concerning the defendant's threatening hand gestures toward witnesses during trial. According to the reviewing court, "[e] vidence of threats made by defendant to witnesses may be 'probative of defendant's consciousness of guilt' and thus may be admissible on that ground."[111]

In some instances, comments made by the defendant after being taken into custody for a crime are admissible. Demonstrative of this point is the case in which the defendant possessed an awareness of guilt as evidenced by his words to a television reporter during his transport from a sheriff's office to a county jail. When asked whether the defendant had been attempting to commit a robbery when the alleged victim was shot, the defendant replied, "No comment." The reviewing court approved the introduction of the defendant's answer because the police did not ask the question that elicited it, and the defendant's comments were freely offered. Postarrest silence following the giving of ***Miranda* warnings** cannot be used against a defendant because the defendant may simply be exercising the rights that the warnings cover.[112] In a situation that was the opposite of speech, a North Dakota appellate court noted that "a prosecutor's use of a defendant's post-arrest silence after receiving *Miranda* warnings to impeach a defendant's exculpatory story, told for the first time at trial, violates the defendant's right to due process."[113]

> ***Miranda* warnings** Warnings that must be given to persons who are in custody [arrest] and who police wish to interrogate.

Other instances in which courts have considered the activities of the suspect following the crime are (1) the assumption of a false name after the commission of a crime; (2) the suspect's giving of a false statement; (3) concealment of evidence; and (4) growing a moustache or beard. In a Connecticut case, *State v. Pascal*, the defendant offered a false name and a false date of birth to police. These deceptions were admitted, and the jury was permitted to determine the probative value of the falsities. Despite the defendant's contention that the admission of the evidence was improper, the reviewing court upheld the convictions that resulted.[114] In one bank robbery case, the accused gained weight after his arrest, shaved his beard, and began to wear glasses in an

---

110 *Id.* at 416, 417.

111 People v. Lee, 868 N.Y.S.2d 453, 456, 2008 N.Y. App. Div. LEXIS 8768 (2008).

112 State v. Butler, 2008 N.C. App. LEXIS 1645 (2008).

113 State v. Rivet, 2008 N.D. 145, 2008 N.D. LEXIS 144 (2008).

114 State v. Pascal, 109 Conn. App. 45, 72, 2008 Conn. App. LEXIS 352 (2008).

apparent effort to frustrate courtroom identification by tellers. The court charged the jury that it could consider the defendant's change of appearance as indicating a fear of being identified by tellers, and that the change could help prove consciousness of guilt.[115] The court further stated that it was up to the jurors to determine how much weight to give the evidence.

§ 7.10 —Defenses

While relevancy is the requirement for admitting evidence against a defendant, the same standards generally apply when the defense wants to negate or rebut the prosecution's case. Although a criminal defendant need not introduce any evidence in order to prevail, most defendants attempt to challenge the prosecution's evidence with proof that attempts to rebut the prosecution's case. A defense in a criminal case may involve presenting evidence through defense witnesses, by cross-examining prosecution witnesses, or by combination of the two. Alternatively, a defendant may choose to present evidence of an affirmative defense, such as alibi, entrapment, self-defense, or insanity, and when employing these defenses, the defendant generally has the burden of proof in many jurisdictions. As a general rule, defense evidence must meet the same tests for relevancy and materiality as the prosecution's evidence. Such evidence is usually admissible if it meets general admissibility tests, but there may be additional requirements in some situations. Several commonly offered defenses are discussed here.[116]

A. *Insanity*

A defendant may have a defense of lack of mental capacity if he or she can prove that, at the time of the criminal act, he or she was too mentally deficient to be held responsible for the act. Additionally, in a situation in which the defendant is unable to assist the defense attorney in preparing and presenting a defense, the evidence may show that the defendant is not competent to stand trial. In both cases, the defendant's mental condition becomes relevant. Evidence that proves the defendant met or failed to meet the jurisdiction's test for legal insanity will be relevant and admissible to either prove or disprove the mental condition of the defendant. In many jurisdictions, the insanity defense is considered an affirmative defense, and the burden of proof is placed on the defendant. The defendant may have to introduce evidence that proves

---

115 United States v. Carr, 362 U.S. App. D.C. 303, 373 F.3d 1350, 1353, 2004 U.S. App. LEXIS 14305 (D. C. Cir. 2004). Post-conviction relief denied at United States v. Carr, 2006 U.S. Dist. LEXIS 6368 (D. D. C. 2006).

116 *See* POLLOCK, CRIMINAL LAW (9th ed. 2009) for a discussion of defenses in criminal cases. *See also* Abbe Smith, Promoting Justice through Interdisciplinary Teaching, Practice, and Scholarship: The Difference in Criminal Defense and the Difference It Makes, 11 WASH. U.J.L. & POLICY 83 (2003). *See also* Daniel S. Medwed, Actual Innocents: Considerations in Selecting Cases for a New Innocence Project, 81 NEB.L. REV. 1097 (2003).

insanity beyond a reasonable doubt or by clear and convincing evidence. The second issue concerning mental health occurs at the time of trial and requires that the defendant possess sufficient mental competency to meaningfully assist and communicate with his or her attorney in presenting a defense.

The concept of legal insanity is recognized as a defense in most jurisdictions, while temporary insanity is recognized as a defense in some jurisdictions. Some jurisdictions allow a judge or jury to find that a person was not insane, but was suffering from a mental illness and "may be found guilty but mentally ill."[117] Arizona recently restricted the insanity defense under the traditional *M'Naghten* rule by removing the part of the test that addressed cognitive capacity and leaving the basic "right–wrong" part of the test.[118] Although not a favored defense, some states recognize the concept of temporary insanity that may have arisen from the chemical effects of alcohol or other drugs and will permit evidence in court to prove this defense.[119] Some states recognize a type of temporary insanity caused by voluntary intoxication, but use it in mitigation of the penalty attached to the offense for which the defendant has been convicted.[120] The Texas code prohibits voluntary intoxication from being asserted as a defense to the commission of any crime, but it provides that "[e]vidence of temporary insanity caused by intoxication may be introduced by the actor in mitigation of the penalty attached to the offense for which he is being tried."[121] States that do not recognize temporary insanity may allow evidence of the condition to be used as mitigating factors to be asserted during a capital or other sentencing proceeding.[122] As a general rule, to qualify for the defense of temporary insanity based on alcohol consumption, there must be some evidence to show that the insanity was caused by intoxication, and a judge commits error if the judge offers a jury instruction in the absence of evidence of voluntary intoxication.[123]

B. Voluntary Intoxication

Intoxication may be roughly equated to a type of voluntary insanity, and as a general rule, a defendant's own conduct in becoming intoxicated will not excuse that individual from criminal responsibility. The Texas Code is representative of most jurisdictions when it states "[v]oluntary intoxication does not constitute a defense to the commission of crime."[124] It is generally accepted that a defendant's voluntary intoxication is neither an excuse for the commission of crime, nor a defense to a prosecution for it,[125]

---

117 *See* 720 ILL. COMP. STAT. 5/6-2(c) (2013). *See also* OR. REV. STAT. §§ 161.319 and §161.295 (2012).

118 *See* Clark v. Arizona, 548 U.S. 735, 2006 U.S. LEXIS 5184 (2006).

119 People v. Washington, 2009 Mich. App. LEXIS 308 (2009). *See* § 3.11 of this book for a discussion of the burden of proving sanity. *See also* 18 U.S.C.S. § 17, Insanity Defense, for the text of the insanity defense available in federal criminal trials.

120 TEX. PENAL CODE § 8.04 (2013).

121 *Id.* § 8.04(b).

122 Williams v. State, 273 S.W.3d 200, 2008 Tex. Crim. App. LEXIS 692 (2008).

123 Sakil v. State, 2008 Tex. App. LEXIS 4230 (Tex. 2008).

124 TEX. PENAL CODE § 8.04 (a) (2013).

125 Leppla v. State, 277 Ga. App. 804, 811, 627 S.E.2d 794, 800, 2006 Ga. App. LEXIS 75 (2006).

but may provide some mitigation of the penalty.[126] This general rule of the common law is contained in the statutes of many states and exists by judicial decision in the federal courts, but some state and federal jurisdictions recognize limited exceptions.

An exception to the general rule exists in some jurisdictions when a defendant has been accused of a crime that involves some specific intent or requires the operation of a more complicated mental process such as deliberation or premeditation, and evidence that would support such concepts may be admissible. If the evidence discloses that a defendant was extremely intoxicated to the point that the correct *mens rea* could not be formed, some jurisdictions will take the lack of a specific intent into consideration as a demonstration that a particular crime has not been committed or as a mitigating factor. For example, in Alabama, voluntary intoxication may be a defense in a battery case where the intoxication amounts to insanity and incapacitates a person to the extent that he or she cannot form the proper intent.[127]

Not all jurisdictions agree that voluntary intoxication may operate as a mitigator or as a partial defense. In Arizona, the statute states that "[t]emporary intoxication resulting from the voluntary ingestion, consumption, inhalation or injection of alcohol, an illegal substance... or other psychoactive substances or the abuse of prescribed medications does not constitute insanity and is not a defense for any criminal act or requisite state of mind."[128] In a Florida case,[129] a defendant failed to win a reversal of his murder conviction, because the reviewing court found that his intoxication, although based partly on prescription medication, involved consumption far beyond the prescribed dosages, involved significant consumption of alcoholic beverages, and was characterized as voluntary intoxication. Florida law provides that "[v]oluntary intoxication resulting from the consumption, injection, or other use of alcohol or other controlled substance... is not a defense to any offense proscribed by law."[130] The statute also refuses to allow the admission of evidence to evaluate what effect voluntary intoxication might have had on *mens rea* or any required mental intent. Taking a similar approach, an Ohio reviewing court refused to reverse a vandalism conviction where the intoxicated defendant used a bulldozer to smash the windshield and the hood of a police cruiser.[131] The defendant was heavily intoxicated (.244 on a **Breathalyzer test**) on alcohol, but could operate the bulldozer and had control over it. The state's law did not take into consideration what effect intoxication might have on a required mental state. The approach demonstrated by these two examples is consistent with the position of the

Breathalyzer test Test to determine alcohol content of blood in one arrested for operating a motor vehicle under the influence of alcohol.

126 TEX. PENAL CODE § 8.04 (b) (2013).
127 Saunders v. Alabama, 2007 Ala. Crim. App. LEXIS 236 (2007).
128 ARIZ. REV. STAT. § 13-503 (2013).
129 Stimus v. State, 995 So. 2d 1149, 1151, 2008 Fla. App. LEXIS 18376 (2008).
130 FLA. STAT. § 775.051 (2013).
131 State v. Armstrong, 2007 Ohio 6405, 2007 Ohio App. LEXIS 5609 (2007).

Supreme Court of the United States under its holding that a state can prohibit a criminal defendant from offering evidence of voluntary intoxication to negate the requisite *mens rea*, without violating the due process clause of the Fourteenth Amendment.[132]

Where intoxication is recognized as a defense to a specific intent crime, the result may not always be acquittal, but rather conviction of a lesser degree of the offense for which no proof of specific intent is necessary. In a prosecution for aggravated sodomy by a drunk defendant, the reviewing court noted that the crime involved a specific intent and that a conviction could not stand unless there was proof of the proper intent.[133] The court upheld the conviction on the strength that the jury could have found the presence of a specific intent.

C. *Other Defenses*

Evidence of other affirmative defenses may be relevant if introduced for the purpose of establishing defenses such as entrapment, alibi, self-defense, defense of others, mistake of fact, mistake of law, lack of knowledge sufficient to commit the crime, and others. The evidence to support these defenses must meet the other tests of admissibility in addition to the relevancy and materiality tests.

§ 7.11 —Character Evidence

Rule 404

CHARACTER EVIDENCE; CRIMES OR OTHER ACTS

(1) Prohibited Uses. Evidence of a person's character or character trait is not admissible to prove that on a particular occasion the person acted in accordance with the character or trait.

(2) Exceptions for a Defendant or Victim in a Criminal Case. The following exceptions apply in a criminal case:

(A) a defendant may offer evidence of the defendant's pertinent trait, and if the evidence is admitted, the prosecutor may offer evidence to rebut it;

(B) subject to the limitations in Rule 412, a defendant may offer evidence of an alleged victim's pertinent trait, and if the evidence is admitted, the prosecutor may:

(i) offer evidence to rebut it; and

(ii) offer evidence of the defendant's same trait; and

(C) in a homicide case, the prosecutor may offer evidence of the alleged victim's trait of peacefulness to rebut evidence that the victim was the first aggressor.

(3) Exceptions for a Witness. Evidence of a witness's character may be admitted under Rules 607, 608, and 609. [134]

---

132 Montana v. Egelhoff, 518 U.S. 37, 56, 1996 U.S. LEXIS 3878 (1996).

133 State v. Langholz, 2009 Kan. App. Unpub. LEXIS 195 (2009).

134 FED. R. EVID. 404.

The character of a defendant should assist a jury or judge in making determinations about a defendant. In ordinary social and business situations, people make judgments about others based on character, a trait of character, or reputation. This approach works quite well in ordinary human affairs where money or relationships may be involved. However, when evaluating whether someone might be guilty of a crime, reliance on character evidence could mislead a finder of fact into making an erroneous decision that affects the freedom of the accused. Taken alone, the defendant's bad reputation or a particular character trait does not necessarily mean that the defendant always follows that trait or that he or she followed the trait on a particular occasion. Clearly, a good reputation should not be used to assist a defendant when a jury might ignore some evidence and acquit due to proof of a good reputation. Alternatively, justice might not be served if we partially substitute character for more demanding and more reliable evidence of criminality. If the state was permitted to prove that a person's character is bad, it could contend that this fact had some slight probative value in determining whether that person actually committed the charged offense. The reputation of an accused for a particular character trait might be relevant, but the jury might also use the reputation for that trait to convict in a close case where, in the absence of the trait evidence, it would have acquitted. As is sometimes stated in legal circles, proof of character might prove too much, and the jury might convict to punish the defendant for his bad character, rather than the issues presented at trial. In order to protect the accused from the possibility of conviction based on bad character, a general rule has evolved that evidence showing the bad character of the accused is usually not admitted.

Federal Rule 404(a) codifies the common-law rule that evidence that tends only to show a propensity to act in a particular manner, evidence of a criminal defendant's general bad character, and evidence of a witness's good character are not admissible.[135] This basic prohibition is often called the "propensity" rule. Under this rule and under the general evidence provisions, a person's character or propensity to act in a certain way may not be offered as a basis for the inference that, on a specific occasion, a person acted in conformity with the propensity or the character trait. The prosecution may not use evidence of a defendant's negative character trait to show that the defendant may have a propensity to commit the crime for which the defendant is currently on trial.[136] While the text of Federal Rule 404(a) generally excludes character evidence of the defendant or of a victim, the rule recognizes exceptions where the defendant offers evidence of personal character.[137]

While the prosecution cannot introduce evidence of the bad character of the accused during its case-in-chief, the courts apply a different rule when the criminal defendant places his or her character at issue by introducing evidence in support of good character. Because a jury might give a defendant with good character the benefit of the doubt in a close case, he or she has the opportunity to introduce evidence of

---

135 State v. Buie, 671 S.E.2d 351, 353, 2009 N.C. App. LEXIS 48 (2009).

136 Ohio v. Bronner, 2002 Ohio 4248, 2002 Ohio App. LEXIS 4413 (2002).

137 *See* 24 TEX. JUR. *Criminal Law* § 3468 (2008) and FED. R. EVID. 404(b).

general good character to show that it was improbable that he or she committed the charged crime. If a defendant introduces evidence of good character by inquiring of a witness concerning the witness's knowledge of the defendant's good reputation in the community, the defense has "opened the door" to the issue of character, and the prosecution may inquire into the matter using the same type of evidence.[138]

Where the defense offers evidence of good general character, the prosecutor may offer evidence that disputes the good character evidence. Therefore, if a defendant asks a witness during cross-examination if she was aware of the defendant's reputation in the community, the prosecution may ask about specific instances of the defendant's misconduct to test the witness's credibility.[139] A prosecutor may inquire about a defendant's character only after a defendant places it at issue. A South Carolina trial court was in error when it permitted an inquiry into some of the defendant's prior difficulties with the legal system, after the defendant testified that he hated to see a woman cry.[140] Such testimony permitted an inquiry into defendant's prior crimes involving dishonesty as impeachment, but did not "open the door" to permit inquiry concerning criminal domestic violence and criminal sexual conduct, identical crimes for which he was currently on trial.

Even when the defendant has not "opened the door" to his or her character, and the prosecution improperly reveals to the jury that the defendant had a prior felony conviction, any resulting conviction will not automatically be reversed. If there is overwhelming evidence of guilt, or if the judge issues an immediate curative jury instruction, the conviction will not be disturbed based solely on a violation of erroneous admission of character evidence against an accused.[141]

While the prosecution generally cannot introduce adverse character evidence about the defendant during its case-in-chief, a defendant may bring forth relevant evidence of the alleged victim's tendency to show a particular trait. Federal Rule 404 generally excludes character evidence from admission, but provides an exception that provides that "a defendant may offer evidence of the defendant's pertinent trait."[142] For example, when a defendant's wife claimed self-defense in a domestic homicide case, the trial judge refused to allow her to introduce evidence that her deceased husband had a reputation as a violent and dangerous man. On appeal, the defendant contended that the trial court erred when it prevented her from introducing proof that her husband had a violent character. Specifically, the court excluded evidence that the victim-husband had grown angry with a car dealership and subsequently broke the windows of several cars in the dealership's inventory. In self-defense cases, the victim's violent character becomes relevant only to the extent that it relates to the defendant's fear of harm from the victim. The reviewing court granted the defendant a new trial because the trial court should have allowed the introduction of evidence of the victim's

---

138 State v. Braswell, 2008 Tenn. Crim. App. LEXIS 43 (2008). *See also* FED. R. EVID. 405(a).

139 *Id.*

140 State v. Young, 378 S.C. 101, 106, 2008 S.C. LEXIS 153 (2008).

141 Nickleson v. State, 2005 Tex. App. LEXIS 6658 (2005).

142 FED. R. EVID. 404(a)(1).

violent character, including specific instances of violence, because it was clearly relevant to the issue of self-defense.[143]

If it bears upon the case, the character of the ordinary witness—one who is not accused, including the victim—can also be shown by evidence. As a general rule, every person who testifies as a witness places his or her character for truthfulness at issue. If a defendant testifies, the credibility of the defendant becomes relevant and subject to impeachment. As in the case of other types of character evidence, once the door is opened, the other side may introduce evidence to rebut the evidence introduced by the first party.

The reason a defendant can always introduce evidence of good general character is that such evidence may be sufficient to create reasonable doubt concerning whether a defendant is guilty of the crime charged. The defendant is permitted to present evidence that he or she possesses a positive general reputation, but the defendant cannot introduce evidence that is irrelevant to general reputation. For example, a trial judge properly excluded a defendant's offer, through his witnesses, to prove that he was an honest person when the defendant had not taken the witness stand and the case involved a murder prosecution.[144]

In referring to Alaska's version of Federal Rule 404(a)(1), a state trial court noted that the accused in a criminal case has an option to introduce evidence of his or her good character by personal testimony or through other defense witnesses, but the prosecution may meet the evidence of the defendant's good general character with proof of specific incidents that have the effect of rebutting the defendant's evidence.[145] In a case involving sexual abuse of girls, the defendant testified that he had a benevolent nonsexual attitude toward children and had been employed as a counselor to teenagers who had been victims of sexual abuse. The trial court properly allowed the Alaska prosecutor to introduce evidence that the defendant had made sexual comments about 10- to 14-year-old girls as rebuttal evidence.[146] As with any other testifying witness, every defendant who testifies places his or her credibility at issue and is subject to efforts to impeach, but merely testifying does not place at issue all other sorts of character traits or the defendant's general reputation.[147]

§ 7.12 —Proof of Other Crimes, Wrongs, or Acts

Rule 404

CHARACTER EVIDENCE; CRIMES OR OTHER ACTS

* * *

(b) Crimes, Wrongs, or Other Acts.

---

143 State v. Everett, 630 S.E.2d 703, 2006 N.C. App. LEXIS 1302 (2006).

144 Marschke v. State, 185 S.W.3d 295, 307, 2006 Mo. App. LEXIS 280 (2006).

145 Bryant v. State, 115 P.3d 1249, 1253, 2005 Alaska App. LEXIS 62 (2005).

146 *Id.* at 1254.

147 Gage v. State, 2005 Tex. App. LEXIS 531 (2005).

(1) Prohibited Uses. Evidence of a crime, wrong, or other act is not admissible to prove a person's character in order to show that on a particular occasion the person acted in accordance with the character.

(2) Permitted Uses; Notice in a Criminal Case. This evidence may be admissible for another purpose, such as proving motive, opportunity, intent, preparation, plan, knowledge, identity, absence of mistake, or lack of accident. On request by a defendant in a criminal case, the prosecutor must:

(A) provide reasonable notice of the general nature of any such evidence that the prosecutor intends to offer at trial; and

(B) do so before trial—or during trial if the court, for good cause, excuses lack of pretrial notice.

* * *

In essence, Federal Rule 404(b) in restates the general rule that evidence of other crimes, wrongs, or acts may not be admissible to prove the character of a person in order to show action that would be in conformity with the character trait. It may, however, be admissible against a defendant for other purposes, such as proof of motive, opportunity, intent, preparation, plan, knowledge, identity, or absence of mistake or accident.[148] Federal Rule 404(b) was amended in 1991 to provide for a notice requirement to criminal defendants, where use of character evidence was contemplated.

When a trial court is faced with deciding whether to admit prior acts against a defendant currently on trial, the judge must make sure that the prior acts are not admitted to prove that the defendant has a predisposition to commit the charged crime or that the evidence proves the defendant is a bad person. In a District of Columbia prosecution against a defendant who had been selling counterfeit compact discs, the prosecution wanted to prove that the defendant knew that the discs were counterfeit. The jewel cases that contained the discs had a thin piece of paper inside that indicated the artist for each disc, and the jewel cases were wrapped in plastic wrap. The defendant had been previously convicted of selling compact discs without a district vending license, under circumstances that clearly showed he knew the compact discs were counterfeit. So, the prosecution wanted to admit the prior offense. The reviewing court noted that evidence of prior acts and crimes was presumptively inadmissible due to the danger of unfair prejudice, but in this case, the court approved the admission of prior crime evidence because it tended to show that the defendant had knowledge that the compact discs were counterfeit.[149] The two crimes were so similar in many aspects that proof of one tended to prove the other.

---

[148] Idaho v. Siegel, 137 Idaho 538, 541, 50 P.3d 1033, 1036, 2002 Idaho App. LEXIS 30 (2002).

[149] Jackson v. United States, 856 A.2d 1111, 1114, 2004 D.C. App. LEXIS 413 (D.D.C. 2004).

As a general rule, evidence of prior misconduct is inadmissible if intended to suggest that the defendant might be guilty of a crime for which the defendant is presently standing trial. In a case in which a minor, adopted child had accused her father of sexual offenses, the court was in error when it permitted the defendant's adult daughters from a prior marriage to testify that, 30 years earlier, the defendant had sexually abused them by touching them inappropriately. In reversing the convictions, the reviewing court noted that "[e]vidence is legally relevant if its probative value outweighs its costs."[150] In this case, the earlier allegations took place too long ago and allegedly involved only touching, while in the present prosecution, the allegation involved statutory rape and sodomy. To be admissible, evidence of prior uncharged sexual activities must be nearly identical to the crime charged in the current case and so unusual that the prior acts operate as a virtual signature of the defendant's method of committing the crime. The prejudicial value of the prior, 30-year-old uncharged acts outweighed any probative effect in the present case, so the appellate court reversed the convictions.[151]

Evidence of other crimes or prior misconduct by the defendant is generally not admissible to prove that a defendant is guilty of a crime for which he or she is currently on trial. Where an exception to this general rule applies, the evidence of prior crimes may be admissible if the evidence demonstrates a defendant's knowledge to commit the crime, common scheme or plan, motive, intent, or lack of mistake. In an Arkansas case[152] in which the defendant had been accused of selling methamphetamine to an undercover officer, the trial court permitted the prosecution to admit evidence that he had made a similar sale to an undercover officer ten days prior to the date of the sale for which he was on trial. The defendant's identity was not at issue, and the sale was a routine sale of methamphetamine. According to the defendant, none of the reasons for admitting prior crimes supported admission in his case, and if the prior sale evidence was relevant, he contended that the prejudicial value of that evidence outweighed its probative effect. The Supreme Court of Arkansas reversed the defendant's drug sale conviction because it could not perceive a valid reason for admitting that prior drug sale other than to show that he was a drug dealer likely to have sold drugs in the instance for which he was being tried. Over a dissenting opinion, the court noted, "[t]his is precisely the type of evidence that Rule 404(b) was designed to exclude."[153] It should be stressed that many courts would take a different view and would hold that the crimes are so similar that the earlier crime evidence should have been admitted under a common scheme or plan exception.

When the prosecution introduces evidence of other crimes, wrongs, or acts committed by the defendant under Rule 404(b) or the state equivalent, the burden of proof of the fact of the prior act must be clear and convincing[154] and have a logically relevant

---

150 State v. Berwald, 186 S.W.3d 349, 359, 2005 Mo. App. LEXIS 1917 (2005).

151 *Id.*

152 Phavixay v. State, 373 Ark. 168, 2008 Ark. LEXIS 234 (2008).

153 *Id.* at 171.

154 State v. Stokes, 673 S.E.2d 434, 2009 S.C. LEXIS 35 (2009).

connection to the crime for which the defendant is on trial. For example, in a North Carolina case[155] where the defendant had been charged with selling methamphetamine to a police officer working undercover, he alleged that proof of two prior sales to the same officer were erroneously introduced by the prosecution. The defendant argued that the sales were far apart and not necessarily related. One sale occurred six days prior to the date of the sale for which he was on trial, and one occurred ten months prior to the other sale. In upholding the trial court's admission of prior bad acts, the reviewing court noted that in this case, the sales were made to an undercover female officer, the sale occurred in the same neighborhood as the other sales, the defendant was identified as the seller, all three sales were made by a man standing on the street to the officer sitting in a car, the quantity of methamphetamine was the same, and the price was the same. The court noted, "[i]n sum, after careful review, we hold that the trial court did not abuse its discretion by admitting the challenged evidence under Rule 404(b) for the limited purpose of showing defendant's intent, identity, and common plan or scheme."[156]

In determining whether a trial court properly admitted evidence of other acts under Rule 404(b), the United States Court of Appeals for the Tenth Circuit considers four factors: "(1) whether the evidence is offered for a proper purpose, (2) whether the evidence is relevant, (3) whether the probative value of the evidence is substantially outweighed by its prejudicial effect, and (4) whether a limiting instruction is given if the defendant so requests."[157] The Court of Appeals for the Fifth Circuit employs a slightly different test for admissibility of other act evidence, but overall, a similar result emerges. The Fifth Circuit employs a two-pronged analysis for the admissibility of evidence under Rule 404(b). First, the evidence of "other crimes, wrongs, or acts" must be relevant to an issue other than the defendant's character,[158] and, second, the evidence of other crimes or acts must possess probative value that is not outweighed by the danger of unfair prejudice to the defendant.[159] An example of a state test for other act evidence is demonstrated by Idaho, which also directs its courts to follow a two-pronged test in determining whether to admit the evidence.[160] The court first asks whether there is a sufficient level of evidence to establish the fact of the prior act, and then the court must determine relevance to a disputed issue in the crime for which the defendant is presently being charged. In all of these tests for prior act admission or exclusion, the courts are attempting to screen out earlier crimes and acts that, in all fairness, should not be admitted against a defendant in an unrelated trial, while allowing admission of prior acts that have sufficient relevance to the current case.

---

155 State v. Welch, 666 S.E.2d 826, 829, 830, 2008 N.C. App. LEXIS 1741 (2008).

156 *Id.* at 831.

157 United States v. Parker, 553 F.3d 1309, 1314, 2009 U.S. App. LEXIS 359 (10th Cir. 2009).

158 United States v. Percel, 553 F.3d 903, 912, 2008 U.S. App. LEXIS 26428 (5th Cir. 2008).

159 *Id.*

160 State v. Palmer, 2009 Ida. App. LEXIS 17 (2009).

In 1988, in *Huddleston v. United States*, the Supreme Court was asked to clarify the application of an earlier, but similar, version of Rule 404(b).[161] In this case, the petitioner had been charged under federal law with knowledge of the possession and sale of stolen videotapes. At the trial, the district court allowed the government to introduce, as evidence of "similar acts" under Rule 404(b), evidence of the petitioner's involvement in a series of sales of allegedly stolen televisions and appliances from the same suspicious source as the tapes. On appeal, the defendant conceded that "similar acts" evidence was admissible to show his knowledge that the tapes had been stolen, but he argued that the grave potential of "similar acts" evidence for causing undue prejudice called for a preliminary determination by the court that the defendant committed such acts before the jury should be allowed to hear that evidence. In a footnote to that case, the Supreme Court noted that there was inconsistency in the circuit courts, because six circuits apparently required a preliminary finding of the trial court that the government has proven commission of the similar act.

The United States Supreme Court then decided that the trial court had properly admitted evidence of the prior acts. According to the Court, there is no need for a preliminary finding by the trial court that the government has proven the commission of the similar acts, as such a requirement is inconsistent with the legislative history behind Rule 404(b). In referring to the relevancy issue, the Court included this statement:

> Evidence is admissible under Rule 404(b) only if it is relevant. "Relevancy is not an inherent characteristic of any item of evidence but exists only as a relation between an item of evidence and a matter properly provable in the case." In Rule 404(b) context, similar act evidence is relevant only if the jury can reasonably conclude that the act occurred and that the defendant was the actor.[162]

Many states have adopted rules that are either identical or fairly similar to Federal Rule 404. Each year, cases that interpret these rules reach state reviewing courts. Some of these decisions, which state the rules of the respective states and explain the reasoning of the courts in applying the rules, are included in Part II of this book.

The philosophy underlying the general exclusion of evidence of an accused's past acts "is meant to prevent the State from punishing people for their character."[163] If most prior misconduct is allowed into evidence, its admission "endangers the defendant of being convicted because he or she is a person of bad character generally, or has criminal tendencies."[164]

Applying the general rules relating to other acts evidence, the Supreme Court of Rhode Island reversed a defendant's second murder conviction, because the trial court admitted evidence that the defendant had been convicted of murder in a prior case.[165] Which inescapably led the second jury to understand that the defendant had

---

[161] Huddleston v. United States, 485 U.S. 681, 108 S. Ct. 1496, 96 L. Ed. 2d 771 (1988).

[162] *Id.*

[163] Bassett v. State, 795 N.E.2d 1050, 1053, 2003 Ind. LEXIS 750 (2003).

[164] Samaniego-Hernandez v. State, 839 N.E.2d 798, 802, 2005 Ind. App. LEXIS 2450 (2005).

[165] State v. Pona, 948 A.2d 941, 2008 R.I. LEXIS 69 (2008).

committed a prior murder. While there was some connection between the two murder cases, the primary effect of the evidence from the first murder was to brand the defendant as a murderer who might have a propensity for criminal activity or, in particular, murder. The other crime evidence introduced at the second trial deprived the defendant of a fair trial.

Thus, prior crimes and misconduct may be excluded when the connection to the charged crime is largely irrelevant and unfairly prejudicial. In an Indiana case, the victim had been wearing brass knuckles when he initiated a fight with the defendant, who had then used a knife to puncture the victim's heart. The defendant objected to the use of prior act evidence at his homicide trial. The trial judge permitted the prosecutor to introduce evidence that the defendant used marijuana, had rolling papers, had Xanax and alcohol in his blood, and had indicated that he wanted to cut another man's throat at a different time. In reversing the homicide conviction, the appellate court held that the other crime and misconduct evidence was not properly admitted to show the defendant's state of mind or to refute self-defense. The other evidence involved different people and occurred at different times from the fatal altercation, unfairly suggesting that the defendant had a criminal propensity and may have engaged in the illegal conduct.[166]

§ 7.13 —Experimental and Scientific Evidence

While the progress of science and its application to crime solving cannot be overemphasized, the concepts involving relevancy require additional attention to assure the admission of scientific results. Scientific evidence that is excluded from trial does not assist the party seeking to introduce it. The most prominent recent development in science that has positively influenced criminal justice professionals involves variations of DNA testing for identification purposes. The professionals conducting criminal investigations must be aware of the rules regarding the care, custody, and admissibility of scientific evidence and evidence resulting from experiments. This includes weapons tests, ammunition identification, fingerprints, DNA collection and care protocols, photographs, motion pictures, X-rays, tape recordings, maps, drawings, blood-alcohol tests, and results from computer hard drive examinations. Using specialized tracking software to gather data from the Internet and the interpretation of metadata from e-mail and Web sites have become necessary forms of evidence collection in some investigations. Without a full understanding of the processes involved, such evidence may not be properly secured for introduction in court. Most often, experiments and scientific test results will be conducted by experts and introduced in court by expert witnesses, but, in some situations, specially trained technicians who may not precisely fit the traditional definition of "expert" may present the evidence in court. The following chapters discuss these types of evidence more thoroughly, especially Chapter 14, "Real Evidence."

---

166 Gillespie v. State, 832 N.E.2d 1112, 1117, 2005 Ind. App. LEXIS 1505 (2005).

When properly conducted, the admissibility of all scientific or technical evidence should be a foregone conclusion because the results contain no bias and only reveal truth. The contention could be made that scientific evidence should always be admissible because of relevancy in criminal cases. Each scientific result must meet individual tests of logical and legal relevancy prior to being considered for admission, and the expert witness must be qualified as an expert. In the exercise of discretion, the trial judge may exclude some scientific evidence to avoid possible unfair prejudice to the accused. Moreover, the court may impose a limit on the prosecution's demonstrations to avoid procedures that may unduly arouse, mislead, or confuse the jury. The admission or exclusion of scientific or technical evidence rests with the trial judge, whose decision will not be disturbed by an appellate court, unless it finds a clear abuse of discretion.

As a preliminary matter concerning the admissibility of the results of scientific tests or experiments, the trial court must determine whether the results will meet the tests for relevancy. According to Federal Rule of Evidence 702, "[i]f scientific, technical, or other specialized knowledge will assist the trier of fact to understand the evidence or to determine a fact in issue, a witness qualified as an expert by knowledge, skill, experience, training, or education, may testify thereto in the form of an opinion or otherwise." The burden of proving admissibility of evidence under Rule 702 is placed on the party offering evidence by the standard of clear and convincing evidence.[167] As a general rule, before scientific evidence is admitted, the party seeking to introduce the evidence must lay a foundation for the evidence by introducing proof that "(1) the underlying theory is generally accepted as valid; (2) the procedures used are generally accepted as reliable if performed properly; [and] (3) the procedures were applied and conducted properly in the present instance."[168]

In 1993, after reviewing the ***Frye* test**[169] of the admissibility of scientific evidence, as established in previous cases, the United States Supreme Court reconsidered whether the *Frye* test had continued usefulness in federal courts. Under the *Frye v. United States* standard,[170] courts required that a scientific principle and its related tests had gained "general acceptance" in a particular scientific or technical field before a court should consider admitting the results of those tests. The *Frye* standard gradually gained acceptance in federal and many state jurisdictions. The adoption of the Federal Rules of Evidence brought some challenges to the *Frye* standard, and in *Daubert v. Merrell Dow Pharmaceuticals*,[171] the Supreme Court determined that *Frye* should no longer be followed in federal courts.

> ***Frye* test** The standard originally offered in *Frye v. United States* (1923) that regulated the admissibility of scientific tests into evidence.

[167] Frankenfield v. State, 2008 Tex. App. LEXIS 7920 (2008).

[168] State v. Escobido-Ortiz, 109 Haw. 359, 367, 126 P.3d 402, 410, 2005 Haw. App. LEXIS 520 (2005).

[169] Frye v. United States, 54 D.C. App. 46, 293 F. 1013, 1923 U.S. App. LEXIS 1712 (1923).

[170] *Id.*

[171] Daubert v. Merrell Dow Pharmaceuticals, Inc., 509 U.S. 579, 1993 U.S. LEXIS 4408 (1993).

Daubert established the following nonexclusive list of factors to guide lower federal courts in assessing the reliability of scientific evidence:

1. Whether a scientific theory or technique can be (or has been) tested;
2. Whether the theory or technique has been subjected to peer review or publication;
3. The known or potential rate of error and the existence and maintenance of standards controlling the technique's operation;
4. Whether the technique is generally accepted. (But it is not an absolutely necessary precondition to the admissibility of scientific evidence.)

The Court in *Daubert* emphasized that the inquiry in determining the reliability of scientific evidence is flexible and should focus on the principles and methodology offered as evidence. Where the evidence would assist the finder of fact and has sufficient reliability, the evidence should be admitted, even under circumstances when the *Frye* test would have excluded the scientific evidence.[172] In effect, following the *Daubert* rule, judges serve a "gatekeeping" role and must determine whether the expert's proffered testimony of scientific, technical, or other specialized knowledge will help the trier of fact to understand or determine a fact or principle at issue.[173]

§ 7.14 —Relevancy of Cybercrime Evidence

Almost no limits exist to the different criminal acts that can be either committed with computers or facilitated by the use of computers. Trespassing into the computers of others for the purpose of creating computer problems, accessing and stealing valuable data, and transferring money from bank or corporate accounts are just a few of the possible crimes attributed to cybercriminals. Cybercriminals often spam thousands of e-mail addresses, alleging that money is available provided the recipient will provide checking account routing numbers, and occasionally, such spamming efforts lead to success. Individuals interested in child pornography commit cybercrime when they create, produce, and transfer the images to willing recipients via the Internet. Computers that control heating, ventilating, and cooling have been hacked for various purposes, and hospital record systems involving critical patient care have also been breeched. Although not an everyday occurrence, convicted criminals have even been known to commit new cybercrimes while still incarcerated. In a case involving a prisoner in a county correctional facility, the inmate who was supposed to be using a protected computer for legal research discovered how to circumvent the limits and gain entrance, for himself and for others, into the personnel records of the institution, including the Social Security numbers of current and prior employees.[174] A federal prosecutor procured an

---

[172] *See* Chapter 15 for a comprehensive discussion of the admissibility of the results of examinations and tests.

[173] Burton v. CSX Transportation, 269 S.W.3d 1, 2008 Ky. LEXIS 236 (2008).

[174] *See* United States v. Janosko, 2011 U.S. App. LEXIS 7433 (1st Cir. 2011).

indictment against the inmate that included charges of causing damage to a protected computer and damage to the network system. The defendant pled guilty to violations of the federal Computer Fraud and Abuse Act.[175]

Proving guilt of the various cybercrimes, whether state or federal, requires proof based on relevant evidence gathered from a variety of lawful sources, and collecting this evidence may require warrants directed to Internet service providers[176] or to the owners or possessors of personal computers. In a significant number of computer crime cases, Fourth Amendment search and seizure issues create hurdles for the prosecution to overcome in the initial phases of the case, or they require the prosecution to defend the conviction on appeal.[177] When a defendant prevails in a Fourth Amendment suppression motion, the evidence might be logically relevant, but the court deems it to be legally irrelevant and inadmissible. In one case in which the defendant had consented to federal agents searching his computer, he objected to the introduction of photographs printed from a forensic image of his hard drive.[178] Although he contended that the printed pictures lacked a proper foundation to be relevant to the case, the reviewing court held that sufficient authentication existed and allowed them to be introduced. Cybercrime involving child pornography or an attempt by a defendant to meet with an underage child is often discovered when state or federal law enforcement agents use searchable peer-to-peer file sharing software to locate actual posted child pornography or when officers engage in dialogue with predators seeking to meet children.[179] The admissibility of this relevant evidence does not normally pose a significant legal issue because the officer had a direct involvement in acquiring the evidence.

In determining whether evidence stored on a computer meets the test of relevancy, care must be taken to determine whether the defendant was the responsible person or whether the data could have been created, stored, or downloaded by another person. In a Texas case, an appellate court reversed some of the defendant's convictions for possession of child pornography, because the defendant purchased the desktop computer at a

---

175 *See* 18 U.S.C. § 1030 *et seq.* Cell phones are included under the federal definition of "computer" even if the particular phone used has no Internet connection capability and may subject the cybercriminal to prosecution under this statute. United States v. Kramer, 631 F.3d 900, 902, 2011 U.S. App. LEXIS 2367 (8th Cir. 2011).

176 *See* United States v. Pires, 2011 U.S. App. LEXIS 7019 (1st Cir. 2011), and United States v. Warshak, 631 F.3d 266, 2010 U.S. App. LEXIS 25415 (6th Cir. 2010).

177 United States v. Simpson, 2011 U.S. Dist. LEXIS 20752 (N.D. Tex. 2011).

178 United States v. McNealy, 625 F.3d 858, 864, 2010 U.S. App. LEXIS 23111 (5th Cir. 2010). Other computer users consent to allowing anyone to use and copy designated files with the LimeWire®, Shareaza®, or other peer-to-peer sharing software, and law enforcement officials are legally permitted to enter any consenting computer system without a warrant. *See* Brown v. State, 912 N.E.2d 881, 2009 Ind. App. LEXIS 1487 n.3, "The basic Lime Wire program is designed to allow computer users to share files with others and is available on-line for download to anyone searching for or looking to share files by key word, category, or name."

179 Wenger v. State, 292 S.W.3d 191, 194, 2009 Tex. App. LEXIS 4859 (2009).

flea market, and the forensics examiner could not determine who placed the offending photographs on the hard drive or when they were last accessed.[180] In addition, there were viruses present on the computer that were capable of covertly placing images on the hard drive. The examiner also indicated that the images had been deleted at some unknown time, and they were not available to be viewed by anyone. Because the prosecution was not able to prove a connection between the defendant and the offending photographs, the appellate court reversed the counts of possession of child pornography that were based on the desktop computer hard drive.

Computers used by criminals in committing cybercrime have a particularly interesting characteristic: they create and store significant amounts of metadata concerning Internet locations that have been visited, the times and durations of the connections, and the identity/address of the initiating computer. When a cooperating witness can be motivated into assisting law enforcement agents, the production of legally relevant evidence can be assured. In a South Carolina federal investigation, a potential defendant decided to cooperate and assist officers in investigating and identifying individuals using the Internet to commit identity theft and credit card fraud.[181] Secret Service agents targeted a particular online community that trafficked in personal information, by having the cooperating witness engage in online chats with other criminals offering to sell data from the backs of credit and debit cards. When the cooperating witness purchased some stolen identity data, the Secret Service electronically deposited the payment in the bank account of the online criminal, creating a data trail that eventually helped convict the defendant for five counts of wire fraud and two counts of identity theft. The computers used by the defendants and by the cooperating witness created a data trail of relevant evidence sufficient for a guilty verdict.

In considering cybercrime and the various methodologies that may be used to combat it and to convict those involved with cybercrime, new tools will be constantly evolving that will collect data that will be considered relevant and admissible in court. Another variable in this context is that criminals will also evolve in their abilities to engage in electronic crime and to confuse or hide the data necessary to convict them. Therefore, the acquisition and production of legally relevant evidence necessary to combat cybercrime will continue to be a challenge for police and prosecutors.

§ 7.15 Summary

In a criminal trial, the primary objective is to determine the truth as to the issues presented. Over the years, the courts have developed rules of exclusion, including rules concerning relevancy and materiality. If the evidence does not meet the tests

---

180 *See* Wise v. State, 2011 Tex. App. LEXIS 1583 (2011). *See* case in Part II.

181 *See* United States v. Giannone, 360 F. App'x. 473, 2010 U.S. App. LEXIS 326 (4th Cir. 2010).

of relevancy and materiality, it will not be admitted. Evidence that has even a slight tendency to prove or disprove a pertinent fact in issue will be considered relevant, but some relevant evidence may be excluded if its tendency to prove or disprove a fact at issue is unfairly prejudicial. Evidence that goes to substantial matters in dispute and has an effective influence or bearing on the decision of the case is material.

The trial court has great latitude in determining the admissibility of the evidence and whether it has legal relevancy or materiality. The court's interpretation as to what evidence is relevant is usually given great weight, and its determination will be final unless there is a clear abuse of discretion.

State constitutions and the federal Constitution, along with state and federal court decisions and relevant statutes, must be considered in determining what evidence meets the relevancy and materiality tests. The following general rules have been developed through this procedure:

- Evidence that tends to establish the identity of persons involved is admissible as relevant and material. This, of course, is subject to the other rules of admissibility.
- Evidence that concerns the identity of things connected with the crime is considered relevant, although there are some exceptions.
- Evidence that helps prove or disprove elements of the crime is considered relevant and material.
- Generally, evidence that relates to the circumstances and events that precede or follow the crime is admissible as relevant to the issues.
- Evidence relating to the defenses claimed by the defendant, such as mental disease, coercion, self-defense, and alibi, is generally admissible if it meets the other admissibility tests, in addition to the relevancy and materiality tests.
- Evidence regarding the character and reputation of the accused or other crimes committed by the accused is sometimes recognized as relevant and material, but it is often excluded because of overriding dangers of unfair prejudice to the defendant's case. For this reason, only certain evidence of this type is admissible.
- Evidence of other crimes, wrongs, or acts is not admissible to show criminal propensity, but may be admissible to show the existence of a continuing or common plan, scheme, motive, intent, identity, lack of mistake, lack of knowledge, or conspiracy of which the crime charged is a part.
- Evidence concerning experimental and scientific evidence is also usually considered relevant, but it must pass other tests before it can be admitted into court.

It is obvious that, even though the parties may succeed in excluding evidence that is irrelevant and immaterial, there is certainly no reciprocal assurance that the court will necessarily admit evidence that is relevant and material. In future chapters, some of the other requirements are discussed, and relevancy and materiality as they relate to specific types of evidence are also explored in more detail.

CHAPTER SEVEN: QUESTIONS AND REVIEW EXERCISES

1. How is relevant evidence defined under Rule 401 of the Federal Rules of Evidence? What is logical relevance? What is legal relevance? In a murder case, should a judge admit crime scene and autopsy color photographs that are arguably gruesome? Analyze in terms of logical and legal relevancy.
2. Materiality is a similar, if not parallel, to relevancy. "Material evidence is evidence, fact, statement, or information that, if believed, would tend to influence or affect the issue under determination."[182] Evidence that is material must not be unfair or unduly prejudicial to introduce against a defendant. Should a judge admit into evidence as material the fact that the defendant has a conviction for driving under the influence that occurred 15 years prior to the defendant's trial for larceny or theft? Explain briefly.
3. Evidence is not always admissible because it meets the concept of logical relevancy. What are some examples of evidence that might be logically relevant but legally irrelevant due to constitutional errors in obtaining the evidence? Would rape shield laws exclude potentially relevant evidence as a way to further a particular public policy?
4. Under Rule 403 of the Federal Rules of Evidence, evidence can be excluded when its value in revealing the facts of the case are substantially outweighed by dangers of unfair prejudice, confusing the issues, misleading the jury, or for other reasons. Construct a hypothetical example where a defense argument could be made that evidence should have been refused admission by the trial judge because of any of the reasons in Rule 403. Should a judge refuse a prosecutor's request to put six witnesses to the same criminal act on the stand, if those witness will offer virtually the same exact evidence? Assume logical relevance exists.
5. Concerning concepts of relevancy as it relates to identity, should a witness who has identified a defendant from an in-person lineup, but who is not totally sure of her identification, be permitted to indicate her belief that the defendant was the perpetrator of the crime against her? Could this shaky identification be excluded as constituting unfair prejudice to a defendant?
6. Circumstances that occurred prior to the crime may be admissible as relevant. Where a defendant has been accused of murdering his "off and on again" girlfriend, should a court admit evidence that the defendant had beaten the woman two weeks prior to her

182 United States v. Bonsu, 291 Fed. App. 505, 2008 U.S. App. LEXIS 17998 (4th Cir. 2008).

death and that on the day of the murder, the defendant procured the murder weapon from his sister's kitchen?

7. Where a defendant has alleged an affirmative defense, evidence that helps prove or disprove the defense should generally be admissible. If a defendant pleads insanity, what kind of evidence should be admissible as meeting the tests of logical and legal relevancy?
8. As a general rule, a person's character or propensity to act in a certain way may not be offered as a basis for the inference that, on a specific occasion, a person acted in conformity with that propensity or character trait. When a defendant has a habit of acting in a particular way or manner, why should evidence of that trait be excluded from use against a defendant, when it seems as if the relevant character or trait would enlighten the jury concerning the accused's criminal conduct?
9. With reference to question 8, under what circumstances can a judge allow the evidence, excluded previously, into evidence for different purposes other than showing that the defendant is merely a "bad person"?
10. Scientific evidence and the results of testing substances to reveal their identity may be admissible against a defendant. What is the foundation that must be demonstrated before scientific evidence will be deemed relevant and, therefore, admissible?

Competency of Evidence and Witnesses

8

The terms "relevancy," "competency," and "materiality" are frequently used conjunctively in such manner as to suggest that they are synonymous, yet it is obvious upon second thought that a matter which may be relevant to an issue of the case may be rendered incompetent and inadmissible as to the established rules of evidence, such as the rule which excludes hearsay evidence or requires the production of the best evidence. . . . In other words evidence must be not only logically relevant, but of such a character as to be receivable in courts of justice

20 AM. JUR. Evidence 253

Chapter Contents

KEY TERMS AND CONCEPTS	
Admissibility of Scientific Tests	*Daubert* Test
Authenticating Phone	*Frye* Test
Conversations Best Evidence Rule	Incompetent Evidence by Law
Competency of Children	Mental Competency
Competency of Judge	Negative Evidence
Competency of Juror	Privileged Communications
Competency of Spouses	Witness Competency

§ 8.1 Introduction

While the preceding chapters discuss some of the rules concerning relevancy and materiality, this chapter focuses on the competency of both witnesses and evidence. Even when evidence has been deemed to be relevant and material or logically and legally relevant, it still must clear the third hurdle, competency, before it can be considered admissible. Evidence is inadmissible if it is incompetent, but evidence may be admissible when it is competent[1] and when it meets the standards of relevancy and materiality.[2]

Evidence that is competent, relevant, and material is admissible. The complexity of applying the rules concerning competency of evidence and witnesses has troubled courts, judges, and attorneys, and, for that reason, many writers and even some legal encyclopedias fail to adequately explain the competency restrictions. Therefore, this chapter considers the rules relating not only to the competency of witnesses but also to the competency of evidence. The fact that a witness meets the threshold of competency to testify does not necessarily mean that the evidence that the witness may offer meets the standard of competency. Similarly, evidence may meet the tests of

---

1 Peterson v. State, 274 Ga. 165, 167 (2001); State v. Stanley, 131 N.M. 368, 373, 37 P.3d 85, 91 (2001).

2 State v. Martinez, 149 N.C. App. 553, 560, 561 S.E.2d 528, 533 (2002); Robbins v. State, 88 S.W.3d 256, 259, 2002 Tex. Crim. App. LEXIS 208 (2002).

relevancy, materiality, and competency, but the witness who wishes to offer the evidence may not be legally competent as a witness because of some state law provisions.[3]

§ 8.2 Definitions

Black's Law Dictionary defines competent evidence by reference to admissible evidence as "evidence that is relevant and is of such a character (e.g., not unfairly prejudicial or based on hearsay) that the court should receive it."[4] Competent evidence is also defined as evidence that tends to establish the fact in issue and does not rest on mere surmise or conjecture.[5]

Perhaps the definition of competent evidence can be better understood by defining incompetent evidence. In *Black's Law Dictionary*, incompetent evidence is defined as "[e]vidence that is for any reason inadmissible."[6] A Kentucky court recognized that evidence was defective and thus incompetent where the proof indicated that a defendant was a persistent felony offender. The penalty had to be reversed because the evidence proving the persistent offender status had not been properly authenticated at the trial, and the incompetent evidence had been introduced against the defendant.[7] Here, if the trial judge had determined that the evidence failed the test of competency, the court would have excluded the evidence from admission.

In seeking answers about what evidence should be deemed incompetent, and therefore inadmissible, many avenues are open, and volumes of material are available. Much of this book is devoted to determining what evidence is considered incompetent and therefore inadmissible in court.

§ 8.3 General Categories of Incompetent Evidence

If evidence is found to be incompetent, the courts have usually found that it falls within one of the following three categories.

---

3 *See* § 735 ILL. COMP. STAT. 5/8-201 (2013) "In the trial of any action in which any party sues or defends as the representative of a deceased person or person under a legal disability, no adverse party or person directly interested in the action shall be allowed to testify on his or her own behalf to any conversation with the deceased or person under legal disability or to any event which took place in the presence of the deceased . . ." *And see* CAL. VEH. CODE § 40803 (2014). Admissibility of speed trap evidence. In some situations, a police officer is deemed incompetent to testify to what he or she has observed involving speeding motorists.

4 BLACK'S LAW DICTIONARY 636 (9th ed. 2009).

5 31 A C.J.S. *Evidence* § 3 (1996).

6 BLACK'S LAW DICTIONARY 637 (9th ed. 2009).

7 Merriweather v. Commonwealth, 99 S.W.3d 448, 2003 Ky. LEXIS 39 (2003). *See also* Young v. Commonwealth, 47 Va. App. 616; 625 S.E.2d 691; 2006 Va. App. LEXIS 42 (2006).

A. *Wrongfully Obtained Evidence*

Evidence that has been obtained in violation of the Constitution, such as evidence obtained by an illegal search, will often not be admitted because the courts have reasoned that admitting such evidence would encourage the state to disregard the constitutional rights of citizens. Demonstrative of this principle, the Supreme Court held that where the police operated roadblocks to screen all drivers for crime, in the absence of individualized suspicion, the practice violated the Fourth Amendment.[8] In addition, evidence obtained directly or indirectly as a result of an involuntary confession should not be admitted because the process used in obtaining the evidence violated the due process clauses of the Constitution.[9] As a general rule, a conviction cannot stand where police violate the principles of *Miranda v. Arizona* to obtain evidence in a manner that is inconsistent with the intent of the required custody warnings.[10] Evidence seized because of illegal police activity is inadmissible, not because it is irrelevant or immaterial, but because it is incompetent as determined by the courts.

B. *Statutory Incompetency*

Some evidence is admissible as competent evidence because a statute provides that it is competent evidence, and, similarly, some evidence is not admissible because a state or federal statute prohibits the admission of the evidence. For example, § 2515 of the Omnibus Crime Control and Safe Streets Act of 1968,[11] as amended, provides that evidence obtained by **wiretapping** or eavesdropping, when conducted in violation of the statute, is inadmissible in any court or other official proceeding. An Ohio statute also provides that a police officer is incompetent to testify as a witness in a misdemeanor prosecution against a driver charged with violating the vehicle or traffic laws, if, at the time of the arrest or citation, the officer was using a motor vehicle that was not distinctively marked and did not have a flashing light mounted outside the police vehicle.[12] Some states have statutes that protect the interests of decedents' estates when the law specifically states that some

> **Wiretapping** A form of electronic eavesdropping in which, upon a court order, law enforcement officials surreptitiously listen to land and cell phone conversations, e-mail, text messages, and similar communications.

8 *See* City of Indianapolis v. Edmond, 531 U.S. 32 (2000). *See also* Mapp v. Ohio, 357 U.S. 643 (1961).

9 *See* Arizona v. Fulminante, 499 U.S. 279, 111 S. Ct. 1246, 113 L.Ed.2d 302 (1991); the exclusion of illegally obtained evidence is discussed in Chapter 16. *See also* KANOVITZ, CONSTITUTIONAL LAW (13th ed. 2012) and WALKER AND HEMMENS, LEGAL GUIDE FOR POLICE: CONSTITUTIONAL ISSUES (7th ed. 2005).

10 State v. Seibert, 542 U.S. 600, 2004 U.S. LEXIS 4578 (2004).

11 Omnibus Crime Control and Safe Streets Act of 1968 tit. III, 18 U.S.C. § 2510 *et seq.*

12 City of Parma Heights v. Nugent, 92 Ohio Misc. 2d 67, 700 N.E.2d 430, 1998 Ohio Misc. LEXIS 32 (1998); *See* OHIO REV. CODE § 4549.14 (2014), Incompetency of officer as witness, in conjunction with OHIO REV. CODE § 4549.13 (2014), Motor vehicles used by traffic officers and OHIO R. EVID. 601(C) (2014), General rule of competency.

people are not competent as witnesses in listed legal actions.[13] Evidence produced in contravention of these and similar statutes will be excluded from court use, not because it is irrelevant or immaterial, but because the statutes specifically provide that the evidence is not admissible or usable in court.

C. Evidence Excluded Because of a Court-Established Rule

Although many rules of evidence have now been codified, most evidence is excluded because the courts, over a period of years, have established certain rules regarding the admissibility of evidence. Some excellent examples, which are discussed more thoroughly in the forthcoming chapters, are rules that prohibit the admission of certain opinion testimony, hearsay evidence, and **privileged communications.** The Federal Rules of Evidence prevent a judge who is sitting in the case from being a witness in that case, and a juror who is hearing a case is considered incompetent as a witness in the same case.[14] Where court rules exclude evidence, the courts generally have a sound reason for rejecting the evidence, whether the purpose relates to the public policy of supporting confidential relationships or preventing the admission of evidentiary errors involving hearsay evidence.

Privileged communications Statements made by one person to another when both parties share a necessary relation of trust and confidence. Because of this relationship, the person receiving the statements cannot be legally compelled to disclose them.

§ 8.4 Competency of Evidence—Documentary Evidence

Legal evidence in open court includes not only oral testimony and physical objects introduced in evidence by witnesses but also all kinds of documents and records. The concept of documents includes traditional written documents, as well as films, videotapes, CD and DVD data, electronically stored documents, jump drive documents, Web pages, and stored cell phone data. These methods of storing and observing information are roughly classified as documentary evidence. Evidence meeting the definition of documentary evidence is subject to the same rules of relevancy, materiality, and competency as other types of evidence. Documentary evidence must pass all the competency tests, such as the hearsay test, the opinion evidence test, and the various constitutional tests. In addition, documentary evidence must meet other qualifications before it is admissible. The party desiring to offer documentary evidence must authenticate the document by demonstrating that it is genuine. Documentary evidence must

---

13 *See* IND. CODE ANN. § 34-45-2-4 (2013). When executor or administrator is party.

14 *See* FED. R. EVID. 605 and 606.

also meet the requirements of the **best evidence rule** and comply with requirements that are peculiar to "questioned documents."[15]

Best evidence rule Also called the original document rule, this rule requires that proof provides the greatest certainty of the fact to be proven, or the most reliable evidence.

§ 8.5 —Tests and Experiments

The results of scientific tests and experiments may assist the trier of fact in evaluating the evidence in a criminal case and assist the jury in reaching a correct verdict. Evidence showing the outcome of an experiment or test may be admissible to aid in determining the issues in a case in which it is shown that the conditions under which the experiment or test was made are substantially similar to the circumstances prevailing at the time of the occurrence. Evidence obtained as a result of tests and experiments made during a trial, or conducted out of the courtroom, has been challenged as being incompetent evidence based on alleged improper administration, improper conduct, and testing under different circumstances.[16] Generally, where it is necessary to show the condition or quality of a certain article or substance, the item itself may be introduced in evidence to supplement the testimony of the witness, or as direct evidence when properly identified. Some scientific tests are designed to reveal the identity of a substance, a chemical, or drug, while other tests reconstruct how an event occurred or connect people or objects to a crime. The actual objects tested may be introduced as evidence, but in some cases, only the results of testing are available. For instance, most drug analysis tests and some experiments may prove destructive to the item being tested, a factor that will prevent the actual object or item from being introduced as physical evidence.

In order to determine whether the results of a test or experiment should be admitted as evidence, a trial court must evaluate whether the test will produce relevant evidence that is reliable and fair. Until the Supreme Court of the United States decided the *Daubert v. Merrell Dow Pharmaceuticals* case (1993), a great number of courts, both federal and state, followed the old *Frye* standard. *Frye v. United States* (1923) generated a test for admissibility of scientific evidence, suggested by the District of Columbia Court of Appeals, that other state and federal courts adopted. In determining whether to admit scientific evidence and tests, the *Frye* Court considered that:

> Just when a scientific principle or discovery crosses the line between the experimental and demonstrable stages is difficult to define. Somewhere in this twilight zone, the evidential force of the principle must be recognized, and while courts will go a long way in admitting expert testimony deduced from a well-recognized scientific principle or discovery, the thing from which the deduction is made must be sufficiently

---

15 The rules relating to the admissibility of documentary evidence are discussed fully in Chapter 13.

16 Holt v. State, 2006 Tenn. Crim. App. LEXIS 107 (2006).

> established to have gained general acceptance in the particular field in which it belongs.[17]

In *Daubert v. Merrell Dow Pharmaceuticals*, the issue arose concerning whether the *Frye* standard governed in federal cases, or whether the Federal Rules of Evidence should take precedence because the Federal Rules were enacted long after the *Frye* decision. According to *Daubert*, Federal Rule 702 generally controls the admissibility of scientific or technical knowledge in federal courts.[18] Rule 702, Testimony of Experts, states:

> If scientific, technical, or other specialized knowledge will assist the trier of fact to understand the evidence or to determine a fact in issue, a witness qualified as an expert by knowledge, skill, experience, training, or education, may testify thereto in the form of an opinion or otherwise, if (1) the testimony is based upon sufficient facts or data, (2) the testimony is the product of reliable principles and methods, and (3) the witness has applied the principles and methods reliably to the facts of the case.

Even though the *Frye* test was displaced upon adoption of the Federal Rules of Evidence, it did not mean that Rule 702 placed no limits on the admissibility of scientific evidence and tests. The trial judge must be certain that any and all scientific evidence admitted is both relevant and reliable. Although Rule 702 does not mention the "general acceptance" standard of *Frye*, many judicial evaluations used to determine the admissibility of evidence from scientific tests and experiments under Rule 702 will consider some of the following factors as a commonsense approach: (1) whether the scientific evidence has been tested and the methodology by which it has been tested, (2) whether the evidence has been subjected to peer review or publication, (3) whether the potential rate of error is known, (4) whether the evidence is generally accepted in the scientific community, and (5) whether the experts' research in the field has been conducted independent of litigation.[19] Consistent with the concept of federalism, courts that follow a state adoption of the Federal Rules of Evidence are free to interpret them differently from the *Daubert* decision and could follow a state version of the *Frye* standard or some other version consistent with due process. Examples of scientific tests and experiments that may be admissible are blood grouping tests, blood-alcohol testing, fingerprint comparisons, **ballistics experiments,** and DNA tests.[20]

Ballistics experiments The science of gun examination, frequently used in criminal cases, especially cases of homicide, to determine the firing capacity of a weapon, its fireability, and whether a given bullet was fired from a particular gun.

---

17 Frye v. United States, 54 D.C. App. at 47, 293 F. at 1014, 1923 U.S. App. LEXIS 1712 (D.C.C.A. 1923).

18 Daubert v. Merrell Dow Pharmaceuticals, Inc., 509 U.S. 579, 1993 U.S. LEXIS 4408 (1993).

19 State v. Begley, 956 S.W.2d 471 (1997).

20 The rules relating to admissibility of evidence concerning tests and experiments are discussed in detail in Chapter 15.

§ 8.6 —Conduct of Trained Dogs

Evidence produced by observing the conduct of trained dogs may be admissible against a defendant in a variety of contexts. Law enforcement officials may use dogs to discover the identity of a suspect, to discover the suspect, to find lost objects, to detect the presence of controlled substances, to alert to the presence of arson accelerants, to discover cadavers, and to identify objects containing explosives. The training for each dog in a particular field tends to be unique considering a drug-detection dog may be trained to scratch, a feature that would not be advisable in an explosives-detection dog. In order to be admissible, a foundation detailing the particular animal's training is generally required.

In a firearm possession by a felon case initiated by a Virginia state police officer and his dog, the animal alerted to the presence of drugs in a lawfully stopped motor vehicle. No drugs were ever found, giving the defendant a basis for arguing that the dog evidence was erroneous and did not establish probable cause to search his car. In denying the defendant's motion to suppress the drug evidence, the federal prosecutor constructed a foundation for the admission of the dog-produced evidence. A trainer at the Virginia State Police academy testified concerning the procedures followed when training a canine officer and a particular dog. In addition, the state trooper who handled the dog in question explained how he and the dog received training together. The Virginia program involved the officer and the dog completing a 13-week, 520-hour canine and canine handler drug detector course. Before being allowed to actually work out on the street with the police officer, the dog had to pass a certification test with his police officer handler. The dog-and-officer team then had to complete four hours of field training every week, as well as three full days of training at the Virginia State Police training academy under the supervision of a certified dog trainer. The handling officer indicated that the particular dog occasionally failed to find narcotics, but had not offered false positives in any training scenario. In admitting the evidence of the firearm, the judge determined that probable cause existed, even though no drugs were ever discovered. The general rule is that if a drug-sniffing dog is reliable, the positive reaction to the presence of drugs produces probable cause for a search for the controlled substance. In this case, the extensive training of the dog and his human handler were deemed sufficient to support the search and the admission of the evidence.[21]

The conduct of a dog in tracking a suspect, as interpreted by the animal's handler, has been held to produce competent and admissible evidence in both civil and criminal cases.[22] "[M]any courts have ruled that in general, evidence of tracking a defendant is

---

[21] *See* United States v. Brooks, 589 F. Supp. 2d 618, 2008 U.S. Dist. LEXIS 102201 (E.D. Va. 2008).

[22] Washington v. Loucks, 98 Wash. 2d 563, 656 P.2d 480, 1983 Wash. LEXIS 1333 (1983); *see also* Washington v. Hunotte, 2001 Wash. App. LEXIS 1941 (2001), and Commonwealth v. Hill, 52 Mass. App. 147, 153 (2001).

admissible, subject to establishment of a proper foundation"[23] to assist in proving identity, as long as a proper foundation regarding the animal's training and the handler's skills with the dog have been proven. For example, Washington requires that the party offering the dog-tracking evidence establish foundation requirements. A precondition for dog-tracking evidence to be admitted requires that:

> (1) the handler was qualified by training and experience to use the dog, (2) the dog was adequately trained in tracking humans, (3) the dog has, in actual cases, been found by experience to be reliable in pursuing human track, (4) the dog was placed on track where circumstances indicated the guilty party to have been, and (5) the trail had not become so stale or contaminated as to be beyond the dog's competency to follow.[24]

Washington courts generally require that the dog-tracking evidence have some minimal corroboration to be admissible. Dog-tracking evidence should include a cautionary jury instruction that dog-tracking evidence by itself cannot support a conviction in the absence of other evidence.[25]

Evidence of the conduct of a dog in tracking the accused from the scene of a crime to the place where the police arrested him has been found competent and admissible. In a Connecticut case where the defendant had been charged with armed robbery, a police dog followed a human scent from the crime scene to a cap and then on to a car in which the defendant was sitting. After a break for water, the dog again went from the cap to the car where the defendant had previously been sitting. Over the defendant's objection that some extensive scientific foundation must be provided to explain dog-scent-tracking, the trial court refused to suppress the circumstantial evidence of identity. The court noted that properly trained dogs have been used in Connecticut for an extensive period and that courts have routinely admitted dog-tracking evidence. In this particular case, the dog had sufficient training, making the evidence properly admissible.[26]

The Court of Criminal Appeals of Alabama approved the use of trained dogs for identifying persons suspected of a store burglary. The owner of the store fired several shots at the departing men he knew to be the guilty parties. Shoes and socks believed to belong to the culprits were found in the parking lot and were used to give the canines a sniff of the goal of their search. Four miles down the road, the dogs identified the defendant's odor as matching the scent from the clothing at the parking lot. The prosecution appealed a trial court order suppressing the canine identifications on the ground that dog-tracking evidence cannot establish probable cause to arrest. In overturning the trial court's decision on the motion to suppress, the reviewing court held that such evidence could equal probable cause if the training and reliability of the dog is established, the

---

23 *See* Jay M. Zitter, Annotation, *Evidence of Trailing by Dogs in Criminal Cases*, 81 A.L.R. 5TH 563 (Updated 2004).

24 State v. Lathim, 2006 Wash. App. LEXIS 936 (2006).

25 State v. Burnice, 2006 Wash. App. LEXIS 45 (2006).

26 *See* State v. Kelly, 2009 Conn. Super. LEXIS 98 (2009). *See also* Jones v. Commonwealth, 277 Va. 171, 2009 Va. LEXIS 10 (2009).

trainer and handler have proper qualifications, and the circumstances indicate reliability of the evidence. Citing cases that extended over a century, the court held that dog-tracking evidence was admissible for identification purposes.[27]

Canine detection of accelerants used in arson cases has also been approved in appropriate cases. In a Tennessee case in which fire investigators suspected the use of an accelerant in a fatal fire in a trailer home, they procured the assistance of a dog trained to alert to the presence of hydrocarbons.[28] The investigator testified that he had been tracking with the dog for nearly nine years, that the dog had worked hundreds of fire scenes, and that the dog and the investigator trained 365 days a year. The investigator indicated that the dog alerted to the presence of hydrocarbons in two specific places, indicating that an ignitable fluid had been on the floor area. The dog's conclusions were corroborated by a state investigatory agency. The reviewing court upheld the admission of the dog evidence of accelerants and, as a result, the conviction for aggravated arson and felony murder.

§ 8.7 —Telephone Conversations

A completed telephone call may be considered competent and admissible as evidence, along with other data that a call generates. The data, the fact of the conversation, and the content must be relevant to be admissible in court, however. In the case of voice recordings of phone conversations pursuant to a lawful wiretap or other recording, the voice must be authenticated as being genuine. The concept of authentication means that the party wishing to introduce evidence of a telephone conversation must be able to prove who was actually talking on the telephone and, in some cases, prove the identities of all parties to the conversation. Identification of the speakers may occur through the use of either direct evidence offered by one of the parties to the conversation who knew with whom he or she was speaking, or by facts and circumstantial proof that indicates the identity of one or more of the speakers. In addition, where the conversation evidence has been obtained by wiretap, law enforcement authorities must have properly observed relevant federal and state laws, or the evidence may be excluded.[29] Beyond the data generated by traditional phones, newer phone systems and cell phones generate tremendous amounts of nonverbal data and metadata that are routinely stored for long periods by the cell phone carrier and in the handset. Most cell phones store text messages, pictures, Web pages, information on personal contacts, as well as calendar and appointment data and global positioning information. Most of this data is also linked to the time and date of the activity. Police and prosecutors have just begun to mine this

---

27 State v. Montgomery, 2006 Ala. Crim. App. LEXIS 36 (2006).

28 *See* State v. Virga, 2009 Tenn. Crim. App. LEXIS 161 (2009).

29 18 U.S.C. § 2511 *et seq.*, Title III of the Omnibus Crime Control and Safe Streets Act of 1968, as periodically amended, generally prohibits the interception of wire, electronic, and oral communications by anyone, unless done in compliance with the Act.

nonverbal data, and that process and the results it produces will generate new admissibility issues.

For evidence of telephone conversation contents to be admitted, the identities of participants must be authenticated. Such identity may be proved through voice identification, where the recipient is familiar with the caller's voice, or through circumstantial evidence, where the caller gives sufficient specific information that only he or she would know, such as a name, telephone number, address, and Social Security number.[30] Proper **authentication** of a telephone conversation can be deemed sufficient when evidence shows that a call was made to the number that the telephone company assigned to a particular person under circumstances, including self-identification by the recipient, indicating that the answering party was the person who was called.[31] In one case where the defendant denied knowing the other person or talking to him, conversations between drug traffickers were authenticated when the cooperating drug trafficker explained 16 intercepted phone calls between him and the defendant. During the calls, the two discussed using a hidden compartment in a motor vehicle, as well as payment options for the drugs allegedly supplied by the defendant to the cooperating drug trafficker. The substance of the conversation and the cooperating drug trafficker's specialized knowledge had the effect of authenticating the caller as being the defendant.[32] Telephone conversations may be authenticated where one party to the conversation recognizes a person based on distinctive accents or speech patterns. The requirement of direct voice recognition is not an absolute requirement for authentication, but where the caller or the person called can recognize the other, this tends to authenticate the other party to the conversation.

Authentication An attestation made by a proper officer, by which he or she certifies that a record is in due form of law, and that the person who certifies it is the officer appointed so to do.

When a caller places a call to another person, the fact that the caller self-identified does not serve as sufficient authentication of the identity of the caller,[33] unless the recipient recognized the voice. Caller Identification (Caller ID) is a device that displays the caller's number and other incoming call data to the recipient, and it may play a role in authenticating a caller. Although Caller ID may be admitted to prove the source of the call, and while Caller ID cannot authenticate the identity of the caller, it may be admissible to prove the location and source of the call. In a Tennessee murder case, the defendant's girlfriend testified that the defendant called her from the victim's home, because she had Caller ID on her phone, and the readout indicated that the call originated from the victim's phone. Naturally, because she was intimately familiar with the voice of her boyfriend, the combination of the Caller ID and his voice authenticated

30 Angleton v. State, 686 N.E.2d 803 (1997).

31 Broadhead v. State, 981 So. 2d 320, 326, 2007 Miss. App. LEXIS 809 (2007).

32 United States v. Avila, 557 F.3d 809, 2009 U.S. App. LEXIS 4940 (7th Cir. 2009).

33 Wells v. Liddy, 37 F. App'x 53, 2002 U.S. App. LEXIS 3356 (4th Cir. 2002).

the call as being from her boyfriend, who was using the soon-to-be homicide victim's telephone.[34] Thus, in conjunction with other information, Caller ID may provide the additional information necessary to authenticate a caller and disclose the origination location.

In a prosecution for second-degree rape of a child, the defendant appealed his conviction based on the admission of a telephone conversation that he allegedly had with one of his young victims, because, allegedly, the conversation had not been properly authenticated. When adults became aware of allegations that the defendant had consummated sexual relations with one or more children, one adult directed a victim to call the defendant's telephone number and engage him in a conversation that implicated the defendant in the crimes for which he was later convicted. The trial court permitted the adult to relate to the jury the substance of the conversation that the adult witness overheard between the victim and the defendant. The appellate court agreed that the adult could authenticate the defendant as being the voice on the telephone making incriminating statements, because the defendant and the adult witness were neighbors, the witness was familiar with the quality of the defendant's voice, and the victim dialed the defendant's number in full view of the adult witness.[35]

Related to audio telephone conversations are text messages that are sent from one cell phone to another. As often is the case, these messages may be stored on a cell phone computer server and/or sent directly and immediately to the recipient's cell phone. These activities create significant metadata that is available to support authentication, if traditional avenues of authentication are not sufficient. In order to introduce these text messages, they must be authenticated to show that the message is what it purports to be. As an Indiana court noted, "We see no reason why the writings or recordings generated and saved inside of a cellular telephone should be exempted from the. . .authentication requirement."[36] In a case involving terroristic threats and felony domestic assault, a Minnesota court concluded that text messages received by the victim had been properly authenticated when the recipient indicated that the number associated with the text messages came from the telephone number assigned to the defendant. She possessed knowledge of the defendant's phone number because she once dated him and had lived with him for a period of time. In addition, the defendant helped authenticate the text messages, because in one of them, he displayed an intimate knowledge of the domestic situation by ridiculing her for getting law enforcement involved.[37]

In summary, telephone and text messages must be properly authenticated as being genuine prior to their admissibility into evidence. As long as the method of authentication proves that the message is what it purports to be, it should be admitted where otherwise relevant.

---

34 *See* State v. Flannel, 2008 Tenn. Crim. App. LEXIS 821 (2008).

35 State v. Brown, 2006 Wash. App. LEXIS 1092 (2006).

36 Hape v. State, 903 N.E.2d 977, 2009 Ind. App. LEXIS 637 (2009).

37 *See* State v. Haines, 2008 Minn. App. Unpub. LEXIS 1479 (2008).

§ 8.8 Negative Evidence as Competent Evidence

In *Black's Law Dictionary*, **negative evidence** is defined as "[e]vidence suggesting that an alleged fact does not exist, such as a witness's testifying that he or she did not see an event occur."[38] Evidence is negative when the witness states that he or she did not see or know of the existence of a certain circumstance or fact.[39] Virtually all courts have recognized "that negative evidence is admissible, where the attending circumstances indicate that it has some probative force, such as concerning what the witness did not see or did not hear"[40] when there would have been an opportunity for the witness to have seen or heard. Trial courts have broad discretion to admit evidence that something did not happen[41] and must determine whether the probative value outweighs the prejudicial nature of the evidence. Testimony concerning negative evidence is admissible where the circumstances demonstrate that the negative evidence has some probative force, the proponent establishes the competency of the witness, and the witness has personal knowledge that something did not occur.[42]

Negative evidence Testimony that an alleged fact does not exist or that an event did not occur; an absence of evidence.

An effective use of negative evidence involves allowing an opposing witness to testify freely and completely concerning matters within his or her knowledge, then noting, for later cross-examination purposes, matters that he or she would logically have related to others at a prior time. If the witness added new matters during the **direct examination,** covering new topics that he or she had not discussed earlier and bringing out his or her previous silence on that topic, or absence of evidence, have the effect of impeaching the witness's direct testimony. In one case involving alleged sexual misconduct, a complaining witness noted both to police and on direct examination that she wrote in her diary concerning the acts that the defendant perpetrated against her. On cross-examination, the defense attorney elicited from the witness that the existing diaries did not mention the alleged sexual assault. The absence of mention in the diaries would indicate that, perhaps, her recent testimony was fabricated.[43] The prior silence in the diaries appeared to be

Direct examination The initial questioning of a witness by the party who calls him or her to testify. The questioning party uses direct questions in which the form of the question does not suggest the desired answer.

38 BLACK'S LAW DICTIONARY 638 (9th ed. 2009).

39 31A C.J.S. *Evidence* § 165 (1994).

40 29 AM. JUR. 2D *Evidence* § 327 (2013).

41 Brown v. Classic Inns, 2002 Wis. App 134, 255 Wis. 2d 832, 646 N.W.2d 854 (2002).

42 29A AM. JUR. 2D *Evidence* § 318 (1994).

43 State v. Arcia, 111 Conn. App. 374, 379, 380, 2008 Conn. App. LEXIS 529 (2008). On redirect as a method of rehabilitation, the prosecutor had the witness tell that she had other diaries that were in police custody that did contain statements of sexual abuse by the defendant.

inconsistent with the recent trial testimony, suggesting that the trial testimony might be a recent contrivance by the witness. Questions arise when the witness fails to mention the substance of the testimony at a time when it would have been natural to speak on the topic. Therefore, the absence of evidence—negative evidence—may be relevant and competent to prove a recent fabrication by the witness.[44]

The failure of a drug-sniffing dog to alert to the presence of controlled substances within a motor vehicle constitutes negative evidence, providing an indication that drugs were not present, and that the lack of evidence does not help in developing probable cause to search. If the same canine subsequently makes a false positive indication of recreational drugs in the same vehicle, then the false positive can similarly serve as negative evidence of the presence of the prohibited substances.[45]

Some writers and courts have noted that, with all other things being equal, a general rule of evidence states that positive evidence carries more weight than negative evidence,[46] but a court would be in error if it instructed the jury that positive evidence should be given greater weight.[47] To indicate that negative evidence carries less weight than positive evidence invades the province of the jury. One court indicated that, where there are two witnesses of equal credibility in direct contradiction on a question of fact, the positive testimony would be given preference.[48]

In summary, while negative evidence is regarded by some authorities as entitled to less weight than positive evidence, negative evidence is valuable and admissible when a proper foundation has been laid, provided that the competency of the witness and his or her knowledge of the matter are established.

§ 8.9 Evidence Competent for Some Purposes but Not for Others

When evidence may be admissible based upon one theory and excludable under another, courts have generally decided that the evidence is admissible. For example, Texas holds that "[w]hen evidence which is admissible as to one party or for one purpose but not admissible as to another party or for another purpose is admitted, the court, upon request, shall restrict the evidence to its proper scope and instruct the jury accordingly."[49] If, however, the evidence has so strong a prejudicial value as to outweigh the advantages of receiving the evidence, a judge has discretion in deciding whether to admit or refuse it. When evidence is logically relevant and admissible under one theory, but inadmissible under a different theory, the judge should qualify the admission of the

---

44 Connecticut v. Vines, 71 Conn. App. 359, 371 A.2d 918, 926, 2002 Conn. App. LEXIS 406 (2002).

45 Longshore v. State, 399 Md. 486, 531, 532, 2007 Md. LEXIS 344 (2007).

46 29A AM. JUR. *Evidence* § 1438 (1994); *see also* Randall v. Norfolk S. Ry. Co., 800 N.E.2d 951, 959, 2003 Ind. App. LEXIS 2406 (2003).

47 Tafoya v. Chapin, 2003 Neb. App. LEXIS 64 (2003).

48 State v. Bentley, 499 So. 2d 581 (La. 1987); 29A AM. JUR. 2D *Evidence* § 318 (1994).

49 *See* TEX. R. EVID. 105 (2013). *See also* Arcement v. State, 2009 Tex. App. LEXIS 1096 (2009).

evidence with an instruction that the jury can consider the evidence for one purpose, but not for another.[50] There is contrary authority that a judge should not give a cautionary instruction in the absence of a request, because "a party might well intentionally forego a limiting instruction as part of its deliberate strategy."[51] If desired, the defendant's counsel can request a second cautionary instruction prior to jury deliberations. The Federal Rules of Evidence note that, when evidence is admissible for one purpose but not another, "the court, upon request, shall restrict the evidence to its proper scope and instruct the jury accordingly."[52]

In a Texas case demonstrative of this rule, the defense introduced evidence of the defendant's prior felony convictions that involved moral turpitude, because the defense knew that the prosecution would bring up the seven convictions during cross-examination. The proof of the prior convictions had the effect of impeaching the defendant's testimony. Under the Texas rules that govern evidence, when evidence is admissible for one purpose but not for some other purpose, a defendant may request a limiting instruction from the judge that restricts the use of the evidence to its proper scope. However, a trial court has no obligation to offer the limiting instruction on its own motion, and in this case, the defendant never requested such an instruction. Therefore, no error was committed when the court failed to tell the jury that the evidence could be used for impeachment but not for substantive evidence.[53]

Constitutional reasons may have the effect of excluding evidence when offered for one purpose, but permitting admission of that evidence as competent when used for a different purpose. In a New York criminal case, the prosecution was prevented from using the defendant's statements made after his arrest, due to a *Miranda* warning violation. When the defendant took the witness stand in his own defense and offered a story that was inconsistent with his postarrest statement, the trial court permitted the prosecution to introduce the inconsistent postarrest statement over the defendant's objection, for the limited purpose of impeaching the defendant and not to prove his guilt.[54] According to Chief Justice Burger, "[t]he shield provided by *Miranda* cannot be perverted into a license to use perjury by way of a defense, free from the risk of confrontation with prior inconsistent utterances."[55] If the Court had suppressed the postarrest statement from evidence, the effect would have been to permit the defendant to commit perjury without suffering any adverse consequences.

Before moving to the discussion of the competency of witnesses, it should be mentioned that there are many other evidentiary rules of exclusion that are not addressed here, not because they are not pertinent, but because they are discussed in detail in other chapters.

---

50 Mackey v. Russell, 148 F.. App'x 355, 2005 U.S. App. LEXIS 16933 (6th Cir. 2005). *See also* OHIO EVID. R. 105.

51 Oursbourn v. State, 259 S.W.3d 159, 180, 2008 Tex. Crim. App. LEXIS 686 (2008).

52 FED. R. EVID. 105.

53 Reyes v. State, 2013 Tex. App. LEXIS (2013).

54 *See* Harris v. New York, 401 U.S. 222 (1971).

55 *Id.* at 226.

§ 8.10 Competency of Witnesses

Rule 601

COMPETENCY TO TESTIFY IN GENERAL

Every person is competent to be a witness unless these rules provide otherwise. But in a civil case, state law governs the witness's competency regarding a claim or defense for which state law supplies the rule of decision.[56]

The Federal Rules of Evidence start with the presumption that all witnesses are competent to offer testimony unless a particular rule of evidence provides otherwise or there exists some defect in the four elements of competency of the witness that renders the witness incapable of offering proper evidence.[57] Because federal courts often sit as state civil courts in diversity of citizenship cases, Rule 601 defers to state law to determine whether a witness is competent when adjudicating state cases. Ohio's enhanced version of Rule 601 holds that every "person is competent as a witness except"[58] "[a] spouse testifying against the other spouse charged with a crime,"[59] unless the trial concerns crimes against the child or the testifying spouse, or unless the witness spouse is willing to testify against the other spouse. In state courts, witnesses are generally presumed to be competent, and the party alleging otherwise has the burden of proving that a witness is incompetent. In the interests of clarity, a distinction must be made between the competency of a witness and the competency of evidence. A witness may meet the personal tests of competency and yet not be authorized to testify concerning evidence that is incompetent, such as certain hearsay evidence or illegally seized evidence.

One of the common tests of witness competency looks to see whether four factors have been met. Every witness must take the oath or a substitute, have original perception, be able to remember the facts, and have an ability to communicate to the court. A collateral test of the competency of a witness requires that the witness be able to communicate relevant material and that the witness have the ability to understand that there is an obligation to communicate truthfully. When considering the issue of a witness's competency, "[p]recedence instructs that the question of a witness's competency is to be determined by the trial judge, and a reviewing court may not disturb that determination absent a clear abuse of discretion."[60] The question of competency is almost

---

56 FED. R. EVID. 601.

57 *Id.*

58 OHIO R. EVID. 601 (2013). Rule 601 also provides for some other situations involving incompetency.

59 *Id.*

60 People v. Harris, 2009 Ill. App. LEXIS 118 (2009).

always one of fact, and thus will not be reversed unless clearly erroneous.[61] Although witness competency involves a question of law for the judge to determine, the jury must determine the credibility of any particular witness and the evidence that the witness offers.[62]

In determining whether the witness is competent to testify at the trial, the better practice is to make the determination prior to the trial and out of the hearing of the jury,[63] thus avoiding the chance that a jury might believe that a court had determined that a witness was to be believed rather than being determined minimally competent to testify. Where the trial is to the judge, a determination of witness competency may be done at the time the witness is called to the witness stand.[64]

When a person has been called as a witness to give testimony in front of a grand jury, the usual tests for competency apply, but a witness's competency is rarely contested, because a grand jury meets in secret with no opposing party to offer an objection. In one New York case, an indictment was quashed because the prosecutor made no attempt to determine whether the four-year-old complaining witness met the requirements of competency,[65] even though that prosecutor had the power to make a ruling on the competency of a grand jury witness, as if the prosecutor were a trial judge.[66] As one court noted, "[a] more stringent standard than that applied to trial proceedings certainly cannot be applied to determine competency of a witness to testify before a Grand Jury, whose function is primarily investigative."[67] In the grand jury context, one state considers children competent to testify without taking the oath, as long as the jurors are aware that the witness is not under oath and met the other requirements for competency.[68]

The tests for determining competency of a witness before a grand jury are (1) the witness must understand the obligation of an oath and the obligation to tell the truth before the grand jury, and (2) the witness must be capable of giving a reasonably correct account of the matters that he or she has seen or heard in reference to the questions being asked. Where the competency of a grand jury witness has been raised, these two issues must be determined by the court's own examination and upon the testimony of witnesses who may be called by the prosecution or by the witness's counsel. The court cannot avoid this duty merely by referring to or quoting from the statements of medical experts. The court must make its own determination and its own

---

61 Commonwealth v. Garmache, 35 Mass. App. 805, 626 N.E.2d 616 (1994). *See also* United States v. Gates, 10 F.3d 765 (11th Cir. 1993), in which the court held that the court has the power to rule that the witness is incapable of testifying, and in an appropriate case it has a duty to hold a hearing to determine that issue.

62 *See* Barrientos v. State, 1 So. 3d 1209, 2009 Fla. App. LEXIS 793 (2009).

63 Norman v. Georgia, 269 Ga. App. 219, 223, 603 S.E.2d 737, 742, 2004 Ga. App. LEXIS 1120 (2004). *See also* Medina v. Diguglielmo, 373 F. Supp. 2d 526; 2005 U.S. Dist. LEXIS 10672 (E.D. Pa. 2005).

64 *See* Ohio v. Cotterman, 2001 Ohio App. LEXIS 3322 (2001).

65 People v. Esaw, 2002 N.Y. Slip Op. 40045U, 2002 N.Y. Misc. LEXIS 201 (2002).

66 *See* N.Y. CRIM. PROC. LAW § 190.30(6) (2011).

67 In re Loughran, 276 F. Supp. 393, 430, 1967 U.S. Dist. LEXIS 7589 (C.D. Cal. 1967).

68 People v. Miller, 295 A.D.2d 746, 747, 2002 N.Y. App. Div. LEXIS 6511 (2002).

examination. The court must also be assured that the physical and mental health of the witness will not be damaged, impaired, or harmed in any significant way.[69] Because the defendant has no representation at a grand jury proceeding, questions about the competency of grand jury witnesses do not frequently arise, and where they do, the witness often raises the issue.

Where the competency of expert witnesses is at issue, courts generally have broad discretion in determining whether to allow the testimony. Where expert witnesses are concerned, the issues of competency and qualifications appear to overlap somewhat. Every witness must meet the traditional standards of competency, but an expert needs to meet additional standards. The California Evidence Code provides that "[a] person is qualified to testify as an expert if he [or she] has special knowledge, skill, experience, training, or education sufficient to qualify him as an expert on the subject to which his testimony relates. Against the objection of a party, such special knowledge, skill, experience, training, or education must be shown before the witness may testify as an expert."[70] The opposing side may ask questions designed to probe the qualifications of the offered expert. When there is an issue concerning qualifications, the jury is bound by the judge's determination that a person is qualified as an expert witness is binding on the jury, but the weight to be assigned to the expert's testimony rests with the finder of fact.

In the sections immediately following, the specific grounds for challenging the competency of witnesses are discussed.

§ 8.11 —Mental Incapacity

In state and federal courts, feeble-mindedness, mental illness, and insanity are not enough to prevent a witness from being considered competent. However, in evaluating the mental status of witnesses, "there are few particularized standards governing the assessment of a person's mental capacity."[71] In the Notes of Advisory Committee on (federal) Rules, the committee asserted that "[a] witness wholly without capacity is difficult to imagine."[72] Therefore, in once case, a teenage witness who was suffering from post traumatic stress disorder related to sexual abuse could be considered a competent witness where she had the capacity to perceive, recollect, and understand the necessity of telling the truth. Nothing indicated that her mental challenges had any effect on her testimony, and the trial judge concluded that she possessed capacity as a witness.[73]

---

69 *Id.*

70 CAL. EVID. CODE § 720 (2014).

71 Bornstad v. Honey Brook Twp., 2005 U.S. Dist. LEXIS 19573 (E.D. Pa. 2006).

72 FED. R. EVID. 601.

73 *See* United States v. Street, 531 F.3d 703, 2008 U.S. App. LEXIS 14729 (2008), *cert. denied*, 129 S. Ct. 432, 2008 U.S. LEXIS 7688 (2008).

In *District of Columbia v. Armes*, the United States Supreme Court established the basic standard or rule to be applied when considering the mental capacity of an adult witness to testify:

> The general rule is that a lunatic or a person affected with insanity is admissible as a witness if he has sufficient understanding to apprehend the obligation of an oath, and to be capable of giving a correct account of the matters which he has seen or heard in reference to the questions at issue; and whether he has that understanding is a question to be determined by the court, upon examination of the party himself, and any competent witnesses who can speak to the nature and extent of his insanity.[74]

In *Armes*, the Court upheld the admissibility of the testimony of an acute melancholic who was confined to an asylum and had attempted suicide several times. The Court stressed that "the existence of partial insanity does not prevent individuals so affected. . .from giving a perfectly accurate and lucid statement of what they have seen or heard."[75]

The issue of mental competency not only arises with adult witnesses; it clearly applies to juveniles as well. In an Illinois case involving alleged aggravated sexual abuse by a juvenile, the state's witnesses were all children who attended a therapeutic school with the defendant. One of the witnesses was placed in a psychiatric institution shortly after the alleged delinquent acts took place. To determine the competency of the juvenile witnesses, the child facing delinquency accusations questioned the competency of the government's juvenile witnesses and wanted to have the judge conduct an *in camera* review of their school records in order to determine whether competency was at issue. Because the juvenile court refused to conduct any review of the witnesses' records, the appeals court reversed the finding of delinquency based on the concern that the undisclosed school records may have contained crucial evidence relevant to competency.[76]

Even though a trial court or jury might accept arcane psychiatric concepts of mental condition or illness as a basis for measuring criminal capacity and responsibility, a judge will not blindly accept such theoretical concepts when evaluating the competency of witnesses. Despite mental difficulties, the test of a witness's competency includes the capacity to communicate relevant material and to understand the obligation to do so truthfully. In upholding the admission of evidence offered by a witness in a murder case, an Illinois court noted that having bipolar disorder and a significant history of drug abuse did not disqualify a witness.[77] This history would be disqualifying only where the drug use or mental illness impaired the witness's mental capacity to the extent that the witness could not meet the traditional requirements of a witness. In Illinois, a person is disqualified as a witness when he or she is not capable of expressing the matter in an understandable fashion or fails to understand the duty to tell the truth.[78]

---

[74] 107 U.S. 519, 2 S. Ct. 840, 27 L. Ed. 618 (1882).

[75] *Id.*

[76] People v. K.S., 387 Ill. App. 3d 570, 2008 Ill. App. LEXIS 1333 (2008).

[77] People v. Nowicki, 385 Ill. App. 3d 53, 87, 88, 2008 Ill. App. LEXIS 869 (2008).

[78] *See* 725 ILL. COMP. STAT. 5/115-14 (2013).

Most courts in state and federal cases allow testimony of a witness, even though the witness has been found to be drug addicted and taking psychiatric medicine for mental problems. This has been reflected in the Federal Rules of Evidence, as interpreted by various courts. For example, in one federal trial, a prosecution witness was permitted to testify that she was a drug addict, and she admitted to having smoked significant quantities of crack cocaine on the day she was witnessed several crimes. The witness had suffered a gunshot wound to her head and had auditory and visual hallucinations. She was also under a doctor's care, which resulted in multiple psychiatric medications being prescribed. Despite all of these problems that might relate to her competency, the trial court properly permitted her to testify against the defendant.[79] In a different federal case, the judge ordered the prosecution's principal witness to be examined by a court psychiatrist because there was some concern about his capacity.[80] The doctor reported that the proposed witness had a history of being hospitalized for mental illness and that he had a "severe personality disorder" and a "character disturbance," but had no present mental illness. In considering the witness's competency, the examining doctor noted that the witness had previously been diagnosed as a paranoid schizophrenic with conduct and adjustment disorders, but that the doctor did not believe such problems would affect competency. The trial judge's decision in favor of competency of this mentally challenged witness was not disturbed on appeal.

In making a determination of the competency, a judge could not solely use the fact that a proposed witness had substance abuse issues and an unspecified learning disability to disqualify a person. Even the facts that the witness was also suffering from severe bipolar disorder, which required long-term medical care, would not necessarily indicate that the individual lacked competency.[81] When a person has been adjudicated as an incompetent in the sense of managing his or her own affairs, the individual may still qualify as a witness, so long as the person has knowledge of the facts of the case and understands the duty to tell the truth.[82]

However, there are occasions when mental illness and psychiatric problems may require a trial court to conduct close scrutiny of how the mental challenges affect a particular witness's capacity. In a case involving a juvenile adjudication of delinquency for an act that would have been rape if committed by an adult, the trial court committed error when it failed to conduct a more complete competency hearing.[83] The complaining witness was a 12-year-old girl who attended special education classes, had imaginary friends, and had been previously diagnosed with schizophrenia, and her ability to remember even routine information proved to be limited. The juvenile court conducted an examination of the witness, but failed to follow up on answers that

---

79 United States v. Williams, 445 F.3d 724, 728, 2006 U.S. App. LEXIS 9639 (4th Cir. 2006).

80 Bryant v. United States, 859 A.2d 1093, 1101, 2004 D.C. App. LEXIS 526 (Dist. Col. 2004).

81 Witherspoon v. United States, 2008 U.S. Dist. LEXIS 94601 (W.D.N.C. 2008).

82 *Id.*

83 In re J.M., 2006 Ohio 1203; 2006 Ohio App. LEXIS 1088 (2006).

might have created doubt concerning her competency. In reversing the adjudication, the reviewing court noted:

> There is no indication in the record that the court questioned B.D. regarding her capacity to recount the events accurately or even that she understood the nature of the proceedings. After the trial court questioned B.D. regarding routine questions such as the day, month, and year and received inaccurate or confusing responses from her, the court merely proceeded to the next set of questions without delving further into the key issue of competency.
>
> The lack of more detailed evidence supporting or refuting B.D.'s competency should be clear on the record. Since such evidence is lacking, we find that the trial court abused its discretion in failing to conduct a more complete competency hearing.[84]

As a general matter of procedure, when the competency of a witness arises, the trial judge must make a preliminary determination concerning competency. When the judge finds a proposed witness competent, the jury must evaluate credibility of the witness, and the jury determines the value to be assigned to the testimony.[85] Concerning the procedure in making an evaluation of a challenged witness, a Maryland court, under state Rule 601, commented that holding a competency hearing outside of the hearing of the jury is not required, but is up to the sound discretion of the trial judge. The court believed that, as long as the trial judge was satisfied with the competency of a challenged witness, competency was sufficiently established,[86] and the value of the testimony rested with the finder of fact.

In summary, a witness is generally considered competent to testify unless evidence is introduced to show that incompetency exists. Where one party has concerns that an adverse witness may lack some of the elements of competency, many state statutes or evidence codes provide that the party must make a motion to the trial court before the witness testifies, placing the burden of proof on the moving party[87] to establish that the witness lacks competency. To meet that burden, the challenging party must establish the witness's inability to understand the obligation of the oath and to comprehend the obligation imposed by it, the witness's lack of understanding of the consequences of false swearing, or the witness's inability to perceive accurate impressions and to retain them.

§ 8.12 —Children

Where the competency of a child to be a witness becomes an issue for either party, the trial judge has the duty to evaluate whether the child possesses the elements of competency. Even where neither party objects to the competency of a child witness, the trial judge generally has the discretion to determine whether competency exists.[88] In most

---

84 *Id.*

85 United States v. Phibbs, 999 F.2d 1053 (6th Cir. 1993). *See* case in Part II.

86 *See* Perry v. State, 381 Md. 138, 848 A.2d 631, 2004 Md. LEXIS 246 (2004).

87 *See* 725 ILL. COMP. STAT. 5/115-14(c) (2013).

88 Haycraft v. State, 760 N.E.2d 203, 209, 2001 Ind. App. LEXIS 2225 (2001).

jurisdictions, a child may not be required to take a formal oath as long as the witness's duty and ability to tell the truth can be established.[89] As one court noted, "trial judges are required to make a preliminary determination as to the competency of all witnesses, including children, and that absent an abuse of discretion, competency determinations of the trial judge will not be disturbed on appeal."[90] According to a reviewing court, one trial judge conducted a proper examination of a six-year-old child witness when the judge's questions to the child were:

> Sufficient to establish the child was capable of "receiving just impressions of the fact and transactions" and "relating them truly." Although [she] showed some confusion about the actual terms "right" and "wrong" and "truth" and "lie," she clearly demonstrated she knew the difference between telling the truth and telling a lie, and knew the consequences of telling a lie.[91]

While some state statutes are similar to Ohio's in providing that "children under ten years of age, who appear incapable of receiving just impressions of the facts respecting which they are examined, or of relating them truly"[92] are incompetent as witnesses, there is no fixed age at which a child is considered to be a competent witness. Other states follow the principles used in the Arkansas rules of evidence, stating that "[e]very person is competent to be a witness except as otherwise provided in these rules."[93] When making determinations of the competency of a particular witness, an Arkansas reviewing court suggested that "[t]he criteria for determining whether a witness is competent to testify are (1) the ability to understand the obligation of an oath and to comprehend the obligation imposed by it; or (2) an understanding of the consequences of false swearing; or (3) the ability to receive accurate impressions and to retain them, to the extent that the capacity exists to transmit to the fact finder a reasonable statement of what was seen, felt, or heard."[94] Using this standard, the reviewing court upheld allowing an eight-year-old girl to testify about a defendant's acts of slamming her 23-month-old sister into a wall.[95] The trial court had spoken to the eight-year-old concerning the duty to tell the truth, and she appeared to understand the difference between truth and falsity and that lies were wrong and could merit punishment. On this record, the reviewing court found no abuse of discretion on the part of the trial court.

In a variety of cases, children much younger than 10 years of age have been considered competent witnesses while other cases have refused to allow some young

---

89 10 DEL. CODE ANN. § 4302 Competency to Testify (2014). "No child under the age of 10 years may be excluded from giving testimony for the sole reason that such child does not understand the obligation of an oath. Such child's age and degree of understanding of the obligation of an oath may be considered by the trier of fact in judging the child's credibility."

90 In re J.M., 2006 Ohio 1203, 2006 Ohio App. LEXIS 1088 (2006).

91 State v. Patterson, 2005 Ohio 6703; 2005 Ohio App. LEXIS 6050 (2005).

92 OHIO R. EVID. 601(A) (2013).

93 ARK. R. EVID. 601 (2013).

94 Lyons v. State, 2008 Ark. App. LEXIS 430 (2008).

95 *Id.*

children to testify. A determination of competency of child witnesses depends upon the facts in each case and on the maturity of the individual child. In Pennsylvania, all witnesses are considered competent, including children, but witnesses under 14 years of age may face special scrutiny. In one case involving juvenile sexual abuse by an adult, the trial court permitted a six-year-old girl to testify.[96] Against the presumption of competency, the defendant must first demonstrate some defect in competency to cause the court to hold a "taint" hearing. This process examines whether events or other people have tainted the child's memory and perception. In evaluating whether a defendant has presented evidence sufficient to hold the "taint" hearing, the court considers the totality of the circumstances surrounding the child's allegations, including:

> (1) the age of the child; (2) the existence of a motive hostile to the defendant on the part of the child's primary custodian; (3) the possibility that the child's primary custodian is unusually likely to read abuse into normal interaction; (4) whether the child was subjected to repeated interviews by various adults in positions of authority; (5) whether an interested adult was present during the course of any interviews; and (6) the existence of independent evidence regarding the interview techniques employed.[97]

Where a Pennsylvania defendant fails to produce sufficient evidence to warrant a "taint" hearing, the trial court will permit the child's testimony without additional analysis or consideration.

Pennsylvania's "taint" hearing appears to be a different approach from most jurisdictions, but in determining a child's competency as a witness, most courts do consider the child's ability to perceive just impressions of the facts at the time that the events occurred, while evaluating his or her capacity to communicate that information at the time of the trial. Of crucial importance is the child's competency or incompetency as of the date that the child provides testimony, and not at the time that the incidents originally occurred.

On occasion, courts have permitted very young children to serve as witnesses following a determination of competency. In the District of Columbia, a trial court permitted a six-year-old boy to testify concerning injuries that a defendant inflicted upon his mother when the boy was only five years old.[98] The child was able to recall that the attack took place at night and that the attacker was the defendant. He remembered that the attack on his mother took place in his bedroom and in a nearby bathroom and that he had attempted to defend her using a toy plastic sword. In approving the admission of the boy's testimony, the District of Columbia Court of Appeals noted that competency of a child required that there be proof that the child had an ability to recall the events in question, could understand the difference between truth and falsehood, and could appreciate the need to tell the truth.

---

[96] Commonwealth v. Judd, 2006 Pa. Super. 84, 897 A.2d 1224, 2006 Pa. Super. LEXIS 538 (2006).

[97] *Id.* at 1230.

[98] Scott v. United States, 953 A.2d 1082, 1092, 1093, 2008 D.C. App. LEXIS 379 (D.C.C.A. 2008).

A Mississippi court noted that the test for admissibility of child testimony required that the trial judge: "determine that the child witness (1) has the ability to perceive and remember events, (2) understand and answer questions intelligently, and (3) comprehend and accept the importance of truthfulness."[99] In that case, the child had been six years of age at the time of the crime, but was eight at the time of the proposed testimony. The potential witness knew her birthday, where she went to school, her teachers' names, and her home telephone number. Additionally, the girl stated that it was a bad thing to tell a lie. Not only did the judge observe the child answering the questions, but he also observed her carriage and demeanor, all factors in reaching the conclusion that the child was competent as a witness.[100]

The preferable course is to accept a child's testimony if the competency tests are met. However, the testimony should not be allowed if evidence indicates that the child lacks competency. For example, an Ohio appellate court reversed a conviction for two counts of gross sexual imposition involving two children, one a three-year-old and a child who had just turned four years old at the time of the alleged crime. The trial court failed to conduct a competency hearing or voir dire exam of the children prior to allowing them to testify. The prosecutor's examination revealed numerous defects in memory and recollection and demonstrated a general lack of understanding of events or an understanding of the concept of time. One child did not know when she would have her next birthday and did not know the year she was born. The court of appeals reversed the conviction on the basis of plain error in permitting the testimony of children who had not been determined to be competent as witnesses.[101]

To be considered a competent witness, a child need not understand the concept of perjury, but must know the difference between telling a lie and telling the truth. In an Arkansas prosecution for sexual crimes against a child, the judge conducted a competency hearing with the alleged victim, who was five years old at the time of the offense and seven at the time of trial . Outside of the presence of the jury, the prosecutor asked the child witness about the difference between a lie and the truth and gave several examples that the child understood. From the prosecutor's questions, it appeared that the child knew her colors, the difference between a dog and a cat, understood the need to tell the truth, and seemed to understand the significance of an oath. In upholding the trial judge's decision to allow the child to testify, the appellate court noted that, "[a]s long as the record is one upon which the trial judge could find a moral awareness of the obligation to tell the truth and an ability to observe, remember, and relate facts, we will not hold there has been a manifest error or abuse of discretion in allowing the testimony."[102]

---

99 Borsarge v. State, 786 So. 2d 426, 430, 2001 Miss. App. LEXIS 227 (2001).

100 *Id.*

101 State v. Holland, 2008 Ohio 3450, 2008 Ohio App. LEXIS 2914 (2008); *see Competency and Credibility: Double Trouble for Child Victims of Sexual Offenses*, 9 SUFFOLK J. TRIAL & APP. ADV. 113 (2004), for a discussion of problems involving competency of children in sexual assault cases.

102 Warner v. State, 2005 Ark. App. LEXIS 875 (2005).

In summary, child witnesses present challenges related to determining whether they are competent. Individual determinations based on the unique facts of each child and each case will assist the court in evaluating each proposed child witness. When the child meets the elements of competency of original perception and recollection, and is able to communicate the story to the finder of fact, the judge should rule that the particular child is a competent witness. In the case of children, the final element of competency, the oath, is generally excused as long as the judge is satisfied that the child understands the duty to tell the truth.

§ 8.13 —Husband and Wife

The common law rule held that husbands and wives were incompetent as witnesses for or against each other because the spouse had an interest in the case and could not serve as an unbiased witness. The rule appears to have its genesis in medieval times and seems to have developed "from two canons of medieval jurisprudence: first, the rule that an accused was not permitted to testify in his own behalf because of his interest in the proceeding; second, the concept that husband and wife were one, and that since the woman had no recognized separate legal existence, the husband was that one."[103] In *Hawkins v. United States*, the Supreme Court provided additional justification, stating that "the rule rested mainly on a desire to foster peace in the family and on a general unwillingness to use the testimony of witnesses tempted by strong self-interest to testify falsely."[104]

Courts began to erode this early rule, however, when the logic and philosophy supporting the concept began to fail, especially when the rule gave protection to the wrong interests. Thus, in the 1839 federal case of *Stein v. Bowman*, the United States Supreme Court noted that the rule of spousal incompetency "is subject to some exceptions; as where the husband commits an offence against the person of his wife."[105] Consistent with this logic, modern law in all states considers one spouse to possess competency to testify against the other where one spouse has been charged with a crime against the person or property of the other, or has been charged with a crime against a child of either spouse or a crime involving the child's property.[106] As with some other jurisdictions, Wisconsin includes a "domestic partner" as having the same rights as a spouse concerning competency,[107] even though Wisconsin law does not provide for same-gender marriages.

---

103 People v. Sinohui, 28 Cal. 4th 205, 210, 47 P.3d 629, 2002 Cal. LEXIS 3777 (2002) (quoting Trammel v. United States, 445 U.S. 40, 44 (1980)). *See* 1 COKE, COMMENTARY UPON LITTLETON 6b (19th ed. 1832). *See also* Chapter 10 for a discussion of the husband-wife marital testimonial privilege.

104 Hawkins v. United States, 358 U.S. 74, 75, 1958 U.S. LEXIS 115 (1958).

105 38 U.S. 209, 221, 1839 U.S. LEXIS 431 (1839).

106 WIS. STAT. § 905.05(3)(b) (2013).

107 *Id.*

In 1933, the United States Supreme Court rejected the common law rule that excluded testimony by spouses in favor of each other,[108] but the new interpretation of the common law rule applied only to federal actions. In *Hawkins v. United States*, the Court:

> Recognized that the basic reason underlying the exclusion [of one spouse's testimony on behalf of the other] had been the practice of disqualifying witnesses with a personal interest in the outcome of a case. Widespread disqualifications because of interest, however, had long since been abolished both in this country and in England in accordance with the modern trend which permitted interested witnesses to testify and left it for the jury to assess their credibility. Certainly, since defendants were uniformly allowed to testify in their own behalf, there was no longer a good reason to prevent them from using their spouses as witnesses. With the original reason for barring favorable testimony of spouses gone the Court concluded that this aspect of the old rule should go too.[109]

While spouses were considered competent to testify as interested individuals, the jury could evaluate the value of the testimony and the credibility of the spouse-witness, recognizing that the evidence came from an interested individual.

Marriage does not make the spouse incompetent in civil or criminal cases, and spouses may testify freely, unless prevented by defects in the elements of competency: oath, original perception, recollection, and an ability to communicate. Typical of the modern trend, Maine evidence statutes consider both a husband and a wife as competent witnesses. The Maine Revised Statutes provide that "[t]he husband or wife of the accused is a competent witness except in regard to marital communications."[110] What has emerged is that the spouses are generally considered competent for all purposes, but some marital privileges exist that may have the effect of allowing one spouse to refuse to give testimony. In a few states, both the husband and the wife are holders of the marital testimonial privilege, and a defendant spouse can effectively prevent a witness spouse from testifying against the defendant spouse, absent injury to the spouse, children, or the property of either.[111]

Spousal competency as witnesses has been accepted in all jurisdictions, but spousal testimony may be rejected where a marital testimonial or confidential communication privilege exists. For example, in a murder case in which the defendant spouse had been accused of killing the victim and his DNA had been found on the woman's body, the prosecution wanted his then wife to testify against him concerning his whereabouts

---

108 Funk v. United States, 290 U.S. 371, 54 S. Ct. 212, 78 L. Ed. 369 (1933). *See* this case in Part II in Cases Relating to Chapter 1.

109 358 U.S. 74, 76 (1958).

110 15 ME. REV. STAT. ANN. § 1315 (2013).

111 Iowa Code § 622.9 (2013). "A husband and wife shall be competent but not be compellable to give evidence in any criminal proceeding for or against each other." *See* GA. CODE ANN. § 24-5-503 (2013). Preventing the testimony of a spouse against another is most likely to occur in a situation in which the defendant spouse has communicated with the proposed witness spouse under circumstances in which the defendant spouse was relying on the intimate and close marital relationship.

on the night of the victim's death. It was a foregone conclusion that the then wife was a competent witness, but the defendant argued that a marital privilege, the confidential communication privilege, prevented her from telling the jury that he left their home in the middle of the night in question. The trial court held that the defendant's act of leaving the marital home did not qualify as a confidential communication with his then wife because it was not much of a communication and it was not done in confidence, given that other people outside the marital home would have been able to view his presence outside the home. Thus, because no privilege prevented her testimony, and her competency was not an issue, the witness spouse properly testified against her husband.[112]

Statutes in most states permit spouses to testify against each other in prosecutions for only certain types of crimes. For example, under Ohio law, a husband and wife are competent to testify on behalf of each other in all criminal prosecutions and against each other subject to the law that recognizes exceptions to statutory privileges. Under the Ohio Revised Code, spouses are considered competent witnesses who may give testimony against each other in (1) prosecutions for personal injury of either by the other, bigamy, rape of one by the other, felonious sexual penetration, other sexual offenses against each other, and in cases involving violations of personal protection orders; (2) prosecutions for bigamy; and (3) prosecutions for failure to provide for, for neglect of, or for cruelty to their minor children under 18 or their physically or mentally handicapped children under 21 years of age.[113]

Following a similar legal theory, the Georgia code provides that both husband and wife are competent to testify against the other in any criminal proceeding when either one desires to testify against the other. The spouses cannot be compelled to offer testimony against the other, except where either the husband or wife has been charged with a crime against any minor child, a crime against the other spouse, or crimes against the property of the spouse or child.[114] In interpreting this statute, the Court of Appeals of Georgia noted that the trial court committed error when it virtually required a wife to testify against her spouse in a case in which her husband had been accused of assaulting his girlfriend. Under the Georgia statute, the witness spouse is considered competent to give evidence against a spouse, but cannot be compelled to do so.[115] In a Georgia case involving a homicide witnessed by the defendant's wife, the court allowed the prosecutor to question the wife about the events despite her assertion of the statutory privilege. Although the wife was competent as a witness, the court failed to recognize her marital privilege not to testify against her spouse. The reviewing court reversed the conviction and remanded the case for additional proceedings.[116] According to Georgia law, as interpreted, the spouse is competent to testify against the accused in a criminal

---

112 State v. Bates, 2003 Me. 67, 822 A.2d 1129, 2003 Me. LEXIS 77 (2003).

113 OHIO REV. CODE ANN. § 2945.42 (2013).

114 GA. CODE ANN. § 24-5-503 (2013).

115 Phillips v. State, 278 Ga. App. 439, 441, 629 S.E.2d 130, 132, 2006 Ga. App. LEXIS 350 (2006).

116 Webb v. State, 284 Ga. 122, 127, 2008 Ga. LEXIS 564 (Ga. 2008).

case, but to require such testimony would constitute error due to her spousal privilege not to testify.

The Texas Rules of Evidence follow a legal theory similar to the one used by Georgia, granting a privilege to the spouse of the accused not to be called as a witness for the prosecution. However, the Texas rules do not prohibit voluntary spousal testimony on behalf of the prosecution. In Texas, the potential witness spouse, though competent as a witness, is a holder of a privilege not to testify against the other spouse where nonconfidential matters are involved.[117] Therefore, a witness spouse may testify voluntarily for the state about nonconfidential matters, even over the objection of the accused, but the evidence rule contains some exceptions that require adverse spousal testimony.[118] In a murder case where the defendant was alleged to have killed his "off and on" girlfriend with a knife, he alleged that his common-law wife was being forced to testify against him, in violation of the Texas spousal privilege.[119] The trial court took evidence that established a valid marriage existed between the defendant and his common-law wife, but the court rejected the defendant's argument that she could not testify against him. According to the common-law wife's testimony, she was not being coerced and was willing, if not eager, to voluntarily testify, and she indicated that she would have come to the courthouse and testified freely, even if the prosecution had not served her with a subpoena. Under the Texas rule of evidence, Rule 504(B)(1), the common-law wife's testimony against the defendant was appropriately accepted and could serve as the basis for a reversal on appeal, according to the reviewing court. Under the current Texas rule of evidence, the wife was competent as a witness and could voluntarily testify against her husband.

Some states have made changes that slightly reduce the value to a defendant of spousal privileges. As is the case in many states, the Commonwealth of Pennsylvania, offers competent spouses a privilege not to testify against a current spouse in criminal proceedings, but the privilege can be waived. And following the traditional route, the privilege does not apply in some circumstances involving an alleged crime against the spouse or children or their property, but no privilege exists when the criminal charges that are pending against the defendant spouse involve *any* "murder, involuntary deviate sexual intercourse, or the crime of rape."[120]

Federal evidence rules do not address in any detail the concept of marital privileges,[121] and a federal court of appeals has noted that the marital privilege recognized by federal courts really involves two privileges. The first is the marital testimonial privilege, which permits a witness spouse from having to testify against the defendant spouse during the existence of the marriage, and the second privilege allows one spouse to prevent the other from giving testimony relating to confidential communications

---

117 TEX. R. EVID. § 504 (2013).

118 *Id.*, Rule 504(b)(4).

119 Gonzalez v. State, 2012 Tex. App. LEXIS 5215 (2012).

120 42 PA. CONS. STAT. §5913 (2013).

121 *See* FED. R. EVID. 501.

made between them during the existence of the marriage.[122] As one Indiana court noted, the purpose of the marital privileges are "grounded at least in significant part not on a policy of promoting disclosure but on concern for the health of the ongoing relationship between husband and wife and the policy of preventing further conflict between them by forcing one to testify against the other."[123]

Modern legal theory holds that spouses are competent to testify for or against each other. Even though legal competency exists, through the exercise of the marital testimonial and confidential communication privileges, either spouse may refuse to testify against the other. These privileges are subject to some exceptions involving crime against the person of the other spouse, the children, or the property of either. The ability to exercise a privilege to testify for or against the other spouse depends on case law and the provisions of federal or state statutes. Although spouses may testify on behalf of each other in all jurisdictions, some jurisdictions do not require one spouse to testify against the other spouse in any criminal case, while in others, the spouse is required by statute to testify against the accused spouse when the spouse is accused of specified crimes. If the statute makes wives and husbands competent to testify against each other regarding a specific crime, and there is no privilege to assert, then a spouse may be compelled to testify. Under these circumstances, if the spouse refuses to testify, he or she may be found to be in civil contempt of court.

§ 8.14 —Conviction of Crime

Under English common law, a person convicted of a felony was considered incompetent to testify as a witness in court.[124] In the Republic of Texas, prior to its admission into the federal union, the English common law was followed, and all persons who had been convicted of a felony anywhere were considered incompetent as witnesses. This practice continued following statehood.[125] Nevada followed this theory and refused to admit testimony from felons during the 1800s.[126] States gradually removed this disability on the theory that a felony conviction did not by itself make an individual an untruthful person for all time and some felonies do not involve any dishonesty.

Pursuant to state law and in agreement with the common law, a Tennessee appellate court reversed a conviction for assault with intent to commit murder, because one of the prosecution witnesses had previously been convicted of petit larceny. The appellate court ordered a new trial in 1872 because the state of the law at that time was such that people who had been convicted of specific crimes were deemed to be incompetent as witnesses in courts. "The rule of exclusion grew out of the common law doctrine that a

---

122 United States v. Montague, 421 F.3d 1099, 1103, 2005 U.S. App. LEXIS 14593 (10th Cir. 2005).

123 Glover v. State, 836 N.E.2d 414, 421, 2005 Ind. LEXIS 983 (2005).

124 Logan v. United States, 144 U.S. 263, 1892 U.S. LEXIS 2080 (1892).

125 *Id.*

126 State v. Foley, 15 Nev. 64, 1880 Nev. LEXIS 16 (1880).

party to the record, or one interested in the result, with certain exceptions, which were engrafted upon the rule from supposed necessity, was not competent as a witness, because of the temptation to perjury."[127]

In states following the English common law theory, a felony conviction meant that the individual was incompetent to testify as a court witness. As times changed, the legal theory supporting legal incompetency evolved. More than 91 years ago, the United States Supreme Court decided that "the dead hand of the common law rule," disqualifying a witness who had been convicted of crime, should no longer be applied in criminal cases in the federal courts.[128] Under modern legislation, states have acted legislatively and have removed any defect in competency from those who have criminal records. Demonstrative of this principle, Arizona legislation provides that "[a] person shall not be incompetent to testify because he is a party to an action or proceeding or interested in the issue tried, or because he has been indicted, accused or convicted of a crime. . ."[129]

Legislation may make a person presumptively competent as a witness, but defects in the elements of competency may defeat this presumption. Aside from competency, issues relating to credibility are matters to be determined by the trier of fact. Because some crimes may, by their nature, lead to questions about a person's honesty or credibility, proof of some prior crimes committed by a witness, including a defendant-witness, may be permitted based on the theory that prior convictions may have a legitimate bearing on the jury's perception of the witness's truthfulness. Most jurisdictions permit a showing of the fact of a witness's felony conviction or conviction of a crime of moral turpitude for the purpose of impeaching the credibility of the witness.[130]

State and federal statutes enacted during the past 70 years, as well as court interpretations, have made it quite clear that a criminal conviction does not render a witness incompetent to testify, but may create concerns about a witness's credibility. Demonstrative of this concept, New York provides that "[a] person who has been convicted of a crime is a competent witness; but the conviction may be proved, for the purpose of affecting the weight of his testimony, either by cross-examination, upon which he shall be required to answer any relevant question, or by the record."[131] The general rule is that prior convictions of a witness affect the weight and credibility of the witness's testimony, but do not disqualify the witness.[132]

---

[127] State v. Kennedy, 85 S.C. 146, 150, 67 S.E. 152, 1910 S.C. LEXIS 219 (1910).

[128] Rosen v. United States, 245 U.S. 467, 1918 U.S. LEXIS 2150 (1918).

[129] ARIZ. REV. STAT. § 12-2201(2013).

[130] For the rules regarding impeachment of witness, see Chapter 9. *See also* FED. R.EVID. 609.

[131] N.Y. CRIM. PROC. LAW § 4513 (2013).

[132] United States v. Reynolds, 2006 U.S. App. LEXIS 18115 (4th Cir. 2006). *See also* People v. Hinton, 37 Cal. 4th 839, 887, 126 P.3d 981, 1018, 38 Cal. Rptr. 3d 149, 193, 2006 Cal. LEXIS 336 (2006).

§ 8.15 —Religious Belief

Fearing that nonbelievers would have no incentive to be truthful, many American jurisdictions once prevented persons who had no religious belief from serving as witnesses in court. In an old case, the Supreme Court of Kansas once noted that, "[u]nder the common law, as well as in some of the states, atheists and persons without religious belief are deemed insensible to the obligations of an oath and incompetent as witnesses."[133] But the Supreme Court of Alabama noted in an earlier (1841) case that oaths had nothing to do with Christianity because they were more ancient than the Christian religion.[134] Under modern law, state constitutions or state and federal statutes affirmatively provide that no person shall be rendered incompetent to testify as a witness on account of his or her religious opinions or for want of any religious belief.[135] An Arizona statute is representative of modern state evidence codes on religious tests for witness competency and states that "[a] person shall not be incompetent to testify because. . .of his religious opinions, or because he does not have any religious belief."[136] Consistent with this view is Federal Rule of Evidence 610, which holds "[e]vidence of the beliefs or opinions of a witness on matters of religion is not admissible for the purpose of showing that by reason of their nature the witness's credibility is impaired or enhanced." If the witness is able to understand the obligation of an oath and the consequences of false swearing, the witness is competent, even if there is no evidence that he or she has a religious background.[137] Also improper is using religion as a tool to bolster a witness's credibility. Assuredly, it would be error to enhance witness testimony to suggest in a closing argument in a drug case that the police officer walked into a hotel "alone, armed *with a cross on his belt* and a gun on his side, into the belly of the beast like a surgeon aiming for the cancer as he came across it."[138]

However, "[n]ot all religious inquiries are forbidden"[139] if an aspect of religion might have an effect on bias or motive for impeachment purposes. Yet, it would be improper to state in a closing argument that a defendant "had the nerve to tell (the jury) 'I pray.'"[140] The Commonwealth of Massachusetts allows persons other than Christians to be sworn as witnesses using the ceremonies of their respective religion. A person with a belief in some notion of a supreme being and "[a] person not a believer in

---

133 Atchison, T. & S. F. R. Co. v. Potter, 60 Kan. 808, 811, 58 P. 471, 1899 Kan. LEXIS 143 (1899).

134 Blocker v. Burness, 2 Ala. 354, 355, 1841 Ala. LEXIS 357 (1841).

135 Under Federal Rule of Evidence 610, Religious Beliefs or Opinions, evidence of the beliefs or opinions of a witness on matters of religion is not admissible for the purpose of showing that by reason of their nature the witness's credibility is impaired or enhanced.

136 ARIZ. REV. STAT. § 12-2201 (B) (2013).

137 Chapell v. State, 710 S.W.2d 214 (1986).

138 United States v. Rogers, 556 F.3d 1130, 1141, 2009 U.S. App. LEXIS 5236 (10th Cir. 2009).

139 Slagle v. Bagley, 2006 U.S. App. LEXIS 20240, 2006 Fed. Appx. 0283P (6th Cir. 2006).

140 *Id.*

any religion shall [still] be required to testify truly under the penalties of perjury," and the "evidence of his disbelief in the existence of God may not be received to affect his credibility as a witness."[141]

The courts and state statutes have been consistent in providing that one's religious belief or lack thereof should not be a basis upon which a court or jury should evaluate testimonial capacity or credibility.[142] Michigan takes a strong stand against interjecting religion into trials and has "determined that when religious beliefs and their relationship to the veracity of a defendant or witness have been improperly raised by a prosecutor during trial, reversal is necessitated regardless of whether there is a demonstration of prejudice because of the questioning."[143]

§ 8.16 Competency of the Judge as a Witness

Rule 605

JUDGE'S COMPETENCY AS A WITNESS

The presiding judge may not testify as a witness at the trial. A party need not object to preserve the issue.[144]

For some years, the matter of whether a judge should be incompetent to testify as a witness in a trial over which he or she presides has been debated. One argument states that, where a judge both sits as a judge and serves as a witness in the same case, the impartiality of the judge may be called into question.[145] Additional issues would arise if a judge served as a witness, especially those involving who should rule on objections, who would compel the judge to answer questions, and what would occur during cross-examination. A party attorney could be reluctant to attempt impeachment of a judge because that attorney would have future cases before that judge, an obvious conflict of interest. However, these issues have been rendered moot by 28 U.S.C. § 455, which mandates that federal judges disqualify themselves in cases in which they are serving or

---

141 MASS. GEN. LAWS ANN. ch. 233, § 19 (2013).

142 *See* MICH. COMP. LAWS § 600.1436 (2011), which removed any religious test for competency and provided that religion-related interrogation of the witness could not be the subject of inquiry.

143 People v. Bell, 2008 Mich. App. LEXIS 2307 (2008).

144 FED. R. EVID. 605.

145 Elmore v. State, 13 Ark. App. 221, 227, 682 S.W.2d 758, 762, 1985 Ark. App. LEXIS 1735 (1985). The failure of a witness judge to recuse him- or herself does not always constitute reversible error. *See also* 22 A.L.R.3d 1198 (2003).

have served as material witnesses or in which they may have bias or prejudice.[146] Rule 605 of the Federal Rules of Evidence follows the federal statute that deems federal judges incompetent to testify in cases in which they are sitting. This rule has been so well followed that a Texas court was prompted to state, "[n]ot surprisingly, there are few reported federal or state cases involving Rule 605 violations."[147]

A federal case that did involve a Rule 605 violation occurred when a transcript of a suppression hearing, in which the judge offered some conclusions concerning a defendant's suppression witness, was admitted at the trial on the merits.[148] A pretrial motion of the suppression-hearing transcript included the judge's comments concerning the lack of credibility of the defense witness. According to the reviewing court, "the introduction of the trial judge's suppression-hearing comments amounted to impermissible to suppress, the trial judge expressed his opinion concerning the credibility of a defense witness in fairly clear terms. The same judge permitted the prosecutor at trial to read part judicial testimony"[149] and effectively made the judge a witness in the very trial over which he was presiding, violating Rule 605.

A violation of Rule 605, or a comparable state rule, does not require an automatic reversal of any verdict. In a federal case involving a border crossing reentry into the United States by an illegal alien, a judge interjected some of his own knowledge regarding the location and number of the stop signs along the border road where the aliens were captured, as well as the narrowness of the road. The judge stated these facts at a time in the suppression hearing when these facts had yet to be introduced to the record. The real effect in this case was that the judge was testifying as an unsworn witness. The Court of Appeals concluded that the suppression judge violated Rule 605, which makes judges incompetent to testify when the judge is presiding over the proceeding, but noted that the error could be considered on the harmless error standard. Because sufficient admissible evidence was present to convict the illegal alien of reentry, the court upheld the conviction.[150]

Many states have adopted the federal rule either by statute or by court decision. For example, an Indiana evidence statute that mirrors Federal Rule 605 provides that a judge may not testify in any trial over which the judge is presiding.[151] In a speeding prosecution, a defendant, serving as his own attorney, questioned the court's subject matter jurisdiction in the cause and wanted to ask the judge questions concerning whether there was personal jurisdiction over the defendant.[152] During the trial, the judge did not answer the defendant's questions concerning issues of jurisdiction, a

---

146 28 U.S.C. § 455.

147 Bradley v. State ex rel. White, 990 S.W.2d 245, 248, 1999 Tex. LEXIS 33 (1999).

148 *See* United States v. Blanchard, 542 F.3d 1133, 2008 U.S. App. LEXIS 19151 (7th Cir. 2008).

149 *Id.* 1149.

150 United States v. Berber-Tinoco, 510 F.3d 1083, 1091, 2007 U.S. App. LEXIS 29301 (9th Cir. 2007), *cert. denied*, 2008 U.S. LEXIS 7266 (2008). *See also* Henderson v. State, 2005 Tenn. Crim. App. LEXIS 667 (2005).

151 IND. R. EVID. 605 (2013).

152 Banfield v. State, 2013 Ind. App. Unpub. LEXIS 886 (2013).

practice that was applauded by the reviewing court, since it noted that Indiana judges are not competent as witnesses in the very trial over which a judge is sitting. Generally, a defendant cannot use Rule 605 to force a judge to recuse him- or herself from a trial or from a postconviction proceeding by placing the judge on a witness list.[153] In a Florida federal case that involved alleged improper assignment of cases to federal judges, one judge removed the name of a different federal judge from a witness list offered by one of the attorneys, because the judge was not considered competent in a case in which that same judge would be required to make findings of fact or other rulings.[154] Even though the judge is not considered competent as a witness in the case over which that judge presides, he or she need not disqualify himself or herself as a judge in order to testify in such a case.[155] However, judges may testify in separate but related proceedings. In one case where the parties came to a settlement in the presence of the judge, but the agreement was not immediately reduced to a writing, the judge can be called as a witness in a separate proceeding to give evidence concerning the agreement.[156]

§ 8.17 Competency of Juror as Witness

Rule 606

JUROR'S COMPETENCY AS A WITNESS

(a) At the Trial. A juror may not testify as a witness before the other jurors at the trial. If a juror is called to testify, the court must give a party an opportunity to object outside the jury's presence.
(b) During an Inquiry into Validity of Verdict or Indictment.
   (1) ***Prohibited Testimony or Other Evidence.*** During an inquiry into the validity of a verdict or indictment, a juror may not testify about any statement made or incident that occurred during the jury's deliberations; the effect of anything on that juror's or another juror's vote; or any juror's mental processes concerning the verdict or indictment. The court may not receive a juror's affidavit or evidence of a juror's statement on these matters.
   (2) ***Exceptions.*** A juror may testify about whether:
      (A) extraneous prejudicial information was improperly brought to the jury's attention;
      (B) an outside influence was improperly brought to bear on any juror; or
      (C) a mistake was made in entering the verdict on the verdict form.[157]

---

[153] State v. Sims, 272 Neb. 811, 826, 827, 2006 Neb. LEXIS 185 (Neb. 2006).
[154] See Bettis. v. Toys 'R' Us, 646 F. Supp.2d 1273 (2009).
[155] Ginsberg v. Evergreen Sec., Ltd., 570 F.3d 1257, 2009 U.S. App. LEXIS 12535 (11th Cir. 2009).
[156] McMillin v. Davidson Industries, 2005 Ohio 224, 2005 Ohio App. LEXIS 221 (2005).
[157] FED. R. EVID. 606.

Although many older cases are to the contrary, the general rule is that a juror may not testify as a witness in the trial of a case in which he or she is sitting. In addition, jurors are not allowed to call into question the way that the case is deliberated. According to the Tenth Circuit Court of Appeal,

> The rule against impeachment of a jury verdict by juror testimony as to internal deliberations may be traced back to "Mansfield's Rule," originating in the 1785 case of *Vaise v. Delaval*, 99 Eng. Rep. 944 (K.B. 1785). Faced with juror testimony that the jury had reached its verdict by drawing lots, Lord Mansfield established a blanket ban on jurors testifying against their own verdict.[158]

Years ago, the Supreme Court of the United States noted that "[f]ull and frank discussion in the jury room, jurors' willingness to return an unpopular verdict, and the community's trust in a system that relies on the decisions of laypeople would all be undermined by a barrage of post-verdict scrutiny of juror conduct."[159]

In preventing most juror testimony, "[c]onsiderations that bear upon the permissibility of testimony are similar to those invoked when a judge is called as a witness."[160] The juror could argue against any personally impeaching evidence and rehabilitate his or her testimony in the perception of other jurors in a way not open to other witnesses. A juror-witness would have an unfettered opportunity to unfairly sway the jurors with personal historical knowledge of the case that may have been inadmissible at trial. The chances are too great that the testimony of the juror would have an undue influence on the verdict. This rule of exclusion was codified in the Federal Rules of Evidence, which, without exception, prohibit the members of a jury from testifying in the case in which they sit as jurors. If an attorney attempted to call a sitting juror, objection may be made outside the hearing of the jury.[161]

Section (b) of Federal Rule 606 generally holds that jurors are incompetent as witnesses and may not testify "about any statement made or incident that occurred during the jury's deliberations; the effect of anything on that juror's or another juror's vote; or any juror's mental processes concerning" the decision. However, the rule allows jurors to testify about whether outside influences improperly affected jury deliberations. This rule makes a juror incompetent to testify concerning the facts used to prove the case, as well as activities that took place during the jury's deliberations. This incompetency stems from the old maxim that "a juror may not impeach his own verdict." The rule has been justified on a variety of theories including the need for the preservation of the secrecy of internal jury deliberations and to protect the verdict against attack for corrupt reasons.[162] Significant considerations support the rationale of Rule 606(b) that

---

158 United States v. Benally, 546 F.3d 1230, 1233, 2008 U.S. App. LEXIS 23555 (10th Cir. 2008).

159 Tanner v. United States, 483 U.S. 107, 120-121, 107 S.Ct. 2739, 97 L.Ed.2d 90, 1987 U.S. LEXIS 2868 (1987).

160 FED R. EVID 606(a),

161 FED. R. EVID. 606(a).

162 People v. Grider, 246 Cal. App. 2d 149, 153, 54 Cal. Rptr. 497, 501, 1966 Cal. App. LEXIS 1013 (1966).

"include verdict finality, maintaining the integrity of the jury system, encouraging frank and honest deliberations, and the protection of jurors from subsequent harassment by a losing party."[163]

Were this rule to permit inquiry into the mental deliberations and processes of the jurors, every verdict would be susceptible to being undermined by post-trial jury tampering and harassment of jurors. One court noted that, if every defendant had the power to make former jurors into witnesses against a previous verdict, the procedure "would allow defendants to launch inquiries into jury conduct in the hope of discovering something that might invalidate the verdicts against them"[164] and result in the destruction of openness and freedom of discussion in the jury room. Under federal evidence rules, the protection from making jurors into witnesses extends to each of the components of the deliberation, including arguments, statements, discussions, mental and emotional reactions, and any other feature of the deliberation process.[165] Interestingly, where the inquiry of reasoning and deliberation concern the judge and improper extraneous factors used in reaching a verdict in a bench trial, no prohibition on an investigation of judicial reasoning exists.[166]

In a case where a defendant wanted a reversal due to alleged juror misconduct, a court of appeal had to consider the report about one juror who had allegedly determined his vote prior to the time the prosecution finished and another juror who indicated that, if it were 11 to 1 in favor of guilty, the other jurors should just roll over and vote so they can get out of the jury room quickly.[167] The reviewing court indicated that few jury trials were without some problems here and there and that the federal rule prohibits jury testimony in court consideration of internal deliberations by any jury. Federal Rule 606(b) does not forbid judicial consideration of evidence of juror statements or conduct, but it does prohibit consideration of evidence about how such statements may have affected actual deliberations. The court noted that reviewing courts must "ignore any evidence about the supposed actual effects of the statements or conduct on the jurors, and must rely instead on precedent, experience, and common sense to gauge whether the statements or conduct should be *presumed* prejudicial."[168] The reviewing court applauded the trial court because it found that the statements made by the jurors were not presumptively prejudicial and that the trial judge did not abuse judicial discretion. The court noted that it is almost impossible for jurors not to form some preliminary opinions about the merits of any case. While a case unfolds during its presentation, it is natural that some jurors may attempt to share that opinion or conclusion with other jurors. But, so long as the early opinion was not an irrevocable final

---

163 United States v. Delatorre, 572 F. Supp. 2d 967, 2008 U.S. Dist. LEXIS 77787 (N. D. Ill. 2008).

164 United States v. Siegelman, 2009 U.S. App. LEXIS 5369 (11th Cir. 2009).

165 United States v. Crosby, 294 F.2d 928 (2d Cir. 1961).

166 Stewart v. Southwest Foods, 688 So. 2d 733, 735, 1996 Miss. LEXIS 643 (1996).

167 United States v. Farmer, 717 F.3d 559, 2013 U.S. App. LEXIS 10932 (7th Cir. 2013).

168 *Id.*,at 565.

opinion, the jury verdict should stand. Additionally, in this particular case, there were no allegations of improper external influences whatsoever.

Rule 606 (b) makes an exception that authorizes the juror to testify on the question of whether extraneous prejudicial information was improperly brought to the jury's attention or whether any outside influence was improperly brought to bear upon any juror. The purpose of this measure is to allow the courts to determine whether there were any irregularities, such as the introduction of a prejudicial newspaper account into the jury room or statements by the bailiff concerning the case. Mistakes and misconduct of the jury during its deliberations that do not involve external influences are not generally subject to inquiry.[169]

In a Wisconsin case, there was an allegation that some of the jury members had become extrajudicially aware that the defendant had prior criminal convictions. At postconviction relief hearings, the defense counsel alleged that there had been jury misconduct that required a reversal and a new trial. As the reviewing court noted, pursuant to Wisconsin law, "the party seeking to impeach the verdict must demonstrate that a juror's testimony is admissible by establishing that: (1) the juror's testimony concerns extraneous information (rather than the deliberative process of the jurors), (2) the extraneous information was improperly brought to the jury's attention, and (3) the extraneous information was potentially prejudicial."[170] Under this daunting procedure, if the appellant establishes that the juror is permitted to testify, the appellant must then demonstrate that one or more jurors heard the statements or engaged in the alleged conduct, and, finally, the court must determine whether sufficient prejudice occurred to justify overturning the conviction.[171] In this case, the defendant managed to meet the first three hurdles, but the court did not find by clear and convincing evidence that any jurors were exposed to the prejudicial information about the defendant's prior convictions. Therefore, the reviewing court refused to disturb the jury verdict. Simply stated, the process to overturn a jury verdict based on outside influence almost always proves unsuccessful to any criminal appellant.

While jurors are not competent to be witnesses at the trial in which they are sitting, jurors may discuss the case with anyone and everyone following their discharge by the judge. During the trial, a strong general rule prohibits jurors from talking about the case with anyone or with each other until they begin their deliberations. In implementing this rule, judges routinely order jurors not to discuss the case at any time with anyone other than with fellow jurors during regularly scheduled deliberations, and judges may remind the jurors of this instruction during the trial.[172] Once a trial has concluded, and the jurors have been officially discharged, they are free to speak with attorneys in the case, as well as print, broadcast, and Internet media, or to choose not to speak with anyone or any organization. In this context, information concerning the internal

---

[169] Williams v. Price, 343 F.3d 223, 2003 U.S. App. LEXIS 18662 (3d Cir. 2003).

[170] State v. Searcy, 288 Wis. 2d 804; 709 N.W.2d 497; 2005 Wis. App. LEXIS 1124 (2005).

[171] *Id.* at 828, 507.

[172] United States v. Camacho, 555 F.3d 695, 704, 2009 U.S. App. LEXIS 3592 (8th Cir. 2009).

deliberations, discussions, and behaviors of the jury may be revealed at the individual discretion of the juror.[173]

Because discharged jurors have the right to refuse any comment concerning a case, states are permitted to keep much juror information private and can refuse to disclose it unless a defendant-appellant makes a strong case for disclosure.[174] In an assault with a deadly weapon case, the convicted defendant petitioned the court to release some juror information pursuant to the California statute.[175] In arguing the need for juror information, the defendant-appellant contended that one juror had been overheard to state that it would have helped the defendant's case had he at least denied committing the crime. The reviewing court noted that the attorney for the appellant offered a vague declaration provided no context for the juror's comment, and noted that the juror's comment did not show that the jury improperly considered defendant's failure to testify in reaching its verdict. The appellate court refused to hold that the lower court should have revealed juror identities and addresses in the absence of a stronger showing of juror misconduct.[176] The California statute allows some protection for jurors against unreasonable contact with the defendant or someone working on behalf of the defendant because the identity is sealed unless a judge orders a different result.[177] Similarly, under Florida law, a party who believes a verdict may be subject to legal attack, must notify the court to request an order permitting the party to interview a juror or jurors to determine if the belief is supported by facts.[178] According to the Florida criminal rules, following "notice and hearing, the trial judge, upon a finding that the verdict may be subject to challenge, shall enter an order permitting the interview, and setting therein a time and a place for the interview of the juror or jurors, which shall be conducted in the presence of the court and the parties."[179] Essentially, following the trial, jurors are free to discuss the case at any and all levels or to remain silent. Some jurisdictions limit contact, unless judicially approved, if the initiator is the defendant, counsel, or another person connected to the original case.

§ 8.18 Summary

To be admissible in a trial in a criminal case, evidence must be competent in that it meets the tests of logical and legal relevancy. The item of evidence must help prove or disprove a fact in issue, and the probative value of the evidence must be greater than its prejudicial effect. The evidence is then considered competent. Even though the

---

173 Stoker v. Stemco, LP, 2013 U.S. Dist. LEXIS 99461 (E.D, Tex. 2013).

174 *See* CAL. CIV. PROC. CODE § 206 (2013).

175 *See* People v. Mejia, 2012 Cal. App. Unpub. LEXIS 2145 (2012).

176 *See* CAL. CIV. PROC. CODE §§ 206, 237 (2013).

177 *Id.*

178 *See* FLA. R. CRIM. P. 3.575 (2013).

179 *Id.*

evidence has passed the relevancy and materiality tests, it will be excluded if the court finds that it is incompetent for other legal reasons, such as a statutory or constitutional violation.

Care must be taken to avoid confusion concerning the rules regarding competency of the evidence and competency of the witness. A witness may be competent by meeting the four elements of competency, and yet the evidence to be introduced by the witness may be ruled incompetent, and thus excludable.

From a general point of view, evidence is incompetent if (1) law enforcement officials have obtained it wrongfully or illegally; (2) a statute declares it to be incompetent; (3) it has been declared incompetent by the courts; or (4) it has insufficient or no connection to the case.

Documentary evidence must meet the usual competency tests so that it possesses sufficient connection to the case, but it also must comply with special requirements. For example, it must be authenticated to show that it is genuine. Likewise, real evidence may be excluded as incompetent if specific requirements are not met.

Through court decisions and statutes, rules have evolved that require a witness to meet the four elements of competency prior to being permitted to testify in court. These elements are oath (or a substitute), original perception, recollection, and an ability to communicate. While competency rules have been liberalized in recent years, there are still certain requirements that, if not met, may make a witness incompetent to testify in court or may prevent a prospective witness from testifying through reliance on a privilege.

Even though a person may not have normal mental capacity, he or she may be allowed to testify if he or she can understand the obligation of an oath and can give a correct account of the matters seen or heard. Some jurisdictions hold that a child is generally presumed competent to testify, while other jurisdictions hold that, below a specified age, the presumption is against competency. As a general rule, a child can be proved to be competent where the child demonstrates the capacity to observe events and to recollect and communicate them, as well as the ability to understand questions and to make intelligent answers, based on an understanding of the duty to speak the truth.

Under common law, neither husband nor wife was permitted to testify for or against the other. All states by statute have made both husband and wife competent to testify on behalf of an accused spouse, but with varying exceptions, depending on the jurisdiction. It is generally provided that the prosecution may not force a spouse to testify against the accused spouse.

A criminal conviction for a felony generally does not render a witness or a defendant incompetent to testify. While considered competent to testify, a defendant who has been previously convicted of a crime, especially a felony, can choose to forgo testifying because it opens the door for impeachment based on the introduction of evidence of prior felonies and misdemeanors involving moral turpitude. However, certain convictions may be relevant if they are introduced to show that the defendant had a common scheme or plan, motive, intent, identity, knowledge sufficient to commit the crime, or lack of mistake in committing the crime.

The competency of a judge to testify in a case the judge is presently hearing has severe limitations. Under the modern rules of evidence, and consistent with Rule 605 of the Federal Rules of Evidence, judges in federal courts and states that have adopted versions of the Federal Rules are incompetent to testify as to any matter in a trial over which they preside. A juror is also incompetent to act as a witness at a trial, while serving as a juror in the trial of that case. In addition, under Federal Rule 606, jurors may not testify about the verdict or the manner in which the jury decided the case, except when the inquiry relates to external influence or external prejudicial information that may have been improperly brought to the jurors' attention.

As a practical matter, justice personnel should be fully aware of the rules that make testimony or other evidence inadmissible because of competency rules. In some instances, a case may be resolved based on one piece of real evidence or testimony that an attorney attempts to get the court to admit or exclude.

CHAPTER EIGHT: QUESTIONS AND REVIEW EXERCISES

1. Incompetent evidence is generally not admissible in court. The category of incompetent evidence includes wrongfully obtained evidence, statutorily incompetent evidence, and evidence that is excludable because of court-established rules. Explain what is meant by the three types of incompetent evidence and give one example of each.
2. Documentary evidence is a category that includes traditional writings, as well as other methods of storing data. What are some of the other methods of storing data that are included within the concept of a document for evidence purposes?
3. Tests and experiments are included within competent evidence, provided they meet the tests of relevancy and are not constitutionally or statutorily prohibited. How does the old *Frye v. United States* (1923) test for admissibility of scientific evidence compare to the more recent case that set a new test for scientific test admissibility, *Daubert v. Merrell Dow Pharmaceuticals* (1993)?
4. Telephone conversations, text messages, and sometimes the mere fact that a message was sent or that a phone call was made, may be important in a criminal case. Cellular phones typically store a wealth of data including the number called, length of call, pictures, and GPS information. With respect to a voice telephone call that one person made to another, construct a hypothetical situation in which a telephone conversation can be authenticated by one of several methods.
5. As a general rule, all witnesses are considered competent, thus meeting the four elements of competency. Name and explain

the four elements of adult witness competency.

6. Mentally challenged and mentally ill individuals may often be considered competent witnesses. What are some attributes that a mentally ill individual might possess that might disqualify that person from testifying as a witness?
7. Young children are frequently called to testify as witnesses. How should an attorney proceed in establishing the competency of a young child? What are the kinds of questions that the attorney theoretically could ask a child that would help establish the elements of competency, except for the oath?
8. Although modern law considers that spouses are competent witnesses both for and against each other, the common law did not permit them to testify because neither one could be an unbiased witness against the other. What are some of the circumstances under which one spouse may refuse to testify either for or against the other? Do these situations involve a lack of competency or a privilege not to testify?
9. Under modern law, neither conviction of a crime nor a lack of religious belief prevents a person from being considered competent as a witness. What were the reasons for determining that a conviction should render someone incompetent as a witness? Similarly, under outdated theory, why should a person who did not believe in any supreme being be prohibited from testifying in court?
10. According to the Federal Rules of Evidence, a judge who is presiding over a case and a person sitting as a juror in that case are considered incompetent as witnesses. What is the rationale behind a blanket decision that neither the judge nor a juror can be considered competent as a witness in a case in which they are involved?

Evidence via Witness Testimony

Examination of Witnesses

9

For two centuries past, the policy of the Anglo-American system of Evidence has been to regard the necessity of testimony by cross-examination as a vital feature of the law. The belief that no safeguard for testing the value of human statements is comparable to that furnished by cross-examination, and the conviction that no statement (unless by special exception) should be used as testimony until it has been probed and sublimated by that test, has found increasing strength in lengthening experience.

Wigmore, Evidence, Vol. 5 § 1367 (3d ed. 1940)

Chapter Contents

Section

KEY TERMS AND CONCEPTS	
Affirmation	Oath
Cross-examination	Past Recollection Recorded
Direct Examination	Present Memory Revived
Hostile Witness	Prior Inconsistent Statement
Impeachment of Witness	Recross-examination
Judicial Control	Redirect Examination
Leading Question	Sequestration

§ 9.1 Introduction

With the exceptions of judicial notice, stipulations, and the use of inferences and presumptions, the evidence in criminal trials must be introduced through the testimony of witnesses who orally describe what happened and what they observed. No physical evidence—such as a firearm, knife, or the results of a chemical test—can be introduced except through actual witnesses. Even with the use of judicial notice, inferences, presumptions, and stipulations, it would be impossible to present a criminal case without trial witnesses. The function of the witness is to present the evidence to the trier of fact so that it may make a determination of what these facts indicate or what deductions may be made from the facts. Properly presented, the evidence will indicate what happened, whether a crime occurred, whether that person should be held criminally responsible, or whether an affirmative defense has been proved. On the assumption that a criminal trial has as its sole purpose the determination of whether an accused person is guilty or innocent of the crime charged, it would seem appropriate to assume that all evidence related to the case should be admissible where there is any possible connection to the particular case in front of the court. However, there are various constitutional, statutory, and sound public policy reasons that limit some of the evidence that is highly related to the crime; the evidence may be prohibited from admission and never revealed to the trier of fact.

In conducting the typical criminal trial, the prosecution has the duty to present evidence that it believes proves the offense charged by the level of proof known as *beyond a reasonable doubt.* In so doing, the prosecution calls a series of witnesses and then proceeds to ask them questions. The defendant may cross-examine the prosecution's witnesses, and the prosecution may do the same to the defense witnesses. After the prosecution has presented its case, the defense has an opportunity to put its own witnesses on the stand and introduce evidence that follows the defense's theory of the case.

As a preliminary matter, each witness must be qualified as a witness, but a "witness is presumed to be competent unless it is shown that she does not have personal knowledge of the matter about which she testifies, does not have the ability to recall, or does not understand the oath."[1] The qualifications of a witness include that the witness take an oath to tell the truth, have personal knowledge of the historical facts of the case, have memory and recollection of those facts, and have an ability to communicate. Even after the witnesses have been qualified, their testimony is subject to many rules that will be discussed in this chapter and in future chapters.

This chapter focuses on the general rules regulating the qualification of witnesses and witness examination by the prosecution and the defense. Specifically, the sections in this chapter cover the qualifications of the witnesses, the requirement of the oath or affirmation, the separation of witnesses, the direct and cross-examination of witnesses, and the process of witness impeachment and rehabilitation. Later chapters will discuss in great detail the rules that limit the admissibility of testimonial evidence while giving due recognition to some of the more complex and arcane rules and their exceptions. This category includes testimonial privileges, opinion testimony, and the **hearsay rule**, with its exceptions.

Hearsay rule Statements offered by a witness that are based upon what someone else has told him or her and not upon personal knowledge or observation.

§ 9.2 Essential Qualities of a Witness

Rule 602

NEED FOR PERSONAL KNOWLEDGE

A witness may testify to a matter only if evidence is introduced sufficient to support a finding that the witness has personal knowledge of the matter. Evidence to prove personal knowledge may consist of the witness's own testimony. This rule does not apply to a witness's expert testimony under Rule 703.[2]

In order to meet the threshold witness requirements and to be eligible to testify, a witness must have a personal connection with the relevant occurrence, coupled with mental and physical faculties sufficient to be able to observe and understand the events at the time of their occurrence and to recollect and relate them to the jury or a court in a manner that renders the testimony relevant.[3] In other words, the witness must be

[1] United States v. Barbee, 524 F. App'x. 15, 20, 2013 U.S. App. LEXIS 9074 (4th Cir. 2013).

[2] FED. R. EVID. 602. Rule 703, which is referenced in Rule 602, provides that the expert witness need not have personal knowledge of facts or data.

[3] People v. Hooker, 253 Ill. App. 3d 1075, 625 N.E.2d 1081 (1993).

qualified. Generally, "[a] witness is presumed to be competent unless it is shown that she does not have personal knowledge of the matter about which she testifies,"[4] but when an issue arises that questions the competency of a particular witness, the witness may be required to demonstrate that the witness had original perception, remembers what happened, can communicate this knowledge, and is willing to take the oath or a substitute. When a judge makes a determination about competency, the witness is either competent or incompetent. There are no degrees of competency where one witness would have more competency than another.[5]

The rationale for Federal Rule 602 is based on the concept that lay testimony that has not been based on personal information is useless for proof of guilt, and a witness cannot provide information about a matter about which he or she has no knowledge.[6] In a probation revocation hearing, a detective testified that the victims of an alleged break-in told him that they thought a named probationer was involved. In an appeal of the revocation, the probationer contended that the detective had no firsthand knowledge and was incompetent to testify about the alleged new crime. In reversing the revocation of probation, the appellate court indicated that the state failed to present a witness who had any personal knowledge of the charged offense and the detective was not competent to testify that the probationer was the person who had committed the new crime.[7]

The requirement of firsthand knowledge or original knowledge will allow a person to be considered competent as a witness for a particular case. In a prosecution for a series of motor vehicle burglaries, security video revealed an individual who had broken into several motor vehicles over a period of time in a hospital parking garage. Each of the owners of the motor vehicles testified that they had viewed the surveillance video prior to testifying at trial, where they identified items taken from their respective vehicles and provided descriptions as to each of their motor vehicles. The victims also indicated that the surveillance video accurately depicted the damage to their vehicles. The defendant argued that none of the witnesses should have been allowed to testify concerning their motor vehicles, the thefts from them, and vehicle damage, because none of them had personal firsthand knowledge of the crime and that their knowledge came from the video. According to the reviewing court, the testimony of the five victims, who had viewed the video, was sufficient to support a judicial determination that each witness possessed personal knowledge under Mississippi's Rule 602.[8]

As a general rule, the party offering the testimony must prove that the witness had an opportunity to observe the incident about which he or she is testifying. This does not necessarily mean that a witness must have observed every facet of the event in question, especially when the witness may be considered an expert. For example, in a stabbing

---

4 United States v. Barbee, 524 F. App'x. 15, 2013 U.S. App. LEXIS 9074 (2013). *See also* ARIZ. REV. STAT. § 13-4061 (2013) and FED. R. EVID. 601.

5 Hawai'i v. Jones, 98 Haw. 294, 2002 Haw. App. LEXIS 65 (2002).

6 United States v. Allen, 10 F.3d 405 (7th Cir. 1993).

7 Wescovich v. State, 2013 Ala. Crim. App. LEXIS 99 (2013).

8 Bunch v. State, 123 So.3d 484 ¶30, 2013 Miss. App. LEXIS 602 (2013).

altercation outside an apartment complex, the court permitted a responding police officer to testify that the victim's stab wounds were consistent with someone fleeing an aggressor.[9] An emergency room doctor testified to the same conclusion, although neither the doctor nor the officer observed the fight. They obtained their personal knowledge by observing the situation and the victim and coming to a conclusion. The appellate court approved the admission of evidence by the two witnesses on the theory that each one was an expert and was properly allowed to offer a conclusion even though neither one observed the fight. The police officer had specific training as a police officer and had additional training as a military police officer.

Personal knowledge may be somewhat fleeting and still meet the requirements of firsthand knowledge. In one case, the defendant took flight in his motor vehicle when police indicated that he should stop, and he had a collision with another vehicle. At the conclusion of the vehicle chase, the witness indicated that she had an excellent opportunity to view the defendant; she had looked directly at the defendant driver of the white Mitsubishi as he careened into the left front fender of the witness's vehicle. The woman positively identified the defendant from a photo lineup array. Despite the defendant's contention of lack of personal knowledge, the reviewing court held that the woman witness had sufficient firsthand information to be found competent as a witness to identify the defendant under Rhode Island's version of Rule 602.[10]

In criminal cases, witnesses are frequently called upon to testify about events that were only casually observed, such as recounting events that were not thought to be important at the time of observation or making an identification. It is permissible under the firsthand knowledge requirement for a witness to testify that, to the best of the witness's belief, the defendant committed the criminal act, while still acknowledging that he or she may be mistaken as to the identity of the defendant.

§ 9.3 Oath or Affirmation Requirement

Rule 603

OATH OR AFFIRMATION TO TESTIFY TRUTHFULLY

Before testifying, a witness must give an oath or affirmation to testify truthfully. It must be in a form designed to impress that duty on the witness's conscience.[11]

---

[9] Vasquez v. State, 2006 Tex. App. LEXIS 500 (2006).

[10] State v. Hall, 940 A.2d 645, 2008 R.I. LEXIS 7 (2008).

[11] FED. R. EVID. 603.

As a general rule, every witness is required to take an oath or make a clear affirmation that he or she will offer the truth. Consequently, as one of the elements of competency, every witness, including child witnesses, is required to state that he or she will testify truthfully and with an awareness of the importance of offering truth. As one court phrased it, courts require that the prospective witness take an oath or affirmation that is "calculated to awaken the witness' conscience and impress the witness' mind with the clear duty"[12] to tell the truth. A trial court may use an oath that contains language such as "solemnly swear" to tell the truth rather than asking each witness about using the term "affirm to tell the truth," unless the defendant or a witness objects. The inadvertent failure to swear a witness does not necessarily require a reversal of conviction where the witness was under the impression that she had to tell the truth.[13]

Most states have statutes that allow the witness to make an affirmation rather than an oath. The affirmation need not take a particular form; the concept of affirmation is designed to afford some flexibility when dealing with religious adults or children.[14] This alternative to the formal oath is provided for those who lack the requisite belief in God and for those who are forbidden by conscientious scruples to take an oath. Under these statutes, the witness must explicitly state that the scruple exists.

Because of First Amendment protection of the freedom of religion, federal courts do not require the witness to swear or to affirm to God in the court's administered oath. In a case in which a Mennonite defendant swore to tell the truth prior to offering his trial testimony, but later complained of the process during a posttrial motion, the reviewing court noted that if he were morally opposed to swearing, he could have affirmed to tell the truth instead of swearing the oath and had, therefore, waived any right that he had in the matter.[15]

If the witness claims a First Amendment right not to be sworn, the court's interest in administering the precise form of oath must yield to the witness's First Amendment rights.[16] In the case of *United States v. Ward*, the reviewing court held that the defendant had a right to substitute the phrase "fully integrated honesty" for the word "truth" in taking the oath and that the rule governing the form of the oath was sufficiently flexible to permit modifications of the oath. Rule 603 and similar state statutes were developed with a view to affording flexibility when dealing with adults, atheists, conscientious objectors, mentally challenged persons, and children.[17]

When a potential witness refuses to take an oath to tell the truth and completely refuses to testify in any form, trial courts face a problem. If the potential witness made an out-of-court statement, that statement might provide needed evidence. However, a

---

12 Esguerra v. State, 2005 Alaska App. LEXIS 2 (2005).

13 *See*, State v. Hiatt, 834 N.W. 2d 82(¶12), 2013 Iowa App. LEXIS 451 (2013).

14 North Carolina v. Beane, 146 N.C. App. 220, 225, 226, 552 S.E.2d 193, 196, 197, 2001 N.C. App. LEXIS 852 (2001).

15 Izac v. United States, 2008 U.S. Dist. LEXIS 80013 (N.D.W.VA. 2008).

16 United States v. Ward, 989 F.2d 1015 (9th Cir. 1992).

17 *See* the advisory Notes accompanying Federal Rule 603.

constitutional problem arises under this situation because the defendant is denied the right under the Sixth Amendment to confront the adverse witness. These types of situations have no easy answer and may result in evidence that is inadmissible.[18]

In the exercise of judicial discretion, a court may dispense with the formal oath when one of the parties presents a young child as a witness. As a substitute for the oath, the court must be satisfied that a young witness understands the consequences of not telling the truth. Ohio courts do not require an oath from children, but do require that children be shown to understand the duty to tell the truth and know the difference between a lie and the truth.[19] In California, a child under the age of 10 is not required to swear an oath or affirmation but, at the judge's discretion, may testify where the child promises to tell the truth.[20] In Connecticut courts, children as witnesses are not automatically rejected based on age, but may be subjected to a modified version of the adult oath and may, in some cases, give testimony without any oath.[21]

An oath may not be required in some other judicial proceedings that do not involve young children. For example, in a capital case, an Ohio court permitted a death-eligible convicted defendant to offer an unsworn statement to the court in an effort to present mitigating evidence to avoid the death penalty.[22] Under the criminal rules in Ohio, whether under oath or not, any criminal defendant has the right to "make a statement in his or her own behalf or present any information in mitigation of punishment."[23]

Rule 603 of the Federal Rules of Evidence requires that every witness declare "that he or she will testify truthfully by oath or affirmation, administered in a form calculated to awaken the witness' conscience and impress the witness' mind with the duty to do so."[24]

All state jurisdictions have adopted this or follow a similar rule. Where a witness has neither taken the oath nor otherwise affirmed to tell the truth, a failure to object immediately by the opposing party has generally been viewed as a **waiver.** In one California case, a prosecution witness refused to take the oath, even though the judge indicated that the witness had been told to swear to tell the truth. The prosecution offered questions to the witness that the witness answered. The reality was that the witness never took the oath or any substitute. The reviewing court held that the defendant has waived any complaint concerning the lack of oath and that the witness's evidence had been properly admitted.[25]

Waiver A positive act by which a known legal right is relinquished or abandoned.

---

18 *See* Crawford v. Washington, 541 U.S. 36, 2004 U.S. LEXIS 1838 (2004).

19 *In re* J.M., 2012 Ohio 1467, 2012 Ohio App. LEXIS 1283 (2012). In Ohio, all persons over the age of ten years are presumed to be competent witnesses. *See* OHIO R. EVID. 601(A).

20 CAL. EVID. CODE § 710 (2014).

21 State v. Vincent M., 43 A.3d 839, 853, 2012 Conn. Super. LEXIS 855 (2012). *See* § 8.12 for a discussion of the competency of child witnesses.

22 State v. Turner, 105 Ohio St. 3d 331, 2005 Ohio 1938, 826 N.E.2d 266, 2005 Ohio LEXIS 961 (2005).

23 OHIO CRIM. R. 32 (2013).

24 FED. R. EVID. 603.

25 People v. Prentiss, 2008 Cal. App. Unpub. LEXIS 8119 (2008).

§ 9.4 Judicial Control of Testimony

Rule 611

MODE AND ORDER OF EXAMINING WITNESSES AND PRESENTING EVIDENCE

(a) Control by the Court; Purposes. The court should exercise reasonable control over the mode and order of examining witnesses and presenting evidence so as to:
(1) make those procedures effective for determining the truth;
(2) avoid wasting time; and protect witnesses from harassment or undue embarrassment.[26]

Each party is permitted to call witnesses who give evidence favorable to that party. The attorney for each side poses questions to the sworn witness that help present that side's view and theory of the case as the usual manner of introducing evidence in a criminal trial. Whether the testimony takes the form of a narrative response to open-ended questions or individual responses to specific questions is ultimately a matter to be decided by the trial judge under the particular circumstances. Unless a party raises an objection, as a general rule, the judge does not interfere with the attorney's approach to interrogation of witnesses. Only where there is some danger that improper or incompetent evidence might be admitted that creates unfairness or could spark a reversal of an eventual verdict does a trial judge intervene in the questioning of witnesses. The judge has the authority and, in fact, the responsibility to exercise reasonable control over the mode and order of interrogating witnesses and presenting evidence. Proper judicial oversight and control facilitate the interrogation process and assist in evidence presentation that is effective for the ascertainment of the truth, for avoiding needless consumption of time, and for the protection of witnesses from undue harassment.

The trial judge enjoys wide discretion in ruling on the forms of questions and how the attorneys examine the witnesses. The judge may not only rule on objections to questions, but also may instruct a witness to answer the questions as asked. A judge may order that witnesses not argue with the attorneys or the judge and give answers that are responsive to the actual question asked. The judge has the ultimate responsibility for the orderly reception or rejection of evidence, and a reviewing court will usually uphold judicial decisions in relation to the control of testimony unless the trial judge has abused his or her discretion.

Under Federal Rule of Evidence 614 and similar state rules,[27] judges have the right to ask questions of either party's witnesses and to call witnesses on the judge's own motion. In prosecutions under the Uniform Code of Military Justice, a judge may ask questions of any witness and has wide latitude in the subject matter; however,

26 FED. R. EVID. 611.

27 State v. Dougherty, 2009 N.C. App. LEXIS 485 (2009).

but military judges, like their civilian counterparts, must not appear to be siding with either the prosecution or defense.[28] Judicial questions must generally be designed to clarify ambiguities and factual gaps in the evidence rather that assist one of the parties. Consistent with this concept, regarding a beating that resulted in a second-degree murder conviction, the trial judge asked questions of the prosecution's three main witnesses to the event.[29] The problem with this episode of judicial questioning was that the questions emphasized, highlighted, and summarized certain important parts of the prosecution's case, making the judge an active participant in the presentation of evidence. The reviewing court reversed the conviction because the judge's questions created reversible error by being fundamentally unfair to the defendant.

In federal trials, judges possess wide latitude and discretion in the role that they determine to play in a trial and, consequently, may interject during direct or cross-examination to clarify an issue, require an attorney to lay a foundation, or encourage an examining lawyer to get to a point.[30] However, wide discretion in controlling court activity does not imply unfettered freedom, and appellate courts may reverse any case under the abuse of discretion standard. For example, in an Eighth Circuit case, the defense counsel wished to inquire about a mental disability of a prosecution witness. It was known to the defense attorney that the witness had a short-term memory problem. When the witness answered that he had "diabetes" as a disability, the trial court refused to allow additional inquiry relative to mental disability. The court refused to hear any evidence of the witness's mental disability and limited the cross-examination by the defendant. On appeal, the court held that the refusal to inquire about a mental disability of the prosecution witness violated the defendant's right of confrontation necessitating a reversal of the conviction[31] under the abuse of discretion standard.

Rule 611 of the Federal Rules of Evidence and similar adoptions by the states make it clear that trial judges exercises control over the examination of witnesses in determining what evidence shall be admitted and in what order. The judge must take care to control a case in a fair and impartial manner or risk being reversed on appeal. For example, in a state case where the defendant had been accused of selling cocaine to a confidential undercover informant, the defendant's attorney wanted to cross-examine the informant concerning prior convictions and other misconduct.[32] The trial judge limited the defense attorney's cross-examination of the confidential informant so that his credibility could not be fully tested. In this case, the cross-examination that was limited by the judge resulted in a reversal by the reviewing court because the confidential informant's testimony and his credibility or lack thereof were a crucial part of both the government's and the defendant's case.

---

28 United States v. Norman, 2013 CCA LEXIS 679 (A.F. 2013).

29 State v. Thomas, 114 So.3d 684, 2013 La. App. LEXIS 1122 (2013).

30 Johnson v. General Board of Pension, 733 F.3d. 722, 733, 2013 U.S. App. LEXIS 21463 (7th Cir. 2013).

31 United States v. Love, 2003 U.S. App. LEXIS 10756 (8th Cir. 2003).

32 Anthony v. State, 108 So.3d 394, 397, 2013 Miss. LEXIS 7 (2013).

§ 9.5 Separation of Witnesses

Rule 615

EXCLUDING WITNESSES

At a party's request, the court must order witnesses excluded so that they cannot hear other witnesses' testimony. Or the court may do so on its own. But this rule does not authorize excluding:
(a) a party who is a natural person;
(b) an officer or employee of a party that is not a natural person, after being designated as the party's representative by its attorney;
(c) a person whose presence a party shows to be essential to presenting the party's claim or defense; or
(d) a person authorized by statute to be present.[33]

Statutes or court rules in all jurisdictions authorize trial judges to exclude persons from the courtroom who are on witness lists for either party and who are expected to be called to testify. In many jurisdictions, the exclusion of witnesses is mandatory upon request by a party; however, in some states, it is discretionary by the court.[34] Naturally, when the witness is called to the stand, the witness may enter the courtroom for purposes of giving testimony. Some court orders may allow witnesses who have completed their testimony to remain within the courtroom following their testimony, especially when the witnesses are not subject to recall. The procedure is variously called separation, exclusion, **sequestration,** or "putting witnesses under the rule." The Federal Rules of Evidence and state derivatives take the position that sequestration of witnesses is a matter of right; the rule states "[a]t the request of a party the court shall order witnesses excluded so that they cannot hear the testimony of other witnesses."[35] Some jurisdictions permit the judge upon his or her own motion to order sequestration of witnesses.[36] The purpose of the sequestration rule is to prevent witnesses from being influenced by hearing the testimony of other witnesses and subsequently adjusting their testimony,[37] whether consciously or

Sequestration Separating or setting apart; excluding witnesses from the courtroom except when testifying to prevent one witness from being influenced deliberately or subconsciously by hearing what another witness says.

[33] FED. R. EVID. 615.
[34] *See* State v. Sampson, 301 P.3d 276, 2013 Kan. LEXIS 450 (2013).
[35] FED. R. EVID. 615.
[36] GA. CODE ANN. § 24-6-615 (2013).
[37] Tennessee v. Coleman, 2002 Tenn. Crim. App. LEXIS 84 (2002).

inadvertently. Other purposes of Rule 615 are "to discourage and expose fabrication, inaccuracy, and collusion and to minimize the opportunity that each witness will have to tailor testimony to the testimony of other witnesses."[38]

In a Georgia case involving driving while impaired by alcohol, the defendant asked for witness sequestration during a pretrial motion *in limine* that involved whether she had rescinded her initial refusal to take a blood-alcohol test.[39] The concern was that officers who sat in the courtroom during her testimony would be able to more effectively oppose her position with their testimony. The trial court rejected her sequestration motion on the ground that mandatory sequestration did not apply until the first witness was called for trial. The reviewing court held that the ability to exclude witnesses who were expected to testify included not only the trial but pretrial proceedings as well and that the failure to exclude the officers constituted reversible error. A new trial was ordered.[40]

Pursuant to federal Rule 615 and state adaptations, several categories of persons are excluded from an order of sequestration. Natural persons who are parties to the action cannot be excluded from the courtroom as doing so would violate the Sixth Amendment right of confrontation and create Fifth or Fourteenth Amendment due process problems. In most instances, an investigative officer designated by the prosecution may remain in the courtroom to assist in the orderly presentation of evidence, even if the officer may be called to testify.[41]

In a federal prosecution in which the judge had placed the other witnesses "under the rule" by ordering them to be sequestered, the defendant complained at trial and on appeal that one of the arresting officers had been permitted to stay at the counsel table with the federal prosecutors.[42] The defendant argued that the officer was not absolutely necessary for the presentation of the government's case. In rejecting the defendant's argument, the Court of Appeals for the First Circuit held that Rule 615 permitted the government to designate the officer as the officer or an employee of a party that is not a natural person and to remain in the courtroom.

In interpreting Rule 615 of the Tennessee Rules of Evidence, the defendant requested that the police officer who was designated to assist a prosecutor testify first when the judge had given a witness sequestration order. The trial court rejected the defendant's motion, and the police officer testified as the third witness for the prosecution. In rejecting the defendant's argument for a new trial, the reviewing court noted that nothing in the record indicated that the police officer had changed his testimony after hearing the testimony of two prior police officers, and there was no proof that the defendant had been prejudiced by not having the designated police officer testify first.[43]

---

38 *See* FED. R. EVID., 615,181 A.L.R. FED. 549 (2003).

39 Smith v. State, 749 S.E.2d 395, 2013 Ga. App. LEXIS 803 (2013).

40 *Id.*

41 *Id.*

42 United States v. Charles, 456 F.3d 249, 2006 U.S. App. LEXIS 19619 (1st Cir. 2006).

43 State v. Naïve, 2013 Tenn. Crim. App. LEXIS 710 (2013).

In determining whether a witness can be excluded from a sequestration order, the judge has some discretion. In a case involving possession of an unregistered submachine gun that the defendant claimed malfunctioned and should have fired only in semi-automatic mode, the defendant wanted his firearms expert witness to hear the government's experts testify during the prosecution's case-in-chief.[44] Because an expert may render an opinion based on facts or data made known to the expert during trial, the defendant argued that the presence of his firearms expert was essential to the presentation of his case. In the exercise of discretion, the trial judge rejected that argument and sequestered the defendant's firearms expert. In upholding the trial judge's decision, the Seventh Circuit Court of Appeals held that even if an expert may base his opinion upon matters known at trial, that argument alone did not exempt the expert from the Rule 615 exclusion. Additionally, the defendant had indicated that he would have "liked to have" his expert present, but that was insufficient to indicate that the expert was central to the presentation of the defendant's case. As a general rule, the exemption of an expert witness from the sequestration order is up to the discretion of the trial judge, especially where the judge finds that the presence of the expert witness is crucial to the presentation of one of the parties.[45]

In criminal cases, witnesses who are found to have violated a sequestration order will generally be allowed to testify even if they failed to follow the rules, although courts may consider sanctions.[46] Where there has been a violation of the sequestration order, the remedy may turn upon whether it was a willful violation or an accidental or negligent violation.[47] One approach, if the witness did not deliberately attempt to evade the order, allows the opposing counsel an opportunity to vigorously cross-examine the witness concerning the details of his or her sequestration order violation, but allow the witness to testify. Following a different approach, where there has been connivance by the witness's party, it is possible to exclude the witness from giving testimony where the judge determines that the testimony would result in probable prejudice to the opposing party. However, if exclusion would prevent the defendant from mounting any defense, any order of exclusion of the witness would likely be a violation of due process or an abuse of judicial discretion. In one state prosecution for a felon in possession of a firearm, a defense witness inadvertently violated the judge's Rule 615 sequestration order and walked into the courtroom near the conclusion of a defense witness's testimony.[48] As a sanction against the defendant, the witness was prevented from testifying. The state appellate court noted that a failure to comply with a sequestration order does not necessarily or automatically prevent a

---

44 United States v. Olofson, 2009 U.S. App. LEXIS 9433 (7th Cir. 2009).

45 *See* Hernandez v. State, 4 So. 3d 642, 2009 Fla. LEXIS 149 (Fla. 2009) for a discussion of the principles prior to the adoption of the Florida version of the Federal Rules of Evidence and the changes brought by the new rules.

46 People v. Melendez, 102 P.3d 315; 2004 Colo. LEXIS 1006 (2004). *See* case in Part II.

47 *See* White v. State, 2013 Miss. LEXIS 577 (2013).

48 Clark v. State, 2013 Miss. LEXIS 553 ¶10 (2013).

witness from testifying, but striking the witness's testimony might be appropriate where the witness connived with the defendant to create prejudice to the prosecution's case. The court additionally noted that exclusion of a witness's testimony is appropriate only in cases where probable prejudice would result of the other party. In this case, the appellate court found that there was no evidence that the state would have been prejudiced by the witness's testimony and her violation of the sequestration order was clearly inadvertent and not by design. In addition, there was no indication that she altered her testimony to conform to the testimony of the witness she had overheard and, therefore, the witness should have been permitted to testify for the defendant. Since the exclusion of this witness may have affected the outcome of the trial, the reviewing court ordered a new trial.[49]

Most sequestration violations do not result in orders for new trials. Demonstrative of this principle, in a Minnesota state case that involved a gang-related murder, one of the prosecution witnesses did not abide by the sequestration order and, over the defendant's objection, was allowed to testify for the prosecution.[50] The defendant argued that this witness was crucially important to the prosecution because the witness had been present at the crime scene and identified the defendant as being present at the time of the killing. In addition, the witness who violated the sequestration order testified about the physical location of the shooters at the crime scene. By virtue of violating the sequestration order, the defendant alleged that the prosecution witness was able to tailor his testimony to closely the match that of the other crime scene witness who he had heard give testimony. As a remedy, the trial court permitted the defendant to impeach the witness by asking him questions concerning his violation of the order and his improper presence in the courtroom. When the state appellate system offered no relief, the defendant filed a petition for a writ of *habeas corpus* in a federal district court and argued that the violation of the sequestration order may have affected the outcome of the trial. In reviewing the allegations and denying the writ, the federal district court concluded that the defendant failed to demonstrate a violation of federal due process because he failed to show how the outcome would have been different had the witness not been allowed to testify.[51]

In summary, where there has been a violation of a judge's sequestration order that is not affirmatively attributable to either the prosecution or the defense, a trial court will be reluctant to exclude the testimony, especially where the exclusion may do more harm to justice than any other remedy. Under the theory of judicial discretion, reviewing courts will normally uphold the decision of a lower court in rulings dealing with exclusion of witnesses under Rule 615. If an exclusion effectively removes a defendant's ability to mount a defense, a trial court will be most reluctant to apply such a remedy and would apply a different remedy.

---

[49] *Id.* ¶25.

[50] Martin v. Symmes, 2013 U.S. Dist. LEXIS 147965 (D. Minn. 2013).

[51] *Id.*

§ 9.6 Direct Examination of Witnesses

When a witness is called to offer testimony and there is no objection to the competency of the witness, as a general rule, the witness will be allowed to give evidence in response to questions. Where there is an initial objection to the witness's competency or other challenge to giving testimony,[52] the judge will have to make an inquiry and make a determination concerning competency. After the court has determined that a witness is qualified to testify, the witness has observed any sequestration order as required, and the witness has been administered the oath or affirmation, the direct examination of the witness begins. Direct examination usually begins by having the party who called the witness ask the witness his or her name, address, and occupation. Even though everyone in the courtroom may know this information, it is necessary to complete the court records. After these preliminary background questions are completed, the general questioning of the witness begins.

If the witness cannot understand or speak English, or is not able to communicate in the usual manner for some other reason, a language or sign interpreter will help the witness communicate with the attorneys and the jury. According to Rule 604, the interpreter must meet the qualifications of an expert and must take an oath to interpret materials correctly. An interpreter may also translate documentary evidence for admission into evidence.[53] The interpreter is not permitted to give his or her individual conclusions with respect to the answers of the witness, but must give a literal interpretation of the language employed by the witness.[54]

Even after the case has progressed to this stage, there are still rules that apply during the direct examination of the witness. For example, **leading questions,** which suggest the desired answer, are usually not authorized on direct examination, although some may be permitted concerning preliminary matters and when speaking with child witnesses. Limiting procedures have evolved regarding allowing a witness to refer to records in an effort to revive memory, or to use memoranda of past recollection as a substitute for memory. These are discussed in the sections that follow.

> **Leading question** An inquiry of a witness that by its form suggests the answer that the attorney would prefer to hear.

52 Other challenges to a witness could involve one of the marital privileges, attorney–client privilege, Fifth Amendment privilege, or a challenge under the Fourth Amendment.

53 Boim v. Quranic Literacy Inst., 340 F. Supp. 2d 885, 916, 2004 U.S. Dist. LEXIS 22745 (N.D. Ill. 2004).

54 FED. R. EVID. 604.

§ 9.7 —Leading Questions

Rule 611

MODE AND ORDER OF EXAMINING WITNESSES AND PRESENTING EVIDENCE

(c) Leading Questions. Leading questions should not be used on direct examination except as necessary to develop the witness's testimony. Ordinarily, the court should allow leading questions:
(1) on cross-examination; and
(2) when a party calls a hostile witness, an adverse party, or a witness identified with an adverse party.[55]

Redirect examination An examination of a witness by the direct examiner following the cross-examination by the opposing party.

Hostile witness A person who is called to give evidence and is unfriendly and/or opposed to the position of the party whose attorney called him or her and is, or may be, really allied with the opposing party.

The use of leading questions on direct or **redirect examination** is, with certain exceptions, not proper, and the opposing counsel has the right to object to prevent the use of such questions.[56] The policy reason for this rule is to prevent a questioner from substituting his or her personal opinion or language in the place of the thoughts and testimony of a witness concerning a material fact at issue. However, trial courts are allowed wide discretion in deciding whether to allow the use of leading questions on direct examination[57] where necessary to develop a particular witness's testimony. This is especially true where the witness exhibits ignorance or is an adverse party or identified with an adverse party, or a **hostile witness**.[58]

"A 'leading question' is a question that suggests to the witness the answer that the examining party desires."[59] In order to elicit the facts, a trial lawyer may find it necessary to direct the attention of a witness to the specific matter about which his or her testimony is desired, and if the question does not suggest the answer, it is not leading. Even though the question may call for a "yes" or "no" answer, it is not impermissibly

55 FED. R. EVID. 611.
56 For reasons that will be explained in later sections, leading questions are permitted on cross-examination.
57 Jones v. State, 982 N.E.2d 417, 430, 2013 Ind. App. LEXIS 62 (2013).
58 Slater v. Ballard, 2013 W.Va. LEXIS 968 (2013).
59 CAL. EVID. CODE § 764 (2013).

leading unless it is unduly suggestive under the circumstances[60] and unless it is so worded that, by permitting the witness to answer yes or no, the witness would be testifying in the language of the interrogator rather than his or her own language.[61] A leading question suggests to the witness "how to answer or puts into his mouth words to be echoed back."[62]

The alternative question, "State whether or not. . ." or "Did you or did you not. . ." is free of this defect of form because both affirmative and negative answers are presented for the witness's equal choice. Nevertheless, such a question may become leading insofar as it rehearses lengthy details that the witness may not otherwise have mentioned and thus supplies him or her with full suggestions, which he or she would incorporate—without any effort—by the simple answer "I did" or "I did not." Such a question may or may not be improper, according to the amount of palpably suggestive detail that it embodies.[63]

As a general rule, a trial court has broad discretion in permitting leading questions on direct examination[64]; this gives the trial judge discretion to allow an attorney to develop a witness's testimony.[65] However, the fact that a prosecutor used several leading questions on direct examination that sparked objections that the judge sustained does not constitute sufficient prosecutorial misconduct sufficient to require a retrial.[66] A leading question was proper in directing a witness to identify a defendant sitting at the counsel table because a computer monitor blocked the witness's original view of the complete courtroom.[67] In one case, a prosecutor conducted the state's case-in-chief by consistently using leading questions in paraphrasing the testimony of the witnesses as he moved to the next leading question. This leading question tactic, coupled with other errors, can contribute to a reversal of a criminal conviction.[68]

Although the general rule is that leading questions may not be used on direct examination, there are well-known exceptions to this rule. These exceptions are based upon necessity, and the right to lead is given only to the extent reasonably required to meet the necessity. The best-known exceptions are as follows.

---

60 People v. Pearson, 56 Cal. 4th 393, 297 P.3 793, 2013 Cal. LEXIS 2131 (2013).

61 *See* Newsome v. State, 829 S.W.2d 260 (1992), in which the court held that the mere fact that a question may be answered by a simple yes or no will not render it impermissibly leading. The question is impermissibly leading only when it suggests the answer that is desired or when it puts words to be echoed back into the witness's mouth.

62 Ohio v. Boden, 2002 Ohio 5043, 2002 Ohio App. LEXIS 5060 (2002), quoting BLACK'S LAW DICTIONARY 888 (6th ed. 1990).

63 State v. Scott, 20 Wash. 2d 696, 149 P.2d 152 (1944).

64 State v. Burton, 2013 Wash. App. LEXIS 1513 (¶61) (2013).

65 Moore v. State, 2005 Ark. LEXIS 245 (2005).

66 State v. Serrano, 91 Conn. App. 227, 232, 880 A.2d 183, 188, 2005 Conn. App. LEXIS 390 (2005).

67 People v. Williams, 2008 Cal. App. Unpub. LEXIS 7807 (2008).

68 Chambers v. State, 924 So. 2d 975, 977, 2006 Fla. App. LEXIS 5058 (2006).

A. *Introductory Matters*

Leading questions relating to the name of the witness, his or her address, and other matters that are introductory such as age, family, and school or work are authorized. One Minnesota court approved the use of leading questions on preliminary matters and noted that "[a]n attorney is allowed some scope in examination, particularly as to preliminary matters."[69] These permissible, introductory leading questions, however, must always stop short of an inquiry into the disputed facts.

B. *Hostile Witnesses*

Anyone who has attended a trial or watched television court battles recognizes the rule that leading questions are authorized whenever the party has called a hostile witness, an adverse party, or a witness identified with an adverse party even though he or she is the witness of the party that called the witness.[70] Leading questions can be posed to the hostile witness to the extent deemed necessary where the witness, although called by the prosecution, is related to the defendant and has exhibited a change in testimony to assist the defendant's case.[71]

The rule permitting leading questions of hostile witnesses is of special significance in criminal matters in which the state must often rely on reluctant or hostile witnesses to prove its case. As a general rule and upon objection, the trial judge must rule that the witness is hostile or reluctant before leading questions may be asked, but "where the record shows that a witness has reason to be adverse to the calling party, no formal declaration of a witness's hostility is required."[72]

The rule will permit a prosecutor who must call a witness with strong ties to the defendant to use leading questions during the direct examination. An example of this rule is a Louisiana case involving the rape and molestation of a minor female child. Her pretrial allegations had been retracted by the time of trial, and she became allied with her defendant stepfather.[73] Although at trial she maintained that the defendant was innocent, the state called her as a witness and questioned her about her previous allegations against the defendant. The trial judge deemed her to be a hostile witness over the defendant's objection and permitted her examination using leading questions. Upon appeal, the defendant contended that the prosecution should not have been permitted to

---

[69] State v. Nankoo, 2009 Minn. App. Unpub. LEXIS 68 (2009).

[70] Lampkins v. Indiana, 778 N.E.2d 1248, 1250, 2002 Ind. LEXIS 892 (2002).

[71] *See* State v. Clay, 2009 Ohio 1204, 2009 Ohio App. LEXIS 1012 (2009), in which the reviewing court held that the trial court has the discretion to allow leading questions during direct exam when the witness was the defendant's good friend and has altered his testimony to be favorable to the defendant.

[72] North Carolina v. Robinson, 2002 N.C. App. LEXIS 2403 (2002).

[73] State v. Alfaro, 2013 La. App. LEXIS 2200 (2013). The defendant also complained that his Sixth Amendment right of cross-examination was violated when the judge required his attorney to use direct examination when interrogating the complaining witness because she was allied with the defense.

examine its own witness using leading questions; however, the reviewing court held that under the circumstances, the child witness was properly described as "hostile" and leading questions were permitted under the Louisiana Rules of Evidence.[74]

In determining whether a witness is reluctant, unwilling, or hostile, the judge takes into consideration many factors. In some instances, the determination is not difficult: it is apparent that the witness is hostile. In others, the judge must take into consideration the demeanor and actions of the witness. For example, in a prosecution for murder, the prosecution called a witness who had indicated in pretrial discussions with the prosecutor that the witness had observed the defendant fire a weapon numerous times during the shooting affray that resulted in multiple deaths. On the witness stand, the prosecution witness changed his story and indicated that he had put the original story together from rumors and that during the time of the crime, he actually got down on the floor and took cover and did not observe anything. The prosecutor received permission from the court to treat the witness as a hostile witness and was permitted to ask leading questions that probed the witness's contrary pretrial discussions with the police. The reviewing court upheld the trial judge's ruling that the witness had surprised the prosecutor by changing his testimony and was properly considered a hostile witness.[75]

C. Obviously Erroneous Statements

Where it appears that the witness has inadvertently answered a question incorrectly, or that he or she did not understand the question, a leading question may be used on direct examination to afford the witness an opportunity to correct the mistake.[76] For example, if a police witness inadvertently gave a date as 2003 when answering a question, the prosecutor would be allowed to say, "You mean 2013, don't you?" According to an Ohio appellate court, "the parties can use leading questions when necessary to develop a witness's testimony, and the trial court has discretion to allow such questioning."[77]

The exception to the rule that disallows leading questions also applies when the defense attorney is the one to ask questions. When the witness made erroneous statements in a federal case, the reviewing court found no problem with the lower court allowing defense counsel to ask leading questions of the defendant on cross-examination when the prosecution had been "particularly egregious" in questioning the witness, causing the witness to misunderstand the prosecutor's questions.[78]

---

74 See LA. CODE EVID. ANN. art. 611(C) (2013).

75 State v. Kimmie, 2013 Ohio App. LEXIS 4231 (2013).

76 *See* State v. White, 259 S.E.2d 281 (1979), which held that a witness may be interrogated with leading questions on direct examination when it appears that he or she has exhausted his or her memory or has trouble understanding the questions.

77 State v. Glenn, 2011 Ohio 829, 2011 Ohio App. LEXIS 737 (2011).

78 Woods v. Lecureux, 110 F.3d 1215 (6th Cir. 1997).

D. *Child Witnesses, Mentally Handicapped Witnesses, and Witnesses with Slight Command of the English Language*

If adult witnesses who rarely or never testify in court find themselves under stress or in a situation where worry and discomfort overtakes them during their testimony, it is understandable that witnesses who are children are completely out of their element, and the unfamiliar environment of the courtroom makes their testimony difficult to offer. Many witnesses may have mental challenges that do not render them incompetent as witnesses, but that result in their reluctance to testify completely and openly. Extremely shy witnesses or witnesses who may face embarrassing questions may have difficulty giving testimony when questioned under direct examination. In order to facilitate the testimony of these individuals, courts will permit leading questions on direct examination in cases involving children as witnesses or where the inquiry is directed at delicate topics such as sexual matters, where a witness may have difficulty testifying in the absence of prompting leading questions.[79]

In a Massachusetts case, a defendant had been accused of the rape of his own nine-year old female child, among other alleged errors; he complained on appeal that the trial court erred in allowing the prosecutor to examine the child using leading questions.[80] When the prosecutor used open-ended questions, the alleged victim answered them appropriately and proved able to explain the allegations in the case. The appellate court considered that the use of leading questions by the prosecutor was perfectly appropriate for the developmental level of the particular nine-year-old witness, and the court refused to reverse the defendant's two-count rape conviction. Consistent with the theory of allowing leading questions where there is a specific justification, in a Michigan case, the trial court allowed the use of leading questions in a rape case where the 21-year-old victim was mentally disabled and had the mental development of a nine-year-old with an IQ of 56. The reviewing court cautioned the use of so many leading questions on direct examination but expressed the view that the practice in a case like this was permissible. In upholding the rape convictions, the court noted that leading questions were necessary to develop her testimony because of her level of retardation.[81]

A Maine appellate court ruled that the trial court did not abuse its discretion when it permitted a child who was almost five years of age to testify through the use of leading questions.[82] The defendant, who had been charged with murdering the child witness's brother, contended that he did not get a fair trial because the prosecution used more than 40 leading questions to develop the child's testimony. The reviewing court found no unfair prejudice to the defendant and noted that it was a classic example of a situation where leading questions may be necessary.

---

79 *See,* State v. Smith, 741 S.E.2d 927, 2013 N.C. App. 441 (2013).

80 Commonwealth v. Truesdell, 83 Mass. App. Ct. 839, 2013 Mass. App. LEXIS 113 (2013).

81 People v. West, 2007 Mich. App. LEXIS 1344 (Mich. 2007). Unpublished opinion.

82 Osborne v. State, 2006 Miss. App. LEXIS 134 (2006).

§ 9.8 —Refreshing Memory—Present Memory Revived

To a greater or lesser extent, all human memory fades with the passage of time; many witnesses experience difficulty recalling all the relevant details that were once fresh in their mind. Despite preparation by attorneys, trial witnesses frequently do not remember all the facts, especially after a long period between the events and the trial. Memory may be additionally complicated by witnesses who have impaired intelligence, were under the influence of drugs at the relevant time, or have an injury or disease that has complicated their memory. It is also apparent that referring to a written statement may revive or refresh the memory of an experience so that a witness can testify from present memory. In other words, by referring to statements or other past experiences, the witness's recollection may be refreshed to the point that he or she is able to testify from present memory. If the witness has absolutely no recollection regarding the matters being contested, he or she obviously is not competent to testify concerning those matters.

However, if the witness remembers the transaction in general but not the essential details, or if he or she remembers recording the transaction, some evidence concerning the transaction is admissible. This process involves two concepts that have become known as **present memory revived** (or present memory refreshed) and **past recollection recorded** (or past memory recorded). These two concepts differ in theory; therefore, the tests for admissibility differ. In the first instance, where present memory has been refreshed, the witness is able to testify from present memory; this testimony serves as the evidence rather than anything the witness wrote or any reference he or she used to refresh his or her memory. In the second instance, where the witness originally recorded the event in writing at a time when it was fresh in his or her memory, the writing—not the oral testimony—is the evidence.

Present memory revived The act of a witness who consults his or her documents, memoranda, or books to clarify his or her recollection of the details of past events or transactions about which he or she is testifying.

Past recollection recorded
A memorandum or record concerning a matter about which a witness once had knowledge but now has insufficient recollection to enable him or her to testify fully and accurately; shown to have been made or adopted by the witness when the matter was fresh in his or her memory and to reflect that knowledge correctly; and is not excluded by the hearsay rule, even though the declarant is available as a witness.

In this section, the first of these two concepts—present memory revived or, as it is sometimes called, present memory refreshed—will be discussed. In the next section, we will address the concept of past recollection recorded.

In order to stimulate, revive, or refresh a witness's memory, a trial court allows a witness to refer to records, accounting sheets, or reports while testifying. It is of no importance what helps revive the memory because the testimony, when offered, is based solely on the witness's then present memory. Generally, doctors, engineers, accountants, and other experts as well as criminal justice officials and ordinary fact witnesses are allowed to refer to data on their reports or other writings while they are testifying as a means of refreshing their memory. As a practical matter, it is impossible for law enforcement personnel, who make daily investigations of alleged violations of law, to remember the names, dates, and what took place without referring to notes made by them at the time or immediately thereafter. However, trial courts must exercise caution to assure that the witness is testifying from present memory that has recently been refreshed. The court should be careful to ensure that the memorandum is not a written summary made specifically for use in court and that the law enforcement officer is actually testifying from a refreshed memory and not merely testifying from a written record.

When a witness has a lapse of memory while testifying, the court allows him or her to refer to some form of memorandum to refresh or revive his or her recollection of the facts. A witness is "permitted to refresh and assist his memory, by the use of a written instrument, memorandum or entry in a book, and may be compelled to do so if the writing is present in court. It is not necessary that the writing has been made by the witness himself, nor that it is an original writing, provided that, after inspecting it, he or she can speak to the facts from his own recollection."[83] After the witness's memory is revived or refreshed and he or she presently recollects the facts and swears to them, his or her testimony, and not the writing, is the evidence. When a party uses a prior statement generated by his or her own witness as the vehicle to refresh the memory of the witness, the only evidence that is actually presented is the testimony given by the witness, whose memory has been refreshed.

Under the Federal Rules of Evidence and state adaptations, Rule 612 allows the opposing party to have a piece of writing that a party is planning to use to refresh the memory of a witness produced at trial, to be able to inspect it, and to cross-examine the witness concerning the writing. If the writing contains unrelated matter, the trial judge should order that the particular unrelated portion be deleted. Any portion of the writing that the judge orders withheld over objections shall be preserved and made available to the appellate court in the event of an appeal. If a piece of writing is not produced or delivered pursuant to order under this requirement, the court shall make any order justice requires; however, in criminal cases when the prosecution elects not to comply with the judge's order, the order shall strike the witness's testimony or, if the court in its discretion determines that the interests of justice so require, declare a mistrial.[84]

Documents shown to a witness for the purpose of reviving or refreshing his or her recollection may not be read by the witness to the court under the pretext of refreshing the witness's memory or shown to the jury: the documents themselves are not evidence

---

[83] Brockenbrough v. Commonwealth, 2003 Va. App. LEXIS 243 (2003), quoting Harrison v. Middleton, 52 Va. 527, 544 (1854).

[84] FED. R. EVID. 612.

and have no independent evidentiary value. The fact that a defense attorney might seek to introduce that material on cross-examination rather than the prosecutor on direct examination is not a significant difference. The fact that a tape-recording rather than a written document is involved also does not affect the result.[85]

In one case involving the aggravated sexual abuse of a child, the trial court allowed the mother of the complaining witness to testify after having her memory refreshed by reviewing a transcript of her previous interview with law enforcement officers.[86] Before reading the transcript, the witness could not remember all the details, but after reviewing the transcript, she testified from present memory. The reviewing court rejected the defendant's argument that she was really testifying from the document because her memory had not truly been refreshed. In another use of present memory refreshed, an Ohio murder defendant complained that both the coroner and a DNA expert consulted their written reports during their direct examination by the prosecutor.[87] The coroner referred to his report to refresh his memory of the decedent's age while the DNA expert consulted his report concerning the genetic profile obtained from an examination of the defendant's right shoe. When a convicted defendant makes a contention of this nature, the court must determine whether the witness had an independent recollection of the event and was merely using the memorandum to refresh details or is using a memorandum as a testimonial crutch for something beyond the witness's recollection. In both cases, the witnesses testified from present memory that had been refreshed. According to the reviewing court, the defense attorney was not deficient in not objecting at trial and the failure to object did not prove to be ineffective assistance of counsel.

The use of hypnosis has been approved in some cases in which a witness or victim possesses no present recollection. A set of guidelines mentioned by the U.S. Supreme Court suggested that hypnosis be performed by a psychologist or psychiatrist who has received special training and who is independent of the investigation, that the hypnosis procedure occur in a neutral setting, and only the subject and the hypnotist should be present.[88] Although trial courts have discretion in determining whether hypnotically refreshed testimony is admitted, a *per se* rule excluding all hypnotically refreshed testimony infringes impermissibly on a criminal defendant's right to testify on his or her own behalf.[89] In a federal *habeas corpus* case arising out of a homicide in Tennessee, the convict contended that the use of the victim's wife's testimony should have been excluded from trial because she had undergone hypnosis; he contended that they hypnosis bolstered her confidence in identifying him as the murderer of her husband.[90] The *habeas corpus* proponent contended that the hypnotically refreshed testimony should

85 United States v. McKeever, 271 F.2d 669 (2d Cir. 1959); *see also* United States v. Booz, 451 F.2d 719 (3d Cir. 1971); People v. Parks, 485 P.2d 257 (1971).

86 State v. Cook, 2009 N.C. App. LEXIS 268 (2009).

87 State v. Neeley, 2006 Ohio 418, 2006 Ohio App. LEXIS 349 (2006).

88 *See* Rock v. Arkansas, 483 U.S. 44, 107 S. Ct. 2704, 97 L. Ed. 2d 37 (1987).

89 *Id.*

90 Thomas v. Carlton, 2013 U.S. Dist. LEXIS 41940 (E.D. Tenn. 2013).

be rendered inadmissible unless a contemporaneous recording of the hypnotic sessions had been made and provided to the defense. The only portions of the hypnotic sessions that were not recorded were the "induction" part, when she was actually and initially being placed under hypnosis. The doctor who hypnotized the victim's wife met with her six times. Four of those meetings were hypnosis sessions, two of which were audio-taped. Two other sessions that dealt with the events on the day of the murder were also taped. According to the *habeas corpus* court, there was no evidence that the victim's wife brought out previously unremembered key facts or enhanced her description of the defendant in any way that did not exist prior to her hypnosis. In addition, there was such strong overwhelming evidence of guilt, that the trial, taken as a whole, did not deprive the defendant of due process. The district court refused to issue the writ of *habeas corpus*, partly because the hypnotically enhanced evidence had appropriately been introduced at the trial.

In an effort to regulate hypnosis-related evidence, a California statute provides that such evidence for recollection can be admitted where it conforms to state law. Among other things, California limits the revived testimony to written records that were made prior to the hypnosis that document the subject's description of the event. Additionally, the law mandates that the prehypnotic memory be preserved in some written or taped form; that the witness gave consent; that the pre- and post-hypnosis interviews be recorded by video; and that the sessions be conducted by a licensed medical doctor, psychologist, or social worker trained in hypnosis.[91]

In all cases of refreshed memory, the trial judge has a duty to prevent a witness from putting into the record the contents of an otherwise inadmissible writing under the guise of refreshing recollection. Counsel should lay a foundation for the necessity of refreshing the witness's memory, show the witness the writing, remove the writing from the witness, and ask questions about the refreshed memory. Under this theory, showing the witness the writing should be all that is required to refresh memory.[92] When using a writing to refresh memory, the defendant has the right to compel the production of the document used to refresh the witness's memory. Where the document is not produced, the judge may order the refreshed memory testimony to be stricken, even where the document could not be introduced as evidence.

In supporting the concept that writing used to refresh memory must be available for inspection by the opposing counsel, the court of appeals in an Ohio felony-murder case involving arson indicated that in using writing to refresh a prosecution witness's memory, there must be proof that the memory of the witness is exhausted or nearly nonexistent and that the writing actually does refresh the recollection of the witness.[93] In addition, the court noted that the opposing party must be given a chance to inspect the writing, and if so desired, to cross-examine the witness about the writing. The reviewing court noted that the writing or an audio or video recording used to refresh

---

[91] *See* CAL. EVID. CODE § 795(a)(3) (2014).

[92] Tennessee v. Pylant, 2003 Tenn. Crim. App. LEXIS 405 (2003).

[93] State v. Jewett, 2013 Ohio 1246, 2013 Ohio LEXIS 1135 (2013).

memory does not have to have been prepared by the witness who has his or her memory refreshed. The defense had an opportunity to inspect and view the document used to refresh memory. In this case, the court permitted an emergency responder to refresh his memory with a summary document written by another public official who was at the crime scene at the same time as the emergency responder. The paramedic responder then testified in substance from his refreshed memory as to what a codefendant had orally stated at the crime scene. The court of appeals concluded that the memory of the witness had been properly refreshed and no reversible error had occurred.

§ 9.9 —Past Recollection Recorded

Rule 803

EXCEPTIONS TO THE RULE AGAINST HEARSAY—REGARDLESS OF WHETHER THE DECLARANT IS AVAILABLE AS A WITNESS

The following are not excluded by the rule against hearsay, regardless of whether the declarant is available as a witness:

(5) Recorded Recollection. A record that:

(A) is on a matter the witness once knew about but now cannot recall well enough to testify fully and accurately;

(B) was made or adopted by the witness when the matter was fresh in the witness's memory; and

(C) accurately reflects the witness's knowledge.[94]

When a witness's memory cannot be refreshed by any technique and where the evidence has been recorded by some permanent method, the video or audio recording or writing may become a substitute for the witness's memory and, where it meets all the requirements, be introduced as substantive proof of the facts that it contains. However, the proponent of the recorded memory must lay a foundation before the writing will be admitted.

To meet the accepted standards of admissibility, a Florida court noted that a memorandum or record must exist about which the witness had knowledge at one time when at the time of trial the witness possesses insufficient recollection to be able to testify fully and completely. The memorandum or record must be shown to have been made by the witness, or at the witness's direction, when it was fresh in the witness's memory, and the witness must indicate that the record reflects that knowledge correctly. A party is permitted to read into evidence the memorandum or audio or video record, but the

94 FED. R. EVID. 803(5).

memorandum or other record is not admissible as an exhibit unless it is offered by the adverse party.[95]

The trial judge must be satisfied that the writing was made from firsthand knowledge at a time when the events were fresh in the writer's mind, and the witness must verify the writing's authenticity and truthfulness. The witness must have insufficient recollection to testify fully. In a Florida burglary/home invasion robbery case, the Supreme Court of Florida reversed the convictions because the use of past recollection recorded was erroneously admitted.[96] According to the high court, one requirement for allowing past recorded recollection into evidence is that the witness must first vouch for the accuracy of the record or recorded memorandum. In this case, the complaining witness clearly was afraid of the defendants, did not want to testify, and, initially, could not identify any of the perpetrators. When shown a copy of her earlier statement, she indicated that she had never read it and refused to testify. After a brief discussion with the judge in the absence of the jury, she remembered more and testified that three men broke into her home; however, she could not remember what she said to the intruder. She admitted that the sworn prior statement was hers, but that the events were not fresh in her mind when she gave the initial statement because she was under pressure by police. At trial, she never adopted the statement as a true statement of what happened in her home. The Florida Supreme Court, in reversing the convictions, held that in order to be admissible under Florida's version of federal Rule 803(5), past recollection recorded statements must be acknowledged by the original declarant as being accurate and truthful at the time they were made. In this case, in open court, the witness never indicated that the recorded sworn statement was truthful, which meant that it was reversible error to have admitted it against the defendants.[97]

Under modern police practice, the written document may not have been created in the traditional manner; it may have originally been an entry written by an officer on a computer system. In a North Carolina case, *State v. Love*, the complaining witness's spouse told police that her husband had repeatedly threatened to beat her. This information, as well as other relevant data, was recorded by a police officer on a computer. The officer allowed the witness to review what she had told him in order to correct any typing errors that he had made. She stated at the time that the report was accurate and that she did not wish to change anything. At trial, the witness could not remember what she had told the officer but did remember making a statement to police that was read back to her. She stated that it was true when made. The appellate court approved the trial court decision allowing the officer to read to the trier of fact the statement made by the complaining witness.[98]

---

95 McNeal v. State, 109 So.3d 268, 2013 Fla. App. LEXIS 3201(2013).

96 Polite v. State, 116 So.3d 270, 271, 2013 Fla. LEXIS 1163 (2013).

97 *Id.,* at 274, 275.

98 North Carolina v. Love, 576 S.E.2d 709, 712, 713, 2003 N.C. LEXIS 114 (2003).

Federal and state courts have not developed set rules concerning precisely when the evidence must be recorded following an event.[99] Generally, the recording of a statement occurs fairly soon after the event that becomes the focus of the future court trial. An Iowa appellate court approved the use of past recollection recorded when the witness recorded the information in writing 31 days after observing the facts of the case.[100] As is typical, a trial court approved the admission of a previously recorded statement when it was reduced to writing on the day the events occurred.[101] The Supreme Court of Hawai'i approved the admission of a record qualifying as past recollection that was prepared a day after the events in question, and the high court noted with approval a prior case where the information was recorded a month after the relevant events.[102] In a federal case, the officer interviewed the defendants but did not make a written memorandum of the interview until eleven days later. The delay did not affect admissibility, according to the Court of Appeal for the Seventh Circuit.[103]

Despite arguments to the contrary, the application of past recollection recorded does not deprive the accused of the opportunity to cross-examine the witness as guaranteed by the Sixth Amendment[104] because the witness with the faulty memory must be in court and testifying about having created the writing. Cross-examination may be somewhat limited given the faulty memory of the witness, but the right to confront and cross-examine the witness will generally not pose a problem of constitutional dimensions. In a 1975 California murder case that was uncovered by the use of DNA database testing, the appellate court rejected the defendant's contention that his Sixth Amendment right to confront an adverse witness had been violated when the court allowed a recorded witness statement made in 1975 to be admitted at his 2011 murder trial. According to the court, the witness statement met all the requirements for past recollection recorded, especially the requirement that the testifying witness did not have sufficient memory to testify fully.[105] The U.S. Court of Appeals for the Seventh Circuit held that a memorandum of a telephone conversation between an Internal Revenue Service (IRS) agent and a tax defendant was properly admitted at trial.[106] The court indicated that it "would seem, as the government argues, that the report satisfies the criteria for admissibility as a recorded recollection under federal Rule 803(5)." The agent, in laying a foundation, had testified that the history sheet

---

99 *See* Isler v. United States, 2003 D.C. App. LEXIS 291 (2003), in which the appeals court permitted admission of past recollection recorded when it was recorded at the first trial of the issue some five months after the original event occurred.

100 Iowa v. Stevenson, 2001 Iowa App. LEXIS 752 (2001).

101 Faust v. State, 95 So.3d 421, 2012 Fla. App. LEXIS 13575 (2012).

102 *See*, State v. Keohokapu, 127 Haw. 91, 276 P.3d 660, 2012 Haw. LEXIS 158 (2012).

103 United States v. Green, 258 F.3d 683, 688, 2001 U.S. App. LEXIS 16770 (7th Cir. 2001).

104 United States v. Dingle, 2007 U.S. Dist. LEXIS (D. Conn. 2007). Witness had a drinking problem, but the tape of information was made on the same date as the observed crime.

105 People v. Johnson, 2013 Cal. App. LEXIS 1347 (2013).

106 United States v. Sawyer, 607 F.2d 1191 (7th Cir. 1979); *see also* United States v. Ray, 768 F.2d 991 (8th Cir. 1985).

was prepared immediately after the conversation but that he no longer recalled the details of the conversation.

§ 9.10 Cross-Examination of Witnesses

Rule 611

MODE AND ORDER OF EXAMINING WITNESSES AND PRESENTING EVIDENCE

(b) Scope of Cross-Examination. Cross-examination should not go beyond the subject matter of the direct examination and matters affecting the witness's credibility. The court may allow inquiry into additional matters as if on direct examination.[107]

Testing the credibility of adverse witnesses helps promote a search for the truth; therefore, the right to confront and question adverse witnesses has been deemed a critical component in fact-finding at trial.[108] The right to personally confront adverse witnesses is guaranteed by the Sixth Amendment to the U.S. Constitution[109]; this right has been applied to the states,[110] so state courts must also follow this portion of the Sixth Amendment. Every witness places his or her credibility at issue by taking the witness stand and offering testimony.[111] According to the Supreme Court, "The right to cross-examination, protected by the Confrontation Clause is essentially a 'functional' right designed to promote reliability in the truth-finding functions in a criminal trial."[112] The rationale for allowing comprehensive cross-examination of witnesses has been noted in both federal and state cases and is designed, among other things, to assist in discerning whether witnesses have been truthful in their testimony. Confrontation protects both parties against personal bias that might involve witness perception issues, memory, narration, and sincerity.[113] As a federal district judge noted concerning the reasons for allowing cross-examination:

> Basic to the right of cross-examination is the opportunity to impeach adverse witnesses. Impeachment is a challenge to the witness's inclination to tell the truth and her ability to do so. The cross-examiner must be allowed to examine defects

---

107 FED. R. EVID. 611(b).

108 United States v. McKeithan, 2002 U.S. App. LEXIS 23408 (3d Cir. 2002).

109 The Sixth Amendment applies to the states. South Carolina v. Mizzell, 349 S.C. 326, 563 S.E.2d 315, 2002 S.C. LEXIS 68 (2002) (quoting Pointer v. Texas, 380 U.S. 400, 402 (1965)).

110 *See* Pointer v. Texas, 380 U.S. 400 (1965).

111 Pearce v. Commonwealth, 53 Va. App. LEXIS 113, 2008 Va. App. LEXIS 545 (2008).

112 Kentucky v. Stincer, 482 U.S. 730,737, 1987 U.S. LEXIS 2727 (1987).

113 United States v. Duron-Caldera, 2013 U.S. App. LEXIS 24899 (5th Cir. 2013).

> in the witness's ability to perceive and remember events, clear up ambiguities, test the witness's ability to communicate accurately, and explore character defects or motives that might induce the witness to shade her testimony or to lie. The Sixth Amendment's Confrontation Clause guarantees the accused the right to cross-examine adverse witnesses to uncover possible biases and expose the witness's motivation for testifying.[114]

As the U.S. Supreme Court noted in a prior case, cross-examination as part of the confrontation in a lawsuit presupposes:

> Personal examination and cross-examination of the witness in which the accused has an opportunity, not only of testing the recollection and sifting the conscience of the witness, but of compelling him to stand face to face with the jury in order that they may look at him, and judge by his demeanor upon the stand and the manner in which he gives his testimony whether he is worthy of belief.[115]

The right to observe or to see one's accusers is of little value unless one can question the accuser. For that reason, the right of cross-examination is included in the Sixth Amendment right of an accused to confront adverse witnesses.[116] No one experienced in trying lawsuits would deny the critical value of cross-examination in exposing falsehood and revealing the facts. The fact that this right appears in the Sixth Amendment to the Constitution reflects the framers' belief in those liberties and safeguards whereby confrontation was a fundamental right essential to a fair trial in a criminal prosecution.

A full cross-examination of a witness on the subjects of his or her direct examination is a right and not a mere privilege of the party against whom the witness is called. The denial of this right is reversible error except in certain limited circumstances. For example, in the usual case where the defendant has no opportunity to confront his accuser, the evidence should not be admitted. In *Giles v. California*,[117] the defendant could not cross-examine his accuser ex-girlfriend involved in a dispute, because she had died by the time of the trial. The court permitted prosecutors to introduce statements that the defendant's ex-girlfriend had made to a police officer during his response to the radio dispatch call. The Supreme Court did not accept the prosecutor's contention that the defendant had forfeited the right of cross-examination, because he had murdered his ex-girlfriend accuser, and therefore, it was his fault that he could not cross-examine her. In reversing the murder conviction, the Court held that the theory of forfeiture by wrongdoing did not constitute an exception to the Sixth Amendment requirement of confrontation. However, the denial of this right is not necessarily

---

114 Vanlandingham v. McGhee, 2008 U.S. Dist. LEXIS 67934 (E.D. Mich. 2008).

115 Mattox v. United States, 156 U.S. 237, 242, 15 S. Ct. 337, 339, 39 L. Ed. 409, 411, 1895 U.S. LEXIS 2131 (1895).

116 United States v. Villarman-Oviedo, 325 F.3d 1, 2003 U.S. App. LEXIS 5694 (1st Cir. 2003).

117 554 U.S. 353, 208 U.S. LEXIS 5264 (2008). This case contains a decent overview of the doctrine of forfeiture by wrongdoing and why it is not an exception to the right of confrontation in a criminal case.

reversible error when a witness, having given his or her direct testimony, dies prior to cross-examination. In such cases, the judge often allows the direct examination to stand and gives precautionary instructions to the jury. Where the cross-examination has been curtailed following proper direct examination covering material issues because of a witness's valid claim of privilege, the trial court may strike the witness's direct testimony in an effort to preserve the Sixth Amendment right of confrontation and cross-examination.[118]

The extent of cross-examination, with respect to an appropriate subject and length of an inquiry, is within the sound discretion of the trial judge. Courts retain wide latitude to impose reasonable limits on cross-examinations based on issues of witness harassment, prejudice to either party, confusion of the issues, and marginal usefulness of the cross-examination. Judges have significant discretion regarding how long and in what direction a cross-examination may proceed. As a general rule, the courts give cross-examiners fairly wide latitude, but that latitude does not mean that attorneys conducting cross-examinations may make all the decisions about witness questioning; rather, a judge may place reasonable limits on the examination related to relevance and repetition.[119]

However, effective cross-examination in a criminal case is the primary means by which the credibility and truthfulness of witnesses can be tested. The trial court may not preclude all inquiry into a subject appropriate for cross-examination, but it may and should exercise such control over the scope of the examination as is necessary to prevent the parties from unduly burdening the record with cumulative or irrelevant matters or wasting time.[120]

The determination of whether and to what extent to cross-examine a particular witness rests with the defendant's counsel. Where the attorney for the defendant chooses, as a part of trial strategy, not to cross-examine a witness, the effect is to waive the Sixth Amendment right of cross-examination.[121]

Although proper cross-examination should not exceed the subject matter of direct exam, the scope is largely within the trial court's discretion. The general rule is that cross-examination should stay within the bounds of the direct examination and may include matters that affect the witness's credibility.[122] One exception to this rule is that cross-examination may be permitted to test the capacity of the witness to observe, remember, and recount, and the cross-examination may also test the sincerity and truthfulness of the witness. This may be done with respect to subjects not strictly relevant to the testimony given by the witness on direct examination. Inquiry may be made concerning bias, interest, or prejudice of the witness as long as it goes to testing credibility.

---

[118] Combs v. Commonwealth, 74 S.W.3d 738, 744, 2002 Ky. LEXIS 98 (2002).

[119] United States v. Green, 2008 U.S. App. LEXIS 18678 (2d Cir. 2008).

[120] FED. R. EVID. 611(b).

[121] United States v. McKeithan, 2002 U.S. App. LEXIS 23408 (3d Cir. 2002).

[122] United States v. Musk, 719 F3d 962, 2013 U.S. App. 13479 (8th Cir. 2013).

Although under the traditional rules of the limited scope of cross-examination, the prosecution usually may not cross-examine on matters not brought out on direct examination, the attorney may and should make the opposing witness the prosecution's witness at the proper time, and ask additional questions of the witness if necessary to get all the facts before the court. However, Rule 611(b) allows a trial court, in the exercise of discretion, to permit questioning on matters beyond the scope of direct examination, but the questioner must inquire as if on direct examination. When direct examination opens a particular subject, the consequent cross-examination may probe into any related area covered on direct examination and may inquire into specific facts developed by the opposing counsel on direct examination. The cross-examination is not restricted to identical details developed during the direct examination, but extends to the entire related subject matter limited by the concepts or relevance.[123]

In a case before the U.S. Court of Appeals for the Fifth Circuit, the court agreed that the trial court has the discretion to impose reasonable limitations on cross-examination of witnesses in a criminal trial.[124] The appeals court noted that, even though the Sixth Amendment guarantees a defendant the right to cross-examine government witnesses, the right can be satisfied even when a trial court limits cross-examination to basic information concerning an adverse witness's prior convictions and restricts inquiry into the facts that led up to the witness's prior convictions. In this case involving possession and distribution of methamphetamine, the defendant contended that his Sixth Amendment right to cross-examine had been improperly curtailed when the defendant wanted to introduce evidence concerning the details of a government witness's convictions for unauthorized use of a credit card, obtaining money under false pretenses, and theft in excess of $1,500. The reviewing court explained that confrontation has been satisfied when a jury has sufficient information to evaluate the bias and motives of the adverse witnesses and to draw inferences concerning the witness's reliability. Going into the underlying details of prior convictions is not necessary and can be curtailed by a trial court.

One common exception to the rule that cross-examination should be limited to subject matter brought out on direct examination is the exception that permits cross-examination on matters relating to the names and addresses of witnesses. Under virtually all circumstances, this information must be divulged. In a landmark case, *Smith v. Illinois*, the Supreme Court held that when

> the credibility of a witness is in issue, the very starting point in "exposing falsehood and bringing out the truth" through cross-examination must necessarily be to ask the witness who he is and where he lives. The witness's name and address open countless avenues of in-court examination and out-of-court investigation. To forbid this most rudimentary inquiry at the threshold is effectively to "emasculate the right of cross-examination itself."[125]

---

123 Stotler v. Florida, 834 So. 2d 940, 943, 2003 Fla. App. LEXIS 445 (2003).

124 United States v. Galaz-Perez, 524 F. App'x. 95, 97, 2013 U.S. App. LEXIS 8722 (5th Cir. 2013). *See* United States v. Spivey, 841 F.2d 799 (7th Cir. 1988) in Part II.

125 Smith v. Illinois, 390 U.S. 129, 131 (1968).

Because the witness's name and address open countless avenues of in-court examination and out-of-court investigation, the name and address of the witness generally must be given when the witness testifies at trial. Consistent with *Smith*, in an appellate ruling in California involving a special-circumstance murder, the reviewing court indicated that the prosecution and defense must reveal the names and addresses of potential witnesses because the very starting point in exposing falsehood and bringing out the truth in cross-examination necessarily involves asking the witness for information about him or herself and identifying the circumstances under which he or she lives.[126] The purpose of the inquiry regarding the witness's address and present employment is to make known to the jury the setting or context in which to judge the character, veracity, or bias of the witness, and it is necessary to show that the witness was in custody in order to make such inquiry, even if there may be some danger to the witness or his family.

As is true with many rules of evidence, this rule is not without alternatives. Where there is a threat to the life of the witness, the pretrial right of the defendant or the defendant's counsel to have the witness's true name and address is not absolute.[127] In a California death penalty case, one witness, who was crucial to the prosecution, received numerous death threats and moved to a new location following each threat. The trial court determined that the prosecution demonstrated that her health and well-being could be jeopardized if her address was ever revealed. Following a conviction and appeal, the Supreme Court of California agreed, indicating that there was good cause shown as proved by an investigator who swore that the witness's life would be in danger if her address were revealed.[128] Various judicial and legal tools exist to prevent or minimize threats to witnesses, such as housing relocation, establishing new identities, state witness protection programs, and transfer of an incarcerated witness to a different prison or a different jurisdiction. Typical of many state laws, a California statute attempts to protect witness by enhancing murder convictions to "death or imprisonment in the state prison for life without the possibility of parole"[129] when a witness has been killed by a defendant to prevent testimony or in retaliation for having served as a witness.[130] When a request has been made to keep a witness's identity private prior to trial, a judge must consider whether disclosure of a witness's identity to the opposing party would pose a significant threat or danger to the safety of a "witness, possible loss or destruction of evidence, of possible compromise of other investigations by law enforcement."[131] Revealing the identity of a testifying witness is generally required when the

---

126 Holland v. California, 2013 Cal. App. Unpub. LEXIS 4523 (2013).

127 People v. Williams, 2013 Cal. LEXIS 10184 (2013). *See, e.g.*, OHIO CRIM. R. 16, Discovery and inspection. (2014).

128 *Id.*

129 CAL. PENAL CODE § 190.2 (2014).

130 *Id.* § 190.2(a) (10).

131 People v. Hernandez, 178 Cal. App.4th 1510, 101 Cal. Rptr. 3d 414, 2009 Cal. App. LEXIS 1798 (2009).

witness was present at the scene of the crime or was otherwise shown to be a material witness to the criminal transaction.[132]

The rules relating to cross-examination for purposes of impeachment are discussed in other sections of this chapter.

§ 9.11 Redirect and Recross-Examination

"In theory, redirect examination should be limited to explanations and replies to any new matters brought up during cross-examination, while recross-examination should be further limited to new matters brought up during redirect."[133] After a witness has been cross-examined, the party calling the witness may, by redirect examination, afford the witness the opportunity to make a full explanation of his or her testimony that occurred during cross-examination, allowing him or her to rebut the discrediting effect of the witness's testimony on cross-examination and to correct any improper impressions that may have been created. On redirect examination, a witness may give the reasons for his or her actions in order to refute unfavorable inferences from matters that have been mentioned on cross-examination. He or she may state the circumstances of the inquiry covered on cross-examination, even where the facts revealed on redirect examination may be detrimental to the other party. As explained in a Florida case, under the doctrine of completeness, redirect testimony is admissible to qualify, limit, or explain testimony given on cross-examination.[134]

Considering the scope and extent of redirect examination, a trial judge enjoys wide discretion in allowing or excluding evidence during redirect examination; however, this discretion is not unlimited. The general rule in many jurisdictions holds that the scope of redirect examination is "largely within the discretion of the trial court, [and] it is limited to matters brought out during cross-examination."[135]

Redirect examination may be appropriate where the "door has been opened" by an attorney for one of the parties on cross-examination, by pursuing a line of inquiry that exceeded the scope of the direct examination. For example, in a case in which the defendant was being prosecuted for a homicide, the defense counsel during cross-examination inferred through his questioning of prosecution witnesses that some of the witnesses might have recently fabricated their trial stories.[136] It was then appropriate for the prosecution to bolster the testimony of the witnesses whose credibility had been called into question. The defense attorney opened the door to such testimony

---

132 Banks v. Dretke, 540 U.S. 668, 694, 124 S.Ct. 1256, 1274, 157 L. Ed. 2d 1166, 1192, 2004 U.S. LEXIS 1621 (2004). *See also* Roviaro v. United States, 353 U.S. 53, 77 S. Ct. 623, 1 L. Ed. 2d 639, 1957 U.S. LEXIS 1125 (1957).

133 MARYLAND EVIDENCE HANDBOOK, § 1207 at 573 (4th Ed. 2010).

134 Pacheco v. State, 698 So. 2d 393 (Fla. 1997).

135 Christmas v. State, 2009 Miss. LEXIS 144 (2009).

136 Warren v. Conway, 2008 U.S. Dist. LEXIS 106309 (E.D.N.Y. 2008).

during the cross-examination because otherwise bolstering the witnesses' credibility would have been inappropriate and beyond the scope of the cross-examination. Under the circumstances, the court, in hearing the defendant's *habeas corpus* motion, believed that the prosecutor's introduction of new matter, which otherwise would have been beyond the scope of cross-examination, was appropriate.

Although it is beyond dispute that a defendant has a constitutional right to cross-examine adverse witnesses and that the extent of cross-examination is based on the sound discretion of the trial judge, there is not any general constitutional right to conduct **recross-examination.**[137] The decision whether to allow recross-examination is typically left to the discretion of the judge and is normally limited to new matters brought out on redirect examination. If a court refused to allow recross-examination on new matters developed during redirect examination, the party is effectively denied any cross-examination covering the new matter. A court should not by rule or by following a predetermined policy prohibit all recross-examination of a witness about new matters brought out on redirect examination. A court commits error and abuses its discretion when it prohibits recross-examination under circumstances when new material has been disclosed on redirect examination.[138]

Recross-examination An examination of a witness by a cross-examiner subsequent to a redirect examination of the witness.

§ 9.12 Impeachment of Witnesses

Rule 607

WHO MAY IMPEACH A WITNESS

Any party, including the party that called the witness, may attack the witness's credibility.[139]

The value of testimony and evidence given by any witness depends upon whether that witness has credibility or is believed to have been telling the truth. It is the duty of the trier of fact, whether a judge or the jury, to determine whether to believe or disbelieve any witness, including the defendant. In cases where a defendant never testifies, the credibility of the defendant as a witness does not arise because only witnesses are ever subject to impeachment.[140] The task of giving the trier of fact the information

137 Poole v. United States, 929 A.2d 413, 2007 D.C. App. LEXIS 470 (2007).

138 Thurman v. State, 211 Md. App. 455, 470, 65 A.3d 730, 739, 2013 Md. App. LEXIS 48 (2013).

139 FED. R. EVID. 607.

140 *See* State v. Johnson, 2008 VT 135, 2008 Vt. LEXIS 200 (2008).

necessary to evaluate the worth of the testimony of each witness falls to the parties, who must offer sufficient information concerning the believability and reliability of each witness. The judge or jury must determine whether to believe any witnesses and which witnesses to believe.[141] One case referred to *McCormick on Evidence*, which suggests:

> Impeachment is a technique used to attack the truth-telling capacity of a witness. Impeachment may be accomplished by demonstrating the witness' bias, self-contradiction, poor character, defect in perceptive capacity, prior convictions or bad acts, or by contradicting the witness on specific facts in her testimony.[142]

Impeachment has also been defined as an attack on the credibility or believability of a witness and can involve explaining away a witness's testimony concerning facts at issue in the trial.[143] Every witness who takes the oath to tell the truth places his or her credibility at issue,[144] and relevant evidence that affects the credibility should generally not be excluded. There are various methods and techniques of impeaching adverse witnesses, some of which will be discussed in the following sections.

A party's decision to impeach a witness in a criminal case is subject to a discretionary limitation by the trial judge,[145] but a judge should not unfairly limit the process. In determining whether the trial judge abused his or her discretion in limiting a defendant's impeachment of the complaining witness, the pertinent issue is whether the rejection of a defendant's efforts to impeach the credibility of the trial witness withheld from the jury information necessary to make a discriminating appraisal of the witness's trustworthiness. Thus, denying impeachment of the complaining witness by refusing to allow a defendant to inquire about swastikas tattooed on the body of a prosecution witness was an abuse of discretion affecting substantial rights of the defendant. The tattooed witness may have harbored feelings against other racial or ethnic minority groups of one of which the defendant was a member. Based on a failure to allow proper impeachment, the reviewing court reversed the conviction.[146] In any case, a party may impeach any witness who has any felony convictions or other convictions involving dishonesty or false statement.[147]

A witness may not be impeached by evidence that merely contradicts his or her testimony on an issue or matter that is collateral (and is not legally relevant) to any issue in the trial.[148] For example, where a prosecution witness has stated that the defendant was wearing a blue shirt at the crime scene, impeachment by a defense witness that the

---

141 Brown v. Maryland, 368 Md. 320, 327, 793 A.2d 561, 565, 2002 Md. LEXIS 95 (2002).

142 Colorado v. Trujillo, 49 P.3d 316, 2002 Colo. LEXIS 569 (2002), citing 1 JOHN W. STRONG, MCCORMICK ON EVIDENCE § 33 (5th ed. 1999).

143 *See* United States v. Luke, 69 M.J. 309, 2011 CAAF LEXIS 78 (2011).

144 *See* United States v. Ratliff, 346 F. App'x. 473, 2009 U.S. App. LEXIS (11th Cir. 2009).

145 Connecticut v. Abernathy, 72 Conn. App. 831, 836, 837, 806 A.2d 1139, 1145, 1146, 2002 Conn. App. LEXIS 519 (2002).

146 United States v. Figueroa, 548 F.3d 222, 227, 2008 U.S. App. LEXIS 23697 (2d Cir. 2008).

147 FED. R. EVID. 609(a)(2).

148 State v. Merida, 2008 R.I. LEXIS 118, n.14 (2008).

defendant was wearing a red shirt demonstrates an example of collateral evidence that could be excluded. The rule precluding impeachment of a witness by otherwise admissible evidence directed to collateral issues serves policies such as the prevention of confusion, waste of time, and surprise.

"When a defendant chooses to testify at trial, he has opened his [or her] credibility to attack like any other witness"[149] and becomes subject to cross-examination to the same extent as any other witness and must face the possibility of impeachment as may any other witness,[150] except where there are overriding constitutional or statutory provisions that limit such impeachment.[151] For example, the defendant may have a Fifth Amendment privilege with respect to other uncharged crimes, the questions may relate to illegally seized wiretap evidence, evidence taken in violation of ***Miranda* warnings**, or may involve a confidential marital communication.

> ***Miranda* warnings** Warnings that must be given to persons who are in custody [arrest] and who police wish to interrogate.

§ 9.13 —Own Witness

Although largely eroded by statute or judicial decision, the traditional rule holds that a party vouches for the credibility of witnesses it may call to offer evidence. Therefore, a party may not impeach his or her own witness under the theory that a party would never present a witness if there were doubts about that person's credibility. However, modern evidence theories as well as Rule 607 of the Federal Rules of Evidence and similar state provisions permit any party to attack the credibility of its own witnesses without showing any proof of surprise, hostility on the part of the witness, or that the witness is allied with the opposing side.

With respect to state evidence law, some jurisdictions follow provisions identical or similar to Rule 607 and allow impeachment of one's own witness, while other states follow the traditional rule and permit limited impeachment of a party witness.[152] Consistent with the federal rule of evidence, under Florida evidence law, any party may impeach any witness when the witness's testimony involves a prior inconsistent position, when the testimony shows that the witness may be biased, and when there may be defects in the elements of competency.[153] The witness may be impeached by any party

---

149 Hall v. Vasbinder, 563 F.3d 222, 232, 2009 U.S. App. LEXIS 8265 (6th Cir. 2009).

150 Robinson v. Texas, 2000 Tex. App. LEXIS 5792 (2000), and Hampton v. Texas, 2003 Tex. App. LEXIS 3984 (2003).

151 Lopez v. Texas, 990 S.W.2d 770, 777, 1999 Tex. App. LEXIS 871 (1999).

152 For example, compare N.Y. CRIM. PROC. LAW § 60.35(1), rules of evidence; impeachment of own witness by proof of prior contradictory statement (2013) (demonstrating the limited situations [generally surprise] in which a party may impeach its own witness), with FED. R. EVID. 607 (allowing any party to impeach any witness—including its own—for any reason or no reason).

153 FLA. STAT. § 90.608 (2013).

without regard to whether the witness's testimony constitutes surprise to the calling party. As a slight limitation concerning impeaching a party's own witness, Alabama does not allow a party to call a witness known to be allied with the opposing side for the sole purpose of impeaching the witness just so that the party can introduce impeaching hearsay evidence against an opposing party.[154] In contrast, a New York statute follows the traditional rule and does not permit the party who called the witness to impeach unless the witness in a criminal case gives material evidence that is adverse to the position of the party calling the witness. In that event, the surprised "party may introduce evidence that such witness has previously made either a written statement signed by him or an oral statement under oath contradictory to such testimony."[155] The reality seems to be that any party may impeach its own witness when the witness exhibits unexpected hostility or the party is unfairly surprised by the witness's testimony, regardless of which theory of impeachment the jurisdiction follows.

One technique that appears to involve impeaching one's own witness may be considered damage control rather than impeachment. When a prosecutor plans to place a witness on the stand and the witness has been cooperative in exchange for certain leniencies, such as dropping criminal charges, or has received a favorable plea bargain from the government, the prosecutor may wish to disclose the substance of a plea deal or other favorable disposition of a criminal case between the prosecution's witness and the government. Otherwise, the defendant would impeach the witness by showing bias or favorability toward the prosecution because of the accommodation. Generally, any plea agreement with a cooperating witness will be required to be disclosed to the defendant under pretrial discovery rules. Demonstrative of this principle, Minnesota requires that the prosecution reveal this potential impeachment evidence to the defendant.[156] Sharing this evidence displays honesty on the part of the prosecution so the jury does not learn of a plea bargain for the first time when revealed by the defense counsel on cross-examination.[157] Open disclosure may benefit either party in a criminal case and is usually the most appropriate path to follow when using a witness who has prior legal problems.

In a criminal case, the government may impeach its own witness by presenting his or her prior inconsistent statements; however, there are limits on this authority.

---

154 *See* Jackson v. State 2013 Ala. Crim. App. LEXIS 15 (2013), where the defendant alleged that his father was called by the prosecution for the purpose of impeaching the father with evidence that would not have been admissible otherwise. The reviewing court disagreed, noting that the father, although somewhat hostile, did give significant substantive evidence that favored the prosecution and that the prosecution did not call the father for the primary purpose of introducing otherwise inadmissible hearsay evidence as impeachment.

155 N.Y. CRIM. PROC. LAW § 60.35(1) (2013).

156 State v. Miller, 754 N.W.2d 686, 706, 707, 2008 Minn. LEXIS 424 (2008). *See also* Colo. Crim P.16, Rule 16, Discovery and Procedure Before Trial. Among other things, this rule dictates that the prosecutor reveal any criminal convictions of any potential prosecution witnesses.

157 United States v. Valuck, 286 F.3d 221 (5th Cir. 2002).

> **Prior inconsistent statement** In evidence, prior statements made by the witness that contradict statements made on the witness stand may be introduced to impeach the witness after a foundation has been laid concerning where and when the inconsistent statement was uttered and an opportunity given to the witness to affirm or deny whether such prior statements were made.

A federal prosecutor may not pursue impeachment by introducing a **prior inconsistent statement** by calling a witness for the purpose of impeaching the witness to obtain evidence in front of the jury that would not normally be admissible.[158] Many state courts adhere to the same rule prohibiting the admission of prior inconsistent statements under the guise of impeachment for the primary purpose of placing otherwise inadmissible evidence before the jury.[159] In addition, the government may not impeach its own witness merely because the witness refused to give testimony that the government hoped he or she would give.[160]

The state or the defendant may impeach its own witness to lessen the blow of a cross-examination by the opposing counsel. For example, where the government informant's past would likely have come out on cross-examination, the government had a legitimate reason to explore the subject on direct examination,[161] and a testifying defendant may elect to lessen the blow of his prior convictions by disclosing them during direct examination.[162]

§ 9.14 —Bias or Prejudice

One of the most effective ways to impeach a witness is to show bias on the part of that witness. "Bias is a term used in the 'common law of evidence' to describe the relationship between a party and a witness that might lead the witness to slant, unconsciously or otherwise, his testimony in favor of or against a party. Bias may be induced by a witness's like, dislike, or fear of a party, or by the witness' self-interest."[163] In criminal cases, great latitude is generally permitted in the cross-examination of a witness in order to test his or her credibility and to develop facts that may tend to show bias, prejudice, or any other motive that the witness may have for giving testimony. It is

158 *See* United States v. Letner, 273 Fed. App. 491, 2008 U.S. App. LEXIS 8375 (6th Cir. 2008). *See also* King v. State, 2008 Miss. App. LEXIS 765 (2008), where the prosecution used impeachment of its own witnesses to bring otherwise inadmissible evidence into court. The conviction was reversed.

159 *See* James v. State, 124 So.3d 693, 2013 Miss. App. LEXIS 217 (2013).

160 United States v. Ince, 21 F.3d 576 (4th Cir. 1994).

161 *Id.*

162 State v. Derby, 800 N.W.2d 52, 57, 2011 Iowa Sup. LEXIS 39 (2011).

163 Coles v. United States, 808 A.2d 485, 489, 2002 D.C. App. LEXIS 556 (2002).

a well-established principle that the bias of a witness is subject to inquiry at trial and is almost always considered relevant as potentially discrediting the witness or otherwise affecting the weight of his or her testimony.[164] A court commits constitutional error if it unreasonably limits a defendant's cross-examination of a prosecution witness regarding that witness's bias, interest, prejudice, or motive for testifying.[165] However, reasonable limits may be placed on cross-examination where it may constitute harassment of the witness, confuse the issues, or waste the court's time. Examples of situations in which cross-examination was allowed to show bias or prejudice follow.

In a California case involving a defendant who was a gang member and had been convicted of murder and shooting into an occupied motor vehicle, the defendant argued on appeal that his right to due process had been violated by the trial court when it instructed the jury that it could consider evidence of gang activity and membership in evaluating witness credibility. According to the reviewing court, "it is well established that gang membership evidence may be used to evaluate witness credibility when the gang membership is relevant on such issues as the witness's fear or bias."[166] Generally, the use of gang membership evidence for witness impeachment proves appropriate because the gang membership creates a reason why a witness might be untruthful due to gang retaliation or gang fellowship.

As a general rule, a prosecution witness may be cross-examined to show bias if promises of leniency were made by the prosecution. A witness may have a bias or an interest when he has a pending criminal charge or even when there is a prospect of criminal charges, and this is true even if he has made no plea bargain with the prosecutor. In a Louisiana armed robbery case, the court prohibited the defendant from inquiring about a pending criminal charge that one of the witnesses faced. The reviewing court noted that it was clear error in limiting the cross-examination of the witness with respect to his pending criminal charge but that under the circumstances the error was categorized as harmless.[167] As a general rule, the attorney attempting to impeach a witness by demonstrating bias must have a reasonable and well-founded suspicion that the evidence of bias has a basis in fact. The bias should be reasonably inferable from the facts presented by the attorney.[168]

Examples of cases in which evidence has been allowed to show bias are many. A few are briefly summarized here. A defense witness who possessed exculpatory evidence prior to trial immediately knew of the defendant's legal difficulties, never attempted to convey the information to the police, and only offered the evidence at trial in support of the defendant could be impeached by a showing of bias in favor

---

164 Wilson v. State, 950 A.2d 634, 2008 Del. LEXIS 263 (2008).

165 People v. Gonzales-Quevedo, 203 P.3d 609, 614, 615, 2008 Colo. App. LEXIS 1832 (2008).

166 People v. Flowers, 2009 Cal. App. Unpub. LEXIS 525 (2009).

167 State v. Bradley, 995 So. 2d 1230, 1235, 2008 La. App. LEXIS 1307 (2008).

168 Joyner v. United States, 818 A.2d 166, 172, 2003 D.C. App. LEXIS 133 (2003).

of the defendant based on recent fabrication of exculpatory evidence.[169] Clear instances of possible bias occur when the witness is a spouse of a defendant or other close relative, or a fellow fraternity member, or when a witness is in business with the defendant.

In a demonstration of the use of bias to impeach, in a Georgia murder case, the defense counsel cross-examined a prosecution witness who was the girlfriend of the deceased victim in a manner that tended to show potential bias regarding testimony that she had offered on direct examination.[170] The defendant's attorney established bias on behalf of the witness by bringing out the fact that she had been dating the deceased for almost three years and that she lived with the deceased, who was the father of her two children and the father of the child with whom she was pregnant at the time. The defense counsel also elicited the fact that the deceased financially supported the prosecution witness and her children and got her to admit that she was trying to help the police with the prosecution of the case. Illuminating the witness's potential bias against the defendant by demonstrating her connection to the deceased victim demonstrated a proper method of impeaching a witness. Under such circumstances, revealing a witness's biases will allow a jury to pour properly evaluate the credibility of a witness.

In another case[171] involving witness bias or prejudice directed against a defendant, a former girlfriend accused the defendant of sexual battery, which in Florida is the same as rape. According to her story, she allowed the defendant to enter the apartment that they had one shared, whereupon he eventually forced her to have sexual relations. The case was somewhat complicated by the fact that the defendant appeared to have developed a homosexual relationship with his employer, which served to deteriorate the relationship with the girlfriend. During the trial, the court excluded evidence that the girlfriend was financially motivated to lie about being sexually battered by the defendant, and the defendant offered some evidence to impeach the complaining witness that she was seeking money to drop the charges and had discussed obtaining money from his employer for that purpose. As a general rule, matters that demonstrate bias may include prejudice, an interest in the result of the case, and any other motivation that might cause a witness to testify untruthfully. According to the reviewing court, the trial judge committed reversible error by excluding evidence that there may have been a financial motivation to fabricate the charge in the first place and an offer to drop the charges for the purpose of obtaining money from the defendant's employer. The court reversed the conviction and ordered a new trial.[172]

---

169 Massachusetts v. Cintron, 435 Mass. 509, 522, 759 N.E.2d 700, 711, 2001 Mass. LEXIS 771 (2001).

170 Romer v. State, 293 Ga. 339, 344, 745 S.E.2d 637, 642, 2013 Ga. LEXIS 600 (2013).

171 Mardis v. State, 122 So.3d 950, 952, 2013 Fla. App. LEXIS 15908 (2013).

172 *Id.*, at 954.

§ 9.15 —Character and Conduct

Rule 608

A WITNESS'S CHARACTER FOR TRUTHFULNESS OR UNTRUTHFULNESS

Reputation or Opinion Evidence. A witness's credibility may be attacked or supported by testimony about his or her reputation for having a character for truthfulness or untruthfulness, or by testimony in the form of an opinion about that character. But evidence of truthful character is admissible only after the witness's character for truthfulness has been attacked.

(b) Specific Instances of Conduct. Except for a criminal conviction under Rule 609, extrinsic evidence is not admissible to prove specific instances of a witness's conduct in order to attack or support the witness's character for truthfulness. But the court may, on cross-examination, allow them to be inquired into if they are probative of the character for truthfulness or untruthfulness of:

(1) the witness; or

(2) another witness whose character the witness being cross-examined has testified about.

By testifying on another matter, a witness does not waive any privilege against self-incrimination for testimony that relates only to the witness's character for truthfulness.[173]

Every person who testifies as a witness in a criminal trial places at issue his or her character for truthfulness or believability, including all defendants. Consistent with Federal Rule 608 and similar state derivatives, a party to a lawsuit may inquire on cross-examination about specific instances of the adverse witness's past conduct or another opposing witness for the purpose of attacking or supporting the witness's character for truthfulness as long as any specific instances of conduct that are mentioned are related to or are probative of the character of the witness for truthfulness or untruthfulness. In this context, the Supreme Court of Mississippi noted that "instances of past misconduct offered solely to attack a witness's credibility 'must be such as to reflect upon the witness's character for truthfulness. If the past conduct did not involve lying, deceit, or dishonesty in some manner, it cannot be inquired into of cross-examination.'"[174] Merely by taking the witness stand, the only character trait that the witness places at issue is that of his or her credibility unless the witness gives testimony that is supportive or destructive of a relevant character trait of the defendant.

---

173 FED. R. EVID. 608

174 Anthony v. State, 108 So.3d 394, 401, 2013 Miss. LEXIS 7 (2013).

A defendant who has not taken the witness stand generally has not placed his or her character trait for truthfulness at issue.

As a general rule, the prosecution may not introduce evidence of a defendant's general character or habit unless the defendant has placed his general character at issue by taking the stand and testifying to a relevant character trait or calling a witness to testify concerning the defendant's general reputation or his or her reputation for a particular character trait. In a case involving federal medical care fraud, a defendant attempted to call his mother as a witness to testify to his general trait for being a law-abiding citizen; however, the trial judge refused to allow her testimony. This was an error: evidence of a defendant's law-abiding character is always relevant and should have been admitted.[175] Alternatively, a defendant might wish to place his or her general reputation at issue by introducing what is loosely described as a "character" witness, who, from the witness stand, would personally offer evidence of good character. By using such a witness, he or she places his or her general character at issue and is said to have "opened the door" for the prosecution to test the credibility of the witness. The prosecution may inquire on cross-examination whether the witness had knowledge of specific facts that, if known generally, would tend to detract from the summary of the defendant's reputation offered by the character witness. Allowing the character witness's knowledge of the defendant's character to be tested by such means is fraught with great danger. Unless circumscribed by rules of fairness and grounded in good faith on the part of the prosecution, the result may be unfairly prejudicial to the defendant, thus causing a miscarriage of justice.

If the prosecution attempts to attack the observations offered by a character witness or to cast doubt on the credibility of the defendant's character witnesses, there should be a prior demonstration, out of the hearing of the jury, establishing to the trial judge's satisfaction the truth of the basis for such inquiry. Moreover, cautionary instructions should be given to the jury, preferably at the time of the inquiry and in the jury instructions at the close of the case.

In *Michelson v. United States,*[176] the U.S. Supreme Court carefully considered the manner and extent of cross-examination of character witnesses in criminal cases in general and in *Michelson* specifically. The Court stated:

> Wide discretion is accompanied by heavy responsibility on trial courts to protect the practice from any misuse. The trial judge was scrupulous to so guard it in the case before us. He took pains to ascertain, out of the presence of the jury, that the target of the question was an actual event, which would probably result in some comment among acquaintances if not injury to defendant's reputation. He satisfied himself that counsel was not merely taking a random shot at a reputation imprudently exposed or asking a groundless question to waft an unwarranted innuendo into the jury box.

When the defendant has called character witnesses and those character witnesses have been cross-examined through inquiry about whether the character witnesses had

---

175 United States v. DeLeon, 728 F.3d 500, 504, 2013 U.S. App. LEXIS 18108 (5th Cir. 2013).

176 335 U.S. 469, 69 S. Ct. 213, 93 L. Ed. 168 (1948).

knowledge of specific facts that, if generally known, would tend to detract from the character testimony, the jury must be carefully cautioned that the testimony refers solely to reputation and not to the truth of collateral facts.[177] The prosecution may explore the basis and scope of the witness's knowledge of the defendant's reputation by asking the witness whether he or she has *heard* various reports about the defendant, provided that the questions have a foundation; for example, in the sense that arrests or accusations have been rumored and discussed. In a Pennsylvania prosecution involving an attempted homicide, the defendant called a witness to the stand and inquired if the defendant's arrest on the specific charges seemed to be out of character. The witness answered in the affirmative that the defendant's character was of a law-abiding nature sufficient to cause her to be surprised by his arrest. In this instance, the defendant placed his law-abiding character trait at issue, which permitted the prosecution to ask on cross-examination if the witness had heard or was aware of the defendant's past criminal record.[178] Unless the defendant had placed his law-abiding character before the court, the prosecution could not have inquired concerning specific instances of the defendant's criminal misconduct.

The prosecution's cross-examination regarding specific instances of conduct has limitations. It is permitted only to evaluate the character witness's credibility and knowledge of a defendant and cannot be used to prove that a defendant has a propensity to commit a crime.[179] Of course, the prosecutor may not simply ask a question without any basis in fact; the government must have a good faith belief that the specific instances of misconduct occurred. The danger lurking in this impeachment process is that in constructing an intelligible question, the cross-examiner's query often gives details of specific misconduct affecting general reputation, which would not otherwise be admissible.[180]

Because a defendant's character witnesses generally convey the collective community opinion concerning the defendant's overall character, the prosecutor may inquire on cross-examination whether a defendant's character witness "has heard" of the defendant's prior arrests or convictions. Some jurisdictions allow questions concerning whether the witness "knows" of any of the defendant's misdeeds. Such cross-examination is not admitted to establish the truth that such events took place, but only to test the foundations and reliability of the witness's testimony.

Under Rule 608, evidence is not admissible to establish the defendant's bad character or his or her propensity to commit the crime charged, but the evidence might be admissible under a different legal theory. The typical rationale for permitting such questions, even when they refer to a defendant's prior arrests, is that they enable the

---

177 Gross v. United States, 394 F.2d 216 (8th Cir. 1968); United States v. Lewis, 482 F.2d 632 (D.C. Cir. 1973).

178 Commonwealth v. Cox, 2013 Pa. Dist & Cnty. Dec. LEXIS 74 (2013).

179 State v. Staggs, 2013 Tenn. Crim. App. LEXIS 499 (2013).

180 *See* North Carolina v. Calloway, 2002 N.C. App. LEXIS 2438 (2002), in which the appellate court held that cross-examination concerning prior acts of the defendant was not proper under Rule 608(b), but was admissible under North Carolina Evidence Rule 404(b), dealing with exceptions to proof of other crimes to prove conduct.

jury to better evaluate the character testimony that has been offered. If a witness has heard these damaging rumors and adheres to his or her statement that the defendant's reputation is good, some light and some doubt will have been shed upon the standards the witness has employed; alternatively, if he or she has not heard of these rumors that have some basis in fact, some doubt will have been cast upon his or her ability to speak on behalf of the collective opinion of the community concerning the defendant's relevant trait. Because of this method of impeachment, some potential witnesses for a defendant may not be called in court. In a Texas case involving an appeal because of the alleged ineffective assistance of counsel, the attorney for the defense had purposely not called some potential defense witnesses because the defendant's attorney knew the prosecutor would ask the "have you heard?" types of questions concerning specific instances of the defendant's conduct. The attorney believed that the answers would not benefit the defendant's case. The appellate court affirmed the conviction.[181]

In one case in which the prosecution's character witness was to be cross-examined, the court found no prejudicial error in refusing to permit questions concerning whether the witness had been involved in drug dealing because "drug dealing is not the type of conduct that necessarily bears on a witness's character for truthfulness."[182] Alternatively, when a defendant had testified on direct examination, the prosecutor properly used the defendant's prior convictions for writing a check on insufficient funds, defrauding an innkeeper, writing a check when he had no bank account, and tax fraud for impeachment evidence.[183]

Since every witness who testifies placed his or her reputation for being truthful at issue, "[t]he truthfulness or untruthfulness of a witness may be attacked by opinion or reputation evidence, without any proffer of evidence of a good character for truthfulness."[184] The credibility of a witness may be attacked or supported by evidence in the form of reputation or opinion, but this is subject to several limitations. Under Rule 608 (a), the evidence may refer only to character for truthfulness or untruthfulness, but evidence to support truthful character is admissible only after the truthfulness of the witness has been attacked by opinion or reputation evidence or otherwise. Where a witness denies specific instances of personal misconduct, other than for the conviction of crime, no additional inquiry may be made under Rule 608(b). Thus, specific instances of dishonesty or untruthful prior conduct committed by any witness that are mentioned for the sole purpose of attacking the witness's character or reputation for truthfulness on cross-examination may not be proven by extrinsic evidence. This means that the questioner is stuck with the answer and may not introduce any other evidence to prove the specific instance of dishonesty or untruth.[185] If the rule were otherwise, courts would

---

[181] Bean v. State, 2007 Tex. App. LEXIS 8914 (2007).

[182] United States v. Walker, 47 F. App'x. 639, 2002 U.S. App. LEXIS 19817 (4th Cir. 2002).

[183] United States v. Arhebamen, 2006 U.S. App. LEXIS 24564 (6th Cir. 2006).

[184] United States v. Sangiovanni, 2013 U.S. Dist. LEXIS 73001 (D. N. Mex. 2013).

[185] State v. Bergerud, 2013 Ida. App. LEXIS 78 (2013).

be getting into matters that detract from the central issue in a criminal case by having a mini-trial over relatively unimportant issues.

In applying the rules relating to the admissibility of evidence concerning character and conduct of a witness, including a defendant, the element of time is normally given consideration when the conviction occurred more than 10 years before. In a state prosecution for murder, the trial court permitted the impeachment of a defendant who took the witness stand by allowing the prosecution to use prior convictions that were more than 10 years old.[186] The trial court judge indicated that he had evaluated the facts and circumstances and determined that the probative value outweighed the prejudicial effect of using convictions that were older than 10 years, but made no findings considering the specific facts and circumstances that led to his decision. Although the reviewing court held that it was an error to have admitted as impeachment evidence proof of crimes that occurred more than 10 years ago, the court found the error to be harmless under the circumstances of the case. In a case in which a police officer lied to the defendant during interrogation, the trial court properly refused to allow cross-examination concerning the officer's lies. Generally, a witness's credibility may be attacked by specific instances of conduct if they are probative of the witness's character for truthfulness or untruthfulness. In this case, the trial court held that because the use of false statements by police during questioning is a routine practice, the evidence was not admissible to impeach the police officer's testimony at trial. According to the court, it had not found any authority suggesting that use of deception as a police interrogation tactic implicated an officer's credibility under oath.[187]

If evidence of prior crimes is admissible to impeach, the defendant cannot prevent the prosecution from introducing evidence to that effect by offering to stipulate to the existence of the prior felony convictions. In another case involving a felon in possession of a firearm, the defendant stipulated that he had prior felony convictions.[188] Once the defendant became a witness in his own defense, he placed his character trait for honesty at issue, and the district court did not abuse its discretion in allowing the prosecution to cross-examine the defendant concerning his prior felony convictions.

§ 9.16 —Conviction of Crime

Rule 609

IMPEACHMENT BY EVIDENCE OF A CRIMINAL CONVICTION

(a) In General. The following rules apply to attacking a witness's character for truthfulness by evidence of a criminal conviction:

---

186 State v. Brown, 741 S.E.2d 925, 2013 N.C. App. LEXIS 452 (2013).

187 Minnesota v. Martinez, 657 N.W.2d 600, 602, 603, 2003 Minn. App. LEXIS 252 (2003).

188 United States v. Kilgore, 151 F. App'x. 799, 802, 2005 U.S. App. LEXIS 20690 (11th Cir. 2005).

(1) for a crime that, in the convicting jurisdiction, was punishable by death or by imprisonment for more than one year, the evidence:

(A) must be admitted, subject to Rule 403, in a civil case or in a criminal case in which the witness is not a defendant; and

(B) must be admitted in a criminal case in which the witness is a defendant, if the probative value of the evidence outweighs its prejudicial effect to that defendant; and

(2) for any crime regardless of the punishment, the evidence must be admitted if the court can readily determine that establishing the elements of the crime required proving—or the witness's admitting—a dishonest act or false statement.

(b) Limit on Using the Evidence After 10 Years. This subdivision (b) applies if more than 10 years have passed since the witness's conviction or release from confinement for it, whichever is later. Evidence of the conviction is admissible only if:

(1) its probative value, supported by specific facts and circumstances, substantially outweighs its prejudicial effect; and

(2) the proponent gives an adverse party reasonable written notice of the intent to use it so that the party has a fair opportunity to contest its use.

(c) Effect of a Pardon, Annulment, or Certificate of Rehabilitation. Evidence of a conviction is not admissible if:

(1) the conviction has been the subject of a pardon, annulment, certificate of rehabilitation, or other equivalent procedure based on a finding that the person has been rehabilitated, and the person has not been convicted of a later crime punishable by death or by imprisonment for more than one year; or the conviction has been the subject of a pardon, annulment, or other equivalent procedure based on a finding of innocence.

(2) the conviction has been the subject of a pardon, annulment, or other equivalent procedure based on a finding of innocence.

(d) Juvenile Adjudications. Evidence of a juvenile adjudication is admissible under this rule only if:

(1) it is offered in a criminal case;

(2) the adjudication was of a witness other than the defendant;

(3) an adult's conviction for that offense would be admissible to attack the adult's credibility; and

(4) admitting the evidence is necessary to fairly determine guilt or innocence.

(e) Pendency of an Appeal. A conviction that satisfies this rule is admissible even if an appeal is pending. Evidence of the pendency is also admissible.[189]

---

189 FED. R. EVID. 609.

As a general rule, because a case should be decided on relevant evidence that either proves or fails to prove the specific crime or crimes charged, it would be unfair to introduce evidence to show that a defendant in a criminal case had previously committed other crimes. The concern when a judge admits evidence of a prior crime or crimes is that a jury might, in a close case, convict the defendant because the defendant had committed prior crimes or because the defendant might just be a bad person. A jury might determine that if the defendant had committed one prior crime, then he or she might be guilty of others, including the crime for which the defendant was presently being prosecuted. The concern with prior crime evidence is that juries might use a defendant's prior convictions as evidence of the defendant's general propensity or likelihood to commit crime.[190] When any witness, including any defendant, takes the stand and testifies, he or she puts her credibility directly at issue.[191] The ordinary witness may usually be asked, for purposes of impeachment, whether he or she has been convicted of a felony, infamous crime, or crime involving moral turpitude. A defendant witness places his credibility at issue by testifying. When a defendant testifies in his or her own defense, he or she is said to have placed his or her credibility at issue, and the prosecution is entitled to introduce a certified copy of a felony conviction[192] or a conviction involving dishonesty or ask the defendant questions concerning the fact of prior convictions that are felonies or involve any dishonesty. Therefore, such evidence of prior difficulties with the law may be admitted for whatever effect the prior offenses might have on his credibility.

A defendant may be said to have "opened the door" to impeachment with prior convictions by becoming a defense witness. In an Iowa case involving domestic violence allegedly committed by the defendant against his then girlfriend, the defendant testified in his own defense.[193] During the defense case presentation, his attorney ineffectively attempted to elicit evidence of the defendant's nonviolent character from some of his witnesses. Because the defendant placed his credibility at issue by taking the witness stand, the government was properly allowed to impeach his testimony using his two prior felony convictions, one for interference with official acts with a weapon, and the other involving a prior assault against another former girlfriend. Had he not taken the witness stand, his credibility would never have been placed at issue and it is unlikely that the prior felony convictions would have been admissible. The reason for exposing a criminal record is to call into question the reliability and credibility of the witness.

Under Rule 609, criminal offenses that are remote in time to the current trial may be excluded where they are older than 10 years or are considered too remote in time, even if within the 10-year period. In determining whether a prior conviction's probative

---

190 North Dakota v. Stewart, 2002 N.D. 102, 646 N.W.2d 712, 715, 2002 N.D. LEXIS 140 (2002).

191 United States v. Murphy, 172 F. App'x. 461, 462, 2006 U.S. App. LEXIS 7827 (3d Cir. 2006). *See also* Thomas v. State, 2009 Miss. App. LEXIS 192 (2009).

192 People v. Clinton, 2013 Ill. App. Unpub. Unpub. LEXIS 2356 (2013).

193 State v. Jones, 2013 Iowa App. LEXIS 1263 (2013).

value outweighs its prejudicial effects, a Texas court listed five factors that it used to evaluate whether to allow the admission of prior crimes as impeachment evidence.[194] The court indicated that it would consider the impeachment value of the prior crime, the temporal proximity of the past crime relative to the charged offense and the witness's subsequent criminal history, the similarity of the prior crime to the currently charged offense, the relative importance of the witness's testimony, and the importance of the credibility of the witness. The court indicated that these factors were not exclusive considerations because several factors relevant to assessing probative value often run in different directions. Texas courts consider crimes involving deception or dishonesty to possess a greater impeachment value than a crime or crimes of violence.[195]

As a general rule, a witness may not be impeached by inquiry into prior misdemeanors unless those misdemeanors involve dishonesty that can be equated as involving moral turpitude. In California, case law indicates that a misdemeanor conviction is admissible to impeach a witness, including a defendant, when the misdemeanor involved moral turpitude,[196] but that misconduct resulting in a misdemeanor conviction is less probative of dishonesty than a felony conviction. Where a prior misdemeanor involved a crime of moral turpitude such as theft, such a crime involves dishonesty and may be used for impeachment purposes. According to an Illinois appellate court, in a case in which the credibility of the defendant was crucial to guilt or innocence, "theft is a crime that speaks directly to a person's truthfulness," and the jury should have been allowed to fully assess his credibility.[197]

A witness generally may not be impeached by the introduction of evidence regarding a pending charge that has not been tried, but not all jurisdictions follow this rule. In one case, where the defense wanted to cross-examine a prosecution witness who was facing charges of impersonating a police officer, the trial judge would not permit the line of questioning because there was no conviction, only a pending charge.[198] However, in Tennessee and in many jurisdictions, the credibility of a prosecution witness who has pending charges or is under criminal investigation may be impeached by introducing information concerning pending legal problems that have yet to be resolved.[199] When there is proof that a witness is or may be facing criminal charges and is cooperating with the prosecution, the witness may have something to gain by testifying for the prosecution and is a factor that a jury should be permitted to evaluate.

In federal cases and state jurisdictions that have adopted a version of the federal evidence rules, the trial judge initially determines whether the probative value of admitting evidence outweighs its prejudicial effect (Rule 609(a)(1)). The trial judge's decision will not be disturbed unless there is a clear abuse of discretion.

---

[194] Leyba v. State, 2013 Tex. App. LEXIS 10067 (2013).
[195] Mixon v. State, 2007 Tex. App. LEXIS 4310 (2007).
[196] People v. Gant. 2013 Cal. App. Unpub. LEXIS 9045 (December 16, 2013).
[197] Illinois v. Diehl, 335 Ill. App. 3d 693, 704, 783 N.E.2d 640, 650, 2002 Ill. App. LEXIS 1060 (2003).
[198] *See* State v. Myricks, 2009 Ohio 5304, 2009 Ohio App. LEXIS 4485 (2009).
[199] State v. Morris, 2013 Tenn. Crim. App. LEXIS 783 (2013).

Whether in state or federal courts, trial judges have broad discretion to determine the admissibility of evidence relating to prior convictions. Rule 609 must be read by the trial court in conjunction with Rule 403, which requires that the trial judge balance the probative value of the impeachment evidence against the risk of unfair prejudice. In a case involving Rule 609, a trial court refused to allow a defendant to attempt to impeach a government witness concerning the witness's past criminal activity, and the appellate court upheld the decision.[200] The government's witness had a misdemeanor conviction that was more than 10 years old and did not involve dishonesty. The felony conviction similarly occurred more than a decade prior to the trial, and the district court determined that the probative value of admitting the witness's prior felony was exceeded by the danger of unfair prejudice to the government. Courts are especially hesitant to admit evidence relating to convictions of witnesses that occurred long before the crime that is the subject of a current trial. State courts have followed much of this same theory and philosophy when interpreting their respective versions of Rule 609.

Following are a few examples of cases in which criminal convictions were used for the purpose of attacking a witness's credibility. In a prosecution for possession of more than five grams of cocaine, the trial court did not abuse its discretion in admitting the defendant's prior conviction for conspiracy to import heroin and aiding and abetting the distribution of heroin.[201] There was no abuse of discretion in admitting evidence of two prior convictions for possession of unauthorized weapons when the defendant was on trial for two counts of distributing crack cocaine.[202] According to the Supreme Court of North Dakota, evidence of the defendant witness's prior convictions for the felony of unauthorized use of a motor vehicle, unlawful possession of a firearm by a felon, and reckless endangerment were considered probative of the defendant's character for truthfulness and admissible for impeachment purposes in a prosecution for driving under the influence and aggravated reckless driving involving a death.[203] A Minnesota court properly admitted evidence of a defendant's prior robbery conviction that occurred less than six years before as impeachment evidence in a trial for attempted second-degree murder. The appellate court noted that the evidence of the robbery conviction helped the jury obtain a better view of the whole person in assessing his truthfulness.[204]

Although subject to many exceptions, Rule 609 generally prohibits the use of evidence of a conviction when the person has been pardoned or the conviction is the subject of annulment or certificate of rehabilitation. In *United States v. McMurrey*, convictions for which the witness had been pardoned to restore rights of citizenship were inadmissible as impeachment evidence even though the pardons were not based

---

200 United States v. Loma, 2006 U.S. App. LEXIS 24599 (9th Cir. 2006).

201 United States v. Conway, 53 F. App'x. 872, 876, 877, 2002 U.S. App. LEXIS 26341 (10th Cir. 2002).

202 United States v. Broadwater, 2003 U.S. App. LEXIS 10873 (7th Cir. 2003).

203 North Dakota v. Stewart, 2002 N.D. 102, 646 N.W.2d 712, 715, 716, 2002 N.D. LEXIS 140 (2002).

204 State v. Flores, 2006 Minn. App. Unpub. LEXIS 390 (2006).

on rehabilitation or innocence.[205] However, according to the comments associated with Rule 609, a pardon granted solely for the purpose of restoring the defendant's civil rights lost by virtue of a felony conviction has no relevance where a party desires to inquire into the character of the pardoned individual. If the pardon or other proceeding includes a finding of rehabilitation, the result under federal Rule 609, and many state jurisdictions, is to render the conviction inadmissible for impeachment purposes.[206] An alternative policy could allow each party to introduce proof of the conviction and rehabilitation, but this procedure presents challenges with respect to reasons of policy, economy of time, and difficulties of evaluating the pardon and whether rehabilitation has occurred. Due process requires that federal courts give full credit to state pardons.

Absent exceptional circumstances, the cross-examiner, in making inquiries about a witness's prior convictions, generally may not inquire into collateral details and circumstances of the earlier conviction or convictions. Permitted areas of inquiry include the general nature of the conviction, its date, and its punishment, but little detail beyond this line of questioning is proper.[207] However, when a defendant/witness has mentioned details of prior convictions on direct exam or has attempted to rehabilitate himself or herself by explaining and offering details of the prior convictions, the door has been opened to allow the prosecutor to inquire concerning the details of the prior conviction[s].[208]

§ 9.17 —Prior Inconsistent Statements

Rule 613

WITNESS'S PRIOR STATEMENT

(a) Showing or Disclosing the Statement During Examination. When examining a witness about the witness's prior statement, a party need not show it or disclose its contents to the witness. But the party must, on request, show it or disclose its contents to an adverse party's attorney.

(b) Extrinsic Evidence of a Prior Inconsistent Statement. Extrinsic evidence of a witness's prior inconsistent statement is admissible only if the witness is given an opportunity to explain or deny the statement and an adverse party is given an opportunity to examine the witness about it, or if justice so requires. This subdivision (b) does not apply to an opposing party's statement under Rule 801 (d)(2).[209]

---

205 United States v. McMurrey, 827 F. Supp. 424 (S.D. Tex. 1993), *aff'd*, 48 F.3d 149 (1993). *See also* State v. Baker, 956 S.W.2d 8 (Tenn. 1997).

206 FED. R. EVID. 609.

207 United States v. Osauzuwa, 564 F.3d 1169, 1175, 2009 U.S. App. LEXIS 10918 (9th Cir. 2009).

208 Love v. State, 302 Ga. App. 106, 109, 690 S.E.2d 246, 249, 2010 Ga. App. LEXIS 62 (2010).

209 FED. R. EVID. 613.

When a witness, including a defendant, has taken the stand and made a statement or adopted the statement at trial that is inconsistent with an earlier statement, or adoption, or act, both the present position and the prior position cannot both be correct or true. When the prior statement adoption or act calls into question the witness's present position and the inconsistency has not been explained, the effect is to impeach the witness's testimony. Generally, a witness who speaks or acts inconsistently is thought to have reduced credibility when compared to a person who speaks and acts in a consistent manner. The theory of Rule 613 and similar state adaptations indicates that the testimony of a witness may be impeached by showing prior or declarations, statements, or testimony from another case made by that witness (and never another person) that contradict or are inconsistent with the witness's testimony offered at trial. Prior inconsistent statements include written statements actually signed by the maker, statements adopted or approved by a witness or a party-witness, mechanical recordings of statements or their exact transcription, and accurate statements recited in a continuous narrative form.[210] Under the Federal Rules, the statement need not be shown or played for or to the witness, but on request shall be shown or disclosed to opposing counsel. The witness should be informed of the statements and the conditions, time, place, and circumstances under which they were made. In a rape prosecution, the trial court admitted into evidence a prior recorded conversation between the defendant's ex-wife and the complaining victim. The ex-wife testified that the victim had apologized for making false accusations against the defendant concerning the alleged rape, and the ex-wife denied making a phone call to the victim supporting her ex-husband's prosecution for rape. Outside of the jury's presence, the prosecution played the tape of the phone conversation. Upon retaking the witness stand, the ex-wife stated that she was lying on the tape-recording of the phone call. The reviewing court upheld the trial court's allowing the jury to hear the tape of the prior conversation to determine whether the ex-wife's testimony at trial was truthful and did not allow the jury to consider the out-of-court phone conversation as substantive evidence.[211]

In a prosecution for Medicare fraud, a defense witness testified that he had never discussed or met with anyone from Medicare or had any discussion with any Medicare official concerning the relevant transaction. In addition, the defense witness indicated that he had not told anyone that he had met with a Medicare official. In using a prior inconsistent statement, the prosecution elicited from a different witness the fact that the defense witness admitted to meeting with a Medicare official and speaking with him. Obviously, the first witness cannot have both met and never met the same Medicare official. And the defense witness could not have both spoken with a Medicare official and also not spoken with the same official at the same time. The inconsistency has the effect of calling into doubt the testimony of the first witness. In approving of the use of this impeachment technique, the reviewing court noted that the evidence offered by the

---

210 Ohio v. Linder, 2002 Ohio 5077, 2002 Ohio App. LEXIS 5113 (2002).

211 Winkle v. State, 374 Ark. 128, 134, 2008 Ark. LEXIS 433 (2008).

second witness was not offered for the truth of the matter asserted, but to impeach the testimony of the first witness.[212]

Previous contradictory statements introduced for the purpose of impeachment generally are not admissible as substantive evidence due to their nature as hearsay evidence. Many jurisdictions hold that it is incumbent on the defendant to request a cautionary statement from the judge that the prior inconsistent statement can only be used to evaluate the credibility of that particular witness.[213] However, contradictory statements may become substantive evidence if the witness recants the testimony that he or she gave at the grand jury or at trial and admits that his or her prior statements contained the truth. Such an admission would make the prior statements a part of the witness's present testimony[214] and the witness would be available for cross-examination. In an exception to the general rule holding that prior inconsistent statements are to be considered for impeachment use only, Colorado law permits the use of a prior inconsistent statement as substantive proof if "[t]he witness, while testifying, was given an opportunity to explain or deny the statement or the witness is still available to give further testimony in the trial"[215] and the previous inconsistent statement purports to contain information and relates to a matter within the witness's personal knowledge.

§ 9.18 —Defects of Recollection or Perception

An effective method of impeaching a witness involves demonstrating to the judge or jury that a witness had a defect in perception, recording of facts, recollection, narration, or perception concerning matters about which he or she testified. The judge or jury possesses the duty to determine the impeachment value of the defects of in perception, memory, and sincerity of trial witnesses.[216] For example, a witness whose hearing or eyesight is impaired may be impeached by calling the impairment to the attention of the jury or judge or by demonstrating it in court. The opposing party may attempt to impeach the witness's testimony by showing that he or she has a poor memory and was unable to recall events of similar importance. Witnesses may have reduced perception and recollection where recreational pharmaceuticals have been used by the witnesses: one court noted that it was a settled area of law that a party may attack a witness's testimony by showing that his or her capacity to observe, remember, or narrate has been impaired by drug use.[217] The use of contradiction to impeach, while different from prior inconsistent statements as an impeachment tool, involves evidence that shows that all or part of a different prior witness's testimony is

---

212 United States v. St. Junius, 2013 U.S. App. LEXIS 25155 (5th Cir. 2013).

213 Polk v. Indiana, 783 N.E.2d 1253, 1267, 1258, 2003 Ind. App. LEXIS 313 (2003).

214 Commonwealth v. Ragland, 72 Mass. App. Ct. 815, 2009 Mass. App. LEXIS 1039 (2008).

215 COLO. REV. STAT. 16-10-201 (2013).

216 Jackson v State, 119 So.3d 1156 (¶13), 2013 Miss. App. LEXIS 489 (2013).

217 Montoya v. Village of Cuba, 2013 U.S. Dist. LEXIS 173610 (D. N. Mex. 2013).

incorrect.[218] For example, if a defendant had testified on cross-examination and portrayed himself as an individual who had never possessed firearms and avoided being around guns, the prosecution could properly impeach the defendant with his prior arrests for being a felon in possession of a firearm under the theory of impeachment by contradiction.[219] As in other matters involving admitting challenged evidence, the trial judge has discretion in determining whether to admit, and the trier of fact has the duty to determine the weight to be given to defects in memory or perception as well as to determine the impeachment value of inconsistencies or contradictions.[220]

A witness's consumption of alcohol or other drugs at the time hat he or she perceived events or immediately prior to testifying can be introduced as impeachment evidence, if the consumption impaired the witness's memory and perception of the event.[221]

In attempting to impeach a witness, the party is permitted to test the credibility of that witness by delving into the testimony of the witness to test his or her ability to perceive and to test the ability to remember the facts. However, judges have wide latitude in determining limits in the attempt to impeach a witness to prevent harassment of the witness, prejudice to either party, or confusion of the issues.[222]

§ 9.19 —Use of Confession for Impeachment Purposes

A free and voluntary confession, properly offered, that has been recanted prior to or at trial allows the prosecution to use the earlier confession as an impeachment tool and as substantive evidence as an exception to the hearsay rule.[223] However, if a defendant's statement or statements were made involuntarily, they should be completely suppressed and may not be used as substantive evidence or for any other purpose.[224]

Since the *Miranda v. Arizona* decision in 1966, a body of case law has developed concerning the use of improperly taken confessions when offered solely for impeachment purposes. In the *Miranda* case, the U.S. Supreme Court held that when an individual is taken into custody and is not free to leave under circumstances in which police wish to question him or her, the police must inform the arrestee that he or she has the right to consult with an attorney and does not have to speak with police about the reason

---

218 Barber v. City of Chicago, 725 F.3d 702, 709 (7th Cir. 2013).

219 United States v. Weicks, 362 F. App'x. 844, 849-50, 2010 U.S. App. LEXIS 1487 (9th Cir. 2010).

220 Singleton v State, 2009 Miss. App. LEXIS 169 (2009).

221 Maynard v. Government of the Virgin Islands, n.17, 2009 U.S. Dist. LEXIS 35132 (D.V.I. 2009).

222 Newton v. Kemna, 354 F.3d 776, 781, 2004 U.S. App. LEXIS 232 (8th Cir. 2004).

223 A voluntary confession is generally admissible against a defendant, whether as an exception to the hearsay rule or as nonhearsay by definition. Under Federal Rule 801, a voluntary confession or a prior statement by definition is not considered hearsay and will be admitted unless some other legal doctrine calls for exclusion under the circumstances.

224 People v. Zadran, 2013 CO 69 (¶13), 2013 Colo. LEXIS 928 (2013).

for the arrest.[225] In that decision, the Court indicated that unless such warnings were properly given at the time when custody and the desire to interrogate coexisted, no evidence received from the subject would be admissible. Under *Edwards v. Arizona*, the moment an arrestee asks to consult with an attorney, all interrogation must immediately stop, and information taken thereafter is not admissible as substantive evidence.[226] Unless a proper *Miranda* waiver has been demonstrated by the prosecution at trial, direct evidence and most derivative evidence obtained as a result of interrogation cannot be used against the defendant. When a defendant understands the warning and remains silent, generally, the fact of silence cannot be used against him or her at trial because the defendant was merely following the *Miranda* principles by remaining silent.[227] Were the decision otherwise, the defendant would be informed that he or she has the right of silence; however, the exercise of that right would prove costly if the prosecutor could use the fact of silence as a tool against the defendant by asking a testifying police officer about the defendant's silence or mentioning it during a closing argument.

In an early post-*Miranda* prosecution, a defendant in custody made an unwarned confession in violation of *Miranda* and realized the prosecution could not use the confession to prove guilt. Believing that no use could be made of his unwarned statements, the defendant concluded that he could tell a different story at trial, secure in the knowledge that his prior inconsistent confession would not be admitted. The prosecution used portions of his earlier unwarned confession to impeach him. However, in upholding the conviction, in *Harris v. United States*, the U.S. Supreme Court determined that a voluntary extrajudicial confession obtained without properly administering the *Miranda* warnings could be used for impeachment purposes.[228] The Court reasoned that a defendant, having voluntarily taken the stand, has an obligation to speak truthfully and accurately, and the prosecution properly introduced the non-*Mirandized* confession as impeachment evidence. If the trial court had excluded the unwarned statement, it would have given the defendant a "license to commit perjury" when he told one story to police and a separate, untruthful story to the court. In a recent application of the principle that unwarned confessions or admissions can be used to impeach, in a District of Columbia prosecution of aggravated assault, the defendant's rights under *Miranda* were not honored when he requested an attorney and police continued to badger him to talk.[229] His subsequent confession was taken in violation of *Miranda* and the *Edwards* rule. The reviewing court reversed his conviction and indicated that the confession could not

---

225 Miranda v. Arizona, 384 U.S. 436, 86 S. Ct. 1602, 16 L. Ed. 2d 694 (1966). The Supreme Court reaffirmed the *Miranda* case in 2000 when it ruled that the warnings were required by the Constitution and that Congress could not overturn the *Miranda* decision by changing federal law. *See* Dickerson v. United States, 530 U.S. 428, 2000 U.S. LEXIS 4305 (2000).

226 451 U.S. 477, 101 S. Ct. 1880, 68 L. Ed.2d 378, 1981 U.S. LEXIS 96 (1981).

227 Doyle v. Ohio, 426 U.S. 610, 96 S. Ct. 2240, 49 L. Ed. 2d 91 (1976).

228 Harris v. New York, 401 U.S. 222, 91 S. Ct. 643, 28 L. Ed. 2d 1 (1971), *see also* Oregon v. Hass, 420 U.S. 714, 915 S. Ct. 1215, 43 L. Ed. 2d 570 (1975).

229 Dorsey v. United States, 60 A.3d 1171, 2013 D.C. App. LEXIS 3 (2103).

be used as substantive evidence; however, the confession could be used to impeach the defendant if he took the stand in his own defense in the subsequent trial because the confession had not been coerced, but rather obtained in violation of *Miranda* and *Edwards*.

If a confession has been taken in violation of *Miranda* or secured from the arrestee by less than free and voluntary means, it may not be used for impeachment purposes or as substantive proof. In *Mincey v. Arizona* (1978), the U.S. Supreme Court refused to extend the *Harris* reasoning to a confession obtained in violation of the **free and voluntary rule**.[230] If voluntary confessions have been obtained without administering the *Miranda* warnings or in violation of the right to counsel under the Sixth Amendment, they may be used only for impeachment purposes when the defendant takes the witness stand and directly contradicts the known confession. In *Kansas v. Ventris*, the prosecution placed an informant into the defendant's cell and obtained the defendant's admission/confession to a burglary and robbery.[231] The Supreme Court upheld the use of the cell block confession for use as impeachment evidence to counter the defendant's inconsistent trial testimony. Under these circumstances, the evidence will be received not as substantive evidence of guilt, but solely as impeachment evidence. If the statement has been obtained involuntarily, it would not be inadmissible for any purpose due to doubts concerning its reliability.

Free and voluntary rule The confession of a person accused of a crime is admissible against the accused only if freely and voluntarily made, without fear, duress, or compulsion in its inducement and with full knowledge of the nature and consequences of the confession.

While the *Miranda* case excludes unwarned custodial answers to questions, police may not make an end run around the warning requirement. For example, in one case, an officer interrogated the suspect without giving any warnings while the subject was in custody. After she confessed to murder, the officer took a break for a short time and returned to give the *Miranda* warnings for the first time. The officer managed to get the subject to confess to murder for a second time. This process violated *Miranda,* and the confession, although it was voluntary by traditional standards, violated the requirement mandated by the original *Miranda* case.[232]

According to the Supreme Court in *Doyle v. Ohio*,[233] a defendant's post-*Miranda* silence cannot be used to convict, impeach, or otherwise call into question his or her assertion of a constitutional right, but the silence must be the exercise of a constitutional right. In a Maryland murder case, the police had the defendant in custody and

---

230 Mincey v. Arizona, 437 U.S. 385, 1978 U.S. LEXIS 115 (1978).

231 Kansas v. Ventris, 556 U.S. 212, 2009 U.S. LEXIS 3299 (2009).

232 Missouri v. Seibert, 542 U.S. 600, 2004 U.S. LEXIS 4578 (2004).

233 Doyle v. Ohio, 426 U.S. 610, 618-619, 96 S. Ct. 2240, 2244, 49 L.Ed.2d 91, 97, 1976 U.S. LEXIS 66 (1976).

had given him his *Miranda* rights twice, which he apparently understood. Subsequently, the defendant spoke with police officers briefly during their attempts to interrogate him and he eventually indicated that he was present at the crime scene. At some point during the interrogation, the defendant began to remain silent despite accusations concerning his involvement. Police testimony during the trial indicated at least 30 times that the defendant chose to remain silent and did not say anything further. The defendant's counsel failed to object during any of the instances in which the police commented on the defendant's post-*Miranda* silence. The reviewing court reversed the defendant's murder conviction because the police improperly used the defendant's post-*Miranda* silence as evidence and his attorney failed to meet the standards required of the Sixth Amendment right to counsel.[234]

In summary, statements that have been taken properly and qualify as admissions or confessions may be used for impeachment purposes and present no problem when the evidence is admitted against the person who uttered them. However, if the statement has been taken in violation of the principles of *Miranda* or involuntarily, the admission or confession is prohibited from admission to prove guilt. Where the statement was voluntarily offered, even though the *Miranda* warnings should have been offered or the right to counsel was violated, the statement may only be used for impeachment purposes when the defendant gives a contradictory statement during the defense case-in-chief. The fact that a subject exhibited silence before the *Miranda* warnings were necessary is admissible; however, after the warnings are required, the fact of silence should not bring a comment from a government witness or prosecutor because it constitutes error.

§ 9.20 Rehabilitation of Witness

"Evidence of a witness's prior consistent statement is admissible to rehabilitate the witness when the statement is offered to rebut a charge of recent fabrication, bias, or improper motive."[235] As a general rule,[236] to be admissible, a prior consistent statement must be offered after a witness's inconsistent statement has been admitted to attack that witness's credibility and where the consistent prior statement was made before the inconsistent statement. Alternatively, a prior consistent statement may be admitted where there is an express or implied charge that the witness's trial testimony was recently fabricated and that the statement was made prior to the fabrication. Following efforts to impeach a witness through the use of his or her prior inconsistent statements, offering prior consistent statements or acts serves to rehabilitate the witness. For example, in Pennsylvania, a court may permit the introduction of a prior consistent statement of a witness for the purpose of rehabilitation where the statement is being presented to

---

234 Coleman v. State, 434 Md. 320, 325, 75 A.3d 916, 919, 2013 Md. LEXIS 592 (2013).

235 Commonwealth v. Busanet, 54 A.3d 35, 66, 2012 Pa. LEXIS 2476 (2012).

236 *See* People v. Lopez, 56 Cal. 4th 1028, 301 P.3d 1177, 2013 Cal. LEXIS 4702 (2013).

rebut an inference of recent "fabrication, bias, improper influence or motive, or faulty memory" and where "the statement was made before" the issue being litigated occurred.[237] In an appeal of a murder conviction, a Pennsylvania defendant contended that a prosecution witness had been improperly rehabilitated after the defense had questioned the witness concerning his motivation for being a prosecution witness. The defendant contended that the witness was testifying in order to obtain a lenient treatment for his own criminal problems with the prosecutor. The trial court allowed the prosecution to introduce a prior consistent statement made by the witness; during the investigation, he told police officers that he had followed the defendant down the street and seen the defendant commit the murder. On the redirect examination, the prosecution introduced a written statement that the witness had given to a police investigator 15 days after the murder; this statement was consistent with the witness's trial testimony. Under the circumstances, the Supreme Court of Pennsylvania upheld the use of the prior consistent statement because it was originally made before any motive to lie existed and was being used as rehabilitation and not for the proof of its contents.[238]

As a general rule, when a witness's credibility has been attacked by the opposing party, evidence that tends to rehabilitate that witness will be admissible. In a Wyoming murder case, the defense offered the theory that both prosecution witnesses had lied from the outset and falsely implicated him in the murder to get personal leniency from the prosecutor. Here, the witnesses' credibility was attacked as the defendant characterized them as untruthful when they implicated him in the murder. In order to rehabilitate the prosecution witnesses, the judge allowed a police officer to relate what the prosecution witnesses had stated to him at the beginning of the murder investigation, facts that were consistent with the prosecution witnesses' trial testimony.[239] Rehabilitation of a witness through the use of appropriate evidence may be viewed as according due process to the opposing side; each party is thus provided with a fundamental opportunity to meet the evidence offered by the other side.

§ 9.21 Summary

Although the testimony of witnesses is essential in criminal cases, not all witnesses who have information about the facts of the case are permitted to testify. Moreover, witnesses who are authorized to testify are limited as to the manner and extent of the testimony they may give. The trial judge has a responsibility to apply the rules of evidence in determining whether a witness may testify at all and, if so, the extent of his or her testimony. Usually, the trial judge has a great deal of discretion in making

---

237 *See* PA. R. EVID. 613 (c)(1) (2013).

238 *See* Commonwealth v. Busanet, 54 A.3d 35, 2012 Pa. LEXIS 2476 (2013).

239 Proffit v. State, 2008 WY 103, 191 P.3d 974, 982, 2008 Wyo. LEXIS 108 (2008).

this determination, and a reviewing court will not reverse a trial judge except on abuse of discretion.

Generally, to be eligible to testify, a witness must have a personal connection to the relevant occurrence—in addition to sufficient mental and physical faculties to observe the events at the time of their occurrence—and must be able to recollect and relate the events to the jury or court in a manner that renders the testimony relevant. Before the witness gives substantive information, he or she is required to state under oath or affirmation that he or she will testify truthfully.

To prevent witnesses from being influenced by the testimony of other witnesses, the judge has the discretion to separate the witnesses during the trial so that they are in the courtroom only when called upon to testify and cannot coordinate their testimony with other witnesses. As a general rule, police officers and other government agents are considered officers of the court and are allowed to remain in the courtroom despite the fact that they will be called as witnesses. This is not an absolute rule, however.

After a witness has been sworn, the attorney representing the party calling him or her as a witness will conduct the questioning. This is known as the direct examination of the witness. As a general rule, leading questions are not permitted on direct examination, although there are exceptions. Leading introductory questions are permitted in these circumstances: to ask a witness's address; with hostile witnesses; to correct an obviously erroneous statement; and with children of a tender age and others who have difficulty expressing themselves.

Although it is preferable for witnesses to testify from memory in all situations, it is clear that witnesses do not always remember the facts after a substantial period of time has passed. Recognizing this human limitation, witnesses are allowed in some instances and under very controlled conditions to refresh their memories by referring to written statements. This is known as refreshing memory or, in some courts, as "present memory revived."

When the witness has no present recollection of the events or has a deficient memory that does not allow for a proper and full testimony about what occurred at the time, information that has been preserved in writing may be admissible. Where the witness remembers that he or she recorded the facts concerning the action, the writing or memorandum of past recollection is admitted when the proponent has laid a proper foundation.

For years, the right of cross-examination has been considered a constitutional right alongside the right of confrontation. The purpose of cross-examination is to give the opposing party an opportunity to challenge the credibility of statements given by the witness on direct examination. With some exceptions, cross-examination of the witness is limited to the scope of matters brought out on direct examination. On rare occasions, especially in cases involving sex offenses and small children, direct confrontation may be curtailed as long as the overall right of confrontation and its purposes have been met.

After a witness has been cross-examined, the party calling him or her may ask questions on redirect examination to explain matters brought out on cross-examination.

Following this, the opposing party may then ask questions on recross-examination; however, such questions are limited to new matters brought out on redirect examination.

Impeachment is the process of attempting to diminish the credibility of a witness by convincing the jury or court that the testimony may not be truthful or is unreliable. Common techniques in the impeachment process are to show bias, interest, or prejudice on the part of the witness; to introduce evidence of conviction of certain crimes; and to introduce evidence of prior inconsistent statements. In some instances, a confession may be used for impeachment purposes even though the *Miranda* warnings were not administered. However, if a confession was not made freely and voluntarily, it will not be admitted even for impeachment purposes because of questions concerning the truthfulness of the confession.

An impeached witness may be rehabilitated and evidence may be admitted to contradict the impeaching testimony through the use of an explanation or by introducing a prior consistent statement or act.

Those involved in the criminal justice process are often confused and disappointed when they are not allowed to testify about what they think is pertinent, but the rules of evidence have created methods of achieving fundamental fairness while accommodating socially important goals. If the rules of evidence are fully understood and justice personnel are familiar with the reasons for limiting the use of evidence, they will be more confident and better prepared for giving testimony.

CHAPTER NINE: QUESTIONS AND REVIEW EXERCISES

1. Explain why having firsthand knowledge or original knowledge is a requirement for competency as a witness.
2. An additional element of witness competency is oath or affirmation. Why is the making of an oath or affirmation considered so important? Young children are often permitted to testify and are not required to give an oath. How is a young child determined to be competent if he or she does not take an oath?
3. At the request of a party or upon the judge's own motion, courts generally have the power to order witnesses who have yet to testify to remain outside the courtroom. Rule 615 of the Federal Rules of Evidence and similar state provisions permit sequestration of witnesses. What is the rationale behind keeping witnesses who have not testified from being present in the courtroom prior to offering their testimony? When witnesses violate a judge's order and remain in the courtroom prior to testifying, what remedy might the judge consider?
4. As a general rule, courts do not permit leading questions during the direct examination of a party's witness. However, there are occasions when they are permitted. Describe at least three

occasions during direct examination when they are considered to be appropriate.

5. When a witness has a problem remembering certain aspects of his or her testimony, there are two techniques to relay this information to the jury. An attorney for a party may attempt to refresh the memory of the witness or use a theory known as past recollection recorded. Explain these two techniques and describe how they operate.
6. The Sixth Amendment to the U.S. Constitution provides that a defendant has the right "to be confronted with the witnesses against" him or her. Why is the right to confront and cross-examine one's accusers so important to fairness and justice?
7. What does the phrase "impeach a witness" mean? Is a party who called the witness permitted to impeach that witness? Give an example of impeachment of a witness by demonstrating the witness's bias or prejudice to the opposing party.
8. All witnesses, including all defendants who take the witness stand, place at issue their character trait for credibility. Assume that the defendant has taken the witness stand and testified fully on direct examination. In this hypothetical case, the prosecutor had a factual basis to inquire about a defendant's prior convictions for writing an insufficient funds check, for defrauding an innkeeper, for writing a check when he had no bank account, and a conviction for tax fraud. Would such an inquiry concerning all or some of the prior convictions be appropriate during cross-examination? Why or why not?
9. One method of impeachment involves a prior statement that is inconsistent with that witness's trial testimony. Create a factual example of the use of a prior inconsistent statement that would be admissible as impeachment evidence.
10. Assume that a defendant made a confession following a lawful arrest and appropriate *Miranda* warnings. After deciding to speak with an attorney, the defendant indicated that the confession was untrue and inaccurate. Since the defendant repudiated the confession, can the prosecutor use the confession as impeachment evidence if the defendant takes the witness stand and offers testimony that is contrary and inconsistent to the out-of-court confession? Could the prosecutor use the confession as substantive evidence?

Privileges

10

For more than three centuries it has now been recognized as a fundamental maxim that the public. . .has a right to every man's evidence. When we come to examine the various claims of exemption, we start with the primary assumption that there is a general duty to give what testimony one is capable of giving, and that any exemptions which may exist are distinctly exceptional, being so many derogations from a positive general rule.

United States v. Bryan, 339 U.S. 323, 331 (1950)
(quoting 8 J. Wigmore, Evidence § 2192)

Chapter Contents

Section

KEY TERMS AND CONCEPTS

Assertion of Privilege	Holder of a Privilege
Attorney–Client Privilege	Marital Confidential Communication Privilege
Doctor–Patient Privilege	Marital Testimonial Privilege
Duration of Privilege	Privileged Communication
Exception	Scope of Privileges
Exclusionary Rule	Waiver of Privilege

§ 10.1 Introduction

Rule 501

PRIVILEGE IN GENERAL

The common law—as interpreted by U.S. courts in the light of reason and experience—governs a claim of privilege unless any of the following provides otherwise:
- the United States Constitution;
- a federal statute; or
- rules prescribed by the Supreme Court.

But in a civil case, state law governs privilege regarding a claim or defense for which state law supplies the rule of decision.[1]

Generally, the rules of evidence are designed to allow the introduction of evidence that proves truthful, is not unfair, and is not confusing. Most of the rules of evidence operate to reveal the truth of what they contain; however, in some instances, the rules may exclude evidence where there is a higher value to be protected. This happens not only in constitutional areas involving the Fourth Amendment's **exclusionary rule** and the rules relating to *Miranda* warnings and interrogation, but in the area that is the focus of this chapter: rules of privilege. For example, our society values the institution

[1] FED. R. EVID. 501.

Exclusionary rule This rule requires that when evidence has been obtained in violation of the privileges guaranteed by the United States Constitution, the evidence must be excluded at the trial. Evidence that is obtained by an unreasonable search and seizure is excluded from evidence under the Fourth Amendment to the United States Constitution, and this rule applies to the states.

of marriage and works to protect existing marriages by limiting the testimony that one spouse can be forced to offer against another spouse. By not requiring one spouse to testify against another, one avenue of marital discord is removed, or at least, not created. It is believed that the social policy behind not requiring spouses to testify against each other outweighs the benefits for society that the truthful testimony of one spouse against another might generate.

Concepts of privileged communication recognize that there are many occasions in which humans issue communications that they would expect or desire to be kept confidential or private or, at least, not have them forcibly disclosed within the context of a lawsuit. In the absence of a recognized privilege, many individuals would be reluctant to fully disclose information to a physician, a priest, an attorney, or other individual that might well be crucial to the relationship or to the ability of one individual to help someone else resolve a problem. Where a privilege is recognized, the perception is that society benefits from maintaining the confidentiality that exists in that relationship by not forcing its disclosure to the public.

A privilege has the effect of preserving the confidentiality of particular relationships by excluding from court highly believable and trustworthy evidence for social policy reasons even though such exclusion clouds the truth. In many cases, courts refuse to admit otherwise relevant evidence due to the operation of legal privileges that promote particularly important relationships, interests, and rights. According to the U.S. Supreme Court, "[t]he lawyer–client privilege rests on the need for the advocate and counselor to know all that relates to the client's reasons for seeking representation if the professional mission is to be carried out."[2] The rule that protects the rights of persons in certain relationships to refuse to give information acquired as the result of the relationship and to refuse to disclose the identity of an informant in some instances is known in law as the testimonial privilege rule, or the privileged communications rule. However, most privileges come from a legislative enactment or have developed through case law. For example, there is no privilege under the First Amendment that would allow journalists to refuse to identify sources or that would permit a news reporter to refuse to divulge information given in confidence by a source,[3] and where a journalist has a privilege it is usually the result of a

---

2 Trammel v. United States, 445 U.S. 40, 51 (1980). *See* case in Part II, Chapter 2.

3 *See* Branzburg v. Hayes, 408 U.S.665, 92 S. Ct. 2646, 33 L. Ed. 2d 626, 1972 U.S. LEXIS 132 (1972). *See also* Atlanta Journal-Constitution v. Jewell, 251 Ga. App. 808, 810, 555 S.E.2d 175, 179, 2001 Ga. App. LEXIS 1153 (2001).

legislative enactment. However, "forty-nine of the fifty United States. . .have recognized some form of reporter's privilege, whether by statute or in case law."[4]

In most instances in which the law recognizes a privilege, one person has communicated information to another person that was intended to be kept confidential by both parties, and the privilege not to disclose generally serves an important social interest. For example, where a penitent confesses to a priest or rabbi as part of religious faith and practice and the information was intended to be kept private, society allows this confidentiality because it recognizes the benefit to society of religious teachings and practices in promoting a harmonious social order. A society hostile to religion would reject this confidence and order the information to be disclosed in a court proceeding regardless of the effect on the individuals or society. Similarly, police are often permitted to decline a defense request to reveal the identity of secret informants, unless the informant will be offering testimony in court. Society values the informant who is willing to assist law enforcement and, as an encouragement, permits the identity to remain secret to protect the informant and to encourage additional assistance in the future. In both of these examples, it is believed that the balance of benefits to society is on the positive side of the ledger and that to refuse to recognize such a privilege would not serve society as well.

Privileged communications Statements made by one person to another when there is a necessary relation of trust and confidence between them, which the person receiving them cannot be legally compelled to disclose.

The **privileged communications** rule includes information beyond items gathered from informant sources and may cover the identity of the person who gave the privileged information. It can be more accurately stated that there are really three categories of privileges: (1) those that protect privileged communications resulting from relationships, such as husband–wife and attorney–client; (2) those relating to disclosing the identity of persons who made the communications, such as not revealing the identity of an informant, and (3) those that permit a defendant to not give the prosecutor constitutionally protected information and allow governments to keep from divulging secrets that are deemed essential or otherwise confidential. The privilege that exists between spouses actually involves two distinct privileges: one covering confidential communications[5] made to each other during the marriage and the other involving a privilege of the potential witness spouse not to testify against the other during the duration of the marriage. The second category permits the peace officer and the prosecutor to refuse to divulge the name of an informant and, in some

---

4 United States v. Sterling, 732 F.2d 292, 295, 2013 U.S. App. LEXIS 20897 (4th Cir. 2013).

5 Communication includes speech and, in some jurisdictions, conduct that one spouse performs in full view of the other while relying on the confidentiality of the relationship. When a husband killed a man in full view of his wife, the acts were not deemed to constitute confidential communication. *See* Roland v. State, 882 So. 2d 262, 265, 2004 Miss. App. LEXIS 911 (2004).

jurisdictions, may allow news reporters the privilege of not revealing the identity of their confidential information sources.[6]

The rules regarding privileges have evolved over a long period through case law and legislative enactments.[7] Concern with privileges and their effects have energized critics who have been both numerous and vocal. Some authorities argue that the reasons for excluding valuable testimony because of these privilege rules are no longer valid and should be abandoned, or at least modified. As the late Chief Justice Burger once observed, "Whatever their origin these exceptions to the demand for everyman's evidence are not lightly created nor expansively construed, for they are in derogation of the search for truth."[8] Those who oppose the use of the privilege argue that prohibiting the use of some evidence because of certain relationships alters the normal mode of proof in a trial by denying the trier of fact some of the information that he or she otherwise would have been able to present to the court. These arguments have had some influence on judicial behavior, and because these rules are either in derogation of the common law or are statutory enactments, there is a tendency on the part of the courts to construe the rules narrowly.[9]

As a general rule, most privileges that are based on confidences are narrowly construed,[10] because privileges may inhibit the search for truth by shielding potentially reliable and relevant evidence in an effort to protect human relationships.[11] Therefore, privileges based on confidential relationships are not easily recognized or endorsed by the courts. However, a contrary view exists that some privileges should be liberally construed because they have been founded on constitutional principles.[12] In a civil case involving potential criminal fraud in the avoidance of corporate income taxes, the court ordered a former executive of a company to produce documents sought by the Internal Revenue Service.[13] According to the court, the documents had to be produced because the attorney–client privilege was narrowly construed and the executive did not carry the burden of proof that the privilege applied. A Washington court held that a conversation between a woman and her social agency counselor could be divulged by the counselor to the court when the substance of the counseling involved the woman's admissions of child neglect. Washington had a counselor–patient privilege, but that privilege did not

---

6 Persky v. Yeshiva University, 2002 U.S. Dist. LEXIS 23740 (S.D.N.Y. 2002); *and see* United States v. Hively, 202 F. Supp. 886, 889, 890 (E.D. Ark. 2002) for a brief discussion of the news reporters' privilege in federal courts.

7 For example, *see* 10 DEL. CODE ANN. § 4322 (2013). This statute offers a privilege to reporters who may refuse to reveal the identity of a source who had been expressly or impliedly told that the relationship would remain confidential or would significantly impair the reporter in the maintenance of his or her source relationship, so long as the reporter obtained the information within the scope of the reporter's professional activities.

8 United States v. Nixon, 418 U.S. 683, 94 S. Ct. 3090, 41 L. Ed. 2d 1039 (1974).

9 *See* Cavallaro v. United States, 153 F. Supp. 2d 52, 58, 2001 U.S. Dist. LEXIS 11232 (D. Mass. 2001).

10 United States v. Banks, 556 F.2d 967, 981, 2009 U.S. App. LEXIS 3696 (9th Cir. 2009).

11 Cassel v. Superior Court, 2011 Cal. LEXIS 2, n.12 (2011).

12 People v. Williams, 43 Cal. 4th 584, 613, 2008 Cal. LEXIS 4818 (Cal. 2008).

13 United States v. Trenk, 2009 U.S. Dist. LEXIS 15333 (D.N.J. 2009).

survive when the court looked at the exceptions contained in another part of the Washington code.[14]

Under the common law, there was no accountant–client privilege, so where such a privilege exists, it does so based on statutory enactments. Similarly, there is not an accountant–client privilege under federal law,[15] except for the limited privilege granted under the Internal Revenue Code.[16] States that have an accountant–client privilege generally follow a statutory framework that allows a public accountant to refuse to divulge information in court that has been obtained by virtue of the employment relationship. Because statutory privileges are narrowly construed, the accountant–client privilege dictates that to be considered confidential and covered by a privilege, the communication must arise from actual accounting services and not have been generated from consulting or other related activities.[17]

When the United States Supreme Court began drafting the Federal Rules of Evidence, it initially included extensive rules related to testimonial privileges. The U.S. Congress did not approve of the rules relating to privileges; as a result, they never survived to become part of the Federal Rules of Evidence. What resulted was Rule 501, which noted "the privilege of a witness, person, government, State, or political subdivision thereof shall be governed by the principles of the common law as they may be interpreted by the courts of the United States in the light of reason and experience." Thus, Congress determined that the federal case law respecting privileges was not to be frozen by detailed federal rules, but allowed to develop on a case-by-case basis. As a result, Congress never enacted the proposed comprehensive codifications, and only the general provision regarding privileges, noted earlier, remained in the version that was finally adopted by both houses of Congress.[18]

Notwithstanding the fact that Congress rejected the draft prepared by the U.S. Supreme Court and deleted the articles relating to privileges, the definitions and requirements developed in the document are well worth studying. Some of these definitions are used in this chapter.

In the sections that follow, the relationships recognized by law in which the exchange of confidential information is encouraged are discussed first. These relationships include (1) attorney–client, (2) physician–patient, (3) husband–wife, and (4) communications to clergy. A later section examines the law relating to privileges that protect the identity of informants and the news media–informant privilege.

---

14 Hamilton v. Department of Social and Health Services, 109 Wash. App 718, 730, 37 P.3d 1227, 1233, 2001 Wash. App. LEXIS 2810 (2001).

15 United States v. Bisanti, 414 F.3d 168, 170, 2005 U.S. App. LEXIS 13575 (1st Cir. 2005).

16 *See* 26 U.S.C. § 7525.

17 PepsiCo, Inc. v. Baird, Kurtz & Dobson LLP, 305 F. 3d 813, 815, 2002 U.S. App. LEXIS 192 (8th Cir. 2002).

18 Trammel v. United States, 445 U.S. 40, 47, 1980 U.S. LEXIS 84 (1980). *See* case in Part II, Cases Relating to Chapter 2.

§ 10.2 Reasons for Privileged Communications

The theoretical basis for privileges involving communication reflects concern for the protection of important personal relationships and the recognition of significant other legal rights and social interests that may be at stake. When the protection and importance of these relationships philosophically outweigh the need for the evidence, courts tend to uphold the privilege and exclude the evidence to protect perceived higher social values. These statutory privileges have been created by statutory enactments because they are regarded as serving more important public interests than the need for full disclosure. As a general rule, in most jurisdictions testimonial privileges are given a rather narrow construction because they have the effect of removing relevant evidence from the trier of fact and therefore somewhat undermine the search for truth in a criminal case.[19]

The rationale for the privileged communication rules is that when people occupy certain confidential relations, the law, on public policy grounds, will not compel, or in some instances even allow, one of them to violate the confidence reposed in him or her by the other. This rule of privileged communications is not a rule of substantive law, but rather a rule of evidence that does not affect the general competency of a witness but merely renders him or her able to refuse to testify about particular matters covered by the privilege.

Traditionally, the courts recognize and protect the following relationships: (1) husband–wife, (2) attorney–client, (3) physician–patient, and (4) clergy–penitent. Some jurisdictions by statute recognize confidential communication privileges involving counselor–client, accountant–client, psychologist–client, and news reporter–source. In each instance there are specific rules regarding the scope of the privilege, who is considered a "holder" of the privilege, who is eligible to claim the privilege, and when, how, and in what context the privilege may be asserted. There are also some general requirements that apply in all instances. First, the exchange must be between two people whose relationship is recognized by law. Second, the communication must have been exchanged because of the confidential nature of the relationship. Third, the communication must be such that the interests of society will benefit to a greater degree than the opposing party by keeping information secret rather than by revealing it.

Communications made in confidence do not carry a privilege not to reveal the substance merely because the parties expected the communication to remain confidential. A special confidential relationship that is recognized by the courts or by statute must exist, and a communication intended to remain confidential must have occurred between the proper parties for the communication to be covered by a privilege.

The presence of an unnecessary third party will prevent the communication from being recognized as one made in confidence. Therefore, if a third party who was not a member of the privileged relationship overhears the privileged communication,

[19] State v. J.G., 201 N.J. 369, 383, 990 A.2d 1122, 1130, 2010 N.J. LEXIS 381 (2010).

whether by accident or design, that person may testify about the substance of the communication. For example, an attorney who speaks with a client on a jail phone known to be monitored and recorded by third-party correctional workers does not create a confidential communication, and the person overhearing can testify against the jail inmate.[20] However, when agents of the prosecution intentionally overheard defense attorneys speaking with clients under circumstances where the parties reasonably could have expected confidentiality, the active presence of the officers may not destroy the confidentiality of the communication and the officer's testimony should be rejected.[21]

The sections that follow explore the specific rules that apply to the respective privileged communications.

§ 10.3 Communications Between Husband and Wife

Protection of confidential communications between spouses has origins in the common law and "is premised upon the belief that the marital union is sacred and that its intimacy and confidences deserve legal protection."[22] Historically, the privilege existed to preserve marital harmony by encouraging open spousal communication through allowing spouses to confide in each other freely, thus protecting the privacy of marriage. As an early Supreme Court case noted:

> This rule is founded upon the deepest and soundest principles of our nature. Principles which have grown out of those domestic relations, that constitute the basis of civil society, and which are essential to the enjoyment of that confidence which should subsist between those who are connected by the nearest and dearest relations of life.[23]

Common law rules that become obsolete in practice or for which a questionable basis emerges are subject to judicial revision or rejection. For example, in the case of *Funk v. United States*,[24] the U.S. States Supreme Court stated that a rule of evidence thought necessary at one time should yield to the experience of a succeeding generation whenever experience has clearly demonstrated the fallacy of the proposition or where changed circumstances suggest an invalidation of the old rule. At no place is this more evident than in the law relating to the husband–wife testimonial privilege. In the 1980 case *Trammel vs. United States*,[25] the Supreme Court set aside rules for federal courts

---

20 McWatters v. State, 36 So.3d 613, 636, 2010 Fla. LEXIS 406 (2010).

21 See People v. Shrier, 190 Cal. App. 4th 400, 118 Cal. Rptr. 3d 233; 2010 Cal. App. LEXIS 1997 (2010).

22 State v. Rollins, 2009 N.C. LEXIS 348 (N.C. 2009).

23 Stein v. Bowman, 38 U.S. (13 Pet.) 209, 223, 10 L. Ed. 129 (1839).

24 290 U.S. 371, 54 S. Ct. 212, 78 L. Ed. 369 (1933). *See* case in Part II, in Cases Relating to Chapter 1.

25 Trammel v. United States, 445 U.S. 40, 100 S. Ct. 906, 63 L. Ed. 2d 145 (1980).

that had been established in the 1958 case of *Hawkins v. United States.*[26] As a result of *Trammel* and its influence on state jurisprudence, it is necessary to approach the husband–wife privilege from two perspectives.

A. Statement of the Rules

Rule 1. Marital communications are privileged, but only to the extent that the communications were made in the expectation of confidence.[27] This rule is followed in both federal and state courts and was not changed by the decision in *Trammel*, which applied only to federal courts.

Rule 2. A witness spouse cannot testify against a defendant spouse regarding any acts observed or regarding any nonconfidential communication that occurred before or during the marriage unless both spouses agree. Under this theory, both spouses hold the marital testimonial privilege and may assert it to prevent the witness spouse from giving testimony. This rule was established for federal courts in *Hawkins v. United States*,[28] but the *Trammel* case had the effect of reversing the *Hawkins* decision and held that only the witness spouse was a holder of the marital testimonial privilege who had the option to exercise the right to refuse to testify against a defendant spouse in a federal court.[29] The older *Hawkins*-style rule is still followed in some states, as demonstrated by a Minnesota statute that prohibits either spouse from being examined for or against the other in the absence of the other's consent, whether during the existence of the marriage or thereafter.[30]

B. Scope of the Privilege

At common law, neither spouse possessed competency as a witness to give testimony, either for or against the other. This rule was based on the premise that husband and wife were one, and at common law, where one spouse was a party to a suit, whether civil or criminal, the other was not permitted to testify due to the obvious bias. This restrictive rule was gradually abolished by court decisions and statutes; it was replaced by the rule that a spouse may testify on behalf of the other in a criminal

---

26 Hawkins v. United States, 358 U.S. 74, 79 S. Ct. 136, 3 L. Ed. 2d 125 (1958).

27 United States v. Dunbar, 553 F.3d 48, 58, 2009 U.S. App. LEXIS 1639 (1st Cir. 2009).

28 Hawkins v. United States, *supra* n.26.

29 *See* the footnotes by the court in the *Trammel* case cited *supra* n.23. Where a spouse holds the privilege not to testify, asking the potential witness spouse to exercise the privilege does not constitute witness tampering when the request comes from the defendant spouse. *See* United States v. Doss, 2011 U.S. App. LEXIS 708 (9th Cir. 2011).

30 For example, MINN. STAT. § 595.02 (2013) contemplates that both spouses are holders of the marital testimonial and marital communication privilege. Similarly, in the absence of any statutory exception, Arizona requires consent of the defendant spouse prior to testimony by the other either for or against the defendant spouse. ARIZ. REV. STAT. § 13-4062 (2013). The positions of these two states appear to be distinctly minority positions.

proceeding, but in some instances a spouse may not testify against the other if either spouse objects.

The *Trammel* case involved a husband who had been indicted on federal drug charges while his wife had been named in the indictment as an unindicted conspirator. The trial court ruled that confidential communications between Mr. Trammel and his wife were privileged and therefore inadmissible; however, the wife was permitted to testify to any act she observed before or during the marriage and to any communication made in the presence of a third person. The Court in *Trammel* referred to studies that revealed that in 1958, when *Hawkins* was decided, 31 states allowed a defendant the privilege of preventing adverse spousal testimony; the Court indicated that the number had declined to 24 in 1980. The Court then said, "Here we must decide whether the privilege against adverse spousal testimony promotes sufficiently important interests to outweigh the need for probative evidence in the administration of criminal justice."[31] With respect to nonconfidential communications within a marriage, the Supreme Court decided "that the existing rule should be modified so that in federal courts, the witness-spouse alone has a privilege to refuse to testify adversely; the witness may be neither compelled to testify nor foreclosed from testifying. This modification—vesting the privilege in the witness-spouse—furthers the important public interest in marital harmony without unduly burdening legitimate law enforcement needs."[32] *Trammel* affected only federal courts.

Prior to *Trammel*, in the case of *Blau v. United States*,[33] the Supreme Court reaffirmed the rule that in federal courts, confidential communications between husband and wife are privileged. The *Trammel* Court noted that the *Trammel* case did not change the *Blau* recognition of the marital confidential communication privilege in federal courts.[34] This meant that neither spouse could be required to testify concerning confidential communications made during the existence of the marriage, nor would the other be permitted to testify if the other objected.

This case did not decide, however, the issue of whether the spouse may be permitted to testify to an act observed before or during the marriage, nor did it settle the issue of communications made in the presence of a third party. The lower court in *Trammel* agreed that confidential communications between husband and wife were privileged and therefore inadmissible, but the privilege permitted the wife to testify about any acts that she observed before and during the marriage, and about any communications made in the presence of a third person.

---

31 Trammel v. United States, *supra* n.25.

32 *Id.*

33 Blau v. United States, 340 U.S. 332, 71 S. Ct. 301, 95 L. Ed. 306 (1950).

34 *See* Trammel v. United States, n.5 of the Court's decision.

After discussing the arguments for and against permitting a spouse to testify about criminal acts observed during a marriage or nonconfidential communications, the *Trammel* Court concluded:

> Accordingly, we conclude that the existing rule should be modified so that the witness spouse alone has the privilege to refuse to testify adversely: the witness may be neither compelled to testify nor foreclosed from testifying. This modification—vesting the privilege in the witness spouse—furthers the important public interest in marital harmony without unduly burdening legitimate law enforcement needs.[35]

Federal and most state courts recognize two separate marital privileges: the marital confidential communications privilege and the marital testimonial privilege.[36] In federal courts, the witness-spouse alone has the privilege to testify or refuse to testify adversely regarding criminal acts observed and nonconfidential communications occurring during the marriage. In other states, where the rule has not been changed by statute or court decision, an accused may object not only to a spouse testifying about confidential communications, but also to that spouse's testimony about any act observed before or during the marriage. However, with respect to the marital confidential communication privilege, generally both spouses are holders of this privilege and each may assert it independently of the other.

Demonstrative of the rules pertaining to the marital confidential communication privilege, husbands and wives are generally not required to testify and may prevent the other from testifying about confidential communications made to each other because of the confidence resulting from their intimate marital relationship.[37] The communication must have been made in the absence of third parties and cannot include coercion of one spouse by the other. In addition, where the communication was intended to be conveyed to third parties or where one spouse revealed a threat made by the other spouse, the privilege not to testify does not exist. Some jurisdictions limit the availability of the marital confidential communication privilege to the point that its existence must be determined on a case-by-case basis. Tennessee recognizes the confidential marital privilege in civil cases but, in a criminal proceeding, the communication must have originated in a communication that the parties believe will not be disclosed and the confidentiality is essential to the maintenance of the relation between the persons.[38] In addition, the element of confidentiality must be essential to the full and satisfactory maintenance of the relationship between the husband and the wife, the relationship must be one that, in the opinion of the community, should be fostered, and the injury

---

35 Trammel v. United States, *supra* n.25. *See also* United States v. Medina-Castellanos, 359 Fed. Appx. 404, 2010 U.S. App. LEXIS 29 (2010), where the court implicitly recognized and spoke of two different marital privileges applicable in federal courts: one bars testimony concerning statements confidentially communicated between spouses; and the other permits one spouse to refuse to testify against his or her spouse about anything so long as the couple are married at the time of trial.

36 United States v. Espino, 317 F.3d 788, 795, 2003 U.S. App. LEXIS 261 (8th Cir. 2003).

37 *See* Williams v. State, 2010 Ind. App. Unpub. LEXIS 598 (2010).

38 See TENN. CODE ANN. § 24-1-201 (2013).

to that relationship that would be caused by the disclosure of the confidential communication must outweigh the benefit gained for the correct result in the disposal of litigation.

In some jurisdictions, written communications between spouses[39] and physical acts done in full view of the spouse may constitute confidential communications from which a testimonial privilege may arise. Private communications between spouses does not always occur behind closed doors and may be made openly when other persons are not able to hear or observe. In a murder prosecution, the trial court admitted conversations between the witness spouse and the defendant spouse in which the defendant spouse made incriminating confidential statements to the wife. In reversing the conviction, the Supreme Court of Kentucky noted that some of the conversations were completely private with no third party in a position to overhear; one conversation occurred in a hay barn away from other people. The reviewing court held that the trial court should not have permitted the wife to testify concerning those private conversations. The court also questioned the trial court ruling that permitted the testimony of the wife concerning her feeling a gun when she hugged her husband, because that communication could be considered conduct as well as privileged communication.[40] In a different case, an appellate court held that numerous confidential cell phone communications made between spouses was privileged, remained privileged, and could not be revealed by a police officer who overheard the verbal marital conversations while listening on a lawful wiretap, even though the officer's presence was unknown and he was not an essential party to the conversations.[41] As a limitation, the activities of one spouse that could easily be observed by other individuals may not qualify as a confidential communication. In a murder case, the wife was required to testify concerning the time that the defendant arrived home on a particular night, which effectively negated his alibi.[42] Neighbors or other people outside of the home could have observed the defendant's arrival, and so his entry at a particular time was not a confidential communication and the wife lawfully could be compelled to testify against her then husband.

To summarize, marital privileges can be distinguished from each other in a variety of ways. The marital communication privilege applies only to communications between spouses of a confidential nature made during the marriage and in the absence of any third party. This privilege exists during the marriage and survives the dissolution or other end of the marriage, with both parties being holders of the privilege. The testimonial privilege applies to nonconfidential communication and observations made during the marriage, but this privilege may be asserted only during the existence of the marriage in both civil and criminal cases. The strong trend in the marital testimonial

---

39 United States v. Montgomery, 384 F.3d 1050, 1056, 2004 U.S. App. LEXIS 19322 (2004).

40 St. Clair v. Commonwealth, 174 S.W.2d 474, 480, 2005 Ky. LEXIS 334 (2005).

41 *See* State v. Terry, 430 N.J. Super. 587, 66 A. 3d 177, 2013 N.J. Super. LEXIS 71 (2013). See this case in Part II, Chapter 10.

42 Winstead v. Commonwealth, 2010 Ky. LEXIS 102 (2010).

privilege area holds that the witness spouse is the only one who may assert this privilege; however, some states allow either the defendant spouse or the witness spouse to be considered holders.[43]

The part of the marital confidential communication privilege that concerns confidential communications during the marriage has periodically come under scrutiny. It has been argued that if the marriage is in "utter shambles," the force behind the rule no longer exists, and the spouse should be required to testify. In a federal prosecution on three counts of making false statements to a federally insured financial institution, the defendant contended that the trial court erred in allowing her estranged husband to testify concerning documents and conversations indicating the criminal behavior of the wife that he had acquired while visiting the former marital residence. The husband took his information to federal authorities and agreed to wear a concealed recording device to record incriminating statements that his wife might make. The wife made several statements to the husband that indicated her consciousness of guilt in making the false loan statements. Over the objection, the trial court allowed the husband to testify concerning confidential matters he learned from his wife. The trial court held that the marital communication privilege should not be applied to communications made while the spouses, while still technically married, were living separate lives with no reasonable expectation of reconciliation or reunification as a happily married couple.[44]

However, Arizona statutory law presently provided that neither a husband can be examined "against his wife without her consent, nor a wife for or against her husband without his consent, as to events occurring during the marriage, nor can either, during the marriage or afterwards, without consent of the other, be examined as to any communication made by one to the other during the marriage."[45] According to the statute, "[t]hese exceptions do not apply in a criminal action or proceeding for a crime committed by the husband against the wife, or by the wife against the husband, nor in a criminal action or proceeding against the husband for abandonment, failure to support or provide for or failure or delay to furnish the necessities of life to the wife or the minor children."[46] Arizona courts have interpreted the statute to forbid any testimony by a spouse concerning any confidential communication between them that occurred during the marriage, whether the marriage is intact at the time of the testimony or not, unless the other spouse gives consent to the testimony.[47] However, Arizona courts do not hold that the communication privilege protects nonconfidential communications or noncommunicative acts carried out when the other spouse may be in a position to observe. In one Arizona case involving a conspiracy to commit murder, the defendant's then ex-wife was properly permitted to testify about conduct of the defendant observed

---

43 *See* State v. Riley, 258 Ore. App. 246, 257 2013 Ore. App. LEXIS 1001 (2013).

44 United States v. Singleton, 260 F.3d 1295, 1297, 1298, 2001 U.S. App. LEXIS 17694 (11th Cir. 2001).

45 ARIZ. REV. STAT. § 13-4062(1) (2013).

46 *Id.*

47 State ex rel. Woods v. Cohen, 173 Ariz. 497, 501, 502, 844 P.2d 1147, 1151, 1152, 1992 Ariz. LEXIS 104 (1992).

during the marriage when the acts were not intended as confidential communicative activities.[48] While the principle that the marital confidential communication privilege should not apply if a marriage was an utter shambles at the time the communication was made is probably still a minority view, the trend appears to be in that direction, especially in the federal courts.

An essential prerequisite for the assertion of the marital confidential communication privilege requires proof of the existence of a valid marriage at the time the spouse uttered the private communication,[49] and where the communication was made to a future spouse before the marriage, no privilege exists.[50] People who cohabitate and who do not qualify for common law marriage status, or who are of the same gender, are generally not considered married (although some exceptions exist) and cannot assert marital privileges.[51] However, some states extend marital privileges to "domestic partners" as is demonstrated by Washington where "a spouse or domestic partner shall not be examined for or against his or her spouse or domestic partner, without the consent of the spouse or domestic partner."[52] The same Washington statute also permits both spouses and partners to prevent the other spouse or partner from testifying concerning communications made to each other during the existence of the marriage or partnership. As same-gender marriages are permitted in more jurisdictions, the marital privileges will most likely be construed to cover such partners in these relationships to the same extent as has been recognized in traditional marriages.

The marriage is considered valid if there has been a formal ceremony as recognized by a state and the marriage has not been dissolved. If a couple or one member of a couple contends that the two have matured a common law marriage, the marriage must have been initiated in a state that recognized common law marriages and the burden to prove the existence of the marriage rests with the person making the allegation of marriage.[53] In the states that permit common law marriages to come into existence, certain requirements must be met. If those requirements are followed and the common law marriage is recognized in that state, a defendant in a criminal case could invoke either the marital communication privilege or the marital testimonial privilege in that state or any other.

In the absence of proof of a common law or formal marriage, no marital privilege attaches to any communication between a particular man and woman. When a valid

48 Arizona v. Harrod, 200 Ariz. 309, 26 P.3d 492, 498, 499, 2001 Ariz. LEXIS 104 (2001).

49 *See* Reese v. Lamas, 2013 U.S. Dist. LEXIS 110880 (W.D. Pa. 2013).

50 *See* State v. Kleine, 2011 Mo. App. LEXIS 28 (2011), where a future spouse admitted to his soon-to-be bride that he had killed two people at a prior time, no marital confidential communication privilege existed.

51 *See* A.L.R. 4TH 422 (2008). Some states recognize same-sex marriage; these states remain in a minority, even though the trend decidedly is moving in the direction of state and federal recognition of same-sex marriage or civil unions.

52 REV. CODE WASH. § 5.60.060. (2013).

53 Perrotti v. Meredith, 2005 Pa. Super. 57, 868 A.2d 1240, 1243, 2005 Pa. Super. LEXIS 148 (2005).

common law marriage exists, other states are generally bound to recognize the marriage and treat it as equal to a marriage contracted in a traditional ceremony. For example, in Texas, where common law marriages are recognized, there was a common law marriage between the defendant and the witness, and the defendant could invoke the marital communication privilege.[54] The court decided that because the defendant and witness had lived together in Texas and held themselves out to the public as a married couple, and as the witness testified that she and the defendant agreed to live together as husband and wife and indicated on an employment application and tax records that she was married, and because the defendant and witness exchanged wedding rings, this was sufficient indication of a common law marriage and the defendant could invoke the marital communication privilege.

Unless validly married under local law, marital confidential communication privileges generally do not extend to homosexuals in "spousal relationships."[55] This type of limitation on privileges of married couples may be affected by the Supreme Court's decision in *Lawrence v. Texas*, in which laws regulating private sexual activity between persons of the same sex were ruled to be unconstitutional.[56] However, litigation in California that recognized same-sex marriages[57] was called into question by a voter-initiated [Proposition 8] amendment to the California constitution that prohibited same-sex marriages. Litigation on the issue of same-sex marriage resulted in a federal district court ruling that Proposition 8 was unconstitutional, but an appeal to the Ninth Circuit resulted in a referral to California state courts for clarification concerning the standing of some of the litigants and the uncertainty continues.[58] However, New York recently recognized that same-sex marriages created in other states would be recognized by New York[59]; spousal privileges probably come with this recognition, although no reported case yet exists.[60] Spousal privileges similar to traditional marriages or some similar legal theory may eventually be statutorily devised or created by case law that protects same-gender relationships in ways similar to current marriage practice, although some of the litigation indicates that the extension of this type of privilege may be a long way into the future.[61]

---

54 People v. Badgett, 30 Cal. Rptr. 2d 152 (1994).

55 Greenwald v. H & P 29th Street Associates, 659 N.Y.S.2d 473 (N.Y. 1997). *And see* Hernandez v. Robles, 2005 N.Y. SLIP OP. 9436, 805 N.Y.S.2d 354, 2005 N.Y. App. Div. LEXIS 13892 (2005), determining that same-sex individuals were not eligible in New York to obtain marriage licenses.

56 *See* Lawrence v. Texas, 539 U.S. 558, 2003 U.S. LEXIS 5013 (2003).

57 *In re* Marriage Cases, 43 Cal. 4th 757, 2008 Cal. LEXIS 5247 (Cal. 2008).

58 *See* Perry v. Schwarzenegger, 2011 U.S. App. LEXIS 153 (9th Cir. 2011).

59 See Lewis v. New York State Department of Civil Service, 2009 NY SLIP OP. 283, 2009 N.Y. App. LEXIS 415 (N.Y. 2009). See also Varmi v. Brien, 763 N.W.2d 862, 2009 Iowa Sup. LEXIS 31 (2009) (holding that gays and lesbians may have full access to civil marriage).

60 Research has not revealed any attempt to assert a spousal privilege in New York litigation since the state decided to recognize out-of-state same-sex marriages.

61 *See* Wilson v. Ake, 354 F. Supp. 2d 1298, 2005 U.S. Dist. LEXIS 755 (2005), and Li v. State, 338 Or. 376, 110 P.3d 91, 2005 Or. LEXIS 490 (2004).

C. *Exceptions*

1. The privilege is generally limited to confidential communications

The marital privilege protects information privately disclosed between husband and wife that at the time was intended to be a confidential communication and can generally be asserted by either spouse.[62] A communication from one spouse to the other is considered confidential if it was made privately and was not intended for disclosure to any other person. Where no other people are able to hear a communication between spouses, the husband–wife confidential communication privilege should be recognized. In an Arkansas case, the husband and wife were in a car when the husband shot at people in a nearby car. While he paused, the wife asked him what he was doing, and he told her that he was reloading to kill another person. The court determined that a valid marital privilege existed that should have prevented the admission of the wife's testimony about his intent because the street discussion occurred in reliance on the confidential nature of their marital relationship.[63] The presence of unnecessary third parties prevents confidential communication between spouses, such as where a prisoner sends a letter to his wife.[64] If other persons are present at the time of the communication, but are not able to overhear the conversation, the privilege exists. In one case, one side of a telephone conversation was privileged while the other one was not.[65] The defendant, who had been accused of killing his wife's boyfriend's family, spoke to her on a telephone within earshot of her family members on the wife's side of the conversation. The court ruled that the husband's speech to his wife was considered confidential, while the wife's speech to the husband that was overheard by her family members was not considered as privileged under the confidential communication theory.

In a Florida case, the defendant's "communication" was by his conduct in front of his wife. At a murder trial, the ex-wife was properly permitted to testify that she had witnessed her then husband dump a human body into a ditch and, that upon return to their trailer home, observed blood on curtains, walls, and blinds. The Supreme Court of Florida noted that the marital communication privilege does not apply to observations made by the witness spouse.[66]

2. Communications overheard by third parties or made to third parties

Another exception to the marital privilege concerns the testimony of a third party who was in a position to overhear communications between spouses or when one

[62] United States v. Montgomery, 384 F.3d 1050, 1057, 2004 U.S. App. LEXIS 19322 (2004). The court noted (n.1) that 33 states and the District of Columbia allow either spouse to assert the confidential communication privilege.

[63] Walker v. State, 2005 Ark. App. LEXIS 471 (2005).

[64] United States v. Griffin, 440 F.3d 1138, 2006 U.S. App. LEXIS 6393 (9th Cir. 2006).

[65] *See* State v. Serrano, 346 Ore. 311, 210 P.3d 892, 2009 Ore. LEXIS 33 (2009).

[66] Bolin v. State, 117 So. 3d 728, 736, 2013 Fla. LEXIS 271(Fla. 2013).

spouse divulges the confidence to a third party. As a general rule, when a third party has overheard an otherwise confidential communication between spouses, the third party may testify. In a federal case involving a convicted felon possessing a firearm, at the defendant's pretrial bail hearing, his spouse was asked if the defendant knew about the presence of firearms in the marital home. In the absence of any objection from the defense counsel, the wife was permitted to testify that the defendant told her to take two guns from their home and put them in a car. The federal district court determined that the marital confidential communication privilege had been waived by the fact that the wife testified in open court without objection concerning the defendant's relationship with the guns, and such testimony constituted a waiver.[67]

The privilege protecting confidential marital communication generally does not exist where the original communication was made in the presence of an unnecessary third party, where one spouse observed criminal conduct of the defendant spouse, or where communication occurred between spouses using an employer's e-mail system that offered warnings that e-mail was subject to monitoring.[68] In a Tennessee case involving charges of rape and incest, the defendant verbally communicated with his wife inside the courthouse, in a room that also included the defendant, his mother, the defense counsel, two other inmates, and a police officer. The appellate court approved the introduction of the defendant's incriminating statement offered by the police officer who had overheard the defendant's communication directed toward his wife. Under such circumstances, the defendant could not have had any expectation in a confidential communication with his wife.[69]

3. Prosecution against one spouse for acts against the other spouse or their child

It would be a miscarriage of justice and inconsistent with the rationale for the marital privilege for the rule to prevent one spouse from testifying against the other when the spouse or their child[70] or a person living in their household was the victim of the aggressor spouse.[71] This exception applies in prosecutions for child abuse, bigamy, adultery[72] and in cases involving criminal injury to the person or property of a family member.

In a court ruling that demonstrated the exception concerning criminal acts committed against a household member, spouse, children, or their property, an Arkansas appellate court indicated that no husband–wife privilege existed where the defendant

---

67 United States v. Brock, 724 F.3d 817, 2013 U.S. LEXIS 15574 (2013).

68 *See* Bonds v. Leavitt, 647 F. Supp. 2d 541, 2009 U.S. Dist. LEXIS 72287 (2009).

69 State v. Fann, 2012 Tenn. Crim. App. LEXIS 542 (2012).

70 Jackson v. State, 2005 Tex. App. LEXIS 3631 (2005), *and see* TEX. R. EVID. 504 (2010). There is no spousal privilege where there is an accusation that the defendant committed a crime against the spouse or minor child or in furtherance of crime or fraud.

71 KY. R. EVID 504(c) (2013).

72 United States v. Taylor, 62 M.J. 636, 2006 CCA LEXIS 9 (2006).

privately communicated to his wife that he had killed his girlfriend, who had been residing with the defendant and his wife in their marital home.[73] The reviewing court cited the exception to the Arkansas statute that provided no husband–wife privilege of any sort existed were a crime has been charged against one spouse where the victim resided in the household of either spouse. In a different case but consistent with the crime or harm exception, a Minnesota appellate court, in a case where the wife had been accused of arson of property jointly owned by the couple, agreed with the prosecutor that no marital privilege existed because the prosecution involved allegations of arson destruction of the husband's property by the wife.[74]

The marital privilege not to testify has a recognized exception when the criminal victim is the child of a defendant or, in most cases, a witness spouse. In a Georgia case, the defendant, who was separated from his wife, went to her apartment, threw her phone out a window, and started to choke her in front of a minor child.[75] Georgia law provided that a husband and wife shall not be compelled to testify in any criminal proceeding for or against each other.[76] Georgia law also made it illegal to commit crimes in front of the children on the theory that it causes mental stress. Although the wife had a privilege not to testify against her husband, even though she had been a victim, the court forced her to testify concerning the fact that children were present during the family violence, which helped prove cruelty to children. According to the reviewing court, a charge of cruelty to children in the third degree under state law triggered the exception to the marital privilege for a crime against the person of a minor child.

Interestingly, some defendant spouses may prevent the adverse use of their spouse's voluntary statements when the statements have been offered to police prior to trial, where the wife was not a victim, but merely was a witness to her husband's criminal activity. In a case in which the wife made a tape-recorded statement to police that implicated her husband in criminal activity, the prosecution wanted to play the tape to the jury. Over the husband's objection and the wife's refusal to testify about the alleged assault with intent to commit murder of a third party, the trial court allowed the wife's evidence to be recounted via tape during the trial. The defendant raised a Sixth Amendment objection, contending that he was unable to cross-examine his wife at his trial because she refused to testify. The Supreme Court of the United States reversed the conviction and sent the case back to the trial court. The Court held that by playing the wife's tape-recorded statement at the trial, the defense was unable to cross-examine the defendant's wife, which violated the defendant's constitutional rights under the confrontation clause of the Sixth Amendment. According to the Court, the confrontation clause demanded that the testimonial evidence from the wife given to police had to be tested by the crucible of cross-examination. When testimonial evidence was at issue and where there was no prior opportunity to cross-examine the wife,

---

73 Collins v. State, 2013 Ark. App. 339, 2013 Ark. App. LEXIS 408 (2013).

74 State v. Andvik, 2013 Minn. App. Unpub. LEXIS 464 (2013).

75 Sherman v. State, 2010 Ga. App. 312, 690 S.E.2d 915; 2010 Ga. App. LEXIS 112 (2010).

76 GA. CODE.ANN. § 24-9-23 (2013).

the admission of her police-recorded statement constituted reversible error under the Sixth Amendment as applied to the states.[77]

4. Conspiracy

Where a husband and wife have jointly engaged in a criminal conspiracy, the defendant spouse cannot claim the marital testimonial privilege to prevent adverse testimony by the other spouse in a federal prosecution. In an Eighth Circuit case, the court allowed the testimony of a defendant's spouse in a prosecution for conspiracy to distribute methamphetamine. The defendant and his wife had allegedly engaged in drug trafficking, but the prosecution offered her a possibility of a reduced sentence in her personal drug prosecution if she testified against her husband. In permitting the defendant's wife to testify, the trial court was careful to prevent any confidential communications that had occurred between her and her husband from being introduced, but allowed the witness-wife to testify about their ongoing drug conspiracy and the defendant's actions, when it involved drug trafficking.[78]

Minnesota has taken a completely different route concerning marital privileges where spouses conspire with each other to commit criminal activities. According to Minnesota law,

> A husband cannot be examined for or against his wife without her consent, nor a wife for or against her husband without his consent, nor can either, during the marriage or afterwards, without the consent of the other, be examined as to any communication made by one to the other during the marriage.[79]

In offering an interpretation of the law and ordering a new trial, the state's top court held that a wife, over her husband's objection, should not be required to testify against her husband and, presumably, *vice versa*. In this case, the two spouses allegedly engaged in a conspiracy to commit a murder of a potential witness against them in a separate criminal proceeding. Minnesota requires the consent of the witness-spouse and of the defendant spouse prior to offering any testimony concerning matters adverse to a defendant spouse as long as the crime was not against the other, their children, or property.[80]

D. Duration of the Privilege

The Supreme Court opinion in *Trammel*[81] allowing the witness-spouse to decide whether to testify adversely makes the question of the duration of the marital

---

77 *See* Crawford v. Washington, 541 U.S. 36, 2004 U.S. LEXIS 1838 (2004).

78 United States v. Espino, 317 F.3d 788, 795, 796, 2003 U.S. App. LEXIS 261 (8th Cir. 2003).

79 MINN. STAT. § 595.02(a) (2013).

80 Minnesota v. Gianakos, 644 N.W.2d 409, 418, 419, 2002 Minn. LEXIS 350 (2002). The defendant was later convicted in a related federal prosecution involving the same conduct. *See* United States v. Gianakos, 404 F.3d 1065 (2005), which was affirmed, 415 F.3d 912 (8th Cir. 2005) and ultimately upheld, 560 F.3d 817, 2009 U.S. App. LEXIS 6391 (8th Cir. 2009).

81 Trammel v. United States, *supra* n.25.

testimonial privilege less important in federal trials. The majority of the states appear to have adopted the view that only the witness-spouse is a holder of the marital testimonial privilege. However, when the marital confidential communication privilege is implicated, the better view is that both marriage partners are holders and may assert the privilege in an appropriate setting. The confidential communication privilege exists during the marriage and continues for an indefinite time following the end of a marriage[82] and continues following divorce or the death of one of the marital partners and may be asserted by the holder's guardian, conservator, or personal representative.[83] In a Kentucky case in which the defendant had requested his then spouse to offer a false alibi that gave him cover in a murder case, the marital confidential communication privilege remained even after the parties were divorced, and could properly be asserted by the defendant at his trial for murder. In this particular case, the defendant's original request that his then spouse give a false alibi while protected under the marital communication privilege did not prevent the witness spouse from testifying concerning what she *actually* told the police and whether her statement to the police was true or false.[84]

Although in most American jurisdictions the marital privilege continues after divorce with respect to statements made in confidence between spouses during the existence of the marriage,[85] an argument could be made that the reason for the rule no longer applies after the divorce. When spouses are divorced at the time of the trial, allowing a willing former spouse to testify against the defendant spouse would not affect any present relationship. A commonsense approach allows a spouse or former spouse to testify about nonconfidential matters and also allows a defendant spouse to prohibit a spouse or former spouse from testifying against a defendant with respect to confidential matters discussed or communicated during the marriage.[86]

The protection offered by either spouse does not apply when the defendant is merely living with the person who is called as a witness[87] unless there is a recognized common law marriage.[88] In a state that considers marriages between first cousins "void," that state generally will recognize marriages between first cousins as valid where the marriage occurred in a state that approves of first-cousin marriages,[89] a prerequisite for permitting an assertion of a marital privilege.

---

82 *See*, for example, IOWA CODE § 622.9 (2013).

83 *See*, KY. R. EVID. 504(b) (2013).

84 Day v. Commonwealth, 2011 Ky. Unpub. LEXIS 95 (2011).

85 Commonwealth of Pennsylvania v. Weiss, 565 Pa. 504, 776 A.2d 958, 2001 Pa. LEXIS 1574 (2001), in which the court held that disclosure of confidential communications made during a marriage is prohibited even following the dissolution of the marriage.

86 Louisiana v. Nash, 821 So. 2d 678, 683, 684, 2002 La. App. LEXIS 1928 (2002).

87 Dermody v. State, 2002 Tex. App. LEXIS 6639 (2002); *see also* Arboleda v. Newland, Warden, 2003 U.S. Dist. LEXIS 513 (N.D. Cal. 2003).

88 *See* Bevan v. Bevan, 2006 Ohio 2775, 2006 Ohio App. LEXIS 2605 (2006), for the essentials of common law marriage.

89 Cook v. Cook, 209 Ariz. 487, 104 P.3d 857, 2005 Ariz. App. LEXIS 6 (2005).

§ 10.4 Communications Between Attorney and Client

A. Statement of the Rule

Confidential communications made in the course of professional employment between an attorney or one reasonably believed to be an attorney and his or her client may not be divulged by the attorney without the consent of the client. The privilege protects confidential communications between the client and the attorney that have been made to facilitate the delivery of legal advice and services. Absent a waiver of the privilege, neither the attorney nor the client can be compelled to testify regarding such communications. This privilege has been recognized as the oldest privilege relating to confidential communications, and its purpose is to encourage honest and full communication between attorneys and their clients, with the effect of promoting a broader public interest in the administration of justice.[90] The Supreme Court once noted that "the attorney–client privilege has been recognized in federal courts not only to protect professional advice given to those who can act upon it, but also the privilege gives information to a lawyer to enable him or her to give sound and informed advice."[91]

This privilege has limitations; it is not absolute and only extends to confidential communications between the two individuals when made for the purpose of seeking legal advice and counsel. The privilege is also applicable when a potential client initially consults an attorney, even though no professional relationship develops.

The privilege regarding confidential communications between client and attorney was recognized at common law and by state statutes,[92] but no federal constitutional provision created or established the attorney–client privilege.[93] As a general rule, the privilege applies only when statements are made to an attorney where there is an expectation that the information will remain confidential, but the privilege does not exist when a defendant spoke in such a loud voice that other people could hear him.[94] In situations involving representation in a criminal or civil matter, the privilege prevents the attorney from being required to be an adverse witness. In fact, in the absence of the attorney–client privilege, the Sixth Amendment right to counsel would become a hollow shell. Although the privilege has the effect of preventing significant evidence from being offered in the search for the truth, good public policy holds that

---

90 *See* Alomari v. Ohio Department of Public Safety, 2013 U.S. Dist. LEXIS 131270 (Ohio 2013).

91 Upjohn Co. v. United States, 449 U.S. 383, 101 S. Ct. 677, 66 L. Ed. 2d 584 (1981).

92 For example, see ARIZ. REV. STAT. § 13-4062 (2) (Arizona 2013). The statute reads: "A person shall not be examined as a witness in the following cases: (2). An attorney, without consent of the attorney's client, as to any communication made by the client to the attorney, or the attorney's advice given in the course of professional employment."

93 People v. Alexander, 49 Cal.4th 846, 888, 235 P.3d 873, 912, 113 Cal. Rptr. 3d 190, 236, 2010 Cal. LEXIS 6754 (2010).

94 People v. Urbano, 128 Cal. App. 4th 396, 26 Cal. Rptr. 3d 871, 2005 Cal. App. LEXIS 572 (2005).

the interests protected by the privilege outweigh the desirability of placing all facts known to the client's attorney before the judge or jury.

The protections extend only to communications and interactions with the attorney and not to facts that are merely known by the client. The client need not disclose what he or she told the attorney, but the client or the attorney might have to reveal facts known by the client that are not otherwise privileged. As a strong general rule, a party cannot conceal a fact under a claim of privilege merely by revealing or conveying it to his or her lawyer. In a Kansas case involving an alleged kidnapping, the defendant had a friend send a car rental contract to the defendant's attorney to help show that the car he drove on the day in question was different from the car's description given by the complaining witness. As part of discovery, the defense attorney shared the contract with the prosecutor prior to the kidnapping trial, at which the defendant was convicted. On appeal, the reviewing court rejected the defendant's claim of a violation of the attorney–client privilege [due to sharing the contract with the prosecutor] because the rental contract was never covered by the attorney–client privilege merely by being conveyed to the defense attorney.[95]

B. *Scope of the Privilege*

The privilege is subject to statutory regulations and limitations based on court decisions. While it is desirable to protect communications between an attorney and his or her client, unless the facts demonstrate that such a relationship exists, the rule should not apply. As a general proposition, the burden to prove that an attorney–client relationship has developed rests with the defendant, who must show that an attorney has been hired, that the defendant was the client, that confidential communications involving the seeking or offering of legal advice were made between the two, and that no unnecessary third parties were present. In addition to client–attorney communication, the privilege generally covers other communications made by the client with people who are necessary to support the attorney in the rendition of legal services. These others include office personnel such as secretaries, law clerks, and investigators hired by the attorney. The privilege may also include a client's communications with a medical doctor or accountant employed by his attorney when made for the purpose of enabling the attorney to comprehend the client's fact situation in order to give appropriate legal advice.[96]

A classic comment from a landmark case illuminating the scope and attributes of the privilege is found in *United States v. United Shoe Machinery Corp.*[97] In that case, the Court commented:

> The privilege applies only if (1) the asserted holder of the privilege is or sought to become a client; (2) the person to whom the communication was made (a) is a

---

95 State v. Young, 297 P.3d 1194, 2013 Kan. App. Unpub. LEXIS 270 (2013).

96 *In re* Grand Jury Subpoenas, 2003 U.S. Dist. LEXIS 9022 (S.D.N.Y. 2003).

97 89 F. Supp. 357 (D. Mass. 1950); *see also* United States v. Schmidt, 360 F. Supp. 339 (M.D. Pa. 1973), for a discussion of the scope of the privilege.

member of the bar of a court, or his subordinate and (b) in connection with this communication is acting as a lawyer; (3) the communication relates to a fact of which the attorney was informed (a) by his client (b) without the presence of strangers (c) for the purpose of securing primarily either (i) an opinion on law or (ii) legal services or (iii) assistance in some legal proceeding, and not (d) for the purpose of committing a crime or tort; and (4) the privilege has been (a) claimed and (b) not waived by the client.

After referring to previous cases, a federal court reiterated that the attorney–client privilege is intended to be construed within the narrowest possible limits consistent with the logic of its principle. In one case, a defendant had been arrested and released and his attorney moved to withdraw from the case. The client failed to appear at the withdrawal hearing and was indicted for failure to appear. Over his objection, his former attorney testified that she had forwarded notice of the hearing date to the defendant. The court ruled that she was not testifying in violation of the attorney–client privilege but was testifying concerning nonprivileged information.[98]

As generally recognized, the privilege applies only when the person to whom the communication was made was a member of the bar or was reasonably believed to be a member of the bar or to the attorney's subordinate or agent. Because the attorney–client privilege is intended to encourage full disclosure between the client and the attorney, the client's belief, even if reasonably mistaken, that the person with whom he or she is consulting is an attorney generally is considered to be sufficient to justify application of the privilege.[99]

Included within the attorney–client privilege are statements made to an attorney's essential employee by a person seeking legal services from the attorney. In most situations in which the presence of third parties is necessary, or at least useful to assisting attorney–client communication, the presence of those persons does not destroy the privilege.[100] These situations include interpreters, support staff, and others who are important to communicating properly with the client.

However, where individuals who are not necessary for an effective attorney–client relationship are present, generally, no attorney–client relationship will exist or be created. No attorney–client relationship developed when a potential client spoke to persons who were known to be attorneys, but under circumstances where they were highly unlikely to be hired by the client. In one case, a defendant who was in court awaiting a criminal proceeding in a different matter spoke with prosecutors in a casual manner concerning what he could expect for a sentence involving a drive-by shooting.[101] The defendant admitted to possession of a firearm and shooting once in the air, evidence that was later used against him at his criminal trial. Other court personnel and law enforcement agents were present in the courtroom within earshot of the

---

[98] State v. Kemper, 158 Ohio App. 3d 185, 187, 2004 Ohio 4050, 814 N.E.2d 540, 541, 2004 Ohio App. LEXIS 3677 (2004).

[99] CAL. EVID. CODE § 950(2014).

[100] Cavallaro v. United States, 284 F.3d 236, 246, 2002 U.S. App. LEXIS 5366 (1st Cir. 2002).

[101] State v. Rice, 2011 Wash. App. LEXIS 248 (2011).

defendant. The trial court and appellate courts rejected his contention that he developed an attorney–client privilege with the attorney prosecutors during his casual banter with them while the court was not in session. Additionally, other persons unessential to the attorney–client relationship were present, so the attorney prosecutors were permitted to testify against the defendant.

The primary purpose of the privilege is to protect communications between attorney and client. Documents that the attorney has requested that the client generate to assist the attorney in representing that client are often covered by the attorney–client privilege. In one case, where a client's daughter had alleged abuse by the client, the attorney requested that the client generate some materials to be given to the attorney. Before the materials could be given to the attorney, police officers executing a search warrant seized the materials and conveyed them to the prosecutor. These papers were held to be covered by the attorney–client privilege because their generation had come from the attorney as part of the representation of the client: the papers and notebooks were prepared and made to obtain legal advice, outline overall strategy, and prepare a criminal defense.[102] In addition, the privilege has been construed to include e-mails and online chat records generated by discussions between a client and his attorney even where the government has obtained its information through a search warrant served on Google directed at the defendant's online communications.[103] When made, the communication between lawyer and client did not involve any third parties who were able to discover or read or hear what the attorney and client discussed and the information remained covered by the attorney–client privilege.

Exchanges between a client and an accountant, under circumstances in which the accountant enables communication with the attorney by translating complex accounting concepts into information that could be understood by the attorney, will be covered by the attorney–client privilege to the extent that the accountant's information is provided in connection with legal representation.[104] However, when the federal government wanted information from a taxpayer's accountant in a case that had criminal overtones, the taxpayer could not shield information from the federal government by claiming an accountant–client privilege because the federal courts do not recognize an accountant–client privilege and the information would be privileged only if covered by an attorney–client privilege.[105]

Although the attorney–client privilege has existed for several hundred years and is recognized in all courts, not all the relationships are protected in all contexts. Some of the situations in which the confidential communication protection does not apply are discussed in the following sections.

---

102 State v. Perrow, 156 Wn. App. 322, 328–330, 231 P.3d 853, 855-856, 2010 Wash. App. LEXIS 1106 (2010).

103 United States v. Nunez, 2013 U.S. Dist. LEXIS 116145 (S.D. N.Y. 2013)

104 RCC, Inc. v. Cecchi, 2010 Md. Cir. Ct. LEXIS 8 (2010).

105 United States v. Pflueger, 2012 U.S. Dist LEXIS 90281 (D. Haw. 2012).

C. Exceptions

1. Identity of client

The identity of the attorney's client has not been considered a privileged matter because it usually reveals little concerning the nature of the relationship or what has been discussed between the two individuals. As a general rule, the mere existence of an attorney–client relationship and the identity of the client is not a privileged communication, unless the identity of the client is the last piece of evidence needed to initiate a criminal prosecution or the disclosure would reveal a confidential communication.[106] The privilege pertains to the subject matter and not the fact of the employment as attorney, and as it presupposes the relationship of attorney and client, it does not attach to the creation of that relationship. Either the client or the attorney may be compelled to testify regarding his or her employment as an attorney, the fee or how it was paid, and certain services performed for the client but not concerning the substantive matters of the advice given. For example, through a summons, a federal prosecutor wanted to discover the source of money that an attorney had placed in his attorney trust account to determine whether the attorney had paid the proper amount of taxes. The third-party bank records generated by deposits and withdrawals of client funds or of the attorney's funds were held not to constitute confidential communications of clients to the attorney; were not privileged; and had to be divulged pursuant to the summons.[107]

Absent a unique situation or special circumstances, client identity and fee information are not privileged because neither the fact of employment nor the amount of the fee paid has any bearing on the matters discussed between the client and the attorney. In one closed murder case, an investigative reporter for a newspaper requested that the trial court unseal court records so that the reporter could gain access to data concerning costs and fees paid to the indigent defendant's counsel. In approving the release of information by the trial judge, the reviewing court noted that the request involved court records and held that the identity of an attorney's indigent client and the fees charged for representation are not considered privileged information.[108] In an attorney's bankruptcy proceeding, under circumstances where the attorney had not kept clear records concerning what was owed, the trustee wanted information concerning fee arrangements, fees charged, and fees that had been paid from clients. The court rejected the attorney's contention that the records were privileged and the attorney was ordered to produce them or face sanctions by the court.[109]

Clarifying the rule for federal courts that the identity of the attorney's client is not subject to secrecy under the attorney–client privilege, as well commenting on the limitations on this exception, a federal district court noted that the identity of the client

---

106 Nester v. Jernigan, 908 So. 2d 145, 149, 2005 Miss. LEXIS 467 (2005).

107 Gjerde v. United States, 2012 U.S. Dist. LEXIS 114689 (E.D. Cal. 2012)

108 State v. Mendez, 157 Wn. App. 565, 585, 238 P.3d 517, 526, 2010 Wash. App. LEXIS 1878 (2010).

109 Hood v. Bennitt, 200 Bankr. LEXIS 3950 (2010).

and the amount of the fee or the form of payment of the fee are not usually considered privileged.[110] The attorney's time records and billing statements are not considered covered by the attorney–client privilege, at least where the records and statements do not contain detailed accounts of the services performed.[111] With respect to confidentiality of information received by an attorney practicing in Massachusetts, the requirements dictate that an attorney "should keep in confidence information relating to representation of a client except so far as disclosure is required or permitted by the Rules of Professional Conduct or other law."[112]

2. Advice in furtherance of crime

There is no privilege if either the attorney or the client has involved the other in a criminal endeavor or if the legal advice of the lawyer has been sought or obtained to advance any criminal plan.[113] According to California law, which is representative of most states, no attorney–client privilege comes into existence "if the services of the lawyer were sought or obtained to enable or aid anyone to commit or plan to commit a crime or a fraud."[114] Under the crime-fraud exception to the attorney–client privilege, Florida law provides that, "if a client consults an attorney for advice which will aid in the commission of a crime or in the planning of a future criminal activity, the attorney–client privilege does not exist."[115] In explaining this principle, one court noted, "Only when a client knowingly seeks legal counsel to further a continuing or future crime does the crime-fraud exception apply."[116] Under such circumstances, the attorney and the "client" may be forced to divulge any communication between them that relates to actively "covering up" an old crime or embarking on new criminal behavior. For example, the privilege does not exist under circumstances where a husband and his wife met with an attorney to have her will prepared in the presence of their attorney and a legal assistant; the will preparation was part of a plan to alleviate the defendant's financial problems by later pushing his well-insured wife over a cliff to her death.[117]

The interests of public justice require that no shield be interposed to protect a person who takes counsel on how he or she can safely commit a new crime. However, this exception to the attorney–client privilege does not apply when a person has committed a crime, prior to consulting an attorney concerning what the client's legal rights may be, and inquired how the crime may be lawfully adjusted. But the crime-fraud exception prevents a privilege from being recognized when a "client" who, having committed a

---

110 Estate of Reiserer v. United States, 229 F.R.D. 172, 179, 2005 U.S. Dist. LEXIS 17597 (W.D. Wash. 2005).

111 DiBella v. Hopkins, 403 F.3d 102, 120, 2005 U.S. App. LEXIS 5332 (2d Cir. 2005).

112 MASS. R. PROF. CONDUCT, ALM Sup. Jud. Ct. Rule 3:07(3) (2013).

113 For example, *see* CAL. EVID. CODE § 956 (2013).

114 CAL. EVID. CODE § 956.5 (2013).

115 Brugmann v. State, 117 So. 3d 39, 47, 2013 Fla. App. LEXIS 9297 (Fla. 2013).

116 United States v. Doe, 429 F.3d 450, 2005 U.S. App. LEXIS 25256 (3d Cir. 2005).

117 *See* People v. Richardson, 2010 Mich. App. LEXIS 2105 (2010), Leave to appeal denied, 489 Mich. 940, 2011 Mich. LEXIS 952 (2011)

crime, seeks advice on how he or she can initiate or complete a "cover-up" of the offense. For example, when a prospective client asked the attorney to hide a murder weapon or otherwise aid in the disposition of a murder weapon, such conduct falls far outside of the attorney–client privilege.[118] In a similar fashion, the act of a jailed inmate, who called an attorney on a monitored line and spoke about whether he should trust a fellow inmate to arrange for a hit man to murder witnesses and maybe kill the prosecutor, fell into the crime-fraud exception to the attorney–client privilege. The acts contemplated need not be successful; the mere communication of criminal plans takes the communication outside the protections of the attorney–client privilege.[119]

Although the crime-fraud exception to the attorney–client privilege may have a narrow construction, in order to prevail on an allegation of crime-fraud, the burden of proving the exception rests with the party wishing to invade the attorney–client relationship. Where the prosecution wants to invoke the crime-fraud exception, it must make a prima facie demonstration that (1) the client was committing a fraud or crime and that (2) the communications between the attorney and the client were made in furtherance of the alleged crime-fraud.[120] In a case in which the prosecution believed that the client was destroying e-mail communication necessary to a prosecution, the reviewing court found that the crime-fraud exception to the attorney–client privilege applied to the attorney's communication with his defendant regarding the types of e-mails the prosecution was seeking in a discovery request. The communication permitted the client to know which e-mails to destroy from the hard drive to keep them from being turned over to the government.[121]

3. Communications not intended to be confidential

While the attorney–client privilege protects confidentiality, there may be occasions between the client and the attorney made for the purpose of rendering legal services, where the communication is confidential under the attorney–client privilege only when it is not intended to be disclosed to any third party. A communication will remain confidential if an attorney or client needs to divulge information to an accountant, a private investigator, or similar person assisting the attorney in understanding or interpreting the facts. If the communication does not fall into these categories, it may not be considered confidential and the rationale for the attorney–client privilege does not exist. For example, where a defendant was supposed to make a court appearance while out on bail, and he called his attorney to explain that he would not be present at the hearing because of a migraine headache, such disclosure was not intended to be kept in confidence but to be communicated to the court and was not covered by the attorney–client confidential communication privilege.[122]

---

[118] Mixon v. State, 179 S.W.3d 233, 235, 2005 Tex. App. LEXIS 9079 (2005).

[119] United States v. Lentz, 419 F. Supp. 2d 820, 829 (E.D. Va. 2005).

[120] *In re* Grand Jury Proceedings, 445 F.3d 266, 274, 2006 U.S. App. LEXIS 10041 (2006).

[121] *Id.* at 275.

[122] State v. Freeman, 2009 Wash. App. LEXIS 1359 (2009).

Where the communication is not intended to be confidential, no privilege exists concerning that information. In a federal bank robbery prosecution, the defendant mailed a letter to his attorney that contained a second sealed letter to a family member. The attorney became suspicious and opened the letter to discover that it contained instructions to the family member to construct a false alibi for the defendant in order to obstruct justice. The defendant's attorney turned the letter over to the government and withdrew as his counsel. Following the defendant's conviction, he appealed contending that there was a violation of the attorney–client privilege when the original attorney divulged the letter to the government. The Court of Appeals for the Seventh Circuit rejected the defendant's contention and held that there was no violation of the attorney–client privilege because the defendant was neither soliciting legal advice nor providing information that his lawyer might use in constructing his defense.[123]

Where an unnecessary third party was present at the time the communications were made, the attorney–client privilege generally does not exist. Demonstrative of this principle is a Florida case in which a jailed defendant called his sister, who initiated a three-way conference call with his lawyer. At the beginning of the call from the jail, an audible warning automatically notified the defendant that the conversation might be monitored and recorded. At trial, the court admitted into evidence a number of taped telephone conversations initiated by the defendant on the monitored line. One of the taped conversations that included incriminating information occurred among the defendant, his attorney, and his sister on the three-way conference call. The appellate court upheld the admission of the authenticated tape of the incriminating conversation as well as other taped conversations on the theory that the attorney–client privilege only covers communications that are neither overheard by nor intended to be disclosed to third persons.[124]

4. Statements of the attorney relating to the client's mental or physical condition

The privilege does not extend to information received by the attorney that does not relate to communications, even though it was obtained while he or she was acting as an attorney. For example, testimony at the trial by the defendant's previous counsel from another proceeding concerning the defendant's mental competency may not violate the attorney–client privilege.[125] The court in *Clanton v. United States* stated:

> Here the attorney's testimony did not relate to private, confidential communications with his client during the time of communications prior to and at the entry of the pleas of guilty. He was qualified as a layman to express a view as to his client's mental competency.

---

123 United States v. Williams, 698 F.3d 374, 380, 2012 U.S. App. LEXIS 19030 (2012).

124 State v. Black, 920 So. 2d 668, 670, 2006 Fla. App. LEXIS 48 (2006), *reh'g denied*, 2006 Fla. App. LEXIS 3673 (2006).

125 Clanton v. United States, 488 F.2d 1069 (5th Cir. 1974).

However, an attorney has a duty of confidentiality to the client regardless of whether the information is available from other public or private sources. Such duty to preserve confidences extends beyond information that may be covered by a narrow interpretation of the attorney–client privilege.[126]

5. Posthumous revelation exception

Does a compelling need for important evidence in criminal cases outweigh the confidentiality claims involving the attorney–client privilege? This issue received national attention in the 1990s when Whitewater special prosecutor Kenneth Starr asked a federal grand jury to issue subpoenas for handwritten notes made by the attorney who represented Vincent W. Foster Jr., a deputy White House counsel for President Clinton who had committed suicide by the time the subpoenas were issued.

A federal grand jury issued subpoenas for the notes and litigation resulted when the district court refused to require that the attorney–client privilege be breached even following the client's death. The Court of Appeals for the District of Columbia circuit reversed and held that the notes could be viewed by the grand jury, effectively holding that, in this case, the attorney–client privilege did not survive the death of the client.

The United States Supreme Court granted certiorari to hear the case and ultimately disagreed with the reasoning of the Court of Appeals, holding that the petitioner's notes were protected by the attorney–client privilege. The Supreme Court admonished that the relevant case law demonstrated that the privilege survives the client's death in federal cases.[127] The Supreme Court emphasized that "knowing that communications will remain confidential even after death serves a weighty interest in encouraging a client to communicate fully and frankly with counsel; posthumous disclosure of such communication may be as feared as disclosure during the client's lifetime."[128] "Balancing *ex post* the importance of the information against client interests, even limited to criminal cases, introduces substantial uncertainty into the privilege's application, and therefore must be rejected."[129] Without a doubt, the attorney–client privilege survives the death of the client in federal courts.

Consistent with the concept of a durable attorney–client privilege, one Ohio case involved the disappearance and probable death of a nine-year-old girl, in which authorities believed that a deceased woman had communicated information to her attorney. Her attorney refused to divulge what the client had communicated to her, citing an Ohio law[130] that provided a durable attorney–client privilege after death. The privilege could only be waived by a surviving spouse or personal representative. Numerous state and federal courts heard aspects of the case,[131] but the principle that an attorney–client

---

126 Sealed Party v. Sealed Party, 2006 U.S. Dist. LEXIS 28392 (2006).

127 Swidler & Berlin v. United States, 524 U.S. 399, 1998 U.S. LEXIS 4214 (1998).

128 *Id.* Headnote.

129 *Id.*

130 OHIO REV. CODE § 2317.02 (2013).

131 Ohio v. Doe, 433 F.3d 502, 2006 U.S. App. LEXIS 481 (6th Cir. 2006).

privilege survives the death of the client-holder of the privilege remained intact. This principle is consistent with other jurisdictions in determining that the privilege survives the death of the holder and may be asserted or waived by the decedent's personal representative.[132] The interests served by extending the attorney–client privilege beyond the life of the holder allows living holders of the privilege security in the knowledge that embarrassing or personal information shared with an attorney will remain private under most situations.

D. Assertion and Waiver

The party who asserts the attorney–client privilege has the burden of establishing that the privilege existed in the first instance and that there has been no waiver.[133] A client may waive the attorney–client privilege by putting discussions with counsel at issue, by making an unprivileged disclosure, or by failing to object at the proper time.[134] Where a court recognizes the existence of the privilege, the privilege prohibits disclosure of information that has been confidentially disclosed to an attorney. The information remains personal to the client or successor who is the holder of the privilege and is the proper person to assert the privilege. However, if asked about matters covered by the privilege, a client's attorney has a duty to inform the court of the privilege and must not divulge the confidences.[135] However, if the client is neither present nor available during the proceeding in which the attorney's testimony has been ordered, the attorney must honor the client's wishes and should assert the privilege on behalf of the client but is not asserting on his or her own behalf.[136] Although the attorney–client privilege belongs to the client, the attorney has an obligation to assert it in the absence of the client. A convicted defendant generally waives the attorney–client privilege when he or she raises a claim of ineffective assistance of counsel in an appellate setting or in a petition for a writ of *habeas corpus*.

Recent decisions have reaffirmed the general rule that the waiver of the attorney–client privilege rests solely with the client, not the counsel. The attorney or agent may exercise that power only when acting with the client's authority.[137] A convicted defendant generally waives the attorney–client privilege when he or she raises a claim of ineffective assistance of counsel in an appellate setting or in a petition for a writ of habeas corpus. In an appeal, where the defendant essentially argued incompetency of trial counsel, such contention had the effect of waving the attorney–client privilege

---

132 *See* Estate of Putnam v. State, 2009 Conn. Super. LEXIS 3519 (2009).

133 United States v. Ary, 2005 U.S. Dist. LEXIS 21958 (D. Kan. 2005).

134 United States v. Brock, 724 F.3d 817, 821, 2013 U.S. App. LEXIS 15574 (7th Cir. 2013).

135 For example, *see* CAL. EVID. CODE § 951 (2013) and HLC Properties, Ltd. v. Superior Court, 35 Cal. 4th 54, 62, 105 P.3d 560, 565, 2005 Cal. LEXIS 1607 (2005), where the court held that "the attorney–client privilege belongs only to the client, whether the client is a natural person, an unincorporated organization, or some other entity."

136 Martin Marietta v. West Virginia, 227 F.R.D. 382, 2005 U.S. Dist. LEXIS 8379 (2005).

137 State v. Davis, 116 N.J. 341, 561 A.2d 1082 (1989).

and allowing the defendant's former attorney to explain to the court how the plea bargain had been thoroughly reviewed by the attorney and explained to the defendant, and that the defendant fully understood its terms prior to accepting the plea bargain. By asserting that his counsel had not properly explained the government's plea offer, the defendant had waived the attorney–client privilege.[138]

In a Louisiana case, a defendant alleged that his counsel had been incompetent in advising him to waive a trial by jury and to plead guilty.[139] Over the defendant's objection based on the attorney–client privilege, the reviewing court approved allowing the defendant's attorney to testify about the attorney's conversation with the client concerning whether the client should plead guilty or go to trial. By alleging ineffective representation by his counsel, the defendant waived any attorney–client privilege relating to that claim, but the defendant retained the privilege concerning all other subjects covered by the attorney–client privilege.

In addition to waiver by initiating an appeal, an individual may waive the attorney–client privilege by signing a written waiver that allows his or her attorney to speak openly about otherwise confidential information. In a Massachusetts case, a defendant successfully argued for a new trial based on new evidence that his uncle gave considering the uncle's guilt of homicides and on information that the uncle's attorney offered to authorities following the waiver of his attorney–client privilege.[140]

Once a client has effectively waived the attorney–client privilege, the attorney may be compelled to testify regarding matters that were within the scope of the privilege, because the privilege was for the client's benefit, and once the privilege has been waived, it ceases to exist.[141] However, an attorney, while testifying in the absence of a client's consent, may not disclose any privileged communication made to the client or received by the attorney.[142]

Unless a holder of the attorney–client privilege makes a positive effort to assert or claim the privilege, the benefits will be lost. Under the general rule, a failure to object constitutes waiver. For a holder of the privilege to avoid waiver, a claim of privilege must be promptly raised or the court will rule that the privilege has been waived. A holder waives the privilege when he or she places a confidential communication at issue that goes directly to a claim or defense, whether at trial or upon appeal.[143]

Voluntary testimony or disclosure by the client without compulsion, or a public communication by the attorney, that discloses a portion of the confidential communication, constitutes a waiver as to the remainder of the particular communication. A holder waives the privilege by voluntarily divulging privileged information to a third party,[144] whether in court or otherwise. If a client alleges that his or her attorney's

---

[138] United States v. Cunningham, 467 F. App'x 219 (4th. Cir. 2012).

[139] State v. Dominquez, 2010 La. App. LEXIS 1662 (2010).

[140] Commonwealth v. Fickling, 27 Mass. L. Rep. 51, 2010 Mass. Super. LEXIS 68 (2010).

[141] See OHIO REV. CODE § 2317.02 (2013).

[142] Arizona ex rel. Thomas v. Schneider, 130 P.3d 991, 994, 2006 Ariz. App. LEXIS 44 (2006).

[143] Jackson v. City of Chicago, 2005 U.S. Dist. LEXIS 32538 (N. D. Ill. 2005).

[144] United States v. Lentz, 419 F. Supp. 2d 820, 827, 2005 U.S. Dist. LEXIS 41084 (E.D. Va. 2005).

representation in a criminal case constituted ineffective assistance of counsel, the client has waived the attorney–client privilege to the extent of the allegation.[145]

§ 10.5 Communications Between Physician and Patient

A. Statement of the Rule

The general purpose of the physician–patient privilege is to ensure that open and complete communication between the doctor and patient results in the best medical outcome by encouraging patients to give full disclosure of their problems, symptoms, and conditions. The zone of privacy prevents third-party disclosures of information that might prove embarrassing or otherwise cause anguish to the patient. This privilege protects the doctor–patient relationship and ensures that the communications between the two remain confidential because, in the absence of this privilege, some individuals would avoid medical care or be less than honest with their physicians. Like other privileges, this privilege has the effect of shielding relevant evidence from the court in an effort to protect the doctor–patient relationship, and because of this fact, the statutes establishing the physician–patient privilege are narrowly construed.[146] The physician–patient privilege did not exist at common law but in jurisdictions where it now exists, it has been created by statute[147] or court decision.[148] Therefore, courts may interpret legislative intent of the doctor–patient privilege statutes but are not free to completely ignore legislative intent.[149] Although the text of the Federal Rules of Evidence have not provided for specific privileges, federal courts are permitted to define new privileges by interpreting federal common law principles in light of reason and experience.[150] Historically, federal common law did not recognize a privilege between patients and physicians, and presently, there is no federal statutory doctor–patient privilege.[151] However, federal court decisions have recognized a limited federal doctor–psychotherapist confidential communication privilege that protects the confidences of a patient and his or her psychotherapist or licensed clinical social worker pursuant to Federal Rule of Evidence 501. The case involved a police officer who, in the line of duty, had killed a participant in a fight and had subsequently sought mental health assistance to deal with job-related stress. The Committee Notes to Rule 501 of the Federal

---

145 LeCroy v. Secretary, Florida Dept. of Corrections, 421 F.3d 1237, 1253, 2005 U.S. App. LEXIS 18570 (11th Cir. 2005), n.11.

146 People v. Doers, 2010 Mich. App. LEXIS 1197 (2010).

147 *See*, MICH. COMP. LAWS SERV. § 600.2157 Physician–patient privilege; waiver (2013).

148 Jaffee v. Richmond, 518 U.S. 1, 15, 1996 U.S. LEXIS 3879 (1996). The Supreme Court recognized that a psychotherapist–patient privilege existed under Rule 501 for federal courts.

149 D'Amico v. Delliquardri, 114 Ohio App. 3d 579, 683 N.E.2d 814 (1996). *See also* State v. Hardin, 569 N.W.2d 517 (Iowa 1997).

150 *See* FED. R. EVID. 501, Notes of the Committee.

151 Aguilar v. Immigration and Customs Enforcement Division, 2009 U.S. Dist. LEXIS 99815 (S.D.N.Y. 2009).

Rules of Evidence contemplated that federal courts would define new testimonial privileges consistent with developing federal common law as new experiences and needs arose. In recognizing the new privilege, the Court observed that all fifty states had previously implemented laws to protect some sort of psychotherapist–patient privilege and that the need and rationale for such a privilege was the same as for the marital and attorney–client privileges.[152]

Even in the absence of an evidentiary privilege that specifically covers communications between a doctor and a patient, the Supreme Court has held that confidential communications between a licensed psychotherapist and patients in the course of diagnosis or treatment are protected from compelled disclosure under Federal Rule of Evidence 501.[153] As the Supreme Court noted, "the physician must know all that a patient can articulate in order to identify and to treat disease; barriers to full disclosure would impair diagnosis and treatment."[154]

While the statutes of the various states inconsistently define which professional groups are covered by the physician–patient privilege, most modern statutes include psychologists and psychotherapists. Some statutes specifically include marriage counselors and social workers. Because state laws differ significantly, it is essential that the prosecutor or law enforcement official consults the statutes and analyzes the cases interpreting the statutes. Of importance to prosecutors is the concept that, where the patient's conduct creates an express or implied waiver, the medical information will usually be admissible because it is no longer privileged.[155] In addition, some states do not recognize any doctor–patient privilege with the result that medical information may be admitted into criminal trials.[156] If the relationship is not specifically stated in the statute or covered by case law interpretation, the privilege will not be recognized.

California has a statute that provides that a patient has a privilege to refuse to disclose, and to prevent others from disclosing, any confidential communication made to a physician, as long as the privilege is claimed by the patient privilege holder or a person authorized by the holder to make such a claim. A person who was a physician[157] at the time of the confidential communication may claim the privilege only during the life of the patient, unless released by the patient.[158]

---

152 *See* Jaffee v. Richmond, 518 U.S. 1, 116 S. Ct. 1923 (1996).

153 *See* United States v. Lawrence et al., 2013 U.S. Dist. LEXIS 77384 (2013).

154 Trammel v. United States, 445 U.S. 40, 51, 1980 U.S. LEXIS 84 (1980).

155 State v. Bergmann, 2009 Iowa App. LEXIS 54 (Iowa 2009). *See* case in Part II.

156 Veasley v. State, 275 Ga. 516, 518, 2002 Ga. LEXIS 852 (2002), Cert. denied, 538 U.S. 1002, 2003 U.S. LEXIS 3309 (2003). *See also* Alsip, et al. v. Johnson City Med. Ctr., 197 S.W.3d 722, 725, 2006 Tenn. LEXIS 557 (2006). Tennessee does not recognize a doctor–patient privilege.

157 A physician for purposes of California law is defined as a "person authorized, or reasonably believed by the patient to be authorized, to practice medicine in any state or nation." *See* CAL. EVID. CODE § 990 (2013).

158 CAL. EVID. CODE § 994 (c) (2013). The California Code also recognizes a patient–physician privilege between the patient and a medical or podiatry corporation, partnership, or limited liability company.

At first impression, the California provision appears to offer complete coverage to confidential medical communications. However, § 998 of the California Evidence Code provides that "there is no privilege under this article in a criminal proceeding" for the doctor–patient privilege.[159] Similarly, there is no application of the medical privilege when the services of a physician were sought to enable a person to plan or to commit a crime or a tort (civil wrong) or to escape detection or apprehension following the commission of either one.[160] When medical information that might prove embarrassing is weighed against the interests of justice and potential loss of freedom to a defendant, the confidential medical evidence will be admitted as a matter of public policy as expressed in California law.

In contrast, the California psychotherapist–patient privilege law covers many more counselors by including physicians, psychiatrists, psychologists, licensed clinical social workers, school psychologists, licensed marriage and family therapists, and numerous other support workers in the mental health and family counseling fields.[161] Persons who are considered holders of this privilege include the patient, a patient's guardian or conservator, and the personal representative of the patient in cases where the patient is deceased. In a slightly more expansive manner, Mississippi permits greater protection of the patient–medical provider relationships because it holds that medical and even pharmacological records are privileged in civil and criminal proceedings and cannot be divulged without the patient's consent.[162]

B. *Scope of the Privilege*

The privilege exists for the protection of the patient, not the physician, and for that reason the patient is considered the holder of the privilege and may assert this privilege.[163] However, although not a holder, a physician called to testify should alert the court that a medical privilege exists. The rationale for the rule is to shield the patient from disclosures that might be undesirable. There is no intent to protect third persons or other family members, although others may benefit incidentally. For the privilege to apply, the physician–patient relationship must have existed at the time that the physician acquired the information that he or she is called upon to disclose. Interestingly, the federal courts do not recognize a physician–patient privilege, but federal courts do recognize a psychotherapist–patient privilege under federal common law.[164]

Utah's provision concerning the physician–patient privilege is typical of rules followed in other jurisdictions.[165] A doctor or physician is defined as any person who is

159 CAL. EVID. CODE § 998 (2014).
160 CAL. EVID. CODE § 997 (2014).
161 CAL. EVID. CODE § 1010 (2014).
162 Cox v. Mississippi, 2003 Miss. LEXIS 103 (2003).
163 State v. Miles, 211 Ariz. 475; 123 P.3d 669, 673, 2005 Ariz. App. LEXIS 161 (2005).
164 Doe v. Oberweis Dairy, 2004 U.S. Dist. LEXIS 9204 (D. Ill. 2004) and Sterner v. DEA, 2005 U.S. Dist. LEXIS 18467 (2005).
165 UTAH R. EVID. 506 (2013).

licensed or reasonably believed by the patient to be licensed to practice medicine in any state. The patient is defined as a person who consults a physician, was examined, or was interviewed by a physician or a mental health therapist. In order to be privileged, the information must have been communicated in confidence and for the purpose of diagnosing or treating a patient, include information gathered by a physical examination of the patient, and cover information obtained from guardians or members of the patient's family who are giving the information because it is reasonably necessary for delivery of medical services. The Utah medical privilege endures so long as the patient is alive or until the patient waives the privilege. In Utah, the privilege is assertable in either a civil or criminal proceeding; however, in some states, it may be asserted only in civil cases. As for exceptions under Utah law, no privilege exists concerning any communication relevant to an issue of physical, mental, or emotional condition of the patient in any court proceeding or otherwise in which the condition medically is an element of any claim or defense. In addition, if the mental health therapist believes that a patient needs to be hospitalized, communications relevant to that issue are not considered privileged. Finally, communications made in the course of a court-ordered examination of a patient, whether physical, mental, or emotional, produce no physician–patient privilege.

Florida takes a blanket approach and holds that no provision exists under Florida law that would allow any breaching of the confidentiality accorded to doctor–patient confidences. In one case, a defendant charged with attempted murder wanted to obtain all the victim's psychiatric records from her psychiatrist, which he believed were necessary to assist in his defense. The court of appeals held that none of the records needed to be disclosed because Florida law failed to contain any statutory authority for revealing the privileged communication and did not offer any legal standard for determining whether or when to reveal confidential communications with a psychiatrist. According to the court of appeals, "there is neither an Evidence Code provision, nor an applicable constitutional principle, which allows the invasion of the victim's privileged communications with her psychotherapist."[166] Confidentiality under these circumstances may encourage people who need psychological assistance to contact medical resources, but it would also foreclose the discovery of important evidence that might be necessary to prevent a miscarriage of justice.

California distinguishes between the doctor–patient privilege, which may be asserted only in civil actions, and the psychotherapist–patient privilege, which sweeps with a much broader stroke and may be asserted in both civil and criminal cases. Under California law, a patient has the privilege to refuse to reveal (and to prevent the doctor from revealing) a confidential communication between the psychotherapist and the patient.[167] Under some circumstances, the psychotherapist–patient privilege may not exist when the psychotherapist reasonably believes that the patient is in such an

---

[166] Florida v. Farmiglietti, 817 So. 2d 901, 907, 908, 2002 Fla. App. LEXIS 6199 (2002).

[167] CAL. EVID. CODE § 1014 (2013). The psychotherapist is considered a holder of the privilege unless released by the patient.

emotional state as to be dangerous to self or others, and, in such cases, the psychotherapist may have a duty to warn or disclose when he or she reasonably believes that the patient poses a danger to another person. As the California statute states, "There is no privilege under this article if the psychotherapist has reasonable cause to believe that the patient is in such mental or emotional condition as to be dangerous to himself or to the person or property of another and that disclosure of the communication is necessary to prevent the threatened danger."[168] Because there would be no privilege under these circumstances, appropriate action, such as notifying police and alerting possible victims, must be initiated if the psychotherapist becomes convinced during the course of treatment that the patient is a menace to himself or others.

C. Exceptions

While many states have created the doctor–patient privilege by statute, the exceptions that have been found necessary in order to obtain information required by the public interest or to avoid fraud are so numerous that the value of the privilege has been reduced in many jurisdictions.[169] In Ohio, among the exceptions from privileged communication under the doctor–patient relationship, the following must be reported to law enforcement authorities and have been statutorily excluded from the doctor–patient privilege: injuries that may cause death, second- or third-degree burn injuries, burn injuries to the respiratory tract, gun and knife wounds, and situations that reasonably are believed to have been caused by domestic violence.[170]

When a physician or other medical provider is required by Ohio law to report to a law enforcement officer evidence of gunshot wounds, deadly weapon wounds, severe burns, or domestic violence, the physician may testify, without violating the physician–patient privilege or other medical privilege. The doctor may convey to law enforcement officials details concerning the condition of the wounded person, the victim's personal information, and the description of the nature and location of such wound and how it occurred. Knowledge in these areas may be obtained by examination, observation, and treatment of the victim.[171]

California takes a different approach and statutorily excludes any assertion of the medical privilege in cases in which the patient, or someone claiming through the patient, placed the patient's condition is at issue.[172] The statutory exclusion also

---

168 CAL. EVID. CODE § 1024 (2013).

169 *See* OHIO REV. CODE ANN. § 2921.22 (2013). All doctors, all professional medical caregivers, and most other people have duties to report the commission of known felonies and cases of serious harms to persons to law enforcement officials even where a medical privilege might otherwise exist.

170 *Id.*

171 *See* OHIO REV. CODE ANN. § 2151.421 (2013). Duty to report child abuse or neglect; investigation and follow-up procedures. *See also* OHIO REV. CODE ANN. § 2317.02 (2013), which may place limitations on duties to report.

172 CAL. EVID. CODE § 1016 (2014).

prevents the use of medical privileges in any criminal proceeding,[173] will contests and related legal proceedings, malpractice cases, and disciplinary hearings as well as in some other limited situations. Thus, the exceptions to the medical privilege leave many situations not covered by any medical privilege.[174] Even when covered by the fairly broad psychotherapist–patient privilege, California recognizes an exception to its psychotherapist–patient privilege if the psychotherapist has reasonable cause to believe that the patient is in such a mental or emotional condition as to be dangerous to himself or herself or to the person or property of another.[175] In that event, the psychotherapist has a duty to disclose the communication when it is necessary to prevent the danger. In order for this exception to apply, there must be more than just a hunch that an individual may be dangerous; without proper proof, the psychotherapist–patient privilege remains. A California appellate court reversed an adjudication that ruled a defendant was a sexually violent predator when nothing in the records of the psychotherapist indicated anything other than mental retardation and no predilection to molest small children.[176] According to the reviewing court, the psychotherapist–patient privilege is to be liberally construed in favor of the patient and the exceptions should apply only when there is clear evidence that the patient met the "dangerous patient" exception to the California psychotherapist–patient privilege.

Florida has a statute covering the psychotherapist–patient privilege that may be asserted by the patient, patient's attorney, patient's guardian, or the psychotherapist on behalf of the patient.[177] Florida law includes within the definition of psychotherapist any medical doctor or a person reasonably believed to be a medical doctor, a person who is licensed or certified as a psychologist or engaged primarily in the diagnosis and treatment of the mental or emotional condition, a person certified as a clinical social worker, marriage and family therapist, or mental health counselor. However, Florida law excludes from privilege any communication related to proceedings to compel hospitalization of a patient for mental illness, communications made during a court-ordered examination of the mental or emotional condition of the patient, and communications related to mental or emotional conditions in proceedings in which the patient is relied upon or has asserted a condition as an element of a claim or defense to a criminal or civil matter. An additional exception to the Florida doctor–patient/patient–psychotherapist privilege occurs when the professional person receives information from the client/patient concerning information involving the perpetrator or alleged perpetrator of known or suspected child abuse, abandonment, or neglect, regardless of the source of the information.[178] These exceptions are typical of many jurisdictions that place a higher value on protecting children than encouraging persons to seek medical or emotional treatment in which they can be completely open with the medical professional.

---

173 CAL. EVID. CODE § 998 (2014).
174 CAL. EVID. CODE § 1016 (2014).
175 *See* CAL. EVID. CODE § 1024 (2013).
176 People v. Gonzales, 2011 Cal. App. LEXIS 91 (2011).
177 FLA. STAT. § 90.503 (2013).
178 FLA. STAT. § 39.204 (2013).

The privilege may be justified only when disclosures are made in confidence. Therefore, when the communication is made in the presence of unnecessary third persons, some jurisdictions hold that the privilege is waived, while others do not. For example, when the crime victim allowed her sister to be present in the emergency room along with a police officer, no doctor–patient privilege existed due to the presence of nonessential persons who overheard the medical information being divulged.[179] In a habeas corpus case, a federal appellate court accepted a state court determination that no physician–patient privilege existed where a patient made incriminating statements to hospital nurses in the presence of police officers. The Oklahoma statute covered nurses and other healthcare providers, but not when police officers, who were not necessary to diagnosis and treatment, were present.[180] New York holds an opposite position and upholds the privilege under similar circumstances if the police officer must be present according to law.[181]

While statements made by a patient to a psychologist in the presence of unnecessary third persons are normally outside the protection of the physician–patient privilege, some jurisdictions permit the presence of third parties whose presence may be necessary or useful to diagnosis and issue treatment. Jurisdictions holding this rationale generally consider that the presence of statutorily listed third parties does not destroy a doctor/psychotherapist–patient privilege. For example, Oklahoma considers a communication to a doctor or psychotherapist confidential if it is not intended to be disclosed to third persons, but the presence of other "persons reasonably necessary for the transmission of the communication, or persons who are participating in the diagnosis and treatment under the direction of the physician or psychotherapist, including members of the patient's family,"[182] does not destroy or create an exception to the confidentiality of the communication.

D. Assertion and Waiver

The psychotherapist–patient privilege and, in some jurisdictions, the psychologist–patient privilege may receive greater protection and be more difficult to defeat than the traditional physician–patient privilege. However, in any of the medically based privileges, the privilege belongs to the patient and a physician may be forced to testify if the patient has waived the privilege or if third parties are involved in its knowledge.[183] State statutes creating a physician–patient privilege usually provide that if the patient

179 State v. Gillespie, 710 N.W.2d 289, 298, 2006 Minn. App. LEXIS 24 (2006).

180 Freeman v. Grubbs, 134 Fed. Appx. 233, 2005 U.S. App. LEXIS 10499 (10th Cir. 2005).

181 People v. Jaffarian, 799 N.Y.S.2d 733, 735, 2005 N.Y. Misc. LEXIS 1640 (2005).

182 *See* OKLA. STAT. tit. 12 § 2503(4) (2013).

183 State v. Cote, 2010 N.J. Super. Unpub. LEXIS 1085 (May 21, 2010); *see also* OHIO REV. CODE ANN. § 2317.02(B)(1) (2013). When the patient is clearly the holder of the privilege, the physician or dentist may be compelled to testify following a patient or guardian waiver or in criminal actions against the medical provider.

voluntarily testifies about privileged matters, the physician may be compelled to testify on the same subject. In civil actions, the physician also may be compelled to testify by express consent of his or her patient or, if the patient is deceased, by the express consent of the surviving spouse, executor, or administrator of the estate of the deceased patient.[184] However, the physician may claim the privilege covering his or her patients' communications in the absence of evidence that the patient has waived the privilege, but a defendant cannot assert the physician–patient privilege on behalf of a crime victim to keep the victim's injuries confidential.[185]

In many jurisdictions, a defendant waives any claim of physician–patient confidentiality or privilege by placing his or her mental condition at issue by offering a not guilty plea by reason of insanity, and a defendant waives any privilege concerning communications made to a doctor or psychologist relevant to the mental condition relevant to trial issues or related to treatment, any hearing on mental condition, or sentencing hearing.[186] Waiver may occur if the defense plans to introduce part of a doctor's report, and, as part of discovery, turns the report over to the prosecution. In a case involving attempted murder, the appellate court held that the trial court correctly ruled that the defendant waived his doctor–patient privilege because his public defender voluntarily turned over the toxicology reports to the prosecution, which bound the defendant.[187]

§ 10.6 Communications to Clergy

A. Statement of the Rule

Statements to clergy are presently covered by privilege; however, the common law, as it came to the American colonies, did not recognize the concept of religious privilege by virtue of historical accidents. The privilege was recognized from the time of the Norman conquest of England in 1066 until King Henry VIII instituted the Protestant Reformation, which created official hostility to the Roman Catholic Church. Given that the privilege sprang from the teachings of the church, official policy dictated a refusal to recognize the religious privilege. Thus, at the time of the American Revolution and acceptance of British common law as the basis for American law, there was no priest–penitent or religious confessor privilege recognized by the common law.[188] As a result, penitential communications must be protected by statutory enactment because they could not be considered as part of the common law. At the present time, all 50 states have privilege statutes that cover confidential communications between religious

---

184 OHIO REV. CODE ANN. § 2317.02(B)(1)(a) and (b) (2013).

185 State v. Sua, 2010 Haw. App. LEXIS 205 (2010).

186 *See*, for example, COLO. REV. STAT. § 16-8-103.6 (2013).

187 State v. Moses, 107 Haw. 282, 285, 112 P.3d 768, 772, 2005 Haw. App. LEXIS 174 (2005).

188 See State v. J.G., 201 N.J. 369, 378, 990 A.2d 1122 1127, 2010 N.J. LEXIS 381 (2010).

leaders and followers[189] and have attempted to be inclusive in order to cover genuine religions and faiths, often giving the religious leader status as a holder of the privilege. Representative of religious privilege statutes is a Colorado law that states that "[a] clergy member, minister, priest, or rabbi shall not be examined without both his or her consent and also the consent of the person making the confidential communication as to any confidential communication made to him or her in his or her professional capacity in the course of discipline expected by the religious body to which he or she belongs."[190] California defines a clergy member to mean a "priest, minister, religious practitioner, or similar functionary of a church or of a religious denomination or religious organization"[191] and provides that a "penitent, whether or not a party, has a privilege to refuse to disclose, and to prevent another from disclosing, a penitential communication if he or she claims the privilege."[192]

In a New Jersey case, the state's supreme court held that under state law, the priest–penitent privilege could be invoked by either the cleric or the penitent and that neither one alone could waive it, except for communications involving future crimes.[193] In order to qualify under this religious privilege, they offered a three-part test as a way of evaluating whether a statutory religious privilege existed in a particular context: "Would an objectively reasonable penitent, under the totality of the circumstances, believe that a communication was secret, that is, made in confidence to a cleric in that cleric's professional character or role as spiritual advisor?"[194] The communication must have been in confidence to a cleric and in the cleric's role as a spiritual adviser. In this New Jersey case, there had been allegations that the defendant had previously molested his two daughters, and his wife wanted the pastor to speak with the father. The pastor contacted the defendant in an effort to protect the children from further abuse; the defendant, in a manner of speaking, admitted to the abuse and spoke with the pastor one additional time concerning the sexual abuse. Although the men spoke privately, the defendant never requested that the conversation remain confidential; the defendant did not belong to the church, although his wife was a member. Given that the intermediate appeals court overruled the original trial court determination that the priest–penitent privilege applied, the New Jersey Supreme Court sent the case back to the trial court for a determination under the test noted previously. In reconsideration, the trial court must determine whether an objective penitent in the defendant's position would reasonably have believed that communication would be confidential, that they met under circumstances of privacy, and that the defendant would have expected the conversation would remain confidential.

---

189 *See* 73 N.Y.U. L. REV. 225, 231 (1998), n.39, noting state statutes that provide for the privilege.

190 COLO. REV. STAT. 13-90-107 (VI) (c) (2013).

191 CAL. EVID. CODE § 1030 (2013).

192 *Id.* § 1033.

193 State v. J.G., 201 N.J. 369, 990 A.2d 1122, 2010 N.J. LEXIS 381 (2010).

194 *Id.* 384, 1131.

Although the New Jersey legislature attempted to illuminate the cleric–penitent privilege by statute and give it clarity, other state statutes and judicial decisions covering confidential communications made to and from clergy or similar religious advisors are rather varied and operate differently in their respective jurisdictions. For example, in Louisiana, the code is very comprehensive; it not only recognizes religious privileges but also includes definitions. It provides:

> A person has a privilege to refuse to disclose and to prevent another person from disclosing a confidential communication by the person to a clergyman in his professional character as spiritual adviser.[195]

The Louisiana legislature included definitions within the statutory formulation covering the priest–penitent privilege. The legislature noted that "A 'clergyman' is a minister, priest, rabbi, Christian Science practitioner, or other similar functionary of a religious organization or an individual believed so to be by the person consulting him."[196] "A communication is 'confidential' if it is made privately and not intended for further disclosure except to other persons present in furtherance of the purpose of the communication."[197] Under this statute, the privilege may be claimed by the person seeking spiritual advice, and/or legal representative, and may be claimed on behalf of the holder by the religious advisor, even after the original holder's death.[198]

The Michigan statute covering clergy–penitent communication offers strong protection to persons seeking religious assistance for conduct that could be characterized as criminal.[199] In a sexual molestation case, where the defendant had admitted during counseling to his minister that he had sexually assaulted his nine-year-old cousin, the cleric–congregant privilege prevented the pastor from testifying against the parishioner who had shared his criminal story. According to the reviewing court, the defendant's statements to his pastor fell within the statutory scope of privileged confidential communication because they were necessary for the pastor to serve in his professional character and had to be excluded from use at a criminal trial.[200]

The Federal Rules of Evidence only indirectly address privileges in federal causes of action. Rule 501, in part, notes that "the privilege of a witness, person, government, State, or political subdivision thereof shall be governed by the principles of the common law as they may be interpreted by the courts of the United States in the light of reason and experience." Only the Court of Appeals for the Third Circuit has explicitly

---

195 LA. CODE Evid. art. 511(B) (2013).

196 *Id.* Art. 511(A)(1).

197 *Id.* Art. 511(A)(2).

198 *Id.* Art. 511(C).

199 MICH. COMP. LAWS. SERV. § 767.5a (2013). The statute provides that "[A]ny communications between . . . members of the clergy and the members of their respective churches, . . . are hereby declared to be privileged and confidential when those communications were necessary to enable . . . members of the clergy . . . to serve as such . . . member of the clergy.

200 People v. Bragg, 296 Mich. App. 433, 462, 2010 Mich. App. LEXIS 874 (2012).

recognized a federal priest–penitent privilege,[201] although other federal courts at times have implicitly recognized the privilege. The Court of Appeals determined that a federal clergy–communicant privilege exists; this privilege protects the disclosure of communications from a communicant to a member of the clergy in his or her spiritual or professional capacity by persons who seek spiritual counseling and who reasonably expect that their words will be kept in confidence.[202]

Similarly, Washington's law regulating religious privileges states that "[a] member of the clergy, a Christian Science practitioner listed in the *Christian Science Journal*, or a priest shall not, without the consent of a person making the confession or sacred confidence, be examined as to any confession or sacred confidence made to him or her in his or her professional character, in the course of discipline enjoined by the church to which he or she belongs."[203] In a case in which a stepdaughter sought to obtain a church's report of disciplinary action against her sexually abusive stepfather in a tort action against the church and the stepfather, the appellate court upheld the defendant's assertion of the clergy–penitent privilege. The reviewing court noted that the church's disciplinary proceeding against the stepfather was conducted under church doctrine and the disciplinary counsel members were ordained clergy.[204]

B. *Scope of the Privilege*

In order for a communication of a church member to a clergy member to be privileged, "communication [must be] made in confidence to a cleric in the cleric's professional character, or as a spiritual advisor in the course of the discipline or practice of the religious body to which the cleric belongs or of the religion which the cleric professes."[205] As used in the statute, the term "cleric" includes a priest, rabbi, minister, or other person or practitioner authorized to perform similar functions of any religion.[206] The privilege generally applies to a voluntary confession, as well as to one made under a mandate of the church, and to observations as well as to communications. However, where the religious practice of a particular church permitted the preacher to report illegality to police and the confessor was aware of the church policy, no clergy–penitent privilege prohibited the preacher from testifying against the confessor.[207] Looking at the scope of the religious privilege, New Jersey specifically extends the privilege to confidential communications made between and among the cleric/priest and "individuals, couples, families, or groups in the exercise of the cleric's professional or spiritual counseling role."[208]

---

201 *In re* Grand Jury Investigation, 918 F.2d 374, 383 (3d Cir. 1990).

202 *Id.* 382.

203 REV. CODE WASH. § 5.60.060(3) (2013).

204 Doe v. Church of Jesus Christ of Latter-Day Saints, 122 Wash. App. 556, 568, 90 P.3d 1147, 1154, 2004 Wash. App. LEXIS 1112 (2004).

205 N.J. STAT. § 2A:84A-23 (2013).

206 *Id.*

207 State v. Hardman, 2010 Mont. Dist. LEXIS 209 (2010).

208 State v. J.G., 201 N.J. 369, 386, 990 A.2d 1122, 132, 2010 N.J. LEXIS 381 (2010).

To be covered under the religious privilege, the communication generally must have been made to a member of the clergy, broadly defined, who has a duty under the discipline or the tenets of the church, denomination, or organization to keep the communications secret; it must have been intended to be in confidence; the communication must have occurred during the course of his or her religious discipline or practice; and he or she must be authorized or accustomed to hearing confidences from parishioners and have a duty under the discipline or tenets of the church to keep the communications secret.

C. Exceptions

In order for a communication to be privileged under most statutes, it must have been made to a clergy member in his or her professional capacity or character. Statements made by a mother to her pastor in which she indicated that her husband was abusing her children were not considered exceptions to the priest–penitent privilege and related confidential communications. While evidence of child abuse would not normally be considered confidential under most circumstances, where a parishioner offered statements to her pastor concerning child abuse, the communication, even though not a confession, was expected to remain confidential and therefore considered privileged. Because the mother sought spiritual guidance, the pastor was under no obligation to report the child abuse to governmental authorities[209]; however, the minister could have been forced to testify if he had learned of the abuse from a nonconfidential source.

In a slightly different context involving an allegation of the existence of a religious privilege, a defendant in a sexual assault case contended that his speaking with a pastor concerning his sexual involvement with the victim should have been covered by the religious privilege. At the time that defendant conversed with his pastor, the pastor's wife was present and heard the complete exchange. According to the Supreme Court of New Hampshire, no priest–penitent or other religious privilege arose because there was an unnecessary third party present that negated any confidentiality between the defendant as a parishioner and the pastor as a religious advisor.[210] The court noted that the presence of an extraneous third party during an otherwise privileged conversation operates to either destroy the privilege or to prevent it from existing at the beginning.

When the communication is not made within the requisite nature of the confidential disclosure of a penitent seeking religious advice or consolation from a clergy member, a court should not recognize the privilege. No priest–penitent privilege existed where a defendant spoke to two preachers, whose wives were present, concerning his sexual activity with an underage female. The defendant made no effort to prevent the wives from hearing the preachers discuss his situation and the preachers did not, at the time, consider the communication and discussion as privileged.[211]

---

209 People v. Prominski, 2013 Mich. App. LEXIS 1445 (2013).

210 State v. Willis, 2013 N.H. LEXIS 91 (2013)

211 Rogers v. State, 2006 Miss. LEXIS 226 (2006).

D. Assertion and Waiver

The majority of the jurisdictions consider the clergy–penitent privilege to be for the benefit of the penitent. Therefore, the penitent may claim the privilege or waive the privilege as he or she sees fit. The general rule is that if the penitent waives the privilege, the clergy member may be required to testify about the communication.[212] On the other hand, in some jurisdictions, the clergy member is deemed also to be a holder of the privilege on the theory that the state should neither force a member of the clergy to violate, nor punish him or her for refusing to violate, church doctrine where the church teaching requires clergy to maintain secrecy as to confidential statements made in the course of a penitential communication.[213] Similarly, New Jersey grants holder status to the priest, rabbi, minister, or other individual authorized to perform similar religious functions and to "the person or persons making the communication" under the cleric–penitent privilege, unless both agree to waive the privilege.[214]

Evidence of statements made in confidence to a member of the clergy is subject to admission in court in certain situations under some statutes. For example, in cases involving abuse or neglect of a child in Texas, communications that normally would be covered by a priest–penitent or other privileges are not considered privileged and are admissible against the accused.[215] Additionally, most jurisdictions hold that the privilege is waived if the holder of the privilege voluntarily discloses privileged material to nonordained unnecessary third parties. California statutes imply a waiver "with respect to a communication protected by the privilege if any holder of the privilege, without coercion, has disclosed a significant part of the communication or has consented to disclosure made by anyone."[216] Waiver of the privilege may also occur when both persons holding the privilege agreed to waive or when the alleged privileged communication concerned the planning of a future crime or crimes.[217]

§ 10.7 Confidential Informant Privilege

Most jurisdictions, by either statute or case law, allow law enforcement officials to protect the identities of confidential informants who offer information concerning criminal activities. According to the teaching of *Roviaro v. United* States, it is an accepted fact that the government has a limited privilege to withhold the identity of

---

212 *See* WASH. REV. CODE § 5.60.060 (2013).

213 CAL. EVID. CODE § 1034 (2014).

214 N.J. STAT. § 2A:84A-23 (2013).

215 *See* TEX. FAM. CODE § 261.202 (2013), where the statute notes: "In a proceeding regarding the abuse or neglect of a child, evidence may not be excluded on the ground of privileged communication except in the case of communications between an attorney and client."

216 *See* CAL. EVID. CODE. § 912 (b) (2013).

217 *See* N.J. STAT. § 2A:84A-23 (2013).

a confidential informant from disclosure.[218] In many cases, informants would not prove motivated and come forth if their identities were mandatorily required to be made known due to fear of reprisal from criminal elements. The rule against disclosure of their identities recognizes that the informants serve as an important resource in effective law enforcement and that their activities should be encouraged. This privilege prompts citizen involvement in alerting police to wrongdoing with the general promise that the citizen's identity will remain undiscovered by criminal suspects unless a defendant demonstrates a strong need for the information.

There are essentially two types of informants: those who were merely observers of criminal events and those who may have been materially involved in the crime to the point at which they may have to be witnesses in criminal trials. The first type merely assists the law enforcement agency in investigating criminal activities; the second type may have to testify in court about what he or she knew or saw. One approach is to consider as privileged the identity of a confidential informant who gives information from which the court can determine "probable cause" for securing an arrest or a search warrant. This is different from the informer who was an integral part of the illegal transaction, whose identity may be demanded by the defense, and who may be called a material witness. The confidential informant in *Roviaro* was the sole participant, other than Roviaro, in the activity for which Roviaro was indicted and was the sole person who could challenge or expand the testimony of prosecution witnesses. The defendant's need was great, and the government should have shared the identity of its confidential informant.[219]

California allows a public entity a privilege not to reveal or disclose the identity of an individual who has furnished information that disclosed a violation of state or federal or local law when a public employee, who has authority, deems it in the public interest not to reveal the identity of the informant.[220] The entity must indicate that the disclosure of the informant's identity would be against the public interest and in the interests of justice.

United States Supreme Court decisions have made it clear that in most instances, the state does not have to disclose the name of a confidential informant who gave information upon which a court found probable cause for a search warrant. In *Illinois v. Gates*, the Supreme Court reemphasized that it is not necessary to disclose the identity of an informant who only gives information that helps establish probable cause.[221] In this case, police obtained a search warrant for a residence and an automobile based on an affidavit setting forth facts contained in an anonymous letter written to police by an undisclosed informant. Police and federal officers corroborated most of the facts contained in the letter but it never appeared that police ever knew the identity of the informant.

---

218 Roviaro v. United States, 353 U.S. 53, 59, 77 S. Ct. 623, 627, 1 L. Ed. 2d 639, 644, 1957 U.S. LEXIS 1125 (1957).

219 *Id.*

220 *See* CAL. EVID. CODE. § 1041 (2013).

221 Illinois v. Gates, 462 U.S. 213, 103 S. Ct. 2317, 76 L. Ed. 2d 527 (1983).

The *Gates* Court, in reaffirming that an informant's identity may be withheld, quoted an older case,[222] and stated that "the magistrate must be informed of some of the underlying circumstances from which the informant concluded that the narcotics were where he claimed they were, and some of the underlying circumstances from which the officer concluded that the informant, whose identity need not be disclosed...was 'credible' or his information 'reliable.'"[223] As a general rule, an informant who provides police with information that the police use to obtain a warrant or to foster an investigation may have his or her identity remain confidential. However, if the informant later testifies at trial, the identity must be disclosed to the defendant for Sixth Amendment confrontation reasons to facilitate cross-examination.

As developed from case law and practice, communications made by informants to public officers engaged in the discovery of crime may be privileged. As the Supreme Court noted in *Roviaro v. United States*:

> The purpose of the privilege is the furtherance and protection of the public interest in effective law enforcement. The privilege recognizes the obligation of citizens to communicate their knowledge of the commission of crimes to law-enforcement officials and, by preserving their anonymity, encourages them to perform that obligation.[224]

This privilege exists in order to conceal the identity of the informant, thereby allowing him or her to continue as a source of future information while protecting the confidential informant from reprisals based on the informant's cooperation with law enforcement. The public policy encouraging citizens to assist police in solving crimes outweighs the damage that may be done to any defendant's case unless the defendant's due process rights become compromised. Where the confidential informant's testimony is not relevant to the defendant's guilt or innocence, where the informant will not be a trial witness, and where the informant did not participate in the crime for which the defendant has been charged, there is no requirement to reveal the identity of the informant. The policy of informant confidentiality has its limits where a nondisclosure rule would frustrate a defendant from fairly presenting a defense. In such a case, the informant's identity may have to be divulged or the prosecution may have to dismiss the case. Where the disclosure is relevant and would be helpful to the defense or might be essential to a fair trial, the government's privilege must give way. In making a decision, trial courts must also consider whether revealing an informant's identity will endanger the informant.[225]

Whether the privilege must yield depends upon the facts and circumstances of the particular case based on the degree of the informant's involvement. The informant who merely observed criminal activity and informed police will rarely have his or her

---

222 Aguilar v. Texas, 378 U.S. 108, 114, 1964 U.S. LEXIS 994 (1964).

223 *Gates* at 278.

224 353 U.S. 53, 59, 1957 U.S. LEXIS 1125 (1959).

225 United States v. Smith, 2005 U.S. Dist. LEXIS 3782 (E.D. Pa. 2005).

identity revealed, whereas an informant who had an active and strong role in the crime may have his or her identity revealed as essential to a fair trial. Cases that fall between noninvolvement and active participation in the crime prove to be the hardest to determine whether disclosure of identity should be revealed to a defendant.[226] But if the informer testifies for the state, the privilege may not be invoked and the identity must be revealed, consistent with the right of confrontation and cross-examination under the Sixth Amendment.

Several examples may help to clarify this exception. In an old but important case decided by the Supreme Court, the justices ruled that the prosecutor was not privileged to withhold the name of the informant when the informant played a direct and prominent part at the crime scene as the sole participant with the accused, Roviaro, in the very offense for which the latter was being tried.[227] The informant had taken a material part in bringing about the petitioner's possession of the drugs and he had been present with the petitioner at the occurrence of the alleged crime and at the arrest.

In deciding whether to require an informant's identity to be revealed to the defendant, courts generally make a detailed inquiry into the facts. The primary issue concerns whether the informant really falls into the category of a material witness. If the witness has been an active and "hands-on" participant in the offense, the prosecution will almost always have to reveal the identity of the witness because it will be crucial to the development of a defense. However, if the informant has been primarily an observer who conveyed information and did not actively participate in the offense, he or she probably will not be labeled an essential witness for the defense and will not be deemed a material witness. The usual burden rests with the defendant to demonstrate the materiality of the witness.

In a California case involving attempted murder, a witness came forth as a confidential informant and told police that he saw the defendant shoot the victim. If the confidential informant proves to be a material witness who might be able to assist the defendant, the identity of the witness must be revealed. According to the appellate court in California, merely because the informant was a percipient witness did not make the revelation of that witness's identity mandatory. Following a review of the evidence in the judge's chambers, the trial court determined that the confidential witness had no information that could be helpful to the defendant in meeting the challenges of the criminal prosecution and, therefore, the reviewing court held that the identity of the witness properly remained confidential.[228]

In order to obtain the identity of confidential informants, the criminal defendant bears the burden of demonstrating the need for disclosure over the desire of the government to keep its confidences. In one federal prosecution for participating in a drug-trafficking conspiracy, investigators captured the voices of confidential informants

---

226 United States v. Harrison, 2005 U.S. Dist. LEXIS 6195 (E.D. Pa. 2005).

227 Roviaro v. United States, 353 U.S. 53, 77 S. Ct. 623, 1 L. Ed. 2d 639 (1957).

228 Davis v. Superior Court, 186 Cal. App. 4th 1272, 1276, 113 Cal. Rptr. 3d 365, 368, 2010 Cal. App. LEXIS 1207 (2010).

whose voices had been recorded when talking to the future defendant.[229] According to the defense motion, the defendant only wanted the substance of the conversations to be revealed by the government, but the prosecution indicated such disclosure would also reveal the identity of the informants. A defendant who seeks the revelation of the identity of confidential informants, or information that would indirectly reveal identities, carries a heavy burden. The defendant was hoping that the wiretap transcripts would reveal the fact that the government had omitted material evidence from the applications for the wiretap warrants and, thus, attack the validity of the wiretap itself. In this case, mere allegations that exculpatory information might be obtained were based purely on speculation and were not shown to be necessary for the accused to prepare a defense. According to the reviewing court, the defendant did not carry the burden to require that the information be revealed to show that the information was crucial to constructing a defense.

If a court decides that disclosure of the informant's identity has been shown to be essential to the defense when a failure to reveal the identity would harm the presentation of a defense, or that the informant was a participant in the crime charged, or that the informant's testimony may be crucial to determining guilt or innocence, the informant's identity must yield to the defendant's need for the evidence.[230] At this point, the government must choose between revealing the informant's name—thereby risking his or her safety and its own investigative efficacy—and forfeiting the informant's testimony. The privilege not to reveal the identity of confidential informants belongs to the governmental authority, whether state or federal, not to the informant, and thus only the prosecution has the power to waive the privilege.

§ 10.8 State Secrets and Other Official Information

Sovereign governments all need, have, and use information that would have negative effects if the data were openly revealed. Covert intelligence operations, state-of-the-art weapons systems, and diplomatic and military information can all be, at some levels, considered secret matters. In an early case, the executor of the estate of a United States spy sued to recover money allegedly owed under a contract to the estate due to the deceased's espionage work for President Lincoln against the Confederate States of America. The Court of Claims dismissed the case because it believed that the work under the contract was a secret service and that the facts surrounding the contract and its results were to be clandestinely secured and privately communicated. Public policy required that the case be dismissed. The Supreme Court affirmed, noting that, "[i]t may be stated as a general principle that public policy forbids the maintenance of any suit in a court of justice, the trial of which would inevitably lead to the disclosure

229 United States v. Cartagena, 593 F.3d 104, 112, 2010 U.S. App. LEXIS 2053 (2010).

230 State v. Francis, 2003 Conn. Super. LEXIS 757 (2003).

of matters which the law itself regards as confidential, and respecting which it will not allow the confidence to be violated."[231]

This principle, which protects military and state secrets, was described as "well established in the law of evidence" in the landmark case of *United States v. Reynolds*.[232] In this case, there were fatalities when a B-29 test aircraft crashed while on a secret test mission that included civilians. The surviving family members sued for damages under the Federal Tort Claims Act. As part of their proof, they wanted a copy of the accident investigation report, among other documents. The Air Force claimed a national secrets privilege that the courts ultimately upheld under a clearly deferential approach to the federal government's assertions. In adjudicating the claim of a state secrets privilege, the court held that:

> The privilege belongs to the Government and must be asserted by it; it can neither be formal claim of privilege, lodged by the head of the department which has control over the matter, after actual personal consideration by that officer. The court itself must determine whether the circumstances are appropriate for the claim of privilege, and yet do so without forcing a disclosure of the very thing the privilege is designed to protect.[233]

The plaintiff's claim in *Reynolds* of necessity was lessened when the Air Force offered to reveal the accident report and related information, but not the secret details of the equipment and the mission of the aircraft. The Supreme Court upheld the validity of the governmental secrets claim of privilege under these circumstances.[234]

The policy basis of the rule is the desirability of encouraging complete candor among executive department employees to discuss secret governmental operations with respect to their exchange of views within the executive branch of the federal government. Moreover, the state secrets privilege is consistent with the Freedom of Information Act.[235]

In order for the privilege to be allowed under the rule stated and under the general laws of evidence, the government must make a claim of a state secrets privilege and demonstrate a need for protecting the secret or other official information. The judge, in an in-camera session, may require a showing of the entire text of the government's statements before granting the privilege. Then, if the privilege is successfully claimed by the government, the effect of such claim makes evidence unavailable as though the witness had died or claimed the privilege against self-incrimination.[236]

---

231 Totten v. United States, 92 U.S. 105, 107, 1875 U.S. LEXIS 1732 (1875).

232 345 U.S. 1, 1953 U.S. LEXIS 2329 (1953).

233 *Id.* at 7.

234 United States v. Reynolds, 345 U.S. 1, 1953 U.S. LEXIS 2329 (1953).

235 5 U.S.C. § 552(a) and (b) (2011). The Freedom of Information Act (FOIA) and the Privacy Act contain exceptions for classified information. 5 U.S.C. § 552(b)(1) (FOIA); 5 U.S.C. § 552a (k) (Privacy Act).

236 For a further discussion of the self-incrimination protection, *see* Chapter 16.

In pointing out the importance of the privilege, the United States Court of Appeals for the District of Columbia Circuit indicated that a ranking of the various privileges recognized in our courts would be a delicate undertaking at best, but that it is quite clear that the privilege to protect state secrets must head that list.[237] In another case, a Fifth Circuit Court of Appeals decision stated that "to the extent that the documents withheld are internal working papers in which opinions are expressed, policies are formulated, and actions are recommended, they are privileged."[238] However, the court went on to say that to the extent that the documents contain purely factual material in a form that can be separated without compromising the privileged portions of the document, the material is not privileged and is subject to discovery.

The state secrets privilege covers matters that, if revealed, might threaten military operations or diplomatic interests of the United States and are absolutely shielded from revelation. The privilege includes a prohibition on revelation of covert operations of intelligence agencies or their future operational plans. The privilege belongs to the federal government, which is the only entity permitted to assert or waive the privilege. The process to assert a state secrets claim begins with the agency or department that has responsibility for the area covered by the request. According to *United States v. Reynolds*:

> There must be a formal claim of [the state secrets] privilege, lodged by the head of the department which has control over the matter, after actual personal consideration by that officer. The court itself must determine whether the circumstances are appropriate for the claim of privilege, and yet do so without forcing a disclosure of the very thing the privilege is designed to protect.[239]

While there should be extreme deference given to the executive department that asserts a privilege, the difficult task is to determine whether the claimed privilege would harm the interests asserted without giving away the secret while still protecting national security. The most strongly articulated need for the information will not, according to the *Reynolds* case, overcome a properly pled government claim of absolute privilege.

A claim of government secrets privilege arose when a covert Central Intelligence Agency Operations Officer sued the Central Intelligence Agency (CIA), its director, and 10 unnamed employees under Title VII of the Civil Rights Act, stating that he had experienced unlawful discriminatory practices at the hands of CIA management and that job expectations of him were much higher than those for white CIA agents. The federal government moved to dismiss the case, citing the state secret privilege. The federal district court conducted a hearing to determine the validity of the government's state secrets contention. Following a thorough review of the merits of each side, the court determined that in order for the plaintiff to properly pursue the racial discrimination case, he would have to disclose the nature of his employment

---

237 Halkin v. Helms, 598 F.2d 1 (D.C. Cir. 1978).

238 Branch v. Phillips Petroleum Co., 638 F.2d 873 (5th Cir. 1981).

239 *Reynolds*, 345 U.S. at 8.

and the place of his employment, as well as similar information about fellow employees, including their duty stations. In fact, the names of most of his superiors were classified, which would have rendered proof of discrimination by comparing positions and duties a breach of national security. Because the court held that divulging government secrets would have been crucial to deciding the core factual questions in the case, the state secrets doctrine compelled dismissal of the case.[240]

In another government secrets case that involved the CIA, a married couple who had served as spies for the United States in their country of origin filed a suit that alleged the government had defaulted on its promises of financial assistance and support in exchange for their spying activities during the Cold War. The couple alleged that the CIA had eventually permitted them to reside in the United States, providing support for many years, but had gradually reduced the level of support as the couple's income rose. When the husband lost his job and was precluded from taking some jobs due to CIA requirements, they alleged that the government would no longer live up to its bargain to support them for life. Two lower courts allowed the suit to continue on the theory that the government secrets privilege did not apply, but the Supreme Court, citing the post-Civil War *Totten*[241] case, reversed on the theory that public policy prevents suits based on covert espionage agreements between the federal government and individuals.[242] Even if all the allegations were true, there is no remedy where state secrets would have to be revealed.

According to settled legal theory, when the federal government validly asserts the state secrets privilege to prevent the release of information during pretrial discovery or the release of any information that, if disclosed, would adversely affect national security, the privilege is absolute.[243] A civil case was brought under the Alien Tort Statute, 28 U.S.C. § 1350, by several individuals who alleged that they had been seized from various foreign locations by the United States government and flown to various locations outside of the United States.[244] According to the Court of Appeals for the Ninth Circuit, "[p]laintiffs allege that the Central Intelligence Agency ("CIA"), working in concert with other government agencies and officials of foreign governments, operated an extraordinary rendition program to gather intelligence by apprehending foreign nationals suspected of involvement in terrorist activities and transferring them in secret to foreign countries for detention and interrogation by United States or foreign officials."[245] Additionally, they contended that they had been tortured by various other governments allegedly on behalf of the United States; the plaintiffs wanted a judgment against the American corporation that flew the private aircraft on which these

---

240 Sterling v. Tenet, 416 F.3d 338, 341, 2005 U.S. App. LEXIS 15945 (4th Cir. 2005).

241 *See* Totten v. United States, 92 U.S. 105, 107, 1875 U.S. LEXIS 1732 (1875), in which secret spy contracts were deemed unenforceable based on state secrets and public policy.

242 Tenet v. Doe, 544 U.S. 1, 3, 2005 U.S. LEXIS 2202 (2005).

243 *See* Ellsberg v. Mitchell, 228 U.S. App. D.C. 225, 709 F.2d 51, 56 (D.C. Cir. 1983).

244 *See* Mohammed v. Jeppesen Dataplan, Inc. 614 F.3d 1070, 2010 U.S. App. LEXIS 18746 (10th Cir. 2010).

245 *Id.* at 1073.

extraordinary renditions occurred. The complaint asserted that the defendant corporation played an integral role in the forced abductions and detentions and provided substantial services to the United States government for its extraordinary rendition program, thereby enabling the clandestine and forcible transportation of terrorism suspects to secret overseas detention facilities to be treated in ways that would not be possible if the facilities had been located within the United States. The United States government intervened in this civil suit and made an allegation through the director of the CIA that the suit should be dismissed because the disclosure of the information covered by the asserted privilege could be expected to cause serious and exceptionally grave damage to the national security of the United States and the information should not be allowed in any court case. The court noted that the privilege of government secrets could only be asserted by the government, which it did in this case. The court then must make an independent determination whether the information is actually privileged without actually knowing the substance of what the government desires to keep private. As a final matter, the court must determine how to proceed in a suit where a government privilege exists. In this case involving extraordinary rendition, the trial court and the circuit court both agreed that the assertion by the government of state secrets carried the day if the case had to be dismissed and could not proceed further. The result may not deliver justice to the individual litigant, but the larger picture of governmental security will not be compromised by allowing government secrets to be divulged.

While the plaintiffs in the extraordinary rendition case needed the evidence to make their case, in a criminal matter, where a defendant alleged that he or she needed access to state secrets to make a defense in court or has access but the government does not want the evidence revealed, the loss of evidence may adversely impact justice. If a court recognizes the existence of a state secrets privilege in a particular case and the privilege serves to exclude evidence that may bear directly upon a substantive defense in a criminal case, it may be necessary to dismiss the case in the defendant's favor.[246]

When the federal government makes an allegation that evidence that a party wants to introduce, or discover, involves a sensitive state secret, the judge should consider whether the proper official invoked the privilege and whether the allegation could conceivably endanger a crucial government interest. Where the judge is convinced that the claim has been properly made and appears to be valid, the proceeding will have to be dismissed if the evidence was critical to the legal action contemplated. When a court holds that the government secrets privilege applies, it is absolute.

§ 10.9 News Media–Informant Privilege

In the absence of a statute or court ruling, a journalist, reporter, or other news gatherer possesses no privilege to refuse to divulge sources of information to courts, grand

[246] United States v. Andolschek, 142 F.2d 503 (2d Cir. 1944).

juries, and other official governmental bodies. Consistent with federal court interpretations, one federal court of appeal noted that there exists no

> ...First Amendment testimonial privilege, absolute or qualified, that protects a reporter from being compelled to testify by the prosecution or the defense in criminal proceedings about criminal conduct that the reporter personally witnessed or participated in, absent a showing of bad faith, harassment, or other such non-legitimate motive, even though the reporter promised confidentiality to his source.[247]

In performing their functions as reporters, members of the print and broadcast media, Internet news outlets, and individual bloggers often find themselves in situations that allow them to gather facts and evidence that ordinary members of the public would not likely discover. Some of this data makes its way to newspapers, news magazines, or to the broadcast arena, but due to space and interest limitations, some of the news is never publicly disseminated. Internet bloggers, people using Twitter®, and posters of YouTube-type snippets and videos are the newest arrivals to the news gathering–dissemination cycle and are increasingly likely to have a presence in news reporter–source litigation.

Unlike traditional journalistic reporting, electronic communication through the Internet leaves a clear trail of file metadata that is often very traceable and legally discoverable and may predict that other legally relevant information may exist that has been neither reported or uploaded. Communication by reporters with their sources via e-mail and social media leave metadata trails on the computers, tablets, and cell phones of both reporters and sources. Statutes have yet to address these new phenomena and existing state statutes may not protect reporter and blogger privileges where a state press shield statute is narrowly construed. News gatherers may find that not only may the judicial system be interested in their sources but police, legislative bodies, and private tort lawyers may develop an intense interest in a particular news source. The reason frequently offered to deny any news gatherer–source privilege concerns the superior interest that the public possesses in the proper administration of the law as opposed to private accommodations or guarantees that have developed between news gatherers and their sources,[248] but such an argument could apply to most other privileges existing in the law of evidence where a case has some public connection.

Consistent with the general rule that a court is entitled to everyone's evidence, the traditional position held that news gatherers should offer their facts to a court as readily as any other citizen called to give evidence. An opposite position holds that if a news reporter were required to divulge every bit of confidential information known to him or her, including news sources, to the police, prosecutors, and the courts, their sources

---

[247] United States v. Sterling, 724 F.3d 482, 2013 U.S. App. LEXIS 14646 (4th Cir. 2013).

[248] *See* 99 A.L.R.3d 37 (Updated Oct. 2005).

would be reluctant to give the information necessary for the public to become informed.[249] The First Amendment[250] as applied to the states and to the federal government arguably gives, or should give, some sort of privilege or shield to gather news without revealing all sources.

In recent years, reporters from the national, regional, and local newspapers and media outlets have litigated hundreds of cases confronting the issue of whether a reporter has the privilege to refuse to testify concerning information acquired in connection with that person's news gathering and publishing. There is no common law dealing with the news media–informant privilege, and earlier cases clearly demonstrated that unless a statute creates a privilege, journalists are under the same duty as every other person to testify when properly called to court or to a grand jury.[251] In developing the law relating to the news media–informant privilege, journalists have refused to testify or otherwise reveal information on the grounds that the First Amendment protects such communications and that statutes enacted by the various states enhanced this theoretical First Amendment protection.

Within the past several years, additional agitation has emerged directed toward enacting a federal reporter shield law; President Obama has announced that he supports such a move by Congress. The president's support comes despite the United States Department of Justice's prosecution of eight leaker officials who gave secret data to news reporters. One Senate bill would create a privilege that would allow journalists to refuse to reveal their confidential sources by setting a legally high bar before the reporter could be ordered to reveal confidences.[252]

Despite recent efforts, the current state of case law that negates a federal reporter's privilege is still good law. The United States Supreme Court first confronted the constitutional issue of whether a reporter has a privilege to shield confidential sources in *Branzburg v. Hayes*.[253] In that case, for which Justice White authored a plurality opinion,[254] the Court acknowledged that news gathering qualified for some First Amendment protection, but found that the First Amendment does not guarantee the press a constitutional right of special access to information not generally available to the public. As Justice White wrote in *Branzburg*:

> We cannot seriously entertain the notion that the First Amendment protects a newsman's agreement to conceal the criminal conduct of his source, or evidence thereof, on the theory that it is better to write about crime than to do something

---

249 This is the same argument that allows police to shield some informants from disclosure of their identities.

250 "Congress shall make no law . . . abridging the freedom of speech, or of the press. . . ." Constitution of the United States, Amendment I.

251 Clein v. State, 52 So. 2d 117 (Fla. 1951).

252 Editorial, *Reporter Shield Law Important Step*, SEATTLE TIMES, 26 Sep 2013. Web. 6 Feb. 2014. <http://seattletimes.com/html/editorials/2021906716_reportershieldeditxml.html>.

253 Branzburg v. Hayes, 408 U.S. 665, 1972 U.S. LEXIS 132 (1972).

254 For a discussion of the opinions of the various judges in the case of *Branzburg v. Hayes*, *see* Liggett v. Superior Court, 260 Cal. Rptr. 161 (1989).

> about it. Insofar as any reporter in these cases undertook not to reveal or testify about the crime he witnessed, his claim of privilege under the First Amendment presents no substantial question.[255]

Reporters receive little protection under the federal Constitution and generally must respond to grand jury subpoenas as any other witness must do as well as answer a United States attorney's questions relevant to a federal criminal investigation. Congress has yet to enact a federal shield law, but efforts directed toward a federal law have been introduced in Congress[256] to no effect at this point. In a case involving a former CIA agent who had been criminally charged with unauthorized retention and disclosure of national defense secrets, the prosecution successfully appealed a lower court decision that quashed a subpoena to a *New York Times* reporter who was working on a book. The ultimate court ruling required the reporter to divulge any information that she received from the defendant, the former CIA employee.[257] According to the reviewing court, the fact that a forced disclosure by the reporter would break the reporter's promise of confidentiality to his source, the defendant, did not enjoy any protection under the First Amendment guarantee of freedom of the press. In this case, "*New York Times* reporter Judith Miller was jailed for refusing to reveal a confidential source, who leaked to her the identity of CIA employee Valerie Plame, to a grand jury."[258] In most situations, the reporter or blogger arguably is in a different position that an attorney or priest; the reporter is not trying to protect confidential information but wants to publish the information but without attribution or recognized sourcing.

In contrast to the federal government, the states have taken a more sympathetic view of the news reporter, blogger, or disseminator because more than half of the states by statute or case law have provided news gatherers either an absolute or qualified privilege from divulging information received in confidence.[259] These statutes have been labeled "shield laws" and they differ in wording and have been interpreted differently by the respective state courts. Some appear to be fairly absolute, while other state statutes refer to the reporter's privilege as a "qualified" privilege and require that the courts balance the need for the information against the importance of keeping the original confidence. In state cases and in pending federal legislation, some controversy has emerged concerning which persons should be covered under a reporter shield law and whether a shield law should cover only gainfully employed reporters and journalists or embrace Internet bloggers and others who disseminate news on the Internet.

California's shield law was first enacted in 1935. This statute has undergone many amendments, and in 1980 the evidence code section relating to the News Gatherers

---

[255] *Branzburg,* 408 U.S. at 692.

[256] *See* 14 COMM. LAW CONSPECTUS 543.

[257] United States v. Sterling, 724 F.3d 482, 2013 U.S. App. LEXIS 14646 (4th Cir. 2013).

[258] David B. Rivkin, Jr. and Lee A. Casey, *Reporters Need a Federal Shield Law.* WALL ST. J.,, 13 Apr 2013. Web. 6 Feb. 2014. <http://online.wsj.com/article/SB10001424127887324030704578424930938783180.html>.

[259] *See* 38 GONZ. L. REV 445, 450, and n.19.

Shield Law was incorporated into the California Constitution.[260] The California Evidence Code provision provides in pertinent part:

> A publisher, editor, reporter or other person connected with or employed upon a newspaper. . .shall not be adjudged in contempt by a judicial, legislative, administrative body or any other body. . .for refusing to disclose. . .the source of any information procured while so connected or employed. . .or for refusing to disclose any unpublished information obtained or prepared in gathering, receiving, or processing information for communication to the public.[261]
>
> As used in this subsection, "unpublished information" includes information not disseminated to the public by the person from whom disclosure is sought, whether or not related information has been disseminated and includes, but is not limited to all notes, out takes, photographs, tapes, or other data of whatever sort not itself disseminated to the public through a medium of communication, whether or not published information based upon or related to such material has been disseminated.[262]

In a case involving Apple Computer and some online news magazines that had gathered and published information obtained from confidential sources to a mass online audience, the owner of the information wanted to find the magazine's sources. The topic of the story involved some stolen Apple Computer trade secrets to develop and release an electronic device that would assist in making live sound recordings on Apple computers. To find out who had stolen the trade secret material, Apple sued the web site to obtain the identity of the alleged criminal. Civil subpoenas were issued to force the operators of the web site to divulge its confidential sources. Although a trial court ordered the persons to comply with the subpoena and refused to grant a protective order, a California appellate court held that any subpoenas demanding unpublished information from the online magazine's owners or employees would be unenforceable. According to the appeals court, any effort to enforce the subpoenas would run afoul of identical provisions of the California Constitution and the California Rules of Evidence § 1070 protecting reporters from having to divulge their secret sources and unpublished confidential material.[263]

Even in states that have shield laws, there may be limitations on the application of the laws. If a reporter or a newspaper fails to assert that the interview in question was conducted under a cloak of confidentiality, a motion to reveal the reporter's notes, transcriptions, memoranda, or tape recordings may be granted. In Pennsylvania, which has a shield law that allows news organizations and their staffs to protect confidential news sources from disclosure,[264] one case involved a newspaper reporter's article about a defendant charged with murder, in which the reporter interviewed the defendant. The reporter did not obtain the information from a confidential or unknown source

---

260 CAL. CONST. art. I, § 2, cl. (b). Amended June 3, 1980.

261 CAL. EVID. CODE § 1070 (a) (2014).

262 *Id.* § 1070 (c).

263 O'Grady v. Superior Court, 2006 Cal. App. LEXIS 802 (2006).

264 *See* 42 PA. CONS. STAT. § 5942 (2013).

and the defendant told only about his own version of the shooting without implicating any confidential source. The prosecutor had no other source from which to obtain the original raw interview data offered by the defendant and could not call the defendant to the witness stand to ask him. According to the trial court, because the newspaper reporter was not covered by the shield law and its privilege, the reporter was required to testify concerning the matters related to him by the defendant.[265]

While Pennsylvania law covers confidential sources, New Jersey's law is an example of a law that has greater coverage and offers significantly more protection to the news media and reporters[266] than that of Pennsylvania. The New Jersey shield law does not require a confidential source to have been the basis or genesis of a story as long as the individual reporter has been engaged in news gathering, procuring, transmitting, compiling, editing, or disseminating news material. However, the reporter shield law does not cover just any random person who posts information on a blog site or apply to every self-appointed news reporter. In a defamation case, the Supreme Court of New Jersey noted that:

New Jersey's Shield Law provides broad protection to the news media and is not limited to traditional news outlets like newspapers and magazines. But to ensure that the privilege does not apply to every self-appointed newsperson, the Legislature requires that other means of disseminating news be "similar" to traditional news sources to qualify for the law's coverage. In one case the New Jersey Supreme Court noted,

> We do not find that online message boards are similar to the types of news entities listed in the statute, and do not believe that the Legislature intended to provide an absolute privilege in defamation cases to people who post comments on message boards.[267]

However, one New Jersey trial court recognized an Internet blog author/news collector as having a newsman's privilege under the state shield law because her blog had the purpose of disseminating news and reported on local government affairs. The court held that the blogger did not have to testify at a grand jury proceeding concerning the identity of govenment employees alleged to have used county property for personal use. The court viewed that the blogger had sufficient connection with news media and had the purpose of gathering and publishing news to the general public.[268]

Maryland has taken an approach midway between Pennsylvania and New Jersey in developing a news gatherer shield that protects a news reporter from revealing stories or news or information procured by the reporter/news gatherer. However, Maryland may

---

265 Commonwealth of Pennsylvania v. Tyson, 2002 Pa. Super. 168, 800 A.2d 327, 2002 Pa. Super. LEXIS 1071 (2002).

266 *See* N.J. STAT. § 2A:84A-21 (2013).

267 Too Much Media, LLC v. Hale, 206 N.J. 209, 216, 2011 N.J. LEXIS 629 (2011).

268 *In re* January 11, 2013 Subpoena by the Grand Jury of Union County, New Jersey, 2013 N.J. Super. LEXIS 124 (2013).

require disclosure of news sources when a court finds that the news or significant information is relevant to a major legal issue before any judicial, legislative, or administrative body, or any body that has the power to issue subpoenas. A requirement to divulge news or data may be ordered when the news or information cannot be obtained from any other source when there is an overriding public interest in disclosure to the court or other public body and the information cannot be produced by alternate means. Even here, the identity of the source of the news remains protected from being divulged.[269] Maryland wants the source to remain private and not to become public while requiring that important information be made public.

Vermont has taken a different route from many state jurisdictions and has opted to follow the strict view that the government is entitled to every person's evidence. While the state has no statute that protects the news media with a privilege not to disclose sources, reporters were believed to possess some protections. Following a college celebration that evolved into a riot, prosecutor's wanted all footage of a television station that covered the raucous party. In reversing the trial court finding of the existence of a privilege, the Supreme Court of Vermont noted:

> In the circumstances of this case, no privilege, qualified or otherwise, excuses [the station] from furnishing the videotape of the riot. Therefore, the State did not have to show that the materials were available from other sources. The facts here are essentially indistinguishable from those in *Branzburg v. Hayes*, 408 U.S. 665, 33 L. Ed. 2d 626, 92 S. Ct. 2646 (1972), in which the United States Supreme Court held that there is no constitutional privilege under the First Amendment that excuses reporters from appearing and testifying before grand juries investigating criminal conduct, even if the source of their information is confidential.[270]

The Supreme Court of Vermont based its decision on the view that every person's evidence should be available, especially where there is a possibility of criminal conduct. The top Vermont court found no privilege in state common law, applicable federal statutes, or the First Amendment, so it ordered the television station to give over its videotape.

In a case that gathered significant public attention at the time, reporters were held in contempt of court for refusing to testify concerning their alleged confidential sources that related to the "leaking" of the identity of a CIA operative, Valerie Plame. In this case, reporters lost their legal arguments in an attempt to establish a reporter's federal privilege by judicial decision. The litigants contended that the First Amendment gave them a privilege not to reveal confidential sources and material and that they had a common law reporter's privilege, among other theories. The Court of Appeals for the District of Columbia circuit rejected their contentions completely and, relying on the Supreme Court's decision in *Branzburg v. Hayes*, upheld their contempt citations. As the Court of Appeals noted, "The Supreme Court in no uncertain terms rejected the existence of such a privilege. As we said at the outset of this discussion, the Supreme

---

269 MD. CODE ANN. § 9-112 (2013).

270 *In re* Inquest Subpoena (WCAX), 2005 Vt. 103, 890 A.2d 1240, 1241, 2005 Vt. LEXIS 244 (2005).

Court has already decided the First Amendment issue before us today."[271] It appears that any federal reporter–news gatherer privilege will have to be based on statutory enactments from Congress or a change in jurisprudence of the Supreme Court of the United States.

§ 10.10 Summary

In arriving at the truth in a criminal trial, all evidence that helps prove or disprove an important point or issue should be admitted. However, our society holds that some relationships deserve protection and privileges that hide the truth. In making the judgment that particular relationships should receive protection, the legislatures and courts have attempted to strike a fair balance between the need for evidence and the protection to be given to important relationships. In resolving these two considerations, courts and legislatures have developed privileges limiting the admission of some types of evidence, while other jurisdictions are more likely to admit evidence unless faced with a statutory or constitutional privilege. In some situations, there are occasions when the protection of the relationship or right is considered more important than the need for the evidence, even when it may create an injustice to another person.

An early privilege that developed over a period of many years is the husband–wife confidential communication privilege; this privilege appears to be extended to same-sex marriages where they are recognized by the particular jurisdiction. The general rule relating to confidential communications between husband and wife is that testimony pertaining to confidential communications arising out of the marital relationship is forever privileged, and a court will not require the conversations to be revealed because both spouses are considered to be holders of the privilege. However, there are several exceptions to this rule where crimes have been committed against family members or their property or the case involves divorce or child custody. With respect to the marital testimonial privilege, the clear trend is to remove the defendant spouse as a holder and permit the potential witness-spouse to decide whether to testify against the other. Some states still give the privilege to both spouses, so that a defendant spouse can prevent the other from testifying even when the witness spouse is willing and the marriage is broken. The marital testimonial privilege prevents a witness spouse from being forced to testify against the defendant spouse, but this privilege endures only as long as the marriage remains in existence.

A second common law privilege protects communications between attorney and client. Confidential communications made in the course of professional employment may not be divulged by the attorney without the client's consent. The privilege may not be claimed when the communication concerns the commission of a crime at some time

---

271 *In re* Grand Jury Subpoena (Miller), 365 U.S. App. D.C. 13, 397 F.3d 964, 2005 U.S. App. LEXIS 2494 (2005).

in the future or how to cover up a prior crime. The client holds the privilege, and he or she may waive the privilege even if the attorney does not agree.

Although at common law there was no physician–patient privilege, most states have enacted statutes creating this testimonial privilege. However, many do not apply this privilege in criminal cases. Where statutes have been enacted, the privilege prohibits disclosure by the physician and allied support staff, when called to testify, of confidential communications made to him or her or information acquired by him or her, in the course of his or her professional attendance upon the patient. The privilege does not apply when a statute requires reports of gunshot wounds or wounds inflicted by deadly weapons. The privilege generally applies in civil cases when the disclosures were made in confidence; however, some states allow medical privileges to be claimed in criminal cases. The patient must claim the privilege and only the patient may grant a waiver.

At common law, there was no privilege as to communications or confessions to a spiritual adviser. However, all 50 states now recognize the privilege. The clergy member, priest, or rabbi may not disclose, over the objection of the party so confiding, the confessions or admissions made as a part of the practice of the particular faith. In order for the communication to be privileged under the statutes, it must be made to the clergy member in a professional capacity where spiritual advice and counseling is the purpose. Generally, the privilege may be claimed only by the communicator, but the existence of the privilege should be raised by the clergy member.

One privilege that is of great concern to criminal justice personnel is the confidential informant privilege. It can be said that, as a general rule, the name of the informant does not have to be disclosed, especially if his or her information relates only to facts from which probable cause can be based. However, if the informant played an integral part in the illegal transaction and his or her disclosure is necessary and relevant to a fair defense, his or her identity may be required to be disclosed. Much discretion in this regard is in the hands of the judge when making a determination concerning whether an informant meets the requirements of a material witness.

Testimony relating to state secrets and other official information is sometimes privileged upon a showing of a reasonable likelihood of danger that the evidence will disclose state secrets or official information. Where this privilege is upheld, it is absolute.

The United States Supreme Court has determined that in the absence of statutes, communications to a newspaper editor or reporter are not privileged in federal courts. In states recognizing the privilege, some courts apply a balancing test that focuses on the need for the information and potential availability from other sources. If collateral sources make the information available, the news media privilege will likely prevail. More than half of the states, by statute or otherwise, have enacted news media privilege laws that attempt to resolve conflicting interests.

Because of the common law privileges, as well as the statutory privileges, it is possible that much relevant evidence may be excluded from trials. However, there are many exceptions that permit much valuable evidence to be obtained, if criminal justice personnel are familiar with the rules and the exceptions.

Courts and legislatures frequently alter the confidential communication privilege rules in order to prevent abuse and to effectuate fair public policy. Changes in evidence rules and laws dictate that law enforcement officials consult the rules of evidence and state case law with a view to ascertaining changes that will affect the practice of criminal justice.

CHAPTER TEN: QUESTIONS AND REVIEW EXERCISES

1. The effect of privileges not to testify is to preserve the confidentiality of particular relationships at the expense of revealing more of the truth in criminal trials. Why should society protect privileged communications? Is society better served by recognizing many of the various privileges to withhold evidence, or would revealing the truth in criminal trials be a better arrangement? Explain your reasoning.
2. In the area of privileged communications between husbands and wives, two distinct privileges have been recognized. Describe the essential attributes of the two separate privileges and give hypothetical examples where courts should recognize each privilege. What are the various views on who is a holder of the privilege?
3. The marital privileges have exceptions in which the privilege is not recognized and individual spouses must, may, or have the option to testify. What are these exceptions? What is the duration of existence of the respective marital privileges?
4. What is the logical rationale that supports the existence of the attorney–client privilege? Are both the attorney and client holders of the privilege? What are some of the limitations concerning what is privileged and what is not privileged in the attorney–client relationship? What are two examples of communication that is not protected by the attorney–client privilege?
5. In the case of the doctor–patient privilege, what is the rationale that supports a patient being permitted to keep medical data private? Can the doctor–patient privilege be asserted in both civil and criminal cases in jurisdictions that recognize this privilege? What are some of the traditionally recognized exceptions or limitations to the doctor–patient privilege?
6. Communications made to religious advisors or clergy members that are consistent with the doctrine of that particular faith are often covered by a confidential privilege. All communications with the religious leader cannot be considered covered by such privilege. So, what are some of the limitations that attach to the penitent–religious

leader privilege? Suggest a hypothetical fact pattern that would allow a penitent to prevent a priest or rabbi from divulging, in court, confidential communication that occurred between the two individuals. Give an example of a communication that would not be covered by the privilege.

7. In many situations, a government may prevent the revelation of the identity of a confidential informant. What is the theoretical rationale for allowing a prosecutor or a police department not to reveal confidential sources? Under what circumstances must the prosecutor or the law enforcement agency reveal the identity of a confidential source?
8. Federal courts have recognized that under the U.S. Constitution, state secrets and other sensitive information may be immune from revelation in a court of law. When properly asserted by the federal executive branch, is this privilege of state secrets absolute or subject to judicial determination concerning whether it has been properly asserted? Why is this privilege important to the United States government?
9. Some state jurisdictions recognize a news media–informant privilege that will protect the identity of an information source. Given that courts have as one of their goals the search for the truth, why should individuals connected to the media, broadly considered, be permitted to refuse in court (or to grand juries) to reveal the original sources of information that is either published or retained by the news organization? Should a news media–informant privilege be applied to the news gatherers who publish on the Internet through blogs, tweets, and similar outlets?

Opinions and Expert Testimony

11

Opinion evidence, to be of any value, should be based either upon admitted facts or upon facts, within the knowledge of the witness, disclosed in the record. Opinion evidence that does not appear to be based upon disclosed facts is of little or no value.

Balaban & Katz Corp. v. Commissioner of Internal Revenue,
30 F.2d 807 (7th Cir. 1929)

Chapter Contents

KEY TERMS AND CONCEPTS

Expert Witness
Lay Witness
Neutron Activation Analysis
Opinion Evidence
Polygraph Examination
Summaries
Ultimate Issue
Admissibility of Polygraph
Chain of Custody
Lay Opinion
Qualification of Expert

§ 11.1 Introduction

All humans form opinions on a variety of subjects that are based on data and information presented to individuals. Opinions are really judgments, inferences, or conclusions that help people organize their lives and create priorities. A court is generally interested in the bare facts and unadorned data that humans use to create their opinions rather that the particular opinion formed based on those raw facts. Therefore, when a witness takes the stand, the testimony is normally restricted to the basic facts and actual circumstances within the personal knowledge and recollection of the witness, as distinguished from opinions, inferences, impressions, and conclusions that the facts may have generated in the mind of the same witness. Because opinions can be considered a type of conclusion and the purpose of the jury is to reach conclusions based on the facts presented, witnesses who are not considered experts are usually restricted from offering their opinions concerning what the evidence actually means.

However, the rule that excludes opinion evidence has exceptions that are based on reason and practical necessity. Frequently, the only possible or practical method of getting proof of a fact in issue is by means of opinion evidence. If, from the nature of the subject matter, no better evidence can be obtained and opinion evidence will aid the members of the jury in their search for the truth, the judge in his or her discretion may admit the evidence even though it consists of an opinion. As one court noted, "[l]ay opinion is admitted when no particular or esoteric knowledge is required or when, as a practical matter, the subject of the testimony is too complex or subtle to enable the witness to accurately convey to the trier of fact his or her observations in any reasonable form other than an opinion. . ."[1] The law does not look with favor on

1 People v. Sneed, 2007 Cal. App. Unpub. LEXIS 10270 (2007).

Lay witnesses Any witness who is not an expert.

Expert witnesses A person who has acquired by special study, practice, and experience, peculiar skill and knowledge in relation to some particular science, art, or trade.

opinion evidence because it invades the province of the factfinder, and, in theory, such evidence should not be admitted unless it is required to prevent a miscarriage of justice.

Over the years, courts and legislatures have approved dozens of exceptions to the opinion evidence rule—to the extent that some opinion evidence is admissible in almost every case. These rules of exception have developed in two areas: (1) opinions of nonexpert or **lay witnesses** and (2) opinions of **expert witnesses.** The rules of evidence treat lay witnesses differently from expert witnesses because lay witnesses are typically discouraged from offering opinions while expert witnesses generally are called to offer opinion evidence.

Occasionally, criminal justice personnel testify as expert witnesses when they possess a particular expertise such as familiarity with drug transaction protocols, serial killer profiles, or fingerprint comparisons. However, in most instances, criminal justice personnel testify as lay witnesses because they offer testimony covering facts within their personal knowledge, observation, or recollection. There is no bright line between lay and expert testimony because every person evaluates information based on individual experiences. Even a lay witness is capable of expressing opinions outside the normal knowledge held by most people without having to be qualified as an expert. When a juror may not fully understand the evidence or not be able to come to a conclusion concerning a fact at issue without the assistance of a person with specialized knowledge, that witness must then be qualified as an expert witness.[2]

The goals of this chapter focus on the general rules related to admissibility of lay opinion evidence and on the protocols required for the use of expert witnesses.[3] The chapter details some of the specific instances that are commonly presented in criminal justice situations and discusses some of the more common rules governing the admission of opinion evidence in criminal cases.

§ 11.2 Definitions and Distinctions

Before discussing the general rules and the exceptions related to opinion testimony of expert and nonexpert witnesses, some definitions are necessary to understand these rules. One court,[4] paraphrasing the Fifth Circuit, noted that the difference between lay

---

2 Williams v. State, 2006 Tex. App. LEXIS 1687 (2006), (quoting Osbourn v. State, 92 S.W.3d 531, 537 (Tex. Crim. App. 2002)). *See* case in Part II.

3 *See* 2005 UTAH L. REV 230 (2005) for a note that clarifies the distinction between lay and expert witnesses with respect to their proper subject matter.

4 Jackson-Flavius v. People of the Virgin Islands, 57 V.I. 716, 732, 2012 V.I. Supreme LEXIS 89 (2012).

and expert witness testimony is that lay testimony is derived from the reasoning processes that people use in everyday life, and expert testimony results from reasoning processes that can be understood and mastered only by specialists in a particular field.

A. Opinion Evidence

Opinion evidence is defined in *Black's Law Dictionary* as a "witness's belief, thought, or inference, or conclusion concerning a fact or facts."[5] The term refers to opinions offered by either lay or expert witnesses while testifying in open court and is distinguished from extrajudicial opinions.

B. Expert Witness

An expert witness is particularly skilled, learned, or experienced in a particular art, science, trade, business, profession, or vocation and has gained a thorough knowledge of a subject that is not possessed by the average layperson. *Black's Law Dictionary*[6] defines an expert as a "person who, through education or experience, has developed skill or knowledge in a particular subject, so that he or she may form an opinion that will assist the fact-finder."[7] It further defines an expert witness as one who is "qualified by knowledge, skill, experience, training, or education to provide a scientific, technical, or other specialized opinion about the evidence or a fact issue."[8] In one old case, an expert witness was defined as one who has acquired the ability to deduce correct inferences from hypothetically stated facts or from facts involving scientific or technical knowledge.[9]

C. Nonexpert Witness

A nonexpert, or lay witness, is one who is not particularly skilled, learned, or experienced in the particular area that is at issue in the court, but who may have knowledge that an average person possesses about many of the things involved in everyday life. A person who is an expert in one field may be considered to be a lay witness when he or she takes the stand to testify about a field in which the witness can claim no expertise. The lay witness bases his or her conclusions on facts personally observed, while the expert witness, who must qualify as such by establishing that he or she has some special skill, knowledge, or experience, may base his or her opinions on facts of his or her own observation or on evidence presented by other witnesses. The lay witness may offer opinions concerning matters about which the average person forms opinions. For example, "[i]t is generally accepted that virtually any lay witness, including a police

---

5 BLACK'S LAW DICTIONARY 638 (9th ed. 2009).

6 BLACK'S LAW DICTIONARY 660 (9th ed. 2009).

7 *Id.*

8 BLACK'S LAW DICTIONARY 1740 (9th ed. 2009).

9 City of Chicago v. Lehmann, 262 Ill. 468, 104 N.E. 829 (1914). "Expert witness" will be further defined in later sections of this chapter.

officer, may testify as to whether an individual appears intoxicated."[10] Similarly, a lay witness may offer testimony concerning the identity of a person.[11] The line between lay and expert testimony is not always easy to discern, and the same witness may offer some evidence as a lay witness and also offer evidence as an expert.[12]

§ 11.3 Admissibility of Nonexpert Opinions

Rule 701

OPINION TESTIMONY BY LAY WITNESSES

If a witness is not testifying as an expert, testimony in the form of an opinion is limited to one that is:
(a) rationally based on the witness's perception;
(b) helpful to clearly understanding the witness's testimony or to determining a fact in issue; and
(c) not based on scientific, technical, or other specialized knowledge within the scope of Rule 702.[13]

Although subject to many exceptions, the general rule provides that "nonexpert" or lay witnesses must state facts or offer evidence based upon their personal knowledge and observations. With some exceptions, lay witnesses cannot give conclusions or opinions, but this rule is tempered by the fact that many items of evidence that could be considered opinions may not be viewed as such through the eyes of the law. For example, when a person testifies as to what he or she observes, hears, or smells, the testimony may be considered a statement of fact and not a conclusion or opinion—even though the statement is actually an opinion of what he or she saw, heard, or smelled.[14] Much effort has been expended to confine the testimony of witnesses to statements of what they saw, heard, or otherwise observed, as distinguished from inferences or opinions formed as a result of such observations. The legal distinction between opinion and fact has not been characterized as a bright line, but can be viewed as shades of gray. For example, one person may testify that the color of a swimming pool was blue, while

---

[10] State v. Clark, 2007 Ohio 3777, 2007 Ohio App. LEXIS 3442 (Ohio 2007).

[11] United States v. Beck, 418 F.3d 1008, 2005 U.S. App. LEXIS 16713 (9th Cir. 2005).

[12] United States v. Ayala-Pizarro, 407 F.3d 25, 2005 U.S. LEXIS 8322 (1st Cir. 2005). *See* State v. Streckfuss, 171 N.C. App. 81, 2005 LEXIS 1190 (2005), in which a police officer was permitted to identify the smell of alcohol and give a lay opinion that the defendant driver was alcohol impaired.

[13] FED. R. EVID. 701.

[14] *See* Livingston v. Texas, 2006 Tex. App. LEXIS 2234 (2006), in which an appellate court upheld the trial court ruling that permitted a lay witness to testify concerning the identity of odors emanating from a boat that smelled "like cigarettes, stale beer, and sweaty sex."

another might refer to the same pool as having an aqua color. Both persons probably view their respective characterizations of color as fact rather than realizing that each one has testified concerning his or her opinion of the color of the pool.

Despite occasional appellate disputes about whether it was proper for a lay witness to give an opinion[15] or whether the opinion offered by a particular witness should have been preceded by testimony establishing the witness's qualifications as an expert, the modern trend appears to allow more lay opinion to be introduced. An Arkansas reviewing court approved of a lay witness police officer giving an opinion that the amount of money found on a suspect, and the fact that the denominations of twenties, tens, and fives, were consistent with making drug sales.[16] In supporting the use of lay opinion testimony, one court noted that lay witnesses are perfectly capable of giving opinion testimony so long as the opinion is rationally based upon the original perception of the witness and the opinion is helpful to a clear understanding of the witness's testimony or aids in the determination of a fact that is at issue.[17] As a general rule, trial judges have broad discretion on the admission of lay witness opinion evidence and a trial court's decision to permit lay opinion will not be reversed unless a clear abuse of discretion appears.[18] As one Texas court noted, "the opinions of lay witnesses, when competent, are admissible concerning estimates of age, size, weight, quantity, time, distance and speed of persons and things."[19] Lay witness testimony should be ruled as inadmissible when it crosses the line and offers testimony that requires special training or expertise.

The lay witness may state a relevant opinion if it is (1) based on the original perception of the witness, (2) generally helpful to the finder of fact to obtain a clear understanding of the issues, and (3) not based on the types of evidence that are reserved for expert testimony.[20] The general rule is that as a condition of stating his or her opinion, the witness must state the facts on which such opinion is based, but if the basis is mentioned on direct examination, the witness will be required to offer it if asked on cross-examination. The enumeration of facts not only goes to show the competency of the witness, but also provides an opportunity to test the reasonableness of the inference, because a witness will not be permitted to state an opinion that is inconsistent with or finds no support in the facts.

The purpose of allowing a lay witness to testify concerning his or her opinion is to help the jury or factfinder obtain a clear understanding of the testimony or to help decide a fact at issue. Consistent with helping a jury decide a controverted fact, in a federal prosecution, a lay witness was permitted to offer an opinion concerning the identity of a voice on a series of telephone recordings of a drug dealer obtained under

---

15 People v. Souva, 2005 Colorado App. LEXIS 1615 (2005).

16 Williams v. State, 2012 Ark. App. 310, 2012 Ark. App. LEXIS 428 (2012).

17 State v. McFeely, 2009 Ohio 1436, 2009 Ohio App. LEXIS 1214 (2009).

18 People v. Brooks, 2010 Cal. App. Unpub. LEXIS 9571 (2010).

19 Scott v. State, 2008 Tex. App. LEXIS 6172 (Tex. 2008).

20 FED. R. EVID. 701.

a wiretap. At trial, the prosecution called a DEA linguist to compare a known voice sample of the defendant obtained from calls recorded at the defendant's lockup in Chicago with the voices in selected calls previously recorded by federal agents. The witness could be considered an expert in translating Spanish to English, but in her lay capacity of familiarity with the defendant's voice, she was permitted to offer her opinion concerning the defendant's identity. As the basis for her testimony, she had listened to tapes of the phone conversations and had listened to voice sample tapes of the defendant which allowed her a sufficient basis to offer her lay opinion that the voice on one tape was that of the defendant. The Court of Appeals upheld the defendant's conviction despite his contention that the linguist was not competent to render a lay opinion concerning identity of his voice.[21] In a case involving falsification of federal permanent resident documents that had similar issues, a police officer was properly permitted to offer a lay opinion concerning the identity of a defendant's voice on an audiotape because the witness need not be an expert witness, just possess familiarity with the voice at issue, which the officer gained by working on the case.[22]

The opinions of lay witnesses are not supposed to invade the function of the jury. Some courts have permitted lay witnesses to come dangerously close to offering an opinion concerning the **ultimate issue.** In one Texas case, the trial court properly permitted a lay witness to offer opinion evidence on the issue of whether a defendant properly used deadly force to protect another person,[23] an opinion that went dangerously close to the core of the case.

Ultimate issue The questions that must finally be answered, such as the defendant's guilt in a criminal action.

Even if the lay witness can describe some of the circumstances that led to an opinion, the witness may still give an opinion even when it is difficult to articulate all the factors. For example, in a theft case in a retail store, a loss prevention security guard was permitted to offer lay opinion evidence concerning whether the defendant intended to deprive Walmart of its property. Although a lay witness cannot possess personal knowledge of what another person may be thinking, he or she may possess personal knowledge of facts from which an opinion regarding the mental state of another person may be drawn. The opinion offered by the lay witness in this theft case was based on her personal perceptions and observations and her opinion was rationally based on knowledge of the events observed.[24]

Using language that expanded the use of opinion evidence by nonexpert witnesses, Federal Rule of Evidence 701(b) allows opinions or inferences if they are merely "helpful" to the jury in understanding the witness's testimony or aid in the determination of a factual issue. Under the rule, the lay witness may now offer an opinion as long

---

21 United States v. Mendiola, 707 F3d 735, 740, 2013 U.S. App. LEXIS 2809 (7th Cir. 2013).

22 United States v. Cruz, 508 F. App'x. 890, 2013 U.S. App. LEXIS 1982 (11th Cir. 2013).

23 Garcia v. State, 2005 Tex. App. LEXIS 4424 (2005).

24 Hines v. State, 2006 Tex. App. LEXIS 3256 (2006).

as it is not based on scientific or specialized knowledge traditionally covered by expert testimony. For example, in a case involving allegations that a felon was in possession of prohibited weapons and body armor, a police officer was properly permitted to testify in the form of an opinion that the attire that defendant wore was body armor. The reviewing court held that because lay witnesses necessarily draw on individualized experience and knowledge, and although the officer had professional experience with body armor, the officer's testimony was still considered lay opinion evidence and properly admissible. The officer had a basis for his opinion because the officer wore similar protection and was familiar with such safety accessories.[25] Rule 701 may broaden the circumstances under which a lay witness may give an opinion or inference based upon personal observation, but limits remain on the conclusions that lay witnesses may draw. In a state case, a police officer should not have been permitted to give an opinion about the credibility of another prosecution witness because it invaded the province of the jury in resolving matters of credibility of witnesses.[26]

Referring to the proper standards for admissibility of lay opinion testimony, a federal court of appeals commented that lay opinion evidence should be admissible when the witness has had sufficient contact with the facts of the case that would render a lay opinion helpful to the judge or jury. In the case, a defendant's probation officer had been permitted to identify the defendant by looking at a still picture taken by a bank's surveillance system. The probation officer had previous significant contacts with the defendant that were considered sufficient to be able to recognize a picture of his client, the accused bank robber. The Court of Appeals for the Ninth Circuit held that a lay witness probation officer's identification testimony was properly admissible within the meaning of Rule 701, where it was based upon personal observation and recollection of concrete facts.[27]

Although allowing some lay opinion evidence, Rule 701, however, does not allow the introduction of opinion evidence when the facts are clear and the jury can draw its own conclusion from the facts that have been presented. To allow lay opinion evidence under such circumstances would present the risk that the testimony might usurp the function of the jury.[28]

While Rule 701 places some limits on the admissibility of opinion testimony by lay witnesses, almost any person, including a police officer, may testify concerning whether an individual appears intoxicated. Consistent with this concept, the Rule allowed an Indiana police officer to offer a lay opinion concerning his conclusion that a defendant was under the influence of alcohol or other drugs because lay witnesses may offer opinions that are rationally based on the perception of the witness[29] and most

---

25 People v. Richardson, 2013 Ill. App. 2d 120119, 2013 Ill. App. LEXIS 565 (2013).

26 Tumblin v. State, 29 So.3d 1093, 100, 2010 Fla. LEXIS 258 (Fla. 2010).

27 United States v. Beck, 418 F.3d 1008; 2005 U.S. App. LEXIS 16713 (2005).

28 United States v. Reneau, 390 F.3d 746, 2004 U.S. App. LEXIS 24837 (2d Cir. 2004), *cert. denied*, 544 U.S. 1007, 2005 U.S. LEXIS 3660 (2005).

29 Duncan v. State, 2013 Ind. App. Unpub. LEXIS 232, 984 N.E.2d 720 (Ind. 2013) February 26, 2013.

adults and older children are competent to render a judgment concerning intoxication. Another court approved allowing a police officer to offer his opinion that a round bruise on a victim's neck was consistent with being struck by a rifle barrel.[30]

It is obvious that significant evidence would be unavailable to the factfinders if all lay opinion evidence were excluded from criminal trials. Examples of proper subject matter for lay opinion testimony are discussed in § 11.4.

§ 11.4 Subjects of Nonexpert Opinions

A. Age

Lay witness opinion testimony is admissible when it is rationally based on personal knowledge and helpful to the trier of fact. It is a foregone conclusion that all humans evaluate other humans with respect to age for various reasons. Competent witnesses with firsthand knowledge will generally be permitted to offer an estimate or opinion as to the age of a person (and a witness may give his or her age), although the age of the witness is not personally known by the lay witness.[31] As one court noted, where age was concerned, it was "particularly appropriate for a lay witness to express an opinion on the subject."[32]

In criminal prosecutions involving possession of child pornography, the prosecution must demonstrate that some of the actors involved are less than 18 years of age. Because many of the films, DVD recordings, and computer files seized do not leave any way to find or discover the actors and their real ages as of the date of the original digital recording, witnesses for the prosecution will have to offer evidence concerning age. In one child pornography possession case where the defendant had left open tabs on a browser in a public library that allegedly contained sexual images of underage children, a police officer was permitted to testify that he observed the images and held the opinion that all of the females depicted in the photographs were under the age of eighteen. The reviewing court noted that lay witnesses are permitted to offer opinions on many subjects, including the age of a person when rationally based on the witness's original perception.[33]

Practical necessity often requires that the opinion of a lay witness as to the age of a person be used because it is often impossible to testify to the exact age of another person or to know the age of a person for certain. In a California drug manufacturing case,[34] a reviewing court upheld a sentencing enhancement because children under sixteen years of age were present at the meth house. Over the defendant's objection, a police officer testified that the children were above the age of one and below the

---

30 Garcia v. State, 2010 Tex. App. LEXIS 3126 (2010).

31 State v. Selmon, 2006 Ohio 65, 2006 Ohio App. LEXIS 50 (2006).

32 United States v. Yazzie, 976 F.2d 1252, 1256 (9th Cir. 1992).

33 Whiddon v. State, 2013 Tex. App. LEXIS 2074 (2013).

34 People v. Romereo-Resendiz, 2006 Cal. App. Unpub. LEXIS 2598 (2006).

age of eight. The court noted that "it has been settled by an overwhelming weight of authority that when a person's age is the subject of judicial inquiry, a witness may give his or her opinion as to that age."[35]

As a general rule, when a witness has previously possessed adequate opportunity to observe the person whose age is at issue, opinion evidence of the lay witness concerning age is admissible. If the exact age of an individual is available from documents or the individual in question, however, the use of that evidence is generally appropriate, sufficient,[36] and preferable to estimation of age by a lay or an expert witness.

B. Appearance

When individuals experience exciting events, become upset, have frightening experiences, or seem scared of another person or situation, an explanation of all the outward manifestations that give rise to the conclusion that a person has experienced excitement, fear, or another emotion are not easily described by another person. How one person's demeanor appears to another is a matter well within the human experience and would not ordinarily call for expert testimony. Assuming a witness meets the requirements of competency and has personally observed another person, a court normally should admit lay testimony concerning the appearance and demeanor of another. For example, in an assault case in which a man threatened his former girlfriend with a firearm, the trial court admitted testimony of a police officer that the victim appeared "fearful" and "excited" at the time he initially encountered her. The appellate court upheld the admission of the testimony describing the victim on the theory that lay testimony can be offered when it is based on the perception of the witness (the officer) and the testimony would be helpful to a clear understanding of the witness's testimony. The officer had firsthand perception and his statements were based on direct involvement and experience in the case.[37]

In a case involving domestic violence and assault, an allegation of self-defense was rebutted by a police officer's testimony that a wound on the defendant was not new and appeared to have been inflicted at an earlier time and definitely not on the day of the assault. The Supreme Court of the Virgin Islands approved allowing the officer to give an opinion as a lay witness concerning the age of the defendant's bruising and prior injury. According to the court, the determination of whether a bruise on a human body was fresh did not require scientific or other specialized knowledge. It noted that lay individuals are generally familiar with bruising and the healing processes of bruises and are permitted to form an opinion concerning the approximate age of a bruise or a cut on the human body.[38]

---

35 *Id.*

36 Commonwealth of Massachusetts v. Montalvo, 50 Mass. App. Ct. 85, 88, 735 N.E.2d 391, 394, 2000 Mass. App. LEXIS 763 (2000).

37 Washington v. Bain, 2002 Wash. App. LEXIS 1863 (2002).

38 Jackson-Flavius v. People of the Virgin Islands, 57 V.I. 716, 732, 2012 V.I. LEXIS 89 (2012).

In a different case, the trial court did not commit error when it allowed a detective's testimony in an assault case to describe the defendant's physical condition at the time of the incident, where he had noticed the defendant was very muscular and had calloused knuckles. This testimony was relevant because it attempted to show, through appearance, that the defendant had the strength and ability to inflict the serious injuries sustained by the victim.[39]

C. Conduct

A lay witness may describe the acts, conduct, and demeanor of a person under investigation if necessary to enable the jury to draw a correct inference. In such a case, the witness should be required—as far as is possible—to state the facts on which he or she based his or her opinions. In a prosecution for public intoxication, a police officer could properly testify that the defendant appeared intoxicated when he had been informed by paramedics that the woman was intoxicated and the officer observed her bloodshot eyes and indicated that she smelled of alcohol. In addition, the defendant told the officer that she was going to urinate in the parking lot. These factors permitted the officer to testify as a lay witness to the fact that he believed that the defendant was under the influence of alcohol in a public place.[40]

Lay opinion concerning the mental state of another person may be admissible in some cases but inappropriate in others. As a general rule, a lay witness may give an opinion concerning the emotional state of another person provided that individual has personal knowledge of the subject's mental state. However, a North Carolina reviewing court approved the exclusion of a lay witness social worker's testimony when she attempted to offer an opinion that a murder defendant "appeared noticeably depressed with flat effect" because such an opinion was more comparable to an expert diagnosis rather than a lay opinion.[41]

An Alabama appellate court in a murder case approved allowing a witness to tell the jury that the victim was afraid of the defendant and had informed the defendant that he could no longer reside in her trailer home and that her demeanor in the presence of the defendant indicated that she feared him. The witness was also permitted to testify that the victim had changed the door locks on the trailer home, which helped support the witness's evaluation that the victim feared the defendant.[42]

Testimony concerning observed conduct may prove crucial when proving criminal activity involving alcohol impairment. In proving a case of aggravated vehicular assault, the trial judge permitted a gas station attendant, who knew the defendant, to testify that, although she could smell no alcohol, the defendant was behaving in an unusual manner. She indicated that he placed his elbows on the counter to support himself; he seemed to omit some words as he spoke; and he asked about lottery tickets that

---

[39] State v. Ames, 950 P.2d 514 (Wash. 1998).

[40] McCutchen v. State, 2010 Tex. App. LEXIS 7760 (2010).

[41] State v. Storm, 743 S.E.2d 713, 718, 2013 N.C. App. LEXIS 727 (2013).

[42] McCray v. State, 2010 Ala. Crim. App. LEXIS 136 (2010).

he normally would know were not sold on that shift. The clerk indicated that, in her opinion, the defendant was intoxicated.[43] In a different Ohio case, police officers observed several subjects around a pickup truck, and one man had his feet on the sidewalk leaning inside the vehicle. One officer testified that from the time of day, the location, the number of people around the vehicle, and considering the defendant's actions and hand movements, the officer believed that a drug transaction was taking place. The appellate court approved of the officers' testimony about the defendant's activities and agreed that they could properly offer their lay opinion that they believed a narcotics deal was being concluded.[44]

A Montana appellate court upheld a trial court decision that permitted police officers to offer lay opinions concerning whether the defendant possessed methamphetamine for the purposes of sale. According to the officers, based on their experience, the quantity of illegal drugs the defendant was carrying indicated possession with the intent to distribute. The officers testified concerning their training, experience, and knowledge of the manner that methamphetamine was typically distributed. The appellate court held that the testimony was rationally based on their perceptions and their opinions helped convey a clear understanding of the facts in the case.[45] In a Texas case, involving a similar rationale, the court upheld the admissibility of a detective's lay opinion that a quantity of methamphetamine was being held for purposes of sale because scales, packaging materials, and a large amount of money were present at the defendant's place of residence.[46] In a different case, a drug user lay witness was properly permitted to offer an opinion on the identity of an alleged controlled substance where she had experience and knowledge of the drug at issue because she had been a long-time user of the particular drug.[47]

While the recent trend has been to permit more lay opinion testimony, many courts still place some limitations on the use of lay opinion, especially where the testimony leans clearly toward being classified as expert testimony. In a case from Hawai'i, the appellate court reversed a murder conviction because a police officer had been permitted to testify that a revolver had been fired recently, meaning within an eight-hour period. On cross-examination, the officer testified that his opinion was based on his personal experience handling firearms. The officer testified that he carried a revolver for 20 years as his primary service weapon and that he had fired thousands of rounds in meeting his quarterly firearm qualification requirement. The reviewing court believed that the testimony concerning the time frame in which the gun had been fired was admitted as lay opinion testimony, for which the court determined that expert testimony would have been required for the offering of such an opinion. The court reversed the murder conviction because the time when the revolver had been fired was crucial to the original conviction.[48]

---

43 State v. DeWulf, 2013 Ohio 2802, 2013 Ohio App. LEXIS 2846 (2013).

44 State v. Farrow, 2005 Ohio 3005, 2005 Ohio App. LEXIS 2799 (2005).

45 State v. Frasure, 323 Mont. 479, 100 P.3d 1013, 204 Mont. LEXIS 558 (2004).

46 Ortiz v. Texas, 2005 Tex. App. LEXIS 6721 (2005).

47 State v. Mielke, 2013 Ohio 1612, 2013 Ohio App. LEXIS 1501 (2013).

48 State v. Torres, 122 Haw. 2, 222 P.3d 409, 435, 2009 Haw. App. LEXIS 781 (2009), *cert. granted*, 2010 Haw. LEXIS 107 (2010).

D. Distance and Space

In criminal cases, it is often necessary to elicit testimony concerning location, distances, and space between objects. While it is preferable to introduce evidence to show exact distances, in some cases this is not practical, and opinion evidence becomes necessary. Adults and older teenagers make these estimates or opinions every day whether driving an automobile, working in a yard, or traveling to a different location, to name a few. Because these individuals have developed a basis on which to offer an opinion, an ordinary witness may give his or her estimate of distances or size, provided that he or she is cognizant of the facts on which the estimate is based. In allowing two lay witnesses to offer their opinion on the speed of a defendant's vehicle immediately prior to a fatal intoxicated driving crash, an Illinois appellate court referred to settled law that a lay witness may testify concerning the speed of vehicle based on the witnesses observation of the moving vehicle.[49] In a criminal appeal, an Alabama court approved the admission of lay witness testimony by a police officer that a butcher knife found at the scene of the homicide had the same width of many of the puncture wounds that had been inflicted on the decedent. The officer testified that the decedent's wounds were consistent with size of the knife found at the crime scene.[50] In a sentencing hearing in a Pennsylvania drug case involving a sentence enhancement based on distance from a school, the defendant objected to the use of Google Earth's accuracy in determining whether the defendant's drug sales were within 1000 feet of a school. The court required that a police officer authenticate the evidence prior to computer-generated satellite-based distance calculations were admissible in court. Authentication can occur when a police officer verifies some of the distance calculations with on-the-scene measurements. In this case, the police officer testified as a lay witness and indicated that he was familiar with Google Earth's Internet Web site and its satellite measurement system and that he had used this tool to determine distances on multiple occasions in the past. Prior to using Google Earth for measuring, he verified its accuracy by physically measuring the distance between two known points and then using Google Earth to calculate the same distance. He testified that it was generally accurate within one foot.[51]

In establishing a person's location, cell phone records may be introduced to indicate the location of the defendant's cell phone. In reversing a defendant's conviction for shooting into the home of his former girlfriend, it was improper for the trial court to allow a police officer to testify as a lay witness explaining how cell phone locations are determined by triangulation and with reference to cell tower locations without being qualified as an expert witness. Therefore, the trial court committed reversible error by allowing the officer to testify how he used using cell phone records to place the defendant near the former girlfriend's home. The officer's lack of training in cell phone theory should have prevented his testimony concerning the location of the defendant's cell

---

[49] People v. Tellez, 2013 Ill. App. 112048-U, 2013 Ill. App. Unpub. LEXIS 986 (2013).

[50] McCray v. State, 2010 Ala. Crim. App. LEXIS 136, 170 (2010).

[51] Commonwealth v. Suarez-Irizzary, 2010 Pa. Dist. & Cnty. Dec. LEXIS 380 (2010).

phone. In this case, an expert should have been offered as a witness because the procedure determining location required specialized skill which the lay witness officer lacked.[52]

The lay witnesses must have a sound foundation for offering an opinion concerning the speed of a vehicle. One court held that a victim-witness should not have been permitted to give an estimate or opinion of the distance that a tractor-trailer truck pushed her car when she was not "sure" and did not "remember" how far the truck pushed her car.[53] In traffic enforcement cases, police are permitted to make an estimate that one vehicle was following another vehicle at too close of a distance and to base a traffic stop on such a conclusion.[54]

E. Time and Duration

Relying on this same rationale, courts have authorized witnesses to make estimates of elapsed time.[55] However, if the witness can give specifics from which the jury can make its own estimate of time, then the opinion evidence regarding the passage of time is inadmissible. In a case in which an alibi defense rested on proof of time, lay witnesses were permitted to offer opinions concerning when the defendant was present at particular locations, some of which supported his alibi with reference to time and some of which did not assist in his alibi defense.[56]

F. Intoxication and Drug Use

When a witness possesses an appropriate foundation to offer lay opinion evidence, the witness may state his or her conclusion without first detailing the facts on which he or she bases such opinion. The subject of the testimony must not encompass topics of a complex nature that would be appropriate only for expert witness testimony. Intoxication is such a matter and is so commonly encountered that almost anyone may discern it.[57] Consistent with this principle, in a Michigan prosecution, a variety of lay witnesses who observed a defendant drinking alcohol at a bar for a period of hours prior to fatally hitting a pedestrian with his motor vehicle were properly permitted to testify concerning the defendant's intoxication generally, and specifically, to his intoxication just prior to the hit and run accident. According to the reviewing court, "Lay witnesses are qualified to testify about opinions they form as a result of direct physical observation."[58] Because opinion evidence of intoxication is not restricted to expert testimony, a police officer may offer lay evidence that a person was impaired where sufficient basis for the

---

52 Wilder v. State, 191 Md. App. 319, 369, 991 A.2d 172, 199, 2010 Md. App. LEXIS 43 (2010). *See also* State v. Patton, 2013 Mo. App. LEXIS 1165 (2013).

53 Heath v. Rush, 259 Ga. App. 887, 578 S.E.2d 564, 2003 Ga. App. LEXIS 287 (2003).

54 Ford v. State, 158 S.W.3d 488, 2005 Tex. Crim. App. LEXIS (2005).

55 Allison v. Wall, 121 Ga. 822, 49 S.E. 831 (1905).

56 Gonzalez v. Texas, 2000 Tex. App. LEXIS 3032 (2000).

57 Warren v. State, 164 Md. App. 153, 168, 882 A.2d 934, 943, 2005 Md. App. LEXIS 189 (2004).

58 People v. Jacques, 2013 Mich. App. LEXIS 488 (2013).

opinion exists. In a driving while impaired prosecution, an officer concluded and was permitted to offer the opinion that the driver of a boat was operating the craft while under the influence of alcohol. The foundation or basis for the officer's opinion was the subject's poor performance on sobriety tests.[59] For any witness to offer an opinion concerning drug or alcohol use, the lay witness must show that he or she had a sufficient firsthand opportunity to observe the defendant while the proponent of the evidence must show that the witness possessed a foundation for the opinion.

While the arresting officer may not give a legal definition of driving while impaired, the officer may give his or her opinion that the defendant was a less safe driver as a result of alcohol consumption, based on the officer's experience with driving under the influence arrests and observations.[60] As a general rule, a police officer may not offer an opinion concerning whether an arrested driver was under the influence of controlled substances because that opinion must be offered by an expert. In an Illinois case, a police officer testified that the defendant had been arrested for driving under the influence of alcohol and other drugs because the driver failed some standard alcohol sobriety tests and there was a strong odor of marijuana coming from the car. However, the defendant had no slurred speech or glassy eyes. This reviewing court noted that most adults are competent to offer lay testimony concerning alcohol intoxication because it is within the common experience of most adults. In a case of drug intoxication, the officer would have to demonstrate that he had relevant skills, experience, or training to render an opinion that someone was under the influence of drugs. The reviewing court reversed the conviction for driving under the influence of alcohol and other drugs because the officer had fewer than two years' experience as a police officer, it was his first arrest for driving under the influence of alcohol and other drugs, and the officer did not have any unique training in drug intoxication recognition.[61] Essentially, the officer possessed no foundation to testify as either a lay or an expert witness with respect to drug intoxication.

As a result of appellate courts reviewing a large number of state criminal drug cases, the courts have developed a body of law concerning drug identification opinion evidence offered by law enforcement agents, confidential informants, and other lay witnesses that has fairly specific application to drug testimony. Generally, these lay witnesses are not permitted to express opinions about matters that are within the scope of the common knowledge and experience of the jury, or matters that are peculiarly within the specialized knowledge of experts. Many lay witnesses and police officers could identify marijuana, whether fresh or burned, but identifying other illegal substances often, but not always, requires expert testimony. However, many courts hold that police officers and other involved witnesses are qualified to testify concerning matters related to the identity and sale of controlled substances if the opinion testimony satisfies the

---

59 Bowling v. State, 275 Ga. App. 45, 47, 619 S.E.2d 688, 689, 690, 2005 Ga. App. LEXIS 808 (2005). *See* case in Part II.

60 Hatcher v. State, 277 Ga. App. 611, 613, 627 S.E.2d 175, 177, 2006 Ga. App. LEXIS 164 (2005).

61 People v. Foltz, 403 Ill. App. 3d 419, 425, 934 N.E.2d 719, 724, 2010 Ill. App. LEXIS 889 (2010).

requirements of firsthand knowledge and if it will be helpful to a jury in developing a clear understanding of the testimony or a fact in issue. In most jurisdictions, police training includes experience with narcotics detection and identification that gives police officers a foundation for some types of drug identification.

In a Texas case, a trial court permitted a police officer to testify that she smelled burned marijuana and found a baggie of marijuana inside an automobile that she had stopped for a traffic offense. She mentioned that she had training in the academy regarding what unburned marijuana looked like and had become familiar with the odor of burning marijuana during other training. The judge allowed the officer to testify as a lay witness with respect to the marijuana. In affirming the conviction, the appellate court noted, "marihuana has a distinct appearance and odor that are familiar and easily recognizable to anyone who has encountered it. So [the officer]'s opinion that appellant possessed marihuana, based on the odor she smelled and the green, leafy substance she saw, was one that a reasonable person could draw from the circumstances. Her testimony regarding the identification of the marihuana was admissible as a lay opinion."[62] A different court approved the testimony of a cooperating steroid drug seller and user who was able to identify and offer an opinion concerning the type of drug being sold as constituting a controlled substance because the witness had a long history of both use and sale of steroid drugs, which provided the foundation for the lay testimony.[63]

In another example, one of the prosecution's lay witnesses was permitted to identify a quantity of suspected drugs as cocaine due to his personal experience and knowledge of cocaine as well as from the circumstances of the transaction. The witness had consumed cocaine hundreds of times and snorted or smoked two to three grams per day for several years. Due to his personal involvement in cocaine use and his familiarity with the drug, the lay witness was properly permitted to identify the controlled substance that was the subject of the trial as cocaine. The court reasoned that the opinion of the lay witness was helpful to the trier of fact and the prosecutor offered a proper foundation to show that the witness was sufficiently familiar with cocaine to be able to identify it.[64]

However, where the factual analysis appears more complicated, a court may reverse a conviction where a police officer's testimony was admitted as lay witness opinion but should have been admitted, if at all, as expert testimony. In a Colorado appellate case, the court reversed a defendant's conviction for possessing pseudoephedrine with intent to manufacture a controlled substance. Police officers had been permitted to testify as lay witnesses that the defendant possessed not only precursor chemicals, but were permitted to explain to the jury how methamphetamine is manufactured by combining the precursor chemicals. The officers' testimony would have been admissible as expert testimony had the prosecutor qualified the officers as

---

62 Osbourn v. Texas, 92 S.W.3d 531, 537, 2002 Tex. Crim. App. LEXIS 236 (2002). *See* case in Part II.

63 State v. Mielke, 2013 Ohio 1612, 2013 Ohio App. LEXIS 1501 (2013).

64 State v. Maag, 2005 Ohio 3761, 2005 Ohio App. Lexis 3461 (2005).

experts, but the admission of the evidence as lay testimony constituted reversible error because the testimony may have substantially influenced the jury.[65]

G. Sanity or Mental Condition

While both expert and lay opinion may be admissible to assist the trier of fact in determining a person's sanity or mental condition, a jury or judge may accept or reject one version of the evidence over the other. In one case, in which the defendant suffered from bipolar disorder, an Axis I disorder, and experienced auditory and paranoid delusions that resulted in commitments to mental facilities more than 15 times, he killed his grandmother in front of witnesses. The trial judge's verdict of guilty but insane was reversed by the Supreme Court of Indiana because all the lay evidence presented at trial did not conflict with any of the expert testimony and all the evidence pointed toward the conclusion that the defendant was legally insane. In reversing the guilty but insane verdict, the Indiana top court pointed to the fact that all the lay evidence (family and associates) supported a straight verdict of not guilty by reason of insanity and had the lay evidence presented been divergent from the expert testimony, there would have been a reason to affirm the guilty but insane verdict.[66] This case demonstrates that lay testimony concerning insanity or sanity is admissible and carries significant weight with the trier of fact.

A nonexpert witness, in response to purely hypothetical questions, may not give an opinion on the question of sanity. Subject to judicial approval, a lay witness may give testimony concerning another person's sanity when that witness clearly has demonstrated that he or she is acquainted with the person whose mental condition is at issue and can detail facts and circumstances relating to his or her acquaintance and the conduct and conversation upon which his or her opinion is based.[67] Before a nonexpert witness is competent to testify as to the sanity, mental condition, or retardation of another person, the witness must demonstrate a foundational level of acquaintance involving close contact and duration as to indicate clearly that the testimony would be of value in determining the mental issue. In a North Carolina homicide case, the defendant, who was mentally retarded, shot and killed a coworker who had been hazing him about his mental condition. The trial court permitted his former live-in girlfriend, with whom he had a child, to testify that the defendant was not retarded. The girlfriend had an intimate relationship with the defendant and had an opportunity to have observed the defendant in a variety of social contexts. She indicated that he performed the typical daily routine and, although he could be quiet sometimes, no one would think that anything was wrong.[68]

---

65 People v. Veren, 2005 Colo. App. LEXIS 1957 (2005), *reh'g denied*, 2006 Colo. App. LEXIS 112 (2006).

66 *See* Galloway v. State, 2010 Ind. LEXIS 806 (2010).

67 Rupert v. People, 429 P.2d 276 (Colo. 1967); McCall v. State, 408 N.E.2d 1218 (Ind. 1980). *See also* United States v. Santos, 131 F.3d 16 (1st Cir. 1997).

68 State v. McClain, 169 N.C. App. 657, 670, 610 S.E.2d 783, 792, 2005 N.C. App. LEXIS 804 (2005).

In the preceding case, where lay evidence of mental condition had been admitted, the North Carolina Court of Appeals suggested some specific conditions that must be applied in determining whether a lay witness may properly testify concerning a defendant's mental condition.[69] That court provided that the following factors are to be considered: (1) the witness's opinion must be rationally based on the personal perception of the lay witness, (2) the testimony must be helpful to the determination of a fact in issue, and (3) the subject of mental condition is an appropriate subject for lay opinion.

As a general rule, there is no requirement as to the length of the acquaintance with a defendant for a lay person to be permitted to offer opinions concerning mental state. In a Washington capital sentencing hearing, the judge permitted a police officer, who interviewed the defendant near the time of the fatal incident, to testify concerning his observations and opinions of the defendant with respect to the defendant's behavior during post-arrest interviews and how the officer had no concerns about the defendant's mental health. He indicated that the defendant followed changing topics in the interview without difficulty and appeared to be normal. Even though the officer had not known the defendant very long, it approved admitting the officer's lay testimony concerning mental health because it was based on firsthand knowledge and experience.[70]

H. Identification

In criminal cases, the identity of the perpetrator is often a contested issue for which proof must be offered or refuted and such proof must often involve lay opinion testimony. Due to issues of perception, visibility, opportunity, uncertainty, and passage of time, the identification of a person need not be made in absolutely positive terms. A witness may testify that an accused "resembles" or "looks like" the person who committed the crime. A witness may testify that in his or her opinion the accused is the person who perpetrated the crime. Courts generally admit lay opinion concerning identity when a witness is sufficiently familiar with the person in question so that the lay witness is better suited to make the identification than the jury.[71]

At trial, proper identification of the perpetrator often serves to resolve the primary issue because, in most cases, there is little doubt that a crime has occurred. In one case in which the identity of the perpetrator proved to be the primary issue, the trial court permitted the victim's boyfriend to make an in-court identification of the defendant. In the crime, the victim's car had been taken in a carjacking when the perpetrator demanded the keys to the vehicle. The victim's boyfriend had a good opportunity to observe the perpetrator when he handed the vehicle keys to him, and the boyfriend naturally had paid close attention to the person with the gun. The reviewing court approved the trial court decision that allowed the victim's boyfriend to make an in-court identification that followed his identification of the defendant from a prior

---

69 *Id.*

70 State v. Davis, 175 Wn.2d 287, 327, 2012 Wash. LEXIS 667 (2012). *Cert. denied,* 2013 U.S. LEXIS 5818 (2013).

71 United States v. Kornegay, 410 F.3d 89, 94, 2005 U.S. App. LEXIS 10707 (1st Cir. 2005).

photographic array.[72] In a felony stalking case, where the identity of the defendant had to be proved as an element of the crime, a trial court permitted the victim's boss to testify concerning the defendant's identity by indicating that the figure on a security tape was actually the defendant.[73] The video had been taken on the premises during the time that the victim's boss had served the defendant in a fast-food restaurant. Although, the reviewing court did not consider this opinion evidence, calling it direct identification evidence, the reality was that the victim's boss was rendering an opinion concerning the defendant's identity as displayed on the video.

The sound of a person's voice also may be the basis of an opinion as to a person's identity.[74] In a prosecution for the sale or attempted sale of military-grade night vision goggles to the government of Iran, an American agent was permitted to offer lay opinion concerning the identity of one of the defendants.[75] The undercover agent had heard the Iranian woman conspirator speak numerous times on intercepted telephone conversations and had one conversation with the defendant directly. The appeals court upheld the use of the agent's lay testimony because the undercover agent had heard her voice many times under circumstances that connected the conversation to the speaker and the testimony was helpful to a clear understanding of a fact at issue, the speaker's identity.

This rule also applies to the identity of things. A person who has tasted alcoholic beverages before may testify as to the nature and odor of a beverage. Police officers are generally permitted to testify concerning the smell of burned marijuana.[76] In a prosecution in which a man had been accused of manufacturing methamphetamine and the chemical endangerment of a child, a police officer was permitted to testify that he observed a plastic bottle and its components within the defendant's house and that those items were consistent with the materials needed to build a methamphetamine lab. The officer also related that the chemical smell coming from the bottle and other odors within the house were consistent with the manufacturing of methamphetamine. According to the reviewing court, scientific evidence and expert testimony is not required to prove the illegal quality of a substance, so long as the evidence is based on the opinion of a knowledgeable layperson. In this case, the officers had significant training in methamphetamine cases and were permitted to offer lay witness testimony to identify the processes and product as involving methamphetamine production and possession.[77]

When lay witnesses are able to make identifications based on their familiarity with personal characteristics of the defendant that are not immediately observable by the jury at the trial, the lay witness testimony is admissible. Demonstrative of this principle is a case involving destruction of federal forest service signs that had been caught on

---

72 Graham v. State, 273 Ga. 187, 189, 614 S.E.2d 815, 818, 2005 Ga. App. LEXIS 442 (2005).

73 State v. Walker, 2013 Minn. App. Unpub. LEXIS 177 (2013).

74 *See* United States v. Norman, 415 F.3d 466, 2005 U.S. App. LEXIS 13149 (5th Cir. 2005).

75 United States v. Gholikhan, 370 F. App'x. 987, 990, 2010 U.S. App. LEXIS 6893 (11th Cir. 2010).

76 *See* Ohio v. Bolling, 2001 Ohio App. LEXIS 3248 (2001).

77 Wallace v. Alabama, 2013 Ala. Crim. App. LEXIS 4 (2013).

videotape from a remote camera. The Tenth Circuit approved of permitting a forest service officer to make an identification of the female perpetrator based on viewing the videotape recording of the destruction of the signage by the actual criminal.[78] The court noted that the forest service officer had several previous encounters with the defendant over several years where he had "observed her backpack and her walking in the forest, [and] he would have had an advantage over the jury in identifying her as the perpetrator, especially considering the less-than-perfect video footage and the person's hidden appearance."[79] In a similar manner, a reviewing court approved of permitting the foster mother of a defendant to identify him in court in a murder case, based on videotape of the crime that had been broadcast on television and that the foster mother had seen. She possessed personal familiarity with the defendant's appearance as one of the perpetrators that was helpful to the determination of facts in the case.[80] However, when the trier of fact is equally able to make an identification from the same evidence observed by a police officer, the lay testimony of an officer should not be admitted. In a pretrial motion, a federal judge prohibited police officers from identifying the defendant, based on bank robbery videotape and still pictures taken at two different banks, when they had no prior relationship with the defendant and had never observed him. In such a situation, the jury is in as good a position to make a decision concerning identity as were the police officers, and as such, the judge prevented the police officers from offering lay opinion concerning the identity of the defendant.[81]

I. Handwriting

As a general rule, any lay witness who has seen a particular person create a handwritten document and has some familiarity with that individual's manner of writing may testify about the identity of the author of the handwriting. Assuming the existence of a proper foundation (familiarity with the person's writing), the opinion of a lay witness concerning the identity of an acquaintance's handwriting may be admissible, provided the familiarity was not acquired for purposes of litigation.[82] In order for a lay witness to offer an opinion concerning the identity a handwriting sample, a foundation must be established to show that the witness had an opportunity to become familiar with the handwriting of the suspected author. In a case involving federal money laundering charges, it was appropriate for the defendant's mother to identify the signature belonging to the defendant.[83] In order to qualify the defendant's mother to offer an opinion about the genuineness of her son's signature, she testified that the defendant lived with

---

78 United States v. Williams, 2010 U.S. App. LEXIS 19964 (10th Cir. 2010).

79 *Id.*

80 People v. Phillips, 2010 Mich. App. LEXIS 228 (2010).

81 United States v. Thompson, 2010 U.S. Dist. LEXIS 26471 (2010). *See also* United States v. Kane, 146 Fed. Appx. 912, 2005 U.S. App. LEXIS 22877 (9th Cir. 2005).

82 FED. RULE EVID. 901(b)(2).

83 United States v. Clouden, 2013 U.S. App. 16126 (3d Cir. 2013).

her from birth until he became an adult, that she observed his signature at different times when he lived with her, and that she simply knew her son's signature. According to the reviewing court, the foundation for offering an opinion concerning the defendant signature was rationally based upon his mother's own perceptions from living with him from birth to adulthood rather than from any technical knowledge or signature familiarity acquired solely for trial. Proof that a witness has a foundation for identifying writing may be accomplished by showing that the witness corresponded with the writer, handled documents written by him or her, witnessed the writer creating his or her signature, or by other means.

While lay witnesses, even with proof of a foundation, are not permitted to offer opinion evidence by comparing a known sample of a signature or more extensive writing, expert witnesses and jurors are permitted to make such a comparison. In a Florida case involving the passing of forged checks, a defendant's conviction was reversed, partly on the basis that a police officer compared signatures in a drivers' license database with signatures on the forged checks and concluded that they were written by the same individual. In this situation, the officer had no background or training in handwriting identification and could not testify as an expert. Although jurors are allowed to compare signatures and handwriting, a lay witness is generally not permitted to compare a known signature with a disputed signature and come to a conclusion. Allowing the Florida officer to testify to his opinion concerning the identity of the defendant's signature on the forged checks constituted reversible error because the police officer had no basis for arriving at such a conclusion and had no familiarity with the defendant's signature or handwriting.[84]

In an appeal of a capital murder conviction, the defendant contended that some documents that were allegedly written by him were improperly identified by his former girlfriend and another associate. The former girlfriend had been involved in a romantic relationship for several years and testified that she was familiar with the defendant's handwriting, that he had written letters to her, and that she could identify his writing style. Another lay witness testified that he was familiar with the defendant's handwriting because he had seen him write notes at various times. In this case, both lay witnesses testified that they were familiar with the defendant's handwriting and that, in their opinion, it matched or was similar to the handwriting on the documents alleged to have been written by the capital defendant. The Alabama reviewing court held that the testimony was valid under Alabama's rule allowing lay witness opinion evidence and Rule 901, which allow for the admission of nonexpert opinion as to the genuineness of handwriting based upon familiarity not acquired for purposes of litigation.[85]

---

84 Proctor v. State, 97 So.3d 313, 2012 Fla. App. LEXIS 15445 (2012).

85 Vanpelt v. State, 2009 Ala. Crim. App. LEXIS 166 (2009).

J. Speed

Most courts admit the testimony of a nonexpert witness relating to the speed of a motor vehicle, provided that the witness had sufficient opportunity to observe the vehicle moving and that the witness has a foundation or basis for being able to estimate speed. In a case involving an automobile accident, a federal judge permitted various eyewitnesses to give estimates concerning the speed of one of the motor vehicles.[86] Each lay witness had somewhat different vantage points and the witnesses had different lengths of time to observe the vehicle, but because all the witnesses appeared to have a foundation for offering an opinion as to speed, the trial judge ordered that they be permitted to give their testimony.

Demonstrative of allowing lay witnesses to give opinions concerning speed, in a driving under the influence case in Chicago involving a fatality, a driver who passed by the car that created the accident was permitted to testify that she was going forty to forty-five miles an hour when the defendant's car passed her doing about seventy miles an hour.[87] The lay witness indicated that the defendant had his foot out the driver's window, resting on the rearview mirror at the time his vehicle passed hers, which was excellent proof that she was in a position to observe the defendant's vehicle and to estimate its speed. The eyewitness also was close enough to the colliding vehicles that she had to slow down to avoid being involved in the collision. A separate eyewitness driving a commercial truck observed the defendant's vehicle speeding in excess of fifty miles an hour immediately prior to the crash. This driver had sufficient driving experience and was close enough to observe the vehicles prior to the crash, which established an excellent foundation for his opinion. In a different vehicular manslaughter case in Texas, the reviewing court approved testimony from eyewitnesses that the defendant was operating her vehicle "fast" and that "it was a red streak" and that the car was "travelling way too fast" for the road conditions.[88] Similarly, in permitting lay opinions concerning speed, the top Ohio court held that the visual observation by a police officer has long been considered a valid means of determining the speed of the moving vehicle so long as the officer had a reliable opportunity to view the vehicle and has had training and experience at visually estimating vehicle speed. The court noted that the foundation for speed estimation in other cases by police officers had been approved where an officer had passed tests at the state police academy, or had 29 years of experience or was otherwise trained in vehicle speed estimation.[89]

As a general rule, the admissibility of an officer's estimate of vehicle speed is so strong that it allows a conviction for speeding, if no contested evidence has been

---

86 Houston v. Smith, 2010 U.S. Dist. LEXIS 118134 (W. Dist. Penn. 2010).

87 People v. Tellez, 2013 Il. App. (1st) 112048-U, 2013 Ill. App. Unpub. LEXIS 986 (2013).

88 Zorn v. State, 315 S.W.3d 616, 627, 2010 Tex. App. LEXIS 4094 (2010).

89 City of Barberton v. Jenney, 126 Ohio St. 3d 5, 11, 929 N.E.2d 1047, 1053, 2010 Ohio LEXIS 1269 (2010).

admitted.[90] A California court upheld the admissibility of a police officer's estimate made from an aircraft that the defendant was speeding at 105 miles per hour despite the defendant's objection that the officer had not been trained to visually estimate vehicle speed on the public highway.[91] Lay witnesses generally are permitted to express opinion estimates of vehicle speed in terms such as "fast," "slow," or "excessive." so long as the testimony concerning the speed of a moving vehicle is more than a hazardous guess.[92] Generally, anyone who has some experience involving motor vehicles possesses a valid basis to offer a lay opinion concerning the speed at which the vehicle was observed traveling. Children who are not of driving age often do not have the experience to possess a proper foundation to estimate speeds, but adult nondrivers are usually permitted to express a conclusion relative to the speed of an observed moving vehicle. The length of time for observation of a moving vehicle or other object does not typically affect the admissibility of the opinion but does affect the weight that the finder of fact might choose to give the opinion.

§ 11.5 Opinions of Experts

Rule 702

TESTIMONY BY EXPERT WITNESSES

A witness who is qualified as an expert by knowledge, skill, experience, training, or education may testify in the form of an opinion or otherwise if:

(a) the expert's scientific, technical, or other specialized knowledge will help the trier of fact to understand the evidence or to determine a fact in issue;

(b) the testimony is based on sufficient facts or data;

(c) the testimony is the product of reliable principles and methods; and

(d) the expert has reliably applied the principles and methods to the facts of the case.[93]

In order to attain the criminal burden of proof beyond a reasonable doubt, criminal case presentations may require the use of expert witnesses to present specialized knowledge to the finder of fact. In the absence of the testimony of experts, it would be difficult for the prosecution to provide the jury with sufficient evidence to meet the burden of proof in cases in which the technical or scientific nature of the evidence

---

[90] In the Interest of B.D.S., 269 Ga. App. 89, 90, 91, 603 S.E.2d 488, 489, 2004 Ga. App. LEXIS 1084 (2004), *aff'd*, 273 Ga. App. 576, 615 S.E.2d 627, 2005 Ga. App. LEXIS 579 (2005).

[91] People v. Zunis, 134 Cal. App. 4th Supp. 1, 36 Cal. Rptr. 3d 489, 2005 Cal. App. 1873 (2005).

[92] Quist v. Commonwealth, 2010 Ky. App. LEXIS 93 (2010).

[93] FED. R. EVID. 702.

exceeds the knowledge of the average person, or in cases in which the expert testimony would assist the jurors in understanding the issues or determining a fact at issue.[94] Expert testimony may be admissible when the subject matter at issue involves concepts with which the average person is not sufficiently familiar, but will generally be excluded where such testimony would add little information for the jury. For example, in a California case involving rape, sodomy, and murder, the trial judge permitted the medical examiner who conducted the victim's autopsy to offer an opinion that the rape and sodomy occurred prior to the death of the victim, facts that would help prove the crimes. The defendant objected that the doctor lacked expertise and that a jury was just as competent to determine whether the sexual offenses happened during life or later. The trial judge's decision, upheld on appeal, to admit the doctor's testimony concerning when the sexual offenses occurred was based on the totality of the factors that the doctor observed on and in the body of the deceased, the manner of death, and his experience as a autopsy doctor over a long period of time dealing with similar cases.[95] Interpretation of laws relating to the use of expert opinion evidence has developed differently from those relating to the use of ordinary lay opinion evidence. While the nonexpert, with some exceptions, may testify only if he or she has firsthand knowledge of the incident, the expert is generally permitted to give an opinion, even if he or she does not have firsthand knowledge. Prior to offering any testimony, the expert may have analyzed the facts that are derived from the event or occurrence and reached a conclusion that the expert will offer to the court in the form of an opinion. Alternatively, an expert may have performed scientific tests or experiments on some of the evidence and drawn a conclusion that would be helpful to the judge or jury. Finally, an expert can testify based on a hypothetical fact pattern or an assumed pattern of facts offered by a party and offer an opinion based on the facts coupled with the witness's special expertise. An expert may consider reports and results of experiments conducted by other experts when such reliance is usual and customary in that field of expertise. Expert testimony is appropriate when the subject of the testimony is beyond the common experiences of most jurors so that testimony of one especially skilled in a particular field would assist the judge or jury in rendering a verdict. It is most certainly needed when the subject matter involves complex technical, medical, or scientific evidence.

When the desirability of or need for expert testimony arises or is proposed to be offered by one of the parties, generally the trial judge must make a decision concerning whether expert testimony will assist the trier of fact and must make a determination that the proposed individual is qualified as an expert. In the District of Columbia, the courts hold that for expert testimony to be considered, the subject matter "must be so distinctively related to some science, profession, business or occupation as to be beyond the ken of the average layman" and the proposed expert "witness must have sufficient skill, knowledge, or experience in that field or calling to make it appear that his opinion" will assist the judge or jury, and that expert testimony cannot be admitted where

---

94 State v. Nesbitt, 185 N.J. 504, 514, 888 A.2d 472, 478, 2006 N.J. LEXIS 7 (2006).

95 People v. Jones, 54 Cal. 4th 1, 55, 275 P.3d 496, 536, 2012 Cal. LEXIS 3995 (2012).

the state of the knowledge does not permit a reasonable opinion to be offered, even by an expert.[96]

If expert testimony is proper and the court deems such testimony would assist the finder of fact, a trial judge must make several additional decisions. For example, the Supreme Court of Nebraska noted that the trial court must evaluate the admissibility of expert testimony in a four-step process. The trial court must first decide whether a witness has the qualifications to testify as an expert through an evaluation of the proposed expert's knowledge, skill, training, and education. The trial judge must next determine whether the reasoning or methodology underpinning the expert testimony is valid and reliable. Then the judge must decide whether the methodology used by the expert was properly applied, that the appropriate protocols were followed, and that any tests were performed properly. Finally, the court must evaluate whether the expert evidence and the opinions offered are more probative than unfairly prejudicial.[97]

When a prosecutor or a defense attorney wants to use an expert witness to present evidence, the trial judge has broad discretion in determining whether to admit the evidence. For example, the Tenth Circuit approved a trial court's determination that an agent could testify as an expert concerning the manner that drug kingpins use to avoid having their identities and drug activities becoming known to law enforcement. The trial court determined that the special agent was qualified as an expert, and it believed that expert testimony would assist the jury in understanding a rather complex drug-selling operation.[98] In considering whether a particular topic was appropriate for the use of expert testimony, California courts appear to allow expert testimony concerning memory pitfalls and effects of uncorroborated eyewitness testimony, especially where the issue of identity is a crucial factor to be determined in a case.[99] California's courts have adopted the view that expert testimony concerning eyewitness identification challenges can be excluded only if there is other evidence that substantially corroborated the in-court eyewitness identification.[100] Other jurisdictions refuse to permit expert testimony concerning the challenges of eyewitness identification testimony and its potential for creating misidentification because courts often consider this issue one for which the jury is completely competent to determine. Some jurisdictions only permit expert eyewitness testimony on a case-by-case basis but do not have a blanket exclusion.[101]

Whether expert testimony shall be admitted or excluded on a particular subject matter has generally been left to the broad discretion of trial courts[102] and will not result

---

96 Hager v. United States, 856 A.2d 1143, 1148, 2004 D.C. App. LEXIS (2004), *cert. denied*, 2006 U.S. LEXIS 2452 (2006).

97 State v. Mason, 271 Neb. 16, 709 N.W. 2d 638, 2006 Neb. LEXIS 23 (2006).

98 United States v. Walker, 2006 U.S. App. LEXIS 11289 (10th Cir. 2006).

99 People v. Datt, 185 Cal. App. 4th 942, 952, 111 Cal. Rptr. 3d 132, 139, 2010 Cal. App. LEXIS 899 (2010).

100 *See* People v. Huang, 2010 Cal. App. Unpub. LEXIS 6251 (2010).

101 United States v. Rodriguez-Berrios, 573 F.3d 55, 71, 2009 U.S. App. LEXIS 16341 (1st Cir. 2009).

102 State v. Vernes, 2006 Mont. 32, 331 Mont. 129, 132, 133, 130 P.3d. 169, 173, 2006 Mont. LEXIS 41 (2006).

in a reversal of a verdict unless an appellate court finds that the trial court abused its discretion in making the decision.[103] When the court has admitted the opinion of an expert, the jury or the judge may consider the witness's qualifications in determining the weight to give to the expert's testimony.[104] Juries are frequently instructed that expert testimony should be given the weight that it deserves, and it may be entirely rejected if the reasons given to support it prove unsound.[105]

Other rules for the use of expert testimony have been handed down in various cases. Generally, an expert may base an opinion on any material or set of facts known to the expert, including hearsay evidence that would not otherwise be admissible. In one case, an Ohio appellate court ruled that both defense and prosecution expert witnesses were properly permitted to testify concerning the mental state of a woman accused of assault on a police officer.[106] In offering testimony, both the defense and prosecution experts had examined the defendant, reviewed hospital records and police reports, and looked at information prepared by other examining doctors. Both parties' expert witnesses were properly permitted to testify concerning their respective opinions relative to the defendant's mental state, even though both experts relied on hearsay evidence from other persons who were not under oath. Generally, expert witnesses may offer opinions that are based partly or wholly on hearsay statements or documents that would not themselves be admissible as substantive evidence. Similarly, where an expert's testimony was based in part upon personal observations and was not completely dependent upon the hospital's medical records, any hearsay objection should be overruled.[107] An expert may base an opinion on tests personally performed and upon reports generated by other persons where "it is the kind of evidence experts customarily rely on as a basis for opinion testimony,"[108] but can be forced to disclose the basis for his or her opinion. Such disclosure permits the finder of fact to evaluate the credibility of the expert witness and to determine the weight that should be granted to the testimony.[109] In the final analysis, the determination concerning the weight to be granted to an expert's opinion and conclusions and the sufficiency of the evidence relied upon by the expert witness are within the province of the finder of fact.[110]

In state jurisdictions that have adopted a variation of the Federal Rules of Evidence, Rule 702 defines the conditions that must be present in order for an expert to testify. The rule states that if the testimony would "assist the trier of fact to understand the evidence or to determine a fact in issue," then an expert witness may testify. Because the expert may testify as to matters that are specialized as well as scientific or

---

103 State v. Villalobos, 235 P.3d 227, 234, 2010 Ariz. LEXIS 26 (2010).

104 United States v. Morris, 576 F.3d 661, 676, 2009 U.S. App. LEXIS 17867 (7th Cir. 2010).

105 State v. Stout, 2010 MT 137, 356 Mont. 468, 477, 237 P.3d 37, 44, 2010 Mont. LEXIS 199 (2010).

106 State v. Sullivan, 2012 Ohio 5107, 2012 Ohio App. LEXIS 4469 (2012).

107 Lewis v. State, 304 Ga. App. 831, 836, 698 S.E.2d 365, 2010 Ga. App. LEXIS 626 (2010).

108 Commonwealth v. Banville, 457 Mass. 530, 541, 931 N.E.2d 457, 466, 2010 Mass. LEXIS 590 (2010).

109 State v. Lyles, 615 S.E.2d 890, 893, 894, 2005 N.C. App. LEXIS 1424 (2005).

110 Potoski v. Wilkes University, 2010 U.S. Dist. LEXIS 99731 (M.D. Penn. 2010).

technical, the rule makes plain its intention to allow expert testimony on matters that are not necessarily beyond the understanding of laypersons. In interpreting this section, the Sixth Circuit Court of Appeals upheld the use of a special agent with the Drug Enforcement Administration as an expert who testified concerning the characteristics of crack cocaine as well as explained the methods that criminals typically use in drug distribution. The agent had approximately 22 years' experience in combating illegal drug use and distribution and was able to make factual distinctions between personal use and possession of quantities that were consistent with distribution. The agent provided an opinion based on his extensive training and experience concerning the items recovered from the defendant's residence and offered an opinion that the items were consistent with drug trafficking. The principle from this case demonstrates that experience from on-the-job training and working in the interdiction of drugs gave the agent an expertise that a typical juror would not possess, and his opinions were helpful to the jury in deciding the case.[111]

In a drug-trafficking case where expert testimony was permitted, a federal agent testified concerning the meaning of coded words or language used in some wiretap transcripts. While many people might have some understanding of the jargon or specialized language used by drug dealers, most people do not, and for that reason, interpreting drug dealing language and its associated jargon is a proper subject for expert testimony.[112] While coded terms are often the subject of expert testimony when trying cases involving narcotics offenses, some of the language would be considered a proper subject of lay testimony and may be offered as such because some of the language has a broader usage and is understood by numerous people. In a prosecution for attempted and actual illegal distribution of Schedule III and IV drugs by a physician, the Eighth Circuit Court of Appeals held that the use of an expert witness physician who explained the protocols and standards of care for writing drug prescriptions was appropriate because the expert witness's testimony was helpful to the jury in understanding the case.[113]

§ 11.6 Qualifications of an Expert

A person who has acquired specialized knowledge of a particular subject matter over which he or she is to testify—either by academic study of the recognized authorities or by practical experience—and who can assist and guide the jury in resolving a problem or issue, may meet the qualifications as an expert witness.[114] Qualification as an expert witness does not require any specific or special education, certification,

---

[111] United States v. Ham, 2011 U.S. App. LEXIS 448 (6th Cir. 2011).

[112] United States v. Reed, 575 F.3d 900, 2009 U.S. App. LEXIS 17283 (Cir. 2010).

[113] United States v. Katz, 2006 U.S. App. LEXIS 11462 (8th Cir. 2006).

[114] People v. Miller, 173 Ill. 2d 167, 670 N.E.2d 721 (1996); *see also* United States v. Sosa, U.S. Dist. LEXIS 2254 (2006), for a review of the foundational requirements for expert testimony.

licensure, or complete mastery of the field of knowledge that is in question. To qualify as an expert, the proposed witness must possess special knowledge or experience in a particular field or calling so that his or her opinion or inference will most likely aid the trier of fact in the search for the truth.[115] The party offering the witness need not demonstrate that the expert is a university-educated professional, such as a physician or scientist possessing one or more advanced degrees. Among the categories of expert witness, the individual might be a doctor, professor, plumber, electrician, carpenter, police officer, or drug dealer who has special expertise. In addition, Federal Rule 702 has no provision that would rank academic training as being superior to demonstrated practical experience and does not require that an expert be highly qualified to offer an opinion on a given topic, but qualifications have some consideration on the weight to be given to a particular expert's testimony. Any specialized knowledge that would not be generally held by the average member of society may qualify a person as an expert in that field.

Whether a proposed witness possesses the qualifications of an expert is a decision that rests within the sound discretion of the trial court and, as a general rule, the decision to admit expert testimony will not be disturbed upon appeal absent an abuse of the trial court's discretion.[116] For example, a California trial court in a prosecution for gang-related criminal activity allowed a police officer to testify as an expert concerning the general history of two particular street gangs.[117] The trial judge rejected a defense contention that the police officer could not be qualified as an expert on gang activities in a particular Los Angeles police division. The officer kept up-to-date on gang activities in his area, had spent almost two years in a gang enforcement division of the police department, and had been a police officer for sixth and a half years. Testimony indicated that the officer had participated in gathering intelligence on gangs in the enforcement division, had engaged in identifying and tracking gang members and their activities, and had worked with other officers and gang detectives, executing searches on gang members and investigating gang-related criminal activities. In addition, the proposed expert had received training on gang awareness, and he had contact with gang members on a daily basis. An appellate court agreed that the officer possessed the expertise to offer general opinions of the general history of the two street gangs involved in the criminal case. The gist of this case illustrates the principle that specialized knowledge is the key to developing expertise and that knowledge can come from any source, even nontraditional learning situations and/or on-the-job training, and is not relegated to formalized university experiences culminating in a doctoral-level degree.

An expert in a criminal case may offer an opinion based wholly upon personal knowledge of the facts disclosed in his or her testimony, or upon facts in evidence assumed in hypothetical questions, but, traditionally, the witness may not properly offer

---

115 United States v. Warren, 2013 U.S. Dist. LEXIS 149571 (E.D. La. 2013).

116 Commonwealth v. Torito, 2013 Pa. Super. 118, 2013 Pa. Super. LEXIS 729 (2013).

117 People v. Valadez, 2013 Cal. App. LEXIS 778 (2013).

an opinion concerning the ultimate issue to be determined by the trier of fact because that opinion invades the function of the jury.[118] In an Ohio case involving vehicular homicide, a prosecution witness was permitted to testify that the defendant was negligent, an element of proof required by the prosecution. The reviewing court noted that the trial court should not have permitted the state's expert to answer the question going to the ultimate issue. The reviewing court refused to reverse the conviction, even though the expert offered an opinion on the ultimate issue, because the court thought the jury was free to disregard the expert's opinion concerning negligence, and the court held that the trial error did not have any significant prejudicial effect sufficient to justify a reversal of a conviction.[119] Even though courts continue to speak of issues invading the province of the jury, increasingly they seem to permit encroachment of the province of the jury, whether by rule changes or through finding a harmless error that does not justify a reversal.

Experts may testify to various levels of certainty concerning their area of expertise and have significant freedom concerning how they phrase their conclusions. Experts need not offer their opinions in terms of absolute certainty but may use terms such as "reasonable medical certainty." Some expert testimony is expressed in terms of percentages or probability because many fields of expertise use mathematical modeling in conducting testing. In a Mississippi homicide case, the DNA expert witness testified that there was a "very high degree of scientific certainty" that the DNA material found under the deceased's fingernails matched the DNA profile of the defendant.[120] Testifying with a bit more precision in a California case, the criminalist who testified as an expert concerning DNA testing, noted that the "odds of another contributor with this DNA pattern were one in 49 million for African-Americans, one in 1 million for Caucasians, and one in 1.6 million for Hispanics."[121] Handwriting experts often express their opinions in probabilities, but there is no exclusion of evidence if an expert notes that a forged document was "probably" authored by the defendant, but such an answer could affect the weight of the testimony.[122]

In outlining the requirements for the admissibility of expert testimony, the federal Fourth Circuit referred to a four-part test that was consistent with Federal Rule 702. These requirements, in one form or another, can generally be applied to state admissibility of expert testimony. According to the Fourth Circuit, the trial judge must first find that the expert's scientific, technical, or other specific knowledge would assist the judge or jury in understanding the evidence or in determining a fact that is of issue in a case. Second, the expert's testimony must be based upon sufficient facts or data that have become known to the expert witness. Third, the testimony offered by an expert must be the product of reliable principles and methodology. Finally, these principles

118 Missouri v. Churchill, 98 S.W.3d 536, 2003 Mo. LEXIS 37 (2003).
119 State v. Boeddeker, 2010 Ohio 106, 2010 Ohio App. LEXIS 97 (2010).
120 Cotton v. State, 2013 Miss. App. LEXIS 472 (2013).
121 People v. Cua, 2011 Cal. App. LEXIS 2 (2011).
122 United States v. Mornan, 413 F.3d 372, 380, 2005 U.S. App. LEXIS 13043 (3d Cir. 2005).

and methodology must have been reliably applied to the facts involved in a particular case.[123]

In qualifying as an expert witness, one who has the necessary education, training, experience, or skill should be recognized as an expert once a minimum threshold for expertise has been established during a *voir dire* of the proposed expert. Once accepted as an expert, the witness who has familiarized him- or herself with the necessary data, who has received facts that constitute a hypothetical situation, or who has listened to the courtroom testimony of other fact witnesses, can form an expert opinion that is useful to the finder of fact. Proposed expert witnesses may share similarities in qualifications or may possess different educational or experiential backgrounds,[124] but as long as a proposed expert crosses the threshold of being qualified as an expert in the relevant field, the trial judge should permit the witness to testify. One court noted that the expert's testimony does not have to be shown to be conclusively reliable or completely valid before it can be admitted into evidence, because the "credibility of and weight to be given to the expert's testimony is a question for the jury, rather than the trial court."[125]

When a party offers a witness as an expert on a matter in issue, in the absence of a stipulation concerning qualifications, the judge must preliminarily determine whether the proposed expert's competency—with respect to education, a special skill or experience, or training—will assist the trier of fact in reaching a verdict. In a Massachusetts criminal case, the prosecution sought to prove the defendant's membership in a gang, and prior to the actual trial, the judge conducted questioning of the proposed gang expert to determine whether he was qualified as an expert on gangs and gang membership. The police officer testified to his extensive interaction with gang members over a two-year period in which he became aware of gang protocols, and the officer noted his observations that the defendant had been seen with other gang members on numerous occasions and lived in a gang territorial area. The officer testified to observations of a personal nature involving the gang and receiving reports by other officers and a confidential informant that assisted the officers in developing expertise concerning the gang in question. The officer indicated his awareness of a feud between the gang in question and a rival, and he was knowledgeable concerning a truce between the two gangs. The trial judge ruled that the officer was qualified to testify concerning various issues involving the defendant and his gang, and an appellate court upheld the decision.[126]

The weight and value of the testimony of an expert witness depend largely upon his or her qualifications as an expert, and these qualifications may be the subject of intensive inquiry by the opposing counsel even after a judge has ruled that witness may testify as an expert.

---

123 United States v. Stanley, 2013 U.S. App. LEXIS 14643 (4th Cir. 2013).

124 Panitz v. Behrend, 2001 Pa. Super. 93, 771 A.2d 803, 2001 Pa. Super. LEXIS 372 (2001).

125 State v. Dew, 738 S.E.2d 215, 222 , 2013 N.C. App LEXIS 228 (2013).

126 Commonwealth v. Gray, 463 Mass. 731, 739, 2012 Mass. LEXIS 1061(2012).

§ 11.7 Selection of Expert Witness

Rule 706

COURT-APPOINTED EXPERT WITNESSES

(a) Appointment Process. On a party's motion or on its own, the court may order the parties to show cause why expert witnesses should not be appointed and may ask the parties to submit nominations. The court may appoint any expert that the parties agree on and any of its own choosing. But the court may only appoint someone who consents to act.

(b) Expert's Role. The court must inform the expert of the expert's duties. The court may do so in writing and have a copy filed with the clerk or may do so orally at a conference in which the parties have an opportunity to participate. The expert:

(1) must advise the parties of any findings the expert makes;

(2) may be deposed by any party;

(3) may be called to testify by the court or any party; and

(4) may be cross-examined by any party, including the party that called the expert.

(c) Compensation. The expert is entitled to a reasonable compensation, as set by the court. The compensation is payable as follows:

(1) in a criminal case or in a civil case involving just compensation under the Fifth Amendment, from any funds that are provided by law; and

(2) in any other civil case, by the parties in the proportion and at the time that the court directs—and the compensation is then charged like other costs.

(d) Disclosing the Appointment to the Jury. The court may authorize disclosure to the jury that the court appointed the expert.

(e) Parties' Choice of their Own Experts. This rule does not limit a party in calling its own experts.[127]

Upon a party's own motion or by motion of both parties, a request may be made that an expert or experts be appointed by the court to evaluate evidence and testify in a case. The parties are free to call their own experts, even if the court appoints one or more expert witnesses. Pursuant to Rule 706, a federal judge may appoint an expert on the court's own motion. To the extent possible, each party will attempt to suggest nominations of an expert who would testify most favorably for his or her side. In some state jurisdictions, and under Federal Rule 706, the judge may appoint expert witnesses based on agreement by the parties, or the court may appoint witnesses based on the judge's preference, especially where there is disagreement. Any expert witness who

---

[127] FED. R. EVID. 706.

receives an appointment will be informed of the expected duties by the judge in writing, and a copy of the letter of appointment will be filed with the clerk. Alternatively, the notice of appointment will be given to the parties at a conference in which the parties have the opportunity to participate. When an expert is appointed by the court, that expert must advise the parties of the expert's opinions and conclusions. The parties may take a deposition of the expert witness, and the expert witness may be called to testify by any party or by the judge. Under Rule 706, although one party may have called the expert to testify, the expert may be cross-examined by counsel for both parties.[128]

Rule 706 of the Federal Rules of Evidence continues the long-established practice of federal judges having authority to appoint expert witnesses. Section (c) of the rule authorizes federal courts and state courts that have adopted a version of the Federal Rules to disclose to the jury the fact that the court appointed the expert witness. Disclosure to the jury that the court appointed the expert witness should give the expert witness more credibility with the jury.

Noting the provisions of an earlier version of Rule 706, one federal district court[129] commented that:

> **Rule 706(a)** of the Federal Rules of Evidence authorizes the district court to appoint an expert witness. Because this authority is discretionary, however, we may overturn the denial of a motion for appointment of an expert only for abuse of discretion. *Duckett v. Mullin*, 306 F.3d 982, 999 (10th Cir. 2002). Under this standard, the district court's "decision will not be disturbed unless the appellate court has a definite and firm conviction that the lower court made a clear error of judgment or exceeded the bounds of permissible choice in the circumstances." *Okla. ex rel. Edmondson v. Tyson Foods, Inc.*, F.3d, 2010 U.S. App. Lexis 19572, 2010 WL 3637041, at *7 (10th Cir. Sept. 21, 2010) (quotation omitted).

While the appointment of an expert is based on a trial court's discretion, a court should not take sides when the prosecution and defense are in dispute over expert testimony. In a civil suit by a California state prisoner alleging that his warden and staff practiced deliberate indifference to his serious medical needs while incarcerated, the plaintiff prisoner requested the appointment of a medical expert who "could help the Court and jury in understanding the medical terminologies, evaluating contradictory evidence and avoiding the potential prejudice of one-sided opinion testimony"[130] from any presentation by the defendant warden. In the exercise of its discretion under Rule 706, the district court refused to appoint a medical expert because it determined that the plaintiff prisoner's medical claims were no different than issues found in similar deliberate indifference cases pending in other federal courts and did not require the assistance of an expert.[131]

---

128 *Id.*

129 Patel v. United States, 2010 U.S. App. LEXIS 21539 (10th Cir. 2010).

130 Brooks v. Tate, 2013 U.S. Dist. LEXIS 111420 (E.D. CA. (2013)

131 *Id.*

§ 11.8 Examination of Expert Witness

Rule 703

BASES OF AN EXPERT'S OPINION TESTIMONY

An expert may base an opinion on facts or data in the case that the expert has been made aware of or personally observed. If experts in the particular field would reasonably rely on those kinds of facts or data in forming an opinion on the subject, they need not be admissible for the opinion to be admitted. But if the facts or data would otherwise be inadmissible, the proponent of the opinion may disclose them to the jury only if their probative value in helping the jury evaluate the opinion substantially outweighs their prejudicial effect.[132]

Rule 704

OPINION ON AN ULTIMATE ISSUE

(a) In General—Not Automatically Objectionable. An opinion is not objectionable just because it embraces an ultimate issue.
(b) Exception. In a criminal case, an expert witness must not state an opinion about whether the defendant did or did not have a mental state or condition that constitutes an element of the crime charged or of a defense. Those matters are for the trier of fact alone.[133]

After the witness has qualified as an expert or if the parties have stipulated to the expert's qualifications, he or she is first examined by the party who called the witness. There are two avenues through which expert evidence may be presented to the jury: (1) through testimony of the witness based on his or her personal knowledge and observation or from reports and results of tests performed by other experts when it is usual and customary to do so in the field of expertise,[134] and (2) through testimony of the witness when the expert witness is asked to assume that hypothetical facts (generally based on the case being tried) are true and to offer an opinion based on the hypothetical fact situation.[135] An expert witness may base his or her opinion partly upon personal knowledge of facts disclosed in his or her testimony and may be partially based on

---

132 FED. R. EVID. 703.

133 FED. R. EVID. 704.

134 State v. Ayers, 2005 Tenn. Crim. App. LEXIS 1108 (2005).

135 State v. Nesbitt, 185 N.J. 504, 511, 888 A.2d 472, 476, 2006 N.J. LEXIS 7 (2006).

factual evidence assumed in a hypothetical question.[136] A hypothetical question need not include all the facts in evidence, nor facts or theories advanced by opposing counsel. A trial judge may properly accept expert testimony predicated on facts that have been previously admitted in evidence as testimony by witnesses who themselves made relevant observations of primary facts. For example, a doctor called to testify may give his or her expert opinion as to whether facts already in evidence support a particular inference, causation, diagnosis, or prognosis. Also, the expert witness may base his or her testimony on information from his or her knowledge of textbooks, treatises, articles, and other publications relevant to the particular field of expertise.

As a rule, expert testimony must be based on facts and evidence presented in the record or on hypothetical facts assumed to be true, but a hypothetical cannot be based on facts unsupported by any evidence.[137] The Federal Rules of Evidence provide, however, that if the external facts or data are of a type reasonably and customarily relied upon by experts in the particular field when forming opinions or inferences on the subject, the external facts or data need not be admissible into evidence.[138] In a bank fraud case involving check kiting, among other violations, a trial court permitted a federal law enforcement officer to give expert testimony based on his analysis of data that he had neither personally collected nor prepared. The federal officer had used information taken from bank records and analyzed the records using a computer program. The Court of Appeals for the Sixth Circuit upheld the admission of the expert opinion because the practice of permitting forensic financial examiners to analyze data collected by other persons prior to trial and to use the information to form an opinion was consistent with the Federal Rules of Evidence.[139] Similarly, a medical examiner may rely on a report prepared by a different medical examiner because reliance on the data prepared by other professionals was a common and standard protocol.[140]

In order to be admissible, the testimony of an expert witness must meet the other rules of evidence (i.e., the evidence must be relevant).[141] In accordance with the traditional teachings concerning the use of opinion testimony, most jurisdictions hold that an expert witness cannot be allowed to invade the province of the jury; that is, an expert's testimony should not give opinions on ultimate issues or evaluate the credibility of other testimony or witnesses.[142] The old common law rule held that experts may

---

136 Lewis v. Virginia, 2004 Va. App. LEXIS 595 (2004).

137 Wells v. State, 913 So. 2d 1053, 1057, 2005 Miss. App. LEXIS 434 (2005).

138 FED. R. EVID. 703.

139 United States v. Abboud, 438 F.3d 554, 586, 2006 U.S. App. LEXIS 3797 (6th Cir. 2006).

140 Sauerwin v. State, 2005 Ark. LEXIS 565 (2005).

141 *See* Richmanv. Sheahan, 415 F. Supp. 2d 929, 2006 U.S. Dist. LEXIS 6667 (N.D. Ill. 2006), in which trial court rejected police use of force expert from testifying concerning medical matters because evidence was not relevant. *See also* United States v. Monteiro, 407 F. Supp. 2d 351, 2006 U.S. Dist. LEXIS 227 (D. Mass. 2006), in which a trial court excluded expert testimony because the trial judge was not convinced of reliability of the particular theory, rendering the expert testimony irrelevant and inadmissible.

142 State v. Favoccia, 119 Conn. App. 1, 986 A.2d 1081, 2010 Conn. App. LEXIS 19 (2010).

give opinions, but not opinions as to the "ultimate issue"; according to this reasoning, only the jury has that responsibility.[143] The Federal Rules of Evidence have rejected the traditional view of opinion on the ultimate issue, stating that "[a]n opinion is not objectionable just because it embraces an ultimate issue."[144] Consistent with Rule 704(a), involving a state version of the rule, in a prosecution for child abuse, an appellate court held that expert medical testimony determining that the cause of a child's injuries involved abuse rather than accidental injury was appropriate even though the doctor's testimony touched on intent and went to the ultimate issue in the case.[145] In approving the testimony, the court made an analogy between the doctor's determination of abuse and intent and the conclusion that could be offered by an arson investigator that a fire had been intentionally started. Similarly, in a Massachusetts prosecution where the allegation was that the defendant possessed crack cocaine with the intention to distribute, the trial court permitted a police officer, who qualified as an expert witness in narcotics crime, to testify that possession of three individually wrapped quantities of crack cocaine was more consistent with distribution than with personal use.[146] The officer based his expert opinion on the manner in which the drugs were packaged, the absence of any smoking apparatus, and the fact that the defendant was arrested in an area with a high incidence of criminal activity.

However, a limitation to Federal Rule 704 and most state counterparts of Rule 704 states that experts who are offering evidence concerning the mental state or condition of the defendant in a criminal case may not testify concerning whether the defendant did or did not possess a correct mental state that constituted an element of the crime for which the defendant was on trial. According to the Rule 704, such an ultimate issues "are for the trier of fact alone."[147]

Just because a witness states an opinion indicating the witness's belief that a defendant possessed a mental state or condition that constituted an element of the crime does not necessarily mean that a case will be reversed due to Rule 704(b) or a similar rule. In a Georgia prosecution involving possession of crack cocaine with intent to distribute, a police officer who qualified as an expert on drug possession, use, and sale was permitted to testify that he had more than 900 hours of special training as a narcotics officer and was familiar with how crack cocaine was packaged when it was ready for sale. He had made numerous drug-related arrests, of which at least fifty involved crack cocaine. According to the reviewing court, the police officer's testimony concerning the defendant's intent to distribute was well within the police officer's special knowledge as an expert.[148]

---

143 People v. Wilson, 25 Cal. 2d 341, 153 P.2d 720 (1944).

144 FED. R. EVID. 704(a).

145 Hildebrand v. State, 2013 Ind. App. Unpub. LEXIS 596, 988 N.E.2d 403 (2013).

146 Commonwealth v. Sepheus, 82 Mass. App. Ct. 765, 2012 Mass. App. LEXIS 280 (2012).

147 FED. R. EVID. 704(b).

148 Thomas v. State, 321 Ga. App. 214, 216, 2013 Ga. App. LEXIS 340 (2013).

§ 11.9 Cross-Examination of Expert Witness

Rule 705

DISCLOSING THE FACTS OR DATA UNDERLYING AN EXPERT'S OPINION

Unless the court orders otherwise, an expert may state an opinion—and give the reasons for it—without first testifying to the underlying facts or data. But the expert may be required to disclose those facts or data on cross-examination.[149]

An expert witness, just like any other witness, must allow a Sixth Amendment confrontation and submit to cross-examination by the opposing party following the expert's direct testimony. An expert may be cross-examined as any other witness and may be queried concerning his or her qualifications, the subject matter, and the reasons for his or her opinion. Traditionally, cross-examination of an expert may encompass the matter on which the expert bases his or her opinion.[150] A skillful cross-examination seeks to challenge the opinion of the expert by questioning the methodology, assumed facts, and reliability of any scientific tests performed and may include an inquiry into fellow experts upon whom the testifying expert may have relied. Although, cross-examination may include an additional inquiry into the witness's qualifications to testify as an expert,[151] such an inquiry could prove counterproductive if the expert manages to buttress his or her qualifications. The rules governing the cross-examination of witnesses generally apply and the trial court has broad discretion in allowing cross-examination of witnesses,[152] including experts, and may place reasonable limits on cross-examination. The failure to allow cross-examination may constitute grounds for reversal if the error could have affected the outcome,[153] but a trial judge has the authority to limit or curtail the cross-examination of an expert where it appears to be a waste of the court's time or where the continued cross-examination would be repetitive, confusing, or of marginal relevance to the case.[154]

On cross-examination, an expert witness may be interrogated concerning the basis for his or her opinion. Cross-examination may include an inquiry relative to the expert's knowledge of textbooks, treatises, articles, and other scholarly publications in the field; he or she may be confronted with excerpts from them, and the expert may be asked whether he or she is familiar with them and whether he or she agrees with them.

149 FED. R. EVID. 705.

150 People v. Pearson, 56 Cal. 4th 393, 436, 2013 Cal. LEXIS 2131 (2013).

151 United States v. Harris, 2010 U.S. App. LEXIS 18180 (6th Cir. 2010).

152 Forbes v. Ricci, 2011 U.S. Dist. LEXIS 480 (Dist. N.J. 2011).

153 United States *ex rel.* Reed v. Gilmore, 1999 U.S. Dist. LEXIS 21525 (N.D. Ill. 1999).

154 People v. Elliott, 53 Cal. 4th 535, 578, 2012 Cal. LEXIS 1147 (2012).

One court observed that it was a well-settled rule that an expert witness may be cross-examined concerning the contents of a book, treatise, or other publication that the expert acknowledged is a standard work in the field.[155] Rule 705 of the Federal Rules of Evidence allows an expert witness to testify on direct examination by offering opinions and conclusions without first having to disclose underlying facts on which the testimony is based. However, on cross-examination, consistent with Rule 705, the opposing party is permitted to challenge the expert's testimony by requiring the expert to reveal the facts and data upon which his or her testimony rests.[156]

In applying the Texas version of Rule 705 on cross-examination, the courts allow a party to request a hearing outside of the presence of the jury, prior to allowing an expert to testify on direct examination. The hearing has two purposes: to permit the defendant to determine the basis of an expert's opinion without any danger of the listing evidence that would be admissible in the jury's presence and to supply the defendant with appropriate information to make a timely objection to the proffered testimony of the expert on the ground that such testimony lacks a sufficient basis for admissibility. In a Texas aggravated sexual assault case, the defendant was permitted to question the basis for the expert witness's testimony out of the hearing of the jury.[157] At the close of the hearing, the trial judge concluded that the expert witness was qualified, and the witness testified at trial. Had the witness for some reason not been qualified as an expert, the jury would not have heard her testimony. Whether the expert testifies in a federal or state court, the basis for the testimony can be revealed to the parties during the pretrial stage or during cross-examination so that the parties may bring the basis for the opinion to the trier of fact so that it can give proper weight to the evidence.

An expert witness who expresses an opinion that significantly relies on his or her readings of scholarly material may be cross-examined as to that opinion by reference to other reputable works in the field. However, in making an effort to impeach an expert witness based on scholarly work or a treatise, the testifying expert can only be questioned over works that the expert recognizes as authoritative in the field. Demonstrative of this principle is a Virginia rule that determined that it constitutes improper cross-examination to use an article as impeachment evidence that the expert witness did not accept as authoritative.[158] The rationale for this rule is that such cross-examination tests the expert witness's credibility and reliability by inquiring into the extent of the expert's familiarity with the accepted authorities in his or her specialty and by asking the expert whether he or she agrees with the recognized authorities.

While the federal Constitution's Sixth Amendment confrontation clause guarantees every defendant the opportunity for confrontation and cross-examination of adverse witnesses, it presents some challenges when expert witnesses testify

---

155 McConnell v. Dunfee, 2010 Phila. Ct. Com. Pl. LEXIS 322 (Penn. 2010).

156 People v. Williams, 238 Ill. 2d 125, 2010 Ill. LEXIS 971 (2010).

157 Shaw v. State, 2010 Tex. App. LEXIS 8902 (2010).

158 Lloyd v. Kime, 79 Va. Cir. 302, 2009 Va. Cir. LEXIS 260 (2009).

concerning the results of tests and experiments done by other experts or technicians who do not appear in court and are not specifically available for cross-examination. The essence of the argument concerns the fact that the person who conducted a test or wrote a treatise was not in court when the information was mentioned by an expert witness and the outside writer or scientist cannot actually be cross-examined. This issue arose in *Melendez-Diaz v. Massachusetts*,[159] where the Supreme Court of the United States held that the Sixth Amendment guarantee of confrontation prohibited a prosecutor from relying upon hearsay evidence offered in the form of "certificates of analysis" that had been prepared by technicians in a crime laboratory that were introduced to prove that the defendant possessed cocaine. The admission into evidence and use of such certificates prevented the defendant from cross-examining the technicians who conducted the tests and who reached the scientific conclusions that were recorded within the certificates. In effect, unsworn testimony that could not be cross-examined was used against Mr. Melendez-Diaz in violation of the Sixth Amendment right of confrontation and cross-examination.

In an Illinois case heard after the Melendez-Diaz case, a defendant had been convicted of rape based partly upon expert testimony that a DNA profile produced by an outside laboratory matched his DNA. The state lab expert testified that the outside lab results from Cellmark matched a DNA profile produced by a state police laboratory that used a blood sample taken from the defendant. The state police analysis of DNA had been properly admitted through the use of expert testimony by a properly qualified expert in DNA analysis. The outside laboratory, Cellmark, unconnected with the state police laboratory, conducted tests on a sample victim vaginal swab that had been sent to it and Cellmark sent the results to the state police lab. The expert from the state police lab was permitted to testify that, in her expert opinion, the two results matched despite the defendant's objection that the he had not been able to confront the Cellmark expert and question that individual. In this case, Cellmark's report was considered for the limited purpose of determining whether two samples of DNA matched, and the relevance of that match was established by independent circumstantial evidence showing that the state police DNA report was based on a blood draw from the defendant while the Cellmark sample was collected from the crime scene. The state police lab expert referred to the Cellmark report, not to prove the truth of the matter asserted in it, but only to establish that it contained a profile that matched the profile deduced from petitioner's blood. According to the Supreme Court of the United States, the defendant could properly confront and cross-examine the state police lab expert and, according the Court, there was no violation of the Sixth Amendment's protections requiring confrontation and cross-examination.[160]

---

159 557 U.S. 408, 451, 129 S. Ct. 2527, 2531, 174 L. Ed. 2d 314, 320, 2009 U.S. LEXIS 4734 (2009).

160 Williams v. Illinois, 132 S. Ct. 2221, 2123, 2012 U. S. LEXIS 4658 (2012).

§ 11.10 Subjects of Expert Testimony

Earlier sections of this chapter presented some of the general rules that regulate the use of expert witness testimony. This particular section will discuss many of the typical topics that are often the subject of expert witness testimony in criminal cases. It should be noted that the subject of expert testimony is not a closed class of topics; information on subjects in one area might have been within the realm of expert testimony but may become common knowledge, while new areas of technology and changes in human endeavor may create new subjects for which expert testimony will become appropriate. For example, at one point in human history, the reason milk may become spoiled would probably have required a scientist to explain the concept of bacteria to a court, while today lay people routinely would have knowledge concerning why milk might become undrinkable. With respect to new areas of expertise, thirty-five years ago the concept of deoxyribonucleic acid and how it might be used for identifying human perpetrators was largely unknown to courts, and even many scientists, and still requires expert testimony for court use at the present time.

Before any person may testify as an expert, a court will require that a proposed expert demonstrate his or her qualifications by indicating education, experience, and knowledge that sets that individual apart from the common knowledge that most persons in society possess. There are numerous subject areas in which persons with specialized knowledge can meet the qualifications and can assist the trier of fact in reaching logical conclusions. Expert testimony generally will be admissible as long as the testimony has a proper foundation, it has been based on reliable principles, and the expert has applied the principles appropriately. Although space limitations make it impossible to discuss all the areas in which expert testimony would be admissible, especially in criminal cases, the following subsections discuss and illustrate some of the most common areas or subjects that will benefit from expert testimony.

A. Automobile Accidents

Testimony of police officers and other trained individuals who may be qualified as accident reconstruction experts may be admissible at criminal or civil trials arising from motor vehicle accidents. In determining whether a witness possesses the qualifications of an expert in automobile crashes, the witness must offer a foundation for his or her expertise. In a New Jersey case involving a vehicular homicide, the accident reconstruction expert was allowed to testify to his credentials that would qualify him as an expert. In establishing a foundation for his expertise, the officer testified that:

> he was educated and certified in the field [accident reconstruction] and belonged to relevant professional organizations. He had been a police officer for twenty-seven years, of which he spent eleven years as a member of the vehicular homicide unit. He was trained as a breathalyzer operator and in detection and enforcement of driving while intoxicated (DWI). He had examined at least 2000 vehicular accident scenes and performed nearly 300 accident reconstructions.[161]

[161] State v. Gentilello, 2013 N.J. Super. Unpub. LEXIS 28 (2013).

Although it could be argued that a better foundation could be required, once the fact of expertise has been established, the expert designation will not usually be disturbed on appeal, absent an abuse of judicial discretion.

In one Florida case, the court reversed a trial court holding that had excluded expert testimony concerning the cause and other details of an automobile crash.[162] The reviewing court noted that the expert's proposed testimony would have been based on simulation calculations relied upon by similar engineering experts in the field and would offer opinions concerning the speed of the vehicles and the movements of one of the litigants within the vehicle during the accident. Experts are permitted to offer testimony based on inferences that have been drawn from facts related to the case and from data supplied by other witnesses.[163] In one case involving a conviction of vehicular homicide, both the prosecution and the defense presented expert testimony concerning how the vehicle left the road. The defendant presented evidence by a mechanical engineer who analyzed skid marks, which supported the defendant's position that the wreck was an accident and that the death was not criminal. Using a more sophisticated approach, the prosecution offered an accident reconstruction expert who used a computer software program—PC-Crash. The prosecution's expert validated the program and testified that it had gained general acceptance in the expert accident reconstruction community. The appellate court upheld the conviction because, even though the two expert witnesses presented opposing conclusions, the jury could determine which version to believe.[164]

In many recent automobile collision cases in which the speed of a defendant's car may be at issue, newer technology, coupled with expert witnesses with cutting-edge knowledge, proves decisive. In a Florida double manslaughter case, at issue was the speed of the defendant's Pontiac Trans Am at the time it hit the victims, who were in a car backing into a public street from a private driveway. The vehicle's "black box," or event data recorder, which also operated the defendant's air bag, recorded the speed at 114 mph in a 30 mph speed zone, while the prosecution's experts estimated the speed to be around 80 mph. According to the appellate court, it was proper for the trial court to allow expert testimony to determine the speed of the vehicle based on the event data recorder because the state's expert testified concerning the reliability of the event data recorder and the fact that such recorders are generally accepted in the accident reconstruction community.[165]

As a general rule, a court does not commit error when it permits a qualified expert witness to reconstruct a motor vehicle accident by basing his or her opinion on photographs, damage repair estimates, personal measurements at the accident scene, police reports, studies of victim injuries, and interviews of witnesses and participants. Where

---

162 Coddington v. Nunez, 2013 Fla. App. LEXIS 14140 (2013).

163 *See* CHARLES W. EHRHARDT, FLORIDA EVIDENCE § 704.1 (2006 ed.).

164 *See* State v. Phillips, 123 Wash. App. 761, 98 P.3d 838, 2004 Wash. App. LEXIS 2296 (2004), *reh'g denied*, 2005 Wash. LEXIS 492 (2005).

165 Matos v. State, 899 So. 2d 403, 405, 2005 Fla. App. LEXIS 4359 (2005). *See also* Matos v. State, 2013 U.S. Dist. LEXIS 4896 (S.D. Fla. 2013).

the expert's reconstruction will assist the trier of fact, the expert's testimony should be admitted,[166] but where the assistance of an expert would not materially assist the trier of fact, the use of an expert can be denied.[167]

B. Airplane Crashes

Under current theory, and recognizing the state-of-the-art of aviation and the usual reliability of airplanes, when aircraft crash there is generally a strong presumption that someone was negligent. Determining the cause of a crash will generally point toward the individual or entity whose negligence contributed to the crash. Because the causes and complexities of aircraft crashes are particularly within the specialized knowledge of experts and due to the technical variables involved in aircraft power plants and air-frames, in order to prove the cause of a particular aircraft crash, expert testimony is generally required to identify the causative factors. Witnesses who have special training, education, and/or experience may qualify as experts in determining the cause of aircraft accidents.[168] In some instances, simple causes can be identified. In one case, a twin-engine Piper aircraft crashed because it ran out of fuel, according to experts who testified in a civil suit concerning crash damages.[169] In identifying the cause in a different aircraft crash, where the plane had not flown in years, contained old fuel, and had been improperly certified as "airworthy," the inspector had a duty to conduct a more thorough inspection before certification. According to the experts, the crash was caused by engine failure, which was, in turn, caused by poor and inadequate maintenance.[170] The expert noted that the inspector did "not indicate that [he] completed the steps necessary to ensure the airworthiness of the fuel system including the carburetor or air intake filter."[171]

Conclusions concerning aircraft crash causation involve evaluation of facts and circumstances that are beyond the knowledge of ordinary witnesses and require an expert to develop an opinion concerning the cause of crash or aircraft mishap.[172] While expert testimony can often identify both cause and the responsible party, expert testimony may be offered to demonstrate that one party was not negligent in an aircraft disaster. In determining responsibility in one crash, a plaintiff alleged that the federal government had been negligent in offering some services to the pilot, including altimeter settings and alternative airports, and negligent in sending rescue equipment;

---

166 Hamilton v. Jones, 2005 Ark. App. LEXIS 92 (2005).

167 Washington v. State, 295 Ga. App. 586, 589, 672 S.E.2d 665, 668, 2009 Ga. App. LEXIS 46 (2009).

168 See Arch Insurance Co. v. United States, 2013 U.S. Dist. LEXIS 95305 (2013). This reported Order and Memorandum Opinion contains detailed information concerning the qualifications of aviation expert witnesses who appeared in one case.

169 Arthur v. Grimmett, 319 S.W.3d 711, 712, 2009 Tex. App. LEXIS 6260 (2009).

170 Mills v. Oberg. 2005 Minn. App. LEXIS 106 (2005), February 1, 2005.

171 Mills v. Oberg, 2005 Minn. App. LEXIS 106 (2005).

172 *Id.*

an expert witness was properly permitted to offer admissible opinion evidence concerning whether the conduct of federal employees amounted to negligence.[173]

C. Physical and Mental Condition

A general practitioner may usually testify concerning matters within a medical specialty if his or her education or experience, or both, involves demonstrable knowledge of the subject. A skilled medical witness generally has no need to be duly licensed to practice medicine[174] and, in most cases, the expert does not have to be licensed in the particular jurisdiction. However, some jurisdictions require a better match between general knowledge and the specialty than merely possessing a medical degree or license. The general rule is that anyone who is shown to have special knowledge and skill in understanding human ailments may have the foundation to testify as an expert qualified to give an opinion on the particular question in issue. For example, medical doctors who are well versed in the effects of insulin, hypoglycemia, and how intoxication might result when insulin protocols were not followed, may be permitted to offer testimony to help establish the defense of involuntary intoxication.[175] In one Ohio case involving alleged felonious assault, a trial court allowed a treating emergency room physician to testify as a prosecution fact witness and not as an expert to the observed physical injuries of the victim.[176] In the same case, the trial court allowed a nontreating physician, who did qualify as an expert witness, to offer an opinion concerning whether the victim sustained serious physical harm and offer an opinion relative to whether the injuries could have been the result of a kick, punch, or receiving an elbow blow to the body.

While expert medical testimony may prove preferable, it is not always essential that an expert medical witness be a medical practitioner. An expert witness in the field of toxicology was permitted to testify in a driving under the influence prosecution that the defendant was a user of marijuana based on the amount of marijuana metabolite found in his blood. She offered testimony concerning amounts of amphetamine, methamphetamine, and mirtazapine, a depressant, but she found no alcohol in the blood sample. Under questioning by the prosecutor, the expert was not able with certainty to say whether the defendant was under the influence or not based on her analysis of his blood chemistry. Even though the expert testified to medical evidence and

---

173 Bieberle v. United States, 255 F. Supp. 2d 1190, 1206, 1207, 2003 U.S. Dist. LEXIS 5427 (D. Kan. 2003).

174 *See* Tenet Healthcare Corp. v. Gilbert, 277 Ga. App. 895, 627 S.E.2d 821, 2006 Ga. App. LEXIS 167 (2006), in which an expert's affidavit had to be attached to a complaint to make the case actionable and the court held that the affidavit was sufficient even though the expert possessed no license to practice at the time of the complaint.

175 People v. Garcia, 113 P. 3d 775, 2005 Colo. LEXIS 562 (2005).

176 State v. Brofford, 2013 Ohio 3781, 2013 Ohio App. LEXIS 3945 (2013).

she was not a medical doctor, her level of expertise was properly admitted in an effort to illuminate the condition of the defendant.[177]

An expert who gives testimony may carry more weight with a jury when explaining physical attributes or mental conditions. For example, a Tennessee court allowed a physician who was an expert in the area of pharmacology and toxicology to testify concerning the physiological effects of drinking ethylene glycol (automobile antifreeze). The court permitted the doctor to explain how ethylene glycol causes a patient's blood to become acidic while metabolizing into oxalic acid, which binds with calcium, causing kidney failure and death.[178] With the detail offered by the doctor, a trier of fact would most likely place great weight on the testimony. In a case involving child rape, a medical doctor who examined the alleged victim was permitted to express an opinion that her physical condition and resulting injuries were consistent with vaginal penetration.[179] The doctor was qualified as an expert in pediatrics and testified that the victim's story of repeated vaginal penetration was consistent with the findings he made during his examination of the victim. Evidence from this physician expert witness generally would be given much more weight by the trier of fact than would be given to a nonmedical child counselor. In a different case, a licensed physician's assistant, who treated the defendant in the hospital's emergency room on the night of the arrest, could be precluded from testifying as an expert about all the medical issues in the case, and his testimony could cover only the examination and treatment of the defendant at the hospital.[180]

Trial courts are given great discretion in deciding how testimony regarding a particular defendant's mental condition should be characterized following its admission. Some courts limit expert testimony relating to the conclusions drawn by an expert because of the danger that the expert's opinion might invade the province of the jury. Other jurisdictions do not exhibit a concern about whether an expert's conclusion might intrude into an area reserved for jury decision making. In an Ohio case, where the female defendant asserted the battered spouse syndrome as an affirmative defense to murder, it was a proper topic for medical testimony involving her mental state.[181] Her retained psychiatrist, who examined her properly, testified on her behalf because most jurors could not understand the mental interplay between a defendant and the concept of the battered spouse syndrome. In this type of case, the state permits the psychiatrist to offer an opinion that the defendant suffered from battered spouse syndrome, an opinion that might intrude into the province of the jury. The federal rules under Rule 704 are similar to the variants adopted by many states and allow an expert to offer an opinion or inference concerning the ultimate issue unless it relates to a mental state or condition of a criminal defendant.[182]

---

[177] State v. Lee, 2005 Tenn. Crim. App. LEXIS 399 (2005).

[178] Tennessee v. Combs, 2002 Tenn. Crim. App. LEXIS 799 (2002).

[179] State v. Streater, 197 N.C. App. 632, 643, 678 S.E.2d 367, 375, 2009 N.C. App. LEXIS 1065 (2009).

[180] State v. Carlson, 559 N.W.2d 802 (N.D. 1996).

[181] State v. Goff, 2010 Ohio 6317, 2010 Ohio LEXIS 3291 (2010).

[182] *See* FED. R. EVID. 704(b).

Expert testimony concerning mental condition often proves both useful and necessary when prosecuting criminal cases and in determining some defenses to criminal activities. In a Texas habeas corpus proceeding, a convicted murder contended that his attorneys were deficient in presenting his defense at trial and at the penalty phase in that they failed to present evidence of his disadvantaged background and neglected to present evidence of his lifelong mental impairment.[183] At various stages prior to, during, and after the murder trial and sentencing proceedings, expert medical practitioners examined the defendant and testified to his mental condition. At the conclusion of the legal wrangling, a United States court of appeal ruled against the defendant in the habeas corpus proceeding, holding that, among other issues, the defendant's challenges concerning mental impairment had been properly presented by expert medical witnesses and that no prejudice to his case existed. In a different Texas case involving a juvenile who fatally shot his father who had extensively and repeatedly abused the defendant throughout his life, it was error to prevent the expert testimony of a psychiatrist who was prepared to tell the jury about the defendant's belief that force was immediately necessary for his defense and that the child suffered from battered child syndrome.[184] The psychiatrist had reviewed the defendant's medical records, was aware of his sexually abusive family situation, and was prepared to testify on behalf of the defendant. The reviewing court determined that the psychiatric testimony was essential to the juvenile defendant's defense and reversed the adjudication.

If the members of the jury can readily observe the defendant's mental condition and base their decision on that observation, expert testimony concerning the condition properly may be excluded. In a California murder case, the reviewing court held that the trial court ruled properly in excluding a medical doctor's proposed testimony that the defendant did not suffer from any clinically diagnosable mental disorder, disease, defect, or other pathological mental condition.[185] As the reviewing court noted, the doctor's testimony was "that the defendant was a slow-witted guy who had caught some bad breaks in life and who was under a lot of stress. A lay jury would be equipped to evaluate this claim; it did not require any expert testimony."[186]

D. *Summaries*

The Federal Rules of Criminal Procedure interface with the Federal Rules of Evidence when, as a precondition of admission of expert testimony, the criminal rules[187] require that both the prosecution and the defense prepare a written summary of any testimony that either side expects to have admitted under Federal Rule of Evidence 702, 703, or 705. As a general rule, the originals of the testimony summarized must be made available to the opposing party for examination in advance of trial or the

183 Jennings v. Stephens, 2013 U.S. App. LEXIS 14864 (5th Cir. 2013).

184 *In re* E.C.L., 278 S.W3d 510, 518, 2009 Tex. App. LEXIS 995 (2009).

185 People v. Villalobos, 2013 Cal. App. Unpub. LEXIS 494 (2013).

186 *Id.*

187 FED. R. CRIM PROC. 16.

expert's testimony may be excluded.[188] Demonstrative of the requirement of providing **summaries** of expected evidence, in a federal prosecution for possessing a prohibited firearm and ammunition, a federal judge ordered the defendant to provide the federal prosecutor with a written summary of any evidence that the defendant intended to offer in his defense involving expert testimony, the basis for the expert opinion, and a disclosure of facts that underlay the opinions of his experts.[189] In a different federal prosecution and consistent with this summary requirement of expert testimony, a federal district judge ordered that the United States attorney provide a defendant, who had been charged with "knowingly possessing with intent to distribute 'five kilograms or more of cocaine hydrochloride,' and 100 kilograms or more of marijuana,"[190] a summary of any scientific expert testimony that the government expected to introduce at the upcoming criminal trial. This information allows a defendant to prepare a defense by having an idea of what the government will attempt to prove and provides a possible avenue for impeachment for the government expert witness.

Summaries of a slightly different kind are covered in § 13.8 Summaries and by Federal Rule of Evidence 1006 that provides that the contents of large writings, recordings of sound or audio, and photographs that cannot be conveniently examined in court can be offered at trial in the form of a summary, chart, or calculation that is displayed for the court. Although the originals can be, pursuant to court order, produced in court, the originals of these items covered by the summary must be reasonably made available to the opposing parties.[191] Trial witnesses may also be permitted to offer summaries of testimony as an aid to the understanding of the jury. For example, following hurricane Katrina, the federal government paid local contractors to remove trees and debris from public right of ways in Wayne County, Mississippi. One contractor allegedly inflated the amount of work and the number of leaning and hanging trees that his company removed pursuant to tickets and orders from the Federal Emergency Management Agency, thus defrauding the federal government. The prosecution was properly allowed to introduce a summary chart of orders and debris tickets to help show the divergence in what was ordered and what was billed. Introducing each debris ticket and matching it to work done or not done would have been cumbersome and using a summary was appropriate, according to the trial court.[192] The summary witness need not necessarily be an expert witness, but in many cases summary witnesses do carry expert witness qualifications.[193]

---

188 FED. R. CRIM PROC. 16.

189 This was a pretrial order issued by the federal judge in United States v. Gardenhire, 2011 U. S. Dist. LEXIS 2391 (S.D. Ga. 2011).

190 United States v. David, et al., 2013 U.S. Dist. LEXIS 46755 (E.D. La. 2013)

191 *See* FED. R. EVID. 1006. States have similar adoptions concerning summaries. *See* TENN. R. EVID. 1006 (2013).

192 United States v. Sturdivant, 2013 U.S. Dist. LEXIS 126780 (E.D. Ms. 2013).

193 *See also* § 13.8 Summaries.

E. Handwriting Comparisons

Analysis of handwriting consists of having an expert compare a known specimen of a person's handwriting to a questioned sample in order to determine whether the same person composed both documents. The scientific theory behind handwriting analysis is that each person's writing technique is different and unique from virtually everyone else.[194] Each time a handwriting expert testifies in court, he or she must demonstrate appropriate qualifications as an expert witness. Testimony that a certain person wrote an individual document is an opinion offered by the expert, but the handwriting analysis need not be absolutely certain as long as principles and proper methodology have been followed. To be qualified, he or she must have expert training and experience in handwriting analysis in general or must be intimately familiar with the handwriting of the individual in question. In a criminal case, expert testimony proved crucial to the prosecution when expert witnesses concluded that a defendant in a drug case had signed a consent-to-search form.[195] Expert testimony that identified the defendant's handwriting on materials involving child pornography assisted the government in gaining a conviction against the defendant for receipt and possession of child pornography.

A lay witness who has no familiarity with a person's handwriting is not qualified to offer an opinion concerning the identity of the writer. For example, a trial court committed error when the judge permitted a police officer to testify that the handwriting at issue belonged to the defendant when the officer had no expertise and was not familiar with the defendant's handwriting prior to the time of the trial.[196] Interestingly, a jury or a judge, when the trial is sent to the judge, is permitted to compare a known example of a writing with a questioned sample and render a conclusion concerning the author of the unknown writing,[197] even though neither the judge nor the jury collectively has any experience as a questioned document examiner.

In contrast, comparison handwriting analysis is generally admissible in court when the evidence comes from a qualified expert. The purpose of allowing expert testimony is to assist the jury in deciding the questioned document and to draw the jury's attention to similarities between the known and the unknown writing sample.[198] When a qualified expert had years of experience in the field of handwriting analysis, he was permitted to offer his opinion that the defendant wrote the document in question,[199] despite the fact that the jury would have to ultimately decide the same question.

---

194 United States v. Prime, 431 F.3d 1147, 1153, 2005 U.S. App. LEXIS 27276 (2005).

195 United States v. Ozuna, 561 F.3d 728, 2009 U.S. App. LEXIS 7034 (7th Cir. 2009).

196 Ohio v. Brennan, 2002 Ohio App. LEXIS 5788 (2002).

197 State v. Williams, 2009 Iowa App. LEXIS 470 (2009). *See also* People v. Rodriguez, 133 Cal. App. 4th 545, 554, 34 Cal. Rptr. 3d 886, 892, 2005 Cal. App. LEXIS 1628 (2005).

198 United States v. Smith, 153 F. App'x. 187, 2005 U.S. App. LEXIS 23798 (4th Cir. 2005) (forensic document examiner who helped develop standards for handwriting analysis was deemed to be qualified as an expert regarding forged instruments).

199 *See* United States v. Brown, 152 F. App'x. 59, 2005 U.S. App. LEXIS 22703 (2d Cir. 2005).

Because handwriting identification cannot be based upon absolute scientific certainty, the opinion of an expert regarding handwriting must meet only the generally accepted standards adopted by questioned document examiners.[200] In a prosecution for mail and wire fraud, the defendant challenged the government's expert witness concerning her "methodology, the bases for her conclusions, and the degrees of certainty with which she was able to reach her conclusions."[201] She testified that her conclusions were within a reasonable degree of scientific certainty that the defendant wrote some of the questioned documents. The judge allowed the testimony, and the jury was permitted to accept or reject the expert's testimony. In a different case, a court permitted the admission of the testimony of a handwriting expert who had "a reasonable degree of certainty that a particular person was the author of the questioned document."[202]

In a case involving the fraudulent recording of an easement, an expert handwriting witness testified that the signatures were not valid while intimate family members who had familiarity with their deceased relatives' signatures were permitted to testify that the signatures were not genuine and were forgeries.[203] In a criminal case, expert testimony proved crucial to the prosecution when expert witnesses concluded that a defendant in a drug case had signed a consent-to-search form.[204]

The Supreme Court of the United States has emphasized that requiring a defendant to provide a handwriting sample for comparison purposes does not violate the privilege against **self-incrimination.**[205] According to the Court, the use of this type of evidence does not run counter to Fifth Amendment constitutional protections because the quality of the handwriting is used for the sole purpose of comparison with a document of uncertain authorship. A handwriting sample reveals the physical characteristics of writing style and does not require a defendant to give actual adverse testimony. "A mere handwriting exemplar, in contrast to the content of what is written, like the voice or body itself, is an identifying characteristic" that is outside the protection of the Fifth Amendment.[206]

Self-incrimination An act or declaration either as testimony at trial or prior to trial by which one implicates oneself in a crime.

Expert testimony may be admissible to determine authorship of a document based not upon handwriting analysis, but upon an evaluation of the style of word selection and textually unique qualities of a writing.[207] Some courts have admitted the testimony of

---

200 United States v. Herrera, 832 F.2d 833 (4th Cir. 1987).

201 United States v. Mornan, 413 F.3d 372, 380, 2005 U.S. App. LEXIS 13043 (3d Cir. 2005).

202 Community Bank v. Stuckey, 2010 Miss. LEXIS 644 (2010).

203 The Berkshires, L.L.C. v. Sykes, 2005 UT App 536, 2005 Utah App. LEXIS 552 (Utah 2005).

204 United States v. Ozuna, 561 F.3d 728, 2009 U.S. App. LEXIS 7034 (7th Cir. 2009).

205 Gilbert v. California, 388 U.S. 263, 265, 1967 U.S. LEXIS 1086 (1967); *see also* United States v. Dionisio, 410 U.S. 1 (1973), in which the Court upheld a federal judge's order that required a suspect to give voice samples for grand jury consideration.

206 Hiibel v. Sixth Judicial District Court of Nevada, 542 U.S. 177, 194, 2004 U.S. LEXIS 4385 (2004), quoting United States v. Wade, 388 U.S. 218, 223 (1967).

207 *See* Sargur Srihari et al., *Individuality of Handwriting*, 47 J. FORENSIC SCI. 856 (2002).

forensic document examiners[208] who look for common artifacts, style, and linguistic markers in questioned documents, while other courts have been somewhat more reticent to take full advantage of this modern method of determining authorship of questioned documents.[209]

F. Typewriter Comparisons

Before the development of inkjet and laser printer technologies, those who could qualify as experts to identify which typewriter might have been used to produce a particular document were more in demand than presently is the case. However, comparisons may still be important in stolen historical document cases and in others where typewritten evidence is relevant. Some of the experts could compare the manner in which a document had been typed to assist in the identity of the writer. However, the need for experts in the typewriter comparison field, while once robust, has diminished in importance but has not completely evaporated. In a recent North Carolina murder case, an examination of a typewriter revealed that a threatening letter had been typed using a specific typewriter ribbon on a typewriter to which the defendant had access.[210] Because some traditional typewriters are still in use, this expertise retains some marginal utility in civil cases as well as in criminal prosecutions.[211] Today, with the more common use of various computer printers that print in a fairly uniform manner, discerning the source of a document has become somewhat more difficult.

Expert evidence is generally admissible to prove that a document was typed on a particular type of machine, such as an Underwood typewriter, even though the police never obtained the specific typewriter. In order to prove that a document was typed on a particular computer printer/typewriter using a specific daisywheel print wheel, courts frequently admit expert testimony.[212] In making comparisons, the expert usually points out the unique characteristics such as dirt particles changing the printed character, damage to a particular character, and any irregularities specifically unique to a particular print wheel. Sometimes, a comparison of documents indicates that they were typed on the same machine even though they purportedly came from separate sources.[213]

More modern methods of printing pose unique problems concerning identification, especially with recyclable inkjet print heads and refillable inks containing different chemical compositions from the original factory ink. Factory inks tend to be homogeneous and do not permit easy typing from batch to batch of ink.

---

208 United States v. Gricco, 2002 U.S. Dist. LEXIS 7564 (E.D. Pa. 2002).

209 United States v. Lewis, 220 F. Supp. 2d 548, 2002 U.S. Dist. LEXIS 17062 (S.D. W.Va. 2002); United States v. Brewer, 2002 U.S. Dist. LEXIS 6689 (N.D. Ill. 2002); United States v. Saelee, 162 F. Supp. 2d 1097 (D. Alaska 2001); United States v. Fujii, 152 F. Supp. 2d 939 (N.D. Ill. 2000).

210 Underwood v. Harkleroad, 2011 U.S. App. LEXIS 614 (4th Cir. 2011).

211 Eta-Ndu v. Gonzales, 411 F.3d 977, 981, 982, 2005 U.S. App. LEXIS 12120 (8th Cir. 2005), in which forensic analysis of typewritten letters proved important in a deportation case.

212 United States v. Johns, 2000 U.S. App. LEXIS 542 (6th Cir. 2000).

213 Caldron v. Ashcroft, 110 F. App'x. 789, 2004 U.S. App. LEXIS 19793 (9th Cir. 2004).

Determining the source of printed documents has taken a step forward because several manufacturers of color laser printers have designed their hardware to print the serial number and manufacturer's code in binary form on each sheet of paper printed by the machine, typically using yellow dots to create the invisible codes. This practice should assist in prosecuting forgers and counterfeiters because the color printer used to create the documents will identify the output in many situations. Documents printed by commercial printing companies will usually carry the same identification marks, as will color prints made from desktop laser printers.[214]

G. Polygraph Examination Results

For a variety of reasons, courts have not generally admitted the results of lie detector, or polygraph, tests because the courts either question the scientific principles behind such tests or have concerns about the reliability of the testing procedures. In any event, because the tests must be interpreted by human beings, there is the concern that the outcome may be somewhat influenced by the polygraph operator and his or her technique. One state court noted, "The general rule in Illinois is to preclude the introduction of evidence regarding **polygraph examinations** and their results because (1) the evidence is not sufficiently reliable, and (2) the results may be taken as determinative of guilt or innocence despite their lack of reliability."[215] The Fourth Circuit has a policy of banning the admission of polygraph evidence, and it continues to refuse admission of test results because of precedent and questions concerning the reliability of the polygraph.[216] In some cases, courts will permit admission of polygraph tests if all parties consent,[217] but when there has been no written stipulation signed by all parties, courts almost uniformly deny the admission of polygraph results.[218] However, when a defendant agrees to take a polygraph test, agrees to be bound by the results, and gives prior consent to the admission of the results, the polygraph operator may testify concerning his or

Polygraph examinations An electromechanical instrument that simultaneously records certain physiological changes in the human body, which are believed to be involuntarily caused by an examinee's conscious attempts to deceive an interrogator while responding to a carefully prepared set of questions.

[214] *Investigating Machine Identification Code Technology in Color Laser Printers.* Electronic Frontier Foundation. 6 February 2014. Available at http://www.eff.org/wp/investigating-machine-identification-code-technology-color-laser-printers. *See also Seeing Yellow,* Computing Counter Culture, MIT Media Lab. 6 February 2014. Available at http://www.seeingyellow.com/.

[215] People v. Washington, 363 Ill. App. 3d 13, 842 N.E.2d 1193, 1199, 2006 Ill. App. LEXIS 24 (2006).

[216] United States v. Prince-Oyibo, 320 F.3d 494, 501, 2003 U.S. App. LEXIS 3568 (4th Cir. 2003), and United States v. Sprague, 134 F. App'x. 607, 2005 U.S. LEXIS 10127 (4th Cir. 2005).

[217] *See* § 6.19 Polygraph Tests. *See also* § 15.5 for a general description of polygraph tests.

[218] *See* Ohio v. DiBlasio, 2002 Ohio 2466, 2002 Ohio App. LEXIS 2691 (2002); *see also* J.R.T. II v. State, 783 N.E.2d 300, 2003 Ind. App. LEXIS 171 (2003).

her opinion of what the examination revealed. In a Georgia murder case, a female defendant agreed to take a polygraph and offered a written stipulation that the results could be admitted. The test results proved damaging to her defense, and the Supreme Court of Georgia upheld the admission of the polygraph results under the circumstances.[219] California by statute bans the admission of polygraph evidence and the opinions of examiners "in any trial or hearing of a juvenile for a criminal offense, whether heard in juvenile or adult court, unless all parties stipulate to the admission of such results."[220]

While polygraph evidence generally is excludable absent agreement, the Supreme Court of Georgia held that there may be occasions in which a polygraph might be admissible in the penalty phase of a death penalty case. In one case, a defendant had passed a polygraph exam conducted a few days after the murder, but the polygraph evidence was not admitted at the guilt phase of the trial. The trial court refused to allow the convicted defendant to present the evidence during his portion of the sentencing. However, the state supreme court reversed the sentence, noting, "When the defendant seeks to introduce unstipulated polygraph test results as mitigation evidence, the trial court must exercise its discretion to determine whether those results are sufficiently reliable to be admitted."[221]

Polygraph examination results are admitted only after a proper foundation has been laid and the examiner's qualifications are established. In California, polygraph results follow the traditional rule of inadmissibility, but in one case a father offered polygraph results to a court that purported to demonstrate that the grandfather had not molested the minor grandchild. The court noted that there was no statutory provision either admitting or excluding polygraph evidence in juvenile *dependency* proceedings, but that the court would not entertain polygraph evidence in the particular case because no proper foundation had been laid by the proponent.[222]

While polygraph results are generally not admissible, statements made to polygraph operators may be admissible where they qualify as admissions or confessions or are otherwise admissible.[223] Therefore, statements that do not transgress other rules of evidence may be admissible.[224] Even where polygraph evidence is not admissible in court, the administration of a polygraph exam may assist police investigators in solving a case, or it may prod a defendant or witness to begin telling the truth once it has been conveyed to the subject that he or she has failed the test.[225]

---

219 Thornton v. State, 279 Ga. 676, 678, 620 S.E.2d 356, 360, 2005 Ga. App. LEXIS 634 (2005).

220 CAL. EVID. CODE § 351.1(a) (2014).

221 Height v. State, 278 Ga. 592, 594, 595, 604 S.E.2d 796; 2004 Ga. LEXIS 958 (2004). *Contra*, United States v. Roman, 368 F. Supp. 2d 119, 2005 U.S. Dist. LEXIS 7772 (2005).

222 Nathan B. v. Superior Court, 2010 Cal. App. Unpub. LEXIS 9063 (2010).

223 *See* Esquibel v. Texas, 2005 Tex. App. LEXIS 6760 (2005). *See also* CAL. EVID. CODE § 351.1(b), "Nothing in this section is intended to exclude from evidence statements made during a polygraph examination which are otherwise admissible" (2014).

224 *See* State v. Damron, 151 S.W. 3d 510, 2004 Tenn. LEXIS 993 (2004).

225 United States v. Sweet, 2011 U.S. App. LEXIS 8, 2011 Fed. App. 0001P (6th Cir. 2011).

H. Neutron Activation Analysis

Neutron activation analysis A testing procedure that determines the presence and amount of certain trace chemical elements.

Although some courts have authorized expert witnesses to testify concerning the results of **neutron activation analysis** or gunpowder residue testing, some of these courts have expressed doubts concerning expert opinions. For example, in an old Minnesota Supreme Court case, neutron activation analysis was used to show that the defendant, who was accused of shooting a police officer, had fired a pistol shortly before his arrest. Swabs were taken of the defendant's hands using a nitric acid solution as a solvent. Results from the Treasury Department in the District of Columbia indicated that suspect had recently fired a firearm.[226] In a Delaware case,[227] in evaluating gunshot residue taken from the person suspected of recently firing a weapon, the police agency sent the samples to a private laboratory for analysis. At the laboratory, the technician removed eight vials of samples received from the police agency and placed them on a scanning electron microscope stage for overnight analysis. At the end of the process, the machine printed out micro images of the particles found within the samples. Other technicians analyzed the evidence separately to verify the existence of gunshot particles such as lead and barium. The positive results suggested that the defendant had recently fired a gun, was near someone who did, or somehow touched gunshot residue. Despite the defendant's contentions concerning the potential adulterizing of the sample or other contamination and a **chain-of-custody** argument, the appellate court approved the admission of the gunshot residue testing.

Chain of custody In evidence, one who offers real evidence must account for the custody of the evidence from the moment when law enforcement officials originally gained custody until the moment when it is offered in evidence.

The absence of test results may have adverse consequences for a defendant who does not cooperate with the police to a minimal degree. In a case in which a defendant refused to submit a sample for neutron activation testing, a trial court permitted the prosecution to comment, during closing arguments, on the refusal because there was no Fifth Amendment privilege to decline to allow a chemical sample to be taken from the defendant's hand.[228] On the other hand, when an arrestee demands to be subjected to a gunpowder residue test, the prosecution is generally under no obligation to conduct such a test and is certainly not under any duty to conduct a residue test to negate probable cause[229] or conduct a test when overwhelming evidence of guilt is present.[230]

226 State v. Spencer, 216 N.W.2d 131 (Minn. 1974).

227 *See* McNally v. State, 980 A.2d 364, 2009 Del. LEXIS 427 (2009).

228 Hubbert v. Mississippi, 759 So. 2d 504, 505, 506, 2000 Miss. App. LEXIS 196 (2000).

229 Vazquez v. Rossnagle, 163 F. Supp. 2d 494, 2001 U.S. Dist. LEXIS 3974 (3d Cir. 2001).

230 *In re* Crossley, 2003 Mich. App. LEXIS 327 (2003).

Neutron activation analysis[231] was once used to determine whether a lead bullet came from a particular batch of lead melt from the lead manufacturer. If a crime scene bullet matched a bullet of similar composition in a cartridge found in the defendant's control, the inference would be that the cartridges containing the lead bullet came from the same source or box of ammunition. As science progressed, the theory that the lead in a particular melt was homogeneous received strong criticism and appears to be an unsupportable theory;[232] even though neutron activation analysis can reveal the trace elements like silver, copper, antimony, or arsenic that are present in bullet lead,[233] the trace elements do not produce a reliable result to link one bullet as having come from a particular lead melt. It is doubtful if any trial court would admit such lead bullet evidence using neutron activation analysis at the present time.[234] However, most courts are extremely reluctant to overturn old convictions in which expert opinion relied upon neutron activation analysis to link bullets taken from crime scenes to the remaining cartridges in the possession of a defendant.[235]

I. DNA (Deoxyribonucleic Acid) Identification

Scientific and technological advances in the past 25 years have made identification of suspects easier and more definite with the application of DNA typing. Deoxyribonucleic acid contains the pattern or unique hereditary "roadmap" for all human beings and determines how humans develop, grow, and mature throughout life. The theory that everyone has unique DNA, except identical twins, has reached scientific certainty, and the ability to translate the science from the laboratory to the courtroom has become routine. Suspects who have left samples of their DNA at the crime scene or on a victim may have their known DNA sample compared to recovered specimens. Where a person would never have had the opportunity to have lawfully been in a specific location to have left DNA evidence or would never have normally occupied a position to leave DNA evidence on or in a victim, the match that can be made may prove decisive in proving guilt. Similarly, wrongly convicted individuals may be able to prove that someone else was the criminal, and, in so doing, free themselves from illegal incarceration.

---

231 The process requires access to a nuclear reactor, where the lead sample is radiated to reveal the trace components contained within the lead.

232 *See Evidence of Injustice.* CBS News: *60 Minutes.* 6 February 2014. Available at http://www.cbsnews.com/stories/2007/11/16/60minutes/main3512453.shtml.

233 *See* Commonwealth v. Daye, 19 Mass. L. Rep. 674, 2005 Mass. Super. LEXIS 368 (2005).

234 The theoretical basis by which neutron activation analysis determines whether one lead specimen matches a different sample depends upon the homogeneous nature of lead in the manufacturing process. Scientific research presently holds that lead samples are not homogeneous, which dooms other scientific efforts to trace lead based on its composition. For a related discussion, *see* Clemmons v. State, 2006 Md. LEXIS 192 (2006). For one case that did permit bullet-lead analysis and was not reversed, *see* Smith v. Secretary, 2007 U.S. Dist. LEXIS 57703 (M.D. Fla. 2007).

235 Commonwealth v. Kretchmar, 2009 PA Super. 63, 971 A.2d 1249; 2009 Pa. Super. LEXIS 79 (2009), and Higgs v. United States, 711 F. Supp. 2d 479, 499, 2010 U.S. Dist. LEXIS 48535 (2010).

In recognition of the accuracy of DNA evidence, Congress passed the DNA Analysis Backlog Elimination Act of 2000, which requires individuals who have been convicted of a qualifying federal offense, and who are in prison or on parole, probation, or other supervised release, to provide DNA samples so that the federal government will be able to add the sample to the national DNA database of convicted felons.[236] One purpose of the database of DNA samples is to help clear older cases in which DNA evidence exists but has not yet been compared to known DNA samples, such as older rape cases in which rape kits have never been analyzed. Demonstrative of this practice, in a homicide case, a baseball cap worn by the shooter and recovered at the robbery scene, and a defendant's DNA taken from a recovered firearm matched a defendant's profile stored in a local CODIS DNA database.[237] The federal district court denied a motion to suppress the DNA evidence.

Although the scientific principle of DNA has been long accepted in American state and federal courts, alleged errors in statistical application and significance, the application of the science, the handling of DNA samples, issues involving alleged contamination,[238] hearsay allegations, and Sixth Amendment confrontation issues drive the litigation efforts of defendants to keep DNA evidence from being admitted at trial.

In a case that involved an allegation of a violation of the right of confrontation, a New York trial court admitted DNA evidence against a defendant where one sample had been taken in 1993, stored, and analyzed years later. The technician compared the stored DNA sample to a recent one taken from the defendant and reported a match. An expert witness in forensic biology and DNA typing testified that she supervised and reviewed the records of the DNA profile performed on the defendant's saliva at the medical examiner's office, and she also reviewed and compared the DNA profile taken from the victim and testified that they all matched. The court found that the admission of the DNA evidence did not violate the defendant's right to confront witnesses and would not result in a reversal of the case on appeal.[239]

In prosecuting sexual assault and rape cases, DNA samples make identifying perpetrators easier, especially where the assailant is unknown to the victim. In a California rape prosecution, four days before the statute of limitations would have expired, prosecutors initiated a rape prosecution in which they identified the defendant only by his 13-loci DNA profile, and a judge issued an arrest warrant based on the DNA description. His identity at that time was unknown and, had the statute of limitations passed, any prosecution would have been forever prohibited. Once the Supreme Court of California determined that initiating a prosecution with a DNA description

---

236 DNA Analysis Backlog Elimination Act of 2000, codified, as amended, at 18 U.S.C. § 3563 and 42 U.S.C.S. §§ 14132, 14135a, 14135e.

237 United States v. Davis, 602 F. Supp. 2d 658, 2009 U.S. Dist. LEXIS 22514 (D. Maryland 2009). This case also contains an excellent description of the science supporting DNA analysis.

238 *See* Jason Borenstein, *DNA in the Legal System: The Benefits Are Clear, The Problems Aren't Always,* 3 Cardozo, PUB. L. POL'Y & ETHICS J. 847 (2006).

239 People v. Brown, 2005 N.Y. Slip Op. 25303, 9 Misc. 3d 420, 423, 801 N.Y.S.2d 709, 711, 2005 N.Y. Misc. LEXIS 1556 (2005).

was sufficient, the prosecutor had properly initiated the criminal case against the suspected rapist.[240]

DNA analysis using restriction fragment length polymorphism (RFLP) testing requires relatively large and nondegraded samples in order to obtain accurate results. The expert usually is able to testify using statistical probability to render an opinion concerning a DNA match. Newer methods, such as the polymerase chain reaction process of DNA testing, enable scientists to amplify or copy DNA samples that are too small to subject to the RFLP process prior to amplification.[241] The expert who has conducted the testing, or the expert who will testify in court in reliance on the work of laboratory technicians, will testify concerning the collection of the evidence and its testing and will interpret the results in a form that will be useful for the trier of fact.

J. Fingerprint Identification

The basic theory that everyone has unique fingerprints, and that fingerprints do not change with time or age, allows identification between a known sample and an unknown impression. Historically, courts have required expert testimony for fingerprint analysis. The standard methodology used in the United States, ACE-V, stands for analysis, comparison, evaluation, and verification.[242] From the first time it was admitted in court in 1911, these principles have generally been accepted by courts as offering a sound method of making reliable identifications.[243] By implementing these principles, law enforcement officers may make identifications using finger, palm, toe, and heel prints, where suspects have generated print impressions. The police officer or evidence technician must testify concerning the recovery process that was used to obtain the visible impression or latent prints from a crime scene, but the analysis and interpretation of the results always must be introduced and interpreted in court by an expert. As required in other fields of expertise, the expert must establish an evidentiary foundation to show that by study, training, and experience, he or she has attained sufficient expertise to offer opinion testimony. For example, in an arson case, the defendant attempted to have a proposed fingerprint expert's testimony ruled as inadmissible. The proffered fingerprint expert had significant experience with fingerprint analysis. The proposed witness was a fingerprint specialist with the Bureau of Alcohol, Tobacco, Firearms, and Explosives Forensic Science Laboratory and had extensive experience in

---

240 *See* People v. Robinson, 47 Cal. 3d 1104, 224 P.3d 55; 104 Cal. Rptr. 3d 727; 2010 Cal. LEXIS 114 (2010).

241 *See* United States v. Morrow, 374 F. Supp. 2d 51, 2005 U.S. Dist. LEXIS 8327 (D.D.C. 2005).

242 Commonwealth v. Patterson, 445 Mass. 626, 628, n.2, 840 N.E.2d 12, 14, n.2, 2005 Mass. LEXIS 765 (2005).

243 Illinois v. Jennings, 252 Ill. 534, 96 N.E. 1077 (1911). More recently, the Court of Appeals upheld the validity of fingerprint identification in United States v. Crisp, 324 F.3d 261, 2003 U.S. App. LEXIS 6021 (4th Cir. 2003), *cert. denied*, 540 U.S. 888, 2003 U.S. LEXIS 6388 (2003). Utah recently upheld the principle of fingerprint identification validity in State v. Quintana, 2004 Utah App. 418, 103 P.2d 168, 169, 2004 Utah App. LEXIS 459 (2004).

fingerprint analysis. The witness had worked for the Federal Bureau of Investigation as a fingerprint examiner, and following that employment, he served as a fingerprint specialist for the United States Secret Service for four years. As part of his education, he completed a two-month course in fingerprint examination and collection at the FBI, and he served as an instructor in processing and comparing fingerprints. The FBI certified him as a fingerprint specialist, and he had been certified by the Secret Service, Alcohol, Tobacco, and Firearms, and the International Association for Identification. In a pretrial motion, the trial judge concluded that the proposed witness was qualified as an expert witness on fingerprint identification and analysis.[244]

While a person must qualify as an expert at interpreting fingerprints in order to properly testify, police personnel or evidence technicians are assigned to collect and preserve fingerprint evidence. When properly obtained and preserved, other experts offer the evidence in court. The FBI and many large law enforcement agencies have experts trained in fingerprint analysis and schooled in courtroom presentation of that evidence. Some cases may present special challenges to obtaining usable fingerprint evidence. In a Virginia case, a police officer used a mixture of equal parts water, black fingerprint powder, and clear Ivory dish soap and applied it to the reverse side of a vehicle identification strip to reveal a defendant's fingerprints. The judge allowed the evidence to be introduced by a fingerprint analyst who testified that the specially revealed fingerprint matched the defendant's prints.[245]

To assist the jury in understanding fingerprint testimony, the expert normally will use enlarged photographs, PowerPoint presentations, or other means to show the points of similarity in the ridges and lines on which the expert has based his or her conclusion.

K. Testimony Relating to Drug Operations

Drug manufacturing and distribution operations generally have significant similarities, such that law enforcement officials who have extensive experience in drug-related crime may be permitted to offer expert testimony concerning the modus operandi of drug traffickers. As a limitation, the expert must be careful to explain the usual pattern of drug operation within his or her area of expertise but not to carry the testimony so far as to offer a personal opinion concerning guilt[246] because that is beyond the area of expertise and intrudes on the province of the jury. Experts involved with investigating illegal drug use and sale can be permitted to respond to hypothetical situations posed by the prosecutor where the hypothetical closely mirrors the facts in the case. In a New Jersey case, an officer was asked to assume that a hypothetical was true and to offer an opinion concerning whether a person in the hypothetical would be possessing drugs for personal use or for sale. Qualified experts may be permitted to offer opinion evidence concerning whether a given method of packaging illegal drugs

---

244 United States v. Aman, 2010 U.S. Dist. LEXIS 110545 (E. Dist. Va. 2010).

245 Hasson v. Commonwealth, 2006 Va. App. LEXIS (2006).

246 New Jersey v. Summers, 176 N.J. 306, 323, 324, 823 A.2d 15, 2003 N.J. LEXIS 567 (2003).

indicated possession for sale. In a Texas prosecution, an expert testified that the drug-selling operation was a "poly drug operation," meaning that it offered various drugs for sale and that, in his expert opinion, the cocaine was possessed with intent to distribute and that the marijuana was packaged for resale rather than for personal consumption.[247]

In a different state case, the Supreme Court of New Jersey approved allowing an officer to testify as an expert in illegal drug sale protocols because the officer had extensive experience in investigating drug culture and sales procedures.[248] Expert witnesses may be authorized to testify regarding the identification, use, and value of narcotics, as well as the language used by narcotics dealers.[249] In a Connecticut case involving the alleged sale of narcotics by the defendant, an objection was raised at trial concerning one of the government's expert witnesses.[250] The officer had been on a statewide task force for several years and, through involvement in undercover drug work, had developed specialized knowledge of street-level vocabulary and familiarity with how street-level narcotics are packaged and distributed. The expert also noted that he understood the common practices used by drug dealers in conducting transactions and understood how the language used in drug sales varied from location to location. The reviewing court considered these facts and others and agreed that the trial court properly held that the police officer was qualified as an expert witness, especially in drug language and the protocol of drug selling. All of this demonstrated that he had a special knowledge or experience generally possessed by experts.

A police officer may testify as an expert regarding drug-related practices that drug sellers follow to avoid detection if the evidence introduced indicates that the officer is qualified by experience, training, and education. For example, a reviewing court held that the trial court did not abuse its discretion in a drug-trafficking prosecution by admitting a police officer's expert testimony regarding countersurveillance techniques employed by a drug dealer to avoid detection.[251] To assist lay jurors, qualified law enforcement officers can testify concerning common practices of drug dealers, how sales occur, and that innocent adults are never permitted to be present at the scene of illegal drug sales.[252]

Expert witnesses involving drug sale and use may be able to assist a jury in understanding the testimony. In a Pennsylvania case, defendants had been making telephone calls to each other in which they would use cryptic language. The question "What can you do for me?" is answered by "Tomorrow." A second exchange queried, "Ain't nothing jumpin'," and received the reply, "Goddam boy, whatcha doin'?" The reply to this exchange was "Just waiting around." The trial court ruling, affirmed on appeal,

---

247 King v. State, 2010 Tex. App. LEXIS 2692 (2010).

248 New Jersey v. Nesbitt, 185 N.J. 504, 511, 888 A.2d 472, 478, 2006 N.J. LEXIS 7 (2006).

249 United States v. Walker, 2006 U.S. App. LEXIS 11280 (6th Cir. 2006).

250 *See* State v. Banks, 117 Conn. App. 102, 978 A.2d 519, 2009 Conn. App. LEXIS 415 (2009).

251 United States v. deSoto, 885 F.2d 354 (7th Cir. 1989). *See* case in Part II.

252 United States v. Garcia, 439 F.3d 363, 366, 2006 U.S. App. LEXIS 5032 (7th Cir. 2006).

permitted an expert in drug sales to state that, in his opinion, this type of telephone exchange indicated that one person wanted to buy drugs and that the other person would sell but did not have any drugs to sell but was waiting for a new shipment.[253] In a Maryland case, the trial court found an officer qualified as an expert in the identification and valuation of controlled dangerous substances, and he was permitted to testify with respect to the common practices of narcotics users and dealers.[254] The discovery of "eight balls" in the defendant's possession indicated that an eighth ounce was a common weight to make individual sales and, in the house the police raided, there were no pipes or other appliances used for individual ingestion of drugs.

A paid informant may have sufficient knowledge to qualify as an expert if the informant is able to demonstrate that his or her knowledge, skill, training, or experience allows the witness to offer expert testimony.[255] In one case, the court found that there was no abuse of discretion in allowing a paid informant to testify as an expert witness about drug transactions when the evidence indicated that the informant had participated in more than 50 similar drug sales.[256]

L. *Other Subjects of Expert Testimony*

With the continued popularity of the Internet, the trading of child pornography has accelerated. In an effort to reduce the incidence of harm to children, state and federal prosecutors continue to bring to trial many child pornography cases in which the age of the young subjects is an element to be proved. In a California case, a required proof in a child porn case involved evidence that the image depicted a real minor. The trial court approved of the use of two experts who had special knowledge and were qualified to judge the age of persons depicted in the pornography. According to the trial court:

> Here the testimony of both [experts] was regarding developmental factors beyond the normal experience and knowledge of the average fact finder. The age of the actors was an element of the offense and the testimony of the experts was relevant to the conclusion.[257]

In addition to proof of age, in child pornography cases, the images must be demonstrated to actually be photographs or movies of real minors and not computer-created images. Photographic investigators with extensive child pornography experience can be qualified as expert witnesses to give testimony concerning whether the contested images actually involve real children. In a federal prosecution, the trial court did not abuse its discretion in admitting the testimony of a witness who had 18 years with

---

253 Commonwealth v. Moss, 2004 Pa. Super. 224, 852 A.2d 374, 2004 Pa. Super. LEXIS 1408 (2004).

254 Marshall v. State, 415 Md. 248, 252, 999 A.2d 1029, 1031, 2010 Md. LEXIS 335 (2010).

255 United States v. Garcia, 2006 U.S. App. LEXIS 10955 (11th Cir. 2006).

256 United States v. Anderson, 813 F.2d 1450 (9th Cir. 1987).

257 California v. Kurey, 88 Cal. App. 4th 840, 846, 847, 106 Cal. Rptr. 2d 150, 2001 Cal. App. LEXIS 319 (2001). *See also* United States v. Hamilton, 413 F.3d 1138, 1143-1144, 2005 U.S. App. LEXIS 12790 (10th Cir. 2005).

the FBI, including training, and had 13 years experience in authentication of photographic evidence.[258] In addition, the expert had completed proficiency training and testing in image authentication and had testified as an expert 35 times in the past. In his testimony to prove his qualifications, the witness indicated "exactly the steps he takes in determining the authenticity of images under the approved FBI 'checklist,' including ascertaining an image's resolution and focus, examining its sharpness and depth, comparing it to images in the FBI database, and identifying in the image certain human characteristics—like skin, teeth, ears, and hair—that are difficult to re-create by computer."

Expert testimony has not been limited to oral testimony or oral testimony concerning real objects or substances; computer-generated animations have been permitted when created by crime scene reconstruction experts. The animations must be properly authenticated as depicting what they purport to depict by presenting a fair and accurate representation of the evidence. To be considered for admission, the probative value of computer-generated animations must not outweigh any danger of unfair prejudice to the defendant. In a Pennsylvania case, the trial court permitted the prosecution's expert to offer a frame-by-frame image of how the expert believed that the killer committed the murder of his wife. In approving the admission of the evidence, the appellate court noted that the use of computer-generated animations had to be weighed carefully because of the danger of prejudice. The animation was admissible because it assisted the expert in offering his opinion and served as a graphic representation that illustrated the previously formed opinion of the expert witness.[259]

Expert testimony has no closed categories or fields where specialized knowledge might be admissible. In a case in which the defendant had been charged with robbery of a federally insured financial institution, he proposed to call an expert forensic anthropologist to refute expected eyewitness identification testimony from the prosecution. Over the government's objection, the trial judge concluded that the proposed expert was qualified by training and education and would be permitted to offer testimony concerning ear morphology. The court permitted the anthropologist to testify that the defendant could not have been the bank robber because his earlobes were not attached to his neck while the pictures taken of the robber indicated otherwise.[260]

In another context involving expert testimony, experts may be permitted to testify that footprints at the crime scene match or have a close resemblance to the shoes worn by the accused in a criminal case. In a demonstration of this concept, a trial court permitted a forensic technician to testify that shoe prints left in fireproofing dust from a safe cracked during a burglary matched the shoes worn by the defendant. The court observed that qualified expert testimony could be admitted because shoe print identification does not rest on arcane scientific principles, but on visual comparison of physical samples. An expert could recognize small anomalies in shoe design, wear,

---

258 United States v. Bynum 604 F.3d 161, 167, 2010 U.S. App. LEXIS 9220 (4th Cir. 2010).

259 Commonwealth v. Serge, 2006 Pa. LEXIS 561 (2006).

260 United States v. McClintock, 2006 U.S. Dist. LEXIS 201 (E.D. Pa. 2006).

or physical traits characteristic of a particular shoe that might escape a nonexpert. The judge ruled that such information could assist the jury and should be admitted.[261] In an Ohio case, an appellate court approved the admission of the testimony of a criminalist as an expert in the analysis of shoe prints. In demonstrating his qualifications as an expert, the witness indicated that he had a master's degree in forensic science and had received training in footwear analysis as an extern with the Michigan State Police. He had participated in two separate training classes in shoe print analysis, both as to characteristics of classes of shoes and to individual characteristics. In addition he had worked for the Toledo [Ohio] Police Department for six years, spending 15 to 20 percent of his time on footwear analysis. There was no error to allow the expert to testify that the defendant's shoe print matched photographs taken at the murder scene and to offer the opinion that the defendant shoe most likely made the print at the murder scene.[262]

Some of the many other subjects of expert testimony include modus operandi of California street gangs,[263] significance of membership in a gang,[264] significance of manual strangulation,[265] how methamphetamine is made and sold,[266] cause of a fire,[267] cause of an explosion,[268] cause of death,[269] DNA profile identification,[270] blood alcohol content,[271] and tire imprint testimony.[272]

§ 11.11 Experts from Crime Laboratories

Because of the limitations placed on the use of confessions, more reliance is being placed upon the use of real evidence and other evidence obtained by laboratory technicians. With the addition of crime laboratories in all parts of the country, experts from these laboratories have become more readily available. These experts must qualify as do other experts, through experience, training, or knowledge, before they can give opinions concerning the significance of laboratory tests and other scientific evidence, and the evidence must be useful to the finder of fact. Expert testimony of this type is especially important in the field of ballistics—comparing cartridge cases and bullets found

261 *See* Ratiff v. State, 110 P.3d 982, 2005 Alas. App. LEXIS 39 (2005).
262 State v. Jones, 2010 Ohio 4054, 2010 Ohio App. LEXIS 3425 (2010).
263 *See* People v. Sanchez, 2014 Cal. App. LEXIS 44 (2014).
264 *See* People v. McClelland, 2014 Cal. App. Unpub. LEXIS 529 (2014).
265 People v. Jackson, 221 Cal. App. 4th 1222, 1240, 165 Cal. Rptr. 3d 70, 83, 2013 Cal. App. LEXIS 973 (2013).
266 *See* People v. Cerna, 2014 Cal. App. Unpub. LEXIS 81 (2014).
267 Commonwealth v. Lugo, 63 Mass. App. Ct. 204, 824 N.E.2d 481, 2005 Mass. App. LEXIS 296 (2005).
268 Bitler v. A.O. Smith, 400 F.3d 1227, 2004 U.S. LEXIS 28000 (10th Cir. 2004).
269 People v. Edwards, 57 Cal. 4th 658, 673, 161 Cal. Rptr. 3d 191, 213, 2013 Cal. LEXIS 6897 (2013).
270 Brown v. State, 270 Ga. App. 176, 605 S.E.2d 885, 2004 Ga. App. LEXIS 1381 (2004).
271 State v. Taylor, 165 N.C. App. 750; 600 S.E.2d 483, 2004 N.C. App. LEXIS 1519 (2004).
272 Rodgers v. State, 2006 Tex. Crim. App. LEXIS (2006).

at the scene with those fired from a known weapon or DNA analysis—connecting a defendant to a victim or a location.

Ordinarily, one expert can rely upon reports and analyses of other experts where that is commonly done in that field. However, a recent United States Supreme Court case, *Melendez-Diaz v. Massachusetts* in 2009, has cast some doubt on the ability to introduce reports from technicians or other experts who have done their work outside of the courtroom.[273] In this case, the Commonwealth offered notarized laboratory certificates attesting to the fact that the defendant had possessed cocaine of a certain level of purity. The witness offering the certificates had not conducted the chemical analysis or tests of the confiscated sample but simply offered the notarized certificate that attested to the presence of cocaine. The Supreme Court of the United States reversed the conviction on the ground that the defendant had the Sixth Amendment right to confront and cross-examine the individual who has conducted the tests. What this means for the future is that the experts in crime laboratories are more likely to be called as witnesses in criminal trials so that they may be cross-examined concerning technique, accuracy, bias, and any other matter that might cast doubt upon the test or the credibility of the witness. Once this testing evidence has been accepted in court, expert witness testimony may additionally be necessary to explain the significance of the laboratory tests.

No attempt will be made here to list all the other areas in which a crime laboratory expert can testify, but these include tool mark comparisons and testimony concerning glass and glass fractures, enhancing latent fingerprint evidence with cyanoacrylate fuming, clothing, hairs, and fibers.

§ 11.12 Summary

Because most witnesses testify as lay witnesses, generally witnesses should confine their testimony to "who," "what," "where," and "when" types of answers and not "how" or "why" answers. Because humans typically form opinions in matters of everyday life, there is no absolute bar to admitting lay opinion evidence. The general rule excluding opinion evidence gives way in a variety of settings for lay witnesses and almost disappears when expert witnesses are concerned. The rule excluding lay opinion evidence is based on the principle that the witnesses are to furnish the facts and the jury has the responsibility of reaching conclusions based on these facts.

There are, however, necessary exceptions to the general rule limiting lay opinion testimony. These common-sense exceptions have been developed so that the jury will have better information and because the courts have recognized that it is often impossible to give facts to describe all situations. For example, it is difficult to give facts that explain a person's emotional state or to explain that a person was "nervous," "upset," or "acted suspiciously."

---

273 129 S. Ct. 2527, 174 L. Ed. 2d 314, 2009 U.S. LEXIS 4734 (2009).

The rules relating to the exceptions to the opinion rule are discussed in two categories: those relating to nonexpert opinions and those relating to expert opinions. If the ordinary lay witness cannot adequately or accurately describe the facts so as to enable the jurors to draw an intelligent conclusion, the witness may be permitted to offer a lay opinion. For example, a lay witness, in the usual case and with certain limitations, may give opinion testimony as to age, smell, appearance, conduct, distance, mental condition, handwriting, identification, and speed of a vehicle.

An expert witness, when properly qualified, may offer opinions where the opinions will assist the trier of fact in situations where lay opinion would not be permitted. However, this exception possesses a different logical basis; therefore, the rules are different. This opinion testimony is allowed because the expert, due to training, experience, or knowledge, can give information on a specific subject that is substantially superior to the knowledge possessed by the average person. The opinion of the expert witness does not have to be, and usually is not, based on direct observation of prior incidents that brought about the trial. An expert's opinion may be based on scientific testing performed by the expert him- or herself, testing conducted by other experts, questions based on hypothetical assumed facts, or on facts presented by other witnesses in the trial.

Some examples of subjects of expert testimony are (1) speed of automobile, (2) identification of vehicle from tire marks, (3) cause of death, (4) handwriting comparisons, (5) typewriter comparisons, (6) DNA identification, (7) fingerprint comparison identification, and (8) firearms and ballistics identification.

Although sworn justice personnel will not normally present the case in court, because many officers will offer crucial portions of testimony, it is important to understand the lay opinion rule and the exceptions to it. While ordinary law enforcement personnel may actually qualify as expert witnesses due to specialized training and experience, most police officers will be testifying as lay witnesses in criminal trials where lay opinion evidence has limitations.

CHAPTER ELEVEN: QUESTIONS AND REVIEW EXERCISES

1. How do the qualifications for a lay witness differ from the qualifications expected of an expert witness?
2. As a general rule, lay witnesses are not expected to offer opinions and must stick to observed facts when offering testimony. Under what circumstances may lay witnesses offer opinions?
3. As lay witnesses, most adults would be permitted to offer testimony concerning the age of a person, an individual's appearance, and the conduct exhibited by a particular person. Because these categories seem to involve opinions, why should adults be permitted to offer opinions concerning age, color, demeanor of an individual, that an individual tried to kill a police officer, or that the individual appeared to flee the scene of the crime?

4. Lay witnesses may be permitted to offer opinions concerning distance, space, time, intoxication, and drug use. A lay witness must have a basis for offering such an opinion. What foundation would be required for a lay witness to estimate distance or alcohol intoxication or whether a person was under the influence of drugs?
5. Courts routinely permit lay witnesses to offer opinions concerning the identity of a defendant, the identity of another person, or whether a smell involved marijuana or tobacco. What foundation would be required for a lay witness to offer opinions concerning these categories?
6. Explain what distinguishes an expert witness from a lay witness. An expert witness offers opinions that are not always based on the expert's firsthand observation. What is the rationale or basis for permitting expert witnesses to offer in court testimony that is based on scientific testing or experiments done long after the historical facts in the case occurred?
7. Could a police officer who had extensive experience in undercover drug investigations testify as an expert concerning whether the facts observed by the officer indicated that a particular defendant possessed drugs with the intention of distribution? Support your answer with an explanation.
8. After having testified on direct examination by offering opinions, on cross-examination must the expert be required to disclose the underlying facts or data upon which the expert's opinion was based?
9. What are some topics or fields of knowledge for which the testimony of an expert would prove particularly valuable and to which lay testimony would probably not be permitted?
10. Under recent interpretations of the right of confrontation under the Sixth Amendment, the Supreme Court limited the ability of an expert to rely on reports generated by technicians and other experts. How does this interpretation affect expert testimony in criminal cases that depends on reports by other individuals outside of the courtroom? Will experts from crime labs be required to appear in court to testify to the results of their work?

Hearsay Rule and Exceptions

12

The determination that a statement is hearsay does not end the inquiry into admissibility; there must still be a further examination of the need for the statement at trial and the circumstantial guaranty of trustworthiness surrounding the making of the statement.

Zippo Mfg. Co. v. Rogers Imports, Inc.,
216 F. Supp. 670 (S.D.N.Y. 1963)

Chapter Contents

Section

KEY TERMS AND CONCEPTS	
Business Records Exception	Hearsay Evidence
Confession Exception	Hearsay Rule
Declaration Against Interest	Nontestimonial Utterance
Dying Declaration	Pecuniary Interest
Excited Utterance Exception	Penal Interest
Family History Exception	Reported Testimony
Former Testimony	Spontaneous Utterance

§ 12.1 Introduction

Many people have heard of hearsay evidence, whether from books, films, television shows, Internet news sources, or newspapers, and the public recognizes that such evidence should be excluded from use in court. However, it is difficult for most people to understand how the rule operates because of the many exceptions that allow hearsay evidence to be introduced. As the hearsay rule has so many exceptions, the rationale behind the rule may challenge logical thinking. Even those who have some understanding of the rule are probably unaware that the exceptions to the hearsay rule may allow more evidence to be admitted than the rule excludes. When a rule or a court recognizes an exception, and the theory admits hearsay evidence, there are usually powerful reasons and justifications for trusting the truthfulness and reliability of the evidence. If the hearsay rule was to be applied without exceptions in criminal cases, it would be very difficult for prosecutors to present sufficient facts to prove guilt or for a defendant to mount a defense, and certainly much reliable evidence would be excluded from consideration.

As a practical matter, determining what kind of testimony is hearsay provides the starting point for developing an understanding of this rule of exclusion. When a witness on the stand repeats another person's out-of-court statement, the evidence that the witness utters in court may be excluded on the ground that it constitutes hearsay evidence. To be properly considered hearsay evidence, the substance of the out-of-court statement must have been offered in court to prove its truth. If police found a robbery demand note in a suspected bank robber's automobile, the note could be admitted and would not be considered hearsay evidence because it would not be admitted as proof of the truth of the note's contents but rather as proof that a note had been written and proof of the defendant's intention. Courts tend to exclude hearsay evidence because subtle alterations in wording, demeanor, inflection, or other body language may change the meaning of spoken words. Every time a story is retold by and to new people, the essence of the story changes slightly, with a detail added or unconsciously deleted, causing the meaning to shift. The general rule excluding hearsay statements is justified on these and other grounds. It is important to be aware of the historical justifications for the rule in order to understand the exceptions. If the reasons for the rule do not exist in a particular situation, then the evidence should be admitted to assist in determining the facts of the case. The following paragraphs discuss some of the reasons for the exclusion of evidence under the hearsay rule.

1. "Traditionally, testimony that is given by a witness who relates not what he or she knows personally, but what others have said, and that is therefore dependent on the credibility of someone other than the witness."[1]
2. "Hearsay evidence is objectionable because the person who makes the offered statement is not under oath and is not subject to cross-examination."[2] Although the witness in court was under oath when repeating what someone else said, the person who actually made the original statement was not under oath so that hearsay statements generally lack trustworthiness.
3. When the witness comes to court to tell what was stated outside the court, the judge or jury cannot observe the demeanor or conduct of the person who originally made the statement. Evaluating demeanor proves important when judging credibility of witnesses and is an important aspect of the right of confrontation.[3]
4. There is a danger that the in-court witness who is reporting what was said by an out-of-court declarant may repeat the statement inaccurately. The proponent of the evidence "essentially asks the jury to assume that the out-of-court declarant was not lying or mistaken when the statement was made."[4]
5. One of the primary justifications for the exclusion of hearsay is that the adversary has no opportunity to cross-examine the absent declarant to test the accuracy and completeness of the testimony. In addition, the declarant is not under oath at the time of the statement.[5]

In explaining some of the reasons for excluding hearsay evidence from court, a Louisiana appellate court stated that "[h]earsay evidence is excluded because the value of the statement rests on the credibility of the out-of-court asserter who is not subject to cross-examination and other safeguards of reliability."[6] Similarly, the Supreme Court of Connecticut offered related reasons for the hearsay rule when it stated:

---

1 BLACK'S LAW DICTIONARY 790 (9th ed. 2009).

2 Missouri v. Mozee, 2003 Mo. App. LEXIS 940 (2003) (quoting State v. Bowens, 964 S.W. 2d 232, 240, 1998 Mo. App. LEXIS 383 (1998)).

3 *See* In re Kentron D., 101 Cal. App. 4th 1381, 125 Cal. Rptr. 2d 260, 2002 Cal. App. LEXIS 4629 (2002).

4 Armstead v. State, 255 Ga. App. 385, 389, 565 S.E.2d 579, 582, 2002 Ga. App. LEXIS 633 (2002).

5 *See* Louisiana v. Harry, 11 So.3d 1244, 2009 La. App. Unpub. LEXIS 382 (2009).

6 State v. Moore, 2010 La. App. LEXIS 1373 (2010).

> The declarant might be lying; he might have misperceived the events which he relates; he might have faulty memory; his words might be misunderstood or taken out of context by the listener. And the ways in which these dangers are minimized for in-court statements—the oath, the witness' awareness of the gravity of the proceedings, the jury's ability to observe the witness' demeanor, and, most importantly, the right of the opponent to cross-examine—are generally absent for things said out of court.[7]

Some forms of hearsay evidence prove more reliable than others, and, for that reason, some hearsay will be admitted based on recognized and standardized hearsay exceptions, such as the out-of-court declarant being unavailable.[8] The courts seek to allow as much evidence into court as possible while sifting out unreliable evidence, and, to this end, the courts have developed many exceptions to the hearsay rule. For each exception, however, there is a clear justification designed to assure the trustworthiness of the evidence. In situations in which none of the well-known exceptions permits admission of the hearsay evidence, the federal rules allow a party to argue that the interests of justice would be promoted by admission of the hearsay evidence where the "statement has equivalent circumstantial guarantees of trustworthiness,"[9] so long as the evidence is not otherwise excluded by some hearsay rule of evidence and would be probative on the point for which it is offered.[10]

However, in a different hearsay context, using the **dying declaration** exception,[11] the Court permitted police officers to offer hearsay evidence against the defendant in a murder case by revealing the circumstances under which the victim explained to police officers how he received his fatal injuries at the hands of the defendant.[12] Although the defendant had no chance to cross-examine the victim because the victim died, the Court approved the use of the dying declaration hearsay exception. According to the Court, the informality of the exchange between the dying victim and the police suggested that the officers' purpose was to address what appeared to be an ongoing emergency and determine the necessary response. The circumstances of the dying declaration lacked any formality that would have alerted the victim to any future use of his statements and contained the usual guarantees of reliability that exist in a

Dying declaration Hearsay evidence of what a person said when aware of his or her imminent death. The statement in question must relate to the way the declarant received his or her fatal injuries.

---

7 Connecticut v. Cruz, 260 Conn. 1, 792 A.2d 823, 2002 Conn. LEXIS 127 (2002).

8 *See* Illinois Jurisprudence, CRIMINAL LAW AND PROCEDURE § 18:29 (2011). Unavailability of the declarant is generally required for dying declarations, declarations against pecuniary or penal interest, statements of family history or pedigree, and declarations made in prior or former testimony.

9 *See* FED. R. EVID. 807.

10 *Id.*

11 *See* § 12.9, Dying Declarations, Criminal Evidence 12ed.

12 *See* Michigan v. Bryant, 661 U.S. 196, 131 S. Ct. 1143, 2011 U.S. LEXIS 1713 (2011).

dying declaration. Exactly where the Supreme Court of the United States is headed with its analysis of hearsay exceptions and constitutional limitations is not known and will have to wait for future cases to explain the ultimate direction and destination of this jurisprudence.

While this chapter emphasizes many hearsay exceptions, other chapters of this book also discuss evidence that may be challenged as excludable hearsay. For example, an out-of-court confession that is repeated by another person in court is, technically, hearsay in many jurisdictions. However, this evidence is often admissible under one of the exceptions discussed in Chapter 16. The hearsay exception of "past recollection recorded" and its rationale are discussed in Chapter 9. Official records, ancient documents, and learned treatises are generally admissible as hearsay exceptions and are considered in Chapter 13.

This chapter presents the hearsay rule of exclusion and introduces the important exceptions and exclusions that permit such evidence to be admitted in criminal courts. Among the exceptions treated within this chapter are declarations against interest, the business records exception, dying declarations, spontaneous and excited utterances, and family history.

§ 12.2 Definitions and Statement of the Hearsay Rule

Rule 801

DEFINITIONS THAT APPLY TO THIS ARTICLE; EXCLUSIONS FROM HEARSAY

(a) "Statement" means a person's oral assertion, written assertion, or nonverbal conduct, if the person intended it as an assertion.
(b) Declarant. "Declarant" means the person who made the statement.
(c) Hearsay. "Hearsay" means a statement that:
  (1) the declarant does not make while testifying at the current trial or hearing; and
  (2) a party offers in evidence to prove the truth of the matter asserted in the statement
(d) A statement that meets the following conditions is not hearsay:
  (1) A Declarant-Witness's Prior Statement. The declarant testifies and is subject to cross-examination about a prior statement, and the statement:
    (a) is inconsistent with the declarant's testimony and was given under penalty of perjury at a trial, hearing, or other proceeding or in a deposition;
    (b) is consistent with the declarant's testimony and is offered to rebut an express or implied charge that the declarant recently fabricated it or acted from a recent improper influence or motive in so testifying; or
    (c) identifies a person as someone the declarant perceived earlier.

(2) An Opposing Party's Statement. The statement is offered against an opposing party and:
(a) was made by the party in an individual or representative capacity;
(b) is one the party manifested that it adopted or believed to be true;
(c) was made by a person whom the party authorized to make a statement on the subject;
(d) was made by the party's agent or employee on a matter within the scope of that relationship and while it existed; or
(e) was made by the party's coconspirator during and in furtherance of the conspiracy.

The statement must be considered but does not by itself establish the declarant's authority under (c); the existence or scope of the relationship under (d); or the existence of the conspiracy or participation in it under (e).[13]

During the course of both civil and criminal litigation, many courts have resolved and refined hearsay problems by explaining the concepts, defining hearsay, and evaluating the admissibility of hearsay evidence. Although these explanations are worded differently, the general meaning of hearsay emerges. Some of these definitions are included here as examples:

- Hearsay is defined as an out-of-court statement offered to prove the truth of the matter asserted.[14]
- "Hearsay" is a statement, other than one made by the declarant while testifying at the trial or hearing, offered in evidence to prove the truth of the matter asserted.[15]
- "Hearsay" means a statement that (1) is not made by the declarant while testifying at the trial or hearing; and (2) is offered in evidence to prove the truth of the matter asserted.[16]
- Hearsay is defined as a statement that the declarant does not make while testifying at the current trial or hearing, and which the proponent offers in evidence to prove the truth of the matter asserted in the statement.[17]

As litigants have raised legal questions and identified problems, the federal courts have have responded by interpreting and explaining the Federal Rules of Evidence. For example, one court decided that evidence was "not hearsay," as defined in Rule 801(d)(1)(A), when a witness testifying at the trial claimed no recollection of the underlying events described in his prior grand jury testimony or of providing the grand jury

---

13 FED. R. EVID. 801.
14 State v. Vazquez, 311 P.3d 1115, 1119 2013 Ariz. App. LEXIS (Ariz. 2013).
15 White v. State, 2013 Ala. Crim. App. LEXIS 71 (2013).
16 IND. R. EVID. 801(c) (2013).
17 United States v. Monserrate-Valentin, 729 F.3d 31, 52 (2013).

testimony itself.[18] The trial court did not abuse its discretion in admitting the declarant-witness's prior grand jury testimony under Rule 801(d)(1)(A), which pertains to prior inconsistent statements. When prior inconsistent statements come within the rule, they are not considered hearsay and may be admitted as substantive evidence.

Under Federal Rule 801(d)(1)(A), if an out-of-court statement is inconsistent with the declarant's trial testimony and was given under the penalty of perjury at a deposition, trial, hearing, or similar proceeding, while subject to cross-examination, the prior statement may be received as evidence and is not considered hearsay. For purposes of this rule, the word "inconsistent" is not limited to statements that are diametrically opposed, but the term can also indicate a witness's manifest reluctance to testify, changes in position, or the forgetting of particular facts at trial.[19]

According to one court, the rationale for the admission of prior consistent statements, as provided in Rule 801(d)(1)(B), is that the statements are considered relevant and necessary.[20] Where a defendant alleged that a witness had a reason to testify untruthfully and that the lie involved recent fabrication, a witness's earlier statement made long prior to trial should be admissible to refute a charge of recent fabrication.[21]

Section 801(d)(1)(B) of the Federal Rules of Evidence provides that a statement is not hearsay if consistent with the declarant's testimony and offered to rebut an express or implied charge against the declarant of recent fabrication or improper influence or motive. In *Tome v. United States*, the Supreme Court debated the interpretation of this provision.[22] In *Tome*, the government initiated charges against the defendant involving the sexual abuse of his four-year-old daughter. The defense argued that the allegations were concocted so that the mother would obtain custody and the child would not be returned to her father. After the initiation of the case and the alleged motive to fabricate arose, the child made out-of-court statements to witnesses. At the trial, the judge permitted the admission of some of these witness statements, despite the fact that they were made and introduced after charges of recent fabrication had been asserted. The United States Supreme Court reversed the conviction, deciding that Rule 801(d)(1)(B) did permit the introduction of a declarant's consistent out-of-court statements, if those statements were intended to rebut a charge of recent fabrication, improper influence, or motive, but, in order to be admitted, those statements must have been made *before* the fabrication, influence, or motive arose.

Determining that the statements made by the child to other witnesses were made after the defendant's charge of fabrication, the Supreme Court remanded the case for further proceedings. The majority explained that to allow the out-of-court statements

---

18 United States v. DiCaro, 772 F.2d 1314 (7th Cir. 1985).

19 United States v. Gerard, 507 F. App'x 218, 222, 2012 U.S. App. LEXIS 25875 (3rd Cir. 2012). *See also* State v. Pusyka, 592 A.2d 850 (R.I. 1991), in which the court held that a witness's prior statement must be sufficiently inconsistent with the witness's in-court testimony to be admissible. This determination is within the sound discretion of the trial judge.

20 State v. Gardner, 490 N.W.2d 838 (Iowa 1992).

21 United States v. Belfast, 611 F.3d 783, 816, 2010 U.S. App. LEXIS (11th Cir. 2010).

22 Tome v. United States, 513 U.S. 150, 115 S. Ct. 696, 130 L. Ed. 2d 574 (1995).

made after the in-court charge of fabrication would shift the emphasis of the trial to the out-of-court statements rather than the in-court statements.

Consistent with the logic of the Supreme Court, a defendant in a Medicare/Medicaid fraud case contended that the court improperly excluded government wiretap evidence in which the defendant appeared to advise other doctors in his podiatry practice to bill only for services actually rendered.[23] The government's position was that the defendant billed for services never performed, and the defendant podiatrist contested the prosecution's allegations. The podiatrist wanted the wiretap information admitted as a prior consistent statement under Rule 801(d)(1)(B). Apparently, the doctor became aware of the investigation and then made the intercepted phone call after he had developed a motive for fabrication. According to one court of appeal, a party wishing to introduce a prior consistent statement must establish four elements consistent with Federal Rule 801(d)(B): "(1) the declarant must testify at trial and be subject to cross-examination; (2) there must be an express or implied charge of recent fabrication or improper influence or motive of the declarant's testimony; (3) the proponent must offer a prior consistent statement that is consistent with the declarant's challenged in court testimony; and, (4) the prior consistent statement must be made prior to the time that the supposed motive to falsify arose."[24] In this case, the conversation with the other podiatrists occurred after the defendant became aware of the federal investigation, indicating that the prior consistent statement made on the wiretap occurred after the defendant podiatrist developed a motive to testify falsely.

Rule 801(d)(1)(C) allows the admission of prior identifications of a person made by a witness who was present at the earlier time (when the witness's memory was fresh), so long as there was virtually no opportunity for other individuals to influence the prior identification. At or near the time of trial, other persons may have attempted to convince or compel the witness to testify that the earlier identification was erroneous or did not occur.[25]

Rule 801(d)(2)(E) of the Federal Rules, which has been made part of the rules of evidence in many states, provides that a statement is not hearsay if made by a conspirator during the course of a conspiracy in order to further the conspiracy's goals. Under this rule, such statements made by a conspirator are not considered hearsay if the conspirator has the authority to speak for and bind other conspirators. An out-of-court statement made by a conspirator and offered in court for its truth does fit the traditional definition of hearsay, but this rule of evidence simply decrees that it is not to be considered hearsay. In explaining the rule's purpose, one reviewing court noted that, under the conspirator exception to hearsay defined by Rule 801(d)(2)(E), statements by one conspirator are admissible against other members of the conspiracy, so long as the

---

23 United States v. Holden, 2013 U.S. Dist. LEXIS 70128 (E.D. Wash. 2013).

24 Id., citing United States v. Bao, 189 F.3d860, 864 (9th Cir. 1999).

25 Cardoso v. Roden, 2010 U.S. Dist. LEXIS 141767 (2010). Court determined to permit witness's grand jury testimony concerning defendant's identity as substantive nonhearsay evidence when witness later denied being truthful at the grand jury, but insisted that her trial evidence of nonidentification was correct.

government proves by a preponderance of evidence that the defendant and the person making the statement were both members of the same conspiracy, and that the statement made by the conspirator was made in furtherance of the goals of conspiracy.[26]

Rule 802

THE RULE AGAINST HEARSAY

Hearsay is not admissible unless any of the following provides otherwise:
- a federal statute;
- these rules; or
- other rules prescribed by the Supreme Court.[27]

As defined in Rule 801 of the Federal Rules of Evidence, hearsay is a statement that "(1) the declarant does not make while testifying at the current trial or hearing; and (2) a party offers in evidence to prove the truth of the matters asserted in the statement."[28] California defines hearsay evidence as "evidence of a statement that was made other than by a witness while testifying at the hearing and that is offered to prove the truth of the matter stated."[29] For example, if a police officer testified about the meaning of numbers on a fast food receipt based on knowledge gained by speaking with an employee of that establishment, the officer's testimony would constitute hearsay evidence because it depends on the veracity and credibility of the fast food employee who was not in court or under oath.

Hearsay evidence Statements offered by a witness, based upon what someone else has told him or her, and not upon personal knowledge or observation.

While **hearsay evidence** may be excluded, out-of-court statements that are not offered for their substantive truth may be admissible because they do not meet the definition of hearsay. In a prosecution for importing fake Nike shoes, the court permitted the prosecution to admit evidence of e-mails between the defendant's then girlfriend and a customer who claimed the shoes were "knock offs" of real Nike shoes.[30] The evidence was not admitted to show the truth of the customer's allegations. Instead, it was admitted to show that, when the defendant's then girlfriend informed him of the customer's e-mail complaints, he did not protest, but ordered the girlfriend to refund the customer's money. The e-mails were admitted to provide context by allowing the prosecutor to show that the defendant had been informed that he might be peddling counterfeit Nike shoes. When used for

---

26 United States v. Robinson, 2010 U.S. App. 25543 (7th Cir. 2010).

27 FED. R. EVID. 802.

28 *Id.*

29 CAL. EVID. CODE § 1200 (2013).

30 United States v. Neuman, 2010 U.S. App. 26384 (10th Cir. 2010).

this purpose, the e-mails were properly admitted because the e-mails were not offered for their truth and thus did not qualify as hearsay.

The term "statement," as used in the hearsay definition, consists of: (1) an oral or written assertion or (2) nonverbal conduct of a person, if it is intended by him or her as an assertion or is a substitute for speech. Therefore, a statement may be an actual verbal statement, a written statement, or nonverbal conduct, such as pointing, to identify a suspect in a lineup. In the context of a lineup, the act of pointing to indicate a choice operates as a substitute for speech. Thus, if a police officer later attempted to testify in court about the out-of-court witness's indication, the defense would object because the officer would be attempting to bring the out-of-court, nonverbal assertion into court as a hearsay statement. A "declarant," as used in the hearsay definition, is a person who makes a statement.

Admitting hearsay evidence generally involves having the out-of-court declarant's statement or evidence introduced in court with the result that the defendant cannot actually cross-examine that actual declarant. Cross-examination of the witness in court is certainly possible, but the person actually offering the evidence is not in court, creating constitutional issues that intermix with hearsay jurisprudence. In interpreting the Sixth Amendment right of confrontation and cross-examination, the Supreme Court overruled the assertion that evidence of a testimonial nature should not be admitted unless there is an opportunity to engage in personal confrontation with the adverse witness.

In *Crawford v. Washington,*[31] the defendant had been convicted of assaulting a man who attempted to rape the defendant's wife. The prosecution used evidence drawn from the wife's statement to police shortly after the events occurred. The statement by the wife, recorded by the police and introduced by the prosecution, did not assist the defendant's case. The defendant's wife invoked her marital testimonial privilege and did not testify against the defendant, with the result being that the trial judge allowed the wife's statement to the police to be used against the defendant. The trial judge followed the then current theory and allowed the testimony because the judge understood that the defendant's wife's testimony was unavailable, and the judge considered the wife's out-of-court statement to be "reliable." The statement called into question the defendant's contention of self-defense. The Supreme Court reversed the decision of a top Washington court that had reinstated the trial court conviction, and the Supreme Court of the United States held that Crawford's Sixth Amendment right to confront and cross-examine adverse witnesses had been violated. The Court found a Sixth Amendment violation because, where testimonial evidence was at issue, the playing of the wife's testimony by audiotape prevented the defendant from confronting or conducting any cross-examination of the wife. The Court held that the Sixth Amendment demanded both unavailability and, at minimum, a prior opportunity to cross-examine the witness. In this case, the defendant had no opportunity to ever cross-examine his wife. The rule to be distilled from the *Crawford* case is that, when testimonial evidence is involved, the parties must have had an opportunity to cross-examine the witness during trial or a proper earlier proceeding, and there must be proof of unavailability of the

---

31 Crawford v. Washington, 541 U.S. 36, 2004 U.S. LEXIS 1838 (2004).

witness.[32] The case did not put an end to hearsay exceptions, but it did reinstate the right to confront and cross-examine witnesses where prior testimony is involved.

In applying the *Crawford* rationale to a later Washington case, *Davis v. Washington,*[33] the alleged victim in a domestic violence case made a 911 call to report an assault by her former boyfriend. He was under a no-contact domestic order and had just fled the victim's dwelling, and she had some fear for her safety. When the case came to trial, the former girlfriend-victim did not testify against her attacker, but the trial court admitted an audiotape of the 911 call against the defendant, over his Sixth Amendment objection. The defendant appealed his resulting conviction through Washington courts with unsuccessful results. The Supreme Court of the United States affirmed the lower courts' rulings, after determining that the 911 call was not testimonial in nature, and the use of the audiotape did not create a confrontation and cross-examination issue under the Sixth Amendment. The victim was speaking with an emergency operator while the events were in progress, describing current circumstances that necessitated a police response. As the Court noted in making a distinction between testimonial statements and nontestimonial statements, "Statements are nontestimonial when made in the course of police interrogation under circumstances objectively indicating that the primary purpose of the interrogation is to enable police assistance to meet an ongoing emergency. They are testimonial when the circumstances objectively indicate that there is no such ongoing emergency, and that the primary purpose of the interrogation is to establish or prove past events potentially relevant to later criminal prosecution."[34] The victim's statements were not testimonial, because the statements were necessary to enable the police to resolve the ongoing emergency, rather than to reconstruct what had happened in the past. Because the Court characterized the 911 call as nontestimonial, the Sixth Amendment was not implicated.

Consistent with the *Crawford* case rationale, when the Supreme Court finds that the hearsay evidence possesses aspects of testimonial evidence, it generally excludes the evidence on Sixth Amendment grounds. In *Melendez-Diaz v. Massachusetts* in 2009,[35] the Court reversed a conviction for distribution and trafficking of cocaine, because the trial court permitted the admission of a notarized certificate from a drug laboratory that indicated that cocaine was the drug seized from the defendant. The witness who brought the drug-attesting hearsay certificate to court had not personally performed the drug tests on the suspected cocaine, resulting in the defendant's inability to cross-examine the real witness concerning details of his or her laboratory work. According to the Court, the certificates were really affidavits containing hearsay, which were within the class of testimonial statements covered by the Sixth Amendment's confrontation clause. In addition, the certificates had been created under circumstances

---

32 *Id.*

33 Davis v. Washington, 547 U.S. 813, 2006 U.S. LEXIS 4886 (2006).

34 *Id.* at 822.

35 Melendez-Diaz v. Massachusetts, 557 U.S. 661, 174 L. Ed. 2d 314, 2009 U.S. LEXIS 4734 (2009). *See* case in Part II, Chapter 16.

that would have led an objective witness reasonably to believe that they had been developed for admission and use in a criminal case, so the conviction had to be reversed.

In a subsequent case dealing with the hearsay and confrontation issues, the Court in *Michigan v. Bryant*[36] held that a mortally wounded victim could offer statements to police concerning who shot him and how his injuries occurred. The Court approved allowing police officers to testify about what the victim told them because the victim's identification and description of the defendant and the location where the shooting occurred were not considered testimonial statements. The Court felt that the police were reacting to an ongoing emergency in informally speaking with the victim, and given that police did not know the extent of the threat or who was a target, they were merely collecting information and not putting together a prosecutable case at the moment they spoke with the dying man. The victim's statement was not considered "testimonial" in nature, partly due to its informality, and as a result, it was not considered to violate either the Sixth Amendment or the rule against hearsay testimony.

Although the rule that hearsay evidence is inadmissible is generally true, significant hearsay evidence is admitted based on exceptions to the general rule of exclusion and despite Sixth Amendment confrontation and cross-examination issues. The exceptions to the hearsay rule are so numerous that the argument could be made that most hearsay evidence may be admissible, while some hearsay evidence may be excluded. In the sections that follow, this chapter considers some of the well-recognized exceptions, as well as the reasoning for those exceptions.

§ 12.3 History and Development of the Hearsay Rule

In an article that appeared in the *Minnesota Law Review*, the authors included a thumbnail sketch of the history of the use of the hearsay rule.[37] This article included the following history:

> The hearsay rule was not the creation of some clever legal philosopher or rules-drafting committee. Rather, it was a byproduct of jury-based common law adjudication. It was molded and remolded over the course of more than four centuries by lawyers pursuing the business of representing clients and by judges seeking to ensure proper verdicts. As a consequence of its incremental development, the rule, like so much in Anglo-American jurisprudence, does not have a single goal or express a single viewpoint. It reflects a variety of objectives sought at different times by participants in the courtroom contests.
>
> Medieval English jury adjudication was, in essence, based upon hearsay. Juries in the thirteenth and fourteenth centuries decided cases on the basis of rumor, gossip, and community opinion to which they were exposed before the trial commenced. While reservations about hearsay were articulated as early as 1202, it was not until the latter half of the 1500s that serious concerns were voiced about its use in litigation.

---

36 Michigan v. Bryant, 131 S. Ct. 1143, 2011 U.S. 1713 (2011).

37 Richard F. Rakos and Stephen Landsman, *The Hearsay Rule as the Focus of Empirical Investigation*, 76 MINN. L. REV 655 (1992).

Hearsay rule Rule prohibiting the admission of hearsay evidence—evidence of a statement that was made out-of-court by a person other than the witness testifying as to the contents of the statement. The testimony is offered to prove the truth of the matter stated.

The **hearsay rule** as we know it had its origin in England in the sixteenth century. Prior to that time, juries were permitted to obtain evidence by consulting persons who were not called as witnesses. Jurors did not decide the case on the basis of testimony given in open court, but were, in fact, chosen because they had some knowledge of the case.

In 1813, Chief Justice Marshall explained the justification for the hearsay rule, stating, "Our lives, our liberty, and our property, are all concerned in the support of these rules, which have been matured by the wisdom of ages, and are now revered from their antiquity and the good sense in which they are founded. One of these rules is that hearsay evidence is by its own nature inadmissible." Justice Marshall went on to say that "[i]ts intrinsic weakness, its incompetency to satisfy the mind of the existence of the fact, and the frauds which might be practiced under its cover, combine to support the rule that hearsay evidence is totally inadmissible."[38]

As courts began to select jurors who had no knowledge of the case that would influence their decision, the hearsay rule began to develop. By 1700, the rule prohibiting the admission of hearsay statements was formulated in criminal cases. Over the centuries, exceptions to the hearsay rule have developed because of the strict exclusionary nature of the rule.

§ 12.4 Exceptions to the Hearsay Rule—General

Although Chief Justice John Marshall argued that hearsay evidence should not be admitted in federal courts because of its intrinsic weakness and incompetency, and despite the fact that he concluded that "[t]his court is not inclined to extend the exceptions further than they have already been carried,"[39] state and federal courts have made exceptions, and the exceptions have been extended over the years in all American courts.

In Rules 803 and 804 of the Federal Rules of Evidence, there are at least 28 specific exceptions, and Rule 807 contains one broad category of residual exceptions for situations not specifically covered by Rule 803 or Rule 804. Rule 807 provides for recognition of other exceptions when there are "equivalent circumstantial guarantees of trustworthiness."[40]

---

38 Mima Queen and Child v. Hepburn, 7 U.S. (3 Cranch) 290 (1813). *See also* Donnelly v. United States, 288 U.S. 243, 33 S. Ct. 449, 57 L. Ed. 820 (1913), for a discussion of the history of the rules.

39 Mima Queen and Child v. Hepburn, *supra* n.31.

40 FED. R. EVID. 807. The exceptions noted in Rules 803 and 804 are not included in this section. Rule 807 covers situations that are not specifically mentioned in Rules 803 and 804. These rules are included in the appendix, and they should be reviewed before continuing.

In the first instance, the logical basis for the rule excluding hearsay evidence has been based on the facts that that (1) the declarant was outside of the court at the time of making the statement, and was not under oath to speak the truth; (2) the demeanor of the person who actually made the statement cannot be observed by the judge and jury; (3) there is a danger that the person who heard the statement may repeat it inaccurately; and (4) generally the declarant cannot be cross-examined despite the defendant's rights under the Sixth Amendment. The argument for admitting evidence under exceptions to the rule holds that, if the purpose and rationale for excluding evidence under the hearsay rule do not exist in a specific case, and if the interests of justice will be best served by admitting the statement into evidence, then the evidence should be admitted as an exception to the hearsay rule.

As a general rule, most hearsay exceptions have been categorized into fairly recognizable and repeating fact patterns addressed by the rules of evidence. Attorneys are able to intelligently argue the advantages and disadvantages of following a well-known exception by arguing the merits of the introduction of hearsay evidence. Thus, when hearsay statements fall within firmly rooted hearsay exceptions, or occur under circumstances with particularized guarantees of trustworthiness,[41] such statements are adequately reliable to be admissible in criminal cases,[42] provided they are consistent with the concepts encountered in *Crawford v. Washington*.[43]

In the following sections, the text discusses some of the hearsay exceptions that are most frequently encountered by criminal justice personnel and explains the rationales for the exceptions.

§ 12.5 —Spontaneous and Excited Utterances

Rule 803

EXCEPTIONS TO THE RULE AGAINST HEARSAY—REGARDLESS OF WHETHER THE DECLARANT IS AVAILABLE AS A WITNESS

The following are not excluded by the hearsay rule, even though the declarant is available as a witness:

(2) Excited utterance. A statement relating to a startling event or condition, made while the declarant was under the stress of excitement that it caused.[44]

---

41 *See* FED. R. EVID. 807.

42 United States v. Barrett, 8 F.3d 1296 (8th Cir. 1993), United States v. Matthews, 20 F.3d 358 (2d Cir. 1994).

43 Crawford v. Washington, 541 U.S. 36, 2004 U.S. LEXIS 1838 (2004). *See* § 12.2.

44 FED. R. EVID. 803(2).

As a general rule, when hearsay evidence will be admitted as substantive evidence, facts and circumstances that demonstrate the reliability and trustworthiness of the evidence must be present. Speech that has been immediately prompted by stressful or exciting events may be admissible as a hearsay exception if it qualifies as a spontaneous exclamation or excited utterance. The circumstances under which spontaneous or excited utterances occur offer reason to believe that statements made under severe stress will be truthful. An excited utterance caused by the stress or excitement of the situation must be made without mental reflection or deliberation. Under Florida's version of Rule 803(2), three requirements for an excited utterance exist: (1) there must have been a startling event sufficient to cause nervous excitement, (2) the statement must be made before the declarant had time to contrive, concoct or misrepresent, and (3) the statement must have been made while the declarant was under the stress or excitement cause by the startling or exciting event.[45] The theory of this exception is that circumstances produce a condition of excitement that temporarily halts the mental capacity for reflection and produces utterances that are free of conscious and considered fabrication. Another way to indicate the spontaneity of such speech is to think of a stimulus that produces an instant human response without an opportunity for significant reflection.

In order for a spontaneous or excited utterance to be admissible, an Arkansas court suggested that courts should conduct an analysis of the lapse of time between the stress and the statement, consider the age of the declarant, look at the physical and mental condition of the declarant, evaluate the characteristics of the event, and consider the subject matter of the statement made by the declarant. The court also noted that the declaration must be made soon enough after the stressful event that it can be reasonably considered to be a product of the stress and excitement, rather than of reflection or deliberation.[46] In the Arkansas case, which involved the rape, robbery, and kidnapping of the victim, the reviewing court approved the use of the excited utterance exception, noting,

> the victim's account of the crimes that she told [the officer] in the hospital was made shortly after the crimes occurred and while she was under the stress of excitement they caused. He testified that she was upset when he talked to her at [the crime scene]—shaking, teary-eyed, and "very excited in her mannerisms," as shown by hand gestures, rapid speech, and deep breathing—and that he could make little sense of what she was trying to say about the incident. He transported her from [the crime scene] to the hospital. With the curtains drawn and a female nurse present, the victim was still upset but calmed down a bit and was able to give a more coherent statement.[47]

In another case, the victim was walking along a street, and the defendant drove over to her in an attempt to pick her up. When she ultimately rebuffed his advances, he

---

45 *See* Thomas v. State, 2013 Fla. App. LEXIS 7863, 38 Fla. L. Weekly D. 1069 (2013).

46 Dillard v. State, 2013 Ark. App. 87, 2013 Ark. App. LEXIS 86 (2013).

47 *Id.*

pulled his van ahead of her and was standing on the sidewalk when he grabbed her and tried to throw her into the van. The victim managed to get away and ran through traffic, pounding on cars, trying to get help. The defendant stood nearby, pointed a gun at her and threatening to shoot her. The victim managed to get to her house and call 911, but when police arrived, she was hysterical and could not speak coherently. It took the officers 15 or 20 minutes to calm her down to the point where she could speak with them. Over the defendant's objection, the officers were permitted to render to the court what the hysterical victim had said to them while under the stress and the excitement following her assault. The reviewing court upheld the admission as an excited utterance, noting that there was a startling event, there was no time to contrive or misrepresent, and the statement was made while the victim was certainly under stress.[48]

In another situation that involved stress, anger, and excitement, a victim spoke with a 911 operator and, after identifying himself, told the operator that his uncle, whose voice could be heard in the background, had head butted him, tried to stab him, was currently carrying two knives, was following the victim, and refused to leave the home.[49] When the police arrived on the scene in response to the 911 call, they saw the victim exit the house. In the process of exiting the house, the victim concluded his 911 call and came toward police in an apparent excited state. Holding a cell phone, with blood on his hand, face, and shirt, the victim proceeded to point at a man later identified as the defendant. The victim then yelled to the police that the defendant had head butted and cut him. In determining whether to admit the statements the victim gave to police and the tape of the 911 call, the reviewing court analyzed the steps necessary for admission. Analysis of the circumstances of the out-of-court statements should consider whether the utterances were made contemporaneously or immediately after the startling series of events, and this analysis must show that the declarant was under the influence of the excitement caused by that event, leading the declarant to lack the reflective capacity essential for fabrication, and thus indicating that the victim's utterances must have been spontaneous and trustworthy. The court concluded that the victim's call indicated excitement and that an individual who has been head butted and chased around with knives would not likely be able to reflect and fabricate during the course of an ongoing spontaneous startling series of events. The described events were continuing during the 911 call and lasted until the officers arrived on the scene. The court concluded that the 911 call and the officer's testimony concerning what the victim said met the requirements for admission under the **spontaneous utterance** exception.

In an Indiana case, police arrived at the scene of a reported criminal battery. The victim was crying and shaking, and her appearance and overall demeanor indicated that she was very upset. She was talking rapidly and showed signs of fresh physical injuries, including a bleeding cut above her eye. Her left eye was swollen, and she was holding an ice pack to her eye. The attack had left marks on her neck that appeared to have been

---

48 Bell v. State, 847 So. 2d 558, 2003 Fla. App. LEXIS 8767 (2003). *See* case in Part II.

49 People v. Robinson, 27 Misc. 3d 1216A, 910 N.Y.S.2d 764, 2010 N.Y. Misc. LEXIS 919 (2010).

Spontaneous utterance A statement relating to a startling event or condition made while the declarant was under the stress of excitement cause by the event or condition.

caused by someone grabbing her around the neck. Over the defendant's objection that the woman's report to the officer was not a **spontaneous utterance**, the trial court permitted the police officer to tell the court what the victim had told him at the scene concerning her injuries. An Indiana appellate court held that the woman's statement to police met all the requirements for the excited utterances exception to the hearsay rule and was properly admitted.[50]

As a general rule, to be admissible a spontaneous statement need not be completely spontaneous and may be made in response to a question by a police officer or other person.[51] The fact that the statement goes beyond a mere description of the event may be considered in deciding whether the statement was sufficiently related to the event to be spontaneous, as required by the excited utterance exception to the hearsay rule, or whether the statement was a product of conscious reflection.[52]

The fact that an excited witness spoke of other crimes that occurred earlier in the day during her kidnapping does not exclude the admissibility of her statements under the excited utterance exception to the hearsay rule.[53] A prostitute who had been kidnapped and held for six hours in the back of a van, where she was forced to commit sexual acts with the strangers, made an excited utterance upon her release to several police officers. Police rescued the victim following the defendant's shootout with the police officers. During the stressful kidnapping where the men threatened her with death if she did not have sex with them, they forced her to drive the van while they committed at least two robberies, and she remained present in the van during the shootout with police. As the reviewing court observed, "Being inside a van that becomes the target of police gunfire certainly qualifies as a serious occurrence."[54] Her first words to an officer involved her rape allegations, even though those acts occurred earlier than the shootout. The trial court admitted her first statement made to police under the excited utterances exception to the hearsay rule on the theory that it was her first chance to comment about her ordeal; that there were sufficient events to cause stress; that she had not had an opportunity to fabricate; and that her remarks indicated the spontaneity of her speech. Her comment to another officer a few moments later that she had been kidnapped and repeatedly raped were properly admissible, even though they were made shortly after her rescue. The court held that the lapse of time is a factor to consider in determining spontaneity, but in this case, the lapse was rather short for both of the separate utterances to the police and both were properly admissible.

---

50 Cox v. State, 774 N.E.2d 1025, 2002 Ind. App. LEXIS 1533 (2002). *See* case in Part II.

51 *See* Melendez v. United States, 2011 D.C. App. LEXIS 106 (2011), where a child was present during a murder and excitedly told the first friendly adult what the defendant had done and also excitedly responded to questions about the killing from the adult.

52 United States v. More, 791 F.2d 566 (7th Cir. 1986).

53 Bryant v. United States, 859 A.2d 1093, 1106, 2004 D.C. App. LEXIS 526 (2004).

54 *Id.*

According to accepted practice, "there is no lapse of time beyond which the excited utterance exception is unavailable,"[55] but the evaluation of a statement under this exclusion requires an inquiry concerning whether the statement is inherently reliable because the person making the declaration remained incapable of thoughtful reflection. The general rule is that an utterance following an exciting event must be made soon enough thereafter so that it can be reasonably considered a product of the stress of the excitement, rather than of reflection or deliberation.

In a case where there was an interval between the exciting event and the declarant's statement, a Texas court admitted testimony of a police officer and a tape of a 911 call in a case involving attempted murder.[56] The facts indicated that the defendant had driven a truck off of the road and between houses in an effort to kill the victim. After she escaped death by going under a house, the victim made the 911 call to summon police, but she remained under stress. Her voice quivered as she spoke, and she sounded upset, scared, and excited. The trial court allowed the 911 call to be admitted and permitted a police officer to tell the court what the victim told him an hour after the event, as her statement described the attempted murder. The officer testified that, when he spoke with the victim, she was "very shaken, very upset, scared, excited, and crying" as she told him what the defendant had done to her. Even though some time had passed from the exciting event, the appellate court approved the admission into evidence of both of the victim's excited utterances.

In making an evaluation concerning whether the elapsed time between the startling event and the declaration to another is too long for the statement to be an excited utterance, the trial court focuses on the declarant's state of mind at the time the alleged excited statement was made. For the statement to be deemed admissible, the stress and influence of the event must be present at the time that a declarant makes a statement to a third party. For example, in a case in which the defendant had been charged with lewd conduct with a minor under 16 years of age, the trial court permitted a sister of the victim to tell the court what the victim told her.[57] In a later conversation, the child told her mother substantially the same story. According to the evidence, the conduct occurred while the defendant was babysitting the victim when he placed his finger in her private area. The child stayed at the defendant's home that night, went to school the next day, and returned to stay at the defendant's house the next night. On the second day, the child's father picked her up and drove her to her mother's home. The child disclosed no details of the incident to anyone until the evening, when her sister questioned her concerning whether something was wrong. At that time, the child told her sister about the illegal conduct, and subsequently she told her mother about the encounter with the defendant. Over an objection by the defendant's attorney, the judge permitted the sister and the mother of the victim to tell the jury what the victim told them, on the theory that the excited utterance exception to the hearsay rule permitted admission of

---

55 Shepherd v. State, 2013 Ind. App. Unpub. LEXIS 1414 (2013).

56 Dixon v. State, 2011 Tex. App. LEXIS 1745 (2011).

57 State v. Field, 2006 Idaho App. LEXIS 44 (2006).

their testimony. In finding error in the admission of the child's story through the sister and mother, the reviewing court noted that an excited utterance requires that the declarant be under the stress of the event when making the statement. The court stated that:

> "[i]n considering whether a statement constitutes an excited utterance, the totality of the circumstances must be considered, including the nature of the startling condition or event, the amount of time that elapsed between the startling event and the statement, the age and condition of the declarant, the presence or absence of self-interest, and whether the statement was volunteered or made in response to a question."[58]

The reviewing court agreed with the prosecution that the event would be classified as startling or shocking, but that stress would, for the purposes of the excited utterance exception, last for hours and not days, as was contended in this case. In finding that the declarant was not offering an excited utterance, the court stated that "at some point, the time span between a startling event and a subsequent statement simply becomes too great for the statement to be considered an excited utterance even when the declarant is a child."[59] If the situation indicates a lapse of time sufficient to manufacture or formulate a statement and if a statement lacks spontaneity, a trial court should not admit the alleged spontaneous statement.[60]

§ 12.6 —Business and Public Records

Rule 803

EXCEPTIONS TO THE RULE AGAINST HEARSAY—REGARDLESS OF WHETHER THE DECLARANT IS AVAILABLE AS A WITNESS

The following are not excluded by the hearsay rule, even though the declarant is available as a witness:

(6) Records of a Regularly Conducted Activity. A record of an act, event, condition, opinion, or diagnosis if:
- (A) the record was made at or near the time by—or from information transmitted by—someone with knowledge;
- (B) the record was kept in the course of a regularly conducted activity of a business, organization, occupation, or calling, whether or not for profit;
- (C) making the record was a regular practice of that activity;
- (D) all these conditions are shown by the testimony of the custodian or another qualified witness, or by a certification that complies with **Rule 902(11)** or **(12)** or with a statute permitting certification; and

---

58 *Id.*

59 *Id.*

60 North Carolina v. Riley, 54 N.C. App. 692, 695, 572 S.E.2d 857, 859, 2002 N.C. App. LEXIS 1531 (2002).

(E) neither the source of information nor the method or circumstances of preparation indicate a lack of trustworthiness.

(7) Absence of a Record of a Regularly Conducted Activity. Evidence that a matter is not included in a record described in paragraph (6) if:

(A) the evidence is admitted to prove that the matter did not occur or exist;

(B) a record was regularly kept for a matter of that kind; and

(C) neither the possible source of the information nor other circumstances indicate a lack of trustworthiness.

(8) Public Records. A record or statement of a public office if:

(A) it sets out:

(i) the office's activities;

(ii) a matter observed while under a legal duty to report, but not including, in a criminal case, a matter observed by law-enforcement personnel; or

(iii) in a civil case or against the government in a criminal case, factual findings from a legally authorized investigation; and

(B) neither the source of information nor other circumstances indicate a lack of trustworthiness.[61]

Businesses, partnerships, corporations, nonprofit organizations, and government agencies collect and compile records generated during their ordinary and usual operations to meet internal needs, tax requirements, and governmental reporting dictates. The requirements of business and organization dictate that these entities collect and create these records with a view toward accuracy and, most assuredly, with no motive to falsify. Because of the way the records are generated, there is a presumption that they contain true and reliable information because these entities act based on the recorded data. Recognizing the accuracy principle, many states have adopted the Uniform Business Records Act, which facilitates the admission into evidence of records of regularly conducted operations of government and private entities. For example, Washington has adopted its own state version of the Uniform Business Records Act as a hearsay exception, and it provides that the "record of an act, condition or event, shall in so far as relevant, be competent evidence if the custodian or other qualified witness testifies to its identity and the mode of its preparation, and if it was made in the regular course of business, at or near the time of the act, condition or event, and if, in the opinion of the court, the sources of information, method and time of preparation were such as to justify its admission."[62]

The purpose of the statute is to provide, as an exception to the hearsay rule, an acceptable substitute for the specific authentication of records kept in the ordinary

---

61 FED. R. EVID. 803. *See also* FED. R. EVID. 803(9) and (10) in Appendix I.

62 WASH. REV. CODE § 5.45.020 (2013).

course of business. The underlying rationale permitting this exception is that business records have the "earmark of reliability" or "probability of trustworthiness," because they reflect events occurring in the day-to-day operations of the enterprise, and business entities rely on their ordinary records in the conduct of business.

The Federal Rules of Evidence have greatly expanded the uniform law regarding records.. According to these rules, various business and public records may be the source of admissible evidence as hearsay exceptions. Some of these databases include but are not limited to records of regularly conducted activity, public records and reports, and records of vital statistics. Not only is information from the records admissible, but negative evidence may also be introduced to prove the absence of public records or entries or the absence of an entry in records of regularly conducted activities, so long as the record was regularly kept or created for data of that kind.[63]

As a general rule, all regularly kept business records are admissible under this rule, but they are subject to exclusion if the sources of the information or other circumstances indicate a lack of trustworthiness. In interpreting the Washington Rules of Evidence, one court approved the admission of business records in a case where the defendant was convicted of theft of rental or lease-purchased property, after he rented some furniture, but never made any payments.[64] The reviewing court held that the trial court did not err in admitting documents under the business record exception to the hearsay rule, section 5.45.020 of the Washington Revised Code. At trial, the rental store manager provided the proper foundation to admit the documents when he explained how each transaction or contact with customers was always logged in the computer system and how the system automatically time- and date-stamped the entries. The manager testified that he was familiar with all of the store's business documents and how they were generated. The business records exception assisted in proving the fact that the defendant had received the property, had not responded to attempts to contact him, and had retained the property.

In reviewing a trial court decision in another case, a Washington court upheld the admission of a business record of a trespass notice issued by a Wal-Mart store to the defendant, barring the defendant from the store in the future.[65] In its business records, Wal-Mart had kept a record of the issuance of the no trespass order. Subsequent to the issuance of the no trespass document to the defendant, he entered the Wal-Mart store in violation of the order and attempted to return merchandise. The defendant contended that his attorney had been deficient in failing to object to the admission of the no trespass order, which helped the prosecutor prove a criminal trespass charge of entering Wal-Mart. The reviewing court noted that the no trespass order was clearly admissible as a business record under the Washington statute because it had been generated in the usual and ordinary course of business, and there was no reason to doubt its authenticity.

---

[63] FED. R. EVID. 803(7).

[64] State v. Fleming, 155 Wn. App. 489, 495-496, 228 P.3d 804, 807, 2010 Wash. App. LEXIS 744 (2010).

[65] State v. Reek, 2012 Wash. App. LEXIS 2921 (2012).

Business records that have been created with litigation in mind may potentially reflect some bias of the preparer and do not generally qualify for admission under the business records exception to the hearsay rule. In a federal prosecution for growing marijuana, the reviewing court held that the business records showing that the defendant was the account holder for the electrical power bill should not have been admitted as a business record exception.[66] The electric company's representative testified that the document, while based on records kept in the ordinary course of business, was specially prepared for litigation and was inadmissible hearsay. In a New York prosecution for driving while impaired, the defendant had given a urine sample that was subsequently tested for drug metabolites. Called to the stand to comment on the test, a doctor testified at the trial that he was a general supervisor at his lab and also indicated that his laboratory and other subordinate staff prepared reports in anticipation of litigation, providing those reports to the local prosecutor. The doctor further testified that he had no personal knowledge concerning the tests performed on the sample from the urine container. The prosecutor unsuccessfully attempted to get the litigation package that the lab had prepared into evidence. The case had to be dismissed because, without the business record prepared by the lab, there was no admissible proof that the urine contained prohibited substances.[67] The same result *most likely* would be required in similar cases following the ruling in *Melendez-Diaz v. Massachusetts*,[68] because the report would be considered testimonial in nature and would be excluded on Sixth Amendment confrontation grounds. On a cautionary note, the Supreme Court more recently decided *Williams v. Illinois*, in which the state used a comparison between two different samples of DNA, but did not introduce the comparison test results into evidence.[69] The state presented a DNA expert witness who offered an opinion that the private DNA laboratory result was consistent with a state police laboratory result of a test of the defendant's DNA. The DNA expert witness further stated that the two results were consistent with each other. Although there was no majority in the Supreme Court, the Court essentially held that the expert's testimony concerning the private laboratory result was not offered to prove the truth of its contents, only that the results matched the results from another laboratory. According to the Court, there was no problem with the confrontation clause of the Sixth Amendment, because the DNA results were not considered to be testimonial in nature. As the Court noted, "[o]ut-of-court statements that are related by the expert solely for the purpose of explaining the assumptions on which that opinion rests are not offered for their truth and thus fall outside the scope of the Confrontation Clause."[70] Although the Court did not deal explicitly with the hearsay issue of the report as a business record, the argument was made that the private DNA laboratory

---

66 United States v. Niebla, 2013 U.S. App. LEXIS 23285 (11th Cir. 2013).

67 People v. Levy, 2008 NY Slip Op 51878U (N.Y. 2008).

68 *See* Melendez-Diaz v. Massachusetts, 557 U.S. 661, 129 S.Ct.2527, 2009 U.S. LEXIS 4734 (2009).

69 Williams v. Illinois, ___ U.S. ___, 132 S. Ct 2221, 2012 U.S. LEXIS 4658 (2012).

70 *Id.* at 2228.

did not produce its result in anticipation of litigation, because the defendant had not been identified at the time of the private lab DNA testing.

Some types of business records that are routinely created as a usual business practice may fail to qualify for admission under the business records exception, especially when they may include hearsay on hearsay. Although police reports containing statements concerning the cause of or responsibility for an accident are in a sense business or public records, they are often excluded because the person making the report is relying on what someone else told him or her, and the record does not reflect what the officer personally observed from firsthand perception. However, some public record police reports may be admissible where they contain only firsthand information or have been prepared in the usual course of business. For example, records created during the process of booking an arrestee into jail are routine, ministerial, and typical, and there is no motivation on behalf of anyone to interject untrue data when booking a prisoner.[71]

In determining whether a government document offered for admission is either an investigative report or a compilation of factual findings that do not come within the public record exception of the hearsay rule, the court considers: (1) whether the document contains findings that address materially contested issues in the case, (2) whether the record or report contains factual findings, and (3) whether the report was prepared for advocacy purposes or in anticipation of litigation.[72]

Applying this test, an Indiana court concluded that a diagram of the scene of a single-vehicle accident in which a passenger died did not contain any interpretative factual findings, despite being prepared by an accident investigator for the state police. Thus, the diagram was admissible under the public records exception to the hearsay, and it was subsequently used in the prosecution of a motorist for operating the vehicle while intoxicated. The court explained that the diagram was merely a recording of physical conditions that were observed by the investigator, and the fact that the statute, which makes accident reports filed by persons involved in automobile accidents confidential, did not bar the admission of a Standard Crash Report filed by the officer who investigated the accident, because the statute contains an exception for such reports.

Some police reports are admissible as exceptions to the hearsay rule where the reports are required to be made as part of a police department's regularly conducted activities. In Louisiana, a parish sheriff has a duty to seek out and obtain fingerprint evidence and record them as part of criminal investigations. In a case involving attempted armed robbery,[73] a defendant contended that the officer who lifted a latent fingerprint from the crime scene had to personally testify to that fact and that any other expert who so testified would be offering hearsay evidence. In rejecting the defendant's contention that the testifying officer would be offering hearsay, the reviewing court noted that the Supreme Court of Louisiana had previously ruled that fingerprints on file with a police agency fall under the public documents exception to the hearsay rule,

---

71 Fowler v. State, 929 N.E.2d 875, 879, 2010 Ind. App. LEXIS 1120 (2010).

72 Shepherd v. State, 690 N.E.2d 318 (Ind. 1997).

73 State v. Arita, 900 So. 2d 37, 44, 2005 La. App. LEXIS 501 (2005).

and, in this case, the fingerprint evidence was properly introduced to show that the crime scene fingerprint matched the print of the defendant.

In some jurisdictions, police reports and other public records may be admissible as business or public records in civil cases, but inadmissible in criminal cases where the report or record was generated by information "observed by police officers and other law enforcement personnel."[74] An autopsy report may meet the requirements of a business record exception to the hearsay rule, but may be excluded on constitutional grounds. In an Alabama homicide case,[75] the defendant objected to the introduction of an autopsy report when it was introduced by a doctor who had not performed the autopsy, but had read the public records generated by the actual autopsy doctor. Under Alabama law, an autopsy report is generally admissible as a business records exception to the hearsay rule.[76] However, the defendant made a Sixth Amendment right of confrontation argument that the actual declarant doctor giving the information was not present in court for cross-examination. According to the Alabama reviewing court, the Sixth Amendment prevents the admission of an autopsy report in a criminal case when it is not offered by the doctor who performed the procedure. Taking a completely different view, a Michigan reviewing court upheld the use of an autopsy report offered by an expert witness, despite the fact that the presenter did not conduct or review the autopsy in question.[77] The Michigan reviewing court held that the doctor performing the autopsy was not preparing for a trial, and the report was essentially a nontestimonial business record of the doctor's own findings and conclusions.

It is well known that business and public records are commonly entered and stored on computer systems and that police departments are moving toward generating fewer paper records. Computer records stored on servers or personal computers are unavailable and useless, except by accessing the data on a display or printing the data on paper. In admitting computer-generated printouts, which reflect the records stored on the computer, courts are actually following the best evidence rule. This is not departing from the business records hearsay rule, because the data contained must meet any hearsay hurdles that are presented, in addition to meeting the requirements of authentication of a writing. In a California case in which the defendant was found guilty of robbery and burglary, the conviction was based in part on records of traffic between the defendant's cell phone and his accomplice's cell phone and testimony about the cell phone records.[78] According to court testimony, the Sprint telephone system records custodian indicated that the computer system records information on each phone call at the time it is made and then sends the data to a call detail record archive that the Sprint system

---

74 *See* TEX. R. EVID. 803(8) (2014).

75 Smith v. State, 898 So. 2d 907, 2004 Ala. Crim. App. LEXIS 93 (2004).

76 *Id.* at 916.

77 People v. Raby, 2010 Mich. App. 622 (2010). *See also* NOTE, *Prosecutorial Use of Forensic Science at Trial: When Is a Lab Report Testimonial?*, 93 MINN. L. REV. 1058 (2009).

78 People v. Zavala, 216 Cal. App. 4th 242, 244, 245, 2013 Cal. App. LEXIS (2013).

maintains for billing purposes, and thus, those records are kept the ordinary course of business. The Court of Appeal upheld the admission of the cell phone records. According to the court, even though the records admitted in court consisted of a compilation of cell phone data that was produced for the trial in the form of a spreadsheet, those records were based on data that was automatically recorded and stored by computer program in the regular course of business.

Computer-generated maps may fall under the definition of business records stored on electronic computing equipment and should be admissible in evidence if they are relevant and material, without the necessity of identifying, locating, and producing as witnesses the individuals who made the entries in the regular course of business. In a prosecution for manufacturing crack cocaine within 1,500 feet of a school zone, the trial court allowed the introduction into evidence of a computer-generated map of the jurisdiction intended to demonstrate that a school existed within 1,500 feet of the crack laboratory. Before admitting an electronic map as a business record, the court must determine whether the map was made in the regular course of business, whether it was the regular course of business to produce this record (a map), and whether the map must have been prepared at the time described in the report. In this case, the custodian of the map data personally prepared the map from computer-stored data, had sufficient knowledge of the methods used to generate city maps, and was well acquainted with the technology used to produce city maps. Thus, the trial court held that the city map produced by the witness in the usual course of business could be admitted under the business records exception to the hearsay rule to help prove that the crack lab was within 1,500 feet of a school.[79]

The absence of a business record when it normally would have been recorded may constitute negative evidence of an event or evidence that the event most likely did not happen. The foundational showing that the business or entity normally records and keeps such records and that a due diligence search has not revealed the entry where it would normally have been entered allows the custodian of the records to note the nonexistence of the data.[80] Demonstrative of this principle is a California case in which the defendant claimed to be a lieutenant colonel in the Marine Corps when he testified under oath in a separate case.[81] This testimony sparked an investigation into the defendant's military status. In a subsequent prosecution for perjury for that statement, an officer in the Naval Criminal Investigative Service testified that one of his duties was to determine whether individuals were actually on active duty in the military, and he had searched the databases kept by the military for that information, finding no record of the defendant's military service. The negative information helped convict the defendant of perjury due to the lack of a military business record.

---

79 *See* Connecticut v. Polanco, 69 Conn. App. 169, 797 A.2d 523, 2002 Conn. App. LEXIS 187 (2002).

80 Washington v. Knott, 2002 Wash. App. LEXIS 392 (2002).

81 State v. Knott 2002 Wash. App. LEXIS 392 (2002)

§ 12.7 —Family History and Records (Pedigree)

Rule 803

EXCEPTIONS TO THE RULE AGAINST HEARSAY—REGARDLESS OF WHETHER THE DECLARANT IS AVAILABLE AS A WITNESS

The following are not excluded by the hearsay rule, even though the declarant is available as a witness:

(11) Records of Religious Organizations Concerning Personal or Family History. A statement of birth, legitimacy, ancestry, marriage, divorce, death, relationship by blood or marriage, or similar facts of personal or family history, contained in a regularly kept record of a religious organization.

(12) Certificates of Marriage, Baptism, and Similar Ceremonies. A statement of fact contained in a certificate:

(A) made by a person who is authorized by a religious organization or by law to perform the act certified;

(B) attesting that the person performed a marriage or similar ceremony or administered a sacrament; and

(C) purporting to have been issued at the time of the act or within a reasonable time after it.

(13) Family Records. A statement of fact about personal or family history contained in a family record, such as a Bible, genealogy, chart, engraving on a ring, inscription on a portrait, or engraving on an urn or burial marker.

(19) Reputation Concerning Personal or Family History. A reputation among a person's family by blood, adoption, or marriage—or among a person's associates or in the community—concerning the person's birth, adoption, legitimacy, ancestry, marriage, divorce, death, relationship by blood, adoption, or marriage, or similar facts of personal or family history.[82]

By its nature, evidence of one's family history and other information that existed prior to any human's birth involves hearsay. No individual has an actual awareness of his or her date of birth, except through hearsay information, and all family history prior to one's birth falls into the same category. Almost all evidence relating to pedigree, genealogy, and family history consists of hearsay, but family history evidence will usually be admissible as an exception to the general rule excluding hearsay evidence. The family history exception to the hearsay rule is based in part on the inherent trustworthiness of a declaration by a family member regarding matters of family history and on the often unavailability of other evidence. The one exception for family history can involve DNA testing to prove paternity, maternity, and lineage issues. In a Texas case where the grandmother had passed away, she had given birth to

82 FED. R. EVID. 803.

three children who would normally share in her intestate estate. One of the grandmother's children was long deceased, but he had fathered a daughter that he always indicated was his. Testimony concerning family history consistently indicated that the daughter was the child of her deceased father throughout her life, and there had been no information or contention to the contrary until the grandmother died. Of course, the deceased grandmother and her son were unavailable for testimony. All family members treated the child as being the child of the deceased father in all respects and without question during the life of the grandmother. Only when the grandmother died and her interstate estate was claimed by the deceased's two living children did the granddaughter of the deceased have to make a contest to establish her claim as heir to the share to which her deceased father would have been entitled had he outlived his own mother. During the trial, the daughter of the deceased father testified that *all* family members accepted her as the child of her deceased father, and her deceased grandmother treated her as her grandchild. However, the two known children of the deceased grandmother testified concerning family history that the wife of the deceased father had been unfaithful during the time when the child would have been conceived. However, DNA evidence obtained from the exhumed body of the child's father indicated a 99 percent chance that the potential heir was the child of her father. Family history was somewhat in dispute, but the greater weight of evidence pointed toward the child being the child of the deceased whose grandmother had recently died, and the DNA evidence was the final bit of evidence that established the child as heir of her father who succeeded to the position her father would have occupied had he outlived his mother.[83] Without the family history hearsay exception and DNA testing, the child of the father would have experienced a difficult time proving her lineage and pedigree.

Oral declarations by a family member regarding matters of family history are admissible as an exception to the hearsay rule, while other evidence of family history may be admissible where the information has been recorded in a manner that suggests reliability. Oral declarations of the names of uncles, aunts, and cousins and their point of origin in Eastern Europe may be accepted as family history sufficient to make a claim to an intestate relative's estate.[84] Virtually no family would record a birth record in a family Bible if the birth never occurred, a factor that gives reliability to family histories contained within religious books. Family records contained within the family bible are admissible when a proper showing is made as to the authority or authenticity of entries of the family record, especially when better evidence is not available. Such matters as births, deaths, and marriages are competent as evidence.

Family history may become important in criminal prosecutions involving sexual activity with persons beneath a certain age. In a New Hampshire prosecution, the underage victim was asked to state her age under direct examination by the

---

83 In re Estate of Wallace, 2013 Tex. App. LEXIS 10863 (2013).

84 *See* In re Estate of Doris Rosen, Deceased, 2003 Pa. Super. 96, 819 A.2d 585, 2003 Pa. Super. LEXIS 364 (2003).

prosecutor.[85] The age of the victim was crucial to the case because one of the elements of the particular offense required that the victim had been sexually molested when she was under the age of thirteen. The defendant objected on hearsay grounds when the alleged victim offered that she was twelve years of age when the defendant molested her. She knew her age because she always celebrated her birthday on that particular day of the year and had a birthday party on that date every year. Additionally, she stated that she had recently seen her birth certificate and knew that she was twelve years of age at the relevant time. Where there is some practical basis for the knowledge of intimate family history, especially one's age, the hearsay rule does not prevent a person from expressing her age. In some jurisdictions, entries in family Bibles are declared admissible by statute,[86] while some states recognize the hearsay exception for family records that have been included in family Bibles.[87]

Federal Rule of Evidence 803(11) provides that regularly kept records of a religious organization may be consulted in order to find family information, and if this information meets the legal requirements, it should be admissible in court as an exception to the hearsay rule. Although many people do not have close ties to organized religion, many people are intimately involved with their religion in situations in which careful records of church membership, birth, baptism, bar mitzvah, and wedding information are generated. Because there is every desire to record this information in an accurate manner and no reason to erroneously enter the information, there is a presumption that the records are accurate. In interpreting this rule, one federal court explained that the exception is limited to personal information and does not authorize evidence of statements of monetary contributions to a church, because these do not fall within the religious records exception to the hearsay rule.[88]

Under Federal Rule of Evidence 803(19) and its state equivalents, family relationships that exist by blood, adoption, or marriage may be proved by persons who have intimate knowledge of the family or by associates of family members concerning family history. For example, a father or mother could give the date of birth of their respective parents, even though they could not possibly know this information from firsthand knowledge. And a father could testify to the birth date of his son or daughter, even though the father was not present at the birth or even in the geographical area of the birth. In a case involving an illegal alien who had been convicted of attempted reentry into the United States, one of his defenses was that he [the son] was a citizen of the United States.[89] The trial court rejected testimony by the defendant's father that he had told the defendant that the son was born in the United States. While the father could testify personally that his son was born in the United States, he was not permitted to

---

85 State v. Tayag, 159 N.H. 21, 24, 977 A.2d 510, 514, 2009 N.H. LEXIS 80 (2009).

86 FED. R. EVID. 803.

87 2004 Phila. Ct. Com. Pl. LEXIS 134 (Pa. 2004).

88 Hall v. C.I.R., 729 F.2d 632 (9th Cir. 1984).

89 United States v. Ullah, 282 F. App'x 923, 925, 2008 U.S. App. LEXIS 14030 (2008). *Post-conviction relief denied*, 210 U.S. Dist LEXIS 1976 (W.D.N.Y. 2010)

state that he had told his son that he [the son] was born in the United States. What the father told the illegal alien son about the circumstances of the son's birth did not fall within the exception under Rule 803(19). Consistent with the family history exception, a federal prosecution of a rather complex nature involved men who had sexual relationships with at least two young Somali women alleged to have been under the age of 18 at the time.[90] Subsequent post-trial evidence emerged from relatives of two of the women that they were not children when the sexual acts happened, but were adults, a factor that was crucial to the original conviction. On a retrial and consistent with Rule 803, the court determined that close tribal and family members should be permitted to testify concerning the age of the alleged under aged female victims. People who do not have a close association with the family or group are not permitted to offer this sort of hearsay in court, however. For example, in a prosecution for aggravated driving under the influence of an intoxicant while a person under 15 years of age was in the vehicle,[91] the trial court permitted the arresting officer to relate to the court that the father of one of the car's occupants told the officer that his son was only 13 years old. The officer who testified had no personal knowledge concerning the age of the child, had not been a member of the family's community, and was a stranger to the child and his father. Because the family history related to an element of the crime, the appellate court reversed the conviction.

§ 12.8 —Former Testimony

Rule 804

EXCEPTIONS TO THE RULE AGAINST HEARSAY—WHEN THE DECLARANT IS UNAVAILABLE AS A WITNESS

(b) The Exceptions. The following are not excluded by the rule against hearsay if the declarant is unavailable as a witness:
  (1) Former Testimony. Testimony that:
    A. was given as a witness at a trial, hearing, or lawful deposition, whether given during the current proceeding or a different one; and
    B. is now offered against a party who had—or, in a civil case, whose predecessor in interest had—an opportunity and similar motive to develop it by direct, cross-, or redirect examination.[92]

---

90 United States v. Adan, 913 F. Supp.2d 555 (M.D. Tenn. 2012).

91 State v. May, 210 Ariz. 452, 455, 112 P.3d 39, 42, 2005 Ariz. App. LEXIS 73 (2005).

92 FED. R. EVID. 804.

Every criminal defendant has a Sixth Amendment right to confront and cross-examine adverse witnesses, and not having the opportunity to confront and cross examine a trial witness will likely lead to the reversal of a conviction. Consequently, when evidence has been introduced against a defendant in a manner that prevented or limited meaningful cross-examination, the trial judge should exclude the evidence. A literal construction of the Sixth Amendment would prevent virtually all hearsay evidence from being considered for admission, and a result, this strict interpretation would have the effect of making trials difficult. When a substitute for cross-examination exists or circumstances existed where the defendant originally had motive, opportunity, and incentive to conduct cross-examination at a prior proceeding between the same parties, the evidence may be admitted even though it constitutes hearsay testimony. This exception does not require that the defendant actually have conducted cross-examination of the witness at the earlier proceeding, only that the defendant had the opportunity, motive, and incentive. As a general rule, to have an opportunity to use testimony given in a prior proceeding, the parties to the lawsuit must be identical, the now-absent witness must have been under oath in the first proceeding, the absent witness must now be unavailable for testimony, and the lawsuit must cover the same issues covered in the first proceeding. Federal Rule 804 and state equivalents emphasize that the declarant must be unavailable for testimony. The unavailability may involve a witness assertion of a constitutional or other privilege, witness absence beyond the power of the court to command attendance, witness refusal to testify through no fault of the offering party, witness testimony stating a lack of memory, or death of the witness. If a hearsay exception absolutely conflicts with the Sixth Amendment provision that states, "in all criminal prosecutions, the accused shall enjoy the right to be confronted with the witnesses against him," the evidence will not be admissible.

In a sexual assault case in which the complaining witness, A.S., had disappeared after the first trial but prior to the second trial, the defendant objected to the use of his accuser's original trial testimony.[93] There was opportunity to cross-examine A.S. at the first trial. At the retrial, the judge permitted a law clerk to read the first trial testimony to the jury, but the jury likely gave more credibility to the testimony because the original testimony was accompanied by long pauses, slow responses, and evasive answers, while the law clerk delivered a smoother version than the original. According to the reviewing court, even if there is recorded testimony from a prior trial, the prosecution must exercise due diligence in an effort to discover the whereabouts of such an important witness. In this particular case, officers went to where the woman was thought to be located, but no in-depth effort to identify her whereabouts appeared to be evident. The appellate court noted

> The only new information secured by the detective and advocate concerned the ex-boyfriend in Waukegan and A.S.'s enrollment in beauty school, neither of which were noteworthy or particularly helpful to the investigation. While the detective

93 Cross v. Hardy, 632 F.3d 356, 2011 U.S. App. LEXIS 651 (7th Cir. 2011).

> drove to the ex-boyfriend's house in Waukegan, it does not appear that any effort was made to contact A.S.'s current boyfriend—whom she was with just moments before the alleged assault—or any of her other friends in the Chicago area. And with respect to the beauty school, there is no indication that the advocate or the detective (to whom the advocate passed along the information) asked for the name or location of the school, much less made any attempt to contact the school to inquire about whether anyone had seen A.S. In our view, the state's failure to investigate these leads does not comport with a showing of reasonable good faith.[94]

Former testimony Testimony given by a witness at another hearing or in a deposition taken in compliance with law. The testimony was given during the current proceeding or during a different proceeding, and the party against whom the testimony is offered in the current proceeding, or the predecessor of interest in a civil action or proceeding, had an opportunity and motive to develop the testimony by direct, cross, or redirect examination.

According to the Court of Appeals, without extensive efforts to find the important witness, the **former testimony** exception to the hearsay rule was not sufficient by itself to permit the government to read the complaining witness's testimony to the second trial. The court further determined that the Sixth Amendment right of the defendant to be able to confront his accuser at trial was sufficiently important that the conviction was reversed, and the case remanded. As the court noted, "We do not lightly reach our conclusion that the state court unreasonably applied federal law, but under the circumstances of this case, where A.S.'s testimony was critical and the state neglected to subpoena her despite knowing that she was extremely reluctant to testify, we find that the state did not sufficiently demonstrate that it acted in good faith."[95]

In one case, a California reviewing court approved the admission of a complaining witness's preliminary hearing testimony against a defendant who had allegedly violated California statutes against domestic violence.[96] The court noted that the prosecution had exercised due diligence in attempting to locate the witness. Due diligence involves a persevering application, untiring efforts in good earnest, and efforts of a substantial character directed toward finding the absent witness. In this case the district attorney's investigator promptly initiated an investigation to locate the witness and serve her with a subpoena; he visited her last known address and returned there on three different occasions. The investigator talked to former neighbors of the witness and requested that those individuals make an effort to find the missing witness. In addition, he accessed the DMV records, conducted a Lexis-Nexis search, and contacted other state agencies with no success. None of these efforts bore fruit, and the trial court properly allowed the earlier testimony from the preliminary hearing to be admitted into court over the defendant's objection that he did not have the same motive and incentive to

---

94 *Id.*

95 *Id.*

96 People v. Puerto, 2011 Cal. App. Unpub. LEXIS 2303 (2011).

deeply cross-examine at the preliminary hearing. The reviewing court noted that the defendant had been represented by counsel and that the trial court made no rulings restricting the defendant's cross-examination of the witness at the preliminary hearing. Therefore, the trial rejected his complaint based on hearsay and the confrontation clause, as did the appellate court.[97]

Some jurisdictions and legal authorities assert that former testimony is actually not hearsay, because it was given under oath and subject to cross-examination. The Federal Rules of Evidence and derivative state adopters recognize former testimony as hearsay, but hold that it is admissible under an exception to the hearsay rule. Under either approach, when a witness for the prosecution or defense is unavailable and cannot be produced at the present trial, or when a present witness refuses to testify, courts will generally admit the recorded testimony of such witness from a prior criminal proceeding where it meets the other qualifications for this hearsay exception. A witness who is expected to assert some constitutional or statutory privilege is not considered to be unavailable until the witness is placed on the witness stand and formally asserts a privilege not to testify or simply refuses to testify even though no legal basis exists for the refusal.[98]

In admitting **reported testimony**, a Tennessee reviewing court approved the admission into evidence of prior testimony from a witness who had testified at the preliminary hearing, but was deceased at the time of the trial.[99] The court noted that two issues were involved—the right of confrontation and whether a hearsay exception applied. The court noted that the defendant had ample opportunity and motive to conduct effective cross-examination of the witness at the preliminary hearing and that a preliminary hearing is precisely what the rules of evidence contemplate when Rule 804 mentions former testimony.

Reported testimony Testimony given by a witness at a prior hearing or in a deposition taken in compliance with law. The testimony occurred during the current proceeding or during a different proceeding, and the party against whom the testimony is now offered, or a predecessor in interest in a civil action or proceeding, must have had an opportunity and motive to develop the testimony by direct, cross, or redirect examination.

Under circumstances where the requirements for admission of reported testimony are absent, a trial court should reject the evidence. In a District of Columbia federal prosecution involving marijuana trafficking where three involved individuals had been killed in Maryland and two cooperating government witnesses had fully testified in the Maryland state grand jury proceeding, the defendant in the federal portion of the case wanted to use some of their testimony from the state grand jury

---

97 *Id.*

98 *See* Edmonds v. State, 2006 Miss. App. LEXIS 311 (2006).

99 State v. Bowman, 2009 Tenn. Crim. App. LEXIS 35 (2009).

hearing to assist him in defending the federal charges.[100] United States marshals and defense investigators were unable to locate the two state grand jury witnesses. In rejecting the use of the reported testimony exception, the federal district court judge ruled that the original testimony, out of the Maryland grand jury investigation, could not be used in the federal proceeding because the United States and the state of Maryland did not have an identity of motive when interrogating the grand jury witnesses in the state grand jury proceeding. In addition, the party against whom the grand jury reported testimony would be offered would be the United States, which was not a party to the Maryland grand jury proceeding, and did not have any control of the Maryland investigation. Therefore, the same incentive to question the witnesses at the grand jury stage did not exist, and there was not an identity of parties between the earlier proceeding in the state court system and the proceeding in the federal trial court. Therefore, the federal district judge ruled that the reported testimony exception under Rule 804 did not apply.[101]

In summary, when a party wants to admit into evidence earlier testimony offered at prior proceedings, there should be an identity of parties, as well as identity of issues between the parties at the prior proceeding and the present one. For the former testimony exception to be permitted, there must also have been ample motive, incentive, and opportunity for the adverse party to have developed sufficient cross-examination of a witness who must have been under oath. Where all the statutory and legal issues are met involving former testimony, "[o]nly the absence of an opportunity for the trier to observe the witness's demeanor detracts from the ideal conditions for giving testimony."[102]

§ 12.9 —Dying Declarations

Rule 804

EXCEPTIONS TO THE RULE AGAINST HEARSAY—WHEN THE DECLARANT IS UNAVAILABLE AS A WITNESS

(b) The following are not excluded by the hearsay rule if the declarant is unavailable as a witness:

(2) Statement Under the Belief of Imminent Death. In a prosecution for homicide or in a civil case, a statement that the declarant, while believing the declarant's death to be imminent, made about its cause or circumstances[103]

[100] United States v. Carson, 2013 U.S. Dist. LEXIS 135877 (D. Col. 2013).

[101] *Id.*

[102] 5-804 WEINSTEIN'S FEDERAL EVIDENCE § 804.04 (2014).

[103] FED. R. EVID. 804.

Dying declaration Hearsay evidence of what a person said when he or she was aware that his or her death was imminent. The evidence must relate to the way the declarant received final injuries.

In state criminal prosecutions, for a statement to be admissible as a **dying declaration** exception to the hearsay rule, the victim of a homicide must make a statement that describes the receipt of the infliction of fatal final injuries, and the statement or circumstances must indicate that the victim has no hope of surviving and is aware that death is imminent, and the victim must actually die. From ancient times, dying declarations in homicide cases have been admitted in evidence either (1) because of solemnity—the solemnity of the occasion and the fear that one would not want to meet one's maker with a lie on one's lips, or (2) because of necessity—due to the fact that the victim of the homicide cannot testify at trial, it is necessary to protect the public against homicidal criminals and to prevent a miscarriages of justice. Under the common law, the person making the dying declaration must actually die,[104] but the federal courts do not require death in order for the declaration to be admissible, and many states that have adopted a version of the Federal Rules do not require that death actually occur. Consistent with the position of many states and the Federal Rules, a Tennessee appellate court recently noted.

> [t]hat a statement must satisfy the following five elements to qualify as a dying declaration: (1) The declarant must be dead at the time of the trial; (2) the statement is admissible only in the prosecution of a criminal homicide; (3) the declarant must be the victim of the homicide; (4) the statement must concern the cause or the circumstances of the death; and (5) the declarant must have made the statement under the belief that death was imminent.[105]

From the legal perspective, the dying declaration has the same effect and carries the same presumptive weight as testimony given under oath, although a jury is free to give any weight it might desire to such evidence.

In order for a judge to admit a dying declaration, the declarant's statement must describe the circumstances and events immediately surrounding or leading up to the defendant's conduct that caused death of the declarant. The person making a dying declaration generally does not have to unequivocally and unambiguously state that the victim knows death is imminent, but the awareness of impending death may be inferred from the character of the wounds, the language used by the declarant, the facts and surrounding circumstances, or what has been told to the victim by medical personnel. The expectation of imminent demise may be shown by the circumstances of his or her condition or by his or her acts, such as sending for a minister or rabbi before making the declaration or requesting last rites from a minister or priest.

---

104 If the person survived, the individual could personally testify or the statement might be admissible as an excited utterance.

105 State v. Smith, 2010 Tenn. Crim. App. LEXIS 508 (2010).

In a recent Mississippi case, the court reviewed the requirements for the admissibility of a dying declaration. The state courts generally require at least three elements to be present prior to the admission of a dying declaration: (1) The wounded person must be in extremis and must die after making the statement; (2) The dying declarant must realize that he is mortally wounded; and (3) The individual has no hope of recovery.[106] In the Mississippi case, the victim had received a gunshot wound allegedly from the defendant and had been taken to the hospital where a trachea breathing tube had been inserted in his throat, preventing the victim from speaking. An officer who was present and who knew the victim asked him a series of questions to which the victim responded by nodding his head up and down to respond affirmatively. The questions were aimed at identifying the shooter, and when the police officer asked if the defendant was the person who shot the soon-to-be deceased, the hospitalized victim nodded emphatically in the affirmative. Shortly thereafter, the victim died. According to the trial court, it was clear that the victim was in extremis and did actually die. The court also concluded that the victim must have realized that his wound was mortal and that he had no true hope of recovery, a fact that could be inferred from the nature and extent of this gunshot wounds. The fact that the victim was responsive to the officer's questions indicated that the victim was of sound mind at the time. The defendant did not contest the assertion that the victim believed his death was imminent, but instead contended that the trial judge abused his discretion in admitting the decedent's statement as a dying declaration. The reviewing court rejected the defendant's contentions and upheld the admission of the dying declaration even in the face of a Sixth Amendment confrontation argument based on the case of *Crawford v. Washington*[107] and subsequent cases.[108]

In a different case with a different outcome, the proffered dying declaration was ruled as inadmissible because the victim probably expected to live, even though he died a day and a half later.[109] A police officer interviewed a gunshot victim immediately prior to surgery and, afterwards, in the hospital recovery room. They discussed the circumstances immediately prior to the shooting. The officer and the victim spoke about the person (the defendant) who had hit the victim in the head and then used a 9-millimeter pistol to shoot the victim in the torso. The officer indicated that the victim might need to talk to him later because the victim's mouth was too dry to easily understand his voice. No one told the victim he was dying, and the victim never expressed the view that he did not have long to live. According to the court, the victim probably "regarded his survival as far from assured. But that would not be the same as believing his death was inevitable and imminent."[110] The trial judge's decision denying admission of the victim's statements as a dying declaration was upheld on an interlocutory pretrial appeal.

---

106 Grindle v. State, 2013 Miss. App. LEXIS 535 (2013).

107 Crawford v. Washington, 541 U.S. 36, 52, 2004 U.S. LEXIS 1838 (2004).

108 *Id.*

109 People v. Jenkins, 2013 Il. App. (4th) 120628, 2013 Ill. App. LEXIS 135 (2013).

110 *Id.*

Inherent in hearsay evidence is an argument that the defendant has been deprived of the Sixth Amendment right to confront and cross-examine adverse witnesses. Over the past several years, the Supreme Court of the United States has taken several cases that address confrontation issues that relate to confrontation and the admissibility of dying declarations. In a 2011 case, *Michigan v. Bryant*,[111] the Supreme Court revisited the constitutional issues that surround admission of dying declarations that relate to what evidence is considered testimonial, specifically the Sixth Amendment right to confront and cross-examine adverse witnesses. In an earlier case, *Crawford v. Washington*,[112] a pure confrontation case, the Court held to directly confront the declarant in court. In *Crawford*, the defendant's wife had made a statement to police during her interrogation that occurred shortly after the time of the alleged crime. The wife was not permitted to testify at trial because of a marital privilege, but the trial court erroneously allowed admission of the wife's statement made earlier to police. The *Crawford* Court reversed the husband's conviction due to the Sixth Amendment confrontation violation. In *Michigan v. Bryant*, the victim had received a fatal gunshot wound prior to his encounter with police officers. Upon realizing that a gunshot victim was in poor shape, the officers who had arrived at the scene of the emergency tried to make sense of what had happened. Addressing the victim, police asked him "what had happened, who had shot him, and where the shooting had occurred."[113] The police did not know if other persons had been harmed or would be harmed or where the shooter might be located, and they needed answers rapidly. The victim offered responsive answers to the police, and those answers were later admitted at Bryant's murder trial as a dying declaration. According to the *Bryant* Court, when the primary purpose of an interrogation or inquiry is to enable police to meet an ongoing emergency, the resulting statements by a dying victim are generally considered nontestimonial and do not trigger a Sixth Amendment right of confrontation concerning the utterance of those words. This finding is different than the result in the *Crawford* case because, in *Crawford*, the police were calmly conducting a station-house interview with the arrestee's wife, and they were clearly attempting to put a case together for prosecution.[114]

---

111 Michigan v. Bryant, 512 U.S. 298, 2011 U.S. LEXIS 1713 (2011).

112 Crawford v. Washington, 541 U.S. 36, 124 S. Ct. 1354, 158 L. Ed. 2d 177, 2004 U.S. LEXIS 1838 (2004).

113 Michigan v. Bryant, 483 Mich. 132, at 143, 768 N.W.2d, at 71 (2009).

114 In a later case, *Williams v. Illinois*, 132 S.Ct. 2221, 2012 U.S. LEXIS 4658 (2012), the Supreme Court did little to clarify what could be considered "testimonial" and what did not qualify as "testimonial." The court upheld the use of an expert who did not identify a DNA sample used for a laboratory analysis and did not establish how it was handled or tested by the lab and did not vouch for the accuracy of the DNA profile produced. She was permitted to indicate that there was a computer match of a male DNA profile taken from a sexual assault victim and a male DNA profile developed by a state police lab that the lab stated came from the defendant. The expert witness referred to the report, not to prove the truth of the matter that it contained but only to establish that it contained a profile that matched the defendant's DNA sample. Justice Alito noted that "[t]he report was sought not for the purpose of obtaining evidence to be used against petitioner, who was not even under suspicion at the time, but for the purpose of finding a rapist who was on the loose." He concluded that the contents of the DNA report comparisons were not "testimonial" in nature and did not implicate the Sixth Amendment.

Following the lesson of *Michigan v. Bryant*, when determining the admissibility of dying declarations, courts must determine whether police officers and other individuals who speak with dying declarants are trying to ascertain or understand what has occurred, as opposed to asking questions with a view toward preserving oral evidence and building a case for admission of the oral statements at a later trial. In *Michigan v. Bryant*[115] the Court mentioned Davis v. Washington in noting that

> "interrogations by law enforcement officers fall squarely within [the] class" of testimonial hearsay, we had immediately in mind (for that was the case before us) interrogations solely directed at establishing the facts of a past crime, in order to identify (or provide evidence to convict) the perpetrator. The product of such interrogation, whether reduced to a writing signed by the declarant or embedded in the memory (and perhaps notes) of the interrogating officer, is testimonial.[116]

Under the modern Federal Rules of Evidence, the dying declarant need not actually die, but many states still hold that the dying declaration is not admissible unless the declarant has died and limit the declarations to homicide prosecutions. Even with the guidelines established by federal and state statutes, the Supreme Court of the United States, and state supreme courts, lower courts are required to apply the test to specific cases. For example, are the victim's statements admitted as dying declarations if they are elicited by questions? Must the victim affirmatively state that he or she is dying? Must the person actually die?

A case from Michigan offers some answers to these questions. In a case where the defendant had been convicted of assault with intent to commit murder, he contended that a statement by the victim should not have been admitted as a dying declaration.[117] Michigan permits the use of dying declarations where a declarant is unavailable, if the statement was made while the declarant believed his or her death was imminent and the statement concerns the cause or circumstances surrounding how the victim received his or her final injuries. The victim must be unavailable for testimony, but not necessarily deceased. In this case, when police arrived, the victim was lying on a mattress, bleeding, with a gunshot wound to her chest and two gunshot wounds to her lower leg. The officer testified that she was sighing, crying, and appeared to be in extreme pain, and her statement related to how she received those injuries. The trial court found that the female victim in this case concluded that her death was imminent due to the seriousness of her injuries and the difficulty she had in breathing, and this mindset seemed supported by her statement concerning the cause of what she believed to be her impending death. She did not testify at trial, as the prosecution was unable to locate her, despite due diligence. The reviewing court felt that, under Michigan's version of Rule 804, the woman's statements qualified as a dying declaration, even though she did not die from the defendant-inflicted wounds, and alternatively, the statement could also have been admitted properly as an excited utterance. The event proved to be a startling event that caused great stress and removed the ability to fabricate a story.[118]

---

115 Michigan v. Bryant, 562 U.S. ____, 131 S. Ct. 1143, 179 L. Ed. 2d 93, 2011 U.S. LEXIS 1713 (2011).

116 547 U.S., at 826, 126 S. Ct. 2266, 165 L. Ed. 2d 244 (2006).

117 People v. Brown, 2013 Mich. App. LEXIS 1445 (2013).

118 *Id.*

When an injured person does not believe that he or she is going to die or the proof may be uncertain that the victim has that belief, the statement may be admissible as an excited utterance, even if it does not qualify as a dying declaration. In a Texas case, friends of the victim discovered him in a parking lot, suffering from a tremendous beating that included a broken neck. According to six witnesses, while in the parking lot, the victim had responded to a question by identifying the defendant as the person who had beaten him. The appellate court approved the admission of the victim's statement as an excited utterance or as a dying declaration. It was clear that the victim had suffered an exciting traumatic event, and other evidence indicated that he knew he was in precarious shape. When the victim was about to be removed from a ventilator, he indicated to others that the defendant had given him his final injuries, and it was clear to the victim that he would not live very long once removed from the ventilator.[119]

As a matter of logic, a dying declaration must be made between the infliction of the fatal injury and the death of the declarant. For admission as a dying declaration, the length of time a declarant lives after making a dying declaration is immaterial in determining whether the statement qualifies as a dying declaration for purposes of the hearsay exception.

While the typical dying declaration is usually offered orally and later reduced to a writing, a dying declaration may be written or oral. It must, however, relate to final injuries suffered by the declarant prior to his or her death, and it may never explain the death of a third party. Due to the typical police response to reported homicides, many dying statements are made to law enforcement officers and emergency medical responders. Law enforcement officers are generally trained to recognize that, while a statement by a declarant may not qualify as a dying declaration, it may be admissible under the excited utterance exception to the hearsay rule. Police officers should take care to record the substance of a statement and the circumstances under which it was uttered as soon as possible in order to clearly convey the final statements regarding a victim's final injuries. Cross-examination by defense attorneys should also be anticipated at the time the dying declaration is offered in court by the police officer or other third party, so that the witness will be prepared to give accurate testimony about what he or she heard.

§ 12.10 —Declarations Against Interest

Rule 804

EXCEPTIONS TO THE RULE AGAINST HEARSAY—WHEN THE DECLARANT IS UNAVAILABLE AS A WITNESS

(b) Hearsay exceptions.—The following are not excluded by the hearsay rule if the declarant is unavailable as a witness:

---

119 Sadlier v. State, 2009 Tex. App. LEXIS 2962 (2009). *See* case in Part II.

(3) Statement against interest. A statement that:

(A) a reasonable person in the declarant's position would have made only if the person believed it to be true because, when made, it was so contrary to the declarant's proprietary or pecuniary interest or had so great a tendency to invalidate the declarant's claim against someone else or to expose the declarant to civil or criminal liability; and.

(B) is supported by corroborating circumstances that clearly indicate its trustworthiness, if it is offered in a criminal case as one that tends to expose the declarant to criminal liability. [120]

A. Declarations Against Pecuniary Interests

Under the common law, confessions or partial confessions to crimes by third parties were not considered admissible into evidence as declarations against interest, because the courts feared that they would be flooded with witnesses who would testify falsely to confessions that were never actually made. Gradually, many courts relaxed this common law rule, because it tended to prevent exoneration of innocent defendants by a guilty person who was not a defendant, but who had made an out-of-court statement.[121] Consistent with present evidence codes and case law, any time a person makes an oral or written statement that could have the effect of harming his or her pecuniary or monetary interests, such statement *may* qualify as an exception to the hearsay rule, provided circumstances indicate trustworthiness. Because most individuals are somewhat self-serving in what they say to others about themselves, declarations against **pecuniary interests** are probably true. A statement qualifying as a declaration against interest may be admissible as an exception to the hearsay rule because declarations against interest have been found to offer a high probability of truthfulness. Admission into evidence has become acceptable out of necessity; most individuals decline to repeat such statements while under oath in a court of law because admitting a declaration against interest may have an adverse result. The legal theory holds that a person does not make statements against his or her own pecuniary interest unless the statements generally are true, and courts have thus considered such statements trustworthy, even though there may be no opportunity to confront or to cross-examine the witness.

Pecuniary interests A direct interest related to money in an action or case as would, for example, require a judge to disqualify him- or herself from sitting on a case if he or she owned stock in a corporate party.

120 FED. R. EVID. 804.

121 Moore v. State 2013 Wy. 146, 2013 Wyo. LEXIS 152 (2103) (citing 2 MCCORMICK ON EVIDENCE § 318 (2013)).

Privity A situation where two or more individuals have a sufficiently close legal relationship that legal matters affecting one of the individuals may have a similar legal effect on another person. Two persons involved in a contract with a third person are said to be in privity with the other.

A declaration against interest by a person who is not a party or in **privity** with a party to an action is admissible in evidence when (1) the person making such declaration is either dead or unavailable as a witness due to sickness, insanity, or absence from the jurisdiction; (2) the declarant had peculiar means of knowing the facts that he or she stated; (3) the declaration was against his or her pecuniary or proprietary interest; and (4) he or she had no probable motive to falsify the facts stated.[122] Applying the declaration against interest theory, an Arkansas court revoked a prior judgment ordering a trustee to pay child support to a child beneficiary's custodian.[123] The trustee refused to comply with the court's original order when the trustee gained knowledge that the custodial father and the noncustodial mother appeared to have colluded to defraud the court and the trust. The mother, who could not be found for the hearing, told the trustee that she and the custodial father had concocted a scheme to get $2,000 per month from the trustee for the benefit of the child and that the mother and father were planning on splitting the $2,000 each month. At the time of the court's hearing, the mother was absent, and the statement was clearly against her pecuniary interest because if the trustee acted properly, knowing the truth about the fraud, her share of the monthly child support would not likely be paid. She must have known that the statement was against her pecuniary interest when it was made, and her absence permitted the hearsay use of her statement. In admitting the mother's declaration against interest, under Ark. R. Evid. 804(a)(4), the appellate court stated, "Here, Ms. Salmon was unavailable because no one knew her location and attempts to find her had proved unavailing." Moreover, Ms. Salmon's statements that she had colluded with Mr. Osborne (the father) were admissible because such statements were declarations against the pecuniary interest of her estate.[124]

A hearsay statement may qualify as a declaration against interest if the statement, at the time of its original utterance, was contrary to the declarant's pecuniary, proprietary, or social interest; tended to subject the declarant to civil or criminal liability; or tended to render invalid the declarant's claim against another, so that a reasonable person in the declarant's position would not have uttered the statement unless that person believed the statement to be true.[125] A statement may qualify as a declaration against the interest when the statement threatens loss of employment or reduces chances for future employment. For example, when a lessee's employee made a hearsay statement to a fire investigator that he and others were smoking on the leased premises a few

[122] Gichner v. Antonio Troiano Tile Co., 410 F.2d 238 (D.C. Cir. 1969).

[123] Osborne v. Salmon, 2006 Ark. App. LEXIS 266 (2006).

[124] *Id.*

[125] New Jersey v. Brown, 170 N.J. 138, 148, 784 A.2d 1244, 1251, 2001 N.J. LEXIS 1409 (2001).

hours before the fire started, that statement was against the employee's pecuniary and proprietary interests, and because the statement also concerned a subject of which the employee was personally cognizant and there was no conceivable motive to falsify, the statement was admitted as a declaration against the interest of the employee. In that case, the court agreed, however, that the statement would not be admitted unless the employee was unavailable to testify at the trial.[126]

In a Texas case, the trial court first acknowledged the rule relating to declarations against interest and reviewed the admissibility requirements, including the fact that the statement must have adverse consequences to the one making the statement. When police executed a search warrant of a residence where the defendant was present, the police discovered a quantity of cocaine in the presence of the defendant and a friend. Several days later, after posting bail for an associate, the defendant stated to his girlfriend that he knew the cocaine belonged to the friend who had been present during the search, because the defendant admitted selling the cocaine to the same friend. In approving the admission of the declaration made to his girlfriend, the reviewing court noted, "The voluntary statement, although made several days after the arrest, was not the product of coercion or questioning. . . . McElroy's incriminating statements were made to his live-in girlfriend, and thus, he had no reason to believe that statements made to her would be used against him."[127] In this case, the original declarant, the defendant, was unwilling to repeat his statement on the witness stand and therefore was "unavailable" to testify within the meaning of the statute governing the inadmissibility of declarations against interest.

B. Statements Against Penal Interests—Confessions and Admissions

The general exception to the hearsay rule introduced earlier includes an exception concerning admissions and confessions. To qualify as a third party statement against penal interest, the third party must be unavailable as a witness, the statement must be criminally inculpatory, and there must be proof of corroborating circumstances that demonstrate the trustworthiness of the out-of-court statement.[128] As used in criminal law, a confession consists of a suspect admitting responsibility for all the elements of the crime or crimes, and it constitutes a complete acknowledgment of guilt by one who has committed a crime or crimes. The confession is the admission of the criminal act itself, not an admission of a fact or circumstances from which guilt may be inferred. An admission, as distinguished from a confession, consists of the suspect admitting to some involvement or responsibility for some elements of a crime or admitting to facts that, when linked to other facts, may show guilt. However, the statement falls short of a complete confession for the criminal act itself. To qualify as a statement against penal

---

126 Gichner v. Antonio Troiano Tile Co., *supra* n.113.

127 Risher v. Texas, 85 S.W.3d 839, 842, 2002 Tex. App. LEXIS 6086 (2002).

128 Moore v. State, 2013 WY 146¶ 13 , 2013 Wyo. LEXIS 152 (2013).

interest, the admission or confession must have been made by a person who was not a defendant in the case in which the statement is desired to be introduced.

In a Michigan case, a man was robbed at gunpoint while using a public phone. The two assailants went through the victim's pockets and took his watch and pager, but were upset when he did not have anything else of value. At that moment, one of the felons shot the victim in the back. Police officers encountered the defendants a few minutes after the incident, because the officers had noted that the defendants appeared to be acting in a suspicious fashion. At the moment of contact, a radio broadcast alerted police of the robbery and shooting, and when one of the officers asked to have the robbers' descriptions repeated, the defendant blurted out, "I did it—I'm the shooter!" According to the Supreme Court of Michigan, the defendant's statement was properly introduced against the defendants as a declaration against penal interest, because at that time, the defendant knew that admitting to a robbery and a shooting was not in his best interest.[129]

When determining whether to admit or exclude alleged declarations against penal interest, courts often use a three-step process in analyzing the prospects for admissibility. Courts generally consider whether the alleged declarant actually made a statement that was against his or her penal interest, determine whether the declarant is actually unavailable for testimony, and evaluate whether there are corroborating circumstances that support the trustworthiness of the statement. The statement must have had the tendency to subject the declarant to a criminal penalty, and the declarant must have been aware of that fact. Also, courts want some proof that the declarant understood that the statement was against his or her penal interest at the time it was made. For a judge to determine that a declarant is unavailable, an assertion of the Fifth Amendment privilege will be sufficient in some jurisdictions, but if the witness cannot be found, subpoenaing the witness and providing proof of a serious attempt to locate the witness is generally required.[130] In a Virginia strong-arm robbery case where money was taken from a victim, the defendant attempted to have his girlfriend testify that the defendant had told her that he sold drugs, and that he planned a drug sale in the near future.[131] She was to tell the court that the defendant had later admitted that he had an issue with a drug sale that went "bad.". The theory was that the defendant's statement to his girlfriend had subjected the defendant to criminal penalties for drug dealing, that he was aware of that fact that it was an out-of-court statement, and that he [the defendant] was unavailable as a witness due to his invocation of the Fifth Amendment privilege against self-incrimination. If the declaration would have been admitted, it might have helped defend against the robbery allegation because it would show that robbery was not the motive, and that a sale of illegal drugs was the primary goal. In rejecting the defendant's offer through his girlfriend of a declaration against penal interest, the trial court indicated that the statements offered by the girlfriend were inadmissible because of questions

---

129 *See* State v. Washington, 664 N.W.2d 203, 2003 Mich. LEXIS 1465 (2003). *See* case in Part II.

130 United States v. Weekes, 611 F.3d 68, 71, 2010 U.S. App. LEXIS 14010 (1st Cir. 2010).

131 Baily v. Commonwealth, 749 S.E.2d 544, 2013 Va. App. LEXIS 314

concerning the reliability of those statements. The reviewing court upheld this theory regarding the unreliability of the statements, but indicated that the declarant was not unavailable as required by this hearsay exception. According to the rule of evidence, because he was present and could have testified, had he not invoked the Fifth Amendment privilege, the defendant was not "unavailable." As the reviewing court noted, if it allowed a defendant to make himself "unavailable,"

> [s]uch a defendant would be able to have his alleged prior statement admitted into evidence for the truth of its content while simultaneously insulating himself from cross-examination about it. We will not interpret the hearsay rule to allow a defendant to invoke his Fifth Amendment right not to testify as a shield to protect and insulate him against cross-examination only to simultaneously employ that right as a sword to obtain the admission of his alleged extrajudicial prior self-serving hearsay statements.[132]

Under these circumstances, the declaration against penal interest did not apply, and the girlfriend's offer of what the defendant allegedly stated was properly excluded as evidence.

In applying Federal Rule 804(b)(3), one federal trial court properly refused to admit a statement by the father of the defendant that the gun in question belonged to the father.[133] The son was being prosecuted for being a felon in possession of a firearm, and theoretically, the father's claim could have subjected him to criminal prosecution, thus helping the son. However, at the time of his son's arrest, the father had stated that the gun belonged to his son, before later trying to claim ownership of the firearm himself, perhaps in anticipation of assisting his son with his considerable legal problems. The father was unavailable because he would have refused to repeat the statement under oath. However, there was no corroboration of the father's declaration that would have given it an indication of believability. The Court of Appeals approved the trial court decision on refusing to admit the father's statement as a declaration against penal interest.[134]

When declarants who are not defendants in a case make out-of-court confessions that could subject them to criminal prosecution, the confessions qualify as hearsay evidence and may be admitted as declarations against the interests of the individuals making the declarations. Such evidence may be admissible as an exception to the hearsay rule when the evidence meets the requirements of the declaration against interest.[135] The reason for admitting the confession as an exception to the hearsay rule is that a reasonable person in such a position would not have made the incriminating statement constituting a confession or a statement against pecuniary or propriety interest, unless he or she believed it to be true, and if the confession or other declaration is not true, the

---

132 *Id.*

133 United States v. Halk, 2011 U.S. App. LEXIS 4749 (8th Cir. 2011).

134 *Id.*

135 *See* Chapter 16 for a discussion of the constitutional issues concerning confessions and admissions. *See also* KAN. STAT. ANN. § 60-460(j) (2012).

defendant is free to explain why he or she made a false confession or other utterance. Accused persons offer confessions for a variety of reasons, including efforts to protect other people, attacks of conscience and honesty, and other unknown reasons.

Before leaving the declaration against interest exception to the hearsay rule, a couple of warnings should be noted. First, the federal rule, as well as most state rules, requires corroboration of the trustworthiness of both the declarant and the statement. The party who seeks to introduce the unavailable witness's statement against penal interest has a duty to introduce sufficient proof that a rational juror could believe in the statement's truth. In order to determine whether a declarant's statement is sufficiently trustworthy, a judge should focus on whether there are corroborating circumstances that clearly demonstrate the trustworthiness of the declarant's statement.[136] In other words, the party offering the declaration against penal interest must demonstrate sufficient corroboration of the statement in context with other facts in the case in order for the declaration to be admissible.

Moreover, there is no declaration against penal interest if the declarant has not mentioned facts that, if true, would most assuredly implicate the declarant in crime. Early stage criminal planning or merely thinking about a crime is not a crime in itself. In a Michigan case, the court held that a declarant's statements implicating the defendant in a scheme to burn down the defendant's house were not against the declarant's penal interest as required for admission under the hearsay exception. Because the arson or significant steps toward its completion had not taken place, the statements only demonstrated an intent to commit a crime in the future.[137]

§ 12.11 —Other Exceptions—Residual Exceptions

Rule 807

RESIDUAL EXCEPTION

(a) In General. Under the following circumstances, a hearsay statement is not excluded by the rule against hearsay even if the statement is not specifically covered by a hearsay exception in **Rule 803** or **804**:

(1) the statement has equivalent circumstantial guarantees of trustworthiness;

(2) it is offered as evidence of a material fact;

(3) it is more probative on the point for which it is offered than any other evidence that the proponent can obtain through reasonable efforts; and

(4) admitting it will best serve the purposes of these rules and the interests of justice.

---

[136] United States v. Franklin, 415 F.3d 537, 547, 2005 U.S. App. LEXIS 14540 (5th Cir. 2005).

[137] People v. Brownridge, 225 Mich. App. 291, 570 N.W.2d 672 (1997).

(b) Notice. The statement is admissible only if, before the trial or hearing, the proponent gives an adverse party reasonable notice of the intent to offer the statement and its particulars, including the declarant's name and address, so that the party has a fair opportunity to meet it.[138]

Most hearsay exceptions fall into set patterns that arise time and time again and are covered by the rules of evidence dealing with specific exceptions, including those listed in Federal Rules 803 and 804. Rule 807, on the other hand, covers hearsay evidence that is not regulated by the previously discussed rules, given the unique circumstances surrounding the evidence in contention. The federal rules and similar state evidence codes have recognized that, merely because some of the exceptions are listed, such listing does not close the door to the use of other nontypical hearsay evidence as exceptions to evidence that might otherwise be excluded. It would be presumptuous to assume that all possible desirable exceptions to the hearsay rule have been catalogued or that accused individuals might never create any unique fact patterns in which there is reason to trust hearsay evidence. Therefore, Rule 807 specifically provides for other exceptions when certain conditions are met.[139]

In order to admit a statement under Rule 807, one court noted that:

> [T]here must be a showing that (1) the statement has equivalent circumstantial guarantees of trustworthiness to the other hearsay exceptions; (2) the statement is offered as evidence of a material fact; (3) the statement is more probative on the point for which it is offered than any other evidence which the proponent can procure through reasonable efforts; (4) the general purposes of the rules and the interests of justice will best be served by its admission; and (5) adequate notice must be given to the opposing party.[140]

To summarize, admissibility under Rule 807 must overcome five hurdles, including trustworthiness, materiality, probative importance, the interests of justice, and timely notice to the opposing party.

Interpreting the rule authorizing evidence to be admitted under the exceptions of Rule 807, one commentator noted that such a rule is necessary because not every possible contingency can be covered by detailed rules of evidence; the rule allows exceptions to the hearsay rule to continue to evolve; and the rule allows hearsay evidence that does not precisely fit into one of the listed exceptions to be used where its probative value is great.[141] Courts in a variety of jurisdictions have repeatedly indicated that the

---

138 FED. R. EVID. 807.

139 The provisions of former Rule 803 (24) and former Rule 804, (b)(5) have effectively been transferred to Rule 807 effective December 1, 1997, and remain in the latest 2013 revision of the federal rules.

140 United States v. Peneaux, 432 F.3d 882, 891, 2005 U.S. App. LEXIS 28877 (8th Cir. 2005).

141 *See* 5-807 WEINSTEIN'S FEDERAL EVIDENCE § 807.02[1] (2014).

residual hearsay exception under Rule 807 "is to be used rarely and in exceptional circumstances so that the exception does not swallow the hearsay rule."[142]

In an income tax evasion case in which the prosecution had been permitted to introduce foreign bank records that had been seized from the home and office safes of the defendant's conspirator, the defendant contended that the prosecution failed to prove that the documents had exceptional guarantees of trustworthiness as required by Rule 807, the residual hearsay exception.[143] The reviewing court noted that the bank documents had been relied upon by the defendants and had been seized from their collective possession. There was no indication that a break in the chain of custody occurred between the possession by the conspirators and the government. In addition, the reviewing court observed that the district court relied upon the way the records appeared and noted their internal consistency with respect to their contents and the circumstances of their discovery. The documents had the official appearance of bank records and some had the conspirator's address and had been received in response to messages sent by the conspirators. The reviewing court also noted that none of the defendants attempted to identify any document from the foreign banks that might be a forgery or might in any way contain inaccuracies. Accordingly, the Court of Appeals held that the defendant's arguments, under Rule 807, lacked merit and that the trial court did not err in concluding that the documents possessed sufficient indications of trustworthiness to be properly admitted against the defendant.

In applying Rule 807, a federal district court properly excluded an investigator's report from evidence when the report was designed to help the remaining defendant.[144] One conspirator pleaded guilty to robbery charges and testified against the other conspirator in the robbery of an armored truck driver. An investigator for the defendant had conversations with a third Brinks employee, which could have been used to impeach the government's conspirator witnesses who had already pled guilty. The conversations that the investigator wanted to relate to the jury were hearsay, but the defendant did not effectively show why the words spoken to the defendant's investigator would have any independent indicia of reliability or trustworthiness. There was no proof that the statements had been made under oath, and no proof that they were videotaped or voluntarily made. The reviewing court upheld the trial court's determination that the hearsay evidence should not have been admitted under Rule 807.

In a landmark case, *Crawford v. Washington*,[145] the Supreme Court of the United States dealt a harsh blow to prosecution efforts to successfully get evidence admitted under Rule 807 and related state evidence rules. In the *Crawford* case, a trial court convicted the defendant of assault of a man who had tried to rape the defendant's wife. At trial, the court permitted his wife's recorded out-of-court statement given to police to be admitted against him. The defendant's wife did not testify at trial after the defendant

---

142 United States v. Stern, 2013 U.S. Dist. LEXIS 164455 (E.D. Wisc. 2013).

143 United States v. Turner 718 F.3d 226,¶ 14-17, 2013 U.S. App. LEXIS 8870 (3rd Cir. 2013).

144 United States v. Rodriguez, 2009 U.S. App. LEXIS 4506 (9th Cir. 2009).

145 Crawford v. Washington, 541 U.S. 36, 52, 2004 U.S. LEXIS 1838 (2004).

invoked his state marital privilege to prevent her testimony, but the prosecution used her recorded out-of-court statements made to investigators as substantive evidence against him. Because his wife did not testify, he was effectively prevented from confronting and cross-examining her. The Supreme Court reversed the assault conviction with the view that, in allowing the use of the wife's statement and the testimonial evidence it contained, the trial court prevented the defendant's exercise of his Sixth Amendment right to confront and cross-examine an adverse witness. Only in exceptional situations will testimonial evidence be admitted when confrontation and cross-examination are impossible. In the *Crawford* case, the Court noted that statements taken by police during investigations are generally considered testimonial in nature and can be excluded on Sixth Amendment grounds.[146]

After *Crawford* and a couple of subsequent Supreme Court cases, courts trying to follow the requirements of *Crawford* still admitted evidence under Rule 807 and state equivalent provisions that cover hearsay evidence that may be admissible, even though such evidence does not fit well-defined hearsay exceptions.[147] In a Minnesota homicide case, a married woman who was leaving a nightclub with her boyfriend recognized her husband's car and remarked to other members of her party, "[l]ook at my husband over there, stalking me again."[148] Even though he was not visible inside the car due to the darkness, the woman had noticed that her husband appeared to have parked his white Cadillac across the street from the nightclub entrance. A short time later, someone shot the woman's boyfriend in the back as he arrived at his place of residence, an occurrence that took the boyfriend's life. Over the defendant's objection that the evidence was hearsay, the trial court permitted the prosecution to introduce the statement made by the wife concerning her husband's white Cadillac and its presence near the nightclub. Minnesota case law indicated that evidentiary rulings are made within the sound discretion of the trial court, and appellate courts should not reverse those rulings unless there is a clear absence of judicial discretion. Under Rule 807, Minnesota courts, in admitting or excluding evidence, consider the voluntariness of the statement, whether it was given under oath, and whether it was subject to cross-examination under the penalty of perjury. In addition, the court considers the declarant's personal knowledge, relationship with other parties in the case, the declarant's motivation to make such a statement, the existence of other evidence that might corroborate the statement, and the character of the declarant for truthfulness and honesty. The court should also consider the importance of the material offered and whether the out-of-court statement is more probative on the point that it is intended to support than other available evidence. In this case, the wife's statement that her husband was stalking her again was made to friends as she exited the nightclub with her boyfriend, and this statement possessed circumstantial guarantees of trustworthiness because she reaffirmed her statement to police, and she had no motive to be untruthful. During a police interview and later,

---

146 *Id.*

147 State v. Griffin, 834 N.W.2d 688, 2013 Minn. LEXIS 359 (2013).

148 *Id.* at 689.

she never disavowed the statement at any time. The reviewing court also indicated that the statement was offered as evidence of an important fact in the case because other witnesses saw the shooter fleeing the actual murder scene in a white Cadillac, and the defendant had a motive because his wife was dating the decedent. Under the circumstances, the Supreme Court of Minnesota concluded that the evidence, though hearsay, contained sufficient indications of reliability to be admitted under the catch-all hearsay exception of Minnesota's version of Rule 807.[149]

In a slightly different context, a lower Minnesota appellate court approved the admission of evidence under the state's version of Rule 807 in a case involving a defendant's alleged criminally assaultive and sexual conduct with his wife's minor child from a prior marriage.[150] The injuries concerned pattern burns that were indicative of the handle ends of silverware in the home being placed on multiple parts of the minor's body. Initially, the child-victim would speak with no one about the incident, except his grandmother, in whom he fully confided at his first opportunity. Because the child was ruled incompetent as a witness, the trial court permitted the grandmother to testify concerning the conversation she had with the grandchild in reference to his injuries. The reviewing court considered the defendant's contention that the residual exception should not have been used to allow the testimony of the grandmother, because it did not have circumstantial guarantees of trustworthiness. After rejecting the defendant's argument concerning the right of confrontation and cross-examination, the appellate court indicated that the child's statement to the grandmother concerned a material fact, that the statement was more probative on the facts that than any other available, and that the admission of the hearsay statement by the grandmother served the interests of justice. The court noted with approval that the child's original statement was spontaneous, short, and in response to his burn pains when he hugged his grandmother, and that few persons around him spoke Somali. Even though the child later told other relatives the same story, Rule 807 permitted the admission of the hearsay evidence in this case.

If the reasons for excluding hearsay evidence are not strong, and the interests of justice would best be served by admission of a hearsay statement into evidence, the proponent must assert logical rationales that support admitting the evidence under the residual exception theory to the hearsay rule. Admitting evidence under the residual exception rule has a chance of court approval where there are special cases involving unique circumstances.

§ 12.12 Nontestimonial Utterances

While the previous sections discuss the hearsay rule of exclusion and demonstrate some of the well-known exceptions that allow admission of evidence, some expressions by humans are not intended as testimony and are not considered hearsay. Courts

---

[149] *Id,* at 694.

[150] *See* State v. Ahmed, 782 N.W.2d 253, 2010 Minn. App. LEXIS 70 (2010).

recognize the legal principle stating that, if an out-of-court statement is offered to show what was said or to prove a statement was uttered, rather than to establish the truth of what was stated, that statements is not considered hearsay. Demonstrative of this principle is a case where undercover officers were using a confidential reliable informant (CRI) to purchase methamphetamine from the defendant.[151] The officer requested that the CRI make a phone call to the defendant in order to arrange the purchase of methamphetamine at a Home Depot store. At court, the officer testified concerning what he requested of the CRI, and the officer also testified concerning what the CRI said to the defendant on the telephone. A drug purchase resulted for which the defendant was placed on trial. The trial court properly allowed the police officer to tell what the CRI did in response to the officer's request that the CRI make a drug deal with the defendant and what the CRI said to the defendant after having dialed his telephone number. On appeal, the defendant complained that allowing the police officer to tell what the CRI said on the telephone constituted hearsay that should have been excluded. The prosecution contended that the words of the CRI constituted verbal acts, which are not considered hearsay because they are not assertions intended as a substitute for speech, and they were not introduced to prove the truth of the matter contained within the words. Essentially, the police officer explained what he had observed, and part of what he had observed was the verbal utterances of the CRI when she ordered methamphetamine from the defendant. The officer's testimony was not offered to prove that the CRI actually ordered methamphetamine, only that she uttered the words to a telephone that had dialed the defendant's telephone number. As such, this was a verbal act and not subject to hearsay exclusion according to the reviewing Court of Appeals.

A Virginia court advised that whether an out-of-court statement or act constituted hearsay depended on the purpose for which the statement was offered at trial; a statement that was offered for proof of its truth qualified as hearsay, but a statement or act that has been offered for the purpose of explaining or throwing light on the conduct of an individual to whom the statement was directed was not considered hearsay.[152] When a witness testified that she called police after observing a larcenist leaving her store, she mentioned that the reason the man piqued her interest was that another store employee gave her a detailed description of the repeat larcenist. The statement describing the appearance of the repeat larcenist was not offered for proof of its truth; it was offered only to explain why the witness scrutinized the behavior of the particularly described customer.[153] However, "a nod of the head in response to a question calling for a 'yes' or 'no' answer, or a gesture pointing to a particular person when asked to identify a perpetrator, are examples of assertive conduct"[154] that qualifies as hearsay evidence.

[151] United States v. Tenerelli, 614 F.3d 764, 771, 2010 U.S. App. LEXIS 15959 (8th Cir. 2010).

[152] Farrar v. Commonwealth, 2006 Va. App. LEXIS 301 (2006).

[153] *Id.*

[154] People v. Jurado, 38 Cal. 4th 72, 129, 131 P.3d 400, 438, 41 Cal. Rptr. 3d 319, 365, 2006 Cal. LEXIS 4391 (2006).

"A verbal act is an utterance of an operative fact that gives rise to legal consequences. Verbal acts, also known as statements of legal consequence, are not hearsay, because the statement is admitted merely to show that it was actually made, not to prove the truth of what was asserted in it."[155] The hearsay rule does not apply to verbal acts when the evidence has not been offered for its truth. In an Ohio aggravated menacing case, defendant's conduct could have been construed as conduct that was a substitute for words, and therefore hearsay, or it could have operated as a threat, as no one knew whether the defendant intended to take action on his threat.[156] A witness had discovered the witness slashing tires and breaking car windows with a baseball bat, at which time the witness told the defendant that she was going to call the police. Immediately, the defendant approached the witness with a knife, which he pointed at her face and then waved at the throats of two other individuals and a two-year-old child, telling all of them to get inside their house. The defendant stated, "Bitches, you ain't seen *hit, get back in the house."[157]Upon being asked to identify the apprehended perpetrators by the police, the witness approached a squad car in which the defendant and a conspirator were seated, appearing rather hostile. The defendant looked at the eyewitness, who he had earlier threatened by conduct with the knife, and he drew his finger like a knife across the front part of this neck in a slashing motion, while his conspirator stated, "Bitch, wait until we get out, I'm going to slash your throat!"[158] The witness was allowed to testify to these verbal and conduct threats by the defendants, although they argued the statements constituted inadmissible hearsay. The trial court held that the threats offered by the defendants' conduct were verbal acts that were not hearsay. According to the reviewing court, these threats were admitted and offered to prove only that the defendants spoke the words rather than to prove the truth of the statement; whether or not the defendants actually intended to perform the threatened throat cuttings would be immaterial. The court of appeal upheld the defendant's convictions.

Under what is sometimes referred to as the verbal act doctrine, a statement that accompanies conduct is admissible because it gives legal significance to the act, but the statement is not offered as proof of its truth. Where the evidence is offered only to show that words were spoken and not for proof of the truth of what was said, the evidence is not hearsay. For example, words uttered to offer another person a bribe constitute verbal acts that possess their own special significance and are not considered hearsay.[159] In an Ohio case, where the defendant had been convicted of a sexual offense against a woman,[160] he asserted that the woman had solicited him and that he went to her apartment for oral sex, but she claimed that she had invited him into her home so that he could eat

---

[155] 5-801 WEINSTEIN'S FEDERAL EVIDENCE § 801.11[3] (2014).

[156] State v. Skipper, 2013 Ohio 4508, 2013 Ohio App. LEXIS 4748 (2013). Each defendant was able to speak or act for the other due to the proof that they were engaged in a conspiracy that, under Ohio law, had not completely ended at the time they were seated in the police cruiser.

[157] *Id.* ¶ 3.

[158] *Id.* ¶ 5.

[159] United States v. Fofana, 2013 U.S. App. LEXIS 23600 (6th Cir 2013).

[160] State v. Ciacchi, 3020 Ohio 1975, 2010 Ohio App. LEXIS 1642 (2010).

his takeout food that he was carrying. The trial court sustained objections to questioning and testimony concerning what the victim stated to the defendant on the street. The court permitted the defendant to testify that the victim propositioned him on the street and that he went to her apartment after paying her $20 for oral sex. However, the trial judge prohibited the defendant from providing additional details concerning the conversation that occurred on the street. According to the reviewing court, the rejected testimony concerning what the victim said to the defendant was not hearsay, but the statements in question were verbal acts that were offered to support the defense theory that the victim engaged him through an act of prostitution and to prove consent. The appellate court reversed the defendant's conviction and remanded for a new trial. Verbal acts may be admitted to explain an actor's conduct in reaction to the statements, to show the effect on the hearer, and to show the mental state of the declarant.

§ 12.13 Summary

As a general rule, hearsay evidence is not admissible in court, because of the concern that such evidence may not be reliable or truthful and has usually not been given under oath. Hearsay evidence is defined as oral testimony presented in court by a witness, when the statement offered was originally uttered out of court by another person and when the statement is intended to prove the truth of matters asserted within the statement. Hearsay evidence can include evidence that was written outside of court and brought into court and offered for proof of its truth. Thus, evidence that relies on the credibility of the out-of-court declarant will be classified as hearsay and excluded. Although this general rule is universally applied and based on sound reasoning, there are many exceptions. If evidence meets the requirements of a recognized hearsay exception or qualifies under the residual exception, it may be admissible, even though it is classified as hearsay. Some evidence codes classify evidence that would historically be considered hearsay as non-hearsay and admit the evidence.

Examples of exceptions to the hearsay rule include spontaneous and excited utterances, some business and public records, family history and records, former testimony, dying declarations, declarations against interest, confessions, and exceptions under the residual exception rule. Under each of the traditional hearsay exceptions evidence may be admitted for substantive proof; however, it must meet the specific requirements that have been established for the particular exception, because these requirements help assure trustworthiness. Once hearsay evidence has been admitted, it is reviewed only for abuse of discretion by the trial judge and will only result in a reversal of a conviction where the error was outcome determinative.

The Sixth Amendment to the United States Constitution guarantees defendants the right to confront and cross-examine the witnesses against them. When out-of-court hearsay statements are admitted as evidence in court, the defendant may not have the opportunity to cross-examine or even confront the adverse declarant whose evidence is introduced by the one who overheard the declarant speak. Given that the Supreme Court recently held that testimonial evidence normally requires that actual confrontation and cross-examination must be permitted, some hearsay exceptions have come under more intense scrutiny by trial courts.[161] Care must be taken to determine whether the hearsay exception involves testimonial evidence or will be classified as nontestimonial and thus be admissible through a recognized hearsay exception.[162] While preserving of the rights of confrontation for defendants, the interests of justice require that a balance exist between the rights of defendants and the necessities of justice and fairness for society.

The hearsay rule does not exclude evidence when the out-of-court statements are offered solely as evidence that a statement was made, and not for the substantive content of the statement. Witnesses to out-of-court statements who repeat them in court, not for the substantive truth of the statement, but to indicate the person's physical or mental condition, will be permitted to offer testimony. Statements that qualify as verbal acts may be admissible as non-hearsay evidence where the purpose for admitting is to show that a statement was made or was made by a particular person.

From the foregoing discussion, it is clear that although some hearsay evidence is not admissible in court, significant exceptions to the hearsay rule have been recognized. The exceptions to the rule may result in most evidence classified as hearsay being admitted and very little evidence being excluded, but where courts admit hearsay evidence, the requirements of the exceptions assure truthfulness. In order to offer the greatest level of admissible evidence to the prosecutor, good practice dictates that criminal justice personnel be familiar not only with the rules that exclude hearsay evidence, but also with the hearsay exceptions and their individual requirements, which permit the admission of hearsay evidence in court.

CHAPTER TWELVE: QUESTIONS AND REVIEW EXERCISES

1. What is the definition of hearsay evidence? Based on general principles, why should hearsay evidence be excluded from criminal trials? Offer an example of hearsay evidence that should be excluded from a trial within the context that you develop.
2. As with most legal principles, the hearsay rule has many exceptions. Under the excited utterance exception to the hearsay rule, some statements made out of court may be repeated inside of court. What is the rationale that an excited utterance is probably truthful? Construct a hypothetical example where an excited utterance made under the stress of the moment should be admissible in a criminal trial.

---

161 *See* Crawford v. Washington, 541 U.S. 36, 2004 U.S. LEXIS 1838 (2004).

162 *See* Michigan v. Bryant, 661 U.S. 196, 131 S. Ct. 1143, 2011 U.S. LEXIS 1713 (2011).

3. Under the business records exception, courts frequently admit hearsay evidence in criminal cases. What is the basis for believability of a record that qualifies as a business record? Give an example of a business record that should be admitted in a criminal trial as a hearsay exception. A public record or report may also be admissible as a hearsay exception. What are the requirements to admit a public record or a public report in a court of law?
4. Records of family history that explain blood, birth, and marriage relationships are often important in criminal trials. Starting with the obvious fact that no person knows exactly when or where he or she was born, important data concerning families may be available only from hearsay sources. Create at least two examples where family history or a family record should be admitted in a criminal trial even though such information would clearly be considered hearsay evidence.
5. Even though every criminal defendant has a Sixth Amendment right to confront and cross-examine adverse witnesses, testimony from a prior case or hearing may be admissible against a defendant under the hearsay exception of former testimony or prior testimony. Identify some constitutional challenges that a defendant might make to the use of reported or former testimony. Develop a hypothetical fact situation in which a witness's former testimony should be admissible against a defendant in a criminal case.
6. The use of a dying declaration as a hearsay exception requires that certain elements be proven. As a general rule, what are the requirements that the attorney must demonstrate prior to a court admitting a dying declaration? What is traditionally the main difference in the dying declaration exception in state courts as compared to federal courts? Develop a fact situation in which you believe that a state court should allow the admission of a dying declaration against a criminal homicide defendant.
7. Declarations against interest (whether monetary or penal) may be admitted as hearsay exceptions. What is the theoretical basis for believing that a person who has made a statement against his or her financial interest has been truthful when doing so? Similarly, what is the rationale for allowing an out-of-court statement that a witness made that had the effect of subjecting the individual to possible incarceration? Construct a hypothetical example of a declaration against penal interest that should be admissible against a defendant at his or her criminal trial.
8. One of the exceptions to the hearsay rule covers a defendant's confession made out of court that the prosecution would like to admit, despite the defendant later

repudiating it. Assume that a particular defendant has made a pretrial out-of-court confession and a trial judge has allowed its admission into evidence. Why should a finder of fact believe the out-of-court confession? Give an example of a confession that a judge should allow into evidence against a criminal defendant.

9. Federal Rule of Evidence 807 provides for residual exceptions to the hearsay rule of exclusion and will permit some hearsay evidence that fails to fall into a typical category of hearsay exception. What is the logic of allowing nonstandard exceptions into evidence? Offer one example that you believe a judge might seriously consider admitting into evidence under Rule 807.

10. Humans often communicate nonverbally. Nonverbal communication includes offering a "thumbs up" or "thumbs down," nodding approval or disapproval, and appearing excited or calm. Where another individual has observed these nonverbal communications of a person outside of court and wishes to relay them to a judge or jury, such evidence might be considered hearsay if offered for proof of its truth. In most cases, these nonverbal communications or verbal acts are offered for nonhearsay purposes. Develop a hypothetical fact pattern that involves nonverbal communication that would not be admissible for proof of its truth but would be admissible for other purposes.

Documentary Evidence

13

Although writings must be authenticated before they are received into evidence or before secondary evidence of their contents may be received, a document is authenticated when sufficient evidence has been produced to sustain a finding that the document is what it purports to be. As long as evidence would support a finding of authenticity, the writing is admissible.

Jazauero et al. v. Mao, 174 Cal. App. 4th 301, 321,
2009 Cal. App. LEXIS 859 (2009)

Chapter Contents

Section

KEY TERMS AND CONCEPTS

Authentication
Authentication of Public Records
Authentication of Private Writings
Best Evidence Rule
Duplicate Original
Learned Treatise
Secondary Evidence
Self-Authentication
Use of Summaries

§ 13.1 Introduction

Prosecutors and defense attorneys must introduce evidence that either helps prove or disprove their respective case or their theory of the case. The evidence that the attorneys offer at a trial can be classified into in three general categories: (1) oral testimony that witnesses offer in open court, (2) documentary evidence introduced and authenticated by witnesses, and (3) real evidence that has tangible essence, which is offered and authenticated by witnesses who make its introduction possible. While the discussion in previous chapters related primarily to oral evidence, this chapter focuses on the broad category of documentary evidence. This type of evidence encompasses evidence beyond what the term "documentary evidence" would normally bring to mind. Documentary evidence includes evidence furnished by written instruments, inscriptions, and documents of all kinds. The term is broad enough to encompass every form of writing and applies to both public and private documents. Under the Federal Rules of Evidence, a writing or recording has been defined as including "letters, words, numbers, or their equivalent set down in any form."[1] Originally, a document provided a way of storing information in a fairly permanent manner, but that concept has grown to include movies, phonograph records, video- and audiotapes, computers and their mass storage devices, and photographs. Because the general rules of admissibility apply to all types of evidence, documentary evidence must meet these usual requirements of relevancy. In addition, there are certain rules that apply uniquely to documentary evidence. These rules are discussed in this chapter. In Chapter 14, the rules relating to the introduction of real evidence will be discussed and explained.

Under the law of evidence, the word *document* is a term of art and has a rather broad definition that encompasses many items that are not ordinarily considered documents. A document may be defined as any message that has been expressed,

---

1 Fed. R. Evid. 1001(1).

described, inscribed, embedded, saved, or recorded in or upon any substance by means of letters, figures, or marks and that is intended to be used for the purpose of recording that matter. Examples of private documents are letters, photographs, computer data, videotape data, digital video recordings, text messages, films, deeds, wills, agreements, and personal and commercial contracts. Birth records, death records, marriage records, registrations of various kinds, some police records, and licensing records are examples of public documents.

To be admitted into evidence, documentary evidence must meet the same rules of evidence as oral testimony concerning relevancy and materiality. In addition, the party that introduces a document must lay a foundation for the introduction of the documentary evidence to demonstrate that it is genuine and that the document is what it purports to be. As a threshold matter, the proponent must offer sufficient evidence to authenticate, verify, or identify the document offered as being the genuine article. Once a document meets the minimum foundational requirements of admissibility, any shortcomings or defects in evidence supporting authentication goes to the weight to be given to the document. The level of evidence needed to meet the requirement of authentication is fairly low. Meeting the requirements for authentication and the best evidence rule are two tests that relate primarily to documentary evidence. The following sections of this chapter address the general rules relating to these tests and their requirements, and demonstrate the principles by offering some specific examples.

§ 13.2 Authentication

Rule 901

AUTHENTICATING OR IDENTIFYING EVIDENCE

(a) In General

To satisfy the requirement of authenticating or identifying an item of evidence, the proponent must produce evidence sufficient to support a finding that the item is what the proponent claims it is.

(b) Examples

The following are examples only—not a complete list—of evidence that satisfies the requirement:

(1) Testimony of Witness with Knowledge

Testimony that an item is what it is claimed to be.

(2) Nonexpert Opinion About Handwriting

A nonexpert's opinion that handwriting is genuine, based on a familiarity with it that was not acquired for the current litigation.

(3) Comparison by an Expert Witness or the Trier of Fact

A comparison with an authenticated specimen by an expert witness or the trier of fact.

(4) Distinctive Characteristics and the Like

The appearance, contents, substance, internal patterns, or other distinctive characteristics of the item, taken together with all the circumstances.

(5) Opinion About a Voice

An opinion identifying a person's voice—whether heard firsthand or through mechanical or electronic transmission or recording—based on hearing the voice at any time under circumstances that connect it with the alleged speaker.

(6) Evidence About a Telephone Conversation

For a telephone conversation, evidence that a call was made to the number assigned at the time to:

(A) a particular person, if circumstances, including self-identification, show that the person answering was the one called; or

(B) a particular business, if the call was made to a business and the call related to business reasonably transacted over the telephone.

(7) Evidence About Public Records

Evidence that a writing authorized by law to be recorded or filed and in fact recorded or filed in a public office, or a purported public record, report, statement, or data compilation, in any form, is from the public office where items of this nature are kept.

(A) A document was recorded or filed in a public office as authorized by law; or

(B) A purported public record or statement is from the office where items of this kind are kept.

(8) Evidence About Ancient Documents or Data Compilations

For a document or data compilation, evidence that it:

(A) is in a condition that creates no suspicion about its authenticity;

(B) was in a place where, if authentic, it would likely be; and

(C) is at least 20 years old when offered.

(9) Evidence About a Process or System

Evidence describing a process or system and showing that it produces an accurate result.

(10) Methods Provided by Statute or Rule

Any method of authentication or identification allowed by a federal statute or a rule prescribed by the Supreme Court.[2]

A writing that lacks any connection to a criminal case has no ability to influence the existence or nonexistence of any of the elements that must be proved or disproved and is not admissible because has no relevance of any sort. As a fundamental rule of evidence, no writing, as broadly defined, may be admitted into evidence without some proof that it is genuine or authentic and that it is what it purports to be. As one early

---

2 FED. R. EVID. 901.

writer stated, "A writing, of itself, is evidence of nothing, and therefore is not, unless accompanied by proof of some sort, admissible in evidence."[3] An Arkansas appellate court recently remarked that requirements for authentication "are satisfied if the trial court, in its discretion, concludes that the evidence presented is genuine and, in reasonable probability has not been tampered with or altered in any significant manner."[4] The requirement of authentication does not demand that the proponent of a document conclusively prove that the document or article is genuine, but only that the document or article has enough evidence presented by the proponent that supports the finding that the item is what its proponent claims it to be.[5] According to the rationale behind this rule, absent a showing that the evidence is what the proponent alleges, it has no logical or legal relevance. The required proof may be contained within the document itself, in that the document may become, by authority of statute or otherwise, **self-authenticating**. Otherwise, outside proof is required to lay a foundation for admission of the documentary evidence. Authentication merely means that there must be preliminary proof of genuineness, authenticity, or identity of the document sufficient to prove that the evidence is what its proponent purports the evidence to be.

Self-authentication Documents that have within their contents proof of their genuine status and are what they are purported to be.

Under Rule 901(a), authentication or identification is a condition precedent to admissibility and is intended to ensure that an item of evidence is what it purports to be. Therefore, a proponent need only introduce evidence that would allow a reasonable judge to conclude that the document or article is the genuine item and that it is what it appears to be. Another way of phrasing the requirement of authentication is to have the proponent "present foundational evidence that is sufficient to constitute a rational basis for a jury to decide that the primary evidence is what its proponent claims it to be."[6]

While authentication is necessary for admission of documentary evidence, the proponent may use a variety of evidence to demonstrate its genuine quality, including direct or circumstantial evidence.[7] In an Arkansas case, the prosecution needed to authenticate an audio recording of an illegal drug transaction. In, in a prearranged drug purchase by an informant, police gave their confidential operative marked money and placed a hidden audio cassette recorder on the informant's person prior to engaging in the drug purchase. The informant was outside the view of the officer at some times, but returned with the recording of the transaction and the purchased drugs. The confidential informant testified under oath that the tape-recording was a genuine and accurate recording of the drug transaction, and the officer testified that the recorder had been in

3 Stamper v. Griffin, 20 Ga. 312 (1856).
4 Buffalo v. State, 2010 Ark. App. 127, 2010 Ark. App. LEXIS 118 (2010).
5 State v. Anglemyer, 269 Neb. 237, 243, 691 N.W.2d 153, 160, 2005 Neb. LEXIS 35 (2005).
6 Ohio v. Payton, 2002 Ohio App. LEXIS 496 (2002).
7 State v. Carpenter, 275 Conn. 785, 856, 882 A.2d 604, 648, 2005 Conn. LEXIS 396 (2005).

the police vault since it was originally returned. The reviewing court upheld the admission of the sound recording because it had been properly authenticated as a writing under the state's version of Rule 901 by the officer and the informant.[8]

Depending on the character of the document that a proponent seeks to have introduced into evidence, the requirements vary concerning authentication. The proponent of documentary evidence usually offers sworn testimony by a witness concerning the source and genuineness of the writing. Having the witness identify the writing and swear to its authenticity while under oath will typically suffice to authenticate a writing. In some instances, however, such specific testimony is not required. Demonstrative is a recent case involving paperwork generated for a sham marriage designed to evade federal immigration law where one of the men involved identified a "Borrower Statement" as a receipt for partial payment for one of the parties to the "marriage."[9] The witness testified that he recognized the document and that it was a receipt that the witness personally created to document the finance portion of the sham marriage transaction. The witness even knew why the document did not carry a date because the process for getting residency took three years. According to the Court of Appeals, the document was properly authenticated and was properly admitted. In a Tennessee case, the reviewing court held that an abstract of a driving record that contained a certification of authenticity, but bore no seal of the office or official, was not self-authenticating and therefore should not have been admitted.[10] Formal proof of authenticity will not be necessary if the parties to the case agree to stipulate to the authenticity of a particular writing.

In an effort to promote judicial economy, statutes have been designed to do away with the formal authentication requirements when such requirements obviously serve little purpose. Even when such statutes are in effect, the opposing party is not foreclosed from disputing authenticity by introducing evidence that the documents fail to meet the requirements or are not authentic. Rule 901 of the Federal Rules of Evidence lists ten examples of authentication or identification that conform to the rule. Some of these examples deal with real evidence, which is discussed in the next chapter, while some refer to documentary or oral evidence.

In authenticating written documents under Rule 901(b)(2), state courts have universally agreed that a nonexpert witness may properly identify a signature or handwriting if the witness is sufficiently familiar with the writing of another person so that the testimony would aid the jury. A witness cannot have developed familiarity with a person's handwriting just for the purposes of litigation and so must have gained the knowledge by observing him or her write on previous occasions. This knowledge could have been acquired from a social setting, interactions at work, or through personal correspondence. However, knowledge of another person's writing may be acquired by any means, as long as it is not obtained especially for the trial.[11] Courts have not

---

[8] Wilkerson v. State, 2005 Ark. App. LEXIS 12 (Ark. 2005). *See* case in Part II.

[9] United States v. Ruiz, 2013 U.S. App. LEXIS 17349 (11th Cir. 2013).

[10] State v. Troutman, 2008 Tenn. Crim. App. LEXIS 899 (Tenn. 2008).

[11] *See* FED. R. EVID. 901(b)(2).

set a minimum number of occasions or encounters with examples for familiarity to be sufficient for authentication purposes. However, evidence must be introduced to show that the witness possessed sufficient familiarity with the handwriting. In an Ohio drug case, a reviewing court approved the authentication of the defendant's handwriting on a ledger by a cooperating witness. The witness had known the defendant for an extensive period, had been romantically involved with him for a period of time, and had exchanged letters with him during the period, and she was storing a truck for him. The reviewing court held that the witness's level of familiarity with the defendant's handwriting provided a sufficient foundation to authenticate the ledger book as being the genuine article.[12]

In authenticating a voice sample under federal Rule 901(b)(5) and similar state enactments, the rule permits a lay opinion concerning the identification of a person's voice by anyone who has heard the voice on a first-hand basis and who has sufficient familiarity with the alleged speaker. In one federal prosecution, an expert Spanish language translator was permitted to testify as a lay witness for purposes of identifying the defendant's voice.[13] The reviewing court mentioned that the bar for voice familiarity is not a high one and held that where the translator had listened to known and authenticated samples of the defendant's voice and to recorded conversations purported to be of the defendant, she was properly permitted to offer a lay opinion concerning the identity of the defendant on the uncertain recordings. An opinion concerning identity was especially helpful to the jury because the known sample voices and the recorded voices were in Spanish and the English-speaking jury would not easily be able to make the same comparisons. The reviewing court found that the translator met the "minimum familiarity test" under the federal rule and that she properly authenticated the unknown sample as being the defendant's voice. The court affirmed the conviction for drug trafficking.

In federal prosecutions, wiretap recordings must be authenticated under Rule 901 (b)(6) in order to be admitted in court. In one case, the judge allowed a detective to authenticate a recorded voice conversation alleged to be the defendant speaking. The officer's familiarity with the defendant's voice was somewhat limited because it was based on 62 words spoken by the defendant at a pretrial hearing and from hearing the defendant and his attorney speak for 15 minutes prior to trial. While the appellate court had some difficulty with the minimal familiarity of the detective with the defendant's voice, it upheld the authentication of the wiretapped conversation and allowed it to be admitted.[14]

Rule 901(b)(7), Evidence about Public Records, provides that the requirement of authentication of a public record or report, as a condition precedent to admissibility, is satisfied if evidence is introduced to show that the writing was authorized by law to be recorded or filed in a public office and was actually filed or recorded. Under this

---

12 State v. Jones, 2010 Ohio 2704, 2010 Ohio App. LEXIS 2198 (Ohio 2010).

13 United States v. Mendiola, 707 F.3d 735, 739, 2013 U.S. App. LEXIS 2809 (7th Cir. 2013).

14 United States v. Jones, 600 F.3d 847, 860, 210 U.S. App. LEXIS 7160 (7th Cir. 2010).

section, the proponent of the evidence need only demonstrate that the office from which the party obtained the records served as the legal custodian of the records or operated as the official repository. Demonstrative of this principle is an Arizona drug possession prosecution where the defendant objected to the introduction of a booking fingerprint card based on an allegation that it had not been authenticated properly.[15] The officer who took the prints and prepared the card did not testify, while a different officer retrieved the card from the police repository of fingerprints and brought the card to court of use. The reviewing court noted that, in this case, the fingerprint card was properly authenticated. As the court explained,

> the fingerprint card is a public record that is self-authenticating. In addition to his fingerprints, the card had [the defendant's] name and identifying information such as height, weight, tattoos, social security number, date of offense, and birth date. The card also contained a stamp from the custodian of records for the sheriff's office that certified that the fingerprint card was "a true and correct copy of the fingerprints on file in this office."[16]

Old or ancient writings may pose special problems concerning authentication because the people who could identify and authenticate older documents often have defects of memory or may no longer be alive. Older legal teaching required that the documents be 30 years of age or older and relate to real property. For practical reasons, requirements have been relaxed concerning the authentication of older or ancient documents. Rule 901(b)(8) of the Federal Rules of Evidence liberalizes the common law "ancient document" rule by providing that a document may be authenticated when requirements pertaining to age, nonsuspicious condition, and appropriate custody are satisfied. Under this rule, a document must be demonstrated to be at least 20 years old. States that have variations of the Federal Rules follow the same requirements for ancient document authentication, including the 20-year period necessary to qualify as an ancient document,[17] but some jurisdictions adhere to the 30-year requirement.[18]

In states following the 30-year provision, the rules dictate that the document "must on its face be free from suspicion and must come from proper custody."[19] The requirement that the document be free from suspicion relates to whether the document is genuine but does not address concerns related to the document's contents. Questions as to the document's content and completeness bear on the weight to be given to the evidence and do not affect the threshold issue of authenticity.

In interpreting the "ancient document" authentication rule, a trial court in Hawai'i properly permitted a lease for land that had been executed in 1872 to be admitted in a trial court in a dispute over title to land on Maui. The opponent contended that the internal language of the document failed to mention a particular parcel of land and that

---

15 State v. Friedman, 2013 Ariz. App. Unpub. LEXIS 373 (Ariz. App. 2013).

16 *Id.*

17 *See*, for example, WIS. STAT. § 909.015 (2013).

18 TENN. R. EVID. 803(16) (2013).

19 29A AM. JUR. 2D *Evidence* § 1204 (2008).

the ancient document dealing with the disputed land was not relevant. The Intermediate Court of Appeals of Hawai'i disagreed and held that, under the ancient document rules of Rule 803 (hearsay exceptions) and the effect of Rule 901 that required the document to be older than 20 years, the document had been properly authenticated.[20] Most assuredly, no one who was a party to the original lease was alive to help otherwise authenticate the document.

As the business use of computers has become necessary and commercial transactions are virtually always recorded in computer databases, courts have been forced to determine when and under what circumstances computer-generated data should be and can be authenticated. Federal Rule of Evidence 901(b)(9) offers an example of authentication identification conforming to the requirements of this rule. This section provides that evidence describing a process or system used to produce a result, and a showing that the process or system produces an accurate result, conforms to the authentication requirements of this rule. Data from global positioning satellite truck tracking systems have been admitted to show location and speed of vehicles because the process can be demonstrated to produce accurate information.[21] In a prosecution under the Uniform Code of Military Justice, a defendant complained under the military version of Rule 901 that evidence of her alleged fraud had been obtained by using software to link her computer access to another individual's accounts and that the results could not be properly authenticated.[22] In upholding admission of the evidence, the reviewing court mentioned that the software that gathered and compiled the incriminating information from various servers and computers used no operator discretion in its data searches and presumably produced accurate results. The admission of the computer-generated data was approved as properly authenticated. Other examples of evidence that has been held admissible under this subsection involve X-rays, computer output, electrocardiograms, surveys and polls, and statistical samples. Evidence generated by a process or automated computer system may be presented and authenticated by individuals who understand the system and who may fall into the category of either expert or lay witness, depending upon the sophistication of the retrieval process.

More recently, courts have admitted computer printouts in accordance with this provision. In a state prosecution in which an automatic teller machine technician had been accused of illegally removing money from the machine, electronically and automatically generated evidence stored on a computer was admitted against him. The trial court rejected his lack of authentication argument. In admitting the computer-generated records, the court held that they met the standards for authentication, especially because the records were based on automatic data inputs and were not dependent on human interaction. The appellate court noted that computer business records have a level of trustworthiness that the individually prepared records lack.[23]

---

20 Makila Land Co. v. Kapu, 2006 Haw. App. LEXIS 181 (2006).

21 Houston v. Smith, 2010 U.S. Dist. LEXIS 118135 (W.D. Pa. 2010).

22 United States v. Lubich, 72 M.J. 170, 2013 CAAF LEXIS 479 (C.A. Armed Forces 2013).

23 State v. Huehn, 53 P.3d 733, 737, 2002 Colo. App. LEXIS 21 (2002). *See* case in Part II.

Even though evidence generated or gathered by means of a process or system is often highly technical and complex in nature and can be accurately retrieved, authentication must meet minimum standards under this rule, or that evidence will be excluded from introduction in court. In a Kentucky murder case, where cell phones were used to lure a victim, the prosecutor introduced cell phone records that had been produced by Cingular and delivered to the police for trial purposes. The Cingular records were not introduced by the company's records custodian, and the detective who brought the records to court had no personal knowledge concerning how they were produced or how Cingular maintained its cell phone records and thus could not attest to their veracity Although the conviction was not overturned under the harmless error standard, the top court held that the records should not have been admitted.[24]

§ 13.3 Self-Authentication

Rule 902

EVIDENCE THAT IS SELF-AUTHENTICATING

The following items of evidence are self-authenticating; they require no extrinsic evidence of authenticity in order to be admitted:

(1) Domestic Public Documents That Are Sealed and Signed. A document that bears:

(A) a seal purporting to be that of the United States; any state, district, commonwealth, territory, or insular possession of the United States; the former Panama Canal Zone; the Trust Territory of the Pacific Islands; a political subdivision of any of these entities; or a department, agency, or officer of any entity named above; and

(B) a signature purporting to be an execution or attestation.

(2) Domestic Public Documents That Are Not Sealed But Are Signed and Certified. A document that bears no seal if:

(A) it bears the signature of an officer or employee of an entity named in Rule 902(1)(A); and

(B) another public officer who has a seal and official duties within that same entity certifies under seal—or its equivalent—that the signer has the official capacity and that the signature is genuine.

(3) Foreign Public Documents. A document that purports to be signed or attested by a person who is authorized by a foreign country's law to do so. The document must be accompanied by a final certification that certifies the genuineness of the signature and official position of the signer or attester—or of any foreign official whose certificate of genuineness relates to the signature or attestation or is in a chain of certificates of genuineness relating to the signature or attestation. The certification may

---

24 Dalton v. Commonwealth, 2010 Ky. Unpub. LEXIS 45 (2010).

be made by a secretary of a United States embassy or legation; by a consul general, vice consul, or consular agent of the United States; or by a diplomatic or consular official of the foreign country assigned or accredited to the United States. If all parties have been given a reasonable opportunity to investigate the document's authenticity and accuracy, the court may, for good cause, either:

(A) order that it be treated as presumptively authentic without final certification; or

(B) allow it to be evidenced by an attested summary with or without final certification.

(4) Certified Copies of Public Records. A copy of an official record—or a copy of a document that was recorded or filed in a public office as authorized by law—if the copy is certified as correct by:

(A) the custodian or another person authorized to make the certification; or

(B) a certificate that complies with Rule 902(1), (2), or (3), a federal statute, or a rule prescribed by the Supreme Court.

(5) Official Publications. Books, pamphlets, or other publications purporting to be issued by public authority.

(6) Newspapers and Periodicals. Printed materials purporting to be newspapers or periodical.

(7) Trade Inscriptions and the Like. An inscription, sign, tag, or label purporting to have been affixed in the course of business and indicating origin, ownership, or control.

(8) Acknowledged Documents. A document accompanied by a certificate of acknowledgment that is lawfully executed by a notary public or another officer who is authorized to take acknowledgments.

(9) Commercial Paper and Related Documents. Commercial paper, a signature on it, and related documents, to the extent allowed by general commercial law.

(10) Presumptions Under a Federal Statute. A signature, document, or anything else that a federal statute declares to be presumptively or prima facie genuine or authentic.

(11) Certified Domestic Records of a Regularly Conducted Activity. The original or a copy of a domestic record that meets the requirements of Rule 803(6)(A)-(C), as shown by a certification of the custodian or another qualified person that complies with a federal statute or a rule prescribed by the Supreme Court. Before the trial or hearing, the proponent must give an adverse party reasonable written notice of the intent to offer the record—and must make the record and certification available for inspection—so that the party has a fair opportunity to challenge them.

(12) Certified Foreign Records of a Regularly Conducted Activity. In a civil case, the original or a copy of a foreign record that meets the requirements of Rule 902(11), modified as follows: the certification, rather than complying with a federal statute or Supreme Court rule, must be signed in a manner that, if falsely made, would subject the maker to a criminal penalty in the country where the certification is signed. The proponent must also meet the notice requirements of Rule 902(11).

Courts have developed a substantial body of decisional law governing instances in which authenticity may be viewed as sufficiently established without extrinsic evidence. In addition, updates to modern evidence codes have provided somewhat simpler methods of authenticating documents. However, under older case law and pursuant to older rules of evidence, there were only a few self-authenticating documents, such as ancient documents, documents bearing a certificate of acknowledgment, and replies to letters.[25] However, to enhance the speed of judicial process, the number of types of documents that are self-authenticating has grown in most jurisdictions. For example, the Federal Rules of Evidence now lists 12 types or categories of writings that are presently considered self-authenticating. Rule 902 of the Federal Rules of Evidence provides that extrinsic evidence of authenticity as a condition precedent to admissibility is not required with respect to the following: (1) domestic public documents that are sealed and signed, (2) domestic public documents that are not sealed but which are signed and certified, (3) foreign public documents that are signed or attested by the proper authorized official, (4) copies of public or official records certified by the custodian of the original record, (5) official publications issued by public authority, (6) newspapers and periodicals, (7) trade inscriptions and similar labels affixed in the usual course of business, (8) documents acknowledged by a notary public or other officer authorized by law to take acknowledgments, (9) commercial paper and related documents, (10) documents or signatures that a federal law declares genuine or authentic, (11) certified domestic records of regularly conducted activity, and (12) certified foreign records of regularly conducted activity.[26]

Consistent with Rule 902(1), governments and their subdivisions may authenticate documents that are under seal, and courts should recognize their authenticity. In a Tennessee felony driving while intoxicated case, where the prosecutor wanted to introduce evidence of two prior offenses, the appellate court approved the admission of court records of two previous DUI judgments that had raised court seals and the notation, "CERTIFIED COPY I certify that this is a true copy of the original order/pleading filed in the Circuit-General Sessions-Juvenile Courts of Franklin County, TN."[27] Both of the documents were signed and dated by a deputy clerk of courts as required under Rule 902(1).

Rule 902(2) regulates the methods of authenticating public documents that are not under seal, but purport to contain the signature of a person with official capacity under the authority of the United States, any state of the United States, or of other specific subentities of the United States. Demonstrative of the concept that public documents that are not under seal may be properly authenticated is a federal district court case involving authentication of documents from the federal Bureau of Prisons. In a proceeding involving the calculation of sentence length, a federal prisoner contended that documents from the Bureau of Prisons were not properly authenticated as genuine. The trial court accepted documentary evidence from a custodian of records who attested

---

[25] JOHN E. TRACY, HANDBOOK OF THE LAW OF EVIDENCE (1952).

[26] *See, generally,* FED. R. EVID. 902.

[27] State v. Adkins, 2010 Tenn. Crim. App. LEXIS 721 (Tenn. 2010).

verbally and in writing that they were true and accurate records contained in the ordinary course of the business of the Bureau of Prisons. The Bureau of Prisons administrative assistant who made the attestation was one of the official custodians of the records and introduced government exhibits and testified that they were authentic. Under the circumstances of the case, a federal magistrate judge ruled that the documents had been properly authenticated and were therefore admissible.[28]

Rule 902(3) governs the authentication and admissibility of foreign public documents in federal courts. As a matter of practice, a federal appeals court noted that there are two requirements for the authentication of foreign public documents.[29] First, some proof must be introduced that the document is what it purports to be, executed by a proper official in his or her official capacity and, second, there must be some indication that the public official of the foreign government vouching for the document is who he or she purports to be. In a Department of Homeland Security–initiated prosecution involving a defendant who allegedly engaged in sexual activities with underage children, where a United States citizen was alleged to have had traveled to a foreign country to engage in such activity, proof of the age of the victim was part of the prosecution's case. In this case, the defendant complained about the authenticity of a birth certificate from the Philippines that indicated one of defendant's sexual partners was underage. First, in order to be admissible in court, a foreign public document, such as a birth certificate, had to appear to be genuine on its face. Secondarily, the rules dictate that one of a specified group of foreign officials has to issue a final certification attesting to the genuine quality of the signature and title of the person executing the original document. In this case, a federal investigator obtained a copy of the birth certificate from the Philippines National Census and Statistics Office and had it certified at the United States Embassy. In this case, the reviewing court held that the birth certificate appeared to be genuine and properly issued and was properly deemed as authenticated by the trial court.[30]

In a Texas prosecution where the defendant had been convicted of cocaine possession with intent to sell and the prosecution desired an enhanced habitual offender sentence based on prior criminal convictions, the prosecution introduced two penitentiary packets (pen packets) that contained a variety of documents, including an affidavit from the Texas Department of Criminal Justice.[31] Under Texas law, it has frequently been held that pen packets are admissible as an exception to the hearsay rule if they are properly authenticated as public records. Each of the pen packets introduced by the prosecutor were accompanied by an affidavit of the Chairman of Classification and Records for the Texas Department of Criminal Justice, Correctional Institutions Division, certifying that the attached information concerning the defendant were true and correct copies of the original records on file in the Texas Department of Criminal

---

28 Felix v. Rios, et al., 2009 U.S. Dist. LEXIS 83121 (Dist. Minn. 2009).

29 United States v. Deverso, 518 F.3d 1250, 1256, 2008 U.S. App. LEXIS 4629 (11th Cir. 2008).

30 *Id.*

31 Carr v. State, 2013 Tex. App. LEXIS 13396 (2013).

Justice and were maintained in the regular course of business. The pen packet contained the defendant's past criminal history, photograph, weight, hair, and eye color along with his date of birth. The pen packets contained fingerprint cards, which matched a fingerprint cards introduced with expert testimony during the trial. The reviewing court upheld the admission of the pen packets and noted, "based on the foregoing, the certification of the pen packets by the TDCJID Chairman of Classification and Records provides sufficient evidence to support a finding that the pen packets are what the State claimed them to be, and as such, the pen packets were properly authenticated under Rules of Evidence 901 and 902(4) ('Certified Copies of Public Records')."[32]

Not everything that is certified may qualify as properly authenticated. For example, in a Texas criminal case, where the defendant possessed a juvenile record, a Texas Youth Commission self-authenticating business record packet, which included juvenile adjudications that were not certified, should not have been admitted. The packet certification could not cover or certify adjudications of documents that were merely placed within the business record packet. The complier of the juvenile packet was not the custodian of the original juvenile judgments and could not attest to the genuine correctness of the documents.[33] A different court held that a copy of a driving record obtained from a state's bureau of motor vehicles (BMV) that failed to contain any official certifying signature should not have been admitted in court because it failed to meet standards for authentication. There was no indication on the BMV record that a custodian or authorized individual certified the record.[34]

In a case where the defendant, along with other individuals, obtained loans for residential houses that were inflated in value and involved other individuals who falsified documents to make the loan transactions appear to be genuine, the defendant objected at trial and on appeal that the federal district court improperly admitted various lending documents as self-authenticating business records. The documents admitted against the defendant included residential loan applications, appraisals, offers to purchase, verifications of rent and employment, and other documents related to the mortgage loan applications that the defendant submitted to various lending institutions. Some of the documents were created by financial institutions and others were submitted by the defendant as part of his joint scheme. At the trial, the prosecution provided written declarations by the custodians of the documents that attested to the authenticity of those records in a way that met the foundational requirements of Rule 902(11) covering the admission of certified domestic records of regularly conducted activity. Under Rule 902(11), both the prosecution and defense may authenticate a business record through a written declaration by a qualified custodian that the record met the necessary foundational requirements that the business made the record at or near the time of the transaction, proof that the business generated the record in the usual course of business, and proof that the business kept the record in the usual course of business. According to the

---

32 *Id.*

33 Rangel v. State, 2009 Tex. App. LEXIS 1555 (Tex. 2009).

34 State v. Lee, 2010 Ohio 6276, 2010 Ohio App. LEXIS 5259 (Ohio 2010).

Seventh Circuit Court of Appeals, it rejected the defendant's argument that the prosecution had not properly established the authenticity of the business records. The court approved the introduction of the self-authenticating records because the documents had been certified by their respective custodians as accurate renditions of the records generated by their respective business organizations.[35]

Under Federal Rule 902 and similar state rules of evidence, extrinsic evidence is not required for documents within the self-authenticating group, and such documents are admissible without further authentication. The opposing party may introduce evidence that disputes a judge's preliminary ruling on authentication and may attempt to have perfectly authenticated documentary evidence rejected based on arguments that the authenticated documents possess insufficient relevancy to the case.

§ 13.4 Methods of Authentication

To be admissible as evidence, all documents and items that qualify as writings must meet the test of minimal authentication. When written documents are not self-authenticating, the proponent of a writing must offer a sufficient evidentiary foundation to support its admission. Generally, one of four methods may be followed in offering sufficient proof of authenticity: (1) proof of signing, (2) proof of signature, (3) comparison of signatures, and (4) circumstantial evidence.[36] Requirements include proof of the genuineness and proper execution of the document and that the document correctly states what the party claims. If a writing is not going to be introduced into evidence but may be used for some other purpose, there is no requirement that the evidence be authenticated.

In order to authenticate a written document, the most common method involves offering proof of the document's signing. One avenue is for the authenticating witness to testify that he or she saw the person sign the document in question. The next most common method of authentication is proof of the signature. In a case involving gross sexual imposition and rape of children, the grandmother of one of the complaining child witnesses was permitted to authenticate a letter written by one of the victims. Although the grandmother did not see the child sign the letter, she was familiar with the handwriting sufficiently to identify the signature. The reviewing court concluded that the letter had been sufficiently authenticated and had been appropriately introduced in evidence.[37]

Some written documents may be self-authenticating under Rule 901(7) covering trade inscriptions, signs, and tags. In an Indiana prosecution for possession of methamphetamine precursor chemicals, the trial court approved the admission of several boxes

---

35 United States v. Lock, 2010 U.S. App. LEXIS 24382 (7th Cir. 2010). *See also* FED. R. EVID. 902(11), app'x I.

36 TRACY, HANDBOOK OF THE LAW OF EVIDENCE (1952).

37 State v. Hupp, 2009 Ohio 1912, 2009 Ohio App. LEXIS 1622 (2009).

Self-authentication Documents that have within their contents proof of their genuine status and are what they are purported to be.

that originally contained pseudoephedrine hydrochloride, a chemical used in the manufacture of methamphetamine. The original packaging contained printed data that told the weight of the drugs within the box and the state offered the labels under the Indiana rule of evidence, which allow **self-authentication** for "inscriptions, signs, tags, or labels purporting to have been affixed in the course of business and indicating ownership, control, or origin."[38] In a Texas case, a deferred adjudication of burglary was revoked during a hearing at which a copy of an Oklahoma penitentiary packet that exhibited fax transmission information, a copy of the Oklahoma information filed against the defendant, an Oklahoma seal, and certification as a true copy of the record maintained by the clerk. The reviewing court held that the material received by Texas could be considered self-authenticating under the Texas Rules of Evidence, Rule 902.[39]

A tape-recording or a 911 call recording constitutes a writing and must be authenticated in order to be introduced at trial. In one case involving a multiple murder by the father of one of the victims, a child managed to call the 911 operator. The emergency operator was able to hear a child's screaming voice saying, "Daddy, stop it; Daddy, stop it," along with the sound of blows being landed by the attacker. A federal district court held that the 911 tape had been properly authenticated by the 911 operator who took the call. The operator was able to state that the call came from the number registered to the murder scene and the words of the child were offered at the very time the call transpired.[40]

In a case from Hawai'i, a federal jury found the defendant guilty of defrauding a financial institution by making false statements using a phone in an application for a car loan.[41] The credit union clerk entered the data into the financial institution's computer during a phone call purportedly involving the defendant, but the defendant contended that the telephone conversation that he allegedly had with the finance company had not been properly authenticated. According to the trial court, the telephone conversation was properly authenticated as having originated with the defendant because the person on the phone verified the defendant's access account number, his date of birth, and the last four digits of his Social Security number, and he knew about his pending loan application. The reviewing court noted that a phone conversation may be authenticated as having originated from a particular person by virtue of the individual's ability to offer information that would be known uniquely to him or her.

With respect to a written document, if a witness who can state that he or she witnessed the signing of the document, that testimony would authenticate the document. However, just because an individual claims to have witnessed the writing of the

38 Reemer v. State, 835 N.E.2d 1005, 1007, 2005 Ind. LEXIS 955, n.4 (Ind. 2005).

39 Ford v. State, 2013 Tex. App. LEXIS 6028 (2013).

40 Timmons v. Lee, 2010 U.S. Dist. LEXIS 99847 (E.D.N.Y. 2010).

41 United States v. Manibusan, 2013 U.S. App. LEXIS 12496 (9th Cir. 2013).

document and is familiar with the victim's handwriting does not mean that a court will accept a document as having been authenticated. In a New Mexico case involving battery on a household member, the defendant attempted to introduce letters allegedly written by the female victim that indicated the victim was lying to the 911 operator about the defendant's attack and that she hurt herself within the home by her clumsiness.[42] Defendant explained that having lived with the victim, he was sufficiently familiar with her handwriting to be able to identify and to authenticate the exculpatory letters in question. He offered no known samples of the victim's handwriting for comparison and presented no expert testimony. The appellate court approved the exclusion of the letters as lacking indicators of reliability due to the circumstances and upheld the exclusionary ruling that they lacked proper authentication. When an eyewitness is not available, a handwriting expert may authenticate a document by comparing known sample signatures with the questioned document's signature. In determining admissibility of questioned documents, trial judges have considerable discretion in determining what evidence is admissible for proving the authenticity of a questioned document.

To have a witness authenticate a writing, there must be a foundation presented to show the reasons the witness has familiarity with a signature or writing. The procedure generally followed in qualifying a witness to identify a writing, a signature, or a tape-recording is to place the witness on the stand and ask the witness foundational questions that will assure the jury and the judge that the witness is familiar with the writing and demonstrates how the witness gained the familiarity. The witness may be asked, "Will you state whether you are acquainted with the handwriting (or voice) of the writer?" If the witness answers in the affirmative and details how he or she is acquainted, the witness will then be asked to look at the letter or signature and tell whether it is the handwriting of the purported writer. In addition, the witness may be asked questions that could confirm whether he or she is or is not qualified. As an example, in a prosecution for preparing fraudulent tax returns, a government agent was permitted to authenticate the defendant's signature on a questioned document because the agent had gained familiarity with the defendant's signature card at a bank and a fingerprint card, both of which possessed indicators of reliability sufficient to permit the agent to authenticate a document containing the defendant's signature.[43]

As writings, videotape and DVD recordings must be authenticated prior to being introduced into evidence using authentication procedures familiar from other contexts. Generally, authentication requires that the proponent of the evidence prove who operated, controlled, or oversaw the device that recorded or videotaped the event and when and where the recording occurred. An appellate court in Mississippi upheld the prosecutor's use of a video showing the defendant in the act of burglarizing several cars in a Walmart parking lot against the defendant's allegation that the video evidence had not been properly authenticated. One Walmart employee who was familiar with the contents of the video authenticated it by offering proof that as an assistant manager of

---

42 State v. Solliz, 2013 N.M. App. Unpub. LEXIS 274 (2013).

43 United States v. Ali, 616 F.3d. 745, 754 (8th Cir. 2010).

the Walmart store, he was the employee who was custodian of all surveillance video at that Walmart, and he noted that the videos were recorded for security purposes in the normal course of their business. The Walmart employee testified that the video copies presented and identified by him at the trial both fairly and accurately depicted what was on the original video taken by the security cameras.[44] In a different case, a Georgia court upheld a conviction for being a felon in possession of firearms where the defendant and his brother were secured in the back of a police cruiser. The brothers engaged in a conversation that was videotaped by a cruiser-cam that included audio. Although the video had been received from an unnamed officer from a different jurisdiction, and might have presented authentication problems, the nondefendant brother testified for the prosecution and identified his voice and the voice of his brother. Because the cooperating brother admitted that the tape accurately reflected the conversation with his defendant brother, the reviewing court held that the videotape had been properly authenticated as genuine and had been properly admitted into evidence.[45]

§ 13.5 Specific Examples of Documentary Evidence

Social and business interactions in the modern world produce a variety of evidentiary items that are classified as "writings" but do not fall into the category of paper documents, as traditionally understood. From electronic checks, computer data, web pages and their accompanying metadata, cell phone data, global positioning system coordinate data stored in cars and phones, to actual paper documents, these "writings" are preserved on individual hard drives and servers and explain much of human activity. Few people give much consideration to the fact that cell phones record the location of every person who carries one, who the individual texted, or where the person "phone surfed" on the Internet. Modern "smart" cell phones transmit and store data by "pinging" cell towers and reading global positioning satellites to render location data even when not being used so long as they are in the "on" position. Although human memories will eventually fade, documents and data created in the course of human events remain for significant periods of time to assist in the reconstruction of a person's recent past location and activity. When the human endeavors involve crime, these documents may help prove or disprove elements in criminal cases. Even though the primary amount of evidence introduced into courts consists of oral evidence, documentary evidence plays an important part in recreating the full picture for the finder of fact. Documentary evidence includes written proof of laws; judicial records and proceedings; public records; private documents such as business records, account books, corporate records, letters, telegrams, and other correspondence; books; church records; hospital records; hotel registers; and many others. In each instance, the general rules of evidence, as well as the authentication requirements discussed in this chapter, must

---

44 Bunch c. State, 2013 Miss. App. LEXIS 602 (2013).

45 Smallwood v. State, 296 Ga. App. 16, 2009 Ga. App. LEXIS 115 (Ga. 2009).

be considered when arguing for or against admission. Court decisions and statutes in various states must be consulted for more precise rules concerning the introduction of documentary evidence.

In order to develop an understanding of some of the rules relating to documentary evidence, examples of specific types of such evidence are included here. These examples have been selected as those most likely to be encountered by criminal justice personnel[46] and are not exclusive to problems related to the admission of documentary evidence.

A. Public Records and Documents

Writings that have been deposited in public offices or were created by those public offices are generally easier to authenticate than some private writings. In many cases, because a public official is under a duty to keep records or make reports of acts or transactions occurring in the course of his or her official duty, records or reports so made by or under the supervision of the public official are admissible as prima facie evidence of facts stated.[47] In Texas, and in some other states, a public record is considered to be authenticated when it has been accompanied by a certificate from the custodian or manager of the public records office who certifies the document as a true and correct copy of the original on file in the particular office.[48] A public officer or official may be a county recorder, coroner, tax assessor, member of a board of elections, or a law enforcement official, either elective or appointive.

Labeling a document as a "public document" or "public record" does not make the document admissible in court. A publicly recorded document may include opinion, conclusions, and hearsay evidence and, although properly authenticated, it may be excluded, or portions of it may not be admissible on relevancy or other grounds. The fact that a document contains opinions and conclusions may create particular problems for the admission of some police records because hearsay evidence commonly is included in police reports.

In a variety of situations, police officers and law enforcement personnel may have a duty record or may create records of transactions that occur in the usual course of their work. The official records and writings made by such officers, or under their supervision, are of a public nature and are ordinarily admissible in evidence as proof of their contents, even though not proved by the person who actually made the entries. The extraordinary degree of confidence reposed in such documents is founded principally upon the fact that they have been made by authorized, accredited officers and deputies appointed for that purpose. As a cautionary note, public records created by law enforcement officials that have been properly authenticated may contain hearsay

---

46 *See* Chapter 14, Part I, for a discussion of the use of photographs, diagrams, maps, and models.

47 People v. Hudson, 655 N.Y.S.2d 219 (1997).

48 Smith v. State, 401 S.W. 3d 915, 918, 2013 Tex. App. LEXIS 6416 (2013).

evidence, which typically raises other evidentiary questions that may prevent the evidence from being admitted or dictate that the inadmissible parts be deleted.

Following this rationale, in an Arizona prosecution, a trial court admitted a fingerprint card prepared when the defendant was initially booked for possession of marijuana for sale and possession of drug paraphernalia.[49] Fingerprints found within plastic wrap covering the marijuana were compared to his booking prints. The defendant complained that the booking fingerprint card was not properly authenticated. The reviewing court found that the booking card was a public record that was self-authenticating. The card contained a stamp from the custodian of records at the sheriff's office that certified that the card was a true and correct copy of fingerprints on file with the sheriff's office and contained the defendant's name and identifying information such as height, weight, tattoos, Social Security number, date of offense, and birth date. The court held that under Arizona Rule of Evidence 901(b)(7), the fingerprint card had sufficient indications of being a public record so that the trial court and jury could conclude that the fingerprint card was authentic.[50]

When properly authenticated and relevant, police training and policy manuals may be admissible under the public document provisions of statutes. In a murder prosecution resulting in a conviction for the manslaughter of a police officer, the police department manual was admissible to demonstrate that the victim, an off-duty police officer who had been shot during a robbery attempt, was under a duty to apprehend felons at all times.[51] A Mississippi court noted that calibration certificates, bearing the seal of the Mississippi Crime Laboratory and containing the signature of the calibrating and attesting official, who certified that the proper calibration of Intoxilyzer® machines had occurred, were considered public records for which authentication existed as a matter of law. However, the government only needed to demonstrate that the certificates had been prepared by the proper person, who would attest that any copy offered was a true copy of the original.[52]

Many public records, including death certificates and autopsy reports, contain undisputed facts that have occurred; they are generally considered public documents that may be admissible as self-authenticating. For example, admitting court records of prior convictions for violating domestic relations no-contact orders was proper even if the records did not have the seal of the court as required. The appellate court noted that there was no abuse of discretion in admitting the certified records and there was evidence the court found the records sufficiently authenticated.[53]

While copies of most public records and documents are generally admissible without extrinsic evidence of authenticity, they must comply with the requirements as set out in state and federal rules of evidence. Evidence rules for the particular jurisdiction

49 State v. Friedman, 2013 Ariz. App. Unpub. LEXIS 373 (2013).

50 *Id.*

51 Michell v. State, 689 So. 2d 1118 (Fla. 1997).

52 Drabicki v. City of Ridgeland, 2013 Miss. App. LEXIS 404 (2013).

53 State v. Lux, 2005 Wash. App. LEXIS 980 (2005).

must be examined to determine whether any additional conditions must be met to ensure admissibility, such as offering a certified copy of a public record, giving reasonable notice of intent to use the evidence, or by delivering a copy to the adverse party in a reasonable time before the trial.[54]

B. *Private Writings*

Many evidentiary items that are classified as "private writings" encompass a wide variety of documents, broadly defined. They include personal correspondence, e-mail, text messages, blog and other Internet postings, videos on cameras and tablets, many business records, and individual business contracts. Credit card receipts, ATM receipts, telephone bills, and cash register tapes from retail stores qualify as private writings, as do legal writings such as wills and trust instruments. Consistent with the requirement of authentication, in order for a private writing to be admissible in court, it must be proven to be genuine and also that it is what it appears to be. The genuineness may be proven by the testimony of anyone who saw the writing executed, by indirect or circumstantial evidence, or from testimony that an automated process generated the writing. However, if circumstantial evidence is used to establish the authenticity of a document, it must be of such force and character that the person's authorship or the identity of the person responsible for the creation of the writing can be legitimately deduced from its contents or from attendant circumstances.

The internal contents of the letter may authenticate it is genuine and point to the author as well. Circumstantial evidence that helps pinpoint the origin nation of a letter may also assist in its authentication. In a Georgia criminal case where the defendant had been charged with rape and aggravated assault, among other crimes, the defendant objected to the introduction of a letter, allegedly written by the defendant, but which he claimed lacked authentication.[55] The letter had been sent to the person who initially called police while overhearing screams during the attack. The reviewing court noted that a letter may be authenticated by circumstantial evidence, and in this case, the letter bore the defendant's name and jail booking number. The envelope in which the letter arrived exhibited a stamp that appeared to be from the county jail where the defendant was being held prior to trial. In addition, the internal contents of the letter related a detailed account of what happened during the attack inside the house where the defendant and the victim were alone, and the contents were consistent with the defendant's version of events. The reviewing court concluded that under the circumstances, it was very unlikely that anyone other than the defendant could have written this letter containing the specific contents. Therefore, the court held that the letter properly had been authenticated and admitted in evidence at the trial.

---

[54] *See* FED. R. EVID. 1005 for an example of other requirements that may assist in admitting copies of public records into evidence. Meeting the hearsay rules also may influence the admission of evidence under Rule 902.

[55] Johnson v. State, 322 Ga. App. 612, 614, 744 S.E.2d 903; 2013 Ga. App. LEXIS 573 (2013).

Expert and lay witnesses may testify to their opinions respecting authorship or genuineness of writings provided they are properly qualified and the proponent has offered a proper foundation. An Ohio court noted, "[t]estimony by a non-expert witness who is familiar with the alleged author's handwriting can authenticate a document."[56] The proponent of the document usually establishes that the witness gained the necessary familiarity with the handwriting by observing the person write or by receiving letters or other written material from the purported author. In this case, the grandmother had a familiarity with the granddaughter's handwriting from prior exchanges of letters and testified that both the letter and the signature were written by her granddaughter. According to the reviewing court, the letters were properly authenticated.[57] If a party offers an expert witness to authenticate a document, the expert must be qualified as having expertise with handwriting prior to offering opinions concerning the known sample and the questioned sample of writing.

Authenticating e-mails, letters, and text messages may be done in a variety of ways. In a Colorado case[58] involving a defendant's violation of a personal protection order, there was evidence that he had sent the victim an e-mail in the very early morning that the violation hearing was to be held. Preliminarily, the reviewing court noted that

> We conclude that e-mails may be authenticated (1) through testimony explaining that they are what they purport to be; or (2) through consideration of distinctive characteristics shown by an examination of their contents and substance in light of the circumstances of the case.[59]

In this case, the prosecutor showed the victim a copy of e-mail, which she identified as being a true and accurate copy of the e-mail she received that carried the e-mail address of the defendant. She also noted that the contents of the e-mail mentioned their previous relationship and commented on the fact that the victim was scheduled to testify later in the same day. Under these circumstances, the reviewing court held that the e-mail was properly authenticated and that the trial court did not abuse its discretion in admitting it.

Text messages and other cell phone data are considered private writings and frequently contain evidence that may be relevant but must be authenticated prior to admission into evidence. Some courts enforce a higher standard for authentication than do others. An Indiana court held that the authentication of data from a cell phone is the same as for data obtained from a personal computer, and authentication can be proved where images or text messages were recovered from a defendant's cell phone.[60] In an example of failure to authenticate due to more strict standards, a defendant sent text

---

56 State v. Hupp, 2009 Ohio 1912, 2009 Ohio App. LEXIS 1622 (Ohio 2009); FED. R. EVID. 901(b)(2). This federal rule specifies that the familiarity not be acquired for purposes of the litigation when a lay witness provides the authentication.

57 *Id.*

58 People v. Bernard, 2013 COA 79, 305 P.3d 433, 2013 Colo. App. LEXIS 775 (2013).

59 *Id.*

60 Toran v. State, 2013 Ind. App. Unpub. LEXIS 1210 (2103).

messages to a cell phone that indicated some evidence of a conspiracy to commit murder.[61] The defendant, who was clearly not the shooter, did not deny that he sent the text messages that police found on his phone, but there was no proof of who sent the reply texts even though the reply cell number was known. The court noted that an author of a received text may be unknown because other people are known to use an individual's cell phone with some frequency to chat and to text. Additional evidence is required to authenticate a text message such as context or content of the message where the return message contains information unique to the two parties. In this case, the messages were extremely cryptic, the replies were not clearly unique to the defendant's outgoing message, and the phone was not registered to anyone. In rejecting authentication of the incoming message, the court noted, "the messages are only relevant to the extent that the State can authenticate that the Defendant authored all of the outgoing messages and that the alleged shooter authored the incoming messages." In a different case, involving bank fraud and identity theft, federal authorities lawfully seized a cell phone from the defendant and successfully authenticated some of the text messages contained within it.[62] The appeals court noted that the prosecution's foundation needed only to meet a slight burden of proof demonstrating that the evidence is what the government claims it to be. The internal content of the text messages indicated that the defendant was the user and also the receiver of the texts on the cell phone because some of the messages were directed toward the defendant's co-conspirator and were textually responsive to the co-conspirator's prior faxes. Incoming text messages mentioned the defendant's name, and outgoing texts identified the defendant's girlfriend by name. According to the reviewing court, the content of the text messages and trial testimony combined to authenticate the text messages on the defendant's phone.

Documents on private computers and publicly accessible servers can be properly authenticated by following one of several techniques. In a felony murder case, in which the defendant had been convicted of murder as a party to the crime due to his gang involvement, one of the grounds of his appeal was that a police officer had been improperly allowed to offer a screenshot printout of a MySpace® page that the officer accessed to help prove gang membership.[63] At trial, the officer had been permitted to introduce the publicly available screenshot of a person using the defendant's nickname, which described him as a Murk Mob member from New York. In the printout, the defendant's image depicts him wearing a bandanna in a color associated with the Murk Mob and making a gang sign. The defendant contended that the officer could not say who created the profile or who owned the profile page, and there was no proof that the defendant owned or created the data. The reviewing court noted that the defendant was known by the nickname, "Oops," and that he was a member of the Murk Mob and was originally from New York. Testimony prior to the admission of the MySpace® page by in-court witnesses proved his mob name and his affiliation. According to the Supreme

[61] State v. Zachary, 2013 Del. Super. LEXIS 285 (2013).

[62] United States v. Mebrtatu, 2013 U.S. App. LEXIS 22093 (3rd Cir. 2013)

[63] Burgess v. State, 292 Ga. 821, 823, 824, 742 S.E.2d 464, 467; 2013 Ga. LEXIS 369 (2013).

Court of Georgia, "In this case, there was sufficient circumstantial evidence to authenticate the printout from the MySpace profile page."[64]

Private letters, e-mails, and text messages may be authenticated by the use of the "reply letter doctrine" where a letter or other correspondence mailed or sent to another provokes a response that is genuine on its face and is responsive to the original letter. When these facts have been proved, the received letter is deemed to be authenticated and is generally admissible without any further proof.[65]

Business records that are generated in the ordinary and usual course of business may be authenticated and introduced in court. In one state case, the defendant had been convicted of two counts involving deception to obtain a dangerous prescription drug.[66] As authorized by state law, a centralized state pharmacy board created a drug database to monitor misuse and wrongful diversion of controlled substances. State-licensed pharmacies, when filling prescriptions for specified controlled substances, were required to report information about the prescriptions to the state pharmacy board database. Reports generated from the state database are considered public records generated in the usual and ordinary course of the business of the pharmacy board, but they need authentication to be admissible. In this case, the detective, who had access to the database, testified that he routinely ran reports from the state pharmacy database and that he ran a report on the defendant after he received information that she might be abusing drugs. The detective testified regarding what data from filled prescriptions the pharmacies must send to the pharmacy board and how the data in the state pharmacy board database are compiled. One of the doctors involved noted that he is familiar with the state pharmacy board drug reports and uses them in his medical practice. The detective noted that he ran a state pharmacy board database request on the defendant that revealed multiple prescriptions for the same scheduled drug. According to the reviewing court, both the detective and the doctor properly testified concerning the authentic nature of the business record generated by the state pharmacy board that indicated the defendant's criminality. In one case involving a sexual assault and the admission of authenticated business records,[67] the defendant contended that a doctor's report concerning her examination of the alleged rape victim should not have been admissible because it lacked authentication. The original report was authenticated by a nurse (who had been present at the victim's examination and who had signed the original report) and a different doctor, and the report had been originally made at or near the time of the examination and kept in the usual course of a regularly conducted business. While there were other evidentiary issues in this case, the report by the doctor was deemed to have been properly authenticated and had been properly admitted in court.

---

64 *Id.*, 824.

65 *See* Varkonyi v. State, 276 S.W.3d 27, 2008 Tex. App. LEXIS 3353 (Tex. 2008).

66 State v. Toudle, 2013 Ohio 1548, 2013 Ohio App. LEXIS 1459 (2013).

67 Johnson v. State, 117 So.3d 1238, 2013 Fla. App. LEXIS 10982 (Fla. 2013).

§ 13.6 Best Evidence Rule

Rule 1002

REQUIREMENT OF ORIGINAL

An original writing, recording, or photograph is required in order to prove its content unless these rules or a federal statute provides otherwise.[68]

In a criminal case, where the contents of a writing, broadly construed, helps prove or disprove a fact at issue, there is a preference that the original writing be tendered for use as evidence of the disputed fact. Under modern law, a writing includes a traditional document on paper, as well as almost any item that may contain data, such as a digital video, a taped video, a sound recording, a movie, a jump or thumb drive, a hard drive, and similar items that can store data.[69] The Hawai'i rules of evidence define a writing as consisting of "letters, words, sounds, or numbers, or their equivalent, set down by handwriting, typewriting, printing, Photostatting, photographing, magnetic impulse, mechanical or electronic recording, or other form of data compilation."[70] As a general rule, the preference for the original writing serves to enhance the truth because secondary evidence of what a writing contained may be less precise or actually inaccurate or otherwise imperfect when compared to the original.[71] In order for secondary evidence of the contents of a writing to be admissible, generally the party must show that it was not at fault in the destruction or loss of the document, or it may prove that the document is beyond the jurisdiction of the court, and, in such cases where the original writing cannot be produced, secondary evidence of the writing's contents may be admissible. Where secondary evidence can be admitted because of the nonproduction of the original writing, evidence may be oral or contained in a separate writing that helps prove or disprove the fact at issue. In order for the writing to be considered at issue in a case, the substantive contents contained within the writing must affect the probabilities of a fact that can be proven or disproven.

As the rule has commonly, but imperfectly, been stated, the best evidence that is obtainable under the circumstances of the case must be presented to prove any disputed fact. Where proof is to be made of a fact that is recorded in a writing, the best evidence and probably the most accurate rendition of the contents of the writing involve the production of the original document. The label "best evidence" is not exactly correct

---

68 FED. R. EVID. 1002.

69 *But see* Cobb v. Commonwealth, 2013 Va. App. LEXIS 301 (2013), where the Commonwealth of Virginia law applied only to traditional writings and was not applied to photographs and video recordings taken from hard drives.

70 H.R.E. chap. 626, H.R.S., Rule 1001 (Hawai'i 2013).

71 State v. Robinette, 2013 Tenn. Crim. App. LEXIS 850 (2013).

because, although the rule generally prefers that the original of documentary evidence should be introduced, it does not require the production of the original, and other secondary evidence may be offered to prove the contents of the missing original.[72] A Florida reviewing court noted that when the best evidence rule requires the original or a qualified substitute, a court should accept no secondary evidence if the secondary evidence serves merely as a substitute for the original.[73] Contrary to the Florida view, one federal court noted that where digital video from a public surveillance camera had been lost, that DEA agents who had viewed the video prior to its being accidentally "dumped" during a transfer from a server to a hard drive, could testify concerning what data had originally been recorded by the camera.[74]

Drafters of the Federal Rules of Evidence included this note regarding the best evidence rule:

> Traditionally the rule requiring the original centered upon the accumulations of data and expressions affecting legal relations set forth in words and figures. This meant that the rule was one essentially relating to writings. Present day techniques have expanded methods of storing data, yet the essential form which the information ultimately assumes for useable purposes is words and figures. Hence the considerations underlying the Rule dictate its expansion to include computers, photographic systems and other modern developments.[75]

The real purpose of, and reasons for, the best evidence rule were classically stated by Dean Wigmore:[76]

> (1) As between a supposed literal copy and the original, the copy is always liable to errors on the part of the copyist, whether by willfulness or by inadvertence; this contingency wholly disappears when the original is produced. Moreover, the original may contain, and the copy will lack, such features of handwriting, paper, and the like, as may afford the opponent valuable means of learning legitimate objections to the significance of the document. (2) As between oral testimony, based on

---

72 Ostalaza v. People of the Virgin Islands, 58 V. I. 531, 564, 2013 V.I. Supreme LEXIS 27 (2013).

73 McKeehan v. State, 838 So. 2d 1257, 1259, 2003 Fla. App. LEXIS 3367 (2003). *See* case in Part II. *But see* Commonwealth v. Leneski, 66 Mass. App. Ct. 291, 294, 846 N.E.2d 1195, 1198, 2006 Mass. App. LEXIS 525 (2006), in which the court noted that the best evidence rule does not apply in that jurisdiction to photographs, videotapes, or films. In referring to the best evidence rule in Ohio, one court noted that "This rule has been generally abrogated, though, by Evid. R. 1003, which states: '[a] duplicate is admissible to the same extent as an original unless (1) a genuine question is raised as to the authenticity of the original or (2) in the circumstances it would be unfair to admit the duplicate in lieu of the original.'" The current federal version (2011) of this rule reads substantially the same. *See* State v. Dobrovich, 2005 Ohio 1441, 2005 Ohio App. LEXIS 1405 (2005). Virginia takes a different view and one that is similar to that of Massachusetts and does not apply the best evidence rule to anything but a traditional writing; videotapes are not considered writings and are not covered by the best evidence rule. *See* Brown v. Commonwealth, 2009 Va. App. LEXIS 226 (2009).

74 United States v. Ortiz, 2013 U.S. Dist. LEXIS 2939 (E.D. Pa. 2013).

75 These original drafters' comments were included with Rule 1001 of the Federal Rules of Evidence.

76 IV WIGMORE, EVIDENCE § 1179 (3d ed. 1940). *See also* United States v. Holton, 116 F.3d 1536 (D.C. Cir. 1997).

recollection, and the original, the added risk, almost the certainty, exists, of errors of recollection due to the difficulty of carrying in the memory literally the tenor of the document.

The focus of the best evidence rule concerns only the substantive content of a writing and does not regulate or apply to other evidence, especially evidence that exists independently of the writing. Therefore, testimony as to other facts about a writing may be admissible. Thus, in a case involving attempted murder in the state of New York, a security videotape in the custody of police was inexplicably lost and could not be produced for trial. Instead, the trial court allowed testimony from three detectives regarding the contents of the lost videotape, allegedly violating the best evidence rule.[77] The defendant argued that the witnesses should not have been permitted to testify what presumably was on the videotape without the production of the videotape itself. In a federal habeas corpus case, the trial judge rejected the defendant's best evidence rule argument primarily because the individual witnesses were permitted to testify concerning what they actually observed.

"The [best evidence] rule is inapplicable when content is not at issue."[78] When a document actually exists and when witnesses possess the same knowledge that was incorporated into the writing or video, witnesses may testify independently of the introduction of the document or even when the document/writing/video was never introduced in court as long as they do so from personal knowledge. In a proceeding involving the revocation of supervised release, a federal agent observed, in real time, the defendant make a sale of some illegal recreational pharmaceuticals and the officials recorded the transaction on video. At the hearing, a federal officer testified concerning his real-time observation via video camera/monitor of the defendant's activities, but the video recording of the drug transaction was never introduced into court. In rejecting the defendant's best evidence rule argument, the trial judge ruled that the best evidence rule did not apply because the federal agent based his testimony on monitoring a live video feed and not from observing a video recording of the same drug transaction.[79] In this case, the substantive content of the writing/video was never at issue in the revocation proceeding.

On some occasions, the best evidence rule will apply, and the original or a duplicate original and other secondary evidence may be admitted. In one North Carolina case, the police videotaped a defendant's admissions of responsibility in a rape case and introduced an audio copy, made from the videotape and a transcript of the conversation, into evidence. The defendant's contention that this practice constituted plain error under the best evidence rule was dismissed. As the reviewing court noted, "[a]lthough the audio recording was the 'best evidence' of defendant's interview, the

---

77 Blake v. Martuscello, 2013 U.S. Dist. LEXIS 95369 (E.D. N.Y 2013).

78 6 JACK B. WEINSTEIN ET AL., WEINSTEIN'S FEDERAL EVIDENCE § 1002.05[1] (2d ed. 2002).

79 United States v. McKenzie, 505 F. App'x. 843, 2013 U.S. App. LEXIS 1942 (11th Cir. 2013). The court observed that the federal Rules of Evidence do not apply in supervised release revocations, but due process considerations did apply.

admission of the transcript did not prejudice defendant. The transcript only reiterated the evidence presented through the audio recording."[80]

§ 13.7 Secondary Evidence

Rule 1003

ADMISSIBILITY OF DUPLICATES

A duplicate is admissible to the same extent as the original unless a genuine question is raised about the original's authenticity or the circumstances make it unfair to admit the duplicate.[81]

Under the best evidence rule, a duplicate of a writing may be called a duplicate original or, as phrased in Rule 1001, an original. As defined in Rule 1001(4), an original is a "writing or recording itself or any counterpart intended to have the same effect by the person who executed or issued it." The rule defines a duplicate as a "counterpart produced by a mechanical, photographic, chemical, electronic, or other equivalent process or technique that accurately." If the original has been lost or destroyed through inadvertent conduct of the proponent of the evidence, secondary evidence may be admitted where the loss or destruction of the original was not the fault of the proponent and where there is no reason to doubt the accuracy of the secondary evidence or duplicate original.[82] In allowing secondary evidence in a shooting case, a reviewing court approved of the use of recordings made on a cell phone of a playback of a store's security camera that recorded some of the defendant's criminal activities.[83] The detective had personal knowledge of the original video and the duplicate made on her iPhone correctly reproduced the original store security video, although there were some still photographs that were taken from the video. The detective also attached some of the video recordings to an e-mail to her supervisor. The duplicate videos and still photos were authenticated as accurately depicting the original recordings. Under Ohio's version of Rule 1003, a duplicate is as admissible as the original unless a real question is raised concerning the authenticity of the original or if it would be unfair to allow use of the duplicate. The reviewing court concluded that duplicate original videos could be used along with the still frame photographs because the defendant did not sufficiently raise questions concerning their trustworthiness. It appeared that the cell phone

---

80 State v. Fernandez, 2008 N.C. App. LEXIS 1828 (N.C. 2008).

81 *See* FED. R. EVID. 1003.

82 United States v. Codrington, 2008 U.S. Dist. LEXIS 35859 (E.D.N.Y. 2008). Fifteen seconds missing from surveillance tape does not make duplicate original inadmissible.

83 State v. Taylor, 2012 Ohio 5421, 2012 Ohio App. LEXIS 4710 (2012).

recording of the original video was necessary because the security would automatically record over earlier videos on a 36-hour loop.[84] The rationale for Rule 1003 is that when the only concern is with introducing the words or other contents before the court with accuracy and precision, a counterpart serves equally as well as the original if the counterpart or duplicate original is the product of a method that ensures accuracy and authenticity.[85]

Applying this rationale to the California version of Rule 1003, a court permitted the admission of a printout of an e-mail that one witness had sent to another who forwarded the e-mail to a police officer. The printout of the e-mail on the police officer's computer was permitted to be introduced into evidence. The sender of the e-mail indicated from the witness stand that she had no present memory of writing it, but the original recipient testified concerning her receipt of the message and authenticated the source of the e-mail. The reviewing court held that it was sufficiently authenticated by its original recipient admitting to using e-mail to communicate with the other, there was no dispute concerning the terms of the writing, and it had properly been admitted as secondary evidence.[86]

Rule 1004

ADMISSIBILITY OF OTHER EVIDENCE OF CONTENT

An original is not required and other evidence of the content of a writing, recording, or photograph is admissible if:

(a) all the originals are lost or destroyed, and not by the proponent acting in bad faith;

(b) an original cannot be obtained by any available judicial process;

(c) the party against whom the original would be offered had control of the original; was at that time put on notice, by pleadings or otherwise, that the original would be a subject of proof at the trial or hearing; and fails to produce it at the trial or hearing; or

(d) the writing, recording, or photograph is not closely related to a controlling issue.

As a concession to necessity, in situations when the original writing has been lost or destroyed, secondary evidence of its contents may become admissible when absence of the original has not occurred through the culpable fault of the offering party. The party desiring to offer secondary evidence may be required to show that a reasonable search has been made for the lost writing in the place where it was last known to have been, and the offering party should inquire of persons most likely to have custody or

---

84 *Id.*

85 Notes of the Advisory Committee on the Proposed Federal Rules of Evidence.

86 People v. Whicker, 2007 Cal. App. Unpub. LEXIS 5197 (Cal. 2007). Unpublished opinion.

who might have some knowledge of its whereabouts. Rule 1004 of the Federal Rules of Evidence provides that the original is not required and secondary evidence of the contents of a writing (or recording or photograph) is admissible if (1) originals are lost or destroyed (not in bad faith); (2) the original is not obtainable; (3) the original is in the possession of an opponent; or (4) the writing, recording, or photograph is not related to the controlling issue. When an original is not available, there is generally no preference concerning proof by secondary evidence of what the original contained.[87]

In a criminal case where the original writing has been lost, destroyed, or otherwise becomes unavailable, secondary evidence may be admissible under Rule 1004 and state equivalent provisions or under the common law. In a murder case from the Virgin Islands, a police security camera produced a record of the defendant's vehicle passing the police station going to and from the murder scene at the relevant time.[88] Due to technical complications, the original could not be saved and was not available for trial, but one officer had played the video on a police monitor and used a camcorder to make a copy of the screen movie shots of the defendant's vehicle as it passed the police department offices. Another off-duty officer who worked at the business where the homicide occurred identified the vehicle occupied by the defendant as the one involved in the shooting based on his observations at the crime scene and from the viewing the duplicate video. Despite the defendant's best evidence argument to exclude the secondary evidence, the Supreme Court of the Virgin Islands approved the admission of the camcorder's rendition of the original police security tape.[89] In justifying its position, the court noted that there was no evidence of fault on behalf of the police agency, no argument that the secondary video did not accurately depict what it was purported to depict, and no evidence of bad faith by police or the prosecutor. According to the court, once the requirements of Rule 1004 covering secondary evidence have been met, the prosecutor may prove the contents of the writing/video by any kind of secondary evidence.

In some situations, courts require the original. In an unpublished opinion, an Arkansas appellate court ruled that the original surveillance tape from a convenience store should have been introduced in court against a defendant accused of shoplifting. The clerk-witness did not observe the theft directly, but immediately played the surveillance tape that revealed the theft by the defendant. The defendant objected to the clerk-witness testifying to what the videotape recording showed, contending that the clerk-witness had no personal knowledge and that the videotape was the original copy that had to be produced because its contents were at issue in the case. The court of appeals reversed the conviction on the ground that the original writing (the videotape)

---

87 Ostalaza v. People of the Virgin Islands, 58 V. I. 531, 2013 V. I. Supreme LEXIS 27 (2013).

88 *Id.*

89 *Id., Contra*, Brown v. Commonwealth, 2009 Va. App. LEXIS 226 (Va. 2009), where the court noted that the best evidence rule was not to be applied to videotape evidence because Virginia only recognized the concept as having application to traditional written instruments.

must be admitted, rather than secondary evidence, because the original had not been lost or destroyed and the prosecution had not accounted for its absence.[90]

The state of Nevada, as well as many other states, has codified the common law best evidence rule.[91] Nevada's statute is substantially the same as Rule 1004 of the Federal Rules of Evidence. In *Stephans v. State*, the Supreme Court of Nevada reversed a defendant's grand larceny conviction for lifting six bottles of cologne from Abercrombie & Fitch because of a failure of proof concerning the value of the stolen merchandise.[92] A store loss prevention officer testified concerning his remembrance of the price tags on each bottle, but the original price tags were never introduced. The prosecution had to prove that the value exceeded two hundred fifty dollars in order to make the case into grand larceny. The Supreme Court of Nevada reversed the grand larceny convictions because there was no excuse for not producing the original price tags and the witness had no knowledge concerning the value except what he had once read on the price tag.

While all states allow the admission of secondary evidence, the proponent of the evidence must lay a foundation that explains why the original evidence disappeared and support the admission of secondary evidence. The party must satisfy the judge that the original evidence has been lost, destroyed, or is otherwise unavailable through no fault of the moving party and that one of the reasons contained in Rule 1004 applies. In a Texas case,[93] the police or the judiciary lost the last page of an affidavit for a search warrant at some point after the warrant had been served. An unsworn but true copy of the last page of the affidavit was offered as secondary evidence of the terms of the original writing. The secondary evidence did not have the magistrate's signature or the affiant officer's signature but was admitted into evidence. The appellate court approved the admission of secondary evidence of the affidavit because there was no proof of bad faith as the reason for the loss or destruction of the original writing and the reviewing court did not address the issue of prosecutorial or police negligence in mishandling the affidavit page.

When the original writing cannot be located and appropriate justifications have been proffered, proper secondary evidence may be admissible. A common misconception concerns the type of secondary evidence that should be admitted in place of the original. Although some support for the next best evidence may be found in some cases, generally any type of secondary evidence may be admitted as long as it meets the authentication and relevancy tests.

Modern developments with the use of desktop, laptop, and tablet computers, cloud storage, and the use of network server computers have created additional challenges concerning what really constitutes the original, the duplicate original, and what serves

---

90 Bradley v. State, 2003 Ark. App. LEXIS 756 (2003). *See also* People v. Jimenez, 796 N.Y.S.2d 232, 2005 N.Y. Misc. LEXIS 1114 (2005).

91 NEV. REV. STAT. ANN. § 52.255 (2013).

92 Stephans v. State, 262 P.3d 727, 733, 2011 Nev. LEXIS 80 (2011).

93 McCormick v. State, 2006 Tex. App. LEXIS 1619 (2006).

as secondary evidence. Printouts or computer screen captures are the best evidence because of the impossibility in practice of reading the original, which is a piece of magnetic disc, a compact disc, solid-state drive, jump drive, or a digital video or audio recording.[94] In a Georgia case involving attempted child molestation, a detective conversed with the defendant in an Internet chat room, while posing as a 15-year-old girl who might be available.[95] The detective copied each chat that she conducted with the defendant into a word-processing program by cutting and pasting with her mouse, but she did not change any of the text material that she received. Each of the printouts from the word-processing program were placed in the file being kept for the investigation. The detective did not print out text material that originally showed up on her computer screen as they were conversing over the Internet, but she could have. The transcripts of the conversations introduced at trial were photocopies of the ones originally placed in the investigation file and were allowed to be introduced at trial despite the defendant's objection under the best evidence rule. According to the reviewing court, the Georgia version of the best evidence rule does not prohibit the introduction of photocopies so long as there is satisfactory accounting of the originals. In this case, the originals were known to exist because they had been placed in the case file, and the court noted that there was no evidence that the trial court abused its discretion in allowing accurate duplicate secondary evidence into court under the circumstances. In an Indiana case involving a thumb drive, a detective downloaded surveillance footage taken during a robbery at a gasoline station onto his thumb drive and made copies of the surveillance video by taking a video of the surveillance footage directly from the gas station computer monitor screen. He sent both videos to his office e-mail account but was unable to burn them onto a CD format disc due to technical difficulties. The detective received a promotion prior to the trial and, in cleaning out his computer, accidentally deleted the video footage from the gas station. The trial court permitted him to testify concerning what he had seen on the videos as secondary evidence over a best evidence rule objection. Because there was accountability for why the original was not available, whether on a thumb drive or the cell phone video, the reviewing court held that secondary evidence offered orally by the detective was permissible under the circumstances.

The rules relating to best and secondary evidence generally apply to recordings and photographs as well as documents. For example, in a case originating in a domestic dispute, police were allowed to read the transcript of an audiotape containing details of the dispute that the complaining witness had given to police officers. The officer used a duplicate of the original recording and read the transcript of that recording to the jury over the objection of the defendant based on the best evidence rule. The prosecution presented no evidence as to when, where, how, or by whom the original audiotape was made. According to the reviewing court, the trial court abused its discretion when they admitted the audiotape and the transcript because a proponent of secondary

---

94 Fed. R. Evid. 1004 and 1001(d).

95 Castaneira v. State, 321 Ga. App. 418, 427, 426, 2013 Ga. App. LEXIS 280 (2013).

evidence must first authenticate the original writing and establish that the proffered evidence is secondary evidence of the original.[96]

The proven fact that a person recorded a conversation does not automatically implicate the best evidence rule or serve to exclude oral testimony concerning the issue. In a North Carolina case, police videotaped the defendant's confession and had a transcript prepared. At the trial, an audiotape of the confession and a printed transcript were introduced over the defendant's objection. According to the reviewing court, "the admission of the transcript did not prejudice defendant. The transcript only reiterated the evidence presented through the audio recording."[97] As would be required in all such cases, the proponent offering the transcript would have to lay a foundation demonstrating the accuracy of the transcript.

When a fact may be subject to proof in more than one manner, the proponent may choose the method that best suits the party. In the course of introducing evidence sufficient to demonstrate that a defendant had committed a robbery, the prosecutor had a police officer introduce photographs of the actual currency seized from the defendant. Over an objection that the money was a writing and the originals should have been introduced, the defendant contended that the admission of the money violated the best evidence rule and secondary evidence of the money should not have been permitted. In approving the trial court's admission of the photographs, the appellate court noted that a witness can testify concerning tangible objects (such as money) without introducing the actual objects and without violating the best evidence rule.[98] Another way of considering a case like this is to note that, other than the fact that the writing on the currency denoted its value, it was the fact that money was taken in a robbery, and not precisely how much, that was important.

§ 13.8 Summaries

Rule 1006

SUMMARIES TO PROVE CONTENT

The proponent may use a summary, chart, or calculation to prove the content of voluminous writings, recordings, or photographs that cannot be conveniently examined in court. The proponent must make the originals or duplicates available for examination or copying, or both, by other parties at a reasonable time and place. And the court may order the proponent to produce them in court.[99]

---

96 People v. Dicharry, 2007 Cal. App. Unpub. LEXIS 5538 (Cal. 2007).
97 State v. Fernandez, 2008 N.C. LEXIS 1828 (N.C. 2008).
98 Wingfield v. State, 2005 Ark. 574 (2006).
99 FED. R. EVID. 1006.

The evidentiary rule allowing the use of summaries is consistent with the common law and permits the use of summaries of evidence when that method may be the only practical way to present the evidence to a court.[100] The admissibility of summary evidence is a matter that rests within the sound discretion of the trial court, but standards have evolved to guide courts in exercising their discretion. As a general rule, a proper foundation must be offered with regard to the admissibility of the originals. Under a prior version of this rule, the Sixth Circuit held that there are five requirements for admission of a summary under Rule 1006.

> [T]he Rule imposes five requirements for the admission of summary evidence: (1) the underlying documents are so voluminous that they cannot be conveniently examined in court; (2) the proponent of the summary must have made the documents available for examination or copying at a reasonable time and place; (3) the underlying documents must be admissible in evidence; (4) the summary must be accurate and nonprejudicial; and (5) the summary must be properly introduced through the testimony of a witness who supervised its preparation.[101]

Failure to meet these or substantially similar requirements in other jurisdictions may result in summary evidence being refused by the trial judge or a reversal on appeal.

According to one New Jersey court, there are three kinds of evidentiary summaries that are often admitted in court. The first can be called a primary evidence summary and is used to condense large amounts of material that could not otherwise be grasped by a court or jury. The second type of summary involves a pedagogical device summary, which serves as a demonstrative aid to present or clarify drawings, charts, calculations, or models and can simplify evidence already admitted in a case. The final type can be called a secondary evidence summary because it is a combination of the first two types of summaries. This summary assists the jury in accurately understanding complex evidence that they would otherwise have difficulty placing in context or understanding its importance.[102]

The purpose of using a summary or a chart is to assist the jury in understanding the evidence without being bombarded with so much data that making logical sense of it might strain the mind. The summary might be what a college student might consult in learning to understand a Shakespeare play. Similarly, political science and scientific journals often present an abstract of each article that offers a window to the reader concerning what the article contains. The purpose of a summary or a chart under Rule 1006 is to assist in educating the jury and allowing it to comprehend and place in context a large body of evidence that has been presented. A summary that has been prepared for a jury must be fair and accurate and be presented in a correct and nonmisleading

---

[100] Washington v. Dudley, 2003 Wash. App. LEXIS 1551 (2003).

[101] United States v. Moon, 513 F.3d 527, 2008 U.S. App. LEXIS 879 (6th Cir. 2008) (quoting United States v. Jamieson, 427 F.3d 394, 409, 2005 U.S. App. LEXIS 23337 (6th Cir. 2005)).

[102] *See* Heinzerling v. Goldfarb, 359 N.J. Super. 1, 8, 818 A.2d 345, 349, 2002 N.J. Super. LEXIS 531 (2002).

manner.[103] In the interests of fairness, the summaries should be supplied to the opposing party at a reasonable time prior to courtroom use so that the party has time to check to see if the summaries or charts are accurate.[104]

The preparation and submission to the jury of summaries prepared by an expert is almost indispensable to the understanding of a long and complicated set of facts. When summaries are used and physically given to the jury, the court must ascertain with certainty that they are based upon, and fairly represent, competent evidence already before the jury. Such summaries, if given to the jury, must be accompanied by appropriate instructions concerning their nature and use. The jury should be advised that the summaries do not, in and of themselves, constitute evidence in the case, but only purport to summarize the documentary and detailed evidence already admitted; that the jury should examine the basis upon which the summaries rest and be satisfied that they accurately reflect other evidence in the case; and that, if the jury is not so satisfied, the summaries should be disregarded. In addition, broad cross-examination should be permitted upon the summaries to afford a thorough test of their accuracy.

Summaries may be used to assist the jury in understanding large amounts of information or to place large amounts of data in perspective, but the summaries are generally not considered evidence unless specifically admitted.[105] In a federal prosecution involving a bank robbery and three other attempts, the government wanted to use a summary presentation of the defendants' cell phone traffic from Sprint® and AT&T because of the burden an impracticality of having the jury study and construe the voluminous cell phone records in the case.[106] The government was planning to use a PowerPoint presentation, which it submitted to the trial court. The PowerPoint presentation of the prosecution appeared to present the AT&T and Sprint cellular phone records and geolocation plotting of defendant's phone calls made to and from three separate telephones. The prosecution argued that the evidence was also self-authenticating as a business record under Rule 902(11). Among other things, the prosecution argued that the databases from which some of the information was derived were too complex and too voluminous to present in court. The defendant objected, arguing that rather than summarizing the electronic records, the PowerPoint slides included the defendants' addresses, the location of the banks at issue, distances, routes, and elapsed times, which were not included in the cell phone records and that the defendant did not even own some of the cell phones. The court felt that the admissibility of the evidence turned upon two factors: (1) whether the evidence was too voluminous and (2) whether review of all the evidence by the jury would be inconvenient. The trial court officially rejected the government's offer of a summary presentation because the PowerPoint slides went far beyond merely summarizing electronic telephone records; the PowerPoint slides essentially summarized and argued the government's case; and the PowerPoint

---

103 United States v. Wainwright, 351 F.3d 816, 2003 U.S. App. LEXIS 24731 (8th Cir. 2003).

104 United States v. Dukes, 242 Fed. Appx. 37, 2007 U.S. App. LEXIS 15961 (4th Cir. 2007).

105 United States v. Green, 428 F.3d 1131, 1134, 2005 U.S. App. LEXIS 24583 (8th Cir. 2005).

106 United States v. Saunders, 2013 U.S. Dist. LEXIS 83297 (E.D. LA. 2013).

presentation went beyond the underlying data. In this case, the prosecution was attempting to put some evidence before the jury in a manner that was unfair to the defendant's case, and the trial judge rejected the proposal.

Courts "cannot rationally expect an average jury to compile summaries and to create sophisticated flow charts to reveal patterns that provide important inferences about the defendant's guilt."[107] It does not have to be demonstrably impossible to examine all the underlying records before a summary chart may be utilized under Rule 1006, but only that in-court examinations would be an inconvenience.

In interpreting Rule 1006, the Fifth Circuit Court of Appeals approved the use of summary charts in a case involving mail fraud in conjunction with perjury in receiving workers' compensation. The defendant was collecting disability payments for a back injury while he worked as a pilot for several charter airline companies. The government presented summaries in the form of a timeline chart comparing the dates that the defendant worked and payments received to the dates of fraudulent forms filed with the government to continue his disability benefits. The defendant claimed that the trial court erred when it admitted the timeline summary chart along with a government witness who explained the summary chart. The reviewing court noted that summary evidence is admissible based on the court's discretion, and past practice permits a summary witness in a limited way to explain voluminous records. The court rejected the defendant's complaints because pursuant to the defendant's trial objection, the chart was never admitted into evidence and the court did not allow the summary chart to go to the jury room. In affirming the conviction, the Court of Appeals found no error in the use of the summary under Rule 1006.[108] However, when summary charts are erroneously admitted in a manner that substantially affects the legal rights of a defendant, such admission may result in a reversal of a trial jury decision and the awarding of a new trial.[109]

Obviously, the admission of summary exhibits must be conditioned on the requirement that the items of evidence upon which they rest must be admissible. For example, in a federal case[110] involving conspiracy to import and harbor illegal aliens, the defendant contended that the summary spreadsheet exhibit offered by the prosecution, which tracked the status of illegal aliens working on the farms of defendant's clients, was unnecessary because the data were not voluminous, his counsel had not been permitted a chance to examine the underlying documents, and the items of evidence on which the summary spreadsheet was based involved inadmissible hearsay. The reviewing court rejected the defendant's arguments and noted, "[t]he spreadsheet was introduced to establish the alienage of the workers. As the government demonstrates, however, even without the admission of the summary exhibit, the evidence of the alienage of the

107 United States v. Buck, 324 F.3d 786, 791, 2003 U.S. App. LEXIS 4820 (5th Cir. 2003).

108 United States v. Harms, 442 F.3d 367, 375, 2006 U.S. App. LEXIS 6622 (5th Cir. 2006).

109 United States v. Hart, 295 F.3d 451, 2002 U.S. App. LEXIS 11246 (2002).

110 United States v. Matousek, 131 F. App'x. 641, 2005 U.S. App. LEXIS 9063 (10th Cir. 2005).

persons involved was uncontested."[111] Even if there was any error, which the court did not find, any error was harmless.

Even when the underlying documents have not been introduced under Rule 1006, the charts or summaries are admissible. In a federal embezzlement case involving employees of a labor union, the reviewing court rejected the defendant's contention that charts were not permissible when the opposing party had not actually introduced them, but had offered certifications for the underlying documents. As the court noted, "the point of Rule 1006 is to avoid introducing all the documents."[112]

While Rule 1006 allows the use of summaries when all the conditions are met, a court should exclude summaries when the proponent of the summary fails to meet the requirements or where hearsay evidence has been included as one of the bases of the summary. In a prosecution for selling cocaine base, the trial court permitted the federal government to introduce summaries of the numbers of defendant's cell phone calls, and to whom they were made, when the evidence that supported the summaries was never authenticated. In addition, some of the evidence was hearsay; the government failed to make the cell phone records available for examination and copying; and the government failed to give written notice to the defendant that it was going to use cell phone records in a summary. The reviewing court noted that the summaries should not have been admitted because the summaries did not meet the requirements for admission. However, in affirming the conviction, the court viewed the other evidence as sufficiently strong that the admission of the summaries constituted harmless error.[113]

A federal district court, following the directive of the Sixth Circuit, suggested that when summaries or charts are used under Rule 1006, they should be accompanied by a limiting instruction that informs the jury of the purpose of the summary or the chart and that the summary or chart does not constitute evidence.[114] In a different case, the appellate court grudgingly allowed a verdict to stand where the prosecution had permitted one of its own witnesses to summarize trial testimony just before the government rested its case. The Court of Appeals noted that under Rule 1006 there is no provision that addresses summary witnesses who summarize trial testimony, but some courts have permitted summary testimony in a limited capacity. The court took the position that while the use of summary evidence often serves an important purpose, one of the purposes of Rule 1006 is to not permit the prosecution to repeat its entire case-in-chief shortly before jury deliberations and prior to final arguments.[115]

---

111 *Id.*

112 United States v. Hemphill, 514 F.3d 1350, 2008 U.S. App. LEXIS 2786 (D.C. Cir. 2008).

113 United States v. Laguerre, 119 F. app'x. 458, 2005 U.S. App. LEXIS 213 (4th Cir. 2005).

114 O'Brien v. Ed Donnelly Enterprises, 2007 U.S. Dist. LEXIS 92973 (S.D. Ohio 2007).

115 United States v. Fullwood, 342 F.3d 409, 2003 U.S. App. LEXIS 16309 (5th Cir. 2003), cert. *denied*, 540 U.S. 1111 (2004).

§ 13.9 Learned Treatises

Medical reference books or treatises covering engineering or science or other specialized professional fields like history or art, even though properly identified and authenticated and shown to be recognized as standard authorities on the subjects in the learned areas to which they relate, are not generally admissible in evidence due to their hearsay status. According to the common law rule, proponents of evidence are not permitted to use learned treatise passages as substantive proof of their contents.[116] However, the federal courts do not use the hearsay rule to exclude learned treatises from use as substantive evidence so long as an expert witness relied upon the treatise, where the treatise has been established as a reliable authority by admission by that witness or another witness or by the use of judicial notice.[117] Rule 803 permits a statement in a learned treatise that has been identified as authoritative to be read into evidence, but the statement cannot be received as an exhibit in court.[118] Prior to using a learned treatise in court, generally an expert must adopt a published work as being authoritative in the field. In a District of Columbia prosecution involving burglary, part of the government's proof involved the presence of the defendant's fingerprints at the crime scene that was presented by a fingerprint expert. The defendant wished to cross-examine the government's fingerprint expert by using an alleged learned treatise that the government expert would not agree to or recognize as a learned treatise. The defendant did not call his own fingerprint expert who could have adopted the work as a learned treatise. Because no expert testified in court that the proposed work involving fingerprint analysis qualified as a learned treatise, it was never authenticated as a learned treatise. Therefore, it could not be used in cross-examining the government's expert, and its passages could not be used for any other purpose at trial. The reviewing court upheld the trial court exclusion of the "learned treatise." Many state courts follow a version of the federal rules, as does Ohio, where learned treatises can be used as substantive evidence rather than being restricted to impeachment and rehabilitation evidence.[119] Some state courts and rules often treat learned treatises different from federal courts. For example, according to Pennsylvania case law, "learned writings which are offered to prove the truth of the matters therein are hearsay and may not properly be admitted into evidence for consideration by the jury."[120]

A few states have adopted the rule that a published treatise, periodical, or pamphlet on a subject of history, science, or art may be admitted in evidence in some limited types of cases to prove the truth of a matter stated therein if the judge takes judicial notice or an expert witness in the subject area testifies that the writer of the treatise,

---

116 Aldridge v. Edmunds, 561 Pa. 323, 331, 750 A.2d 292, 296, 2000 Pa. LEXIS 1059 (2000).

117 *See* FED. R. EVID. 803(18).

118 *Id.*

119 Moretz v Muskkassa, 2012 Ohio App. LEXIS 1034 (2012). *See also*, Filippelli v. St. Mary's Hospital, 141 Conn. App., 594, 610, 2013 Conn. App. LEXIS 163 (2013).

120 Calandra v. St. Agnes Med. Ctr., 2005 Phila. Ct. Com. Pl. LEXIS 254 (2005).

periodical, or pamphlet is a recognized authority on the subject. Under a Massachusetts statute, as a prerequisite to the admission of a treatise as evidence in contract, tort, or medical malpractice actions, the proponent of such evidence must demonstrate for the trial judge that the offered treatise statements are relevant and that the "writer of such statements is recognized in his profession or calling as an expert on the subject."[121]

§ 13.10 Summary

In addition to oral testimony, documentary evidence may be used in court to assist the jury and judge in determining the ultimate facts. Documentary evidence includes all kinds of documents, records, and writings. The concept of a writing proves to be an expansive idea and many jurisdictions include computer data wherever and however stored, movies, videotapes, digital video disc and compact disc storage, as well as almost anything that contains data under the definition of a writing. To be admissible, documentary evidence must meet the same requirements of relevancy, competency, and materiality, as does oral evidence, and must meet other requirements specifically related to writings. As a prerequisite to admission, documentary evidence must also be authenticated by one of several processes. As a rule, competent evidence must be introduced to show that the writing is what it purports to be.

In the interests of judicial economy, courts have recognized practical and simplified methods of authentication that are to be used in specific instances. Domestic public documents under seal are often deemed to be self-authenticating, while documents that have been certified as accurate copies of documents on file by the official custodian are similarly considered to be self-authenticating. Official publications by government agencies, including statutes and official regulations, may be self-authenticating because the concept of authentication is only a threshold consideration that the document is what it purports to be. Given that authentication is a rather low standard, the opposing party may introduce evidence that disputes the judge's initial determination that a document has been authenticated and the ultimate decision concerning whether the document has evidentiary value belongs to the finder of fact.

Although these are not necessarily exclusive, there are four general methods of authenticating a document: (1) proof of signing; (2) proof of signature; (3) comparison of signatures, usually by an expert; and (4) circumstantial evidence. The degree of proof varies with the type of document. As a general rule, public records and documents are admissible into evidence as exceptions to the hearsay rule without the same degree of authenticity as is required for private writings. This is allowed because of the extraordinary degree of confidence reposed in documents drafted by authorized and accredited officers or required by law to be filed publicly. This same degree of confidence is not placed in private writings, and such writings must be proven by slightly more exacting standards to be genuine before they are admissible as evidence.

---

121 ALM GL ch. 233 § 79C (Mass. 2013).

To prevent the admission of forgeries, fabrications, and false writings, the best evidence rule accepts the principle of law that there is a decided preference for the original document where the contents of the writing are at issue. Although the rule permits several types of secondary evidence to be considered acceptable to the courts, many jurisdictions recognize several significant exceptions to producing the original. When the original cannot be obtained through any judicial process or has been lost or destroyed through no fault of the proponent, courts will frequently accept secondary evidence. The historical basis for this rule assumes that a copy is more likely to have errors and that a typewritten or computer-generated copy will lack such features as handwriting and original paper impressions and could be more easily manipulated. Without individual characteristics of the original, an opponent has few means to detect alteration or fraud on secondary evidence. Currently, most modern writings are produced in ways that allow many duplicate originals that have not been produced by the human hand and are indistinguishable from each other. For this reason, many of the rationales for requiring the original are no longer valid, and exceptions have been included in statutes and codes, consistent with the interests of justice.

CHAPTER THIRTEEN: QUESTIONS AND REVIEW EXERCISES

1. All documents that are introduced as evidence in court must be authenticated. Explain the concept of authentication. How must authenticated documents meet the other rules concerning admission of evidence?
2. Items of evidence classified as documents or documentary evidence include many more types of evidence than a traditionally typed document. What are some of the other examples of documentary evidence that do not meet the traditional definition of a document?
3. Some documents are said to be self-authenticating. Within this category are regularly published newspapers and periodicals. What are three other examples of documents that tend to self-authenticate?
4. In authenticating a writing or a document, one of four methods are traditionally followed in offering sufficient proof of authenticity. What are these four methods? Give an example of each one.
5. With respect to the authenticating of public records and documents, authentication is not ensured merely because the document may be referred to as a public record or document. Where a birth certificate or a death certificate needs to be authenticated, what would the proponent of the evidence have to prove?
6. Private writings must also be authenticated as one step toward admission in a criminal trial. Assume that a defendant has allegedly violated a no-contact order from a prior stalking

case by writing the victim a letter. Offer at least one method by which this letter could be authenticated as having been written by the defendant.

7. The "reply letter doctrine" can be used to authenticate private letters, e-mails, and text messages. Explain what is meant by the reply letter doctrine. How could its theory be used to authenticate an e-mail or text message?
8. The best evidence rule is a codification of an evidence concept that dates to the common law but does not actually require what its name might imply. What is the legal rationale that supports the best evidence rule? Explain how the best evidence rule operates. Under what circumstances may a court permit secondary evidence to be admitted? Construct an example where secondary evidence admission would be appropriate.
9. Under Federal Rule of Evidence 1006, summaries of voluminous writings, recordings, or photographs that cannot conveniently be examined in court may be presented in the form of a chart, summary, or calculation. What kind of a foundation should the proponent of a summary of data offer to the court in order to have the summary admitted into evidence?
10. In most instances, a learned treatise, such as a well-recognized medical book or other authoritative scientific work, is considered hearsay evidence and therefore not admissible as substantive evidence. Such a work could be used for impeachment purposes. The federal courts have taken a different position and may admit this type of evidence as substantive evidence. What would the foundation for admission of a learned treatise include?

Real Evidence

14

Stains of blood, found upon the person or clothing of the party accused, have always been recognized among the ordinary indicia of homicide. The practice of identifying them by circumstantial evidence and by the inspection of witnesses and jurors has the sanction of immemorial usage in all criminal tribunals. . . . the degree of force to which it is entitled may depend upon a variety of circumstances to be considered and weighed by the jury in each particular case; but its competency is too well settled to be questioned in a court of law.

People v. Fernandez, 35 N.Y. 49 (1866)

Chapter Contents

KEY TERMS AND CONCEPTS

Admissibility of Evidence
Authentication of Audio Recordings
Authentication of Digital Video Recordings
Authentication of Photographs
Authentication of Weapons
Brady Material
Chain of Custody
Gruesome Photographs
Real Evidence
Weight of Evidence

§ 14.1 Introduction

Real evidence is evidence that is addressed directly to the senses such as by sight, hearing, or taste, and it is without the intervention of witnesses other than to authenticate and explain the significance of the evidence. This type of evidence has a physical and tangible existence as compared to oral testimony alone. Real evidence has often been referred to as "demonstrative" or "physical" evidence. Some authorities distinguish between demonstrative and real evidence by defining real evidence as that which involves the introduction of an object that had a direct part in the incident, such as the exhibition of injured parts of the body or an actual weapon or a quantity of drugs involved in a crime. On the other hand, demonstrative evidence involves the production in court of such things as models made for the trial, maps, photographs taken for use in litigation, X-rays, films, and weapons that are used only for demonstrative purposes and were not actually used in the crime. The term "demonstrative real evidence" generally refers to a physical object that had no historical connection to the crime but will be used to show how a similar item was actually used in the crime or how a similar object reacted to events or forces that occurred during the crime.[1] Demonstrative evidence possesses no probative value in itself but serves as a visual aid to the finder of fact in understanding the testimony of witnesses.[2] When demonstrative evidence is admitted, the decision is based on judicial discretion and, like the admission of all evidence, is reviewable under an abuse of discretion standard.[3] For example, in a murder prosecution in which a man had been killed while in his girlfriend's bed, the trial court permitted the government to bring a mannequin head to help the jury understand the testimony of the medical examiner. To further the jury understanding, the court permitted a

1 Torres v. Texas, 2003 Tex. App. LEXIS 6580 (2003).
2 See People v. Flores, 2010 Ill. App. LEXIS 1386 (2010).
3 Hartsock v. State, 322 S.W.3d 775, 778, 2010 Tex. App. LEXIS 6853 (2010).

wooden dowel to be inserted in the mannequin's head to demonstrate the trajectory of the bullet. The medical examiner authenticated the head and dowel representing the trajectory as accurately depicting the original crime scene. The Supreme Court of Georgia approved of using this demonstrative real evidence because the mannequin head served to illustrate the medical examiner's testimony.[4] In this and the following chapter, real evidence includes tangible evidence that has a physical connection to the crime and evidence that is also tangible, but which has no historical connection to the case and is used for demonstration purposes only.

In admitting real evidence, courts must carefully weigh the probative value against the risk of unfair prejudice because real evidence is generally considered an especially persuasive class of evidence. In a Texas case, the court permitted the prosecution to dress a dummy in the bloody clothes of the deceased over the objection of the defendant that the danger of unfair prejudice outweighed any probative value of the dummy. Demonstrative real evidence must accurately depict what it purports to depict, and in this case the dummy appeared much smaller than the size of the deceased. Even though the defense unsuccessfully contended that having the dummy in court in the defendant's bloody clothes would prejudice the defendant, it failed to mention the size discrepancy. The reviewing court upheld the original trial court ruling.[5]

Court decisions have emphasized the necessity of developing more sophisticated methods of obtaining and utilizing real evidence in criminal cases. Because of the constitutional limitations placed upon the use of confessions, more emphasis is placed upon the use of real evidence. For example, in the case of *Schmerber v. California,*[6] the United States Supreme Court held that the Fifth Amendment self-incrimination protection applied to evidence of a testimonial or communicative nature, but not to real evidence. In that case, the Court stated:

> On the other hand, both federal and state courts have usually held that it [the Fifth Amendment] offers no protection against compulsion to submit to fingerprinting, photographing, or measurements, to write or speak for identification, to appear in court, to stand, to assume a stance, to walk, or to make a particular gesture.

The Court also noted that:

> Compulsion which makes a suspect or accused the source of real or physical evidence does not violate it [the Fifth Amendment].

In rendering the *Schmerber* decision, the Court upheld the collection of real evidence derived from the suspect personally and indicated that the evidence could be used

---

4 Moss v. Georgia, 274 Ga. 740, 559 S.E.2d 433, 2002 Ga. LEXIS 48 (2002).

5 Runnels v. State, 193 S.W.3d 105, 107, 2006 Tex. App. LEXIS 17 (2006). The trial court might not have admitted the dummy if the defense had objected to its use because it did not properly depict the size of the victim.

6 384 U.S. 757, 86 S. Ct. 1826, 16 L. Ed. 2d 908 (1966). *See* case in Part II. *See* Chapter 16 for discussion of constitutional safeguards that regulate the admissibility of evidence.

against that same defendant. Similarly, deoxyribonucleic acid (DNA) samples can be compelled and forcefully taken without violating a person's Fifth Amendment privilege against self-incrimination because the evidence is neither testimonial nor communicative in nature.[7]

The sections that follow discuss the tests for general admissibility relating to real evidence and offer some examples of the types of real evidence of particular concern to criminal justice personnel. In Chapter 15, emphasis is placed on the use of results of experiments and tests conducted in and out of court.

§ 14.2 Admissibility Requirements

To be admissible, real evidence must generally meet the same requirements of relevancy, competency, and materiality as documentary evidence and oral testimony. In addition, a foundation proving authenticity must be laid before real evidence is admissible. Generally, the foundation is offered by an attorney calling a witness, showing the real evidence to the witness, and asking questions relating to the real evidence to be introduced. To provide a proper foundation, the real evidence offered must be identified as being the same evidence or object involved in the alleged crime, and it must be shown that the object has not undergone any important or material change.[8] In many instances, criminal justice personnel are most familiar with the evidence and can most correctly connect the evidence with the crime and the accused by using several authentication techniques. Occasionally, a defendant may be willing to stipulate facts that support admission of adverse evidence.[9] Finally, the prosecuting attorney may call upon the victim to take the stand to establish the identity and relevance of the real evidence.

As a general rule for real evidence to be admissible at trial, the proponent must show that it is sufficiently connected with case through the defendant, the victim, or the crime.[10] The state must demonstrate a reasonable probability that tampering, substitution, or alteration of the evidence did not occur. Trial courts may assume and appellate courts will concur, "absent a showing of bad faith or ill will, that the officials charged with custody of the evidence properly discharged their duties and did not tamper with the evidence."[11]

The party offering an item in evidence bears the burden of presenting evidence sufficient to support a finding that the matter in question is what the party claims, and in satisfying its burden, the party may authenticate the item either by having a witness visually identify the item as the one that was involved in the crime or by

---

7 Smith v. State, 2009 WY 2, 2009 Wyo. LEXIS 2 (2009).

8 State v. McClure, 2006 N.C. App. LEXIS 47 (2006).

9 *See* People v. Garth, 353 Ill. App. 3d 108, 817 N.E.2d 1085, 2004 Ill. App. LEXIS 1192 (2004).

10 People v. Hogan, 114 P.3d 42, 51, 2004 Colo. App. LEXIS 2001 (Colo. 2004), *reh'g denied*, 2005 Colo. Lexis 597 (2005).

11 State v. Goff, 191 S.W.3d 113, 116, 2006 Mo. App. LEXIS 712 (2006).

establishing a chain of custody that indirectly establishes the identity and integrity of the evidence by tracing its continuous location. During a trial, a decision concerning whether an item of evidence has been sufficiently authenticated for admission rests with the trial judge, whose decision is subject to review on the basis of an abuse of discretion standard.[12] Once the proponent of the real evidence has laid a minimally sufficient foundation, "a lack of positive identification or a defect in the chain of custody goes to the weight of the evidence rather than the admissibility."[13]

Four general rules regarding the admissibility of real evidence are often applied. They are: (1) establishment of a chain or continuity of custody; (2) necessity; (3) relationship to crime; and (4) proper identification.

A. *Establishment of a Chain or Continuity of Custody*

Chain of custody In evidence, one who offers real evidence (such as narcotics in the trial of a drug case) must account for the custody of the evidence from the moment when law enforcement officials originally gained custody until the moment when it is offered in evidence.

In establishing a **chain of custody**, the proponent of the real evidence must demonstrate that item is the actual object that was associated with the crime and that the evidence has not been subject to tampering or other change. In a perfect world, the proponent of the evidence would have to prove where the evidence has been from the time it gained a connection to the case until the moment it was offered in evidence, but a perfect chain is not required. Proving the chain of custody is one way to demonstrate the authenticity of real evidence.[14] Chain of custody applies to evidence that a defendant would want to introduce, but normally the issue is one for the prosecution because it will be introducing most of the real evidence. The necessity of proving chain of custody exists because many people may handle the evidence from the time of its original collection. Proof of where the evidence has been minimizes the chances that someone tampered with the evidence, substituted evidence, lost and replaced it, or otherwise allowed it to be altered in some manner.[15] A failure to make a chain-of-custody objection at the time the evidence is introduced generally waives any chain-of-custody argument.[16] Proving the chain of custody ensures authenticity of the evidence, and without authentication, the evidence would be inadmissible unless authenticated by a different process. While it is preferable to introduce evidence to show that the chain

---

[12] People v. Lee, 2005 Mich. App. LEXIS 3186 (2005).

[13] State v. Housley, 922 So.2d 659, 665, 2006 La. App. LEXIS 116 (2006).

[14] Oritz v. State, 2013 U.S. Dist., LEXIS 48270 (E.D. Ny. 2013). *See also,* State v. Cowans, 336 Ill. App. 3d 173, 782 N.E.2d 779, 2002 Ill. App. LEXIS 1170 (2002), *appeal denied,* 2003 Ill. LEXIS 649 (2003). *See* case in Part II.

[15] Tennessee v. Woods, 2001 Tenn. Crim. App. LEXIS 797 (2001).

[16] Miller v. State, 2004 Tex. App. LEXIS 11547 (2004).

of custody was not broken at any time, in offering proof of the chain of custody, the prosecution need not eliminate each and every possibility of tampering with the evidence. As one court noted, "A lack of positive identification of demonstrative evidence or its chain of custody goes to the weight of the evidence, not to its admissibility, and the connection of that evidence to the case is a factual matter to be determined by the trier-of-fact."[17] In proving sufficient chain of custody, the prosecutor is not "required to foreclose every possibility of tampering; it need only show reasonable assurance of the identity of the evidence."[18]

In a Tennessee rape prosecution, the defendant contended that pantyhose from the victim did not meet the chain-of-custody requirements and should have been excluded from evidence. Testimony demonstrated that the hospital personnel routinely cleaned each emergency room prior to the admission of the next patient so that any clothing placed the underwear bag and transferred into the rape kit would be from the patient being examined.[19] The rape kit was examined by a state lab, which found DNA from both the victim and the defendant. The reviewing court concluded that the pantyhose introduced in court met the requirements of real evidence authentication, and that the concept of chain of custody assumes that multiple individuals will handle evidence from the time it is collected until the time it is introduced in a criminal trial.

In a driving under the influence case, the defendant appealed, alleging that the chain of custody for his blood draw was deficient and that the results of the scientific testing used to determine his blood alcohol content should have been excluded from his trial.[20] The defendant contended that there was one break in the chain of custody and that defect should prevent authentication of the real evidence, the blood sample. While there is language in some court cases that there must be established a completely unbroken chain of custody to show that there has been no tampering loss or substitution concerning the evidence, the prosecution is not required to establish facts beyond all doubt concerning the chain of custody. In this case, a police officer observed a hospital laboratory technician draw a sample of the defendant's blood, and that officer took the blood sample from the laboratory technician and delivered it to an evidence custodian. There was proof that the evidence custodian hand-delivered the blood sample to the police laboratory at the state capital. Evidence also indicated that a forensic technician retrieved the sample from the dropbox at the state police laboratory and processed the contents and delivered the blood sample to a different state agent, who tested it and disclosed that the blood alcohol content was .21. The final state agent indicated that there was nothing unusual about the blood sample and nothing to imply that the sample had been adulterated or mishandled. Under these circumstances, the reviewing court felt compelled to state that the chain of custody had been properly met and that the blood evidence had been properly authenticated.

---

17 State v. Castro, 40 So.3d 1036, 2010 La. App. LEXIS 793 (2010).
18 Franklin v. State, 2006 Ga. App. LEXIS 1111 (2006).
19 State v. Cannon, 2012 Tenn. Crim. App. LEXIS 982 (2102).
20 State v. Holden, 2013 Tenn. Crim. App. LEXIS 204 (2013).

Chain of custody need not be perfect in every respect; it is sufficient that once the prosecution introduces evidence that strongly suggests the presence of virtually every link in the chain, any gaps go to the weight to be given to the evidence rather than to its admissibility.[21] When the chain of custody covers an extended period, but the chain has been sufficiently proved to be unbroken, the evidence should be admitted.

However, the failure to follow proper chain-of-custody procedures or a failure to allege and prove them in court will have serious consequences for the prosecution. For example, an Illinois appeals court reversed a probation revocation based on the defendant's delivery of a controlled substance within 1,000 feet of a church, where the defendant had sold crack cocaine to an undercover police agent. The officer stated that when he received the crack, he inventoried the item but offered absolutely no other evidence concerning chain of custody. The prosecution failed to present any evidence concerning the handling and safekeeping of the evidence between the time the state received the crack from the defendant and the delivery of some substance to the state forensic scientist; thus, proof of the chain of custody failed. Because the state either failed to follow the proper procedures or failed to prove that it followed them, the appellate court reversed the case.[22]

In a federal bank robbery case, the perpetrators restrained the victims with Zip® ties, and one of the robbers made a deposit of his DNA on the Zip® tie tip as he cinched them on the victims' wrists. Police officers cut the Zip® ties and placed them on the bank floor prior to collecting them for scientific testing. The defendant contended that other DNA may have been deposited on the Zip® tie ends or they were otherwise contaminated because they remained on the bank floor for a period of time and were not actually in the custody of police during part of the investigation. In all other respects, chain of custody existed for the Zip® ties from the time they were collected at the bank until they were tested for DNA. The reviewing court held that the chain of custody was sufficiently demonstrated and that any gaps in custody of the Zip® ties went to the weight of the evidence and not its admissibility.[23]

Notwithstanding the fact that the courts have been reluctant to prohibit the use of evidence even if there has been a gap in the chain of custody, it is quite clear that unless a serious question arises concerning the chain of custody, or of contamination or alteration, most courts will admit evidence as having been properly authenticated. In admitting such evidence, most courts suggest that deficiencies that are not fatal to the chain of custody can have an effect on the weight that the trier of fact may give to the evidence.

---

[21] Troxell v. Indiana, 778 N.E.2d 811, 814, 2002 Ind. LEXIS 888 (2002), *and see* Hawkins v. Arkansas, 105 S.W.3d 397, 2003 Ark. App. LEXIS 334 (2003).

[22] Illinois v. Moore, 335 Ill. App. 3d 616, 781 N.E.2d 493, 2002 Ill. App. LEXIS 1058 (2002).

[23] United States v. Brooks, 727 F.2d 1291, 1299, 2013 U.S. App. LEXIS 18140 (10th Cir. 2013).

B. Necessity

Because of the weight that may be placed upon the use of real evidence, courts have reasoned that it should not be admitted unless a valid reason for its admission is offered. While real evidence does not require absolutely perfect links in the chain of custody to qualify for admission in evidence,[24] the admission or exclusion of real evidence rests largely within the sound discretion of the trial judge.[25] In some instances, the party offering a demonstration of the real evidence is required to give good reason for its acceptance into evidence. As one court stated, the evidence should be admitted when it is both relevant and highly probative, better evidence cannot reasonably be anticipated, and the dangers are small in comparison to the advantages.[26]

While the admission of certain evidence is not improper merely because it may tend to influence the emotions, it should be excluded when it appears to be designed to appeal to the emotional and sympathetic tendencies of a judge or jury. In a trial for having her husband murdered, the court initially excluded a sexually suggestive photograph of the defendant, found in the possession of the defendant's paramour, as being unfairly prejudicial.[27] The trial court later reversed its ruling and admitted the explicit photo after the defendant testified that she had not had a consensual sexual relationship with the government witness who hired the hit man to kill her husband. Once her testimony was on the record as denying her relationship with her lover, the photograph became more relevant and less prejudicial to explain her relationship with her paramour, who hired the hit man.

When photographs of a murder victim serve only to inflame the passion of the jury, their prejudicial effect outweighs their probative value and admission is improper even when there are no issues with authentication. However, to win an argument that the photographs of victims should be excluded, a strong case of unfair prejudice must be demonstrated, which can be difficult to accomplish. In a Georgia murder prosecution, the court permitted the admission of pre-autopsy photographs that indicated the victim had been held against his will, bound with duct tape, and dismembered.[28] In the same case, the court permitted the introduction of post-autopsy photographs that showed injuries beneath the scalp. According to the reviewing court, all photographs were introduced for a particular purpose, and the trial court did not abuse its discretion. Similarly, in a triple murder case where the defendant had been accused of shooting his girlfriend and her two small children, photographs of the victims at the crime scene and during the autopsies were proper because the use of each photo had a necessary purpose.[29]

---

24 People v. Conner, 2005 Mich. App. LEXIS 653 (2005).

25 *See* Washington v. Delgado, 2003 Wash. App. LEXIS 87 (2003), which held that a judge in his or her discretion may admit or exclude real evidence in the form of photographs.

26 Commonwealth v. Inhabitants of Holliston, 107 Mass. 232 (1871).

27 United States v. Brudette, 86 Fed. Appx. 121, 2004 U.S. App. LEXIS 804 (6th Cir. 2004).

28 McKibbins v. State, 2013 Fulton County D. Rep. 3224, 2013 Ga. LEXIS 873 (Ga. 2013).

29 Miller v. State, 2010 Ark. 1, 2010 Ark. LEXIS 3 (2010).

C. Relationship to Crime

Evidence may be excluded at the discretion of the judge when facts that the prosecution seeks to prove are only remotely connected to the issues. In other words, the evidence that a party seeks to have admitted must tend to prove or disprove a fact at issue, and when the effects of an item of evidence are marginal, it should be excluded. In addition, if the evidence would be likely to mislead or confuse the jury, a judge may refuse to allow the evidence.[30] In a California case involving the deaths of two police officers, the trial judge refused to allow the jury to view the scene of the alleged murders because the lighting at the crime scene was different during the trial due to the fact that the trial occurred during the summer, whereas the crime happened during the winter. According to the court, there was other evidence in the case that it was a very dark night and that it was difficult to see at the crime scene, and a view of the scene would add very little to the knowledge of the jury.[31]

In cases in which the prosecution wants to introduce a physical object (such as a weapon) connected with the commission of a crime, it may properly be admitted into evidence where it has been authenticated and shown to have a sufficient connection to the crime charged. In a habeas corpus case, a federal judge approved a state court decision that allowed a knife and a rock to be admitted into evidence in a murder case where police found the knife and the rock at the location where the defendant admitted the killing occurred.[32] The coroner testified that the fatal wounds were consistent with a single edge knife and indicated that the knife found on a rock had human blood on it. If there is insufficient evidence to show that the article is properly connected with the crime, it should not be admitted and, in this case, even though an argument could be made to exclude, the reviewing courts did not require it. For example, in a child sexual misconduct case, the prosecution had a plastic bag containing hair taken from the defendant's possession marked as an exhibit, but it never introduced the bag of hair into evidence.[33] The prosecution had planned to ask the defendant about the hair if he took the witness stand, but the opportunity never arose. A reviewing court concluded that the bag of hair did not make any fact that was of consequence to the case more or less probable than it would have been without it. The reviewing court concluded the hair was improperly introduced because it may have encouraged jury speculation, but the appellate court thought that the hair evidence constituted harmless error and did not reverse the convictions.

Although the burden is on the party introducing the evidence to show that it complies with the requirements, in most instances the court will admit real evidence if it has any logical bearing upon the case. The judge has the discretion as to whether the

---

30 People v. Burst, 225 Cal. App. 4th 108, 2014 Cal. App. LEXIS 298 (2014).

31 People v. Russell, 50 Cal.4th 1228, 242 P.3d 68, 117 Cal. Rptr. 3d 615, 2010 Cal. LEXIS 11346 (2010).

32 Goodwill v. Palmer, 2013 U.S. Dist. LEXIS 140930 (W.D. Mich. 2013).

33 State v. Jacobson, 87 Conn. App. 440, 450, 866 A.2d 678, 687, 2005 Conn. App. LEXIS 64 (2005).

evidence is related to the crime, and his or her decision is not subject to review unless there has been a clear abuse of this discretion.

D. *Proper Identification*

When the prosecution wants to introduce an object, article, tool, weapon, or similar tangible item in evidence to prove a fact to which it is connected from a previous time or event, the item is not properly authenticated as evidence unless it is first identified as being the same object that was originally recovered and is shown to be in substantially the same condition as it was during the time or event to which it is claimed to be related.[34] A Texas court noted that in identifying evidence, "[t]he chain of custody is conclusively proven if an officer is able to identify that he or she seized the item of physical evidence, put an identification mark on it, placed it in the property room, and then retrieved the item being offered on the day of trial."[35] The requirement that physical objects be identified or authenticated as genuine serves to prevent the introduction of false evidence or evidence that has been subjected to tampering. In a Delaware case involving a juvenile who possessed a firearm with an obliterated serial number, the juvenile alleged that the gun had not properly been identified by the police.[36] In support of showing proper identification, police officers testified that they saw the juvenile duck behind a car at which time they heard a dull thud and retrieved the firearm from where the juvenile had been standing. One officer took the firearm from the crime scene, placed it in a sealed container that was opened and later resealed by an officer trained in ballistics. Each time the firearm was removed from the sealed container and returned, a notation was made on the outside of the container. Additionally, the firearm exhibited a unique rust stain that was visible in a crime-scene picture and that same rust stain was observable on the firearm introduced into evidence. Under the circumstances, the Supreme Court of Delaware held that the firearm had been properly identified at trial and met the requirements of authentication and had been properly admitted.[37]

Generally, physical evidence is properly admitted if it is readily identifiable by some unique feature or other identifying mark.[38] When a real or physical object is offered as evidence in a criminal prosecution, an adequate foundation for admission

---

34 Gutman v. Industrial Comm., 71 Ohio App. 383, 50 N.E.2d 187 (1942); *see also* State v. Campbell, 103 Wash. 2d 1, 691 P.2d 929, *cert. denied*, 471 U.S. 1094, 105 S. Ct. 2169, 85 L. Ed. 2d 526 (1984), which held that before a physical object connected with the commission of a crime may properly be admitted into evidence, it must be satisfactorily identified and shown to be in substantially the same condition as it was when the crime was committed. The factors to be considered include the nature of the article, circumstances surrounding its preservation and custody, and the likelihood of intermeddlers tampering with it.

35 Bridges v. State, 2005 Tex. App. LEXIS 10389 (2005).

36 Davis v. State, 74 A.3d 653, 2013 Del. LEXIS 439 (2013).

37 *Id.*

38 United States v. Abreu, 952 F.2d 1458 (1st Cir.), *cert. denied*, 503 U.S. 994, 112 S. Ct. 1695, 118 L. Ed. 2d 406 (1992).

requires testimony that the object identified at trial is the same object that was involved in the alleged incident, and the condition of the object is substantially unchanged.[39]

In a case involving identification of money, the state of Florida met the identification requirement in a buy/bust scheme operated by the police, in which the defendant obtained marked money during a drug purchase and later dropped it at the point of his arrest.[40] Previously, police had photocopied the money and also marked the bait money in a distinctive manner. At trial, police officers testified that the photocopied money matched the marked money used in the operation and that the marked money was found in the proximity of the defendant's person in the staircase where he was arrested. A second officer also identified the marked money on the photocopied sheet as being the $20 bill that he recovered on the staircase at the point of the defendant's arrest.

Objects and articles are sometimes admitted into evidence even though a slight alteration or change has occurred. For example, a court admitted the serrated blade of a knife discovered at a murder scene after a fire had altered some of the evidence. In this case, a surviving victim stated that the defendant had cut his throat with a complete knife while the victim was in the living room,[41] even though the fire investigator found a serrated knife blade and knife handles on the living room floor. A different court admitted two mangled bullets recovered from a wall that a ballistics expert stated were fired from the same gun.[42]

§ 14.3 Exhibition of Person

When the prosecution of the defendant is based on physical harm to the victim, it would seem that the best evidence of such harm would be the exhibition of the person of the victim to the jury. Such a witness would be more valuable in determining what happened than would oral testimony, photographs, or even X-rays, in some instances. Courts as a rule will allow the display of injuries to the jury—often in spite of the fact that the injury is gruesome.

The trial judge has a great deal of discretion in determining whether the physical display of the injury is so inflammatory as to unduly influence the jury. Such decisions are seldom overruled, unless there is a clear abuse of discretion. However, if the judge determines that the display of the person and the injury is so inflammatory that it may prejudice the jury, the judge may refuse to allow the display of a crime-related injury. In a California case, a judge permitted the jury to view a videotape of a man who was in a hospital after being attacked with a hammer by the defendant. He was in poor condition after the attack and was so elderly that he died prior to the defendant's trial. There were questions concerning the reliability of the witness's statement, but the judge allowed the

[39] United States v. Miller, 994 F.2d 441 (8th Cir. 1993).

[40] Gray v. Secretary, Florida Department of Corrections, 2013 U.S. Dist. LEXIS 3995 (M.D. Fla. 2013).

[41] Commonwealth v. Edwards, 2006 Pa. LEXIS 1529 (2006).

[42] Grayson v. King, 2006 U.S. App. LEXIS 21215 (11th Cir. 2006).

jury to observe the man and hear his story on videotape, which had been recorded after the attack.[43]

Although the judge in his or her discretion may permit the witness to be exhibited at the trial in a criminal case in order to determine the extent of injury, the judge runs the risk of committing reversible error if he or she compelled a defendant to appear at a trial in handcuffs or shackles. In one case, the court of appeals reversed a drug conviction because the trial judge ordered that the defendant be shackled if he insisted upon serving as his own defense attorney.[44] It was not clear whether the jury could see the shackles, but the court's policy of having every individual who served as his or her own defense attorney submit to shackling was in error. The prosecution produced no evidence that exhibiting the defendant in shackles did not affect the trial's outcome. In a separate federal prosecution involving the importation of the drug, ecstasy, the trial court required that the defendant be shackled for the duration of the trial and for no apparent reason that appeared on the record.[45] When the defendant, who had no prior criminal history, took the witness stand, the jury could clearly see the restraints worn by the defendant, and the defense counsel referred to the defendant's shackles during summation. The Court of Appeal reversed the conviction for several cumulative errors, including the use of shackles during trial. In a Missouri capital prosecution, in the penalty phase, the trial court ordered that the defendant be shackled with visible leg irons, handcuffs, and a belly chain. According to the Court, "the Fifth and Fourteenth Amendments prohibit using physical restraints visible to the jury absent a trial court determination, in the exercise of its discretion, that restraints are justified by a state interest specific to the particular defendant on trial."[46] The Supreme Court of the United States reversed the death penalty, noting that the visible restraints almost certainly affected the jury's perception of the defendant's character.[47] However, when a defendant was restrained during the trial but made no objection to being shackled, and where the shackling did not affect the verdict beyond a reasonable doubt, any conviction and sentence will not be disturbed.[48]

§ 14.4 Articles Connected with the Crime

Any item of evidence that has tangible existence, in whatever form, may be admitted as evidence in a criminal trial, provided that the prosecutor can properly connect each of the items of evidence to the crime itself. Weapons, tools, drugs and drug

---

43 *See* California v. Tatum, 108 Cal. App. 4th 288, 133 Cal. Rptr. 2d 267, 2003 Cal. App. LEXIS 629 (2003).

44 United States v. Banegas, 600 F.3d 342, 346, 2010 U.S. App. LEXIS 4993 (5th Cir. 2010).

45 United States v. Haynes, 729 F.3d 178, 2013 U.S. App. LEXIS 18453 (2d Cir. 2013)

46 Deck v. Missouri, 544 U.S. 622, 626, 2005 U.S. LEXIS 4180 (2005).

47 *Id.,* at 628.

48 *See* United States v. Brantley, 342 F. App'x 762, 2009 U.S. App. LEXIS 19270 (3rd Cir. 2009).

paraphernalia, paper records, sound and video recordings, photographs, and anything with tangible essence that will help prove or disprove a case has a chance to be admitted into evidence. All items of real evidence must be reasonably identified or authenticated as being the thing or object the party offering the evidence represents it to be. If the object is one that a witness can particularly identify from memory by its appearance or attributes, it will be sufficiently authenticated. Alternatively, an item of evidence may be authenticated by creating a chain of custody that is largely intact.[49] Federal Rule of Evidence 901(a) notes that "authentication or identification as a condition precedent to admissibility is satisfied by evidence sufficient to support a finding that the matter in question is what its proponent claims." Examples of types of articles that have been acquired by investigators and submitted for consideration are discussed in the sections that follow.

A. Weapons

To be admitted as evidence, weapons must be authenticated and must have sufficient relevancy to the matters at issue. In a case in which the prosecution failed to establish that a firearm had any connection to the murder case, the .45 caliber revolver should not have been admitted in evidence.[50] Five years after the murder, the defendant's then-girlfriend told police that the defendant admitted that he committed the murder, and she told officers that he had a gun in a backpack inside a closet where they lived. The weapon was entirely unconnected to the crime charged, but the trial court allowed the introduction of the gun from the backpack. There was no precise evidence concerning the caliber of the murder weapon, and its location was unknown. The state referenced the unconnected gun during closing arguments. Under the circumstances of this case, the reviewing court held that the .45 caliber revolver, which admittedly had no connection to the murder, should never have been introduced at the murder trial.

A weapon that appears to have virtually no connection with a homicide can be excluded from evidence when it lacks relevance to the facts of a case. Under the circumstances, a judge may refuse to permit a firearm to be authenticated and introduced into evidence. In a Mississippi homicide case, police arrested the defendant, who was wearing bloody clothes and sleeping on top of a .32 pistol and a .380 handgun. At the trial, the defendant wanted to introduce evidence that he also possessed the .380 handgun at the time of his arrest.[51] The deceased had been fatally shot with the .32 caliber pistol possessed by the defendant, but there was never any evidence that the .380 handgun had been present at the murder scene. In arguments to the trial judge, the defendant's counsel contended that the .380 had been at the murder scene, but neither party introduced any actual evidence that the .380 handgun had any role in the homicide. The Supreme Court of Mississippi upheld the trial judge's exclusion of the extra firearm,

---

49 Commonwealth v. Herring, 66 Mass. App. Ct. 360, 365, 2006 Mass. App. LEXIS 569 (2006).
50 Agatheas v. State, 77 So.3d 1232, 1240, 2011 Fla. App. LEXIS 2880 (2011).
51 Flora v. State, 925 So. 2d 797, 813, 2006 Miss. LEXIS 49 (2006).

noting that the judge did not abuse his discretion. In this case, it might be argued that the defendant wanted to "muddy the waters" in an effort to create some confusion on the part of the jury.

In a proper situation, a firearm may be authenticated in a variety of ways, including recognition of unique features exhibited by a particular firearm. In a Texas robbery case, in order to help prove that the defendant was guilty of the robbery, part of the proof involved identifying a gun taken during the crime that one of the victims placed in a bag given to the robber.[52] Police recovered a .38 caliber revolver from the defendant's automobile that was the same type taken in the robbery. Under Texas evidence law, Rule 901, one manner of authenticating a piece of real evidence involves recognition of unique or distinctive characteristics. In this case, three victims of the robbery identified the gun at issue as the one given to the robber because it looked like the gun and all three witnesses noted that the hammer on the revolver had been broken, just like the one placed in the bag given to the robber. The appellate court held that the gun had been properly authenticated as being the one involved in the robbery and found no error in admitting the firearm in evidence.

For many types of weapons, proof of a chain of custody will not be the only method of proving a sufficient connection to a particular crime. All modern firearms must have serial numbers stamped on the frame of the weapon so that a firearm identified at the crime scene by a serial number may be authenticated at trial by reference to the same number. Even when the serial number has not been used, the failure to establish a chain of custody is not essential if the weapon introduced is clearly identified by one or more witnesses or through expert ballistics evidence. Demonstrative of these principles for authentication, in an Arkansas aggravated robbery case, a witness identified a .22 Ruger® pistol that the prosecution introduced by its appearance as the gun that the witness had given the defendant.[53] The witness testified that the serial number on the .22 Ruger was the identical number that had been on the pistol the witness had transferred to the defendant. In this case, the witness was able to identify the gun by its overall appearance as well as by its serial number, sufficiently authenticating the gun for use as evidence against a suspected armed robber.

In addition to firearms, other weapons used to commit crimes may be introduced into evidence if properly identified. In a Massachusetts assault and battery prosecution, authentication of the knife used in the crime proved to be an essential element.[54] The defendant admitted to having a foldable knife and that he had been inside the crime-scene apartment with such a knife. Police testified concerning details of the knife and its recovery from the defendant's vehicle. In upholding the trial court determination that the knife had been properly authenticated, the reviewing court stated, "[t]he matching description and discovery of the knife during a valid search of the defendant's vehicle, which had blood splattered on the interior, supplied the inference required to

52 Traylor v. State, 2010 Tex. App. LEXIS 3611 (2010).
53 Looney v. State, 2005 Ark. LEXIS 326 (2005).
54 Commonwealth v. Sadeghi, 2009 Mass. App. Unpub. LEXIS 1130 (2009).

authenticate the knife."[55] In a different prosecution, an appellate court held that a knife was properly introduced when its authenticity was established by the testimony of a police officer who took the knife from the defendant and provided proof of chain of custody until its introduction at the defendant's trial.[56]

B. Instruments Used in the Crime

Instruments associated with crimes, such as burglary tools, screwdrivers, guns, knives, explosives, lock picks, and other implements adapted to crime, especially burglary, are admissible if reasonably identified, although more weight will be given to the evidence if identification is certain. If the witness is uncertain concerning the identification of an item of real evidence, the witness's uncertainty goes only to the weight of the physical evidence and not to its admissibility.[57]

In a Hawai'i case, an apartment manager observed a subject with a bicycle and a backpack attempting to gain entry into the apartment's parking garage by prying on the steel-framed locked door.[58] When asked why he did not use a key, the subject noted that he did not have a key. Upon additional inquiry, the manager realized the subject was an interloper who had a rope, a cord, and a chisel in his hand. A shoving match between the two men followed, in which the backpack fell to the ground, revealing screwdrivers, pliers, and a pair of scissors. The defendant argued on appeal that physical evidence did not support the proof of possession of burglary tools and that the eyewitness did not give believable testimony. The reviewing court rejected the defendant-appellant's contention because it thought that reasonable minds could find guilt beyond a reasonable doubt based on the manager's testimony concerning the real evidence.

In a state prosecution breaking and entering and being in possession of criminal tools, the defendant contended that there was insufficient evidence to prove his guilt of the charges.[59] Police apprehended the defendant in front one unit of a commercial store and lock storage facility, with the bolt cutter and the other tools, wearing heavy dark clothing and gloves. Police observed him going from one unit to the next and opening at least one unit. During the trial, the prosecution proved the chain of custody for the broken padlock, bolt cutters, and a flashlight that had been with the defendant at the time of his arrest. The burglar tools were seized by police at the crime scene and remained in their custody until their introduction at trial. In this case, the proof of the chain of custody was properly met, and the reviewing court did not reverse the convictions.

Evidence that has a strained chain of custody may pose difficult challenges for the prosecution and, in some cases, may ultimately not be admissible against the defendant. In a prosecution in Idaho involving gang activity and an alleged violation of the federal

---

55 *Id.*

56 Maranda v. State, 253 S.W.3d 762, 2007 Tex. App. LEXIS 9285 (2007).

57 *See* Commonwealth v. Crork, 2009 Pa. Super. 24, 2009 Pa. Super. LEXIS 31 (2009).

58 State v. Tetu, 2005 Haw. App. LEXIS 435 (2005).

59 State v. Southam, 2012 Ohio 5943, 2013 Ohio App. LEXIS 5134 (2012).

RICO statute, police recovered a firearm that was linked to a drive-by shooting.[60] Ballistics tests matched the firearm to the crime, but a couple of years later, the police department returned the firearm to its rightful owner, who was not the defendant. Subsequently, the owner sold the firearm to a different individual, who eventually allowed the government to take the gun back almost 6 years after the shooting. The defendant contended that the prosecution could not show a chain of custody because of the several-year gap when the firearm was in the hands of two different owners. When there is a gap or break in the chain of custody, to properly authenticate the gun, the prosecution must demonstrate proof such that a reasonable juror could find the firearm was in substantially the same condition as when it was originally seized after the attempted murder. The federal district court did make a definitive decision at the pretrial stage of the case on the defendant's contention that the government could not show that the gun was in substantially the same condition as it was on the day of the crime. The judge also refused to dismiss the indictment pending the government's effort to introduce evidence that the firearm had not been altered in the time it was not in police custody. This case illustrates the difficulties in some cases of using a chain-of-custody theory to authenticate a firearm to show that it was the actual item involved and that it had not been altered substantially from the time it was used in the crime until the time it was scheduled to be introduced at trial.

C. Clothing

Clothing that a witness identifies as having been worn by the accused or the victim during the commission of the crime may be scientifically tested, identified, and submitted to the jury for inspection. For example, in one case involving a residential robbery, burglary, and kidnapping, one of the perpetrators wore a T-shirt fragment as a mask covering his nose and below to the neck.[61] During this home invasion, one of the defendants tripped on the edge of a bed, fell to the floor, dropped his gun, and lost his mask. Later, one of the victims found the mask in a bathtub and delivered the cloth mask to police, who had it tested, revealing the predominant DNA of the defendant. Testimony demonstrated that the T-shirt mask did not belong to any family members and no one had ever seen it prior to the incursion by the defendants. DNA experts testified concerning scientific testing of the T-shirt mask and how other, less predominate DNA could be deposited on the cloth. Accordingly, the reviewing court noted that the trier of fact could also reasonably conclude, based on the witness testimony and the scientific evidence establishing that (1) the defendant's DNA matched the major contributor on the DNA profile from the T-shirt and (2) such a match would occur only once in 117 sextillion individuals, that the defendant had worn the mask and was one of the men who participated in the home invasion.[62]

---

60 United States v. Garcia, 2012 U.S. Dist. LEXIS 181362 (2012).

61 State v. Brown, 2013 Ohio 2690, 2013 Ohio App. LEXIS 2679 (2013).

62 *Id.*

Demonstrating chain of custody involving clothing may be used to connect a potential defendant to involvement in criminal activity. In an Arkansas murder case, the victim had received a fatal gunshot wound while lying in her bed.[63] Her husband contended that she was alive and well at the time he went to work but he found her dead when he returned to the marital home. At some point in the investigation, and with the defendant's consent, police officers retrieved the clothing that the defendant allegedly wore on the night of his wife's death. Testing indicated the presence of gunpowder residue on the clothing, and the prosecution introduced the clothing and its significance at trial. The defendant objected based on a lack of authentication under the chain-of-custody theory. One of the officers explained how he retrieved the shirt and blue jeans and offered testimony that the items of clothing introduced into evidence were the items that he had retrieved and that the defendant admitted wearing on the night of the homicide. The reviewing court found that there was sufficient evidence identifying and authenticating the clothing as the clothing the defendant was wearing when he found his wife's body, and the appellate court found no abuse of discretion in admitting the defendant's clothing against him.

In putting together a prosecutable case, police may have to integrate clothing as well as scientific testing to implicate a particular defendant. In a case involving the robbery of a bank teller, the robbers left a trail of money, some clothing, a boot, and other evidence, including a burned-out getaway vehicle.[64] At trial, one of the defendants objected to the introduction of various clothing items against him, contending that chain of custody had not been proven. Officers testified that they responded to a radio report indicating the direction of the getaway vehicle and followed it until they encountered clothing along the roadway and eventually the motor vehicle. Officers testified that they collected the clothing, boot, and other articles and bagged and tagged them. Other officers testified concerning the method in which the evidence was secured both in a safe and in an evidence locker, while other paperwork indicated where the evidence was sent for testing and when it was returned. A laboratory employee testified that there was no obvious tampering from the FedEx box when it was shipped to the laboratory for DNA testing. In rejecting the defendant's contention that a proper chain of custody for the clothing items had not been laid, the reviewing court noted that

> [t]he production of every person, who handled the evidence at every moment is not required to establish a chain of custody. However, in this case, the testimony of the officers indicated that there was an accounting of every person who had handled the evidence at every moment of the investigation and its analysis. In addition, [the defendant] failed to produce any evidence that suggested there had been any tampering with the evidence.[65]

---

[63] *See* Gill v. State 2010 Ark. App. 524, 2010 Ark. App. LEXIS 568 (2010).

[64] Craig v. State, 45 So.3d 699, 709, 2010 Miss. App. LEXIS 525 (2010).

[65] *Id.* at 710.

The DNA testing connected the defendant to the boot found at the site of the abandoned vehicle, a factor that constituted a separate method of authenticating the boot as being connected to the defendant and properly authenticated.

In another case where scientific testing of clothing proved to be crucial to the prosecution's, success, a Texas appeals court did not disturb a trial court's admission of DNA testing results of underwear that the defendant had been wearing on the night that a child in his care was raped.[66] From a single stain on defendant's underwear, experts determined that the stain tested positive for blood from the infant victim and semen from the defendant. The trial court also admitted a washcloth used at an emergency room that had been used to wipe the infant's private area that contained presence of semen. Because the real evidence in the case appeared to meet all the requirements of authentication by chain of custody, the appeals court affirmed the conviction for aggravated sexual assault on a child.

D. Bloodstains

The practice of identifying blood and criminals by circumstantial evidence and by the inspection of witnesses and jurors has had the sanction of immemorial usage in criminal tribunals.[67] With the development of modern blood testing, science generated new data on types and subtypes of blood, yielding additional information from blood analysis. Within the past 25 years, the use of DNA as a method of identifying the source of blood left at crime scenes opened new avenues of identification of criminals, as well as screening the innocent away from prosecution. The testing has also evolved to the point at which extremely small samples of blood may be used to reveal DNA information that previously would not have been available. Blood is only one type of body fluid that contains DNA for which law enforcement officers may find use.

The discovery of the presence of blood on the person or clothing of the accused party or the victim has been recognized as being among the ordinary indicia of homicide and lesser criminal injury. Blood-related evidence left by the perpetrator at the scene of the crime may be used to prove that a particular defendant has been present at the crime scene and may help indicate when a person was present. When a victim's blood is discovered on a defendant or on his or her possessions, that fact tends to prove proximity to the victim. In an Alabama robbery-murder case, proof that the victim's blood was on the defendant's blue jeans and on a cigarette pack possessed by the defendant was circumstantial evidence of the defendant's presence at the liquor store robbery.[68] Blood pattern evidence may indicate what occurred and how long ago the acts took place. Blood evidence may be visible to law enforcement officers or may require enhancement by chemicals introduced at the scene. Police and evidence technicians have used Luminol®[69] as a screening test to detect latent evidence of blood

---

66 Smith v. State, 2004 Tex. App. LEXIS 11851 (2004).

67 People v. Gonzales, 35 N.Y. 49 (1866).

68 Riley v. State, 2013 Ala. Crim. App. 75 (2013).

69 A chemical compound that reacts with blood and semen and chemically changes to emit a blue glow.

since 1955, when it was first used in the investigation of a crime scene and introduced in court.[70] A recent challenge to the use of Luminol® was rejected by the Supreme Court of California, noting that presumptive tests for the presence of blood have been appropriately admissible, even where laboratory-grade positive blood tests have not been performed.[71]

The use of blood-obtained information and bloodstain evidence will generally require expert collection, expert evaluation, and expert testimony. In one murder case, the victim had been killed by an unknown assailant, but blood testing pointed toward the perpetrator. The body of a young woman was found by her sister in their home. A medical examiner determined, based on an examination of the body at the scene and an autopsy, that the deceased had been beaten and stabbed multiple times with a screwdriver as well as sexually assaulted. Evidence in the form of bloodstained clothes and a partial Walkman® headset were found at the defendant's home. The headset part matched one part found under the body of the deceased. A Walkman® and bloodstained underwear were found in the defendant's bedroom. The prosecution introduced DNA evidence obtained from blood at the crime scene. The DNA evidence demonstrated that the DNA profile of blood samples taken from the defendant's screwdriver and personal property found at his home matched the victim's DNA profile and that semen samples taken from the victim's body matched the defendant's DNA profile. Despite a challenge concerning whether the science involved met Minnesota requirements,[72] the reviewing court determined that the testing met the state's strong general scientific acceptance standard.[73]

Evaluating crime-scene blood splatter patterns helps to corroborate truthful oral evidence or challenge witness statements that may be false, misleading, or erroneous. Blood spatter analysis involves mechanical scrutiny based on the physics of fluid flow and an evaluation of impact angles at which the spatters hit other objects rather than only concerning microscopic scientific analysis. For example, a significant number of state jurisdictions have held that blood spatter analysis is reliable and may be admitted where the witness qualifies as an expert through training, education, and experience. Blood splatter analysis has been recognized as known and accepted scientific discipline by many courts because of its logical and scientific basis.[74] In a Virginia case involving expert testimony covering blood splash patterns, the high court accepted the principles on which bloodstain pattern interpretation has been based and noted that expert testimony is recognized to explain the pattern of bloodstains. The court observed that:

---

[70] People v. Wooten, 283 A.2d 931, 933, 725 N.Y.S.2d 767, 770, 2001 N.Y. App. Div. LEXIS 4659 (N.Y. 2001).

[71] People v. Alexander, 49 Cal.4th 846, 904, 235 P.3d 873, 923, 113 Cal. Rptr. 3d 190, 249, 2010 Cal. LEXIS (2010).

[72] *See* Minnesota v. Roman Nose, 649 N.W.2d 815, 2002 Minn. LEXIS 554 (2002).

[73] Minnesota v. Roman Nose, 667 N.W.2d 386, 2003 Minn. LEXIS 513 (2003).

[74] Hudson v. State, 95 Ark. 85, 102, 146 S.W.3d 380, 390, 2004 Ark. App. LEXIS 124 (2004). *See also* State v. Torres, 137 N.M. 607, 113 P.3d 877; 2005 N.M. App. LEXIS 56 (2005).

> Many of the specific physical elements of blood spatter analysis are capable of being tested using the laws of physics and chemistry, and by employing principles of gravity, inertia, and viscosity. In accordance with other jurisdictions, we adhere to the view that this form of scientific analysis can form a basis for admissible proof upon an appropriate foundation.[75]

As a general rule, if the prosecution needs to explain bloodstain patterns as a way to prove how a crime occurred, expert testimony will be essential. The prosecution is required to show that evidence concerning the impact of bloodstain evidence is based upon a well-recognized scientific principle or technique that has gained general acceptance in the particular field to which it belongs.[76] Consistent with the Virginia view described earlier, a Michigan trial court properly allowed an expert witness to explain how a deceased female did not commit suicide and, therefore, was probably murdered.[77] The expert analyzed the crime scene, analyzing the significance of a high-velocity mist pattern of blood spatter on fitted sheets and pillows, and concluded that a void in the pattern was consistent with something having been present at the time the shots were fired that intercepted the high-velocity blood mist. The expert noted that the void was consistent with someone firing the fatal shots while standing behind the victim. A conviction for murder was upheld on direct appeal and was not disturbed by the defendant's petition for a writ of habeas corpus. Similarly, in a Georgia murder case in which the defendant alleged that the victim committed suicide, expert crime-scene investigators testified that blood spatter evidence and the bullet's trajectory indicated that the victim's head was pressed against a couch at the time of the fatal injury and the victim was not sitting up in an erect position, as the defendant claimed.[78] The expert witnesses testified that the fatal gunshot injury could not have occurred as explained by the defendant. Investigators found the victim with a muzzle stamp on her head while holding a gun in her left hand, although she was known to be right-handed. The evidence was completely inconsistent with the defendant's information that he originally offered to investigators.

E. Narcotics and Narcotics Paraphernalia

Drug-related crimes involving major trafficking, possession with intent to sell, and simple possession have increased in the recent past to such an extent that a large percentage of local, state, and federal agents' time is devoted to investigating such crimes and testifying against the accused persons. Naturally, the high level of litigation that surrounds drug prosecutions generates a significant number of court decisions in which

---

75 Smith v. Commonwealth, 265 Va. 250, 576 S.E.2d 465, 2003 Va. LEXIS 36 (2003).

76 *See* Frye v. United States, 54 App. D.C. 46, 293 F. 1013 (1923), which followed the general scientific acceptance approach and many state jurisdictions followed the logic. When the Supreme Court decided Daubert v. Merrell Dow Pharmaceuticals, 509 U.S. 579 (1993), it ruled that Federal Rule of Evidence 702 had superseded the *Frye* standard for federal courts.

77 Duyst v. Rapelje, 2011 U.S. Dist. LEXIS 11960 (E.D. Mich. 2011).

78 Hester v. State, 292 Ga. 356, 357, 736 S.E.2d 404, 406, 2013 Ga. LEXIS 10 (2013).

defendants test the rules for admission and exclusion of drug-related evidence. As a general rule, courts require a more conclusively established chain of custody for proof of authentication where interchangeable items like drugs or blood are involved,[79] a factor that may help some drug defendants.

A 2009 case decided by the Supreme Court presents some new constitutional challenges to police and prosecutors because it changed prior practice concerning admitting the results of drug identification and testing. In a cocaine trafficking case, *Melendez-Diaz v. Massachusetts*, the Court determined that the admission of sworn certificates prepared by drug technicians that indicated the type of drug and quantity based on scientific testing violated a defendant's Sixth Amendment right to confront and cross-examine adverse witnesses.[80] According to the Court, unless the actual person doing the testifying was the individual who conducted the scientific tests, the defendant cannot effectively cross-examine the actual person who performed the tests concerning the merits of the testing procedures and the accuracy of the results obtained. It now appears that the individuals who work in the scientific testing labs will be required to personally testify directly in court concerning their tests and results.

Although defendants routinely challenge the admissibility of narcotics and other recreational pharmaceuticals, prosecutors must be ready to meet the legal theories and prevail in getting the evidence introduced in court. Constitutional mandates, state evidence codes, and case law require that precise and documented steps be followed to ensure admissibility. Deficiencies in meeting these rigorous procedures may result in evidence not being admitted. Although trial and appellate courts have generally approved the admissibility of narcotics, there is a fine line between what is admissible and what is inadmissible.

While there are several legal theories that will permit seized drugs to be admitted as evidence, one typical way is for the prosecution to prove a chain of custody of the drug as a prerequisite to admission in evidence. In a federal prosecution involving the smuggling of cocaine via airliners, federal agents X-rayed a suitcase and then seized it because it contained an odd package.[81] Following a drug dog alert to the suitcase, the officer opened it and discovered what appeared to be cocaine. The officer transferred control of the suspected drugs to a special agent of ICE. The ICE agent testified that the narcotics seized from the airliner were turned over to him and that they were transferred to the main office in Newark, New Jersey, and placed within the drug evidence room. At trial, the same agent identified the suitcase but was not asked to identify the drugs themselves. A DEA chemist stationed in New York City related to the court that she conducted drug analysis of seized substances that she took from the main vault and

---

79 Thompson v. State, 2006 Ark. App. LEXIS 364 (2006).

80 *See* 557 U.S. 107, 129 S. Ct. 2527, 174 L. Ed. 2d 314, 2009 U.S. LEXIS 4734 (2009). *See also* Bullcoming v. New Mexico, 131 S.Ct. 2705, 2011 U.S. LEXIS 4790 (2011), which effectively reaffirms Melendez-Diaz v. Massachusetts. For a slightly different analysis and view of the confrontation clause of the Sixth Amendment as it is applied to scientific tests, *see* Williams v. Illinois, 132 S.Ct. 2221 (2012).

81 United States v. Rawlings, 606 R.3d 73, 84, 2010 U.S. App. LEXIS 10719 (3d Cir. 2010).

determined that the objects contained a particular weight of cocaine. The defendant complained that the drugs were stored in New Jersey and the DEA chemist testified that she removed them from a vault. It was never established whether the DEA chemist based in New York got the cocaine from New Jersey-based ICE agents or where the drugs were actually located at all times before she tested them. Her testimony was that she did test the substance; it was cocaine; and the sample introduced at trial was same one that she had tested. The court of appeals rejected the defendant's broken chain-of-custody argument and noted that, due to the various agents' testimony, there was a "reasonable probability" that the cocaine package seized from the suitcase, stored in New Jersey, and tested and introduced in court, involved the same drug.[82] The court further noted that any weaknesses in the chain of custody generally affects the weight of the evidence but not its admissibility.

However, in an Ohio case, police arranged for a controlled buy using a confidential informant who they carefully searched prior to sending him to meet the seller to make the buy.[83] The informant was also fitted with audio and video recording devices. The police officer observed the confidential informant enter and leave the defendant's apartment and observed the confidential informant from time he left the apartment until the officers searched the confidential informant to reveal the expected drugs that the informant purchased. The police agents followed the standard departmental pre-purchase and post-purchase protocols established by the department. The suspected drug sample obtained during the purchase was delivered and locked into a drug safe in the police department and later removed and sent to the state laboratory for testing. The state laboratory technician who tested it found that the sample involved crack cocaine, and the written report was entered into evidence. The trial court allowed, and the appellate court approved, the admission of the crack cocaine into evidence because the proper chain of custody had been demonstrated, and the conviction was not disturbed.

Generally, courts have authorized the introduction of not only narcotics seized from the defendants or from their residences, but also related objects such as drug paraphernalia, containers used for packaging, records, pagers, and other "tools of the trade." Some examples will highlight the types of evidence that have been introduced and the conditions surrounding the introduction of the evidence.

Concerning drug-related evidence in a Tennessee case, a trial court admitted three aerosol cans that originally contained engine starting fluid, one component of which was ether, used in manufacturing methamphetamine. Police initially stopped the defendant's vehicle because he had been reported to have recently purchased large quantities of Sudafed, an over-the-counter decongestant that can be used as a precursor chemical in the production of methamphetamine. A problem with admission of the three starter fluid cans occurred when one deputy sheriff checked two cans from the property room and used them to clean the carburetor on his personal boat motor. Because the original

---

82 *Id.* at 85.

83 State v. Bell, 2013 Ohio 1299, 2013 Ohio App. LEXIS 1210 (2013).

officer identified the three starting fluid cans at trial as being the ones he seized from the defendant, the appellate court did not find error in the chain of custody and stated, "The identification or chain of custody is sufficient if the facts establish a reasonable assurance of the identity of the evidence and its integrity."[84]

F. Other Types of Evidence

Other articles connected with a crime are also admissible if they meet the general tests. For example, in a murder case that involved crossing state lines and triggered federal jurisdiction, an expert in analytical chemistry was permitted to testify at trial concerning paint chips found at the murder scene and a sample taken from a burned motor vehicle involved in the crime.[85] Matching the paint chip from the crime scene with the vehicle involved in the murder had the tendency to connect the defendants to the killings. The defendants objected to the scientific theory behind paint chip comparison, alleging that the comparison process was unreliable, methods of peer review were unreliable, and there was a lack of proper data regarding rates of error in chip comparison. Chain of custody of the paint chips was not contested, with the result that the reviewing court sustained the convictions.

In a burglary-robbery case, the defendant raised a question concerning the prosecutor's proof of the chain of custody of a tobacco sample.[86] The perpetrator entered a woman's home and secured the victim with a bathrobe that he placed over her head and cinched with the bathrobe's terry belt so that she could not observe him. He removed some of her clothing and touched her in intimate areas and then gathered the victim's truck keys, firearms, jewelry, and other valuables and put the items in the victim's truck, which he used to drive away from the scene of the crime. The victim thought she recognized the voice of the perpetrator and communicated this to police, who quickly arrested the defendant. The DNA evidence, a chewing tobacco plug that was discovered in a trash bag that had been removed from the victim's bathroom and recovered from the stolen truck, matched the defendant's DNA profile. The break in the chain of custody occurred when the victim removed the trash bag from the recovered pick-up truck and put it in a shed on the victim's property until it was transferred to police. The defendant contended that something could have happened to the DNA sample during the time that it was placed in the shed until the police retrieved it and subjected it to DNA testing. The trial court found that the defendant only offered mere speculation that something might have occurred to the saliva sample and, therefore, the chain of custody, though possessing a slight gap, was not sufficiently broken to prevent the admission of the DNA sample against the defendant.

In an unpublished California arson case, a court convicted a grandmother and her grandson of committing arson of their residential home and insurance fraud.[87]

---

84 State v. Long, 2005 Tenn. Crim. App. LEXIS 199 (2005).

85 United States v. Whitmore, 386 Fed. Appx. 464, 2010 U.S. App. LEXIS 14599 (5th Cir. 2010).

86 Newman v. State, 2012 Ida.App. Unpub. LEXIS 354 (Idaho. 2012).

87 People v. Mead, 2006 Cal. App. Unpub. LEXIS 3150 (2006).

Firefighters responded to a report of the fire and discovered several old burn areas on floors and an active fire in a linen closet that they later concluded had been intentionally set. When other evidence aroused additional suspicion by firefighters that the fire might have been intentionally set, they procured a criminal search warrant. In executing the warrant, investigators

> [f]ound bills indicating [defendant] was past due on her mortgage and a credit card account. They also found receipts from Wal-Mart for the recent purchase of storage containers and garbage cans. In a motor home on the property, investigators found storage containers matching the type on the receipts. They also found several cats in small cages, clothing, food, and a computer. Further, they located receipts for three storage units at a self-storage facility. A search of these units revealed clothing, furniture, and household furnishings in good condition. Some items in the units were contained in storage bins matching the type on the receipts.[88]

The trial court permitted the evidence of prefire planning and other real evidence to be introduced against both defendants, and a jury rendered a guilty verdict on all counts. The court of appeals upheld the convictions, noting that any rational trier of fact could have found that all the essential elements of the crimes had been proven beyond a reasonable doubt.

§ 14.5 View of the Scene

As a strong general rule, a trial court has the discretion concerning whether to allow a jury to have a view of the scene of the alleged crime, and the trial court's decision will only be reversed on appeal based on a showing of an abuse of the judge's discretion when the judge has acted in an arbitrary or capricious manner.[89] Generally, the defendant and legal counsel must be permitted to accompany the jury to a view of the scene, and a failure to permit their presence may be reversible error.[90] The trial judge may act on a motion by either party or may order the jurors to be escorted to a place where a material fact occurred or an offense was committed, without a motion of either party. In Connecticut, in deciding whether to allow a view of the scene, a judge may consider whether a view of the scene would be helpful to the jury in determining any factual issues and may order that the jury be conducted to the scene or location of the crime at any time before closing arguments.[91] The Connecticut court should consider whether the viewing of the scene is necessarily important in order to understand

---

88 *Id.*

89 People v. Russell, 50 Cal. 4th 1228, 1246, 242 P.3d 68, 83, 117 Cal. Rptr. 3d 615, 633, 2010 Cal. LEXIS 11346 (2010).

90 *See* People v. Garcia, 36 Cal. 4th 777, 115 P.3d 1191, 31 Cal. Rptr. 3d 541, 2005 Cal. LEXIS 8226 (2005). *But see* State v. Engelhardt, 280 Kan. 113, 123, 119 P.3d 1148, 1159, 2005 Kan. LEXIS 462 (2005), holding that a defendant may have no right to be present at a jury view of the scene.

91 State v. Boutilier, 144 Conn. App. 867, 872, 2013 Conn. App. LEXIS 409 (2013).

the evidence, but a view of the scene should be invoked only after the judge becomes satisfied that the conditions at the scene are substantially the same or similar to those that existed on the day of the incident or crime.[92]

A New York statute regulates jury views of the scene of a crime and permits a jury viewing when the judge is of the opinion that a viewing or observation by the jury of the premises or place

> where an offense on trial was allegedly committed, or of any other premises or place involved in the case, will be helpful to the jury in determining any material factual issue, it may in its discretion, at any time before the commencement of the summations, order that the jury be conducted to such premises or place for such purpose.[93]

As a strong general rule, the jury must be kept together as a group under the supervision of the court, and the parties have the right to be actually present. The purpose of a view of the scene is to allow visual observation by the jury of the premises or place in question so that the jury may see places or objects that are relevant to the case and thus to provide them with a mental picture of the locality.[94] There exists a conflict in law as to whether a view constitutes independent evidence; however, the resulting difference in opinion has little operational effect because the jury has the power to give a view of the scene whatever weight it chooses.

The procedure for viewing the premises varies from state to state, and the manner of viewing the scene is often regulated by statute or rule of the court. Good practice dictates that the trial judge attend the viewing with the members of the jury, although it may not constitute reversible error if the judge does not view the scene.[95] Consistent with the general rule, under the New York view, in conducting a view of the scene, "the jury must be kept together throughout under the supervision of an appropriate public servant or servants appointed by the court, and the court itself must be present throughout."[96] As a general rule, the parties and their counsel are allowed to be present; however, they are not permitted to discuss their case with members of the jury, and jurors are not allowed to discuss the case in any manner. For example, Kansas law provides that while conducting a view of the scene, generally "no person other than the officer and the person appointed to show them the place shall speak to them on any subject connected with the trial"[97] and, even then, only to the extent that it is necessary to conduct the jury to the place and to identify the places, things, or objects that are relevant to the case. In addition, Kansas criminal procedure allows, but does not require, a judge to permit a defendant to be present.[98]

---

92 *Id.*

93 N.Y. CRIM. PROC. LAW § 270.50 (1) (2013).

94 *Id.* at (2), (3).

95 State v. Campbell, 2006 Tenn. Crim. App. LEXIS 584 (2006).

96 N.Y. CRIM. PROC. LAW § 270.50 (2) (2013).

97 KAN. STAT. ANN. § 22-3418 (2013).

98 *Id.*

In criminal cases, most states permit the accused to be present; in others, the presence of the accused is within the discretion of the judge. For example, in one state, if a view of the scene is permitted, "[t]he accused has the right to attend such view by the jury, but may waive this right."[99] While most jurisdictions do not permit jurors to ask questions at the scene, there are situations in which a judge may permit juror questions. Inevitably, what the jurors see at a view of the scene will be used in reaching a verdict; therefore, viewing the scene must be carefully planned, and the activities at the scene must be kept under close supervision. A defendant may base an appeal on crime-scene views if prejudice to the case resulted from the viewing.[100]

§ 14.6 Photographs

As mentioned in previous sections, it is often possible to exhibit the person of the victim to the jury or judge, to introduce actual articles and items connected with the crime, or to have the jury view the scene of the crime. When it is not practical to bring tangible real evidence before a court, using photographs or video representation may be used. On the other hand, it is often impossible to define tangible evidence and properly convey its importance by words alone. An old saying that a picture is worth a thousand words may well constitute one reason for using pictures in criminal courts. Photographs frequently convey information to the court and jury more accurately than words and, when properly taken and explained, present this type of evidence in a convenient fashion. Although photos arguably are merely graphic representations of the oral testimony of witnesses, they often have far greater value than words and may pose a risk of unfair prejudice because of the chance that jurors may be swayed by emotion or vindictiveness and have only a defendant upon whom to vent these feelings.

When an attorney for a party determines that a picture would advance his or her case, the attorney must convince the judge that the photographic evidence has sufficient relevance to be introduced. Because a trial judge has discretion concerning whether to admit or exclude a photograph, the proponent must make the argument that the probative value of the photographs outweighs any potential unfair prejudice to the other party. Consistent with the concept of relevancy, a trial court can exclude evidence that possesses some logical relevance (including photographs), where "its probative value is substantially outweighed by a danger of one or more of the following: unfair prejudice, confusing the issues, misleading the jury, undue delay, wasting time, or needlessly presenting cumulative evidence."[101] Judicial decisions to admit or exclude photographic evidence must be based on the sound discretion of the judge and will not result in error, unless there is proof of an abuse of discretion. Precisely how this calculation is made varies with the case, the need for the evidence, and the perception of the judge.

---

99 OHIO REV. CODE ANN. 2945.16 (2013).

100 State v. Matthis, 970 So. 2d 505, 2007 La. LEXIS 2389 (2007).

101 FED. R. EVID. 403.

In considering the admissibility of photographs, the Supreme Court of Arkansas suggested that:

> When photographs are helpful to explain testimony, they are ordinarily admissible. Further, the mere fact that a photograph is inflammatory or is cumulative is not, standing alone, sufficient reason to exclude it. Even the most gruesome photographs may be admissible if they assist the trier of fact in any of the following ways: by shedding light on some issue, by proving a necessary element of the case, by enabling a witness to testify more effectively, by corroborating testimony, or by enabling jurors to better understand the testimony. Other acceptable purposes are to show the condition of the victims' bodies, the probable type or location of the injuries, and the position in which the bodies were discovered. Absent an abuse of discretion, this court will not reverse a trial court for admitting photographs into evidence.[102]

This passage offers some standards to judge whether to admit a photograph and does not simply mean that any and all photographs should be admitted into evidence. For a photograph to be properly considered for admission, the trial judge must evaluate the probative value of that photograph and consider its prejudicial effect in the exercise of judicial discretion. Photographs may be admissible even where a defendant offers to stipulate concerning what they would demonstrate and even under circumstances that involve undisputed facts.

Unless photographs were part of the crime, such as would be the case in child pornography or extortion by use of a photograph, these images are generally inadmissible as original or substantive evidence. However, as demonstrative real evidence, photographs should be admissible where they help the witness explain testimony or assist the jury in understanding the testimony of a witness. As a general rule, so long as they assist the trier fact, even gruesome photographs are generally admissible in evidence, provided that the prejudicial value is not too high.

The proponent of photographic evidence must supply the court with a proper foundation prior to admission into evidence. Federal Rule of Evidence 901 requires authentication or identification that an item of evidence is what its proponent claims. In the case of a photograph, the person who took the photo presumably could offer evidence concerning where, when, how, and under what circumstances he or she took the photo. A photo may be authenticated by anyone who has sufficient knowledge to prove that the contents of a photo depict what it purports to depict. For example, in a stabbing case, the defendant objected to the admission of photographs by a police officer who did not take the picture but was able to state that he was present and observed the stab wounds and that the wounds were accurately depicted in the photographs at issue.[103] Additionally, the prosecutor obtained the officer's testimony that he observed the victim's wounds when he first arrived at the crime location and when medical personnel treated the victim, both at the crime scene and at the hospital. The reviewing court rejected the defendant's arguments concerning lack of proper foundation and noted that the

---

102 Davis v. State, 350 Ark. 22; 86 S.W.3d 872; 2002 Ark. LEXIS 528 (2002).

103 State v. High Elk, 330 Mont. 259, 265, 127 P.3d 432, 436, 2006 Mont. LEXIS 6 (2006).

admission of photographic evidence lies within the sound discretion of the trial court. To be admissible, a photograph must first be made a part of a qualified person's testimony. Someone, often a law enforcement officer, must serve as its testimonial sponsor; in other words, it must be verified. A photograph may not be received by itself, but must be brought to court by a witness and authenticated as genuine and correctly representing what it purports to represent.[104]

A trial court has broad discretion to determine the admissibility of photographs and videotapes by weighing the probative value of such evidence against its unfair prejudicial effect.[105] For example, autopsy photographs may be admissible when they help explain the evidence in a case. In a California murder case, the reviewing court approved the admission, over the defendant's objection, of close-up photographs of three men who had been sitting in an automobile when they were shot to death, and the reviewing court also allowed autopsy photographs of the men's bodies that showed the location of the wounds on the male victims.[106] The court indicated that the probative value of the photographs helped the jury determine whether the defendant's contention of self-defense was credible. In a different case that involved issues of habeas corpus that arose out of a situation where a father allegedly killed his own daughter, the trial court admitted a variety of autopsy photographs that were admittedly gruesome.[107] The child died after being folded in half by her father, breaking her spine and tearing her aorta, all the details of which were presented in photographs that the trial court admitted into evidence. Photographs depicted the victim's broken spine and indicated a separation between some of the vertebrae. Other photographs involved close-up views of organs removed from the child's torso with the aorta remaining in place and some photographs included the victim's face and chest on the autopsy table, taken prior to the actual autopsy. The prosecution contended that the photographs were corroborative of the testimony in the case rather than unfairly prejudicial to the defendant's position. The trial court agreed with the prosecution, a position upheld on appeal, and sustained in the habeas corpus action. Although gruesome photographs in this case demonstrated what happened, they did not prevent the defendant father from receiving a fair trial, according to the federal habeas corpus court.

In addition to being properly verified or identified, photographic evidence will not be admitted unless it is relevant and necessary. Photographs are generally admissible to prove facts at issue in a criminal case, if they have a tendency to prove or disprove some disputed point or if the photographs offer corroboration of other evidence. Even photographs that might inflame the passions of the jury may be admissible where there is a need for the evidence. In a case involving a capital murder sentencing trial, the evidence

---

104 3 WIGMORE, EVIDENCE § 794 (3d ed. 1970); *see also* Phillips v. State, 550 N.E.2d 1290 (Ind. 1990), which held that photographs are generally admissible if they depict an object or scene that a witness would be permitted to describe in his or her testimony.

105 State v. Davlin, 272 Neb. 139, 158, 719 N.W.2d 243, 2006 Neb. LEXIS 123 (2006).

106 *See* People v. Duff, 2014 Cal. LEXIS 637 (2014). *See* this case in Part II, Chapter 14.

107 Cole v. Trammell, 2013 U.S. App. LEXIS 23188 (10th Cir. 2013).

revealed that the defendant attacked his female victim at a public recreation center in a particularly violent manner.[108] The victim ran toward the center's innermost staff offices, where the defendant cornered her. The evidence revealed that the defendant beat the victim using his fists, a compass, a golf club, and a wooden coat rack. The forensic evidence, including evidence on her nude body, established that she was moving about during the attack until the coat rack pierced her skull and ended her life. At trial, and over the defendant's objection, the trial court permitted a variety of crime-scene photographs showing the deceased's partially nude and beaten body, 11 autopsy photographs, and 30 general crime-scene photographs that were fairly gruesome. Noting that the admissibility of photographs is a matter generally allotted to the trial court's discretion, the reviewing court observed that photographs are admissible if they have some probative value and are not unduly prejudicial in an unfair manner. The appellate court approved of the use of these photographs by various expert witnesses who testified concerning blood spatter characteristics as well as evidence from the medical examiner relative to the cause of death. Because the photographs assisted the jury in understanding the nature of the wounds and how they were inflicted on the deceased, the reviewing court ruled that the trial court had not been in error when it admitted them. Even where autopsy photographs might be somewhat cumulative, they are not always excluded.

A defendant cannot prevent the prosecution from using photographs by conceding or admitting that a deceased died from a gunshot wound, or from a beating, or from specific injuries. It has often been stated that there is no rule that requires a prosecutor to try a case based on stipulations,[109] so by removing some issues from the contest, a defendant cannot defeat the use of photographs by the prosecution. Even after an offer of a stipulation, the prosecution may introduce photographs because they help present the true story of a case and may be helpful to a jury in rendering a verdict or a sentence and therefore remain relevant.[110]

In some situations, photographs are evidence of the crime itself. In a prosecution for several child pornography offenses, the court allowed images of children in sexual poses to be admitted against the defendant.[111] The photographic images had been obtained from servers belonging to Yahoo! and Google and delivered to the government. Legal assistants for both companies testified concerning the reliability of servers and their accuracy and indicated their familiarity with the records collection process of both companies. They testified that the photographic evidence offered by the prosecution from both of the company's servers involved the same images as those produced during a search of Yahoo! and Google's servers and that the images were properly attributable to the defendant. The district court allowed the introduction of the evidence because it was what the prosecution claimed and it was properly linked to the defendant.

---

108 Mitchell v. State, 2010 OK CR 14, 235 P.3d 640; 2010 Okla. Crim. App. LEXIS 13 (2010).

109 Green v. Commonwealth, 197 S.W.3d 76, 2006 Ky. LEXIS 140 (2006) (quoting Payne v. Commonwealth, 623 S.W.2d 867, 877 (Ky. 1981)).

110 Green v. Commonwealth, 197 S.W.3d 76, 2006 Ky. LEXIS 140 (2006).

111 United States v. Cameron, 2011 U.S. Dist. LEXIS 4721 (Dist. Me. 2011).

In several cases, the question has arisen as to whether it is necessary to follow the rules relating to the chain of custody as discussed in § 14.2. Still photographs and video movies are treated differently from instrumentalities of the crime or fungible drugs that do not necessarily have unique qualities. In a prosecution in which a security camera captured the crime and getaway, the prosecution played the video for the jury and made a few still photos from the video that were introduced over the defendant's objection on chain-of-custody grounds. The video and the still photographs did not require any proof of chain of custody because witnesses authenticated the pictures by testifying to their genuine quality.[112] The fact that it is not necessary to establish the chain of custody of a photograph, however, does not mean that it may be used without authentication. Evidence must be introduced to demonstrate that the photograph constitutes a genuine representation of the object or scene depicted.

Not all photographs are admissible, even when a proper foundation is laid. If, in obtaining a photograph, the state violates the Constitution, the defendant has constitutional grounds to object to its admissibility. In the case of *California v. Ciraolo*, police officers took an airplane flight over the defendant's backyard and photographed marijuana under cultivation.[113] The United States Supreme Court held that the photographs were lawfully taken from a public vantage point and no constitutional violation occurred. However, when officers use infrared photography without a warrant to scan a home or apartment to reveal extra heat escaping from the building that might indicate the presence of a marijuana grow house, the image produced should have been suppressed from use to obtain a search warrant for the home because taking the image violated the defendant's expectation of privacy under the Fourth Amendment.[114]

A. Posed Photographs

Some courts will allow the introduction into evidence of staged or posed photographs of attempted reproductions of crime scenes showing posed persons, dummies, or other objects. However, one court held that posed photographs of trial witnesses that were prepared for the sole purpose of allowing the jury to take the photos to the jury room to associate a name with a witness's face constituted error.[115] Some posed photographs are actual evidence of the crime. A federal court upheld a state court's admission of nudity-oriented, posed-child photographs that the defendant had arranged and taken of children that played in his own home.[116] According to the federal court that ruled on defendant's habeas corpus petition, there was no federal constitutional

---

112 State v. Thomas, 158 S.W.3d 361, 2005 Tenn. LEXIS 135 (2005).

113 California v. Ciraolo, 476 U.S. 207, 106 S. Ct. 1809, 90 L. Ed. 2d 210, 1986 U.S. LEXIS 154 (1986).

114 State v. Detroy, 102 Haw. 13, 72 P.3d 485, 2003 Haw. LEXIS 314 (2003). *See also* Kyllo v. United States, 533 U.S. 27, 2001 U.S. LEXIS 4487 (2001).

115 State v. Chomnarith, 654 N.W.2d 660, 666, 2003 Minn. LEXIS 2 (2003).

116 Dolman v. Coleman, 2013 U.S. Dist. LEXIS 79053 (N.D. Ohio 2013).

deficiency in his prosecution. Some posed photos were of preteen girls who modeled some clothing provided by the defendant, and some were younger girls in scanty clothing, one as young as seven posed in panties and socks. Police obtained these photographs and others of nude children by executing a valid search warrant on the defendant's home, where computers, cameras, CDs and DVDs and VHS tapes were found. No issues of evidence authentication of the images arose during the prosecution. An Ohio court upheld a posed photo of a defendant handcuffed on his stomach with money and crack cocaine placed on his back by police. The Ohio Court of Appeals noted that "[w]e agree with appellant that the photographs had limited probative value but we do not find them misleading or prejudicial as argued by the appellant."[117] In a different case, the Supreme Court of Georgia approved the use of a staged photograph of a police officer holding a particular stance to demonstrate the trajectory of a fatal bullet. According to the court, there was no abuse of discretion by the trial court.[118] In recent years, posed photographs have seen diminished use in criminal trials, probably because of computer-generated animations (CGAs) and some reluctance of courts to admit posed photographs.

B. *Gruesome Photographs*

As a general rule, trial courts are rarely reversed based on abuse of discretion in the admission of photographs that might be classified as gruesome or inflammatory. There is the requirement that the probative value of the photographs outweigh the risk of unfair prejudice, but that measuring concept remains a rather subjective device so that appellate courts often choose to defer to the trial court judgment. And in federal habeas corpus cases, reviewing courts do not normally review state court admission or exclusion of evidence issues, including photographs. An Arkansas court noted:

> Even the most gruesome photographs may be admissible if they assist the trier of fact by shedding light on some issue, by proving a necessary element of the case, by enabling a witness to testify more effectively, by corroborating testimony, or by enabling jurors to better understand the testimony. Other acceptable purposes are to show the condition of the victim's body, the probable type or location of the injuries, and the position in which the body was discovered.[119]

On the other hand, a different court held that photographs that are gruesome or inflammatory and lack any evidentiary purpose should be excluded.[120] After making this general observation, a Mississippi court noted that when deciding on the admissibility of gruesome photographs, the trial judge must consider (1) whether the proof is absolute or in doubt as to the identity of the guilty party and (2) whether the photographs are necessary evidence or simply a ploy on the part of the prosecutor to arouse

---

117 State v. Owings, 2006 Ohio 4281 (2006).

118 Rowe v. State, 276 Ga. 800, 582 S.E.2d 119, 2003 Ga. LEXIS 549 (2003).

119 Garcia v. State, 2005 Ark. LEXIS 559 (2005).

120 Underwood v. State, 708 So. 2d 18 (Miss. 1998).

passion and prejudice in the jury. Arkansas takes the view that introduction of a particular gruesome photograph does not constitute an abuse of discretion if a photograph helps inform the jury on some issue of the case, helps prove a necessary element of the case, allows a witness to testify more fully or more effectively, corroborates testimony, or allows the jury to better understand the testimony that has been offered.[121] In addition, the photographs cannot have an unfair prejudicial effect that would outweigh the probative value. Consistent with this basic theoretical foundation, an Arkansas appellate court approved the introduction of crime-scene and autopsy photographs of a man who had been beaten to death with a baseball bat by his son-in-law. The prosecution wanted to show the extent of the victim's head injuries and indicated that if the victim's skin was not separated from the skull, the jury would be unable to see the full extent of the victim's injuries visible in an autopsy photograph. According to the reviewing court, the photographs were not unfairly prejudicial and were offered for an appropriate purpose, and therefore, the trial court committed no abuse of discretion in admitting them.

While many defendants base their appeals partially on alleged error in the admission of prejudicial photographs, few are ever successful on this ground because reviewing courts rarely find that the trial judge has abused judicial discretion. The line between photographs that are inadmissible because they unduly arouse passion or prejudice and those that have sufficient probative value remains a gray area rather than a bright line. For example, a Michigan court allowed the admission of a black-and-white photograph of the female decedent's body lying naked on her back with her arms crossed, revealing a stab wound to her neck.[122] In a California gang retaliation killing case, the trial court permitted the prosecution to introduce a photograph that showed the abdomen of the victim after being stabbed and showed the extrusion of the intestines of the victim from inside the body.[123] Even though it was a gruesome photograph, it depicted the condition of the victim at the time he was first attended by paramedics and thereafter at the coroner's office. Other gruesome photos were allowed because they were relevant to issues like intent, malice, premeditation, and deliberation. The same court excluded some other photographs because the trial judge felt that the cumulative effect if they were admitted would be unfairly prejudicial to the defense and would outweigh any probative value that would accrue to the prosecution.

In an Arizona murder case, a reviewing court considered whether photographs had been properly introduced over the defendant's objection.[124] In approving the admission of photographs that depicted blood spatter and blood pools on the floor beneath the decedent's body, the court noted that the photographs corroborated the expert opinion of a government witness that the person who slit the decedent's throat stood behind the decedent's chair to accomplish the mission.

---

121 Nunn v. State, 2013 Ark. App. 282, 2013 Ark. App. LEXIS 309 (2013).

122 People v. Benore, 2005 Mich. App. LEXIS 2718 (2005).

123 People v. Khek, 2013 Cal. App. Unpub. LEXIS 2870 (2013).

124 State v. Lynch, 234 P.3d 595, 603, 2010 Ariz. LEXIS 25 (2010).

If photographs of this type do not result in reversal because they help prove the case, most photographs will be admitted unless there is no apparent reason to introduce them. In explaining admissibility of rough photographs, one court noted that gruesome photographs have evidentiary value in homicide cases when they assist in describing the circumstances of a killing, describe the location where the body was found, indicate the cause of death, and supplement or explain the clarity of witness testimony.[125]

The general rule that can be discerned from the case law suggests that if photographs are relevant to facts in issue and are not so inflammatory or prejudicial as to substantially outweigh their probative value, the mere fact that they are somewhat inflammatory or even gruesome does not bar their admission. If, however, the photographs have the potential to distort the deliberative process and unfairly skew the trial's outcome, their prejudicial effect outweighs their probative value, and admission is improper.

C. *Time of Taking*

In authenticating photographs for admission in criminal cases, the photograph must accurately depict what it purports to depict so that the picture is not misleading either because too much time has passed between the event in question and the time the photograph was taken or because the picture may not accurately capture the situation as it existed on the relevant date. To be admissible, a photograph must be sufficiently identified as a true and accurate representation of what it is supposed to represent. Therefore, if the time between the incident and the taking of the photograph is so great as to make it unlikely that the photograph actually portrays the situation as it existed at the time of the incident, such a photograph cannot be authenticated as accurately portraying the reality of the original event or scene and should not be admissible. A driving while intoxicated case from Alaska is demonstrative of the principle that a photograph must capture an image that is roughly the same as it was at the time of the crime and substantially unchanged and not materially different in order for it to be admitted into evidence.[126] The defendant had been captured following a high-speed motorcycle chase and a subsequent excursion of the motorcycle from the highway. The defendant appeared intoxicated with bloodshot eyes and slurred speech patterns. He claimed that he was not the driver and that the actual driver was somewhere around the area, but police could never find anyone else. At trial, the defendant attempted to introduce photographs that had been taken immediately prior to trial that indicated minimal vegetation that would have allowed the alleged actual driver to escape without matting down grasses or leaving evidence of his presence near the motorcycle. The prosecutor successfully resisted the admission of photographs because the defendant's pictures were taken in May prior to the beginning of the Alaskan growing season, but the actual DWI incident occurred during the prior August when the vegetation looked very different

---

125 McIntosh v. State, 917 So. 2d 78, 84, 2005 Miss. LEXIS 754 (2005).

126 Marriott v. State, 2013 Alas. App. LEXIS 93 (2013).

and was robust because it was the top of the growing season. In addition, a construction project had widened the path taken by the motorcycle since the incident, and the area looked very different at the time of trial than it did at the time of the apprehension. The reviewing court upheld the trial judge's decision to exclude the photographs on the grounds that, because of vegetation and topography changes, the photos did not fairly and accurately depict the scene at the time of the DUI arrest and that they were actually misleading.[127]

In a case involving criminal property damage, police took pictures of the automobile that had been damaged to both indicate the state of damage and to preserve the crime scene with a photograph.[128] The pictures were taken shortly after the crime had occurred and accurately depicted the condition of the motor vehicle immediately after the crime, according to the complaining witness. No error was found in the admission of the pictures under these circumstances.

Demonstrative of the principle that pictures must be taken at the appropriate time, in an Arizona case where the defendant had been charged with being a felon who possessed a deadly weapon contrary to law, he alleged that a photograph showing him holding a Ruger pistol was not what it appeared.[129] He contended that the "gun" in the picture was not real but was an Airsoft® replica pistol, and so the photograph should not be used in evidence against him to prove his prohibited possession. An additional factor that made the photo relevant was the fact that the defendant admitted that he *knew* that he could not possess firearms and the picture appeared to have been taken *after* his disqualifying earlier felony conviction. A police search of the defendant's home produced two Ruger firearms, similar to the one in the picture. The defendant's pretrial motion to exclude the photograph showing him holding what appeared to be a pistol was rejected because the judge felt that the probative value of the photo outweighed the danger of unfair prejudice to the defendant's case. Part of the judge's reasoning appeared to have been influenced by the fact that the defendant spoke with his mother on an unsecured jailhouse phone in an attempt to get her to say that he lived elsewhere and did not live in the home where the police discovered the firearms. The reviewing court upheld the trial judge's decision admitting the photograph of the defendant holding the alleged weapon.[130] So long as the photographs accurately appear to depict what they purport to show and are not otherwise misleading, most courts will admit the photographs.

D. Color Photographs

While, color photographs, color slides, PowerPoint presentations, and other methods of displaying photographs are admissible in evidence and are subject to the same limitations and restrictions placed on black-and-white photographs, there is an

---

127 *Id.*

128 *See* State v. Pang, 2010 Haw. App. LEXIS 123 (2010).

129 State v. McCormick, 2013 Ariz. App. Unpub. LEXIS 999 (2013).

130 *Id.*

argument that color presentations contain more information and may have a tendency to inflame a jury to a greater extent than black-and-white pictures. Even though color photographs are often more lifelike and consequently may be more grotesque and revolting, the fact that a picture is in color constitutes a factor in determining whether it can be admitted.[131] In an Illinois murder prosecution, where the deceased was killed outside a bar with a firearm, a forensic pathologist who performed the autopsy on the victim brought several color photographs to court for admission to explain the fatal injuries.[132] In one of the photographs, the left lung of the deceased with a gunshot wound was shown as completely detached from the body and resting on a wooden surface on which there were some smears of blood. In another color photograph, the deceased's larynx and vocal chords and associated body parts were visible on the same wooden surface. Among other photographs, the doctor used a green rod that demonstrated the overall path of one of the bullets through vital organs. Although the defendant did not object to allowing the jury to see the photographs, he did object to sending some of the photographs into the jury room during deliberations. On appeal, the defendant argued that plain error had occurred and the photograph should not have been admitted into evidence, even though this argument had not been preserved specifically for appeal. In dismissing the appellant's contentions, the reviewing court noted that it was "not error to allow the jury to view, even gruesome photographs, where they are probative of the issues of the cause of the victim's death and the aforesaid manner in which the injuries were inflicted and where they corroborate the pathologist testimony concerning nature and the extent of the injuries suffered."

In another case involving color photography, where the color images were presented on a large screen within the courtroom, a reviewing court approved the use of the color images of the autopsy photographs and rejected the defendant's objection to the introduction of allegedly gruesome photographs taken during the autopsy of the deceased, a Pennsylvania state trooper.[133] One photograph that depicted the interior of the deceased officer's skull was necessary to show the bullet's trajectory and to demonstrate the neurological damage that the bullet caused. Other expert testimony, using the photographs, indicated that a second shot caused additional damage and supported the Commonwealth's position that the defendant executed the state trooper. The photographs that were introduced, according to the reviewing court, were admitted for relevant purposes and, while somewhat gruesome, did not create undue prejudice, especially where the trial court cautioned the jury concerning not allowing emotions to affect their thoughts.

Although the use of color photographs that may be somewhat gruesome arguably create some prejudice to a defendant's case, where there are valid reasons for introducing such photographs, trial courts will rarely have their admission decisions reversed.

---

131 Wilson v. State, 2009 Texas App. LEXIS 2954 (2009).

132 People v. Sanders 2013 IL App (2d) 120672-U, 2013 Ill. App. Unpub. LEXIS 2648 (2013).

133 Commonwealth v. Mollett, 2010 Pa. Super. 153, 5 A.3d 291, 301, 2010 Pa. Super. LEXIS 2621 (2010). *Appeal denied*, 2011 Pa. LEXIS 212 (2011).

E. Enlargements and Aerial Photographs

Photographs that have been enlarged in the same aspect ratio generally will be admitted if a smaller print or a photo on a computer screen would have been admissible. In a California felon in possession of a firearm case, the prosecution used an enlarged photo of a Raven Arms .25 caliber pistol that had been taken from the defendant's picture collection saved on his cell phone to help prove the gun belonged to him.[134] Although a defendant will typically object to the use of an enlarged picture on the grounds that the larger picture may cause unfair prejudice, courts routinely admit enlarged pictures because they help the jury better understand the evidence. In a proceeding involving child pornography photos discovered by the defendant's girlfriend on his cell phone, he objected to the admission of enlarged child porn photographs at trial.[135] The photos were recovered after being deleted from the cell phone and were the smallest ones available to be printed, being just a bit larger than those presented on the screen on the phone. The reviewing court approved the use of the enlarged photographs on the ground that the jury had been told that the photos were enlargements and that they were not distorted or misleading and to allow the jury to view the phone's actual images would have allowed the jury to observe other recovered photos that were not part of the prosecution. A different court, commenting on medical use of enlarged photographs observed, "Enlarged photographs facilitate medical experts in explaining injuries to juries as a group, and the practice has a legitimate evidentiary purpose."[136]

In an Arkansas murder trial, the prosecution had been allowed to introduce 17 enlarged pictures of the deceased victim who had been stabbed to death by her former boyfriend. Over objections by the defendant that the photographs were gruesome and ghoulish, the trial court permitted the prosecution to use photographs of the victim's body taken at the crime scene and other photographs that had been taken during the autopsy. One of the autopsy photos showed the victim's intestines protruding from a knife wound. In showing the photographs to the jury, the court permitted the prosecution to present enlarged photographs so that the jury could better understand the testimony. In approving the admission of the photographs, the Supreme Court of Arkansas noted,

> [W]e are convinced that the circuit judge did not abuse his discretion on [admission]. The trial court carefully examined each photograph offered for admission and weighed the appropriate balancing test. It exercised considerable discretion and restraint in deciding what photographs to admit into evidence. Further, the court individually pointed out its basis for allowing in each photograph, whether because it accurately depicted the crime scene, the extent of Katie's injuries, the condition of Katie's body following the attack, or was essential for a full understanding of the State's forensic and investigatory witnesses.

---

134 People v. Weathers, 2013 Cal. App. Unpub. LEXIS 4159 (2013).

135 Frye v. State, 2013 Ind. App. Unpub. LEXIS 1277, 995 N.E.2d 730 (2013).

136 Dalton v. Commonwealth, 2010 Ky. Unpub. LEXIS 45 (2010).

In this case, the photographs taken at the scene of the crime and enlarged at trial were introduced during the crime-scene technician's testimony to illustrate how the body was found, the injuries to the body, and how the scene appeared when the police arrived. The prosecution had the autopsy photographs introduced during the testimony of the forensic examiner, who testified concerning the nature of the injuries and the cause of death.[137] Enlarged photographs are frequently used in cases involving the comparison of handwriting or to show the place of an accident or the scene of a crime.

There seems to be no distinction between aerial and other types of photographs insofar as their admissibility is concerned, but authentication may be an issue. In a case in which a defendant had been charged with selling and delivering illegal recreational pharmaceuticals within 1,000 feet of a school, aerial photographs from the jurisdiction's planning department were authenticated and introduced to demonstrate that the defendant drug-selling activity was within the prohibited area.[138] In another case, the prosecution used an aerial photograph, with an officer's accompanying testimony, to indicate the area where police recovered a firearm involved in the crime of a felon being in possession of a weapon.[139] The admission of aerial photography is not uncommon, and such photographs are usually admitted into evidence for the purpose of giving the jury an accurate view of an object or geographic scene that is relevant to a fact in issue; however, they may be excluded from evidence at the discretion of the court when the court has previously admitted other evidence covering the same issues.[140]

§ 14.7 Motion Pictures, Videotapes, and Digital Video Recordings

Motion pictures, videotape recordings, DVD or CD video recordings, and accurate copies are admissible in evidence "once a proper foundation has been laid if the [recording] is a true, authentic, and accurate representation of the event taped without distortions or deletions."[141] The proponent of admission of a videotape recording or of a traditional movie film must lay a foundation that demonstrates that the film or video properly depicts what it purports to depict. The questions concerning authenticity are similar to those involved when laying the foundation for admission of a still photograph. The party desiring to introduce recorded motion pictures must establish that the contents of the motion pictures are relevant to an issue and that they accurately demonstrate what they purport to show. The authentication process also must demonstrate that the pictures are accurate, genuine, and that no tampering has occurred. In some

---

137 Marcyniuk v. State, 2010 Ark. 257, 2010 Ark. LEXIS 296 (2010).

138 *See* State v. Bryant, 2010 Tenn. Crim. App. LEXIS 897 (2010).

139 People v. Wilson, 2013 Il. App. 112272-U, 2013 Ill. App. Unpub. LEXIS 1422 (2013).

140 *See* United States v. Chiquito, 175 Fed. Appx. 215, 2006 U.S. App. LEXIS 8724 (10th Cir. 2006) and Helmig v. Kemna, 2006 U.S. App. LEXIS 22564 (8th Cir. 2006).

141 Parkinson v. Kelly, 2006 U.S. Dist. LEXIS 54661 (N.D.N.Y. 2006).

cases, the admissibility of motion pictures depends upon testimony by the operator of the camera that the film or video accurately portrays what he or she observed at the time and place of the action in question. Although modern evidence rules permit the admission of film, DVD, or still photos taken in sequence that some banks use, by permitting authentication by a person who can identify the contents of the recording,[142] some jurisdictions require a more formal presentation of a foundation. In one case involving forgery, an Indiana court noted the method of proving a foundation for film cameras requires that "there should be evidence as to how and when the camera was loaded, how frequently the camera was activated, when the photographs were taken, and the processing and chain of custody of the film after its removal from the camera."[143] In this forgery case, the bank camera recorded transactions, and it included one from the defendant teller forging a withdrawal record from a customer's account. The appellate court approved the admission of the bank surveillance tape showing the defendant's crime because the bank manager removed the videotape and a police officer checked it to identify the proper date of the tape. The officer watched that same videotape to match transaction numbers to customer accounts with representations that were depicted on the video. In addition, the custodian of the bank's records signed an affidavit that the surveillance taping was a regularly conducted business activity of the bank and that the custodian had verified the trustworthiness of the tape. This evidence proved to sufficiently lay the foundation for the video evidence.[144]

In determining whether photos and related matter should be admitted into evidence, a Georgia statute provides:

> Subject to any other valid objection, photographs, motion pictures, video recordings, and audio recordings produced at a time when the device producing the items was not being operated by an individual person or was not under the personal control or in the presence of an individual operator shall be admissible in evidence when the court determines, based on competent evidence presented to the court, that such items tend to show reliably the fact or facts for which the items are offered, provided that, prior to the admission of such evidence, the date and time of such photograph, motion picture, or video recording shall be contained on such evidence, and such date and time shall be shown to have been made contemporaneously with the events depicted in such photograph, motion picture, or video recording.[145]

In applying the statute, a Georgia appellate court approved the introduction of a videotape unknowingly made by the defendant when he committed larceny of tradesmen's tools at the front door of the Savannah office of the United States attorney.[146] Security cameras showed the victim and his tools, and later, the defendant and his

---

142 *See* FED. R. EVID. 901.

143 McHenry v. State, 820 N.E.2d 124, 128, 2005 Ind. LEXIS 4 (2005) (quoting Edwards v. State, 762 N.E.2d 128, 136, 2002 Ind. App. LEXIS 50 (2002)).

144 McHenry v. State, 820 N.E.2d 124, 128, 2005 Ind. LEXIS 4 (2005). *See* case in Part II.

145 GA. CODE ANN. § 24-9-923(c) (2013).

146 Sheppard v. State, 300 Ga. App. 631, 634, 686 S.E.2d 295, 298, 2009 Ga. App. LEXIS 1235 (2009).

friend, who took the tools, appeared in the video and made off with the stolen tools for parts unknown. The defendant contended that the trial court erred when it admitted the videotape from the surveillance camera because, he alleged, the prosecution failed to provide a proper foundation under the Georgia law, noted earlier. The security device recorded automatically and placed a date and time stamp on the video recording. The victim viewed the videotape prior to trial and, at trial, identified himself as being in the picture prior to the time his tools were stolen. Under the circumstances, the trial court felt that the videotape had been properly authenticated to depict what it purported to depict, and the reviewing court did not disturb the trial court's decision.

With respect to authentication and introduction of videotapes made by an automatic surveillance system, a Texas trial court admitted a video recording of an actual murder containing the moment the defendant discharged a firearm into the back of the head of the unsuspecting victim.[147] The defendant was a former employee of a taxicab company who knew where the safes were located, but who appeared to be unaware of the surveillance video recording system when he subsequently looted the two safes. When the body of the decedent was discovered, the surveillance system recorded that episode as well. The owner of the taxicab company viewed the video recording and indicated that it appeared to have properly recorded what happened within the company's building. The taxicab driver who discovered the body was also familiar with the recording system and testified that it was working properly on the day of the murder and appeared to have made an accurate rendition of the scene as the murder occurred up until the time the witness discovered the victim. The technician who installed the video system testified concerning how it worked and how it recorded, including the fact that there were four video cameras that fed data into a recording system and also presented the data in real-time to a quad screen office monitor. Almost immediately, the video surveillance system was taken by the police and was in their custody until the time of trial. After hearing the foregoing evidence, the trial court determined that the surveillance video had been properly authenticated and allowed it into evidence, and the ruling was upheld by the Texas Court of Appeals. In an Arizona case, authentication of a video copied to a DVD was relatively simple in a case involving sexual activity with minors when the defendant originally videotaped all but one of the crimes for which he was on trial.[148] His former girlfriend found the original videotape and burned it to a DVD, which she turned over to police. At trial, she identified the defendant and the victims' mothers identified the victim daughters in the video. The prosecution made a second DVD and added a chapter menu so that it was easier to find various vignettes of the defendant's alleged crimes. He did not object to the admission of the first DVD and argued on appeal that it should have been excluded, but the reviewing court found no plain error that would require a reversal.

---

147 Turnbull v. Texas, 2013 Tex. App. LEXIS 13167 (2013).

148 State v. Cervantes, 2011 Ariz. App. Unpub. LEXIS 1561 (2011). *Review denied* by State v. Cervantes, 2012 Ariz. LEXIS 146 (2012).

When video recordings have been edited or otherwise altered, proper authentication as substantive evidence may prove troublesome, and some courts will not admit the evidence. In an Illinois prosecution for a ninth offense of driving without a license, a neighbor had made a videotape of the defendant driving a van on public streets.[149] The neighbor who made the videotape made a copy of the original on a VCR and through a process of erasure, some of the videotape content that related to more personal matters was eliminated on the copy. The witness was somewhat evasive in explaining the editing process and how it occurred, but the trial court admitted the videotape as being properly authenticated. The tape that the court admitted clearly was a copy that omitted portions of the original, and the reviewing court held that it was error to admit the edited version. According to the reviewing court, an altered videotape copy that has been produced by an unexplained process is not acceptably authenticated for use as substantive evidence. The shift to digital visual recordings and the prevalence of image-altering computer programs serves to put a burden on trial judges to apply real evidence standards in ways that addresses the technological context of present-day video recorders.

In case involving a Texas Justice of the Peace, allegations had been made that the justice committed larceny when he removed new computer monitors from the courthouse where he worked.[150] A woman who worked in information technology, and who was familiar with the way their security cameras operated, testified that she made copies of recordings made by a motion detector camera that was triggered by the defendant's appearance when he entered the area where he took the monitors. The witness IT professional initially made a backup of the hard drive to preserve its original condition and then separately pulled various segments from the digital video recording system that depicted the defendant removing the monitors. She testified that she did not alter any of the images but that she did give a filename to each so that it would be possible to discern what each file contained. Texas Rule of Evidence, Rule 1003, in effect at the time of the case, held that copies of an original recording are admissible to the same extent as an original unless there is some question concerning the authenticity of the original, or it would otherwise be unfair to admit a duplicate original. A copy of the original hard drive was made available to the defendant prior to trial. The trial court rejected the defendant's argument based on the best evidence rule and his contention that the digital video recording used in court was nothing more than an abbreviated and altered copy of the original. The reviewing court rejected the allegations and concluded that the secondary recording made by the IT professional had been sufficiently authenticated by her and had been properly introduced in evidence.[151]

Newer cases may involve CGAs that incorporate the opinions of one or more expert witnesses in a manner that appears as a re-creation of a how a crime happened. The use of CGAs in criminal cases requires that the jury be informed that the

---

149 *See* People v. Flores, 2010 Ill. App. LEXIS 1386 (2010).

150 Williams v. State, 2013 Tex. App. LEXIS 9376 (2013).

151 *Id.*

animation constitutes only a demonstrative exhibit or an illustration that will be used to demonstrate the prosecution's theory of a case that is based on interpretation of actual evidence in the case. In one Pennsylvania case that involved a police officer as a defendant in a homicide prosecution involving the demise of his wife, the trial court permitted the Commonwealth to show the jury a CGA that incorporated the expert opinion of a forensic pathologist and a crime-scene reconstructionist that was based on the forensic and physical evidence found at the actual crime scene.[152] The trial court required the prosecution to properly authenticate the CGA as being a fair and accurate representation of the experts' reconstruction of the crime. Following the police officer's conviction of the murder of his wife, he appealed, contending that the CGA was unfairly prejudicial, lacked authentication, presented cumulative evidence, and should not have been admitted. The Supreme Court of Pennsylvania concluded that the admission or exclusion of CGAs should be governed by the concepts of authentication and relevancy, by weighing the chance for unfair prejudicial value against the probative effect of the evidence. The top court of the Commonwealth affirmed the police officer's conviction for first-degree murder because, among other issues, the admission of the CGA did not create unfair prejudice to his case and provided relevant evidence. Subsequently, the convicted police officer filed a petition for a writ of habeas corpus, which was rejected by a federal district court. The defendant argued that there was insufficient evidence to support the depictions in the CGA concerning how the victim fell, where her arm would have been located, and the position of the defendant, among other complaints. The habeas court found that the CGA was not inflammatory and was admitted only after an extensive limiting instruction by the court to the jury.[153] In a separate case involving a CGA issue that had a different outcome, the Court of Criminal Appeals of Oklahoma reversed a murder conviction in which a CGA attempted to demonstrate how the defendant killed her fiancé with a firearm.[154] The court overturned the conviction because the CGA failed to accurately and properly demonstrate what actually occurred. Insufficient data existed to tell which positions each person occupied during the event, and there were no data to explain the trajectory of the bullet. Essentially, the CGA filled in the gaps of evidence with what amounted to speculation. The prejudicial effect clearly outweighed any probative value offered by the animation.

Traditional motion pictures, videotape recordings, DVD recordings, and virtual movies constructed by the use of "padding" must be authenticated as accurately portraying what they purport to depict, as a threshold for admission into evidence. Video evidence and CGA must be relevant to a fact that is at issue in the case, and the prejudicial value cannot outweigh the probative value in order for a judge to allow the video evidence as proof in a case.

---

[152] Commonwealth v. Serge, 896 A.2d 1170, 1178, 2006 Pa. LEXIS 561 (2006).

[153] Serge v. Superintendent, 2012 U.S. Dist. LEXIS 122669 (M.D. Pa. 2012).

[154] *See* Dunkle v. State, 2006 Okla. Crim. 29, 139 P.3d 228, 2006 Okla. Crim. App. LEXIS 29 (2006).

§ 14.8 X-rays, CAT Scans, and MRI Images

For purposes of admission, the Federal Rules of Evidence generally treat X-ray evidence much like traditional photographs for purposes of authentication,[155] although some slightly different admission problems may arise. The purpose of an X-ray "picture" is to reveal inner portions of the body that cannot be seen by the naked eye by passing X-ray radiation through the human body to place an image on film that is sensitive to radiation produced by X-rays. Because no person ever really sees the body part depicted on X-ray film, it cannot be verified in the same manner as an ordinary photograph—that is, by testimony that it is a correct representation of the object that it purports to depict.

In a decision involving the potential termination of a parent's rights due to extreme child abuse, the mother contended that X-ray images taken at a hospital should not have been admitted to show broken bones of her child because the government had not authenticated them properly. The evaluating doctor testified that he is a specialist in the area of interpretation of pediatric imaging studies. He also testified that he was the radiologist who evaluated the child's X-ray images and that the images were appropriate for use. The doctor helped authenticate the X-rays by testifying that the images taken had the child's name and the date of the X-ray on them.[156] The Supreme Court of Texas held that the trial court properly admitted the X-ray image stored on the computer and did not abuse its discretion.[157]

In a case involving an alleged medical maltreatment of a New York state prisoner, the judge made a pretrial ruling excluding images produced by X-ray, bone scan, and a CAT (computer-assisted tomography) scan for use at trial because the images had been taken long after the alleged injury had occurred and lacked relevancy to the case.[158] The judge did not indicate that there was any particular problem with the admission of these types of images as a general principle, provided they were properly authenticated, but in this case they were not relevant to show injuries that occurred a long time prior to the creation of the present images.

The foundation for authentication of X-ray evidence is usually done by the testimony of an X-ray technician or a radiologist. Some jurisdictions hold that an X-ray has been sufficiently authenticated if the evidence shows that the X-ray was taken by a qualified expert who is familiar with X-ray techniques and procedures and that the X-ray is a true depiction of what it purports to represent.

Professional medical witnesses may illustrate X-rays, CAT scan images, and MRI (magnetic resonance imaging) images through a view screen, PowerPoint display, or other appropriate projection device. In addition, enlargements of X-ray angiograms from smaller images already authenticated should not be excluded from evidence

---

155 FED. R. EVID. 1001(c).

156 In the Interest of J.P.B., 2005 Texas App. LEXIS 1159 (2005).

157 In the Interest of J.P.B, 180 S.W.3d 570, 575, 2005 Tex. LEXIS 912 (2005).

158 Colon v. Porliar, 2012 U.S. Dist. LEXIS 2924 (N.D. NY. 2012)

where the enlargements were accurate representations of the evidence portrayed.[159] Using X-rays in a different manner, a computer tomography imaging system (CT or CAT scan) provides excellent images of living tissue, bone, and blood structures, and the resulting images can be admitted into evidence upon a proper foundation. MRI offers better views of some types of living tissue, and experts frequently testify once the doctor or other professional has provided a proper foundation. Similar issues of authentication arise with MRI and CT scan data that accompany traditional X-ray evidence.

§ 14.9 Sound Recordings, Phone Voice Messages, and Texts

Public sound recordings generally present few constitutional issues due to a lack of any Fourth Amendment or statutory expectation of privacy that exists when speaking in public,[160] and sounds or speech voluntarily uttered generally do not implicate Fifth Amendment self-incrimination allegations and should be admissible. Surreptitious recordings may present both constitutional issues as well as concerns relating to authentication of the voices that may be present on a wiretap recording. Recording conversations by one party to a phone conversation may be legal in many jurisdictions but not in others, where all persons must be aware and consent to the recording.[161] For example, recording a prisoner's nonlawyer phone calls does not transgress state or federal law, and the recording may be admissible against a prisoner.[162] In a Georgia case, the arrestee made several phone calls from jail during which he implicated himself more deeply in the crime for which he had been arrested.[163] At the start of each call, a warning issued that the call might be monitored or recorded, and the arrestee ignored the warning. The reviewing court approved the admission of the recorded calls against the arrestee.

Wiretapping A form of electronic eavesdropping in which, upon a court order, law enforcement officials surreptitiously listen to land and cell phone conversations, e-mail, text messages, and similar communications.

Federal law and many state statutes regulate **wiretapping** and surreptitious recording of conversations but provide for methods to properly record and to admit

[159] Arlton v. Schraut, 936 N.E.2d 831, 837, 2010 Ind. App. LEXIS 2063 (2010).

[160] *See* Commonwealth v. Rivera, 445 Mass. 119, 833 N.E.2d 1113; 2005 Mass. LEXIS 491 (2005), in which a convenience store robbery suspect failed in his argument to suppress video and audio of his conduct and words during a murder.

[161] *See* GA. CODE ANN. § 16-11-62 (2013). *See also* Bolton v. State, 2011 Tex. App. LEXIS 514 (2011), where a police investigator privately recorded a conversation with a suspect during a telephone call that was later admitted in court.

[162] *See* Sanchez v. State, 2005 Tex. App. LEXIS 5084 (2005).

[163] Boykins-White v. State, 305 Ga. App. 827, 829, 701 S.E.2d 221, 224, 2010 Ga. App. LEXIS 823 (2010).

the fruits of a wiretap[164] when done with a warrant by law enforcement agents. Through these laws and through constitutional protections, privacy rights are generally protected despite the advances in the ability of law enforcement agents and private citizens to record almost anything at any time. Despite defense bar concerns that extensive law enforcement use of recording devices raises serious constitutional questions, sound recordings are frequently admitted into evidence.

Recordings of 911 emergency telephone calls provide an excellent source of evidence that may be admissible at criminal trials.[165] In an Indiana case involving the illegal production of methamphetamine, a person with knowledge of the crime made a 911 call, which brought the police to the scene of the home of the defendant.[166] At his trial, the defendant objected to the admission of the audio of the 911 call because he contended it had not been properly authenticated. The trial court rejected his contention because one of the witnesses who knew the 911 caller, and who was present at the very moment the other witness made the 911 call, testified that he had listened to the recording of the 911 call prior to trial, verified its accuracy, and placed his initials on the compact disc of the recording after he listened to it. The same witness also identified the caller's voice on the 911 call in open court. The reviewing court held that the 911 call had been properly authenticated and properly admitted in evidence. Another method of authenticating 911 calls has been called the silent witness theory. This method of authentication allows an audio or video recording to essentially speak for itself as a method of authentication. An Alabama court suggested that this particular type of authentication required:

1. A showing that the device or process or mechanism that produced the item being offered as evidence was capable of recording what a witness would have seen or heard had a witness been present at the scene or event recorded.
2. A showing that the operator of the device or process or mechanism was competent.
3. Establishment of the authenticity and correctness of the resulting recording, photograph, videotape, etc.
4. A showing that no changes, additions, or deletions have been made.
5. A showing of the manner in which the recording, photograph, videotape, etc., was preserved.
6. Identification of the speakers or persons pictured.
7. For criminal cases only, a showing that any statement made in the recording, tape, etc., was voluntarily made without any kind of coercion or improper inducement.[167]

---

164 *See* OHIO REV. CODE ANN. § 2933.52 (2013).

165 *See* Crawford v. Washington, 541 U.S. 36, 2004 U.S. LEXIS 1838 (2004), where out-of-court evidence that is determined to be testimonial in nature cannot be admitted because of Sixth Amendment confrontation concerns.

166 Warren v. State, 982 N.E.2d 484, 2013 Ind. App. Unpub. LEXIS 78 (2013).

167 Calhoun v. State, 932 So. 2d 923, 2005 Ala. Crim. App. LEXIS 101 (2005), *cert. denied*, 2006 U.S. LEXIS 5233 (2006).

Authentication for 911 tapes may in actual practice be an easier task than authenticating recordings involving surreptitious audiotaping or wiretapping, where acquiring evidence to authenticate an unknown voice may prove difficult. The fact that the proponent of an audio recording has sufficiently authenticated it does not mean that the substantive content will be admissible; the concept of authentication is a preliminary hurdle that must be overcome prior to considerations of admission of the internal content. In authenticating a 911 call from a Washington domestic violence victim, who was speaking with the operator and the alleged perpetrator, the defendant argued that the recorded 911 audio had not been properly authenticated and should have been excluded from his criminal trial.[168] In Washington, a tape-recording can be authenticated by calling a witness who has personal knowledge of the conversation, and by one who has knowledge of its contents, by one who testifies that the audio recording accurately portrayed the original conversation, or by one who identifies each relevant voice heard on the tape.[169] The 911 conversation was sufficiently authenticated in a couple of different ways. In this case, circumstantial evidence indicated the victim made the call from the particular address because when the officers arrived at the address associated with the 911 call, the victim was present. While the victim did not testify at trial, the trial court itself made a direct comparison between the voices on the 911 recording and some jailhouse recordings made by the defendant. In one of the jailhouse recordings, the defendant referred to the victim by name and indicated that they had a daughter together, a fact that helped authenticate the defendant's voice as well as the voice of the victim. According to the trial court and the reviewing court, circumstantial evidence was sufficient to authenticate the 911 emergency call as having been made by the victim.

One method of authenticating audiotapes requires that informants and police officers be able to identify voices from the recordings. In a case where the defendant solicited other individuals to murder his codefendant in a separate case, the individuals who had been solicited involved law enforcement officials.[170] Later, police placed a recording device on one of these individuals who engaged the defendant in a conversation in which the defendant indicated that he wished to have his codefendant blown up using propane tanks placed under his codefendant's house trailer. Included in the conversation was the method of detonating the propane tanks and dealing with the victim's dogs. At the trial, the defense objected to the introduction of the recording because its audibility had been enhanced by the United States Secret Service and the defendant contended that it could not be properly authenticated. One of the solicited individuals who was a party to the original recorded conversation stated that he had listened to the recording, and it accurately reflected the conversation concerning solicitation for murder that he had with the defendant concerning plans to murder the codefendant. A detective involved in the case, who monitored the original conversation, testified that

---

168 State v. Hurtado, 173 Wn. App. 582, 294 P.3d 838, 2013 Wash. App. LEXIS 342 (2013).

169 *Id.*

170 See State v. Robinette, 2013 Tenn. Crim. App. LEXIS 850 (2013).

the recording, even the enhanced version, was an accurate representation of the conversation that was originally recorded. The trial court concluded that the recording in its enhanced version had properly been authenticated, and the judge permitted it to be played for the jury. The reviewing court agreed that the recording had been properly authenticated by those who knew the voices and were participants to the original conversation, and therefore, the audio recording had been properly admitted into evidence and the convictions were not disturbed.

In determining whether to admit a properly authenticated audiotape recording, the judge must consider whether the probative value of the audiotape outweighs the danger of unfair prejudice to the defendant. In a California murder case, the female victim and the defendant lived in an apartment building where their close neighbors were aware of their domestic disputes.[171] The defendant pushed the victim out of a sixth floor window in front of witnesses who observed the victim trying to avoid leaving the building through the window. Several 911 calls were made about the time of the killing, the contents of which were admitted against the defendant. One objection made by the defendant involved the admission of a 911 call made several weeks prior to her death by the homicide victim in which the victim told the 911 operator that the defendant was threatening her by saying that he was "going to do something" to her, "was going to find her," and "have other people do stuff to her."[172] In contending that the earlier 911 tape should not be admitted, the defendant contended that the unfair prejudicial effect against his case largely outweighed any minimal probative value that the evidence of the 911 call might possess. The reviewing court approved the admission of the audio of the 911 call because it helped to show that the defendant was the person who pushed the victim from her window, and the 911 call made fewer than three weeks before the victim's death that reported the defendant's threat to harm her were very probative of the fact that he may have harmed her.

The use of recording devices to overhear conversations beyond the area in which they might normally be heard does not in itself require the evidence to be suppressed. Section 2511 of the United States Code states in detail the procedures that must be followed when using electronic surveillance devices to overhear and record conversations. Informants and undercover law enforcement agents may use hidden recorders or wear wire transmitters to tape or record a conversation, and the same agents can invite unsuspecting criminals into bugged locations controlled by police without violating 18 U.S.C. § 2515. In federal courts, as long as one party to the conversation consents to the electronic recording of the conversations, they will not be excluded unless other rules of evidence prevent admission.[173]

If there is not at least one party to the conversation who consents to an audio recording, the procedures specified in the statute must be followed to the letter if

---

171 People v. Green, 2011 Cal. App. Unpub. LEXIS 446 (2011).

172 *Id.*

173 *See* 18 U.S.C. § 2510 *et seq.*

the recording is to be free from challenge on constitutional grounds.[174] Federal law prohibits the use of illegally seized audio information in court. For example:

> § 2515. Prohibition of use as evidence of intercepted wire or oral communications
>
> Whenever any wire or oral communication has been intercepted, no part of the contents of such communication and no evidence derived therefrom may be received in evidence in any trial, hearing, or other proceeding in or before any court, grand jury, department, officer, agency, regulatory body, legislative committee, or other authority of the United States, a State, or a political subdivision thereof if the disclosure of that information would be in violation of this chapter [18 U.S.C. § 2515].[175]

Noncompliance with the statute renders otherwise excellent evidence inadmissible in court. Even with a valid warrant to intercept telephone calls, federal or state agents are generally required to conduct their eavesdropping in such a way as to minimize the interceptions of communications that are not otherwise subject to interception, i.e., those that are not pertaining to criminal activity.[176] For telephone calls that do not appear to be criminally related, federal agents are not supposed to intercept them except to conduct spot checks to see if the conversation has turned to criminal activities. In a recent case, a federal appeals court suppressed evidence of one phone call that the target made in which he spoke for nearly an hour, which the government monitored, and in which the conversation did not turn to criminal matters until the last few minutes. The appeals court felt that the government failed to comply with the statutory minimization requirements when monitoring one of the target's phone conversations and ordered the conversation's criminal components suppressed.[177]

Related to sound recordings are text messages, as well as e-mail correspondence that may be sent and received on cell phones, personal digital assistants, iPods®, iPads®, and other digital devices. Criminals have embraced the new technology to make criminal activities more difficult to detect while providing better communication to facilitate criminal activities. Generally, courts have determined that the Federal Wiretap Act, 18 U.S.C. §§ 2510 et seq., governs only the "acquisition of the contents of electronic communications that occur contemporaneously with their transmission,"[178] and the Act does not regulate data that are acquired from electronic storage by information service providers. To obtain text messages and other stored electronic data, Title II of the Electronic Communications Privacy Act of 1986, 18 U.S.C. § 2701 et seq., states that federal officials must apply for a warrant based on probable cause that is consistent with the Federal Rules of Criminal Procedure. The warrant requires

---

174 *See* 18 U.S.C. § 2515.

175 *Id.*

176 18 U.S.C. § 2518(5).

177 United States v. North, 2013 U.S. App. LEXIS 21656 (5th Cir. 2013).

178 United States v. Jones, 2006 U.S. Dist. LEXIS 56473 (D.D.C. 2006) (citing United States v. Steiger, 318 F.3d 1039, 1048-49 (11th Cir. 2003)).

the provider or storing entity to disclose the contents of wire or electronic communication that the holder has in storage to the federal government.[179]

Consistent with this view, in the context of private e-mail messages, the Sixth Circuit held that an e-mail user with an Internet service provider has an expectation of privacy in sent and received e-mail messages that cannot be breached by the federal government in the absence of a warrant.[180] According to the court, to the extent that the Stored Communications Act purported to allow the federal government to obtain the e-mails without a warrant, the Act was unconstitutional. Additionally, the Sixth Circuit held that "[t]he government may not compel a commercial ISP to turn over the contents of a subscriber's e-mails without first obtaining a warrant based on probable cause."[181]

Text messages sent by a public employee on government-provided pagers may carry no expectation of privacy concerning the content of the text pages. In the *City of Ontario v. Quon*,[182] the Supreme Court held that the city did not violate an employee's Fourth Amendment rights or rights under the Stored Communications Act[183] by obtaining and reviewing stored text messages sent by police officers on city-issued text pagers, some of which were personal messages and some which were business related. Essentially, since the city had notified the employees that they had no privacy on their text pagers, the city could review all messages because they were not private without violating any law or practice.

Private text messages sent by smart phones or tablet computers may have a better argument concerning privacy than texts sent on publicly owned devices. Once police or a prosecutor gain lawful access to the substantive text message, authentication may be fairly easy due to the internal contents of the text messages and with reference to who controlled the smart phone or other device at the time the texts were sent or received.[184] In an Arkansas murder case, the defendant objected to the introduction of several text messages because, he alleged on appeal for the first time, that the use of a subpoena rather than a warrant violated the federal Stored Communications Act.[185] The trial court properly permitted a Verizon Wireless employee to testify concerning the damaging contents of three text messages sent by the defendant from the phone assigned to him on the day prior to the homicide. Because the defendant failed to make an argument and offer a specific objection based on the Stored Communications Act[186] at the trial,

---

179 *Id.*

180 United States v. Warshak, 2010 Fed. App. 0377P, 2010 U.S. App. LEXIS 25415 (6th Cir. 2010).

181 *Id.*

182 117 U.S. 743, 130 S. Ct. 2619, 177 L. Ed. 2d 216, 2010 U.S. LEXIS 4972 (2010).

183 *See* 42 U.S.C. § 1983, 18 U.S.C. § 2701 *et seq.*

184 *See* United States v. Mebrtatu, 2013 U.S. App. LEXIS 22093 (3rd Cir. 2013), where the court approved authentication of text messages because the defendant was the sender and receiver of the text messages and the texts were responsive to messages sent via FAX by a conspirator. Other text messages contained content that reinforced the authentication of the relevant messages.

185 Gulley v. Arkansas, 2012 Ark. 368, 2012 Ark. LEXIS 393 (2012).

186 *See* 18 U.S.C. § 2701 *et seq.*

the issue had been forfeited. However, part of the defendant's objection concerned the argument that the texts had not been properly authenticated as having been written and sent by the defendant from his phone and not by someone else. Two texts were threatening to the deceased and one indicated that the defendant was going to be at the crime scene. Other text traffic over the defendant's phone to others indicated the author was the defendant, and there was evidence that the defendant was seen exiting a car near the homicide scene after he texted that he was getting dropped off over at that location. Such information sufficiently authenticated the text messages as having been written and sent by the defendant, according to the trial court. Over the defense attorney's objection that text messages were as private as phone conversations and required warrants to obtain, the trial court admitted the substance of the incriminating texts. The reviewing court approved the admission of the three text messages that were damaging to the defendant's case, and the court upheld the convictions. Thus, there are occasions when text messages will be admissible in court despite arguments against their admission that might cite federal law or the Fourth Amendment.

§ 14.10 Diagrams, Maps, and Models

As a general rule, trial courts possess broad discretion to admit demonstrative evidence such as diagrams, maps, and charts to illustrate a witness's testimony, and allowing a witness to explain his or her testimony by visual illustration usually will assist the jury. However, unless the illustration is helpful or essential to an understanding of the testimony, the opposing party may contend that such evidence is largely cumulative and should be excluded, but the admission or exclusion rests within the discretion of the trial judge. A prosecutor could use a map to help a witness illustrate his or her testimony, and it could either be used only as an exhibit or the proponent could move for it to be admitted into evidence. In a murder case, the court permitted the prosecution to use a map that was not drawn to scale as an exhibit, but the witness described it as essentially accurate. The trial court later admitted the map into evidence over the defendant's objection. The fact that the map was not a genuine map and was not to scale went to its weight and did not affect admissibility.[187]

Maps may be used to demonstrate where a defendant's cell phone has traveled and when it has been used. In a Florida capital murder case where it was important and relevant to demonstrate the location of the defendant at the time of the homicide, the trial court allowed the testimony of a Nextel engineer concerning maps of the cell towers, their respective coverage areas, and specific calls made by the defendant's cell phone.[188] The trial court noted that the principles of cellular technology have been widely accepted and admitted into evidence in prior cases, including testimony about cell phone records and comparing them to locations that existed on cell site maps.

---

187 Calhoun v. State, 932 So. 2d 923, 951, 2005 Ala. Crim. App. LEXIS 101 (2005).

188 Gosciminski v. State, 38 Fla. L. Weekly S 638, 2013 Fla. LEXIS 1988 (2013).

Although not testifying as an expert, the Nextel engineer explained the map coverage areas of cell towers, discussed the propagation of cell tower information, and provided information concerning specific cell phone calls made or received by the defendant's cell phone. The engineer detailed how he developed the diagrams that demonstrated the cell phone tower locations and their coverage for each area, and he testified about which cell tower handled the defendant's calls that had originated from his cell phone based upon which tower picked up the signal first. The cell phone and tower data and the coverage map area helped place the defendant at or near the scene of the homicide at the time that it appeared to have occurred. Because the defense had ample opportunity to cross-examine the Nextel engineer concerning his testimony, the Supreme Court of Florida held that the evidence had been properly admitted by the trial court, and the court did not disturb the conviction and death sentence.[189]

Authenticated maps may be admissible to demonstrate drug-free zones around schools and other locations. In an Indiana case, police had a confidential informant purchase drugs from the defendant from his home on several occasions.[190] The defendant lived within 1,000 feet of a public park when he sold cocaine to the police operative. At his trial involving three counts of dealing in cocaine within the 1,000-foot boundary of the public park, the court permitted the prosecutor to introduce a map produced by the city engineer, using a software program known as AutoCAD, that showed the location of the defendant's residence and its proximity that was within the prohibited radius of the public park.

Charts may be used to show relationships and organizational structure if properly introduced and used for a limited purpose. In addition, Rule 1006 permits the use of charts to summarize evidence of voluminous writings, recordings, or photos that cannot be conveniently presented in court. Generally, charts should show factual data and not advocate one party's legal position. In order to permit admission of a chart that purports to be a summary of a larger set of books or data, the larger body of data must be shown to be admissible on its own merits. For instance, a chart made from a larger body of data would not be admissible unless the larger body of data would qualify for admission. In a federal income tax evasion case, the trial court refused to permit a chart whose introduction was attempted by the taxpayer's accountant, partly because the defendant did not make the actual documents summarized in the chart available for the prosecution. In addition, the accountant indicated that the defendant had prepared the chart and the accountant had no first-hand knowledge concerning the data on the chart. The reviewing court upheld the exclusion of the chart under Rule 1006, based on the fact that the data might have been unreliable and the underlying documents had not been made available to the prosecution.[191]

Models, when properly identified and authenticated, may be used for illustration purposes if the evidence offered as a result of the use of a model is relevant and material

---

189 *Id.*

190 *See* Jenkins v. State, 2009 Ind. App. Unpub. LEXIS 2007 (2009).

191 United States v. Smith, 516 Fed. App'x 592, 2013 U.S. App. LEXIS 4705 (6th Cir. 2013).

to the ultimate fact to be demonstrated.[192] Neither an exact model nor a full-size model is required if the original is substantially represented so the model will not prove misleading to the jury or judge. If a replica of the original is used, the jury should be instructed that the object is not the one used in the crime and that it is to be considered as evidence that demonstrates or illustrates the object used in the crime. In a Virginia murder prosecution involving the Virginia, Maryland, and District of Columbia sniper shootings of 2002, the prosecution used a model of the trunk of the car from which the Commonwealth alleged the shooting took place. The defendant objected that the model was "not complete" and "was out of context." The appellate court upheld the trial judge's decision to allow the model of the car trunk to be used as demonstrative evidence because it sufficiently represented the original Caprice trunk in most important aspects.[193]

Plastic models of the human skeleton and of the heart, brain, kidney, or other organs—when criminal injury to one of them is involved—are frequently used to illustrate the testimony of a coroner or other medical expert.

§ 14.11 Courtroom Demonstrations and Experiments

Although it is usually more convenient to videotape or photograph demonstrations or experiments that are performed outside of court, in some instances, courtroom demonstrations are logically permitted because they more convincingly depict the situation to the jury. In order for a courtroom demonstration to be admissible as evidence, the party wishing to conduct the demonstration must convince the trial judge that the demonstration will be relevant and will be conducted under conditions that are substantially the same as the actual event to which it relates.[194] As a general rule, virtually all the same foundational and legal requirements and elements affecting the admissibility and use of demonstrative evidence apply to courtroom experiments and demonstrations.

For a courtroom demonstration to be admissible as evidence, the party offering the demonstration, like the proponent of any evidence, must show that the demonstration is relevant. An experiment or demonstration may be permitted by the judge where it clearly resembles the actual event presents evidence connected to the issues in the case. In a California first-degree murder case in which the defendant did not deny committing the killing of his male paramour, the prosecution procured a manikin and had the defendant reenact and demonstrate the strangulation of his boyfriend in the courtroom.[195] The two men had met through Craigslist® and had engaged in an unprotected

---

[192] State v. Mitchel, 56 Wash. App. 610, 784 P.2d 568 (1990). *See also* Taylor v. State, 640 So. 2d 1227 (1994), in which the court noted that demonstration exhibits may be used at the trial as an aid to the jury's understanding, but only if the exhibits constitute an accurate and reasonable reproduction of the object involved.

[193] Muhammad v. Commonwealth, 611 S.E.2d 537, 576, 2005 Va. LEXIS 39 (2005).

[194] United States v. Williams, 2006 U.S. App. LEXIS 21337 (4th Cir. 2006).

[195] People v. Rivera, 201 Cal. App. 4th 353. 2011 Cal. App. LEXIS 1499 (2011).

sexual relationship until the victim informed the defendant that the victim had tested positive for HIV. This anger precipitated the killing. According to the reviewing court, having the jury watch the defendant strangle a manikin was more likely to inflame their emotions and have them react inappropriately, while at the same time having very little probative value of the issues in the case. Despite the clear error in conducting the demonstration, the other evidence in the case was so overwhelmingly strong against the defendant, and his own statements offered little to support either self-defense or a heat of passion killing, the appeals court upheld the murder conviction.[196] This was a demonstration that should never have been permitted in open court.

To be legally relevant, demonstration or experiment must meet the test of "similarity of conditions," but it is not necessary that the conditions be exactly the same because this would generally be difficult or impossible. One California court noted, "Experimental evidence may be admitted if (1) it is relevant, (2) its conditions and those existing at the time of the alleged occurrence are shown to be substantially similar, and (3) the evidence will not consume undue time or confuse or mislead the jury."[197] In a murder case, the trial court permitted the prosecution to introduce evidence of an experiment conducted by police officers in which they proved it was possible to drive from one location where it was known the defendant was located to the murder scene area in time to have committed the killings.[198] Additionally, detectives test-drove a second route from the murder scene area to a second location where the defendant's cell phone indicated he was present within the time frame that fit the prosecution's theory of the case. Essentially, the prosecution's demonstration was necessary to prove the defendant could have traveled from point A to the murder scene and to point B after the killing in a set amount of time. The test-drive evidence was relevant and therefore admissible if it tended to prove the two legs of the drive could have been completed within the timeframe available to defendant. The reviewing court upheld the demonstrative evidence of the test drive and indicated that any defects would go to the weight of the evidence and not its admissibility.

§ 14.12 Preservation and Disclosure of Evidence Favorable to the Defense

In the classic case of *Brady v. Maryland*, the United States Supreme Court decided that a defendant has a due process right to request and obtain from the prosecution evidence that is either material to the guilt, innocence, or punishment of the defendant.[199] The *Brady* material that must be disclosed includes impeachment evidence that could be useful to a defendant.[200] In the *Brady* case, the prosecution knew of an extrajudicial

---

196 *Id.*

197 People v. Scherer, 2013 Cal. App. Unpub. LEXIS 6163 (2013).

198 *Id.*

199 Brady v. Maryland, 373 U.S. 83, 1963 U.S. LEXIS 1615 (1963).

200 United States v. Bagley, 473 U.S. 667, 677, 1985 U.S. LEXIS 130 (1985).

confession to murder by Brady's accomplice, and Brady was never informed. The rationale of disclosure supports the view that fundamental fairness requires that the government not affirmatively hide evidence known to it that could be helpful to the rendering of actual justice. The *Brady* Court cautioned that failure to disclose such evidence following a defense request denies due process—irrespective of the good or bad faith of the prosecutor.

According to the Supreme Court in *United States v. Agurs*, the prosecution has a duty to disclose evidence that might be exculpatory for the defendant, even if the defendant does not request discovery of exculpatory evidence. Fundamental fairness requires that the prosecution seek justice and not be interested in winning the case at the cost of injustice.[201]

In *Moore v. Illinois*, the Court observed that:

> We know of no constitutional requirement that the prosecution make a complete and detailed accounting to the defense of all police investigatory work on a case.[202]

In one case, the Supreme Court reviewed a West Virginia prosecution involving withheld *Brady* discovery material that involved evidence known to a police officer but not known to the prosecution. Case law holds that knowledge by police is knowledge by the prosecution, even where the prosecutor has no actual knowledge. The conviction involved a sexual assault conviction in which the defendant maintained his innocence consistently. Following the trial and conviction, a defense investigator discovered that two of the victims had written a graphically explicit note that taunted the defendant for being played for a fool and one "victim" thanked him for oral sex. The letter squarely supported the defendant consent theory of the encounter and, if believed, could have changed the outcome of the case. A state trooper had seen the note and not only declined to take possession of it but also suggested that it be destroyed. Evidence favorable to the accused under *Brady* appeared to have been suppressed. The Supreme Court sent the case back for a determination of whether the exculpatory note required reversal of the conviction based on the *Brady* principles of discovery,[203] and the Supreme Court of Appeals of West Virginia ordered a new trial on all the issues in the case.[204]

The Supreme Court noted that to establish a *Brady* violation, a defendant must show that (1) material information was in the possession of the prosecutor or the actual police who were involved in the investigation and presentation of the case, (2) the information tends to cast doubt on the defendant's guilt, and (3) the prosecutor failed to disclose the evidence to the defense.[205] In a California murder case involving rival gang members, one of whom had killed a person on a municipal bus, an eyewitness saw an

---

201 United State v. Agurs, 427 U.S. 97, 1976 U.S. LEXIS 72 (1976).

202 Moore v. Illinois, 408 U.S. 786, 92 S. Ct. 2562, 33 L. Ed. 2d 706 (1972).

203 Youngblood v. West Virginia, 547 U.S. 867, 2006 U.S. LEXIS 4884 (2006).

204 State v. Youngblood, 221 W. Va. 20, 42, 650 S.E.2d 119, 2007 W. Va. LEXIS 23 (2007).

205 *Brady* at 87.

individual who met the defendant's description at the scene of the crime.[206] The eyewitness also observed the defendant carrying a gun at the time of the killing and called police the next day when he overheard two of the defendants bragging about the killing and the defendant taking credit for the murder. The eyewitness gave a statement implicating the defendant and testified reluctantly at trial, but claimed that he had a bad memory and was also afraid of gang retaliation. A police officer was permitted to tell the court what the witness had told the police officer at the time the eyewitness made his initial contact with police.[207] After the trial, the defendant's counsel became aware that the eyewitness had a prior felony conviction that had not been revealed to the defense. California law,[208] as well as under the principles of the *Brady* case, requires that the prosecution disclose to the defendant the existence of any felony conviction of any material witness whose credibility is likely to be important to the outcome of the criminal trial. In this case, if the attorney for the defendant had been aware of the witness' prior felony record, he would have used the prior conviction to impeach the only witness who could place a gun in the hands of the defendant. The prosecution had not disclosed the witness's prior felony conviction to the defense counsel and had not revealed that the prosecution witness was on probation for that offense at the time he testified against the defendant. Because credibility was a crucial issue in the case, the federal habeas corpus court ordered a new trial because the important *Brady* material (witness's prior felony conviction) had not been revealed to the defense. For a *Brady* violation to be recognized, the police or the prosecution must understand the importance of the evidence; otherwise, they could not be expected to reveal it to the defense team. For example, in a Massachusetts case, no *Brady* violation occurred when police came into possession of firearms used in a murder case that was about to go to trial when they had no knowledge that the guns might be related to the murder case.[209] The guns had been seized in an unrelated case, and police did not become aware that the guns might have been involved in the first case until after the trial in the first case had concluded. In affirming the guilty verdicts, the reviewing court found no reason to disturb the original convictions when the defendants could not demonstrate any *Brady* violation.

From these cases emerges the rule that due process requires disclosure, upon the defendant's request, of evidence favorable to the defendant, but unless a criminal defendant can show bad faith on the part of the police, failure to preserve potentially useful evidence does not constitute a denial of due process of law. When the interests of justice clearly require it, the police and prosecutor have an obligation to preserve the evidence. If the evidence is destroyed through bad faith, a due process protection has occurred that may constitute reversible error.

---

206 Amado v. Gonzalez, 2013 U.S. App. LEXIS 22088 (9th Cir. 2013).

207 *Id.*

208 Cal Pen Code § 1054.1 (2013).

209 *See* Commonwealth v. Caillot, 454 Mass. 245, 909 N.E.2d 1, 2009 Mass. LEXIS 331 (2009).

§ 14.13 Summary

In addition to the use of oral testimony and documentary evidence, real evidence may be introduced to help the jury or judge in determining what happened in a particular case. Real evidence may involve the actual historical objects from the crime or crime scene, or they may be called demonstrative real evidence when the objects consist of sample or duplicate items such as guns or knives or when one of the parties had the evidence constructed or developed for trial, such as models or charts. In many instances, real evidence accompanied by witness testimony may prove persuasive and is thought to assist the jury more in reaching a just decision.

With the use of real evidence, judicial scrutiny proves essential to ensure that the probative value of such evidence does not pose a risk of unfair prejudice. This may be a special concern when using demonstrative real evidence that has no historical connection to the case. To avoid unfair prejudice, certain rules have been established and must be followed if such evidence is to be admitted. For example, the prosecution must show that there is a connection between the instrument or article introduced and the accused, that the article is relevant to the particular case, and that the object is substantially in the same condition as it was when it was used in connection with the crime—or the change in condition, if any, is explained. Also, with real evidence, the prosecution must show a chain or continuity of custody concerning the article to be introduced, while a break in the chain may affect the weight to be given to the evidence. Alternatively, to authenticate the evidence, the proponent may properly connect the evidence to the case by identifying a unique mark or serial number on the object.

There are various types of real evidence that have been held admissible, and for each type, certain conditions must be met. In some instances, the exhibition of the person of the witness may be the best way to explain a criminal wrong or an injury. In this event, the judge in his or her discretion may allow such exhibition, even though it may be somewhat gruesome.

The prosecution or defense can introduce articles connected with the crime, such as weapons or clothing, as real evidence if the party can show that there was or is a connection between the properly authenticated article and the case. Also, the judge has discretion to allow the jury to visit and view the scene of the alleged crime if the view will help the jury in understanding and determining the facts of the case.

A jury's view of the scene may be presented by the use of still pictures or a video that is played for the jury. As an alternative to bringing all the evidence into court, photographs of important objects are admissible as a form of real evidence. Before a photograph may be introduced, a foundation must be laid; that is, a competent witness who has personal knowledge of the area or thing photographed must testify that the picture is an accurate representation of the object or person depicted. In addition to still photographs, motion pictures, DVDs, X-rays, CT scans, MRI scans, and sound recordings may be introduced. As in the case of photographs, a foundation must be laid before such evidence is admitted into court.

With the use of demonstrative real evidence, it is possible for witnesses to more effectively explain the events that occurred by using guns, knives, diagrams, maps, charts, and models. When references are made to such a diagram, map, or model, a witness must testify that it is a correct portrayal of the situation or thing represented.

Due process requires disclosure, especially upon the defendant's request, of evidence of any sort favorable to the defense, and the prosecution has a duty to disclose exculpatory evidence even without a request. Evidence known to police or prosecutors, even where known only to one and not the other, is deemed to be known by the government for disclosure purposes unless the government is completely ignorant of the connection between the evidence and a different prosecution.

CHAPTER FOURTEEN: QUESTIONS AND REVIEW EXERCISES

1. Real evidence has a physical and tangible existence as compared to oral testimony. In order for real evidence to be admissible at trial, what must the proponent demonstrate? In other words, what type of foundation is generally required to admit real evidence?
2. Would a firearm that was actually used in the crime be considered real evidence? How could a weapon that had no historical connection to the case be used as demonstrative real evidence? Explain and give an example.
3. Explain what is meant by the term "chain of custody" as it relates to the introduction of real evidence. Why is proof of the chain of custody important to the introduction of real evidence?
4. In order to introduce real evidence, many courts require a demonstration of necessity. For example, a photograph of a deceased murder victim, as an item of real evidence, has the possibility of generating unfair prejudice against a defendant. How could the use of such a photograph be argued to constitute a necessity?
5. When would it be appropriate to exhibit the physical person of the victim to the jury to show injury or damage that has been inflicted allegedly by a defendant? Are there risks if a defendant is required to wear visible restraints during a trial? Could unfair prejudice result from such a procedure?
6. Articles that constitute real evidence and are connected with the crime may be introduced in evidence. If a prosecutor wanted to introduce a firearm that was actually used in the crime, what would the prosecutor have to prove in order to get a judge to admit the firearm?
7. As an item of real evidence, clothing that has a sufficient connection to the crime may be introduced in evidence, provided that an

appropriate foundation is offered. Assume that a prosecutor wanted to introduce bloody clothing that had been worn by a homicide victim. What would the prosecutor have to prove in order to convince the judge to allow the clothing to be admitted in evidence?

8. Allowing a jury to view the physical scene where the crime occurred or to view a videotape of the crime scene may be appropriate. Under what circumstances should a judge permit a jury to view the crime scene? What is the typical procedure that the court would follow in arranging a crime-scene visit?
9. Photographs of persons, places, and things may be admitted following a proper foundation. When should a court allow photographs of an autopsy in a homicide case? Offer a fact pattern involving a gruesome photograph that a judge should allow to be admitted under the circumstances of your hypothetical fact pattern. Should it make any difference if the photographs were black-and-white or if they were color prints or enlargements shown on the screen by the use of PowerPoint slides?
10. Sound recordings of telephone calls, especially 911 calls, may be admissible against a defendant or in support of a defendant's case. What are the requirements for admission of a sound recording? Can wiretap recordings be admitted? Are there several different ways to authenticate sound recordings? Offer some examples.
11. Diagrams, maps, and models of objects may be admitted as demonstrative real evidence under proper circumstances. What steps should a prosecutor take to have a map of a drug-free school zone admitted into evidence? Could a coroner use a replica of a human skull in offering testimony concerning how a bullet entered a decedent?

Results of Examinations and Tests 15

It is now well established that a witness who qualifies as an expert in the science of ballistics, may identify a gun from which a particular bullet was fired by comparing the markings on that bullet with those on a test bullet fired by the witness through the suspect gun.

Roberts v. Florida, 164 So. 2d 817 (Fla. 1964)

Chapter Contents

Section

KEY TERMS AND CONCEPTS	
Admissibility Test	Frye Test
Ballistics Experiments	Horizontal Gaze Nystagmus Test
Ballistic Identification	Implied Consent
Breathalyzer Test	Laser Speed Detection
Daubert Test for Admissibility of Scientific Testing	Polygraph Examinations
DNA Testing	Radar
Fingerprint Identification	Scientific Evidence

§ 15.1 Introduction

Chapter 14 considers the general rules concerning the collection, protection, and introduction of real evidence. Evidence is characterized as real evidence if it is the result of experiments and tests either in or out of court even though, in many cases, the evidence is of little value unless it is accompanied by oral testimony.

Although a comparatively small part of the evidence produced at the usual criminal trial results from out-of-court tests and examinations, it is often very convincing and is certainly important in helping the factfinders to determine what actually occurred. Convictions for drug possession and related activities are often decided on the results of tests administered out of court. Prosecutions are initiated following out-of-court tests, such as having a drug detection dog sniff a car and obtaining a positive result,[1] testing residue found in trash that reveals the presence of illegal drugs,[2] and testing powders found in a prison cell that indicate the presence of drug contraband.[3] Juries and judges rely on the admission of these drug tests in deciding whether to convict because most tests prove to be quite convincing. Prosecutors use scientific testing results to prove that a driver of a vehicle has been driving under the influence of alcohol. Similarly, DNA testing in rape cases carries significant weight with factfinders in many cases, especially where a stranger has been charged with adult sexual assault, or the test indicates illegal contact between relatives.[4]

---

1 Illinois v. Caballes, 543 U.S. 405, 2005 U.S. LEXIS 769 (2005).

2 See United States v. Faust, 456 F.3d 1342, 2006 U.S. App. LEXIS 18366 (11th Cir. 2006).

3 See Garcia v. Martinez, 2006 U.S. App. LEXIS 24199 (7th Cir. 2006).

4 McGregor v. State, 2004 Tex. App. LEXIS 3365 (2004).

While evidence concerning the results of examinations and tests has a great impact in criminal cases, such evidence is admissible only when it clears several evidence hurdles. First, forensic evidence must meet the same tests as most other evidence, such as the tests of relevancy, materiality, and competency. Before such evidence is admitted, a foundation must be laid. For example, as demonstrated by a Georgia case, the foundation for admission of scientific test results related to a seized sample requires that care be taken that the correct sample is tested.

> Evidence such as suspected cocaine, seized from a crime scene, is typically placed in a sealable evidence bag that can be marked with the date, time, location, suspect, arresting officer, and other particulars. The evidence should be promptly delivered to a safe, suitable storage site that provides "reasonable assurance" that the evidence will not be tampered with or corrupted. Evidence may be sent by certified mail, return receipt requested, to a crime lab and sent to the prosecutor in the same manner. The mail receipts, once identified by the witness, are admissible to help prove the chain of custody. For fungible evidence that has been tested, it generally is sufficient to provide the testimony of the police officer who seized and transported the evidence, according to the department's routine, and the lab technician who tested the evidence and recorded the results according to the crime lab's routine.[5]

If a sample is not labeled properly, a significant break in the chain of custody has occurred, and a trial court may rule that the proper foundation has not been made for the introduction of the results of the scientific testing.[6]

If the courts have not previously accepted the results of a novel scientific test or a test that has not reached general scientific acceptance, the party seeking to introduce the evidence must demonstrate that the new or different test or experiment meets the test required for introduction in that particular jurisdiction.[7]

Frye test The standard, originally offered in *Frye v. United States* (1923), that regulates the admissibility of scientific tests into evidence.

For many years, state and federal courts followed the ***Frye* test** or standard when evaluating the admissibility of scientific tests and experiments. The test gradually gained national acceptability following the decision in *Frye v. United States*.[8] In that case, the court stated:

> Just when a scientific principle or discovery crosses these lines between the experimental and the demonstratable stages is difficult to define. Somewhere in this twilight zone the evidential force of the principle must be recognized, and while courts will go a long way in admitting expert testimony deduced from a well-recognized scientific principle or discovery, the thing from which the deduction is made must be sufficiently established to have gained general acceptance from the particular field in which it belongs.[9]

---

5 Wilson v. State, 271 Ga. App. 359, 362, 609 S.E.2d 703, 706, 2005 Ga. App. LEXIS 41 (2005).
6 *Id.*
7 Kanani v. Phillips, 2004 U.S. Dist. LEXIS 20444 (S.D.N.Y. 2004).
8 Frye v. United States, 293 F. 1013 (D.C. Cir. 1923).
9 *Id.* at 1014.

In the ensuing years, the majority of state and federal jurisdictions adopted the *Frye* "general acceptance" test, discussing, defining, and attempting to refine it as new and more complex forms of novel evidence have surfaced in the legal arena.[10] Many states have not adopted the different test for **scientific evidence admissibility** required in the federal courts by the Supreme Court decision in *Daubert v. Merrell Dow* and have retained the *Frye* standard. Among these states are Alabama and Florida, where the arguably slightly more rigorous *Frye* standard remains good law and is applied to the full range of scientific testing when court admissibility is desired.[11]

Scientific evidence admissibility
Admissibility of scientific evidence rests on several considerations: whether a scientific theory or technique can or has been tested; whether the theory or technique has been subjected to peer review and publication; the known or potential rate of error and the existence and maintenance of standards controlling the technique's operation; whether the technique is generally accepted.

In the case of *Daubert v. Merrell Dow Pharmaceuticals, Inc.*, the United States Supreme Court held that the Federal Rules of Evidence supersede the *Frye* test for cases involving federal law.[12] The Court held that the admissibility of expert opinion testimony concerning novel scientific evidence is no longer limited solely to knowledge or evidence "generally accepted" as reliable in the relevant scientific community. The Court did not, however, sanction the wholesale abandonment of standards for admission of expert opinion or knowledge, but stated:

> That the *Frye* test was displaced by the Rules of Evidence does not mean, however, that the Rules themselves place no limits on the admissibility of purportedly scientific evidence. Nor is the trial judge disabled from screening such evidence. To the contrary, under the Rules the trial judge must ensure that any and all scientific testimony or evidence admitted is not only relevant but reliable.

The Court in *Daubert* held that Rule 702 is the "primary locus" of a trial judge's screening of purportedly scientific evidence for relevancy and reliability under Rule 104(a) for federal trials.[13] The *Daubert* Court stated, "'General acceptance' is not a necessary precondition to the admissibility of scientific evidence under the Federal Rules of Evidence, but the Rules of Evidence—especially Rule 702—do assign to the trial judge the task of ensuring that an expert's testimony both rests on a reliable

---

10 United States v. Martinez, 3 F.3d 1191 (8th Cir. 1993). *See also Fifty Years of* Frye *in Alabama: The Continuing Debate over Adopting the Test Established in* Daubert v. Merrell Dow Pharmaceuticals, 35 CUMB. L. REV. 231 (2004/2005).

11 *See* Arnold v. Florida, 807 So. 2d 136, 2002 Fla. App. LEXIS 743 (2002), and Slay v. Keller Industries, 823 So. 2d 623, 2001 Ala. LEXIS 439 (Ala. 2002).

12 Daubert v. Merrell Dow Pharmaceuticals, 509 U.S. 579, 1993 U.S. LEXIS 4408 (1993).

13 FED R. EVID. 702. Rule 702 provides that "if scientific, technical or other specialized knowledge will assist the trier of fact to understand the evidence or to determine a fact in issue, a witness qualified an expert by knowledge, skill, experience, training, or education may testify thereto."

foundation and is relevant to the task at hand. Pertinent evidence based on scientifically valid principles will satisfy those demands."[14] The concept of requiring proof of a scientific foundation guarantees that admissible evidence will have a firm grounding in scientific methods and practices.

The *Daubert* Court established the following nonexclusive list of nonexclusive factors to guide lower federal courts in assessing the reliability of scientific evidence:

- Whether a scientific theory or technique can be (or has been) tested
- Whether the theory or technique has been subjected to peer review and publication
- The known or potential rate of error and the existence and maintenance of standards controlling the technique's operation
- Whether the technique is generally accepted or has widespread acceptance.[15]

The *Daubert* Court emphasized that the inquiry to determine the reliability of scientific evidence is a flexible one, focusing on the principles and methodology proffered as evidence rather than the conclusions they generate. The *Daubert* principles are to be read in conjunction with Rule 702, which permits expert scientific witnesses where their testimony "will assist the trier of fact to understand the evidence or to determine a fact in issue." In addition, the evidence must be based on reliable principles and scientific methods, and the expert witness must be shown to have applied the scientific principles properly.[16] Under *Daubert*, scientific evidence brought to court by expert witnesses must be both relevant and reliable and meet the other standards in order to be properly admitted in evidence.[17]

A Colorado appeals court referred to both the *Frye* test and the Federal Rules of Evidence as links to the *Daubert* case and stated the applicable law in these terms:

> Under the *Frye* test, novel scientific evidence is not admissible unless its proponent shows that the theory supporting the proffered conclusion exists and is generally accepted in the scientific community, the techniques that are generally accepted in the scientific community exist and are capable of producing reliable results, and accepted scientific techniques were performed.[18]

The Colorado court noted that the ***Daubert* test** superseded the *Frye* test for federal trials.

> ***Daubert* test** Under *Daubert v. Merrell Dow Pharmaceuticals*, 509 U.S. 579 (1993), the Court adopted a revised test to regulate the admission of scientific evidence.

> Under the federal counterpart of CRE 702, the admissibility of scientific evidence, "novel" or otherwise, now rests on several considerations, including: (1) whether the theory or technique is or can be tested; (2)

---

[14] *Daubert* at 597.

[15] *Daubert* at 593.

[16] Smith v. Cangieter, 2006 U.S. App. LEXIS 23085 (8th Cir. 2006).

[17] United States v. McGinnis, 2006 U.S. App. LEXIS 24451 (5th Cir. 2006) (quoting Pipitone v. Biomatrix, Inc., 288 F.3d 239, 244-45 (5th Cir. 2002)).

[18] People v. Brooks, 950 P.2d 649, 652, 1997 Colo. App. LEXIS 183 (1997).

> whether a theory or technique has been subjected to peer review and publication; (3) whether a technique has a known or potential rate of error; (4) whether a technique's operation is controlled by existing and maintained standards; and (5) whether the theory or technique is generally accepted in the scientific community.[19]

According to the Colorado court, where scientific expertise was not helpful or where the evidence could be presented by laypersons or nonscientific experts, any test for admissibility of scientific evidence did not apply. The Colorado court noted:

> If the proffered evidence does not depend upon any scientific device, method, or process, neither the Frye nor the *Daubert* test for admissibility applies.[20]

The proponent of the scientific evidence has the burden of proving its relevancy as well as its scientific reliability, both of which are deemed proven where a particular court has previously approved the use of a particular scientific test.[21]

Once a test for admissibility of scientific evidence has been approved in a substantial number of courts, the trial judge may judicially notice (without receiving evidence) that the procedure has been established with verifiable certainty, or that it rests on the laws of nature.[22]

§ 15.2 Examination of the Person

When conducted in a reasonable manner, examination of the body of the defendant in a criminal case is not considered violative of his or her constitutional right of privacy or his or her privilege against self-incrimination. Both federal and state courts have usually held that the privilege against self-incrimination, as protected by the Fifth Amendment to the United States Constitution, offers no protection against being compelled to submit to fingerprinting, photographing, or measurements; to write or speak for identification; to appear in court; to stand; to assume a stance; to walk; or to make a particular gesture.[23] For purposes of identification, the courts have allowed procedures that involve minor interferences with the person of individuals charged with crimes. Numerous cases uphold reasonable out-of-court identification procedures against claims of violation of the Fifth Amendment. Such reasonable procedures have included requiring the prisoner to try on a blouse that fit him,[24] requiring the accused to submit to a lineup,[25] ordering an accused to give a voice sample at trial for identification

---

19 *Id.*

20 *Id.*

21 United States v. Dien Vy Phung, 127 F. App'x 594, 2005 U.S. App. LEXIS 6146 (3d Cir. 2005).

22 Gentry v. State, 443 S.E.2d 667 (Ga. Ct. App. 1994).

23 Schmerber v. California, 384 U.S. 757, 86 S.Ct. 1826, 16 L. Ed. 2d 908 (1966). *See* case in Part II at cases relating to Chapter 14. See also Chapter 16 for additional discussion of the privilege against self-incrimination.

24 Holt v. United States, 218 U.S. 245, 31 S. Ct. 2, 54 L. Ed. 1021 (1910); State v. Lerner, 308 A.2d 324 (R.I. 1973).

25 United States v. Gaines, 2006 U.S. App. LEXIS 22584 (7th Cir. 2006).

purposes,[26] examination of a defendant's body for traces of blood,[27] ordering a subject to give his name,[28] examination of the body for marks and bruises,[29] and requiring the defendant to remove items of clothing or to assume poses.[30] Similarly, taking saliva samples from a convicted defendant does not violate the Fifth Amendment,[31] and requiring a person convicted of theft to give a saliva sample as a condition of federal probation violates no constitutional provision.[32]

In both homicide and wrongful death cases, the results of an autopsy of the body of the deceased by a trained pathologist can be introduced as evidence in a court. The pathologist may offer testimony concerning the condition of the body, the cause of death, and the injuries sustained. Examination of the body generally includes photographs that the doctor may have taken during an autopsy. Crime scene pictures taken by the medical examiner may be introduced to illustrate the injuries sustained by a deceased and to support an expert opinion on the cause of death. The medical examiner's report is admissible as to his or her anatomical findings, anatomical diagnosis, and cause of death.

§ 15.3 Intoxication Tests

Intoxication may be scientifically determined by testing the subject's blood, breath, urine, or saliva. Evidence resulting from such out-of-court tests is usually admissible. Types of tests and limitations on the use of such evidence are discussed in the following paragraphs.

The Supreme Court of the United States has heard a number of cases involving blood tests and constitutional issues spawned by the collection of blood and introduction into evidence of blood results. Litigants in these cases complained of search-and-seizure and self-incrimination violations. Over the past 50 years, most of the important constitutional issues have been decided with the result that legal issues involving driving while intoxicated cases have been determined and can be considered settled law.

Early blood testing sparked defendants to argue that constitutional violations occurred in the drawing and testing of blood. In *Breithaupt v. Abram*,[33] police officers had medical staff draw and test the blood of an unconscious driver who, when sober, contended that his due process rights had been violated. The Supreme Court held that

---

26 Hubanks v. Frank, 392 F.3d 926, 932, 2004 U.S. App. LEXIS 26791 (7th Cir. 2004).

27 McFarland v. United States, 150 F.2d 593 (D.C. Cir. 1945), Brattain v. Herron, 309 N.E.2d 150 (Ind. 1974).

28 *See* Hiibel v. Sixth Judicial District Court, 542 U.S. 177, 2004 U.S. LEXIS 4385 (2004), and United States v. Doe, 128 Fed. Appx. 179, 2005 U.S. App. LEXIS 5707 (2d Cir. 2005).

29 Leeper v. Texas, 139 U.S. 462 (1891).

30 Gilbert v. United States, 366 F.2d 923 (9th Cir. 1966), United States v. Robertson, 19 F.3d 1318 (10th Cir. 1994).

31 Wilson v. Wilkinson, 2009 U.S. Dist. LEXIS 31895 (S.D. Ohio 2009).

32 *See* United States v. Hand, 2006 U.S. App. LEXIS 17715 (11th Cir. 2006).

33 352 U.S. 432, 77 S. Ct. 408, 1 L. Ed. 2d 448 (1957).

the unconscious blood draw did not offend fundamental concepts of due process under the Fourteenth Amendment. In a landmark case, *Schmerber v. California*,[34] the Supreme Court held that the extraction and testing of blood samples from the accused while he was in the hospital, after being arrested for driving under the influence of intoxicating liquor, had been conducted in a reasonable manner and did not violate his rights under the Fourth Amendment to be free from unreasonable searches. The Court also decided that the physician's withdrawal of a blood sample at the direction of a police officer and the admission of the blood analysis against Schmerber did not deny him due process of law. Finally, the Court rejected Schmerber's contention that the blood evidence should be excluded on the theory that it violated his Fifth Amendment privilege against self-incrimination, because he had been compelled to be a witness against himself. The Court held that the blood evidence was not of a testimonial nature, but was simply evidence of a scientific fact.

A. Blood Tests

Statutes in the several states have amended their driving while intoxicated statutes to hold that a driver is considered to be in violation of the law when the blood-alcohol content is 0.08 percent or higher. Many states formerly did not recognize intoxication until it reached 0.15 percent blood-alcohol content. Demonstrative of this change in state law is the Alaska statute.

> Sec. 28.35.030. Operating a vehicle, aircraft or watercraft while under the influence of an alcoholic beverage, inhalant, or controlled substance
>
> (a) A person commits the crime of driving while under the influence of an alcoholic beverage, inhalant, or controlled substance if the person operates or drives a motor vehicle or operates an aircraft or a watercraft
>
> (1) while under the influence of an alcoholic beverage, intoxicating liquor, inhalant, or any controlled substance, singly or in combination; or
>
> (2) and if, as determined by a chemical test taken within four hours after the alleged operating or driving, there is 0.08 percent or more by weight of alcohol in the person's blood or 80 milligrams or more of alcohol per 100 milliliters of blood, or if there is 0.08 grams or more of alcohol per 210 liters of the person's breath.[35]

Under subsection (a)(1), a driver may be proven to violate the Alaska law by objective evidence that the driver was under the influence of an intoxicant by proving behavior consistent with impairment in the absence of blood or breath testing. This provision becomes particularly useful when a problem exists in a blood or breath test, and the results are excluded from evidence. Under the latter subsection, Alaska law requires

---

[34] Schmerber v. California, 384 U.S. 757, 1966 U.S. LEXIS 1129 (1966). *See the Schmerber* case in Part II at cases relating to Chapter 14. *See also* Winston v. Lee, 470 U.S. 753, 105 S. Ct. 1611, 84 L. Ed. 2d 662 (1985), in which reference was made to the balancing test approved in *Schmerber*.

[35] ALASKA STAT. § 28.35.030 (2013).

that a chemical or blood test prove that the prohibited 0.08 blood-alcohol content existed at the time the person operated the motor vehicle.[36]

Other states follow Alaska's concept in permitting proof of impairment to be made by introducing evidence of objective conduct by the driver or by a finding of a prohibited level of alcohol in the driver's blood. In 2010, a Missouri court of appeals reversed a reinstatement of a driver's license, based on proof that the defendant driver had a 0.08 percent or greater blood-alcohol content at the time of arrest. Proof of a valid probable cause arrest for driving in violation of an alcohol-related offense and proof of a 0.08 percent or greater blood-alcohol content creates the presumption that the driver was intoxicated.[37]

B. Breath Tests

A doctor, chemist, or medical technician with the proper equipment can determine the level of alcohol in the blood from a blood sample. Due to the inconvenience and cost of obtaining and analyzing a blood sample, other means have been invented to determine blood-alcohol content without actually taking blood. The law enforcement use of breath samples has become common and has the advantage of being more convenient and less painful. In developing probable cause for arrest, many jurisdictions use a preliminary blood-alcohol test that a motorist generally may refuse without consequence and that can only be used to establish the existence of probable cause to arrest.[38] The breath test that police use is more accurate than the preliminary portable roadside models and is admissible if conducted according to the manufacturer's instructions. The admissible breath test has the advantage of being administered by a law enforcement officer, while generally a physician or nurse is needed when blood is to be drawn.

In the use of devices such as Breathalyzers, Intoxilyzers, Alcosensor IV, and other alcometers, the blood-alcohol content is determined by a formula applied to a test of the breath of the subject, who is required to blow deep lung or alveolar air into a collection device. Different detectors operate on separate scientific theories. For example, the modern Breathalyzer brand alcohol detectors require the subject to breathe into the device. The breath, thus captured, is allowed to expel itself through a tube containing a mixture of sulfuric acid, potassium dichromate, silver nitrate, and water. The sulfuric acid removes the alcohol from the air and forms a liquid solution, and the alcohol reacts with the potassium dichromate to create a color change in the solution that can be compared to a control solution. This change of color is directly related to the amount of alcohol in the breath sample, and the Breathalyzer operator can determine the amount of alcohol by manipulating the machine's controls.[39]

---

36 Valentine v. State, 215 P.3d 319, 326, 2009 Alas. LEXIS 116 (2009).

37 *See* Bouillon v. Director of Revenue, 306 S.W.3d 197, 2010 Mo. App. LEXIS 317 (2010).

38 *See* WIS. STAT. § 343.303 (2013). *But see* Blank v. State, 2006 Alaska App. LEXIS 144 (2006), where the Alaska statute regulating chemical testing refers only to the time of administration.

39 *See* Craig Freudenrigh, *How Breathalyzers Work*, http://electronics.howstuffworks.com/gadgets/automotive/breathalyzer3.htm (2014). *See also Breathalyzer Accuracy in Actual Enforcement* Practice, 32 J. FORENSIC SCI. 1235 (1987), in which it was found that the blood-alcohol concentration tended to be underestimated by the Breathalyzer.

The major emphasis on apprehending, punishing, and deterring the drinking driver has led to novel methods of attacking the problem. While driving while intoxicated or driving under the influence of alcohol continues to be addressed criminally, some states have devised alternative methods to remove drinking drivers from the road. For example, Illinois provides that a person suspected of driving under the influence may be asked to take a preliminary breath test, which the driver may refuse.

The results of the preliminary blood test are not admissible against the driver in a driving while intoxicated prosecution. If the officer has probable cause to arrest even in the absence of the preliminary breath test, the officer may arrest and request that the motorist take the admissible breath test. In many states, and Illinois in particular, if the motorist refuses to take or complete tests, the statute provides for a twelve month "statutory summary suspension for a refusal or failure to complete a test or tests to determine the alcohol, drug, or intoxicating compound concentration,"[40] and the driver may still be prosecuted for driving under the influence. If the driver consents and takes the test, leading to results indicating a prohibited blood-alcohol level, that test may be admitted against the arrestee in court.[41]

Before evidence regarding breath test results is admissible in a criminal prosecution, the party offering the evidence must establish a proper foundation for the machine, that the machine was operated properly, and that the machine had been approved by appropriate state regulatory agencies.[42] The standards for each machine are somewhat different, and states have protocols to assure that breath analysis machines are working properly. For example, in establishing a proper foundation for breath evidence, a Georgia statute requires that all chemical analysis of blood must be performed in accordance with Georgia Bureau of Investigation rules requiring an approved machine operated properly by an individual who both completed a training course on that specific machine model and held a valid state permit to operate the machine.[43] In one Georgia case, consistent with the statute, the prosecution introduced a certificate indicating that the Intoxilyzer 5000 had been tested and found to be in good working order before and after the officer used the machine to take a sample of the defendant's breath. Additional foundational evidence indicated that the machine passed its own diagnostic self-test and appeared to be in good working order at the time. According to the appellate court, a proper foundation had clearly been laid for the introduction of the evidence of intoxication.[44]

---

40 625 ILL. COMP. STAT. 5/6-208.1 (2013).

41 *See* People v. Lynn, 388 Ill. App. 3d 272, 2009 Ill. App. LEXIS 82 (Ill. 2009).

42 *See* GA. CODE ANN. § 40-6-392 (2013). *See also* Goethe v. State, 294 Ga. App. 232, 234, 2008 Ga. App. LEXIS 1157 (Ga. 2008).

43 Lancaster v. State, 294 Ga. App. 12, 17, 2008 Ga. App. LEXIS 1094 (2008). A later Georgia case rejected a claim that the testing certificate for the machine was hearsay and should have been excluded under *Melendez-Diaz v. Massachusetts*, 07 U.S. 159, 129 S. Ct. 2527, 174 L. Ed. 2d 314 (2009), because the court held that the certificate was not generated for a particular case or defendant. See Jacobson v. State, 306 Ga. App. 815, 817, 703 S.E.2d 376, 378, 2010 Ga. App. LEXIS 1055 (2010).

44 *Id.*

In a different case, a defendant questioned the foundational requirements for admission of evidence produced by the Intoxilyzer 5000.[45] The officer allegedly met all the foundational requirements for properly operating the Intoxilyzer so that it would produce admissible evidence. The defendant contended in her appeal that the Kansas Department of Health and Environment (KDHE) protocols had been breached, because she had her tongue pierced the day prior to the Intoxilyzer test, and there was an excellent likelihood that the breath test could have been contaminated by the presence of blood from her tongue piercing. The reviewing court rejected her claim and noted that the foundation for a breath test requires the prosecution to introduce evidence that the testing equipment had been certified by the KDHE, that the testing procedures performed by the officer met the requirements of the KDHE, and that the operator was certified under the KDHE protocols. In compliance with these requirements, the officer had the defendant remove her tongue ring, and the officer checked her tongue and mouth area for foreign objects, observing nothing unusual.

According to the court, under the circumstances, a proper foundation had been made for the introduction of the **breathalyzer test** results, and the court affirmed the conviction.[46] These steps are designed to provide accurate information on the blood-alcohol level and to protect persons who are tested from having inaccurate information used against them.

> **Breathalyzer test** Test used to determine alcohol content of blood in one arrested for operating a motor vehicle under the influence of alcohol.

In many jurisdictions, the test designated the Preliminary Breath Test (PBT) has been considered sufficiently reliable to indicate the presence of alcohol consumption, but is not usually admitted in court as substantive evidence.[47] However, the PBT can be used by a police officer as a screening tool to help determine whether a person has consumed alcohol and may assist in making the decision concerning whether probable cause exists.[48] In one such case, the court held that these tests, if positive, create a rebuttable presumption that the defendant has engaged in the prohibited activity. With respect to the preliminary breath test, at least one state will admit the PBT as trial evidence if an arrest followed, and the traditional admissible test for blood-alcohol content indicated intoxication.[49] Most jurisdictions will allow evidence of a refusal to take either a PBT[50] or the traditional intoxication tests following an arrest.

When a person is charged with the offense of operating a motor vehicle while under the influence of intoxicating liquor, there is no deprivation of constitutional rights involving search and seizure or the privilege against self-incrimination when that

---

45 State v. Schmidt, 240 P.3d 626, 2010 Kan. App. Unpub. LEXIS 740 (2010).

46 *Id.*

47 State v. Whitney, 889 N.E.2d 823, 2008 Ind. App. LEXIS 1344 (Ind. 2008). *See also* People v. Bock, 357 Ill. App. 3d 160, 168, 827 N.E.2d 1089, 1095, 2005 Ill. App. LEXIS 386 (2005).

48 *Id.*

49 *See* State v. Pollman, 286 Kan. 881, 2008 Kan. LEXIS 450 (Kan. 2008).

50 State v. Logan-Price, 197 P.3d 904, 2008 Kan. App. Unpub. LEXIS 976 (Kan. 2008).

person voluntarily submits to a test to determine blood-alcohol level. States use the concept of **implied consent** to permit the collection of blood, breath, or urine samples for analysis. Statutes typically note that, if a person has been driving on the roads within a jurisdiction and probable cause exists to believe that the person has operated or been in control of a motor vehicle while in violation of the statutes prohibiting impaired driving or other triggering conditions, the act of driving indicates that the driver has given prior consent, by operation of law, "to the withdrawal of specimens of the person's blood, breath, or urine and to a chemical test or tests of the specimens for the purpose of determining the alcohol concentration or presence of a controlled substance or other drugs."[51]

Implied consent Various state laws provide that any person who operates a motorized vehicle in the state is deemed to have given consent to a chemical test of substances collected from his or her person, such as blood, breath, urine, and saliva, for the purpose of determining the alcohol content of his or her blood, so long as that person appeared to be driving or exerting any physical control over a motor vehicle in the state, while under the influence of intoxicating beverages.

C. Urine Tests

Although the analysis of urine to infer blood-alcohol content has some advantages, it also has disadvantages. One disadvantage is that the concentration of alcohol or drug metabolites in the urine lags behind the alcohol concentration in the blood, so that an impaired person's urine might not indicate the level of impairment. Demonstrative of this principle is a Kentucky case that showed the defendant's urine contained bare traces of drugs, while a blood test indicated an absence of drugs.[52] Further, the test results can be rendered unreliable by the fact that dilution is greater or lesser according to the amount of urine in the bladder, and the person conducting the test has no way of knowing this information. In a Florida federal case, the expert witness testified that a defendant had Xanax, cocaine, marijuana, opiates, and methadone in his urine, but the amount or dosage that the defendant consumed could not be determined by the urine tests.[53] Expert testimony in one case indicated that the first urine sample was not reliable for alcohol content, and the second sample was the one to be used for testing purposes.[54] As contrasted with blood collection, obtaining a urine sample can be compromised by psychological stress or, in one case, physical problems. In an Ohio case, a breath machine indicated that suspect had a 0.07 percent blood-alcohol content, so the officer wanted a urine sample.[55] The man proved unable to provide a sample due

---

51 *See* IOWA CODE § 321J.6 (2013). *See also* ALA. CODE § 32-5-192 (2013).

52 Thompson v. Commonwealth, 177 S.W.3d 782, 783, 2005 Ky. LEXIS 370 (Ky. 2005). *See also* State v. Smith, 2006 Tenn. Crim. App. LEXIS 145 (2006).

53 United States v. Hughett, 2010 U.S. Dist. LEXIS 108005 (M. Dist. Fla. 2010).

54 State v. Watson, 2007 Ohio 2804, 2007 Ohio App. LEXIS 2565 (2007).

55 State v. Norman, 2006 Ohio 3362, 2006 Ohio App. LEXIS 3254 (2006).

to an enlarged prostate. On appeal, the court reversed the administrative revocation of his driving privileges because the man did not refuse to provide a sample; he was unable to produce one.

One advantage of urine testing for drugs is that, while the percentage of alcohol content is usually required and is reported by standard blood-alcohol tests, the amount of legal or illegal drugs that affects motor control is not typically reported.[56] The lab reports the presence of the metabolites produced by various drugs, but not the amount, and mere presence of the metabolites does not prove or disprove impairment. Because courts generally admit the fact of the presence of other drugs, this evidence helps the prosecution because a jury can give these drug tests any weight that a jury deems appropriate.

D. *Horizontal Gaze Nystagmus Tests*

With the development of the **horizontal gaze nystagmus test** (HGN), police officers have one more field diagnostic test available to assist them in the determination of whether probable cause to arrest exists in a particular case. The basis of the test is the inability of the eyes to maintain visual fixation as they are turned to the side following consumption of alcohol. In 2006, the Supreme Court of New Hampshire described the HGN test in these terms:

> **Horizontal gaze nystagmus test** Horizontal gaze nystagmus is the inability of the eyes to maintain visual fixation as they are turned to the side from the center.

> In summary, it is a standardized field sobriety test designed to detect nystagmus, i.e., an involuntary, rapid, back-and-forth jerking of the eyes. The administering police officer positions a stimulus, such as a pen, penlight, or finger, approximately twelve to fifteen inches in front of the suspect's eyes and gradually moves the stimulus laterally towards the suspect's ear. The officer observes the suspect's eyeballs to detect the following three signs, which could indicate intoxication: (1) the inability of the eye to smoothly track the stimulus; (2) the presence of nystagmus at the eye's maximum horizontal deviation; and (3) the point at which nystagmus, if present, begins as the stimulus is moved. The officer tests each eye and gives the suspect a point for each sign observed; therefore, a total of six points is possible.[57]

Nystagmus is a well-known physiological phenomenon caused by, among other things, ingestion of alcohol. The courts in virtually all American jurisdictions have recognized that the HGN test is based on scientific principles and, when properly performed, produces reliable and admissible evidence. Because the HGN test is based on science, the HGN testing must be performed by an expert trained in its use and interpretation. A Florida appellate court reversed a driving under the influence of alcohol conviction,

---

56 State v. Tripathi, 226 Or. App. 552, 555, 2009 Or. App. LEXIS 147 (2009).

57 State v. Cochrane, 897 A.2d 952, 955, 2006 N.H. LEXIS 48 (2006).

because the officer had not been qualified as an expert when he testified in court, and other evidence in the case was not sufficiently strong to make the error harmless.[58]

As a general rule, an officer who has been properly trained with respect to the administration and interpretation of the HGN test, and who was properly qualified in court, is permitted to testify concerning whether an individual was intoxicated.[59] Although some evidence exists to demonstrate that a police officer can estimate the blood-alcohol content from a subject's performance, a Georgia court reversed a motorist's conviction for the crime of DUI less safe to drive a vehicle. When the only evidence of blood alcohol presented in court was a police officer's estimate following the HGN test that the defendant was at 0.25 percent blood-alcohol content. According to the reviewing court, the state failed to establish the scientific validity and reliability of percent blood-alcohol estimation through the use of the HGN test.[60] A Maryland court earlier held a similar view that the HGN test could not be used to estimate a specific blood-alcohol content.[61]

E. Implied Consent Statutes

Many states have enacted statutes providing that a driver, whether licensed locally, unlicensed, or licensed in another state, is deemed to have given his consent, by the individual's act of driving in the state, to submit to an alcohol test if probable cause exists to believe that he or she is driving while intoxicated. Therefore, if he or she refuses to take the test, his or her license may be suspended. For example, California law provides:

> A person who drives a motor vehicle is deemed to have given his or her consent to chemical testing of his or her blood or breath for the purpose of determining the alcoholic content of his or her blood, if lawfully arrested for an offense committed in violation of [the law].[62]

California law also provides that a failure to take or complete the required chemical testing will result in a fine, possible imprisonment, and a one-year suspension of driving privileges.[63] Since there has been an implication of consent, Fourth Amendment search and seizure issues will not likely prevent the evidence from being admitted, provided the testing evidence otherwise meets the rules of evidence.

In most jurisdictions, following an arrest, a driver who is advised of his or her rights under a state's implied consent law and who declines to submit to a chemical test to determine his or her blood-alcohol content is deemed to have refused the test. As a general rule, an administrative suspension, either immediate or within a few days, will be imposed on the refusing driver.[64] Florida law provides that the officer shall

---

58 Robinson v. State, 982 So. 2d 1260, 2008 Fla. App. LEXIS 8099 (2008).

59 State v. Hicks, 791 N.W.2d 89, 98, 2010 Iowa Sup. LEXIS 120 (2010).

60 Bravo v. State, 304 Ga. App. 243, 248, 696 S.E.2d 79, 83, 2010 Ga. App. LEXIS 507 (2010).

61 State v. Blackwell, 2009 Md. LEXIS 62 (Md. 2009).

62 CAL. VEH. CODE §§ 23612 (a)(1)(A), 23612 (a)(1)(B) (2013).

63 *Id.*, (a)(1)(D).

64 *See* FLA. STAT. § 322.2615 (2013).

suspend the driver's license at the moment of refusal, substitute it with a temporary permit that expires within 10 days, and notify the state licensing department.[65] According to a Pennsylvania law,[66] the suspension of a driver's license will follow a refusal to submit to a breath, urine, or blood test. The officer must have reasonable grounds for arrest, and the driver must have been arrested and have refused to take the test suggested by the police officer. The administrative suspension lasts at least 12 months. The fact of refusal and circumstances surrounding the defendant's refusal are statutorily deemed to be admissible in any civil or criminal proceeding, a fact that might support either or both a civil and a criminal penalty.

Some individuals who had lost driving privileges believed that the implied consent laws violated their federal constitutional rights, and one impaired driver managed to have the Supreme Court review his constitutional arguments. In *South Dakota v. Neville*, the Court examined not only the implied consent statutes, but also the constitutionality of prosecutors using closing arguments to comment on the failure of defendants to take a blood-alcohol test.[67] In *Neville*, the defendant was arrested for driving while intoxicated. The arresting officer asked him to submit to a blood-alcohol test and warned him that he would lose his license administratively if he refused. The South Dakota trial court granted a motion to suppress all evidence, and the South Dakota Supreme Court affirmed this ruling on the ground that the statute permitting the introduction of evidence of refusal to take the blood-alcohol test violated the Fifth Amendment privilege against self-incrimination as applied to the states. The United States Supreme Court granted certiorari, accepting the case.

First, the United States Supreme Court stated that the reason for the implied consent law wash to deter drinkers from driving by making it easier for South Dakota law enforcement officials to obtain evidence from the drinking driver. The United States Supreme Court held that the Fifth Amendment's self-incrimination clause was not implicated because the results of blood-alcohol tests were not testimonial in nature so it was permissible to introduce evidence of a refusal to take a blood-alcohol test and for a prosecutor to comment on that failure.

As to the constitutionality of commenting on the failure to take the test, the Court stated that it was not fundamentally unfair or in violation of due process to use a defendant's refusal to take a blood-alcohol test as evidence of guilt, even though the police failed to warn him that the refusal could be used against him at trial. In making this decision, the Court explained, "the offer of taking the blood-alcohol test is clearly legitimate, and the action becomes no less legitimate when the state offers a second option of refusing the test, with the attendant penalties for making that choice." Summarizing the opinion, the Court concluded "that a refusal to take a blood-alcohol test, after a police officer has lawfully requested it, is not an act coerced by the officer, and thus is not protected by the privilege against self-incrimination."[68]

---

65 *Id.*

66 *See* 75 PA. C.S. § 1547 (2013).

67 South Dakota v. Neville, 459 U.S. 553, 1983 U.S. LEXIS 129 (1983).

68 *Id.* at 564.

§ 15.4 Blood Grouping Tests and Blood Comparisons

In the days prior to DNA testing becoming highly sophisticated and regularly admitted as evidence, general blood grouping tests often served a very useful identification purpose in criminal prosecutions for rape,[69] assault and battery,[70] or paternity.[71] In a rape and murder case, the defendant argued on appeal that the trial court erred in admitting evidence of a serologist that the defendant was one of 35 percent of the male population who are type O secretors.[72] The evidence was offered to show that the defendant could have been the male who had sexual contact with the victim. The reviewing court agreed that this was not improper evidence, because it only indicated that the defendant fell into the suspect percentage of the population who could have been the perpetrator. The appellate court ordered exclusion of the evidence upon retrial, however, because the risk of unfair prejudice outweighed the probative value of the evidence.

Some other examples of the use of blood comparisons in criminal cases indicate the importance of this type of test. In a prosecution for kidnapping and for engaging in lewd and lascivious conduct with a child, blood grouping evidence taken from the victim's clothing indicated a high probability that the sample came from the defendant. According to expert testimony that helped convict the defendant, the defendant's blood matched the factors contained within the sample tested because the blood "had to have come from either an ABO type B secretor or a nonsecretor who is PGM two plus."[73] DNA testing of semen from the victim's shirt matched the defendant's DNA profile.[74] In another case, the trial court admitted results from electrophoretic typing of aged, dried bloodstains from the defendant's tennis shoes over his objections that the electrophoretic testing did not have scientific acceptance.[75] Electrophoresis results reveal the type of individual blood protein and enzyme patterns found in a blood sample by a method that separates electrically charged molecules, but those results do not evaluate DNA. The reviewing court noted that "electrophoresis is generally accepted in the scientific community and, once a scientific procedure such as electrophoretic testing of bloodstains has become generally accepted, mere variations in technique or procedure go to the weight of the evidence, not its admissibility."[76]

Some pre-DNA era testing cases are still moving through the criminal justice system, where convictions were obtained based on older blood grouping methodology. A California capital case is demonstrative of prosecutions involving older blood

---

69 Shanks v. State, 185 Md. 437, 45 A.2d 85 (1945).

70 Commonwealth v. Statti, 16 Pa. Super. 577, 73 A.2d 688 (1950).

71 See Eubanks v. Moss, 2010 Conn. Super. LEXIS 1073 (2010).

72 State v. Duncan, 698 S.W.2d 63 (Tenn. 1985).

73 California v. Funston, 2002 Cal. App. Unpub. LEXIS 3513 (2002).

74 *Id.*

75 People v. Cook, 40 Cal. 4th 1334, 2007 Cal. LEXIS 5070 (Cal. 2007).

76 *Id.* at 1345.

identification science that are continuing to be litigated.[77] In this case, police discovered the eight-year-old female child's body inside the defendant's suitcase, which was in the defendant's apartment. Ordinarily this type of evidence might prove to be devastating to a defendant, but police and the prosecutor's office also pursued blood-grouping tests that were commonly available in 1994. Using older technology, one of the criminalists typed the victim's blood as ABO type A, and another criminalist identified the defendant's blood as ABO type B. In the defendant's apartment, police found the sheet in which the victim had been wrapped and found bloodstains of ABO type AB, semen, and amylase, a component of saliva. A forensic serologist testified at trial that the sample, ABO type AB, could be a mixture of the defendant's blood and the victim's blood or it could have come from an unknown third person. Police found stained tissue paper in the defendant's wastebasket that, upon analysis, revealed that the tissue paper exhibited semen stains consistent with the defendant and high amylase activity consistent with saliva from the victim. Expert testimony indicated that the stains were consistent with the result of oral copulation. The blood evidence alone might have been sufficient to convict, but at that time in history, with the blood evidence being less than certainly conclusive on the issue of identity, the non-blood evidence mentioned and other extensive evidence resulted in a guilty verdict and a death sentence.

Older science that provided much-needed evidence of identification has largely been supplanted by DNA testing because the DNA testing proves much more definitive in making identifications and is able to discriminate among different donors of blood and body material when human material becomes commingled.

§ 15.5 Polygraph Examinations[78]

The polygraph, also known as the lie detector, is an electronic device that, when properly connected to the human body, graphically records changes in blood pressure, heart rate, and respiration in response to questions posed to the test taker. The basic features may be supplemented with a unit for recording what is known as the galvanic skin reflex, based on changes in the activity of the sweat pores that alters the electrical conductivity of the skin, and another unit for recording muscular movements and pressures.

As an investigative technique, the use of the polygraph is based on the assumption that lying leads to conflict; that conflict causes fear and anxiety; that this mental state is

---

77 People v. Panah, 35 Cal. 4th 395, 414, 107 P.3d 790, 803, 25 Cal. Rptr. 3d 672, 689, 2005 Cal. LEXIS 2712 (Cal. 2005).

78 Kevin Muenster, *See* Chapter 6, *supra*, for discussion of admissibility of polygraph results on stipulation. *See also The Re-Lie-ability of Polygraph Evidence: An Evaluation of Whether Texas's Per Se Rule Against the Admissibility of Polygraph Evidence Is Violative of the Texas Rules of Evidence*, 58 BAYLOR L. REV. 265 (2006).

the direct cause of measurable physiological changes that can be accurately recorded; and that the polygraph operator, by a study of these reactions, can tell whether the subject is being deceptive or truthful. The polygraph presents problems concerning reliability, scientific acceptability, consistency, and accuracy among examiners, and operation of the polygraph still cannot answer the questions that it purports to answer, without engaging detractors who present good arguments against admissibility.

An early blow to the admissibility of polygraph evidence occurred in a famous case, *Frye v. United States*, where the court of appeals held that polygraph evidence was not admissible because the field of polygraph testing had not been "sufficiently established to have gained general acceptance in the particular field in which it belongs."[79] Despite general inadmissibility, two federal appellate circuits have seen fit to allow the mention, if not the admission, of polygraph evidence in particular situations.[80] According to the Supreme Court of New Mexico, as of 2004, 27 states apply a per se rule of exclusion to the admission of polygraph evidence.[81] As the court noted, "These per se states ban polygraph evidence, including test results, offers to take the test, as well as refusals to take the test, for a variety of reasons. These courts found that the polygraph has not been proven valid or reliable or that it has not been generally accepted in the scientific community."[82] If the polygraph produces unreliable evidence that should not be admissible in court, it seems interesting that virtually all law enforcement agencies in the nation use the machine in some capacity, while some prosecutors and defense attorneys similarly find the polygraph useful.

Consistent with many jurisdictions, an Arizona appellate court determined that the trial court did not have to hold hearings concerning the reliability of the polygraph because the state's position on admissibility had not changed from its earlier refusal to admit polygraph results.[83] A murder defendant believed that the results of his polygraph examination would assist his defense to a charge under Arizona's felony-murder statute. The trial court ruled that, in general, polygraph results were not admissible, and therefore, the court refused to hold a hearing concerning admissibility or to admit the evidence. The trial court noted that "Arizona courts have concluded that, absent a stipulation by the parties, such test results are categorically inadmissible."[84] The reviewing court upheld the ruling of the trial court, which was consistent with the majority of court jurisdictions.

Contrary to most jurisdictions, the Supreme Court of New Mexico considered the admission of polygraph evidence and, in principle, approved the admission of polygraph evidence in state courts.[85] The court reviewed the theory of the polygraph.

---

79 293 F. 1013, 1014, 1923 U.S. App. LEXIS 1712 (D.C. Cir. 1923).

80 See 80 TEMP. L. REV. 711, n.27 (2007).

81 Lee v. Martinez, 136 N.M. 166, 96 P.3d 291, 2004 N.M. LEXIS 378 (2004).

82 *Id.* at 185.

83 State v. Perez, 308 P.3d 1189, 1193, 2013 Ariz. App. LEXIS 183 (2013).

84 *Id.*

85 Lee v. Martinez, 136 N.M. 166, 2004 NMSC 27, 96 P.3d 291, 2004 N.M. LEXIS 378 (2004).

> The polygraph instrument records "physiological responses that are believed to be stronger during acts of deception than at other times." These physiological responses include cardiovascular activity, electrodermal activity (electrical conductance at the skin surface), and respiratory activity. In general, a polygraph examination consists of "a series of yes/no questions to which the examinee responds while connected to sensors that transmit data on these physiological phenomena by wire to the instrument, which uses analog or digital technology to record the data. ... The record of physiological responses during the polygraph test is known as the polygraph chart." The polygraph examination is based on the theory that "a deceptive response to a question causes a reaction—such as fear of detection or psychological arousal—that changes respiration rate, heart rate, blood pressure, or skin conductance relative to what they were before the question was asked." [Internal citations omitted.][86]

The Supreme Court reviewed the three general types of polygraph examination techniques and eventually focused on the second theory for use in New Mexico courts.

> Three different polygraph questioning techniques have been developed. First, in the "relevant/irrelevant" technique, the examinee is asked two different types of questions—"the relevant questions are typically very specific and concern an event under investigation"; whereas, "the irrelevant questions may be completely unrelated to the event and may offer little temptation to deceive." A deceptive person is expected to have a stronger physiological response to the relevant questions than to the irrelevant questions. Second, in the "control question technique" or "comparison question technique," instead of coupling the relevant questions with irrelevant questions, the irrelevant questions are replaced with control questions "intended to generate physiological reactions even in nondeceptive examinees." An example of a control question might be, "Have you ever lied to a friend?" Truthful examinees are expected to experience stronger physiological responses to the control questions; whereas, deceptive examinees are expected to experience stronger physiological responses to the relevant questions. Third, in the "guilty knowledge polygraph test," the examinee is asked a number of "questions about details of an event under investigation that are known only to investigators and those with direct knowledge of the event." Examinees are expected to experience the greatest physiological responses to those questions that accurately describe the event. [Internal citations omitted.][87]

Under the New Mexico rules regulating the admission of evidence, the judge must assure that any and all scientific evidence or results meet the tests of reliability and relevancy. The trial judge must also determine whether the scientific methodology is really based on science and whether that science will support conclusions based on probability rather than mere guess or conjecture.

> In making this determination, we consider: "(1) whether a theory or technique can be (and has been) tested; (2) whether the theory or technique has been subjected to peer review and publication; (3) the known potential rate of error in using a particular scientific technique and the existence and maintenance of standards controlling the technique's operation; and (4) whether the theory or technique has been generally accepted in the particular scientific field." [Internal citations omitted.][88]

---

[86] *Id.* at 170.

[87] *Id.*

[88] Id. at 173.

The court reviewed some of the reasons for admitting this sort of testimony and noted that the research that has been conducted shows that the basic science demonstrated support for the theories on which the polygraph examination is based. The court considered the perceived rate of error related to polygraph examinations and evaluated the fact that a number of polygraph validation studies had been conducted with adequate results. Additionally, the court surveyed some of the peer-reviewed scholarly publications that addressed polygraph issues and testing, some of which cautioned that polygraph studies were not yet supported by the high level of research desired in scientific inquiry, but it noted that some studies have appeared in high-quality research journals. According to the court, professional standards have been developed by the leading professional association, the American Polygraph Association, which, when followed, should produce reliable evidence. The court concluded that the control question polygraph examination technique proved to be appropriate to admit if general standards for admission of evidence were followed.[89]

In its decision, the Supreme Court of New Mexico pointed out the fact that the very groups and individuals wanting to keep polygraph evidence from admission in New Mexico courts were those who used polygraph examination results in their own governmental pursuits. "Often the same government officials who vigorously oppose the admission of exculpatory polygraphs of the accused find polygraph testing to be reliable enough to use in their own decision making. Federal and state governments rely upon the results of polygraph examinations for a variety of law enforcement purposes, even in jurisdictions where polygraph evidence is inadmissible."[90] The court mentioned that polygraph results have been used to determine probable cause, whether to prosecute, or whether to arrest, and judges have considered the results in deciding whether to issue an arrest warrant. In order for polygraph results to be admitted, each trial judge must evaluate the situation and make an individual determination based on the facts of each case, but the clear thrust of this case was to permit, and not to absolutely prohibit, the admission of polygraph evidence that has been conducted by licensed examiners who have followed the standards of the professional associations and meet the criteria established by the Supreme Court of New Mexico.

In a recent case, the Supreme Court of New Mexico upheld the use of a polygraph examination that had been administered to one of the defendant's relatives.[91] The top New Mexico court indicated that polygraph evidence was generally admissible and would be disturbed only due to an abuse of discretion by the trial judge. According to the court, any doubt concerning the admissibility of scientific evidence should be resolved in favor of admitting the evidence. The defendant's remedies include aggressive cross-examination, the presentation of rebuttal evidence, and final arguments to the jury. In this case, the defendant had ample opportunity to cross-examine the state's polygraph examiner and to inquire about the validity of his conclusions. In fact, in

---

[89] *Id.* at 171.

[90] *Id.* at 181.

[91] State v. Holly, 2009 NMSC 4, 2009 N.M. LEXIS 3 (N.M. 2009).

rebuttal, the defendant introduced evidence from his own polygraph examiner in an effort to show that the method of scoring the state's polygraph test was erroneous.

Prior to the *Lee* decision, the Supreme Court of the United States had an opportunity to liberalize the admission of polygraph evidence in federal courts, but determined not to go in that direction. The case that provided the opportunity was decided in 1998, and it involved an appeal from the Court of Appeals for the Armed Forces in which an airman had been accused of ingesting methamphetamine, and he contended that he absolutely had not taken any drugs.[92] In this case, *United States v. Scheffer*, the trial court refused to admit polygraph evidence based on a unique military rule of evidence. Military Rule of Evidence 707 provides, among other things, that "[n]otwithstanding any other provision of law, the results of a polygraph examination, the opinion of a polygraph examiner, or any reference to an offer to take, failure to take, or taking of a polygraph examination, shall not be admitted into evidence."[93] The available evidence resulted in a conviction at court-martial. On appeal, the Court of Appeals reversed the conviction, noting that, in that case, the per se exclusion of the polygraph evidence violated the Sixth Amendment right to put on a defense. The Supreme Court considered the case and rejected the Sixth Amendment argument while stating:

> Rule 707 serves several legitimate interests in the criminal trial process. These interests include ensuring that only reliable evidence is introduced at trial, preserving the jury's role in determining credibility, and avoiding litigation that is collateral to the primary purpose of the trial. The rule is neither arbitrary nor disproportionate in promoting these ends. Nor does it implicate a sufficiently weighty interest of the defendant to raise a constitutional concern under our precedents.[94]

The Supreme Court mentioned that the defendant was not categorically prohibited from introducing a defense because he could introduce any factual evidence he possessed and nothing prohibited him from taking the witness stand in his own defense. Writing for the majority, Justice Thomas noted, "[t]he contentions of respondent and the dissent notwithstanding, there is simply no consensus that polygraph evidence is reliable."[95] From the perspective of the Supreme Court, it appears that a general approval for the admission of polygraph evidence in federal courts may be a long time coming, if ever. The *Scheffer* Court upheld Military Rule 707, totally excluding polygraph evidence in military trials, but the case does not prohibit a federal district judge from using discretion to allow polygraph evidence. It simply means that there is no constitutional right to have the evidence admitted.

According to one law review article, when the Supreme Court heard arguments in the *Scheffer* case, "twenty-two states allowed for the admission of polygraph evidence to some degree, and twenty-seven states plus the District of Columbia did not allow for

---

92 United States v. Scheffer, 523 U.S. 303, 1998 U.S. LEXIS 2303 (1998).

93 *Id.* at 306-307.

94 *Id.* at 309.

95 *Id.*

polygraph evidence in criminal trials."[96] The author noted that, in 2000, only two federal circuits, the Fourth Circuit and the District of Columbia Circuit, continued to hold that polygraph evidence was per se inadmissible.[97] With customary inertia, jurisdictions that refuse to allow any polygraph evidence tend to continue on the same path, while jurisdictions that permit polygraph under some circumstances tend to remain open to polygraph evidence on a case-by-case basis.

In conformity with the practice that most state and federal courts tend to exclude polygraph evidence, the Court of Appeals for the Seventh Circuit supported a trial court decision to prohibit polygraph evidence from being offered by a defendant.[98] In a case involving a defendant who lied to federal authorities concerning his purchase of firearms on behalf of another individual, the trial court exercised its discretion and refused to admit evidence that the defendant had offered to take a polygraph examination, because of concern that it might confuse the jury. The Court of Appeals noted that it reviews evidentiary decisions by trial judges based on an abuse of discretion standard. In this case, the Court of Appeals could find no abuse in the trial court decision to exclude evidence concerning the defendant's offer to take a polygraph examination.

A substantial minority of courts admits polygraph evidence upon stipulation of the parties subject to judicial discretion. For the most part, this result has been achieved by court decision, although statutory provisions may achieve the same result. A few courts recognize a trial court's discretion to admit polygraph evidence even in the absence of stipulation. The Seventh Circuit Court of Appeals has adopted this approach.

There are generally three identifiable approaches to the admissibility of polygraph evidence. The first holds that the evidence is inadmissible per se, the second approach allows the evidence upon the stipulation of all the parties, subject to the judicial discretion, and the third approach permits polygraph evidence in the absence of stipulation when certain circumstances exist such as impeachment or corroboration. The approaches in the various jurisdictions are discussed as follows, with the caveat that the decisions of each jurisdiction must be examined to determine the law applicable in that jurisdiction.

1. Some states take the position that polygraph evidence is inadmissible per se and under all circumstances. Whether the intent of admission is to impeach, corroborate, or use as substantive evidence, the results of a polygraph test cannot be used in court.[99] Evidence is not admissible by either party, either as substantive evidence or as relating to the credibility of the witness. Demonstrative of this principle, the Intermediate Court of Appeals of Hawai'i noted that polygraph examination

---

96 *See* Dorian D. Peters, *Per Se Prohibitions of the Admission of Polygraph Evidence as Upheld in* Scheffer *Are Both Violative of the Constitution and the Federal Rules of Evidence as Applied by* Daubert, 27 AM. J. CRIM. L. 249 (2000).

97 *Id.*

98 United States v. Dinga, 609 F.3d 904, 908, 2010 U.S. App. LEXIS 13688 (7th Cir. 2010).

99 ARK. CODE ANN. § 12-12-704 (2013). *But see* Rollins v. State, 2005 Ark. LEXIS 293 (Ark. 2005), in which stipulations by both parties have been admitted.

results are not admissible in the state's courts.[100] In this case, the trial court did not commit reversible error when it refused to grant a continuance in a prostitution case to permit the defendant to find a witness who would have testified to the results of the defendant's polygraph test.

2. Any reference to polygraph evidence is excluded unless both parties stipulate to the evidence's admissibility. For example, in California courts, according to statute, "the results of a polygraph examination, the opinion of a polygraph examiner, or any reference to an offer to take, failure to take, or taking of a polygraph examination, shall not be admitted into evidence in any criminal proceeding, including pretrial and postconviction motions and hearings, or in any trial or hearing of a juvenile for a criminal offense, whether heard in juvenile or adult court, unless all parties stipulate to the admission of such results."[101] Similarly, in Ohio courts, polygraph "results are admissible only if both the prosecution and defense jointly stipulate that an accused will take a polygraph test and that the results will be admissible."[102]
3. Polygraph evidence is admissible in the absence of a stipulation when certain circumstances exist. For example, in a carjacking-murder case, the defendant took a lie detector test, as suggested by the police, but he failed. At trial, the defense counsel made it seem as if police had coerced the defendant on a one-on-one interrogation. To rebut the inference of coercion, the prosecutor was permitted to have a police officer explain that the one-on-one interrogation involved defendant's consensual polygraph examination. The officer who conducted the polygraph was permitted to explain to the jury much of what the defendant had told him. The resulting conviction was affirmed on appeal.[103]

In jurisdictions in which the results of polygraph examinations are inadmissible in court, police still use the polygraph during investigations and as a tool to encourage admissions and confessions. Even though the results may be useless in court, statements made before, during, and after an examination may be admissible. In a Tennessee court, where polygraph results are inadmissible, a suspect in a child rape case agreed to take a polygraph test concerning the facts.[104] After the examiner finished asking questions, he told the subject that he had observed deception on a few questions and stated to the subject that the child contended that she had been forced to engage in sexual intercourse. The subject noted to the examiner, "she was not forced." At the trial, the court permitted the polygraph examiner to tell the court that the defendant stated that, in reference to the sexual activity with the alleged victim, that "she was not forced." The defendant appealed and offered the argument that "Tennessee courts have held repeatedly that polygraph test results, testimony concerning such results, and testimony concerning a defendant's willingness or refusal to submit to a polygraph test are

---

100 State v. Cho, 2009 Haw. App. LEXIS 98 (2009).

101 *See* CAL. EVID. CODE § 351.1(a) (2014).

102 State v. Dunlap, 2007 Ohio 1624 (Ohio 2007).

103 United States v. Blake, 571 F.3d 331, 347, 2009 U.S. App. LEXIS 14609 (2009).

104 State v. Damron, 151 S.W.3d 510, 515, 2004 Tenn. LEXIS 993 (2004).

inadmissible."[105] The reviewing court held that the evidence had been properly introduced against the defendant because, according to the general rule followed in a majority of jurisdictions in the United States, the introduction of voluntary statements made during a polygraph examination are admissible because the reliability of a voluntary statement does not depend on the accuracy or reliability of the polygraph.

Absent a stipulation of the parties, if the state court has held that polygraph results are generally inadmissible, if only for impeachment purposes, the prosecutor has commited a due process violation when he or she failed to disclose to the defense that an important prosecution witness failed a polygraph test concerning whether she actually saw the shooting that was a centerpiece of the prosecution's case.[106] In *Bartholomew v. Wood*, the defendant claimed that the state denied him due process by failing to disclose that a crucial witness on the issue of premeditation had failed a polygraph test. The Ninth Circuit Court of Appeals agreed with the defendant that failure to disclose to the defendant that the witness had failed the test was a due process violation of the kind condemned in *Brady v. Maryland*.[107]

Evidence or mention of the fact that the defendant or a witness either took, refused to take, or passed a lie detector examination is generally not admissible[108]and could create reversible error if mentioned by a witness. An Ohio reviewing court noted that polygraph evidence is not generally admissible and mention of a defendant's willingness to submit or refuse a polygraph examination is not admissible and can create reversible error.[109] In this Ohio case, the prosecutor asked the question that involved the polygraph on direct examination. Naturally, there would be a difference in directly soliciting a witness to mention polygraph evidence and an inadvertent mention by a witness who answered a question while casually mentioning polygraph evidence. A cautionary instruction may suffice to reduce any damage, but courts often disagree on this point.

The polygraph examiner should receive his or her training in the lie detector technique under the guidance of an experienced examiner with a sufficient volume of actual cases to permit the trainee to make frequent observations of lie detector tests and to conduct tests him- or herself under the instructor's personal supervision. In addition, the trainee should read and take courses in the pertinent areas of psychology and physiology and should examine and interpret a considerable number of lie detector test records in verified cases.[110] Some states now require licensing of polygraph operators.

---

105 *Id.* at 516.

106 Tennison v. California Victim Comp. & Government Claims Board, 152 Cal. App. 4th 1164, 62 Cal. Rptr. 3d 88, 2007 Cal. App. LEXIS 1097 (2007).

107 Brady v. Maryland, 373 U.S. 83; 83 S. Ct. 1194; 10 L. Ed. 2d 215; (1963) U.S. LEXIS 1615. *See* § 4.9 for a discussion of the *Brady* rule.

108 *See* CAL. EVID. CODE § 351.1 (2014). California will permit polygraph evidence if all parties stipulate to admissibility. *See also* People v. May, 2008 Cal. App. Unpub. LEXIS 7458 (2008).

109 State v. Banner, 2010 Ohio 5592, 2010 Ohio App. LEXIS 4713 (2010).

110 F.E. Inbau and J.E. Reid, *The Lie-Detector Technique: A Reliable and Valuable Investigative Aid*, 50 A.B.A.J. 470 (May 1964).

To practice in Illinois, the law requires that the examiner possess a state license. To qualify, an Illinois polygraph examiner must have good moral character, have passed the state examination, have at least a baccalaureate degree, and have completed six months of study in detection of deception.[111] A Vermont statute requires that polygraph examiners establish personal honesty, truthfulness, integrity, and moral fitness and have not been convicted of a felony or misdemeanor involving moral turpitude. The examiner must have passed an approved course of study with a six-month internship.[112] Evidence generated by such an individual has a chance of being admitted into a Vermont court.

From the foregoing, it is apparent that the laws relating to the use of polygraph evidence in court are still changing. Some courts now hold that the polygraph has attained a degree of validity and reliability, and that such evidence may be admitted under specified conditions or by stipulation. Future cases and legislation will determine whether this trend toward recognition will continue.

§ 15.6 "Truth Serum" Results

The term "truth serum" has no precise medical or scientific meaning.[113] To refer to sodium amytal or sodium pentathol as "truth serum" is a misnomer, as they have no propensity or chemical effect to cause a person "to speak the truth." These drugs do not induce a state of mind in which a person tells the truth, but instead cause the subject to speak more freely than he or she might otherwise. The use of sodium amytal can produce any one of four results: truth, falsehood, fantasy, or response to suggestion.[114] Constitutionally, any substance that might be administered as a way of recovering or discerning the truth will require the consent of the defendant, and as a result, if any truth serum drug is to be administered, it is the defense rather than the prosecution that has an opportunity to consider this avenue. Research concerning recent usages of the various "truth serums" has not revealed any recent state or federal cases where the results of such tests were considered admissible.

An admission or a confession induced by the administration of drugs is constitutionally inadmissible where it was not the product of a rational free will and intellect.[115]

---

111 225 ILL. COMP. STAT. 430/11 (2009).

112 26 U.S.A VT. STAT. ANN. § 2904 (2013).

113 *See* Townsend v. Sain, 372 U.S. 293, 83 S. Ct. 745, 768, 9 L. Ed. 2d 770 (1963) (Stewart, J., dissenting).

114 Freeman v. New York Central R. Co., 174 N.E.2d 550 (Ohio Ct. App. 1960), a civil action in which the plaintiff told his psychiatrist that he was unable to recall the events leading up to his accident, and asked the doctor to try to restore his memory. The doctor administered a treatment of sodium amytal, which placed the plaintiff in a hypnotic or semiconscious state during which the doctor conversed with the plaintiff and made a record of the questions and answers. At the trial, the plaintiff's testimony was based upon his medically refreshed memory. The court did not expressly decide on the propriety of this method of refreshing one's memory.

115 Hanna v. Price, 2005 U.S. Dist. LEXIS 30380 (W.D. Mich. 2005).

In a prosecution for murder, police questioned the defendant at the hospital after he had been shot by police three times. At the time, he was recovering from surgery performed hours earlier, he was on significant amounts of pain medication, and he had not eaten for several days. In addition, he was in the intensive care unit, he had tubes in his nose and mouth, and he was suicidal. The court felt that the interrogation conducted by police under these circumstances did not produce a free and voluntary confession. Allegedly, the defendant's answers to police questions were delusional, and a doctor testified that he was not sane or competent to waive any rights. Officers noted that he waived his *Miranda* rights, so they continued to question him. The answers were mostly unintelligible. Other medications were withheld from the defendant, leading the federal district court to conclude that withholding medication must be considered coercive. The drugs given the defendant may have had "truth serum" properties, but the federal district court granted the writ of habeas corpus because of the dangers of interrogating a person in the drugged state in which the police found the defendant.

Although excessive alcohol causes people to talk and say things that they might not ordinarily say when sober, the mere fact that a subject is intoxicated does not make a waiver of rights improper or interrogation constitutionally suspect. In an Ohio case, a court of appeals upheld a conviction when the defendant made an allegation that he was too drunk to understand *Miranda* warnings.[116] The court reviewed the defendant's tape-recorded statements that he understood his rights and that he had read them, and as a result, the court held that the effects of alcohol did not render the statement invalid or coerced.

In a case involving drug use prior to a confession, a federal court of appeals refused to disturb a verdict of murder and a sentence of death in an Alabama state prosecution where the defendant alleged that his confession had been involuntarily taken.[117] He contended that he was under the influence of marijuana and alcohol and suffering a withdrawal from alcohol at the time he made incriminating comments to police. During a postconviction hearing, medical experts in psychiatry, forensic psychiatry, and drug abuse testified that the defendant would have been in a mixed state of marijuana and alcohol intoxication and may have understood the basic questions being asked of him, but would have been in a situation that made it more difficult for him to control impulses. One expert indicated that the drugs used by the defendant would have acted like a truth serum and would have reduced his control over his volitional and willful processes. The state court rejected the argument that the confession was involuntarily taken and held that even if the medical testimony had been offered at the suppression hearing, the result would have been no different. The federal court of appeals upheld the state court's factual determination, because it was not objectively unreasonable, thus refusing to issue a writ of habeas corpus.

In a Texas murder case, which was not exactly a "truth serum" case because the drugs were introduced by treating physicians, the defendant was a heroin addict, and

116 State v. Hill, 2006 Ohio 1408 (2006).

117 Parker v. Allen, 2009 U.S. App. LEXIS 8275 (11th Cir. 2009).

she gave several statements to police at different times that were used against her at trial.[118] After her initial arrest, and while she was under the self-induced influence of heroin, police conducted an interrogation of her. When she began to exhibit signs of heroin withdrawal, she was taken to a hospital where she was given morphine and methadone. Police officers continued their interrogation at the hospital. The next day the defendant complained of heroin withdrawal and was given the drug Librium under a doctor's order. Police subsequently interrogated her again, and during this interrogation, she made statements that were not in her best interest. Prior to trial the defendant filed a motion to suppress all three of her recorded statements, as having been involuntarily made. In support of her motion, the defendant offered a physician board-certified in psychiatry and addiction medicine who explained the effects of the various medications given to the defendant, noting that the high dose of methadone given would have made an average person unconscious. In his testimony, the doctor did not conclude that any of the medications or their combination would act as a truth serum, even though he did offer the opinion that she was intoxicated with heroin during the initial interrogation. The reviewing court upheld the trial court's decision not to suppress the statements, despite the defendant's allegation that her statement should have been suppressed because the drugs acted as a truth serum, leading her to provide a series of involuntary statements. According to the reviewing court, "[w]e recognize that appellant's drug abuse was significant, and her medical treatment considerable. Nevertheless, the record supports the trial court's ruling that appellant was capable of making an informed decision to waive her rights."[119]

The use of a truth serum or truth-inducing drug by the prosecution on a defendant has doubtful utility because of questions involving self-incrimination, voluntariness, and the overall issue of relevance. From the defense perspective, the use of so-called truth serums have generally not produced an outcome in the defendant's favor, whether at trial stage or during posttrial appellate proceedings.

§ 15.7 Fingerprint Comparisons

The use of fingerprints as a means of identification seems to have originated in Assyria, and artifcast related to this process have been preserved in clay tablets in the British Museum. The British used fingerprints as early as 1858 in Bengal to curb check forgeries by natives.[120] In referring to the seminal case, *United States v. Kelly*, 55 F.2d 67 (CA2 1932), in a newer case,[121] the Supreme Court noted with approval that, in *Kelly*, Judge Augustus Hand wrote that "routine fingerprinting did not violate the

---

118 Paolilla v. State, 2011 Tex. App. LEXIS 1516 (2011).

119 *Id.*

120 Moon v. State, 22 Ariz. 418, 424, 198 P. 288 (Ariz. 1921) (quoting People v. Sallow, 100 Misc. 447, N.Y. Misc. LEXIS 809 (N.Y. 1917)).

121 Maryland v. King, 133 S.Ct. 1958, 1976, 186 L. Ed. 2d 1, 39, 2013 U.S. LEXIS 4165 (2103).

Fourth Amendment precisely because it fit within the accepted means of processing an arrestee into custody." The Supreme Court noted that, by the middle of the 20th century, it was considered elementary that people in lawful custody could be required to submit to fingerprinting, among other identification procedures.[122] Courts take judicial notice of the fact that fingerprint identification is one of the surest methods of identification and that no two persons have identical fingerprints. The primary purpose of fingerprinting is the positive identification of an accused. Another purpose of fingerprinting is evidentiary. For example, technicians compare the fingerprints of the defendant with fingerprints left at the scene of the crime or on an object connected to the crime. The evidentiary purpose may or may not be present in a given case.

According to Supreme Court interpretations of the Fifth Amendment, the taking and using of fingerprint evidence does not violate the Fifth Amendment privilege against compelled testimonial self-incrimination. Furthermore, warrantless fingerprinting of individuals who have been validly arrested or formally charged with a crime does not constitute an unreasonable search and seizure within the meaning of the Fourth Amendment.[123]

In a criminal case, to compare two or more samples of fingerprint evidence with a view to making an identification or an exclusion, the person comparing the prints must qualify as an expert to the satisfaction of the trial court. In response to one defendant's challenge that a police officer was not qualified as an expert and should not have been permitted to offer evidence, a court found that the evidence showed that the officer was able to explain the traditional rules for fingerprint identification, which included the number of matching points required to offer a positive identification. The trial judge made additional inquiries into the officer's expertise and ultimately determined that the officer was sufficiently qualified to offer testimony.[124] In a different case, a woman was declared qualified to testify regarding fingerprint identification, after it was shown that the woman had been doing fingerprint identification for 24 years, during which time she had compared more than three million fingerprints, with no misidentifications.[125] Whether a witness has the requisite qualifications of a fingerprint expert is a question within the discretion of the trial court.

Evidence of palmprints left at the scene of a crime is admissible under the same standards as those used for fingerprints, and palmprint identification is just as reliable and accurate as identification by fingerprints. In a California case involving burglary and petty theft, police evidence technicians discovered a palmprint that was later linked

---

122 *Id*, at 40.

123 United States v. Laub Baking Co., 283 F. Supp. 217 (N.D. Ohio 1968); Schmerber v. California, 384 U.S. 757, 86 S. Ct. 1826, 16 L. Ed. 2d 908 (1967). *See* KANOVITZ, CONSTITUTIONAL LAW (13th ed. 2012) and WALKER AND HEMMENS, LEGAL GUIDE FOR POLICE (8th ed. 2008). *See also* Wright v. Quarterman, 2009 U.S. Dist. LEXIS 128897 (N.D. Tex. 2009) (noting that "[f]ingerprints are not testimonial, and the taking of fingerprints is not protected by Fifth Amendment privileges.").

124 State v. Lewis, 990 So. 2d 109, 116, 2008 La. App. LEXIS 1120 (La. 2008), *writ denied*, 6 So. 3d 811, 2009 La. LEXIS 379 (La. 2009).

125 United States v. Cruz, 2006 U.S. App. LEXIS 18353 (10th Cir. 2006).

to the defendant, by comparing the palmprint to the database in California.[126] Expert testimony revealed that a comparison of the palmprint photograph with the computer database indicated that the defendant's palmprint was the closest match of all the "hits," and the expert subsequently made an individual human-based comparison. The fingerprint expert testified that all of the proper comparison points on the defendant's file print matched the crime scene palmprints, and there were no discrepancies between the two prints. Upon appeal, the court rejected the defendant's argument that the palmprint by itself was insufficient to convict the defendant, indicating that there were numerous prior appellate cases where in fingerprint and palmprint evidence alone was considered sufficient to prove the case beyond a reasonable doubt.

A court that orders a defendant to submit a fingerprint or palmprint after he or she has been indicted has not interfered with a defendant's rights under the Fourth Amendment or the Fifth Amendment. In a prosecution involving the allegation that the defendant was a felon found in possession of a firearm, the defendant ultimately refused to stipulate as to his prior conviction.[127] As a result, the prosecution wanted a new copy of his fingerprints to compare with the fingerprints that existed in his prior felony prosecution to prove that he was a felon in possession of a firearm. The defendant objected, but was ordered to submit to fingerprinting. Following his conviction, in a motion to vacate the conviction, he contended that he should not have been forced to give his fingerprints to the prosecutor. The motion judge refused to disturb the conviction and sentence, because he noted that the compelled display of identifiable physical characteristics such as fingerprints does not infringe on any interest protected by the Fifth Amendment privilege against self-incrimination and that the Fourth Amendment protection against unreasonable searches and seizures does not apply because the defendant was lawfully in custody.

A search warrant is not necessary to take the fingerprints, footprints or palmprints, of a person lawfully in custody. The fact that the person is under arrest permits the taking of a print as part of ordinary booking procedures and removes any Fourth Amendment search and seizure issue.[128] A search warrant or consent would be necessary for a person not in custody, however.

Although the police or evidence technicians may collect fingerprint evidence at the crime scene that an expert may use to make comparisons at trial, the government is under no duty to gather fingerprint evidence and has "no duty to conduct fingerprint tests."[129] Even if the defendant argues that the police destroyed evidence, this argument alone may not create reversible error. In a case in which no evidence of the defendant's fingerprints was obtained from materials that constituted a methamphetamine lab, there was no duty on behalf of law enforcement to attempt to find fingerprints that they

---

126 People v. Morgan, 2013 Cal. App. Unpub. LEXIS 7379 (2013).

127 United States v. Williams, 2010 U.S. Dist. LEXIS 40912 (E.D. Pa. 2010).

128 See Williams v. State, 2013 Tex. App. LEXIS 14753 (2013).

129 Smith v. United States, 966 A.2d 367, 2009 D.C. App. LEXIS 35 (D.C. App. 2009).

did not know existed or that they did not believe were necessary.[130] In this particular case, the police called the hazardous materials team to dispose of hazardous waste at the meth lab and did not attempt to collect fingerprint evidence. The court noted that, when police have not collected fingerprint evidence and have not conducted any analysis, there is no duty to preserve what amounts to nonexistent evidence.

Fingerprint and palmprint evidence that has been validly collected and appropriately preserved may be introduced against a defendant to prove guilt, and where proof of prior convictions may be used to enhance a sentence or elevate a charge, fingerprint evidence that links the defendant to the prior convictions is admissible.[131] The fingerprint evidence is used to make certain that the defendant actually did commit prior offenses. Comparisons of fingerprint samples require the use of expert witnesses who have to be qualified as such in order to testify in a court of law.

§ 15.8 Ballistics Experiments

The field of ballistics possesses a general acceptance in the criminal forensics community, but there have been some defendants and writers who have attempted to rebut the general concepts that encompass ballistics.[132] The science of forensic ballistics concerns the techniques that experts use to determine whether a particular projectile was fired from a particular firearm. It involves, among other factors, the analysis of the size or caliber of the projectile and weapon, as well as marks made on the projectile, and it may include consideration of the cartridge and its tool markings. The application of this technology may determine the brand or class of firearm by analyzing the remains of a projectile and comparing it to known firearm classes and subclasses.[133] The field of ballistics and **ballistic identification** often involves test firings of recovered weapons to produce a sample projectile that can be the basis for comparison with a crime scene projectile. Rifle barrels produce markings on each projectile as the bullet twists through the barrel during the firing sequence, but the markings made by all guns will change over the life of the firearm, depending on firearm care, how many rounds have been fired, and the type of projectile fired. These markings, called striations, often aid or enable the forensic

> **Ballistic identification** The use of machine markings, produced on gun projectiles from being fired from the weapon, to identify the source of the projectile or from the projectile, to identify the particular gun that was used.

130 State v. Best, 2008 Tenn. App. LEXIS 744 (Tenn. 2008).

131 Bowley v. State, 310 S.W.3d 431, 432, 2010 Tex. Crim. App. LEXIS 553 (2010).

132 *See* United States v. United States v. Willock, 2010 U.S. Dist. LEXIS 27473 (D. Md. 2010), n.24, and Mouzone, 696 F. Supp. 536, 2009 U.S. Dist. LEXIS 100718 (D. Md. 2009).

133 A projectile's class characteristics include caliber and the number of the land and groove impressions.

examiner to determine which particular gun or brand of gun fired the questioned projectile. In addition to striation marks on a bullet, firearms leave marks on brass shells that are ejected from many guns by automatic extractors, and even revolvers may sometimes leave telltale signs and scratches on the cartridges used in the gun.

An expert in ballistics may be permitted to offer testimony to show that a firearm used in one crime was also involved in a separate shooting. In one case, the defendant, who was on trial for murder, denied being the gunman. Testimony by a ballistics expert linked the defendant to both the murder and a different shooting when he concluded that the same firearm was used in both and that it was the defendant's gun.[134] Before a witness may testify in regards to the identification of firearms and bullets, the attorney for one of the parties must qualify the person as an expert by demonstrating the background, experience, and education of the proposed expert to give such scientific and opinion testimony. If the proponent of the expert demonstrated that the witness had specialized training and experience as an employee of a crime laboratory or can be qualified as an independent expert in forensic ballistics, the court will allow the witness to testify as an expert.

For example, in appealing convictions for murder and narcotics trafficking, one defendant questioned the validity of the field of forensic ballistics, but the trial court rejected the challenge and noted that, under Rule 702, which deals with expert testimony, the field of ballistics possesses demonstrated reliability for its techniques.[135] In this case, to demonstrate the witness's qualifications as an expert, the prosecution had the proposed expert explain those qualifications to the court. The expert had served as a firearms examiner in a county crime lab for 12 years, had received hands-on training from her section supervisor, had attended seminars on firearms identification, was a member of a nationally recognized firearms and toolmark identification organization, had published in the field, had given numerous presentations, had examined approximately 2,800 different types of firearms, and had provided expert testimony in a trial setting between 20 and 30 times. The trial court properly determined that she was qualified as an expert witness in the field of forensic ballistics and appropriately offered testimony in the murder and narcotics trafficking case.[136]

A ballistics expert may testify that the firing-pin marking on cartridge shells remaining in a revolver or on spent cartridges found in a defendant's possession corresponds to the marking on a test shell fired from the defendant's revolver.[137] Ballistics evidence may be able to prove that particular bullets came from the same firearm,[138] due to microscopic markings placed on a bullet by the effect of the rifling lands and

---

134 Daniels v. Wilson, 2010 U.S. Dist. LEXIS 122452 (W.D. Pa. 2010).

135 United States v. Williams, 506 F.3d 151, 2007 U.S. App. LEXIS 24726 (2d Cir. 2007), *cert. denied,* 2008 U.S. LEXIS 2859 (2008).

136 Id.

137 Sanchez v. State, 2005 Tex. App. LEXIS 5084 n.2 (2005).

138 State v. Burnes, 997 So. 2d 906, 2008 La. App. Unpub. LEXIS 715 (La. 2008).

grooves as it twists down the barrel[139] or due to unique markings made on spent cartridges ejected from the gun.[140] Likewise, a ballistics expert witness who is also trained in toolmark analysis[141] may testify that an empty shotgun shell found at the scene of a homicide had been fired from the defendant's shotgun, that a bullet did not come from a defendant's gun, or that the toolmarks are not conclusive for any purpose either to include or exclude.[142] The brand of a firearm can often be identified, or sometimes excluded, by careful observation of the lands and grooves.[143] In some situations, ballistics experts will be permitted to offer expert opinion concerning the probable trajectory of a bullet fired from a firearm based on forensic evidence in a particular case.[144]

In some case, a qualified expert can use gunpowder burn patterns on clothing or bare skin to determine whether a gun was fired at a close range or from a distance.[145] The burn pattern can also determine whether a wound was an entry or an exit wound.[146] With respect to powder burns, an expert in firearms, toolmarks, and gunshot residue could identify gunshot residue in a pair of underwear to indicate that a gun had been fired within an inch of the person wearing them.[147] Powder burns may indicate who recently fired the gun.[148] Experts can evaluate the presence of stippling, small abrasions on skin that are made by powder and other particles that travel with a bullet when it strikes skin, to determine a gun's distance from the wound at the time it was fired.[149]

In order for an expert to give opinion testimony concerning ballistics test results, the opinion must be based upon facts within the knowledge of the expert, or the expert may give an opinion based upon a hypothetical question that is itself based on facts already in evidence. This does not necessarily mean that real evidence itself must be admitted. For example, in the case of *Hinton v. State*, test bullets fired by the state's ballistics expert were compared with the bullets recovered from the crime scene. Even though the test bullets were not admitted into evidence, the reviewing court found that the decision of the lower court was not error, because the experts used the test bullets only in analyzing the pieces of evidence that they were asked to examine.[150]

---

139 Hinton v. State, 2006 Ala. Crim. App. LEXIS 72 (2006).

140 United States v. Hicks, 389 F.3d 514, 523, 2004 U.S. App. LEXIS 22688 (5th Cir. 2004).

141 United States v. Green, 405 F. Supp. 2d 104, 118, 2005 U.S. Dist. LEXIS 34273 n.26 (D. Mass. 2005).

142 United States v. Williams, 506 F3d 151, 159, 159, 007 U.S. App. LEXIS 24726 (2d Cir. 2007).

143 *See* Maine v. Cookson, 2002 Me. Super. LEXIS 256 (2002), for discussion of the merits and techniques of ballistics.

144 Ronquillo v. Washington, 2001 Wash. App. LEXIS 2615 (2001).

145 State v. Reardon, 2009 N.C. App. LEXIS 306 (N.C. 2009).

146 State v. Austin, 2005 Tenn. Crim. App. LEXIS 815 (2005).

147 State v. Foulk, 2009 Tenn. Crim. App. LEXIS 16 (Tenn. 2009).

148 State v. Georgekopoulos, 2005 Ohio 5106, 2005 Ohio App. LEXIS 4624 (2005).

149 Ayala v. Quarterman, 2009 U.S. Dist. LEXIS 13019 (S.D. Tex. 2009).

150 *See* Hinton v. State, 2006 Ala. Crim. App. LEXIS 72 (2006).

Radio Detection and Ranging (RADAR) Used in law enforcement to measure distance and speed of motor vehicles by evaluating the frequency shift of radio waves that have bounced back from the target motor vehicle.

§ 15.9 Speed Detection Readings

The principle of **Radio Detection and Ranging (RADAR)** applies exact laws of science and nature in the measurement of distance and speed. The radar speed-detecting devices commonly used in traffic control operate on what is known as the Doppler effect and utilize a continuous beam of microwaves emitted at a fixed frequency. An observer can experience the Doppler effect by listening to the sound of a train horn when it is approaching and then noting how the sound changes as the train and its horn pass into the distance. The frequency shift in the sound of the horn is an example of the Doppler effect. The operation depends upon the physical law that when such waves are intercepted by a moving object, the frequency changes in such a ratio to the speed of the intercepted object that, by measuring the change of the frequency, the speed may be determined.[151] The scientific principle is so universally accepted that courts routinely take judicial notice of the reliability of the principles upon which radar is based.[152] Where difficulty in enforcing speed laws with radar units arises, defendants normally attack the operational techniques of the officers using the equipment or the calibration and maintenance of the machines, because the principles are not easily refuted.

In operation, traffic enforcement police use a vehicle in which the radar speed detection system has been installed in such a way as to beam radio waves toward the motoring public. Modern radar devices are designed to be calibrated at set intervals of time to assure that the units are operating properly. When a moving vehicle enters the radar unit's broadcast radio beam, the returned radio wave has a frequency shift that registers with the radar unit, in which the speed of the vehicle is then instantly computed. If the driver appears to be violating the speed limit, the officer may initiate a stop or radio to another officer to make the traffic stop.

For many years, the public, especially those who have been ticketed, have been aware of the widespread use of radio, microwaves, and other electronic devices in detecting the speed of motor vehicles and other moving objects. While the intricacies of such devices are not fully understood by all drivers, their general accuracy and effectiveness had few scientific or legal challenges after courts in the several states accepted the basic scientific principles. Once the principles of radar as applied to speed detection gained general legal acceptance, courts then took judicial notice of the scientific principles and did not require expert testimony on the principles before admitting evidence produced by radar units. In most jurisdictions, to establish the foundation for admission of radar-produced speed evidence, there must be expert testimony or judicial notice of

---

151 Kopper, *The Scientific Reliability of Radar Speedmeters*, 33 N.C.L. REV. 343 (1955).

152 Cleveland Heights v. Katz, 2001 Ohio App. LEXIS 5394 (2001). *See* case in Part II.

the construction and accuracy of the device, evidence that the device is in good working order, and evidence that the officer using the device is qualified by training and experience.[153]

In laying a proper foundation for admission of radar-produced evidence, the officer must explain his or her training, the calibration of the machine, and that it was used properly during the event being litigated. In one Nebraska case, the officer explained that he had used the same type of radar unit since becoming a trooper, he was certified to use the particular type of radar, and his training certificate was up-to-date.[154] The officer testified to the use of tuning forks to assure proper operation of the radar unit and that the radar unit itself had a current certificate of calibration. At the start of each shift, the officer presses a switch on the unit to conduct a self-test and the unit runs a self-test every 10 minutes while in operation. The unit indicated that it was functioning properly by a four-count beep. He also noted that a technician checks the accuracy of the tuning forks once a year and that the radar units are checked for accuracy by the technician on a yearly basis. The reviewing court held that the prosecution had established a sufficient foundation for admitting the evidence of speed produced by the Stalker Dual SL radar unit.

Although radar speed detection remains one of law enforcement's tools for regulating the speed of motorists, laser detection has become a strong companion tool for police officers. Laser detection of speed poses different challenges than those posed by the use of radar, and the theoretical accuracy may make this system a superior law enforcement tool. Before any new scientific tool may be used, the proponent must prove that it accurately does what it says it will do. Initially, a foundation concerning the principles of laser speed detection had to be introduced by experts. Then, as the science and its application became known, judicial notice of the principles behind the use of lasers in speed detection gained acceptance, and some jurisdictions, like Georgia, specify by statute the types of speed detection devices that are permissible to use, and those that will be admitted in court. In the case of laser detection, the courts initially had to be convinced by expert testimony that the principles were scientifically sound and that the device that purported to apply the science did so regularly and routinely.

In *State v. Stoa*, the Intermediate Court of Appeals of Hawai'i upheld the use of laser speed detection where the prosecution did not produce any expert witnesses to testify concerning how the **laser speed detection** system operates.[155] The Intermediate

> **Laser speed detection** A device that measures the speed of objects by bouncing light energy off of the object to be checked for speed. The device records the time required for the light to leave and return to the laser detector. Making such recordings hundreds of times a second, the device compares changes in the length of time the light takes to return to the detector, thus enabling a speed to be calculated.

---

153 *See* City of Cleveland v. Tisdale, 2008 Ohio 2807, 2008 Ohio App. LEXIS 2372 (Ohio 2008).

154 State v. Huff, 2004 Neb. App. LEXIS 117 (2004).

155 2006 Haw. App. LEXIS 397 (2006).

Court of Appeals of Hawai'i rejected the defendant's arguments that expert witnesses were required to prove the principles supporting laser speed detection. The court noted that (1) the science of laser speed detection is based on well-understood principles; (2) the accuracy and reliability of laser speed-detection devices for monitoring traffic speed have been approved in other jurisdictions (Maryland, Minnesota, and New Jersey as well as a municipal court in the state of Ohio); and (3) the laser device used in this case met all the requirements of the Hawai'i Supreme Court for accuracy. However, in a different case, the Supreme Court of Hawai'i partially overruled *Stoa* when it overturned a reviewing court in a case involving laser speed detection. In *State v. Assaye*, the Supreme Court reversed a speeding case based on laser detection, when the officer testified that he had been trained and certified by another officer on the particular laser machine, but there was no evidence that the training of the officer-witness met the manufacturer's requirements for training on that specific machine.[156]

To facilitate police use of laser equipment, some states have passed statutes that permit police use and court admissibility of laser-generated information concerning speed.[157] To facilitate the admission of laser speed detection evidence into Georgia courts, the legislature passed a statute that operates like a rule of evidence and, generally, permits evidence of laser-detected speed to be admitted in court. The law provides:

> § 40-14-17. Laser devices; reliability and admissibility of evidence
>
> Evidence of speed based on a speed detection device using the speed timing principle of laser, which is of a model that has been approved by the Department of Public Safety shall be considered scientifically acceptable and reliable as a speed detection device and shall be admissible for all purposes in any court, judicial, or administrative proceedings in this state. A certified copy of the Department of Public Safety list of approved models of such laser devices shall be self-authenticating and shall be admissible for all purposes in any court, judicial, or administrative proceedings in this state.[158]

As a result, laser speed detection evidence should be admissible where a law enforcement officer operates the approved laser speed detection unit according to the manufacturer's instructions and uses a Georgia-approved laser speed detection device that has been properly calibrated according to the manufacturer's specifications. Similar procedures permit admissibility of the evidence in other jurisdictions.

In one case, a defendant who had been convicted of speeding appealed based on the alleged inaccuracy of an LTI 20/20 laser speed measuring system used to clock the speed of his car.[159] Although there was no evidence offered in the trial court concerning the scientific accuracy of the LTI 20/20, the reviewing court held that the trial court

---

156 121 Haw. 204, 216, 216 P.3d 1227, 1239, 2009 Haw. LEXIS 239 (2009).

157 Odum v. Georgia, 255 Ga. App. 70, 564 S.E.2d 490, 2002 Ga. App. LEXIS 478 (2002). The trial court admitted laser-generated evidence of speed upon proof that the officer and officer's use of the device met state standards.

158 GA. CODE ANN. § 40-14-17 (2013).

159 State v. Kim, 2008 Ohio 6928 (Ohio 2008).

properly took judicial notice that another trial court found that the device was scientifically accurate because the other trial court actually heard testimony from a qualified expert witness where the expert explained how the LTI 20/20 worked and concluded that it offered reliable data concerning speed of vehicles. Five months before stopping the defendant, the police officer had been recertified to use the LTI 20/20, and his state certification was demonstrated to be current. Under the circumstances, the defendant's conviction was upheld, given that the device was accurate, was working properly, and was being operated by a certified police officer.

There are some different methods of detecting speed of motor vehicles that involve global positioning satellites and computers that are nested in modern motor vehicles. For example, onboard computers of currently manufactured motor vehicles record the last few seconds of the vehicle's speed and store the data, purge that data, and then store the most recent data and repeat the process. Recently manufactured motor vehicles often contain an onboard diagnostics computer system, OBD II, that captures various information about the performance of the individual motor vehicle, such as whether seat belts were fastened, when brakes were last applied, when the air bag deployed, and the speed of the motor vehicle. In General Motors cars since 1990, an SDM, or sensing diagnostic module, records, among other parameters, the:

> Acceleration or deceleration and makes decisions every 10 milliseconds whether or not to deploy the passive restraint system in the vehicle. The system also stores vehicle data such as vehicle speed, engine RPM, throttle percentage and brake data, change in velocity or delta V and seat belt usage, all in one second increments for a period of five seconds.[160]

Information stored in a sensing and diagnostic module (SDM) that regulates deployment of vehicle air bags may be useful in reconstructing vehicle accidents and speed of vehicles. For example, data from a General Motors event data recorder, the SDM module, recorded a defendant's Pontiac Firebird excessively speeding in a 30 mph residential zone.[161] The Florida trial court admitted the computer-generated speed evidence in a double manslaughter case involving the deaths of two 16-year-old girls whom the defendant killed while he was driving down a residential street at 114 mph. An expert witness testified concerning information stored on the vehicle's event data recorders. The prosecutor introduced evidence that insurance companies and accident crash investigators rely on this type of collected data because it is believed to be accurate and reliable. For these reasons, the Florida reviewing court upheld the admissibility of the data collected from the motor vehicle computer.

In a Massachusetts case involving the death of a passenger in an automobile, police believed that the automobile had been going too fast for the slushy road conditions

---

[160] People v. Christmann, 3 Misc. 3d 309, 311, 776 N.Y.S.2d 437, 439, 2004 N.Y. Misc. LEXIS 45 (N.Y. 2004).

[161] Matos v. State, 899 So. 2d 403, 405-406, 2005 Fla. App. LEXIS 4359 (2005).

immediately prior to leaving the road and colliding with a large tree.[162] In order to determine the speed of the automobile immediately prior to the impact, police obtained a warrant to download data from the SDM, the electronic data recorder in the Chevrolet Tahoe. The police officer, an expert in accident reconstruction, obtained data from the SDM that indicated the motor vehicle was traveling at 58 mph five seconds before the crash and 40 mph one second prior to impact. This information, along with other information generated by the officer, was admitted against the defendant and resulted in a conviction for motor vehicle homicide.

In order to assure that electronically stored data from motor vehicles will be admissible in court, compliance with constitutional search and seizure issues proves critical. In one California vehicular homicide case, at the direction of the prosecutor, two officers warrantlessly downloaded information from a motor vehicle's computer after it had been involved in a hit and run accident, despite the absence of probable cause.[163] The evidence included data concerning engine speed, vehicle speed, vehicle deceleration, throttle percentage, breaking, air bag deployment, and the restraint system. Following a guilty verdict, a court of appeals reversed the conviction based on the fact that probable cause to search the car's computer was missing. As the court noted, "the prosecution failed to show that the objective facts known to the police officers at the time of the download constituted probable cause to search the SDM for evidence of crime."

§ 15.10 Neutron Activation Analysis

Neutron activation analysis is a process by which the chemical composition of materials can be determined, but it has been eclipsed by some newer technologies. The admission of the results of this process was approved in a federal case that involved sending a package bomb through the mail.[164] In this case, the court approved the explanation of the process, which appeared in *American Jurisprudence's* "Proof of Facts," stating[165]:

> One of the newest and most promising techniques of forensic science is neutron activation analysis. The ability of this nuclear method to detect traces of elements in minute samples enables it to solve many problems of identification that have heretofore been considered hopeless. . . . The process is essentially one whereby the material to be analyzed is first made radioactive—i.e., it is "charged" so that it will give off or emit radiation in the form of gamma rays. This radioactive sample is then exposed to a scintillation crystal; and every time a gamma ray from the radioactive material interacts with the crystal, it emits a flash of light, which is converted into an electrical pulse whose voltage is proportional to the energy of the gamma rays. An electronic device called a multichannel differential analyzer then sorts the electrical impulses into different energy

---

[162] *See* Commonwealth v. Zimmermann, 70 Mass. App. Ct. 357, 2007 Mass. App. LEXIS 1050 (Mass. 2007).

[163] People v. Xinos, 192 Cal. App. 4th 637, 661, 2011 Cal. App. LEXIS 153 (2011).

[164] United States v. Stifel, 433 F.2d 431 (6th Cir. 1970).

[165] *Id.* at 436.

> groups and adds up the pulses in each group. The result is a graph shown on an oscilloscope screen. The graph contains information related to the kind and amount of elements in the radioactive sample and can be transcribed immediately or stored on magnetic tape or punched paper tapes for future reference.
>
> Virtually no sample of material is too small to be analyzed by activation analysis. A single hair, a shred of marijuana, or a fleck of automobile paint no longer than the period at the end of this sentence can be analyzed and correctly identified. Furthermore, activation analysis' high sensitivity allows quantitative measurement of elements in the parts per million and parts per billion range. For instance, if one thimbleful of arsenic poison were diluted in ten tankcars of water, the exact amount of arsenic present could be determined by activation analysis. In most cases, the analysis is also nondestructive, so that material evidence may be preserved for presentation in court or saved for analysis by another method.

One use for neutron activation analysis that arose and that was championed by the FBI was called Comparative Bullet Lead Analysis (CBLA), which was believed to be able to match various batches of lead, thus allowing investigators to determine if a bullet was from the same batch and then to to link unused bullets to crime scene bullets. The theory was that trace elements in lead batches could be used as a lead "fingerprint." Many courts allowed CBLA evidence to be used for proof in criminal trials.

However, several studies involving comparisons of lead composition from a crime scene to other lead bullets recovered from defendants using neutron activation analysis called into question whether the concept was accurate.[166] In November 2007, the FBI offered a press release that also indicated its concerns with the concept of CBLA, and in the press release, the Bureau indicated that it would work with the defense bar to rectify any injustices that had occurred due to inaccurate evidence produced by the process,[167] although that may not be working out in actual practice.[168]

A Pennsylvania case illustrates the use of neutron activation testing to match a bullet fragment with other bullets taken from a case of cartridges from defendant's apartment.[169] The gun used in the homicide was never recovered. CBLA using neutron activation analysis demonstrated that the bullets recovered from the victim's body "matched" in trace metal content those in the box of ammunition recovered from defendant's apartment. The reviewing court duly noted the existence of arguments challenging the exactness of comparative bullet lead analysis, but it decided to affirm the defendant's conviction despite the fact that the case was primarily a circumstantial evidence case, more questions on the reliability CBLA had been raised, and the FBI had abandoned its use in 2005.[170]

---

166 *See* Higgs v. United States, 711 F. Supp. 2d 479, 2010 U.S. Dist. LEXIS 48535 (D. Md. 2010), n.5, n.6.

167 *See* the FBI Press Release of 17 November 2007 that questions the reliability of comparisons of lead. Available at: http://www.fbi.gov/pressrel/pressrel07/bulletlead111707.htm.

168 *See* Higgs, *supra.*

169 Commonwealth v. Kretchmar, 2009 Pa. Super. 63, 2009 Pa. Super. LEXIS 79 (2009).

170 *See* http://www.fbi.gov/news/pressrel/press-releases/fbi-laboratory-announces-discontinuation-of-bullet-lead-examinations. 10 March 2011.

Some crime scenes may not prove conducive to either neutron activation analysis or to a related test, atomic-absorption analysis, especially where numerous potential defendants have been present at the crime scene and have similar contaminants on their persons. Therefore, the limits of the testing process indicate that it will not solve all gun-firing crime issues. In a variety of contexts, however, neutron activation analysis will be able to indicate who has fired a weapon if the testing is conducted promptly.

Although the neutron activation analysis cannot conclusively establish whether the subject has recently fired a weapon, a different test, the Atomic Absorption Test, is commonly adopted to offer similar evidence. In a recent Ohio case, a defendant contended that the Atomic Absorption Test exhibited reliability problems, and the evidence that one of his gloves indicated that he had recently fired a weapon while wearing the glove should not have been admitted at his murder trial.[171] Newer testing processes, the defendant contended, would indicate whether the chemical components on his glove were from powder combustion or were simply indicative of certain chemical elements normally associated with gunpowder. The reviewing court refused to disturb his conviction based on his allegation of the need for more accurate chemical testing.

A newer technology than neutron activation analysis that offers some promise is called inductively coupled plasma-optical emission spectroscopy" (ICP).[172] The process is able to distinguish discrete components of different products, such as lead. The goal of distinguishing different components of lead would, in theory, allow scientists to compare lead from one batch of lead bullets to see if it matched other bullets possessed by a defendant. Comparative bullet lead analysis would permit a recovered bullet's chemical composition to be compared with remaining bullets contained in a defendant's remaining cartridges. Ultimately, the FBI abandoned the process because the science did not allow the reliable chemical bullet matching that had originally been anticipated.[173]

§ 15.11 Deoxyribonucleic Acid (DNA) Tests

Researchers have made a significant breakthrough in using the deoxyribonucleic acid (DNA) code present in human cells, blood, and other body fluids to link evidence, such as bloodstains or semen specimens, to a specific individual, while excluding all others. According to an article that appeared in a National Institute of Justice publication dated October 1987, DNA patterns are so different between people who are not identical twins so as to provide virtually definite identification. In recent years,

---

171 State v. Johnson, 2010 Ohio 4117, 2010 Ohio App. LEXIS 3486 (2010).

172 "In 1993, the technique of FBI choice was changed to inductively coupled plasma, atomic emission spectroscopy" (ICP). *See* State v. Behn, 375 N.J. Super. 409, 426, 868 A.2d 329, 341, 2005 N.J. Super. LEXIS 73 (N.J. 2005).

173 *See* Clemmons v. State, 392 Md. 339, 896 A.2d 1059, 2006 Md. LEXIS 192 n.8 (Md. 2006). *See also* Commonwealth v. Daye, 19 Mass. L. Rep. 674, 2005 Mass. Super. LEXIS 368 (Mass. 2005). *See also* http://www.cbsnews.com/stories/2007/11/16/60minutes/main3512453.shtml for a *60 Minutes* exposé on lead bullet analysis.

smaller and smaller samples of fluids containing DNA have been required because the science has advanced in the area of amplification of samples to usable levels. Some legal issues are still being litigated concerning Fourth Amendment concerns, including the collection of DNA samples from convicted persons and in some cases from arrestees.[174]

In *Maryland v. King*, the Supreme Court reviewed the current state of the art with respect to DNA identification and its evidential reliability. According to the Court:[175]

> The current standard for forensic DNA testing relies on an analysis of the chromosomes located within the nucleus of all human cells. "The DNA material in chromosomes is composed of 'coding' and 'noncoding' regions. The coding regions are known as *genes* and contain the information necessary for a cell to make proteins. . . .

The King Court continued to explain the science of DNA analysis and usage by citing passages from District Attorney's Office V. Osborne, 557 U.S. 52 (2009):

> Many of the patterns found in DNA are shared among all people, so forensic analysis focuses on "repeated DNA sequences scattered throughout the human genome," known as "short tandem repeats" (STRs). *Id.*, at 147-148. The alternative possibilities for the size and frequency of these STRs at any given point along a strand of DNA are known as "alleles," *Id.*, at 25; and multiple alleles are analyzed in order to ensure that a DNA profile matches only one individual. Future refinements may improve present technology, but even now STR analysis makes it "possible to determine whether a biological tissue matches a suspect with near certainty." Osborne, supra, at 62, 129 S. Ct. 2308, 174 L. Ed. 2d 38.[176]

A California case demonstrates the significant advances that have occurred in the years since the DNA testing revolution changed criminal investigations forever. In this case, a woman was raped by someone she knew. The rapist injured the woman sufficiently that her DNA and the attacker's DNA became mixed together so that the rape testing kit contained multisource DNA. Blood samples were taken from the victim and from the attacker, and these samples were sent, along with DNA samples collected from a sexual assault kit, to a DNA laboratory.

As the court explained part of the theory of DNA testing:

> Deoxyribonucleic acid is material present in each cell of the human body that determines an individual's characteristics. Virtually all deoxyribonucleic acid is the same from one human to another. However, a small percentage of the deoxyribonucleic acid is different in each individual. Cellmark Diagnostics tests deoxyribonucleic acid by comparing an unknown sample from a crime scene to that from known individuals. The tests serve to either include or exclude an individual as a possible source of the biological sample. As will be explained in more detail below, the polymerase chain reaction is a technique that has been used in the field of molecular biology

174 *See* Maryland v. King, 133 S.Ct. 1958, 186 L.Ed.2d 1, 2013 U.S. LEXIS 4165 (2013).

175 Id. at 1966.

176 *Id.* at 1967.

> since the 1980s to copy small specific regions of deoxyribonucleic acid. The deoxyribonucleic acid is isolated into a form that can be copied. Then copies of that deoxyribonucleic acid sequence are copied. Finally, the actual deoxyribonucleic acid types are examined and compared to other samples to determine whether they could be included or excluded as a donor source for the sample.[177]

The evidence demonstrated that the lab followed extremely strict protocols to avoid contamination of samples or inaccurate results. The results demonstrated that the nonsperm DNA fraction had a primary source that was female and was consistent with the profile from the victim, while the sample of DNA taken from the sperm fraction indicated the source was from a male. In addition, the interpretation of the results demonstrated that the defendant was the source of the male fraction taken from the victim using the sexual assault kit.

In a hearing consolidated from several California cases with similar issues, a judge made a determination that the science has progressed to the point that DNA at a crime scene can be properly compared with samples donated by suspects and victims to see if a match can be declared, and such results would be admissible. The evidence discussed included STR (short tandem repeat) testing and PCR (polymerase chain reaction) testing and found that both theories had scientific validity for the purposes in question. The court ruled that DNA testing, based on analysis and separation of mixed samples, was generally accepted in the scientific community, and the results could be admitted against the defendant in the rape case.[178]

With the general admissibility of DNA evidence permitted under the *Daubert* or the *Frye* standards for admission of scientific evidence, the battle for prosecutors and for the defense bar moved from challenging the concept to challenging the methodology and admissibility of the newest advances in DNA testing. For example, in a quadruple murder case involving four rapes and strangulations, the defendant mounted an attack on the admissibility of the DNA evidence that the defense expected would be offered by the prosecution.[179] He challenged the testing laboratory's methodology in dealing with mixed DNA samples and alleged that the lab violated generally accepted protocols. The defendant alleged that the laboratory failed to perform its tests properly and to report them accurately. In addition, the defendant contended that the lab failed to adhere to the conservative protocols of the DNA test kit manufacturer. In the math area of DNA testing, he contended that the use of the product rule to make frequency calculations for mixed samples was faulty. Finally, the defendant contended that the database used by the lab proved inadequate for frequency calculations. The Supreme Judicial Court of Massachusetts serially addressed each of the defendant's contentions and upheld the trial court's rejection of all of his arguments. The posture of this type of

---

177 California v Smith, 107 Cal. App. 4th 646, 131 Cal. Rptr. 2d 230, 2003 Cal. App. LEXIS 475 (2003), *petition for review denied,* 2003 Cal. LEXIS 3547 (2003). For additional enlightenment, this case has a scientifically interesting account of DNA information contained within the opinion.

178 *Id.*

179 Commonwealth v. Gaynor, 443 Mass. 245, 263, 820 N.E.2d 233, 249, 2005 Mass. LEXIS 7 (Mass. 2005). *See* case in Part II.

case demonstrates that defendants are contesting the application of the science of DNA testing, rather than arguing about the basic validity of the concept that each person (except identical twins) carries a unique DNA profile.

As courts approved the admission of DNA results and approved different types of testing procedures, the prosecution and defense bars have embraced the use of DNA evidence where appropriate. The defense bar adopted the concept of DNA testing for the purpose of establishing actual innocence in older death penalty cases in which a convicted defendant alleged that the wrong person had been convicted. DNA testing has resulted in some people being removed from death row, by excluding them as the source of DNA at homicide scenes. In a Maryland case that involved an assault for missing a group of people with a shotgun, the defendant was forced to give a DNA sample by allowing a buccal swab of the inside of his mouth.[180] A Maryland statute required that persons arrested for specific crimes were required to give a DNA sample to be added to the state database unless the case is dropped or a person is acquitted. Subsequent processing of the sample indicated that his DNA matched DNA taken from a rape victim, and the identified defendant was subsequently convicted of the earlier unsolved rape offense. The Supreme Court upheld the collection of the DNA sample and its introduction into evidence against an allegation that the collection and use constituted a violation of the Fourth Amendment. The Court noted that "[w]hen officers make an arrest supported by probable cause to hold for a serious offense and they bring the suspect to the station to be detained in custody, taking and analyzing a cheek swab of the arrestee's DNA is, like fingerprinting and photographing, a legitimate police booking procedure that is reasonable under the Fourth Amendment."[181]

As the science of DNA testing has become generally accepted and admissible, other legal challenges have involved proper collection, storage, and contamination prevention of samples,[182] rather than arguing against the science. Proper handling of DNA samples in conformity with established procedures is essential before DNA evidence can be considered reliable.[183] Convicted defendants have demanded that older evidence be tested to exclude them from guilt by attempting to force the prosecution to conduct DNA tests on evidence that neither the police nor the prosecution had reason or desire to test.[184]

A collateral issue concerning the collection and use of DNA data arises when former convicts, probationers, and parolees are ordered to submit a DNA sample to be added to state and local DNA databanks or the federal databank, the Combined DNA Index System of the Federal Bureau of Investigation (CODIS). Most jurisdictions require persons convicted of felonies or sexual offenses to submit a DNA sample for inclusion in national and state databanks.

---

180 Maryland v. King, 133 S. Ct. 1958, 186 L. Ed.2d 1, 2013 U.S. LEXIS 4165 (2013).

181 *Id.* at 1980.

182 United States v. Morrow, 374 F. Supp. 42, 46 (D.D.C. 2005).

183 Commonwealth v. Blasioli, 685 A.2d 151 (Pa. 1996).

184 *See* United States v. Fasono, 2008 U.S. Dist. LEXIS 64055 (S.D. Miss. 2008), in which appellant wanted various personal articles tested to see if another person's DNA and not the defendant's might have been present.

In a case from the District of Columbia, government agents ordered that a probationer give a DNA sample for inclusion in the CODIS databank.[185] The authority for the order came from a federal statute stating that officials "shall collect a DNA sample from each individual under the supervision of the Agency who is on supervised release, parole, or probation who is, or has been, convicted of a qualifying District of Columbia offense. . . ." Under the DNA Analysis Backlog Elimination Act of 2000, persons with former convictions were required to give DNA samples. When his probation was about to be revoked for failure to give his sample, one probationer sued in federal court, alleging that requiring him to give a sample violated his constitutional rights. Over his argument dealing with the Fourth Amendment search and seizure provision and the Fourteenth Amendment's due process clause, the trial court ruled in favor of the federal government. The court noted that probationers have a reduced expectation of privacy and that future searches of the database would not be a search of the probationer. Because DNA profiles can be collected from probationers, such evidence can also be collected from parolees because they are similarly situated for Fourth Amendment purposes. The 2013 decision in *Maryland v. King* further solidifies the practice of having parolees or probationers submit DNA samples.[186]

The Combined DNA Index System may assist wrongly convicted defendants in proving their allegations of actual innocence. In the face of the FBI's refusal to run a DNA database search of this system to assist an inmate who alleged that he had wrongly been convicted, a federal district court in Illinois concluded that the FBI had acted arbitrarily and ordered it to run the DNA comparison on behalf of the convicted defendant.[187]

§ 15.12 Other Examinations and Tests

As other techniques and procedures have met the requirements for admission by way of expert testimony, courts have recognized the new tests and have admitted evidence based on those tests. For example, in a New Jersey case, the trial court permitted an expert witness to testify that the bullets taken from the crime scene were tested using the Plasma Atomic Emission Spectroscopy testing process, as were the bullets from live cartridges possessed by the defendant, and the lead composition of all tested bullets was the same. The plasma atomic emission spectroscopy testing method determines what trace elements are contained in a lead sample and compares that result to another sample bullet. If they are of the same composition, the conclusion is that they came from the same original source. On a petition for habeas corpus, the federal district court held that

---

[185] Johnson v. Quander, 370 U.S. App. D.C. 167, 440 F.3d 489, 499, 2006 U.S. App. LEXIS 6601 (D.C. Cir. 2006). *Accord*, United States v. Sczubelek, 402 F.3d 175, 2005 U.S. App. LEXIS 4568 (3d Cir. 2006).

[186] 133 S. Ct. 1958, 186 L. Ed. 2d 1, 2013 U.S. LEXIS 4165 (2013).

[187] Rivera v. Mueller, 596 F. Supp. 2d 1163, 2009 U.S. Dist. LEXIS 9308 (N.D. Ill. 2009).

the admission of the expert testimony did not violate any federal constitutional right.[188] The process of using plasma atomic emission spectroscopy probably analyzes the trace metals in lead properly, but there has been some concern in other jurisdictions and among some experts that the original source of lead for bullets fails to have the consistency of composition that is required for this type of bullet matching to be valid.[189]

A Florida trial court admitted expert testimony in a homicide case that used plasma atomic emission spectroscopy analysis to demonstrate that the lead in a bullet fragment taken from the victim matched other lead bullets that were linked to the defendant.[190] The state's witness testified as an expert in neutron activation analysis and inductively coupled plasma atomic emission spectrometry and indicated that his conclusions were correct. The defense offered rebuttal expert witnesses who testified somewhat differently, but did not dispute the scientific concept behind plasma atomic emission spectroscopy. The Supreme Court of Florida upheld the admission of the expert testimony and the conviction,[191] and a federal district court denied a writ of habeas corpus.[192]

In contrast to these cases, comparative bullet lead analysis originally had been admitted against a defendant to help prove that the bullets recovered from the homicide matched the lead in other bullets remaining in his gun's unfired cartridges, and the reviewing court reversed.[193] Using inductively coupled plasma-optical emission spectroscopy as a successor to neutron activation analysis might reveal the constituents of a lead bullet, but that information may still remain irrelevant. To make valid comparisons of lead in different bullets and then to establish that they came from a common source would require that the common source be a completely homogeneous source of lead. The best testimony indicated that, within each run of lead used to make bullets, significant differences exist in the constituent trace metals. The reviewing court held that the use of any of the different methods of conducting comparative bullet lead analysis should not have been admitted because, under the *Frye* test for admission of scientific evidence, several fundamental assumptions were not generally accepted by the relevant scientific community.[194]

Whether plasma atomic emission spectroscopy analysis will eventually meet general scientific acceptability and be generally admissible in most of the nation's state courts remains to be seen. As mentioned in section 15.11, the Federal Bureau of Investigation Laboratory used this method of bullet analysis until its discontinuation.

In discussing a scientific procedure used to analyze cement dust in another court, a defendant questioned the reliability of the Fourier Transform Infrared Spectroscopy

---

188 *See* Noel v. Hendricks, 2006 U.S. Dist. LEXIS 41374 (D.N.J. 2006).

189 *See* Clemmons v. State, 392 Md. 339, 896 A.2d 1059, 2006 Md. LEXIS 192 n.8 (Md. 2006). *See also* State v. Behn, 375 N.J. Super. 409, 868 A.2d 329, 2005 N.J. Super. LEXIS 73 (N.J. 2005).

190 Smith v. Secretary, Department of Corrections, 2007 U.S. Dist. LEXIS 57703 (M.D. Fla. 2007).

191 Smith v. State, 931 So. 2d 790, 2006 Fla. LEXIS 388 (Fla. 2006).

192 Smith v. Secretary, Department of Corrections, 2007 U.S. Dist. LEXIS 57703 (M.D. Fla. 2007).

193 *See* Clemmons v. State, 392 Md. 339, 896 A.2d 1059, 2006 Md. LEXIS 192 n.8 (Md. 2006). *See also* Commonwealth v. Daye, 19 Mass. L. Rep. 674, 2005 Mass. Super. LEXIS 368 (Mass. 2005).

194 *Id.*

(FTIR) analysis procedure. The issue concerned whether the FTIR analysis was based upon scientific principles that are generally accepted as reliable within the relevant scientific community. The process at issue used advanced materials science analysis to compare safe cement linings that deposited its dust on a safe-cracker's tools, clothing, and other articles personal to the alleged safecracker. The trial court found that this scientific test of cement residue was admissible in criminal proceedings.[195] The use of FTIR analysis has not been litigated in the reported cases since 1997. In this case, the expert testimony evidence tended to prove that cement dust samples taken from the crime scene, from the remains of the victims' safe, and from the defendant's tools were all consistent with safe lining cement, which could have come from the victim's safe, and were sufficiently reliable to be admissible in a burglary prosecution.

§ 15.13 Summary

Real evidence is often not admitted directly into court, but is used for experiments and tests conducted out of court. General rules have been established regarding the admissibility of testimony concerning the results of experiments and tests, and the use of evidence such as charts and graphs resulting from experiments and tests. In recent years, the trend has been for the courts to allow and encourage the use of such evidence, and this has been held to be consistent with the rights of the accused.

As a general rule, examination of the body for evidence such as marks and bruises, and the taking of samples (saliva, urine, and blood) from the body do not violate the privilege against self-incrimination. Such evidence is admissible if proper standards concerning the testing of this type of evidence are met. Also, the common practice of determining blood-alcohol content by testing the suspect's blood, breath, or urine has been approved when law enforcement officials meet the conditions dictated by the Constitution, by the courts, and by legislative bodies.

Blood grouping test results provide useful information, but are increasingly replaced by DNA testing, which is both more reliable and very precise. Blood-based evidence is generally used for purposes of identification when that element is at issue in criminal prosecutions involving rape, assault, homicide, and in civil and criminal paternity actions. For the results of blood-based testing to be admissible, it must be demonstrated that a qualified person conducted the test, that a qualified technician observed proper protocols during the testing procedure, and that the testing methods revealed no discrepancies in the results.

Courts are divided concerning the admissibility of polygraph evidence, with a strong bias in favor of exclusion. Three approaches have been taken by various federal and state courts: (1) the traditional approach of per se inadmissibility; (2) polygraph evidence is admissible only when both parties so stipulate; and (3) polygraph evidence is admissible even in the absence of stipulation when special circumstances exist.

---

[195] People v. Roraback, 666 N.Y.S.2d 397 (1997).

The reasoning that has been applied in the use of the polygraph is similar to that of most courts in finding that so-called truth serum tests are not admissible for or against the defendant in a criminal case because of the lack of scientific certainty about the results. However, the courts take an entirely different view as to fingerprint comparisons. The results of fingerprint comparisons made out of court may be introduced to compare the fingerprints of the defendant with fingerprints left at the scene of the crime. This procedure has become so well recognized that the courts will take judicial notice of the fact that fingerprint identification is one of the most accurate methods of personal identification.

The science of forensic ballistics is also a well-recognized subject of expert testimony. The courts will generally allow such expert testimony to show, for example, that the bullet that entered the body was fired from a weapon belonging to the defendant in the case. Before such evidence is admissible, the introducing party must show that approved procedures were followed and that the person testifying is qualified as an expert in the field.

The use of speed detection devices using the principle of radar are universally approved, and testimony concerning the readings on such devices is generally accepted in evidence. However, test results are not admissible in court unless there is proof that the equipment was properly calibrated and the witness is qualified to testify concerning the meaning of such tests. Many jurisdictions have approved the use of laser-based speed detection, as long as police use approved laser units and follow proper protocols provided by the manufacturer.

Neutron activation analysis provided strong evidence to detect trace compounds but has fallen into disuse in criminal cases in recent times. Evidence concerning the results of such analysis will face challenges where lead bullet identification is concerned.

Scientific research has resulted in the development of forensic DNA analysis as a scientific technique that reveals distinctive patterns in human genetic material in blood and some body fluids, hair, and tissue. Courts routinely admit the results of this "DNA fingerprint" test to prove identity and to exclude suspects because this science has general acceptance by the experts in the field. Generally, proof that the experts have properly applied the technology assures admission into evidence.

Because criminal justice personnel conduct many of the out-of-court examinations and tests, it is essential that such personnel be aware of the value of such evidence and be familiar with the requirements designed to protect the rights of those who are accused of crime.

CHAPTER FIFTEEN: QUESTIONS AND REVIEW EXERCISES

1. When considering the admissibility of scientific tests, the federal courts and many state courts followed the *Frye* standard derived from *Frye v. United States* (1923). Due to the adoption of the Federal Rules of Evidence and the changes that they initiated, the Supreme Court adopted a new standard for federal courts in

Daubert v. Merrell Dow Pharmaceuticals (1993). Describe the requirements for admissibility of scientific evidence under *Frye* and compare those requirements to the new rules under *Daubert*. If you wanted to get results from a new technical or scientific procedure admitted, under which standard would you be most likely to have a judge consider the evidence?

2. Scientific tests that measure the percentage of alcohol in the blood are generally admissible in evidence, despite arguments of various defendants who have challenged admissibility on constitutional grounds. What were the two general constitutional objections to the use of blood evidence results that defendants have historically raised? Do you agree with the results of cases that have gone to the Supreme Court of the United States?
3. One method of measuring blood-alcohol for impaired vehicle drivers is to use one of the commercially available machines that measure the alcohol that is expelled from a driver's lungs. Give an example of the foundational requirements to introduce results from a breath measuring device that indicated a driver was over the legal blood-alcohol content limit.
4. What is the Horizontal Gaze Nystagmus test for blood alcohol? Can this test provide sufficient evidence for an officer to arrest a driver for driving under the influence of alcohol?
5. Explain what the term *implied consent statute* means with respect to operating a motor vehicle. As a general rule, must the driver who is suspected of impairment be under arrest in order for the concept of implied consent to operate?
6. The admission of the results of polygraph examinations in criminal courts is rather limited. What is the basis or theoretical rationale for admission of polygraph evidence? In Chapter 6, the concept of a stipulation is introduced. If both parties to a criminal suit stipulate concerning the admissibility of polygraph evidence, should a trial court allow the results into evidence?
7. What is the theory behind the admissibility of fingerprint evidence? Must a witness be specially qualified as an expert prior to being permitted to testify concerning fingerprint evidence? Is a search warrant necessary to obtain the fingerprint from a person who is in custody? Would it be different if the suspect was not under arrest?
8. Explain the concept of ballistics as it relates to firearms identification. What other marks may a firearm make on a brass shell case? In order to offer testimony and a trial, an individual who has done ballistics tests on a firearm must be qualified as an expert witness. What are some of the qualifications that a proposed ballistics expert witness should demonstrate?
9. Radar and laser speed detection has been sufficiently developed

and its scientific principles are well known. What sort of foundation would a police officer have to offer in order to be permitted to give evidence that a laser radar detector has recorded concerning a defendant's motor vehicle speed?

10. What is the basic scientific principle behind DNA testing of human tissue? From what you have learned, would properly obtained and analyzed DNA evidence be admissible under the *Frye* standard or the *Daubert* standard or both? Can convicted defendants legally be required to give a DNA sample for inclusion in state or federal databases?

Exclusion of Evidence on Constitutional Grounds

Evidence Unconstitutionally Obtained

16

Today we once again examine Wolf's constitutional documentation of the right of privacy free from unreasonable state intrusions, and, after its dozen years on our books, are led by it to close the only courtroom door remaining open to evidence secured by official lawlessness in flagrant abuse of that basic right, reserved to all persons as a specific guarantee against that very same unlawful conduct. We hold that all evidence obtained by searches and seizures in violation of the Constitution is, by that same authority, inadmissible in a state court.

Mapp v. Ohio, 367 U.S. 643, 81 S. Ct. 1684,
6 L. Ed. 2d 1081 (1961)

Chapter Contents

KEY TERMS AND CONCEPTS	
Delay in Arraignment Rule	Open Fields Doctrine
Due Process	Patriot Act
Eavesdropping	Plain View Doctrine
Exclusionary Rule	Privilege Against Self-incrimination
Fourth Amendment	Protective Sweep
Free and Voluntary Rule	Search Incident to Arrest
Impoundment	Self-incrimination
Knock-and-Announce Requirement	Wiretapping
Miranda Warnings	

§ 16.1 Introduction

In a democracy, where the rule of law is of paramount importance, the state and federal governments must follow the law so that fundamental fairness and predictability of behaviors serve as the norm for the governmental entities and their citizens. Fair dealing is a rough equivalent to due process, which everyone should be able to expect and all are entitled to receive from all levels of government. On the rare occasion when a local, state, or the federal government fails to follow the policy of due process and fairness, a remedy should be readily accessible for that constitutional violation. In the discussion of the rules of evidence in Chapter 2, the text indicates that some judicially created rules exclude evidence that has been obtained in violation of the rights protected by the Constitution. This is not because the evidence is not relevant or material; the exlusion is intended to reduce any incentive for future improper governmental behavior, so that the executive branch law enforcers observe the rule the next time the situation arises. In fact, in many instances, the evidence obtained in violation of the constitutional provisions is highly relevant and material and would be admissible under the traditional rules of evidence. The courts have reasoned that, even though the evidence is otherwise admissible and would help prove or disprove a fact at issue, illegally obtained evidence should not be admitted because authorizing the use of illegally obtained evidence would encourage violation of citizens' rights as enumerated in the federal and state constitutions and give a judicial stamp of approval for future law enforcement violations of the Constitution.

Although the exclusionary rules relating to the various types of evidence have been extended greatly in recent years, and the rules are constantly being slightly altered by the Supreme Court, frequent issues arise concerning what evidence will be excluded and what will be admissible. Under recent United States Supreme Court decisions, evidence is primarily excluded when the seizure of evidence violates the rights protected by the Fourth, Fifth, or Sixth Amendments to the Constitution. The general rules concerning search and seizure, self-incrimination, right to counsel, and other constitutional provisions cannot be discussed comprehensively because of space limitations.

However, this chapter does briefly discuss the rules relating to the admission or exclusion of the evidence obtained by conduct that infringes on these rights.[1]

Following the 2001 attacks involving passenger aircraft, the World Trade Center, and the Pentagon, Congress passed a series of laws and revisions to older laws called the USA PATRIOT Act (Uniting and Strengthening America by Providing Appropriate Tools Required to Intercept and Obstruct Terrorism Act of 2001), often referred to as the Patriot Act. Various interest groups have continually expressed concerns that the effect of the legislation was to violate or restrict many civil liberties previously enjoyed by all Americans; this legislation generally does not provide for the exclusion of evidence when obtained pursuant to the Act. Parts of the Patriot Act made permanent changes to statutory law while others contained sunset provisions, meaning that if they were not renewed, they would cease to be law. Since the initial post-911 reforms occurred, Congress has made some provisions permanent, but others remained subject to sunset limitations. Several of the controversial sunset statutes have been regularly, if not grudgingly, renewed after legislative fights and issues with the executive branch.

Section 215 of the Patriot Act allows the federal government access to various business records when those records allegedly relate to foreign intelligence and international terrorism investigations. In effect, the federal government, through the FBI, is permitted to ask the Foreign Intelligence Surveillance Act court to approve subpoenas that order the production of items of evidence alleged to be related to powers granted under the Foreign Intelligence Surveillance Act. According to the statute, the FBI "may make an application for an order requiring the production of any tangible things (including books, records, papers, documents, and other items) for an investigation to obtain foreign intelligence information not concerning a United States person or to protect against international terrorism or clandestine intelligence activities, provided that such investigation of a United States person is not conducted solely upon the basis of activities protected by the first amendment to the Constitution."[2] One provision that caused some civil libertarian groups concern involved the dictate that a person or entity who received a subpoena to give information to the government was prohibited from divulging receipt of the subpoena or releasing any information concerning the substance of the information requested, unless it was on an absolute need-to-know basis.[3]

---

[1] For a more comprehensive discussion of the constitutional limitations, see KANOVITZ, CONSTITUTIONAL LAW (13th ed. 2012) and WALKER AND HEMMENS, LEGAL GUIDE FOR POLICE (9th ed. 2010).

[2] 50 U.S.C. § 1861(a)(1).

[3] *Id.* § 1861(d)(1).

The Patriot Act under Sec. 206, Roving Surveillance Authority, amended the Foreign Intelligence Surveillance Act of 1978, to authorize the federal government to apply for warrants to monitor telephones, computers, and other electronic communication devices. Under circumstances when an individual target would roam or switch devices, the statute granted the federal government the ability and authority to monitor the alternative means of communication without applying for a new warrant. Pursuant to 50 U.S. C. §1805(c)(2)(B), statutorily specified communication or other common carriers, landlords, property custodians and other individuals were required to furnish assistance to the government in the carrying out of the surveillance or other activity. This roving wiretap authorization applied in situations when the government offered an allegation, in any affidavit presented to the Foreign Intelligence Surveillance Court that the target's actions could have the effect of thwarting the surveillance if the power to monitor multiple different communications devices was not granted.[4] This broad wiretap authority and the provision for roving communication interception created concerns for many civil libertarian groups, but the federal government prevailed, and the provision granting the authority to conduct roving wiretaps has been renewed to the present time.

The Intelligence Reform and Terrorism Prevention Act (IRTPA) of 2004[5] statute, as amended, takes aim at "lone wolf" or "individual unaffiliated terrorists," defining them as being within the definition of a "foreign power." An "agent of a foreign power" means "any person other than a United States person, who acts in the United States as an officer or employee of a foreign power, or as a member of a foreign power,"[6] any person who engages in "clandestine intelligence gathering on behalf of a foreign power or who engages in sabotage or international terrorism,"[7] or "engages in international terrorism or activities in preparation therefore,"[8] among other statutory descriptions. Essentially, "agent of a foreign power" is intended to encompass anyone who acts on behalf of or in support of a foreign government or part of a foreign government and who is involved in doing almost anything that would be contrary to the interests of the federal government.

The individual provisions of the Patriot Act that remain subject to the sunset provisions have been extended several times. The President of the United States signed a bill on January 5, 2010, that extended the USA Patriot Improvement and Reauthorization Act of 2005 and the Intelligence Reform and Terrorism Prevention Act of 2004 until February 28, 2011. When no long-term agreement could be reached between the executive and the legislative branch, the President signed a three-month extension of the 2010 extension before its scheduled sunset in February 2011. In the near term, it is not clear whether the sunset provisions of the Patriot Act will be made permanent, or whether the Congress and the executive branch will continue to disagree on some of the terms, but it is unlikely that the federal government will lose the ability to obtain information from

---

4 *Id.* § 1805(c)(2)(B).

5 50 U.S.C. § 401.

6 *Id.* § 1801(a) and (b).

7 *Id.* § 1801(b)(1)(B).

8 *Id.* § 1801(b)(1)(C).

companies and governmental bodies concerning terrorists, and the power to investigate the lone wolf terrorist will probably remain intact in some form or another. To the extent that terrorists are brought to trial, federal court suppression of any evidence obtained under the Patriot Act is extremely unlikely, given the fact that courts have thus far rejected exclusion of evidence.[9]

Exclusionary rule This rule requires that when evidence has been obtained in violation of the privileges guaranteed by the United States Constitution, the evidence must be excluded at the trial.

§ 16.2 Development of the Exclusionary Rule

Comparatively speaking, the search and seizure **exclusionary rule** is of recent origin. This rule provides very succinctly that, when evidence has been illegally obtained, or obtained in violation of the Constitution, it will be excluded from use in court.

First, it should be pointed out that this exclusionary rule is not universally applied. Today, in England and in most other countries that follow Anglo-Saxon legal tradition, evidence is admitted even if obtained illegally. The principle that evidence should not be excluded merely because the constable has blundered in obtaining it was followed in about one-half of the states as late as 1961. An English judge justifies this rule, also known as the common law "English Rule," by explaining:[10]

> I think it would be a dangerous obstacle to the administration of justice if we were to hold that because evidence was obtained by illegal means, it could not be used against the party charged with an offense. It therefore seems to me that the interests of the state must excuse the seizure of documents, which seizure would otherwise be unlawful, if it appears in fact that such documents were evidence of a crime committed by anyone.

As it relates to searches in violation of the Constitution, the exclusionary rule was mentioned by the United States Supreme Court as far back as 1886, but it was not until 1914 that the Supreme Court, in the case of *Weeks v. United States*,[11] made the exclusionary rule applicable in federal courts in this country. The Supreme Court held that, in a federal prosecution, the Fourth Amendment barred the use of evidence secured through an illegal search and seizure.

The reason for adopting the exclusionary rule is that the rule (according to the *Weeks* Court) was the only way for the judiciary to ensure that police and prosecutors will not violate or encourage violation of Fourth Amendment rights protected by the Constitution. If courts allowed illegally seized evidence to be introduced for jury

---

9 *But see* Robert M. Bloom and Hillary Massey. Accounting for Federalism in state courts: Exclusion of evidence lawfully obtained by Federal agents. 79 U. COLO. L. REV. 381 (2008) for an article dealing with the use in state court of evidence seized lawfully under federal law but that contradicts state law.

10 Elias v. Pasmore, 2 K.B. 65 (1934).

11 232 U.S. 383, 34 S. Ct. 341, 58 L. Ed. 2d 652 (1914).

consideration, the courts could be considered tainted by the illegality that they would be condoning. Excluding illegally obtained evidence has been extended to other violations of the federal constitution over the years. The rationale for excluding evidence becomes most clear when one lawbreaker, the criminal, is prosecuted by evidence obtained by another lawbreaker, the police officer, who obtained evidence illegally and transmitted it to the prosecutor. While the English courts argue that the remedy is action against the officer who violates these provisions, the courts in this country emphasize that only exclusion of the tainted evidence can sufficiently protect the defendant's privileges set forth by the Constitution. By removing illegally seized evidence from admissibility, the incentive for law enforcement agents to violate the law or the Constitution is substantially diminished. A civil action for damages against the offending officer by the injured party may also be a possibility under state law or pursuant to a federal *Bivens* action, which may allow a civil suit against federal officers.[12]

"The ordinary remedy in a criminal case for violation of the Fourth Amendment is suppression of any evidence obtained by the illegal police conduct."[13] Exclusion of evidence serves as a judicially created sanction that indirectly enforces the Fourth Amendment by removing any reward for its violation.[14] The primary purpose of the exclusionary rule is to remove the incentive for police to disregard the provisions of the Fourth Amendment.[15] When the illegally seized evidence is excluded, the prosecutor may no longer have a prosecutable case, the degree of seriousness of the case may be reduced, or the case may have sufficient legal evidence remaining to enable a successful prosecution.

Although the language used would seem to imply that all evidence illegally seized will always be suppressed from courtroom use, the recent trend has been to allow some illegally seized evidence into court. In effect, the exclusionary rule is not applied to every Fourth Amendment or other constitutional violation. In *Hudson v. Michigan*, the Supreme Court held that applying the exclusionary rule for violations of the knock-and-announce requirement of the Fourth Amendment would not be an appropriate remedy[16] because of the social costs of applying the exclusionary rule. The Court of Appeals for the Seventh Circuit recently refused to use the fact that the arresting officers used excessive arrest force, a Fourth Amendment violation, as a basis for excluding evidence.[17]

---

12 Bivens v. Six Unknown Named Agents of Federal Bureau of Narcotics, 403 U.S. 388, 1971 U.S. LEXIS 23 (1971).

13 United States v. Olivares-Rangel, 2006 U.S. App. LEXIS 20595 (10th Cir. 2006).

14 State v. Klosterman, 114 Ohio App. 3d 327, 683 N.E.2d 100 (1996).

15 Hudson v. Michigan, 547 U.S. 586, 2006 U.S. LEXIS 4677 (2006).

16 *Id.* at 598.

17 United States v. Collins, 714 F.3d 540, 2013 U.S. App. LEXIS 7774 (2013). The Court also noted that the defendant dropped the evidence before being elbowed, kicked in the stomach and groin, pepper sprayed, and hit with a Taser. In an older case, United States v. Leon, 468 U.S. 897 (1984), the Court approved using evidence obtained by the use of an invalid search warrant since the officers were acting in objective "good faith" that the warrant was valid.

Although the exclusionary rule has been applied in federal courts since 1914,[18] it was not until 1961 that the Supreme Court determined that the Fourth Amendment and the exclusionary rule were applicable against the states in search and seizure cases.[19] The extension of the exclusionary rule to the states had to do with the doctrine of selective incorporation of many rights from the Bill of Rights into the due process clause of the Fourteenth Amendment, which made those federal guarantees applicable to the states.

Wiretapping A form of electronic eavesdropping in which, upon a court order, law enforcement officials surreptitiously listen to land and cell phone conversations, e-mail, text messages, and similar communications.

Eavesdropping Knowingly and without authority entering into a private place with the intent to surreptitiously listen to a private conversation or to observe the personal conduct of any other person or persons therein conducted by personal listening or electronic collection of sounds.

Partially on the basis of the Fourth Amendment and the exclusionary rule, and consistent with statutory requirements, **wiretapping** and **eavesdropping** evidence is often excluded if government conduct has failed to meet legal dictates. However, if the wire or telephone intercept meets the requirements of state and federal wiretap laws, evidence obtained by wiretapping and eavesdropping is admissible.[20] Following the events of September 11, 2001, Congress strengthened the ability of the federal government to conduct wiretaps under the Foreign Intelligence Surveillance Act (FISA) to allow enhanced electronic intelligence gathering that might affect the United States.[21] The target of the surveillance must be a foreign power or an agent for a foreign power, and where a criminal prosecution results, there is no provision for exclusion of evidence under FISA. Individual civil suits attacking the FISA provisions have not generally seen success in either getting the eavesdropping to cease or in getting cases to trial where damages or other remedies have been sought.[22]

The United States Supreme Court has determined that involuntary confessions and statements taken in violation of the *Miranda* warnings should not be admitted in court. Coerced confessions violate the concept of due process and the Fifth Amendment protections against self-incrimination, and coerced statements call into question the reliability and truthfulness of a confession. Statements taken in violation of *Miranda* actually may be reliable, but are excluded under public policy decisions made by the Supreme Court. More recently, the courts have applied exclusionary reasoning

---

18 Weeks v. United States, 232 U.S. 383, 1914 U.S. LEXIS 1368 (1914).

19 Mapp v. Ohio, 367 U.S. 643, 81 S. Ct. 1684, 6 L. Ed. 2d 1081 (1961).

20 See United States v. Moore, 452 F.3d 382, 2006 U.S. App. LEXIS 14152 (5th Cir. 2006), for a case in which wiretapping in a federal prison did not require suppression of evidence seized since it complied with the Federal Wiretap Act.

21 50 U.S.C. § 1801.

22 *See* ACLU v. National Security Agency, 493 F.3d 644, 2007 U.S. App. LEXIS 16149 (6th Cir. 2007).

to exclude evidence obtained in violation of the right to counsel provisions of the Sixth Amendment to the Constitution.

Before leaving the introductory discussion of the exclusionary rule, it is important to emphasize that the rule applies not only to evidence obtained directly as a result of unlawful action by enforcement personnel, but also to "derivative evidence." When an original search proved to be unlawful, but the results pointed toward other evidence that would have been discovered only because of the original illegality, that other evidence is also excluded[23] in order to ensure that the prosecution is not enjoy advantages it would not have gained if the illegality had not transpired.[24] However, if the prosecution can show that the evidence ultimately or inevitably would have been discovered by lawful means,[25] the exclusionary rule serves no deterrent purpose and does not apply.[26] The degree of application of these rules of exclusion is discussed in the following sections.

§ 16.3 Search and Seizure Exclusions

The Fourth Amendment to the Constitution provides:

> The right of the people to be secure in their persons, houses, papers, and effects, against unreasonable searches and seizures, shall not be violated, and no Warrants shall issue, but upon probable cause, supported by Oath or affirmation, and particularly describing the place to be searched, and the persons or things to be seized.[27]

The amendment that is now known as the Fourth Amendment was part of the first 10 amendments proposed as a means of inducing the necessary number of states to ratify the proposed Constitution of the United States. The first 10 amendments became known as the Bill of Rights and were designed to place limitations on the national government. At this point in history, the Fourth Amendment and the other amendments in the Bill of Rights did not apply to state officials, but were added to prohibit the officials of a strong central government from abridging the rights of the citizens of the various states.

Initially, in the case of *Weeks v. United States*,[28] the Supreme Court of the United States devised the exclusionary rule to help enforce the Fourth Amendment by excluding evidence from federal courts when federal officials had obtained evidence through illegal searches. In a later reconsideration of the coverage of the Fourth Amendment during *Mapp v. Ohio* (1961), the Supreme Court extended the rule to cover state

---

[23] Wong Sun v. United States, 371 U.S. 471 (1963).

[24] State v. Seager, 571 N.W.2d 204 (Iowa 1997). See *also* United States v. Watson, 118 F.3d 1315 (9th Cir. 1997).

[25] See Murray v. United States, 487 U.S. 533 (1988), and Nix v. Williams, 467 U.S. 43 (1984).

[26] State v. Ballon, 703 So. 2d 130 (La. 1997).

[27] U.S. CONST. amend. IV.

[28] 232 U.S. 383, 1914 U.S. LEXIS 1368 (1914).

and local courts because the Court believed that the rule was needed to enforce the due process clause of the Fourteenth Amendment.[29] By making the exclusionary rule applicable to the states, the Court made it necessary for state police agencies, state prosecutors, and state judges to consider and follow the decisions of the Supreme Court of the United States to meet the minimum federal constitutional search and seizure standards.

In *Mapp v. Ohio*, the Supreme Court's decision closed the last door to the use of illegally seized evidence. Where a proven illegality existed with respect to the Fourth Amendment, any seized evidence was excluded if offered against a person whose rights were violated. However, in 1984, the Supreme Court adopted the good faith exception to the exclusionary rule. In the case of *United States v. Leon*, police officers acting in good faith executed a search warrant instructing them to search residences for controlled substances.[30] Although it was later determined that the search warrant was invalid due to lack of probable cause, the evidence seized pursuant to the warrant could be admitted in court. The *Leon* Court made this comment:

> We conclude that the marginal or nonexistent benefits produced by suppressing evidence obtained in objectively reasonable reliance on a subsequently invalidated search warrant cannot justify the substantial costs of exclusion.

The Supreme Court acknowledged that the exclusionary rule had been modified, but included this warning:

> We do not suggest, however, that exclusion is always inappropriate in cases where an officer has obtained a warrant and abided by its terms. Nevertheless, the officer's reliance on the magistrate's probable cause determination and on the technical sufficiency of the warrant he issues must be objectively reasonable . . . and it is clear that in some circumstances the officer will have no reasonable grounds for believing that the warrant was properly issued.

The original intent of the Fourth Amendment's exclusionary rule was to deter illegal police conduct. When the wrong came not from the police but from a judge, the police could not have been deterred from using a facially valid search warrant because they would have no reason to question its validity. When, under particular circumstances, there could be no deterrent effect on the police, there would be no rationale for applying the exclusionary rule.

In *Massachusetts v. Shepherd*, which was decided on the same day as *Leon*, the Supreme Court upheld a search for real evidence when the officers executed the search in good faith.[31] The Court determined that the evidence should be admitted, even though a reviewing court later found that the description in the search warrant did not meet constitutional standards, and the error had been made by the judge and not the police.

---

[29] 367 U.S. 643, 1961 U.S. LEXIS 812 (1961).

[30] 468 U.S. 897, 104 S. Ct. 3405, 1984 U.S. LEXIS 153 (1984).

[31] Massachusetts v. Shepherd, 468 U.S. 897, 104 S. Ct. 3424, 82 L. Ed. 2d 677 (1984).

In both the *Leon* and *Shepherd* cases, police officers executed what they reasonably believed to be valid warrants. Soon after these cases were decided, the question arose as to whether the "good faith" rationale would be applied to situations in which officers acted without a warrant. In the case of *Illinois v. Krull*, officers, acting pursuant to a statute, warrantlessly inspected an automobile wrecking yard and discovered several stolen cars.[32] The state statute, similar to those in many other states, regulated the business of buying and selling motor vehicles, parts, and scrap metal. The day after the warrantless search, a federal court ruled that such a statute was unconstitutional, and at the trial a motion was made to exclude the evidence obtained by the officers, even though the officers acted in good faith under the statute. On review, the United States Supreme Court reversed the lower court decision and decided that the evidence should have been admitted. Under the circumstances, the application of the exclusionary rule would have offered little deterrent effect on police conduct because police cannot foretell which laws might be later ruled unconstitutional. In fact, the police made no error; the Illinois legislature erred in passing the unconstitutional statute. With reference to both *Leon* and *Shepherd*, the basic deterrent effect would not operate to affect judicial behavior because the intent of the exclusionary rule was to modify police behavior not judicial activity. As Justice O'Connor once stated, "Where the rule's deterrent effect is likely to be marginal, or where its application offends other values central to our system of constitutional governance or the judicial process, we have declined to extend the rule to that context."[33] The Court applied Justice O'Connor's sentiments in *Arizona v. Evans*, a case where the defendant had been arrested based on a warrant entry that remained in a police computer, but which should have been removed.[34] The police acted in good faith on the apparent existence of the warrant and the drug evidence obtained incident to arrest remained good evidence because exclusion would not have affected the particular police officers and would not affect future police conduct.

Although the court in the *Krull* case did not extend the "good faith" exception, it did clarify the reasoning and logic underpinning the exclusionary rule with these comments:

> Application of the Exclusionary Rule "is neither intended nor able to cure the invasion of the defendant's rights which he has already suffered". . . . Rather, the rule "operates as a judicially created remedy designed to safeguard Fourth Amendment rights generally through its deterrent effect, rather than as a personal constitutional right of the party aggrieved". . . . As with any remedial device, application of the exclusionary rule properly has been restricted to those situations in which its remedial purpose is effectively advanced.[35]

---

32 Illinois v. Krull, 480 U.S. 340; 107 S. Ct. 1160; 94 L. Ed. 2d 364; (1987) U.S. LEXIS 1061. *See* KANOVITZ, CONSTITUTIONAL LAW (13th ed. 2012) for a more thorough discussion of the search and seizure requirements.

33 Duckworth v. Eagan, 492 U.S. 195, 208 (1989).

34 Arizona v. Evans, 514 U.S. 1, 1995 U.S. LEXIS 1806 (1995).

35 Illinois v. Krull, 480 U.S. 340, 347, 1987 U.S. LEXIS 1061 (1987).

These cases indicate a trend in the Supreme Court to apply less technical rules in search and seizure cases. However, the exclusionary rule still applies in a majority of cases when evidence has been obtained illegally. Therefore, it is essential that the rules concerning the constitutionality of searches be followed.

Stops and brief searches on less than probable cause may create constitutional issues when police are looking for drugs rather than impaired drivers. In *Indianapolis v. Edmond*, the defendant had been stopped based on absolutely no suspicion at a city-wide checkpoint in an effort to locate drivers and passengers who possessed illegal substances. The court held that while brief stops to detect drunk drivers constituted a reasonable approach under the Fourth Amendment,[36] stopping people for general crime control on absolutely no suspicion could not be squared with the Constitution.[37] However, for a specific important purpose, such as a roadblock designed to obtain more information about a recent hit-and-run offense and not to investigate any particular driver, a checkpoint can be reasonable under the Fourth Amendment.[38] Police contact with motorists consisted of an information request, and they gave each motorist an informational flyer.

When police proceed without probable cause or a warrant, there may be some limitations on searches and seizures. Clearly, in the absence of a warrant, exigent [emergency] circumstances, or probable cause, physically entering a private residence may run afoul of the doctrine of the *Mapp* case, but the thermal imaging of a dwelling from the street involves no physical intrusion. However, evidence obtained from heat scans of residential buildings should not be used as part of probable cause to obtain a warrant. In *Kyllo v. United States*, the Court held that using a thermal-imaging device to scan the heat signature of a residence in search of marijuana cultivation constituted a Fourth Amendment search for which a warrant or a substitute was constitutionally required.[39] In the case of warrantless searches of vehicle drivers, the Supreme Court recently altered the previously settled routine of searching for the blood alcohol content of suspected impaired drivers by suggesting that warrants are required in the absence of emergency or exigent circumstances.[40] According to the Court, while the natural metabolization of alcohol might support a finding of exigent circumstances in some cases, the average intoxicated driving will not allow a blood test for alcohol absent a warrant. The existence of an emergency must be tested by the totality of the circumstances.

The exclusionary rule is not without exceptions, and several have been recognized. For example, exigent or emergency circumstances permit warrantless police entries to a home or other location to save a life, to prevent serious bodily injury, and, in some cases, to prevent the destruction of evidence. In a Third Circuit case, police officers had been sent to the apartment building by a dispatcher, who informed the officers that,

---

36 See Michigan v. Sitz, 496 U.S. 444 (1990).

37 Indianapolis v. Edmond, 531 U.S. 32 (2000).

38 See Illinois v. Lidster, 540 U.S. 419, 2004 U.S. LEXIS 656 (2004).

39 Kyllo v. United States, 533 U.S. 27 (2001).

40 Missouri v. Neely, 133 S.Ct. 1552, 1561, 2013 U.S. LEXIS 3160 (2103).

due to a 911 call, a female was being held against her will at the defendant's apartment.[41] Upon arriving at the scene, the police spoke with a woman standing on the street outside of the apartment, who told the officers that she had received text messages on her cell phone from a friend inside the defendant's home, who was in fear of her life because the defendant was acting violently. The woman indicated that her friend seemed to be in distress, while being held against her will. According to the Third Circuit, this information was sufficient to create exigent circumstances that allowed the officers to gain a warrantless entry into the defendant's apartment and to detain him briefly, at which time police discovered a hidden firearm on his person. The defendant had a prior felony conviction, making his possession of the firearm illegal. The Third Circuit Court of Appeal rejected the defendant's contention that no emergency existed and approved the police entry into his apartment because the officers had an objectively reasonable basis to believe a person might have been seriously injured and detained against her will. Evidence so acquired is admissible and is not excluded by the *Mapp* doctrine.

Other exceptions to the exclusionary rule include the independent source rule, in which evidence is admitted when the Fourth Amendment has been violated, but there is a separate avenue by which the evidence could be legally obtained.[42] In one Supreme Court case, officers illegally entered a building to determine whether some of the evidence they sought was still inside the premises, but they included only good, untainted evidence on an affidavit for a search warrant and did not mention their earlier illegal entry inside the building. The illegal entry did not taint the warrant, because there was sufficient evidence of probable cause separate from the tainted evidence that the officers did not mention on the application for the warrant. According to the reviewing court, a good independent source for probable cause existed sufficient to support the warrant.[43]

As an exception to the *Mapp* exclusionary principle, the inevitable discovery rule allows the admission of the results of an illegal search and seizure to be used as evidence when the evidence would have been disclosed or found by lawful means within a reasonable time period.[44] In a case that demonstrates this principle, an officer violated the principles of *Miranda* to obtain the location of the body of a murder victim, but the evidence of the body was not excluded because the police were searching in the area where the body had been hidden and would inevitably have found the body lawfully within a reasonable time.[45] In a different case, police officers illegally, and in violation of the Fourth Amendment, entered a defendant's motel room without a warrant but with probable cause to arrest.[46] Once inside, the officers encountered some guns in

---

41 United States v. Wood, 2013 U.S. App. 20220 (3rd Cir. 2013).

42 Murray v. United States, 468 U.S. 796 (1984).

43 *Id.*

44 Nix v. Williams, 467 U.S. 431, 1984 U.S. LEXIS 101 (1984).

45 *Id.*

46 United States v. Stokes, 2013 U.S. App. LEXIS 17276 (2nd Cir. 2013).

the possession of the defendant/arrestee, who had a prior felony conviction and was not eligible to possess any firearms. The trial court applied the rule of inevitable discovery because it reasoned that the defendant would have left the motel room at some point, and at that time, he would have been subject to a search. In reversing the trial judge, the reviewing court noted that, although the defendant might have left the motel room with a weapon, he also might not have been carrying one, and so there was no certainty that the officers would have found the firearms lawfully.

A different exception exists under the doctrine of attenuation. Under this exception, when the police illegality is separated or attenuated from the illegal collection of evidence by time and distance, the evidence is not excluded.[47] In determining whether to apply this doctrine, courts often consider the length of time between the original illegality and the newer evidence, the presence of intervening circumstances, and the purpose behind the official misconduct. In a case involving attenuation, the defendants voluntarily went to police to confess and make what they believed was a plea bargain several days after an alleged illegal search of their homes. The Supreme Court considered the fact that the original illegality and the lawful confession evidence were separated by an independent act of free will, as well as by time and distance, and the confessions should not be excluded on Fourth Amendment grounds.[48] In one large-scale drug undercover operation, federal and state police officers used a GPS system that was warrantlessly attached to several vehicles, but police visually tracked the vehicles at different times before making traffic stops and searches based on probable cause.[49] The federal district court held that, regardless of whether the use of GPS tracking devices violated the Fourth Amendment rights of the several defendants, the visual tracking, police observations, and other evidence were sufficiently separated or attenuated from any possible illegality involving the warrantless GPS tracking device usage. Accordingly, the evidence seized from the vehicles was constitutionally admissible in court.

One type of search, which is universally recognized as legal, is a search with a warrant. Both the United States Constitution and the constitutions of the various states describe the circumstances under which search warrants may be issued.

In order for a search warrant to be valid, it must meet certain requirements. Some of the requirements are enumerated in the Constitution. Others have been added by legislation or court interpretation. In order for a search warrant to be enforceable, the following requirements must be met:

1. The warrant must be issued on probable cause.
2. The warrant must be supported by oath or affirmation.
3. The proper judicial official must issue the warrant.

---

47 *See* Wong Sun v. United States, 371 U.S. 471, 1963 U.S. LEXIS 2431 (1963).

48 *Id.*

49 United States v. Powell, 2013 U.S. Dist. LEXIS 64804 (E.D. Mich. 2013).

4. The place to be searched and the things to be seized must be particularly described.[50]

The United States Supreme Court, as well as other courts, has encouraged the use of a search warrant in making a search. In 1983, the Court reinforced this preference and in indicated a trend to approve less technical procedures when it modified the probable cause requirements for a search warrant. In previous cases, the Court had approved the use of undisclosed informants in determining probable cause and had established what was known as the "two-pronged" test.[51] Under this test, the judge must be given facts from an informant that equal probable cause, and the judge must estabish clear reasons why the informant is to be believed. When an informant's tip will be used to justify a search warrant, the standard test for the tip's credibility requires (1) that the magistrate must be given some of the underlying circumstances from which the affiant concluded that the informant was credible or that his or her information was reliable, and (2) that the magistrate must be given some of the underlying circumstances from which the informant reached the conclusion conveyed in the tip.

In *Illinois v. Gates*, the Supreme Court reconsidered the use of informants to help establish probable cause, abandoning the two-pronged test in which probable cause depended on an informant's information in favor of the "totality of circumstances" test.[52] While agreeing with the Illinois Supreme Court that an informant's veracity, reliability, and basis of knowledge were all highly relevant in determining whether an informant's report equals probable cause, the Court indicated that the totality of circumstances approach was far more consistent with the Court's prior treatment of probable cause. Under this test, the issuing judicial official must consider all the circumstances set forth in the affidavit and then make a practical, commonsense decision that there is a fair probability that contraband or evidence of a crime will be found in a particular place. State courts are free to require a higher standard for informant-based probable cause under state laws or constitutions, and some states follow the old two-pronged test.[53]

Even though a warrant has been issued correctly, the evidence can be made inadmissible by improper execution of the warrant. In executing the warrant, the officer must follow these guidelines:

1. The warrant must be executed by the officer named in it, or the officer must come within the class of officers designated.

---

50 *See* WALKER AND HEMMENS, LEGAL GUIDE FOR POLICE: CONSTITUTIONAL ISSUES (8th ed. 2008) and U.S. CONST. amend. IV.

51 Aguilar v. Texas, 378 U.S. 108, 84 S. Ct. 1509, 12 L. Ed. 2d 723 (1964). See also, Spinelli v. United States, 393 U.S, 410, 1969 U.S. LEXIS 2701 (1969).

52 462 U.S. 213, 103 S. Ct. 2317, 76 L. Ed. 2d 527 (1983). *See also* People v. Jack, 70 Cal. Rptr. 2d 676 (1997).

53 *See* People v. Chisholm, 21 N.Y. 3d 990, 2013 N.Y. LEXIS 1728 (2013) (Smith, J., dissenting). New York adopted the two-pronged test in People v. Griminger, 71 N.Y.2d 635, 1988 N.Y. LEXIS 604 (1988).

2. The warrant must be executed within certain time limitations.
3. Only necessary force may be used in executing the warrant.
4. Prior notice and demand shall usually precede forcible entry.
5. Only the property described may be seized under the warrant.

One of the requirements of the Fourth Amendment is that searches and seizures must be reasonable in the way they are executed. One of the common law hallmarks indicating reasonableness was the concept that the officers should knock-and-announce before resorting to breaking into a house. The knock-and-announce rule serves to protect the privacy of the individual, avoids needless destruction of property, and reduces confusion, shielding police and occupiers from attack by each other. Notwithstanding the statutes and case law requiring prior notice and demand, the courts have recognized an exception for exigent circumstances, such as immediate physical danger, flight, or clear potential for destruction of evidence. In the case of *Wilson v. Arkansas*, the United States Supreme Court noted that "this Court has little doubt that the Amendments' framers thought that whether the officers announced their presence and authority before entering a dwelling was among the factors to be considered in assessing a search's reasonableness."[54] The Court recognized, however, that there are exceptions to the rule, "including the threat of physical harm to the police, the fact that an officer is pursuing a recently escaped arrestee, and the existence of reason to believe that evidence would likely be destroyed if advance notice were given may establish the reasonableness of unannounced entry."

The Court retreated from a preference for the knock-and-announce requirement when faced with a clearly guilty defendant who wanted evidence suppressed based on an admitted violation by police of the knock-and-announce principle. In this case,[55] under the authority of a search warrant, the police announced their presence and entered, all within the space of three to five seconds. The defendant's door was unlocked at the time the police entered to find narcotics and guns that were illegal for the felon to possess. The prosecution conceded that the police had violated the *Wilson v. Arkansas* rule, but contended that suppression of the evidence was not the appropriate remedy. The Supreme Court noted, "[t]he common-law principle that law enforcement officers must announce their presence and provide residents an opportunity to open the door is an ancient one,"[56] but the Court was not inclined to suppress the evidence just because there was a Fourth Amendment violation. It noted that the knock-and-announce rule did not protect the citizen in his efforts to keep the government from seeing evidence described in a warrant. The deterrence effect on police must outweigh the substantial social costs of suppression, and the Court believed that the deterrent effect was small, and every litigant would be contesting the failure to knock-and-announce if the result of a win would be suppression of all the evidence. What the Court

---

[54] 514 U.S. 927, 115 S. Ct. 1914, 131 L. Ed. 2d 976 (1995).

[55] Hudson v. Michigan, 547 U.S. 586, 2006 U.S. LEXIS 4677 (2006).

[56] *Id.*

stated in *Wilson v. Arkansas* had been difficult to apply in practice, and the Court will not require that evidence be suppressed when police violate the knock-and-announce principle. The present rule seems to suggest that knock-and-announce may be proper, but that, if police fail to knock-and-announce, they run little risk of having a court suppress the evidence from use by the prosecutor.

Although preference is given to the search warrant as a means of making a search, and the search warrant is the only such means mentioned in the Constitution as proper, Supreme Court jurisprudence has recognized the necessity of conducting some searches without warrants, especially in emergency situations[57] or when the officer might be facing an unclear danger.[58] Case law illuminates and illustrates the typical exceptions to the general necessity of a warrant. In each instance, an exception applies only when certain requirements are met. The paragraphs that follow discuss the most important examples of these exceptions.

A. *Search Incident to a Lawful Arrest*

The right to make a search incident to a lawful arrest has been recognized by all courts, including the United States Supreme Court,[59] but this right does require an actual lawful arrest prior to conducting a valid search.[60] Such a search is designed to protect the arresting officers and to safeguard evidence. In addition to a valid arrest, the **search incident to arrest** requires that the search be made contemporaneously with the arrest, or immediately after, and that the search be reasonable in scope. Naturally, the arrest must be made in good faith that probable cause for the arrest exists.[61] If police made an erroneous entry into a law enforcement database, that entry might falsely disclose an active warrant, leading to an arrest, a subsequent search, and the discovery of criminal evidence. In such a situation,, the evidence would not be excluded because excluding the evidence would not alter police practice in the future.[62] Even if the law of the jurisdiction does not permit

> **Search incident to arrest** Once a person has been arrested, police may search the person of the arrestee, his or her immediate effects, and the physical area within his or her immediate control. Probable cause to search is not required.

[57] *See* Warden v. Hayden, 387 U.S. 294 (1967), and New York v. Quarles, 467 U.S. 649 (1984).

[58] *See* United States v. Arellano-Ochoa, 2006 U.S. App. LEXIS 22466 (9th Cir. 2006), in which the court permitted a warrantless entry where an officer could not see through the screen of a house trailer door under circumstances in which the officer might have been dealing with an armed drug trafficker.

[59] Chimel v. California, 395 U.S. 752, 89 S. Ct. 2034, 23 L. Ed. 2d 685 (1969).

[60] *See* Knowles v. Iowa, 525 U.S. 113, 1998 U.S. LEXIS 8068 (1998).

[61] Arizona v. Evans, 514 U.S. 1, 1995 U.S. LEXIS 1806 (1995). *See also* United States v. Miller, 382 F. Supp. 2d 350 (N.D.N.Y. 2005).

[62] Herring v. United States, 555 U.S. 135, 2009 U.S. LEXIS 581 (2009). An arrest is not illegal even where police acted based on outdated information contained with a computer system. The evidence seized will not be excluded from trial or other use.

the arrest, an arrest is lawful as long as police have probable cause to believe the individual has committed a crime, and police do not otherwise violate the Fourth Amendment.[63] Under these circumstances, police can conduct a search incident to the lawful arrest, and evidence is not excluded under the Fourth Amendment.

The United States Supreme Court has left no doubt that a search of the person incident to a lawful arrest may occur slightly before the actual arrest if the arrest occurs contemporaneously with the search, but it is preferable to conduct a search incident to an arrest following the arrest.[64] In the case of *Smith v. Ohio*, the United States Supreme Court was asked to answer the single question of "whether a warrantless search, which provides probable cause for an arrest, can nonetheless be justified as an incident of that arrest."[65] In this case, when asked by an officer to "come here a minute," the defendant threw a paper grocery sack that he was carrying on to the hood of his car. Before making the arrest, the officer pushed the defendant's hand away from the bag and opened it, observing drug paraphernalia among its contents.

The search was illegal because the defendant was not arrested until after the contraband was discovered. Therefore, the contraband could not serve as a part of the justification for a lawful arrest and could not support a lawful search incident to an arrest. The Supreme Court of the United States reversed the top Ohio court and concluded that:

> The exception for searches incident to arrest permits the police to search a lawfully arrested person and areas within his immediate control. . . . it does not permit police to search any citizen without a warrant or probable cause so long as an arrest immediately follows.[66]

Because a search incident to a lawful arrest is intended to protect the searching officer and to prevent the destruction of evidence, the scope of the area of the search can be limited. In the case of physical searches, they may be limited generally to the "lunge area" where a weapon could be obtained or evidence destroyed.

Many searches incident to arrest produce cell phones and small tablet computers. In situations involving data from these devices, officer safety cannot provide a good argument, and limitations may exist. The Supreme Court has yet to definitively address data searches incident to arrests. However, in a Boston drug sales case where the arrestee possessed a working cell phone that the officers searched, the Court of Appeals for the First Circuit held that

---

63 Virginia v. Moore, 553 U.S. 164, 177, 2008 U.S. LEXIS 3674 (2008). Police arrested the defendant for a crime for which Virginia authorized the issuance of a summons. A search incident to the arrest revealed the presence of illegal drugs.

64 Rawlings v. Kentucky, 448 U.S. 98, 111, 1980 U.S. LEXIS 142 (1980). *Accord*, United States v. Montgomery, 377 F. 3d 582, 2004 U.S. App. LEXIS 15438 (6th Cir. 2004).

65 Smith v. Ohio, 494 U.S. 541, 110 S. Ct. 1288, 108 L. Ed. 2d. 464 (1990).

66 Smith v. Ohio, 494 U.S. 541, 543, 1990 U.S. LEXIS 1198 (1990).

> the search-incident-to-arrest exception does not authorize the warrantless search of data on a cell phone seized from an arrestee's person, because the government has not convinced us that such a search is ever necessary to protect arresting officers or preserve destructible evidence.[67]

With respect to searches incident to arrest involving physical objects, the case of *Chimel v. California* has been considered a leading case. In *Chimel*, the Supreme Court defined the proper scope of a search incident to arrest as "the area within his immediate control—construing that phrase to mean the area from which he might gain possession of a weapon or destructible evidence."[68] In the actual case, officers lawfully arrested Chimel inside his home but searched the entire house without a warrant on the ground that the search was incident to a lawful arrest.

However, in applying the *Chimel* rule when the search is made of a residence incident to a lawful arrest, police may not search the interior of the arrestee's home when the arrest occurred on the sidewalk outside of the home. In one case, the search of the arrestee's home was unreasonable because it was not conducted incident to his arrest and was not confined to a cursory inspection. The Fourth Amendment allows a sweep if the officers lawfully enter an arrestee's home, but where the officers have no right to enter, there can be no lawful sweep.[69] If an arrest is made in one part of the house, the Fourth Amendment permits a properly limited protective sweep in conjunction with the in-home arrest, when the searching officers possess a reasonable belief, based on specific and articulable facts, that the area to be swept harbors an individual posing a danger to those on the arrest scene. However, the fact that an arrest is made in the living room does not justify a full warrantless search of the whole house absent the consent of one in control of the premises.[70] In making a protective sweep, police may look anywhere in a home that a person might be hiding. There must be articulable facts along with rational inferences that would warrant a prudent officer in believing that the sweep area harbors an individual who poses a danger.[71]

In a Pennsylvania domestic violence case that demonstrates the **protective sweep** principle related to the search incident to arrest theory, police had reason to enter a defendant's apartment. Neighbors had complained, and the police heard the sound of a violent argument when they arrived on the scene. To ensure that the female occupant was not in danger, the officers requested admission to the premises.[72] Upon being admitted by defendant's girlfriend, they observed him run into a bedroom and shut the door, but were able to coax him out of the room. One of the officers did a protective bedroom sweep to make sure no one else was inside the bedroom when he observed a

---

[67] United States v. Wurie, 728 F.3d 1, 13, 2013 U.S. App. LEXIS 9937 (1st Cir. 2013).

[68] Chimel v. California, 395 U.S. 752; 89 S. Ct. 2034; 23 L. Ed. 2d 685; (1969) U.S. LEXIS 1166; *see also* United States v. Robinson, 414 U.S. 218 (1973), which held that the authority to search incident to a lawful arrest includes the right to search the person arrested for evidence not related to the crime.

[69] *See* United States v. Rios-Ramirez, 2004 U.S. Dist. LEXIS 26573 (D.P.R. 2004).

[70] Maryland v. Buie, 494 U.S. 325, 110 S. Ct. 1093, 108 L. Ed. 2d 276 (1990).

[71] *Id.*

[72] Commonwealth v. Potts, 2013 Pa. Super. 236, 2013 Pa. Super. LEXIS 2635 (2013).

Protective sweep A legal theory that permits police officers to make a quick and limited search of a building, apartment, or room premises incident to an arrest and conducted in a manner that protects the safety of police officers and others who may be present and potentially harmed. Generally articulable facts which, taken together with rational inferences, would lead an officer to conclude that the area to be swept may harbor an individual who poses a danger to those on the arrest scene.

black suitcase filled with a large amount of marijuana. The reviewing court concluded that the trial court was correct in holding that the officers could have reasonably believed that the area of the bedroom to be swept could harbor a weapon or an individual posing a danger to those on the arrest scene. Given that marijuana was in plain view of an officer when he was in a place he lawfully occupied, authorities could lawfully seize the marijuana and use it as evidence against the defendant.

In *Arizona v. Gant*,[73] the Supreme Court considered a case involving a search incident to arrest in a motor vehicle context, overruling earlier cases that had permitted a search of the interior of a motor vehicle following a lawful arrest of a driver or passenger. In *Gant*, police had arrested the driver for driving under a suspended license, and the arrestee and some other people who were his friends had been handcuffed and secured in patrol cars when the vehicle search occurred. No arrestee could destroy evidence or endanger the officers while in the police car. Under the new Fourth Amendment interpretation of a search incident to a lawful arrest involving a motor vehicle, as well as the search incident to arrest theory, the police may search a vehicle's interior only if there is reason to believe that the arrestee might access the car, or if the police believe that the vehicle contains evidence of the offense for which the driver or occupant has been arrested. In this particular case, there was no expectation that evidence of the crime of driving with a suspended license would be found, and there was no chance that the arrested individuals could gain access to the motor vehicle. Therefore, the search of its interior was unreasonable, and seized evidence should have been suppressed from trial.

In a slightly different application of a search following an arrest, rather than pursuant to the traditional search incident to an arrest, police in Maryland used a swab to take a DNA sample from the mouth of an arrestee, as was pursuant to a state statute. The DNA results implicated the defendant in a completely different crime, a cold-case rape. Following his conviction for the rape, the defendant pursued his appellate remedies, but was ultimately unsuccessful in his efforts to suppress the DNA evidence from his rape case. According to the Supreme Court, the collection of DNA evidence following an arrest for a violent felony was very similar to taking a defendant's fingerprints following an arrest. Given the fact that a state has an interest in definitively identifying arrestees, the taking of a DNA sample in this case was deemed to have been reasonable under the Fourth Amendment, especially when compared with drawing a blood sample for a DUI arrest. Given the fact that the defendant was already in custody, taking a DNA

[73] Arizona v. Gant, 556 U.S. 332, 2009 U.S. LEXIS 3120 (2009). *See* case in Part II.

sample with a cotton swab of the mouth was more similar to fingerprinting or giving deep lung air samples for a DUI prosecution, and, as such, the swabbing did not represent an unreasonable search issue under the Fourth Amendment.[74]

B. Search After a Waiver of Constitutional Right

In accordance with the general principles allowing a person to waive his or her constitutional rights, an individual may waive the rights protected by the Fourth Amendment to the Constitution, as well as state provisions concerning search and seizure. In order for this exception to the warrant rule to apply, the prosecution must show that the consent was voluntarily and freely given, and that the person who gave the consent had the capacity and authority to consent. As a general rule, authorities must obtain consent from a person who has dominion and control over the premises or effects and who may give valid consent against the absent nonconsenting person with whom the authority is shared.[75] Consent may not be obtained, however, if the nonconsenting person is present and refuses to grant consent.[76] In one case, a couple shared dominion and control over the marital residence, and a domestic dispute brought the police. The wife alleged that the defendant had drugs within the home and consented to a police search of the marital home. The husband refused to grant consent to search, and the Supreme Court held that one spouse had no recognized authority in law or in social practice to prevail over the other spouse who was present and refused consent to search. The police had no better claim to reasonably enter the marital premises than any other person when joint consent was not available.[77] In a different case, apparent "shared authority" permitted the girlfriend of a defendant bank robber to consent to a search of the defendant' motor vehicle in his absence.[78] The girlfriend had permission to drive the car; she had driven the car; she had possession of the only keys; and the defendant had no driver's license. There was no coercion [just a few officers were present] on the part of police officers when she offered search consent for the search. The test for a waiver of constitutional rights under the consent theory of searches encompasses the totality of the circumstances, including the consenting party's age, education, and possible legal education, as well as the coerciveness of the atmosphere, the party's arrest status, and the party's knowledge of the right to refuse without facing adverse consequences.[79]

In considering the waiver of constitutional rights, the police and the courts must carefully observe any limitations placed upon the consent. A general consent to search

---

74 See Maryland v. King, ___ U.S. ___, 133 S. Ct. 1958, 186 L. Ed. 2d 1 (2013). See case in Part II, Chapter 16.

75 United States v. Matlock, 415 U.S. 164, 94 S. Ct. 988, 39 L. Ed. 2d 242 (1974). *See* KANOVITZ, CONSTITUTIONAL LAW (13th ed. 2012) for a discussion of the authority of a spouse, a minor child, and a parent to consent to a search.

76 Georgia v. Randolph, 547 U.S. 103, 2006 U.S. LEXIS 2498 (2006).

77 *Id.*

78 United States v. Scott, 2013 U.S. App. LEXIS 21367 (8th Cir. 2013).

79 *See* Schneckloth v. Bustamonte, 412 U.S. 218 (1973).

for drugs in a vehicle usually extends to any part of the vehicle where the drugs might reasonably be hidden,[80] so long as a limitation is not asserted by the consenting party.[81] There is some authority stating that a person may revoke the consent during the process of the search.[82] If the consent is revoked, evidence obtained from a continuing search is not admissible unless justified on other grounds.

To be constitutionally adequate, the consent must be given without force, duress, or compulsion of any kind.[83] Where the government agent used subtle or overt coercion, the consent may be ruled as inadequate and involuntary. In a case in which an officer used pressure to gain consent to search a car, the consent was not valid,[84] and where police officers illegally entered a trailer home and then asked for consent to search, the consent was ruled invalid.[85] The government has the burden of proving that the consent was truly voluntary and unfettered by coercion, whether express or implied.[86] However, the Fourth Amendment does not require that a lawfully seized motorist detainee be affirmatively advised that he or she is "free to go" before his or her later consent to search will be recognized as voluntary.[87]

Some situations exist when the consent to search may not be completely voluntarily given, but evidence seized remains admissible. In the context of probation or parole, a convict may be forced to agree to a reduction or waiver of some Fourth Amendment rights as a condition of release. In one California case,[88] as a condition of release, the parolee was forced to agree in writing to allow any probation or law enforcement officer to conduct a search and seizure of his person, property, place of residence, and any other location where he might have an expectation of privacy at any time, with or without a warrant. A warrantless search of the parolee's person found methamphetamine, and a reviewing court upheld the validity of the consent originally given as a condition of parole. Taking a completely different view based on the Iowa state constitution, the Supreme Court of Iowa held that purported blanket consent authority to search forcibly granted by parolees was considered coercive and could not support a later consent search analysis.[89]

The Court looks at the totality of circumstances when determining whether an alleged consent to search has been voluntary in fact,[90] and if consent is not sufficiently

---

80 Florida v. Jimeno, 500 U.S. 248, 1991 U.S. LEXIS 2910 (1991).

81 United States v. Gregoire, 425 F.3d 872, 880, 2005 U.S. App. LEXIS 21398 (10th Cir. 2005).

82 *Id.* at 881. *See also* United States v. Flores-Ocampo, 173 F. App'x 688, 691, 2006 U.S. App. LEXIS 8367 (10th Cir. 2006), in which a general consent to search a car included gas tank and sun roof area.

83 Schneckloth v. Bustamonte, 412 U.S. 218 (1973).

84 Ohio v. Robinette, 519 U.S. 33 (1996).

85 United States v. King, 2013 U.S. Dist. LEXIS 89047 (E.D. Ky. 2013).

86 Commonwealth v. Rogers, 444 Mass. 234, 344, 827 N.E.2d 669, 677, 2005 Mass. LEXIS 216 (Mass. 2005).

87 Ohio v. Robinette, 519 U.S. 33, 177 S. Ct. 417, 136 L. Ed. 2d 347 (1996).

88 Samson v. California, 547 U.S. 843, 2006 U.S. LEXIS 4885 (2006).

89 State v. Baldon, 829 N.W.2d 785, 789, 790, 2013 Iowa Sup. LEXIS 42 (2013).

90 *See* United States v. Drayton, 536 U.S. 194, 2002 U.S. LEXIS 4420 (2002), in which officers were "working the buses" and obtained consent to search luggage from interstate bus passengers.

proven to be an act of the free will, thus purging the primary taint of the illegal search warrant, then the results of the search must to be suppressed as "fruit of a poisonous tree."[91]

C. Search of a Vehicle that Is Moving or About to Be Moved

Recognizing a difference between the search of a dwelling house, for which a warrant can be readily obtained, and the search of an automobile, ship, wagon, airplane, or other movable object, for which securing a warrant may not be practical because of the mobility of the vehicle, courts have determined that some vehicles may be searched without a warrant as long as probable cause exists.[92] Two requirements must be met in order for a search of this type to be valid: (1) the officer must have probable cause that would justify the issuance of a search warrant if the facts were presented to a judge, and (2) the vehicle must be readily movable. In such a case, the decision concerning whether to seize the vehicle while a warrant is obtained, or to conduct an immediate warrantless search is left to the determination of the officer involved. According to the Supreme Court in *Chambers v. Maroney*, 399 U.S. 42, 51 (1970),

> [W]e see no difference between on the one hand seizing and holding a car before presenting the probable cause issue to a magistrate and on the other hand carrying out an immediate search without a warrant. Given probable cause to search, either course is reasonable under the Fourth Amendment.

Given that a person who owns or leases a motor vehicle generally has an expectation of privacy in that automobile, that person could argue that the exclusionary rule should permit suppression of evidence. The Supreme Court has ruled that a police stop of a motor vehicle results in the seizure of every occupant in the vehicle.[93] Therefore, any occupant has the right to challenge the legality of the stop of the vehicle and may be able to suppress evidence subsequently seized if a court determines that the stop was not justified.

In determining the extent of an automobile search, the United States Supreme Court reconsidered some prior case law governing the scope of the search under the moving vehicle doctrine and held that police may search every part of the vehicle, including closed containers in the trunk, that might conceal the contraband for which

---

91 United States v. Cowdin, 984 F. Supp. 1374 (D. Kan. 1997). In this case, a revolver obtained as a result of a search without voluntary consent was held inadmissible. *See also* Wong Sun v. United States, 371 U.S. 471 (1963).

92 Chambers v. Maroney, 339 U.S. 42, 90 S. Ct. 1975, 26 L. Ed. 2d 419 (1970). The genesis for this theory seems to have been Carroll v. United States, 267 U.S. 132, 1925 U.S. LEXIS 361 (1925), in which police conducted a warrantless search of a moving automobile that had been stopped where there was probable cause to search. See also Wyoming v. Houghton, 526 U.S. 295 (1999), in which the United States Supreme Court, after referring to United States v. Ross, held that police officers with probable cause to search a car may inspect passengers' belongings found in the car that are capable of concealing the object of the search.

93 *See* Brendlin v. California, 551 U.S. 249, 2007 U.S. LEXIS 7897 (2007).

the police have probable cause.[94] However, officers may not search the trunk of a vehicle where there is no probable cause to believe that seizable property is contained within.[95] Under the stop-and-frisk standard, officers may briefly stop, ask questions, and request consent to search when there is a reasonable basis to suspect that criminal activity might be afoot.[96] When subjects fit a drug courier profile, police may stop and talk to occupants of automobiles.[97]

The scope of the search under the moving vehicle doctrine depends upon the object of the search and the places in which there is probable cause to believe the object may be found. Where there is probable cause to search an entire car, it would be permissible to search a woman's purse found within the car.[98] For example, if probable cause exists to believe that a container placed in an automobile contains contraband,[99] the vehicle search theory permits an immediate warrantless seizure and search of the container.[100] Consistent with this concept, an Indiana state trooper properly opened a soap box inside a vehicle without a warrant, after developing probable cause to think that a vehicle contained illegal recreational pharmaceuticals.[101]

As a general rule, the movable vehicle doctrine, which authorizes the search of a vehicle that is in movable condition, applies to automobiles, boats, and airplanes if the criteria are met and if probable cause to search exists. Naturally, probable cause to search exists at the moment the search begins and cannot be based on what contraband might be discovered. Where a driver has been removed from a vehicle and secured away from the vehicle, the vehicle may be warrantlessly searched incident to an arrest when there is reason to believe that the vehicle may contain seizable property *that relates to the reason for the arrest*. No search of the vehicle may occur where no evidence relating to the reason for the arrest is expected.[102]

Some vehicle stops may be initiated on less than probable cause,[103] and some cursory searches may mature into full probable cause vehicle searches. In one case, border patrol officials determined that a vehicle had tripped a sensor on a road typically used by drug smugglers. As a federal official interdicted the minivan, he noticed that the occupants did not want to look at him, and the children had their legs up on some cargo on the backseat floorboards. Probable cause to search did not exist, but the officer followed the *Terry* stop-and-frisk protocol, as applied to motor vehicles, to make a stop and brief inquiry. Following the stop, the story offered by the driver of the heavily

---

94 United States v. Ross, 456 U.S. 798, 1982 U.S. LEXIS 18 (1982).

95 United States v. Jackson, 367 U.S. App. D.C. 320, 415 F.3d 88, 92, 2005 U.S. App. LEXIS 14951 (D.C. Cir. 2005).

96 *See* Alabama v. White, 496 U.S. 325 (1990).

97 Orlenas v. United States, 517 U.S. 690 (1996).

98 Wyoming v. Houghton, 526 U.S. 295 (1999).

99 California v. Acevedo, 500 U.S. 565 (1991).

100 *Id.*

101 United States v. Glover, 2013 U.S. Dist. LEXIS 119254 (S.D. Ind. 2013).

102 *See* Arizona v. Gant, 556 U.S. 332, 2009 U.S. LEXIS 3120 (2009). *See* case in Part II.

103 Alabama v. White, 496 U.S. 325, 1990 U.S. LEXIS 3053 (1990).

loaded minivan did not make sense, and eventually, probable cause developed, allowing a warrantless search that revealed that the driver was smuggling recreational drugs.[104] Various factors considered on an individual basis may not lead to a reasonable basis to suspect criminal activity under the stop-and-frisk standard or to probable cause for a search or arrest, but when considered under a totality of the circumstances, the stop-and-frisk standard may mature, or probable cause for a vehicle search may be present.[105]

D. The Seizure of Evidence When No Search Is Required (Plain View)

The **plain view doctrine** allows seizures of objects that either offend the law by their mere presence or are objects that, under the circumstances, appear to constitute criminal evidence. In an earlier case, *Coolidge v. New Hampshire*, the Court seemed to require that seizures under the plain view doctrine must have been discovered inadvertently from a vantage point where the police officer had the legal right to be.[106] In one sense, the plain view doctrine does not involve a search; the law enforcement officer merely observes the seizable object in full view without any need to conduct a search. The officer must legally occupy a position from which the officer is able to observe the object, and the object's nature must be either incriminating or be evidence that, under the circumstances, is subject to seizure. For example, in one case, a police officer was lawfully inside an apartment investigating a gunshot when he observed expensive electronic equipment that looked out of place in the shabby apartment. He moved one item to secure a serial number from the rear of the unit. This was held to be a search and could not be justified under the plain view doctrine.[107] In a typical situation, the officer is merely on the premises and, unexpectedly, the officer observes an object that seems to indicate that a crime has been committed. For example, the plain view doctrine would come into play when an officer on a domestic call observed white powder and a scale or when a parole officer who was meeting with a parolee observed a gun on a bed.

> **Plain view doctrine** A rule of law creating an exception to the requirement that police officers have a search warrant, when the police, while conducting themselves lawfully (e.g., while patrolling the streets or executing a search warrant for something else), observe incriminating evidence, and it is immediately apparent to the police that they have evidence of a crime. In such a situation, the evidence may be seized without a warrant if the officer physically occupies the place where the contraband is situated.

[104] United States v. Arvizu, 534 U.S. 266, 2002 U.S. LEXIS 490 (2002).
[105] *Id.*
[106] 403 U.S. 443, 469, 1971 U.S. LEXIS 25 (1971).
[107] *See* Arizona v. Hicks, 480 U.S. 321, 1987 U.S. LEXIS 1056 (1987).

The gloss of inadvertence as a requirement of the plain view doctrine ended when the Supreme Court decided *Horton v. California*.[108] In that case, the police executed a warrant at Horton's home in an attempt to locate proceeds from an armed robbery. The warrant mentioned some objects but did not describe a gun that the officers expected to find and did find. The *Horton* Court held that inadvertence was not a necessary condition under this warrant exception. The Court considered the gun to have been lawfully seized, even though its presence was expected. The United States Supreme Court reiterated that the warrantless seizure of an object in plain view is valid if the following conditions are met: (1) the officer did not violate the Fourth Amendment when entering the place where the object was seen; (2) the object's incriminating character was immediately apparent; and (3) the officer had lawful access to the object itself. The *Horton* Court added that the concept of inadvertency as part of this warrant exception was never an essential part of the holding in *Coolidge v. New Hampshire*, even though most plain view doctrine seizures occur due to the unexpected finding of contraband. "The normal Fourth Amendment rule is that items discovered in plain view are admissible if the officers were legitimately on the premises"[109] as long as there was probable cause to seize the evidence at the time it was encountered.

In a Massachusetts case that involved the plain view doctrine,[110] officers observed an automobile being driven erratically and stopped the vehicle. Officers observed that the vehicle was occupied by a female driver, a girl, and the defendant, who was passed out. One officer rousted the defendant and then assisted him from the car. One trooper noticed the butt of a gun protruding from the defendant's jacket pocket, in plain view, so the officer secured the firearm. At the defendant's trial for having a firearm under a felon's disability, he unsuccessfully contended that he had not consented to the roadside stop or search and that the gun was inside his pocket and not in plain view. This case proved to be a classic example of the plain view doctrine; the officer was physically where he had the right to be and observed the firearm, and probable cause existed to seize the firearm.

Officers may not lawfully use the plain view doctrine where they have no lawful access to a defendant's premises. In a Georgia case, officers procured the consent of a landlord to enter a defendant's rented trailer. As the officer opened the door, he observed growing marijuana plants. Using the evidence gathered under the plain view doctrine, the officer procured a search warrant and later seized the plants. The court of appeals held that the plain view doctrine did not produce good evidence because the officer had no legal right to enter the trailer home, given that the right was based on the landlord's "consent," and, therefore, the officer was not lawfully on the premises.[111]

Generally, state and federal courts have agreed that the use of an officer's flashlight to illuminate a darkened area in an automobile does not constitute a search, and thus

---

108 496 U.S. 128, 141, 1990 U.S. LEXIS 2937 (1990).

109 Georgia v. Randolph, 547 U.S. 103, 137, 2006 U.S. LEXIS 2498 (2006). *See* case in Part II.

110 United States v. Clintron, 724 F.3d 32, 34, 2013 U.S. App. LEXIS 14661 (1st Cir. 2013).

111 Looney v. State, 293 Ga. App. 639, 2008 Ga. App. LEXIS 1039 (2008).

triggers no Fourth Amendment protection.[112] One court reasoned that an officer who uses a flashlight for illumination and safety, while peering into the interior of a vehicle during a traffic stop, commits no Fourth Amendment wrong.[113]

E. Seizure of Evidence from Premises Not Protected by the Fourth Amendment (Open Fields)

In 1984, the United States Supreme Court confirmed the rule that only "houses, papers, and effects" are protected by the Constitution and that a search of open fields does not violate the Fourth Amendment.[114] The closing paragraph of the Supreme Court opinion in this case summarizes the decision with these words:

> We conclude that the open fields doctrine, as enunciated in Hester, is consistent with the plain language of the Fourth Amendment and its historical purposes.

While the Constitution protects houses, including the area around a house known as the curtilage,[115] evidence obtained from outside the curtilage is admissible, even if entry amounts to a trespass in the civil or criminal sense. In the case of *United States v. Dunn*, the United States Supreme Court suggested some guidelines that could be applied in determining whether an area is within the curtilage for Fourth Amendment purposes.[116] The *Dunn* Court enumerated four factors to be considered in determining extent-of-curtilage questions:

1. The proximity of the area to the home
2. Whether the area is within an enclosure surrounding the home
3. The nature and uses to which the area is put
4. The steps taken by the resident to protect the area from observation by passersby

Applying these criteria, the Court ruled that a barn, located 50 yards from the house, behind several animal fences, and not within the area enclosed by a fence surrounding the house, was not within the curtilage of the home. Additionally, the government had evidence that the barn was not being used for intimate family purposes.

In a federal case out of Virginia, the prosecutor charged a landowner with taking or possessing migratory birds without a permit in violation of federal law.[117] The property owner had placed traps that snared the migratory birds, which the defendant later killed.

---

112 People v. Brown, 2006 Cal. App. Unpub. LEXIS 4196 (2006).

113 State v. Young, 895 So. 2d 753, 757, 2005 La. App. LEXIS 536 (2005).

114 Oliver v. United States, 466 U.S. 170, 104 S. Ct. 1735, 80 L. Ed. 2d 214 (1984) (reaffirming Hester v. United States, 265 U.S. 57 (1924)).

115 BLACK'S LAW DICTIONARY (9th ed. 2009) defines curtilage as "[t]he land or yard adjoining a house, usu. within an enclosure." At common law, the curtilage is the area around an individual dwelling house that might reasonably be fenced, if a fence were installed.

116 United States v. Dunn, 480 U.S. 294, 107 S. Ct. 1134, 94 L. Ed. 2d 326 (1987). *See also* State v. Moley, 490 N.W.2d 764 (Wis. 1992).

117 United States v. Vankesteren, 2009 U.S. App. LEXIS (4th Cir. 2009).

Evidence in the case came from a surveillance camera placed on the private property by Commonwealth game officials, who had entered the property without a warrant to install the camera. The cameras were a mile or more from the defendant's home and were clearly outside the curtilage. The court of appeals held that the occupier of the land had no expectation of privacy in the open fields and that the use of concealed cameras was not significantly different from observations that government agents might make if they walked on the defendant's land.

Although occurring close to the home, some human conduct indicates that individuals may no longer assert or expect privacy when placing refuse for collection at the curb of their homes. Placing an end to significant inconsistent state and federal court decisions, the United States Supreme Court concluded that the Fourth Amendment does not prohibit the warrantless seizure of garbage and trash left for collection outside of the curtilage.[118] In a California case, the defendant had indicated that he wanted to make no additional use of the trash and that he had abandoned it by placing it at the curb and beyond the curtilage of his home. When the police arranged to have private trash haulers collect the evidence from the trash at the curb in front of the defendant's home, they committed no Fourth Amendment wrong, and the evidence of drug possession and use was properly admitted against the resident defendant.

F. Search by a Private Individual

The Fourth Amendment provisions apply to government officials, not to private individuals who are not acting as agents of the government or with participation or knowledge of any government official. In the case of *United States v. Jacobsen* in 1984, the Supreme Court held that employees of a private carrier who examined a package did not violate the Fourth Amendment; therefore, the evidence obtained in the examination was admissible.[119]

This exception to the warrant requirement applies to private conduct when there is either no official governmental involvement or only minimal entanglement. In order to show that private activity in conducting searches has so much government connection that it cannot be deemed private, "two elements must be shown in order to treat ostensibly private action as a state-sponsored search: (1) the police must have instigated, encouraged, or participated in the search; and (2) the private individual must have engaged in the search with the intent of assisting the police."[120] Private conduct that did not implicate the Fourth Amendment was held to exist when hotel employees smelled burning marijuana and reported it to supervisory staff, who contacted the local police. The police requested that the trash from each room be kept separate and labeled. After police inspected the trash, they obtained a search warrant, using the evidence from the trash pulls. The defendant contended that the hotel employees were acting as police agents, but the reviewing court noted that the hotel employees were asked

118 California v. Greenwood, 486 U.S. 35, 1988 U.S. LEXIS 2279 (1988). *See* the case for a review of lower court decisions.

119 466 U.S. 109, 104 S. Ct. 1652, 80 L. Ed. 2d 85 (1984).

120 United States v. Bruce, 396 F.3d 697, 705, 2005 U.S. App. LEXIS 1712 (6th Cir. 2005).

by the police only to label and not commingle the trash from the respective rooms. In addition, private individuals working at the hotel first contacted the police and not the other way around. The Court held that the evidence obtained had been properly admitted because the evidence had been obtained solely through private conduct.[121] However, if the government initiated the searching process, the activity would probably be considered to be governmental conduct, and the Fourth Amendment would apply.

If a private individual, without the prior knowledge of a law enforcement agent, makes a private search of another person's personal computer and anonymously sends the information to a local police agency, the search of the hard drive will not be considered a search by a government agency and will not be suppressible under the Fourth Amendment.[122] In a similar case, a private individual obtained a videotape that depicted his girlfriend's father engaged in sexual activities with underage females. As the individual who seized the video tape was not operating under police direction, the private search of the videotape did not offend the principles of the Fourth Amendment, and the evidence was properly admitted against the defendant who appeared in the video.[123]

In an early case concerning the status of public school officials, the United States Supreme Court held that teachers and administrators are considered government officials for Fourth Amendment purposes. The Court justified the search of students when there are reasonable grounds for suspecting that the search would turn up evidence that either the law or a rule of the school had been violated.[124] With parental consent, public schoolchildren can be tested for drugs as a condition of participating in extracurricular sports or related academic activities, even in the absence of any individualized suspicion.[125] As a general rule, these results are not used for purposes of criminal prosecution. Even though the Fourth Amendment applies, these searches are considered "reasonable" because the tests cannot be performed unless parents consent and because the purpose of the testing is to reduce drug use by public school students. Private schools are not covered by Fourth Amendment principles and may require students to submit to drug testing consistent with school policy and parental consent.

Probation officers are also considered government officials for Fourth Amendment purposes. As one court recognized, "[i]t is well-settled that conditions that allow probation officers to conduct visits to and searches of the residences of probationers are valid under the Fourth Amendment."[126] In order to be reasonable, the entry must be authorized by law, a regulation, or an agreed-upon condition of probation. The reason may be routine or may involve suspicion or probable cause to believe that the probationer has violated some condition of probation.[127]

---

121 *Id.*

122 United States v. Kline, 112 Fed. Appx. 562, 2004 U.S. App. LEXIS 20759 (9th Cir. 2004), *cert. denied*, 544 U.S. 950, 2005 U.S. LEXIS 2818 (2005).

123 State v. Robinson, 653 S.E.2d 889, 2007 N.C. App. LEXIS 2556 (N.C. 2007).

124 New Jersey v. T.L.O., 469 U.S. 325, 105 S. Ct. 733, 83 L. Ed. 2d 720 (1985).

125 Board of Education v. Earls, 536 U.S. 822, 2002 U.S. LEXIS 4882 (2002).

126 Cass v. County of Suffolk, 2005 U.S. Dist. LEXIS 8623 (E.D.N.Y. 2005).

127 *Id.*

In some jurisdictions, a private police officer may carry sufficient authority of the state so that the officer must comply with the Fourth Amendment. In Michigan, private security officers employed by a casino possessed state-granted powers to detain errant patrons, as well as full arrest powers. When a dispute involving the Fourth Amendment arose, the trial court held that, as a matter of law, the security officer was a state actor subject to the restraints of the Fourth Amendment.[128]

G. Search After Lawful Impoundment

Impoundment Seizing and taking into custody of the law or a court.

Inventory searches have been approved when objects or vehicles come into the control of police following an **impoundment**, but inventory searches are improper and will not produce admissible evidence unless the police department has a policy regulating such searches.[129] The general rule is that "[e]vidence discovered during an inventory search conducted pursuant to standardized procedures is admissible, unless the police acted in bad faith or for the sole purpose of investigation."[130] Often the police have the duty and responsibility to impound a car that has been abandoned, is blocking traffic, is illegally parked, or has been left without a driver after the driver has been arrested. In such instances, law or departmental regulations usually require the officer to search the vehicle and make a list of its contents before impounding it. Provided that the police department has and follows an inventory policy routinely and not just when police think something incriminating might be discovered, evidence seized during an inventory search will be admissible against the occupier of the vehicle.[131] The issues of the reasonableness of inventory seizures reached the United States Supreme Court in the case of *Colorado v. Bertine* in 1987.[132] In approving the opening of closed containers found in a van that was lawfully impounded, the Court held that inventory searches served important government interests. An inventory search protects the citizen from loss of property by police or their agents, while it protects the police from false claims of loss. In addition, an inventory search prevents police from harboring a vehicle that might contain

128 Romanski v. Detroit Entertainment, L.L.C., 428 F.3d 629, 635, 2005 U.S. App. LEXIS 23336 (6th Cir. 2005).

129 Florida v. Wells, 495 U.S. 1 (1990). *See also* State v. Hensley, 2005 Minn. App. LEXIS 233 (2005), in which an inventory search did not produce admissible evidence because the sheriff's department had no inventory policy.

130 United States v. Thompson, 2006 U.S. App. LEXIS 12734 (3d Cir. 2006).

131 South Dakota v. Opperman, 328 U.S. 364, 96 S. Ct. 3092, 49 L. Ed. 2d 1000 (1976); Arkansas v. Sullivan, 532 U.S. 769, 2001 U.S. LEXIS 4118 (2001), in which the court approved an inventory search following the driver's arrest.

132 Colorado v. Bertine, 479 U.S. 367, 107 S. Ct. 738, 93 L. Ed. 2d 739 (1987). *See also* Florida v. Wells, 495 U.S. 1, 110 S. Ct. 1632, 109 L. Ed. 2d 1 (1990), in which the United States Supreme Court discussed the necessity of having a departmental policy regarding inventory searches, and United States v. McKnight, 17 F.3d 1139 (8th Cir. 1994).

harmful cargo, contraband, or dangerous items, and it prevents vandalism to the vehicle. Two caveats apply here:

1. The police must follow standard procedures in carrying out the search.
2. The police must perform the inventory search for the purpose of actually obtaining an inventory and not for the sole purpose of conducting a criminal investigation.[133]

In following a departmental inventory search policy, police may look for incriminating items that might be present, as long as their sole purpose is not to investigate a crime.[134] Therefore, police may not use the inventory search theory as a justification for supporting a search that was simply a search for incriminating evidence.

H. Stop-and-Frisk Search

Any discussion concerning the admissibility of search and seizure evidence must include a consideration of the stop-and-frisk limited search. In 1968, the United States Supreme Court authorized the admission of evidence obtained by a police officer who stated that, in the incident in question, he was "frisking" a person because he suspected that person was "casing a job."[135] The Court explained the limitation of such a seizure in this language:

> The sole justification of the search in the present situation is the protection of the police officer and others nearby, and it must, therefore, be confined in scope to an intrusion reasonably designed to discover guns, knives, clubs, or other hidden instruments for the assault of the police officer.

As authorized by the *Terry v. Ohio* case, a frisk is limited to a search for weapons when an officer has reasonable suspicion that the person with whom he is dealing may be armed and dangerous. When there is no reasonable suspicion that a subject may be armed and dangerous, a frisk does not appear to be warranted. When an officer who has made a valid *Terry* stop has reasonable suspicion that the person with whom he or she is dealing may be armed, the officer may frisk the outer garments of the detainee to search for weapon-like lumps. Applying the *Terry* reasoning, the Supreme Court upheld the investigatory stop of a motorist and the search of a paper bag located in his car.[136] The Court reasoned that the protective search of the driver and of the passenger compartment was reasonable under the principles articulated in *Terry*. A pat-down may be conducted where the facts would allow a reasonable officer to conclude that the person may be armed or have arms close at hand and, as a result, may pose a serious and present danger to the safety of the officer. The Supreme Court held that if a *Terry* detainee refuses to identify him- or herself, and where state law permits, the detainee may be arrested

---

133 State v. Hensley, 2005 Minn. App. LEXIS 233 (2005).

134 United States v. Kennedy, 427 F.3d 1136, 1143, 2005 U.S. App. LEXIS 23962 (8th Cir. 2005).

135 Terry v. Ohio, 392 U.S. 1, 88 S. Ct. 1868, 20 L. Ed. 2d 720 (1968).

136 Michigan v. Long, 463 U.S. 1032, 103 S. Ct. 3469, 77 L. Ed. 2d 1201 (1983), *and see* California v. Acevedo, 500 U.S. 565 (1991).

and subjected to a search incident to a lawful arrest.[137] In that case, a police officer received a phone call reporting that a man was engaged in an assault on a woman inside a red and silver pick-up truck on a particular road. When he arrived, the male subject was not cooperative, said that he had done nothing wrong, and refused to produce any identification or to orally identify himself. The officer arrested the driver for refusing to produce identification. According to the Court, the arrest was proper, and any evidence obtained in the search incident to the arrest would be admissible against the motorist.

The *Terry* rule was also applied to a decision that law enforcement agents may temporarily detain luggage on reasonable suspicion, which is less than probable cause, that the luggage contains narcotics.[138] The Supreme Court noted that, if an officer's observation leads him or her to reasonably suspect that a traveler may be carrying luggage that contains narcotics, the officer may detain the luggage briefly to investigate the circumstances that aroused his or her suspicion, provided that the investigative detention is properly limited in scope. In this case, the 90-minute time span between the luggage seizure and its exposure to a search by a trained narcotics detection dog was unreasonable under the circumstances; therefore, the Court suppressed the evidence.

In the *Terry* case, the United States Supreme Court approved the practice of frisking suspects on less than probable cause when there were reasonable grounds to believe that criminal activity might be afoot. The Court noted, however, that the frisk had to be confined in scope to an intrusion reasonably designed to discover guns, clubs, knives, or other hidden instruments for the assault of the police officer. Several years after that decision was handed down by the Supreme Court, the Court considered whether, while in the process of searching for a weapon on a person, officers could seize other articles that were not dangerous, so long as the other articles came into plain view or under the "plain feel" doctrine.[139]

In the case of *Minnesota v. Dickerson*, the officer observed the suspect's seemingly evasive actions when approached by police officers and the fact that he had just left a building known for narcotics trafficking. Based on these observations, the officer decided to investigate further and ordered the suspect to submit to a pat-down search because the suspect might be a drug trafficker who was armed. The officer who conducted the search testified that he felt a small lump in the suspect's jacket, and after rolling it between his thumb and fingers, he believed the lump to be crack cocaine. The search then revealed a small bag of cocaine. According to the Court, the rolling of the crack between the thumb and index finger constituted a search beyond the scope of a frisk, and the rock of cocaine should not have been admitted at his trial.[140] In a different case,[141] an officer who had responded to another officer's traffic stop

---

137 *See* Hiibel v. Sixth Judicial District Court, 542 U.S. 177, 2004 U.S. LEXIS 4385 (2004).

138 United States v. Place, 462 U.S. 696, 103 S. Ct. 2637, 77 L. Ed. 2d 110 (1983).

139 Minnesota v. Dickerson, 508 U.S. 366, 1993 U.S. LEXIS 4018 (1993).

140 *Id.*

141 State v. Bennett, 2008 Ohio 3969, 2008 Ohio App. LEXIS 3349 (2008). People v. Sanders, 2006 Mich. App. LEXIS 2 (2006).

observed a man across the street watching the event. As the officer walked over to the traffic stop, the man across the street turned away and put his hand in his mouth. Two officers walked over to the subject to frisk him, and at that time, one officer observed drugs in the subject's mouth. Under the circumstances, there was no reason for a stop or a frisk, because the subject's behavior did not appear to be criminal, and the trial court properly suppressed the evidence from trial.

From the foregoing, it is obvious that some evidence, such as the rock of cocaine in the *Dickerson* case, obtained in an illegal search is logically relevant and material to a case, and as a result, such evidence would be admissible under the rules of evidence if no other considerations were involved. For constitutional reasons and consistent with Court-generated rules designed to enforce constitutional provisions, some evidence cannot be admitted. Evidence will be excluded if the search is illegal or if the search does not come within one of the recognized exceptions.

§ 16.4 Exclusion of Evidence Obtained by Illegal Wiretapping or Eavesdropping

At one time, the United States Supreme Court refused to include wiretapping within the scope of the Fourth Amendment. In the case of *Olmstead v. United States*,[142] after reviewing the historical context in which the Fourth Amendment was adopted, the Court concluded that the proscription was limited to search and seizure of material things, and therefore, it did not apply to evidence procured by the sense of hearing. However, in a later decision, *Nardone v. United States*,[143] the Supreme Court held that, although wiretapping did not violate the Constitution, it did violate the Federal Communications Act of 1934, and the Court ruled that evidence obtained by officers who violated the provisions of this Act was inadmissible in federal court. This rule was not originally applied to the state courts, but many states adopted the rule, either by legislation or by court interpretation. In a landmark decision in 1967, *Katz v. United States*,[144] the Supreme Court rejected the contention that surveillance without trespass and without the seizure of material fell outside the purview of the Constitution. This and other decisions make it clear that wiretapping and electronic or mechanical eavesdropping are within the protection of the Fourth Amendment.

In 1968, after several efforts, Congress finally enacted a comprehensive scheme designed to regulate eavesdropping and wiretapping on a uniform nationwide basis.[145] This law, as amended, must be studied thoroughly in order to understand the requirements for wiretapping or eavesdropping. Broadly speaking, the interception of wire or

---

142 277 U.S. 438, 48 S. Ct. 564, 72 L. Ed. 944 (1928).

143 302 U.S. 379, 58 S. Ct. 275, 82 L. Ed. 314 (1937).

144 389 U.S. 347, 88 S. Ct. 507, 19 L. Ed. 2d 576 (1967).

145 *See* Omnibus Crime Control Act of 1968, ch. 119, 18 U.S.C. § 2510 (amended by PUB. L. NO. 99–508 (1986), and codified at 18 U.S.C. § 2510 *et seq.*).

oral communications is illegal unless conducted in conformity with statutory procedures. To be admissible, evidence obtained by wiretapping or eavesdropping must comply with the standards established by federal law, as interpreted by the courts.

Title 18 of the United States Code §§ 3121-3126 sets forth the procedures for electronic interception of data using pen registers and trap and trace devices as authorized by a warrant. Federal warrants may be obtained pursuant to § 3121 *et seq.* and under the Foreign Intelligence Surveillance Act of 1978 (50 U.S.C. § 1801 *et seq.*). Title 18 of the United States Code § 2511 *et seq.* contains the general federal law that prohibits the interception and disclosure of wire, oral, or electronic communications, except when in compliance with the detailed statutory procedure. § 2516 governs the procedures by which a federal investigative agency may apply for an order authorizing the interception of a wire or oral communication. In effect, this portion of the statute authorizes designated federal and state officers to apply for warrants to intercept wire or oral communications, under procedures similar to the process for traditional search warrants.

In addition, some evidence obtained by means of wiretapping and eavesdropping is admissible if one party to the conversation consents. Section 2511(2)(c) authorizes federal law enforcement officers to intercept wire, oral, or electronic communications with the consent of one party and without a court order, unless a state statute prohibits such interception.

While federal law and some state laws include an exception that allows interception of communications if one party consents, the consent must be voluntary.[146] It is not voluntary if it is coerced by either explicit or implicit means or by an implied threat or covert force. Where federal prisoners are permitted to make telephone calls, the prisoner must consent to having the calls recorded, or telephone privileges will not be extended. In one case, the prisoner continued to run a heroin importation ring using a prison phone, following his imprisonment for prior crimes.[147] The phone calls that the prisoner made were monitored with his consent, and some of the tapes of the calls were used at his subsequent trial for conspiracy to distribute heroin. The trial court and the court of appeals rejected his contention that the government taping violated section 2515 of the Federal Wiretap Act,[148] and the phone evidence should have been excluded from his trial. The defendant offered the theory that consent was not sufficient to allow admission, and the conversations should have been excluded because they were not collected in the ordinary course of law enforcement. According to the Court of Appeals for the Fifth Circuit, consent by one party is all that is required to render a telephone recording admissible in a federal court.

Cases interpreting and explaining the provisions of the federal law have been voluminous. When law enforcement officers circumvent the requirements of the wiretap authorization statute, courts must suppress evidence obtained from the illegal wiretap.

---

146 United States v. Antoon, 933 F.2d 200 (3d Cir.), *cert. denied*, 502 U.S. 907, 112 S. Ct. 300, 116 L. Ed. 2d 243 (1991).

147 United States v. Moore, 452 F.3d 382, 2006 U.S. App. LEXIS 14152 (5th Cir. 2006).

148 18 U.S.C. § 2515.

For example, in a drug conspiracy case, a state judge had issued a wiretap order for the defendants' digital beepers, which required the police to record and store the data recovered on tape or another storage device. The police did not follow the court order, instead recording the data recovered in handwriting. Due to the police's disregard of the judge's order, the evidence was suppressed. The federal government wanted to try the defendants for the same act under federal law, and the defendants contended that the evidence should be suppressed because 18 U.S.C. § 2510 contains virtually identical language to the state statute violated by state officers, and suppression is a remedy when the government violates the law. The federal district judge suppressed the evidence because the government failed to follow the judicial order, and if the evidence was allowed, it could encourage law enforcement officials to sidestep other requirements for electronic eavesdropping.[149]

While states may enact wiretap and eavesdrop statutes that are more restrictive than the federal statutes, they may not enforce statutes that are less restrictive. But if the federal government's wiretap procedure complied with the federal law, evidence obtained thereby is admissible in federal courts, even if those procedures violated the more restrictive state law and the evidence would be excludable if offered in a state court.[150]

Pen register An electronic device that, when properly connected to the telephone system, has the ability to record all the outgoing telephone numbers placed from that telephone.

Detecting and recording phone numbers and other data associated with phone communications were originally viewed as not violating any expectation of privacy possessed by users of telecommunication facilities,[151] and law enforcement agencies were free to collect such data. Recognizing that collecting the information might constitute a violation of privacy, Congress addressed the **pen register** and the trap-and-trace device issue to prohibit the warrantless use of such devices, subject to limited exceptions.[152] Later, as part of the USA Patriot Act, Congress modified 18 U.S.C. § 3121, redefining pend register and, thereby, expanding the coverage of pen registers and similar devices. Under the revised statute, "the term 'pen register' means a device or process which records or decodes dialing, routing, addressing, or signaling information transmitted by an instrument or facility from which a wire or electronic communication is transmitted, provided, however, that such information shall not include the contents of any communication."[153] Presently, pen registers and trap-and-trace devices must be used with court orders where the goal is to obtain cell phone numbers, web addresses, e-mail addresses, and similar noncontent data. The statute defined a

149 United States v. Amanuel, 418 F. Supp. 2d 244; 2005 U.S. Dist. LEXIS 30108 (W.D.N.Y. 2005), *Adhered to*, on reconsideration by United States v. Amanuel, 418 F. Supp. 2d 244, 2006 U.S. Dist. LEXIS 3890 (W.D.N.Y. 2006).

150 United States v. Padilla-Pena, 129 F.3d 457 (8th Cir. 1997).

151 Smith v. Maryland, 442 U.S. 375 (1979).

152 18 U.S.C. § 3121.

153 18 U.S.C. § 3127(3).

trap-and-trace device as "a device or process which captures the incoming electronic or other impulses which identify the originating number or other dialing, routing, addressing, and signaling information reasonably likely to identify the source of a wire or electronic communication," but the captured information may not contain the contents of any communication.[154] *One possible limitation concerns cell phone tower usage, which could reveal where the person making or taking the call was located. In a federal case, the government sought such evidence, but was rebuffed by a federal district court in 2005.*[155]

In the case of *United States v. Jones* in 2012, the Supreme Court determined that global positioning satellite (GPS) tracking devices that government agents attach to motor vehicles require probable cause and warrants.[156] Prior to this case, state and federal courts had issued different rulings concerning the use of GPS tracking devices attached to motor vehicles.

In *Jones*, District of Columbia officials became interested in the defendant's activity with respect to potential drug trafficking and narcotics sales, and the auhtorities obtained a warrant to attach a GPS tracking device to a motor vehicle frequently driven by Mr. Jones, though owned by his spouse. The warrant had been issued by a District of Columbia federal court and allowed the tracking device to be installed within 10 days, but federal officials did not install the device until 11 days had elapsed, completing the installation in the state of Maryland and not within the District of Columbia. Federal agents tracked vehicle's movements for 28 days. By monitoring the GPS system's communication through an attached cell phone system, they were able to determine the vehicle's location within 50 to 100 feet, and, along with other evidence, the defendant's travels indicated that he was involved with drug trafficking. The warrant could not be considered valid, because the time for its execution had expired, and it was served outside the jurisdiction of the court that issued it. At the subsequent conspiracy and drug trafficking trial, the GPS-derived data, along with other evidence, resulted in the defendant's conviction, however, and he was sentenced to life imprisonment. The United States Court of Appeal for the District of Columbia reversed the conviction, and the prosecution received certiorari from the Supreme Court.

Writing for a unanimous Court, Justice Scalia indicated that the government physically occupied private property [the Jeep] for the purpose of obtaining information that was considered a search within the meaning of the Fourth Amendment. The District of Columbia contended that Mr. Jones had no expectation of privacy on the undercarriage of his motor vehicle, but the unanimous Supreme Court decided otherwise, although the justices did not all agree on the precise logic.[157] The Court did find that the use of the GPS-and-cell-phone tracking system constituted a search. Justice Scalia rejected a government argument that the placing of the GPS device was like a police officer

---

154 *Id.* § (4).

155 In re Application of the United States of America for an Order Authorizing the Installation and Use of a Pen Register, 402 F. Supp. 2d 597 (D. Md. 2005).

156 United States v. Jones, 132 S.Ct. 945, 2012 U.S. LEXIS 1063 (2012). See case in Part II, Chapter 16.

157 *Id.*

entering an open field where no expectation of privacy would exist. In addition, Justice Scalia distinguished a couple of prior cases that dealt with government-installed tracking beepers placed inside objects that came into the possession of defendants as not being controlling in this case.[158] The Court did not accept the government's contention that, even if the use of the device was considered a search, it was a reasonable search, and the evidence was properly admitted at the trial court. The Court refused to consider the government's contention, because the prosecution had not advanced that argument at trial or in briefs below the Supreme Court. The reversal of the criminal case against Mr. Jones and his co-defendants by the Court of Appeals was upheld when the Supreme Court affirmed the lower court's judgment.

While a future prosecutor might argue that the use of a GPS system without a warrant might be legal under the Fourth Amendment, the better practice would be to obtain a warrant and follow the guidelines of the Supreme Court in *United States v. Jones*. If the evidence is obtained in violation of the federal Fourth Amendment, the *Mapp* exclusionary rule prevents admission into court to prove guilt.[159]

Federal statutes relating to cellular phone usage generally follow the federal wiretap act and the *Mapp* rule with respect to inclusion or exclusion of seized evidence of content voice transmissions. However, cellular phones generate significant amounts of data, when compared to traditional telephone land lines, giving in federal and state authorities a potential treasure trove of information concerning usage and location, even when a law enforcement agent is not interested in intercepting the telephone conversations. Until recently, many criminals appeared to be ignorant of the interceptable data produced by cell phones used in their enterprises. In one federal prosecution, the defendant used to pay-as-you-go cellular phones and traditional cell phones to facilitate his transportation of drugs between Arizona and Tennessee.[160] The large-scale operation used some phones that were identified with the defendant and other phones that were so-called "throwaway phones," for which a person need not give his own, or even a real name, to acquire. Federal agents, doing drug undercover work, managed to discover some of the practices this particular defendant followed to move drugs across the country, and federal agents became aware that he was using cellular telephones to facilitate the transportation. A federal magistrate judge then issued federal wiretap warrants for some of the phones used by the defendant and his associates. The judicial official authorized the phone company to release subscriber information, cell site information, GPS real-time location, and "ping" data for the phones in order to determine locations and routes that the defendant was using to transport his drugs. With help of the cellular phone service, the agents were able to "ping" the phones to determine location of the phones near the drugs and ultimately made multiple arrests. Despite the defendant's contention that the

---

[158] See United States v. Knotts, 460 U.S. 276, 1983 U.S. LEXIS 135 (1983) and United States v. Karo, 468 U.S. 705, 1984 U.S. LEXIS 148 (1984).

[159] For further discussions of the use of wiretap and eavesdrop evidence see KANOVITZ, CONSTITUTIONAL LAW (13th ed. 2012). *See also* WALKER AND HEMMENS, LEGAL GUIDE FOR POLICE: CONSTITUTIONAL ISSUES (8th ed. 2008).

[160] United States v. Skinner, 680 F.3d 772, 2012 U.S. App. LEXIS 16920 (6th Cir. 2012).

GPS evidence resulting from the "pinging" of the phones violated his constitutional rights, the trial court determined that the GPS location information emitted from cell phones did not constitute a Fourth Amendment search and that he had no expectation of privacy with respect to the GPS information that revealed the location of his drug activity. Although intercept warrants were procured in this case, according to the reviewing court, the defendant had no expectation of privacy in the data given off by his voluntarily procured pay-as-you-go cell phone. The court noted, "If a tool used to transport contraband gives off a signal that can be tracked for location, certainly the police can track the signal. The law cannot hold that a criminal is entitled to rely on the expected untrackability of his tools."[161] In a separate case within a different federal circuit, a trial court approved the use of a warrantless emergency "ping" designed to locate an armed and dangerous drug dealer and murder suspect.[162] The concern was that, after the homicide occurred, the potential defendant might encounter civilians or law enforcement officials with deadly results. The Sprint Nextel cell company cooperated with law enforcement agents, "pinged" the potential defendant's phone, and revealed his location, which resulted in his arrest.[163] If the Supreme Court of the United States eventually adopts the principle that no one has an expectation of privacy concerning metadata generated by cell phones, law enforcement interests will have been enhanced, but this must be balanced with the requirements of the Fourth Amendment.

§ 16.5 Exclusion of Confessions Obtained in Violation of Constitutional Provisions

Although a confession or an admission of guilt would seem to be the best kind of relevant evidence, evidence of a confession is not admissible in many cases because the officer obtaining the confession violated certain constitutional provisions. In making a determination of whether a confession has been voluntarily taken consistent with the Fifth Amendment, the ultimate question to be answered is "whether, under the totality of the circumstances, the challenged confession was obtained in a manner compatible with the requirements of the Constitution."[164] In most instancses, a confession that has been secured following a violation of the Fourth Amendment cannot be used against the person due to the Fourth Amendment exclusionary rule, unless the confession can be shown to be an act of free will sufficient to purge the taint of the original illegality.[165]

---

161 *Id.* at 777.

162 United States v. Caraballo, 2013 U.S. Dist. LEXIS 112739 (D. Vt. 2013).

163 See 18 U.S.C. § 2702(c)(4). Federal law allows cell phone companies to provide information concerning a customer to a governmental entity if the company believes in good faith that an emergency involving a danger of death or serious bodily injury requires immediate disclosure.

164 Miller v. Fenton, 474 U.S. 104, 112, 1985 U.S. LEXIS 144 (1985).

165 Kaupp v. Texas, 538 U.S. 626, 632, 2003 U.S. LEXIS 3670 (2003). An illegal arrest without probable cause quickly followed by a confession will ordinarily result in the confession being suppressed under the Fourth Amendment.

It is essential that both federal and state laws be examined when considering the admissibility rules. Although the federal courts have established minimum standards to be applied, states may employ more stringent standards concerning the admissibility of confessions than the due process requirements pronounced in federal cases. Less stringent state standards are prohibited, however.[166]

A. The Free and Voluntary Rule

In early common law, courts permitted the use of admissions or confessions as evidence of guilt despite the fact that they were products of force or duress. The rule allowing the admissibility of such evidence was abandoned because experience indicated that persons accused of a crime would admit to committing the crime in order to avoid torture. As a result, the courts developed what came to be known as the "free and voluntary" rule.

Free and voluntary rule The confession of a person accused of crime is admissible against the accused only if the accused freely and voluntarily makes that confession, without fear, duress, or compulsion in its inducement, and with full knowledge of the nature and consequences of the confession.

The **free and voluntary rule** states that the confession of a person accused of crime is admissible against the accused only if the accused freely and voluntarily makes that confession, without fear, duress, or compulsion in its inducement. Excluding coerced confessions made logical sense because involuntary confessions might not be reliable, and courts insisted on the requirement of voluntariness because the Fifth Amendment, which required that no person shall be compelled in a criminal case to be a witness against himself, seemed to dictate the rejection of coerced confessions.[167] *Within the trial context, when a defendant contests the voluntariness of a confession, the burden to prove whether the confession was voluntarily and freely given rests upon the prosecution.*[168] *A determination of the voluntariness of a confession requires that the trial court consider various factors, including the defendant's age, intelligence, and level of education. The court must factor into the decision the length of the defendant's detention and the length and nature of the interrogation, whether the police advised the defendant of constitutional rights, and whether the defendant had been subject to any physical coercion.*[169] *Additional considerations may include the location of the interrogation, as well as the suspect's education, mental health, and physical condition.*[170]

---

166 Griffin v. State, 230 Ga. App. 318, 496 S.E.2d 480 (1998).

167 Bram v. United States, 168 U.S. 532, 18 S. Ct. 187, 42 L. Ed. 2d 568 (1897).

168 United States v. Jett, 2006 U.S. Dist. LEXIS 27829 (N.D. Ind. 2006) (citing Lego v. Twomey, 404 U.S. 477, 489, 1972 U.S. LEXIS 100 (1972)).

169 United States v. Lopez, 437 F.3d 1059, 1063, 2006 U.S. App. LEXIS 4052 (2006).

170 Withrow v. Williams, 507 U.S. 680, 693, 1993 U.S. LEXIS 2980 (1993).

Although the free and voluntary rule was formulated more than a century ago, the courts continue to define the rule. In 1991, the United States Supreme Court upheld the reversal of a murder conviction by Arizona's top court on the ground that the defendant had been coerced into a confession. A fellow inmate, who was working for the government inside the prison, offered protection from harm from other inmates if the defendant confessed to the government's inmate agent. The Supreme Court of Arizona held that the first confession had been involuntarily given under coercion,[171] because without the confession, the abuse by fellow inmates would have continued.

The test for the voluntariness of a confession is whether, under the totality of circumstances, the statement was made freely, without compulsion or inducement, with consideration given to the characteristics of the accused and the details of the interrogation. Under the totality of the circumstances, the "[f]actors to be considered include: the defendant's age, intelligence, background, experience, mental capacity, education and physical condition at the time of questioning, the legality and duration of the detention, the duration of the questioning, and any physical or mental abuse by the police, including any threats or promises. No single factor is dispositive."[172]

In 1985, the United States Supreme Court reaffirmed its authority to review state cases in which the confession was admitted as part of the evidence. The Court noted that the voluntariness of a confession is a matter that is subject to review by federal courts.[173] Although, in the case in question, the New Jersey Supreme Court had determined that the petitioner's confession was voluntary, the United States Supreme Court announced that it was not bound by a state court finding as to voluntariness and would reconsider the facts.

Regardless of which historical approach is most persuasive, a judicial or extrajudicial confession obtained by force, duress, or promises of reward should not be admitted.[174] The issue to be determined in each case is whether the defendant's will was overborne at the time that the defendant made the confession.[175]

For example, the Ninth Circuit Court of Appeal determined that a defendant's confession should have excluded because it could not have been considered voluntary, where the federal agents clearly indicated that if he did not cooperate and talk, that he

---

171 Arizona v. Fulminante, 499 U.S. 279 (1991).

172 Bridges v. Chambers, 447 F.3d 994, 997, 2006 U.S. App. LEXIS 11763 (7th Cir. 2006), quoting People v. Bridges, 2003 Ill. App. LEXIS 888 (2003).

173 Miller v. Fenton, 474 U.S. 104, 106 S. Ct. 445, 88 L. Ed. 2d 405 (1985).

174 The United States Supreme Court in the case of Arizona v. Fulminante, 499 U.S. 279, 113 L. Ed. 2d 302, 111 S. Ct. 1246 (1991), ruled that defendants whose coerced confessions were improperly used as evidence are not always entitled to a new trial. The use of such confessions may be considered "harmless error" if other trial evidence was sufficient to convict the defendant. In this case, the Supreme Court affirmed the Arizona Supreme Court's decision that harmless error analysis could not be used to save the conviction, because a potentially admissible second confession was tainted by the first confession, which was deemed illegally taken. The Court remanded the case for a new trial without the use of the first confession.

175 United States v. Yukins, 444 F.3d 713, 719, 2006 U.S. App. LEXIS 8160 (6th Cir. 2006).

would receive a harsher sentence and other treatment.[176] A different Court of Appeals concluded that government agents are permitted to make some representations to a defendant, and may discuss cooperation without making any subsequent confession involuntary.[177] However, in the event that an involuntary confession has been erroneously admitted, any conviction resulting from the admission should be tested by the harmless error standard. Generally, a court must be able to conclude that, even if a coerced confession had not been admitted, the verdict would be the same, tested by the standard of beyond a reasonable doubt.[178]

Judges in various courts have often disagreed as to the amount of evidence required to determine whether a confession is voluntary. When an allegation has been made and some evidence demonstrated, the prosecution has the burden of proof to demonstrate that the confession was given freely and voluntarily. In *Lego v. Twomey*,[179] the judge in the lower court found the confession voluntary "beyond a reasonable doubt," and the defendant argued that this made the admission of the confession erroneous. The Supreme Court disagreed, however. The Court explained that the defendant is presumed innocent, and that the burden falls on the prosecution to prove guilt beyond a reasonable doubt. However, the Court continued, "[t]his is not the same burden that applies in determining the admissibility of a confession." The Court agreed that the prosecution must prove the confession to be free and voluntary by a preponderance of the evidence, but that it was not required to prove the confession to be free and voluntary "beyond a reasonable doubt."

B. The Delay in Arraignment Rule

Under *Riverside v. McLaughlin*, when police make a warrantless arrest, the arrestee must be taken before a judicial official for a determination of probable cause within 48 hours. If a warrant has provided the basis for arrest or if the arrest followed an indictment by a grand jury, a judicial official need not make a second determination of probable cause. When a person has been arrested without any judicial involvement or grand jury action, it becomes imperative that a judicial official make a decision regarding whether probable cause exists within the allotted time.[180] In *Corley v. United States*,[181] federal officials arrested the defendant but did not present him to a judicial official for almost 30 hours, during which he made inculpatory statements. Federal Rule of Criminal Procedure 5 requires that federal law enforcement officials take any arrestee to a judicial official within a reasonable time. Federal prosecutors

176 United States v. Casillas, 2013 U.S. App. LEXIS 17098 (9th Cir. 2013).

177 United States v. Buensalida, 2013 U.S. App. LEXIS 16332 (4th Cir.2013).

178 See Arizona v. Fulminante, 400 U.S. 279, 1991 U.S. LEXIS 1854 (1991). But see State v. Cramer, 129 Haw. 296, 2013 Haw. LEXIS 151 (2013), where Hawai'i considers admission of an involuntary confession to be reversible error without any consideration of the harmless error rule.

179 Lego v. Twomey, 404 U.S. 477, 92 S. Ct. 619, 30 L. Ed. 2d 618 (1972).

180 Riverside v. McLaughlin, 500 U.S. 44 (1991).

181 Corley v. United States, 556 U.S. 303; 129 S. Ct. 1558; 173 L. Ed. 2d 443; (2009) U.S. LEXIS 2512.

Delay in arraignment rule This rule provides that, if there has been a delay in bringing the accused person before a magistrate, and if a confession has been obtained during this unnecessary delay, the confession may not be admitted, even though voluntarily made.

contended that the defendant's confession should be admissible because it was voluntarily given by traditional measures. The government cited a section of federal law that seemed to indicate admissibility, but the Supreme Court ruled that the confession was not admissible based on Federal Rule 5 and the *McNabb-Mallory* rule.[182] Older case law gave rise to the concept that an unreasonable delay required the suppression of a confession, and the Supreme Court felt that Rule 5, read in conjunction with the *McNabb-Mallory* rule, required that the confession had to be excluded where the **delay in arraignment rule** had been violated.

C. *The* Miranda *Rule*

The Supreme Court expanded restrictions concerning the use of unwarned confessions and admissions, by limiting their use as evidence in 1966. The confessions in *Miranda v. Arizona* and its three companion cases were declared inadmissible by the Supreme Court, because the suspects were not given the constitutionally required warnings prior to being interrogated. The Supreme Court held that, for a confession or an inculpatory statement to be deemed admissible, the person who has been taken into custody or otherwise deprived of his or her freedom of action in any significant way must be warned before questioning that (1) the individual has a right to remain silent; (2) if the subject does make a statement, anything he or she says can and will be used against him or her in court; (3) the individual has the right to have an attorney present or to consult with an attorney; and (4) if he or she cannot afford an attorney, one will be appointed prior to any questioning if he or she so desires.[183]

Although the earlier cases interpreting the requirements of *Miranda* held that the warning must be given in exact terms, as stated in the case, the Supreme Court has retreated from that position in recent cases. In a state case, Florida v. Powell,[184] police officers read an arrestee the standard Tampa Police Department *Miranda* warning:

> You have the right to remain silent. If you give up the right to remain silent, anything you say can be used against you in court. You have the right to talk to a lawyer before answering any of our questions. If you cannot afford to hire a lawyer, one will be appointed for you without cost and before any questioning. You have the right to use any of these rights at any time you want during this interview.[185]

---

182 *Id.* This rule provides that, subject to some qualifications, a federal defendant's confession is inadmissible if given after an unreasonable delay in bringing him before a federal judge or magistrate judge. See McNabb v. United States, 318 U.S. 332 (1943) and Mallory v. United States, 354 U.S. 449 (1957).

183 Miranda v. Arizona, 384 U.S. 436, 16 L. Ed. 2d 694, 86 S. Ct. 1602 (1966).

184 Florida v. Powell, 559 U.S. 83, 130 S. Ct. 1195, 2010 U.S. LEXIS 1898 (2010).

185 *Id.*, at 83.

Florida courts held for the arrestee because they concluded the warning did not inform him adequately of his right to have an attorney present throughout all the interrogation, but the United States Supreme Court disagreed and reversed the state courts. The Court determined that the advice given to the defendant, although not containing clear language, combined to adequately convey to the defendant that he could consult an attorney prior to any questioning and that he could invoke the right at any time.

There are many occasions when police encounter individuals who are well aware of the substance of the *Miranda* warnings and have heard them on numerous occasions. However, even when an arrestee states that he "knows" the warnings, police must administer the warnings; otherwise, the oral evidence obtained will generally be suppressed for use in proving guilt.[186]

The *Miranda* warnings are only required where the individual has been placed in custody and the police expect or want to interrogate the subject. Determining whether a suspect is in custody for *Miranda* purposes requires the authorities to identify whether there is a formal arrest or whether the subject's freedom of action has been curtailed to a degree normally associated with a formal arrest. Courts often consider whether a person in the suspect's position would have understood that his or her situation was one of custody.[187]

In considering the existence of custody in an Alaska case, the Supreme Court evaluated the surrounding facts to make a determination on the factors essential to custody. In *Thompson v. Keohane*, the police interrogated the defendant for a period of time and allowed him freely to leave the police station after he admitted killing his ex-wife. Following his allegation that he had been in custody for *Miranda* purposes and that his statements should have been suppressed, the Supreme Court sent the case back for a decision concerning custody,[188]and the Ninth Circuit found that Keohane was not in custody, and *Miranda* warnings were not necessary.[189] In another case, where *Miranda* warnings were not given and where custody was found to exist, the Court of Appeals for the Fourth Circuit reversed a defendant's conviction involving child pornography.[190] Police executed a search warrant at the defendant's home using a SWAT-style raid, accosted the defendant at gunpoint, and removed him to the basement where they interrogated him for three hours. Although the door to the basement storage room used for interrogation was open, and police told him he was free to leave at any time, the reality was that he could not leave. Police told him they must keep an eye on him at all times. The Fourth Circuit held that the defendant was in custody and was interrogated in the absence of any *Miranda* warning, and therefore, the substance of what he told police concerning child pornography should have been excluded from evidence.

---

186 United States v. Patane, 542 U.S. 630, 639, 2004 U.S. LEXIS 4577 (2004).

187 United States v. Ford, 2010 U.S. App. LEXIS 24549 (4th Cir. 2010).

188 Thompson v. Keohane, 516 U.S. 99 (1995).

189 Thompson v. Keohane, 1998 U.S. App. LEXIS 9432 (9th Cir. 1998).

190 United States v. Hashime, 2013 U.S. App. LEXIS 22044 (4th Cir. 2013).

The twin factors of custody and the desire to interrogate dictate that the initial warnings must be given, but the subject must also understand that the right to cease talking or to consult an attorney may be exercised at any time during questioning. If the accused indicates in an unambiguous manner that he or she wants to speak with an attorney, interrogation must cease immediately and not be attempted later.[191] However, if an arrestee clearly initiates new contact and wants to talk, the conduct indicates a waiver of *Miranda*. In a case in which the subject wants to talk and answer questions, but refuses to sign or make a written statement, the oral statements generally constitute admissible evidence.

At any time during custody, the individual may waive his or her rights and make a statement or submit to questioning, even if the arrestee has previously expressed a desire not to talk or has requested to speak to an attorney. When an arrestee merely responds to additional police-initiated interrogation following an initial request for counsel, there has been no valid waiver.[192] But where the arrestee has indicated a desire for an attorney after receiving the original *Miranda* warnings, and an officer read the warnings a second time as part of the custodial booking process, the subject's subsequent indications of a desire to talk normally constitute a waiver.[193] The burden of proving a *Miranda* waiver is on the prosecution by a preponderance of the evidence.[194] If an accused, after invoking his right to counsel under *Miranda*, does not initiate new discussions with law enforcement agents, any later statement procured by law enforcement efforts as a result of interrogation is not admissible for proof of guilt. However, in *Maryland v. Shatzer*, the Supreme Court departed from some prior *Miranda* principles and permitted secondary interrogation in some situations.[195] In this case, Shatzer, who was then in prison, was approached by a police officer and given *Miranda* warnings. The officer was investigating Shatzer for sexual abuse of his own son. Shatzer invoked his right to legal counsel, and the interview ceased. Approximately three years later, a different police officer approached Shatzer who was still in prison on an unrelated conviction, offered the *Miranda* warnings, and indicated a desire to question the prisoner concerning the crime of sexual abuse of the convict's own son, about which Shatzer had, three years prior, refused to speak to police. This occasion led to a waiver of the *Miranda* warnings, and the prisoner offered damaging remarks that were later used against him in a sexual abuse case. The Supreme Court of the United States rejected his contention that, once he had requested an attorney he could not be interrogated on that subject again, and dismissed his contention that nothing else had changed in the three year period, so that attempting to reinterrogate him on the same subject violated his rights under *Miranda*. The Court disagreed with the defendant's position and held that, following the initial attempt at interrogation by police, there was a return to the

---

191 Edwards v. Arizona, 451 U.S. 477 (1981).

192 *Id.*

193 United States v. Morgan, 2013 U.S. App. LEXIS 14210 (9th Cir. 2013).

194 Colorado v. Connelly, 479 U.S. 157, 168, 986 U.S. LEXIS 23 (1986).

195 Maryland v. Shatzer, 559 U.S. 331, 130 S. Ct. 1213, 2010 U.S. LEXIS 1899 (2010).

normal life of a prisoner and that he was not in custody for *Miranda* purposes beyond the initial interview. According to the Court, the evidence of the second effort at questioning was perfectly admissible. In what amounted to judicial rulemaking, the *Shatzer* Court held that a 14-day break between *Mirandized* interrogations, where the individual was not in custody in the interim for *Miranda* purposes, would permit a renewed second reading of the *Miranda* warnings in an effort to get a person to talk.[196] In the *Shatzer* case, there was the three-year break between interrogations.

Despite the rules that restrict how confessions and statements damaging to a defendant's case may be obtained, confessions continue to be a useful investigative tool and provide evidence that a prosecutor can use during the government's case-in-chief. In fact, the Supreme Court in the *Miranda* case stated that confessions remained a proper element in law enforcement and that any statement given freely and voluntarily without any compelling influence was admissible in evidence.[197] In a subsequent case, the Court held that a person may volunteer any statement, even one prompted by mental problems, and the statement will not be excluded on *Miranda* grounds, as long as the police did not coerce the subject.[198] In this case, when a person with mental problems approached a police officer to confess to a homicide, the officer properly listened to the confession, and the confession was not considered to have been involuntarily taken under *Miranda*. The Court held that "coercive police activity is a necessary predicate to the finding that a confession is not 'voluntary' within the meaning of the Due Process Clause of the Fourteenth Amendment."[199] Therefore, it is clear that confessions continue to be admitted into evidence, and the skilled and informed investigator can obtain confessions or statements and still comply with the requirements established by the courts. Even if police fail to meet the strict requirements of *Miranda*, as long as the confession is voluntarily given, the evidence may be admitted for impeachment purposes where a defendant takes the stand and offers testimony contradictory to an otherwise inadmissible *Miranda* statement.[200]

In the case of *Harris v. New York*, the defendant was charged with selling heroin, and at the trial, he took the stand in his own defense. Following his arrest, he had made some incriminating statements that were not admissible to prove guilt due to a failure to properly warn him under *Miranda*. The prosecution did not offer the defendant's admission or confession during its case-in-chief, because it had been taken in violation of the principles of *Miranda*. After the defendant testified by telling a story that was in direct conflict with his voluntary statement taken in violation of *Miranda*, the prosecution offered the original confession to impeach the testimony of the defendant, however. The United States Supreme Court allowed the admission of the confession even though

---

196 *Id.*

197 Miranda v. Arizona, 384 U.S. 436, 1966 U.S. LEXIS 2817 (1966).

198 Colorado v. Connelly, 479 U.S. 157, 1986 U.S. LEXIS 23 (1986).

199 *Id.* at 167.

200 Harris v. New York, 401 U.S. 222, 91 S. Ct. 643, 28 L. Ed. 2d 1 (1971); Oregon v. Hass, 420 U.S. 714, 91 S. Ct. 1215, 43 L. Ed. 2d 570 (1975).

Miranda warnings had not been given, and the Court held that a confession may be used for impeachment purposes if it has been freely and voluntarily made. In so doing, the Court reasoned that:

> Having voluntarily taken the stand, petitioner was under an obligation to speak truthfully and accurately, and the prosecution did no more than utilize the traditional truth-testing devices of the adversary process.

In a more recent application of the *Harris* principle, in *United States v. Gomez*,[201] a defendant, who had been arrested on a charge of importing drugs from Mexico, refused to talk after being given the *Miranda* warnings because he noted that someone would kill his family in Mexico if he gave information to police. The trial court would not allow the prosecution to introduce the statement, "I can't say anything because my family . . . my family will get killed,"[202] as proof of guilt. At trial the defendant testified that he was not aware that drugs were in his car, so the prosecutor introduced the above statement to impeach the defendant's testimony. He would not have feared for his family if he had no knowledge of the drugs that he was importing. Silence after the *Miranda* warning cannot be used against a person, but this defendant was not silent; he gave a reason why he would not talk, and that evidence could be used to impeach his testimony that he was ignorant of the presence of drugs in his car.

Alternatively, if a confession has been coerced and was not voluntarily made, even though *Miranda* warnings were given, the confession is not admissible into evidence, even for impeachment purposes, due to concerns involving reliability.[203]

A failure to follow the exact requirements of the *Miranda* warnings may not always result in the exclusion of evidence. In one case involving an emergency situation where the suspect was interrogated while in custody, the Supreme Court of the United States permitted the evidence to be introduced against the defendant. The subject was in custody following an allegation of a sexual offense by a woman who said that he had a firearm. Following a frisk, the firearm was not located, and the police were permitted to ask where the gun had been hidden. The gun evidence was admissible against the defendant on a firearm charge, even though there had been custodial interrogation without a *Miranda* warning. The Supreme Court recognized a "narrow exception" to the *Miranda* principles, which held that statements elicited from an arrestee, as well as real evidence obtained by exploiting such statements, may be admitted against the arrestee–defendant even if the officers failed to recite the *Miranda* warnings before asking the questions, as long as the officer's safety or the safety of others appeared to be in jeopardy.[204] In recognizing a "public safety" exception to the *Miranda* rule, the Court concluded that, if the officer or the public may be in life-threatening danger, the threat to the public safety outweighs the need for the rule protecting the Fifth

---

201 725 F.3d 1121, 1125, 2013 U.S. App. LEXIS 16229 (9th Cir. 2013).

202 *Id.*

203 Mincey v. Arizona, 437 U.S. 385, 98 S. Ct. 2408, 57 L. Ed. 2d 290 (1978).

204 New York v. Quarles, 467 U.S. 649, 104 S. Ct. 2626, 81 L. Ed. 2d 550 (1984).

Amendment privilege against self-incrimination, and evidence resulting from questions not preceded by *Miranda* warnings is admissible under these limited circumstances. In a newer case, police gained custody of a domestic dispute subject in a bedroom prior to questioning the subject concerning guns in plain view on a living room couch.[205] The officer asked, "What are those doing there?" and the subject admitted that he was trying to hide them because he knew the police were coming. The subject had a prior felony conviction and was not lawfully permitted to have the firearms. Under the circumstances, the subject's answer to the officer's pre-*Miranda* question constituted admissible evidence against him due to the emergency in getting control of the domestic dispute situation.

Following the original *Miranda* decision, the Congress demonstrated its disagreement with the ruling by passing the Omnibus Crime Control and Safe Streets Act of 1968, which contained a provision intended to reverse the effects of the *Miranda* decision in federal courts. The applicable part of this Act is 18 U.S.C. § 3501(c), which reads as follows:

> In any criminal prosecution by the United States or by the District of Columbia, a confession made or given by a person who is a defendant therein, while such person was under arrest or other detention in the custody of any law enforcement officer or law enforcement agency, shall not be inadmissible solely because of delay in bringing such person before a commissioner or other officer empowered to commit persons charged with offenses against the laws of the United States or of the District of Columbia if such confession is found by the trial judge to have been made voluntarily.[206]

The clear intention of the statute was to undermine the *Miranda* warnings by statutorily overruling the Supreme Court. Congress may change laws that it has passed and nullify Supreme Court decisions that have interpreted those laws, but it has no power to overrule Supreme Court decisions when the Court has interpreted a provision of the Constitution of the United States. In the case of *Dickerson v. United States*, the Supreme Court found that § 3501 was an unconstitutional exercise by Congress of its powers, because the Court held that the *Miranda* decision and its accompanying warnings were of constitutional dimension.[207] That is to say, the Court held that the *Miranda* warnings were required by the Constitution and that Congress had no power to attempt to change a decision of constitutional dimensions. In the *Dickerson* case, the defendant, a bank robber, had been arrested by federal agents and interrogated voluntarily without being given his *Miranda* warnings. By all objective measures, the interrogation and incriminating statements were given in a completely voluntary manner; the only problem with their use was the *Miranda* decision. The trial court suppressed

---

205 *See* United States v. Martinez, 406 F.3d 1160, 1163, 2005 U.S. App. LEXIS 8624 (9th Cir. 2002).

206 A delay in bringing an arrestee before a judge or magistrate may cause a detainee to file a civil suit, but generally, it does not seem to have resulted in the dismissal of a criminal case. See Turner v. City of Taylor, 412 F.3d 629, 2005 U.S. App. LEXIS 11233 (6th Cir. 2005), and Bryant v. City of New York, 404 F.3d 128, 2005 U.S. App. LEXIS 5376 (2d Cir. 2005).

207 Dickerson v. United States, 530 U.S. 428, 440, 2000 U.S. LEXIS 4305 (2000).

the statement, but in reversing and remanding the case, the Court of Appeals for the Fourth Circuit noted that the requirements of § 3501 had been met and that the confession was voluntarily made. After granting *certiorari*, the Supreme Court reversed the Fourth Circuit, holding that *Miranda* warnings were required by the Constitution and that any voluntariness standard suggested by the statute would not square with the *Miranda* decision and the federal Constitution.[208] The attempt by Congress to overturn the *Miranda* decision failed, and the accused robber's confession could not be used in court.

It is apparent from this discussion concerning confessions and other statements that although courts have established strict rules concerning how to evaluate their admissibility, confessions and admissions constitute admissible evidence and continue to be valuable tools in the prosecution of criminal activity. Generally, voluntary statements obtained in accordance with the requirements of the Fifth Amendment, *Miranda*, and other rules established by the Supreme Court will be admissible evidence.

§ 16.6 Self-incrimination and Related Protections

Often evidence is challenged because, in obtaining evidence, the officer violated the Fifth Amendment privilege against self-incrimination. The pertinent section concerning self-incrimination provides that "No person . . . shall be compelled in any criminal case to be a witness against himself." As with the Fourth Amendment search and seizure provision, the self-incrimination provision was included as a part of the Bill of Rights and became a part of the Constitution in 1791. The Fifth Amendment restrictions were not made applicable to the states until 1964, when the Supreme Court held that the due process clause of the Fourteenth Amendment included protections against self-incrimination.[209] In deciding *Malloy v. Hogan*,the United States Supreme Court stated:

> We hold today that the Fifth Amendment's exception from compulsory self-incrimination is also protected by the Fourteenth Amendment against abridgement by the states.

This means that the Fifth Amendment standards applied by states are the standards determined by the Supreme Court for federal courts and not the standards developed by state courts. In the case of *Schmerber v. California*,[210] the Supreme Court resolved many conflicting decisions when it clearly limited the application of the privilege against self-incrimination to evidence that can be categorized as "testimonial" in nature.

---

208 *Id.*

209 Malloy v. Hogan, 378 U.S. 1, 84 S. Ct. 1489, 12 L. Ed. 2d 653 (1964).

210 384 U.S. 757, 86 S. Ct. 1826, 16 L. Ed. 2d 908 (1966). *See* case in Part II in Cases Relating to Chapter 14.

> We hold that the privilege protects the accused only from being compelled to testify against himself, or otherwise provide the state with evidence of a testimonial or communicative nature, and that the withdrawal of blood and use of the analysis in question in this case did not involve compulsion to these ends.

Even though no Fifth Amendment privilege exists involving blood alcohol evidence, under a recent case, *Missouri v. McNeely*, the Court indicated that a warrant may be needed to draw blood for testing in order to be in compliance with the Fourth Amendment involving search and seizure.[211] The issue presented in *McNeely* involved whether the natural metabolism of alcohol in a human body would generally support an emergency, nonwarrant-based testing of blood where probable cause existed. The Court held that authorities must consider the totality of circumstances when deciding whether an emergency existed, and an emergency would not be the norm in most impaired driving prosecutions.

Following the *Schmerber* interpretation under the Fifth Amendment, obtaining and using physical evidence from a defendant's person, such as evidence from a lineup, taking blood or DNA samples, and taking handwriting samples, does not constitute testimonial self-incrimination. As the *Schmerber* Court noted, the Fifth Amendment, as applied to the states, "offers no protection against compulsion to submit to fingerprinting, photographing, or measurements, to write or speak for identification, to appear in court, to stand, to assume a stance, to walk, or to make a particular gesture."[212] On the other hand, if an accused was forced to take a lie detector test or was coerced into providing other evidence of a communicative nature, such as a response to a subpoena that has hallmarks of being testimonial in nature,[213] the Fifth Amendment's self-incrimination provisions can be violated, and evidence so obtained may be ruled as inadmissible.

As a general rule, when a defendant invokes a constitutional right, the claim of this right cannot be used as a sword against the defendant by commenting on it or highlighting its invocation. However, when there is no constitutional right to withhold evidence under the Fifth Amendment, a prosecutor may properly inform jury of the defendant's withholding during closing arguments. In the case of *South Dakota v. Neville*, the United States Supreme Court approved the admission of evidence that the defendant refused to submit to a blood-alcohol test.[214] Summarizing its opinion, the Court stated:

> We hold, therefore, that a refusal to take a blood alcohol test, after a police officer has lawfully requested it, is not an act coerced by the officer, and thus is not protected by the privilege against self-incrimination.

Thus, the prosecutor may ask a police officer if the subject refused a test for alcohol and may comment on that fact during closing arguments.

---

211 569 U.S. ___, 133 S.Ct. 1552, 1563, 2013 U.S. LEXIS 3160 (2013).

212 *Schmerber v. California*, 384 U.S. 757, 764 (1966).

213 United States v. Ponds, 454 F.3d 313, 319, 2006 U.S. App. LEXIS 17718 (D.C. Cir. 2006).

214 South Dakota v. Neville, 459 U.S. 553, 103 S. Ct. 916, 75 L. Ed. 2d 748 (1983).

The Fifth Amendment self-incrimination provision neither prohibits the compelled display of identifiable physical characteristics, such as tattoos, bodily scars, or deformities, that help identify a person, nor does it protect against the compelled provision of saliva and hair samples to a grand jury.[215] Echoing the *Schmerber* case, the Supreme Court of the United States, in *Maryland v. King*, found no problem with a Maryland law that requires a DNA sample be collected from every person arrested for a crime of violence or burglary, or an attempt at one of these crimes.[216] The state statute provided that the sample may not be added to the DNA database before an arrestee is arraigned and must be destroyed if the person is acquitted. The *King* Court spent some time discussing Fourth Amendment search and seizure concepts, but virtually assumed that no Fifth Amendment self-incrimination problem existed in obtaining or using DNA swab evidence. Such logic is completely consistent with the *Schmerber* case and raises no self-incrimination issue. Requiring a handwriting sample from a defendant does not violate the Fifth Amendment or a similar state provision because the sample is an identifying physical fact and nothing more.[217]

Although it is not generally a violation of the Fifth Amendment self-incrimination provision to require a suspect to give handwriting specimens or voice exemplars for comparison or identification purposes, and it is not a violation for a prosecutor to comment on the failure to provide such a sample, the prosecutor does violate the Fifth Amendment when commenting to the jury on the failure of the accused to testify at trial.[218] However, in a non-custody situation where *Miranda* warnings are not necessary prior to voluntarily answering questions, a suspect must affirmatively invoke the protections of the Fifth Amendment if he or she suddenly does not want to answer a particular question.[219] In remaining silent, the subject runs the risk that such silence may be considered a tacit admission of guilt or an adverse probable answer to the question posed by police. Thus, the prosecutor may bring out this silence at trial. According to the Supreme Court, the Fifth Amendment privilege under these circumstances is not self-executing, and any witness who wants to have such protection must claim it.[220]

In Wisconsin, when reasonable suspicion exists that an individual may be driving under the influence of alcohol or other drugs, there is no self-incrimination clause protection to allow a driver to refuse to take field sobriety tests, and introducing evidence of such a refusal does not violate the driver's Fifth Amendment privilege.[221] Wisconsin courts hold that the results of a field sobriety test are not testimonial in nature, and the

---

215 *See* People v. Watson, 214 Ill. 2d 271, 825 N.E.2d 257, 2005 Ill. LEXIS 2 (Ill. 2005).

216 Maryland v. King, 133 S. Ct. 1958, 186 L. Ed. 2d 1, 2013 U.S. LEXIS 54165 (2013). See case in Part II, Chapter 16.

217 State v. Wiggins, 2004 Del. Super. LEXIS 64 (Del. 2004). The Delaware courts have interpreted the DEL CONST. of 1897, art. I, § 7, dealing with self-incrimination to be coextensive with the federal Fifth Amendment.

218 Griffin v. California, 380 U.S. 609, 85 S. Ct. 1229, 14 L. Ed. 2d 106 (1965).

219 Salinas v. Texas, 133 S.Ct. 2174, 2178, 2013 U.S. LEXIS 4697 (2013).

220 *Id.*

221 State v. Schmidt, 2012 Wi. App. 137, 345 Wis.2d 326, 331, 2012 Wisc. App. LEXIS 905 (2012).

subject is not intending to convey a statement. Likewise, in an Arkansas case, where a city employee refused to give a urine sample in a drug and employment case, the government did not violate any Fifth Amendment provision against self-incrimination because the results were not considered testimonial in nature.[222]

All defendants have the privilege against self-incrimination based on state constitutions or on the federal Fifth Amendment, but it can be successfully asserted only when the evidence would be considered testimonial in nature. Evidence that involves physical attributes, personal characteristics, and scientific data about the defendant may implicate Fourth Amendment search and seizures issues, but rarely involve a violation of the Fifth Amendment.

§ 16.7 Due Process Exclusions

The self-incrimination protections are closely related to the limitations that the due process clause of the Fourteenth Amendment imposes on the conduct of criminal proceedings of the states. In order to illustrate the concept in lay terms, due process could be called the "fundamental fairness" that a government must show toward the persons with which it deals in a criminal context. Demonstrative of the concept of fundamental fairness, if, in obtaining evidence, investigators violate the due process clause of the Fifth Amendment (in federal cases) or of the Fourteenth Amendment (in state cases), evidence obtained thereby should not be used against the person whose rights were violated, as admitting such evidence would constitute an error. As in other instances involving constitutional violations, the reasoning here states that allowing the admission of such evidence would encourage conduct that is prohibited by the Constitution, thus allowing one lawbreaker to use evidence against another lawbreaker.

In determining the extent of the coverage of the due process clause of the Fourteenth Amendment and the rights it protects, it is important to understand that many of the guarantees provided by the first eight amendments in the Bill of Rights (1791) have been incorporated into the due process clause of the Fourteenth Amendment. Facilitated by the Supreme Court, this incorportion was a gradual and selective process that has continued for over a century, since the time early litigants argued that some of the other amendments were included within the due process clause of the Fourteenth Amendment. Some of the incorporated amendments, such as the First Amendment involving religion, speech, and assembly, do not frequently appear in criminal cases. The Fourth Amendment, which deals with searches and seizures, and similar amendments are frequently litigated by criminal defendants, however. The Fifth Amendment dealing with confessions and double jeopardy often has a bearing on criminal cases as well. The Sixth Amendment also offers protections to criminal defendants, including the right to a speedy trial and a public trial conducted in front of a jury, and it contains a provision for the assistance of counsel among other rights. In fact,

---

222 Hess v. Ables, 714 F.3d 1048, 1053, 2013 U.S. App. LEXIS 8493 (8th Cir. 2013).

the Sixth Amendment right to confront adverse witnesses has been incorporated into the due process clause of the Fourteenth Amendment.

The concept of due process is demonstrated by *Melendez-Diaz v. Massachusetts*,[223] which dealt with the right of confrontation under the Sixth Amendment, as applied to the states through the due process clause of the Fourteenth Amendment. *Melendez-Diaz* involved a situation where the defendant had been accused of distributing cocaine. During the state prosecution, the government introduced notarized affidavits from a state laboratory that had analyzed the seized material. The individual who conducted the drug analysis and who had produced the notarized affidavits did not testify, and the affidavits were introduced by a witness who had not personally done the analysis. Following the conviction, the Supreme Court of the United States determined that the certificates of analysis were testimonial in nature and should not have been introduced against the defendant, because he was never able to confront the individual who performed the laboratory analysis of the suspected material, as was his right under the Sixth Amendment.

In a different example of a violation of due process, evidence obtained as a result of an improper lineup or photographic array is inadmissible. If a lineup or other confrontation for the purpose of identification is held in such a way as to be unduly suggestive (i.e., to suggest to the witnesses who make the identification which person in the lineup is the suspect), then the in-court identification would be contaminated.[224] For example, in one case, a police officer accidently placed a photo of the suspect on a table where the witness, a confidential informant, observed it, creating an accidental identification.[225] In rejecting a motion to suppress the identification, the trial court noted that there was no due process violation because there was little chance of irreparable misidentification, due to the fact that the confidential informant knew the defendant well, had dined with him, and had purchased illegal drugs from him in the past. The argument can be made that, when police present photographs to victims for identification purposes in such a way as to be unduly suggestive, the procedure denies due process to the suspect. In one case where the defendant alleged an unduly suggestive photographic array lineup, the court found no due process violation, noting that two of the tree witnesses had failed to identify the defendant, indicating that the array must not have been unduly suggestive.[226] In contrast to suggestive identification activities, the proper taking of blood, breath, saliva, urine samples, does not violate the due process clause, and the introduction of such evidence is appropriate if other evidentiary standards are met, and the disposal of these samples does not violate due process unless done in bad faith by the prosecution.[227]

Under the selective incorporation doctrine, the Supreme Court followed a case-by-case adjudication to determine which enumerated rights in the Bill of Rights should be

---

223 557 U.S. 425, 2009 U.S. LEXIS 4734 (2009). *See* case in Part II.

224 Foster v. California, 394 U.S. 440, 89 S. Ct. 1127, 22 L. Ed. 2d 402 (1969).

225 United States v. Vazquez, 2013 U.S. Dist. LEXIS 133171 (Dist. Vt. 2013).

226 Hall v. Capello, 2013 U.S. Dist. LEXIS 123405 (E.D. Mich. 2013).

227 Ryan v. Warden, 2013 U.S. Dist. LEXIS 144711 (S.D. Ohio 3013).

incorporated against the states through the due process clause of the Fourteenth Amendment. Historically, the Supreme Court of the United States has failed to define completely and specifically what is included in the concept of due process protection. Over the course of many Supreme Court decisions, the rights recognized through the use of the selective incorporation doctrine offer a fairly good understanding of what conduct by police officers will violate due process. However, novel situations might cause the Court to incorporate an additional right from the Bill of Rights or to construe a recognized right in a novel manner.

To summarize, if evidence is obtained by federal agents in violation of the due process clause of the Fifth Amendment, or by state agents in violation of the due process clause of the Fourteenth Amendment, courts will generally exclude such evidence from admission in criminal trials.

§ 16.8 Right to Counsel as It Relates to the Exclusion of Evidence

One of the protections of the Bill of Rights that has been very broadly interpreted in recent years is the section of the Sixth Amendment that provides: "In all criminal prosecutions, the accused shall enjoy the right to have the assistance of counsel for his defense." The Sixth Amendment right to counsel goes into effect at the initiation of adversarial criminal proceedings and is required at all critical stages in the criminal justice process where the results of proceedings may affect the fate of the accused.[228] This right matures when a prosecution is initiated, regardless of whether the proceedings start with an arrest, indictment, or information.

In early decisions, this right was made available to the accused only at the trial and only if a defendant could afford an attorney. Later, the right to representation was extended to require that free lawyers be appointed to defend indigents who were charged with felonies,[229] and eventually, the Supreme Court held that the right to counsel extended to anyone who faced any incarceration if convicted.[230] Subsequently, the Supreme Court determined that the Sixth Amendment right to the assistance of counsel applied during the early stages of any criminal investigation when police focused on an individual suspect to the point where custody existed and interrogation was desired. Under circumstances where the right to counsel has been violated, and the situation produced incriminating evidence, that evidence must be excluded from trial.[231]

---

228 See, 1 *Illinois Jurisprudence - Criminal Law (MB)* CRIMINAL LAW AND PROCEDURE § 2:55.

229 Gideon v. Wainwright, 372 U.S. 335, 1963 U.S. LEXIS 1942 (1963).

230 *See* Argersinger v. Hamlin, 407 U.S. 25 (1972). In a later case, the Supreme Court ruled that an indigent has a right to counsel at an appearance before a magistrate judge to learn of the prosecution's charges. The initiation of adversarial judicial proceedings causes the right to counsel to attach. *See* Rothgery v. Gillespie County, 554 U.S. 191, 2008 U.S. LEXIS 5057 (2008).

231 *See* Miranda v. Arizona, 384 U.S. 436, 1966 U.S. LEXIS 2817 (1966).

In an early case that helped refine the right to counsel, *Escobedo v. Illinois*, the defendant moved to suppress the use of incriminating statements taken after he had requested counsel and had been refused. In this *pre-Miranda* right to counsel case, the Supreme Court held that the Sixth Amendment right to counsel attaches once the police have narrowed their inquiry to a specific subject, have taken the subject into custody, the subject has requested the assistance of an attorney, and police have embarked on efforts to question and elicit incriminating statements. Because Escobedo had been denied his right to the assistance of counsel, his convictions were reversed, and the case remanded.[232]

Although the accused requested counsel in the *Escobedo* case, the Supreme Court in *Miranda*[233] stated that such a request was unnecessary because police must inform the person in custody of an individual's constitutional rights. Under the *Miranda* ruling, if the suspect is in custody when the police desire to conduct interrogation, the burden is placed on the police to inform the suspect of his or her constitutional rights and to refrain from asking any questions unless the accused knowingly waives his or her right to counsel.

From these and other cases, it is obvious that, if the accused in custody requests counsel prior to or during the interrogation, and counsel is not allowed, any statements obtained will not be admissible for proof of guilt. The *Miranda* Court reasoned that there are compelling pressures in any custodial police interrogation, and in order to help a suspect "to combat these pressures and to permit a full opportunity to exercise the privilege against self-incrimination, the accused must be adequately and effectively appraised of his rights and the exercise of those rights must be fully honored."[234] Under the *Miranda* reasoning, if police take a suspect into custody and question him or her with a view to obtaining incriminating statements, the police must advise him or her of his or her right to counsel and to silence, or any evidence obtained will be excluded from trial to prove guilt.

The suspect may waive the right to counsel provided the waiver is made voluntarily, knowingly, and intelligently. However, in *Edwards v. Arizona*, the Supreme Court determined that, if the accused has clearly requested the assistance of counsel, interrogation must cease until counsel has been made available to the accused or until the accused initiates additional communication.[235] The rule under *Edwards* was designed to protect a person who had requested counsel from being talked into waiving the *Miranda* right to silence by police authorities. Although the Court in *Edwards* did not define "initiation of further communications," the Court in a later case determined that the question from the suspect, "Well, what is going to happen to me now?" really amounted to an attempt by the defendant to initiate further questioning, and that

232 *See* Escobedo v. Illinois, 378 U.S. 478, 1964 U.S. LEXIS 827 (1964).

233 Miranda v. Arizona, 384 U.S. 436, 1966 U.S. LEXIS 2817 (1966).

234 *Id.* at 467.

235 Edwards v. Arizona, 451 U.S. 477, 101 S. Ct. 1880, 68 L. Ed. 2d 378 (1981).

ensuing statements given by the defendant, even after he was warned further of his rights, were admissible.[236]

The rationale of *Edwards v. Arizona* generally prohibits efforts by police to get a suspect to talk once the subject has requested an attorney in the *Miranda* context. The Supreme Court has observed a limitation in the recent case, *Howes v. Fields*, where an inmate was in custody in a Michigan prison for earlier offenses.[237] Police were not interested in the conviction for which the defendant was incarcerated, but in an earlier child molestation case over which he had once previously refused to speak, after receiving the *Miranda* warnings. Prison officials allowed outside police officers to use a conference room at the prison to speak with prisoner Fields. Police did not advise him that he did not have to speak with the officers, and they offered no *Miranda* warnings, but he had been told that he was free to return to his cell at any time. Arguably, he was not in custody for *Miranda* purposes. The interrogation lasted about seven hours, during which time he confessed to molesting a twelve-year old boy. The Supreme Court found that the *Miranda* warnings were not necessary, because being in custody for prison purposes was not the same as being in custody for *Miranda* purposes, and so the conviction was ultimately affirmed. The Court noted that its "decisions do not clearly establish that a prisoner is always in custody for purposes of *Miranda* whenever a prisoner is isolated from the general prison population and questioned about conduct outside the prison."[238] The Court reinstated Field's conviction.

Despite the above case, police-initiated interrogation after a defendant's assertion of his or her right to counsel generally runs afoul of the *Edwards* rule, so long as a suspect is in custody for *Miranda* purposes. Once a suspect has been arraigned and has requested counsel at the arraignment or preliminary hearing, a police officer may not initiate questioning. However, where a defendant has merely been arraigned, at which time a judge appointed legal counsel for the defendant, such appointment does not have the same effect as the defendant requesting the assistance of legal counsel immediately following the receipt of the *Miranda* warning. Under the circumstances, where there has been no request for counsel under *Miranda*, and there has been no invocation of the right to silence, the arrestee/defendant may be asked questions by law enforcement officials even after a judge has appointed counsel. In one case, police approached a defendant following his initial court appearance, at which time an attorney had been appointed, and advised him of his *Miranda* rights, which he waived.[239] He agreed to assist police in locating a murder weapon. For *Miranda* purposes, the court appointment of an attorney for trial does not have the same effect as a defendant's

---

236 Oregon v Bradshaw, 463 U.S. 1039, 103 S. Ct. 2830, 77 L. Ed. 2d 405 (1983).

237 Howes v. Fields, 132 S.Ct. 1181, 2012 U.S. LEXIS 1077 (2013).

238 *Id.*, at 1188.

239 *Montejo v. Louisiana*, 556 U.S. 63, 129 S. Ct. 2079, 2009 U.S. LEXIS 3973 (2009). Montejo overruled Michigan v. Jackson, 475 U.S. 625, 1986 U.S. LEXIS 91 (1986), which previously held that defendants could not be interrogated by police following a requested appointment of counsel at an arraignment. Inconsistencies appeared among the states wherein some states automatically appointed counsel for indigents and some did so only upon a defendant's request.

request for an attorney following a reading of the *Miranda* warnings. The Supreme Court indicated that it was somewhat illogical to presume that a defendant's consent to police-initiated interrogation was not voluntary merely because a judge had recently appointed a lawyer for his or her case. According to the Court, "No reason exists to assume that a defendant . . ., who has done *nothing at all* to express his intentions with respect to his Sixth Amendment rights, would not be perfectly amenable to speaking with the police without having counsel present."[240]

When the accused exercised the right to be silent or to have counsel present during a custodial interrogation, the court must determine if that exercise constitutes a waiver of the previously asserted right. To make this determination, the court must first ascertain whether the accused actually invoked the right, and, if so, the court must then establish whether the accused initiated further discussion with the police and knowingly and intelligently waived the previously asserted rights.[241]

Statements that might not be admissible under the *Edwards* case may be used for impeachment purposes. If a defendant chose to present testimony that was materially in conflict with prior statements that had been taken in violation of his or her right to counsel, the prosecution could present the previously excluded statements to cast doubt on a defendant's false or inconsistent testimony. In a 2009 case, *Kansas v. Ventris*, police planted a government witness inside the defendant's cell, and the defendant admitted guilt to murder and robbery to the government witness. The planting of the informant did violate the defendant's right to counsel. However, the prosecution was permitted to introduce evidence of the defendant's prior cellblock admission of guilt for purposes of impeachment, and the Supreme Court upheld the trial court decision.[242] The Court explained that, while the Sixth Amendment prohibits the use of evidence during the prosecution's case-in-chief when the evidence was obtained after the defendant had invoked the Sixth Amendment right to counsel, this shield should not be perverted into a license to commit defensive perjury. The Court had concerns about the effects of permitting exclusion, as those effects related to the integrity of the trial process.

United States v. Wade is a case that remains good law and continues to have an influence on the admissibility of evidence when the right to counsel is at issue.[243] This case concerned the right to counsel during a police lineup. In *Wade*, the Supreme Court stated that both the defendant Wade and his counsel should have been notified of the impending postindictment lineup, and that, unless waived, the defendant had the right to have his counsel present at an in-person lineup. The Court asserted that the best method of enforcing this right to counsel at the lineup is to prohibit in-court identification by witnesses if a trial court finds that the pretrial confrontation or lineup tainted the in-court identification. In other words, the Court reasoned that the postindictment

240 *Id.* at 2086.

241 State v. Lane, 262 Kan. 373, 940 P.2d 422 (1997).

242 *See* Kansas v. Ventris, 51 U.S. 197, 129 S. Ct. 1841, 2009 U.S. LEXIS 3299 (2009). *See also* Michigan v. Harvey, 494 U.S. 344, 110 S. Ct. 1176, 108 L. Ed. 2d 293 (1990).

243 *United States v. Wade*, 388 U.S. 218, 87 S. Ct. 1926, 18 L. Ed. 2d 1149 (1967).

in-person lineup was a critical stage of the proceedings and that counsel should be present if the identifying witness is to testify in court, provided the defendant has not waved his right to representation. In justifying this stand, the Court stated:

> Since it appears that there is a grave potential for prejudice, intentional or not, in the pretrial lineup, which may not be capable of reconstruction at trial, and since presence of counsel itself can often avert prejudice and assure a meaningful confrontation at trial, there can be little doubt that for Wade the post-indictment lineup was a critical stage of the prosecution.[244]

If the accused's attorney is present or if the accused intelligently waives the right to an attorney, then a witness who made an identification of the accused at the lineup may be called upon in court to identify the accused. However, if the attorney was not present at a postinformation or postindictment lineup, and the defendant did not waive the right to counsel, the witness may not be permitted to make an in-court identification of the defendant that mentions the lineup proceeding. However, if the prosecution can establish that an in-court identification will not be based on or tainted by the uncounseled lineup and will be based on a crime scene identification by clear and convincing proof, the identification evidence can be admitted.[245] In a recent case, federal bank robbery witnesses, who identified the defendant at an uncounseled lineup, were permitted to make an in-court identification because the trial judge concluded that they had an independent recollection of seeing the defendant at the bank that was not influenced by the lineup.[246]

In *Kirby v. Illinois*, the United States Supreme Court refused to extend the right to counsel for a face-to-face confrontation between an arrestee and a victim, where neither an indictment had been returned, nor an information had been filed.[247] Police had arrested the subject for a different crime and allowed the victim of a robbery to make an in-person one-on-one identification. Under such circumstances, no attorney need be present for the arrestee, and any identification will not be excluded on grounds that a violation of the right to counsel has occurred. Subjecting a person to an in-person lineup does not involve a deprivation of the privilege against self-incrimination, and the Court further explained that counsel is not required at a prearrest, preindictment identification confrontation. The Court distinguished this one-on-one identification in the *Kirby v. Illinois* situation from the *Wade* postindictment confrontation for identification, holding that a postindictment lineup or confrontation for identification is a critical stage, and the right to counsel attaches if the witness is to identify the accused at trial. However, the prearrest, preindictment, preinformation confrontation is not a critical stage for Sixth Amendment purposes, and identification evidence may be offered at trial even if counsel was not present at the lineup or showup.

---

244 *Id.* at 236.

245 Moore v. Illinois, 434 U.S. 220, 225, 1977 U.S. LEXIS 163 (1977).

246 United States v. West, 2013 U.S. App. LEXIS 12967 (7th Cir. 2013).

247 *Kirby v. Illinois*, 406 U.S. 682, 92 S. Ct. 1877, 32 L. Ed. 2d 411 (1972).

Case law in some states helps clarify when the right to counsel attaches in state prosecutions. For example, in New York, at a prearraignment lineup that occurs prior to the filing of any indictment or information or other formal charge, a defendant does not have a right to counsel, except that the right to counsel will exist and a pre-charging lineup if counsel has actually been retained or been assigned to the matter under investigation.[248] As one New York court noted,

> suspects are not intitled to pre-accusatory, investigatory lineups, but once the right to counsel has attached, that right requires the police to notify defense counsel of an impending investigatory lineup and afford counsel a reasonable opportunity to attend.[249]

Similarly, in Michigan, the right to counsel for in-person lineups does not attach until adversarial judicial proceedings have been initiated.[250] In an additional limitation of the right to counsel at identification procedures, the Supreme Court held that "the Sixth Amendment does not require that defense counsel be present when a witness views police or prosecution photographic arrays."[251] Some jurisdictions, such as the Commonwealth of Pennsylvania, recognize the right to counsel for photographic arrays, however, when the array has been assembled based on the arrest of a suspect.[252] Due process requirements still dictate that a photographic array or photo lineup cannot be unduly suggestive if police want to have the evidence admitted at a defendant's trial.

§ 16.9 Summary

Although the traditional common law doctrine states that relevant evidence is admissible even though obtained illegally, much evidence is not admissible if a federal or state constitutional provision has been violated. Exclusionary rules have developed over time and have been made applicable both to federal and state courts on a piecemeal basis.

Under the present rules, as established by the United States Supreme Court and lower courts, most evidence obtained by search and seizure in violation of the Constitution is inadmissible in both federal and state courts. The cases must be examined thoroughly to determine what is considered an illegal search and under what circumstances the exclusionary rules apply.

---

248 People v. Sharp, 36 Misc.3d 381, 2012 N.Y. Misc. LEXIS 1709 (2012).

249 People v. Washington, 107 A.D.3d 4, 2013 N.Y. App. Div. LEXIS 2539 (2013).

250 People v. Harris, 2005 Mich. App. LEXIS 3264 (2005). Michigan grants the right to counsel for corporeal identifications only at or after the initiation of adversarial judicial proceedings and there is no right to counsel at photographic arrays. *See* People v. Hickman, 470 Mich. 602, 684 N.W.2d 267, 2004 Mich. LEXIS 1544 (2004).

251 United States v. Ash, 413 U.S. 300, 1973 U.S. LEXIS 45 (1973).

252 Commonwealth v. Harrell, 2013 Pa. Super. 8, 2013 Pa. Super. LEXIS 222 (2013).,

Although wiretap evidence was not initially considered to be within the protection of the constitutional provisions, recent cases have held that wiretapping and eavesdropping fall within the protection of the Fourth Amendment, as well as state and federal law. Under the Omnibus Crime Control Act of 1968, certain wiretap and eavesdrop evidence is admissible if the statutory requirements are met or if one party to the conversation consents. Evidence obtained in violation of the statute will not be admitted into court. The Patriot Act expanded the definition of a pen register so that newer methods of transmitting data and communication may be covered when the executive branch obtains a warrant.

Although the admission of physical evidence that helps prove guilt continues to be challenged with arguments that the admission creates a violation of the Fifth Amendment self-incrimination privilege, the Supreme Court has consistently ruled otherwise. Courts have established rules that prohibit the admissibility of confessions obtained in violation of established standards, whether under *Miranda* or involving allegations of force or coercion. Evidence that is of a testimonial or communicative nature is inadmissible unless this protection is waived.

Evidence acquired in violation of the due process clauses of the Fifth and Fourteenth Amendments is also inadmissible. While most due process arguments for excluding evidence fall under specific provisions of the Bill of Rights, some evidence is subject to exclusion under due process standards. Court opinions must be studied to determine what activities constitute a violation, keeping in mind that some states offer greater protection under due process than is required by the federal constitution.

If the right to counsel provision of the Sixth Amendment has been violated, evidence obtained by virtue of the violation is excluded from trial use to prove guilt. It is essential that cases be studied carefully to determine the various courts' interpretations concerning what constitutes a violation of the Sixth Amendment and what use might be made of the evidence with respect to impeachment.

Although courts often exclude illegally obtained evidence to enforce constitutional provisions, and some criminal justice practitioners may view the practice of exclusion as erecting roadblocks to justice, upholding and supporting exclusions have the effect of upholding the rule of law. Proper investigation that follows constitutional requirements and interpretations will result in both protecting the rights of the individual and successful prosecutions of wrongdoers with admissible evidence.

CHAPTER SIXTEEN: QUESTIONS AND REVIEW EXERCISES

1. When police have violated the Fourth Amendment rights of an individual during the process of acquiring evidence, the exclusionary rule generally prohibits the introduction of that illegally seized evidence against the defendant in both state and federal courts. What is the basic rationale for excluding otherwise

reliable evidence for consideration by a jury or by a judge?

2. The exclusionary rule has a variety of exceptions. What is the good faith exception to the exclusionary rule? According to the Supreme Court of the United States, what is the theoretical basis for allowing evidence to be admitted when police, in executing a warrant, made a mistake but did so in good faith?
3. Emergency situations when life or health may hang in the balance often permit officers to enter private premises without warrants. Give an example where police officers may properly enter a private home without a warrant, thus allowing any evidence discovered to be free of exclusion by the exclusionary rule.
4. Searches that are conducted following an arrest do not require separate probable cause to search the individual, his or her immediate possessions, or the area immediately around the arresting. In order for a search incident to an arrest to be considered valid, must the arrest have occurred prior to the search and must the arrest be a lawful one? Would an officer have probable cause to arrest if a dispatcher pulled outdated warrant information from a law enforcement computer and relayed the information to the officer who made the arrest?
5. Most constitutional rights can be waived, if the waiver is made knowingly and intelligently. Assume that a husband and wife were both present when police officers requested permission to search their marital home. Assume that the wife gave consent to search, but the husband refused to give consent. Could police lawfully search the home in the absence of a warrant based on the Fourth Amendment waiver by the wife? Would any evidence seized under such a search be admissible against the husband to prove guilt?
6. Consistent with the Fourth Amendment, may police search vehicles that they have stopped, or that are movable, without a warrant but with probable cause? Would any evidence seized be admissible in a criminal case against the owner-driver?
7. When police seize evidence that appeared in plain view, is there any reason for excluding such evidence from a criminal trial? Are there special requirements for using the plain view doctrine?
8. If law enforcement agents seized evidence from an individual's farm field that they entered without a warrant, would such evidence be admissible against the individual who owned and lived on the farm? What is the "open fields" doctrine?
9. What are the requirements for an inventory search of an automobile in order to produce evidence that will be admissible in court against the owner or lessee of the motor vehicle?

10. Where a police officer sees conduct by a subject that would seem suspicious, can the officer approach the subject and make a reasonable inquiry? Under what circumstances could the officer frisk the individual and produce evidence that would be admissible in court?
11. Is eavesdropping through the use of electronic collection devices not covered by the Fourth Amendment and the exclusionary rule, making evidence generated by these practices always admissible against the defendant involved in the incriminating conversations? If one person consents to eavesdropping or recording a conversation, is that conversation admissible into evidence in federal courts? Some state courts?
12. Constitutionally, coerced confessions are not admissible in criminal trials and should be suppressed under the Fifth Amendment. When deciding whether a confession was freely and voluntarily made, what factors should courts consider? Offer a fact pattern in which a confession should be excluded from evidence as having been involuntarily made.
13. What are the basic *Miranda* warnings that need to be given to an arrestee under circumstances when the police wish to interrogate the individual? If the warnings have been improperly offered, can the oral evidence from the arrestee be introduced in evidence against the arrestee?
14. Identification processes may produce evidence that a prosecutor would want to introduce at trial. When does an accused have the right to have counsel present at a pretrial in-person lineup?

Part II
Judicial Decisions Relating to Part I

Part II: Table of Cases

Cases Relating to Chapter 1
History and Development of Rules of Evidence
Funk v. United States, 290 U.S. 371 (1933)

Cases Relating to Chapter 2
Approach to the Study of Criminal Evidence
Craft v. State, 274 Ga. App. 410 (2005)
Trammel v. United States, 445 U.S. 40 (1980)
State v. Anthony, 218 Ariz. 439 (2008)

Cases Relating to Chapter 3
Burden of Proof
In re Winship, 397 U.S. 358 (1970)
Victor v. Nebraska, 511 U.S. 1 (1994)
State v. Eichelberger, 2005 Wash. App. LEXIS 2429 (2005)
Martin v. Ohio, 480 U.S. 228 (1987)

Cases Relating to Chapter 4
Proof via Evidence
Maddox v. Montgomery, 718 F.2d 1033 (11th Cir. 1983)
Brown v. State, 897 A.2d 748 (Del. 2006)
State v. Jordan, 2002 Ohio 1418 (Ohio App. 2002)

Cases Relating to Chapter 5
Judicial Notice
Commonwealth v. Howlett, 328 S.W.3d 191, 2010 Ky. LEXIS 292 (2010)
City v. Gamez, 2009 N.M. App. Unpub. LEXIS 464 (2009)
Robinson v. State, 260 Ga. App. 186, 2003 Ga. App. LEXIS 366 (2003)
State v. Smith, 2006 Del. C.P. LEXIS 34 (2006)

Cases Relating to Chapter 6
Presumptions, Inferences, and Stipulations
Williams v. State, So.3d 620 (2013)
Graham v. United States, 12 A.3d 1159, 2011 D.C. App. LEXIS 30 (2011)
Bozeman v. State, 931 So. 2d 1006 (Fla. App. 2006)

Cases Relating to Chapter 7
Relevancy and Materiality
Commonwealth v. Prashaw, 57 Mass. App. 19, 781 N.E.2d 19 (2003)

State v. Jackson, 2011 VT 15, 2011 Vt. LEXIS 12 (2011)
Wise v. State, 2011 Tex. App. LEXIS 1583 (2011)

Cases Relating to Chapter 8
Competency of Evidence and Witnesses
United States v. Phibbs, 999 F.2d 1053 (6th Cir. 1993)
State v. Wells, 2003 Ohio 3162 (Ohio App. 2003)

Cases Relating to Chapter 9
Examination of Witnesses
United States v. Drummond, 69 F. App'x 580 (2003)
People v. Melendez, 102 P.3d 315 (Colo. 2004)
State v. Sands, 2008 Ohio 6981 (Ohio App. 2008)

Cases Relating to Chapter 10
Privileges
St. Clair v. Commonwealth, 174 S.W.3d 474, 2005 Ky. LEXIS 334 (2005)
State v. Bergmann, 2009 Iowa App. LEXIS 54 (2009)
New York City Health v. Morgenthau, 98 N.Y.2d 525, 779 N.E.2d 173 (2002)

Cases Relating to Chapter 11
Opinions and Expert Testimony
Bowling v. State, 275 Ga. App. 45, 619 S.E.2d 688 (2005)
Osbourn v. State, 92 S.W.3d 531 (Tex. Crim. App. 2002)
United States v. Delatorre, 309 F. Appx. 366 (11th Cir. 2009)

Cases Relating to Chapter 12
Hearsay Rule and Exceptions
Bell v. State, 847 So. 2d 558 (Fla. App. 2003)
Gonzalez v. State, 195 S.W.3d 114 (Tex. Crim. App. 2006)
Cox v. State, 774 N.E.2d 1025 (Ind. App. 2002)
Sadler v. State, 2009 Tex. App. LEXIS 2962 (2009)
State v. Washington, 664 N.W.2d 203 (Mich. 2003)

Cases Relating to Chapter 13
Documentary Evidence
Wilkerson v. State, 2005 Ark. App. LEXIS 12 (2005)
State v. Huehn, 53 P.3d 733 (Colo. App. 2002)
McKeehan v. State, 838 So. 2d 1257 (Fla. App. 2003)

Cases Relating to Chapter 14
Real Evidence
Schmerber v. California, 384 U.S. 757 (1966)
State v. Cowans, 782 N.E.2d 779, 2002 Ill. App. LEXIS 1170, appeal denied by *People v. Cowans,* 2003 Ill. LEXIS 649 (2003)

Underwood v. State, 708 So. 2d 18 (Miss. 1998)
McHenry v. State, 820 N.E.2d 124 (Ind. 2005)

Cases Relating to Chapter 15
Results of Examinations and Tests
Commonwealth v. Gaynor, 443 Mass. 245, 820 N.E.2d 233 (2005)
People v. Wilkinson, 33 Cal. 4th 821, 2004 Cal. LEXIS 6833 (2004)
City of Cleveland Heights v. Katz, 2002 Ohio 4241 (Ohio App. 2001)

Cases Relating to Chapter 16
Evidence Unconstitutionally Obtained
United States v. Jones, 565 U.S. ___ (2012)
Arizona v. Gant, 556 U.S. 332, 2009 U.S. LEXIS 3120 (2009)
Maryland v. King, ___ 569 U.S. ___. 133 S.Ct. 1958 (2013)
Melendez-Diaz v. Massachusetts, 557 U.S. 305, 129 S. Ct. 2527 (2009)

Cases Relating to Chapter 1

History and Development of Rules of Evidence

FUNK v. UNITED STATES

Supreme Court of the United States, 290 U.S. 371, 54 S. Ct. 212 (1933)

JUSTICE SUTHERLAND delivered the opinion of the Court.

The sole inquiry to be made in this case is whether in a federal court the wife of the defendant on trial for a criminal offense is a competent witness in his behalf. Her competency to testify against him is not involved.

The petitioner was twice tried and convicted in a federal district court upon an indictment for conspiracy to violate the prohibition law. His conviction on the first trial was reversed by the circuit court of appeals upon a ground not material here. 46 F.2d 417. Upon the second trial, as upon the first, defendant called his wife to testify in his behalf. At both trials she was excluded upon the ground of incompetency. The circuit court of appeals sustained this ruling upon the first appeal, and also upon the appeal which followed the second trial. 66 F.2d 70. We granted certiorari, limited to the question as to what law is applicable to the determination of the competency of the wife of the petitioner as a witness.

Both the petitioner and the government, in presenting the case here, put their chief reliance on prior decisions of this court. The government relies on United States v. Reid, 12 How. 361; Logan v. United States, 144 U.S. 263; Hendrix v. United States, 219 U.S. 79; and Jin Fuey Moy v. United States, 254 U.S. 189. Petitioner contends that these cases, if not directly contrary to the decisions in Benson v. United States, 146 U.S. 325, and Rosen v. United States, 245 U.S. 467, are so in principle. We shall first briefly review these cases, with the exception of the Hendrix case and the Jin Fuey Moy case, which we leave for consideration until a later point in this opinion.

In the Reid case, two persons had been jointly indicted for a murder committed upon the high seas. They were tried separately, and it was held that one of them was not a competent witness in behalf of the other who was first tried. The trial was had in Virginia; and by a statute of that state passed in 1849, if applicable in a federal court, the evidence would have been competent. Section 34 of the Judiciary Act of 1789 declares that the laws of the several states, except where the Constitution, treaties or statutes of the United States otherwise provide, shall be regarded as rules of decision in trials at common law in the courts of the United States in cases where they apply; but the court said that this referred only to civil cases and did not apply in the trial of criminal offenses against the United States. It was conceded that there was no act of Congress prescribing in express words the rule by which the federal courts would be governed in the admission of testimony in criminal cases. "But," the court said (p. 363), "we think it may be found with sufficient certainty, not indeed in direct terms, but by necessary implication, in the acts of 1789 and 1790, establishing the courts of the United States, and providing for the punishment of certain offences."

The court pointed out that the Judiciary Act regulated certain proceedings to be had prior to impaneling the jury, but contained no express provision concerning the mode of conducting the trial after the jury was sworn, and prescribed no rule in respect of the testimony to be taken. Obviously however, it was said, some certain and established rule upon the subject was necessary to enable the courts to administer the criminal jurisprudence of the United States, and Congress must have intended to refer them to some known and established rule "which was supposed to be so familiar and well understood in the trial by jury that legislation upon the subject would be deemed superfluous. This is necessarily to be implied from what these acts of Congress omit, as well as from what they contain." (p. 365.) The court concluded that this could not be the common law as it existed at the time of the emigration of the colonists, or the rule which then prevailed in England, and [therefore] the only known rule which could be supposed to have been in the mind of Congress was that which was in force in the respective states when the federal courts were established by the Judiciary Act of 1789. Applying this rule, it was decided that the witness was incompetent.

In the Logan case it was held that the competency of a witness to testify in a federal court sitting in one state, was not affected by his conviction and sentence for felony in another state; and that the competency of another witness was not affected by his conviction of felony in a Texas state court, where the witness had since been pardoned. The indictment was for an offense committed in Texas and there tried. The decision was based not upon any statute of the United States, but upon the ground that the subject "is governed by the common law, which, as has been seen, was the law of Texas . . . at the time of the admission of Texas into the Union as a State." (p. 303.)

We next consider the two cases upon which petitioner relies. In the Benson case two persons were jointly indicted for murder. On motion of the government there was a severance, and Benson was first tried. His codefendant was called as a witness on behalf of the government. The Reid case had been cited as practically decisive of the question. But the court, after pointing out what it conceived to be distinguishing features in that case, said (p. 335), "We do not feel ourselves, therefore, precluded by that case from examining this question in the light of general authority and sound reason."

The alleged incompetency of the codefendant was rested upon two reasons, first, that he was interested, and second, that he was a party to the record, the basis for the exclusion at common law being fear of perjury. "Nor," the court said, "were those named the only grounds of exclusion from the witness stand; conviction of crime, want of religious belief, and other matters were held sufficient. Indeed, the theory of the common law was to admit to the witness stand only those presumably honest, appreciating the sanctity of an oath, unaffected as a party by the result, and free from any of the temptations of interest. The courts were afraid to trust the intelligence of jurors. But the last fifty years have wrought a great change in these respects, and to-day the tendency is to enlarge the domain of competency and to submit to the jury for their consideration as to the credibility of the witness those matters which heretofore were ruled sufficient to justify his exclusion. This change has been wrought partially by legislation and partially by judicial construction." Attention then is called to the fact that Congress in 1864 had enacted that no witness should be excluded from testifying in any civil action, with certain exceptions, because he was a party to or interested in the issue tried; and that in 1878 (c. 37, 20 Stat. 30) Congress made the defendant in any criminal case a competent witness at his own request. The opinion then continues (p. 337):

> Legislation of similar import prevails in most of the States. The spirit of this legislation has controlled the decisions of the courts, and steadily, one by one, the merely technical barriers which excluded witnesses from the stand have been removed, till now it is generally, though perhaps not universally, true that no one is excluded therefrom unless the lips of the originally adverse party are closed by death, or unless some one of those peculiarly confidential relations, like that of husband and wife, forbids the breaking of silence.
>
> . . . If interest and being party to the record do not exclude a defendant on trial from the witness stand, upon what reasoning can a codefendant, not on trial, be adjudged incompetent?

That case was decided December 5, 1892. Twenty-five years later this court had before it for consideration the case of Rosen v. United States, *supra*. Rosen had been tried and convicted in a federal district court for conspiracy. A person jointly indicted with Rosen, who had been convicted upon his plea of guilty, was called as a witness by the government and allowed to testify over Rosen's objection. This court sustained the competency of the witness. After saying that while the decision in the Reid case had not been specifically overruled, its authority was seriously shaken by the decisions in both the Logan and Benson cases, the court proceeded to dispose of the question, as it had been disposed of in the Benson case, "in the light of general authority and sound reason."

> "In the almost twenty [twenty-five] years," the court said [pp. 471, 472], "which have elapsed since the decision of the Benson Case, the disposition of courts and of legislative bodies to remove disabilities from witnesses has continued, as that decision shows it had been going forward before, under dominance of the conviction of our time that the truth is more likely to be arrived at by hearing the testimony of all persons of competent understanding who may seem to have knowledge of the facts involved in a case, leaving the credit and weight of such testimony to be determined by the jury or by the court, rather than by rejecting witnesses as incompetent, with the result that this principle has come to be widely, almost universally, accepted in this country and in Great Britain.
>
> "Since the decision in the Benson Case we have significant evidence of the trend of congressional opinion upon this subject in the removal of the disability of witnesses convicted of perjury, Rev. Stats., § 5392, by the enactment of the Federal Criminal Code in 1909 with this provision omitted and § 5392 repealed. This is significant, because the disability to testify, of persons convicted of perjury, survived in some jurisdictions much longer than many of the other common-law disabilities, for the reason that the offense concerns directly the giving of testimony in a court of justice, and conviction of it was accepted as showing a greater disregard for the truth than it was thought should be implied from a conviction of other crime.
>
> "Satisfied as we are that the legislation and the very great weight of judicial authority which have developed in support of this modern rule, especially as applied to the competency of witnesses convicted of crime, proceed upon sound principle, we conclude that the dead hand of the common-law rule of 1789 should no longer be applied to such cases as we have here, and that the ruling of the lower courts on this first claim of error should be approved."

It is well to pause at this point to state a little more concisely what was held in these cases. It will be noted, in the first place, that the decision in the Reid case was not based upon any express statutory provision. The court found from what the congressional legislation omitted to say, as well as from what it actually said, that in establishing the federal courts in 1789 some definite rule in respect to the testimony to be taken in criminal cases must have been in the mind of Congress; and the rule which the court thought was in the mind of that body was that of the common law as it existed in the thirteen original states in 1789. The Logan Case in part rejected that view and held that the controlling rule was that of the common law in force at the time of the admission of the state in which the particular trial was had. Taking the two cases together, it is plain enough that the ultimate doctrine announced is that in the taking of testimony in criminal cases, the federal courts are bound by the rules of the common law as they existed at a definitely specified time in the respective states, unless Congress has otherwise provided.

With the conclusion that the controlling rule is that of the common law, the Benson case and the Rosen case do not conflict; but both cases reject the notion, which the two earlier ones seem to accept, that the courts, in the face of greatly changed conditions, are still chained to the ancient formulae and are powerless to declare and enforce modifications deemed to have been wrought in the common law itself by force of these changed conditions. Thus, as we have seen, the court in the Benson case pointed to the tendency during the preceding years to enlarge the domain of competency, significantly saying that the changes had been wrought not only by legislation but also "partially by judicial construction"; and that it was the spirit (not the letter, be it observed) of this legislation which had controlled the decisions of the courts and steadily removed the merely technical barriers in respect of incompetency, until generally no one was excluded from giving testimony, except under certain peculiar conditions which are set forth. It seems difficult to escape the conclusion that the specific ground upon which the court there rested its determination as to the competency of a codefendant was that, since the defendant had been rendered competent, the competency of the codefendant followed as a natural consequence.

This view of the matter is made more positive by the decision in the Rosen case. The question of the testimonial competency of a person jointly indicted with the defendant was disposed of, as the question had been in the Benson case, "in the light of general authority and sound reason." The conclusion which the court reached was based not upon any definite act of legislation, but upon the trend of congressional opinion and of legislation (that is to say of legislation generally), and upon the great weight of judicial authority which, since the earlier decisions, had developed in support of a more modern rule. In both cases the court necessarily proceeded upon the theory that the resultant modification which these important considerations had wrought in the rules of the old common law was within the power of the courts to declare and make operative.

That the present case falls within the principles of the Benson and Rosen cases, and especially of the latter, we think does not reasonably admit of doubt.

The rules of the common law which disqualified as witnesses persons having an interest, long since, in the main, have been abolished both in England and in this country; and what was once regarded as a sufficient ground for excluding the testimony of such persons altogether has come to be uniformly and more sensibly regarded as affecting the credit of the witness only. Whatever was the danger that an interested witness would not speak the truth—and the danger never was as great as claimed—its effect has been minimized almost to the vanishing point by the test of cross-examination, the increased intelligence of jurors, and perhaps other circumstances. The modern rule which has removed the disqualification from persons accused of crime gradually came into force after the middle of the last century, and is today universally accepted. The exclusion of the husband or wife is said by this court to be based upon his or her interest in the event. Jin Fuey Moy v. United States, *supra*. And whether by this is meant a practical interest in the result of the prosecution or merely a sentimental interest because of the marital relationship, makes little difference. In either case, a refusal to permit the wife upon the ground of interest to testify in behalf of her husband, while permitting him, who has the greater interest, to testify for himself, presents a manifest incongruity.

Nor can the exclusion of the wife's testimony, in the face of the broad and liberal extension of the rules in respect of the competency of witnesses generally, be any longer justified, if it ever was justified, on any ground of public policy. It has been said that to admit such testimony is against public policy because it would endanger the harmony and confidence of marital relations, and, moreover, would subject the witness to the temptation to commit perjury. Modern legislation, in making either spouse competent to testify in behalf of the other in criminal cases, has definitely rejected these notions, and in the light of such legislation and of modern thought they seem to be altogether fanciful. The public policy of one generation may not, under changed conditions, be the public policy of another. Patton v. United States, 281 U.S. 276, 306.

The fundamental basis upon which all rules of evidence must rest—if they are to rest upon reason—is their adaptation to the successful development of the truth. And since experience is of all teachers the most dependable, and since experience also is a continuous process, it follows that a rule of evidence at one time thought necessary to the ascertainment of truth should yield to the experience of a succeeding generation whenever that experience has clearly demonstrated the fallacy or unwisdom of the old rule.

It may be said that the court should continue to enforce the old rule, however contrary to modern experience and thought, and however opposed, in principle, to the general current of legislation and of judicial opinion, it may have become, leaving to Congress the responsibility of changing it. Of course, Congress has that power; but if Congress fail to act, as it has failed in respect of the matter now under review, and the court be called upon to decide the question, is it not the duty of the court, if it possess the power, to decide it in accordance with present day standards of wisdom and justice rather than in accordance with some outworn and antiquated rule of the past? That this court has the power to do so is necessarily implicit in the opinions delivered in deciding the Benson and Rosen cases. And that implication, we think, rests upon substantial ground. The rule of the common law which denies the competency of one spouse to testify in behalf of the other in a criminal prosecution has not been modified by congressional legislation; nor has Congress directed the federal courts to follow state law upon that subject, as it has in respect of some other subjects. That this court and the other federal courts, in this situation and by right of their own powers, may decline to enforce the ancient rule of the common law under conditions as they now exist we think is not fairly open to doubt.

In Hurtado v. California, 110 U.S. 516, 530, this court, after suggesting that it was better not to go too far back into antiquity for the best securities of our liberties, said:

> It is more consonant to the true philosophy of our historical legal institutions to say that the spirit of personal liberty and individual right, which they embodied, was preserved and developed by a progressive growth and wise adaptation to new circumstances and situations of the forms and processes found fit to give, from time to time, new expression and greater effect to modern ideas of self-government.
>
> This flexibility and capacity for growth and adaptation is the peculiar boast and excellence of the common law. . . . and as it was the characteristic principle of the common law to draw its inspiration from every fountain of justice, we are not to assume that the sources of its supply have been exhausted. On the contrary, we should expect that the new and various experiences of our own situation and system will mould and shape it into new and not less useful forms.

Compare Holden v. Hardy, 169 U.S. 366, 385-387. To concede this capacity for growth and change in the common law by drawing "its inspiration from every fountain of justice," and at the same time to say that the courts of this country are forever bound to perpetuate such of its rules as, by every reasonable test, are found to be neither wise nor just, because we have once adopted them as suited to our situation and institutions at a particular time, is to deny to the common law in the place of its adoption a "flexibility and capacity for growth and adaptation" which was "the peculiar boast and excellence" of the system in the place of its origin.

The final question to which we are thus brought is not that of the power of the federal courts to amend or repeal any given rule or principle of the common law, for they neither have nor claim that power, but it is the question of the power of these courts, in the complete absence of congressional legislation on the subject, to declare and effectuate, upon common law principles, what is the present rule upon a given subject in the light of fundamentally altered conditions, without regard to what has previously been declared and practiced. It has been said so often as to have become axiomatic that the common law is not immutable but flexible, and by its own principles adapts itself to varying conditions. In Ketelsen v. Stilz, 184 Ind. 702; 111 N. E. 423, the supreme court of that state, after pointing out that the common law of England was based upon usages, customs and institutions of the English people as declared from time to time by the courts, said (p. 707):

> The rules so deduced from this system, however, were continually changing and expanding with the progress of society in the application of this system to more diversified circumstances and under more advanced periods. The common law by its own principles adapted itself to varying conditions and modified its own rules so as to serve the ends of justice as prompted by a course of reasoning which was guided by these generally accepted truths. One of its oldest maxims was that where the reason of a rule ceased, the rule also ceased, and it logically followed that when it occurred to the courts that a particular rule had never been founded upon reason, and that no reason existed in support thereof, that rule likewise ceased, and perhaps another sprang up in its place which was based upon reason and justice as then conceived. No rule of the common law could survive the reason on which it was founded. It needed no statute to change it but abrogated itself.

That court then refers to the settled doctrine that an adoption of the common law in general terms does not require, without regard to local circumstances, an unqualified application of all its rules; that the rules, as declared by the English courts at one period or another, have been controlling in this country only so far as they were suited to and in harmony with the genius, spirit and objects of American institutions; and that the rules of the common law considered proper in the eighteenth century are not necessarily so considered in the twentieth. "Since courts have had an existence in America," that court said (p. 708), "they have never hesitated to take upon themselves the responsibility of saying what are the proper rules of the common law."

And the Virginia Supreme Court of Appeals, in Hanriot v. Sherwood, 82 Va. 1, 15, after pointing to the fact that the common law of England is the law of that commonwealth except so far as it has been altered by statute, or so far as its principles are inapplicable to the state of the country, and that the rules of the common law had undergone modification in the courts of England, notes with obvious approval that "the rules of evidence have been in the courts of this country undergoing such modification and changes, according to the circumstances of the country and the manner and genius of the people."

The supreme court of Connecticut, in Beardsley v. Hartford, 50 Conn. 529, 541-542, after quoting the maxim of the common law, cessante ratione legis, cessat ipsa lex, said:

> This means that no law can survive the reasons on which it is founded. It needs no statute to change it; it abrogates itself. If the reasons on which a law rests are overborne by opposing reasons, which in the progress of society gain a controlling force, the old law, though still good as an abstract principle, and good in its application to some circumstances, must cease to apply as a controlling principle to the new circumstances.

The same thought is expressed in People v. Randolph, 2 Park. Cr. Rep. (N. Y.) 174, 177:

> Its rules [the rules of the common law] are modified upon its own principles and not in violation of them. Those rules being founded in reason, one of its oldest maxims is, that where the reason of the rule ceases the rule also ceases.

* * *

Judgment reversed.

MR. JUSTICE CARDOZO concurs in the result.

MR. JUSTICE McREYNOLDS and MR. JUSTICE BUTLER are of opinion that the judgment of the court below is right and should be affirmed.

Cases Relating to Chapter 2

Approach to the Study of Criminal Evidence

CRAFT
v.
STATE

Court of Appeals of Georgia, 274 Ga. App. 410, 2005 Ga. App. LEXIS 778 (2005)

Opinion by Phipps, Judge.

Rodney Craft was tried by a jury and convicted of two counts of child molestation. He was sentenced to forty years, ten in confinement and thirty on probation. On appeal, he claims that the trial court erred in its questioning of two witnesses and in refusing to allow his trial counsel to introduce evidence of the victims' academic records. Craft also charges his trial counsel with ineffective assistance. We conclude that the trial court violated OCGA 17-8-57 by its questioning of one witness. We further conclude that the statutory violation, coupled with the trial court's failure to allow Craft a thorough and sifting cross-examination, constituted plain error. Therefore, we reverse. Because the evidence was sufficient to support the verdict under the standard of Jackson v. Virginia, the case can be retried.

The evidence showed that C. W. and T. J., both 15 years old, were walking to school in Columbus on August 26, 2002. As they walked by Craft's house, Craft said to C. W., "Hey, look over here." C. W. looked in that direction and saw Craft standing naked at his door, masturbating. C. W. told T. J. to look, and T. J. also saw Craft naked and masturbating. They ran the rest of the way to school and reported the incident to the assistant principal, Senobia Moore. After investigation by Columbus police officers, Craft was arrested.

Craft claims that the trial court erred by asking Moore questions about the character of the victims in such a manner as to cause the jury to believe that the court had formed or expressed an opinion about the veracity of the victims, in violation of OCGA 17-8-57.

The following exchange is at issue:

THE COURT: Ms. Moore, I just have a couple of questions for you. Do you know what kind of students these two girls are?

THE WITNESS: Yes. They are very good students. Actually, one is a cheerleader and they are very mannerable, very poli[t]e young ladies. And, again, knowing that they are not ones that are real wild and real, you know, loud in the halls and everything, the way that I saw them that day, you know, caused my attention to go to them.

THE COURT: Are the cheerleaders at [your school] required to make a certain grade-point average?

THE WITNESS: Yes, well, we follow the State, the code that goes with athletes, and if you —

THE COURT: So that's the same requirement?

THE WITNESS: Yes, it is. And if you fail two classes, you cannot participate. So it's the fail-no-participate rule. However, our students are still monitored. All of our athletes are monitored; and if their grades begin to fall low, they can be pulled from a game or pulled from participating for a period of time.

THE COURT: Based on the individual school policy?

THE WITNESS: Yes.

"The credibility and standing of the witness is an issuable fact in every case — a most material fact. Therefore, anything which tends to uphold, to support, to disparage, or to lower the character and the resulting credibility of the witness is vitally connected with the facts of the case." 8 This case was based almost entirely on the testimony of the victims. As a result, their credibility was the most important issue in the case.

Focused on what it calls the court's "leeway" in posing questions during a criminal trial, the dissent misses the point. We do not challenge the trial court's right to "occasional and cautious" questioning of witnesses to develop the truth of a case. Instead, we hold that the specific questioning in this case constituted a violation of OCGA 17-8-57. Contrary to the dissent's argument, we are not breaking new ground or establishing a new rule in holding that a trial court violates OCGA 17-8-57 when it intimates its opinion as to the credibility of a witness — an issue within the sole province of the jury. We are merely applying existing case law to the specific facts of this case — a task performed daily by judges at the trial and appellate levels.

We do not conclude that the trial court's improper questioning, standing alone, constituted plain error. Instead, we consider the issue of plain error in connection with Craft's next claim.

After the court asked Moore questions about the victims' school performance, Craft sought to question her about their academic history and disciplinary history. Craft asked Moore what kind of student C. W. was, Moore admitted that even polite students get into minor trouble and, at Craft's request, Moore explained "administrative detention." The state objected to the line of questioning at that point. Craft's counsel responded that he had documents that contradicted some of Moore's testimony about the victims' school performance and conduct. The court refused to allow Craft to pursue the matter further, stating "you're not going to make these victims look bad." Although this statement was made during a bench conference, it demonstrated that the trial court had reached the conclusion that the state had already proven that the girls were victims. Further, that conclusion likely formed the basis for the trial court's decision to shut down Craft's cross-examination. Craft claims that the trial court's refusal to allow further cross-examination constituted an abuse of the court's discretion.

As noted previously, the testimony elicited by the trial court bolstered the credibility of the victims, which had not previously been challenged. After opening the door to this line of questioning and allowing Moore to testify that the victims were very good students who were well-behaved, the trial court refused to allow Craft to rebut this testimony. Craft had documents showing that C. W. had been disciplined for disrespect and had been placed in administrative detention on two occasions, along with one showing that T. J. had been cited for screaming in the hallway and subjected to in-school suspension. Other documents showed that both victims had failed at least two classes.

The dissent argues that it was sufficient to allow Craft to ask four questions that "inferred to the jury that the two students fell short of perfection." But the limited questioning allowed by the court clearly was not adequate to rebut the critical testimony the court had elicited and did not provide. Craft the thorough and sifting cross-examination to which he was entitled.

The right of cross examination is a substantial right, the preservation of which is essential to the proper administration of justice and extends to all matters within the knowledge of the witness, the disclosure of which is material to the controversy. This right should not be abridged.

Here, not only did the court refuse to allow Craft further questioning of the witness; it refused to allow Craft to introduce the documentary evidence that would have specifically rebutted Moore's testimony regarding the behavior and academic standing of the victims.

We disagree with the dissent's implication that the focus should be on the number of questions asked by the trial court instead of the impact of those questions on the judicial proceedings. The dissent also seems to misunderstand our ultimate conclusion — when the trial court's improper questioning was compounded with the court's refusal to allow Craft to rebut the testimony the court had elicited, it "seriously affected the fairness, integrity, and public reputation" of the judicial proceedings.

Because it is possible that the situation could occur on retrial, we address Craft's claim that the trial court erred when it asked T. J. the following:

THE COURT: Did you have any trouble seeing through the screen door on any of the occasions that you saw him standing behind the screen door?

THE WITNESS: No, ma'am.

THE COURT: Could you be mistaken about what he was doing?

THE WITNESS: No, ma'am.

THE COURT: On any of the times that you saw him?

THE WITNESS: No, ma'am.

Craft argues that the questioning bolstered T. J.'s credibility and revealed a clear bias toward the prosecution, in violation of OCGA 17-8-57.

During direct examination by the state, T. J. testified that she had seen Craft in his boxer shorts on August 19, while she was walking to school. She testified that when she saw him on August 26, he was standing behind a screen door and a light was on behind him. On cross-examination, Craft's counsel asked T. J. numerous questions about what she could and could not see through Craft's screen door.

Because Craft raised no objection to the questioning, he waived his right to assert the issue on appeal. Even if Craft had objected, we find that no error occurred because the trial court merely sought to clarify T. J.'s testimony. The trial court may propound questions to any witness to develop the truth of the case.

Craft's remaining claims are moot.

Judgment reversed. Barnes, J., concurs. Ruffin, C. J., and Blackburn, P. J., concur specially. Andrews, P. J., Johnson, P. J., and Mikell, J., dissent

TRAMMEL v. UNITED STATES

Supreme Court of the United States, 445 U.S. 40, 100 S. Ct. 906,63 L. Ed. 2d 186 (1980)

MR. CHIEF JUSTICE BURGER delivered the opinion of the Court.

We granted certiorari to consider whether an accused may invoke the privilege against adverse spousal testimony so as to exclude the voluntary testimony of his wife. 440 U.S. 934 (1979). This calls for a re-examination of Hawkins v. United States, 358 U.S. 74 (1958).

I.

On March 10, 1976, petitioner Otis Trammel was indicted with two others, Edwin Lee Roberts and Joseph Freeman, for importing heroin into the United States from Thailand and the Philippine Islands and for conspiracy to import heroin in violation of 21 U. S. C.§§ 952 (a), 962 (a), and 963. The indictment also named six unindicted co-conspirators, including petitioner's wife Elizabeth Ann Trammel.

According to the indictment, petitioner and his wife flew from the Philippines to California in August 1975, carrying with them a quantity of heroin. Freeman and Roberts assisted them in its distribution. Elizabeth Trammel then traveled to Thailand where she purchased another supply of the drug. On November 3, 1975, with four ounces of heroin on her person, she boarded a plane for the United States. During a routine customs search in Hawaii, she was searched, the heroin was discovered, and she was arrested. After discussions with Drug Enforcement Administration agents, she agreed to cooperate with the Government.

Prior to trial on this indictment, petitioner moved to sever his case from that of Roberts and Freeman. He advised the court that the Government intended to call his wife as an adverse witness and asserted his claim to a privilege to prevent her from testifying against him. At a hearing on the motion, Mrs. Trammel was called as a Government witness under a grant of use immunity. She testified that she and petitioner were married in May 1975 and that they remained married. She explained that her cooperation with the Government was based on assurances that she would be given lenient treatment. She then described, in considerable detail, her role and that of her husband in the heroin distribution conspiracy.

After hearing this testimony, the District Court ruled that Mrs. Trammel could testify in support of the Government's case to any act she observed during the marriage and to any communication "made in the presence of a third person"; however, confidential communications between petitioner and his wife were held to be privileged and inadmissible. The motion to sever was denied.

At trial, Elizabeth Trammel testified within the limits of the court's pretrial ruling; her testimony, as the Government concedes, constituted virtually its entire case against petitioner. He was found guilty on both the substantive and conspiracy charges and sentenced to an indeterminate term of years pursuant to the Federal Youth Corrections Act, 18 U. S. C. § 5010 (b).

In the Court of Appeals petitioner's only claim of error was that the admission of the adverse testimony of his wife, over his objection, contravened this Court's teaching in Hawkins v. United States, *supra*, and therefore constituted reversible error. The Court of Appeals rejected this contention. It concluded that Hawkins did not prohibit "the voluntary testimony of a spouse who appears as an unindicted co-conspirator under grant of immunity from the Government in return for her testimony." 583 F.2d 1166, 1168 (CA10 1978).

II.

The privilege claimed by petitioner has ancient roots. Writing in 1628, Lord Coke observed that "it hath been resolved by the Justices that a wife cannot be produced either against or for her husband." 1 E. Coke, A Commentarie upon Littleton 6b (1628). See, generally, 8 J. Wigmore, Evidence § 2227 (McNaughton rev. 1961). This spousal disqualification sprang from two canons of medieval jurisprudence: first, the rule that an accused was not permitted to testify in his own behalf because of his interest in the proceeding; second, the concept that husband and wife were one, and that since the woman had no recognized separate legal existence, the husband was that one. From those two now long-abandoned doctrines, it followed that what was inadmissible from the lips of the defendant-husband was also inadmissible from his wife.

Despite its medieval origins, this rule of spousal disqualification remained intact in most common-law jurisdictions well into the 19th century. See id., § 2333. It was applied by this Court in Stein v. Bowman, 13 Pet. 209, 220–223 (1839), in Graves v. United States, 150 U.S. 118 (1893), and again in Jin Fuey Moy v. United States, 254 U.S. 189, 195 (1920), where it was deemed so well established a proposition as to "hardly [require] mention." Indeed, it was not until 1933, in Funk v. United States, 290 U.S. 371, that this Court abolished the testimonial disqualification in the federal courts, so as to permit the spouse of a defendant to testify in the defendant's behalf. Funk, however, left undisturbed the rule that either spouse could prevent the other from giving adverse testimony. Id., at 373. The rule thus evolved into one of privilege rather than one of absolute disqualification. See J. Maguire, Evidence, Common Sense and Common Law 78–92 (1947).

The modern justification for this privilege against adverse spousal testimony is its perceived role in fostering the harmony and sanctity of the marriage relationship. Notwithstanding this benign purpose, the rule was sharply criticized. Professor Wigmore termed it "the merest anachronism in legal theory and an indefensible obstruction to truth in practice." 8 Wigmore § 2228, at 221. The Committee on Improvements in the Law of Evidence of the American Bar Association called for its abolition. 63 American Bar Association Reports 594–595 (1938). In its place, Wigmore and others suggested a privilege protecting only private marital communications, counsell on the privilege between priest and penitent, attorney and client, and physician and patient. See 8 Wigmore § 2332 et seq.

These criticisms influenced the American Law Institute, which, in its 1942 Model Code of Evidence, advocated a privilege for marital confidences, but expressly rejected a rule vesting in the defendant the right to exclude all adverse testimony of his spouse. See American Law Institute, Model Code of Evidence, Rule 215 (1942). In 1953 the Uniform Rules of Evidence, drafted by the National Conference of Commissioners on Uniform State Laws, followed a similar course; it limited the privilege to confidential communications and "[abolished] the rule, still existing in some states, and largely a sentimental relic, of not requiring one spouse to testify against the other in a criminal action." See Rule 23 (2) and comments. Several state legislatures enacted similarly patterned provisions into law.

In Hawkins v. United States, 358 U.S. 74 (1958), this Court considered the continued vitality of the privilege against adverse spousal testimony in the federal courts. There the District Court had permitted petitioner's wife, over his objection, to testify against him. With one questioning concurring opinion, the Court held the wife's testimony inadmissible; it took note of the critical comments that the common-law rule had engendered, but chose not to abandon it. Also rejected was the Government's suggestion that the Court modify the privilege by vesting it in the witness-spouse, with freedom to testify or not independent of the defendant's control. The Court viewed this proposed modification as antithetical to the widespread belief, evidenced in the rules then in effect in a majority of the States and in England, "that the law should not force or encourage testimony which might alienate husband and wife, or further inflame existing domestic differences." Id., at 79.

Hawkins, then, left the federal privilege for adverse spousal testimony where it found it, continuing "a rule which bars the testimony of one spouse against the other unless both consent." Id., at 78. Accord, Wyatt v. United States, 362 U.S. 525, 528 (1960). However, in so doing, the Court made clear that its decision was not meant to "foreclose whatever changes in the rule may eventually be dictated by 'reason and experience.'" 358 U.S., at 79.

II.

A.

The Federal Rules of Evidence acknowledge the authority of the federal courts to continue the evolutionary development of testimonial privileges in federal criminal trials "governed by the principles of the common law as they may be interpreted . . . in the light of reason and experience." Fed. Rule Evid. 501.

* * *

Although Rule 501 confirms the authority of the federal courts to reconsider the continued validity of the Hawkins rule, the long history of the privilege suggests that it ought not to be casually cast aside. That the privilege is one affecting marriage, home, and family relationships—already subject to much erosion in our day—also counsels caution. At the same time, we cannot escape the reality that the law on occasion adheres to doctrinal concepts long after the reasons which gave them birth have disappeared and after experience suggests the need for change. This was recognized in Funk where the Court "[declined] to enforce . . . ancient [rules] of the common law under conditions as they now exist." 290 U.S., at 382. For, as Mr. Justice Black admonished in another setting, "[when] precedent and precedent alone is all the argument that can be made to support a court-fashioned rule, it is time for the rule's creator to destroy it." Francis v. Southern Pacific Co., 333 U.S. 445, 471 (1948) (dissenting opinion).

B.

Since 1958, when Hawkins was decided, support for the privilege against adverse spousal testimony has been eroded further. Thirty-one jurisdictions, including Alaska and Hawaii, then allowed an accused a privilege to prevent adverse spousal testimony. 358 U.S., at 81, n. 3 (STEWART, J., concurring). The number has now declined to 24. In 1974, the National Conference on Uniform State Laws revised its Uniform Rules of Evidence, but again rejected the Hawkins rule in favor of a limited privilege for confidential communications. See Uniform Rules of Evidence, Rule 504. That proposed rule has been enacted in Arkansas, North Dakota, and Oklahoma—each of which in 1958 permitted an accused to exclude adverse spousal testimony. The trend in state law toward divesting the accused of the privilege to bar adverse spousal testimony has special relevance because the laws of marriage and domestic relations are concerns traditionally reserved to the states. See Sosna v. Iowa, 419 U.S. 393, 404 (1975). Scholarly criticism of the Hawkins rule has also continued unabated.

Support for the common-law rule has also diminished in England. In 1972, a study group there proposed giving the privilege to the witness-spouse, on the ground that "if [the wife] is willing to give evidence . . . the law would be showing excessive concern for the preservation of marital harmony if it were to say that she must not do so." Criminal Law Revision Committee, Eleventh Report, Evidence (General) 93.

C.

Testimonial exclusionary rules and privileges contravene the fundamental principle that "the public . . . has a right to every man's evidence." United States v. Bryan, 339 U.S. 323, 331 (1950). As such, they must be strictly construed and accepted "only to the very limited extent that permitting a refusal to testify or excluding relevant evidence has a public good transcending the normally predominant principle of utilizing all rational means for ascertaining truth." Elkins v. United States, 364 U.S. 206, 234 (1960) (Frankfurter, J., dissenting). Accord, United States v. Nixon, 418 U.S. 683, 709–710 (1974). Here we must decide whether the privilege against adverse spousal testimony promotes sufficiently important interests to outweigh the need for probative evidence in the administration of criminal justice.

It is essential to remember that the Hawkins privilege is not needed to protect information privately disclosed between husband and wife in the confidence of the marital relationship—once described by this Court as "the best solace of human existence." Stein v. Bowman, 13 Pet., at 223. Those confidences are privileged under the independent rule protecting confidential marital communications. Blau v. United States, 340 U.S. 332 (1951); see n. 5, *supra*. The Hawkins privilege is invoked, not to exclude private marital communications, but rather to exclude evidence of criminal acts and of communications made in the presence of third persons.

No other testimonial privilege sweeps so broadly. The privileges between priest and penitent, attorney and client, and physician and patient limit protection to private communications. These privileges are rooted in the imperative need for confidence and trust. The priest-penitent privilege recognizes the human need to disclose to a spiritual counsellor, in total and absolute confidence, what are believed to be flawed acts or thoughts and to receive priestly consolation and guidance in return. The lawyer-client privilege rests on the need for the advocate and counsellor to know all that relates to the client's reasons for seeking representation if the professional mission is to be carried out. Similarly, the physician must know all that a patient can articulate in order to identify and to treat disease; barriers to full disclosure would impair diagnosis and treatment.

The Hawkins rule stands in marked contrast to these three privileges. Its protection is not limited to confidential communications; rather it permits an accused to exclude all adverse spousal testimony. As Jeremy Bentham observed more than a century and a half ago, such a privilege goes far beyond making "every man's house his castle," and permits a person to convert his house into "a den of thieves." 5 Rationale of Judicial Evidence 340 (1827). It "secures, to every man, one safe and unquestionable and ever ready accomplice for every imaginable crime." Id., at 338.

The ancient foundations for so sweeping a privilege have long since disappeared. Nowhere in the common-law world—indeed in any modern society—is a woman regarded as chattel or demeaned by denial of a separate legal identity and the dignity associated with recognition as a whole human being. Chip by chip, over the years those archaic notions have been cast aside so that "[no] longer is the female destined solely for the home and the rearing of the family, and only the male for the marketplace and the world of ideas." Stanton v. Stanton, 421 U.S. 7, 14–15 (1975).

The contemporary justification for affording an accused such a privilege is also unpersuasive. When one spouse is willing to testify against the other in a criminal proceeding—whatever the motivation—their relationship is almost certainly in disrepair; there is probably little in the way of marital harmony for the privilege to preserve. In these circumstances, a rule of evidence that permits an accused to prevent adverse spousal testimony seems far more likely to frustrate justice than to foster family peace. Indeed, there is reason to believe that vesting the privilege in the accused could actually undermine the marital relationship. For example, in a case such as this, the Government is unlikely to offer a wife immunity and lenient treatment if it knows that her husband can prevent her from giving adverse testimony. If the Government is dissuaded from making such an offer, the privilege can have the untoward effect of permitting one spouse to escape justice at the expense of the other. It hardly seems conducive to the preservation of the marital relation to place a wife in jeopardy solely by virtue of her husband's control over her testimony.

IV.

Our consideration of the foundations for the privilege and its history satisfy us that "reason and experience" no longer justify so sweeping a rule as that found acceptable by the Court in Hawkins. Accordingly, we conclude that the existing rule should be modified so that the witness-spouse alone has a privilege to refuse to testify adversely; the witness may be neither compelled to testify nor foreclosed from testifying. This modification—vesting the privilege in the witness-spouse—furthers the important public interest in marital harmony without unduly burdening legitimate law enforcement needs.

Here, petitioner's spouse chose to testify against him. That she did so after a grant of immunity and assurances of lenient treatment does not render her testimony involuntary. Cf. Bordenkircher v. Hayes, 434 U.S. 357 (1978). Accordingly, the District Court and the Court of Appeals were correct in rejecting petitioner's claim of privilege, and the judgment of the Court of Appeals is

Affirmed.

STATE v. ANTHONY

Supreme Court of Arizona, 218 Ariz. 439 2008 Ariz. LEXIS 123 (2008)

En Banc

HURWITZ, Justice

On July 7, 2001, Donna Jean Anthony and her two children failed to arrive in Ohio as planned for a family visit. David Lamar Anthony, Donna's husband, was later charged with murdering the three. Anthony was convicted of three counts of first-degree murder after a jury trial in Maricopa County Superior Court; three death sentences were imposed.

This is an automatic appeal pursuant to Arizona Rule of Criminal Procedure 31.2(b) from the convictions and sentences. We have jurisdiction under Article 6, Section 5(3) of the Arizona Constitution and A.R.S. 13–4031 (2001).

I.

At the time of trial, the bodies of the victims had not been recovered. Anthony did not admit to the crimes and there were no witnesses to the murders. The State's case was therefore built on circumstantial evidence. We begin by summarizing that evidence.

A.

Anthony and Donna were married in 1997. Donna had two minor children from a previous marriage - Danielle Romero, born in 1987, and Richard Romero, born in 1988 - both of whom lived with the Anthonys. The Anthony marriage was troubled almost from the outset. Donna and Anthony frequently argued and the evidence suggests that Anthony was unfaithful. Donna apparently did not trust Anthony in financial matters. In late 2000, the family home was refinanced. Donna instructed the mortgage officer not to release the loan proceeds, approximately $ 105,000, to Anthony. She deposited the check into her personal savings account at Bank One, which Anthony could not access.

B.

[On June 25, 200, Donna purchased plane tickets for herself and her children to visit her family in Columbus, Ohio. Three days later somebody changed the PIN on her bank card and later moved the mortgage money from her account to the defendant's account. On July 6, 200, her credit card was used at a gasoline station at a time when she would have been finishing up her second shift. Donna and the children were never seen again and they never boarded the scheduled flight to Columbus, Ohio on 7 July. Defendant contracted to purchase a new truck in late June, but delayed taking delivery until July. He contracted for a carpet cleaning service to clean the home on July 9.]

C.

Anthony was questioned several times by MCSO officers in connection with the family's disappearance. He told detectives that Donna and the children had left for the airport between 5:00 and 5:30 a.m. on July 7. He said Donna customarily carried large amounts of cash and sometimes wore expensive jewelry; he suggested that she may have put herself in danger by driving through the wrong neighborhood. He also speculated that Donna may have driven to the airport, but then decided to drive to Las Vegas. Anthony claimed that "they" had transferred the funds from Donna's account into the joint account; $ 40,000 was to be used for the new truck and the balance to settle a pending lawsuit with neighbors. He denied any marital problems.

* * *

In the master bedroom, small drops of blood (totaling about the volume of one sugar cube) were found on the wall behind the bed. DNA testing identified some of the blood as Donna's. The DNA of a second person was also found; Anthony could not be excluded as the possible contributor. Carpeting to the right of the bed also tested positive for blood.

In the home office, three spots on the carpeting several inches in diameter tested positive for blood. The concrete slab underneath the carpet had a visible stain that tested positive for blood. The blood on the concrete slab was Danielle's.

In Richard's [the son's] room, the side of the mattress, the side of the box springs, a body pillow, and a wall tested positive for blood. The blood on the mattress and on the body pillow was Richard's. Blood from an unidentified person was also found on the side of the mattress; Donna and Danielle could not be excluded as contributors. In the hallway outside the children's rooms, four spots on the wall tested positive for blood. One of the stains contained Richard's DNA, as well as DNA that was consistent with either Donna or Danielle.

A hamper in the children's bathroom tested positive for blood. Blood was found on the coat closet door, on the threshold of the door leading from the kitchen to the backyard, on the exterior wall just outside the door between the kitchen and the backyard, on the back patio, and on a wooden picnic bench on the patio. Several spots in the garage tested positive for blood.

The State's expert testified that the volume of blood discovered in the house was too small to prove either that the victims had died or the cause of any death.

* * *

Anthony was indicted for the first-degree murders of Donna, Danielle, and Richard on August 10, 2001; the State subsequently filed a notice of intent to seek the death penalty. The jury found Anthony guilty on all three counts on April 1, 2002. Penalty proceedings began before a new jury on February 18, 2004.4 On March 2, 2004, that jury found three aggravating circumstances: A.R.S. 13-703(F)(5) (pecuniary gain), -(F)(8) (multiple homicides), and -(F)(9) (victim under the age of fifteen). On March 10, after the penalty phase, the jury returned death verdicts for each murder.

* * *

[DNA examination taken from blood samples from the teenage daughter's bedroom indicated positive for three contributors. It also tested positive for aspermatic semen, the type left by a person with a vasectomy, which the defendant had undergone. Because of this evidence, the state contended that the defendant had molested the teenaged stepdaughter, Danielle, in a sexual manner and that was the reason and the motive for the murders. Following the pretrial hearing, the trial court agreed to admit the blood and DNA evidence as circumstantial evidence that something sexual happened in the bedroom. The prosecution introduced evidence that condoms were found in the septic tank and that the teenaged honor did not like her stepfather. Additional evidence was introduced that indicated the defendant had placed his hands on the teenaged daughter's chest as well as are crotch at different times. During closing arguments, the prosecutor argued the molestation theory and that the defendant had murdered her and the others to cover up hid sexual crimes].

Anthony argues that the superior court erred in allowing the State to argue that he molested Danielle. A defendant's prior bad acts are not admissible "to show action in conformity therewith," but can be used to prove "motive, opportunity, intent, preparation, plan, knowledge, identity, or absence of mistake or accident." Ariz. R. Evid. 404(b). Although the jury must ultimately determine whether the other act is proved, "before admitting evidence of prior bad acts, trial judges must find that there is clear and convincing proof both as to the commission of the other bad act and that the defendant committed the act." State v. Terrazas, 189 Ariz. 580, 582, 944 P.2d 1194, 1196 (1997). Even if the trial judge concludes that the prior act is shown by clear and convincing evidence, the judge must also (1) find that the act is offered for a proper purpose under Rule 404(b); (2) find that the prior act is relevant to prove that purpose; (3) find that any probative value is not substantially outweighed by unfair prejudice; and (4) give upon request an appropriate limiting instruction. Id. at 583, 944 P.2d at 1197.

D.

The trial court concluded that there was "circumstantial evidence that something sexual happened" and that there was a possible "inference to be drawn" of "untoward" activity. The appropriate question under Terrazas [a prior case], however, is whether there was clear and convincing evidence that Anthony molested Danielle. The trial court erred by applying the wrong legal standard to its evaluation of the prior bad acts evidence. State v. Vigil, 195 Ariz. 189, 192, P 16, 986 P.2d 222, 225 (App. 1999).

Analyzing the DNA evidence under the Terrazas clear and convincing evidence standard, we conclude that the allegation that Anthony molested Danielle should have been excluded. Three DNA profiles were in the tested portion of the mattress: Danielle's and possibly those of Anthony and Donna. The State's expert could not opine that the blood found was in fact Danielle's, only that she was the primary DNA contributor. The expert also could not opine that Anthony in fact contributed any DNA to the sample; he testified instead only that Anthony could not be excluded. Nor could the expert conclude that the semen was Anthony's, only that it was aspermatic.

It is reasonable to assume that the aspermatic semen was Anthony's. It is also reasonable to assume that the blood was Danielle's. But even making these assumptions, the forensic evidence at most established that, at some point or points in time, Anthony's semen, Danielle's blood, and the DNA of a third person, perhaps Donna, were left on the mattress. There was no evidence as to when the three individuals left the DNA, let alone whether any two of them left DNA at the same time.

This evidence fell far short of proving either that Danielle was molested or that Anthony had done so. It is clear that Anthony and Danielle were not the only prior users of the mattress; the tested sample also contained DNA of a third contributor, perhaps Donna [the deceased wife]. It is difficult to understand how all three DNA contributions could have been made simultaneously; at least two of three DNA contributors were almost surely on the mattress at different times. This evidence, even taking all inferences in the light most favorable to the State, simply does not establish that Danielle and Anthony were simultaneous occupants of the bed, much less that he molested her.

[The reviewing court noted that the trial court considered only the mattress stain evidence in allowing the allegation of sexual molestation of the teenaged daughter into evidence. The court also noted that it could not conclude that there was sufficient evidence for jury to believe by clear convincing evidence that the defendant had ever molested the stepdaughter and the testimony that some people saw a defendant allegedly touching the teenaged daughter at a basketball game was not very probative of a sexual relationship with the stepdaughter. In this particular case, it might appear that any probative effect that the blood evidence might have toward proving a sexual molestation of the stepdaughter would clearly be outweighed the nature of unfair prejudice to the defendant's case. The defendant was suffered undue prejudice when the jury considered unreliable evidence in coming to a conclusion in this case. In applying the harmless error test the court was *unable* to conclude beyond reasonable doubt that the improperly admitted evidence, dealing with child sexual molestation, did not affect the verdict and therefore the court reversed the conviction and remanded for a new trial.]

Cases Relating to Chapter 3

Burden of Proof

IN RE WINSHIP

Supreme Court of the United States, 397 U.S. 358, 90 S. Ct. 1068, 25 L. Ed. 2d 368 (1970)

MR. JUSTICE BRENNAN delivered the opinion of the Court.

Constitutional questions decided by this Court concerning the juvenile process have centered on the adjudicatory stage at "which a determination is made as to whether a juvenile is a 'delinquent' as a result of alleged misconduct on his part, with the consequence that he may be committed to a state institution." In re Gault, 387 U.S. 1, 13 (1967). Gault decided that, although the Fourteenth Amendment does not require that the hearing at this stage conform with all the requirements of a criminal trial or even of the usual administrative proceeding, the Due Process Clause does require application during the adjudicatory hearing of "'the essentials of due process and fair treatment.'" Id., at 30. This case presents the single, narrow question whether proof beyond a reasonable doubt is among the "essentials of due process and fair treatment" required during the adjudicatory stage when a juvenile is charged with an act which would constitute a crime if committed by an adult.

Section 712 of the New York Family Court Act defines a juvenile delinquent as "a person over seven and less than sixteen years of age who does any act which, if done by an adult, would constitute a crime." During a 1967 adjudicatory hearing, conducted pursuant to § 742 of the Act, a judge in New York Family Court found that appellant, then a 12-year-old boy, had entered a locker and stolen $112 from a woman's pocketbook. The petition which charged appellant with delinquency alleged that his act, "if done by an adult, would constitute the crime or crimes of Larceny." The judge acknowledged that the proof might not establish guilt beyond a reasonable doubt, but rejected appellant's contention that such proof was required by the Fourteenth Amendment. The judge relied instead on § 744 (b) of the New York Family Court Act which provides that "any determination at the conclusion of [an adjudicatory] hearing that a [juvenile] did an act or acts must be based on a preponderance of the evidence." During a subsequent dispositional hearing, appellant was ordered placed in a training school for an initial period of 18 months, subject to annual extensions of his commitment until his 18th birthday—six years in appellant's case. The Appellate Division of the New York Supreme Court, First Judicial Department, affirmed without opinion. The New York Court of Appeals then affirmed by a four-to-three vote, expressly sustaining the constitutionality of § 744 (b). We noted probable jurisdiction. We reverse.

I.

The requirement that guilt of a criminal charge be established by proof beyond a reasonable doubt dates at least from our early years as a Nation. The "demand for a higher degree of persuasion in criminal cases was recurrently expressed from ancient times, [though] its crystallization into the formula 'beyond a reasonable doubt' seems to have occurred as late as 1798. It is now accepted in common law jurisdictions as the measure of persuasion by which the prosecution must convince the trier of all the essential elements of guilt." C. McCormick, Evidence § 321, pp. 681–682 (1954); see also 9 J. Wigmore, Evidence § 2497 (3d ed. 1940). Although virtually unanimous adherence to the reasonable-doubt standard in common-law jurisdictions may not conclusively establish it as a requirement of due process, such adherence does "reflect a profound judgment about the way in which law should be enforced and justice administered." Duncan v. Louisiana, 391 U.S. 145, 155 (1968).

Expressions in many opinions of this Court indicate that it has long been assumed that proof of a criminal charge beyond a reasonable doubt is constitutionally required. [Citations omitted.] Mr. Justice Frankfurter stated that "it is the duty of the Government to establish . . . guilt beyond a reasonable doubt. This notion—basic in our law and rightly one of the boasts of a free society—is a requirement and a safeguard of due process of law in the historic, procedural content of 'due process.'" Leland v. Oregon, *supra*, at 802–803 (dissenting opinion). In a similar vein, the Court said in Brinegar v. United States, *supra*, at 174, that "guilt in a criminal case must be proved beyond a reasonable doubt and by evidence confined to that which long experience in the common-law tradition, to some extent embodied in the Constitution, has crystallized into rules of evidence consistent with that standard. These rules are historically grounded rights of our system, developed to safeguard men from dubious and unjust convictions, with resulting forfeitures of life, liberty and property." Davis v. United States, *supra*, at 488, stated that the requirement is implicit in "constitutions . . . [which] recognize the fundamental principles that are deemed essential for the protection of life and liberty." In Davis a murder conviction was reversed because the trial judge instructed the jury that it was their duty to convict when the evidence was equally balanced regarding the sanity of the accused. This Court said: "On the contrary, he is entitled to an acquittal of the specific crime charged if upon all the evidence there is reasonable doubt whether he was capable in law of committing crime. . . . No man should be deprived of his life under the forms of law unless the jurors who try him are able, upon their consciences, to say that the evidence before them . . . is sufficient to show beyond a reasonable doubt the existence of every fact necessary to constitute the crime charged." Id., at 484, 493.

The reasonable-doubt standard plays a vital role in the American scheme of criminal procedure. It is a prime instrument for reducing the risk of convictions resting on factual error. The standard provides concrete substance for the presumption of innocence—that bedrock "axiomatic and elementary" principle whose "enforcement lies at the foundation of the administration of our criminal law." Coffin v. United States, *supra*, at 453. As the dissenters in the New York Court of Appeals observed, and we agree, "a person accused of a crime . . . would be at a severe disadvantage, a disadvantage amounting to a lack of fundamental fairness, if he could be adjudged guilty and imprisoned for years on the strength of the same evidence as would suffice in a civil case." 24 N.Y.2d, at 205, 247 N.E.2d, at 259.

The requirement of proof beyond a reasonable doubt has this vital role in our criminal procedure for cogent reasons. The accused during a criminal prosecution has at stake interests of immense importance, both because of the possibility that he may lose his liberty upon conviction and because of the certainty that he would be stigmatized by the conviction. Accordingly, a society that values the good name and freedom of every individual should not condemn a man for commission of a crime when there is reasonable doubt about his guilt. As we said in Speiser v. Randall, *supra*, at 525–526: "There is always in litigation a margin of error, representing error in fact finding, which both parties must take into account. Where one party has at stake an interest of transcending value—as a criminal defendant his liberty—this margin of error is reduced as to him by the process of placing on the other party the burden of . . . persuading the factfinder at the conclusion of the trial of his guilt beyond a reasonable doubt. Due process commands that no man shall lose his liberty unless the Government has borne the burden of . . . convincing the factfinder of his guilt." To this end, the reasonable-doubt standard is indispensable, for it "impresses on the trier of fact the necessity of reaching a subjective state of certitude of the facts in issue." Dorsen & Rezneck, In Re Gault and the Future of Juvenile Law, 1 Family Law Quarterly, No. 4, pp. 1, 26 (1967).

Moreover, use of the reasonable-doubt standard is indispensable to command the respect and confidence of the community in applications of the criminal law. It is critical that the moral force of the criminal law not be diluted by a standard of proof that leaves people in doubt whether innocent men are being condemned. It is also important in our free society that every individual going about his ordinary affairs have confidence that his government cannot adjudge him guilty of a criminal offense without convincing a proper factfinder of his guilt with utmost certainty.

Lest there remain any doubt about the constitutional stature of the reasonable-doubt standard, we explicitly hold that the Due Process Clause protects the accused against conviction except upon proof beyond a reasonable doubt of every fact necessary to constitute the crime with which he is charged.

II.

We turn to the question whether juveniles, like adults, are constitutionally entitled to proof beyond a reasonable doubt when they are charged with violation of a criminal law. The same considerations that demand extreme caution in factfinding to protect the innocent adult apply as well to the innocent child. We do not find convincing the contrary arguments of the New York Court of Appeals. Gault rendered untenable much of the reasoning relied upon by that court to sustain the constitutionality of § 744 (b). The Court of Appeals indicated that a delinquency adjudication "is not a 'conviction' (§ 781); that it affects no right or privilege, including the right to hold public office or to obtain a license (§ 782); and a cloak of protective confidentiality is thrown around all the proceedings (§§ 783–784)." 24 N.Y.2d, at 200, 247 N.E.2d, at 255–256. The court said further: "The delinquency status is not made a crime; and the proceedings are not criminal. There is, hence, no deprivation of due process in the statutory provision [challenged by appellant]. . . ." 24 N.Y.2d, at 203, 247 N.E.2d, at 257. In effect the Court of Appeals distinguished the proceedings in question here from a criminal prosecution by use of what Gault called the "'civil' label-of-convenience which has been attached to juvenile proceedings." 387 U.S., at 50. But Gault expressly rejected that distinction as a reason for holding the Due Process Clause inapplicable to a juvenile proceeding. 387 U.S., at 50–51. The Court of Appeals also attempted to justify the preponderance standard on the related ground that juvenile proceedings are designed "not to punish, but to save the child." 24 N.Y.2d, at 197, 247 N.E.2d, at 254. Again, however, Gault expressly rejected this justification. 387 U.S., at 27. We made clear in that decision that civil labels and good intentions do not themselves obviate the need for criminal due process safeguards in juvenile courts, for "[a] proceeding where the issue is whether the child will be found to be 'delinquent' and subjected to the loss of his liberty for years is comparable in seriousness to a felony prosecution." Id., at 36.

Nor do we perceive any merit in the argument that to afford juveniles the protection of proof beyond a reasonable doubt would risk destruction of beneficial aspects of the juvenile process. Use of the reasonable-doubt standard during the adjudicatory hearing will not disturb New York's policies that a finding that a child has violated a criminal law does not constitute a criminal conviction, that such a finding does not deprive the child of his civil rights, and that juvenile proceedings are confidential. Nor will there be any effect on the informality, flexibility, or speed of the hearing at which the factfinding takes place. And the opportunity during the post-adjudicatory or dispositional hearing for a wide-ranging review of the child's social history and for his individualized treatment will remain unimpaired. Similarly, there will be no effect on the procedures distinctive to juvenile proceedings that are employed prior to the adjudicatory hearing.

The Court of Appeals observed that "a child's best interest is not necessarily, or even probably, promoted if he wins in the particular inquiry which may bring him to the juvenile court." 24 N.Y.2d, at 199, 247 N.E.2d, at 255. It is true, of course, that the juvenile may be engaging in a general course of conduct inimical to his welfare that calls for judicial intervention. But that intervention cannot take the form of subjecting the child to the stigma of a finding that he violated a criminal law and to the possibility of institutional confinement on proof insufficient to convict him were he an adult.

We conclude, as we concluded regarding the essential due process safeguards applied in Gault, that the observance of the standard of proof beyond a reasonable doubt "will not compel the States to abandon or displace any of the substantive benefits of the juvenile process." Gault, *supra*, at 21.

* * *

III.

In sum, the constitutional safeguard of proof beyond a reasonable doubt is as much required during the adjudicatory stage of a delinquency proceeding as are those constitutional safeguards applied in Gault—notice of charges, right to counsel, the rights of confrontation and examination, and the privilege against self-incrimination. We therefore hold, in agreement with Chief Judge Fuld in dissent in the Court of Appeals, "that, where a 12-year-old child is charged with an act of stealing which renders him liable to confinement for as long as six years, then, as a matter of due process . . . the case against him must be proved beyond a reasonable doubt." 24 N.Y.2d, at 207, 247 N.E.2d, at 260.

Reversed.

VICTOR v. NEBRASKA

Supreme Court of the United States, 511 U.S. 1, 114 S. Ct. 1239, 127 L. Ed. 2d 583 (1994)

SYLLABUS:

The government must prove beyond a reasonable doubt every element of a charged offense. In re Winship, 397 U.S. 358. In upholding the first degree murder convictions and death sentences of petitioners Sandoval and Victor, the Supreme Courts of California and Nebraska, respectively, rejected contentions that due process was violated by the pattern jury instructions defining "reasonable doubt" that were given in both cases.

Held: Taken as a whole, the instructions in question correctly conveyed the concept of reasonable doubt, and there is no reasonable likelihood that the jurors understood the instructions to allow convictions based on proof insufficient to meet the Winship standard. Pp. 1–20.

(a) The Constitution does not dictate that any particular form of words be used in advising the jury of the government's burden of proof, so long as "taken as a whole, the instructions correctly convey the concept of reasonable doubt," Holland v. United States, 348 U.S. 121, 140. In invalidating a charge declaring, among other things, that a reasonable doubt "must be such . . . as would give rise to a grave uncertainty," "is an actual substantial doubt," and requires "a moral certainty," the Court, in Cage v. Louisiana, 498 U.S. 39, 40, observed that a reasonable juror could have interpreted the instruction to allow a finding of guilt based on a degree of proof below that which is constitutionally required. However, in Estelle v. McGuire, 502 U.S.__, __, and n. 4, the Court made clear that the proper inquiry is not whether the instruction "could have" been applied unconstitutionally, but whether there is a reasonable likelihood that the jury did so apply it. Pp. 1–3.

(b) The instructions given in Sandoval's case defined reasonable doubt as, among other things, "not a mere possible doubt," but one "depending on moral evidence," such that the jurors could not say they felt an abiding conviction, "to a moral certainty," of the truth of the charge. Pp. 3–6.

(c) Sandoval's objection to the charge's use of the 19th century phrases "moral evidence" and "moral certainty" is rejected. Although the former phrase is not a mainstay of the modern lexicon, its meaning today is consistent with its original meaning: evidence based on the general observation of people, rather than on what is demonstrable. Its use here is unproblematic because the instructions given correctly pointed the jurors' attention to the facts of the case before them, not (as Sandoval contends) the ethics or morality of his criminal acts. For example, in the instruction declaring that "everything relating to human affairs, and depending on moral evidence, is open to some possible or imaginary doubt," moral evidence can only mean empirical evidence offered to prove matters relating to human affairs—the proof introduced at trial. Similarly, whereas "moral certainty," standing alone, might not be recognized by modern jurors as a synonym for "proof beyond a reasonable doubt," its use in conjunction with the abiding conviction language must be viewed as having impressed upon the jury the need to reach the subjective state of near certitude of guilt, see Jackson v. Virginia, 443 U.S. 307, 315, and thus as not having invited conviction on less than the constitutionally required proof. Moreover, in contrast to the situation in Cage, there is no reasonable likelihood that the jury here would have understood moral certainty to be disassociated from the evidence in the case, since the instruction explicitly told the jurors, among other things, that their conclusion had to be based upon such evidence. Accordingly, although this Court does not condone the use of the antiquated "moral certainty" phrase, its use in the context of the instructions as a whole cannot be said to have rendered those instructions unconstitutional. Pp. 6–14.

(d) Sandoval's objection to the portion of the charge declaring that a reasonable doubt is "not a mere possible doubt" is also rejected. That the instruction properly uses "possible" in the sense of fanciful is made clear by the fact that it also notes that everything "is open to some possible or imaginary doubt." P. 14.

(e) The instructions given in Victor's case defined reasonable doubt as, among other things, a doubt that will not permit an abiding conviction, "to a moral certainty," of the accused's guilt, and an "actual and substantial doubt" that is not excluded by the "strong probabilities of the case." Pp. 14–16.

(f) Victor's primary argument—that equating a reasonable doubt with a "substantial doubt" overstated the degree of doubt necessary for acquittal—is rejected. Any ambiguity is removed by reading the phrase in question in context: The Victor charge immediately distinguished an "actual and substantial doubt" from one "arising from mere possibility, from bare imagination, or from fanciful conjecture," and thereby informed the jury that a reasonable doubt is something more than a speculative one, which is an unexceptionable proposition. Cage, *supra*, at 41, distinguished. Moreover, the instruction defined a reasonable doubt alternatively as a doubt that would cause a reasonable person to hesitate to act, a formulation which this Court has repeatedly approved and which gives a common-sense benchmark for just how substantial a reasonable doubt must be. Pp. 16–18.

(g) The inclusion of the "moral certainty" phrase in the Victor charge did not render the instruction unconstitutional. In contrast to the situation in Cage, a sufficient context to lend meaning to the phrase was provided by the rest of the Victor charge, which equated a doubt sufficient to preclude moral certainty with a doubt that would cause a reasonable person to hesitate to act, and told the jurors that they must have an abiding conviction of Victor's guilt, must be convinced of such guilt "after full, fair, and impartial consideration of all the evidence," should be governed solely by that evidence in determining factual issues, and should not indulge in speculation, conjectures, or unsupported inferences. Pp. 18–19.

(h) The reference to "strong probabilities" in the Victor charge does not unconstitutionally understate the government's burden, since the charge also informs the jury that the probabilities must be strong enough to prove guilt beyond a reasonable doubt. See Dunbar v. United States, 156 U.S. 185, 199. P. 19.

No. 92–8894, 242 Neb. 306, 494 N.W.2d 565, and No. 92–9049, 4 Cal. 4th 155, modified, 4 Cal. 4th 928a, 841 P.2d 862, affirmed.

STATE v. EICHELBERGER

Court of Appeals of Washington, Division One 2005 Wash. App. LEXIS 2429 (2005)

APPELWICK, J.—Donald Eichelberger was convicted of two counts of trafficking in stolen property in the second degree after he found a suitcase full of compact discs. One count was charged for selling 35 of the CDs the day he found them, and the other count for attempting to sell additional CDs two days later. Eichelberger argues that his conviction for two counts violated his protection against double jeopardy because he committed only one unit of crime, that the State failed to meet its burden of proof beyond a reasonable doubt, and that the trial court erred in determining his offender score because it included a point based on a fact that should have been presented to the jury and found beyond a reasonable doubt. Finding no error, we affirm.

FACTS

Donald Eichelberger was walking through the University District of Seattle in the late afternoon of May 20, 2003. He spotted a black suitcase lying on the ground, in an alley close to a dumpster. There were no people or vehicles around. Eichelberger opened the suitcase and saw that it contained many CDs. He did not inspect the CDs, and from the way they were arranged in the suitcase he could see only the spines of the CDs. Having been a University of Washington student himself, Eichelberger knew that students often move out of their residences and leave behind items that they no longer consider valuable, but that others might. He thought that the former owner of the suitcase had abandoned it and that he was thus entitled to take it. Eichelberger did not notice any identifying information on the CDs or the suitcase, did not attempt to ascertain who owned the CDs, and did not notify the police. Instead, Eichelberger took the bus to CD Trader, a used CD store in Queen Anne where he had previously sold CDs. He sold 35 of the CDs that day for $92. The record contains conflicting evidence about whether Eichelberger left because he was short on time and decided to return later to sell the remaining CDs, or whether he left because the clerk asked him to return later in the week to sell the remaining CDs.

It turns out that many of the CDs had been stolen from Stuart Sanderson during a burglary on May 20. Sanderson had affixed a sticker on many of his CDs that included his name and driver's license number. Sanderson filed a police report after the theft. The police investigation turned up no fingerprints at his home. On May 21, Sanderson called several used CD stores to see if his CDs had turned up. The manager at CD Trader informed Sanderson that several CDs with his sticker on them had been sold to the store the previous day. Sanderson went to the store and identified all 35 of the CDs Eichelberger had sold to CD Trader as his CDs. The manager took the CDs out of inventory and eventually turned them over to the police. Eichelberger returned to CD Trader on May 22 to sell more of the CDs. The manager recognized Eichelberger's name and came up with a ruse to keep Eichelberger in the store while he called the police. The police arrived and arrested Eichelberger. He was charged with two counts of trafficking in stolen property in the second degree. The State had no evidence to link Eichelberger to the burglary of Sanderson's home, and the court specifically instructed the jury not to make any such inference from the evidence or allow it to influence their verdict. The jury convicted Eichelberger on both counts . . . . .

ANALYSIS

I. Eichelberger's Two Convictions Did Not Violate His Protection Against Double Jeopardy.

* * *

We hold that the State was entitled to charge Eichelberger with two counts of trafficking in stolen property in the second degree, and that there was no double jeopardy violation.

II. Eichelberger's Convictions Were Supported By Sufficient Evidence

The test for sufficiency is whether, viewing the evidence in a light most favorable to the State, any rational trier of fact could have found each essential element of the charge beyond a reasonable doubt. State v. Salinas, 119 Wn.2d 192, 201, 829 P.2d 1068 (1992). "A claim of insufficiency admits the truth of the State's evidence and all inferences that reasonably can be drawn therefrom." A reviewing court neither weighs the evidence nor needs to be convinced that it established guilt beyond a reasonable doubt. A trier of fact may properly render a guilty verdict based on circumstantial evidence alone, even if the evidence is also consistent with the hypothesis of innocence. A conviction will not be overturned unless there is no substantial evidence to support it. [Some citations omitted].

To find Eichelberger guilty of trafficking in stolen property in the second degree, the jury had to be satisfied beyond a reasonable doubt that he recklessly trafficked in stolen property. A person "acts recklessly when he knows of and disregards a substantial risk that a wrongful act may occur and his disregard of such substantial risk is a gross deviation from conduct that a reasonable man would exercise in the same situation." RCW 9A.08.010(1)(c). Reckless conduct therefore includes both a subjective and an objective component. State v. R.H.S., 94 Wn. App. 844, 847, 974 P.2d 1253 (1999). A trier of fact is permitted to find actual subjective knowledge if there is sufficient information that would lead a reasonable person to believe that a fact exists. RCW 9A.08.010 (1)(b)(ii); R.H.S., 94 Wn App. at 847.

The evidence here was that Eichelberger came upon a suitcase. He opened the suitcase and saw that it contained CDs. When he saw the CDs, he thought that he would cash them in for money. His next act was to wheel the suitcase down the street, get on the bus, and go to Queen Anne to sell the CDs to CD Trader. He did not notify the police and did not check the CDs to see if they had anyone's name on them. He did not attempt to find out if they actually belonged to someone and were lost. Many of the CDs were labeled with the owner's name and driver's license number, which would have allowed a reasonable person to easily ascertain whether they were actually abandoned, or whether they were in fact lost or stolen.

Taking all inferences in the light most favorable to the state, the evidence was sufficient to permit the jury to find actual subjective knowledge. A reasonable person faced with similar circumstances would know that there was a substantial risk that the CDs were stolen or lost, and would take some steps to determine who the owner was prior to selling the CDs. Thus, the jury was entitled to find that Eichelberger had subjective knowledge of and disregarded the substantial risk that a wrongful act would occur when he converted the CDs to his own use. And, as the court instructed the jury when it asked for the definition of gross deviation, "[t]he law provides no precise definitions of these terms. The jury should rely on their understanding of the common meaning of 'gross deviation.'"

Eichelberger presents plausible explanations for the appearance of the suitcase other than that it was lost or stolen property, and testified that he thought the suitcase was abandoned. But the test is whether there was sufficient evidence to support the jury's verdict, not whether the jury could have reached a different result. We conclude that sufficient evidence supported the jury's verdict.

III. The Trial Court Did Not Err in Calculating Eichelberger's Offender Score

* * *

We affirm.

MARTIN
v.
OHIO

Supreme Court of the United States, 480 U.S. 228, 107 S. Ct. 1098, 94 L. Ed. 2d 267 (1987)

JUSTICE WHITE delivered the opinion of the Court.

The Ohio Code provides that "[every] person accused of an offense is presumed innocent until proven guilty beyond a reasonable doubt, and the burden of proof for all elements of the offense is upon the prosecution. The burden of going forward with the evidence of an affirmative defense, and the burden of proof by a preponderance of the evidence, for an affirmative defense, is upon the accused." Ohio Rev. Code Ann. § 2901.05(A) (1982). An affirmative defense is one involving "an excuse or justification peculiarly within the knowledge of the accused, on which he can fairly be required to adduce supporting evidence." Ohio Rev. Code Ann. § 2901.05(C)(2)(1982). The Ohio courts have "long determined that self-defense is an affirmative defense," 21 Ohio St. 3d 91, 93, 488 N.E.2d 166, 168 (1986), and that the defendant has the burden of proving it as required by § 2901.05(A).

As defined by the trial court in its instructions in this case, the elements of self-defense that the defendant must prove are that (1) the defendant was not at fault in creating the situation giving rise to the argument; (2) the defendant had an honest belief that she was in imminent danger of death or great bodily harm, and that her only means of escape from such danger was in the use of such force; and (3) the defendant did not violate any duty to retreat or avoid danger. App. 19. The question before us is whether the Due Process Clause of the Fourteenth Amendment forbids placing the burden of proving self-defense on the defendant when she is charged by the State of Ohio with committing the crime of aggravated murder, which, as relevant to this case, is defined by the Revised Code of Ohio as "purposely, and with prior calculation and design, [causing] the death of another." Ohio Rev. Code Ann. § 2903.01 (1982).

The facts of the case, taken from the opinions of the courts below, may be succinctly stated. On July 21, 1983, petitioner Earline Martin and her husband, Walter Martin, argued over grocery money. Petitioner claimed that her husband struck her in the head during the argument. Petitioner's version of what then transpired was that she went upstairs, put on a robe, and later came back down with her husband's gun which she intended to dispose of. Her husband saw something in her hand and questioned her about it. He came at her, and she lost her head and fired the gun at him. Five or six shots were fired, three of them striking and killing Mr. Martin. She was charged with and tried for aggravated murder. She pleaded self-defense and testified in her own defense. The judge charged the jury with respect to the elements of the crime and of self-defense and rejected petitioner's Due Process Clause challenge to the charge placing on her the burden of proving self-defense. The jury found her guilty.

Both the Ohio Court of Appeals and the Supreme Court of Ohio affirmed the conviction. Both rejected the constitutional challenge to the instruction requiring petitioner to prove self-defense. The latter court, relying upon our opinion in Patterson v. New York, 432 U.S. 197 (1977), concluded that the State was required to prove the three elements of aggravated murder but that Patterson did not require it to disprove self-defense, which is a separate issue that did not require Mrs. Martin to disprove any element of the offense with which she was charged. The court said, "the state proved beyond a reasonable doubt that appellant purposely, and with prior calculation and design, caused the death of her husband. Appellant did not dispute the existence of these elements, but rather sought to justify her actions on grounds she acted in self defense." 21 Ohio St. 3d, at 94, 488 N.E.2d, at 168. There was thus no infirmity in her conviction. We granted certiorari, 475 U.S. 1119 (1986), and affirm the decision of the Supreme Court of Ohio.

In re Winship, 397 U.S. 358, 364 (1970), declared that the Due Process Clause "protects the accused against conviction except upon proof beyond a reasonable doubt of every fact necessary to constitute the crime with which he is charged." A few years later, we held that Winship's mandate was fully satisfied where the State of New York had proved beyond reasonable doubt each of the elements of murder, but placed on the defendant the burden of proving the affirmative defense of extreme emotional disturbance, which, if proved, would have reduced the crime from murder to manslaughter. Patterson v. New York, *supra*. We there emphasized the preeminent role of the States in preventing and dealing with crime and the reluctance of the Court to disturb a State's decision with respect to the definition of criminal conduct and the procedures by which the criminal laws are to be enforced in the courts, including the burden of producing evidence and allocating the burden of persuasion. 432 U.S., at 201–202. New York had the authority to define murder as the intentional killing of another person. It had chosen, however, to reduce the crime to manslaughter if the defendant proved by a preponderance of the evidence that he had acted under the influence of extreme emotional distress. To convict of murder, the jury was required to find beyond a reasonable doubt, based on all the evidence, including that related to the defendant's mental state at the time of the crime, each of the elements of murder and also to conclude that the defendant had not proved his affirmative defense. The jury convicted Patterson, and we held there was no violation of the Fourteenth Amendment as construed in Winship.

* * *

As in Patterson, the jury was here instructed that to convict it must find, in light of all the evidence, that each of the elements of the crime of aggravated murder has been proved by the State beyond reasonable doubt, and that the burden of proof with respect to these elements did not shift. To find guilt, the jury had to be convinced that none of the evidence, whether offered by the State or by

Martin in connection with her plea of self-defense, raised a reasonable doubt that Martin had killed her husband, that she had the specific purpose and intent to cause his death, or that she had done so with prior calculation and design. It was also told, however, that it could acquit if it found by a preponderance of the evidence that Martin had not precipitated the confrontation, that she had an honest belief that she was in imminent danger of death or great bodily harm, and that she had satisfied any duty to retreat or avoid danger. The jury convicted Martin.

We agree with the State and its Supreme Court that this conviction did not violate the Due Process Clause. The State did not exceed its authority in defining the crime of murder as purposely causing the death of another with prior calculation or design. It did not seek to shift to Martin the burden of proving any of those elements, and the jury's verdict reflects that none of her self-defense evidence raised a reasonable doubt about the State's proof that she purposefully killed with prior calculation and design. She nevertheless had the opportunity under state law and the instructions given to justify the killing and show herself to be blameless by proving that she acted in self-defense. The jury thought she had failed to do so, and Ohio is as entitled to punish Martin as one guilty of murder as New York was to punish Patterson.

It would be quite different if the jury had been instructed that self-defense evidence could not be considered in determining whether there was a reasonable doubt about the State's case, i.e., that self-defense evidence must be put aside for all purposes unless it satisfied the preponderance standard. Such an instruction would relieve the State of its burden and plainly run afoul of Winship's mandate. 397 U.S., at 364. The instructions in this case could be clearer in this respect, but when read as a whole, we think they are adequate to convey to the jury that all of the evidence, including the evidence going to self-defense, must be considered in deciding whether there was a reasonable doubt about the sufficiency of the State's proof of the elements of the crime.

We are thus not moved by assertions that the elements of aggravated murder and self-defense overlap in the sense that evidence to prove the latter will often tend to negate the former. It may be that most encounters in which self-defense is claimed arise suddenly and involve no prior plan or specific purpose to take life. In those cases, evidence offered to support the defense may negate a purposeful killing by prior calculation and design, but Ohio does not shift to the defendant the burden of disproving any element of the state's case. When the prosecution has made out a prima facie case and survives a motion to acquit, the jury may nevertheless not convict if the evidence offered by the defendant raises any reasonable doubt about the existence of any fact necessary for the finding of guilt. Evidence creating a reasonable doubt could easily fall far short of proving self-defense by a preponderance of the evidence. Of course, if such doubt is not raised in the jury's mind and each juror is convinced that the defendant purposely and with prior calculation and design took life, the killing will still be excused if the elements of the defense are satisfactorily established. We note here, but need not rely on, the observation of the Supreme Court of Ohio that "[appellant] did not dispute the existence of [the elements of aggravated murder], but rather sought to justify her actions on grounds she acted in self-defense." 21 Ohio St. 3d, at 94, 488 N.E.2d, at 168.

Petitioner submits that there can be no conviction under Ohio law unless the defendant's conduct is unlawful, and that because self-defense renders lawful what would otherwise be a crime, unlawfulness is an element of the offense that the state must prove by disproving self-defense. This argument founders on state law, for it has been rejected by the Ohio Supreme Court and by the Court of Appeals for the Sixth Circuit. White v. Arn, 788 F.2d 338, 346–347 (1986); State v. Morris, 8 Ohio App. 3d 12, 18–19, 455 N.E.2d 1352, 1359–1360 (1982). It is true that unlawfulness is essential for conviction, but the Ohio courts hold that the unlawfulness in cases like this is the conduct satisfying the elements of aggravated murder—an interpretation of state law that we are not in a position to dispute. The same is true of the claim that it is necessary to prove a "criminal" intent to convict for serious crimes, which cannot occur if self-defense is shown: the necessary mental state for aggravated murder under Ohio law is the specific purpose to take life pursuant to prior calculation and design. See White v. Arn, *supra*, at 346.

As we noted in Patterson, the common-law rule was that affirmative defenses, including self-defense, were matters for the defendant to prove. "This was the rule when the Fifth Amendment was adopted, and it was the American rule when the Fourteenth Amendment was ratified." 432 U.S., at 202. . . . We are aware that all but two of the States, Ohio and South Carolina, have abandoned the common-law rule and require the prosecution to prove the absence of self-defense when it is properly raised by the defendant. But the question remains whether those States are in violation of the Constitution; and, as we observed in Patterson, that question is not answered by cataloging the practices of other States. We are no more convinced that the Ohio practice of requiring self-defense to be proved by the defendant is unconstitutional than we are that the Constitution requires the prosecution to prove the sanity of a defendant who pleads not guilty by reason of insanity. We have had the opportunity to depart from Leland v. Oregon, 343 U.S. 790 (1952), but have refused to do so. Rivera v. Delaware, 429 U.S. 877 (1976). These cases were important to the Patterson decision and they, along with Patterson, are authority for our decision today.

The judgment of the Ohio Supreme Court is accordingly Affirmed.

Cases Relating to Chapter 4

Proof via Evidence

MADDOX v. MONTGOMERY

United States Court of Appeals, Eleventh Circuit 718 F.2d 1033 (11th Cir. 1983)

Fay, Vance and Kravitch, Circuit Judges.

PER CURIAM

Appellant Jimmy Maddox was convicted of rape in a Georgia state court and sentenced to life imprisonment. At the trial, appellant and the alleged victim, Kathy Elder, gave radically different accounts of the events in question. Elder testified that on a number of occasions prior to the alleged rape, appellant had approached her purportedly seeking to sell her an insurance policy. On the morning in question, while Elder was dressing her two sons, appellant appeared at her apartment and again asked whether she wanted the insurance. After explaining that she had discovered that she could get insurance at work, Elder went into the bedroom to retrieve coats for the boys. Elder testified that appellant followed her into the room and forcibly raped her on the bed. Another witness for the prosecution, Debbie Phillips, testified that she had once taken out insurance with appellant, but had dropped it after he had come to her home on a Saturday night. Appellant testified that he and Elder had had voluntary sexual relations on several occasions prior to the alleged rape and that Elder had consented to their sexual relations on the morning in question.

Having unsuccessfully pursued his direct appeal and the state post-conviction remedy, appellant filed a federal habeas corpus petition alleging prosecutorial suppression of exculpatory evidence in violation of the doctrine of Brady v. Maryland, 373 U.S. 83, 83 S. Ct. 1194, 10 L. Ed. 2d 215 (1963). Specifically, appellant asserted that his right to due process was violated by the state's failure to disclose (1) a photograph taken by the police shortly after the alleged rape showing Elder's bed neatly made, (2) the results of a police examination of the bedspread which revealed no blood, semen or other fluid, and (3) a written statement by another witness, Brenda Phelps, that Debbie Phillips had stated that she dropped her insurance with appellant for financial reasons. Appellant appeals the denial of habeas relief. We affirm.

There are four types of situations in which the Brady doctrine applies: (1) the prosecutor has not disclosed information despite a specific defense request; (2) the prosecutor has not disclosed information despite a general defense request for all exculpatory information or without any defense request at all; (3) the prosecutor knows or should know that the conviction is based on false evidence[; (4)] the prosecutor fails to disclose purely impeaching evidence not concerning a substantive issue, in the absence of a specific defense request. United States v. Anderson, 574 F.2d 1347, 1353 (5th Cir. 1978). Inasmuch as appellant filed no pretrial request—specific or general—for exculpatory information, the present case falls within the second category with respect to the photograph of the bed and the results of the police examination of the bedspread and within the fourth category with respect to Phelps' statement.

In order to prevail on a Brady claim, one must establish the materiality of the exculpatory information suppressed by the prosecution. United States v. Kopituk, 690 F.2d 1289, 1339 (11th Cir. 1982), cert. denied, 461 U.S. 928, 103 S. Ct. 2089, 77 L. Ed. 2d 300 (1983); Anderson, 574 F.2d at 1353. The applicable threshold of materiality, however, varies depending on the type of situation. Where, as here, the state failed to disclose substantive evidence favorable to the defendant for which there was no specific request, the standard set forth in United States v. Agurs, 427 U.S. 97, 96 S. Ct. 2392, 49 L. Ed. 2d 342 (1976), governs. In Agurs, the Supreme Court stated that such a failure to disclose violates due process only "if the omitted evidence creates a reasonable doubt that did not otherwise exist." Id. at 112, 96 S. Ct. at 2401; accord United States v. Kubiak, 704 F.2d 1545, 1551 (11th Cir. 1983). In Cannon v. Alabama, 558 F.2d 1211 (5th Cir. 1977), cert. denied, 434 U.S. 1087, 98 S. Ct. 1281, 55 L. Ed. 2d 792 (1978), the former Fifth Circuit explained: Applying this standard requires an analysis of the evidence adduced at trial and of the probable impact of the undisclosed information. In this context, we cannot merely consider the evidence in the light most favorable to the government but must instead evaluate all the evidence as it would bear on the deliberations of a factfinder. Id. at 1213-14.

With regard to the photograph of the bed, we agree with the district court that "the undisclosed photograph does not create a reasonable doubt as to [appellant's] guilt that did not otherwise exist," Order, p. 8, and thus is not material under Agurs. Similarly, the results of the police examination of the bedspread do not give rise to a reasonable doubt and again are immaterial under Agurs. Although both pieces of evidence, if admitted at trial, might conceivably have affected the jury's verdict, the constitutional threshold of materiality is higher. See Agurs, 427 U.S. at 108-09, 96 S. Ct. at 2400. Insofar as this information is merely consistent with appellant's version of the incident and scarcely contradicts the alleged victim's testimony, and in view of the substantial inculpatory evidence in the record, the evidence at issue is not sufficiently material to render the state's failure to disclose unconstitutional.

The standard of materiality in a case, such as this one, involving the prosecution's suppression of impeaching evidence absent a specific request was recently discussed in United States v. Blasco, 702 F.2d 1315 (11th Cir.), cert. denied, 464 U.S. 914, 104 S. Ct. 275, 78 L. Ed. 2d 256 (1983). There this Court noted, "if the suppressed evidence is purely impeaching evidence and no defense request has been made, the suppressed evidence is material only if its introduction probably would have resulted in acquittal." Id. at 1328; accord Anderson, 574 F.2d at 1354. Given the relatively minor role of Phillips' testimony and the limited impact that Phelps' statement would likely have had on the jury's assessment of Phillips' credibility, appellant is unable to demonstrate that the undisclosed evidence probably would have resulted in an acquittal. Accordingly, the evidence is immaterial under Blasco, and its suppression did not violate appellant's due process right.

For the foregoing reasons, the district court's dismissal of appellant's habeas petition is AFFIRMED.

BROWN v. STATE

Supreme Court of Delaware, 897 A.2d 748, 2006 Del. LEXIS 163 (2006)

Before STEELE, Chief Justice, HOLLAND and JACOBS, Justices.

HOLLAND, Justice:

The defendant-appellant, Jeron Brown, appeals from his convictions of Burglary in the Second Degree, Theft, two counts of Receiving Stolen Property, and Criminal Mischief. In this appeal, Brown alleges that the Superior Court erred by: first, denying his motion to suppress evidence obtained during a search incident to his arrest because the police did not have probable cause to arrest him; second, denying his request for a mistrial after the State disclosed potentially exculpatory evidence during the trial; and third, failing to provide, *sua sponte*, a missing evidence jury instruction because a witness was unavailable to testify at trial. We conclude that there was no reversible error. Therefore, the judgments of the Superior Court must be affirmed.

FACTS

On January 20, 2004, the Del-Mar Appliance store and two private residences in Dover, Delaware, were burglarized. After the third burglary, the police reviewed a video surveillance tape from a local 7-11 store that showed an African American male and female attempting to sell items to the store clerk. Anwar Al-Rasul, the third burglary victim, had earlier identified the items on the tape as items that were stolen from his home. Later that day, the police received a tip from Mr. Al-Rasul's wife that an African American man would soon attempt to sell items similar to those stolen from her home at a nearby store, named the Closet.

The police set up surveillance outside the Closet. Jeron Brown approached the store carrying a duffel bag and wearing a jacket similar to the jacket worn by the man whose image was captured in the 7-11 video surveillance tape. Brown was also the same race, height, and build of the man shown in the tape. Brown entered the Closet and left shortly thereafter.

As he exited the store, the police approached Brown and immediately handcuffed him. The officers asked Brown if they could pat him down. They also asked Brown if they could search his jacket and duffel bag. Brown consented to both requests. Mr. Al-Rasul identified the items found by the police in Brown's jacket and duffel bag as his stolen property. The police then obtained a search warrant for Brown's residence, where they searched and seized more stolen property.

Probable Cause Established

[The appellate court agreed that probable cause was properly established.]

Mistrial Properly Denied

On the morning of the third day of Brown's trial, his defense counsel moved for a mistrial because alleged *Brady* material [a request to be notified concerning exculpatory evidence in the hands of the prosecution] was not disclosed by the prosecution until the preceding Friday, following two days of Brown's trial. The alleged *Brady* material at issue was a laptop computer stolen during the January 20, 2004 burglary of the Del-Mar Appliance store in Dover. The stolen laptop computer was recovered by the Delaware Probation Department from an individual named Moustapha Bobbo. After a probation officer took the laptop from Bobbo, it was turned over to Detective Virdin of the Dover Police Department. Detective Virdin then returned the computer to its rightful owner, Bruce Nygard.

Brown contends that, because the State did not inform him of information regarding Nygard's recovered laptop computer and because the computer was found in the possession of Bobbo, not Brown, this prevented Brown from introducing witnesses at trial to trace the whereabouts of the computer after it was stolen from the Del-Mar Appliance store. In denying the mistrial motion, the trial judge noted that Brown's contention concerning the laptop computer related to only one of his three pending burglary charges.

The State tried to mitigate any potential prejudice to Brown by the late disclosure of the information regarding the laptop computer. The State was able to locate both Moustapha Bobbo and Antonio Medina, another witness who had some information as to how the laptop computer came to be in the possession of Bobbo. Both Bobbo and Medina appeared at Brown's trial and testified as defense witnesses.

The Superior Court has a variety of remedies available for a discovery violation under Superior Court Criminal Rule 16(d)(2). As this Court has noted, "In determining the question of whether sanctions should be imposed, the trial court should weigh all relevant factors, such as the reason for the State's delay and the extent of prejudice to the defendant." As we pointed out in *Doran*, "Superior Court Criminal Rule 16 sets forth four alternative sanctions: 1) order prompt compliance with the discovery rule; 2) 'grant a continuance;' 3) 'prohibit the party from introducing in evidence material not disclosed;' or 4) such other order the Court 'deems just under the circumstances.'"

Whether a mistrial should be declared is a matter entrusted to the trial judge's discretion. The trial judge is in the best position to assess the risk of any prejudice resulting from trial events. n16 "A trial judge should grant a mistrial only where there is 'manifest necessity' or the 'ends of public justice would be otherwise defeated.'" The remedy of a mistrial is "mandated only when there are 'no meaningful and practical alternatives' to that remedy."

In this case, the practical alternative to granting a mistrial was to permit Brown to present the testimony of both Moustapha Bobbo and Antonio Medina regarding the stolen laptop computer. Both could testify that Jeron Brown had no ostensible connection with that particular item of stolen property before its seizure by a probation officer and ultimate return to the true owner. In fact, Brown presented testimony to that effect by both of those witnesses.

Brown argues on appeal that, had he known about this information at an earlier date, his trial examinations of Medina and Bobbo would have been different. He fails to explain, however, how their examinations would have been different and how the difference(s), if any, would have mattered. The record reflects that there was no abuse of discretion in the trial judge's refusal to grant Brown's motion for a mistrial.

NO PLAIN ERROR

Finally, Brown contends that the trial judge, *sua sponte*, should have given a missing evidence instruction pursuant to *Deberry* v. State. Brown's request for the *Deberry* missing evidence jury instruction did not involve the physical evidence at issue (the laptop computer), but, rather, related to a missing witness, Laura Johansen, who was not available to testify at Brown's trial. Johansen was the person who gave the stolen laptop computer to Bobbo and presumably could have testified that she purchased the laptop computer from someone other than Brown.

Brown made no request at trial for a *Deberry* missing evidence jury instruction. Therefore, that claim has been waived by Brown and may now be reviewed on appeal only for plain error. To be plain, the alleged error must affect substantial rights, generally meaning that it must have affected the outcome of Brown's trial. In demonstrating that a forfeited error is prejudicial, the burden of persuasion is on Brown.

Brown was found in possession of a digital camera and camera printer taken from the Del-Mar Appliance store when he was arrested by the police. The digital camera and printer that the police discovered in Brown's possession linked him to the stolen property from the Del-Mar appliance burglary. Accordingly, there was an independent evidentiary basis for the jury to conclude that Brown was guilty of receiving that other stolen property.

Brown was not convicted of the Del-Mar Appliance store burglary. He was convicted only of receiving stolen property resulting from that burglary, property that included the digital camera and the printer. Consequently, Brown cannot demonstrate plain error, because even if Johanson had appeared at trial and testified that she purchased the stolen laptop computer from someone other than Brown, the ultimate result at trial would have been the same.

CONCLUSION

The judgments of the Superior Court are affirmed.

STATE
v.
JORDAN

COURT OF APPEALS OF OHIO, THIRD APPELLATE DISTRICT 2002 Ohio 1418, 2002 Ohio App. LEXIS 1469 (2002)

HADLEY, J. The defendant/appellant, Neil L. Jordan ("the appellant"), appeals his conviction by the Seneca County Municipal Court, finding him guilty of three counts of vehicular manslaughter, in violation of R.C. 2903.06(A)(4). Based on the following, we reverse the judgment of the trial court.

Mr. Jordan was returning home from a basketball game on January 21, 2001 when, at approximately 8:30 p.m., his auto collided with another at the intersection of U.S. Route 224 and Hopewell Township Road 113 in Hopewell Township, Seneca County, Ohio. As a result of that accident, Lisa M. Johnson and Daniel P. Shaver, the occupants of the other auto, were killed. The eight to twelve week old fetus that Ms. Johnson was carrying also perished.

The appellant was charged with three counts of vehicular manslaughter. The state alleged that he violated R.C. 4511.43(A), in that he failed to stop at the point nearest the intersecting roadway where he had clear view of approaching traffic on the intersecting roadway before entering it, and that he consequently caused the deaths of Lisa M. Johnson, Daniel P. Shaver, and the unlawful termination of Ms. Johnson's pregnancy, in violation of R.C. 2903.06(A)(4). The appellant was found guilty of all three counts by a jury. He was sentenced to 45 days in jail on each count, to be served consecutively, and fined $375.00, plus costs.

The appellant now appeals his convictions, raising three assignments of error for our review.

ASSIGNMENT OF ERROR NO. I

As a matter of law, the trial judge committed error prejudicial to the defendant-appellant by denying his motion for judgment of acquittal at the conclusion of the State's case, at the conclusion of all of the evidence, and after the return of the verdict, since the State failed to provide any evidence (direct, circumstantial, or otherwise) that the defendant-appellant failed to stop in violation of Revised Code § 4511.43(A).

* * *

The appellant asserts in his first assignment of error that the trial court erred in failing to grant his motions for judgment of acquittal at various stages of his trial because, he alleges, the state failed to prove a material element of the charges against him. We agree with the appellant.

Crim.R. 29 prohibits a court from entering an order of judgment of acquittal if the evidence is such that reasonable minds can reach different conclusions as to whether each material element of a crime has been proved beyond a reasonable doubt. Furthermore, in reviewing a ruling on a Crim.R. 29 motion for judgment of acquittal, a reviewing court must construe the evidence in a light most favorable to the prosecution. Thus, we must determine if, construing the evidence in the light most favorable to the state, evidence was presented before the trial court which would allow reasonable minds to reach different conclusions as to whether the state proved all the material elements of vehicular manslaughter beyond a reasonable doubt.

The portion of R.C. 2903.06 under which the appellant was charged reads, in relevant part:

> A) No person, while operating or participating in the operation of a motor vehicle, motorcycle, snowmobile, locomotive, watercraft, or aircraft, shall cause the death of another or the unlawful termination of another's pregnancy in any of the following ways:
>
> * * *
>
> (4) As the proximate result of committing a violation of any provision of any section contained in Title XLV of the Revised Code that is a minor misdemeanor or of a municipal ordinance that, regardless of the penalty set by ordinance for the violation, is substantially equivalent to any provision of any section contained in Title XLV of the Revised Code that is a minor misdemeanor.

The underlying minor misdemeanor the appellant was found to have violated is R.C. 4511.43 (A), which states:

> Except when directed to proceed by a law enforcement officer, every driver of a vehicle or trackless trolley approaching a stop sign shall stop at a clearly marked stop line, but if none, before entering the crosswalk on the near side of the intersection, or, if none, then at the point nearest the intersecting roadway where the driver has a view of approaching traffic on the intersecting roadway before entering it. After having stopped, the driver shall yield the right-of-way to any vehicle in the intersection or approaching on another roadway so closely as to constitute an immediate hazard during the time the driver is moving across or within the intersection or junction of roadways.

The appellant argues that the state presented no evidence that he failed to stop in violation of R.C. 4511.43(A). Rather, he argues, in order for the jury to find that he failed to stop, it had to draw an inference from another inference.

It is impermissible for a trier of fact to draw "an inference based * * * entirely upon another inference, unsupported by any additional fact or another inference from other facts[.]" If, however, the second inference is based in part upon another inference and in part upon facts, it is a parallel inference and, if reasonable, is permissible. Likewise, a trier of fact may draw multiple inferences from the same set of facts.

There was no direct evidence presented at the trial regarding whether the appellant failed to stop at the stop sign. What follows is a summary of the relevant evidence that was presented:

1. Pictures and descriptive testimony of the crash scene, including evidence that the victims' car was wrapped around a telephone pole and torn almost in half;
2. Testimony regarding the position of the stop sign;
3. Testimony about the point nearest the intersecting roadway where the appellant had a clear view of approaching traffic on the intersecting roadway, which was identified as the point where the fog line on U.S. 224 would traverse 113 if projected into the intersection, and testimony as to the distance between that point and the point of impact;
4. Testimony that the appellant's car was traveling southbound at the time of the accident and the victims' car was traveling westbound;
5. Testimony that the cars traveled in a basically southerly direction after the initial impact;
6. Testimony that no evasive action was taken by either driver prior to impact;
7. Testimony that the final resting point of both cars was the southwest corner of the intersection of U.S. 224 and Township Road 113;
8. And testimony regarding the injuries to and causes of death of the victims.

We agree with the appellant that the only way the jury could have concluded that he failed to stop in accordance with [state law] R.C. 4511.43(A) was to first infer from the evidence that his vehicle was traveling at a high rate of speed at the time of impact. Any further inference beyond this must have been supported by additional facts. The record reveals no other evidence to support an inference that the appellant failed to stop, nor do the facts that were presented independently support it. Thus, the inference that the appellant failed to stop could only be based on an inference that his vehicle was traveling at a high rate of speed, which amounts to an impermissible inference built upon another inference. Thus, we find that the appellant's Crim.R. 29 motion should have been granted because reasonable minds could only find that the State failed to prove beyond a reasonable doubt that the appellant violated R.C. 4511.43(A).

The crucial flaw in the state's case was the lack of expert testimony and scientific evidence, which, if properly presented, would have assisted the jury in understanding the significance of the state's demonstrative evidence. The limited accident reconstruction testimony in this case, in conjunction with photographs and diagrams, established the extent of damage to the vehicles, points of impact, and relative positions of the vehicles following the collision. While this evidence is significant, in order to use it as the cornerstone of their case, the state needed to establish that based on the evidence: 1) the appellant's vehicle must have been traveling at a minimum speed and 2) this speed was greater than the appellant's vehicle could have achieved in any acceleration from a proper stop at either the stop sign or the fog line.

No scientific evidence or expert opinion was placed before the jury to assist them in establishing the speed of appellant's vehicle at the point of impact with the other car. In addition, no scientific evidence or expert opinion was placed before the jury to properly assist them in ascertaining the acceleration capability of appellant's vehicle from either the fog line (approximately three feet from the point of impact) or the stop sign (some 24-27 feet from the point of impact), to the point of impact. In fact there was brief testimony from the state's expert that the acceleration capability of appellant's vehicle to the point of impact might have been anywhere from zero to thirty miles per hour or possibly even zero to sixty miles per hour from a stop at the fog line.

As a result, from the crash scene evidence alone, the jury in this case was permitted to determine for itself, without any expert or other supporting testimony: 1) that the appellant had to be traveling at a certain minimum speed sufficient to create the existing crash scene and 2) that this speed exceeded the capability of appellant's car to accelerate from a lawful stop at the stop sign or the fog line—in order to then determine that appellant did not stop at either location prior to the collision.

In addition to requiring an improper stacking of inferences, the impact-speed and acceleration determinations described above are beyond the knowledge or experience of lay persons and therefore constitute determinations which are not permissible for a jury to make from crash scene evidence alone, without the assistance of expert testimony.

Because we find for the appellant on this assignment of error, we need not address his second or third assignments of error.

Accordingly, the appellant's first assignment of error is well taken and hereby affirmed.

Having found error prejudicial to the appellant herein, in the particulars assigned and argued, we reverse the judgment of the trial court and remand the matter for further proceedings consistent with this opinion.

Judgment Reversed.

SHAW, P.J., and WALTERS, J., concur.

Cases Relating to Chapter 5

Judicial Notice

COMMONWEALTH v. HOWLETT

328 S.W.3d 191, 2010 Ky. LEXIS 292 (2010)

Cunningham, Minton, C.J., Abramson, White, Noble, Schroder and Venters, JJ., concur. Scott, J., dissents by separate opinion.

OPINION OF THE COURT BY JUSTICE CUNNINGHAM: CERTIFYING THE LAW

The Commonwealth, pursuant to Section 115 of the Constitution of Kentucky and CR 76.37(10), petitions this Court for certification of the law regarding the limitations of judicial notice. Specifically, the Commonwealth seeks certification of the law on the following question:

In light of KRE 201's pre-Rules case law and its current Federal equivalent, what if any special prohibitions exist in a bench trial against the use of a judge's taking judicial notice of a fact that comes from the judge's personal knowledge given KRE 201's silence on the matter?

The relevant facts are as follows. On November 26, 2006, Bertrand Howlett was stopped by Sgt. Steve Williams of the St. Matthews Police Department for speeding. Upon approaching the vehicle, Sgt. Williams noticed that Howlett's eyes were bloodshot and that his breath smelled of alcohol. Sgt. Williams administered three field sobriety tests, each of which Howlett failed. Howlett was subsequently arrested and a breath test administered, where he blew a.150. Howlett was charged with speeding, reckless driving, and DUI.

During a two-day bench trial, testimony was offered regarding the necessity of a twenty-minute observation period prior to the administration of the breath test. Howlett testified that he burped during the observation period. When the court convened the following day, Judge Donald Armstrong of the Jefferson District Court, sua sponte, noted the following: "I take judicial notice of the fact that a burp during the operation or observation time needs to start the observation time all over again . . . by the manufacturer of the machine, Smith and Wesson. Therefore, I'm going to find him not guilty of that." Judge Armstrong's concerns over Howlett's burping during the observation period were seemingly based on his prior experience as a DUI prosecutor and his knowledge of the operating instructions for the breathalyzer machine.

Prior to the enactment of KRE 201, our case law on this issue was unambiguous:

> While it may be that the trial judge had information from an undisclosed source that appellant was feigning illness, such information does not constitute evidence, nor would the judge be authorized to act upon such information as constituting a fact within his judicial knowledge. 'It matters not what is known to the judge if it is not known to him judicially,' is a maxim of the doctrine of judicial notice. We have also held that the court must act upon evidence heard in open court and cannot make a private investigation of a matter pending before the court and then base his decision upon information obtained thereby. To hold otherwise would destroy

the very purpose for which our courts are established.

Gray v. Commonwealth, 264 S.W.2d 69, 70-71 (Ky. 1954) (internal citations omitted).

The Commonwealth notes that this Court has not specifically addressed this issue since the adoption of KRE 201 and, therefore, requests a certification of the law for guidance to the bench and bar.

Kentucky Rule of Evidence 201 provides:

(a) Scope of rule. This rule governs only judicial notice of adjudicative facts.
(b) Kinds of facts. A judicially noticed fact must be one not subject to reasonable dispute in that it is either:
    (1) Generally known within the county from which the jurors are drawn, or, in a non-jury matter, the county in which the venue of the action is fixed; or
    (2) Capable of accurate and ready determination by resort to sources whose accuracy cannot reasonably be questioned.
(c) When discretionary. A court may take judicial notice, whether requested or not.
(d) When mandatory. A court shall take judicial notice if requested by a party and supplied with the necessary information.
(e) Opportunity to be heard. A party is entitled upon timely request to an opportunity to be heard as to the propriety of taking judicial notice and the tenor of the matter noticed. In the absence of prior notification, the request may be made after judicial notice has been taken.
(f) Time of taking notice. Judicial notice may be taken at any stage of the proceeding.
(g) Instructing the jury. The court shall instruct the jury to accept as conclusive any fact judicially noticed.

As can be seen, KRE 201 is silent on the subject of judicial notice of a fact peculiarly known to the judge. However, we see no reason to depart from our previous case law on the subject. It is axiomatic that judicial notice is different from judicial knowledge. Shapleigh v. Mier, 299 U.S. 468, 475, 57 S. Ct. 261, 81 L. Ed. 355 (1937). See also R.T.K., Comment Note.—Distinction between judicial notice and judicial knowledge, 113 ALR 258 (1938). In his treatise on Kentucky Evidence, Professor Robert G. Lawson noted that "[the] drafters [of KRE 201] expressed a clear intent to have the provision construed to be in accord with the pre-Rules case law: 'Judicial notice of a fact peculiarly known to the judge is inappropriate.'" Robert G. Lawson, *The Kentucky Evidence Law Handbook*, § 1.00[3][c], at 12 (4th ed. 2003) (quoting *Evidence Rules Study Committee, Kentucky Rules of Evidence—Final Draft*, p.16 (Nov. 1989)). This position is widely accepted among federal courts in cases involving KRE 201's federal counterpart as well. Id. at 13. "While a resident judge's background knowledge of an area may 'inform the judge's assessment of the historical facts,' the judge may not actually testify in the proceeding or interject facts (excluding facts for which proper judicial notice is taken)." U.S. v. Berber-Tinoco, 510 F.3d 1083, 1091 (9th Cir. 2007).

Although KRE 201(a) specifically empowers courts to take judicial notice of "adjudicative facts," we must conclude that the taking of judicial notice which is derived from the court's personal knowledge of a fact peculiarly known to the judge is a fact neither "[g]enerally known within the county from which the jurors are drawn, or, in a nonjury matter, the county in which the venue of the action is fixed; [nor] [c]apable of accurate and ready determination by resort to sources whose accuracy cannot reasonably be questioned." KRE 201(b)(1)(2). Thus, we reaffirm our longstanding position that, under KRE 201, a trial judge is prohibited from relying on his personal experience to support the taking of judicial notice.

Procedurally, we cannot address Section 2 of KRE 201(b). That section allows judicial notice of a proposed fact if it is "[c]apable of accurate and ready determination by resort to sources whose accuracy cannot reasonably be questioned." However, KRE 201(e) states: "A party is entitled upon timely request to an opportunity to be heard as to the propriety of taking judicial notice and the tenor of the matter noticed." But procedurally; the taking of judicial notice on that ground was flawed.

The trial judge, in this case, proclaimed judicial notice without request of either lawyer, and then proceeded to dismiss the case in the same motion. There was no opportunity to make a "timely request" for "an opportunity to be heard." The judge did refer to "Smith and Wesson" as an apparent attempt to cite a source "whose accuracy cannot reasonably be questioned." This was not sufficient.

In a jury trial, when it is requested that judicial notice be taken of a fact, the other party is afforded the opportunity to respond. No less right is afforded parties in a bench trial. Here, there was no opportunity to "reasonably" question the source. "The drafters of KRE 201, following the lead of most commentators, encouraged courts to give advance notification when feasible: 'If a court acts on its own initiative, the parties should be informed of the facts noticed and given an opportunity to respond.'" Lawson, *supra*, § 1.00[5][e], at 20 (quoting *Evidence Rules Study Committee, Kentucky Rules of Evidence—Final Draft*, p. 16 (Nov. 1989)).

Therefore, it was improper for the court to find judicial notice sua sponte and dismiss the case, all in one fell swoop. Judicial notice, as utilized in this case, was inappropriate.

The law is so certified.

SCOTT, J., DISSENTING: I respectfully dissent from the majority's certification limiting a court's judicial notice under KRE 201(b)(2), as the fact in issue in this case was clearly one "capable of accurate and ready determination by resort to sources whose accuracy cannot reasonably be questioned," i.e., the manufacturer's manual, which states, "[d]uring [the observation] period the subject shall not have oral or nasal intake of substances which will affect the test." CMI, Inc., *Intoxilyzer 5000EN Breath Analysis Instrument Operator's Manual (Kentucky Model)* 12 (2000). Moreover, a prior decision establishes that a "burp" constitutes an "oral or nasal intake of substances which will affect the test." See Eldridge v. Commonwealth, 68 S.W.3d 388, 392 (Ky. App. 2001) ("Belching and regurgitating may contaminate the mouth with alcohol volumes from the stomach, and this is a rational basis for re-administering the observation period.").

District Judge Armstrong has been doing this work for many years as a prosecutor and a judge and few would argue about the accuracy of his decision, especially in light of the fact that the trial lasted two days and involved evidence of the necessity of a twenty-minute observation period prior to the administration of the test. Yet, by this decision today, we deprive him and other trial judges of the ability to utilize their professional knowledge [that renders a judge] capable of [an] accurate and [a] ready determination"—in the determination of matters rightly before them. See KRE 201(b)(2). In effect, we are overmanaging our decision maker in a matter that had nothing to do with "fairness"—but now does! Thus, I must dissent.

CITY v. GAMEZ

Court of Appeals of New Mexico, 2009 N.M. App. Unpub. LEXIS 464 (2009)

JUDGES: KENNEDY, WECHSLER, AND BUSTAMONTE

OPINION: KENNEDY, Judge.

Defendant argues the district court erred in denying her motion for directed verdict and in taking judicial notice Defendant was stopped in the City of Clovis. We issued a calendar notice proposing to affirm the district court and Defendant filed a memorandum in opposition. Unpersuaded by Defendant's arguments, we affirm the decision of the district court and hold it was permissible for the district court to take judicial notice Defendant was within the city limits when she was stopped and arrested.

Defendant was arrested and charged with driving with a revoked license, a violation of a City of Clovis ordinance. She pled no contest in magistrate court, reserving her right to appeal to the district court.

At a trial de novo in district court, the City offered evidence one officer was "patrolling eastbound in the City of Clovis," when dispatched. That officer testified he intercepted Defendant at the intersection of Sixth and Sheldon, at 516 Sheldon Street, but failed to indicate Sheldon Street was located within the City of Clovis. Defendant moved for a directed verdict based on lack of proof of jurisdiction. The district court apparently sua sponte took judicial notice documents submitted by the City established jurisdiction based on the location of the streets.

Rule 11-201(B) NMRA states a court may take judicial notice of an adjudicative fact where:

B. Kinds of Facts. A judicially noticed fact must be one not subject to reasonable dispute in that it is either

(1) generally known within the community, or
(2) capable of accurate and ready determination by resort to sources whose accuracy cannot reasonably be questioned, or
(3) notice is provided for by statute.

The district court is permitted to take judicial notice "whether requested or not." NMRA 11-201(C). We have previously held geographical facts are a proper subject for judicial notice. See, e.g., Gallegos v. Conroy, 38 N.M. 154, 29 P.2d 334, 336 (1934) (taking judicial notice that village is located on certain railroad); State v. Tooke, 81 N.M. 618, 619, 471 P.2d 188, 189 (Ct. App. 1970), overruled on other grounds by State v. Ruffins, 109 N.M. 668, 789 P.2d 616 (1990) (reiterating courts may take judicial notice of state and county boundaries).

Defendant's memorandum in opposition argues the geographic location of the streets in question was an improper subject for judicial notice because it could be "reasonably disputed." We disagree. The district court unsurprisingly appears to have been familiar with the geography of the City of Clovis and the streets located therein. That knowledge, especially when coupled with the officer's testimony that he was patrolling in the City of Clovis when dispatched, was sufficient to remove the jurisdictional element from the realm of those facts that could be "reasonably disputed."

We see no reason to disturb the district court's decision and hold the location of certain streets within the boundary of a city is the type of fact "generally known within the community." We hold it was permissible for the district court to take judicial notice that Defendant was stopped within the city limits and affirm the district court's denial of Defendant's motion for directed verdict. State v. Dominguez, 115 N.M. 445, 455, 853 P.2d 147, 157 (Ct. App. 1993) (reiterating that we will affirm the district court's denial of a directed verdict motion where there was substantial evidence to support the charge).

IT IS SO ORDERED.

RODERICK T. KENNEDY, Judge.

ROBINSON v. STATE

Court of Appeals of Georgia, Second Division 260 Ga. App. 186, 2003 Ga. App. LEXIS 366 (2003)

JUDGES: MIKELL, Judge. Johnson, P. J., and Eldridge, J., concur.

OPINION: MIKELL, Judge.

On December 15, 2001, Christina Robinson was charged with driving under the influence of alcohol. A bench trial was conducted on March 28, 2002, in the City of Jonesboro Municipal Court. The court convicted Robinson of DUI and sentenced her to one day in jail, a $963 fine, and sixty hours of community service. The Superior Court of Clayton County affirmed the conviction. Robinson appeals, arguing that her conviction cannot stand because the state failed to prove venue beyond a reasonable doubt. We agree and reverse the conviction.

Our Supreme Court has mandated that "venue is more than a mere procedural nicety; it is a [Georgia] constitutional requirement that all criminal cases be conducted in the county in which the crimes are alleged to have occurred." Graham v. State, 275 Ga. 290, 292 (2) (565 S.E.2d 467) (2002). In Jones v. State, 272 Ga. 900 (537 S. E.2d 80) (2000), the Supreme Court held that the state's failure to prove venue beyond a reasonable doubt warranted reversal of a defendant's felony murder conviction. Id. at 904 (3). The Court reasoned that:

Our Georgia Constitution requires that venue in all criminal cases must be laid in the county in which the crime was allegedly committed. Ga. Const. (1983), Art. VI, Sec. II, Par. VI; O. C.G.A. § 17-2-2 . Venue is a jurisdictional fact, and is an essential element in proving that one is guilty of the crime charged. Like every other material allegation in the indictment, venue must be proved by the prosecution beyond a reasonable doubt. Proof of venue is a part of the State's case, and the State's failure to prove venue beyond a reasonable doubt renders the verdict contrary to law, without a sufficient evidentiary basis, and warrants reversal.

(Punctuation and footnotes omitted.) Id. at 901-902 (2). Accord Walker v. State, 258 Ga. App. 354 (2) (574 S.E.2d 317) (2002) (even when evidence demonstrated that the crimes were committed in the City of Atlanta, convictions must be reversed because the state failed to prove the county in which venue was proper).

We note that this Court is bound by decisions of the Supreme Court; therefore, we are without authority to overlook the requirement that venue be expressly proven, even in a case such as this where the City of Jonesboro is entirely within Clayton County. "The application of the doctrine of stare decisis is essential to the performance of a well-ordered system of jurisprudence." Etkind v. Suarez, 271 Ga. 352, 357 (5) (519 S.E.2d 210) (1999), citing Cobb v. State, 187 Ga. 448, 452 (200 SE 796) (1939).

The only evidence of venue presented in the case sub judice was the testimony of Sergeant Pat Cauchy of the City of Jonesboro Police Department that he observed Robinson driving within the city limits of Jonesboro. "By long-standing precedent, proving that a crime took place within a city without also proving that the city is entirely within a county does not establish venue." (Footnote omitted.) Graham, *supra* at 293 (2). Our research reveals no authority for the presumption that the trial court, acting as the finder of fact in a bench trial, took judicial notice of venue, nor is there any indication in the record that such judicial notice was taken in this case. Accordingly, because the state did not establish the county in which the crime was committed, we reverse Robinson's conviction. We note that retrial would not be barred by the Double Jeopardy Clause. See Jones, *supra* at 905 (4).

Judgment reversed. Johnson, P. J., and Eldridge, J., concur.

STATE v. SMITH

Court of Common Pleas of Delaware, Sussex 2006 Del. C.P. LEXIS 34 (2006)

Rosemary Betts Beauregard

DECISION ON STATE'S APPEAL

Pending before this Court is an appeal by the State of Delaware ("State") from a decision by the Justice of the Peace Court ("J.P. Court") suppressing evidence in favor of the defendant, Mack K. Smith ("Defendant") because it found that the arresting officer did not have probable cause to arrest. This Court set a schedule for briefing on the State's appeal. After reviewing the briefs provided, the Court finds and determines as follows outlined below.

PROCEDURAL BACKGROUND

The Defendant was arrested for committing a violation of 21Del. C. § 4177(a), Driving Under the Influence ("DUI"), and for committing a violation of 21 Del. C. § 4169, Speeding, on November 27, 2004. The State filed the Information in J.P. Court. Thereafter, the court scheduled the motion to suppress and trial for hearing on April 20, 2005. At the hearing, the court granted the Defendant's motion to suppress, and the State certified that the evidence was essential to the prosecution of the case, in accordance with 10 Del. C. § 9902 (b). However, the court did not dismiss the case at the conclusion of the hearing. Instead, upon further inquiry by the State via letter on May 6, 2005, the court properly dismissed the case on May 24, 2005. The State timely filed its appeal pursuant to 10 Del. C. § 9902(c) on June 3, 2005.

STATEMENT OF FACTS

Trooper Mark Little ("Officer") stopped the Defendant on State Route 26 ("SR 26"), west of Dagsboro, Delaware, at 2:52 p.m. on November 27, 2004. The Officer testified that SR 26 has portions that curve and wind and portions that are straight. The Officer stated that he observed and stopped the vehicle as it traveled on a long, straight stretch of the roadway in the opposite direction that the Officer was traveling. Just prior to stopping the Defendant, the Officer observed his vehicle passing several other vehicles. According to the Officer's radar, the Defendant's vehicle was speeding, thus, the Officer stopped the Defendant, who appropriately pulled his vehicle over to the shoulder of the roadway. Upon approaching the vehicle and informing the Defendant that he had stopped him for speeding, the Officer observed that the Defendant had rosy cheeks, bloodshot eyes and that he omitted a moderate odor of alcohol, however, the Defendant spoke well and he appeared to have no trouble producing his license and registration. The Defendant admitted to the Officer that he had been speeding and that he had consumed approximately two beers earlier in the day.

Upon making his observations, the Officer administered a number of routine field sobriety tests to determine whether the Defendant was driving under the influence. First, the Officer administered the alphabet test, wherein the Defendant did not begin or end at the instructed letters and he recited other letters out of order. Second, the Officer asked the Defendant to count backwards from 100 to 85. The Defendant failed to stop at the appropriate number. Next, the Officer had the Defendant perform a finger dexterity test, which the Defendant successfully completed. Thereafter, the Officer asked the Defendant to exit his vehicle, which he did without any visible problem.

Once the Defendant was out of his vehicle, the Officer administered the horizontal gaze nystagmus test ("HGN"), a test on which he had received training during his education with the police academy in 1995, and as a field officer. Additionally, in 2001, the Officer became a certified HGN instructor, which enabled him to assist in instruction at the academy and a special event devised to educate certain members of the legal community. At the hearing, the Officer testified as to how the HGN test is administered, signals that the administrator looks for while conducting the test, and what factors other than alcohol consumption might create nystagmus in the subject, including strobe lights, rotating lights and rapidly moving traffic within close proximity. Furthermore, the Officer testified that when he performed the HGN test on the Defendant, he observed six out of six clues. On cross examination, the Officer admitted that while looking for nystagmus at maximum deviation, which was the second part of the three part test, he only caused the Defendant's eye to be held at the maximum deviation position for two to three seconds, rather than four seconds, which is required by the NHTSA manual. Additionally, the Officer acknowledged that the NHTSA manual states that the HGN test is only validated when it is administered in the prescribed fashion. The Officer also stated that strobe lights, rotating lights and some moving traffic in close proximity where all present when he administered the test.

After conducting the HGN test, the Officer then administered the walk and turn test. Although it is preferred that the test be conducted on a painted line, the Officer had the Defendant complete the test on the side of the road for safety reasons. Thus, the test was administered in an area, which the Officer described as grassy, with a slight slope designed for drainage purposes. According to the Officer, the slight grade did not affect the results of the test. The Officer described the weather as "windy and clear" at the time of the stop. While the Officer explained the test to the Defendant, he observed that the Defendant was unable to maintain his balance while standing with one foot in front of the other. When the Defendant completed the walk and turn test, the Officer perceived that the Defendant took ten steps instead of nine, and he took one large step instead of a series of small steps to make the turn, as instructed. The Defendant accurately took a second series of nine steps back to his original starting point.

Next, the Officer administered the one leg stand test. At that time, the Defendant informed the Officer that one of his feet was weaker than the other. Thus, the Officer suggested that he complete the test using his stronger foot for balance. The Officer observed that the Defendant raised his arms for balance, swayed, and put his foot down at different points throughout the test. Lastly, the Officer administered a portable breath test ("PBT") on the Defendant. Although the J.P. Court permitted such evidence, the State never established the results of that test.

After the court admitted the foregoing evidence, it ruled that the Officer lacked probable cause to arrest. In its decision, the court relied heavily on its personal knowledge of the roadway where a number of the field sobriety tests were administered to find that the area was not an acceptable place to administer the tests.

DISCUSSION

An appeal by the State pursuant to 10 Del. C. § 9902(c) shall be heard on the record. CCP Crim. R. 39(f). When addressing appeals from the J.P. Court this Court sits as an intermediate appellate court. The function of the Court in this capacity is to 'correct errors of law and to review the factual findings of the court below to determine if they are sufficiently supported by the record and are the product of an orderly and logical deductive process.' *State v. Richards*, 1998 WL 732960, *1 (Del. Super.)(citing Baker v. Connell, 488 A.2d 1303 (Del. 1985). Therefore, the Court must apply a de novo standard of review to the lower court's legal determinations and a clearly erroneous standard to findings of fact. State v. Arnold, 2001 WL 985101, *2 (Del. Super.).

The State argues that the J.P. Court inappropriately relied on information outside of the record, and applied the wrong legal standard in its decision on the Defendant's motion to suppress. Accordingly, the first question presented is whether the J.P. Court erred when it considered facts that were not in evidence. The second question at issue is whether the J.P. Court erred when it decided that the Officer did not have probable cause to arrest the Defendant.

The J.P. Court Inappropriately Relied on Facts Not in Evidence

The transcript reflects that as the J.P. Court considered the evidence admitted for purposes of establishing probable cause, the court enlarged the record with its own personal knowledge. The sole witness at the hearing, the Officer who administered the tests, provided that the testing area was grassy, with a slight grade, but hard, not muddy and not rocky. However, upon ruling on the motion, the Court interjected its own knowledge of the area and disregarded the Officer's testimony. Specifically, when determining the probative value of the walk and turn test and the one leg stand test, the court spoke as to its personal knowledge of the roadway. The court noted that the tests were improper because they were conducted,

> "on the side of a road, on a road that I know, and everyone else in Sussex County, knows it is not only a grass shoulder road but a very tapered grass shoulder road into a heavy ditch in low lying swamp ground. We know what that road is. We know why they call it a Nine Foot Road. It was a miraculous piece of construction when they put that concrete road on that piece of road on 26 because it is a low lying piece of swamp that was drained off to put into agriculture. I mean I know all these things. And this is not the place to do that test."

Because the facts depended on by the J.P. Court were not admitted into evidence, the question arises whether reliance on those facts constituted error. The Delaware Rules of Evidence provide that courts are permitted to take judicial notice of an adjudicative fact. D.R.E. 202. However, courts may only take judicial notice of a fact that is not subject to reasonable dispute in that it either is generally known within the territorial jurisdiction of the court, or it is capable of accurate and ready determination in sources whose accuracy cannot reasonably be questioned. D.R.E. 202(b). The doctrine of judicial notice should be applied with due care because if there is even a mere possibility of dispute as to whether the fact asserted is accurate, or of common knowledge, judicial notice is inappropriate and evidence is required to establish the fact. Fawcett v. State, 697 A.2d 385, 388 (Del. 1997).

Although the court stated that "everyone in Sussex County, knows [the area] is not only a grass shoulder road but a very tapered grass shoulder road into a heavy ditch in low lying swamp ground," the Officer's contrary testimony wherein he described the testing area as grassy, with a slight grade, but hard, not muddy and not rocky indicates that the conditions of that area at the time of administration were indeed subject to reasonable dispute. The court did not indicate that it determined the Officer was untrustworthy. Rather, the court relied solely on its own opinion of the conditions that may or may not have been present in the testing area to discredit the tests. The court's opinion is therefore not an adjudicative fact. Accordingly, I find that the J.P. Court committed plain error when it relied on evidence that was outside of the record in its decision finding that the Officer did not have probable cause to arrest the Defendant.

Probable Cause Existed

The State argues that the court improperly "diluted each [of the Officer's probable cause] observation[s] with hypothetically innocent explanations and then rejected them," without considering the Officer's observations under the totality of the circumstances.

* * *

[The Court reviewed the facts supporting a finding of probable cause.]

In conclusion, the Officer made the following observations of the Defendant (1) blood shot eyes, (2) rosy cheeks, (3) moderate odor of alcohol, (4) admission of consuming alcohol, (5) failure to follow instruction and properly perform the alphabet, counting and walk and turn tests, (6) trouble maintaining balance on the walk and turn and one leg stand tests, (7) several clues present upon application of the HGN test and (8) Speeding. Case law suggests that such factors are adequate to establish probable case.

* * *

CONCLUSION

This Court concludes that the J.P. Court inappropriately relied on facts not in evidence. Furthermore, this Court finds that the Officer had probable cause to believe that the Defendant had been driving under the influence when he arrested the Defendant. Thus, the Court hereby reverses the J.P. Court's decision on the Defendant's motion to suppress and remands the case for further proceeding consistent with this Order.

IT IS SO ORDERED, this 6th day of June 2006.

The Honorable Rosemary Betts Beauregard.

Cases Relating to Chapter 6

Presumptions, Inferences, and Stipulations

WILLIAMS v. STATE

Supreme Court of Mississippi, 111 So. 3d 620, 2013 Miss LEXIS 160 (2013)

RANDOLPH, PRESIDING JUSTICE, FOR THE COURT.

Twonia Renee Williams was convicted in the Circuit Court of Harrison County, Mississippi, for the murder of Katrina Sergeant. She was sentenced to life imprisonment in the custody of the Mississippi Department of Corrections. On appeal, Williams contends that jury instructions . . . were given in error.

FACTS

In late November, 2009, Twonia Williams ended her three-and-a-half year relationship with Sean Lindsay. According to Williams, she "put [Lindsay] out" of her home due to his continued infidelity. Almost immediately, Lindsay moved in with his new girlfriend, Katrina Sergeant, her three children, and her niece, Stacey McCall.

McCall testified that, around midnight on December 5, 2010, she and Sergeant drove to the gas station in "[Lindsay's] truck" to purchase "black and mild . . . cigars]." Williams's cousin recognized McCall and Sergeant in Lindsay's truck and called Williams to inform her of what she had seen. Williams admitted being upset by this information because she had "just struggled to get the $2000 to get [the truck] paid off so [Lindsay] could get his title."

Shortly after McCall and Sergeant returned home from the gas station, Williams began calling Lindsay's phone repeatedly. Lindsay placed the calls on speaker phone, and McCall overheard Williams say she was "about to come blow up the house, blow up everybody in there." Williams continued calling until Lindsay turned his phone off, at which point, she got in her car and drove to Sergeant's house. According to Williams, she initially was not going to stop, but, as she drove by, she saw the front "door . . . fly open" and believed that "[Lindsay] was coming out to talk to her." However, Sergeant, and not Lindsay, emerged from the front door. Williams testified that she parked and exited her car with "the gun in [her] hand," and that an argument ensued between her and Sergeant. Williams claimed that she told Sergeant she just "wanted to see [Lindsay]," but that Sergeant told her, "you need to leave, you're not going to talk to [Lindsay], you need to leave." Williams admitted that, at some point in the argument, she shot Sergeant, causing her death.

On July, 26, 2010, Williams was indicted for "willfully, feloniously and without the authority of law kill[ing] and murder[ing] Katrina Sergeant, a human being, with deliberate design . . . ." *See* Miss. Code Ann. § 97-3-19(1)(a)(Rev. 2006). On February 14, 2012, the jury trial commenced. Williams testified on her own behalf, ". . . sometime or another I did pull the trigger . . . I was arguing with [Sergeant] and I was talking with her with my hand. The gun went off, and I heard it pop and saw [Sergeant] go to the ground." Despite acknowledging on direct examination that she "did pull the trigger," Williams claimed that she shot Sergeant by accident. However, two eyewitnesses contradicted Williams's claim. McCall testified that she was outside with Sergeant when the confrontation took place, and that Williams raised the gun up to Sergeant's face and pulled the trigger. McCall also testified that, around the time she pulled the trigger, Williams stated, "I don't give a f***." Furthermore, Sergeant's neighbor, Carsie Durr, testified that he witnessed part of the confrontation from his front yard and that the shot "wasn't like an accident . . . [Williams] deliberately pulled that gun up and shot one time . . . ." In addition to the two eyewitnesses, the State offered two experts whose testimony contradicted Williams's. The State's forensic expert, Dr. Paul McGarry, testified that Sergeant suffered a "close range wound within 12, 18, 20 inches . . . ." Lori Beall, a firearms expert, testified that the type of gun used has certain safety mechanisms that require the trigger be pulled in order to prevent accidental firing.

Williams was found guilty of murder and sentenced to "life imprisonment in the custody of the Mississippi Department of Corrections." After hearing, the circuit court denied Williams's "Motion for New Trial or Judgment Notwithstanding the Verdict (NOV)." Thereafter, Williams filed this "Notice of Appeal."

ISSUE

On appeal, this Court will consider:

Whether the circuit court erred in granting instructions . . . .

ANALYSIS

The jury instructions at issue read, in pertinent part:

> [A] person is *presumed* to have intended the natural and probable consequences of his voluntary and deliberate acts. (Instruction S-4.)
>
> "[D]eliberate design" *may be inferred* through the intentional use of any instrument which based on its manner of use is calculated to produce death or serious bodily injury. (Instruction S-2A.)
>
> [I]f wounds are inflicted upon a person with a deadly weapon in a manner calculated to destroy life then intent *may be inferred* from the use of the weapon. (Instruction S-6.)

"Jury instructions are generally within the discretion of the trial court and the settled standard of review is abuse of discretion." Bailey v. State, 78 So. 3d 308, 315 (Miss. 2012)(citing Newell v. State, 49 So. 3d 66, 73 (Miss. 2010)). "The instructions are to be read together as a whole, with no one instruction to be read alone or taken out of context." Id. (quoting Young v. State, 891 So. 2d 813, 819 (Miss. 2005)). "When read together, if the jury instructions fairly state the law of the case and create no injustice, then no reversible error will be found." Id. (citing Newell, 49 So. 3d at 73).

Williams was indicted for "deliberate design" murder pursuant to Mississippi Code Section 97-3-19(1)(a). "[D]eliberate design connotes an intent to kill . . . ." Brown v. State, 965 So. 2d 1023, 1030 (Miss. 2007). Thus, "intent" was an essential element of the crime upon which the State was required to prove Williams's guilt beyond a reasonable doubt. *See* In re Winship, 397 U.S. 358, 364, 90 S. Ct. 1068, 25 L. Ed. 2d 368 (1970) ("[T]he Due Process Clause protects the accused against conviction except upon proof beyond a reasonable doubt of every fact necessary to constitute the crime with which he is charged."); Hodges v. State, 743 So. 2d 319, 324 (Miss. 1999)("The State is required to prove every element of the offense charged beyond a reasonable doubt.") (citing Heidel v. State, 587 So. 2d 835, 843 (Miss. 1991)). This burden of proof "never shifts from the State to the defendant." Sloan v. State, 368 So. 2d 228, 229 (Miss. 1979).

Williams admits that she shot and killed Sergeant. Her defense at trial was that the shooting was an accident, and, therefore, she lacked the requisite intent to be found guilty of "deliberate design" murder.[2] Consequently, Williams argues that S-4, along with S-2A and S-6, shifted the burden of proof on the only contested issue at trial, *her intent, vel non*.

Williams relies primarily on the United States Supreme Court's holdings in Sandstrom v. Montana, 442 U.S. 510, 99 S. Ct. 2450, 61 L. Ed. 2d 39 (1979), and Francis v. Franklin, 471 U.S. 307, 105 S. Ct. 1965, 85 L. Ed. 2d 344 (1985). In Sandstrom, Sandstrom admitted to the killing, but defended on the grounds that it was not "deliberate." Id. at 512.

Therefore, "[intent] was the lone element of the offense at issue . . . ." Id. at 520-21. The jury was given the following instruction: "[T]he law presumes that a person intends the ordinary consequences of his voluntary acts." Id. at 512. In Francis, the Court again examined a case where "intent" to commit murder was "the only contested issue at trial." Francis, 471 U.S. at 309. The jury was instructed, "[a] person [**8] of sound mind and discretion is presumed to intend the natural and probable consequences of his acts but the presumption may be rebutted." Id. at 311. These two instructions are indistinguishable from S-4. In both cases, the Court emphatically held that the instruction violated the Due Process Clause in that it shifted the burden of proof to the defendant on an essential element of the charged offense, *i.e.*, intent. Sandstrom, 442 U.S. at 521; Francis, 471 U.S. at 325.

This Court has condemned similar presumptive instructions. In Tran v. State, 681 So. 2d 514, 516 (Miss. 1996), the jury was given the following instruction: "Deliberate design may be *presumed* - from the unlawful and deliberate use of a deadly weapon." (Emphasis added.) This Court held that the instruction was given in error because "it relieved the prosecution of its [burden of] persuasion." Id. at 518.

The State counters that, when the instructions are read as a whole, S-4 did not shift the burden of proof. Specifically, the State directs this Court to instructions C-3, C-6, S-8 and S-10. C-3 instructed the jury that Williams was "presume [d] . . . innocent" and that the "State must prove beyond a reasonable doubt" that Williams was "guilty of every material element of the offense." C-5 instructed the jury, in pertinent part, "not to single out any certain . . . instruction and ignore others. The order in which these instructions are given has no significance . . . ." S-8 allowed the jury to find Williams not guilty based on "accident or misfortune," and S-10 encompassed the lesser-included offense of manslaughter.

But Sandstrom and Francis addressed and rejected the very arguments presented by the State. In addition to the erroneous instruction, the Sandstrom "jury was instructed generally that the accused was presumed innocent until proved guilty, and that the State had the burden of proving beyond a reasonable doubt, that the defendant caused the death of the deceased purposely or knowingly." Sandstrom, 442 U.S. at 518 n.7; Francis, 471 U.S. at 311. The general instructions given in Sandstrom and Francisare very similar to those relied on by the State. The Court found that "[t]hese general instructions as to the prosecutor's burden and the defendant's presumption of innocence do not dissipate the error in the challenged portion of the instructions." Francis, 471 U. S. at 319-20.

Comparing the instructions reveals an additional conflict. S-4 conflicts with instruction S-9. S-9 stated, "[t]he Court instructs the jury that an intentional act cannot be excused under the doctrine of accident or misfortune." When S-4 and S-9 are read together, a reasonable juror may have determined that the shooting could not have been an accident because "[Williams was] *presumed* to have *intended* the natural and probable consequences of [her] . . . acts" and "an *intentional* act cannot be . . . [an] accident . . . ."

Additionally, the State argues that instruction S-4 did not employ the mandatory terms "shall" or "will," and, therefore, merely created a permissive inference for the jury. Yet, the absence of "shall" or "will" does not automatically render S-4 permissive. Rather, we consider *HN3* the distinctive differences between "infer" and "presume." "Infer" is defined as "to conclude from certain premises or evidence." Webster's II *New College Dictionary* 567 (2001). By this definition, a jury may not make an inference without evidence adduced at trial to support that inference. However, S-4 did not employ "infer," but instead used "presume," which is defined as "to *assume* to be true without proof to the contrary." Webster's II *New College Dictionary* 875 (2001). "Assume" is analogous to "presume" and "stress[es] the arbitrary acceptance as true of something which has not yet been proved." Webster's *Dictionary of Synonyms* 646 (1942). As a presumption is accepted as true without proof to the contrary, it follows that the burden was shifted to the defendant to provide proof.

The Sandstrom Court addressed the contention that the instruction merely created a permissible inference and stated, "[this] argument[] need not detain us long . . . [,]" for "Sandstrom's jurors . . . were not told that they had a choice, or that they might infer that conclusion; they were told only that the law presumed it." Sandstrom, 442 U.S. at 514-15; *see* Francis, 471 U.S. at 316

("The challenged [instruction is] cast in the language of command.") "It is clear that a reasonable juror could easily have viewed such an instruction as mandatory." Sandstrom, 442 U.S. at 515. S-4 created a mandatory presumption, not a permissible inference, and, therefore, the State's argument must fail.

S-2A and S-6 clearly illustrate the distinction in which the jury is given guidance on what it may infer from the evidence adduced at trial. In contrast to S-4, S-2A and S-6 explicitly used the phrase "may be inferred." In addition to including the permissive "may," the instructions allow the jury *the discretion* to reach a conclusion only if evidence has been presented to support that conclusion, thus creating a true permissive inference. Francis, 471 U.S. at 314 "A permissive inference suggests to the jury a possible conclusion to be drawn if the State proves predicate facts, but does not require the jury to draw that conclusion.") Therefore, S-2A and S-6 "told [the jurors] that they had a choice, or that they might *infer* that conclusion." Sandstrom, 442 U.S. at 515(emphasis added). They did not tell the jurors "that the law presumed it." Id. S-2A and S-6 do not create a mandatory presumption, and, therefore, do not impermissibly shift the burden of proof. *See* Rose v. Clark, 478 U.S. 570, 581, 106 S. Ct. 3101, 92 L. Ed. 2d 460 (1986)("No one doubts that the trial court properly could have instructed the jury that it could *infer* malice from respondent's conduct.") (emphasis in original).

S-4 is practically indistinguishable from the burden-shifting instructions condemned in Sandstrom and Francis and the instruction which relieved the prosecution of its burden of persuasion condemned in Tran. In contrast to the permissive inference established by S-2A and S-6, S-4 created a mandatory presumption which could allow a conviction based upon a presumption as opposed to evidence beyond a reasonable doubt. Therefore, S-4 was given in error.

Having found error, this Court may consider whether such error was harmless. "Error is harmless if it is clear beyond a reasonable doubt that it did not contribute to the verdict." Conley v. State, 790 So. 2d 773, 793 (Miss. 2001)(citing Chapman v. California, 386 U.S. 18, 87 S. Ct. 824, 17 L. Ed. 2d 705 (1967)). Undoubtedly, the State presented substantial evidence of Williams's guilt. However, Williams testified that the shooting was an accident. Her testimony was sufficient to warrant an instruction on accident or mistake, which was granted. Once her defense was placed in issue and the instruction given, it was the duty of the jury to consider Williams's testimony and defense among all the other evidence presented. It was S-4 which created this dilemma, for it is impossible to determine beyond a reasonable doubt whether the jury engaged in this consideration or merely relied on S-4's presumption as to intent. We cannot conclude that is it is "clear beyond a reasonable doubt that [S-4] did not contribute to the verdict." Conley, 790 So. 2d at 793.

CONCLUSION

The circuit court erred in granting instruction S-4, and such error cannot be considered harmless in this case. Therefore, we reverse Williams's conviction and sentence and remand the case to the Circuit Court of Harrison County for a new trial consistent with this opinion.

REVERSED AND REMANDED

Waller, C.J., Dickinson, P.J., Lamar, Kitchens, Chandler, Pierce, King, and Coleman, JJ., Concur.

GRAHAM v. UNITED STATES

District of Columbia Court of Appeals, 12 A.3d 1159, 2011 D.C. App. LEXIS 30 (2011)

JUDGES: Before GLICKMAN, KRAMER, AND BLACKBURNE-RIGSBY. KRAMER delivered the opinion of the court.

Kramer, Associate Judge: David Graham appeals from his convictions for first-degree murder while armed, possession of a firearm during a crime of violence ("PFCV"), and carrying a pistol without a license ("CPWL"). Appellant argues that the jury lacked sufficient evidence to sustain the convictions, that the trial court erred by improperly admitting hearsay evidence, that the trial court erred by giving the jury a flight instruction, and that the trial court's flight instruction itself was erroneous. We affirm.

I. Factual Background

On December 12, 2001, Kamau Walker was shot to death in his home in northwest Washington [District of Columbia]. The government's evidence showed that, prior to the shooting, Graham and Walker had at least one altercation, and on the day of the murder, at least two altercations during which Walker threatened Graham. At trial, the government introduced testimony from a number of witnesses, including Graham's friend Derrick McCray, and Walker's friends Jose Henriquez and Barrington Fowler. Because the testimony was at times contradictory, we summarize the relevant testimony of the key witnesses.

Henriquez testified that prior to the shooting, he was in the house with Graham, Fowler and Walker. Minutes after Graham arrived, Henriquez went to the bathroom, where he heard Walker speak with someone, then heard "firecrackers." When he emerged, Walker was dead, and he fled to get help. He testified that he encountered Fowler by the front door near the stairs, and told him that Walker was "on the floor." Henriquez testified that he believed that the shooter fled via the back door. That night, while giving a statement to police, Henriquez saw Graham across the street and told officers that he "might be the guy."

Fowler testified after Henriquez. He testified that he was outside the home when the shooting occurred, and while running into the home to investigate, met Henriquez in front of the house, where Henriquez, hysterical, told him "Dave [Graham] shot your friend, Kamau [Walker]." Fowler testified that despite knowing that Henriquez was in the house when the shots were fired, he did not believe Henriquez was the shooter. Fowler also testified that after the shooting, he saw Graham walking quickly down the street, in different clothing than he had worn earlier. The night of the shooting, Fowler made a report to the police. At trial, he testified that he told the police the shooter was "Kamau's [Walker's] friend, Dave [Graham]."

McCray testified that on the evening of the shooting, after an altercation with Walker, Graham stated that he should "snuff" Walker. McCray testified that he later followed Graham into Walker's house, where he witnessed Walker's shooting. According to McCray, he was standing behind Graham, who was facing Walker, who in turn was in front of Fowler, when Walker was shot. McCray was behind Graham, thus unable to see whether or not he had anything in his hands. While McCray did not specifically see Graham shoot Walker, he testified that Fowler was definitely not shooting, and therefore he knew that Graham was the shooter. McCray further testified that a few days after the shooting, he met Graham in a parking lot in the northeast part of the city to give Graham clothes from Graham's apartment. Other witnesses testified that Graham was avoiding the area because it was "hot."

The trial judge instructed the jury, including an instruction allowing the jury to consider flight evidence. The jury convicted on all counts, and this appeal followed.

II. Sufficiency of the Evidence

* * *

Graham's primary contention is that the testimony provided by the various witnesses at trial was too contradictory to sufficiently identify him as the shooter. Furthermore, he emphasizes that McCray, the only eyewitness to the shooting, changed his account of events and was influenced by a plea agreement with the government. Nonetheless, viewing the evidence in the light most favorable to the government, we find that the evidence was sufficient to identify Graham as the shooter.

* * *

The testimony of McCray alone, if credited by the jury, was sufficient to convict Graham. McCray testified that on the day of the murder, he heard Graham say that "he should go snuff" Walker. McCray also testified that he witnessed the shooting. While McCray could not testify that he saw Graham holding a gun, he testified that he was standing behind Graham as Walker was shot, and that the only other person present in the room, Fowler, was "definitely not shooting." Based on his observations, he concluded that Graham shot Walker.

We have repeatedly held that the testimony of one witness is sufficient to sustain a conviction. See Gibson, *supra*, 792 A.2d at 1066 "[T]he testimony of a single witness is sufficient to sustain a criminal conviction, even when other witnesses may testify to the contrary."); see also (Kevin) Hill v. United States, 541 A.2d 1285, 1287 (D.C. 1988) "A conviction based upon a single eyewitness identification will not be disturbed if a reasonable juror could find the circumstances surrounding the identification to be convincing beyond a reasonable doubt."). We conclude that a reasonable person could find the identification convincing beyond a reasonable doubt.

* * *

IV. The Flight Instruction

The trial judge issued this flight instruction, over Graham's objection:

> Now a person who hides after, who flees or hides after a crime has been committed or after he has been accused of a crime may be motivated by a variety of factors which are fully consistent with innocence. Flight or concealment does not create a presumption of guilt, nor does it necessarily reflect that the person has feelings of guilt. In addition, because innocent persons sometimes feel guilty, such feelings do not necessarily reflect actual guilt.
>
> On the other hand, you may consider flight or concealment as a circumstance tending to show feelings of guilt and you may also consider feelings of guilt as evidence tending to show actual guilt, but you are not required to do so. However, under no circumstances may you presume that a defendant is guilty, merely because he fled or concealed himself. If you find evidence of flight or concealment, you should consider and weigh such evidence along with all the other evidence in the case and give it the weight that you think it deserves.

The instruction is the standard "Red Book" instruction. Criminal Jury Instructions for the District of Columbia 2.44 (4th Ed. 2004).

"In reviewing a challenge to a jury instruction that was preserved at trial, the central question for this court is whether it is an adequate statement of the law, and whether it is supported by evidence in the case." Wheeler v. United States, 930 A.2d 232, 238 (D.C. 2007) (citing Leftwitch v. United States, 251 A.2d 646, 649 (D.C. 1969)). "This court reviews the trial court's decision to give a requested jury instruction for abuse of discretion, viewing the instruction as a whole." Id. (citing Edwards v. United States, 721 A.2d 938, 944 (D.C. 1998)).

"A flight instruction is improper unless the evidence reasonably supports the inference that there was flight or concealment and that the defendant fled because of consciousness of guilt and actual guilt of the crime charged." Scott v. United States, 412 A.2d 364, 371 (D.C. 1980) (citations omitted). Graham argues that the evidence in the case was insufficient to support the required inference, and as such the instruction was unduly prejudicial. We disagree.

Graham also vaguely argues that the trial court erred by admitting the flight evidence in the first instance. Where a party generally raises an issue on appeal without supporting argument, we deem it abandoned. See generally Bardoff v. United States, 628 A.2d 86, 90 n.8 (D.C. 1993) (citing D.C. App. R. 28 (a)(5) which requires briefs to contain "contentions of the appellant with respect to the issues presented, and the reasons therefore, with citation to the authorities, statutes and parts of the record relied on."). As such, we decline to address the admissibility of the evidence supporting the flight instruction.

Evidence adduced at trial established that Graham left the area quickly after the murder, in different clothing than he had been wearing shortly before. McCray testified that after the incident, he did not see Graham in the neighborhood, and furthermore, that he traveled to another neighborhood to take Graham the clothes from Graham's apartment. This was corroborated by Graham's former girlfriend, who also testified to the grand jury that after the shooting, Graham avoided the neighborhood because it was "hot." This evidence reasonably supports the inference required to issue the flight instruction. See, e.g. Lloyd v. United States, 806 A.2d 1243, 1252 (D.C. 2002) (finding that evidence that the defendant changed clothes and returned to the scene was sufficient to support a flight instruction).

Graham emphasizes that other evidence produced at trial suggests he did not immediately leave the area, and that his reluctance to remain in the neighborhood was consistent with innocence. However, "[a] degree of ambiguity for flight evidence is acceptable; the standard instruction deals with the uncertainties by warning the jury that flight does 'not necessarily reflect' consciousness of guilt and 'may be motivated by a variety of factors which are fully consistent with innocence.'" Comford v. United States, 947 A.2d 1181, 1187 (D.C. 2008) (citation omitted); see also (Curtis) Smith v. United States, 777 A.2d 801, 808 (D.C. 2001) (finding that conflicting explanations for flight are weighed by the jury). Furthermore, to the extent that some evidence suggested Graham did not immediately flee, "contradictions among witnesses at trial are inevitable and are matters for the jury to resolve as they weigh all the evidence." Koonce v. United States, 993 A.2d 544, 551 (D.C. 2010) (quoting Payne v. United States, 516 A.2d 484, 495 (D.C. 1986)). We hold that because the evidence reasonably supported the inference that there was flight, and that the flight reflected consciousness of guilt, the trial court did not abuse its discretion by issuing the instruction.12

V. Adequacy of the Flight Instruction

Graham argues that the language of the flight instruction was improper because it did not clearly inform the jury that finding evidence of flight or concealment is a predicate to weighing such evidence.

* * *

The instruction given at trial included the sentence "If you find evidence of flight or concealment, you should consider and weigh such evidence along with all the other evidence in the case and give it the weight that you think it deserves." (emphasis supplied). Nevertheless, Graham argues that the instruction was flawed because that statement should be prefatory, as reflected in the revised 2008 instruction. We disagree.

Graham relies on Scott v. United States, 412 A.2d 364 (D.C. 1980), where we held that a flight instruction was inadequate where it did not instruct the jury that "it was not bound to consider the flight evidence unless it was convinced that flight had been established." Id. at 372. However, the instruction in Scott failed to give any indication whatsoever that the jury must first find evidence of flight before considering it. Id. Here, while not at the beginning of the instruction, the jury was correctly instructed. In fact, the instruction given here included the clause "If you find evidence of flight or concealment" in direct response to our decision in Scott. Criminal Jury Instructions for the District of Columbia, Comment to No. 2.44 (4th Ed. 2004).

While the 2008 revised instruction did move the language to the beginning of the instruction, this move was for clarification only. Criminal Jury Instructions for the District of Columbia, Comment to No. 2.44 (6th Ed. 2008) ("The Committee did not intend to make any substantive change in the contents of the instruction."). Admittedly, the current formulation of the instruction puts more emphasis on the jury's role in first finding evidence of flight, and may prove to be clearer. Nevertheless, we are unaware of any cases — and Graham points us to none — where the court found the instruction used at Graham's trial erroneous; we decline to find error now. The flight instruction given at trial properly informed the jury that they must first find evidence of flight before weighing such evidence.

VI. Conclusion

Because the testimony of McCray was sufficient to convict Graham, the admission of Fowler's statement of identification was not error, there was enough evidence to support a flight instruction, and that instruction was properly worded, we find no error. Therefore, the judgment is

Affirmed.

BOZEMAN v. STATE

Court of Appeal of Florida, Fourth District 931 So. 2d 1006, 2006 Fla. App. LEXIS 8986 (2006)

Taylor, J. Gunther, J., concurs. Farmer, J., dissents with opinion.

Taylor, J.

Appellant Oliver Bozeman was tried by jury and convicted of grand theft of an automobile. He appeals, arguing that the trial court erred in instructing the jury on the inference to be drawn from possession of recently stolen property. He argues that the evidence was insufficient to show the exclusive possession required for the instruction. We disagree and affirm appellant's conviction.

While on routine patrol in Lauderdale Lakes shortly after midnight, Deputy William Leffew observed a 1990 Mazda pushing a 1967 Chevrolet Malibu. The deputy stopped the two vehicles. Appellant was driving the Mazda. His brother, Antoine McIntyre, was in the front passenger seat. Appellant was using the Mazda to push the Chevrolet Malibu. The Malibu had been stolen from a residence earlier that evening. Joe Bolling was in the driver's seat of the stolen Malibu. The Malibu's headlights were not on and the engine was not running. There was no vehicle tag on the Malibu. Inside, the vehicle's steering wheel column was damaged and there was no key in the ignition. The Malibu's driver side window was shattered and broken glass was on that side of the floorboard. When stopped, appellant told the deputy that McIntyre had purchased the Malibu and that he was merely helping him transport it to McIntyre's house. All three men were arrested at the scene for theft of the Chevrolet Malibu.

Co-defendant Bolling pled guilty to grand theft and possession of burglary tools. When he was sentenced, he told the judge that appellant had nothing to do with the crime. Bolling also testified at appellant's trial. He said that he and McIntyre elicited appellant's help in moving the car without telling appellant that the car was stolen.

During the jury charge conference, defense counsel argued that the standard instruction allowing the jury to infer that the defendant knew that the property was stolen based on his possession of the recently stolen property should not be given because it did not apply. The trial court disagreed and instructed the jury, as follows:

> Proof of possession of recently stolen property, unless satisfactorily explained, gives rise to an inference that the person in possession of the property knew or should have known that the property had been stolen.
>
> *Fla. Std. Jury Instr. (Crim.) 14.1 at 270.*

The jury found appellant guilty of grand theft. He was sentenced to ten years in prison as a habitual felony offender. On appeal, he challenges the above instruction and his sentence.

Appellant argues that the trial court erred in instructing the jury on the inference arising from possession of recently stolen property because the evidence did not demonstrate that appellant possessed the stolen vehicle or that he possessed the vehicle to the extent that he exercised any dominion and control over it.

* * *

As to the defendant's habitual offender sentence, we affirm on the authority of *McBride v. State*, 884 So. 2d 476, 478 (Fla. 4th DCA 2004) (holding that "*Blakely* does not entitle *HN3* a defendant to have a jury determine whether he has the requisite predicate convictions for a habitual felony offender sentence"), and *Washington v. State,* 895 So. 2d 1141, 1143 (Fla. 4th DCA 2005) (holding that "shotgun" notice of intent to seek habitual offender sentence is valid).

At trial, appellant's defense to the grand theft charge was that he did not know that the car was stolen. The jury instruction at issue is a standard jury instruction in theft cases that permits the prosecution to prove by inference that a defendant knew or should have known that property in his possession was stolen. *See Scobee* v. *State*, 488 So. 2d 595, 598 (Fla. 1st DCA 1986). However, before the prosecution can receive the benefit of this jury instruction, it must first produce evidence that the defendant possessed the property. [Citation omitted.] The state must demonstrate that the possession was personal, i.e., involved a distinct and conscious assertion of possession by the accused, and that the possession was exclusive. [Citations omitted].

As the first district explained in *Scobee*:

> The "exclusive" requirement does not mean that defendant's possession must be separate from the possession of all other persons. The joint possession of two or more persons acting in concert is "exclusive" as to any one of them.

Scobee, 488 So. 2d at 598; see *also Walker v. State*, 896 So. 2d 712, 720 n.5 (Fla. 2005) (approving *Scobee's* analysis of the "exclusive" requirement in joint possession cases).

In *People v. White*, 99 Ill. App. 2d 270, 240 N. E.2d 342 (Ill. App. 1968), officers observed the defendant pushing a recently stolen automobile into an alley at 3:00 a.m., and another person sitting at the wheel of the vehicle. When the officers approached, the man at the steering wheel fled. The court stated that the evidence established that "the car was in the joint possession of the defendant and his partner." *Id.* at 343. In finding the facts sufficient to raise a presumption of guilt and warrant a conviction for theft, the court explained that "[a]lthough the defendant was not inside the vehicle, he was exerting control over it by pushing in into the alley." *Id.*

Similarly, in this case, the evidence showed that appellant exercised dominion and control over the Malibu by pushing it while Bolling controlled the car's steering and braking. Without appellant's actions, the car could not have been moved. The two men jointly controlled the car and jointly possessed it. Because this was the sort of possession necessary to support the instruction on inference of knowledge, the trial court did not abuse its discretion in giving this instruction to the jury. It was up to the jury to weigh appellant's explanation for possessing the car and decide whether to accept the correctness of the inference. *See Scobee*, 488 So. 2d at 599.

* * *

Affirmed.
Gunther, J., concurs.
Farmer, J., dissents with opinion.
Farmer, J., dissenting.

* * *

I cannot agree that there is any evidence that this defendant had possession of a stolen automobile when he was simply pushing it with his vehicle.

Cases Relating to Chapter 7

Relevancy and Materiality

COMMONWEALTH v. PRASHAW

Appeals Court of Massachusetts 57 Mass

App. Ct. 19, 781 N.E.2d 19, 2003 Mass. App. LEXIS 5 (2003)

JUDGES: Present: Lenk, Mason, & Berry, JJ.

BERRY, J. In this appeal, the defendant challenges the admission in evidence of photographs depicting her naked in various sexually provocative positions. Balancing the minimal probative value of the pictures with respect to the nonsex-related offenses being tried against the marked prejudice, we conclude that this is one of those exceptional cases where the bounds of the usual grant of wide discretion to a trial judge concerning the admission of photographic evidence were exceeded. Accordingly, we reverse the judgments of conviction.

1. Background facts. On December 26, 1999, a fire broke out in the house in which the defendant and her husband resided. During a "cause-and-origin" survey of the house after the blaze, an investigator saw in plain view in an upstairs bedroom a twelve-gauge shotgun standing in a corner against the wall, and marijuana "roaches" in an ashtray. The shotgun was immediately confiscated. Based on these sightings, the police applied for a warrant to search the house.

The defendant's husband was present in the house both when the fire started and during the fire investigation. The defendant was not at home and had left the house a few days before Christmas following an altercation with her husband during which he beat her and hit her face (this abuse was of a continuing pattern over many years, including past incidents of domestic violence requiring hospital treatment). Following this incident of violence, the defendant sought shelter at her mother's house in New York State. On the day after Christmas, she returned home, only to see the house smouldering from the fire and firefighters and police on the scene.

The defendant entered the house, spoke to an officer, gathered some belongings, and described the assault that had led to her fleeing from the house. The defendant's face had not healed and still bore a bruise from that assault. One of the officers escorted the defendant to the police station, where she applied for, and was granted, a protective order under G.L.C. 209A. Thereafter, she returned to the house, even though she had been previously told by an officer that she could not enter because the police were seeking a search warrant. There were curious aspects surrounding the circumstances of the defendant's return and her explanation of the reasons why she came back to the house. The details do not matter, but of moment is that, when she returned, there was a man with her (whom the officers throughout the trial only described as a black man) and that she had a plan to reenter the house with this man, notwithstanding the police directive not to do so.

While waiting for the search warrant application to be processed, the police had cordoned off the house and stationed an officer as sentry in an unmarked cruiser in front of the house. It was during this time that the defendant and the unidentified man returned to the burned-out house. The man entered the house through the back. When the entry was discovered, another officer was dispatched to the scene to investigate the break-in. A witness, a neighbor, identified the defendant, who was standing nearby, as having "had something to do with this" break-in. The officer approached the defendant, handcuffed her, and conducted a patfrisk. A "crack" cocaine pipe containing cocaine residue was found in her pocket. The defendant was arrested. The man who had entered the house had been arrested by the officer stationed in front of the house.

Thereafter, two search warrants—one for the house and one for a Toyota Four-Runner sport utility vehicle—were executed. Seized from the Toyota were a knife with a seven-inch blade, a small quantity of marijuana, and rolling papers. Seized from the upstairs bedroom were marijuana roaches, a small amount of marijuana in a plastic bag, two bottles that had been crafted into crack cocaine pipes, aluminum foil with marijuana residue, a nonworking postal scale, another scale, the defendant's driver's license and firearm identification card, a joint tax return, and eighteen Polaroid photographs. The photographs depicted the defendant in various sexually explicit poses. In another upstairs room, in a gun cabinet, the police seized two packages of fireworks.

2. The introduction of the photographs. The Commonwealth indicated prior to trial that it would seek to admit all eighteen photographs. In response, the defendant filed a motion in limine. Following a hearing, the trial judge excluded all but three photographs. Although the Commonwealth sought to introduce the three photographs as exhibits, after an unrecorded sidebar conference, only two of the photographs were marked as exhibits and admitted in evidence for the jury's deliberations. In each of the two photographs, the defendant is naked, posing with an object in her hands and displaying the object vis-a-vis her body in a sexually provocative way. The objects being held appear blurry in the pictures. When confronted with the photographs during cross-examination, the defendant described the objects as a cigarette lighter and a billy club; the Commonwealth inferred from its scrutiny that the objects were a handgun and a shotgun. However, as to the latter, the Commonwealth concedes that, even assuming that the object is a shotgun, it is not the same shotgun that was standing in the bedroom and which was the subject of the unlawful storage charge.

The overarching principle is that "the admissibility of photographic evidence is left to the discretion of the trial judge, and [an appellate court] will overturn the judge's decision only where a defendant is able to bear the heavy burden of demonstrating an abuse of that discretion." Commonwealth v. Waters, 399 Mass. 708, 715, 506 N.E.2d 859 (1987). Such judicial discretion has a wide berth, as the trial judge is best positioned to determine evidentiary value and to balance the probative value and relevancy against prejudicial effect. However, notwithstanding this wide latitude, there still are "rare instances in which the probative value of the evidence is overwhelmed by its inflammatory potential." Commonwealth v. Repoza, 382 Mass. 119, 128, 414 N.E.2d 591 (1980). In this case, we determine "whether sexually explicit photographs . . . '[were] so inflammatory as to outweigh their probative value.'" Commonwealth v. Halsey, 41 Mass. App. Ct. 200, 203, 669 N.E.2d 774 (1996), quoting from Commonwealth v. Hrycenko, 31 Mass. App. Ct. 425, 431, 578 N.E.2d 809 (1991). The defendant objected to the admission of the photographs, and, thereby, preserved the issue for appeal. Accordingly, we seek to determine whether there was prejudicial error. We conclude that the answer to that question is in the affirmative. In the balance to be struck, the extraordinary prejudice far overbore the minimal probativeness.

A. Probative value. We begin with an assessment of the evidentiary probativeness of the photographs. As noted, the objects being held by the defendant in the photographs are murky, but, even if viewed by the Commonwealth's lights, and even assuming such additional candle power would have led the beholder to perceive a shotgun of some sort being held in one photograph, it is not, as the Commonwealth concedes, the shotgun identified in the improper storage charge. The Commonwealth, therefore, concedes that neither photograph was relevant to the wrongful storage of a firearm charge and concedes error in admission on that basis. Instead, the Commonwealth argues on appeal, as the sole basis for admission, that the photographs were probative of the defendant's control of the upstairs bedroom where the marijuana, scales, and crack pipes were found.

We note at the outset that there was no dispute that the room was the defendant's bedroom and, in effect, belonged to her. As the prosecutor put it in the closing: "This, ladies and gentlemen, is her room; and there's no question about that. And these things were found in her closet; there's no questions about that, in her bureau, throughout her things; there's no question about the possession, ladies and gentlemen, no question." Precisely so, the defendant's general control over, and association with, the bedroom was well-established by abundant evidence—wholly apart from the photographs. This other evidence included the defendant's clothing, both stored in bureaus and strewn about the bedroom, as well as her driver's license, firearm identification card, and tax return, all of which were found within the bedroom. See Commonwealth v. Rarick, 23 Mass. App. Ct. 912, 912–913, 499 N.E.2d 1233 (1986) (personal effects belonging to the defendant linked her to contraband found in proximity to those effects even though multiple persons shared the dwelling). The strength of this other connective evidence substantially diminished the probative need for introduction of the sexually explicit pictures on the issue of general control of the bedroom, which was not even being disputed. Put another way, that this was the defendant's bedroom was fairly obvious, and the photographs added little but prejudice.

The principal issue with respect to control was limited to the defendant's absence from the house for the five days she stayed with her mother. Given this sojourn, there was a question, it appears from the evidence, as to whether someone else may have used the bedroom for some sort of partying and drinking spree. Indeed, that someone else was in the bedroom during this period might have been inferred from an empty bottle of whiskey and a pizza box which, according to the defendant, were not there before she left for New York, and the fact that, before she left, the photographs were kept in her locked closet. This and other evidence suggest that the defendant did not have control of the room during her absence and that the defendant's estranged, alcoholic husband may well have gone on a drinking binge in that room.

Given this lapse in the defendant's control, the probative value of the photographs, if any, is to be analyzed with respect to this five-day period. Any such probative link between the photographs and this period of time was extremely weak. There was no evidence, and the four corners of the photographs do not manifest, that the pictures were taken within the five-day time frame. Nor was there any evidence that the photographs were taken in the bedroom area where either the drugs or paraphernalia were found or in the corner of the room where the shotgun was standing. Further undercutting the Commonwealth's contention that the photographs showed the defendant's association with, and control over, the bedroom is a handwritten notation, "George's house," on the face of one of the photographs, which suggests that the pictures were taken someplace else. In fact, there was no substantive evidence whatsoever linking the photographs to control of the bedroom by the defendant during her five-day absence. Rather than such authentication, the photographs were simply dropped in evidence as items seized in the search and were not further authenticated by time, place, or manner during the course of trial. "To be admissible in evidence, a photograph must be shown to be accurate and bear enough similarity to circumstances at the time in dispute to be relevant and helpful to the jury in its deliberations." Henderson v. D'Annolfo, 15 Mass. App. Ct. 413, 428, 446 N.E.2d 103 (1983). Thus, on a sliding scale, the probative value of the photographs was minimal. We next consider the prejudice.

B. Prejudicial effect. In this case, the prejudicial effect was depicting the defendant as "a lewd [woman] and to lead the jury to believe that a [woman] of [her] character would be likely to commit the crimes charged." Commonwealth v. Ellis, 321 Mass. 669, 670, 75 N.E.2d 241 (1947). It does not take much imagination to conjure that the purpose and effect of the introduction of the pictures was so that the jury, appalled by the defendant's posing in such a manner, might be swayed to perceive the defendant as not of good moral character and more likely to have committed criminal offenses. Such a prejudicial effect, inherent in sexually explicit depictions, was amplified in this case because the trial did not involve a sex-related offense. Moreover, although only two photographs were published to the jury, one of the officers testified that there were eighteen such Polaroid photographs seized. See, e.g., Commonwealth v. Allen, 377 Mass. 674, 680, 387 N.E.2d 553 (1979) (photograph of the victim's bloody crotch, which was due to natural decomposition, possessed "great potential for inciting jury speculation about possible sexual overtones to the crime" in a murder trial); Commonwealth v. Darby, 37 Mass. App. Ct. 650, 654, 642 N.E.2d 303 (1994) (photograph of the male defendant in a sexually turgid state was unduly prejudicial where impotence or sexual dysfunction was not "directly or inferentially" relevant to the case). As a last resort, the Commonwealth suggests harmless error should cause us to affirm the convictions, but we are unable to say the photographs did not unduly and unfairly influence the jury, or had just a slight effect. In sum, the risk was great that the sexually suggestive pictures, which had little to do with the case at hand, unduly swayed the jury. For these reasons, we conclude that it was error to admit the photographs.

* * *

The judgments of convictions on all the complaints tried are reversed and the verdicts are set aside. The denial of the motion to suppress is affirmed.

So ordered.

STATE v. JACKSON

Supreme Court of Vermont, 2011 VT 15, 2011 Vt. LEXIS 12 (2011)

Before REIBER, DOOLEY, JOHNSON, SKOGLUND, AND BURGESS, JJ., C.J. REIBER, dissenting.

Skoglund, J. Defendant Richard D. Memoli appeals from a judgment of conviction based on a jury verdict of aggravated sexual assault. He contends the trial court erred in: (1) excluding evidence of complainant's use of cocaine during the months preceding and following the assault because it precluded him from presenting his defense that complainant voluntarily exchanged sex for drugs . . .

The record evidence may be summarized as follows. On the evening of December 31, 2007, complainant celebrated New Year's Eve with friends at a bar in Winooski. After consuming several drinks which left her feeling "buzzed," complainant caught a ride to a nearby house party. Complainant smoked marijuana on the ride to the party and drank—by her own estimation—"a lot" of beer while there. Shortly after midnight, complainant left the party with the two friends who brought her, planning to go home. An argument ensued, . . . , and the friends dropped her off on [a public street].

As complainant began to walk home, a sport utility vehicle pulled up and stopped in front of her. Complainant's version of the ensuing events is as follows. She recalled that the driver asked if she was okay, and identified himself as "Rico" and the woman in the passenger seat as "Sam." Complainant gave a false name because she "thought they were undercover cops." Rico, later identified as defendant, offered complainant a ride home. She accepted and entered the rear passenger seat. Complainant also accepted defendant's invitation to join him and Sam at defendant's house for drinks. After parking in defendant's driveway, defendant asked Sam to open the console and she removed what, according to complainant, "looked like a bag of crack." Sam brought the bag inside the house, where she [Sam] and defendant entered a bedroom and closed the door while complainant drank a beer in the living room. Complainant assumed that defendant and Sam were smoking the crack cocaine.

A few minutes later, Sam and defendant came out and invited complainant to enter the bedroom to be "more comfortable." She complied, whereupon Sam closed and locked the bedroom door. Complainant testified that she then observed defendant and Sam smoking crack from an inhaler, and that Sam also blew some of the smoke into her mouth. Complainant further testified that "at some point" her clothes were off but could not recall precisely when or how that occurred. Complainant testified that over the next several hours she was forced to participate in number of sexual activities, including oral sex on defendant. Complainant testified that she was crying, asked to leave, and felt sick and scared throughout much of the ordeal. Eventually defendant told her that she could leave, called her a taxi and told her to be "a good girl and not cry in the cab."

Complainant arrived home shortly after 6:00 a.m., and later that morning called her best friend to report the incident. Complainant also told her mother, who called the police. The investigating officer who arrived at the home observed complainant lying on the bed in a fetal position, crying and hyperventilating. . . .

Defendant and his companion Sam testified and presented a different version of events. Defendant recalled that when complainant entered the car he asked her "if she smoked" and wanted to "hang out with us and get high," she assented, and all three smoked crack cocaine on the ride to defendant's house. Defendant further testified that the three then went straight to the bedroom, where they all smoked a considerable amount of crack cocaine and engaged in consensual sexual relations. Defendant emphatically denied that complainant was forced to smoke or to have sex. He recalled that complainant asked to take some crack with her when she left, and that when he refused, she "wasn't pleased." Defendant's companion testified similarly that complainant voluntarily smoked "a lot" of cocaine, and denied that complainant was forced to do so or compelled to participate in sexual relations.

A jury found defendant guilty as charged. . . . This appeal followed.

Defendant's principal claim on appeal concerns a pretrial ruling excluding all evidence relating to complainant's use of drugs before and after the date of the offense. The ruling arose following the State's in limine motion, which contained no legal argument, but simply asked for exclusion of certain evidence including testimony about complainant's drug use before and after the date of the alleged offense, and a videotaped conversation wherein complainant allegedly buys drugs. Defendant opposed the motion through a written memorandum. At a hearing on the motion, defendant's attorney gave the following proffer of the evidence's relevancy:

> [These two issues] go to the heart of our defense. If we're not allowed to deal with [these issues], we don't have a defense. Our defense is very simple. Our defense is that the complaining witness traded sex for drugs. It's as simple as that, and it's a common occurrence among a certain group of individuals who are addicted to crack cocaine. It's just a fact of life, and so we have a voluntary defense. Our defense is that she voluntarily consented, and the reason that she did was . . . that she was a crack addict, and my client was in a position to give her all the crack that she wanted.

Defendant's attorney explained that he had witnesses who would testify that complainant used and sold crack cocaine within thirty days before and after the incident, and this was both relevant to his defense and to impeach complainant, who in her deposition denied using crack before or after the incident. Defendant's attorney further explained that "if the court restricts everything to just that day, then the jury isn't really going to understand who this person is and the kind of activities that she engages in on a regular basis. Someone who uses crack, you know, shortly before and after and then denies using it on that particular day, I think the jury should be able to hear that."

The State claimed that the evidence should be excluded for lack of relevance because "[t]he fact that she is a crack addict does not mean he has a right to sexually assault her." On the issue of impeachment, the State explained that complainant would testify at trial that she "has been an addict in the past," and so there would be no need to impeach her testimony.

From the bench, the court ruled that complainant's drug use on the night of the incident was admissible, but complainant's subsequent use and "history and reputation as a drug user beforehand is out of bounds." Defendant's attorney again probed whether he could use complainant's drug use to impeach complainant's statement during her deposition that she had not used crack cocaine before or after the night of the incident. The court denied the request, stating that those questions were not directly relevant to the charge and therefore beyond the scope of admissible testimony.

* * *

Thus, in large part, the case came down to a credibility contest between defendant and complainant. In opening statements, defendant's attorney outlined the defense as one of consent, claiming that complainant voluntarily took hits of cocaine and participated in sexual acts. Defendant testified that complainant took around twenty-five hits of crack cocaine voluntarily and was upset when defendant did not give her some crack cocaine to take home. Defendant also testified that complainant willingly participated in sexual acts with Sam and him. Complainant testified that she was forced to take hits of crack cocaine and that the drug use made her feel nauseous.

* * *

Defendant argues that the court's pretrial order was error because it precluded him from presenting his defense. The dissent concludes that defendant waived any objection to the pretrial order because he did not actually raise a sex-in-exchange-for-drugs defense at trial. How could he? The court's pretrial order specifically forbade defendant from eliciting any testimony regarding the complainant's "prior and subsequent use of crack and/or addiction to crack to support an inference that she performed sex for drugs."

* * *

Therefore, we turn to the merits of the court's pretrial order. The trial court cited two grounds for its decision to exclude evidence of complainant's prior and subsequent drug use: the rape shield statute and lack of relevancy to the issue of consent. Neither provides a legal basis for exclusion of defendant's proffered evidence

* * *

Defendant requested to admit evidence of complainant's crack cocaine use, both before and after the incident to demonstrate complainant's affection for the drug. Only then could he argue his defense — that her desire for cocaine was strong enough to motivate her to consent to sexual interactions with him in exchange for the drug. Defendant was not acquainted with complainant prior to that night, had no knowledge of her prior sexual behavior, and did not seek to admit any evidence of her prior sexual encounters.

* * *

Under the plain language of the [rape shield] statute, defendant's request to admit evidence of complainant's drug use should not have been excluded. Complainant's prior addiction to crack cocaine and her use of the drug was not "prior sexual conduct," 13 V.S.A. § 3255(a)(3), and thus outside the statute's evidentiary exclusion. There is no logical reason why this evidence was inadmissible under the policy of the rape shield law, and the court erred in so holding.

* * *

The court's second rationale for exclusion of the evidence—that complainant's drug use, other than on the night of the incident, was not relevant—is also erroneous. Evidence is relevant if it has a tendency to make the existence of a fact in issue more or less probable than without the evidence. V.R.E. 401; see State v. Raymond, 148 Vt. 617, 622, 538 A.2d 164, 167 (1987) (explaining that relevant evidence has some probative value). The trial court has broad discretion in determining the relevance of evidence; however, "this discretion is limited in criminal cases by defendant's constitutional due process rights and right to confront witnesses against him." State v. LeClaire, 2003 VT 4, ¶ 13, 175 Vt. 52, 819 A.2d 719.

The court's decision was erroneous because complainant's drug use within thirty days before and after the charged incident was relevant to the defense that she consented to sexual acts with defendant to obtain crack cocaine. See In re A.B., 170 Vt. 535, 536–37, 740 A.2d 367, 369–70 (1999). In sexual assault cases where the case hinges on the credibility of the complainant, "the presence of an ulterior motive for the victim's making the accusations is often a critical issue." Id. at 537, 740 A.2d at 369 (quotation omitted); State v. Cartee, 161 Vt. 73, 77, 632 A.2d 1108, 1111 (1993) (holding that it was error for trial court to exclude evidence of complainant's motive where case turns on complainant's credibility). Thus, proffered evidence relating to a defense theory of consent is relevant.

The importance of this evidence is highlighted by the State's presentation of its case. At trial, the State underscored that defendant had failed to provide any reason for why complainant would consent to sexual acts with defendant or why she would fabricate her allegations against defendant, reiterating for the jury that complainant found defendant unattractive and that he was older than she was. Specifically, during closing statements, the prosecutor questioned the jury, "Why would [complainant], or anyone, consent to the type of sexual acts that have been described here in this courtroom?" Defendant's one-word answer was cocaine, but the jury never heard it. As defendant proffered at the pretrial hearing, complainant's addiction to, use of, and desire for crack cocaine was essential for defendant to demonstrate his explanation for complainant's motivation—that she participated in sexual acts with defendant in exchange for access to the drug.

* * *

Further, complainant's drug use was relevant for purposes of impeaching her testimony that she did not voluntarily inhale drugs on the night of the incident and that she felt nauseous after being allegedly forced to inhale, thereby implying that she was unfamiliar with the drug. Contrary to the dissent's assertion, defendant adequately preserved this claim of error.

Reversed and remanded for a new trial.

WISE v. STATE

Court of Appeals, Second District 2011, Tex. App. LEXIS 1583 (2011)

Before LIVINGSTON, C.J., McCOY AND MEIR.

I. Introduction

In two points, Appellant Jeffrey Shane Wise appeals his convictions for four counts of sexual assault, one count of indecency with a child, and eleven counts of possession of child pornography. We affirm in part and reverse and render in part.

II. Background Facts

In the spring of 2007, when C.H. was sixteen years old, she began working at a McDonald's restaurant in Wichita Falls. Wise, who was in his forties, was her manager, and because she did not have a car and worked until late at night, he occasionally gave her a ride home. Wise and C.H. began to talk on the phone. One day, Wise took C.H. to his house, where they engaged in sexual intercourse. Wise and C.H. then had many other sexual encounters at various places on later dates. Also, C.H. took pictures of herself naked on a digital camera and on Wise's cell phone and gave them to him.

When the police learned about Wise's relationship with C.H., she agreed to let the police record a phone call from her to Wise. During the call, C.H. told Wise that her parents had discovered her relationship with him and wanted to talk to the police. She and Wise then talked about some details of their sexual acts.

Wichita Falls Police Detective Alan Killingsworth obtained an arrest warrant for Wise and a search warrant for Wise's house. When Detective Killingsworth executed the search warrant a few days after he recorded Wise and C. H.'s phone call, he found Wise at the house. While other officers stayed at the house, Detective Killingsworth arrested Wise and took him to the police station, where he received admonishments about his constitutional rights and gave a confession in an oral statement.

During the search of Wise's house, officers seized, among other items, a digital camera that contained a pornographic image of C.H., pornographic DVDs, a laptop computer, a Gateway desktop computer tower, phone cards, condoms, and a blindfold that Wise used during a sexual encounter with C.H. The police took photographs of the inside of Wise's house and took the laptop and Gateway tower to a forensics computer lab. Detective Killingsworth received a CD containing images that had been copied from the Gateway tower.

A Wichita County grand jury indicted Wise for four counts of sexual assault of C.H. (counts one through four of the indictment), eleven counts of possession of child pornography (count five, based on a picture of C.H., and counts eight through seventeen, based on images stored on the Gateway tower), and two counts of indecency with a child concerning other complainants (counts six and seven). Wise filed a motion to suppress the evidence that police found at his house, contending that the warrant was not supported by an affidavit showing probable cause. After the trial court denied the motion, Wise pleaded not guilty to all counts.

The jury convicted Wise of committing sixteen of the seventeen acts alleged in the indictment; it acquitted him of count seven, which concerned an alleged sexual encounter in 1997. The jury assessed Wise's punishment, and the trial court entered judgment on the verdict: counts one, two, and three—eighteen years' confinement and a $10,000 fine for each count; count four and six—twenty years' confinement and a $10,000 fine for each count; count five—eight years' confinement and a $10,000 fine; and for counts eight through seventeen—ten year's confinement and a $10,000 fine for each count. The trial court ordered that each of Wise's sentences run consecutively. This appeal followed.

III. Suppression

In his first point, Wise argues that the trial court erred by denying his motion to suppress, contending that the facts recited in the search warrant affidavit "were insufficient from the totality of the circumstances" to show probable cause for seizing the computers at his house. [The court held that probable cause to issue the search warrant did exist based upon the alleged victim's telephone call with the defendant where the police officer overheard and recorded their sexual talk; her indication that she had sexual intercourse with the defendant on numerous occasions; that she had taken pictures of herself naked and given them to him on a cell phone and on a camera; and that he had possession of these items; and that he did have a desktop computer in his home. In addition, she had given him three nude pictures of herself that she had taken with the digital camera he had given to her. The court noted that although these facts did not establish that the defendant actually had a computer or digital pornographic images, they were sufficient to establish probable cause for a search warrant for a search of his home and Gateway computer.]

* * *

IV. Evidentiary Sufficiency

In his second point, Wise contends that the evidence is insufficient to support the jury's verdict for possession of child pornography stored on the Gateway tower as alleged in counts eight through seventeen of the indictment. Wise concedes in his appellate brief that the images taken from the tower constitute child pornography. However, he argues that the State failed to prove that he intentionally or knowingly possessed the images. [Wise essentially contended that the images were not logically relevant in his case because there was no proof that he had anything to do with their creation, downloading, storage, or access. If there was no connection to the defendant, the images would be legally irrelevant and not admissible.]

A. Standard of Review

In our due-process review of the sufficiency of the evidence to support a conviction, we view all of the evidence in the light most favorable to the prosecution to determine whether any rational trier of fact could have found the essential elements of the crime beyond a reasonable doubt. Jackson v. Virginia, 443 U.S. 307, 319, 99 S. Ct. 2781, 2789, 61 L. Ed. 2d 560 (1979); Clayton v. State, 235 S. W.3d 772, 778 (Tex. Crim. App. 2007). This standard gives full play to the responsibility of the trier of fact to resolve conflicts in the testimony, to weigh the evidence, and to draw reasonable inferences from basic facts to ultimate facts. Jackson, 443 U.S. at 319, 99 S. Ct. at 2789; Clayton, 235 S.W.3d at 778.

The trier of fact is the sole judge of the weight and credibility of the evidence. See Tex. Code Crim. Proc. Ann. art. 38.04 (Vernon 1979); Brown v. State, 270 S.W.3d 564, 568 (Tex. Crim. App. 2008), cert. denied, 129 S. Ct. 2075, 173 L. Ed. 2d 1139 (2009). Thus, when performing an evidentiary sufficiency review, we may not re-evaluate the weight and credibility of the evidence and substitute our judgment for that of the factfinder. Williams v. State, 235 S. W.3d 742, 750 (Tex. Crim. App. 2007). Instead, we "determine whether the necessary inferences are reasonable based upon the combined and cumulative force of all the evidence when viewed in the light most favorable to the verdict." Hooper v. State, 214

S.W.3d 9, 16–17 (Tex. Crim. App. 2007). We must presume that the factfinder resolved any conflicting inferences in favor of the prosecution and defer to that resolution. Jackson, 443 U.S. at 326, 99 S. Ct. at 2793; Clayton, 235 S.W.3d at 778. The standard of review is the same for direct and circumstantial evidence cases; circumstantial evidence is as probative as direct evidence in establishing the guilt of an actor. Clayton, 235 S.W.3d at 778; Hooper, 214 S.W.3d at 13. In determining the e to show an appellant's intent, and faced with a record that supports conflicting inferences, we "must presume-even if it does not affirmatively appear in the record-that the trier of fact resolved any such conflict in favor of the prosecution, and must defer to that resolution." Matson v. State, 819 S.W.2d 839, 846 (Tex. Crim. App. 1991). If an appellate court finds the evidence insufficient under this standard it must reverse the judgment and enter an order of acquittal. Woodard v. State, No. 01-09-00133-CR, No. 01-09-00134, 2010 Tex. App. LEXIS 9916, 2010 WL 5093848, at *3 (Tex. App.—Houston [1st Dist.] Dec. 9, 2010, no pet. h.).

B. Applicable Law

A person acts intentionally with respect to the nature of the conduct when the person has a conscious objective or desire to engage in the conduct; a person acts knowingly when he is aware of the nature of his conduct. Tex. Penal Code Ann. § 6.03(a), (b) (Vernon 2003). Possession means actual care, custody, control, or management of the thing possessed. Id. § 1.07(a)(39) (Vernon Supp. 2010); Liggens v. State, 50 S.W.3d 657, 659 (Tex. App.—Fort Worth 2001, pet ref'd). Proof of a culpable mental state almost invariably depends upon circumstantial evidence. Krause v. State, 243 S.W.3d 95, 111 (Tex. App.—Houston [1st Dist.] 2007, pet. ref'd); see also Hernandez v. State, 819 S.W.2d 806, 810 (Tex. Crim. App. 1991), cert. denied, 504 U.S. 974, 112 S. Ct. 2944, 119 L. Ed. 2d 568 (1992).

C. Evidence

At trial, Amy Trippel, the digital forensics examiner who searched the Gateway tower, testified that she was asked to look for evidence of "pornography and chat logs and [that the police] were specifically looking for pictures of [C.H.]." Trippel found ten child pornography images in the computer's free space, which is unallocated space that is marked as available for use. Trippel indicated that files go into the free space upon deletion; she described free space as being

like a card catalog in a — in a library. If I take the card out of the card catalog and throw it away, the library book is still there, but I just don't know where to go get it. And that's the same concept. If I delete a file, the file is still there, the operating system just doesn't know where to get it.

Trippel explained that there was no way to know where the image files came from, how they were placed on the computer (for example, whether they were viewed intentionally or popped up automatically while a user was looking at another website), or when they were created, modified, or viewed. Trippel indicated that the Gateway tower contained various viruses and that some viruses could make it possible for pornography to be stored on a computer without the user's knowledge; that anyone using a virus to place the images in free space would not be able to access them; that files placed into free space remain there until they are written over by other files; and that when a cached temporary internet file is deleted, it goes into free space, at which time a forensic examiner cannot tell when the file was viewed. Wise's brother testified that Wise purchased the computer at a flea market in August 2006.

D. Analysis

Wise argues that the evidence is insufficient because the images in question were stored in free space "and the [S]tate failed to show that he had ever seen them or had any access to them." To support his argument, Wise distinguishes this court's previous decision affirming possession of child pornography when images were found in the free space on the defendant's computer. See Perry v. State, No. 02-06-00378-CR, 2008 Tex. App. LEXIS 6446, 2008 WL 3877303, at *1-4 (Tex. App.—Fort Worth Aug. 21, 2008, pet. ref'd) (mem. op., not designated for publication). We agree that Perry is factually distinct from the present case. In Perry, Perry affirmatively uploaded pornographic images of children onto the internet, his computer did not harbor any viruses that could covertly place images on Perry's computer, and there was no evidence that the computer was purchased second-hand, leaving little doubt that Perry accessed and then deleted the pornographic images of children found in his computer's free space. 2008 Tex. App. LEXIS 6446, [WL] at *1, 3, 5.

Here, the uncontroverted testimony that Wise bought the computer second-hand at a flea market and the State's own expert witness's testimony admitting that the computer contained viruses capable of covertly placing images on the computer; that Wise could not access the images; and that it was impossible to determine when the images were placed on to, accessed, or deleted from, the computer, do not meet the State's burden to prove beyond a reasonable doubt that Wise knowingly or intentionally possessed the images. See Lancaster v. State, 319 S.W.3d 168, 173 (Tex. App.—Waco 2010, pet. ref'd). We conclude that this evidence, even when viewed in the light most favorable to the verdict, could not lead a rational jury to find that Wise intentionally or knowingly possessed the child pornography images found in the free space of his computer. See U.S. v. Kain, 589 F.3d 945, 949 (8th Cir. 2009) ("The presence of Trojan viruses and the location of child pornography in inaccessible internet and orphan files can raise serious issues of inadvertent or unknowing possession."). Thus, we hold that the evidence is insufficient to support Wise's convictions in counts eight through seventeen of the indictment, and we sustain Wise's second point.

V. Conclusion

Having overruled Wise's first point and sustained his second point, we affirm the trial court's judgment on counts one through six and reverse the trial court's judgment with respect to counts eight through seventeen and render a judgment of acquittal on those counts.

Cases Relating to Chapter 8

Competency of Evidence and Witnesses

UNITED STATES v. PHIBBS

United States Court of Appeals, Sixth Circuit 999 F.2d 1053 (1993)

Before: GUY and SUHRHEINRICH, Circuit Judges; and DOWD, District Judge.

RALPH B. GUY, JR., Circuit Judge.

Defendants, Raymond Huckelby, Diane Whited, Robert Phibbs, Victor Rojas, and Robert Murr appeal their convictions arising from their participation in a cocaine distribution ring operating in Tennessee and Kentucky. In addition, Phibbs and Rojas challenge the appropriateness of their sentences.

* * *

E. Competency of Jerry Parks and Tommy McKeehan

Whited claims that witnesses Jerry Parks and Tommy McKeehan were incompetent to give testimony on grounds of mental incapacity. In the case of Parks, he had previously been found incompetent to stand trial, had a history of auditory delusions, and had spent time in mental health facilities. As for McKeehan, Whited cites an affidavit filed with the district court by his treating psychiatrist that he could not assist his counsel in an upcoming trial because he suffered from "confusion, agitation, paranoia and hallucinations." This affidavit was dated four days prior to McKeehan having entered into a plea agreement with the government. Because of such information, Whited contends that, at the very least, it was error for the court not to conduct a preliminary examination of Parks' and McKeehan's competency as witnesses.

Under Rule 601 of the Federal Rules of Evidence (General Rule of Competency), "every person is competent to be a witness except as otherwise provided in these rules." The Advisory Committee Notes to Rule 601 explain that "this general ground-clearing eliminates all grounds of incompetency not specifically recognized in the rules of this Article." Accordingly, "no mental or moral qualifications for testifying as a witness" are specified. Id. This is because "standards of mental capacity have proved elusive in actual application." Id.

Thus, the Federal Rules of Evidence strongly disfavor barring witnesses on competency grounds due to mental incapacity. As we wrote in United States v. Ramirez, 871 F.2d 582, 584 (6th Cir.), cert. denied, 493 U.S. 841, 107 L. Ed. 2d 88, 110 S. Ct. 127 (1989):

> What must be remembered, and is often confused, is that "competency" is a matter of status not ability. Thus, the only two groups of persons specifically rendered incompetent as witnesses by the Federal Rules of Evidence are judges (Rule 605) and jurors (Rule 606). The authority of the court to control the admissibility of the testimony of persons so impaired in some manner that they cannot

> give meaningful testimony is to be found outside of Rule 601. For example, the judge always has the authority under Rule 403 to balance the probative value of testimony against its prejudicial effect. Similarly, under Rule 603, the inability of a witness to take or comprehend an oath or affirmation will allow the judge to exclude that person's testimony. An argument can also be constructed that a person might be impaired to the point that he would not be able to satisfy the "personal knowledge" requirement of Rule 602. Again though, it is important to remember that such decisions by a trial judge to either admit or exclude testimony will only be reversed for a clear abuse of discretion.

(Footnote omitted.)

The district court did not rule on Parks' competency before he took the stand; later, in considering a motion for judgment of acquittal, the court indicated that Parks and McKeehan "were not crazy witnesses." Likewise, it addressed the question of McKeehan's mental capacity during a bench conference held after he had begun to testify. The court stated that it had "observed Mr. McKeehan, and he appears to the Court to be sober, cogent. He appears to the Court to know exactly where he is and what he is doing. His testimony has been direct, and his testimony has not been confused." When pressed concerning the psychiatrist's affidavit that McKeehan could not help in his own defense, the court opined that "he sure has made a remarkable recovery . . . [His condition is] fodder for cross-examination, and it would appear that either the psychiatrist made an inaccurate diagnosis September the 5th or the witness has made a remarkable recovery. And the Court observes that—repeats that he does not appear to be confused today."

At a hearing on defendants' post-trial motions, the district court supplemented its findings regarding Parks' and McKeehan's competency, and the need for a special examination of their mental faculties. The court noted that

> one of the reasons I overlooked stating as to my belief that an independent evaluation at this time would be a waste of time is that—is that such a finding, even if they found that they were incompetent here in April of 1992, would not be dispositive as to their competence or mental state when they testified in September of 1991 at the trial of this case or at the hearings that we held in August.
>
> . . ..
>
> Similarly, even if I had such an opinion from a psychiatrist or psychologist or whoever that gave us an independent opinion that these people were—Mr. Parks and McKeehan were total screwballs, I would—I would find those opinions to have little probative value and of little weight, and I would not—I would not accept them as being—as being conclusive on the matter. And I would not let such opinions override my own judgment after having seen—personally witnessed their performance in court.

Hence, the district court did not find that Parks and McKeehan were incapable of understanding their oath and obligation to testify truthfully. Nor did the court find, based on its observations, that their mental abilities were so limited that they did not have sufficient capacity to perceive events, to remember them, and to describe them for the benefit of the trier of fact. See Fed. R. Evid. 602. The court was not required, as Whited would have it, to conduct a special examination into their competency. If either Parks' or McKeehan's behavior raised concerns stemming from Rule 602 or 603, it could have excluded their testimony (or portions thereof) without any examination whatsoever. Furthermore, the court had the additional authority, pursuant to Rule 403, to exclude their testimony in light of their past or present mental state. The court chose not to take any of these measures in the circumstances. Instead, it permitted defense counsel to use the psychiatric records of Parks and McKeehan, as well as other indicia of their mental capacity, to vigorously attack their credibility.

After carefully reviewing the record, we conclude that the district court did not abuse its discretion in doing so. As long as a witness appreciates his duty to tell the truth, and is minimally capable of observing, recalling, and communicating events, his testimony should come in for whatever it is worth. It is then up to the opposing party to dispute the witness' powers of apprehension, which well may be impaired by mental illness or other factors. As we are persuaded that Parks and McKeehan were at least minimally capable of offering reliable evidence, the possible weaknesses in their testimony went to its credibility, and so were to be assessed by the jury. See United States v. Moreno, 899 F.2d 465, 469 (6th Cir. 1990).

Whited also argues that defendants should have been allowed to introduce the psychiatric records of Parks and McKeehan as substantive evidence. They were ruled inadmissible hearsay by the district court. Whited alleges, however, that they were not put forward for the truth of the matters asserted within, but to show how manipulative Parks and McKeehan could be if they were not, in fact, mentally unbalanced. Such use of the records during cross-examination to challenge Parks' and McKeehan's credibility was appropriate. However, we believe that they would have constituted hearsay if employed as part of a substantive defense. They would have to have been offered to show that the psychiatrists making the records actually concluded that Parks and McKeehan were mentally ill. Otherwise, Parks' and McKeehan's deception would have no basis in fact. Consequently, the district court did not err in declining to admit the psychiatric records.

* * *

AFFIRMED.

STATE v. WELLS

Court of Appeals of Ohio, Ninth Appellate District, Summit County, 2003 Ohio 3162, 2003 Ohio App. LEXIS 2840 (2003)

JUDGES: LYNN C. SLABY. SLABY, P. J. CONCURS. BATCHELDER, J. CONCURS. CARR, J. DISSENTS.

This cause was heard upon the record in the trial court. Each error assigned has been reviewed and the following disposition is made:

Per curiam.

Appellant, Jerome Wells, appeals from his conviction in the Summit County Court of Common Pleas of one count of gross sexual imposition. This Court reverses and remands for a new trial.

Wells was indicted on one count of rape, in violation of R.C. 2907.02(A)(1)(b). He allegedly engaged in sexual conduct with a child under thirteen years of age on or about December 9, 2001. The alleged victim of his crime, T.V., was five years old at the time the case proceeded to trial during May 2002. Prior to trial, because T.V. was less than ten years old, a hearing was held to determine whether she was competent to testify. Following an examination by the trial judge, the prosecutor and defense counsel, the trial court determined that T.V. was competent to testify.

Following a jury trial, Wells was convicted of the lesser included offense of gross sexual imposition. Wells appeals and raises five assignments of error.

FIRST ASSIGNMENT OF ERROR

"THE TRIAL COURT ERRED AND ABUSED ITS DISCRETION BY FINDING A FIVE (5) YEAR OLD CHILD COMPETENT TO TESTIFY PURSUANT TO EVID.R. 601 WHERE SHE CLEARLY WAS INCAPABLE OF RECEIVING JUST IMPRESSIONS OF FACTS AND DID NOT COMPREHEND THE CONCEPT OF A LIE OR ITS CONSEQUENCES."

Wells contends that the trial court erred in determining that five-year-old T.V., the alleged victim, was competent to testify because she was not capable of receiving just impressions of fact and did not understand the concept of a lie or the consequences of lying. Evid.R. 601(A) provides:

"Every person is competent to be a witness except * * * children under ten years of age, who appear incapable of receiving just impressions of the facts and transactions respecting which they are examined, or of relating them truly."

The burden falls on the proponent of the witness to establish that the witness exhibits "certain indicia of competency." State v. Clark (1994), 71 Ohio St.3d 466, 469, 1994 Ohio 43, 644 N.E.2d 331. In State v. Frazier (1991), 61 Ohio St.3d 247, 574 N.E.2d 483, syllabus, the Supreme Court of Ohio set forth five factors that the trial court "must take into consideration" when determining whether a child under the age of ten is competent to testify:

> "(1) the child's ability to receive accurate impressions of fact or to observe acts about which he or she will testify, (2) the child's ability to recollect those impressions or observations, (3) the child's ability to communicate what was observed, (4)

the child's understanding of truth and falsity and (5) the child's appreciation of his or her responsibility to be truthful."

These factors "are aimed at protecting the accused by ascertaining that a child witness is trustworthy." State v. Ulch (Apr. 19, 2002), 6th Dist. No. L-00-1355, 2002 Ohio App. LEXIS 1866.

At the hearing to determine whether T.V. was competent to testify in this case, the State failed to meet its burden of presenting sufficient evidence of T.V.'s competency. Specifically, there was not a sufficient inquiry into the fourth or fifth Frazier competency factors: the child's understanding of truth and falsity and the child's appreciation of his or her responsibility to be truthful. "[A] child may be competent to testify even though the child *** initially does not recognize the concept of truth, so long as the voir dire continues on to demonstrate that the child *** generally *** understands the concept of truthfulness." State v. Brooks (Oct. 26, 2001), 2nd Dist. No. 18502, 2001 Ohio 1650, quoting *State v. Boyd* (Oct. 31, 1997), 2d Dist. No. 97 CA 1, 1997 Ohio App. LEXIS 4748.

In this case, however, after T.V. initially demonstrated that she did not understand the concepts of truth and falsity, the further voir dire on this issue was not sufficient to demonstrate that T.V. did, in fact, generally understand the concept of truthfulness or that she appreciated her responsibility to tell the truth. The trial court errs in finding a child witness competent without sufficient evidence before it to consider each of the five Frazier factors. See *State v. Wilson* (Feb. 18, 2000), 4th Dist. No. 99CA672, 2000 Ohio App. LEXIS 677. Because there was not an adequate demonstration on the fourth and fifth *Frazier* factors, the trial court erred in finding T.V. competent to testify.

It has been held that such a deficiency in the hearing on the child's competency can be cured if the child's subsequent testimony at trial demonstrates that the trial court was justified in finding the child competent to testify. See *State v. Wilson*, citing State v. Lewis (1982), 4 Ohio App.3d 275, 4 Ohio B. 494, 448 N.E.2d 487. At the time T.V. testified at trial, however, the State failed to elicit any further testimony regarding her understanding of the concept of truthfulness. Consequently, the error could not have been cured by her later testimony.

Because there was insufficient evidence before the trial court to demonstrate that T.V. had an understanding of the concepts of truth and falsity or that she appreciated her responsibility to be truthful, the trial court exceeded the scope of its discretion by finding that she was competent to testify. See Frazier, 61 Ohio St.3d at 247, syllabus. The first assignment of error is sustained and the judgment is reversed and remanded for a retrial.

The remaining assignments of error have been rendered moot and will not be reached. See App.R. 12(A)(1)(c). The judgment of the trial court is reversed and the cause is remanded for a new trial.

Judgment reversed and the cause remanded.

CONCUR: BATCHELDER, J.

Although I agree with the reasoning of the principal opinion, I write separately to emphasize the lack of the evidence before the trial court regarding T.V.'s competency to testify. There was almost no evidence on the fourth *Frazier* factor, "the child's understanding of truth and falsity" and there was a complete lack of evidence on the fifth factor, "the child's appreciation of his or her responsibility to be truthful." See Frazier, 61 Ohio St.3d at 247, syllabus. As indicated above, the trial judge had an mandatory obligation to consider all five factors. See id.

At the competency hearing, the testimony elicited by the prosecutor from T.V. regarding her understanding of truth and falsity and her appreciation of her responsibility to be truthful was the following:

"Q. Okay. [T,] do you know what it means to have to tell the truth?

"A. (Witness shook head.)

"Q. Okay. You are shaking your head. Which do you mean? If you tell the truth, what do you have to do? Let me ask you a different way. You are wearing a jump suit today, aren't you?

"A. (Witness nodded.)

"Q. Is that a yes?

"A. Yes.

"Q. Okay. If I said your jump suit was green, is that right?

"A. (Witness shook head.) No.

"Q. No? What color is your jump suit?

"A. Pink.
"Q. It is pink. You are right, it is pink. "A. Pink and white.
"Q. Pink and white, you are right. Yes, it is. And who is this right here?
"A. My bear.
"Q. That's a bear. If I told you that this was a kitty cat; is that right?
"A. No.
"Q. No, it is not right, is it. Did you talk with me about having to come to the courtroom today?
"A. Yes.
"Q. Okay. And did I tell you that you would have to tell the truth when you came here?
"A. Yes.
"Q. Okay. And did your mom tell you that, too?
"A. Yes.
"Q. Okay. Did we tell you that that means that you have to tell us what happened and you can't make it up?
"A. Yes.
"Q. Yes, okay."

After T.V. indicated that she did not understand what it meant to have to tell the truth, the prosecutor did not ask any follow-up questions on that specific issue. Instead, the prosecutor asked T.V. questions about what is "right" and "not right," never linking those two concepts to truth and/or falsity. Equating right and not right with truth and falsity is not necessarily something that a five-year-old child is able to do and, absent some demonstration to that effect, the trial court had no reason to presume that this child was able to do so. Further questioning of T. V. failed to even suggest that this child had such an understanding. Although, at the conclusion of the prosecutor's questioning, T.V. agreed that she had been told to tell "the truth" when she came to court, there had been no demonstration that she understood what "the truth" was.

Defense counsel's subsequent questioning of the child only served to demonstrate that the child remained confused:

"Q. [T,] do you remember when [the prosecutor] asked you if you understood what telling the truth was?
"A. Yes.
"Q. Did you shake your head back and forth like a no?
"A. (Witness nodded.)
"Q. You did shake your head back and forth from side to side?
"A. Yes.
"Q. [T.,] do you know what a lie is?
"A. No.
"Q. No? Is that what you are saying?
"A. (Witness nodded.)"

T.V. again indicated a lack of understanding of the concepts of truth and falsity. After these responses by T.V. to direct questions on the issue, there was no follow-up questioning by defense counsel or anyone else to demonstrate that the child was not, in fact, completely confused about the issue.

The trial judge concluded with the following line of questioning:

"Q: [T.,] I am going to ask you a question right now. What you said to me and to [the prosecutor] so far today, have you been telling the truth? She asked you about what the truth is. You have told the truth in this court to this Judge?
"A: Yes.
"Q: Everything you said now is the truth?
"A: (Witness nodded.)
"Q: Is there any question about that in your mind as to whether it is true or not?
"A: Yes.
"Q: There is a question?
"[Prosecutor]: I don't think she understood the question, Judge.
"Q: Okay. You told the truth as far as what happened?
"A. Yes.
"Q: All the questions you answered are—were the truth, right?
"A: Yes.
"Q: And you know what it is to tell the truth, you already answered that.
"A: Yes.
"Q: It is something that really happened, right?
"A: Yes.
"Q: Not something you make up, right?
"A: Yes.
"Q: So you are going to keep telling the truth now from here on, and what you are going to say is what really happened, right?
"A: Yes."

T.V.'s answers to the trial judge's questions might seem appropriate, if viewed in isolation. Given the confusion that T.V. had already demonstrated, however, her answers to the judge's questions failed to demonstrate that she did, in fact, have a general understanding of the concepts of truth and falsity.

Moreover, even if the judge's questioning somehow cured the shortcomings of the confused testimony elicited from T.V. on the fourth Frazier factor, there was absolutely no testimony elicited from T.V. on the fifth mandatory *Frazier* factor, an appreciation of her responsibility to be truthful.

The trial judge had the discretion to find the child competent to testify only upon a consideration of all five of the Frazier factors. Because there was not adequate evidence before the trial court on all five factors, I agree with the principal opinion that the trial judge exceeded the scope of his discretion by finding that this child was competent to testify and I would reverse the judgment of the trial court on that basis.

Cases Relating to Chapter 9

Examination of Witnesses

UNITED STATES
v.
DRUMMOND

United States Court of Appeal, Third Circuit, 69 F. App'x 580, 2003 U.S. App. LEXIS 14819 (2003)

OPINION: OPINION OF THE COURT

ROSENN, Circuit Judge:

This case raises the issue of whether the District Court committed reversible error when it denied the motion in limine of defendant, Alvin Drummond, to compel the Government's case agent to testify first at trial. The purpose of the motion was to prevent the possibility that the case agent might endeavor, when called as a witness, to conform his testimony to that of the preceding Government witness.

On reviewing the matter de novo, we hold that, under the circumstances of this case, the harm to the Government's case that would have resulted from granting Drummond's motion far outweighs any possible harm to Drummond from denying the motion. The District Court did not abuse its discretion in denying the motion. We affirm. Drummond timely appealed.

I.

A jury convicted Drummond on two counts of cocaine distribution. The trial court sentenced him to a 327-month prison term. Before his trial began, he filed a Motion in Limine requesting that the Court order the Government to call its case agent, Detective Ronald Marzec, as its first witness at trial. The District Court denied the motion, holding that, under Federal Rule of Evidence 615, it was outside its authority to control the sequence of the Government's witnesses.

At trial, the Government first called Detective Marvin Charles Mailey, Jr., who testified that, while he was working undercover, Drummond sold him cocaine. Mailey testified to his close contact with Drummond, and unequivocally identified him as the person who sold him cocaine on multiple occasions. Agent Marzec then testified that he witnessed some of the drug-sales transactions between Drummond and Mailey from a distance, sometimes aided by binoculars. Marzec verified that the person present at these transactions was Drummond and, in that respect, his testimony was consistent with Mailey's. Drummond's defense was primarily based on a challenge to the prosecution's identification of Drummond. Drummond's witnesses testified, inter alia, that Drummond had brothers who closely resembled him, and that he often loaned one of his cars—the car in which Mailey and Marzec testified some of the drug sales had occurred in—to others.

Drummond now challenges the District Court's denial of his motion to compel Marzec to testify first.

II.

Our review here is plenary. The District Court is alleged to have misinterpreted the Rules of

Evidence. This is a question of whether it correctly understood the scope of its authority under the Rules. We review the District Court's refusal to require the case agent to testify first for abuse of discretion.

The District Court erred in its exclusive reliance on Rule 615. Rule 615 provides that a court shall order the sequestration of witnesses, upon the request of a party. However, Rule 615 does not permit the exclusion from trial of "an officer or employee of a party which is not a natural person designated as its representative by its attorney." Fed. R. Evid. 615(2). We have held that a case agent for the Government falls within this exemption, and ordinarily cannot be sequestered pursuant to Rule 615. United States v. Gonzalez, 918 F.2d 1129, 1138 (3d Cir. 1990). Thus, Marzec, as the case agent, could not have been validly sequestered under this Rule. The District Court apparently believed that Rule 615 somehow protected the Government against judicial intervention in its sequence of trial witnesses.

However, Rule 611(a) does not exempt case agents. It merely provides: "The court shall exercise reasonable control over the mode and order of interrogating witnesses and presenting evidence so as to (1) make the interrogation and presentation effective for the ascertainment of the truth, (2) avoid needless consumption of time, and (3) protect witnesses from harassment or undue embarrassment." Fed. R. Evid. 611(a). There is no obvious reason why the Rule 615 case agent exemption, designed to allow a representative of the Government to be in the courtroom at all times, would have any relevance to Rule 611.

Accordingly, other courts of appeals have held that case agents, ineligible for sequestration under Rule 615, might nonetheless be forced to testify first at trial, to avoid giving the prosecution unfair advantage. See United States v. Parodi, 703 F.2d 768, 774 (4th Cir. 1983). (permission for the investigating officer to remain in court at trial under Rule 615 may be conditioned on requirement that the officer be forced to testify first); In Re United States, 584 F.2d 666, 667 (5th Cir. 1978) ("The District Court may, in the exercise of its discretion under [Rule 611(a), conclude that the government should be required to present [its case agent's] testimony at an early stage of the government's case."). Thus, the District Court's sole reliance on Rule 615 was error; the language of the Rules of Evidence and the persuasive holdings of our sister courts suggest that Rule 611(a) was applicable.

Drummond next urges that, in determining the standard under which a district court should evaluate a request to have the case agent testify first, we should adopt a rule promulgated by the Court of Appeals for the Fourth Circuit. Under its rule, a Government case agent "should ordinarily be called first so as to avoid giving the prosecution unfair advantage or the appearance that the prosecution is being favored." United States v. Frazier, 417 F.2d 1138, 1139 (4th Cir. 1969). That court went on to state that "this should be the order of presentation unless, in the judge's considered opinion, it would unduly break the continuity and seriously impair the coherence of the Government's proof." Id. At the opposite interpretive pole is the Court of Appeals for the First Circuit. In United States v. Machor, 879 F.2d 945, 954 (1st Cir. 1989), the court held that "good reason should exist before the court intervenes [as to the sequence of witnesses] in what is essentially a matter of trial strategy."

Drummond insists that regardless of the standard we choose, we must set forth some interpretive benchmark as to Rule 611 motions or any other motion regarding the sequencing of case agent witnesses. Because this court has not previously ruled on this issue, he asserts that we must remand to the District Court so that it can apply whatever standard we announce. However, Drummond was not entitled to have Marzec testify first. The Government has an interest in the order of its presentation, cf. (sequencing of witnesses is "essentially a matter of trial strategy"), and here the chief witness was Mailey. It would have been confusing to the jury and harmful to the Government case to force it to have its secondary witness testify first.

Furthermore, in Gonzalez, we observed that there was no prejudice in declining to sequester a case agent, because "[the defendant's] argument that [two Government] agents could coordinate their testimony does not pose a likelihood of prejudice since they had ample time before trial to do that, were they so inclined." 918 F.2d at 1138. Here, the two witnesses were both law enforcement officers, who had worked closely together throughout the investigation, and Drummond gave no other reason for his motion than to prevent deliberate conformity of testimony. If the witnesses were so inclined, and we have confidence that they were not, the two easily could have discussed their testimony before trial.

Therefore, the Government's interests in the orderly presentation of its case far outweighs the negligible possibility of prejudice to Drummond. Although this might be a more difficult issue if Marzec's testimony were not clearly subsidiary to Mailey's, or if there were non-Government witnesses involved for whom pre-trial coordination of testimony would be more difficult, in this case there was no justification for ordering Marzec to testify first. Moreover, Rule 611 only calls for an ordering of witnesses to maximize the "ascertainment of the truth." While there may be instances where the defense is hamstrung by its inability to sequester a case agent, and where it may be justified in requesting that the case agent to testify first, such a measure is not warranted here and would not further the trial's truth-seeking function. The judgment of conviction and sentence is affirmed.

Max Rosenn, Circuit Judge

PEOPLE v. MELENDEZ

Supreme Court of Colorado, 102 P.3d 315, 2004 Colo. LEXIS 1006 (2004)

JUSTICE HOBBS delivered the Opinion of the Court.

EN BANC

We granted certiorari under C.A.R. 49 to review the court of appeals' decision in People v. Melendez, 80 P.3d 883 (Colo. App. 2003). The trial court precluded the testimony of a defense witness who allegedly violated a sequestration order. Because the record does not demonstrate an adequate inquiry by the trial court into whether the sequestration violation actually occurred and because preclusion of the witness's testimony was not harmless error, we affirm the judgment of the court of appeals.

I.

A jury convicted Jorge Melendez of multiple counts of sexual assault in the first and second degrees, aggravated incest, sexual assault on a child, sexual assault on a child-pattern of abuse, and sexual assault on a child under fifteen by one in a position of trust.

Melendez's former step-daughter, a seven-year-old girl, reported to her grandparents that he had sexually assaulted her on several occasions when he was married to her mother. Melendez defended on the basis that the child fabricated the allegations due to emotional problems with her mother, Melendez, and the divorce.

The trial court issued a sequestration order barring witnesses from the courtroom while other witnesses were testifying at trial, but made an exception for Detective Kenneth Brecko, a prosecution advisory witness.

The prosecution proceeded with testimony by Jodi Curtin, the child advocacy center interviewer who had interviewed the child after the police began investigating the allegations. The prosecution showed a videotape of Curtin's interview with the child to the jury. Curtin testified about her observations of the child's behavior during the interview, emphasizing a change in her demeanor when the alleged assaults were mentioned. On cross examination, defense counsel asked Curtin whether false allegations are more common in "high conflict" situations and she answered that they may be. She also said false accusations can occur in interviews but not often, in her experience.

After Curtin's testimony, Brecko, the detective assigned to the Melendez case, testified about general procedures used in investigating sexual assault cases.

* * *

[T]he defense presented testimony from its expert witness, Dr. Spiegle. Spiegle criticized the manner in which Curtin conducted her interview, opining that she had used inappropriately suggestive and leading questions with the child, which may have affected the reliability of the child's answers. He also testified about a study showing that some twenty-three percent of sexual assault allegations by children in the Denver area in a particular time period proved to be false. Spiegle also testified about his evaluation of the child's behavior as seen on the videotaped interview. His view was that various pre-allegation events in her life may have impacted her emotional wellbeing and behavior.

Following Spiegle's testimony, the defense called the director of the child advocacy center where Curtin worked, followed by the officer who had responded to the neglect call. This testimony concluded at the end of the business day.

The defense planned to call Robert Curry the next day. Curry, a friend of Melendez, would have testified to his observations of the child's relationship with Melendez, as well as her behavior with her mother. The trial court precluded Curry from testifying.

The trial court based its preclusion order solely on the prosecution's assertion that Brecko had reported seeing Curry in the courtroom during portions of Curtin's testimony and during bench discussions after the recess.

Defense counsel responded that he was not aware of Curry's presence in the courtroom. He argued that Curry's testimony would not have been tainted by any of Curtin's testimony that he may have overheard, because Curry was planning to testify to completely different matters. Defense counsel made the following offer of proof regarding Curry's testimony:

> Judge, the expected nature of the testimony of Mr. Curry would essentially be that he has observed Mr. Melendez with the alleged victim in this case. He has seen him with the mother in this case. He has seen interactions between parent/child, Mr. Melendez and child. This is essentially the scope of his testimony.

Counsel also asserted that "having [Curry] stricken as a defense witness I believe is a really severe sanction in this case. I think that the Court could inquire or admonish or ask questions of Mr. Curry but not allowing him to testify I think would be a severe prejudice to the defendant."

The prosecutor answered that Curtin testified about the child's behavior and the kinds of behavioral changes to be expected after sexual assaults. The prosecutor argued that this testimony could taint Curry's testimony because it suggested ways to show that the child was emotionally disturbed before she made her allegations. The prosecutor also noted that Brecko had subsequently told her that he had seen Curry talking to the defendant during a break and it sounded as if they were discussing the case. The trial court delayed ruling on the issue until the following morning.

The next day, defense counsel and the prosecutor made essentially the same arguments. The court precluded Curry's testimony, ruling that,

> considering argument of both the defense and the prosecution, noting the length of time the defendant (sic) was in the courtroom, paying particular attention that the witness was in the courtroom during the testimony of Ms. Curtin, the Court is going to not allow the witness to be called for the defense.

The trial court did not ask any questions of Brecko, Curry, or Melendez concerning the alleged sequestration violation.

Defense counsel rested his case after Melendez testified. The jury convicted Melendez on several counts.

On appeal, Melendez argued, inter alia, that the trial court abused its discretion by precluding Curry's testimony and that the error was not harmless. We agree and affirm the court of appeals' judgment.

II.

Because the record does not demonstrate an adequate inquiry by the trial court into whether the sequestration violation actually occurred, and because preclusion of the witness's testimony was not harmless error, we affirm the judgment of the court of appeals.

A. Standard of Review

In proper circumstances, the trial court may sequester witnesses, find that a witness has violated the sequestration order, and impose sanctions for the sequestration violation. See People v. Wood, 743 P.2d 422, 429–30 (Colo. 1987); People v. P.R.G., 729 P.2d 380, 382 (Colo. App. 1986). We review the trial court's determinations for abuse of discretion. People v. Stewart, 55 P.3d 107, 122

(Colo. 2002). If an abuse of discretion occurred, we must then determine whether the error is reversible. See Salcedo v. People, 999 P.2d 833, 841 (Colo. 2000).

B. Sequestration Order Violations

Trial courts shall impose sequestration orders on witnesses at the request of either party. Martin v. Porak, 638 P.2d 853, 854 (Colo. App. 1981); CRE 615. The court may order witnesses to remain outside the courtroom and not discuss the case with each other. People v. Brinson, 739 P.2d 897, 899 (Colo. App. 1987).

* * *

Before it considers sanctions for a sequestration violation, the trial court must first determine that a violation has actually occurred and prejudice will result from unrestricted admission of the testimony. See Wood, 743 P.2d at 429–30.

Sanctions for violations of sequestration orders fall into three general categories: (1) citing the witness for contempt; (2) permitting counsel or the court to comment to the jury on the witness's noncompliance as a reflection on his or her credibility; and (3) precluding the witness's testimony. P.R.G., 729 P.2d at 382; see also J. Weinstein & M. Berger, 4 Weinstein's Federal Evidence § 615.07[2] (2d ed. 2004). Additionally, mistrial is a possible but rarely justified sanction. P.R.G., 729 P.2d at 382.

Disqualifying witness testimony is a severe sanction to be imposed only after careful consideration.

* * *

We have allowed prosecution witnesses to testify despite the allegation of a sequestration violation. See Wood, 743 P.2d at 429 (finding no prejudice to defendant requiring exclusion of witness for sequestration violation); cf. People v. Gomez, 632 P.2d 586, 594 (Colo. 1981) (approving trial court's limitation on scope of testimony by witness who violated sequestration order).

We have not had occasion for over one hundred years to consider the implications of precluding a defense witness from testifying due to a sequestration violation. See Vickers v. People, 31 Colo. 491, 73 P. 845 (Colo. 1903).

Sanctioning a defense witness for violating a sequestration order implicates important rights of the criminal defendant. See Washington v. Texas, 388 U.S. 14, 19, 18 L. Ed. 2d 1019, 87 S. Ct. 1920 (1967) ("The right to offer the testimony of witnesses . . . is in plain terms the right to present a defense, the right to present the defendant's version of the facts as well as the prosecution's to the [fact finder] so it may decide where the truth lies."); People v. Chastain, 733 P.2d 1206, 1212 (Colo. 1987) (noting that a defendant's right to offer testimony at trial is a "fundamental element of due process of law") (internal citations omitted).

While fundamental, the right to present defense evidence is not absolute. A defendant must "make some plausible showing of how [the] testimony would have been both material and favorable to his defense."

* * *

Nevertheless, cumulative evidence that may corroborate the defendant's own statement should ordinarily be admitted. See People v. Green, 38 Colo. App. 165, 553 P.2d 839, 840 (Colo. App. 1976) ("It is manifest that [evidence which is cumulative to some degree] should not be prohibited when it is sought to be introduced to corroborate [the defendant's] statement, which . . . may be, and often is, looked upon by the jury with some degree of suspicion.") (internal quotations omitted); Towner v. State, 685 P.2d 45, 50 (Wyo. 1984) (the only evidence offered to corroborate defendant's testimony was admissible even though duplicative to defendant's own statement).

C. Trial Court's Duty of Inquiry

The trial court has a duty of diligent inquiry into allegations of a sequestration violation. The trial court must first determine whether the violation actually occurred and, if so, whether prejudice will result from allowing the testimony.

* * *

In 1986, the Colorado Court of Appeals . . . set forth three principal factors for trial court consideration in determining a sanction. P.R.G., 729 P.2d at 382. First, the trial court must consider the involvement, or lack thereof, of a party or counsel in the violation of the order by the witness. Id. Second, the trial court should consider the witness's actions and state of mind in his or her violation of the sequestration order, and whether the violation was inadvertent or deliberate. Id. Finally, the trial court should consider the subject matter of the violation in conjunction with the substance of the disobedient witness's testimony and if the testimony is unrelated in substance to the violation of the sequestration order, the court enjoys wide discretion in its ability to allow the witness to testify. Id. We agree, but modify the first factor to require evidence of the party's or counsel's consent, connivance, procurement, or knowledge regarding the violation before a sanction can be imposed against that party. We base adoption of these factors, as modified, on our review of the case law.

* * *

D. Application to This Case

In the case before us, the trial court did not make an adequate inquiry into whether the sequestration violation actually occurred. It simply accepted the prosecution's assertions. The record contains no verification that Curry was actually in the courtroom, let alone any facts regarding the length of his presence or what he heard. Similarly, the record is devoid of any indication that the trial court considered the factors applicable to the choice of appropriate sanction.

* * *

E. Not Harmless Error

The defendant objected to the preclusion of Curry's testimony. Defense counsel argued to the court that: 1) an inquiry could be made to determine the severity of the violation; 2) other sanctions might be imposed, such as admonishment; and 3) that exclusion of Curry would be prejudicial to his client.

We do not require that parties use "talismanic language" to preserve particular arguments for appeal, but the trial court must be presented with an adequate opportunity to make findings of fact and conclusions of law on any issue before we will review it. [Citations omitted.]

Here, defense counsel offered the trial court an adequate opportunity to commence a sufficient inquiry into the violation and the possible prejudice resulting from its exclusion order. Curry's was the only evidence offered to corroborate the defendant's own testimony, as well as the only evidence offered that would link the expert's testimony about factors leading to false allegations with the case at hand. Our review of the record reveals that Curry's evidence would have materially assisted Melendez's case.

A defendant has a fundamental constitutional right to present his or her version of the facts and favorable evidence. See Washington, 388 U.S. at 19. Here, a constitutional error was properly preserved for appeal, and the constitutional harmless error standard applies. See Blecha v. People, 962 P.2d 931, 942 (Colo. 1998). We cannot say beyond a reasonable doubt that the exclusion of Curry's testimony did not contribute to the guilty verdict.

III.

Accordingly, we affirm the court of appeals' judgment. [Reversing the convictions.]

STATE v. SANDS

Court of Appeals, Eleventh Appellate District, 2008 Ohio 6981, 2008 Ohio App. LEXIS 5610 (2008)

MARY JANE TRAPP, J.

Appellant, Joseph A. Sands, appeals from the Lake County Court of Common Pleas judgment of his conviction and sentence for engaging in a pattern of corrupt activity and attempting to commit murder and aggravated arson with public officials as his targets.

As Francis Bacon said, "Revenge is a kind of wild justice, which the more man's nature runs to the more ought law to weed it out." A Lake County jury listened to the revengeful voice of a calculating man outline a chilling plot with his girlfriend and friend to kill a mayor, a prosecutor, and a judge; all because he was aggrieved by prosecutions for various misdemeanor offenses.

Unbeknownst to Mr. Sands, in an effort to stop the plot and weed out the conspirators, Mr. Sands' friend, Mr. Green, became a confidential informant. Over a period of five days he recorded Mr. Sands' detailed plans for the acquisition of materials for the construction of pipe bombs which were to be used to fire bomb officials' homes. The plot had progressed to the point where a dry run for the bombing of the mayor's home was undertaken. When Mr. Green expressed some concern as to any children who would surely be in the mayor's home, Mr. Sands matter-of-factly replied, "[his] kid is going to die with him."

The plot was foiled, the conspirators prosecuted, and the rule of law, not the street, prevailed in the jury's verdict. We affirm the jury's verdict for the reasons that follow.

Substantive and Procedural History

On April 1, 2006, Jason Green contacted Madison Township Detective Mark Parisi and requested that they meet outside of his hometown, North Perry Village. At the meeting, Mr. Green informed him that his friend, Mr. Sands, and Mr. Sands' girlfriend, Dawn Holin, were conspiring to kill four local officials. The intended targets were Painesville Municipal Court Judge Michael Cicconetti, North Perry Police Chief Denise Mercsak, North Perry Mayor Tom Williams, and North Perry Prosecutor Joseph Gurley.

* * *

Both Mr. Green and Mr. Sands had an embattled history over the years with the North Perry Village Police and Mayor Williams, and both believed they were being unfairly harassed. There were incidents and altercations where the police would be called to Mr. Sands' automotive repair shop, JB Performance, which he owned with his girlfriend and co-conspirator, Ms. Holin. Mr. Green also had a lengthy criminal history, and faced various charges in the past few years for theft, menacing, animal cruelty, and littering, to name a few among the many.

* * *

After hearing Mr. Sands lay out this chilling plot, Mr. Green went to the police. Since both Mr. Green and Mr. Sands had been voluntary informants for Detective Parisi in the past, Mr. Green felt he could trust the detective with this information. Mr. Green told the detective that Mr. Sands wanted to kill the victims by building homemade pipe bombs that were going to be loaded with shrapnel and ether, as well as possibly, homemade napalm. The plan was to kill Mayor Williams in the first few weeks of April by throwing a pipe bomb through the bay window of his home. The next target was to be Prosecutor Gurley. Then, after Mr. Sands was sentenced for failing to file his taxes on April 20, they would move on to the judge. By killing Mayor Williams and Prosecutor Gurley, Mr. Sands hoped to intimidate Judge Cicconetti to impose a lesser sentence. [Police set up Mr. Green with recording devices to record his conversations with Mr. Sands.]

* * *

Mr. Sands devised all facets of the plan. His firebombing target was Mayor Williams. He was adamant that Mr. Green would drive, so he could run and throw the bomb into Mayor Williams' home. At the request of the police, Mr. Green suggested involving a third party, but Mr. Sands did not want anyone else involved. Mr. Sands also developed their alibi that they had gotten drunk and the three just stayed at the Sands/Holins' home. Since their history with the village was notorious, Mr. Sands knew they would be under suspicion. Because of that they would hit Prosecutor Gurley a month after Mayor Williams, and then they would possibly have to wait as long as a year to shoot Judge Cicconetti.

Between April 4 and April 9 of 2006, Mr. Green continued to record conversations with Mr. Sands, recording approximately seven conversations. . . . .

* * *

By Friday, April 7, the three had everything they would need with the exception of the wick to light the pipe bomb. To purchase this, Mr. Sands wanted Mr. Green to accompany him to a store some sixty miles away in Ashland, Ohio, called Fin, Fur, & Feather. Like the pipe, he did not want to make the purchase in the local area, where everyone seemed to know each other. Ms. Holin provided them with directions. Unbeknownst to Mr. Sands, ATF, the police, and the FBI were following them, with a plan to arrest the pair upon purchase. On the way to Ashland, Mr. Sands told Mr. Green they could not use the pipe they purchased because it was too identifiable. The police could easily discover that Mr. Green had purchased the pipe, thus, Mr. Sands suggested getting some pipe from his brother-in-law.

At the store, . . . both were arrested and placed in separate vehicles. Mr. Green did not know in advance of the plans for arrest.

At the time of arrest, Mr. Sands consented to a search of his home and business, which produced all of the equipment needed to make a pipe bomb.

* * *

Mr. Sands was subsequently charged with [a variety felonies, including several conspiracy counts, and engaging in a pattern of corrupt activity.]

Mr. Sands, in his defense, testified that the plan was Mr. Green's idea and he was merely a cohort. He was, in fact, trying to "control" Mr. Green to prevent him from carrying out the plan.

After an almost two week trial, the jury found Mr. Sands guilty on six counts of the indictment, finding him guilty of engaging in a pattern of corrupt activity, three counts of conspiracy to commit aggravated murder as they related to Judge Cicconetti, Mayor Williams, and Prosecutor Gurley; as well as two counts of conspiracy to commit aggravated arson as they related to Mayor Williams and his property. . . . [Defendant received a twenty year prison sentence.]

Mr. Sands now timely appeals, raising seven assignments of error:

* * *

[Error # 4.] The Trial Court erred in admitting other acts evidence denying Appellant a fair trial.

Evidence of Other Acts

In his fourth assignment of error, Mr. Sands contends that the trial court abused its discretion in permitting the state to cross-examine him [to impeach him] on other acts [prior criminal activities] that he introduced by way of his direct examination. Specifically, Mr. Sands argues that the trial court erred in allowing the state to question him on an incident in which he forced his thirteen-year old son to file a false police report. Because of the ensuing charge [related to the false police report], Mr. Sands worked as a confidential informant with Mr. Green on a drug case [to get the charge related to the false police report dropped]. We find this argument to be without merit.

"The determination to admit or exclude evidence is within the sound discretion of the trial court and will not be reversed by an appellate court absent a showing of an abuse of discretion." Vinson at P48, citing State v. Sledge, 11th Dist. No. 2001-T-0123, 2003 Ohio 4100, P20, citing State v. Rootes (Mar. 23, 2001), 11th Dist. No. 2000-P-0003, 2001 Ohio App. LEXIS 1391, 4–5, citing Renfro v. Black (1990), 52 Ohio St.3d 27, 32, 556 N.E.2d 150. Abuse of discretion connotes more than error of law or of judgment; it implies that the court's attitude is unreasonable, arbitrary, or unconscionable. [Citation omitted.]

Mr. Sands argues that the essence of the "false charge" testimony implied he was dishonest; thus this was so prejudicial it denied him a fair trial. A review of the record, however, reveals otherwise. The court allowed a limited cross-examination after his counsel objected, specifically because Mr. Sands testified on direct examination that he and Mr. Green were informants for the police in the drug case. Mr. Sands' defense was that Mr. Green was the mastermind behind this conspiracy and that he was set up. Thus, he opened the door as to this line of questioning. The trial court then gave a limiting instruction to the jury before deliberations cautioning that such testimony [about the false police report] could be used only to determine Mr. Sands' credibility.

Evid.R. 401 defines "relevant evidence" as "evidence having any tendency to make the existence of any fact that is of consequence to the determination of the action more probable or less probable than it would be without the evidence."

Furthermore, evidence that is relevant is generally admissible, subject to certain exclusions, and irrelevant evidence is generally inadmissible. [Citation omitted.]

Moreover, Evid.R. 403(A) governs one of the circumstances under which the exclusion of relevant evidence is made mandatory. Id, citing State v. Hamilton, 11th Dist. No. 2000-L-003, 2002 Ohio 1681, P81. "The rule states that the trial court is required to exclude otherwise relevant evidence in cases where the probative value of the evidence is 'substantially outweighed by the danger of unfair prejudice, of confusion of the issues, or of misleading the jury.'" Id., quoting State v. Totarella, 11th Dist. No. 2002-L-147, 2004 Ohio 1175, P34; State v. Entze, 11th Dist. No. 2003-P-0018, 2004 Ohio 5321, P28.

Pursuant to Evid.R. 609 impeachment by evidence of a conviction of a prior crime may be used to attack the credibility of a witness when:

"(A)(3) Notwithstanding Evid.R. 403(A), but subject to Evid.R. 403(B), evidence that any witness, including an accused, has been convicted of a crime is admissible if the crime involved dishonesty or false statement, regardless of the punishment and whether based upon state or federal statute or local ordinance." (Emphasis added.)

Furthermore, "[a]ny time an accused testifies, the accused's prior conviction is admissible, unless the probative value of the evidence is outweighed by its prejudicial effect." Cortner, *supra*, citing State v. Lane (1997), 118 Ohio App.3d 230, 234, 692 N.E.2d 634. Thus, "Evid.R. 609(A)(2) specifically permits the State the ability to conduct a limited cross-examination for the purposes of impeachment." Id., citing State v. Bryan, 101 Ohio St.3d 272, 2004 Ohio 971, P132, 804 N.E.2d 433; State v. Green (1993), 66 Ohio St.3d 141, 147, 1993 Ohio 26, 609 N.E.2d 1253, see, also, State v. Slagle (1992), 65 Ohio St.3d 597, 605, 605 N.E.2d 916, citing Evid.R. 611(B) ("As a general rule cross-examination is 'permitted on all relevant matters and matters affecting credibility.'") "The extent of cross-examination allowed is within the discretion of the trial court, and will not be overturned absent an abuse of that discretion." Id., citing State v. Acre (1983), 6 Ohio St.3d 140, 145, 6 Ohio B. 197, 451 N.E.2d 802.

The state was allowed to cross-examine Mr. Sands on this issue because he testified as to it on direct. This relevant testimony certainly goes to the issue of Mr. Sands' credibility because he claimed Mr. Green was the mastermind in this current plot, and that they had been "snitches" in the past. As to the past incident, however, the state's cross-examination elicited only that Mr. Sands had been facing charges at that time, that Mr. Green had arranged for them to be confidential informants in an effort to help the police and Mr. Sands, and that in exchange, the charges against Mr. Sands were dropped.

Even if we did find this testimony was allowed in error, which we do not, the error would be harmless as "there is no reasonable possibility that exclusion of the evidence would have affected the result of this trial." [Citations omitted.]

This testimony was not so prejudicial as to confuse the jurors. Furthermore, Mr. Sands himself opened the door to this testimony. We do not find an abuse of discretion in permitting this limited cross-examination, or the trial court's giving a limiting instruction as to its use before jury deliberations began.

Mr. Sands' fourth assignment of error is without merit.

* * *

The judgment of the Lake County Court of Common Pleas is affirmed.

Cases Relating to Chapter 10

Privileges

ST. CLAIR v. COMMONWEALTH

Supreme Court of Kentucky, 174 S.W.3d 474, 2005 Ky. LEXIS 334 (2005)

OPINION OF THE COURT BY CHIEF JUSTICE LAMBERT

REVERSING AND REMANDING

FACTS

Appellant, Michael D. St. Clair, was convicted of two counts of receiving stolen property over $ 100, criminal attempt to commit murder, second-degree arson, and capital kidnapping. He was sentenced to death for the kidnapping of Frank Brady, during which Brady was murdered. Appellant waived his right to jury sentencing on the non-capital charges, and agreed to a sentence of twenty years for attempted murder, twenty years for second-degree arson, and five years on each count of receiving stolen property over $ 100, for a total of fifty years. Appellant now appeals to this Court as a matter of right.

This is not the first time this particular defendant is before this Court. In February of 1992, a Bullitt County Grand Jury indicted Appellant for the Capital Murder of Frank Brady. He was tried and convicted in August, and sentenced to death in September of 1998. This Court in a recent decision, St. Clair v. Commonwealth, (hereinafter "St. Clair I"), reversed and remanded for a new penalty phase hearing on Appellant's death sentence. Prior to trial in Hardin County, this Court rendered St. Clair v. Roark, (St. Clair II), in which St. Clair's petition for extraordinary relief to prevent his prosecution for capital kidnapping in Hardin County was denied. In large part a complete recitation of the facts is contained in St. Clair I and St. Clair II, and is relied upon to illustrate the facts relevant to this appeal.

According to the evidence, Appellant escaped from Oklahoma authorities in September of 1991 while awaiting final sentencing for two Oklahoma murder convictions. St. Clair and Dennis Gene Reese stole a pickup truck from a jail employee and fled from the jail in Durant, Oklahoma. The pickup truck eventually ran out of gas and Reese and St. Clair stole another pickup truck, a handgun, and some ammunition from the home of Vernon Stephens and headed for the suburbs of Dallas, Texas. St. Clair's wife at the time, Bylynn St. Clair n4 ("Bylynn"), met with her husband and Reese in Texas, and provided them with money, clothing, and other items. Reese was arrested several months later in Las Vegas, Nevada, and confessed to his involvement in the Kentucky events detailed below.

According to Reese, after escaping from jail in Oklahoma, he and St. Clair traveled to Colorado where they kidnapped Timothy Keeling and stole Keeling's pickup truck. Keeling was later murdered in New Mexico. St. Clair and Reese proceeded to drive Keeling's truck to New Orleans, Louisiana, then through Arkansas and Tennessee before arriving at a rest stop in southern Hardin County, Kentucky. While in Hardin County, they decided to steal Frank Brady's late model pickup truck. They kidnapped Brady and drove him from Hardin County to Bullitt County where St. Clair shot and killed Brady. St. Clair and Reese then returned to Hardin County and set fire to Keeling's truck.

Witnesses to the arson gave the Kentucky State Police a description of the Brady truck seen near the location where Keeling's truck was on fire. Based on that description, Trooper Herbert Bennett stopped Reese and St. Clair while they were still driving Brady's truck through Hardin County. St. Clair fired two shots at Trooper Bennett, one of which penetrated the radiator of the police cruiser. A high-speed chase followed, but Reese and St. Clair escaped when Bennett's cruiser became disabled. Reese was arrested two weeks later in Las Vegas and waived extradition to Kentucky. St. Clair was arrested about two months later in Hugo, Oklahoma.

On December 20, 1991, St. Clair was indicted for two counts of receiving stolen property, criminal attempt to commit murder, and second-degree arson. On January 17, 1992, the Hardin County Grand Jury indicted St. Clair for capital kidnapping. On June 19, 1998, the Commonwealth filed its Notice of Intent to Seek Death Penalty. St. Clair was convicted in February of 2001 of the Capital Kidnapping of Frank Brady, and he was sentenced to death. Additional facts will be presented as necessary. St. Clair argues that his wife Bylynn was improperly allowed to testify to four privileged conversations, and that those conversations should have been excluded by his assertion of the marital privilege under KRE 504. When the statements were made, St. Clair and Bylynn were married.

I. Marital Privilege

The first contested statement given by Bylynn was that when she met St. Clair in Texas before St. Clair reached Kentucky, she hugged him and felt something hard on his belt. Over St. Clair's objection, she testified that when she asked if he had a gun, she testified that he, St. Clair, told her he took a gun off that old man whose house he had broken into (the home of Vernon Stephens in Oklahoma).

Bylynn's second statement concerned her meeting St. Clair in Oklahoma at Frost's Farm in December of 1991, the night before he was arrested. It was there that St. Clair stated to Bylynn that St. Clair and Reese had to leave their belongings and that they burned a truck. St. Clair told Bylynn that he returned to Oklahoma by riding with truck drivers. St. Clair objected and moved for a mistrial on the grounds that this latter statement had not been included in the Commonwealth's notice, and that it was privileged under the marital privilege.

Bylynn's third statement at trial concerned a telephone conversation between her and St. Clair. She testified that St. Clair called her from Louisiana and that Reese was in the bathroom while he was calling. The Commonwealth then elicited that St. Clair told Bylynn that he had to leave some of his things behind in the truck, and that he said something about being in Louisiana. St. Clair objected on the grounds that he was not provided notice of the Commonwealth's intention to introduce evidence relating to his travel to Louisiana, and that it was not an unexpected answer since the Commonwealth asked her if St. Clair had ever said anything about being in Louisiana. The Commonwealth responded that this testimony was not new information since Bylynn had testified to it at the Bullitt County trial.

Bylynn's fourth statement is that St. Clair told her that he was in Louisiana, and that he had told her he had been in Oklahoma for a few weeks before he saw her in December at a friend's house in Durant County, Oklahoma. She stated that he had told her that the Oklahoma State Bureau of Investigation (OSBI) had searched the place, but that he was hiding under some hay and they never saw him. The Commonwealth then asked Bylynn how long St. Clair had told her he had been in Oklahoma and the date of the conversation when he did so. She responded that it was December 17, 1991, the day before his arrest. This testimony was elicited to contradict Reese's anticipated testimony that St. Clair had arrived at his farm on October 1, 1991.

St. Clair objected to the testimony, and the trial court overruled the objection on the grounds that the Commonwealth could cross-examine Bylynn about any subject to which she had previously testified. St. Clair now argues that the introduction of this testimony violated due process, his right to a fair trial and that Bylynn's testimony was admitted in violation of the marital privilege. St. Clair also argues that at the time of trial, KRS 421.210(1) was applicable and allowed one spouse to prohibit the other from testifying to communications made during their marriage, which are confidential in nature. Finally, St. Clair argues that Bylynn's statements that incriminated St. Clair were also inadmissible since they violated RCr 7.24(1).

The Commonwealth contends that the marital privilege does not apply in this case for two reasons. First, the Commonwealth argues that Bylynn and St. Clair were involved in joint criminal activity under KRE 504(c)(1). It posits that no privilege is applicable since the communications testified to occurred during St. Clair's escape from the Bryan County Jail in Oklahoma and that Bylynn provided him with items which he later used to kidnap and kill Brady. Second, the Commonwealth argues that these communications were not confidential because they were made in the presence of Reese.

KRE 504 contains a spousal testimonial privilege, KRE 504(a), a confidential marital communications privilege, KRE 504(b), and exceptions to those privileges in KRE 504(c). Both privileges are designed to protect and enhance the marital relationship at the expense of otherwise useful evidence. KRE 504(c)(1) codifies preexisting law, KRS 421.210(1). KRE 504 provides:

(a) Spousal testimony. The spouse of a party has a privilege to refuse to testify against the party as to events occurring after the date of their marriage. A party has a privilege to prevent his or her spouse from testifying against the party as to events occurring after the date of their marriage.

(b) Marital communications. An individual has a privilege to refuse to testify and to prevent another from testifying to any confidential communication made by the individual to his or her spouse during their marriage. The privilege may be asserted only by the individual holding the privilege or by the holder's guardian, conservator, or personal representative. A communication is confidential if it is made privately by an individual to his or her spouse and is not intended for disclosure to any other person.

(c) Exceptions. There is no privilege under this rule:

  (1) In any criminal proceeding in which sufficient evidence is introduced to support a finding that the spouses conspired or acted jointly in the commission of the crime charged;

  (2) * * *

  (3) In any proceeding in which the spouses are adverse parties.

KRE 504(a) and (b) changed the spousal privilege from KRS 421.210(1) in two significant respects. First, the testimonial privilege in KRE 504(a) was expanded to enable a party spouse to preclude a witness spouse from testifying against him. Second, the marital communications privilege in KRE 504(b) was narrowed by defining the term "confidential" to require that the communication was not intended for disclosure to any other person, i.e., there must have been a positive expectation of confidentiality.

The issue we must first address is whether subsection (c)(1) applies in this situation. We begin our analysis by examining the plain language of KRE 504(c)(1). The plain language of the exception states that there must be "sufficient evidence" to "support a finding that the spouse conspired or acted jointly in the commission of the crime charged." Plainly, this exception to the privilege applies only if each spouse has contributed to or participated in the crime charged. In Gill v. Commonwealth, this Court discussed the application of the marital communications privilege and its exceptions as they existed under KRS 421.210 (1). In Gill, testimony of one spouse was held not privileged where both spouses were accused of being *particeps criminis* with the wife having been indicted for the same crime that her husband had been convicted of committing.

In this case, Bylynn facilitated St. Clair's flight after his prison escape, but there was no evidence that Bylynn conspired or acted jointly in the commission of the crimes with which St. Clair was charged (two counts of receiving stolen property over $ 100, criminal attempt to commit murder, second-degree arson, or capital kidnapping).

This Court has reviewed the record extensively. Statements two and three were undoubtedly made outside the presence of Reese or any other person. Bylynn acknowledged on the stand that statement two occurred in private when she and St. Clair were in a barn loft. She also confirmed that statement three occurred during a phone conversation with St. Clair while Reese was out of the room. As stated in KRE 504(b), "[a] communication is confidential if it is made privately by an individual to his or her spouse and is not intended for disclosure to any other person." St. Clair was running from the authorities, and confided certain information to his wife. His statements implicated him in various crimes, and their sensitive nature combined with the circumstances of their disclosure rendered them confidential. For these reasons statements two and three fall within the ambit of a confidential communication, and should have been excluded by virtue of the marital privilege.

Upon review, there is some doubt as to the confidential nature of statements one and four. Statement one took place at a fair, and apparently was made in full view of the public eye. Moreover, based on the testimony of Bylynn, it is unclear whether St. Clair was alone or with Reese at the time of this statement. However, confidential statements need not be given behind closed doors to retain their confidential character. A hushed or whispered statement from one spouse to another may be considered confidential depending on the circumstances of its disclosure. In this case, the record is insufficient to make a definitive determination as to the confidential nature of statement one. Therefore, upon remand the trial judge should hear additional evidence regarding the circumstances of statement one and make a factual finding.

Whether statement four was confidential is equally unclear. At trial, Bylynn seemed to relate the statement four disclosure to the same telephone conversation in which the statement three disclosure was made. If this is the case, statement four would enjoy the same privileged status as statement three. However, review of the record leaves the Court with enough doubt to require a hearing on the statement four issue.

Accordingly, statements two and three were privileged and should have been excluded at trial. As to statements one and four, a hearing should be held on remand to determine their status.

The admission of the privileged statements was prejudicial because the Commonwealth used this testimony to corroborate Reese's testimony that St. Clair was the ringleader and the shooter. Bylynn was a critical witness as her testimony repeated the details of the jail escape and that St. Clair had stolen the alleged murder weapon. It revealed that she felt a gun on Appellant's person when she met him in Dallas, and her testimony contradicted St. Clair's defense that he had never been in Kentucky because he told her he had burned a truck in Kentucky. Bylynn's testimony was crucial because it contained the only admission by St. Clair of guilt, and one of a few pieces of evidence that placed St. Clair in Kentucky at the time of the kidnapping and murder. Consequently, the admission of Bylynn's testimony was prejudicial error and retrial is required.

II. Jury Instructions

III. Various Other Claims

For the forgoing reasons, we reverse and remand.

DISSENTING OPINION BY JUSTICE WINTERSHEIMER

I must respectfully dissent from the majority opinion because there was no error on the part of the trial judge in permitting the testimony of the ex-wife concerning communications between the accused and her during his escape and other patently criminal activities. The majority opinion construes the marital privilege too broadly.

The marital communications privilege does not apply in this situation because the communications involved aiding St. Clair in patently criminal activity and because the communications sought to be privileged were likely intended to be shared with a third party. Furthermore, the wife's testimony has substantial probative value thereby outweighing the minimal prejudicial effect.

Thus, the majority has interpreted the confidential marital communications privilege too broadly. Privileges are to be interpreted narrowly. [Citation omitted.] Porter, *supra*, states that "privileges 'must be strictly construed and accepted only to the very limited extent that permitting a refusal to testify or excluding relevant evidence has a public good transcending the normally predominate principle of utilizing all rational means for ascertaining truth." 986 F.2d at 1019 *citing* Trammel v. United States, 445 U.S. 40, 50, 100 S. Ct. 906, 63

L. Ed. 2d 186 (1980); United States v. Nixon, 418 U.S. 683, 709–10, 94 S. Ct. 3090, 41 L. Ed. 2d 1039 (1974).

In concluding that statements two and three were confidential, the majority opinion fails to analyze whether the information shared between St. Clair and his wife were "not intended for disclosure to any other person." KRE 504(b). Because St. Clair and Reese escaped and stole a pickup truck together, it is reasonable to infer that they made plans on securing the means to continue their escape. For instance, communications to the wife concerning the need for clothing, money, and other items would be expected to be non confidential because St. Clair would tell Reese from where aid to their escape would come. Accordingly, statements from St. Clair to his wife concerning his and Reese's location, future location, and plans would also fail the "not intended for disclosure to another person" test because Bylynn was a source of aid to them.

KRE 504(c)(1) states that the privilege is excepted "in any criminal proceeding in which sufficient evidence is introduced to support a finding that the spouses conspired or acted jointly in the commission of the crime charged." The majority interprets this to mean that Bylynn must have directly aided in receiving stolen property, criminal attempt to commit murder, or second-degree arson. It is arguable whether aiding and abetting the escape results in conspiring for the purposes of rendering the privilege. Gill v. Commonwealth, 374 S.W.2d 848 (Ky. 1964) states, "when husband and wife are co-conspirators, or when the evidence justifies such a conclusion, a declaration of the husband or wife at the time of the act in question is not privileged". Certainly, under the situation described in these facts, the wife became some part of the criminal activities by her assistance. Furthermore, this analysis is more consistent with the 6th Circuit's interpretation of the joint participation exception to the confidential marital communications privilege. See United States v. Sims, 755 F.2d 1239 (6th Cir. 1985) (Exception to privilege for confidential marital communications arising out of joint criminal activity exists for conversations that pertain to patently illegal activity.). Even though this part of the analysis may be a close call in this case, the communications were not confidential.

The majority opinion states that the evidence of the wife's testimony would be prejudicial. This analysis is incorrect under KRE 403. KRE 403 disallows evidence whose prejudicial value outweighs the probative value. Because her testimony corroborated some other evidence, and especially because her testimony was the critical key to place St. Clair in Kentucky at the time of the criminal commissions, it has significant probative value. Accordingly, the trial judge did not err in admitting the testimony after disallowing the confidential marital communications privilege to apply.

Therefore, there was no confidential marital communications privilege here. The trial judge properly instructed the jury. I would affirm the conviction in all respects.

Graves and Scott, JJ., join this dissent.

STATE v. BERGMANN

2009 Iowa App. LEXIS 54 (2009)

POTTERFIELD, J.

I. Background Facts and Proceedings

On January 11, 2006, Rodney Bergmann was found unconscious in his vehicle, which was in gear with the engine running. Bergmann was roused and taken by ambulance to the hospital. A phlebotomist at the hospital drew Bergmann's blood, which showed a blood alcohol level of .216. [This blood test was separate from another test of Bergmann's blood and urine that was performed pursuant to Iowa Code chapter 321J. The results of that test were suppressed because the specimens were improperly obtained.] Bergmann's attorney sent a letter to Black Hawk County Deputy Sheriff William Locke that contained the medical records for treatment Bergmann received at the hospital. The Black Hawk County Attorney filed a trial information on February 13, 2006, charging Bergmann with operating while intoxicated in violation of Iowa Code section 321J.2 (2005).

Bergmann told rescuers that he took fentanyl for a back injury, and fentanyl was found in his vehicle. A treating nurse noted that Bergmann had refilled a prescription for fentanyl earlier that day. Bergmann asserted that the fentanyl was the cause of his condition and that ingestion of Nyquil caused his elevated blood alcohol level.

The State filed a motion to adjudicate law points seeking to use the analysis of Bergmann's blood that was performed at the hospital as was revealed in the medical records he provided. Bergmann resisted, stating these records were protected by the physician-patient privilege. [Bergmann did not execute a release of information.] The district court found that the records were admissible because Bergmann destroyed the confidentiality between him and his physician when he released his medical records to the sheriff.

On July 3,2007, the State applied for and received, ex parte, a county attorney's subpoena duces tecum commanding hospital personnel to provide the identity and address of the person who had tested Bergmann's blood. The subpoena also ordered the production of related information, which the county attorney obtained orally from the hospital personnel. The court order required the prosecutor to serve defense counsel with the application and order by fax the same day. The State argued the subpoena was necessary so that it could list the individual's name and address in the minutes of testimony as required by the Iowa Rules of Criminal Procedure.

On July 19, 2007, Bergmann filed a motion to quash the information obtained by the subpoena as it was protected by the physician-patient privilege. 3 On July 24, 2007, the district court overruled Bergmann's motion to quash, finding that Bergmann had waived the physician-patient privilege.

Bergmann was convicted by a jury on July 27, 2007. He appeals, arguing the district court erred by: (1) finding that his medical records were admissible and issuing a subpoena; and (2) overruling his motion to quash.

II. Standard of Review

We review the district court's ruling for a correction of errors of law. State v. Henneberry, 558 N.W.2d 708, 709 (Iowa 1997).

III. Admissibility of Medical Records

Bergmann provided the State with medical documents to support his claim that he suffered from a fentanyl overdose. Those documents included the lab report revealing his blood alcohol content. Bergmann argues that, absent his release of additional records, the State should have access to only those medical records that he provided and nothing more.

A doctor is prohibited from disclosing a patient's confidential communications without the patient's consent. Iowa Code 622.10. Unless the physician-patient privilege is waived, the hospital should not provide the State with medical information, including the blood alcohol test results. The patient can waive this privilege by disclosure or consent to disclosure. State v. Demaray, 704 N.W.2d 60, 65 (Iowa 2005). In this case, Bergmann disclosed medical information to the State. "[V]oluntary disclosure of the content of a privileged communication constitutes waiver as to all other communications on the same subject." Miller v. Continental Ins. Co., 392 N.W.2d 500, 504–05 (Iowa 1986). Bergmann cannot waive the physician-patient privilege as to information that benefits his case and invoke the privilege against harmful information. Id. at 505. He can choose to invoke or waive the physician-patient privilege, but his decision is final and applies to all communication on that subject. Id. When Bergmann disclosed his medical records to the State, he waived his physician-patient privilege as to his treatment on that occasion.

The district court did not err in overruling Bergmann's motion to quash.

AFFIRMED.

NEW YORK CITY HEALTH v. MORGENTHAU

Court of Appeals of New York, 98 N.Y.2d 525, 779 N.E.2d 173, 749 N.Y. S.2d 462, 2002 N.Y. LEXIS 3140 (2002)

JUDGES: Opinion by Judge Rosenblatt. Chief Judge Kaye and Judges Smith, Levine, Ciparick, Wesley and Graffeo concur.

OPINIONBY: ROSENBLATT

Hospitals may assert a physician-patient privilege under CPLR 4504 (a) to maintain the confidentiality of patient medical records. The case before us involves the extent to which grand juries may, compatibly with CPLR 4504 (a), acquire medical records for the purpose of identifying criminal assailants.

On May 25, 1998, an unidentified assailant stabbed a man to death in Manhattan. Police could determine only that the assailant was a Caucasian male in his 30s or early 40s and that he may have been bleeding when he fled the scene. Over 2½ years later, still unable to identify him, the District Attorney of New York County conjectured that the assailant may have sought medical treatment at a local hospital shortly after the homicide. In early 2001, the District Attorney served grand jury subpoenas duces tecum on 23 hospitals, including four facilities operated by the New York City Health and Hospitals Corporation (HHC). Those subpoenas sought:

> "any and all records pertaining to any male Caucasian patient between the ages of 30 to 45 years, who was treated or who sought treatment on May 25th, 1998 through May 26th, 1998 for a laceration, puncture wound or slash, or other injury caused by or possibly caused by a cutting instrument and/or sharp object, said injury being plainly observable to a lay person without expert or professional knowledge; said records including but not limited to said patient's name, date of birth, address, telephone number, social security number and other identifying information, except any and all information acquired by a physician, registered nurse or licensed practical nurse in attending said patient in a professional capacity and which was necessary to enable said doctor and/or nurse to act in that capacity."

Citing CPLR 4504 (a), n1 HHC invoked the physician-patient privilege and refused to turn over emergency room triage logs potentially responsive to these subpoenas, claiming that compliance would necessarily breach patient confidentiality in violation of the statute. After the District Attorney moved to hold HHC in contempt, HHC cross-moved for an order quashing the subpoenas. Supreme Court denied both motions but ordered HHC to submit the records for in camera inspection. The Appellate Division unanimously reversed and granted the motion to quash, holding that compliance with the subpoenas would violate the physician-patient privilege because "the assessment of the nature and cause of the injuries triggering production of the relevant documents involves an inherently medical evaluation" (287 AD2d 287, 288, 731 N.Y.S.2d 17 [2001]). This Court granted the District Attorney leave to appeal, and we now affirm.

Our analysis begins with the history and purpose of the physician-patient privilege. Common law did not recognize any confidentiality in communications between patients and medical professionals. New York was the first state to enact a physician-patient privilege statute (see 2 Rev Stat of NY, part III, ch VII, tit III, § 73 [1st ed 1829]; see also Dillenbeck v Hess, 73 N.Y.2d 278, 284, 536 N.E.2d 1126, 539 N.Y.S.2d 707 [1989]; Fisch, New York Evidence § 541, at 356 [2d ed 1977]). The modern codification of the privilege, CPLR 4504 (a), serves three core policy objectives implicated on this appeal (see generally Prince, Richardson on Evidence §§5-301, 5–302, at 246–249 [Farrell 11th ed]). First, the physician-patient privilege seeks to maximize unfettered patient communication with medical professionals, so that any potential embarrassment arising from public disclosure will not "deter people from seeking medical help and securing adequate diagnosis and treatment" (Dillenbeck at 285, quoting Williams v Roosevelt Hosp., 66 N.Y.2d 391, 395, 497 N.Y. S.2d 348, 488 N.E.2d 94 [1985]; see also Matter of Grand Jury Proceedings [Doe], 56 N.Y.2d 348, 352, 437 N.E.2d 1118, 452 N.Y.S.2d 361 [1982]). Second, the privilege encourages medical professionals to be candid in recording confidential information in patient medical records, and thereby averts a choice "between their legal duty to testify and their professional obligation to honor their patients' confidences" (Dillenbeck at 285, citing Fisch § 541; see also Revisers' Reports and Notes, 3 Rev Stat of NY, at 737 [2d ed 1836]). Third, the privilege protects patients' reasonable privacy expectations against disclosure of sensitive personal information (see Martin, Capra & Rossi, New York Evidence Handbook § 5.3.1, at 367 [1997]; Developments in the Law—Privileged Communications, Medical and Counseling Privileges, 98 Harv L Rev 1530, 1544–1548 [1985]).

Though in derogation of the common law, the physician-patient privilege is to be given a "broad and liberal construction to carry out its policy" (Matter of Grand Jury Investigation of Onondaga County, 59 N.Y.2d 130, 134, 450 N.E.2d 678, 463 N.Y.S.2d 758 [1983]; Matter of City Council of the City of N.Y. v Goldwater, 284 NY 296, 300, 31 N.E.2d 31 [1940]).

On this appeal, the District Attorney contends that enforcement of the subpoenas would not offend these policies or violate CPLR 4504 (a). The prosecutor argues that the subpoenas do not seek information acquired by means of medical diagnosis, treatment or expertise, and should be enforced because they purport to seek records only of injuries "plainly observable to a lay person without expert or professional knowledge." We disagree.

The physician-patient privilege generally does not extend to information obtained outside the realms of medical diagnosis and treatment. Indeed, because the policies underlying the physician-patient privilege implicate confidential patient relationships with medical professionals as medical professionals, we have generally limited the privilege to information acquired by the medical professional "through the application of professional skill or knowledge" (Dillenbeck, 73 N.Y.2d at 284 n 4). Accordingly, notwithstanding CPLR 4504 (a), medical professionals have been authorized to disclose observations of a heroin packet falling from a patient's sock (see People v Capra, 17 N.Y.2d 670, 216 N.E.2d 610, 269 N.Y.S.2d 451 [1966]), injuries on a patient's cheek and lip (see People v Giordano, 274 A.D.2d 748, 711 N.Y.S.2d 557 [2000]), and a patient's slurred speech and alcohol-laced breath incident to intoxication (see People v Hedges, 98 A.D.2d 950, 470 N.Y.S.2d 61 [1983]). Likewise, photographs of methadone-treatment patients taken to prevent unauthorized individuals from obtaining the drug (see People v Newman, 32 N.Y.2d 379, 384, 298 N.E.2d 651, 345 N.Y.S.2d 502 [1973], cert denied 414 U.S. 1163, 39 L. Ed. 2d 116, 94 S. Ct. 927 [1974]) and the names and addresses of a medical professional's patients (see In Matter of Albert Lindley Lee Mem. Hosp., 115 F. Supp. 643 [ND NY 1953], affd 209 F.2d 122 [2d Cir], cert denied sub nom. Cincotta v United States, 347 U.S. 960, 98 L. Ed. 1104, 74 S. Ct. 709 [1954]) are outside the ambit of CPLR 4504 (a) and must be surrendered pursuant to a valid subpoena.

We conclude, however, that Onondaga County controls this appeal and directs that the challenged subpoenas be quashed. In Onondaga County, as in the instant case, the victim was stabbed to death under circumstances that led investigators to conclude that the assailant may have left the scene bleeding. Endeavoring to identify the assailant, the District Attorney of Onondaga County issued a grand jury subpoena on a hospital, seeking "all medical records pertaining to treatment of any person with stab wounds or other wounds caused by a knife" (Onondaga County, 59 N.Y.2d at 133). In quashing the subpoena, the Court held that compliance might have "required the hospital to which it is addressed to divulge information protected by the physician-patient privilege" (59 N.Y.2d at 132). The Court concluded that under those circumstances, it was "not . . . possible to comply with a demand for names and addresses of all persons treated for a knife wound without disclosing privileged information concerning diagnosis and treatment" (59 N.Y.2d. at 135).

We perceive no difference of any actual substance between the subpoena quashed in Onondaga County and the ones challenged here. The records potentially responsive to the HHC subpoenas are precisely the same as those sought in Onondaga County. Though the District Attorney crafted the instant subpoenas with Onondaga County in mind by broadening their scope (to include most bleeding wounds rather than only knife wounds) and narrowing their reach (to include only wounds "plainly observable to a lay person"), the subpoenas still run afoul of Onondaga County.

Here, much as in Onondaga County, the challenged subpoenas define the class of records sought by the "cause or potential cause" of injury. Thus, the subpoenas inevitably call for a medical determination as to causation "through the application of professional skill or knowledge" (Dillenbeck, 73 N.Y.2d at 284 n 4). It is precisely this intrusion into the physician-patient relationship that CPLR 4504 (a) seeks to prevent. The inherently medical nature of this judgment is not obviated by attempting to qualify it in terms of what a layperson might plainly observe.

By merely reviewing hospital records after patients obtain emergency medical treatment, hospitals cannot reasonably determine whether particular injuries and their causes would have been obvious to a layperson. Medical records are not organized on the basis of what laypersons—as opposed to medical professionals—might discern. Even if a particular medical record does state the cause of injury, the record may not indicate reliably how the hospital ascertained the cause. Medical professionals may have learned the cause from the patient, or discovered it based on their medical expertise. Hospitals should not face contempt proceedings merely because they cannot distinguish the indistinguishable.

This result is further justified by the policy objectives of the physician-patient privilege and the broad construction of CPLR 4504 (a) required to achieve them. Patients should not fear that merely by obtaining emergency medical care they may lose the confidentiality of their medical records and their physicians' medical determinations. A contrary result would discourage critical emergency care, intrude on patients' confidential medical relationships and undermine patients' reasonable expectations of privacy.

Finally, we note that none of the Legislature's many statutory exceptions to the physician-patient privilege apply here. For example, notwithstanding CPLR 4504 (a), Public Health Law § 2101 (1) obliges physicians to disclose immediately any case of communicable disease (see Thomas v Morris, 286 NY 266, 268–270, 36 N.E.2d 141 [1941]), and Social Services Law § 413 (1) requires all medical professionals to report actual or suspected cases of child abuse (see People v Trester, 190 Misc 2d 46, 48, 737 N.Y.S.2d 522 [2002]). CPLR 4504 (b) exempts from the privilege "information indicating that a patient who is under the age of sixteen years has been the victim of a crime." Likewise, Penal Law § 265.26 requires hospitals and medical professionals to report to law enforcement authorities certain cases of serious burns (see Rea v Pardo, 132 A.D.2d 442, 446, 522 N.Y.S.2d 393 [1987]), and Penal Law § 265.25 obliges hospitals and medical professionals to report every case of a bullet wound, gunshot wound, powder burn and "every case of a wound which is likely to or may result in death and is actually or apparently inflicted by a knife, icepick or other sharp or pointed instrument" (emphasis added; see also Onondaga County, 59 N.Y.2d at 133, 135–136; Donnino, Practice Commentaries, McKinney's Cons Laws of NY, Book 39, Penal Law §§ 265.25, 265.26, at 220, 222).

In as much as the Legislature enacted an exception to CPLR 4504 (a) directing the reporting of potentially life-threatening stab wounds (see Penal Law § 265.25), we reaffirm our conclusion that the Legislature intended CPLR 4504 (a) to protect against disclosure those medical records of patients whose stab wounds are less severe (see Onondaga County, 59 N.Y.2d at 136). Thus, because none of the Legislature's other exceptions to the privilege apply, the records the District Attorney seeks remain privileged under CPLR 4504 (a), and the subpoenas seeking their disclosure must be quashed.

Accordingly, the order of the Appellate Division should be affirmed, without costs.

Chief Judge Kaye and Judges Smith, Levine, Ciparick, Wesley and Graffeo concur.

Order affirmed, without costs.

Cases Relating to Chapter 11

Opinions and Expert Testimony

BOWLING
v.
STATE

Court of Appeals of Georgia, 275 Ga. App. 45, 619 S.E.2d 688, 2005 Ga. App. LEXIS 808 (2005)

Writ of certiorari denied, 2006 Ga. LEXIS 51 (Ga. 2006)

Johnson, Presiding Judge. Ruffin, C. J., and Barnes, J., concur.

Johnson, Presiding Judge.

A jury found Daniel Bowling guilty of operating a boat while under the influence of alcohol to the extent it was less safe for him to do so. He appeals from his conviction, claiming the evidence was insufficient to show that he was a less safe driver, or that he was less safe as a result of being under the influence of alcohol. We disagree and affirm his conviction.

On appeal the evidence is viewed in a light most favorable to the verdict, and an appellant no longer enjoys a presumption of innocence; moreover, this Court determines evidence sufficiency and does not weigh the evidence or determine the credibility of witnesses. The jury's verdict must be upheld if any rational trier of fact could have found the essential elements of the crime beyond a reasonable doubt.

Viewing the evidence in the proper light, it shows that an officer with the Georgia Department of Natural Resources was patrolling Lake Lanier when he observed a boat traveling at night without a stern light. The officer pulled alongside the vessel and told the driver, Bowling, that he was stopping the boat because of the light violation. The officer proceeded to conduct a safety inspection, and asked Bowling to produce a life jacket for each person on board, a "throwable" lifesaving device, a fire extinguisher, and the boat's registration. Bowling had difficulty trying to find some of the items, and was unable to produce the registration or a throwable lifesaving device. The officer testified that Bowling seemed confused while looking for the items. Bowling said he thought the registration card was in the glove compartment, but instead of looking there, he looked around the driver's seat for the card. The officer testified that Bowling asked to use the officer's flashlight, even though Bowling had just looked straight at the floor where there was a large spotlight. The officer noticed an empty wine glass on the floorboard of the boat, and detected an odor of alcohol coming from the boat. He asked Bowling if he had been drinking. Bowling said he had not.

Based on his observations, as well as Bowling's mannerisms and demeanor, the officer asked Bowling to perform field sobriety tests to determine if he was under the influence of alcohol.

With Bowling in his own boat and the officer in the patrol boat, the officer administered the horizontal gaze nystagmus (HGN) test, testing for involuntary jerking of the eyes. Bowling was unable to perform the test properly because he kept moving his head after being told not to do so. The officer testified that Bowling exhibited all six "clues" on the HGN test, though he did not explain for the jury what that meant in terms of intoxication.

The officer asked Bowling to step over into the patrol boat. He noted that Bowling stumbled badly when doing so. The officer noticed an odor of alcohol coming from Bowling's person. When the officer asked Bowling to recite the alphabet without singing, Bowling started reciting it, then stopped, started over, repeated letters, laughed and sang part of the test. He omitted several letters. Bowling was unable to do a finger dexterity exercise or a hand pat exercise as instructed. Bowling refused to submit to an alco-sensor test.

The officer placed Bowling under arrest for boating under the influence, and then read the implied consent notice. Bowling became hostile and demanded to be returned to his boat. Instead, the officer took Bowling to the police station. Once there, Bowling refused to take a breath test. According to the officer, Bowling displayedmood swings throughout the incident, going from belligerent and irritated to calm. When the officer was asked at trial where he believed the odor of alcohol was coming from, he stated that there was a strong odor of alcohol coming from the boat, and a moderate odor of alcohol coming from Bowling. *When asked whether he determined that Bowling "was under the influence to the extent that [it] was less safe to operate that vessel," the officer testified that he concluded after conducting field sobriety tests that Bowling "was a less safe boat operator."* [Emphasis added.]

Bowling contends that the evidence was insufficient to prove beyond a reasonable doubt that he was a less safe driver, or that he was a less safe driver due to the presence of alcohol. He urges that the officer could not recall whether the life jackets and fire extinguisher were eventually found, did not know whether the boat's spotlight worked (which would explain why Bowling asked for a flashlight), and admitted that some operators cannot locate registration documents. He argues further that there was no evidence that he was operating the boat in an unsafe manner, that the hand pat and finger dexterity tests are not part of standard field sobriety exercises, that argumentativeness does not necessarily prove that someone is under the influence of alcohol, that the officer failed to give his opinion of what the six clues of the HGN test indicate about a person's level of intoxication, that a counting test was performed correctly, and that the officer gave inconsistent statements regarding the source and strength of the alcohol odor. Reversal is not required.

In order to obtain a conviction for driving under the influence of alcohol to the extent it is less safe to drive, the state must prove that the defendant had impaired driving ability as a result of drinking alcohol. A trier of fact can find that a driver was "less safe" based on circumstantial evidence, such as where the driver exhibited signs of intoxication. Field sobriety tests are not designed to detect the mere presence of alcohol, but to produce information regarding whether alcohol is present at an impairing level such that the driver is less safe.

Bowling's refusal to submit to chemical tests of his breath is circumstantial evidence of intoxication. And, a jury could have found from Bowling's performances on several of the sobriety tests that he was not as alert or physically capable and was aless safe driver than he would have been had he not consumed alcohol. Moreover, there was evidence that the smell of alcohol emanated from Bowling's person, that he stumbled badly while trying to board the patrol boat, that an empty wine glass lay on the floorboard, and that Bowling was confused. There was also opinion testimony from the officer that Bowling was under the influence to the extent he was a less safe boat operator. This testimony followed a series of questions regarding the officer's detection of the odor of alcohol emanating from the boat and from Bowling's person. A police officer may offer opinion evidence that a person was a less safe driver. We add that, contrary to Bowling's position, the state was not required to prove that he committed an unsafe act in order to show it was "less safe" for him to operate the vessel.

A rational trier of fact could have found from evidence of alcohol on the boat, the odor of alcohol emanating from Bowling's person, Bowling's refusal to submit to chemical tests of his breath, his demeanor and conduct, and his performance on several sobriety tests, that he was impaired and that the impairment was a result of alcohol consumption. The evidence was sufficient for a rational trier of fact to find Bowling guilty beyond a reasonable doubt of operating a boat while under the influence of alcohol to the extent it was less safe for him to do so.

Judgment affirmed. Ruffin, C. J., and Barnes, J., concur.

OSBOURN
v.
STATE

Court of Criminal Appeals of Texas
92 S.W.3d 531, 2002 Tex. Crim. App. LEXIS 236 (2002)

JUDGES: Meyers, J., delivered the unanimous opinion of the Court.

OPINION BY: Meyers

Appellant was convicted in a bench trial of possession of marihuana, a usable amount of less than two ounces. Punishment was assessed at twenty days' confinement in the county jail. The Court of Appeals affirmed the trial court's conviction. We granted review to decide whether the Court of Appeals erred when it held that the arresting officer's identification of marihuana was admissible as a lay opinion under Texas Rule of Evidence 701. We will affirm.

Appellant was the passenger in a vehicle that was stopped by Officer Nicole Saval. During the traffic stop, Saval smelled alcohol and the odor of burning marihuana emanating from the vehicle and suspected that the driver of the vehicle was under the influence. While Saval questioned appellant, another officer performed a field sobriety test on the driver who was subsequently arrested. Saval asked appellant if she and the driver had been smoking marihuana. Appellant first denied that she had been smoking marihuana and claimed that the odor was cigarettes. After Saval explained to appellant that cigarette smoke does not smell like marihuana smoke, appellant admitted that she and the driver had been smoking marihuana. Appellant then told the officer that there was more marihuana in the vehicle, which Saval found in a clear plastic bag between the two front seats.

Saval documented her identification of the marihuana in the offense report that was given to appellant before trial. After receiving the offense report, appellant requested and the court ordered the State to provide notice of its intent to offer expert testimony pursuant to Article 39.14(b) of the Texas Code of Criminal Procedure. The State did not respond to the order.

At trial, Saval testified about her police academy training. She stated that the trainees were shown what different drugs looked like and were able to smell marihuana both before and after it was burned. She stated that although she was not a drug recognition expert and was not certified as one, based on her training at the academy and her experience on the police force, she was able to identify what marihuana looks and smells like.

During Saval's testimony, appellant objected claiming that the State was attempting to qualify Saval as an expert without providing notice. The State responded that Saval was not being offered as an expert under Rule 702, rather as an individual who can identify what marihuana looks and smells like. The court withheld ruling on the admissibility and allowed the testimony to continue. At the end of the trial, the court concluded that the officer was testifying as an expert due to her specialized knowledge, however, the testimony was admissible because the offense report was adequate notice.

On appeal, appellant claimed that the testimony of the officer was improperly admitted due to the State's failure to provide notice of intent to offer expert testimony. Appellant also claimed that without this testimony, the evidence was legally insufficient to support a conviction.

The Court of Appeals concluded that the testimony was admissible as lay opinion testimony under Rule of Evidence 701. Osbourn v. State, 59 S.W.3d 809, 815 (Tex. App.-Austin 2001). Because Saval's testimony was personal knowledge that was rationally based on her perceptions, inferences, and impressions, the Court of Appeals held that she was not testifying as an expert. Id. at 814. Because the trial court found the evidence admissible under the alternative theory that Saval was testifying as an expert, the Court of Appeals also addressed the issue of notice. The court found that because the offense report was made available to appellant prior to the request for notice, appellant could anticipate the content of the testimony of the arresting officer. Since appellant was not surprised by the testimony and the State's actions did not constitute bad faith, the Court of Appeals reviewed the trial court's admission of the testimony for abuse of discretion. Id. at 816. Finding no abuse, the court declined to disturb the trial court's ruling.

Appellant advances two grounds for review but in view of our disposition of the case only ground two will require discussion. The issue raised by the determinative ground of error is whether the Court of Appeals erred when it held that a police officer's identification of marihuana is admissible as a lay opinion under Texas Rule of Evidence 701.

Appellant argues that the Court of Appeals erred when it held that the officer's testimony regarding the identification of marihuana was admissible under Rule of Evidence 701. Because Saval's opinion was based on the training she received at the police academy and the experience she gained during her three years as a police officer, appellant contends that she was an expert witness under Rule 702. Appellant claims that only a witness who testifies based on personal knowledge, rather than experience and training, can identify marihuana as a lay witness under Rule 701.

The State counters appellant's assertion by claiming that expert testimony is not necessary to identify marihuana because appellant herself identified the substance as marihuana. Additionally, the fact that all police officers have training and experience does not necessarily make them expert witnesses. The State contends that since Saval personally observed the marihuana, she was not testifying as an expert.

Both lay and expert witnesses can offer opinion testimony. Rule 701 covers the more traditional witness—one who "witnessed" or participated in the events about which he or she is testifying—while Rule 702 allows for a witness who was brought in as an expert to testify. A witness can testify in the form of an opinion under Rule 701 if the opinions or inferences are (a) rationally based on his or her perceptions and (b) helpful to the clear understanding of the testimony or the determination of a fact in issue. Fairow v. State, 943 S. W.2d 895, 898 (Tex. Crim. App. 1997). Perceptions refer to a witness's interpretation of information acquired through his or her own senses or experiences at the time of the event (i.e., things the witness saw, heard, smelled, touched, felt, or tasted). Since Rule 701 requires the testimony to be based on the witness's perception, it is necessary that the witness personally observed or experienced the events about which he or she is testifying. Id. at 898. Thus, the witness's testimony can include opinions, beliefs, or inferences as long as they are drawn from his or her own experiences or observations. This also incorporates the personal knowledge requirement of Rule 602 which states that a witness may not testify to a matter unless he or she has personal knowledge of the matter. Bigby v. State, 892 S.W.2d 864, 889 (Tex. Crim. App.1994). There is, however, a provision in Rule 602 for opinion testimony by expert witnesses which allows a person testifying as an expert under Rule 702 to base his or her opinion on facts and data that are of a type reasonably relied upon by experts in the field. TEX. R. CRIM. EVID. 703. Thus, expert testimony serves the purpose of allowing certain types of relevant, helpful testimony by a witness who does not possess personal knowledge of the events about which he or she is testifying.

When a witness who is capable of being qualified as an expert testifies regarding events which he or she personally perceived, the evidence may be admissible as both Rule 701 opinion testimony and Rule 702 expert testimony. A person with specialized knowledge may testify about his or her own observations under Rule 701 and may also testify about the theories, facts and data used in his or her area of expertise under Rule 702. Texas Rules of Evidence Manual art. VII-6-7 (6th ed. 2002) states that: "A witness may qualify to give testimony both under Rule 702-because of his or her superior experiential capacity-and under Rule 701, if the witness's testimony and opinion are based upon firsthand knowledge." This court has never addressed the issue of whether someone with training and experience can testify as a lay witness but the Courts of Appeals have admitted such testimony as both lay and expert opinion. See e.g., Harnett v. State, 38 S.W.3d 650, 659 (Tex. App.-Austin 2000, pet. ref'd) (a social worker was permitted to testify under Rule 701 based on her personal observations of the appellant and under Rule 702 based on her training and experience); Thomas v. State, 916 S.W.2d 578, 581 (Tex. App.-San Antonio 1996, no pet.) (police officer qualified as both lay opinion and expert witness to testify regarding the operation of a "crack" house); Ventroy v. State, 917 S. W.2d 419, 422 (Tex. App.-San Antonio 1996, pet. ref'd) (police officer was permitted to testify under Rules 701 and 702 based on his experience and personal knowledge about the scene of an accident); Yohey v. State, 801 S.W.2d 232, 243

(Tex. App.-San Antonio 1990, pet. ref'd) (police officer's testimony regarding time of death was admissible under both Rule 701 and 702); Austin v. State, 794 S.W.2d 408, 409-411, (Tex. App.-Austin 1990, pet. ref'd) (police officer testified under Rules 701 and 702 that, based on his experience and observation, "Swedish Deep Muscle Rub" was a term for prostitution). Thus, although police officers have training and experience, they are not precluded from offering lay testimony regarding events which they have personally observed. See e.g., Reece v. State, 878 S.W.2d 320, 325 (Tex. App.-Houston [1 dist.] 1994, no pet.) (police officer testified that, in his opinion, based on his experience, the actions he observed were consistent with someone selling drugs); State v. Welton, 774 S.W.2d 341, 343 (Tex. App.-Austin 1989, pet. ref'd) (police officer permitted to testify as non-expert opinion witness regarding intoxication based in part on smelling the odor of alcohol).

The ninth circuit has addressed the issue of whether a police officer with experience and training can testify as a lay witness. In United States v. Von Willie, 59 F.3d 922, 929 (9th Cir. 1995) the ninth circuit allowed a police officer who searched appellant's residence to testify as a lay witness about the nexus between drug trafficking and the possession of the type of weapons found during the search. The court stated that "these observations are common enough and require such a limited amount of expertise, if any, that they can, indeed, be deemed lay witness opinion." Id. At 929. Thus, although the police officer testified based on his experience, his testimony was admitted as a lay opinion under Rule 701 because it was rationally based on his perceptions during the search and was helpful to the determination of a fact in issue. Id. at 929. However, not all observations by witnesses with experience and training can be admitted as lay opinion testimony. This Court, in Emerson v. State, 880 S.W.2d 759, 763 (Tex. Crim. App. 1994) declined to admit as a lay opinion an officer's testimony regarding appellant's intoxication. Because the officer's opinion was based on his observations while administering the horizontal gaze nystagmus (HGN) test, this Court held that the testimony could only be admissible as expert testimony under Rule 702. Id. at 763. Although the officer personally perceived the appellant's eye movements during the HGN test, we held that his observations were not considered mere lay opinion because the test is based on a scientific theory. Id. at 763.

A distinct line cannot be drawn between lay opinion and expert testimony because all perceptions are evaluated based on experiences. However, as a general rule, observations which do not require significant expertise to interpret and which are not based on a scientific theory can be admitted as lay opinions if the requirements of Rule 701 are met. This is true even when the witness has experience or training. Additionally, even events not normally encountered by most people in everyday life do not necessarily require the testimony of an expert. The personal experience and knowledge of a lay witness may establish that he or she is capable, without qualification as an expert, of expressing an opinion on a subject outside the realm of common knowledge. United States v. James Earl Paiva, 892 F.2d 148, 157 (1st Cir. 1989). It is only when the fact-finder may not fully understand the evidence or be able to determine the fact in issue without the assistance of someone with specialized knowledge that a witness must be qualified as an expert.

It does not take an expert to identify the smell of marihuana smoke. Testimony as to the identity of an odor is admissible in some instances even though the person testifying is not an expert. Chess v. State, 172 Tex. Crim. 412, 357 S.W.2d 386, 387-388 (1962). While smelling the odor of marihuana smoke may not be an event normally encountered in daily life, it requires limited, if any, expertise to identify. See e.g., Kemner v. State, 589 S.W.2d 403 (Tex. Crim. App. 1979) (airline employee recognized odor of marihuana emanating from appellant's suitcase and informed DEA); Chaires v. State, 480 S.W.2d 196 (Tex. Crim. App. 1972) (airline baggage agent smelled odor of marihuana in appellant's suitcase, opened the suitcase and identified the grassy substance it contained as marihuana); Hattersley v. State, 487 S.W.2d 354 (Tex. Crim. App. 1972) (airline employee determined by sight and smell that appellant's suitcase contained marihuana); Sorensen v. State, 478 S.W.2d 532 (Tex. Crim. App. 1972) (appellant mother testified that she recognized the odor of marihuana when she found it in her son's room); Mumphrey v. State, 774 S.W.2d 75 (Tex. App.-Beaumont 1989, pet. ref'd) (13 year old rape victim testified that she smelled the odor of marihuana on the clothes of appellant). Although it cannot be presumed that everyone is capable of identifying marihuana by smell, a witness who is familiar with the odor of marihuana smoke through past experiences can testify as a lay witness that he or she was able to recognize the odor.

The admissibility of evidence is within the discretion of the trial court and will not be reversed absent an abuse of discretion. Powell v. State, 63 S.W.3d 435, 438 (Tex. Crim. App. 200; Harnett, 38 S.W.3d at 657; Ventroy, 917 S.W.2d at 422. If there is evidence supporting the trial court's decision to admit evidence, there is no abuse and the appellate court must defer to that decision. Powell, 63 S.W.3d at 438; Fairow, 943 S.W.2d at 901. Even when the trial judge gives the wrong reason for his decision, Salas v. State, 629 S.W.2d 796, 799 (Tex. Crim. App. 1981), if the decision is correct on any theory of law applicable to the case it will be sustained. Romero v. State, 800 S.W.2d 539, 543 (Tex. Crim. App. 1990); Moreno v. State, 170 Tex. Crim. 410, 411, 341 S.W.2d 455, 456 (Tex. Crim. App. 1961); Calloway v. State, 743 S.W.2d 645, 651-652 (Tex. Crim. App. 1988). This is especially true with regard to the admission of evidence. Dugard v. State, 688 S.W.2d 524 (Tex. Crim. App. 1985), overruled by Williams v. State, 780 S.W.2d 802 (Tex. Crim. App. 1989); Sewell v. State 629 S.W.2d 42, 45 (Tex. Crim. App. 1982). Taking this into account, we will now determine whether the Court of Appeals erred in upholding the trial court's admission of Saval's testimony.

Using the standard set out above, Saval's observation that the odor she smelled was marihuana did not require significant expertise to interpret. And, her observations were not interpreted based on a scientific theory. Thus, if her testimony meets the requirements of Rule 701, it is admissible as a lay opinion. Rule 701 allows a lay witness to give testimony in the form of opinions or inferences that are rationally based on the witness' perception and helpful to a clear understanding of the witness' testimony or the determination of a fact in issue. Thus, if the witness perceived events and formed an opinion that a reasonable person could draw from the facts, then the first part of the rule is met. If the opinion is also helpful for the trier of fact to understand the witness's testimony or aids in the determination of a fact in issue, then the opinion is admissible under Rule 701. Here, Saval participated in the events about which she testified and her opinion was based on what she perceived at the scene of the traffic stop. That is, she smelled an odor that she recognized as marihuana smoke. And, the testimony was helpful to the determination of a fact in issue (i.e., whether appellant was in possession of marihuana). Her belief or inference that the substance was marihuana was based on identifiable facts that were within her personal knowledge such as the green, leafy appearance and the distinct odor. Unlike other drugs that may require chemical analysis, marihuana has a distinct appearance and odor that are familiar and easily recognizable to anyone who has encountered it. So Saval's opinion that appellant possessed marihuana, based on the odor she smelled and the green, leafy substance she saw, was one that a reasonable person could draw from the circumstances. Her testimony regarding the identification of the marihuana was admissible as a lay opinion under Rule 701.

The record also indicates that appellant objected to Saval's testimony on the basis that her opinion was based on her training and experience as a police officer, making her a Rule 702 expert witness. There are certain fields where a witness may qualify as an expert based upon experience and training, however, use of the terms "training" and "experience" do not automatically make someone an expert. All opinions are formed by evaluating facts based on life experiences including education, background, training, occupation, etc. While Saval may have had the potential to be qualified as an expert because she possessed knowledge, skill, experience and education, she was not testifying as an expert when she identified the marihuana. Rather, she was testifying based on her firsthand sensory experiences. Saval herself smelled the odor that she perceived to be burnt marihuana. The fact that she had smelled marihuana before in the course of her employment as a police officer does not necessarily make her an expert. And, again, even if she was an expert, that would not preclude her from offering a lay opinion about something she personally perceived.

Although the trial court admitted Saval's testimony under a different theory, because evidence supports admission of the testimony under Rule 701, the trial court did not abuse its discretion.

Consequently, the Court of Appeals correctly upheld the trial court's admission of the testimony. The judgment of the Court of Appeals is affirmed.

Meyers, J.

UNITED STATES v. DELATORRE

United States Court of Appeals, Eleventh Circuit 309 F. Appx. 366, 2009 U.S. App. LEXIS 2183 (2009)

[Only the part of the case that relates to opinion and expert testimony is included here.]

PER CURIAM:

Alberto Naranjo Delatorre appeals his convictions for conspiracy to possess with intent to distribute at least five kilograms of cocaine and aiding and abetting possession with intent to distribute at least five kilograms of cocaine. He asserts that there was insufficient evidence for the jury to convict him on either count and that the district court abused its discretion by permitting an expert witness to testify to matters outside the scope of her expertise. After reviewing the record and the parties' briefs, we AFFIRM his convictions.

* * *

At trial, multiple witnesses testified regarding the allegations against Delatorre. Ron Skipper, a Drug Enforcement Agency ("DEA") agent, discussed Delatorre's actions on 27 February 2006. On that date, Skipper was conducting surveillance on a house in Duluth, Georgia that he had reason to believe would be the site of drug transaction. R10 at 30-33. According to Skipper, Villanueva-Naranjo arrived at the house in a green Infiniti car, parked in the driveway, and went inside the building. Id. at 35-36. About one minute later, Delatorre came out of the front door to the house, entered the Infiniti, and backed out of the driveway. Id. at 36-37. Around the same time, a black Ford Focus driven by Villanueva-Naranjo emerged from the garage and backed out of the driveway. Id. at 37-38. Delatorre then parked the Infiniti, approached the Ford, spoke briefly to Villanueva-Naranjo, returned to the Infiniti, and drove off, with the Ford following behind him. Id. at 39. Skipper tailed the two cars. At one point, when the cars had pulled up side-by-side, he observed Delatorre and Villanueva-Naranjo speaking to each other. Id. at 41. Shortly thereafter, Georgia law enforcement conducted a traffic stop on the Ford, based on a request by the DEA, and discovered over sixteen kilograms of cocaine hidden inside the side panels of that car. Id. at 45, 48, 54. A different witness, DEA agent Robert Murphy, testified that he saw Delatorre drive past the traffic stop twice, slowing down on the second occasion to look at the scene.

Jay Mortenson, another DEA agent, testified regarding the 21 April 2006 execution of a search warrant for a house in Lawrenceville, Georgia. Id. at 223, 225, 228. In the course of this search, Mortenson encountered Delatorre, for whom he had two arrest warrants. Id. at 229, 236-37. The agents conducting the search found four cellular telephones in the master bedroom as well as a notebook containing names and telephone numbers and more than $ 16,000 in cash. Id. at 239-43, 247. The assigned phone number for one of the telephones matched a number that was the subject of a DEA investigation. Id. at 241-42. In addition, a separate witness, Maria Cervantes-Suarez, who had lived in the house for two years, testified that Delatorre was a resident of the house and slept in the master bedroom.

Anthony Hall, a former drug dealer, also testified at trial. Id. at 397-98. Hall stated that sixteen kilograms of cocaine would be an amount commensurate with distribution rather than personal use. Id. at 407. He also noted that, when he was a drug dealer, he frequently changed cellular phones to avoid wiretapping and employed coded language when requesting drugs, such as "girls" for cocaine, "paper" for money, and "work" for any type of drug. Id. at 409-12. In addition to these more general topics, Hall also discussed his interactions with Delatorre and Villanueva-Naranjo. Hall first met Villanueva-Naranjo, whom he knew as "Polo," through a mutual acquaintance, Lee Braggs. Villanueva-Naranjo supplied Braggs and Hall with marijuana and cocaine, the latter ranging from two to five kilograms.

* * *

The government also called Spring Williams, who was the DEA case agent for Delatorre's case, as an expert witness on the organization and structure of Mexican drug-trafficking organizations. Delatorre conducted a voir dire examination of Williams, after which he decided not to object to her opinions, and the court deemed her to be a qualified expert in the aforementioned areas. Id. at 572-74. As part of Williams's testimony, she noted her belief that, based on her training and experience, the house in Duluth was a "stash house" – a storing place for drugs in which people might live but without the normal array of furnishings. Id. at 579-80. She also discussed her familiarity with the lingo of the drug trade, including the use of particular code words in both oral conversations and drug ledgers. Id. at 588-90. Relying on this knowledge, she stated the notebook found at the Lawrenceville house was a drug ledger because of the language used in it. Id. at 590-92.

Williams also discussed a wiretapping investigation the DEA conducted for a different case, in which they had recorded various telephone calls involving Delatorre, including one made to "Bucio," a large-scale Atlanta drug distributor. Id. at 608-09. In these telephone calls, she explained, Delatorre used coded words to identify himself as a source of drugs and discussed purchasing and supplying drugs. Id. at 616-618. Williams also testified about a number of other calls which had been wiretapped either for this investigation or another case, in many of which Delatorre was making coded statements regarding the buying, selling, and shipping of drugs. After the completion of Williams's testimony, Delatorre moved for a directed verdict on both counts of the indictment. Id. at 754. The court found that the government had presented sufficient evidence in support of its allegations and thus denied the motion. Id. at 755. Delatorre now appeals this decision as well as his convictions.

II. DISCUSSION

Delatorre raises three issues on appeal. . . . Second, he asserts that the district court erred in allowing Williams to testify as an expert witness about matters beyond the scope of her expertise.

* * *

B. Agent Williams's Testimony

Delatorre argues that the district court erred by permitting Williams to testify as an expert regarding matters outside the scope of her expertise. In particular, he takes issue with Williams's testimony regarding the proper interpretation of language in the wiretapped conversations and notebooks, which she asserted were coded drug references. Delatorre notes that since Williams was not an expert in Mexican drug traffickers, she should not have been allowed to testify regarding the meaning of certain terms allegedly used by such individuals. The government's failure to provide someone involved in the conspiracy who could independently corroborate Williams's interpretations, he asserts, effectively usurped the jury's ability to evaluate accurately and fully the evidence. In addition, Delatorre contends that the probative value of this evidence was outweighed by its prejudicial value and thus should have been inadmissible under Federal Rule of Evidence 403.

We review a district court's decisions regarding the admissibility of expert testimony and the reliability of expert opinions for abuse of discretion See United States v. Frazier, 387 F.3d 1244, 1258 (11th Cir. 2004) (en banc). The Federal Rules of Evidence permit expert witnesses to testify about any form of "specialized knowledge [that] will assist the trier of fact to understand the evidence or to determine a fact in issue" so long as they are "qualified as an expert by knowledge, skill, experience, training, or education." Fed. R. Evid. 702. The testimony is admissible if it is "based upon sufficient facts or data" and "is the product of reliable principles and methods" that the witness has applied reliably to the facts of the particular case. Id. If we find that the district court improperly allowed evidence to be introduced, we then look at whether the error would be harmless in light of the non-problematic evidence produced. See United States v. Carrazana, 921 F.2d 1557, 1568 (11th Cir. 1991) (noting that, even if drug lingo testimony was excluded, there was ample evidence in record to support defendant's drug conspiracy conviction).

Drug enforcement agents can provide expert testimony regarding drug dealing operations because of their ability "to help a jury understand the significance of certain conduct or methods of operation unique to the drug distribution business." United States v. Garcia, 447 F.3d 1327, 1335 (11th Cir. 2006) (quotation marks and citation omitted). For much the same reason, we have found that a district court's admission of expert testimony of policemen interpreting drug codes, slang, and other jargon does not violate Rule 702. See id. Delatorre correctly notes, however, that the officers whom we previously have permitted to testify as experts regarding drug jargon appear to have been more well-versed in the particular drug trafficking schemes at issue than Williams was here. See, e.g., id. (Mexican drug trafficking case in which officer took part in over 50 drug investigations, the majority of which involved Mexican drug traffickers); Carrazana, 921 F.2d at 1567 (officer in Cuban drug case was "a native Spanish speaker with an understanding of slang peculiar to the Cuban dialect"). Nevertheless, we find that Williams's knowledge of and expertise in dealing with drug trafficking schemes was sufficient experience to allow her to testify as an expert about matters relating to such organizations, including drug jargon. See Garcia, 447 F.3d at 1335 (noting that officer's past involvement with drug investigations and familiarity "with the coded language that some drug trafficking organizations use" was sufficient to make him "an experienced narcotics agent") (quotation marks omitted).

Delatorre's Rule 403 argument also fails. Evidence regarding coded drug language can be highly probative because of the often secretive nature of discussions involving drug dealers. See id. This probative value generally is sufficient to outweigh any potential prejudice, and we see no reason to view the value of Williams's testimony any differently. See id.

Accordingly, we find that the district court did not abuse its discretion in permitting Williams to testify about drug jargon based on her own experience, especially since the jury could take into account her expertise in that area. In addition, the government presented ample independent evidence concerning Delatorre's involvement in the drug conspiracy. Any error in admitting expert witness testimony therefore would be harmless.

[The convictions were affirmed.]

Cases Relating to Chapter 12

Hearsay Rule and Exceptions

BELL
v
STATE

Court of Appeal of Florida, Third District, 847 So. 2d 558, 2003

Fla. App. LEXIS 8767 (2003)

COPE, J.

Gary Paul Bell appeals his conviction and sentence for attempted kidnapping. We affirm.

Defendant-appellant Bell argues that the trial court should have excluded as hearsay the officer's testimony regarding the victim's account of the crime. The trial court admitted the testimony under the hearsay exception for excited utterances.

The victim testified that she was walking along the street during the daytime when the defendant twice drove up to her in his van and offered to give her a ride to her destination. She refused. When the victim next saw the defendant he was standing on the sidewalk with his van parked nearby. He grabbed her around the neck, held a gun to her head, and attempted to force her into the van. She broke free, ran into traffic, pounded on cars, and asked for help in getting away. The defendant, standing nearby, pointed his gun and threatened to shoot her.

The victim returned to her house and called the police. They found the victim to be hysterical and very fearful that the defendant may have followed her home. The victim was so upset that she could not speak. It took the officers fifteen or twenty minutes to calm the victim down to the point where she could give them a statement.

The hearsay exception for excited utterances applies to "[a] statement or excited utterance relating to a startling event or condition made while the declarant was under the stress of excitement caused by the event or condition." § 90.803 (2), Fla. Stat. (2001).

The Florida Supreme Court has said:

> The essential elements necessary to fall within the excited utterance exception are that (1) there must be an event startling enough to cause nervous excitement; (2) the statement must have been made before there was time to contrive or misrepresent; and (3) the statement must be made while the person is under the stress of excitement caused by the event.

The spontaneous statement exception and the excited utterance exception often overlap. However, as noted by Professor Ehrhardt:

> The two exceptions differ mainly in the amount of time that may lapse between the event and the statement describing the event. Under Section 90.803(2) it is not necessary that there be contemporaneity between the event and the statement. As long as the excited state of mind is present when the statement is made, the statement is admissible if it meets the other requirements of Section 90.803(2). This excited state may exist a substantial length of time after the event. Factors that the trial judge can consider in determining whether the necessary state of stress or excitement is present are the age of the declarant, the physical and mental condition of the declarant, the characteristics of the event and the subject matter of the statements. Whether the necessary state of mind is

present is a preliminary fact for the court to determine pursuant to Section 90.104. (citation omitted).

The defendant argues that the victim's statements in this case fail the excited utterance test because there was a time delay of approximately 50 minutes between the time of the incident and the time the victim became calm enough to speak. According to the defendant, this was sufficient time for the victim to contrive or misrepresent.

As the Jano decision indicates, however, points two and three of the test are interwoven. The theory of this hearsay exception is that so long as the declarant remains under the stress of excitement caused by the event, the declarant is unlikely to contrive or misrepresent.

In this case the investigating officer described the victim as hysterical when he first reached the house. She kept going to the window and looking outside to be sure that the defendant was not there. She was so upset she could not speak at all. The trial court permissibly concluded that the victim remained sufficiently under the stress of excitement of the event to make this an excited utterance for purposes of the hearsay exception. Henyard v. State, 689 So. 2d 239, 251 (Fla. 1996). Even if there were any error here, and we do not think there is any, we fail to see any harm as the victim herself testified and was subject to defense cross-examination on all of this.

* * *

Affirmed.

GONZALEZ v. STATE

Court of Criminal Appeals of Texas, 195 S.W.3d 114, 2006 Tex. Crim. App. LEXIS 1129 (2006)

COCHRAN

The question presented in this case of first impression is whether appellant forfeited, by his own misconduct of fatally shooting Maria Herrera during a robbery or the burglary of her home, his right to confront Maria in court about hearsay statements she made before she died. We find that he did, and we therefore affirm the judgment of the court of appeals which held the same.

I.

San Antonio police officers, responding to 911 calls, arrived at Maria and Baldomero Herrera's home shortly after 6:00 P.M. on May 3, 2002, and found that both of them had been shot. Maria lay near the front door. She was in shock, scared and bleeding, but she was still conscious and asking for help. Baldomero was sprawled unconscious in an easy chair. When officers asked her what had happened, Maria excitedly said that she and her husband had been shot by "a Latin male, blondish colored hair, and he was about 18 years old." She said "the person that did it is related to the people that live across the street in the rock house." Maria kept repeating that he had colored or bleached hair. She stated "that the guy that shot her took her truck" and "she had recognized him from—from the house across the street that had a rock wall in front of it." Maria said it was "just one person." Baldomero died at their home; Maria died at the hospital a few hours later.

Officers found the license plate number of the Herreras' new white Nissan truck and broadcast it over the police radio. There was only one house with a rock face across the street; appellant's grandmother lived there. Appellant's aunt had left him there earlier in the day. His hair was spiky and blonde on top.

* * *

While appellant was at Sylvia's apartment, a police officer on routine patrol, who had heard the broadcast about the Herreras' stolen truck, saw it parked at [appellant's cousin's] apartment complex. He radioed for assistance, and undercover officers in unmarked cars soon arrived and set up surveillance. Around 7:45 p.m., undercover officers noticed a "bleach blonde Latin," later identified as appellant, and another male walk out to the truck, then they both went back inside. At 9:20 p.m., three people, including appellant, came out of the apartment.

Appellant got into the Herreras' Nissan; the other two people got into the Ford truck. The Nissan then followed the Ford out of the apartment complex. When the SWAT officers followed behind him, appellant raced off in the stolen truck, leading officers on a sometimes high-speed chase that lasted about 15 minutes. Eventually, appellant drove down a one-way street and was blocked in by police cars. Appellant refused to get out of the truck, so he was pulled out, handcuffed, and searched. Officers found a black address book, containing Baldomero's credit cards, in his pocket. Appellant was taken to jail and his clothes, a white shirt, jeans and tennis shoes, were collected. Maria's blood was found on the tennis shoes.

The medical examiner testified that Baldomero died from a single gunshot wound to the chest; Maria, who had been shot from three to five times, died from a gunshot wound to the abdomen.

Appellant was charged with capital murder. In a motion *in limine*, and again at trial, appellant objected to the admission of Maria's statements to the police officers as hearsay and as violating his confrontation rights. The trial court held a hearing outside the presence of the jury to determine if Maria's statements to three different officers were admissible. The State argued that Maria's statements, though hearsay, were admissible under the excited utterance and dying declaration exceptions. Appellant argued that the statements were not dying declarations; he pointed to the officers' testimony that Maria was not aware of the gravity of her condition. He also argued that her statements were not excited utterances because they were not spontaneous; instead, they were answers to police questions. The trial judge doubted that the statements were dying declarations, but he admitted them "mainly under the excited utterance" exception, noting that they also fell under the hearsay exceptions for present-sense impression and then-existing physical condition. The jury convicted appellant of capital murder and sentenced him to life imprisonment.

One of appellant's claims on appeal was that the admission of Maria's out-of-court "testimonial" statements violated his right to confrontation under *Crawford* v. *Washington*, which the Supreme Court had delivered during the pendency of his appeal. The court of appeals held that Maria's statements were excited utterances and decided that it need not resolve whether they were also testimonial because appellant had forfeited his right to confrontation under the doctrine of forfeiture by wrongdoing. Noting that the Supreme Court had stated in *Crawford* that it would continue to recognize the doctrine of forfeiture by wrongdoing, which "extinguishes confrontation claims on essentially equitable grounds," the court of appeals held that "Gonzalez is precluded from objecting to the introduction of Maria's statements on Confrontation Clause grounds because it was his own criminal conduct (in this case, murder) that rendered Maria unavailable for cross-examination."

II.

In all criminal prosecutions, the accused has a Sixth Amendment right to be confronted with the witnesses against him. Even when hearsay offered against a defendant is admissible under evidentiary rules, that evidence may implicate the Confrontation Clause of the Sixth Amendment if the defendant is not afforded the opportunity to confront the out-of-court declarant. In *Crawford v. Washington*, the Supreme Court held that "where testimonial statements are at issue, the only indicium of reliability sufficient to satisfy constitutional demands is the one the Constitution actually prescribes: Confrontation." Nevertheless, the Supreme Court recognized that equitable exceptions to the Confrontation Clause may still apply, and it specifically mentioned the doctrine of forfeiture by wrongdoing which "extinguishes confrontation claims on essentially equitable grounds" as one that it accepts.

The doctrine of for feiture by wrongdoing has been a part of the common law since at least 1666. In early English cases, the doctrine allowed a witness's deposition testimony to be admitted instead of live testimony if the defendant caused the witness's absence from trial. The doctrine is based on the principle that "any tampering with a witness should once for all estop the tamperer from making any objection based on the results of his own chicanery." In other words, the rule is based on "common honesty" and the maxim that "no one shall be permitted to take advantage of his own wrong."

* * *

In 1997, the "forfeiture by wrongdoing" doctrine was codified in the Federal Rules of Evidence as a hearsay exception. By that time every circuit that had addressed the issue had recognized the doctrine of forfeiture by misconduct. The doctrine was added to Rule 804 to clarify that a party forfeits the right to object, on hearsay grounds, to the admission of a declarant's prior statement when that party's deliberate wrongdoing procured the unavailability of the declarant as a witness. As the advisory committee note explained:

> The most obvious situation for employing this exception is where a criminal defendant kills a witness, or has him killed, to prevent him from testifying; by engaging in this conduct, the defendant has forfeited the right to object on hearsay grounds to any of the victim's statements. The Rule was derived from cases that have held that a criminal defendant forfeits his right to confrontation if he causes or acquiesces in the witness' unavailability. If the defendant's conduct is such as to cause a forfeiture of the constitutional objection, it should *a fortiori* be enough to cause a forfeiture of the parallel hearsay objection.

Before the Rule 804(b)(6) hearsay exception can apply, the offering party must show that the opposing party committed the wrongdoing with the intent to prevent the declarant's testimony:

> Under the Rule, it must be shown that the party against whom the evidence is offered acted with intent to procure the unavailability of the declarant as a witness. If the defendant kills a declarant simply because he didn't like him, or because he was burned in a drug deal by him, then the defendant has not forfeited his right to object to the declarant's hearsay statement. It follows that the defendant in a murder case cannot be held to have forfeited his objection to hearsay statements made by the victim. The defendant might have murdered the victim, but he undoubtedly didn't murder the victim to prevent him from testifying in the murder trial.

Some version of the forfeiture doctrine has been adopted in various state courts. While courts have widely accepted the doctrine of forfeiture by wrongdoing to reject both hearsay objections and confrontation claims, the test for determining whether there is a forfeiture has varied. Courts have agreed that forfeiture requires (1) the declarant's unavailability, (2) as a result of the defendant's act of misconduct. Courts have disagreed on whether the defendant must intend that his act of misconduct silence the witness. Courts also have disagreed on whether evidence inadmissible under Federal Rule 804(b)(6) (*i.e.* when the predicate wrongdoing is the same crime for which the defendant is being tried) might nonetheless be admissible over a confrontation clause objection under the forfeiture doctrine.

This debate has taken on new life since the *Crawford* decision. Several courts have used the language in *Crawford* to apply the forfeiture doctrine expansively—when the wrongdoing is the same crime for which the defendant is being tried and without regard to whether the defendant intended to silence the witness. Other courts have held that the forfeiture doctrine does not apply in those situations because (1) the defendant's wrongdoing only indirectly "procured" the witness's absence; (2) the wrongful act was not done with the intent to prevent the witness from testifying; or (3) it is the same wrongful act for which the defendant is on trial.

In *United States v. Mayhew*, the district court cited to the amicus brief filed by a group of law school professors in *Crawford* to apply the forfeiture doctrine even though the defendant was on trial for the very act of murder that caused the declarant's unavailability. In their brief, the professors did not mention the role of the wrongdoer's intent. They simply stated,

> If the trial court determines as a threshold matter that the reason the victim cannot testify at trial is that the accused murdered her, then the accused should be deemed to have forfeited the confrontation right, even though the act with which the accused is charged is the same as the one by which he allegedly rendered the witness unavailable.

* * *

In the present case, the San Antonio Court of Appeals cited state-court decisions that have held the same, including the Kansas Supreme Court in *State v. Meeks* as well as Colorado and California appellate courts in *State v. Moore*, and *People v. Giles*. Some post-*Crawford* decisions have declined to apply the forfeiture doctrine when the defendant's actions did not directly cause the witness's absence or were not intended to make his testimony unavailable. For example, in *People v. Melchor*, the evidence showed that the defendant had intentionally absconded and engaged in an elaborate scheme to avoid the law for ten years, during which time the sole eyewitness to the shooting, Ortiz, died from a drug overdose. The forfeiture doctrine did not apply because there was no causal link between the defendant's misconduct and the witness's unavailability.

In sum, the majority of post-*Crawford* cases have applied the forfeiture by wrongdoing doctrine when the trial court makes a preliminary finding under Rule 104(a) that the defendant's act of misconduct caused the witness's unavailability, although some have also required that the defendant acted with the intent to prevent the witness's testimony.

III.

The determination of whether the forfeiture doctrine applies in the present case appears, at first glance, to depend upon an interpretation of the scope of the "forfeiture by wrongdoing" doctrine. We have been favored with thorough briefing by both the State and appellant. The State cites to the language in *Crawford* and in the law professors' amicus brief, and argues that the court of appeals correctly applied the forfeiture doctrine because forfeiture by wrongdoing, as an equitable doctrine, does not require the prosecution to establish the defendant's motive. Appellant, on the other hand, asserts that the doctrine cannot apply unless the State shows that the defendant engaged in the wrongdoing for the purpose of preventing the witness from testifying at a future trial. Appellant notes that pre-*Crawford*, the doctrine was generally applied only in the context of witness tampering, and that the Supreme Courts in Pennsylvania, Alaska, and New York had expressly held that the doctrine does not apply where the defendant murders the declarant for personal reasons rather than to prevent the declarant from testifying. Appellant faults post-*Crawford* cases applying the doctrine as the court of appeals did in this case for fastening on language in *Crawford* and [another case], without sufficient analysis of the history and intent of the rule.

We need not settle that dispute in this case. An examination of the entire record clearly supports the inference that appellant shot the Herreras to silence them. They knew him. They lived across the street from his grandmother and were friends with her and other members of her family. Appellant entered the Herreras' home without a disguise and with a very distinguishing characteristic—his dark hair dyed blonde. Indeed, there was no sign of forced entry, so he was either welcomed or walked through an unlocked door. Appellant entered the Herreras' home armed. And he shot to kill. Baldomero, who had not even gotten up from his easy chair, was shot through the heart. Maria was also shot in the chest—and when she did not die appellant shot her again and again. Both were shot from beyond two feet. Both were left for dead.

A logical inference is that appellant killed the Herreras because he wanted to steal their truck and their money, and he didn't want any witnesses to his crime—especially witnesses that knew him, and knew where to find him. This case is factually different from the post-*Crawford* cases that the court of appeals relied on. Those cases involved passion or revenge killings—killings for personal reasons. There was no evidence in this case that appellant had any personal grudge against the Herreras; the evidence strongly supports the inference that appellant committed burglary or robbery for financial gain and then murdered the two witnesses who could identify him.

We agree with those post-*Crawford* cases and the *Crawford* amicus brief that the doctrine of forfeiture by wrongdoing may apply even though the act with which the accused is charged is the same as the one by which he allegedly rendered the witness unavailable. The trial court in this case did not make a preliminary ruling on whether appellant killed Maria, at least in part, to prevent her from testifying against him because this case was tried before *Crawford* was decided. Nonetheless, an evidentiary ruling, such as the one admitting Maria's out-of-court statements, will be upheld on appeal if it is correct on any theory of law that finds support in the record. We agree with the court of appeals that the record provides ample support for the admission of Maria's out-of-court statements, despite appellant's Confrontation Clause objection, because appellant forfeited his right to confront Maria by his own wrongful act. The evidence strongly suggests that the procurement of Maria's absence was motivated, at least in part, by appellant's desire to permanently silence her and prevent her from identifying him. We express no opinion on the court of appeals's broader holding that the procurement of a witness's absence need not be motivated by a desire to silence the declarant for the forfeiture by wrongdoing doctrine to apply.

We affirm the judgment of the court of appeals.

Johnson, J., *filed a concurring opinion.*

I concur in the judgment of the Court. First, I think that Mrs. Herrera's statements were admissible as a dying declaration. Despite the police officers' assertions that she was not aware of the gravity of her situation, no one seems to have inquired of her what her perception of her injuries was. Certainly she was aware that she had been shot multiple times, including a gunshot wound to the abdomen. Under such circumstances, it is probable that she understood quite clearly the gravity of her situation. The *Crawford* Court conceded that dying declarations may, by historical imperative, be admissible, despite the lack of an opportunity to cross-examine.

There is also the argument that Mrs. Herrera's statements were not testimonial. Depending on the circumstances, a police officer asking, "What happened?" may or may not be interrogation. Even if her statements were testimonial and the trial court erred in admitting them, I would find the error harmless. The Herreras' truck was missing, a fact easily ascertained from sources other than Mrs. Herrera's statements. The license plate number was also easily ascertainable by law officers. A bulletin about the missing truck was broadcast to police officers. An officer on routine patrol saw the truck and called for assistance. After a chase, officers stopped the truck and arrested appellant, the driver, who had Mr. Herrera's credit cards in his pocket and Mrs. Herrera's blood on his shoes. With such evidence, Mrs. Herrera's statements were superfluous.

I do not think that this is the right case in which to consider expanding the concept of forfeiture by wrongdoing. The basis for such an expansion seems to be based on federal Rule of Evidence 804(b)(4), which by its very terms does not apply in this case. In addition, there is a logical disconnect in saying that a defendant killed a person to prevent them from testifying at the defendant's trial for killing that person; if the defendant did not kill the person, there would be no murder trial and hence no need to suppress damaging testimony, so killing the person creates the reason for killing the person. Such reasoning is circular and should not be incorporated into the law.

COX
v.
STATE

Court of Appeals of Indiana, Second District
774 N.E.2d 1025, 2002 Ind. App. LEXIS 1533 (2002)

JUDGES: ROBB, Judge. RILEY, J., and MATTINGLY-MAY, J., concur.

James Cox was convicted following a bench trial of domestic battery, a Class A misdemeanor. Cox appeals his conviction. We affirm.

Issues

Cox raises two issues for our review, which we restate as follows:

1. Whether the trial court properly admitted hearsay testimony under the excited utterance hearsay exception; and
2. Whether the State presented sufficient evidence to support his conviction.

Facts and Procedural History

Deputy Sheriff Daniel Herrick responded to a radio dispatch of a reported battery on October 12, 2001. When he arrived at the scene, he observed Cox standing in front of an apartment building talking to another police officer. Deputy Herrick found Denise Hogan inside the apartment building a few minutes later. He noticed that she was crying and shaking and appeared to be very upset. He also noticed that she was talking very quickly and showed signs of a fresh injury. Hogan had a cut above her eye which was bleeding, her left eye was swollen and she was holding an ice pack to her eye. Additionally, she had marks on her neck that appeared to have been caused by someone grabbing her on her neck.

Hogan told Deputy Herrick how she sustained the injuries and that it was Cox who injured her. At trial, Deputy Herrick testified to the statements Hogan made to him. Cox objected, asserting that Herrick's testimony was hearsay. The State responded that the statements were being offered under the "excited utterance" exception. The trial court allowed the testimony.

Following the trial, the trial court found Cox guilty of domestic battery. This appeal ensued.

Discussion and Decision

I. Admission of Testimony

A. Standard of Review

Our standard of review in this area is well settled. The admission of evidence is within the sound discretion of the trial court, and the decision whether to admit evidence will not be reversed absent a showing of manifest abuse of the trial court's discretion resulting in the denial of a fair trial. Prewitt v. State, 761 N.E.2d 862, 869 (Ind. Ct. App. 2002). An abuse of discretion involves a decision that is clearly against the logic and effect of the facts and circumstances before the court. Id. In determining the admissibility of evidence, the reviewing court will only consider the evidence in favor of the trial court's ruling and any unrefuted evidence in the defendant's favor. Id.

B. Admission of Deputy Herrick's Testimony

Hearsay is a statement made out-of-court that is offered into evidence to prove the fact or facts asserted in the statement itself. Ind. Evidence Rule 801(c); Craig v. State, 630 N.E.2d 207, 209 (Ind. 1994). In the present case, the contested portions of Deputy Herrick's testimony constitute hearsay. Hogan made the statements out-of-court and Deputy Herrick repeated the statements at trial, for the purpose of proving the facts asserted in the out-of-court statements, namely that Cox struck and choked Hogan. Such hearsay is not admissible at trial unless it fits within some exception to the hearsay rule. Craig, 630 N.E.2d at 207.

Cox contends that the hearsay testimony of Deputy Herrick is inadmissible because it does not fit into any hearsay exception and because Hogan did not appear for trial. Alternatively, he contends that, if the testimony falls under the excited utterance exception, then the State failed to lay a proper foundation for the evidence. We disagree.

The excited utterance exception is found in Evidence Rule 803(2). The rule provides that:

> The following are not excluded from the hearsay rule, even though the declarant is available as a witness.
>
> * * *
>
> (2) A statement relating to a startling event or condition made while the declarant was under the stress of excitement caused by the event or condition.

For a hearsay statement to be admitted as an excited utterance under Evidence Rule 803(2), three elements must be shown: (1) a startling event occurs; (2) a statement is made by a declarant while under the stress of excitement caused by the event; and (3) the statement relates to the event. Jenkins v. State, 725 N.E.2d 66, 68 (Ind. 2000). This is not a mechanical test; it turns on whether the statement was inherently reliable because the witness was under the stress of an event and unlikely to make deliberate falsifications. Id. Additionally, while the time period between the startling event and a subsequent statement is, of course, one factor to consider in determining whether the statement was an excited utterance, no precise length of time is required. Simmons v. State, 760 N.E.2d 1154, 1161 (Ind. Ct. App. 2002).

Cox argues that Hogan's absence makes her statement inadmissible hearsay. However, the language of Rule 803 makes it clear that the exceptions listed are not excluded from the hearsay rule, "even though the declarant is available as a witness." Evid. R. 803. Therefore, Rule 803 lists exceptions which are not hearsay regardless of whether the declarant is available. The fact that Hogan did not appear for trial has no effect on Deputy Herrick's testimony. Hogan's statements to Deputy Herrick fit squarely within the excited utterance exception and were admissible at trial.

Cox also argues that the State failed to lay a proper foundation for the excited utterance exception. We disagree.

We have recently held that a victim's statement made to a police officer after a battery constituted an excited utterance. Gordon v. State, 743 N.E.2d 376, 378 (Ind. Ct. App. 2001). In Gordon, a police officer was dispatched to an apartment complex where he found a woman who was shaking and had redness about her neck. The woman told the officer that her boyfriend had struck her. Because the woman did not testify at trial, Gordon argued that the police officer's testimony was inadmissible hearsay. This court examined the circumstances surrounding the statements made by the victim and held that it was reasonable to infer that the woman was upset because of a startling event and that the event was the physical altercation she described to the officer. Id.

As in Gordon, we find that Hogan's statements to Deputy Herrick satisfy the conditions for excited utterances. The record reflects that Hogan placed a 911 call at 2:21 a.m., that Deputy Herrick was dispatched to the scene at approximately 2:33 a.m., and that he arrived there within minutes of receiving the dispatch. n1 Deputy Herrick testified that Hogan was crying and shaking and appeared to be upset when he spoke with her. It is clear that Hogan was still upset by a startling event, which she had reported in the 911 call only minutes before; it is also reasonable to infer that the startling event that caused her visible distress was the physical altercation with Cox that she described to Deputy Herrick.

Cox also contends that the State failed to lay a proper foundation for the excited utterance exception because he asserts that Hogan was capable of thoughtful reflection when she made the statements to Deputy Herrick. In support of this, Cox compares Hogan's voice on the 911 call with Deputy Herrick's testimony regarding Hogan's emotional state when he interviewed her. Specifically, Cox seems to be arguing that Deputy Herrick testified that Hogan was calm when he interviewed her. However, our review of the record reveals that Deputy Herrick testified that Hogan was upset and crying. The trial court did not abuse its discretion in finding that the State had laid a proper foundation through Deputy Herrick's testimony regarding Hogan's emotional state.

* * *

Our supreme court examined the requirements for a statement to be considered an excited utterance and found the victim's statement met these requirements. 694 N.E.2d at 1140-41. The main question was whether the victim's statement met the requirements for an excited utterance because the victim was answering questions from the officer rather than making his own statements. 694 N.E.2d at 1141. The court noted that the officer did not suggest who the shooter was and there was no evidence that someone had coerced the victim to falsely name Montgomery. Id. Therefore, the court held that the hearsay testimony was properly admitted under the excited utterance exception.

We are presented with facts similar to Montgomery in the present case. Deputy Herrick was the first person at the scene to talk with Hogan. He asked her questions and she identified Cox as the person who had hit her. Cox has presented no evidence that Deputy Herrick suggested Cox's name to Hogan or that someone had coerced Hogan to Identify Cox as her assailant. Therefore, because Hogan's statements to Deputy Herrick satisfy the requirements for excited utterances and Cox has presented no evidence of coercion, the trial court did not abuse its discretion in admitting Deputy Herrick's testimony under the excited utterance hearsay exception.

* * *

Conclusion

The trial court did not abuse its discretion in admitting Deputy Herrick's testimony under the excited utterance hearsay exception. Additionally, there was sufficient evidence to support Cox's conviction. Therefore, Cox's conviction is affirmed.

SADLER v. STATE

Court of Appeal of Texas 2009

Tex. App. LEXIS 2962 (2009)

OPINION BY: Felipe Reyna.

MEMORANDUM OPINION

A jury convicted Michael Shawn Sadler of murder and assessed his punishment at thirty years' imprisonment. Sadler argues on appeal that the court erred by: (1) admitting evidence of an extraneous offense; (2) permitting the State to impeach his fiance on a collateral issue; (3) admitting various hearsay statements which did not qualify under exceptions for excited utterances, statements made for purposes of medical diagnosis or treatment, or dying declarations; (4) admitting a videotaped interview of the victim in violation of Sadler's right of confrontation; and (5) admitting a prior written statement which was not inconsistent with his testimony. We will affirm.

Sadler, Luis Castillo, and others were attending a gathering on a Saturday night at the apartment of Rachel Byrd. At some point, an argument arose between Sadler and Castillo which involved some pushing and shoving. The party ended around 1:30 or 2:00 in the morning. When Sadler left, he called Byrd and told her that Castillo was injured and lying in the parking lot. Byrd and Larry Whatley went out and found Castillo lying on the ground, injured badly, and unable to move his arms or legs. Castillo told them that Sadler had assaulted him. He did not want to seek medical attention so they carried him into Byrd's apartment.

Around 8:00 or 8:30 that morning, Byrd called for an ambulance, and Castillo was taken to the local hospital in Clifton. Because of the extent of his injuries, he was later transported to Scott & White Hospital in Temple. The treating physician at Scott & White testified that Castillo essentially suffered a broken neck. He was placed on a ventilator within a few hours after his arrival at Scott & White.

Clifton Police Chief Rex Childress received a call from Scott & White on Wednesday advising that Castillo was about to be taken off the ventilator at his own request and that he may not survive for long afterward. Childress went to the hospital to conduct a videotaped interview that afternoon. During the interview, Castillo indicated that Sadler had assaulted him.

With limited treatment options available, Castillo was taken off the ventilator. He died about two weeks after the assault.

* * *

Dying Declaration

Sadler argues in his fourth point that the court abused its discretion by admitting the testimony of Beki Bollinger under the dying declarations exception to the hearsay rule. Specifically, Sadler contends that Bollinger's testimony is not admissible under this exception because there is nothing to suggest that Castillo believed his death was imminent when he talked to her.

Bollinger was Castillo's employer. She came to see him at Scott & White on Monday morning. Over objection, Bollinger testified that, when she asked Castillo who had assaulted him, she read his lips to indicate that "Michael" had done it. 5 See TEX. R. EVID. 801(a) (defining in part a "statement" for purposes of the hearsay rule as "nonverbal conduct of a person, if it is intended by the person as a substitute for verbal expression"). Bollinger continued to talk with Castillo about the assault.

> After Luis had been read his last rites, and made the decision to have the ventilator taken off of him and he knew that it was a possibility he was going to pass I was standing by his side and [at] that moment he could speak. And I asked him, "Luis, why did Michael do this to you?"

Over Sadler's objection, Bollinger was permitted to tell the jury Castillo's answer, which was, "Michael probably gottie too much mad."

> A statement meets the dying declaration exception to the hearsay rule if the declarant is unavailable at the time of trial and the statement is "[a] statement made by a declarant while believing that the declarant's death was imminent, concerning the cause or circumstances of what the declarant believed to be impending death." . . . A declarant's belief that death was imminent "may be inferred from the circumstances of the case, such as the nature of the injury, medical opinions stated to him, or his conduct."

Martinez v. State, 17 S.W.3d 677, 689 (Tex. Crim. App. 2000) (quoting TEX. R. EVID. 804 (b)(2); Thomas v. State, 699 S.W.2d 845, 853 (Tex. Crim. App. 1985)) (citations omitted).

Here, Castillo was unavailable at trial because of his death. It is undisputed that his injuries were severe and his prognosis was grim. Given the extent of his injuries, Bollinger's impression that he knew there was a possibility he would die after being removed from the ventilator, and the giving of last rites, we cannot say that the court abused its discretion by admitting Bollinger's testimony under the dying declarations exception to the hearsay rule. See id.; Medrano v. State, 701 S.W.2d 337, 339 (Tex. App.–El Paso 1985, pet. ref'd). Sadler's fourth point is overruled.

* * *

We affirm the judgment.

STATE v. WASHINGTON

Supreme Court of Michigan, 664 N.W.2d 203, 2003 Mich. LEXIS 1465 (2003)

JUDGES: Chief Justice Maura D. Corrigan, Justices Michael F. Cavanagh, Elizabeth A. Weaver, Marilyn Kelly, Clifford W. Taylor, Robert P. Young, Jr., Stephen J. Markman. KELLY, J. (dissenting).

OPINION: PER CURIAM

Defendant was convicted of armed robbery and assault with intent to do great bodily harm less than murder. The Court of Appeals reversed the convictions because the accomplice's statement, in which the accomplice identified himself as the shooter, was improperly admitted against defendant. 251 Mich. App. 520; 650 N.W.2d 708 (2002). It also found that the trial court abused its discretion in denying defense counsel the opportunity to conduct voir dire of a juror in mid-trial. We reverse the judgment of the Court of Appeals and reinstate the verdict.

I.

On May 8, 1998, two men robbed James Turner while he was using a public pay phone at a Detroit gas station. One of the men pulled a gun, pointed it at Turner's head, and demanded money. The other went through Turner's pockets and took his watch and pager. When Turner told his assailants that he didn't have anything else of value, he was shot in the back.

A few minutes later, two police officers saw a car containing defendant and Daniel Mathis drive into an alley behind a gas station that was approximately a mile from the scene of the robbery. The officers decided to investigate because the area was known for drug sales and prostitution. Defendant was uncooperative with the officers and, following a scuffle, he was handcuffed pending further investigation. As the officers returned to talk to Mathis, who had remained in the car, the report of the Turner robbery and a description of his assailants were broadcast over the police radio. When one of the officers asked to have the description repeated, Mathis blurted out, "I did it—I'm the shooter." Turner identified defendant in a lineup as one of his assailants. He failed to identify Mathis.

Defendant and Mathis were charged with armed robbery, MCL 750.529, and assault with intent to murder, MCL 750.83. They were tried separately. On the morning of defendant's trial, the issue whether Mathis's statement was admissible was raised. Without elaboration, the trial court decided that the statement would be allowed into evidence. Defendant was convicted of armed robbery and assault with intent to do great bodily harm less than murder, MCL 750.84.

The Court of Appeals reversed defendant's convictions. It concluded that Mathis's statement was improperly admitted as a statement against penal interest because it was not reliable. According to assertions made by defense counsel, Mathis was mentally ill. n1 In addition, the panel found that the trial court should have allowed defense counsel to question a juror in mid-trial.

II.

The decision to admit evidence is reviewed for an abuse of discretion. People v Starr, 457 Mich. 490, 494; 577 N.W.2d 673 (1998). When the decision regarding the admission of evidence involves a preliminary question of law, such as whether a statute or rule of evidence precludes admissibility of the evidence, the issue is reviewed de novo. People v Lukity, 460 Mich. 484, 488; 596 N.W.2d 607 (1999).

III.

Declarations against penal interest constitute an exception to the general proscription against hearsay provided by MRE 802. MRE 804(b)(3), in pertinent part, defines a declaration against penal interest as

> [a] statement which was at the time of its making . . . so far tended to subject the declarant to civil or criminal liability . . . that a reasonable person in the declarant's position would not have made the statement unless believing it to be true. A statement tending to expose the declarant to criminal liability and offered to exculpate the accused is not admissible unless corroborating circumstances clearly indicate the trustworthiness of the statement.

The exception is based on the assumption that people do not generally make statements about themselves that are damaging unless they are true. People v Poole, 444 Mich. 151, 161; 506 N.W.2d 505 (1993), citing the comment of the Advisory Committee on Federal Rules of Evidence relating to FRE 804(b)(3). Mathis's statement is against his penal interest and, therefore, is admissible.

The inquiry, however, does not stop there because the Confrontation Clauses of the federal and state constitutions are implicated. US Const, Am VI; Const 1963, art 1, § 20. The admission of Mathis's statement as substantive evidence does not violate the Confrontation Clause if the prosecution can establish that Mathis was unavailable as a witness and that his statement bore adequate indicia of reliability. Alternatively, the Confrontation Clause is not violated if the statement fell within a firmly rooted hearsay exception. Poole, *supra* at 163.

Some jurisdictions have held that the hearsay exception for statements against penal interest is a firmly rooted hearsay exception. See, e.g., United States v McKeeve, 131 F.3d 1, 9 (CA 1, 1997), People v Wilson, 17 Cal App 4th 271, 278; 21 Cal. Rptr. 2d 420 (1993), and State v Tucker, 109 Ore. App. 519, 526; 820 P.2d 834 (1991). However, we need not decide that issue because Mathis had been charged with the crimes and was considered unavailable because it was expected that he would assert his Fifth Amendment right not to testify. Additionally, Mathis's statement bears adequate indicia of reliability.

In Poole, *supra* at 165, we instructed:

> In evaluating whether a statement against penal interest that inculpates a person in addition to the declarant bears sufficient indicia of reliability to allow it to be admitted as substantive evidence against the other person, courts must evaluate the circumstances surrounding the making of the statement as well as its content.

The presence of the following factors would favor admission of such a statement: whether the statement was (1) voluntarily given, (2) made contemporaneously with the events referenced, (3) made to family, friends, colleagues, or confederates—that is, to someone to whom the declarant would likely speak the truth, and (4) uttered spontaneously at the initiation of the declarant and without prompting or inquiry by the listener.

On the other hand, the presence of the following factors would favor a finding of inadmissibility: whether the statement (1) was made to law enforcement officers or at the prompting or inquiry of the listener, (2) minimizes the role or responsibility of the declarant or shifts blame to the accomplice, (3) was made to avenge the declarant or to curry favor, and (4) whether the declarant had a motive to lie or distort the truth.

Courts should also consider any other circumstance bearing on the reliability of the statement at issue. See, generally, United States v Layton, 855 F.2d 1388, 1404-1406 (CA 9, 1988). While the foregoing factors are not exclusive, and the presence or absence of a particular factor is not decisive, the totality of the circumstances must indicate that the statement is sufficiently reliable to allow its admission as substantive evidence although the defendant is unable to cross-examine the declarant.

When those precepts are applied to the facts at bar, we find that Mathis's statement to the police officers bears sufficient indicia of reliability to satisfy Confrontation Clause concerns and to allow its admission as substantive evidence at trial. The statement was voluntarily given and made contemporaneously with the events referenced. It was uttered spontaneously by Mathis and without prompting or inquiry by the officers. In fact, the officers had just heard of the robbery when Mathis made the statement. Mathis did not minimize his role in the crimes, admitting that he shot the victim, and he had no motive to lie or distort the truth. In addition, there is nothing in the statement indicating that the declarant was attempting to curry favor at the time he made the statement.

We agree with the dissenting judge of the Court of Appeals that there was no record evidence establishing that Mathis "suffered from mental illness." The unsubstantiated assertions of defense counsel are not substantive evidence and cannot be used to undermine the indicia of reliability contained in the accomplice's statement.

IV.

* * *

V.

We conclude that the accomplice's statement contains sufficient "particularized guarantees of trustworthiness," considering the totality of the circumstances surrounding its utterance, to justify its admission. Poole, *supra* at 164.

* * *

Accordingly, we reverse the judgment of the Court of Appeals and reinstate the judgment of the circuit court. MCR 7.302(F)(1).

Cases Relating to Chapter 13

Documentary Evidence

WILKERSON v. STATE

Court of Appeals of Arkansas, Division Two, 2005 Ark. App. LEXIS 12 (2005)

ROBERT J. GLADWIN, Judge. HART and BAKER, JJ., agree.

ROBERT J. GLADWIN, Judge

Appellant Jeffery Scott Wilkerson seeks the reversal of his conviction for delivering a Schedule VI controlled substance—marijuana. On appeal, appellant argues that the trial court erred: (1) by denying his motion for a directed verdict because there was insufficient evidence to support the conviction; (2) in admitting into evidence a tape recording between a confidential informant and appellant that was not properly authenticated; (3) in failing to suppress evidence where the application for search warrant failed to set forth particular facts bearing on the informant's reliability; (4) by denying his motion to suppress where the search warrant did not indicate that it was based upon either recorded testimony or sworn affidavits. We affirm.

Lonnie Cogburn testified that while he was working as a confidential informant for Officer Chris Martin, he contacted appellant in an effort to purchase marijuana. Officer Martin equipped Cogburn with a micro-cassette recorder and gave him a twenty-dollar bill and a ten-dollar bill as buy money, both of which were photocopied by the police for verification purposes. On or about January 15, 2003, Cogburn met appellant on the road and asked him about the drugs, at which time appellant handed him the marijuana through the car window in exchange for the thirty dollars. Cogburn then returned to Officer Martin and gave him the quarter-bag of marijuana and the micro-cassette recorder and tape.

On or about January 23, 2003, appellant was charged with the delivery of a Schedule VI controlled substance, a Class C felony, pursuant to Ark. Code Ann. § 5-64-401(a)(1)(iv) for allegedly delivering to a confidential informant, directly supervised by an officer with the 18th West Judicial District Drug Task Force, marijuana, the aggregate weight of which, including adulterants or dilutents, was less than one ounce. A trial was held on September 2, 2003, and appellant was convicted by a Montgomery County jury, sentenced to six years in the Arkansas Department of Correction, and ordered to pay a $ 5000 fine. This appeal followed.

Denial of motion for directed verdict

The standard of review in cases challenging the sufficiency of the evidence is well established. We treat a motion for a directed verdict as a challenge to the sufficiency of the evidence. . . . .

Arkansas Code Annotated section 5-64-401 provides that it is unlawful for any person to deliver a controlled substance. "Delivery" is defined as the actual, constructive, or attempted transfer of a controlled substance or counterfeit substance in exchange for money or anything of value. See Ark. Code Ann. § 5-64-101(f). There was testimony from Cogburn, the confidential informant who supposedly bought the marijuana, describing the details of the "buy" from appellant.

There was also a tape recording of the transaction; however, no written transcript of the tape is available to confirm its corroboration of Cogburn's testimony. There was also evidence that the specific twenty-dollar bill and ten-dollar bill that were given to Cogburn as buy money were found in appellant's wallet at the time of his arrest, as verified by the photocopies previously made by the police and by testimony from Officer Martin. Resolution of conflicts in testimony and assessment of witness credibility is for the fact-finder. *Slater* v. *State*, 76 Ark. App. 365, 65 S.W.3d 481 (2002). There was substantial evidence to support appellant's conviction for delivery of a controlled substance.

Admitting into evidence a tape recording between the a confidential informant and appellant that allegedly was not properly authenticated.

Appellant alleges that the micro-cassette recording purporting to corroborate Cogburn's description of the drug buy was erroneously allowed into evidence without proper authentication under Rule 901 of the Arkansas Rules of Evidence. Rule 901(a) specifically states that the requirement of authentication or identification as a condition precedent to admissibility is satisfied by evidence sufficient to support a finding that the matter in question is what its proponent claims. Appellant argues that prior to the admission of the recording, none of the parties speaking on the recording testified that it was a true and accurate depiction of the conversation, and he further contends that Officer Martin was not present when that conversation took place.

Officer Martin testified that after Cogburn left with the thirty dollars and the micro-cassette recorder, there were numerous times during the course of the drug buy that Cogburn was out of his sight. Appellant attempts to distinguish the facts of this case from those in *Smithey v. State*, 269 Ark. 538, 602 S.W.2d 676 (Ark. App. 1980), where the Arkansas Supreme Court found proper authentication where the officer involved testified that he saw the informant talking with the defendant while the officer listened to the conversation electronically and watched a videotape of the parties. In the instant case, Cogburn was the only witness for the State who was present when the recording was made, and he testified that he had never listened to it.

Additionally, Officer Martin testified that he had limited knowledge about the recording, in that he only knew what the recording itself told him about the interaction between Cogburn and appellant. Appellant maintains that this scenario is markedly different from the facts in *Walker v. State*, 13 Ark. App. 124, 680 S.W.2d 915 (1984), where the supreme court found that where one of the undercover officers who was present when the tapes were recorded testified as to their accuracy and authenticity, the officer's testimony was sufficient to authenticate the recordings.

Officer Martin testified that he gave Cogburn the micro-cassette recorder and then followed him around "as best as [he] could" until Cogburn returned with the recorder and the marijuana he purchased from appellant. Officer Martin explained that there were times Cogburn was out of his sight because he could not follow Cogburn too closely, considering that everyone knew the vehicle he drove and that he did not want to put either Cogburn or himself in danger. Officer Martin stated that after receiving the tape and recorder back from Cogburn, he took it to the police department and logged it into the evidence vault. He testified that the transaction lasted only seconds and that he had listened to the tape many times since receiving it from Cogburn. The State reiterates that the tape recording is corroborated by Cogburn's testimony regarding the transaction. The State argues that the authentication requirement of Rule 901(a) is satisfied where a trial judge, in his discretion, is satisfied that the physical evidence presented is genuine and in reasonable probability has not been tampered with. *Guydon v. State*, 344 Ark. 251, 39 S. W.3d 767 (2001).

In evidentiary determinations, a trial court has wide discretion, and we will not reverse a trial court's ruling on the admission of the evidence absent an abuse of discretion. *See Davis v. State,* 350 Ark. 22, 86 S.W.3d 872 (2002). Further, we do not reverse a trial court's evidentiary decision absent a showing of prejudice. *Id.* The tape was properly introduced, and the content of the recording goes to the weight of the evidence rather than to its admissibility. There is also substantial evidence of appellant's guilt, including Cogburn's eyewitness account of the buy, as well as the "buy money" being recovered from appellant's wallet upon his arrest. The tape recording of the drug buy is cumulative, and any error occasioned by the trial court's admission of the recording was rendered harmless beyond a reasonable doubt by the admission of the other evidence. *See Jackson v. State*, __ Ark. __, __ S.W.3d __, 2004 Ark. LEXIS 638 (Nov. 4, 2004).

* * *

[The defendant's other arguments possessed insufficient merit to obtain a reversal of his conviction.]

Affirmed.

HART and BAKER, JJ., agree.

STATE v. HUEHN

Court of Appeals of Colorado, Division Five, 53 P.3d 733, 2002 Colo. App. LEXIS 21 (2002)

JUDGES: Opinion by JUDGE VOGT

Kapelke and Erickson, JJ., concur.

Defendant, Daniel Huehn, appeals the judgment of conviction entered on a jury verdict finding him guilty of theft. We affirm.

On December 24, 1998, technicians responding to a call to service a Key Bank automated teller machine (ATM) discovered that the safe at the bottom of the machine was unlocked and the money cassettes normally found there were missing. The cassettes had been in the safe when the ATM was serviced on the morning of December 23, and customers had withdrawn money from the machine throughout that day. Computer records showed that the safe had been opened at approximately 9:30 p.m. on December 23, although there had been no call for service at that hour.

Defendant, one of the ATM technicians who had access to this machine, admitted in a written statement to his employer that he had opened the safe sometime between 8:30 and 9:30 p.m. on December 23 while at the site on a call regarding another ATM. He claimed, however, that the cassettes were still in the safe at that time.

I.

Defendant first contends that the trial court abused its discretion in admitting into evidence certain computer-generated records that were not sufficiently authenticated. We disagree.

The exhibits at issue are computer records reflecting customer transactions and technician servicing at the ATM on December 23 and 24, 1998. Four of the exhibits were records generated for Key Bank by Money Access Services (MAC), with whom Key Bank had contracted to process its ATM transactions. Defendant objected to admission of these records on the grounds that there was an insufficient foundation for their admission as business records under CRE 803(6) and the records were not authenticated in accordance with CRE 901(b)(9). The trial court overruled the objections and admitted the exhibits.

Although he did not object on this basis at trial, defendant also contends on appeal that Exhibit 14, a portion of a status tape that recorded the openings and closings of the ATM vault on a hard drive inside the machine, should have been excluded for lack of authentication.

A.

As an initial matter, we reject defendant's contention that, because computer-generated evidence is "a species of scientific evidence," the prosecution had to make the showing required under Frye v. United States, 54 App. D.C. 46, 293 F. 1013 (D.C. Cir. 1923), or Daubert v. Merrell Dow Pharmaceuticals, Inc., 509 U.S. 579, 113 S. Ct. 2786, 125 L. Ed. 2d 469 (1993), before the evidence could be admitted. See People v. Shreck, 22 P.3d 68 (Colo. 2001)(CRE 702, rather than Frye, governs admissibility of scientific evidence).

In support of his contention, defendant cites R. Bailin et. al., Colorado Evidentiary Foundations (Miche 1997). However, that authority itself recognizes that, while presentation of scientific evidence usually requires proof of the validity of the underlying theory and the reliability of the instrument, "computers are so widely accepted and used that the proponent of computer evidence need not prove those two elements of the foundation." Colorado Evidentiary Foundations, *supra*, ch. 4(C)(2), at 52; see also Brooks v. People, 975 P.2d 1105, 1112 n.7 (Colo. 1999)(rejecting view that "whenever one can find 'science' by scratching beneath the surface of expert testimony, the validation rules governing scientific evidence would have to apply").

The trial court in this case properly focused its inquiry on whether a sufficient foundation had been laid to warrant admission of the proffered records under the applicable rules of evidence.

B.

The admissibility of a computer printout is governed by the rules of relevancy, authentication, and hearsay. Benham v. Pryke, 703 P.2d 644 (Colo. App. 1985), rev'd on other grounds, 744 P.2d 67 (Colo. 1987). The relevancy of the computer records in this case is not disputed.

The requirement of authentication as a condition precedent to admissibility is satisfied by evidence sufficient to support a finding that the matter in question is what its proponent claims. CRE 901 (a). Whether a proper foundation has been established is a matter within the sound discretion of the trial court, whose decision will not be disturbed absent a clear abuse of that discretion. People v. Slusher, 844 P.2d 1222 (Colo. App. 1992).

* * *

C.

Here, Key Bank's ATM accounting supervisor testified that transactions at the bank's ATMs are electronically communicated to, and recorded by, MAC, which handles the processing of the transactions. MAC's computer-generated reports for each ATM are transmitted daily to Key Bank, stored for three months in Key Bank's computer, then transferred to fiche. The witness testified that Key Bank received and stored the records in the ordinary course of its business, and he identified the exhibits at issue as accurate copies of Key Bank's fiche record of activity at the ATM on the relevant dates.

A representative of the company that serviced Key Bank's ATMs testified similarly that the status tapes for the ATMs are kept inside the ATMs on the hard drive and automatically record each opening and closing of the safe.

It was undisputed that the entries on all the exhibits were made within a reasonable time of the transactions involved.

Defendant contends that this testimony was insufficient to satisfy the requirements for admitting computer records under CRE 803(6) because (1) the first four exhibits were MAC records but were not introduced by anyone from MAC, and (2) the prosecution did not show that the computer input procedures were accurate by complying with the authentication procedure in CRE 901(b)(9). We reject both contentions.

1.

The fact that the records created by MAC were introduced through the Key Bank officer, whose department received and kept the records, did not preclude their admission under CRE 803 (6). See Hauser v. Rose Health Care Systems, 857 P.2d 524 (Colo. App. 1993)(documents created by one business but regularly received, maintained, and relied upon by another may be admitted as business records of the latter); Teac Corp. v. Bauer, 678 P.2d 3 (Colo. App. 1984) (records prepared by another source that are adopted and integrated in regular course of established business procedures into records sought to be introduced are admissible under CRE 803(6), even if identity of person whose first-hand knowledge was the basis of a particular entry is not established).

2.

Defendant also argues that, to establish the accuracy of the input procedures, the prosecution was required to proceed in accordance with CRE 901(b)(9), which permits authentication by "evidence describing a process or system used to produce a result and showing that the process or system produces an accurate result." This showing was not made, he contends, because the Key Bank foundation witness admitted on cross-examination that he did not know how or when the MAC computer had been programmed, whether it had been repaired, or whether procedures were used to ensure the accuracy of the program. Nor did the authentication witness for Exhibit 14, the status list, testify that the system that generated the list produced an accurate result.

Defendant acknowledges that Colorado cases have not previously required compliance with CRE 901(b)(9) as a condition of admitting computer-generated business records. However, he cites Colorado Evidentiary Foundations, *supra*, for the proposition that Colorado courts have been "lax" in applying the authentication requirement to computer records, admitting them with "minimal analysis of authenticity issues," and he argues that we should require such further authentication in this case. We decline to do so.

First, although CRE 901(b)(9) may be used to authenticate computer records, there is no requirement, either in the rule itself or in Colorado case law construing the rule, that computer records be authenticated only in this way.

Second, computer business records have a greater level of trustworthiness than an individually generated computer document such as that at issue in People v. Slusher, *supra*, relied on by defendant, in which a division of this court upheld the exclusion of a purported lease agreement that was apparently created by the defendant on his computer.

Finally, courts have generally declined to require testimony regarding the functioning and accuracy of the computer process where, as here, the records at issue are bank records reflecting data entered automatically rather than manually. See United States v. Moore, 923 F.2d 910 (1st Cir. 1991) (testimony by bank's loan officer was sufficient to authenticate computer-generated loan histories); State v. Veres, 7 Ariz. App. 117, 436 P.2d 629 (Ariz. Ct. App. 1968)(fact that bank's foundation witness was unfamiliar with operation of encoding machine that generated bank records did not preclude their admission as business records), overruled by State v. Osborn, 107 Ariz. 295, 486 P.2d 777 (Ariz. 1971); People v. Lugashi, 205 Cal. App. 3d 632, 252 Cal. Rptr. 434 (Cal. Ct. App. 1988) (where computer record consists of retrieval of automatic inputs rather than computations based on manual entries, testimony on acceptability, accuracy, maintenance, and reliability of computer hardware and software need not be produced for purposes of admitting record into evidence).

In People v. Lugashi, microfiche copies of computer tapes containing credit card account information were introduced in a prosecution for grand theft. In rejecting an authentication argument similar to that made here, the Lugashi court observed that bank statements prepared in the regular course of banking business, in accordance with banking regulations, are in a different category than ordinary business and financial records of a private enterprise. The court also noted that the "bulk of other jurisdictions" had similarly declined to require more extensive authentication of such records. People v. Lugashi, *supra*, 252 Cal. Rptr. at 442 (collecting cases).

We agree with the rationale of those decisions upholding the admission of computer-generated bank records without the additional authentication urged by defendant, and accordingly conclude that the trial court did not abuse its discretion in declining to exclude the computer records in this case based on lack of authentication.

II.

Defendant next contends that admission of an incomplete copy of the status tape that recorded openings and closings of the ATM safe violated the best evidence rule. We disagree.

Under CRE 1002 and 1003, the so-called "best evidence rules," an original is generally required to prove the contents of a writing, but a duplicate is admissible to the same extent as an original unless (1) a genuine question is raised as to the authenticity of the original, or (2) under the circumstances, it would be unfair to admit the duplicate in lieu of the original. CRE 1004(1) further provides that an original is not required if it has been lost or destroyed, unless it was lost or destroyed in bad faith.

Determining the admissibility of evidence offered in lieu of an original writing under these rules is within the trial court's discretion, and that court's determination will not be disturbed absent clear evidence of mistake amounting to an error of law. United Cable Television of Jeffco, Inc. v. Montgomery LC, Inc., 942 P.2d 1230 (Colo. App. 1996).

Mere speculation or supposition that an original document may have contained information that the duplicate did not, or vice versa, does not amount to a showing that it would be unfair to admit the duplicate and thus does not preclude admission of the duplicate under CRE 1003. Equico Lessors, Inc. v. Tak's Automotive Service, 680 P.2d 854 (Colo. App. 1984).

The prosecution's foundation witness for Exhibit 14 identified it as a copy of a portion of the status tape that was kept inside the ATM on the hard drive. The tape was retrieved by a technician who took it off the machine in the presence of the witness. The witness then took the original tape roll and photocopied the portions offered into evidence. At the time of trial, he did not know where the original tape was.

Defendant objected to admission of the copy on the basis that it was incomplete and portions of some entries were cut off at the bottom of the page. He argued that the original tape was required. The trial court disagreed, noting that the critical portion, showing entry into the safe at 9:30 p.m. on December 23, was not cut off.

Admission of the duplicate was not an abuse of discretion. The foundation witness testified that the location of the original tape was unknown, and there was nothing to indicate that the original had been lost or destroyed in bad faith. For the reasons set forth in Part I, above, there is no genuine question as to the authenticity of the original tape. Finally, defendant has not shown that it was unfair to admit the duplicate in lieu of the original. He argues that a cut-off entry at the bottom of the first page of the exhibit might have shown a door opening at 6:56 p.m. on December 23, thereby establishing that the theft could have occurred then. This argument is not only speculative, see Equico Lessors, Inc. v. Tak's Automotive Service, *supra*, but also contradicts defendant's own written statement that the cassettes were in the safe when he opened it between 8:30 and 9:30 p.m. on December 23.

* * *

The judgment is affirmed

McKEEHAN v. STATE

Court of Appeal of Florida, Fifth District, 838 So. 2d 1257, 2003 Fla. App. LEXIS 3367 (2003)

JUDGES: MONACO, J. THOMPSON, C.J., and SAWAYA, J., concur.

The defendant, Ronald McKeehan, was found guilty after jury trial of robbery with a firearm, grand theft, aggravated assault with a firearm, and kidnapping with intent to commit a felony. All of these crimes were purportedly committed at a Sleep Inn Motel in Orlando. McKeehan asserts that the trial court committed error by allowing the State to prove the contents of a videotape with oral testimony, rather than with the tape itself.

During the course of the trial, the State introduced collateral crime evidence of a robbery of an Extended Stay America Hotel that was close to the site of the Sleep Inn that occurred a few days before the crimes related to the present case. A clerk who worked at the Extended Stay Hotel testified and identified McKeehan as the perpetrator of the robbery there. The State then called an investigator with the sheriff's office who investigated both robberies. He testified that he had seen a surveillance videotape of the Extended Stay robbery. When the prosecutor asked him if he saw the defendant on the tape, the defense objected, citing the best evidence rule, and pointed out that the State should be required to introduce the tape. The objection, however, was overruled, and the investigator was permitted to testify that the defendant was shown on the videotape.

During jury deliberations, the jury asked the court by written inquiry two questions concerning the evidence. First, the jury asked why the videotape had not been introduced into evidence. The jury also asked if it was permitted to consider the investigator's testimony concerning his observation of the defendant on the tape "as evidence." The trial judge explained to the jury that he could not answer why the videotape had not been introduced, but that the jury was permitted to consider the testimony of the investigator with regard to the tape.

The best evidence rule is set forth in section 90.952, Florida Statutes (2002), as follows:

Except as otherwise provided by statute, an original writing, recording, or photograph is required in order to prove the contents of the writing, recording, or photograph.

Section 90.954, Florida Statutes, amplifies the preceding statute by providing that:

The original of a writing, recording, or photograph is not required, except as provided in s. 90.953 [concerning duplicates], and other evidence of its contents is admissible when:

(1) All originals are lost or destroyed, unless the proponent lost or destroyed them in bad faith.
(2) An original cannot be obtained in this state by any judicial process or procedure.
(3) An original was under the control of the party against whom offered at a time when that party was put on notice by the pleadings or by written notice from the adverse party that the contents of such original would be subject to proof at the hearing, and such original is not produced at the hearing.
(4) The writing, recording, or photograph is not related to a controlling issue.

The best evidence rule, as codified by statute, requires that if the original evidence or a statutorily authorized alternative is available, no evidence should be received which is merely "substitutionary in nature." Liddon v. Bd. of Pub. Instruction for Jackson County, 128 Fla. 838, 175 So. 806, 808 (Fla. 1937); Sun Bank of St. Lucie County v. Oliver, 403 So. 2d 583, 584 (Fla. 4th DCA 1981). Thus, evidence which indicates that a more original source of information is available should be excluded. Id. In short, unless otherwise excused by the evidence code, the original must be produced unless it is shown to be unavailable for a reason other than the serious fault of the proponent. See Williams v. State, 386 So. 2d 538, 540 (Fla. 1980); Firestone Serv. Stores, Inc. of Gainesville v. Wynn, 131 Fla. 94, 179 So. 175 (Fla. 1938).

This rule is predicated on the principle that if the original evidence is available, that evidence should be presented to ensure accurate transmittal of the critical facts contained within it. See Williams; State v. Eubanks, 609 So. 2d 107 (Fla. 4th DCA 1992). Thus, in Williams it was found to be error for the trial court to permit introduction of oral evidence of what the victim of an attempted murder wrote (which implicated the defendant in the crime), while at a hospital awaiting treatment. The supreme court noted that no effort had been made by the state to explain the absence of the original writing.

The same is true in the instant case concerning the videotape of the Extended Stay Hotel robbery. The State sought to prove the contents of the videotape not by introduction of the tape, but by oral testimony of its contents without ever establishing the videotape's unavailability. Accordingly, the admission of the testimony violated the best evidence rule.

A violation of the best evidence rule may, however, constitute harmless error. In Williams, the supreme court affirmed despite the error, explaining:

Rather than contesting the accuracy of the terms contained in Ms. Marshall's note, appellant's objection was directed to the reliability of the out-of-court identification, an issue not addressed by the best evidence rule. Moreover, counsel had ample opportunity to discredit the identification by cross-examining Ms. Marshall about the events at the hospital. Given this posture, we do not believe that the trial court's technical error injuriously affected the substantial rights of appellant. § 59.041, Fla. Stat. (1975). 386 So. 2d at 540 (footnote omitted).

Under a harmless error analysis, the state must show beyond a reasonable doubt that the error complained of did not contribute to the verdict, or, stated alternatively, that there is no reasonable possibility that the error contributed to the conviction. State v. DiGuilio, 491 So. 2d 1129, 1136 (Fla. 1986); Stires v. State, 824 So. 2d 943 (Fla. 5th DCA 2002). Application of the rule "requires an examination of the entire record by the appellate court including a close examination of the permissible evidence on which the jury could have legitimately relied and, in addition, an even closer examination of the impermissible evidence which might have possibly influenced the jury verdict." DiGuilio, 491 So. 2d at 1135. [**7] As our supreme court has noted, "the harmless error analysis focuses on the effect of the error on the trier of fact." Goodwin v. State, 751 So. 2d 537, 542 (Fla. 1999) (quoting State v. Lee, 531 So. 2d 133, 137 (Fla. 1988)).

The question, therefore, is not whether the evidence against the defendant was overwhelming. Lee, 531 So. 2d at 136-37; Jones v. State, 754 So. 2d 792 (Fla. 1st DCA 2000). A reviewing court "must resist the temptation to make its own determination of whether a guilty verdict could be sustained by excluding the impermissible evidence and examining only the permissible evidence." Goodwin, 751 So. 2d at 542.

In the instant case, the pivotal issue at trial concerned identification of the perpetrator of the Sleep Inn robbery. The sole evidence directly tying the defendant to the Sleep Inn robbery was the desk clerk's eyewitness testimony. The State attempted to bolster the desk clerk's identification with Williams rule evidence linking the defendant to another recent and very similar hotel robbery in the same vicinity. The victim of the second robbery identified McKeehan as the perpetrator of that crime.

The State then presented an investigator's identification of the defendant from the videotape. As this identification confirmed the identification of the defendant made by the victim, it might appear to amount to the erroneous admission of cumulative evidence that would constitute harmless error. [Citations omitted.]

In the present case, however, the jury's inquiry of the court relating, first, to the absence of the videotape, and then to the investigator's identification testimony based on his examination of the tape, makes it quite evident that the jury seriously considered that particular testimony in reaching its verdict. Moreover, the use by the State in this case of evidence less than the original, when there was no demonstration that the original was unavailable, authorizes an inference that the proponent's position would have been defeated if the best evidence had been furnished. Liddon, 175 So. at 808. Under the circumstances, therefore, we cannot say that there is no reasonable possibility that the inadmissible testimony contributed to the conviction. DiGuilio, 491 So. 2d at 1135. Given the questions from the jury, in fact, it is far more likely that the erroneously admitted testimony had an influence on the jury verdict. Accordingly, we reverse the convictions and order a new trial.

REVERSED and REMANDED.

THOMPSON, C.J., and SAWAYA, J., concur.

Cases Relating to Chapter 14

Real Evidence

SCHMERBER v. CALIFORNIA

Supreme Court of the United States, 384 U.S. 757, 86 S. Ct. 1826, 16 L. Ed. 2d 908 (1966)

MR. JUSTICE BRENNAN delivered the opinion of the Court.

Petitioner was convicted in Los Angeles Municipal Court of the criminal offense of driving an automobile while under the influence of intoxicating liquor. He had been arrested at a hospital while receiving treatment for injuries suffered in an accident involving the automobile that he had apparently been driving. At the direction of a police officer, a physician at the hospital then withdrew a blood sample from petitioner's body. The chemical analysis of this sample revealed a percent by weight of alcohol in his blood at the time of the offense which indicated intoxication, and the report of this analysis was admitted in evidence at the trial. Petitioner objected to receipt of this evidence of the analysis on the ground that the blood had been withdrawn despite his refusal, on the advice of his counsel, to consent to the test. He contended that in that circumstance the withdrawal of the blood and the admission of the analysis in evidence denied him due process of law under the Fourteenth Amendment, as well as specific guarantees of the Bill of Rights secured against the States by that Amendment; his privilege against self-incrimination under the Fifth Amendment; his right to counsel under the Sixth Amendment; and his right not to be subjected to unreasonable searches and seizures in violation of the Fourth Amendment. The Appellate Department of the California Superior Court rejected these contentions and affirmed the conviction. In view of constitutional decisions since we last considered these issues in Breithaupt v. Abram, 352 U.S. 432—see Escobedo v. Illinois, 378 U.S. 478; Malloy v. Hogan, 378 U.S. 1, and Mapp v. Ohio, 367 U.S. 643—we granted certiorari. 382 U.S. 971. We affirm.

I.

The Due Process Clause Claim

Breithaupt was also a case in which police officers caused blood to be withdrawn from the driver of an automobile involved in an accident, and in which there was ample justification for the officer's conclusion that the driver was under the influence of alcohol. There, as here, the extraction was made by a physician in a simple, medically acceptable manner in a hospital environment. There, however, the driver was unconscious at the time the blood was withdrawn and hence had no opportunity to object to the procedure. We affirmed the conviction there resulting from the use of the test in evidence, holding that under such circumstances the withdrawal did not offend "that 'sense of justice' of which we spoke in Rochin v. California, 342 U.S. 165." 352 U.S., at 435. Breithaupt thus requires the rejection of petitioner's due process argument, and nothing in the circumstances of this case or in supervening events persuades us that this aspect of Breithaupt should be overruled.

II.

The Privilege Against Self-Incrimination Claim

Breithaupt summarily rejected an argument that the withdrawal of blood and the admission of the analysis report involved in that state case violated the Fifth Amendment privilege of any person not to "be compelled in any criminal case to be a witness against himself," citing Twining v. New Jersey, 211 U.S. 78. But that case, holding that the protections of the Fourteenth Amendment do not embrace this Fifth Amendment privilege, has been succeeded by Malloy v. Hogan, 378 U.S. 1, 8. We there held that "the Fourteenth Amendment secures against state invasion the same privilege that the Fifth Amendment guarantees against federal infringement—the right of a person to remain silent unless he chooses to speak in the unfettered exercise of his own will, and to suffer no penalty. . . for such silence." We therefore must now decide whether the withdrawal of the blood and admission in evidence of the analysis involved in this case violated petitioner's privilege. We hold that the privilege protects an accused only from being compelled to testify against himself, or otherwise provide the State with evidence of a testimonial or communicative nature, and that the withdrawal of blood and use of the analysis in question in this case did not involve compulsion to these ends.

It could not be denied that in requiring petitioner to submit to the withdrawal and chemical analysis of his blood the State compelled him to submit to an attempt to discover evidence that might be used to prosecute him for a criminal offense. He submitted only after the police officer rejected his objection and directed the physician to proceed. The officer's direction to the physician to administer the test over petitioner's objection constituted compulsion for the purposes of the privilege. The critical question, then, is whether petitioner was thus compelled "to be a witness against himself."

If the scope of the privilege coincided with the complex of values it helps to protect, we might be obliged to conclude that the privilege was violated. In Miranda v. Arizona, ante, at 460, the Court said of the interests protected by the privilege: "All these policies point to one overriding thought: the constitutional foundation underlying the privilege is the respect a government—state or federal—must accord to the dignity and integrity of its citizens. To maintain a 'fair state-individual balance,' to require the government 'to shoulder the entire load' . . . to respect the inviolability of the human personality, our accusatory system of criminal justice demands that the government seeking to punish an individual produce the evidence against him by its own independent labors, rather than by the cruel, simple expedient of compelling it from his own mouth." The withdrawal of blood necessarily involves puncturing the skin for extraction, and the percent by weight of alcohol in that blood, as established by chemical analysis, is evidence of criminal guilt. Compelled submission fails on one view to respect the "inviolability of the human personality." Moreover, since it enables the State to rely on evidence forced from the accused, the compulsion violates at least one meaning of the requirement that the State procure the evidence against an accused "by its own independent labors."

As the passage in Miranda implicitly recognizes, however, the privilege has never been given the full scope which the values it helps to protect suggest. History and a long line of authorities in lower courts have consistently limited its protection to situations in which the State seeks to submerge those values by obtaining the evidence against an accused through "the cruel, simple expedient of compelling it from his own mouth. . . . In sum, the privilege is fulfilled only when the person is guaranteed the right 'to remain silent unless he chooses to speak in the unfettered exercise of his own will.'" Ibid. The leading case in this Court is Holt v. United States, 218 U.S. 245. There the question was whether evidence was admissible that the accused, prior to trial and over his protest, put on a blouse that fitted him. It was contended that compelling the accused to submit to the demand that he model the blouse violated the privilege. Mr. Justice Holmes, speaking for the Court, rejected the argument as "based upon an extravagant extension of the Fifth Amendment," and went on to say: "The prohibition of compelling a man in a criminal court to be witness against himself is a prohibition of the use of physical or moral compulsion to extort communications from him, not an exclusion of his body as evidence when it may be material. The objection in principle would forbid a jury to look at a prisoner and compare his features with a photograph in proof." 218 U.S., at 252–253.

It is clear that the protection of the privilege reaches an accused's communications, whatever form they might take, and the compulsion of responses which are also communications, for example, compliance with a subpoena to produce one's papers. Boyd v. United States, 116 U.S. 616. On the other hand, both federal and state courts have usually held that it offers no protection against compulsion to submit to fingerprinting, photographing, or measurements, to write or speak for identification, to appear in court, to stand, to assume a stance, to walk, or to make a particular gesture. The distinction which has emerged, often expressed in different ways, is that the privilege is a bar against compelling "communications" or "testimony," but that compulsion which makes a suspect or accused the source of "real or physical evidence" does not violate it.

Although we agree that this distinction is a helpful framework for analysis, we are not to be understood to agree with past applications in all instances. There will be many cases in which such a distinction is not readily drawn. Some tests seemingly directed to obtain "physical evidence," for example, lie detector tests measuring changes in body function during interrogation, may actually be directed to eliciting responses which are essentially testimonial. To compel a person to submit to testing in which an effort will be made to determine his guilt or innocence on the basis of physiological responses, whether willed or not, is to evoke the spirit and history of the Fifth Amendment. Such situations call to mind the principle that the protection of the privilege "is as broad as the mischief against which it seeks to guard," Counselman v. Hitchcock, 142 U.S. 547, 562.

In the present case, however, no such problem of application is presented. Not even a shadow of testimonial compulsion upon or enforced communication by the accused was involved either in the extraction or in the chemical analysis. Petitioner's testimonial capacities were in no way implicated; indeed, his participation, except as a donor, was irrelevant to the results of the test, which depend on chemical analysis and on that alone. Since the blood test evidence, although an incriminating product of compulsion, was neither petitioner's testimony nor evidence relating to some communicative act or writing by the petitioner, it was not inadmissible on privilege grounds.

* * *

Affirmed. MR. JUSTICE HARLAN, whom MR. JUSTICE STEWART joins, concurring.

In joining the Court's opinion I desire to add the following comment. While agreeing with the Court that the taking of this blood test involved no testimonial compulsion, I would go further and hold that apart from this consideration the case in no way implicates the Fifth Amendment. Cf. my dissenting opinion and that of MR. JUSTICE WHITE in Miranda v. Arizona, ante, pp. 504, 526.

MR. CHIEF JUSTICE WARREN, dissenting.

While there are other important constitutional issues in this case, I believe it is sufficient for me to reiterate my dissenting opinion in Breithaupt v. Abram, 352 U.S. 432, 440, as the basis on which to reverse this conviction.

MR. JUSTICE BLACK with whom MR. JUSTICE DOUGLAS joins, dissenting.

I would reverse petitioner's conviction. I agree with the Court that the Fourteenth Amendment made applicable to the States the Fifth Amendment's provision that "No person . . . shall be compelled in any criminal case to be a witness against himself. . . ." But I disagree with the Court's holding that California did not violate petitioner's constitutional right against self-incrimination when it compelled him, against his will, to allow a doctor to puncture his blood vessels in order to extract a sample of blood and analyze it for alcoholic content, and then used that analysis as evidence to convict petitioner of a crime.

* * *

MR. JUSTICE DOUGLAS, dissenting.

I adhere to the views of THE CHIEF JUSTICE in his dissent in Breithaupt v. Abram, 352 U.S. 432, 440, and to the views I stated in my dissent in that case (id., 442) and add only a word.

We are dealing with the right of privacy which, since the Breithaupt case, we have held to be within the penumbra of some specific guarantees of the Bill of Rights. Griswold v. Connecticut, 381 U.S. 479. Thus, the Fifth Amendment marks "a zone of privacy" which the Government may not force a person to surrender. Id., 484. Likewise the Fourth Amendment recognizes that right when it guarantees the right of the people to be secure "in their persons." Ibid. No clearer invasion of this right of privacy can be imagined than forcible bloodletting of the kind involved here.

MR. JUSTICE FORTAS, dissenting.

I would reverse. In my view, petitioner's privilege against self-incrimination applies. I would add that, under the Due Process Clause, the State, in its role as prosecutor, has no right to extract blood from an accused or anyone else, over his protest. As prosecutor, the State has no right to commit any kind of violence upon the person, or to utilize the results of such a tort, and the extraction of blood, over protest, is an act of violence. Cf. CHIEF JUSTICE WARREN's dissenting opinion in Breithaupt v. Abram, 352 U.S. 432, 440.

STATE v. COWANS

Appellate Court of Illinois, First District, Sixth Division, 336 Ill. App. 3d 173, 782 N.E.2d 779, 2002 Ill. App. LEXIS 1170 Appeal denied by People v. Cowans, 2003 Ill. LEXIS 649 (Ill., Apr. 2, 2003)

JUDGES: JUSTICE O'MARA FROSSARD delivered the opinion of the court. O'BRIEN, P.J., and GALLAGHER, J., concur.

Following a bench trial defendant was found guilty of one count of possession of a controlled substance with intent to deliver. The trial court sentenced defendant to seven years in the Illinois Department of Corrections. On appeal, defendant challenges the sufficiency of the evidence and contends the stipulated facts, together with the entire trial record, fail to establish a complete chain of custody for the controlled substance.

BACKGROUND

The State called Officer McCarthy as a witness and introduced additional evidence through two stipulations. McCarthy testified that around 9:45 p.m. on January 22, 2000, near 4936 West Huron Street, he observed defendant with the aid of binoculars. During a five-minute surveillance McCarthy saw four individuals approach defendant, engage in a brief conversation, and give defendant money. Defendant placed the money in his pants pocket and gave a small object to each individual. When McCarthy was about 15 feet away, defendant looked in his direction and threw a number of small plastic bags to the ground. McCarthy recovered from the ground nine small plastic bags containing what he suspected to be cocaine. Defendant was arrested. McCarthy searched defendant and recovered $ 190 from his pants pocket. McCarthy testified that he later inventoried the nine small plastic bags under inventory number 2295494 and the money under inventory number 2295495. The Nash School was located about one block away.

The State offered two stipulations agreed to by defense counsel. By way of stipulation it was agreed that if Investigator Tansy were to testify he would state that he measured the distance from 4936 West Huron Street to the Nash School and found it was742 feet. It was further stipulated that if forensic scientist Maureen Dully were to testify she would state that she received nine items under inventory number 2295494 and tested five of the nine items, which she found contained 1.2 grams of cocaine.

Defendant and Lonniece Young-Frazier testified in the defense case. Frazier testified that she knows defendant, but does not know him personally. On January 22, 2000, between 9 p.m. and 10 p.m., she was a passenger in a car in front of 4935 West Huron Street. She saw the defendant walking westbound on the north side of Huron Street when two uniformed officers, a male and female, approached him. Defendant put his hands up in the air. Frazier testified that she did not see defendant drop anything on the ground and did not see anyone passing objects for money. She testified that the officers searched defendant, handcuffed him, and placed him in the police car. Frazier testified that the male officer had a flashlight and was looking on the ground all over the area, including under porches two or three houses away.

Defendant testified that he was walking home from the store after playing the lottery. He was on the north side of Huron Street. Officer McCarthy and a female police officer pulled up in a marked squad car. Defendant denied he had anything in his hands or dropped anything; he denied selling drugs or possessing any drugs. Defendant stated that McCarthy searched him, found money, and told the female officer that defendant must be doing something. Defendant was handcuffed and placed in the squad car. McCarthy searched the area with a flashlight. Defendant testified that when McCarthy got into the car he showed defendant a plastic pouch and then drove to the police station.

ANALYSIS

Defendant stipulated to certain facts at trial. Generally, a defendant is precluded from attacking any facts previously agreed to in a stipulation. Defendant does not attack the specific facts agreed to in the stipulation. Defendant, relying on In re R.F., 298 Ill. App. 3d 13, 16, 232 Ill. Dec. 519, 698 N.E.2d 610 (1998), challenges the sufficiency of the evidence and argues that the stipulated facts, together with the entire trial record, fail to establish a sufficiently complete chain of custody.

When a defendant challenges the sufficiency of the evidence, the relevant inquiry is whether, after viewing the evidence in the light most favorable to the prosecution, any rational trier of fact could have found the essential elements of the crime beyond a reasonable doubt. [Citations omitted.] A challenge to the sufficiency of the evidence is not subject to the waiver rule and may be raised for the first time on direct appeal. People v. Enoch, 122 Ill. 2d 176, 119 Ill. Dec. 265, 522 N.E.2d 1124 (1988).

Before real evidence may be admitted at trial, the State must provide an adequate foundation either by way of live testimony or stipulation which establishes that the item sought to be introduced is the actual item involved in the alleged offense and that its condition is substantially unchanged. People v. Cole, 29 Ill. App. 3d 369, 375, 329 N.E.2d 880 (1975). Where an item possesses unique and readily identifiable characteristics and its substance is relatively impervious to change, testimony at trial that the item sought to be admitted in evidence is the same one recovered and in substantially the same condition as when recovered is sufficient to establish an adequate foundation. People v. Gilbert, 58 Ill. App. 3d 387, 15 Ill. Dec. 956, 374 N.E.2d 739 (1978). If the item is not readily identifiable or if it is susceptible to alteration by tampering or contamination, its chain of custody must be established by the State with sufficient completeness to render it improbable that the original item has either been exchanged, contaminated, or subjected to tampering. People v. Winters, 97 Ill. App. 3d 288, 289, 52 Ill. Dec. 763, 422 N.E.2d 972 (1981).

The character of the item determines which method for laying an adequate foundation must be used. [Citation omitted.] Based on the character of the evidence in this case, the chain of custody must be established by the State with sufficient completeness to render it improbable that the original item has either been exchanged, contaminated, or subjected to tampering. Thus, the State was required to establish a chain of custody to demonstrate the connection between the items recovered from the ground by Officer McCarthy after discarded by defendant and the items tested by forensic scientist Maureen Dully.

Regarding that connection, the record contained the testimony of Officer McCarthy and the stipulated testimony of forensic scientist Maureen Dully. The testimony of Officer McCarthy on direct examination by the State regarding recovering and handling the controlled substance was as follows:

"Q. What happened as you were approaching the defendant?

A. He looked in my direction, and he threw to the ground numerous plastic bags. I recovered these bags and found them to be nine clear, plastic bags each containing white, rocky substance that I believed to be crack cocaine.

***

Q. Officer, did you later inventory the U.S. currency and the suspect rock cocaine?

A. Yes.

Q. And did you inventory the nine, clear baggies containing the suspect rock cocaine under inventory number 2295494?
A. Yes."
On cross-examination McCarthy testified as follows:
"Q. And you were 15 feet away from him, and that's when he threw these things down on the ground?
A. I said approximately 15 feet.
Q. And could you see then what those things were?
A. I could tell they were, at least, clear, plastic bags.
Q. Were they tinted at all?
A. Yes.
Q. What color tint?
A. Green."

The agreed stipulation between the State and defense regarding the testimony of forensic scientist Duffy was as follows:

"[711 LAW CLERK FOR THE STATE]: Also, that if Maureen Dully, a forensic scientist employed by the Illinois State Police Division of Forensic Services were to be called, she would testify that on February 7, 2000, she received the following inventory number, 2295494, which contained nine items, and that she tested five of those nine items and that she has determined that—with a reasonable degree of scientific certainty that the five tested items tested positive for 1.2 grams of cocaine. So stipulated?

[DEFENSE ATTORNEY]: Yes."

The testimony of Officer McCarthy and the stipulation regarding the testimony of forensic scientist Dully was in total the evidence produced by the State regarding chain of custody.

In order to prove its case, the State is required to prove a connection between the defendant and the illegal contraband. In doing so the State is required to establish a proper chain of custody. A sufficient chain of custody does not require that every person involved in the chain testify, nor must the State exclude all possibilities that the evidence may have been subject to tampering. Winters, 97 Ill. App. 3d at 295. The State must demonstrate that the evidence has not been changed in any important respect. People v. Hominick, 177 Ill. App. 3d 18, 29, 126 Ill. Dec. 422, 531 N.E.2d 1049 (1988). The State is required to establish that it took reasonable protective measures since the substance was seized. People v. Hermann, 180 Ill. App. 3d 939, 944, 129 Ill. Dec. 656, 536 N.E.2d 706 (1988). The purpose of the protective measures is to ensure that the substance taken from the defendant was the same as the substance tested by the forensic chemist. People v. Ryan, 129 Ill. App. 3d 915, 919, 85 Ill. Dec. 93, 473 N.E.2d 461 (1984).

We are mindful that unless the defendant produces actual evidence of tampering, substitution, or contamination, the State need only establish a probability that tampering, substitution or contamination did not occur, and any deficiencies go to the weight rather than the admissibility of the evidence. Hominick, 177 Ill. App. 3d at 29. In the instant case, defendant did not produce actual evidence of tampering, substitution, or contamination. Therefore, the State is only required to establish a probability that reasonable protective measures were employed to protect the evidence from the time it was seized and that it was improbable the evidence was altered. People v. Bynum, 257 Ill. App. 3d 502, 510, 196 Ill. Dec. 179, 629 N.E.2d 724 (1994). To establish a sufficiently complete chain of custody, the State is required to prove delivery, presence, and safekeeping of the evidence. People v. Gibson, 287 Ill. App. 3d 878, 882, 223 Ill. Dec. 234, 679 N.E.2d 419 (1997).

The State, relying on People v. Irpino, 122 Ill. App. 3d 767, 78 Ill. Dec. 165, 461 N.E.2d 999 (1984), contends that the chain of custody was sufficiently established in this case because the "testimony clearly demonstrated that the evidence seized 'matched' the evidence subjected to chemical analysis." We recognize that if one link in the chain is missing, but there is evidence describing the condition of the evidence when delivered which matches the description of the evidence when examined, the evidence can be sufficient to establish chain of custody. Irpino, 122 Ill. App. 3d at 775.

Officer McCarthy testified he recovered from the ground nine small plastic bags with a green tint that contained suspected crack cocaine after being discarded by the defendant. The record reflects by way of stipulation that the forensic scientist received nine items and tested the contents of five items, which she found to contain 1.2 grams of cocaine. The officer's description includes details about the color, shape and packaging of the items, but not the weight. The forensic scientist's stipulation contains no corresponding details about the color, shape and packaging of the items. The forensic scientist's stipulation includes a weight estimate, but in no way further describes the items.

Here, the only common features in the testimony describing the condition of the evidence when seized and the description of the evidence when tested are the number of items and the inventory number. The stipulation of the testimony provided by the forensic scientist did not include whether the items she received were in plastic bags or whether the bags were colored or clear. The stipulation of the testimony provided by the forensic scientist did not include any description as to size, shape, or color of the items received. Officer McCarthy described the evidence as a white, rocky substance. However, there was no corresponding or "matching" description provided by the forensic scientist in the stipulation as to the shape and color of the substance. While there was evidence that the nine plastic bags retrieved from the ground by Officer McCarthy were distinctive in color, that distinctive color was not included in the description of the items tested by the forensic scientist provided by the State's stipulation. Rather, the stipulation referenced the evidence by use of the generic term "items." The "items" received by forensic scientist Duffy were given no further description in the stipulation.

As noted, where there is evidence describing the condition of the evidence when seized, which matches the description of the evidence when examined, the evidence can be sufficient to establish chain of custody. Irpino, 122 Ill. App. 3d at 775. For the reasons previously discussed, we cannot conclude that the record reflects the condition of the evidence when seized sufficiently matches the description of the evidence when tested. This gap in the chain of custody is not resolved by the record.

Moreover, the record reflects several additional missing links in the chain of custody regarding proof of handling, delivery, presence, and safekeeping of the evidence. To establish a sufficiently complete chain of custody, the State is required to prove delivery, presence, and safekeeping of the evidence. Gibson, 287 Ill. App. 3d at 882. The record reflects no reasonable protective techniques regarding custody, handling, delivery, presence, and safekeeping of the alleged contraband. The State presented no evidence of what procedures, if any, were used in the handling and safekeeping of the evidence between Officer McCarthy's recovery of the plastic bags and the receipt of the evidence by forensic scientist Dully 16 days later. The record contains no evidence either by live testimony or stipulation as to what Officer McCarthy did with the plastic bags he retrieved from the ground after defendant allegedly discarded them, other than the fact that McCarthy inventoried those items under an inventory number. There is no evidence that the plastic bags recovered from the ground from Officer McCarthy were placed in any closed or sealed container or envelope or were initialed or dated by Officer McCarthy; no evidence as to what condition the items were kept in during the 16 days that passed before forensic scientist Dully received them; no evidence that the items received at the crime laboratory were received sealed; and no evidence of the whereabouts of the plastic bags for the 16 days that passed from the time Officer McCarthy recovered the plastic bags on January 22, 2000, and February 7, 2000, when forensic scientist Duffy received the items.

Regarding chain of custody, the State relies on People v. Leemon, 66 Ill. 2d 170, 172, 5 Ill. Dec. 250, 361 N.E.2d 573 (1977), and argues "the court held in Leemon that the police officer's testimony identifying the bag he recovered from the defendant, together with a stipulation between the parties that the contents of the bag were LSD, made a sufficient showing of continuity of possession of custody." In Leemon, Officer Edwards described the bag of LSD he purchased from defendant which he had marked with the date and his initials. That plastic bag containing LSD was received in evidence. Unlike Leemon, the record in this case contains no testimony by Officer McCarthy during trial identifying the baggies he recovered from the defendant, either in the form of live testimony or by way of stipulation. There is no evidence that Officer McCarthy marked the baggies with the date and his initials. In Leemon, the plastic bag containing LSD recovered by the police officer from the defendant was received in evidence. Unlike Leemon, in the instant case the baggies containing the controlled substance recovered by Officer McCarthy were not offered into evidence by the State or received into evidence by the court either through live testimony or by way of stipulation. The controlled substance in this case was never given an exhibit number. Here, the State not only failed to provide an adequate foundation to introduce the contraband into evidence, but it never sought to introduce into evidence the controlled substance either by live testimony or stipulation.

As previously noted, the State must provide an adequate foundation demonstrating the item sought to be offered into evidence is the actual item involved in the alleged offense and its condition is substantially unchanged. McCarthy never identified the narcotics as those retrieved after being discarded by defendant nor did the State establish that fact by way of stipulation. McCarthy never testified that, at the time of trial, the controlled substance was in substantially the same condition as when he inventoried it, nor did the State establish that fact by way of stipulation. The record reflects no evidence by way of live testimony or stipulation that the items recovered by McCarthy were substantially unchanged from the time of the offense to the time of trial. The record contains no evidence either by live testimony or stipulation that Officer McCarthy would identify the items tested by Dully and would testify that these items were in the same or substantially the same condition as when he recovered these items from the ground after they were allegedly discarded by defendant on January 22, 2000. These gaps in the chain of custody are not resolved by the record.

There are additional gaps in the chain of custody. There is no evidence either by way of direct testimony or stipulation regarding delivery of the items to the crime laboratory. The stipulation indicates the items were received on February 7, 2000. However, there is no evidence in the record as to where those "items" were for 16 days from January 22, 2000, until February 7, 2000. There is no testimony, live or stipulated, describing the condition of the items when delivered to the crime laboratory. There is no evidence the items were delivered in a closed or sealed container. There is no evidence of any protective measures the State took from the point the substance was recovered by Officer McCarthy until the point the items were received 16 days later at the crime laboratory by forensic scientist Duffy.

Reversal for evidentiary insufficiency is required when the State fails to prove its case. As recently noted in People v. Moore, "When the issue is one which concerns the sufficiency of the evidence, we are required to reverse outright, whereas the erroneous admission of evidence is a procedural error which allows us to remand for a new trial." People v. Moore, 335 Ill. App. 3d 616, 781 N.E.2d 493, 2002 Ill. App. LEXIS 1058, (November 15, 2002), citing People v. Olivera, 164 Ill. 2d 382, 393, 207 Ill. Dec. 433, 647 N.E.2d 926 (1995). In this case, defendant challenges the sufficiency of the evidence. There is no issue regarding the erroneous admission of the controlled substance, because the State never sought to admit the controlled substance either by live testimony or stipulation.

Moreover, in this case there is no challenge to the stipulated facts and no contention that the stipulations were misstated. See People v. Maurice, 31 Ill. 2d 456, 457–59, 202 N.E.2d 480 (1964) (where stipulation was misstated, court concluded admission of heroin into evidence without sufficient chain of custody required reversal and remand for new trial). Rather, in the instant case, the defendant challenges the sufficiency of the evidence and argues that the stipulated facts, considered together with the entire trial record, fail to establish a sufficiently complete chain of custody. See In re R.F., 298 Ill. App. 3d at 15 (insufficient foundation provided by State for admission of controlled substance required outright reversal).

CONCLUSION

The evidence was insufficient to sustain defendant's conviction because the State failed to establish a sufficient chain of custody for the controlled substance. The State failed to demonstrate that the police took reasonable protective measures to ensure that the substance recovered by Officer McCarthy from the ground after abandoned by defendant was the same or substantially the same as the items tested by forensic chemist Dully.

There was no evidence regarding the handling and safekeeping of the controlled substance from the point in time when Officer McCarthy recovered the evidence until the point in time when forensic scientist Dully received the evidence 16 days later.

Other than the testimony of Officer McCarthy that he inventoried the evidence under inventory number 2295494, the only other evidence offered to prove the chain of custody was the stipulation, which merely established that Duffy tested five of nine "items" assigned to inventory number 2295494, which tested positive for 1.2 grams of cocaine. The State failed to establish a sufficiently complete chain of custody by proof of delivery, presence and safekeeping of the controlled substance. The State failed to establish a probability that reasonable measures were used to protect the evidence from the time that it was seized and that it was improbable the evidence was altered.

For the reasons previously discussed, we find the evidence was insufficient to prove defendant guilty beyond a reasonable doubt.

Reversed.

O'BRIEN, P.J., and GALLAGHER, J., concur.

UNDERWOOD v. STATE

Supreme Court of Mississippi, 708 So. 2d 18 (1998)

En Banc.

SULLIVAN, Presiding Justice, for the Court:

PART ONE: GUILT PHASE

1. Justin Underwood was indicted for capital murder by the grand jury for Madison County during the March Term of 1994. The indictment charged that Underwood had murdered Virginia Ann Harris on or about February 15, 1994, by shooting her with a pistol, during the course of kidnapping, in violation of Miss. Code Ann. § 97-3-19 (2)(e). Underwood pleaded not guilty and proceeded to trial on May 22, 1995, in the Circuit Court of Madison County. The jury returned a verdict of guilty on the charge of capital murder on May 24. The sentencing phase of the trial was held on the following day, and the jury found that Underwood should be sentenced to death. Circuit Judge John B. Toney entered the final judgment of conviction and sentence on May 25, and ordered that Underwood be put to death by lethal injection on July 7, 1995. Following denial of his motion for judgment notwithstanding the verdict, or in the alternative for a new trial, Underwood perfected his appeal to this Court.

STATEMENT OF THE FACTS

2. On February 15, 1994, Lindsay Harris spoke with his wife, Virginia Ann Harris, before leaving their home in Flora to travel to his produce business at the Farmer's Market in Jackson. Mrs. Harris asked her husband to eat dinner in Jackson on his way home from work, because she planned to do some shopping in Jackson that day. Mr. Harris agreed, told his wife goodbye, and left for work at about 6:00 A.M. He worked from 6:30 A.M. until closing time at 4:00 P.M., when he loaded a delivery order in his truck and left for Flora at about 4:30 P.M.
3. When Mr. Harris arrived at his house, he saw his wife's car, a blue Lincoln Towncar, in the garage, but when he entered the home and called her name, there was no answer. He noticed that the lights and television were on in the den, and the curtains were drawn. Walking back to their bedroom, Mr. Harris saw that Mrs. Harris's makeup drawer was pulled open, the lights were on, and a makeup bottle was left upside down on the counter. Mr. Harris and his son Kyle both testified that it was unlike Mrs. Harris to leave the house in such a condition.
4. At about 5:00 P.M., Mr. Harris changed clothes and left to go feed his cattle. When he returned, Mrs. Harris still wasn't home. He showered and dressed for bed, and by 8:00 P.M. he was extremely worried about his wife. He started calling family and friends, but no one knew where she was. At midnight Mr. Harris called the police and reported Mrs. Harris as a missing person. At 12:30 or

1:00 A.M., Officer Ogden Wilson arrived at the Harris home and filled out a missing person report, which he forwarded to the sheriff's department.

5. At 1:30 A.M. Mr. Harris called his son Kyle and told him that Mrs. Harris was still missing. Kyle came over immediately, and the two conducted a search of the house and yard. On their way back into the house through the garage, Kyle noticed that the keys to Mrs. Harris's Lincoln were in the ignition. They also discovered Mrs. Harris's purse on the floor of the front passenger side of the car, which was not Mrs. Harris's custom. Kyle testified that his mother normally kept her purse on the seat beside her. There was no money in the purse, which was unusual for Mrs. Harris, who usually carried at least $40 with her at all times. The only unlocked car door was the driver's door, indicating that only one person had exited the car, because when the ignition was turned, all of the doors automatically locked. The front seat of the car was pushed back to its furthermost position, which was also out of character for Mrs. Harris. Mr. Harris testified that he was 5′9″, and his feet didn't touch the pedals in Mrs. Harris's car with the seat that far back. Charles Scarborough, Master Sergeant Trooper with the Mississippi Highway Patrol, testified that he was 5′11″ and would not be comfortable with the seat in that position. Mr. Harris also testified that he believed the Lincoln was parked in the garage differently than Mrs. Harris usually parked it. Nothing was missing from the house, other than possibly some cash from Mrs. Harris's purse. At this point, Mr. Harris and Kyle agreed that Mrs. Harris must have been kidnapped.
6. At 6:00 A.M. on February 16, the highway patrol, police, and sheriff's department were contacted, and detectives began arriving at the Harris home to take over the investigation. Sergeant Scarborough lifted fingerprints and fibers from Mrs. Harris's Lincoln and took pictures of the car. Only two latent prints of value were lifted from the car, and neither were matched with anyone, including the defendant, Justin Underwood. The fibers taken from Mrs. Harris's car similarly were not linked to anyone, including Underwood. Sergeant Judy Tucker with the Mississippi Highway Patrol Investigation Bureau was called to head up the investigation. Mr. Harris described to Sergeant Tucker the state of the house as he found it on the evening of February 15. He also showed her Mrs. Harris's pill box with two of five pills missing from her February 15 doses, her diet log book showing that she had consumed only two glasses of water on the morning of February 15, and a shopping list left on the kitchen counter of items that Mrs. Harris planned to buy in Jackson on February 15. Based upon the state of the house when Mr. Harris arrived home on February 15, Sergeant Tucker determined that Mrs. Harris had not left the house of her own free will.
7. Sergeant Tucker contacted her supervisors for further instructions, and a search of the area was organized, including an aerial search. The investigators discovered that Mrs. Harris had missed her 11:15 appointment at Jenny Craig Weight Loss Centre and her afternoon nail appointment at Mona's Nails in Jackson. Mona's had called the Harris home at 2:30 P.M. on February 15 with no response. With the help of Mrs. Harris's daughter-in-law, Lynette Harris, they determined that Mrs. Harris's red house shoes, blue robe, and a wide black belt were missing.
8. Around 4:40 P.M. in the afternoon on February 16, Webb Bozeman informed authorities that two of his employees had seen Mrs. Harris's car backed into a cattle gap on his property on old Highway 49, approximately 1.5 miles from the Harris home, between 9:00 and 10:00 A.M. on February 15. Testimony at trial placed Underwood's car, or one very similar to it, in a driveway near the Harris home on February 15 at approximately 10:00 or 10:30 A.M. Based upon the tip from Mr. Bozeman's employees, Sergeant Tucker and other law enforcement officers went to the cattle gap and began searching. At about 5:10, Officer Donny Spell found a black belt in a fire lane on the Bozeman property near Bozeman Lake. Continuing on around the lake shore, at about 5:20, Sergeant Tucker discovered Mrs. Harris's body, clothed in a blue pleated

shirt, black knit pants, and red house shoes. Clumps of grass and weeds were clutched in her hands. Mrs. Harris only had foundation makeup on the right side of her face. At trial, Mr. Harris testified that in more than forty years of marriage, his wife had never left the house without having makeup on or without being properly dressed. After contacting the crime scene unit, Sergeant Tucker accompanied Dudley Bozeman to notify Mr. Harris and his family.

9. Mrs. Harris had been shot four times. Two of the bullets did not exit Mrs. Harris's body, and these were sent to the Mississippi Crime Lab for testing following the autopsy. One bullet traveled from her back through her right lung, diaphragm, and liver. A second bullet struck the right side of her back and penetrated her right lung. Dr. Steven Hayne, who performed the autopsy, testified that either of these first two gunshot wounds would have individually caused death due to extensive internal bleeding. A third bullet struck Mrs. Harris's left ear, went through the ear, struck and went through the left side of her neck, and struck her front right shoulder. Dr. Hayne testified that this gunshot would not have caused death by itself. The fourth bullet entered the front of Mrs. Harris's left arm and exited the inner arm. This gunshot wound was also nonlethal. All four of the gunshot wounds were distant, meaning that the shots were fired more than 1 to 2 feet away, and they occurred at or about the same time. The angles of the gunshot wounds were consistent with Mrs. Harris being on her knees and the shooter standing behind her. Dr. Hayne testified that the manner of Mrs. Harris's death was homicide, and that it would have taken a minimum of fifteen to twenty minutes for Mrs. Harris to die from her wounds.

10. When Mrs. Harris's body was discovered, rigor mortis had set in, indicating that Mrs. Harris had been dead for at least two hours, but no more than forty eight hours. Fly larvae, or maggots, were in both of Mrs. Harris's ears, indicating that she had been dead for at least twelve to twenty four hours. Based upon Sergeant Tucker's testimony that the body was discovered at about 5:20 P.M. on February 16, and Mr. Harris's testimony that he saw his wife alive at about 6:00 A.M. on February 15, this evidence would place the time of death between approximately 6:00 A.M. on February 15, and 5:20 A.M. on February 16. One of the Harris's neighbors, Bill Richardson, testified that he heard three gunshots near Bozeman Lake around 10:15 or 10:20 A.M. on February 15.

11. In late January or February of 1994, Charlie Palmer, Justin Underwood's uncle, discovered that some items were missing from his home, including his pistol and some tools. Mr. Palmer spoke with Chief Deputy Hubert Roberts of the Madison County Sheriff's Department about the stolen items, but did not file an official report, because he thought that his ex-wife might have used the spare keys to enter his home. Mr. Palmer decided to check his nephew's home to find out if Underwood had taken the items. Underwood let his uncle search his car, a light yellow Oldsmobile Cutlass, in which Mr. Palmer found his tools and his pistol. On March 7 or 8, Mr. Palmer went to see Deputy Roberts again, and this time Deputy Roberts filled out a report on the items that Mr. Palmer had discovered were missing over the last month. Included in this report was the RG blue steel .32 caliber revolver, serial number 0207090, that Mr. Palmer had recovered. Although Mr. Palmer was somewhat confused about exactly when he noticed that his pistol was missing, he was certain that it was missing before March 7 or 8, when he gave this report to Deputy Roberts. The statement says that the pistol was missing in late January or early February.

12. When Mr. Palmer gave his statement to Deputy Roberts, he also turned over the pistol and the box of .32 caliber revolver bullets that he used with the gun to the deputy. Deputy Roberts then wrote down the gun's serial number and gave the pistol and bullets to Sergeant Tucker on March 8. No attempts were made to lift fingerprints from the gun, because it had already been handled by Charlie Palmer and Deputy Roberts before he handed it over to Sergeant Tucker. However, Steve Byrd, a forensic scientist specializing in firearms examinations at the crime lab, concluded from

his examination that the bullets taken from Mrs. Harris's body were fired from Charlie Palmer's pistol. His conclusion was corroborated by the findings of a second analyst who initialed Byrd's report.

13. On March 9, Deputy Roberts arrested Underwood for the burglary of Charlie Palmer's residence. Later that afternoon, Underwood gave his statement to Terry Barfield, an investigator with the Madison County Sheriff's Office, and W.H. Hathcock with the Mississippi Highway Patrol. In his statement, Underwood admitted to breaking into Charlie Palmer's home on February 5 and taking items, including the pistol that Charlie Palmer retrieved from Underwood's car on March 7.
14. The next day, March 10, Underwood gave another statement to Officer Barfield and Investigator Larry Saxton in which he admitted to killing Mrs. Harris by shooting her at Bozeman Lake. However, he stated that Mrs. Harris had asked him to kill her because her husband had given her AIDS. Both parties stipulated at trial that Mrs. Harris never had AIDS or HIV. Evidence was presented at trial showing that Mrs. Harris was taking amitriptyline, a medication commonly prescribed for depression. However, Mrs. Harris had undergone a radical mastectomy, so it wouldn't be unusual for her doctor to prescribe an antidepressant. Dr. George Allard, Mrs. Harris's primary care physician testified that amitriptyline could also be prescribed for an intestinal tract problem, which would be consistent with Mrs. Harris's medical history.
15. According to Underwood's March 10 statement made to Officers Barfield and Saxton, Mrs. Harris saw Underwood drive by on February 15 and waved for him to come to her house. Mrs. Harris knew Underwood, because he had done some yard work for her. When he came into the house, Underwood said that Mrs. Harris asked if he had a gun, so he went and got it out of his car, and she offered him money to kill her. Underwood stated that she drove them to the cattle gap, where they got out of the car and walked to the lake, stopping periodically for Mrs. Harris to catch her breath. He said that Mrs. Harris got down on her knees and started praying, so Underwood got down on his knees, and then Mrs. Harris said, "Do it." Underwood got up, closed his eyes, and shot the pistol six times. The pistol was the same one that he had taken from Charlie Palmer's house. Then he left Mrs. Harris lying on the ground, drove her car back to her house, and left in his own car.
16. After presenting the foregoing evidence, the State rested its case. The defense rested without calling any witnesses. Following closing arguments and jury instructions, the jury convicted Underwood of capital murder. At the close of the sentencing phase, the jury found that Underwood should be sentenced to death.

* * *

V.

THE PREJUDICIAL EFFECT OF THE INTRODUCTION OF THE VIDEO TAPE OF THE CRIME SCENE DEPICTING THE VICTIM'S BODY OUTWEIGHED THE TAPE'S PROBATIVE VALUE.

VI.

THE PREJUDICIAL EFFECT OF THE INTRODUCTION OF NUMEROUS GRUESOME PHOTOGRAPHS OUTWEIGHED THEIR PROBATIVE VALUE AND CONSTITUTES REVERSIBLE ERROR BY THE LOWER COURT.

44. Underwood's next two assignments of error are directed toward the trial court's allowing photographs and a video tape of Mrs. Harris's body at the crime scene and photographs of the body prior to the autopsy to be shown to the jury. "Although relevant, evidence may be excluded if its probative value is substantially outweighed by the danger of unfair prejudice, confusion of the issues, or misleading the jury, or by considerations of undue delay, waste of time, or needless presentation of cumulative evidence." Miss. R. Evid. 403. Underwood argues that the photographs and video tape created unfair prejudice in the minds of the jury that outweighed any probative value.

A general rule of this court leaves the admission of photographs into evidence to the sound discretion of the trial judge. Her decision is upheld unless there has been an abuse of that discretion. Stringer v. State, 548 So. 2d 125, 134 (Miss. 1989). "'[P]hotographs which are gruesome or inflammatory and lack an evidentiary purpose are always inadmissible as evidence.'" McNeal v. State, 551 So. 2d 151, 159 (Miss. 1989) quoting McFee v. State, 511 So. 2d 130, 135 (Miss. 1987). Mackbee v. State, 575 So. 2d 16, 31 (Miss. 1990).

When deciding on the admissibility of gruesome photos, trial judges must consider: "(1) whether the proof is absolute or in doubt as to identity of the guilty party, [and] (2) whether the photos are necessary evidence or simply a ploy on the part of the prosecutor to arouse the passion and prejudice of the jury." Holland v. State, 587 So. 2d 848, 864 (Miss.1991) (quoting McNeal, 551 So. 2d at 159).

[T]he lower court's judgment will not be reversed on the ground that photographs are gruesome and prejudicial, unless the lower court has abused its discretion.

Moreover, in a slaying such as the instant case, in which the only eyewitness was the defendant, and it was argued that the slaying was something other than murder, the relevancy of photographs showing the scene and victim is increased. Griffin v. State, 557 So. 2d 542, 549–50 (Miss. 1990) (internal citations omitted). "The same standards applicable to determining the admissibility of photographs are applicable to video tapes." Blue v. State, 674 So. 2d 1184, 1210 (Miss. 1996) (citing Holland, 587 So. 2d at 864).

45. Over Underwood's objection, Judge Toney allowed the prosecution to enter five pictures of Mrs. Harris's body into evidence. State's Exhibit 5 is an 8x10 color photograph of Mrs. Harris's body as found by the lakeshore. It shows the body face down on the ground, wearing a blue shirt, black pants and belt, and red house shoes. There are patches of blood visible on the blue shirt. State's Exhibits 10, 11, and 12 are all 8x10 color photographs of the body just before the autopsy, showing the gunshot wounds. Little or no blood is evident in any of the autopsy photographs. Exhibit 10 shows Mrs. Harris's back with the two gunshot wounds, Exhibit 11 depicts the two arm wounds, and Exhibit 12 is a photograph of the gunshot wound to Mrs. Harris's neck and to the shoulder. State's Exhibit 17 is a 3x4 color photograph taken at the autopsy of Mrs. Harris's hand showing abrasions on her palm and fingers. These pictures are not particularly gruesome or inflammatory so as to shock or prejudice the jury in this case. The photographs were all relevant to show the victim's injuries and to help the jury visualize the crime and crime scene, corroborating the testimony of the investigators and partially corroborating Underwood's confession. Photographs showing Mrs. Harris's body wearing the red house shoes and the scratches on her hands from clutching weeds and grass were relevant to support the prosecution's theory of kidnapping, to refute any theory of assisted suicide, and to corroborate Dr. Hayne's testimony that Mrs. Harris did not die immediately. The trial court did not abuse its discretion in allowing these photographs to be admitted into evidence.

46. Also over Underwood's objection, Judge Toney allowed the prosecution to play a video tape for the jury of Mrs. Harris's body as it was found by investigators. After hearing the arguments from counsel, the judge determined that the jury would not be allowed to take the tape into deliberations, because he instructed the prosecutor to stop the tape before the body was turned over. The portion of the video tape shown to the jury depicts little more than State's Exhibit 5, the photograph of Mrs. Harris's body at the crime scene. The only additional footage is a shot of Mrs. Harris's ear, revealing that maggots had infested her ear. Judge Toney allowed the prosecution to show the tape through a closeup of the ear, because that evidence was used to help establish the time of death. Out of precaution, however, Judge Toney ruled that the remainder of the video tape, showing the investigators' further examination of the body after turning it over, would not be shown to the jury.

47. Underwood specifically points to this Court's decision in McNeal, *supra*, to support his argument that the video depicting maggots in Mrs. Harris's ear was inflammatory and lacked any evidentiary purpose. In McNeal, we held that the admission of closeup color photographs of the victim's decomposed, maggot-infested skull was an abuse of discretion. McNeal, 551 So. 2d at 159. However, the Court described those photographs as "some of the most gruesome photographs

ever presented to this Court." Id. Here, the short segment of video tape showing the inside of Mrs. Harris's ear is not exceptionally gruesome, particularly since there is no visual evidence of decomposition. Furthermore, unlike the photographs in McNeal, the video of the maggots in Mrs. Harris's ear is relevant, because the evidence was used to establish the time of death. Judge Toney properly reviewed this evidence under Rule 403, and did not abuse his discretion in allowing the jury to view that portion of the prosecution's video tape.

* * *

Conviction of murder affirmed.
[Parts of case omitted]

McHENRY v. STATE

Supreme Court of Indiana, 820 N.E.2d 124, 2005 Ind. LEXIS 4 (2005)

Dickson, Justice. Shepard, C.J., and Sullivan, Boehm, and Rucker, JJ., concur.

Dickson, Justice.

Following a jury trial, the defendant, Mirtha McHenry, a bank teller, was convicted of forgery, a class C felony, and theft, a class D felony, as a result of her actions relating to an unauthorized withdrawal of $6,500 from the account of a bank customer. Concluding that the evidence was insufficient to establish her guilt of either crime, the Court of Appeals reversed the convictions and remanded with instructions that she be discharged.

We grant transfer and affirm the trial court.

In her appeal from the convictions, the defendant alleges three grounds for reversal: (1) insufficient evidence; (2) refusal to strike two jurors for cause; and (3) erroneous admission of surveillance videotape.

1. Sufficiency of Evidence

The defendant contends that neither of her convictions were supported by sufficient evidence. Upon a challenge to the sufficiency of evidence to support a conviction, a reviewing court does not reweigh the evidence or judge the credibility of the witnesses, and respects "the jury's exclusive province to weigh conflicting evidence." We have often emphasized that appellate courts must consider only the probative evidence and reasonable inferences supporting the verdict. Expressed another way, we have stated that appellate courts must affirm "if the probative evidence and reasonable inferences drawn from the evidence could have allowed a reasonable trier of fact to find the defendant guilty beyond a reasonable doubt."

Evidence at her jury trial established that the defendant, a bank teller, withdrew $6,500 from the account of Charles Landes. The defendant testified that someone had come to her wanting to make this withdrawal, that she had filled in the withdrawal slip, and that she had the customer sign it and gave him the money. Upon receiving his bank statement and discovering a $6,500 withdrawal from his account, Landes immediately reported the error to the bank and signed an affidavit of forgery stating that the signature on the withdrawal slip was not his and that he did not receive any of the proceeds. The withdrawal slip was time-stamped 4:44 p.m. The bank's videotape showed no one at the defendant's teller window when the transaction occurred. Bank records also disclosed that the defendant had accessed and viewed this customer's account records twice during the two weeks before the withdrawal.

Although reciting that "in reviewing the sufficiency of the evidence, we will not reweigh the evidence or judge the credibility of witnesses," the Court of Appeals reversed the convictions, speculating that the withdrawal slip "may *have been* received earlier and only stamped at 4:44 p.m." and that the defendant's prior inquiries into the customer's account balance "*may have been* precipitated by a phone call request."

In reversing the jury's verdict, the Court of Appeals failed to restrict its consideration to only the evidence and reasonable inferences favorable to the trial court's verdict, but instead reweighed the evidence, improperly substituting its own judgment for that of the jury. While the jury could have drawn the same inferences as the Court of Appeals, they did not. They returned a unanimous verdict of guilt on each count.

The defendant urges that the State failed to present evidence that she intended to defraud the customer or the bank or that she took the money. The State responds (and the defendant concedes) that intent to defraud may be proven by circumstantial evidence, and the State argues that the defendant acknowledged accessing the customer's account and performing the transaction that removed $6,500 from the account—money that the customer did not receive. And the videotape enabled the jury to infer that there was no customer at the defendant's teller window when the withdrawal was made.

Finding that the probative evidence and reasonable inferences drawn from the evidence could have allowed a reasonable trier of fact to find the defendant guilty beyond a reasonable doubt, we conclude that the evidence was sufficient to support the judgment.

2. Failure to Exclude Jurors for Cause

* * *

3. Surveillance Videotape

The defendant also contends that the trial court committed reversible error in admitting the bank's surveillance video. The video shows that no person was at the defendant's teller window at the time she entered the questioned transaction. The defendant objection at trial was that the videotape was not a business record and that there was an inadequate foundation, the particulars of which were not specified. On appeal, the defendant does not present argument as to the business record issue but rather argues generally that because the state did not present information to support the reliability of the surveillance tape other than the affidavit of a records custodian, it failed to lay a proper foundation for the admission of the video.

The parties agree that under a "silent witness" theory, videotapes may be admitted as substantive evidence, but "there must be a strong showing of authenticity and competency" and that when automatic cameras are involved, "there should be evidence as to how and when the camera was loaded, how frequently the camera was activated, when the photographs were taken, and the processing and changing of custody of the film after its removal from the camera."

The State argues that witness testimony established the videotape's authenticity. The bank manager removed the videotape, and a police detective checked it to assure that it was the tape covering the date in question. The detective then watched the tape to match the transactions and customers' account numbers with the representations on the videotape. In addition, the bank's custodian of records verified by affidavit that the tape was a regularly conducted activity of the bank and that she had examined the records to verify its trustworthiness.

Rulings on the admission of evidence are subject to appellate review for abuse of discretion. We are not persuaded that the trial court abused its discretion in admitting the videotape.

Conclusion

We grant transfer and affirm the judgment of the trial court. [Reversed the Court of Appeals.]

Shepard, C.J., and Sullivan, Boehm, and Rucker, JJ., concur.

Cases Relating to Chapter 15

Results of Examinations and Tests

COMMONWEALTH v. GAYNOR

Supreme Judicial Court of Massachusetts, 443 Mass. 245, 2005 Mass. LEXIS 7 (2005)

Judges Present: Marshall, C.J., Greaney, Spina, & Sosman JJ.

SPINA, J. The defendant was convicted of the aggravated rape and murder of four women in Springfield between November 1, 1997, and March 11, 1998. The jury returned verdicts under all three theories of murder in the first degree in each case. On appeal, the defendant asserts error in certain pretrial rulings, including . . . rulings that deoxyribonucleic acid (DNA) evidence taken from mixed DNA samples was sufficiently reliable to be admitted in evidence, and that the database on which Cellmark Diagnostics based its frequency calculations was adequate. . . . Finally, the defendant asks us to grant him a new trial under G. L. c. 278, § 33E. We affirm the convictions and decline to grant relief under § 33E.

1. Facts. *The jury could have found the following facts.*

a. *Victim no.* 1. The victim put her children to bed at 10 P.M. on October 31, 1997. Sometime between midnight and 12:30 A.M., the first-floor tenant at 866 Worthington Street in Springfield heard a "scream of pain" followed by a "thud" from the victim's second-floor apartment. The victim's son discovered her body on the living room couch after he awoke at 7 A.M. on November 1. Her naked body was covered by a blanket and a towel had been placed over her head. Her hands were bound behind her back.

An autopsy revealed that death was caused by asphyxia due to manual strangulation. The victim's blood tested positive for metabolites of cocaine and alcohol. Her anus was widely dilated, consistent with penetration.

The defendant's thumb print was identified on a broken ashtray found in the living room, and his palm print was identified on a hair gel container, also in the living room. Fecal matter was found on a sock and inside the rim of a small vase recovered from the victim's living room. The defendant told his brother that he had had anal intercourse with women he met in the Worthington-Federal Streets section of Springfield, an area known for prostitutes and "crack" cocaine. The defendant's brother had driven him several times in October and November, 1997, to the neighborhood where the victim lived.

Several items collected from the scene and all biological evidence recovered from the first victim's body, as well as blood samples given by the defendant were sent to Cellmark for DNA analysis. Cellmark performed two series of polymerase chain reaction (PCR) tests on DNA samples taken from items submitted in all four cases. The first series of tests were performed at nine genetic loci: DQ Alpha, five polymarker (PM) loci, and three (TPOX, THO1, and CSF) short tandem repeat (STR) loci. In some instances testing was done at a tenth locus, identified as D1S80. Some of these tests were witnessed by a defense expert.

A second series of PCR tests was done on some samples at thirteen core STR loci (including the three STR loci where testing previously had been done) designated for inclusion in the national database that contains DNA profiles of convicted felons, known as the combined DNA index system, or CODIS. See G. L. c. 22E, § 1 (definitions). A defense expert was present during the second series of tests. DNA samples from seven other suspects were examined and all seven were excluded as contributors in each case.

* * *

[Three other murder victims presented similar DNA evidence from murder scenes.]

5. *Admissibility of DNA evidence.* The defendant filed a pretrial motion in which he requested a "*Daubert-Lanigan* hearing" with respect to the admissibility of DNA evidence the Commonwealth was expected to offer in all four cases. See Daubert v. Merrell Dow Pharmaceuticals, Inc., 509 U.S. 579, 125 L. Ed. 2d 469, 113 S. Ct. 2786 (1993); Commonwealth v. Lanigan, 419 Mass. 15, 641 N.E.2d 1342 (1994). Hearings were conducted as to both the first and second series of tests, and the defendant now appeals from rulings that (1) Cellmark's methodology in dealing with mixtures and technical artifacts is generally accepted within the scientific community; (2) Cellmark both performed its tests properly and reported the results accurately; (3) Cellmark's election not to stay within conservative recommendations of test kit manufacturers regarding the minimum quantity of DNA tested did not invalidate the studies; (4) the use of the product rule to make frequency calculations for identifiable primary contributors in a mixed DNA sample is acceptable; and (5) the database used by Cellmark to make frequency calculations is adequate and common within the field.

a. *Mixtures and artifacts.* The defendant first claims that the evidence does not support the judge's conclusion that Cellmark can reliably distinguish technical artifacts from true alleles, or primary from secondary contributors in mixed samples of DNA. He does not challenge the scientific validity of PCR testing. We previously have held that PCR-based DNA analysis, both generally and at the DQ Alpha locus, the PM loci, and the D1S80 locus, is a scientifically valid methodology for developing DNA profile evidence. See Commonwealth v. Vao Sok, 425 Mass. 787, 799, 801–802, 683 N.E.2d 671 (1997). We reached the same conclusion with respect to PCR testing at STR loci identified as CSF1P0, TPOX, and TH01. Commonwealth v. Rosier, 425 Mass. 807, 812–813, 685 N.E.2d 739 (1997). The defendant does not challenge the scientific validity of PCR testing at the other STR loci designated under CODIS. His challenge focuses on the second, or reliability prong of the *Daubert-Lanigan* inquiry.

A determination of the reliability of the testing process entails a fact-based inquiry, including questions of credibility. See Commonwealth v. Vao Sok, *supra* at 797, 798. The analysis calls on a judge to determine whether testing was properly performed, Commonwealth v. McNickles, 434 Mass. 839, 850, 753 N.E.2d 131 (2001), and whether an expert's conclusions based on clinical experience and observations were sufficiently reliable. Canavan's Case, 432 Mass. 304, 313, 733 N.E.2d 1042 (2000). The judge's decision under the reliability prong is reviewed under the abuse of discretion standard. Id. at 312.

Testimony indicated that it is not unusual to find mixtures of DNA (a sample containing DNA from two or more persons) in cases of sexual assault. The presence of a mixture of DNA can create difficulties in interpreting test results. For example, where DNA from two contributors is present in a mixture in relatively equal amounts, the dots or bands (depending on the particular test) produced by the two samples during the testing process will display comparable intensity (darkness). In such cases the Cellmark analyst will report the existence of a combination without attempting to interpret the results.

Similar interpretive challenges arise from the presence of technical artifacts: mistakes in the PCR amplification process that replicates a defined segment of DNA through the use of enzymes. Artifacts typically give faint readings. When a test result suggests either an artifact or a secondary contributor and the difference in intensity between readings is slight, the Cellmark analyst will not attempt to distinguish them but will report the result as not interpretable.

Where DNA from two contributors is present in a mixture in unequal amounts, readings produced by the larger sample will be darker than those of the smaller sample, roughly in direct proportion to the difference between the amounts of the samples. Where the differences are such that intensity readings from the greater sample are dark and those from the lesser sample are faint, the Cellmark analyst may conclude that the darker reading is produced by a primary contributor and report her conclusion in the same way she reports a single source sample, conformably with the recommendation of the National Resource Council (NRC), The Evaluation of Forensic DNA Evidence (1996) at 129. We have treated the reports of the NRC as authoritative works for purposes of determining generally accepted standards within the scientific community for (a) the validity of the underlying scientific theory, or (b) the reliability of the underlying process for developing forensic DNA evidence. See Commonwealth v. Rosier, *supra* at 815; Commonwealth v. Vao Sok, *supra* at 801.

Here, only test results based on a single source of DNA, or, where there appeared to be a mixture, only test results that yielded strong evidence (dark bands or dots) of a primary contributor were used. Consequently, a weak reading of a secondary contributor or technical artifact had no effect on Cellmark's ability to report the result of the primary contributor and calculate a statistic of the probability of a random match to the defendant's DNA profile. The judge's findings that Cellmark's methodology in reporting tests of a mixed sample with an identifiable primary contributor in the same way it reports tests of a single source sample conforms to the recommendation of the NRC, and that Cellmark's methodology in dealing with the presence of mixtures or technical artifacts is generally accepted within the scientific community, were made with record support and well within his discretion.

b. *Conduct of tests.* The defendant suggests other known conditions that could affect the accuracy and reliability of test results, including contamination, loci dropout, allele dropout, differential amplification, stochastic effect, spikes, and peak imbalances. We need not engage in a lengthy discussion about these conditions. For purposes of this appeal, it is sufficient to note that Cellmark analysts considered each of these issues and factored them into their test results. The judge accepted the testimony of Dr. Robin Cotton, Cellmark's forensic laboratory director, with respect to the many controls and safeguards that Cellmark uses to adjust for these challenges, including threshold control dots to detect minimum sample size at the DQ Alpha locus, the use of two different manufacturers' test kits that test DNA at four of the same loci for CODIS testing, controls to ensure against contamination at the PM and D1S80 loci, and others. The judge found that Cellmark follows the standards adopted by the DNA advisory board, a group of individuals authorized by Congress to advise the Federal Bureau of Investigation on DNA testing, and the guidelines published by the Technical Working Group for DNA Analysis Methods (TWGDAM) in 1995, except in cases where those guidelines have been superseded by the DNA advisory board standards. The judge did not abuse his discretion in ruling that the test results were sufficiently reliable to be put before the jury and that the questions raised by the defendant were more appropriately addressed to the weight of the evidence. See Commonwealth v. McNickles, 434 Mass. 839, 850–854, 753 N. E.2d 131 (2001).

c. *Manufacturer's recommendations.* There is no merit to the defendant's contention that Cellmark's failure to comply with the minimum standards for DNA sample sizes set by the test kit manufacturers invalidated the test results. The user's manuals for the Profiler Plus and Cofiler kits, both manufactured by PerkinElmer, Inc., recommended that they not be used with less than one to 2.5 nanograms (one-billionth of a gram) of questioned DNA, but many of the tests were conducted with less than the recommended amounts. The judge found that the manufacturers' recommendations were just that, recommendations. They were intended to ensure optimal results. He found, with record support, that Cellmark had conducted validation studies that supported the reliability of testing based on amounts smaller than recommended by the manufacturers, amounts as small as one-half nanogram. Cellmark had also conducted validation studies indicating that analysts could reliably interpret computerized test results (the second series of tests performed under CODIS) based on readings as low as forty relative fluorescent units (RFUs) rather than the conservative level of 150 RFUs recommended by the manufacturers, and the judge found that Cellmark's readings were reliable. There was no abuse of discretion.

The defendant's expert, Dr. Donald E. Riley, ultimately conceded Cellmark's conclusions (that test results matched the defendant's profile) were supported by the data and that the defendant's and the victims' identified alleles matched those identified by Cellmark's testing. The judge observed that "[a]ll that Dr. Riley can really say is that there is a 'potential' for this system of analysis to miss alleles and distort results. I recognize that the potential for error exists in *any* scientific testing, but I am satisfied that Cellmark has done all that is reasonably possible to eliminate that potential" (emphasis in original). He correctly noted that the issues raised by the defendant went to the weight of the evidence, not its admissibility.

d. *Use of the product rule.* The defendant argues that the judge erred by accepting the proposition that if an analyst can distinguish between a primary contributor and a secondary contributor in a mixed DNA sample, the analyst may properly treat the primary contributor as a single source for statistical purposes. His argument, essentially, is that the "product rule," which has been held to be a scientifically acceptable method for calculating frequency profiles based on results of PCR testing of single source samples, see Commonwealth v. Rosier, *supra* at 816–817, produces unreliable results in mixed samples; and that a "likelihood ratio," which has been held to be a scientifically acceptable method of calculating frequency profiles based on results of testing of mixed samples, should have been used. See Commonwealth v. McNickles, *supra* at 845–848.

Likelihood ratio analysis is appropriate for test results of mixed samples when the primary and secondary contributors cannot be distinguished. Id. at 846. It need not be applied when a primary contributor can be identified. Contrary to the defendant's view, the use of the product rule is scientifically acceptable where the analyst can distinguish between a primary and a secondary contributor in a mixed sample, and thereafter treat the primary contributor as a single source for statistical purposes. See NRC, Evaluation of Forensic DNA Evidence (1996), Executive Summary Recommendation 4.1 at 5; State v. Roman Nose, 667 N.W.2d 386, 398 (Minn. 2003). In any event, at trial, Dr. Christopher Basten, the Commonwealth's statistician in the field of population genetics, recalculated the profile frequencies using likelihood ratios and reached results comparable to those obtained under the product rule.

e. *Cellmark's database.* Finally, the defendant contends that the judge erred in ruling that Cellmark's database was adequate, that the absence of data on African-Americans from Springfield in Cellmark's database was not a matter of concern, and that the results of Cellmark's profile frequency calculations through use of the product rule were reliable and accurate.

The product rule refers to the product, or multiplication, of the frequencies (probabilities) with which each allele in a tested sample of DNA occurs in the population included in the database. The resulting number is the probability of someone's having the same characteristics as the sample tested. See Commonwealth v. Curnin, 409 Mass. 218, 224, 565 N.E.2d 440 (1991). The product rule is based on two assumptions about the nature of genetic variants in the population. Those assumptions are known as the condition of Hardy-Weinberg equilibrium, and the condition of linkage equilibrium. Hardy-Weinberg equilibrium is a condition that is achieved when there is no particular relationship between the occurrence of alleles within a single genetic marker. That is, when a person's parents meet randomly in the general population. Linkage equilibrium is a condition that is achieved when there is no particular relationship between genes. That is, when genes are inherited independently, and not linked to other genes. See id. at 225 n.11; NRC, Evaluation of Forensic DNA Evidence (1996) at 90–91, 106–107.

Dr. Basten testified that he had conducted a study of fifty databases, including Cellmark's, to determine whether the frequencies of alleles at particular loci varied between databases or between racial groups within the databases for the population of the United States. He had presented the details and the results of his study at two scientific conventions. Dr. Basten concluded that there was consistency of allelic frequency between the various databases and within the various racial groups, but that allelic frequency varied between racial groups. He also concluded that the size of Cellmark's database, 103 persons, is adequate and common within the field, and that a database larger than

Cellmark's would produce no significant difference in result. He explained that the reliability of profiling depends more on the number of alleles in the database than the number of persons in the database. Dr. Basten discounted the absence of data on any African-American from Springfield in Cellmark's database because his study of the fifty databases indicated that the African-American population is fairly homogeneous across the United States. He endorsed Cellmark's use of the product rule in making its profile frequency calculations, and verified Cellmark's test results through the use of the theta factor, a statistical adjustment recommended by the NRC when dealing with possible subgroups, or small isolated populations. See NRC, Evaluation of Forensic DNA Evidence (1996) at 29–30. Dr. Basten employed the more conservative of the two theta factors recommended by the NRC. Verification also was made through the use of "confidence intervals." See Commonwealth v. Rosier, *supra* at 814 n.14.

The judge found that Dr. Basten's use of the conservative theta factor and confidence intervals were an "appropriate corrective measure" to account for any possible substructure with the African-American community in Springfield. He acted within his discretion in ruling that Cellmark's database was adequate and that the use of the product rule produced reliable results. See Commonwealth v. Rosier, *supra* at 813–814.

* * *

Relief under G. L. c. 278, § 33E. We have reviewed the transcript, the record, and the briefs, and conclude that there is no reason to reduce the verdicts or grant a new trial pursuant to our power under G. L. c. 278, § 33E.

Judgments affirmed.

PEOPLE v. WILKINSON

Supreme Court of California, 33 Cal. 4th 821, 2004 Cal. LEXIS 6833 (2004)

DISPOSITION: Judgment of the Court of Appeal reversed.

GEORGE, C.J.—Defendant Jaleh Wilkinson was convicted at trial of the offenses of battery on a custodial officer, driving a vehicle under the influence of alcohol, and failing to stop at the scene of an accident. The Court of Appeal reversed defendant's convictions on two unrelated grounds, concluding that (1) the statutory scheme pertaining to battery on a custodial officer violates equal protection principles because the statutes allow battery on a custodial officer without injury to be punished more severely than battery on a custodial officer with injury, and (2) the trial court erred in denying defendant a hearing, pursuant to the Kelly/Frye doctrine (People v. Kelly (1976) 17 Cal.3d 24 [130 Cal. Rptr. 144, 549 P.2d 1240]; Frye v. United States (D.C. Cir. 1923) 54 App. D.C. 46 [293 F. 1013]), regarding the admissibility of polygraph evidence to support defendant's claim that her commission of the charged offenses resulted from her unknowing and involuntary ingestion of drugs. We granted review to consider the Court of Appeal's resolution of both issues.

For the reasons discussed below, we conclude that (1). . ., (2) in light of the categorical prohibition on the admission of polygraph evidence in Evidence Code section 351.1, the trial court did not err in declining to hold a Kelly/Frye hearing regarding the evidence proffered by defendant. Accordingly, we shall reverse the judgment of the Court of Appeal.

* * *

A.

With regard to the second issue before us [whether the trial court should have held hearings concerning the admissibility of polygraph results], the Attorney General contends the Court of Appeal erred by remanding for a Kelly/Frye hearing [concerning the admissibility of scientific evidence], because Evidence Code section 351.1 establishes a categorical prohibition on the admission of polygraph evidence in criminal cases absent a stipulation. Subdivision (a) of section 351.1, which was enacted in 1983, provides: "Notwithstanding any other provision of law, the results of a polygraph examination, the opinion of a polygraph examiner, or any reference to an offer to take, failure to take, or taking of a polygraph examination, shall not be admitted into evidence in any criminal proceeding, including pretrial and post conviction motions and hearings, or in any trial or hearing of a juvenile for a criminal offense, whether heard in juvenile or adult court, unless all parties stipulate to the admission of such results."

* * *

On appeal, defendant contended that, notwithstanding the apparent categorical prohibition of Evidence Code section 351.1, she was entitled to a Kelly/Frye hearing to determine the admissibility of her proposed polygraph evidence under the reasoning of this court's decisions in People v. Jackson (1996) 13 Cal.4th 1164 [56 Cal. Rptr. 2d 49, 920 P.2d 1254] (Jackson), and People v. Fudge (1994) 7 Cal.4th 1075 [31 Cal. Rptr. 2d 321, 875 P.2d 36] (Fudge) (discussed post). The Court of Appeal agreed with defendant that she had "made a sufficient offer of proof to entitle her to a [Kelly/Frye] hearing" under the reasoning of Jackson and Fudge, observing that "we do not see what more such an offer would need to meet the threshold required to convene such a hearing." The court, concluding that the denial of a Kelly/Frye hearing prejudiced defendant, remanded the case to the trial court with directions to conduct such a hearing and to set aside defendant's convictions in the event the trial court "concludes the polygraph evidence is admissible."

B.

Prior to the enactment of Evidence Code section 351.1, the admission of polygraph evidence in California was governed by the test of Frye v. United States, *supra*, 293 F. 1013. Under that test, one who seeks the admission of evidence based upon a new scientific technique must make "a preliminary showing of general acceptance of the new technique in the relevant scientific community." (Kelly, *supra*, 17 Cal.3d at p. 30; see id. at p. 32 ["reaffirm[ing] our allegiance" to the Frye "'general acceptance'" test for new scientific techniques]; see also People v. Leahy (1994) 8 Cal.4th 587, 593–604 [34 Cal. Rptr. 2d 663, 882 P.2d 321] [retaining the Kelly/Frye test as the applicable California standard and declining to adopt the new federal standard set forth in Daubert v. Merrell Dow Pharmaceuticals, Inc. (1993) 509 U.S. 579. Relying upon Frye and its progeny, a long line of California decisions has held or recognized that the results of a polygraph examination are inadmissible at trial absent a stipulation by the parties. (See People v. Carter (1957) 48 Cal. 2d 737, 752, ["Lie detector tests do not as yet have enough reliability to justify the admission of expert testimony based on their results.]

* * *

The legal landscape in California changed with the Court of Appeal's opinion in Witherspoon v. Superior Court (1982) 133 Cal. App. 3d 24 [183 Cal. Rptr. 615] (Witherspoon). The majority in Witherspoon criticized the judicial rule that consistently excludes polygraph evidence as "an almost 'knee jerk' response" "based more on considerations of policy rather than any demonstrated lack of reliability or acceptance of the test" considerations that the majority felt "are more properly matters for legislative rather than judicial determination." (Id. at 29, 31.) The majority, not finding any provision in the Evidence Code expressly barring the admission of polygraph evidence, concluded the defendant was entitled to a hearing to determine the admissibility of the evidence, suggesting that the polygraph evidence should be admitted so long as the evidence was relevant (Evid. Code, 210), its probative value was not substantially outweighed by the probability of undue prejudice (id., 352), and the defendant could satisfy the requirements for the admission of expert testimony (id., 801 [expert opinion testimony]; see also id., 720 [qualification of expert witness]; id., 405 [determination of preliminary fact]). (Witherspoon, *supra*, at pp. 30–35.)

"It was in reaction to Witherspoon that the Legislature enacted Evidence Code section 351.1." (People v. Kegler (1987) 197 Cal. App. 3d 72, 85 [242 Cal. Rptr. 897] (Kegler); In re Kathleen W. (1987) 190 Cal. App. 3d 68, 72 [235 Cal. Rptr. 205].) The Assembly Committee on Criminal Law and Public Safety's analysis of the bill that became section 351.1 expressly stated the bill was "'intended to overrule [Witherspoon] and to create an exception to the truth-in-evidence section of Proposition 8 that bars exclusion of any relevant evidence.' (Assembly Com. on Crim. Law and Pub. Safety, staff comments on Sen. Bill. No. 266 as amended Mar. 16, 1983 (1983–1984 Reg. Sess.), for hg. on June 8, 1983, p. 2.)" (Kegler, *supra*, 197 Cal. App. 3d at p. 84.) Legislative history materials expressed concerns that (1) the Witherspoon procedure would "'substantially increase trial time by requiring courts to litigate collateral issues regarding the reliability of the particular test and qualifications of the specific polygraph examiner in every case,'" (2) polygraph testing procedures lack standardization and cannot be tested for accuracy, and (3) jurors would "'assign too much credence to the results of a polygraph examination.'" (Kegler, *supra*, 197 Cal. App. 3d at p. 89.)

As past decisions make clear, the Kelly/Frye test constitutes a judicially created rule relating to the admissibility of certain types of evidence and, as such, a rule that is subject to legislative revision. . . . . . By enacting Evidence Code section 351.1, the Legislature abrogated the Kelly/Frye rule with respect to the admission of polygraph evidence in criminal cases. As noted, the Legislature enacted section 351.1 to overrule the then recently decided appellate court decision in Witherspoon, *supra*, 133 Cal. App. 3d 24, which had criticized the routine application of the Frye test to exclude polygraph evidence and had suggested that such evidence could be admitted if the proponent made a showing of admissibility under certain provisions of the Evidence Code. Thus, in adopting Evidence Code section 351.1, the Legislature effectively codified the rule set forth in the pre-Witherspoon California cases involving polygraph evidence, namely that such evidence is categorically inadmissible in the absence of the stipulation of all parties.

This understanding of Evidence Code section 351.1 is consistent with numerous cases that subsequently have interpreted the statute to exclude polygraph evidence categorically in criminal cases, absent the stipulation of the parties. (See In re Aontae D. (1994) 25 Cal.App.4th 167, 173 [30 Cal. Rptr. 2d 176]; Kegler, *supra*, 197 Cal. App. 3d at p. 84; In re Kathleen W., *supra*, 190 Cal. App. 3d at p. 72.) Defendant concedes that this is the import of section 351.1, but she argues she nonetheless was entitled to a Kelly/Frye hearing under this court's precedents, in particular the decisions in Jackson, *supra*, 13 Cal.4th 1164, and Fudge, *supra*, 7 Cal.4th 1075 [31 Cal. Rptr. 2d 321, 875 P.2d 36]. Insofar as section 351.1's categorical exclusion is applied to deprive her of the opportunity to demonstrate the current reliability of proffered polygraph evidence under the Kelly/Frye standard, defendant claims the statute infringes upon her right to present a defense at trial, in violation of the federal Constitution. 9

C.

We first address defendant's claim that she was entitled to a Kelly/Frye hearing [concerning the admissibility of scientific evidence, the polygraph in this case] notwithstanding Evidence Code section 351.1. We begin with a review of the relevant portions of the decisions in Jackson, *supra*, 13 Cal.4th 1164, and Fudge, *supra*, 7 Cal.4th 1075, upon which defendant relies. In Jackson, the defendant, at the guilt phase of a capital trial, sought to present evidence that he had "passed" a polygraph test and had stated truthfully in the polygraph session that he had not killed the victim. (Jackson, *supra*, 13 Cal.4th at p. 1212.) The defendant in Jackson contended he was entitled to a Kelly/Frye hearing notwithstanding section 351.1, arguing that the statute's exclusion of such "reliable exculpatory evidence" denied him his right to due process of law under the federal Constitution. (Jackson, *supra*, 13 Cal.4th at p. 1212.) We rejected this claim, reasoning: "Even if defendant's argument were true in the abstract, he has failed to make the proper offer of proof under Kelly/Frye that the polygraph is now viewed in the scientific community as a reliable technique. "'. . . Having failed to make the proper offer of proof, defendant is in no position to assign error in the trial court's ruling." ' " (Ibid., quoting Fudge, *supra*, 7 Cal.4th at p. 1122.)

In Fudge, the defendant attempted to present evidence at the penalty phase of a capital trial that he had "passed" a polygraph examination, arguing that Evidence Code section 351.1 unconstitutionally deprived him of his right to present "relevant mitigating evidence." [Fudge ultimately lost his argument.] (Fudge, *supra*, 7 Cal.4th at pp. 1121, 1122.)

* * *

As the foregoing decisions demonstrate, defendant is correct in observing that, even after the enactment of Evidence Code section 351.1, we have required, as a prerequisite to preserving the claim for appeal, that a challenge to the constitutionality of this statute include an offer of proof that the proffered polygraph evidence is generally accepted under the Kelly/Frye standard. . . . .

The Court of Appeal correctly concluded in the present case that defendant had preserved her constitutional challenge to section 351.1 by making her offer of proof regarding the reliability of polygraph evidence under Kelly/Frye. The court, however, went further and remanded the case to the trial court to conduct a Kelly/Frye hearing, directing the trial court to set aside the judgment if that court found the polygraph evidence to be "admissible" under the Kelly/Frye standard, that is, if defendant demonstrated at the hearing that the polygraph technique employed was generally accepted in the scientific community.

Although our past cases have determined that an offer of proof regarding the reliability of polygraph evidence is a prerequisite for raising a constitutional challenge against Evidence Code section 351.1's categorical exclusion, we never have held that such proof is sufficient by itself to make out such a claim, that is, we never have suggested that evidence that satisfies the Kelly/Frye test must, as a constitutional matter, be admitted in evidence notwithstanding the statutory provision barring such admission. Indeed, in our recent decision in People v. Burgener, *supra*, 29 Cal.4th 833, we cautioned: "Before a criminal defendant can establish a federal due process right to use the results of a polygraph examination, it is necessary (although perhaps not sufficient) to offer proof that the technique has become generally accepted in the scientific community." (Id. at p. 871, italics added.) Thus, the Court of Appeal erred by remanding the case for a Kelly/Frye hearing without specifically addressing the question whether section 351.1's categorical exclusion of polygraph evidence would be unconstitutional in the event defendant is able to satisfy the Kelly/Frye test. Because defendant has preserved her federal constitutional challenge to section 351.1, we now address that issue.

D.

The Attorney General contends that under the reasoning of United States v. Scheffer, *supra*, 523 U.S. 303, the categorical exclusion of polygraph evidence mandated by Evidence Code section 351.1 does not violate the federal Constitution. In that case, the United States Supreme Court rejected a constitutional challenge to Military Rules of Evidence, rule 707(a), which bans polygraph evidence in military trials. The defendant, an airman who faced a military court-martial for alleged drug use, sought the admission of evidence that he had "passed" a polygraph examination, in order to bolster his testimony that he innocently had ingested the drugs. In a portion of the opinion authored by Justice Thomas and joined by seven other justices, the high court noted that "there is simply no consensus that polygraph evidence is reliable," observing that this lack of consensus is "reflected in the disagreement among state and federal courts concerning both the admissibility and the reliability of polygraph evidence." (United States v. Scheffer, *supra*, 523 U.S. at pp. 309–311 (lead opn. of Thomas, J.).) In light of this circumstance, the court concluded that the per se exclusion of polygraph evidence "is a rational and proportional means of advancing the legitimate interest in barring unreliable evidence" and that "[i]ndividual jurisdictions therefore may reasonably reach differing conclusions as to whether polygraph evidence should be admitted. We cannot say, then, that presented with such widespread uncertainty, the President acted arbitrarily or disproportionately in promulgating a per se rule excluding all polygraph evidence." (Id. at p. 312.)

Justice Kennedy, in a concurring opinion joined by three other justices, 12 commented that the "continuing, good-faith disagreement among experts and courts on the subject of polygraph reliability counsels against our invalidating a per se exclusion of polygraph results," and "[g]iven the ongoing debate about polygraphs, I agree the rule of exclusion is not so arbitrary or disproportionate that it is unconstitutional." (United States v. Scheffer, *supra*, 523 U.S. at p. 318 (conc. opn. of Kennedy, J.).) Justice Kennedy, however, expressed doubt "that the rule of per se exclusion is wise, and some later case might present a more compelling case for introduction of the testimony than this one does." (Ibid.)

We recently applied Scheffer in Maury, *supra*, 30 Cal.4th 342, in which the defendant sought the admission of evidence that he had "'passed'" a polygraph examination, in order to bolster his claim that someone else had killed the victim. (Id. at p. 413.) We concluded that in light of Scheffer, "[e]xcluding such evidence does not violate defendant's constitutional right to present a defense." (Ibid.) . . .

We reach the same conclusion here. Scheffer noted that "the scientific community remains extremely polarized about the reliability of polygraph techniques." (United States v. Scheffer, *supra*, 523 U.S. at p. 309 (lead opn. of Thomas, J.).) With respect to the reliability of the "control question technique" employed in the present case, Scheffer observed that studies ran the gamut from showing an 87 percent accuracy rate to a rate "'little better than could be obtained by the toss of a coin,' that is, 50 percent." (Id. at p. 310.) This disagreement in the scientific community in turn has been reflected "in the disagreement among state and federal courts concerning both the admissibility and the reliability of polygraph evidence." (Id. at pp. 310–311.)

Defendant cannot persuasively contend that between the time of the Scheffer decision and defendant's trial, a span of two and one-half years, the deep division in the scientific and legal communities regarding the reliability of polygraph evidence, as recognized by Scheffer, had given way to a general acceptance that would render the categorical exclusion of polygraph evidence "so arbitrary or disproportionate that it is unconstitutional." (United States v. Scheffer, *supra*, 523 U.S. at p. 318 (conc. opn. of Kennedy, J.).) Indeed, defense counsel conceded at oral argument that the disagreement within the scientific community regarding the reliability of polygraph evidence had not been significantly altered in that time period. Further, defendant's offer of proof in the trial court regarding the reliability of polygraph evidence consisted of a publication of the APA that outlined the studies and briefing presented in the Scheffer case—materials which the United States Supreme Court expressly considered and cited in Scheffer in concluding there existed no scientific consensus on the reliability of polygraph evidence in general and the control question technique in particular. Likewise, the legal authorities cited by defendant in the trial court as indicative of a "major reevaluation of the admissibility of polygraph evidence by the federal courts" all predate the Scheffer decision and, in any event, did not consider the constitutionality of a categorical exclusion of polygraph evidence. . . . . In light of the continuing division of opinion regarding the reliability of polygraph evidence, as recognized by Scheffer, the California Legislature has not acted "arbitrarily or disproportionately in promulgating [and retaining] a per se rule excluding all polygraph evidence." (Scheffer, *supra*, 523 U.S. at p. 312 (lead opn. of Thomas, J.); see In re Aontae D., *supra*, 25 Cal. App.4th at p. 177 [exclusion of polygraph evidence under Evidence Code section 351.1 does not deny due process]; Kegler, *supra*, 197 Cal. App. 3d at p. 89 [same].)

* * *

IV.

The judgment of the Court of Appeal is reversed. [The trial court's determination that it did not need to consider whether polygraph evidence should have been admissible was upheld and defendants have no right to introduce polygraph evidence in California, absent stipulation and court consent.]

Baxter, J., Werdegar, J., Chin, J., Brown, J. and Moreno, J., concurred.

CITY OF CLEVELAND HEIGHTS v. KATZ

Court of Appeals of Ohio, Eighth Appellate District, Cuyahoga County, 2002 Ohio 4241, 2001 Ohio App. LEXIS 5394 (2001)

TIMOTHY E. McMONAGLE, P.J.:

Defendant-appellant, Daniel Katz, appeals the judgment of the Cleveland Heights Municipal

Court, entered after a bench trial, finding him guilty of speeding, in violation of Section 333.03 of the Codified Ordinances of Cleveland Heights, and fining him $55.

Cleveland Heights Police Officer Don Roach testified at appellant's trial that at approximately 8:37 p.m. on February 7, 2001, he was parked in a police cruiser in the median at the intersection of Fairmount and Arlington Boulevards in Cleveland Heights. Roach was facing west, monitoring the speed of eastbound vehicles on Fairmount with a radar device. Roach testified that he observed appellant's SUV pulling away from a huge group of cars and approaching him at a pretty good rate. According to Roach, he locked in the radar device on appellant's SUV and then heard a high-pitched tone, which confirmed his visual sighting of appellant's high speed. The reading on the radar unit indicated that appellant was traveling 47 miles per hour in a zone marked 35 miles per hour. Roach testified that appellant's speed was unreasonable for the conditions.

Roach testified that he had received specialized training, including 8 hours of training at the police academy and 40 hours of on-the-road training, regarding operation of the model 96-11KR-10 radar unit he was using on September 7, 2001. Roach also testified that his main function as a police officer since his graduation from the police academy twelve years prior had been operating radar equipment.

Roach testified that he performed a light test, an internal calibration test and an external calibration test on the radar unit prior to using it on September 7, 2001. The light test involved pressing a special button on the unit to make sure that all the lights on the unit were working properly. According to Roach, the internal calibration test involved pressing another designated button on the unit to elicit a preset reading of 32 miles per hour. Roach then used two tuning forks to test the external calibration of the unit. According to Roach, one fork is set at 35 miles per hour and the other is set at 65 miles per hour. When he tapped the forks against a non-metallic object and then placed them in front of the radar unit, they gave readings of 35 miles per hour and 65 miles per hour respectively. Roach testified that the three tests he performed indicated that the radar unit was working properly on September 7, 2001.

Scott Whitmer, a communications and radar technician for the City of Cleveland Heights Police Department, also testified at appellant's trial.

Whitmer testified that one of his job responsibilities was to test the calibration of the radar units used by City of Cleveland Heights police officers, including the unit used by Roach on February 7, 2001. Whitmer testified further that he had received extensive training regarding testing and calibrating radar devices from Simco Electronics, the manufacturer of the devices, and through his service in the United States Air Force.

Whitmer testified that he tests and calibrates all of the radar devices once a year, using three pieces of equipment specifically designed for testing radar equipment.

Whitmer testified that on September 20 and 21, 2000, he calibrated the radar device used by Roach according to the manufacturer's instructions and when the machinery left our precinct, it was working true and accurate. Whitmer testified further that he had no records reflecting that any repairs had been completed on the unit after that time.

The trial court admitted four records created by Whitmer concerning his tests on the unit: 1) an inventory sheet reflecting the model and serial numbers of the unit and its associated tuning forks; 2) a certificate reflecting that Whitmer calibrated the unit on September 21, 2000 at 35 miles per hour, 50 miles per hour and 65 miles per hour; 3) a certificate of accuracy reflecting that one tuning fork associated with the unit was properly calibrated at 35 miles per hour; and 4) a certificate of accuracy reflecting that the other tuning fork associated with the unit was properly calibrated at 65 miles per hour.

Whitmer also testified that the equipment he used to test Roach's radar unit was shipped to Simco Electronics in August 2000 for testing and calibrating.

According to Whitmer, Simco subsequently returned the equipment with certificates of calibration indicating that the test equipment was properly calibrated.

Defense counsel objected to the admission of the certificates of calibration, however, arguing that they were not authenticated. Defense counsel argued further that without the certificates or any testimony by a representative of Simco Electronics that the testing equipment had been properly calibrated, there was no way of knowing whether the equipment used by Whitmer to test the radar device used by Roach was properly calibrated and, therefore, no way of knowing whether the radar device used by Roach to determine that appellant was speeding was accurate. Accordingly, defense counsel asserted that Officer Roach's testimony regarding appellant's speed, as determined by the radar device, was not admissible for consideration by the trier of fact.

In a journal entry filed on April 4, 2001, the trial court ruled that Officer Roach's testimony regarding the radar reading was admissible, finding that the level of proof proposed by appellant, i.e., that evidence of a radar reading is not admissible absent evidence that the equipment used to calibrate the radar device has itself been properly calibrated, was not necessary to the radar reading.

In light of Officer Roach's testimony, the trial court found that appellant was traveling at 47 miles per hour in a zone marked 35 miles per hour and that the speed was unreasonable for the conditions. On April 9, 2001, the trial court fined appellant $ 55 plus costs but stayed the sentence pending appeal.

Appellant raises two assignments of error for our review:

THE CONVICTION AGAINST DANIEL KATZ SHOULD BE REVERSED SINCE THERE WAS INSUFFICIENT TESTIMONY AS TO THE PROPER CALIBRATION OF OFFICER DONALD ROACH'S RADAR EQUIPMENT.

II. THE CONVICTION AGAINST DANIEL KATZ SHOULD BE REVERSED WHERE THE TRIAL COURT DECISION WAS AGAINST THE MANIFEST WEIGHT OF THE EVIDENCE.

In his first assignment of error, appellant asserts that the trial court erred in admitting Officer Roach's testimony regarding his speed because there was insufficient testimony regarding the calibration of Officer Roach's radar equipment.

A court may take judicial notice of the technical theory of operation and the scientific reliability of stationary radar devices. East Cleveland v. Ferell (1958), 168 Ohio St. 298, 154 N.E.2d 630; Cleveland Heights v. Bartell, 1987 Ohio App. LEXIS 7152, (Feb. 19, 1987), Cuyahoga App. No. 51719, unreported. Although not raised in his brief on appeal, at oral argument appellant asserted that the trial court improperly took judicial notice of the scientific reliability of the KR-10 stationary radar device used by Officer Roach. Appellant did not raise this issue in the trial court, however, and therefore has waived it on appeal.

In Cleveland Heights v. Bartell (1987), Cuyahoga App. No. 51719, unreported, the trial court took judicial notice of the scientific reliability of the KR-10 radar unit and this court upheld that finding. Contrary to appellant's argument, our holding did not preclude appellant from further challenging the unit's reliability at trial. If appellant had wanted to challenge the reliability of the KR-10 unit at trial, he could have subpoenaed representatives from the manufacturer of the device and questioned them regarding its reliability. As counsel admitted in oral argument, however, appellant did not do so, and accordingly, there is no evidence in the record to indicate the unit is not reliable. Therefore, the trial court did not err in taking judicial notice of the scientific reliability of the KR-10 radar unit, in reliance on Bartell.

Once judicial notice of the operation and reliability of a radar device is taken, the court must further determine 1) that the radar device was in good operating condition and properly calibrated at the time of use; 2) that the operator of the radar device was properly qualified to use the device; and 3) that the police officer properly operated and read the radar device. Id.

Although appellant concedes that a court may take judicial notice of the reliability and operation of a radar device, as the trial court did here, appellant asks this Court to find that the City failed to prove that the radar device at issue was calibrated properly because 1) Officer Roach should have performed more than three tests on his unit to ascertain its accuracy; and 2) the City did not produce evidence that the equipment used by Whitmer to calibrate the unit and its associated tuning forks was itself properly calibrated.

Appellant argues that the trial court should have required evidence that more than three tests had been performed on Officer Roach's radar unit before concluding that it was properly calibrated because there are limitations to the three tests performed by Officer Roach. Appellant asserts that the light test performed by Roach was insufficient because it merely determined that the light fixtures inside the radar unit were functioning properly. He also asserts that tuning forks may get dented or bent and, if used on a radar unit that is out of calibration, could possibly indicate accuracy when, in fact, the unit is out of calibration.

We refuse to speculate, however, about possible problems with the tests. This court has previously held that as few as two tests (an internal calibration test and an external calibration test) are sufficient to demonstrate that a radar unit is properly calibrated. Lyndhurst v. Danvers, 1988 Ohio App. LEXIS 4621, (Nov. 23, 1988), Cuyahoga App. No. 55537, unreported; Cleveland Heights v. Bartell, *supra*. Moreover, appellant offered no evidence whatsoever that any of the three tests performed by Officer Roach on February 7, 2001 were flawed or produced inaccurate results. Accordingly, there was no reason for the trial court to require evidence of more tests before concluding that Roach's radar unit was accurate.

Appellant also contends that there was insufficient evidence that Roach's radar unit was properly calibrated at the time of use because the City failed to show that Simco Electronics properly calibrated the equipment used by Whitmer to subsequently test and calibrate the unit. Appellant asserts that Whitmer's calibrations of Roach's radar unit were accurate only if the test equipment used to perform the calibrations was itself properly calibrated. Therefore, appellant contends, without testimony from a representative of the manufacturer that the test equipment was properly calibrated, there was no evidence that the radar device used by Roach was functioning properly and, accordingly, Roach's testimony regarding appellant's speed was inadmissible.

* * *

The circumstances of this case demonstrate that it was not necessary for the City to prove that the test equipment used by Whitmer to calibrate Roach's radar unit was itself properly calibrated. First, appellant presented no evidence whatsoever that the testing equipment was not in proper working order. Accordingly, as in Ellison, *supra*, there was no need for the City to produce evidence that the testing equipment was properly calibrated.

Moreover, although no one from Simco Electronics testified regarding the accuracy of the testing equipment, Scott Whitmer testified that the testing equipment was sent to Simco in August 2000 to be tested and calibrated and was subsequently returned with certificates of calibration indicating that the test equipment was properly calibrated. Therefore, contrary to appellant's assertion, there was, in fact, evidence that the testing equipment was in proper working order.

Appellant contends that his argument that the City must demonstrate that the testing equipment was itself properly calibrated has been suggested and followed by the Ohio Supreme Court in State v. Bonar (1973), 40 Ohio App. 2d 360, 319 N.E.2d 388. Appellant's reliance on Bonar, however, is misplaced. First, Bonar was decided by the Seventh Appellate District Court of Appeals, not the Supreme Court of Ohio.

Moreover, Bonar clearly does not support appellant's argument. In Bonar, the defendant was convicted of operating a motor vehicle at a speed of 75 miles per hour in a 60 miles per hour zone. The defendant appealed his conviction, arguing that the State had put on no evidence to indicate that the radar unit that had clocked his speed was functioning properly. The Seventh Appellate District Court of Appeals reversed the defendant's conviction, finding that there was *** no testimony as to whether the radar measuring equipment was properly installed, set up or operating correctly. Accordingly, the Seventh District held that the trial court should have granted the defendant's motion for a directed verdict.

The Seventh Appellate District did not hold, as appellant contends, that in any case involving a radar detector, the State must prove that the equipment used to calibrate the radar detector has itself been properly calibrated. Rather, the Bonar court held that the State must demonstrate, as it did here, that the unit was properly set up, tested and functioning properly.

* * *

Here, in addition to the light test and internal calibration tests, Officer Roach used two individually-calibrated tuning forks to test the external calibration of his radar unit. If in Bechtel the use of two tuning forks was sufficient to demonstrate the accuracy of a radar device, we see no reason in this case to require further proof that the equipment used to calibrate the radar device and tuning forks was itself properly calibrated, especially where there was no evidence that the testing equipment was not functioning properly.

Appellant's first assignment of error is therefore overruled.

In his second assignment of error, appellant contends that because the City failed to prove that the testing equipment used to calibrate Roach's radar unit was itself properly calibrated, it failed to demonstrate the accuracy of Roach's unit and, therefore, Roach's testimony regarding appellant's speed as determined by the radar device was not admissible at trial. Appellant further contends that without Roach's testimony there was no competent evidence produced at trial to establish that he was speeding and, therefore, his conviction was against the manifest weight of the evidence. We disagree.

As set forth in our discussion regarding appellant's first assignment of error, the City was not required to prove that the equipment used to calibrate Officer Roach's radar unit was it self properly calibrated. Rather, Officer Roach's testimony regarding appellant's speed as determined by the radar unit was admissible if the City demonstrated that the radar device was in good operating condition and properly calibrated at the time of use, the operator of the device was properly trained and qualified to use it and did, in fact, properly operate the radar device. See State v. Bechtel, *supra*.

Scott Whitmer testified for the City that Roach's unit had been tested and calibrated on September 20 and 21, 2000 and no repairs were made to the unit after that time. Officer Roach testified that he performed three tests on the unit on February 7, 2001 prior to apprehending appellant and all three tests indicated that the unit was operating properly. He testified further that he had been specially trained in operating the radar device used to determine appellant's speed on February 7, 2001 and that he was properly operating the device at the time of appellant's speeding violation.

This testimony laid a sufficient foundation to establish the accuracy of Roach's radar unit and, therefore, Roach's testimony regarding appellant's speed as established through the radar unit was properly admissible.

In light of this testimony, the trial court did not err in finding appellant guilty of speeding.

Appellant's second assignment of error is therefore overruled.

*** The defendant's conviction having been affirmed, any bail pending appeal is terminated. Case remanded to the trial court for execution of sentence.

Cases Relating to Chapter 16

Evidence Unconstitutionally Obtained

UNITED STATES
v.
JONES

Supreme Court of the United States, 565 U.S. ___, 132 S. Ct. 949, 132 L. Ed. 2d 945, 2012 U.S. LEXIS 1063 (2012)

Justice Scalia delivered the opinion of the Court.

We decide whether the attachment of a Global-Positioning-System (GPS) tracking device to an individual's vehicle, and subsequent use of that device to monitor the vehicle's movements on public streets, constitutes a search or seizure within the meaning of the Fourth Amendment.

I

In 2004 respondent Antoine Jones, owner and operator of a nightclub in the District of Columbia, came under suspicion of trafficking in narcotics and was made the target of an investigation by a joint FBI and Metropolitan Police Department task force. Officers employed various investigative techniques, including visual surveillance of the nightclub, installation of a camera focused on the front door of the club, and a pen register and wiretap covering Jones's cellular phone.

Based in part on information gathered from these sources, in 2005 the Government applied to the United States District Court for the District of Columbia for a warrant authorizing the use of an electronic tracking device on the Jeep Grand Cherokee registered to Jones's wife. A warrant issued, authorizing installation of the device in the District of Columbia and within 10 days.

On the 11th day, and not in the District of Columbia but in Maryland, agents installed a GPS tracking device on the undercarriage of the Jeep while it was parked in a public parking lot. Over the next 28 days, the Government used the device to track the vehicle's movements, and once had to replace the device's battery when the vehicle was parked in a different public lot in Maryland. By means of signals from multiple satellites, the device established the vehicle's location within 50 to 100 feet, and communicated that location by cellular phone to a Government computer. It relayed more than 2,000 pages of data over the 4-week period.

[Information gathered from all sources including the GPS tracking device resulted in a multiple count indictment charging Jones and others with conspiracy to distribute and possess 5 kg or more of cocaine and possessing or distributing 50 g or more of cocaine base, contrary to federal law. Since the warrant to install had expired, the prosecution conceded that the search was warrantless, but contended that a warrant to conduct a GPS search was not required under the Fourth Amendment. Mr. Jones made all the appropriate objections to the admission of the GPS evidence and was overruled by the trial court, but was convicted by a jury and the court sentenced Mr. Jones to life in prison.

The United States Court of Appeals for the District of Columbia Circuit reversed the conviction based on the theory that the admission of the evidence obtained by the warrantless use of the GPS tracking device violated the Fourth Amendment rights of Mr. Jones. The Supreme Court of the United States granted certiorari to hear the government's appeal.]

* * *

II

A

The Fourth Amendment provides in relevant part that "[t]he right of the people to be secure in their persons, houses, papers, and effects, against unreasonable searches and seizures, shall not be violated." It is beyond dispute that a vehicle is an "effect" as that term is used in the Amendment. *United States v. Chadwick*, 433 U. S. 1, 12, 97 S. Ct. 2476, 53 L. Ed. 2d 538 (1977). We hold that the Government's installation of a GPS device on a target's vehicle, and its use of that device to monitor the vehicle's movements, constitutes a "search."

It is important to be clear about what occurred in this case: The Government physically occupied private property for the purpose of obtaining information. We have no doubt that such a physical intrusion would have been considered a "search" within the meaning of the Fourth Amendment when it was adopted. *Entick v. Carrington*, 95 Eng. Rep. 807 (C. P. 1765), is a "case we have described as a 'monument of English freedom' 'undoubtedly familiar' to 'every American statesman' at the time the Constitution was adopted, and considered to be 'the true and ultimate expression of constitutional law'" with regard to search and seizure. *Brower v. County of Inyo*, 489 U. S. 593, 596, 109 S. Ct. 1378, 103 L. Ed. 2d 628 (1989) (quoting *Boyd v. United States*, 116 U. S. 616, 626, 6 S. Ct. 524, 29 L. Ed. 746 (1886)). In that case, Lord Camden expressed in plain terms the significance of property rights in search-and-seizure analysis:

> "[O]ur law holds the property of every man so sacred, that no man can set his foot upon his neighbour's close without his leave; if he does he is a trespasser, though he does no damage at all; if he will tread upon his neighbour's ground, he must justify it by law." *Entick, supra*, at 817.

The text of the Fourth Amendment reflects its close connection to property, since otherwise it would have referred simply to "the right of the people to be secure against unreasonable searches and seizures"; the phrase "in their persons, houses, papers, and effects" would have been superfluous.

[Justice Scalia noted that the Fourth Amendment jurisprudence was once tied to legal concepts of trespass at least until the latter half of the 20th century. He noted that previously, the Court had held that wiretaps attached the telephone wires on the public street did not constitute a Fourth Amendment search because there was no entry of the houses of the defendants. The concept of a trespass did not remain as a requirement for a Fourth Amendment violation as demonstrated in later cases. Scalia mentioned that in an older case, *Katz v. United States* (1967), an expectation of privacy was not always tied to concepts of trespass because Mr. Katz, who was talking on a public telephone that had a police microphone nearby, had an expectation of privacy that what he said would not be overheard, even though Mr. Katz did not own the telephone booth.]

* * *

The Government contends that several of our post-*Katz* cases foreclose the conclusion that what occurred here constituted a search. It relies principally on . . . cases in which we rejected Fourth Amendment challenges to "beepers," electronic tracking devices that represent another form of electronic monitoring. The first case, *Knotts*, upheld against Fourth Amendment challenge the use of a "beeper" that had been placed in a container of chloroform, allowing law enforcement to monitor the location of the container. 460 U. S., at 278, 103 S. Ct. 1081, 75 L. Ed. 2d 55. We said that there had been no infringement of Knotts' reasonable expectation of privacy since the information obtained–the location of the automobile carrying the container on public roads, and the location of the off-loaded container in open fields near Knotts' cabin–had been voluntarily conveyed to the public. 6 Id., at 281-282, 103 S. Ct. 1081, 75 L. Ed. 2d 55. But as we have discussed, *the Katz reasonable-expectation-of-privacy test has been added to, not substituted for* [Emphasis added], the common-law trespassory test. The holding in *Knotts* addressed only the former, since the latter was not at issue. The beeper had been placed in the container before it came into Knotts' possession, with the consent of the then-owner. 460 U. S., at 278, 103 S. Ct. 1081, 75 L. Ed. 2d 55. *Knotts* did not challenge that installation, and we specifically declined to consider its effect on the Fourth Amendment analysis. Id., at 279, 103 S. Ct. 1081, 75 L. Ed. 2d 55, *Knotts* would be relevant, perhaps, if the Government were making the argument that what would otherwise be an unconstitutional search is not such where it produces only public information. The Government does not make that argument, and we know of no case that would support it.

* * *

The Government also points to our exposition in *New York v. Class*, 475 U. S. 106, 106 S. Ct. 960, 89 L. Ed. 2d 81 (1986), that "[t]he exterior of a car . . . is thrust into the public eye, and thus to examine it does not constitute a 'search.'" Id., at 114, 106 S. Ct. 960, 89 L. Ed. 2d 81. That statement is of marginal relevance here since, as the Government acknowledges, "the officers in this case did more than conduct a visual inspection of respondent's vehicle," [Govt. Brief]. By attaching the device to the Jeep, officers encroached on a protected area. In Class itself we suggested that this would make a difference, for we concluded that an officer's momentary reaching into the interior of a vehicle did constitute a search. 475 U. S., at 114-115, 106 S. Ct. 960, 89 L. Ed. 2d 81.

Finally, the Government's position gains little support from our conclusion in *Oliver v. United States*, 466 U. S. 170, 104 S. Ct. 1735, 80 L. Ed. 2d 214 (1984), that officers' information-gathering intrusion on an "open field" did not constitute a Fourth Amendment search even though it was a trespass at common law, id., at 183, 104 S. Ct. 1735, 80 L. Ed. 2d 214. Quite simply, an open field, unlike the curtilage of a home, see United States v. Dunn, 480 U. S. 294, 300, 107 S. Ct. 1134, 94 L. Ed. 2d 326 (1987), is not one of those protected areas enumerated in the Fourth Amendment. *Oliver, supra*, at 176-177, 104 S. Ct. 1735, 80 L. Ed. 2d 214. The Government's physical intrusion on such an area–unlike its intrusion on the "effect" at issue here–is of no Fourth Amendment significance.

* * *

III

The Government argues in the alternative that even if the attachment and use of the device was a search, it was reasonable–and thus lawful–under the Fourth Amendment because "officers had reasonable suspicion, and indeed probable cause, to believe that [Jones] was a leader in a large-scale cocaine distribution conspiracy." Brief for United States 50-51. We have no occasion to consider this argument. The Government did not raise it below, and the D. C. Circuit therefore did not address it. See 625 F. 3d, at 767 (Ginsburg, Tatel, and Griffith, JJ., concurring in denial of rehearing en banc). We consider the argument forfeited. See *Sprietsma v. Mercury Marine*, 537 U. S. 51, 56, n. 4, 123 S. Ct. 518, 154 L. Ed. 2d 466 (2002).

The judgment of the Court of Appeals for the D. C. Circuit is affirmed.

It is so ordered.

JUSTICE SOTOMAYOR, concurring.

I join the Court's opinion because I agree that a search within the meaning of the Fourth Amendment occurs, at a minimum, "[w]here, as here, the Government obtains information by physically intruding on a constitutionally protected area." Ante, at 6, n. 3. In this case, the Government installed a Global Positioning System (GPS) tracking device on respondent Antoine Jones' Jeep without a valid warrant and without Jones' consent, then used that device to monitor the Jeep's movements over the course of four weeks. The Government usurped Jones' property for the purpose of conducting surveillance on him, thereby invading privacy interests long afforded, and undoubtedly entitled to, Fourth Amendment protection. See, *e.g., Silverman v. United States*, 365 U. S. 505, 511-512, 81 S. Ct. 679, 5 L. Ed. 2d 734 (1961).

Of course, the Fourth Amendment is not concerned only with trespassory intrusions on property. See, *e.g., Kyllo v. United States*, 533 U. S. 27, 31-33, 121 S. Ct. 2038, 150 L. Ed. 2d 94 (2001). Rather, even in the absence of a trespass, "a Fourth Amendment search occurs when the government violates a subjective expectation of privacy that society recognizes as reasonable." Id., at 33, 121 S. Ct. 2038, 150 L. Ed. 2d 94; see also *Smith v. Maryland*, 442 U. S. 735, 740-741, 99 S. Ct. 2577, 61 L. Ed. 2d 220 (1979); *Katz v. United States*, 389 U. S. 347, 361, 88 S. Ct. 507, 19 L. Ed. 2d 576 (1967) (Harlan, J., concurring). In *Katz*, this Court enlarged its then-prevailing focus on property rights by announcing that the reach of the Fourth Amendment does not "turn upon the presence or absence of a physical intrusion." Id., at 353, 88 S. Ct. 507, 19 L. Ed. 2d 576. As the majority's opinion makes clear, however, *Katz's* reasonable-expectation-of-privacy test augmented, but did not displace or diminish, the common-law trespassory test that preceded it. Ante, at 8. Thus, "when the Government does engage in physical intrusion of a constitutionally protected area in order to obtain information, that intrusion may constitute a violation of the Fourth Amendment." *United States v. Knotts*, 460 U. S. 276, 286, 103 S. Ct. 1081, 75 L. Ed. 2d 55 (1983) (Brennan, J., concurring in judgment); see also, e.g., *Rakas v. Illinois*, 439 U.S. 128, 144, n. 12, 99 S. Ct. 421, 58 L. Ed. 2d 387 (1978). JUSTICE ALITO's approach, which discounts altogether the constitutional relevance of the Government's physical intrusion on Jones' Jeep, erodes that longstanding protection for privacy expectations inherent in items of property that people possess or control. See post, at 5-7 (opinion concurring in judgment). By contrast, the trespassory test applied in the majority's opinion reflects an irreducible constitutional minimum: When the Government physically invades personal property to gather information, a search occurs. The reaffirmation of that principle suffices to decide this case.

* * *

JUSTICE ALITO, with whom JUSTICE GINSBURG, JUSTICE BREYER, and JUSTICE KAGAN, concurring in the judgment.

This case requires us to apply the Fourth Amendment's prohibition of unreasonable searches and seizures to a 21st-century surveillance technique, the use of a Global Positioning System (GPS) device to monitor a vehicle's movements for an extended period of time. Ironically, the Court has chosen to decide this case based on 18th-century tort law. By attaching a small GPS device to the underside of the vehicle that respondent drove, the law enforcement officers in this case engaged in conduct that might have provided grounds in 1791 for a suit for trespass to chattels. And for this reason, the Court concludes, the installation and use of the GPS device constituted a search. Ante, at 3-4.

This holding, in my judgment, is unwise. It strains the language of the Fourth Amendment; it has little if any support in current Fourth Amendment case law; and it is highly artificial.

I would analyze the question presented in this case by asking whether respondent's reasonable expectations of privacy were violated by the long-term monitoring of the movements of the vehicle he drove.

* * *

ARIZONA v. GANT

Supreme Court of the United States, 556 U.S. 332, 2009 U.S. LEXIS 3120 (2009)

JUSTICE STEVENS delivered the opinion of the Court.

After Rodney Gant was arrested for driving with a suspended license, handcuffed, and locked in the back of a patrol car, police officers searched his car and discovered cocaine in the pocket of a jacket on the backseat. Because Gant could not have accessed his car to retrieve weapons or evidence at the time of the search, the Arizona Supreme Court held that the search-incident-to-arrest exception to the Fourth Amendment's warrant requirement, as defined in Chimel v. California, 395 U.S. 752, 89 S. Ct. 2034, 23 L. Ed. 2d 685 (1969), and applied to vehicle searches in New York v. Belton, 453 U.S. 454, 101 S. Ct. 2860, 69 L. Ed. 2d 768 (1981), did not justify the search in this case. We agree with that conclusion.

Under Chimel, police may search incident to arrest only the space within an arrestee's "'immediate control,'" meaning "the area from within which he might gain possession of a weapon or destructible evidence." 395 U.S., at 763, 89 S. Ct. 2034, 23 L. Ed. 2d 685. The safety and evidentiary justifications underlying Chimel's reaching-distance rule determine Belton's scope. Accordingly, we hold that Belton does not authorize a vehicle search incident to a recent occupant's arrest after the arrestee has been secured and cannot access the interior of the vehicle. Consistent with the holding in Thornton v. United States, 541 U.S. 615, 124 S. Ct. 2127, 158 L. Ed. 2d 905 (2004), and following the suggestion in JUSTICE SCALIA's opinion concurring in the judgment in that case, id., at 632, 124 S. Ct. 2127, 158 L. Ed. 2d 905, we also conclude that circumstances unique to the automobile context justify a search incident to arrest when it is reasonable to believe that evidence of the offense of arrest might be found in the vehicle.

I.

On August 25, 1999, acting on an anonymous tip that the residence at 2524 North Walnut Avenue was being used to sell drugs, Tucson police officers Griffith and Reed knocked on the front door and asked to speak to the owner. Gant answered the door and, after identifying himself, stated that he expected the owner to return later. The officers left the residence and conducted a records check, which revealed that Gant's driver's license had been suspended and there was an outstanding warrant for his arrest for driving with a suspended license.

[When the officers next encountered Gant, he was observed parking his car near the North Walnut Avenue address. Gant had walked about 10 or 12 feet away from his car, when the officers identified him and arrested him for driving with a suspended license. Because several other arrestees from the drug selling house on North Walnut were already in the police cruisers, one officer called for backup. When the additional officers arrived, they placed Gant in the back of a cruiser after handcuffing him. They then proceeded to search his motor vehicle under the doctrine of "search instant to a lawful arrest." The police found a gun and cocaine in a jacket pocket within the car. Gant was charged with possession of a narcotic drug for sale and possession of drug paraphernalia. Gant filed a motion to suppress the evidence taken from the car on the theory that the police could not have reasonably believed that Gant could have any access to gun or cocaine since he was handcuffed in a cruiser and secondarily, police could not have discovered any evidence inside the automobile to support the driving under a suspension charge. The trial court denied his motion to suppress the evidence and he was convicted. After complicated state court proceedings, the Supreme Court of Arizona ruled that the search of his car was unreasonable as incident to a lawful arrest. The Supreme Court granted certiorari.]

II.

Consistent with our precedent, our analysis begins, as it should in every case addressing the reasonableness of a warrantless search, with the basic rule that "searches conducted outside the judicial process, without prior approval by judge or magistrate, are per se unreasonable under the Fourth Amendment – subject only to a few specifically established and well-delineated exceptions." Katz v. United States, 389 U.S. 347, 357, 88 S. Ct. 507, 19 L. Ed. 2d 576 (1967)(footnote omitted). Among the exceptions to the warrant requirement is a search incident to a lawful arrest. See Weeks v. United States, 232 U.S. 383, 392, 34 S. Ct. 341, 58 L. Ed. 652, T.D. 1964 (1914). The exception derives from interests in officer safety and evidence preservation that are typically implicated in arrest situations. See United States v. Robinson, 414 U.S. 218, 230–234, 94 S. Ct. 467, 38 L. Ed. 2d 427 (1973); Chimel, 395 U.S., at 763, 89 S. Ct. 2034, 23 L. Ed. 2d 685.

In Chimel, we held that a search incident to arrest may only include "the arrestee's person and the area 'within his immediate control' – construing that phrase to mean the area from within which he might gain possession of a weapon or destructible evidence." Ibid. That limitation, which continues to define the boundaries of the exception, ensures that the scope of a search incident to arrest is commensurate with its purposes of protecting arresting officers and safeguarding any evidence of the offense of arrest that an arrestee might conceal or destroy. See ibid. (noting that searches incident to arrest are reasonable "in order to remove any weapons [the arrestee] might seek to use" and "in order to prevent [the] concealment or destruction" of evidence (emphasis added)). If there is no possibility that an arrestee could reach into the area that law enforcement officers seek to search, both justifications for the search-incident-to-arrest exception are absent and the rule does not apply. E.g., Preston v. United States, 376 U.S. 364, 367–368, 84 S. Ct. 881, 11 L. Ed. 2d 777 (1964).

In Belton, we considered Chimel's application to the automobile context. A lone police officer in that case stopped a speeding car in which Belton was one of four occupants. While asking for the driver's license and registration, the officer smelled burnt marijuana and observed an envelope on the car floor marked "Supergold" – a name he associated with marijuana. Thus having probable cause to believe the occupants had committed a drug offense, the officer ordered them out of the vehicle, placed them under arrest, and patted them down. Without handcuffing the arrestees, 1 the officer "'split them up into four separate areas of the Thruway . . . so they would not be in physical touching area of each other'" and searched the vehicle, including the pocket of a jacket on the backseat, in which he found cocaine. 453 U.S., at 456, 101 S. Ct. 2860, 69 L. Ed. 2d 768.

* * *

[In Belton,] we held that when an officer lawfully arrests "the occupant of an automobile, he may, as a contemporaneous incident of that arrest, search the passenger compartment of the automobile" and any containers therein. Belton, 453 U.S., at 460, 101 S. Ct. 2860, 69 L. Ed. 2d 768 (footnote omitted). That holding was based in large part on our assumption "that articles inside the relatively narrow compass of the passenger compartment of an automobile are in fact generally, even if not inevitably, within 'the area into which an arrestee might reach.'" Ibid.

* * *

III.

Despite the textual and evidentiary support for the Arizona Supreme Court's reading of Belton, our opinion has been widely understood to allow a vehicle search incident to the arrest of a recent occupant even if there is no possibility the arrestee could gain access to the vehicle at the time of the search. This reading may be attributable to Justice Brennan's dissent in Belton, in which he characterized the Court's holding as resting on the "fiction . . . that the interior of a car is always within the immediate control of an arrestee who has recently been in the car." 453 U.S., at 466, 101 S. Ct. 2860, 69 L. Ed. 2d 768. Under the majority's approach, he argued, "the result would presumably be the same even if [the officer] had handcuffed Belton and his companions in the patrol car" before conducting the search. Id., at 468, 101 S. Ct. 2860, 69 L. Ed. 2d 768.

* * *

Although it does not follow from Chimel, we also conclude that circumstances unique to the vehicle context justify a search incident to a lawful arrest when it is "reasonable to believe evidence relevant to the crime of arrest might be found in the vehicle." Thornton, 541 U.S., at 632, 124 S. Ct. 2127, 158 L. Ed. 2d 905 (SCALIA, J., concurring in judgment). In many cases, as when a recent occupant is arrested for a traffic violation, there will be no reasonable basis to believe the vehicle contains relevant evidence. See, e.g., Atwater v. Lago Vista, 532 U.S. 318, 324, 121 S. Ct. 1536, 149 L. Ed. 2d 549 (2001); Knowles v. Iowa, 525 U.S. 113, 118, 119 S. Ct. 484, 142 L. Ed. 2d 492 (1998). But in others, including Belton and Thornton, the offense of arrest will supply a basis for searching the passenger compartment of an arrestee's vehicle and any containers therein.

Neither the possibility of access nor the likelihood of discovering offense-related evidence authorized the search in this case. Unlike in Belton, which involved a single officer confronted with four unsecured arrestees, the five officers in this case out-numbered the three arrestees, all of whom had been handcuffed and secured in separate patrol cars before the officers searched Gant's car. Under those circumstances, Gant clearly was not within reaching distance of his car at the time of the search. An evidentiary basis for the search was also lacking in this case. Whereas Belton and Thornton were arrested for drug offenses, Gant was arrested for driving with a suspended license – an offense for which police could not expect to find evidence in the passenger compartment of Gant's car. Cf. Knowles, 525 U.S., at 118, 119 S. Ct. 484, 142 L. Ed. 2d 492. Because police could not reasonably have believed either that Gant could have accessed his car at the time of the search or that evidence of the offense for which he was arrested might have been found therein, the search in this case was unreasonable.

* * *

VI.

Police may search a vehicle incident to a recent occupant's arrest only if the arrestee is within reaching distance of the passenger compartment at the time of the search or it is reasonable to believe the vehicle contains evidence of the offense of arrest. When these justifications are absent, a search of an arrestee's vehicle will be unreasonable unless police obtain a warrant or show that another exception to the warrant requirement applies. The Arizona Supreme Court correctly held that this case involved an unreasonable search. Accordingly, the judgment of the State Supreme Court is affirmed.

It is so ordered.

MARYLAND v. KING

Supreme Court of the United States, ___ 569 U.S. ___. 133 S. Ct. 1958, 186 L. Ed. 2d 1 (2013)

JUSTICE KENNEDY delivered the opinion of the Court.

In 2003 a man concealing his face and armed with a gun broke into a woman's home in Salisbury, Maryland. He raped her. The police were unable to identify or apprehend the assailant based on any detailed description or other evidence they then had, but they did obtain from the victim a sample of the perpetrator's DNA.

In 2009 Alonzo King was arrested in Wicomico County, Maryland, and charged with first- and second-degree assault for menacing a group of people with a shotgun. As part of a routine booking procedure for serious offenses [and as required under a Maryland state statute], his DNA sample was taken by applying a cotton swab or filter paper—known as a buccal swab—to the inside of his cheeks. The DNA was found to match the DNA taken from the Salisbury rape victim. King was tried and convicted for the rape. Additional DNA samples were taken from him and used in the rape trial, but there seems to be no doubt that it was the DNA from the cheek sample taken at the time he was booked in 2009 that led to his first having been linked to the rape and charged with its commission.

The Court of Appeals of Maryland, on review of King's rape conviction, ruled that the DNA taken when King was booked for the 2009 charge was an unlawful seizure because obtaining and using the cheek swab was an unreasonable search of the person. [State and federal courts had reached different decisions concerning the constitutionality of obtaining DNA swabs from arrestees.] It set the rape conviction aside. This Court granted certiorari and now reverses the judgment of the Maryland court.

[In Maryland, the DNA results may only be used for identification purposes and may not be analyzed for other personal information.]

***

III

A

Although the DNA swab procedure used here presents a question the Court has not yet addressed, the framework for deciding the issue is well established. The Fourth Amendment, binding on the States by the Fourteenth Amendment, provides that "[t]he right of the people to be secure in their persons, houses, papers, and effects, against unreasonable searches and seizures, shall not be violated." It can be agreed that using a buccal swab on the inner tissues of a person's cheek in order to obtain DNA samples is a search.

***

B

To say that the Fourth Amendment applies here is the beginning point, not the end of the analysis. "[T]he Fourth Amendment's proper function is to constrain, not against all intrusions as such, but against intrusions which are not justified in the circumstances, or which are made in an improper manner." *Schmerber [v. California], supra*, at 768, 86 S. Ct. 1826, 16 L. Ed. 2d 908. "As the text of the Fourth Amendment indicates, the ultimate measure of the constitutionality of a governmental search is 'reasonableness.'" *Vernonia School Dist. 47J v. Acton*, 515 U.S. 646, 652, 115 S. Ct. 2386, 132 L. Ed. 2d 564 (1995).

***

IV

A

The legitimate government interest served by the Maryland DNA Collection Act is one that is well established: the need for law enforcement officers in a safe and accurate way to process and identify the persons and possessions they must take into custody. It is beyond dispute that "probable cause provides legal justification for arresting a person suspected of crime, and for a brief period of detention to take the administrative steps incident to arrest." *Gerstein* v. *Pugh*, 420 U.S. 103, 113-114, 95 S. Ct. 854, 43 L. Ed. 2d 54 (1975).

***

The task of identification necessarily entails searching public and police records based on the identifying information provided by the arrestee to see what is already known about him. The DNA collected from arrestees is an irrefutable identification of the person from whom it was taken. Like a fingerprint, the 13 CODIS loci [specific points on the human genome used for identification purposes] are not themselves evidence of any particular crime, in the way that a drug test can by itself be evidence of illegal narcotics use. A DNA profile is useful to the police because it gives them a form of identification to search the records already in their valid possession. In this respect the use of DNA for identification is no different than matching an arrestee's face to a wanted poster of a previously unidentified suspect; or matching tattoos to known gang symbols to reveal a criminal affiliation; or matching the arrestee's fingerprints to those recovered from a crime scene.

***

[Proper and definitive identification of a perpetrator has many useful aspects. First, in every criminal case, the government must be able to know who is been arrested, and who is being tried. Second, law enforcement officials have a responsibility to ensure that the custody of an arrestee does not present an unreasonable risk for a facility and its staff, and other populations who are present. Third, the government has an interest in ensuring that accused individuals are present for trial. Fourth, an arrestees past conduct is somewhat predictive of the danger posed to the public. Finally, proper identification of one individual may have the effect of freeing a person who has been wrongly imprisoned for the same offense.]

***

V

A

By comparison to this substantial government interest and the unique effectiveness of DNA identification, the intrusion of a cheek swab to obtain a DNA sample is a minimal one. True, a significant government interest does not alone suffice to justify a search. The government interest must outweigh the degree to which the search invades an individual's legitimate expectations of privacy. In considering those expectations in this case, however, the necessary predicate of a valid arrest for a serious offense is fundamental. "Although the underlying command of the Fourth Amendment is always that searches and seizures be reasonable, what is reasonable depends on the context within which a search takes place." *New Jersey* v. *T. L. O.*, 469 U.S. 325, 337, 105 S. Ct. 733, 83 L. Ed. 2d 720 (1985). "[T]he legitimacy of certain privacy expectations vis-á-vis the State may depend upon the individual's legal relationship with the State." *Vernonia School Dist. 47J*, 515 U.S., at 654, 115 S. Ct. 2386, 132 L. Ed. 2d 564.

The reasonableness of any search must be considered in the context of the person's legitimate expectations of privacy. For example, when weighing the invasiveness of urinalysis of high school athletes, the Court noted that "[l]egitimate privacy expectations are even less with regard to student athletes. . . . Public school locker rooms, the usual sites for these activities, are not notable for the privacy they afford." [*Vernonia School Dist. 47J*], at 657, 115 S. Ct. 2386, 132 L. Ed. 2d 564. Likewise, the Court has used a context-specific benchmark inapplicable to the public at large when "the expectations of privacy of covered employees are diminished by reason of their participation in an industry that is regulated pervasively," *Skinner*, 489 U.S., at 627, 109 S. Ct. 1402, 103 L. Ed. 2d 639, or when "the 'operational realities of the workplace' may render entirely reasonable certain work-related intrusions by supervisors and co-workers that might be viewed as unreasonable in other contexts," *Von Raab*, 489 U.S., at 671, 109 S. Ct. 1384, 103 L. Ed. 2d 685.

The expectations of privacy of an individual taken into police custody "necessarily [are] of a diminished scope." *Bell[v. Wolfish]*, 441 U.S., at 557, 99 S. Ct. 1861, 60 L. Ed. 2d 447.

In light of the context of a valid arrest supported by probable cause respondent's expectations of privacy were not offended by the minor intrusion of a brief swab of his cheeks. By contrast, that same context of arrest gives rise to significant state interests in identifying respondent not only so that the proper name can be attached to his charges but also so that the criminal justice system can make informed decisions concerning pretrial custody. Upon these considerations the Court concludes that DNA identification of arrestees is a reasonable search that can be considered part of a routine booking procedure. When officers make an arrest supported by probable cause to hold for a serious offense and they bring the suspect to the station to be detained in custody, taking and analyzing a cheek swab of the arrestee's DNA is, like fingerprinting and photographing, a legitimate police booking procedure that is reasonable under the Fourth Amendment.

The judgment of the Court of Appeals of Maryland is reversed. [The Supreme Court, in effect, held that the DNA evidence had been properly admitted into evidence at the original trial of Mr. King.]

MELENDEZ-DIAZ v. MASSACHUSETTS

Supreme Court of the United States, 557 U.S. 305, 129 S. Ct. 2527, 174 L. Ed. 2d 314, 2009 U.S. LEXIS 4734 (2009)

Justice Scalia delivered the opinion of the Court.

The Massachusetts courts in this case admitted into evidence affidavits reporting the results of forensic analysis which showed that material seized by the police and connected to the defendant was cocaine. The question presented is whether those affidavits are "testimonial," rendering the affiants "witnesses" subject to the defendant's right of confrontation under the Sixth Amendment.

* * *

[Police apprehended Melendez-Diaz in the process of selling white powder believed to be cocaine from his K-Mart work location.]

Melendez-Diaz was charged with distributing cocaine and with trafficking in cocaine in an amount between 14 and 28 grams. Ch. 94C, §§ 32A, 32E(b)(1). At trial, the prosecution placed into evidence the bags seized from Wright and from the police cruiser. It also submitted three "certificates of analysis" showing the results of the forensic analysis performed on the seized substances. The certificates reported the weight of the seized bags and stated that the bags "[h]a[ve] been examined with the following results: The substance was found to contain: Cocaine." The certificates were sworn to before a notary public by analysts at the State Laboratory Institute of the Massachusetts Department of Public Health, as required under Massachusetts law. Mass. Gen. Laws, ch. 111, § 13. Petitioner objected to the admission of the certificates, asserting that our

Confrontation Clause decision in Crawford v. Washington, 541 U.S. 36, 124 S. Ct. 1354, 158 L. Ed. 2d 177 (2004), required the analysts to testify in person. The objection was overruled, and the certificates were admitted pursuant to state law as "prima facie evidence of the composition, quality, and the net weight of the narcotic . . . analyzed." Mass. Gen. Laws, ch. 111, § 13.

The jury found Melendez-Diaz guilty. He appealed, contending, among other things, that admission of the certificates violated his Sixth Amendment right to be confronted with the witnesses against him. The Appeals Court of Massachusetts rejected the claim, affirmance order, relying on the Massachusetts Supreme Judicial Court's decision in Commonwealth v. Verde, 444 Mass. 279, 283–285, 827 N.E.2d 701, 705–706 (2005), which held that the authors of certificates of forensic analysis are not subject to confrontation under the Sixth Amendment. The Supreme Judicial Court denied review. [In 2008].

II.

The Sixth Amendment to the United States Constitution, made applicable to the States via the Fourteenth Amendment, Pointer v. Texas, 380 U.S. 400, 403, 85 S. Ct. 1065, 13 L. Ed. 2d 923 (1965), provides that "[i]n all criminal prosecutions, the accused shall enjoy the right . . . to be confronted with the witnesses against him." In Crawford, after reviewing the Clause's historical underpinnings, we held that it guarantees a defendant's right to confront those "who 'bear testimony'" against him. 541 U.S., at 51, 124 S. Ct. 1354, 158 L. Ed. 2d 177. A witness's testimony against a defendant is thus inadmissible unless the witness appears at trial or, if the witness is unavailable, the defendant had a prior opportunity for cross-examination. Id., at 54, 124 S. Ct. 1354, 158 L. Ed. 2d 177.

There is little doubt that the documents at issue in this case fall within the "core class of testimonial statements" thus described. Our description of that category mentions affidavits twice. See also White v. Illinois, 502 U.S. 346, 365, 112 S. Ct. 736, 116 L. Ed. 2d 848 (1992) (Thomas, J., concurring in part and concurring in judgment) ("[T]he Confrontation Clause is implicated by extrajudicial statements only insofar as they are contained in formalized testimonial materials, such as affidavits, depositions, prior testimony, or confessions"). The documents at issue here, while denominated by Massachusetts law "certificates," are quite plainly affidavits: "declaration [s] of facts written down and sworn to by the declarant before an officer authorized to administer oaths." Black's Law Dictionary 62 (8th ed. 2004). They are incontrovertibly a "'solemn declaration or affirmation made for the purpose of establishing or proving some fact.'" Crawford, *supra*, at 51, (quoting 2 N. Webster, An American Dictionary of the English Language (1828)). The fact in question is that the substance found in the possession of Melendez-Diaz and his codefendants was, as the prosecution claimed, cocaine–the precise testimony the analysts would be expected to provide if called at trial. The "certificates" are functionally identical to live, in-court testimony, doing "precisely what a witness does on direct examination." Davis v. Washington, 547 U.S. 813, 830, 126 S. Ct. 2266, 165 L. Ed. 2d 224 (2006).

Here, moreover, not only were the affidavits "'made under circumstances which would lead an objective witness reasonably to believe that the statement would be available for use at a later trial,'" Crawford, *supra*, at 52, but under Massachusetts law the sole purpose of the affidavits was to provide "prima facie evidence of the composition, quality, and the net weight" of the analyzed substance, Mass. Gen. Laws, ch. 111, § 13. We can safely assume that the analysts were aware of the affidavits' evidentiary purpose, since that purpose–as stated in the relevant state-law provision–was reprinted on the affidavits themselves.

In short, under our decision in Crawford the analysts' affidavits were testimonial statements, and the analysts were "witnesses" for purposes of the Sixth Amendment. Absent a showing that the analysts were unavailable to testify at trial and that petitioner had a prior opportunity to cross-examine them, petitioner was entitled to "'"be confronted with'" the analysts at trial. Crawford, *supra*, at 54.

* * *

The Sixth Amendment does not permit the prosecution to prove its case via ex parte out-of-court affidavits, and the admission of such evidence against Melendez-Diaz was error. We therefore reverse the judgment of the Appeals Court of Massachusetts and remand the case for further proceedings not inconsistent with this opinion.

It is so ordered.

Appendix I

Federal Rules of Evidence

As amended and effective through December 1, 2013
The Committee on the Judiciary
House of Representatives

ARTICLE V
PRIVILEGES

ARTICLE VI
WITNESSES

ARTICLE VII
OPINIONS AND EXPERT TESTIMONY

ARTICLE VIII
HEARSAY

RULE 806. Attacking and Supporting the Declarant's Credibility
RULE 807. Residual Exception
(a) In General
(b) Notice

ARTICLE IX
AUTHENTICATION AND IDENTIFICATION

RULE 901. Authenticating or Identifying Evidence
(a) In General
(b) Examples
RULE 902. Evidence That Is Self-Authenticating
RULE 903. Subscribing Witness's Testimony

ARTICLE X
CONTENTS OF WRITINGS, RECORDINGS, AND PHOTOGRAPHS

RULE 1001. Definitions That Apply to This Article
RULE 1002. Requirement of the Original
RULE 1003. Admissibility of Duplicates
RULE 1004. Admissibility of Other Evidence of Content
RULE 1005. Copies of Public Records to Prove Content
RULE 1006. Summaries to Prove Content
RULE 1007. Testimony or Statement of a Party to Prove Content
RULE 1008. Functions of Court and Jury

ARTICLE XI
MISCELLANEOUS RULES

RULE 1101. Applicability of the Rules
(a) To Courts and Judges
(b) To Cases and Proceedings
(c) Rules on Privilege
(d) Exceptions
(e) Other Statutes and Rules
RULE 1102. Amendments
RULE 1103. Title

Federal Rules of Evidence

Effective July 1, 1975, as amended to December 1, 2013

ARTICLE I: GENERAL PROVISIONS

RULE 101. Scope

(a) Scope. These rules apply to proceedings in United States courts. The specific courts and proceedings to which the rules apply, along with exceptions, are set out in Rule 1101.

(b) Definitions. In these rules

(1) "civil case" means a civil action or proceeding;

(2) "criminal case" includes a criminal proceeding;

(3) "public office" includes a public agency;

(4) "record" includes a memorandum, report, or data compilation;

(5) a "rule prescribed by the Supreme Court" means a rule adopted by the Supreme Court under statutory authority; and

(6) a reference to any kind of written material or any other medium includes electronically stored information. (Amended, eff. Dec. 2011).

RULE 102. Purpose

These rules should be construed so as to administer every proceeding fairly, eliminate unjustifiable expense and delay, and promote the development of evidence law, to the end of ascertaining the truth and securing a just determination. (Amended, eff. Dec. 2011).

RULE 103. Rulings on Evidence

(a) Preserving a Claim of Error. A party may claim error in a ruling to admit or exclude evidence only if the error affects a substantial right of the party and

(1) if the ruling admits evidence, a party, on the record

(A) timely objects or moves to strike; and

(B) states the specific ground, unless it was apparent from the context; or

(2) if the ruling excludes evidence, a party informs the court of its substance by an offer of proof, unless the substance was apparent from the context.

(b) Not Needing to Renew an Objection or Offer of Proof. Once the court rules definitively on the record — either before or at trial — a party need not renew an objection or offer of proof to preserve a claim of error for appeal.

(c) Court's Statement About the Ruling; Directing an Offer of Proof. The court may make any statement about the character or form of the evidence, the objection made, and the ruling. The court may direct that an offer of proof be made in question-and-answer form.

(d) Taking Notice of Plain Error. A court may take notice of a plain error affecting a substantial right, even if the claim of error was not properly preserved.

(e) (*Legislative History* Preventing the Jury from Hearing Inadmissible Evidence. To the extent practicable, the court must conduct a jury trial so that inadmissible evidence is not suggested to the jury by any means. (As amended, eff. Dec. 1 2011.)

RULE 104. Preliminary Questions

(a) In General. The court must decide any preliminary question about whether a witness is qualified, a privilege exists, or evidence is admissible. In so deciding, the court is not bound by evidence rules, except those on privilege.

(b) Relevance That Depends on a Fact. When the relevance of evidence depends on whether a fact exists, proof must be introduced sufficient to support a finding that the fact does exist. The court may admit the proposed evidence on the condition that the proof be introduced later.

(c) Conducting a Hearing So That the Jury Cannot Hear It. The court must conduct any hearing on a preliminary question so that the jury cannot hear it if:
  (1) the hearing involves the admissibility of a confession;
  (2) a defendant in a criminal case is a witness and so requests; or
  (3) justice so requires.

(d) Cross-Examining a Defendant in a Criminal Case. By testifying on a preliminary question, a defendant in a criminal case does not become subject to cross-examination on other issues in the case

(e) Evidence Relevant to Weight and Credibility. This rule does not limit a party's right to introduce before the jury evidence that is relevant to the weight or credibility of other evidence. (Amended, eff. Dec. 1, 2011.)

RULE 105. Limiting Evidence That Is Not Admissible Against Other Parties or for Other Purposes

If the court admits evidence that is admissible against a party or for a purpose — but not against another party or for another purpose — the court, on timely request, must restrict the evidence to its proper scope and instruct the jury accordingly. (Amended, eff. Dec. 1, 2011.)

RULE 106. Remainder of or Related Writings or Recorded Statements

If a party introduces all or part of a writing or recorded statement, an adverse party may require the introduction, at that time, of any other part — or any other writing or recorded statement — that in fairness ought to be considered at the same time. (Amended, eff. Dec. 1, 2011.)

ARTICLE II. JUDICIAL NOTICE

RULE 201. Judicial Notice of Adjudicative Facts

(a) **Scope**. This rule governs judicial notice of an adjudicative fact only, not a legislative fact.

(b) **Kinds of Facts That May Be Judicially Noticed.** The court may judicially notice a fact that is not subject to reasonable dispute because it:
  (1) is generally known within the trial court's territorial jurisdiction; or
  (2) can be accurately and readily determined from sources whose accuracy cannot reasonably be questioned.

(c) **Taking Notice.** The court:
  (1) may take judicial notice on its own; or
  (2) must take judicial notice if a party requests it and the court is supplied with the necessary information.

(d) **Timing.** The court may take judicial notice at any stage of the proceeding.

(e) **Opportunity to Be Heard.** On timely request, a party is entitled to be heard on the propriety of taking judicial notice and the nature of the fact to be noticed. If the court takes judicial notice before notifying a party, the party, on request, is still entitled to be heard

(f) **Instructing the Jury.** In a civil case, the court must instruct the jury to accept the noticed fact as conclusive. In a criminal case, the court must instruct the jury that it may or may not accept the noticed fact as conclusive. (Amended, eff. Dec. 1, 2011.)

ARTICLE III. PRESUMPTIONS IN CIVIL CASES

RULE 301. Presumptions in Civil Cases Generally

In a civil case, unless a federal statute or these rules provide otherwise, the party against whom a presumption is directed has the burden of producing evidence to rebut the presumption. But this rule does not shift the burden of persuasion, which remains on the party who had it originally. (Amended, eff. Dec. 1, 2011.)

RULE 302. Applying State Law to Presumptions in Civil Cases

In a civil case, state law governs the effect of a presumption regarding a claim or defense for which state law supplies the rule of decision. (Amended, eff. Dec. 1, 2011.)

ARTICLE IV. RELEVANCY AND ITS LIMITS

RULE 401. Test for Relevant Evidence

Evidence is relevant if:

(a) it has any tendency to make a fact more or less probable than it would be without the evidence; and the fact is of consequence in determining the action. (Amended, eff. Dec. 1, 2011.)

RULE 402. General Admissibility of Relevant Evidence

Relevant evidence is admissible unless any of the following provides otherwise:

- the United States Constitution;
- a federal statute;
- these rules; or
- other rules prescribed by the Supreme Court.

Irrelevant evidence is not admissible. (Amended, eff. Dec. 1, 2011.)

RULE 403. Excluding Relevant Evidence for Prejudice, Confusion, Waste of Time, or Other Reasons

The court may exclude relevant evidence if its probative value is substantially outweighed by a danger of one or more of the following: unfair prejudice, confusing the issues, misleading the jury, undue delay, wasting time, or needlessly presenting cumulative evidence. (Amended, eff. Dec. 1, 2011.)

RULE 404. Character Evidence; Crimes or Other Acts

(a) Character Evidence:

(1) *Prohibited Uses.* Evidence of a person's character or character trait is not admissible to prove that on a particular occasion the person acted in accordance with the character or trait.

(2) *Exceptions for a Defendant or Victim in a Criminal Case.* The following exceptions apply in a criminal case:

(A) a defendant may offer evidence of the defendant's pertinent trait, and if the evidence is admitted, the prosecutor may offer evidence to rebut it;

(B) subject to the limitations in Rule 412, a defendant may offer evidence of an alleged victim's pertinent trait, and if the evidence is admitted, the prosecutor may:

(i) offer evidence to rebut it; and

(ii) offer evidence of the defendant's same trait; and

(C) in a homicide case, the prosecutor may offer evidence of the alleged victim's trait of peacefulness to rebut evidence that the victim was the first aggressor.

(3) *Exceptions for a Witness*. Evidence of a witness's character may be admitted under Rules 607, 608, and 609.

(b) Crimes, Wrongs, or Other Acts.

(1) *Prohibited Uses*. Evidence of a crime, wrong, or other act is not admissible to prove a person's character in order to show that on a particular occasion the person acted in accordance with the character.

(2) *Permitted Uses; Notice in a Criminal Case*. This evidence may be admissible for another purpose, such as proving motive, opportunity, intent, preparation, plan, knowledge, identity, absence of mistake, or lack of accident. On request by a defendant in a criminal case, the prosecutor must:

(A) provide reasonable notice of the general nature of any such evidence that the prosecutor intends to offer at trial; and

(B) do so before trial — or during trial if the court, for good cause, excuses lack of pretrial notice. (Amended, eff. Dec. 1, 2011.)

RULE 405. Methods of Proving Character

(a) By Reputation or Opinion. When evidence of a person's character or character trait is admissible, it may be proved by testimony about the person's reputation or by testimony in the form of an opinion. On cross-examination of the character witness, the court may allow an inquiry into relevant specific instances of the person's conduct.

(b) By Specific Instances of Conduct. When a person's character or character trait is an essential element of a charge, claim, or defense, the character or trait may also be proved by relevant specific instances of the person's conduct. (Amended, eff. Dec. 1, 2011.)

RULE 406. Habit; Routine

Evidence of a person's habit or an organization's routine practice may be admitted to prove that on a particular occasion the person or organization acted in accordance with the habit or routine practice. The court may admit this evidence regardless of whether it is corroborated or whether there was an eyewitness. (Amended, eff. Dec. 1, 2011.)

RULE 407. Subsequent Remedial Measures

When measures are taken that would have made an earlier injury or harm less likely to occur, evidence of the subsequent measures is not admissible to prove:

- negligence;
- culpable conduct;
- a defect in a product or its design; or
- a need for a warning or instruction.

But the court may admit this evidence for another purpose, such as impeachment or — if disputed — proving ownership, control, or the feasibility of precautionary measures. (Amended, eff. Dec. 1, 2011.)

RULE 408. Compromise and Offers to Compromise

(a) Prohibited Uses. Evidence of the following is not admissible — on behalf of any party — either to prove or disprove the validity or amount of a disputed claim or to impeach by a prior inconsistent statement or a contradiction:

(1) furnishing, promising, or offering — or accepting, promising to accept, or offering to accept — a valuable consideration in compromising or attempting to compromise the claim; and

(2) conduct or a statement made during compromise negotiations about the claim — except when offered in a criminal case and when the negotiations related to a claim by a public office in the exercise of its regulatory, investigative, or enforcement authority.

(b) Exceptions. The court may admit this evidence for another purpose, such as proving a witness's bias or prejudice, negating a contention of undue delay, or proving an effort to obstruct a criminal investigation or prosecution. (Amended, eff. Dec. 1, 2011.)

RULE 409. Offers to Pay Medical and Similar Expenses

Evidence of furnishing or offering or promising to pay medical, hospital, or similar expenses occasioned by an injury is not admissible to prove liability for the injury. (Amended, eff. Dec. 1, 2011.)

RULE 410. Inadmissibility of Pleas, Plea Discussions, and Related Statements

(a) Prohibited Uses. In a civil or criminal case, evidence of the following is not admissible against the defendant who made the plea or participated in the plea discussions:
  (1) a guilty plea that was later withdrawn;
  (2) a nolo contendere plea;
  (3) a statement made during a proceeding on either of those pleas under Federal Rule of Criminal Procedure 11 or a comparable state procedure; or
  (4) a statement made during plea discussions with an attorney for the prosecuting authority if the discussions did not result in a guilty plea or they resulted in a later-withdrawn guilty plea.

(b) Exceptions. The court may admit a statement described in Rule 410(a)(3) or (4):
  (1) in any proceeding in which another statement made during the same plea or plea discussions has been introduced, if in fairness the statements ought to be considered together; or
  (2) in a criminal proceeding for perjury or false statement, if the defendant made the statement under oath, on the record, and with counsel present. (Amended, eff. Dec. 1, 2011.)

RULE 411. Liability Insurance

Evidence that a person was or was not insured against liability is not admissible to prove whether the person acted negligently or otherwise wrongfully. But the court may admit this evidence for another purpose, such as proving a witness's bias or prejudice or proving agency, ownership, or control. (Amended, eff. Dec. 1, 2011.)

RULE 412. Sex-Offense Cases: The Victim's Sexual Behavior or Predisposition

(a) Prohibited Uses. The following evidence is not admissible in a civil or criminal proceeding involving alleged sexual misconduct:
  (1) evidence offered to prove that a victim engaged in other sexual behavior; or
  (2) evidence offered to prove a victim's sexual predisposition.

(b) Exceptions.
  (1) *Criminal Cases*. The court may admit the following evidence in a criminal case:
    (A) evidence of specific instances of a victim's sexual behavior, if offered to prove that someone other than the defendant was the source of semen, injury, or other physical evidence;

(B) evidence of specific instances of a victim's sexual behavior with respect to the person accused of the sexual misconduct, if offered by the defendant to prove consent or if offered by the prosecutor; and

(C) evidence whose exclusion would violate the defendant's constitutional rights.

(2) *Civil Cases*. In a civil case, the court may admit evidence offered to prove a victim's sexual behavior or sexual predisposition if its probative value substantially outweighs the danger of harm to any victim and of unfair prejudice to any party. The court may admit evidence of a victim's reputation only if the victim has placed it in controversy.

(c) Procedure to Determine Admissibility.

(1) *Motion.* If a party intends to offer evidence under Rule 412(b), the party must:

(A) file a motion that specifically describes the evidence and states the purpose for which it is to be offered;

(B) do so at least 14 days before trial unless the court, for good cause, sets a different time;

(C) serve the motion on all parties; and

(D) notify the victim or, when appropriate, the victim's guardian or representative.

(2) *Hearing*. Before admitting evidence under this rule, the court must conduct an in camera hearing and give the victim and parties a right to attend and be heard. Unless the court orders otherwise, the motion, related materials, and the record of the hearing must be and remain sealed.

(d) Definition of "Victim." In this rule, "victim" includes an alleged victim. (Amended, eff. Dec. 1, 2011.)

RULE 413. Similar Crimes in Sexual-Assault Cases

(a) PERMITTED USES. In a criminal case in which a defendant is accused of a sexual assault, the court may admit evidence that the defendant committed any other sexual assault. The evidence may be considered on any matter to which it is relevant.

(b) DISCLOSURE TO THE DEFENDANT. If the prosecutor intends to offer this evidence, the prosecutor must disclose it to the defendant, including witnesses' statements or a summary of the expected testimony. The prosecutor must do so at least 15 days before trial or at a later time that the court allows for good cause.

(c) EFFECT ON OTHER RULES. This rule does not limit the admission or consideration of evidence under any other rule.

(d) DEFINITION OF "SEXUAL ASSAULT." In this rule and Rule 415, "sexual assault" means a crime under federal law or under state law (as "state" is defined in 18 U.S.C. § 513) involving:

(1) any conduct prohibited by 18 U.S.C. chapter 109A;

(2) contact, without consent, between any part of the defend-ant's body—or an object—and another person's genitals or anus;

(3) contact, without consent, between the defendant's genitals or anus and any part of another person's body;

(4) deriving sexual pleasure or gratification from inflicting death, bodily injury, or physical pain on another person; or

(5) an attempt or conspiracy to engage in conduct described in subparagraphs (1)–(4). (Amended, eff. Dec. 1, 2011.)

RULE 414. Evidence of Similar Crimes in Child Molestation Cases

(a) **Permitted Uses.** In a criminal case in which a defendant is accused of child molestation, the court may admit evidence that the defendant committed any other child molestation. The evidence may be considered on any matter to which it is relevant.

(b) **Disclosure to the Defendant.** If the prosecutor intends to offer this evidence, the prosecutor must disclose it to the defendant, including witnesses' statements or a summary of the expected testimony. The prosecutor must do so at least 15 days before trial or at a later time that the court allows for good cause.

(c) **Effect on Other Rules.** This rule does not limit the admission or consideration of evidence under any other rule.

(d) **Definition of "Child" and "Child Molestation."** In this rule and Rule 415:

(1) "child" means a person below the age of 14; and

(2) "child molestation" means a crime under federal law or under state law (as "state" is defined in 18 U.S.C. § 513) involving:

(A) any conduct prohibited by 18 U.S.C. chapter 109A and committed with a child;

(B) any conduct prohibited by 18 U.S.C. chapter 110;

(C) contact between any part of the defendant's body — or an object — and a child's genitals or anus;

(D) contact between the defendant's genitals or anus and any part of a child's body;

(E) deriving sexual pleasure or gratification from inflicting death, bodily injury, or physical pain on a child; or an attempt or conspiracy to engage in conduct described in subparagraphs (A)–(E). (Amended, eff. Dec. 1, 2011.)

RULE 415. Similar Acts in Civil Cases Involving Sexual Assault or Child Molestation

(a) Permitted Uses. In a civil case involving a claim for relief based on a party's alleged sexual assault or child molestation, the court may admit evidence that the party committed any other sexual assault or child molestation. The evidence may be considered as provided in Rules 413 and 414.

(b) Disclosure to the Opponent. If a party intends to offer this evidence, the party must disclose it to the party against whom it will be offered, including witnesses' statements or a summary of the expected testimony. The party must do so at least 15 days before trial or at a later time that the court allows for good cause.

(c) Effect on Other Rules. This rule does not limit the admission or consideration of evidence under any other rule. (Amended, eff. Dec. 1, 2011.)

ARTICLE V. PRIVILEGES

RULE 501. Privileges in General

The common law — as interpreted by United States courts in the light of reason and experience — governs a claim of privilege unless any of the following provides otherwise:

- the United States Constitution;
- a federal statute; or

- rules prescribed by the Supreme Court.

But in a civil case, state law governs privilege regarding a claim or defense for which state law supplies the rule of decision. (Amended, eff. Dec. 1, 2011.)

RULE 502. Attorney-Client Privilege and Work Product; Limitations on Waiver

The following provisions apply, in the circumstances set out, to disclosure of a communication or information covered by the attorney-client privilege or work-product protection.

(a) Disclosure Made in a Federal Proceeding or to a Federal Office or Agency; Scope of a Waiver. When the disclosure is made in a federal proceeding or to a federal office or agency and waives the attorney-client privilege or work-product protection, the waiver extends to an undisclosed communication or information in a federal or state proceeding only if:
  (1) the waiver is intentional;
  (2) the disclosed and undisclosed communications or information concern the same subject matter; and
  (3) they ought in fairness to be considered together.

(b) Inadvertent Disclosure. When made in a federal proceeding or to a federal office or agency, the dis-closure does not operate as a waiver in a federal or state proceeding if:
  (1) the disclosure is inadvertent;
  (2) the holder of the privilege or protection took reasonable steps to prevent disclosure; and
  (3) the holder promptly took reasonable steps to rectify the error, including (if applicable) following Federal Rule of Civil Procedure 26(b)(5)(B).

(c) Disclosure Made in a State Proceeding. When the disclosure is made in a state proceeding and is not the subject of a state-court order concerning waiver, the disclosure does not operate as a waiver in a federal proceeding if the disclosure:
  (1) would not be a waiver under this rule if it had been made in a federal proceeding; or
  (2) is not a waiver under the law of the State where the disclosure occurred.

(d) Controlling Effect of a Court Order. A federal court may order that the privilege or protection is not waived by disclosure connected with the litigation pending before the court–in which event the disclosure is also not a waiver in any other federal or state proceeding.

(e) Controlling Effect of a Party Agreement. An agreement on the effect of disclosure in a federal proceeding is binding only on the parties to the agreement, unless it is incorporated into a court order.

(f) Controlling Effect of this Rule. Notwithstanding Rules 101 and 1101, this rule applies to state proceedings and to federal court-annexed and federal court-mandated arbitration proceedings, in the circumstances set out in the rule. And notwithstanding Rule 501, this rule applies even if State law provides the rule of decision.

(g) Definitions. In this rule:
  (1) "attorney-client privilege" means the protection that applicable law provides for confidential attorney-client communications; and
  (2) "work-product protection" means the protection that applicable law provides for tangible material (or its intangible equivalent) prepared in anticipation of litigation or for trial." (As added. eff. Dec. 1, 2011.)

ARTICLE VI. WITNESS

RULE 601. Competency to Testify in General

Every person is competent to be a witness unless these rules provide otherwise. But in a civil case, state law governs the witness's competency regarding a claim or defense for which state law supplies the rule of decision. (Amended, eff. Dec. 1, 2011.)

RULE 602. Need for Personal Knowledge

A witness may not testify to a matter unless evidence is introduced sufficient to support a finding that the witness has personal knowledge of the matter. Evidence to prove personal knowledge may, but need not, consist of the witness' own testimony. This rule is subject to the provisions of rule 703, relating to opinion testimony by expert witnesses. (Amended, eff. Dec. 1, 2011.)

RULE 603. Oath or Affirmation to Testify Truthfully

Before testifying, a witness must give an oath or affirmation to testify truthfully. It must be in a form de-signed to impress that duty on the witness's conscience. (Amended, eff. Dec. 1, 2011.)

RULE 604. Interpreter

An interpreter must be qualified and must give an oath or affirmation to make a true translation. (Amended, eff. Dec. 1, 2011.)

RULE 605. Judge's Competency as a Witness

The presiding judge may not testify as a witness at the trial. A party need not object to preserve the issue. (Amended, eff. Dec. 1, 2011.)

RULE 606. Juror's Competency as a Witness

(a) At the Trial. A juror may not testify as a witness before the other jurors at the trial. If a juror is called to testify, the court must give a party an opportunity to object outside the jury's presence.

(b) During an Inquiry into the Validity of a Verdict or Indictment.

  (1) *Prohibited Testimony or Other Evidence.* During an inquiry into the validity of a verdict or indictment, a juror may not testify about any statement made or incident that occurred during the jury's deliberations; the effect of anything on that juror's or another juror's vote; or any juror's mental processes concerning the verdict or indictment. The court may not receive a juror's affidavit or evidence of a juror's statement on these matters.

  (2) A juror may testify about whether:

    (A) extraneous prejudicial information was improperly brought to the jury's attention;

    (B) an outside influence was improperly brought to bear on any juror; or

    (C) a mistake was made in entering the verdict on the verdict form. (Amended, eff. Dec. 1, 2011.)

RULE 607. Who May Impeach a Witness

Any party, including the party that called the witness, may attack the witness's credibility. (Amended, eff. Dec. 1, 2011.)

RULE 608. A Witness's Character for Truthfulness or Untruthfulness

(a) Reputation or Opinion Evidence. A witness's credibility may be attacked or supported by testimony about the witness's reputation for having a character for truthfulness or untruthfulness, or by testimony in the form of an opinion about that character. But evidence of truthful character is admissible only after the witness's character for truthfulness has been attacked.

(b) Specific Instances of Conduct.

Except for a criminal conviction under Rule 609, extrinsic evidence is not admissible to prove specific instances of a witness's conduct in order to attack or support the witness's character for truthfulness. But the court may, on cross-examination, allow them to be inquired into if they are probative of the character for truthfulness or untruthfulness of:

(1) the witness; or
(2) another witness whose character the witness being cross-examined has testified about.

By testifying on another matter, a witness does not waive any privilege against self-incrimination for testimony that relates only to the witness's character for truthfulness. (Amended, eff. Dec. 1, 2011.)

RULE 609. Impeachment by Evidence of a Criminal Conviction

(a) In General. The following rules apply to attacking a witness's character for truthfulness by evidence of a criminal conviction:
  (1) for a crime that, in the convicting jurisdiction, was punishable by death or by imprisonment for more than one year, the evidence:
    (A) must be admitted, subject to Rule 403, in a civil case or in a criminal case in which the witness is not a defendant; and
    (B) must be admitted in a criminal case in which the witness is a defendant, if the probative value of the evidence outweighs its prejudicial effect to that defendant; and
  (2) for any crime regardless of the punishment, the evidence must be admitted if the court can readily determine that establishing the elements of the crime required proving — or the witness's admitting — a dishonest act or false statement.

(b) Limit on Using the Evidence After 10 Years. This subdivision (b) applies if more than 10 years have passed since the witness's conviction or release from confinement for it, whichever is later. Evidence of the conviction is admissible only if:
  (1) its probative value, supported by specific facts and circumstances, substantially outweighs its prejudicial effect; and
  (2) the proponent gives an adverse party reasonable written notice of the intent to use it so that the party has a fair opportunity to contest its use.

(c) Effect of a Pardon, Annulment, or Certificate of Rehabilitation. Evidence of a conviction is not admissible if:
  (1) the conviction has been the subject of a pardon, annulment, certificate of rehabilitation, or other equivalent procedure based on a finding that the person has been rehabilitated, and the person has not been convicted of a later crime punishable by death or by imprisonment for more than one year; or
  (2) the conviction has been the subject of a pardon, annulment, or other equivalent procedure based on a finding of innocence.

(d) Juvenile Adjudications. Evidence of a juvenile adjudication is admissible under this rule only if:
  (1) it is offered in a criminal case;
  (2) the adjudication was of a witness other than the defendant;
  (3) an adult's conviction for that offense would be admissible to attack the adult's credibility; and
  (4) admitting the evidence is necessary to fairly determine guilt or innocence.

(e) Pendency of an Appeal. A conviction that satisfies this rule is admissible even if an appeal is pending. Evidence of the pendency is also admissible. (Amended, eff. Dec. 1, 2011.)

RULE 610. Religious Beliefs or Opinions

Evidence of a witness's religious beliefs or opinions is not admissible to attack or support the witness's credibility. (Amended, eff. Dec. 1, 2011.)

RULE 611. Mode and Order of Interrogation and Presenting Evidence

(a) Control by court. The Court shall exercise reasonable control over the mode and order of interrogating witnesses and presenting evidence so as to (1) make the interrogation and presentation effective for the ascertainment of the truth, (2) avoid needless consumption of time and, (3) protect witnesses from harassment or undue embarrassment.

(b) Scope of Cross-Examination. Cross-examination should not go beyond the subject matter of the direct examination and matters affecting the witness's credibility. The court may allow inquiry into additional matters as if on direct examination.

(c) Leading Questions. Leading questions should not be used on the direct examination of a witness except as may be necessary to develop the witness' testimony. Ordinarily, the court should allow leading questions:
   (1) on cross-examination; and
   (2) when a party calls a hostile witness, and adverse party, or a witness identified with an adverse party. (Amended, eff. Dec. 1, 2011.)

RULE 612. Writing Used to Refresh a Witness's Memory

(a) Scope. This rule gives an adverse party certain options when a witness uses a writing to refresh memory:
   (1) while testifying; or
   (2) before testifying, if the court decides that justice requires the party to have those options.

(b) Adverse Party's Options; Deleting Unrelated Matter. Unless 18 U.S.C. § 3500 provides otherwise in a criminal case, an adverse party is entitled to have the writing produced at the hearing, to inspect it, to cross-examine the witness about it, and to introduce in evidence any portion that relates to the witness's testimony. If the producing party claims that the writing includes unrelated matter, the court must examine the writing in camera, delete any unrelated portion, and order that the rest be delivered to the adverse party. Any portion deleted over objection must be preserved for the record.

(c) Failure to Produce or Deliver the Writing. If a writing is not produced or is not delivered as ordered, the court may issue any appropriate order. But if the prosecution does not comply in a criminal case, the court must strike the witness's testimony or — if justice so requires — declare a mistrial (Amended, eff. Dec. 1, 2011.)

RULE 613. Witness's Prior Statement

(a) Showing or Disclosing the Statement During Examination. When examining a witness about the witness's prior statement, a party need not show it or disclose its contents to the witness. But the party must, on request, show it or disclose its contents to an adverse party's attorney.

(b) Extrinsic Evidence of a Prior Inconsistent Statement. Extrinsic evidence of a witness's prior inconsistent statement is admissible only if the witness is given an opportunity to explain or deny the statement and an adverse party is given an opportunity to examine the witness about it, or if justice so requires. This subdivision (b) does not apply to an opposing party's statement under Rule 801(d)(2). (Amended, eff. Dec. 1, 2011.)

RULE 614. Court's Calling or Examining a Witness

(a) Calling. The court may call a witness on its own or at a party's request. Each party is entitled to cross-examine the witness.
(b) Examining. The court may examine a witness regardless of who calls the witness.
(c) Objections. A party may object to the court's calling or examining a witness either at that time or at the next opportunity when the jury is not present. (Amended, eff. Dec. 1, 2011.)

RULE 615. Excluding Witnesses

At a party's request, the court must order witnesses excluded so that they cannot hear other witnesses' testimony. Or the court may do so on its own. But this rule does not authorize excluding:

(a) a party who is a natural person;
(b) an officer or employee of a party that is not a natural person, after being designated as the party's representative by its attorney;
(c) a person whose presence a party shows to be essential to presenting the party's claim or defense; or
(d) a person authorized by statute to be present. (Amended, eff. Dec. 1, 2011.)

ARTICLE VII. OPINIONS AND EXPERT TESTIMONY

RULE 701. Opinion Testimony by Lay Witnesses

If a witness is not testifying as an expert, testimony in the form of an opinion is limited to one that is:

(a) rationally based on the witness's perception;
(b) helpful to clearly understanding the witness's testimony or to determining a fact in issue; and
(c) not based on scientific, technical, or other specialized knowledge within the scope of Rule 702. (Amended, eff. Dec. 1, 2011.)

RULE 702. Testimony by Expert Witnesses

A witness who is qualified as an expert by knowledge, skill, experience, training, or education may testify in the form of an opinion or otherwise if:

(a) the expert's scientific, technical, or other specialized knowledge will help the trier of fact to under-stand the evidence or to determine a fact in issue;
(b) the testimony is based on sufficient facts or data;
(c) the testimony is the product of reliable principles and methods; and
(d) the expert has reliably applied the principles and methods to the facts of the case. (Amended, eff. Dec. 1, 2011.)

RULE 703. Bases of an Expert's Opinion Testimony

An expert may base an opinion on facts or data in the case that the expert has been made aware of or personally observed. If experts in the particular field would reasonably rely on those kinds of facts or data in forming an opinion on the subject, they need not be admissible for the opinion to be admitted. But if the facts or data would otherwise be inadmissible, the proponent of the opinion may disclose them to the jury only if their probative value in helping the jury evaluate the opinion substantially outweighs their prejudicial effect. (Amended, eff. Dec. 1, 2011.)

RULE 704. Opinion on an Ultimate Issue

(a) In General — Not Automatically Objectionable. An opinion is not objectionable just because it embraces an ultimate issue.

(b) Exception. In a criminal case, an expert witness must not state an opinion about whether the defendant did or did not have a mental state or condition that constitutes an element of the crime charged or of a defense. Those matters are for the trier of fact alone. (Amended, eff. Dec. 1, 2011.)

RULE 705. Disclosing the Facts or Data Underlying an Expert's Opinion

Unless the court orders otherwise, an expert may state an opinion — and give the reasons for it — without first testifying to the underlying facts or data. But the expert may be required to disclose those facts or data on cross-examination. (Amended, eff. Dec. 1, 2011.)

RULE 706. Court Appointed Expert Witnesses

(a) Appointment Process. On a party's motion or on its own, the court may order the parties to show cause why expert witnesses should not be appointed and may ask the parties to submit nominations. The court may appoint any expert that the parties agree on and any of its own choosing. But the court may only appoint someone who consents to act.

(b) Expert's Role. The court must inform the expert of the expert's duties. The court may do so in writing and have a copy filed with the clerk or may do so orally at a conference in which the parties have an opportunity to participate. The expert:
   (1) must advise the parties of any findings the expert makes;
   (2) may be deposed by any party;
   (3) may be called to testify by the court or any party; and
   (4) may be cross-examined by any party, including the party that called the expert.

(c) Compensation. The expert is entitled to a reasonable compensation, as set by the court. The compensation is payable as follows:
   (1) in a criminal case or in a civil case involving just compensation under the Fifth Amendment, from any funds that are provided by law; and
   (2) in any other civil case, by the parties in the proportion and at the time that the court direct — and the compensation is then charged like other costs.

(d) Disclosing the Appointment to the Jury. The court may authorize disclosure to the jury that the court appointed the expert.

(e) Parties' Choice of Their Own Experts. This rule does not limit a party in calling its own experts. (Amended, eff. Dec. 1, 2011.)

ARTICLE VIII. HEARSAY

RULE 801. Definitions That Apply to This Article; Exclusions from Hearsay

(a) Statement. "Statement" means a person's oral assertion, written assertion, or nonverbal conduct, if the person intended it as an assertion.

(b) Declarant. "Declarant" means the person who made the statement.

(c) Hearsay. "Hearsay" means a statement that:
   (1) the declarant does not make while testifying at the current trial or hearing; and
   (2) a party offers in evidence to prove the truth of the matter asserted in the statement.

(d) Statements That Are Not Hearsay. A statement that meets the following conditions is not hearsay:

(1) *A Declarant-Witness's Prior Statement.* The declarant testifies and is subject to cross-examination about a prior statement, and the statement:

(A) is inconsistent with the declarant's testimony and was given under penalty of perjury at a trial, hearing, or other proceeding or in a deposition;

(B) is consistent with the declarant's testimony and is offered to rebut an express or implied charge that the declarant recently fabricated it or acted from a recent improper influence or motive in so testifying; or

(C) identifies a person as someone the declarant perceived earlier.

(2) *An Opposing Party's Statement.* The statement is offered against an opposing party and:

(A) was made by the party in an individual or representative capacity;

(B) is one the party manifested that it adopted or believed to be true;

(C) was made by a person whom the party authorized to make a statement on the subject;

(D) was made by the party's agent or employee on a matter within the scope of that relationship and while it existed; or

(E) was made by the party's coconspirator during and in furtherance of the conspiracy.

The statement must be considered but does not by itself establish the declarant's authority under (C); the existence or scope of the relationship under (D); or the existence of the conspiracy or participation in it under (E). (Amended, eff. Dec. 1, 2011.)

RULE 802. The Rule Against Hearsay

Hearsay is not admissible unless any of the following provides otherwise:

- a federal statute;
- these rules; or
- other rules prescribed by the Supreme Court. (Amended, eff. Dec. 1, 2011.)

RULE 803. Exceptions to the Rule Against Hearsay — Regardless of Whether the Declarant Is Available as a Witness

The following are not excluded by the rule against hearsay, regardless of whether the declarant is available as a witness:

(1) *Present Sense Impression.* A statement describing or explaining an event or condition, made while or immediately after the declarant perceived it.

(2) *Excited Utterance.* A statement relating to a startling event or condition, made while the declarant was under the stress of excitement that it caused.

(3) *Then-Existing Mental, Emotional, or Physical Condition.* A statement of the declarant's then-existing state of mind (such as motive, intent, or plan) or emotional, sensory, or physical condition (such as mental feeling, pain, or bodily health), but not including a statement of memory or belief to prove the fact remembered or believed unless it relates to the validity or terms of the declarant's will.

(4) *Statement Made for Medical Diagnosis or Treatment.* A statement that:

(A) is made for — and is reasonably pertinent to — medical diagnosis or treatment; and

(B) describes medical history; past or present symptoms or sensations; their inception; or their general cause.

(5) *Recorded Recollection* A record that:

(A) is on a matter the witness once knew about but now cannot recall

well enough to testify fully and accurately;
(B) was made or adopted by the witness when the matter was fresh in the witness's memory; and
(C) accurately reflects the witness's knowledge.

If admitted, the record may be read into evidence but may be received as an exhibit only if offered by an adverse party.

(6) *Records of a Regularly Conducted Activity.* A record of an act, event, condition, opinion, or diagnosis if:
(A) the record was made at or near the time by — or from information transmitted by — someone with knowledge;
(B) the record was kept in the course of a regularly conducted activity of a business, organization, occupation, or calling, whether or not for profit;
(C) making the record was a regular practice of that activity;
(D) all these conditions are shown by the testimony of the custodian or another qualified witness, or by a certification that complies with Rule 902(11) or (12) or with a statute permitting certification; and
(E) neither the source of information nor the method or circumstances of preparation indicate a lack of trustworthiness.

(7) *Absence of a Record of a Regularly Conducted Activity.* Evidence that a matter is not included in a record described in paragraph (6) if:
(A) the evidence is admitted to prove that the matter did not occur or exist;
(B) a record was regularly kept for a matter of that kind; and
(C) neither the possible source of the information nor other circumstances indicate a lack of trustworthiness.

(8) *Public Records.* A record or statement of a public office if:
(A) it sets out:
(i) the office's activities;
(ii) a matter observed while under a legal duty to report, but not including, in a criminal case, a matter observed by law-enforcement personnel; or
(iii) in a civil case or against the government in a criminal case, factual findings from a legally authorized investigation; and
(B) neither the source of information nor other circumstances indicate a lack of trustworthiness.

(9) *Public Records of Vital Statistics.* A record of a birth, death, or marriage, if reported to a public office in accordance with a legal duty.

(10) *Absence of a Public Record.* Testimony — or a certification under Rule 902 — that a diligent search failed to disclose a public record or statement if:
(A) the testimony or certification is admitted to prove that
(i) the record or statement does not exist; or
(ii) a matter did not occur or exist, if a public office regularly kept a record or statement for a matter of that kind; and
(B) in a criminal case, a prosecutor who intends to offer a certification provides written notice of that intent at least 14 days before trial, and the defendant does not object in writing within 7 days of receiving the notice — unless the court sets a different time for the notice or the objection. Eff. Dec, 1, 2013.

(11) *Records of Religious Organizations Concerning Personal or Family History.* A statement of birth, legitimacy, ancestry, marriage, divorce, death, relationship by blood or marriage, or similar facts of personal or family history, contained in a regularly kept record of a religious organization.

(12) *Certificates of Marriage, Baptism, and Similar Ceremonies.* A statement of fact contained in a certificate:
   (A) made by a person who is authorized by a religious organization or by law to perform the act certified;
   (B) attesting that the person performed a marriage or similar ceremony or administered a sacrament; and
   (C) purporting to have been issued at the time of the act or within a reasonable time after it.

(13) *Family Records.* A statement of fact about personal or family history contained in a family record, such as a Bible, genealogy, chart, engraving on a ring, inscription on a portrait, or engraving on an urn or burial marker.

(14) *Records of Documents That Affect an Interest in Property.* The record of a document that purports to establish or affect an interest in property if:
   (A) the record is admitted to prove the content of the original recorded document, along with its signing and its delivery by each person who purports to have signed it;
   (B) the record is kept in a public office; and
   (C) a statute authorizes recording documents of that kind in that office.

(15) *Statements in Documents That Affect an Interest in Property.* A statement contained in a document that purports to establish or affect an interest in property if the matter stated was relevant to the document's purpose — unless later dealings with the property are inconsistent with the truth of the statement or the purport of the document.

(16) *Statements in Ancient Documents.* A statement in a document that is at least 20 years old and whose authenticity is established.

(17) *Market Reports and Similar Commercial Publications.* Market quotations, lists, directories, or other compilations that are generally relied on by the public or by persons in particular occupations.

(18) *Statements in Learned Treatises, Periodicals, or Pamphlets.* A statement contained in a treatise, periodical, or pamphlet if:
   (A) the statement is called to the attention of an expert witness on cross-examination or relied on by the expert on direct examination; and
   (B) the publication is established as a reliable authority by the expert's admission or testimony, by another expert's testimony, or by judicial notice.

   If admitted, the statement may be read into evidence but not received as an exhibit.

(19) *Reputation Concerning Personal or Family History.* A reputation among a person's family by blood, adoption, or marriage — or among a person's associates or in the community — concerning the person's birth, adoption, legitimacy, ancestry, marriage, divorce, death, relationship by blood, adoption, or marriage, or similar facts of personal or family history.

(20) *Reputation Concerning Boundaries or General History.* A reputation in a community — arising before the controversy — concerning boundaries of land in the community or customs that affect the land, or concerning general historical events important to that community, state, or nation.

(21) *Reputation Concerning Character.* A reputation among a person's associates or in the community concerning the person's character.

(22) *Judgment of a Previous Conviction.* Evidence of a final judgment of conviction if:
   (A) the judgment was entered after a trial or guilty plea, but not a nolo contendere plea;
   (B) the conviction was for a crime punishable by death or by imprisonment for more than a year;
   (C) the evidence is admitted to prove any fact essential to the judgment; and
   (D) when offered by the prosecutor in a criminal case for a purpose other than impeachment, the judgment was against the defendant.

   The pendency of an appeal may be shown but does not affect admissibility.

(23) *Judgments Involving Personal, Family, or General History, or a Boundary.* A judgment that is admitted to prove a matter of personal, family, or general history, or boundaries, if the matter:
   (A) was essential to the judgment; and
   (B) could be proved by evidence of reputation.

(24) [*Other Exceptions.*] [Transferred to Rule 807.] (Amended, eff. Dec. 1, 2013.)

RULE 804. Exceptions to the Rule Against Hearsay — When the Declarant Is Unavailable as a Witness

(a) **Criteria for Being Unavailable.** A declarant is considered to be unavailable as a witness if the declarant:
   (1) is exempted from testifying about the subject matter of the declarant's statement because the court rules that a privilege applies;
   (2) refuses to testify about the subject matter despite a court order to do so;
   (3) testifies to not remembering the subject matter;
   (4) cannot be present or testify at the trial or hearing because of death or a then-existing infirmity, physical illness, or mental illness; or
   (5) is absent from the trial or hearing and the statement's proponent has not been able, by process or other reasonable means, to procure:
      (A) the declarant's attendance, in the case of a hearsay exception under Rule 804(b)(1) or (6); or
      (B) the declarant's attendance or testimony, in the case of a hearsay exception under Rule 804 (b)(2), (3), or (4).

   But this subdivision (a) does not apply if the statement's proponent procured or wrongfully caused the declarant's unavailability as a witness in order to prevent the declarant from attending or testifying.

(b) The Exceptions. The following are not excluded by the rule against hearsay if the declarant is unavailable as a witness:
   (1) *Former Testimony.* Testimony that:
      (A) was given as a witness at a trial, hearing, or lawful deposition, whether given during the current proceeding or a different one; and
      (B) is now offered against a party who had — or, in a civil case, whose predecessor in interest had — an opportunity and similar motive to develop it by direct, cross-, or redirect examination.
   (2) *Statement Under the Belief of Imminent Death.* In a prosecution for homicide or in a civil case, a statement that the declarant, while believing the declarant's death to be imminent, made about its cause or circumstances.
   (3) *Statement Against Interest.* A statement that:

(A) a reasonable person in the declarant's position would have made only if the person believed it to be true because, when made, it was so contrary to the declarant's proprietary or pecuniary interest or had so great a tendency to invalidate the declarant's claim against someone else or to expose the declarant to civil or criminal liability; and

(B) is supported by corroborating circumstances that clearly indicate its trustworthiness, if it is offered in a criminal case as one that tends to expose the declarant to criminal liability.

(4) *Statement of Personal or Family History.* A statement about:

(A) the declarant's own birth, adoption, legitimacy, ancestry, marriage, divorce, relationship by blood, adoption, or marriage, or similar facts of personal or family history, even though the declarant had no way of acquiring personal knowledge about that fact; or

(B) another person concerning any of these facts, as well as death, if the declarant was related to the person by blood, adoption information is likely to be accurate.

(5) [*Other Exceptions.*] [Transferred to Rule 807.]

(6) *Statement Offered Against a Party That Wrongfully Caused the Declarant's Unavailability.* A statement offered against a party that wrongfully caused — or acquiesced in wrongfully causing — the declarant's unavailability as a witness, and did so intending that result. (Amended, eff. Dec. 1, 2011.)

RULE 805. Hearsay within Hearsay

Hearsay within hearsay is not excluded by the rule against hearsay if each part of the combined statements conforms with an exception to the rule. (Amended, eff. Dec. 1, 2011.)

RULE 806. Attacking and Supporting the Declarant's Credibility

When a hearsay statement — or a statement described in Rule 801(d)(2)(C), (D), or (E) — has been admitted in evidence, the declarant's credibility may be attacked, and then supported, by any evidence that would be admissible for those purposes if the declarant had testified as a witness. The court may admit evidence of the declarant's inconsistent statement or conduct, regardless of when it occurred or whether the declarant had an opportunity to explain or deny it. If the party against whom the statement was admitted calls the declarant as a witness, the party may examine the declarant on the statement as if on cross-examination. (Amended, eff. Dec. 1, 2011.)

RULE 807. Residual Exception

(a) **In General.** Under the following circumstances, a hearsay statement is not excluded by the rule against hearsay even if the statement is not specifically covered by a hearsay exception in Rule 803 or 804:

(1) the statement has equivalent circumstantial guarantees of trustworthiness;

(2) it is offered as evidence of a material fact;

(3) it is more probative on the point for which it is offered than any other evidence that the proponent can obtain through reasonable efforts; and

(4) admitting it will best serve the purposes of these rules and the interests of justice. (Amended, eff. Dec. 1, 2011.)

ARTICLE IX. AUTHENTICATION AND IDENTIFICATION

RULE 901. Authenticating or Identifying Evidence

(a) In General. To satisfy the requirement of authenticating or identifying an item of evidence, the proponent must produce evidence sufficient to support a finding that the item is what the proponent claims it is.

(b) Examples. The following are examples only — not a complete list — of evidence that satisfies the requirement:

(1) *Testimony of a Witness with Knowledge.* Testimony that an item is what it is claimed to be.

(2) *Nonexpert Opinion About Handwriting.* A nonexpert's opinion that handwriting is genuine, based on a familiarity with it that was not acquired for the current litigation.

(3) *Comparison by an Expert Witness or the Trier of Fact.* A comparison with an authenticated specimen by an expert witness or the trier of fact.

(4) *Distinctive Characteristics and the Like.* The appearance, contents, substance, internal patterns, or other distinctive characteristics of the item, taken together with all the circumstances.

(5) *Opinion About a Voice.* An opinion identifying a person's voice — whether heard firsthand or through mechanical or electronic transmission or recording — based on hearing the voice at any time under circumstances that connect it with the alleged speaker.

(6) *Evidence About a Telephone Conversation.* For a telephone conversation, evidence that a call was made to the number assigned at the time to:

(A) a particular person, if circumstances, including self-identification, show that the person answering was the one called; or

(B) a particular business, if the call was made to a business and the call related to business reasonably transacted over the telephone.

(7) *Evidence About Public Records.* Evidence that:

(A) a document was recorded or filed in a public office as authorized by law; or

(B) a purported public record or statement is from the office where items of this kind are kept.

(8) *Evidence About Ancient Documents or Data Compilations.* For a document or data compilation, evidence that it:

(A) is in a condition that creates no suspicion about its authenticity;

(B) was in a place where, if authentic, it would likely be; and

(C) is at least 20 years old when offered.

(9) *Evidence About a Process or System.* Evidence describing a process or system and showing that it produces an accurate result.

(10) *Methods Provided by a Statute or Rule.* Any method of authentication or identification allowed by a federal statute or a rule prescribed by the Supreme Court. . (Amended, eff. Dec. 1, 2011.)

RULE 902. Evidence That Is Self-Authenticating

The following items of evidence are self-authenticating; they require no extrinsic evidence of authenticity in order to be admitted:

(1) *Domestic Public Documents That Are Sealed and Signed.* A document that bears:

(A) a seal purporting to be that of the United States; any state, district, commonwealth, territory, or insular possession of the United States; the former Panama Canal Zone; the Trust Territory of the Pacific Islands; a political subdivision of any of these entities; or a department, agency, or officer of any entity named above; and
(B) a signature purporting to be an execution or attestation.

(2) *Domestic Public Documents That Are Not Sealed but Are Signed and Certified.* A document that bears no seal if:
(A) it bears the signature of an officer or employee of an entity named in Rule 902(1)(A); and
(B) another public officer who has a seal and official duties within that same entity certifies under seal — or its equivalent — that the signer has the official capacity and that the signature is genuine.

(3) *Foreign Public Documents.* A document that purports to be signed or attested by a person who is authorized by a foreign country's law to do so. The document must be accompanied by a final certification that certify ies the genuineness of the signature and official position of the signer or attester — or of any foreign official whose certificate of genuineness relates to the signature or attestation or is in a chain of certificates of genuineness relating to the signature or attestation. The certification may be made by a secretary of a United States embassy or legation; by a consul general, vice consul, or consular agent of the United States; or by a diplomatic or consular official of the foreign country assigned or accredited to the United States. If all parties have been given a reasonable opportunity to investigate the document's authenticity and accuracy, the court may, for good cause, either:
(A) order that it be treated as presumptively authentic without final certification; or
(B) allow it to be evidenced by an attested summary with or without final certification.

(4) *Certified Copies of Public Records.* A copy of an official record — or a copy of a document that was recorded or filed in a public office as authorized by law — if the copy is certified as correct by:
(A) the custodian or another person authorized to make the certification; or
(B) a certificate that complies with Rule 902(1), (2), or (3), a federal statute, or a rule prescribed by the Supreme Court.

(5) *Official Publications.* A book, pamphlet, or other publication purporting to be issued by a public authority.

(6) *Newspapers and Periodicals.* Printed material purporting to be a newspaper or periodical.

(7) *Trade Inscriptions and the Like.* An inscription, sign, tag, or label purporting to have been affixed in the course of business and indicating origin, ownership, or control.

(8) *Acknowledged Documents.* A document accompanied by a certificate of acknowledgment that is lawfully executed by a notary public or another officer who is authorized to take acknowledgments.

(9) *Commercial Paper and Related Documents.* Commercial paper, a signature on it, and related documents, to the extent allowed by general commercial law.

(10) *Presumptions Under a Federal Statute.* A signature, document, or anything else that a federal statute declares to be presumptively or prima facie genuine or authentic.

(11) *Certified Domestic Records of a Regularly Conducted Activity.* The original or a copy of a domestic record that meets the requirements of Rule 803(6)(A)-(C), as shown by a certification of the custodian or another qualified person that complies with a federal statute or a rule prescribed by the Supreme Court. Before the trial or hearing, the proponent must give an adverse party reasonable written notice of the intent to offer the record — and must make the record and certification available for inspection — so that the party has a fair opportunity to challenge them.

(12) *Certified Foreign Records of a Regularly Conducted Activity.* In a civil case, the original or a copy of a foreign record that meets the requirements of Rule 902(11), modified as follows: the certification, rather than complying with a federal statute or Supreme Court rule, must be signed in a manner that, if falsely made, would subject the maker to a criminal penalty in the country where the certification is signed. The proponent must also meet the notice requirements of Rule 902(11). (Amended, eff. Dec. 1, 2011.)

RULE 903. Subscribing Witness's Testimony

A subscribing witness's testimony is necessary to authenticate a writing only if required by the law of the jurisdiction that governs its validity. (Amended, eff. Dec. 1, 2011.)

ARTICLE X. CONTENTS OF WRITINGS, RECORDINGS, AND PHOTOGRAPHS

RULE 1001. Definitions

In this article:

(a) A "writing" consists of letters, words, numbers, or their equivalent set down in any form.

(b) A "recording" consists of letters, words, numbers, or their equivalent recorded in any manner.

(c) A "photograph" means a photographic image or its equivalent stored in any form.

(d) An "original" of a writing or recording means the writing or recording itself or any counterpart intended to have the same effect by the person who executed or issued it. For electronically stored information, "original" means any printout — or other output readable by sight — if it accurately reflects the information. An "original" of a photograph includes the negative or a print from it.

(e) A "duplicate" means a counterpart produced by a mechanical, photographic, chemical, electronic, or other equivalent process or technique that accurately reproduces the original. (Amended, eff. Dec. 1, 2011.)

RULE 1002. Requirement of the Original

An original writing, recording, or photograph is required in order to prove its content unless these rules or a federal statute provides otherwise. (Amended, eff. Dec. 1, 2011.)

RULE 1003. Admissibility of Duplicates

A duplicate is admissible to the same extent as the original unless a genuine question is raised about the original's authenticity or the circumstances make it unfair to admit the duplicate. (Amended, eff. Dec. 1, 2011.)

RULE 1004. Admissibility of Other Evidence of Content

An original is not required and other evidence of the content of a writing, recording, or photograph is admissible if:

(a) all the originals are lost or destroyed, and not by the proponent acting in bad faith;

(b) an original cannot be obtained by any available judicial process;
(c) **the** party against whom the original would be offered had control of the original; was at that time put on notice, by pleadings or otherwise, that the original would be a subject of proof at the trial or hearing; and fails to produce it at the trial or hearing; or
(d) the writing, recording, or photograph is not closely related to a controlling issue. (Amended, eff. Dec. 1, 2011.)

RULE 1005. Copies of Public Records to Prove Content

The proponent may use a copy to prove the content of an official record — or of a document that was recorded or filed in a public office as authorized by law — if these conditions are met: the record or document is otherwise admissible; and the copy is certified as correct in accordance with Rule 902(4) or is testified to be correct by a witness who has compared it with the original. If no such copy can be obtained by reasonable diligence, then the proponent may use other evidence to prove the content. (Amended, eff. Dec. 1, 2011.)

RULE 1006. Summaries to Prove Content

The proponent may use a summary, chart, or calculation to prove the content of voluminous writings, recordings, or photographs that cannot be conveniently examined in court. The proponent must make the originals or duplicates available for examination or copying, or both, by other parties at a reasonable time and place. And the court may order the proponent to produce them in court. (Amended, eff. Dec. 1, 2011.)

RULE 1007. Testimony or Written Admission of a Party

The proponent may prove the content of a writing, recording, or photograph by the testimony, deposition, or written statement of the party against whom the evidence is offered. The proponent need not account for the original. (Amended, eff. Dec. 1, 2011.)

RULE 1008. Functions of Court and Jury

Ordinarily, the court determines whether the proponent has fulfilled the factual conditions for admitting other evidence of the content of a writing, recording, or photograph under Rule 1004 or 1005. But in a jury trial, the jury determines — in accordance with Rule 104(b) — any issue about whether:

(a) an asserted writing, recording, or photograph ever existed
(b) another one produced at the trial or hearing is the original; or
(c) other evidence of content accurately reflects the content. (Amended, eff. Dec. 1, 2011.)

ARTICLE XI. MISCELLANEOUS RULES

RULE 1101. Applicability of Rules

(a) To Courts and Judges. These rules apply to proceedings before:
- United States district courts;
- United States bankruptcy and magistrate judges;
- United States courts of appeals;
- the United States Court of Federal Claims; and
- the district courts of Guam, the Virgin Islands, and the Northern Mariana Islands.

(b) **To Cases and Proceedings.** These rules apply in:
- civil cases and proceedings, including bankruptcy, admiralty, and maritime cases;
- criminal cases and proceedings; and

- contempt proceedings, except those in which the court may act summarily.

(c) Rules on Privilege. The rules on privilege apply to all stages of a case or proceeding.

(d) Exceptions. These rules — except for those on privilege — do not apply to the following:
   (1) the court's determination, under Rule 104(a), on a preliminary question of fact governing admissibility;
   (2) grand-jury proceedings; and
   (3) miscellaneous proceedings such as:
      - extradition or rendition;
      - issuing an arrest warrant, criminal summons, or search warrant;
      - a preliminary examination in a criminal case;
      - sentencing;
      - granting or revoking probation or supervised release; and
      - considering whether to release on bail or otherwise.

(e) Other Statutes and Rules. A federal statute or a rule prescribed by the Supreme Court may provide for admitting or excluding evidence independently from these rules. (Amended, eff. Dec. 1, 2011.)

RULE 1102. Amendments

These rules may be amended as provided in 28 U.S.C. § 2072. (Amended, eff. Dec. 1, 2011.)

RULE 1103. Title

These rules may be cited as the Federal Rules of Evidence. (Amended, eff. Dec. 1, 2011.)

Appendix II

Table of Jurisdictions That Have Adopted Some System of Uniform Rules for Regulating the Admission and Exclusion of Evidence—2014[1]

Jurisdiction	Laws	Effective Date	Statutory Citation
Alaska	Sup.Ct. Order 364	8-1-1979	ALASKA. R. EVID. 101 to 1101.
Arizona		9-1-1977	17A A.R.S. Rules of Evid., Rules 101 to 1103.
Arkansas	1975, No. 1143	7-1-1976	ARK. CODE ANN. A4 16-41-101.
Colorado		1-1-1980	COLO. REV. STAT. ANN., Title 13 App., Evid. 101–1102.
Delaware		7-1-1980	DEL. R. EVID. 101 to 1103.
Florida	1976, c. 76–237	7-1-1977	FLOR. STAT. ANN. A4A4 90.101 to 90.958.
Hawai'i	1980, c. 164	1-1-1981	HAW. REV. STAT. A4A4 § 626–1 (HAW. R. EVID. 100 to 1102) to § 626–3.
Idaho		7-1-1985	IDAHO R. EVID. 101 to 1103.
Indiana	Sup.Ct. Order	1-1-1994 8-24-1993	IND. R. EVID. 101 to 1101.
Iowa		7-1-1983	IOWA R. EVID.101 to 1103.
Kentucky	1990, c. 88	7-1-1992	KY. R. EVID. 101 to 1104, Sup.Ct. Order.
Louisiana	1988 Act 515	1-1-1989	LA. CODE EVID. ANN. arts. 101 to 1103.
Maine		2-2-1976	ME. R. EVID. 101 to 1102.
Michigan		3-1-1978	MICH. R. EVID. 101 to 1102.
Minnesota		7-1-1977	50 M.S.A. Evidence, Rules 101 to 1101.
Mississippi	Sup.Ct. Order	1-1-1986 9-24-1985	MISS. R. EVID. 101 to 1103.
Montana	1976, En. Sup.Ct.	7-1-1977	MONT. R. EVID. 100 to 1008. Ord. 12729.
Nebraska	1975, L.B. 279	8-24-1975	R.R.S.1943, A4A4 27–101 to 27–1103.
Nevada	1971, c. 775		NEV. REV. STAT. A4 § 47.929 et seq.
New Hampshire	7-1-1985		N.H. R. EVID. 100 to 1103.
New Jersey			N.J. R. EVID. 101–1103.
New Mexico	1973, S.C. Order	7-1-1973	N.M. R. EVID. 101 to 1102.
North Carolina	1983, c. 701	7-1-1984	N.C. GEN. STAT. A4 § 8C-1, Rules 101 to 1102.
North Dakota		2-15-1977	N.D. R. EVID. 101 to 1103.
Ohio		7-1-1980	OHIO R. EVID. 101 to 1103.
Oklahoma	1978, c. 285	10-1-1978	OKLA. STAT. ANN. tit. 12 A4A4 §§ 2101 to 3103.
Oregon	1981, c. 892	1-1-1982	OR. REV. STAT. §§ 40.010 to 40.585.
Rhode Island		1986	R.I. R. EVID. 100 to 1008.
South Carolina		9-3-1995	S.C. R. EVID.
South Dakota			S.D. CODIFIED LAWS §§ 19-9-1 to 19-18-8.
Tennessee		1-1-1990	TENN. R. EVID. 101 to 1008.
Texas		9-1-1983 9-1-1986	TEX. R. CIV. EVID. 101 to 1008. TEX. R. CRIM. EVID. 101 to 1101.
Utah		9-1-1983	UTAH R. EVID. 101 to 1103.
Vermont		4-1-1983	Titled: Vermont Court Rules, Rules 101 to 1103.
Washington		4-2-1979	WASH R. EVID. 101 to 1103.
West Virginia		2-1-1985	W.VA. R.EVID. 101 to 1102.
Wisconsin	Sup.Ct. Order, 59 W.(2d), page R9	1-1-1974	WIS. STAT. ANN. §§ 901.01 to 911.02.
Wyoming		1-1-1978	WYO. R. EVID. 101 to 1104.

[1] Legal Information Institute, http://www.law.cornell.edu/uniform/evidence.html (2-12-2014).

Appendix III

Table of Contents: Uniform Rules of Evidence (Last Revised or Amended in 2005)[1]

Article I

GENERAL PROVISIONS

Article II

JUDICIAL NOTICE

Article III

PRESUMPTIONS

Article IV

RELEVANCY AND ITS LIMITS

[1] Full text of the Uniform Rules of Evidence with 2005 amendments is available at http://www.law.cornell.edu/uniform/evidence (02-14-2014).

406. Habit; Routine Practice.
407. Subsequent Remedial Measures.
408. Compromise and Offers to Compromise.
409. Payment of Medical and Similar Expenses.
410. Inadmissibility of Pleas, Plea Discussions, and Related Statements.
411. Liability Insurance.
412. Sexual Behavior.

Article V

PRIVILEGES

501. Privileges Recognized Only as Provided.
502. Lawyer-Client Privilege.
503. [Psychotherapist] [Physician and Psychotherapist] [Physician and Mental Health Provider] [Mental Health Provider]-Patient Privilege.
504. Spousal Privilege.
505. Religious Privilege.
506. Political Vote.
507. Trade Secrets.
508. Secrets of State and Other Official Information; Governmental Privileges.
509. Identity of Informer.
510. Waiver of Privilege.
511. Comment upon or Inference from Claim of Privilege; Instruction.

Article VI

WITNESSES

601. General Rule of Competency.
602. Lack of Personal Knowledge.
603. Oath or Affirmation.
604. Interpreters.
605. Competency of Judge as Witness.
606. Competency of Juror as Witness.
607. Who May Impeach.
608. Evidence of Character and Conduct of Witness.
609. Impeachment by Evidence of Conviction of Crime.
610. Religious Beliefs and Opinions.
611. Mode and Order of Interrogation and Presentation.
612. Writing or Object Used to Refresh Memory.
613. Prior Statements of Witness.
614. Calling and Interrogation of Witnesses by Court.
615. Exclusion of Witnesses.
616. Bias of Witnesses.

Article VII

OPINIONS AND EXPERT TESTIMONY

701. Opinion Testimony by Lay Witnesses.
702. Testimony by Experts.
703. Basis of Opinion Testimony by Experts.
704. Opinion on Ultimate Issue.
705. Disclosure of Facts or Data Underlying Expert Opinion.
706. Court Appointed Expert Witness.

Article VIII

HEARSAY

801. Definitions; Exclusions.
802. Hearsay Rule.
803. Hearsay Exceptions: Availability of Declarant Immaterial.
804. Hearsay Exceptions: Declarant Unavailable.
805. Hearsay Within Hearsay.
806. Attacking and Supporting Credibility of Declarant.
807. Statement of Child Victim.
808. Residual Exception.

Article IX

AUTHENTICATION AND IDENTIFICATION

901. Requirement of Authentication or Identification.
902. Self-authentication.
903. Subscribing Witness' Testimony Unnecessary.

Article X

CONTENTS OF WRITINGS, RECORDINGS, AND PHOTOGRAPHS

1001. Definitions.
1002. Requirement of Original.
1003. Admissibility of Duplicates.
1004. Admissibility of Other Evidence of Contents.
1005. Public Records.
1006. Summaries.
1007. Testimony, or Admission in Record of Party. 1008. Functions of Court and Jury.

Article XI

MISCELLANEOUS RULES

1101. Title.

Glossary

Adjudicative facts Facts that concern the immediate parties and are determinative of the outcome of the case.

Affirmation A solemn declaration given in place of an oath. The privilege of affirming in judicial proceedings is now generally extended to all persons who object to taking an oath.

Affirmative defense (1) A defendant's response to a criminal charge intended to relieve the defendant of guilt for the charged offense by proving that the defendant had legally sufficient reason for acting as charged or by proving a legally sufficient reason for doing the act. Affirmative defenses include a plea of self-defense, defense of another, mistake of fact, or an insanity defense. (2) A justification or avoidance.

Alibi A defense in which the accused attempts to prove that he or she could not have committed the crime in question, offering evidence that he or she was in a different place at the time the offense was committed and otherwise had nothing to do with the crime.

Authentication An attestation made by a proper officer for the purpose of certifying that a record is in due form of law and that the person attesting is the officer appointed so to do. In the admission of evidence, authentication is the process of presenting evidence that proves the item to be admitted is what it purports to be or is the genuine article. For example, a police officer testifies that the gun's serial number is the same as the serial number on the gun taken from the arrested defendant.

Ballistics experiments The science of gun examination, frequently used in criminal cases, especially cases of homicide, to determine the firing capacity of a weapon, its fireability, and whether a given bullet was fired from a particular gun.

Ballistic identification The use of machine markings, produced on gun projectiles when fired from the weapon, to identify the source of the projectile. Ballistic identification also uses markings on the projectile to identify the particular gun that fired it.

Best evidence rule Also called the original document rule, this rule requires proof that provides the greatest certainty of the fact to be proven; the most reliable evidence. Ordinarily applied to documents and writings sought to be proven, the best evidence rule usually demands the highest degree of proof; that is, the original document must be presented if it is available, but secondary evidence may be admitted where the loss of the original was not the culpable fault of the party offering the evidence. See Fed. R. Evid. 1004.

Beyond a reasonable doubt Fully satisfied, entirely convinced, satisfied to a moral certainty.

Breathalyzer test A test used to determine the alcohol content of blood in one arrested for operating a motor vehicle under the influence of alcohol. The results of such tests, if properly administered, constitute admissible evidence.

Burden of going forward The obligation resting upon a party to produce prima facie evidence on a particular issue.

Burden of persuasion The burden of persuading the factfinder of the truth of the evidence produced by one side or the other.

Burden of proof The duty of proving facts disputed in the trial of a case by the proper weight of the evidence.

Case-in-chief A party's primary proof supporting his or her claim or defense; the major presentation of evidence for either the defense or the prosecution.

Chain of custody In evidence, one who offers real evidence (such as narcotics in the trial of a drug case) must account for the custody of the evidence from the moment when law enforcement officials originally gained custody until the moment when it is offered in evidence. Minor problems with demonstrating the links in the chain affect the weight to be given to the evidence, not the admissibility.

Circumstantial evidence Evidence of one fact from which a second fact can be reasonably inferred, but not directly proven. Circumstantial evidence is often introduced when direct evidence is not available.

Clear and convincing evidence A flexible term concerning the degree of proof required for certain issues in some civil cases. It is less than the degree required in criminal cases, but more than is required in an ordinary civil action.

Competency (1) The legal fitness or capacity of a witness to testify in the trial of a case that requires an oath, original perception, recollection, and an ability to communicate. (2) Freedom from mental illness or defect that might make a person unable to understand in a reasonable manner the nature and consequences of a transaction, or unable to act in a reasonable manner in relation to the transaction.

Competent evidence The quality of evidence offered that makes it proper to be received.

Conclusive presumption An irrebuttable presumption that once the basic fact has been proven, the existence of the presumed fact is mandatory. In criminal cases, conclusive presumptions are unconstitutional. *Sandstrom v. Montana*, 442 U.S. 510 (1979).

Corroborative evidence Additional testimony intended to reinforce a point that was previously the subject of proof; additional proof that confirms evidence previously admitted on a particular point.

Cross-examination The questioning of a witness by the party opposed to the party who called the witness for direct examination. Cross-examination usually occurs after the direct examination, but on occasion, it may be otherwise allowed. Cross-examination is a Sixth Amendment right of every defendant.

Cumulative evidence Testimony that is offered to prove what has already been proven by other evidence.

***Daubert* test** Under *Daubert v. Merrell Dow Pharmaceuticals*, 509 U.S. 579 (1993), the Court adopted a revised test to regulate the admission of scientific evidence. Prior to *Daubert*, the *Frye v. United States* (1923) test allowed evidence into court only where the involved scientific principle had reached general scientific acceptance. Under the *Daubert* test, however, in determining whether a theory or technique qualifies as scientific knowledge, a court should consider the known error rate and the existence and maintenance of standards controlling the technique's operation. The court should also identify the relevant scientific community and evaluate the particular degree of acceptance within that community. See FED. R. EVID. 702.

Delay in arraignment rule This rule provides that, if there has been a delay in bringing the accused person before a magistrate, and if a confession has been obtained during this unnecessary delay, the confession may not be admitted, even though voluntarily made.

Direct evidence Testimony or other proof that expressly or straightforwardly proves the existence of a fact without the use of an inference or a presumption; the opposite of circumstantial evidence.

Direct examination The initial questioning of a witness by the party who calls him or her to the stand. The calling party uses direct questions structured so as not to suggest the desired answer.

DNA Deoxyribonucleic acid. A long, threadlike chain of molecules found in the nucleus of virtually every cell of the body. DNA chains are tightly coiled into bodies called chromosomes, of which humans have 23 pairs. No two individuals (except for identical twins) have identical DNA. Within a given individual, however, DNA does not vary from cell to cell, except for human chimeras.

Documentary evidence Evidence that is furnished by written documents, records, cell phone text messages, e-mail, computer-generated reports, and other methods of storing data.

Due process (1) A flexible term for compliance with the fundamental rules for fair and orderly legal proceedings. For example, due process includes the defendant's right to be informed of the nature and cause of the accusation, to be confronted by the witnesses for the opposition, to have a compulsory process for obtaining witnesses in your favor, to have the assistance of counsel for defense, and to have a fair and impartial jury. (2) Legal proceedings that observe the rules designed for the protection and enforcement of individual rights and liberties.

Dying declaration Hearsay evidence of what a person said when he or she was aware that his or her death was imminent, so long as that statement relates to the way the declarant received the fatal injuries. Under particular circumstances and in certain cases, a dying declaration is competent evidence in some courts. (2) In a prosecution for homicide or in a civil action or proceeding, the term dying declaration may refer to a statement made by a declarant while believing that his or her death was imminent, so long as the statement relates to the cause or circumstances of what he or she believed to be his or her impending death. Such statements are not excluded by the hearsay rule if the declarant is unavailable as a witness. FED. R. EVID. 804(b)(2).

Eavesdropping Entering into a private place knowingly and without authority, with the intent to surreptitiously listen to a private conversation or to observe the personal conduct of any other person or persons. This action may be conducted by personal listening or the electronic collection of sounds.

Evidence Proof, either written or unwritten, of allegations at issue between parties.

Exclusionary rule This rule requires that, when evidence has been obtained in violation of the privileges guaranteed by the United States Constitution, the evidence must be excluded at the trial. Evidence that is obtained by an unreasonable search and seizure is excluded from evidence under the Fourth Amendment to the United States Constitution, and this rule applies to the states.

Exculpatory circumstances Exonerative facts; excusing evidence; facts tending to clear a defendant from a charge of fault or guilt.

Expert witness (1) A person who has acquired by special study, practice, and experience, particular skills and knowledge in relation to a specific science, art, or trade. (2) A witness who, because of such special knowledge, is called to testify or give his or her opinion in cases depending on questions peculiar to such science, art, or trade.

Federal Rules of Evidence Rules governing the admissibility of evidence at trials in federal courts and before United States magistrate judges.

Former testimony Testimony given by a witness at another hearing of the same or a different proceeding, or in a deposition taken in compliance with the law in the course of the same or another proceeding. This testimony may be admitted into the current trial, if the party against whom the testimony is now offered, or the predecessor in interest in a civil action, had the opportunity and similar motive to develop the original testimony by direct, cross, or redirect examination. Former testimony is not excluded by the hearsay rule if the declarant is unavailable as a witness. FED. R. EVID. 804(b)(1).

Free and voluntary rule The confession of a person accused of crime is admissible against the accused only if freely and voluntarily made, without fear, duress, or compulsion in its inducement and with full knowledge of the nature and consequences of the confession.

***Frye* test** The standard originally offered in *Frye v. United States* (1923) that regulated the admissibility of scientific tests into evidence. *Frye* required that, to admit scientific tests or principles into evidence, the test or principle "must be sufficiently established to have gained general acceptance from the particular field in which it belongs."

Hearsay evidence (1) Statements offered by a witness, based upon what someone else has told him or her, and not upon personal knowledge or observation. Usually, such evidence is inadmissible, but exceptions are made, for example, in questions of pedigree, custom, reputation, dying declarations, and statements made against the interest of the declarant. (2) A statement, other than one made by the declarant while testifying at the trial or hearing, offered in evidence to prove the truth of the matter asserted. FED. R. EVID. 801(c).

Hearsay rule Rule prohibiting the admission of hearsay evidence—evidence of an out-of-court statement originally made by someone other than the witness testifying to it, when that statement is offered to prove the truth of the matter stated.

Horizontal gaze nystagmus test Horizontal gaze nystagmus is the inability of the eyes to maintain visual fixation as they are turned to the side from the center. Nystagmus is a physiological phenomenon that is caused by the ingestion of alcohol, among other things, and law enforcement officers test for the phenomenon to determine whether a person is intoxicated.

Hostile witness A person who is called to give evidence and is unfriendly and/or opposed to the position of the party whose attorney called him. In such cases, the witness may or may not be allied with the opposing party. Such a person is subject to cross-examination by the party calling him or her and may be impeached if necessary by the calling party.

Impeachment of witness Proving that a witness has a bad reputation for truth and veracity and may be unworthy of belief by the finder of fact.

Implied consent Various state laws providing that any person who operates a motorized vehicle in the state is deemed to have given his or her consent to a chemical test (e.g., of his or her blood, breath, urine, or saliva) for the purpose of determining the alcoholic content of his or her blood, so long as the individual is stopped while driving or in any physical control of, a motor vehicle in the state while under the influence of intoxicating beverages.

Impoundment Seizing and taking into custody of the law or a court. For example, the police have a duty and responsibility to impound an automobile that has been abandoned, is illegally parked, or has been left without a driver when the driver has been arrested.

Incriminating circumstances Facts or circumstances, collateral to the fact of the commission of a crime, that tend to show that such a crime has been committed, that some particular person committed it, or both.

Inference A rational conclusion of the existence of a different fact deduced from facts originally proved.

Judicial notice (1) The court's acceptance of certain widely known facts without proof. (2) A judicially noticed adjudicative fact must be one not subject to reasonable dispute, in that it is either (a) generally known within the territorial jurisdiction of the trial court, or (b) capable of accurate and ready determination by resort to sources whose accuracy cannot reasonably be questioned. FED. R. EVID. 201(b).

Laser speed detection The process of measuring the speed of an object by bouncing light energy off the object. As the object moves, the device measures the time the light takes to travel from the laser detector to the object and then back again, and by taking such measurements hundreds of time a second, the detector can calculate the object's speed based on differences in the light's return times.

Lay witness Any witness who is not an expert. A lay witness must simply have the general capacity to testify, record, recollect, narrate, attest to, and affirm certain conditions and facts. Additionally, he or she must have the requisite level of mental capacity and emotional competency to outline in some logical and sensible sequence the facts, conditions, and events before the court.

Leading question An inquiry of a witness that, by its form, suggests the answer preferred by the questioning attorney. A question containing the substance of the correct answer. This type of question suggests a particular answer, and it is generally permissible on cross-examination.

Legal evidence General term meaning all admissible evidence, both oral and documentary, that tends to reasonably and substantially prove the point, while not raising a mere suspicion or conjecture.

Material evidence Evidence that goes to the substantial matters in dispute or has a legitimate and effective influence or bearing on the decision of the case; evidence that may tend to prove or disprove a fact that is at issue in a case.

Materiality Importance; relevance; capability of properly influencing the result of a lawsuit.

***Miranda* warnings** Warnings that must be given to persons who are in custody (arrest) and whom police wish to interrogate. The warnings must include notice of the right to counsel and the right to silence, among other procedural aspects.

Motive The purpose underlying a defendant's conduct; the reason a person forms a criminal intent prior to engaging in a criminal act.

Negative evidence Testimony that an alleged fact does not exist or that an event did not occur; an absence of evidence that can, in itself, serve as evidence.

Neutron activation analysis A testing procedure that determines the presence and amount of certain trace chemical elements.

Oath Various solemn affirmations, declarations, or promises, made by a declarant or a witness, under a sense of responsibility to God, for the truth of what is stated or the faithful performance of what is undertaken.

Objection A resistance or protest on legal grounds. An objection might be made in response to the admissibility of evidence or to the entry of an order or judgment.

Opinion evidence An inference or a conclusion formed or entertained by a witness, as opposed to facts directly seen, heard, or perceived by that witness. Usually, a person's opinions are not competent testimony in a case unless the person has qualified as an expert witness.

Past recollection recorded A memorandum or record concerning a matter about which a witness once had knowledge, but now has insufficient recollection to enable him or her to testify fully and accurately. In order to qualify as an exception to the hearsay rule, even though the declarant is available as a witness, the past recollection must be shown to have been made or adopted by the witness when the matter was fresh in his or her memory, and the recollection must reflect that knowledge correctly. If admitted, the memorandum or record may be read into evidence, but may not itself be received as an exhibit unless offered by an adverse party. FED. R. EVID. 803(5).

Pecuniary interest A direct interest related to money in an action or case. Such an interest might require a judge to disqualify him- or herself from sitting on a case if he or she owned stock in a corporate party.

Pen register An electronic device that, when properly connected to the telephone system, has the ability to record all the outgoing telephone numbers placed from that telephone. "[T]he term 'pen register' means a device or process which records or decodes dialing, routing, addressing, or signaling information transmitted by an instrument or facility from which a wire or electronic communication is transmitted. . ." 18 U.S.C. § 3127(3).

Penal interest Pertaining to or respecting punishment.

Plain view doctrine A rule of law creating an exception to the requirement that police officers have a search warrant, when the police, while conducting themselves lawfully (e.g., while patrolling the streets or executing a search warrant for something else), observe incriminating evidence, and it is immediately apparent to the police that they have evidence of a crime. In such a situation, the police may seize the evidence without a warrant, if the officer physically occupies the place where the contraband is situated.

Polygraph examination An electromechanical instrument that simultaneously records certain physiological changes in the human body, which are believed to be involuntarily caused by an examinee's conscious attempts to deceive an interrogator while responding to a carefully prepared set of questions. If the examination is properly conducted, the operator may be able to determine the truthfulness of the examined subject.

Preponderance of the evidence (1) The greater weight of the evidence, in merit and in worth. (2) Sufficient evidence to overcome doubt or speculation. (3) Any evidence whose weight is greater than 50 percent.

Present memory revived The act of a witness who consults his or her documents, memoranda, or books to clarify his or her recollection of the details of past events or transactions, concerning which he or she is testifying. The witness testifies from present memory.

Presumption A conclusion or inference drawn from the proven existence of some basic fact or group of facts. Example: Proof of the basic fact that person has been missing 7 years, which gives rise to the presumed fact that the person is dead.

Presumption of fact Understandings that are not the subject of a fixed rule, but merely natural presumptions drawn from common experience and arising from the particular circumstances of any case.

Presumption of law An inference or deduction that, in the absence of direct evidence on the subject, the law requires to be drawn from the existence of certain established facts in civil cases. However, the presumption of law is not a deduction that can be enforced in criminal cases. Examples include the presumption of innocence and a presumption that judges act properly.

Prima facie evidence Proof of a fact or collection of facts that creates a presumption of the existence of other facts, or from which some conclusion may be legally drawn. Such a presumption or conclusion may be discredited or overcome by other relevant proof.

Prior inconsistent statement A witness's prior statements entered into evidence that contradict later testimony by the witness. Such prior statements may be introduced to impeach the witness, after a foundation has been laid concerning where and when the inconsistent statement was uttered. The witness in question must also have the opportunity to affirm or deny whether such prior statements were made.

Privileged communications Statements made by one person to another when there is a necessary relation of trust and confidence between them. If such a relationship between parties exists, the person receiving the statements cannot be legally compelled to disclose them. For example, the statements made by a husband to his wife, or a client to his or her attorney might constitute privileged communications.

Privity A situation where two or more individuals have a sufficiently close legal relationship that legal matters affecting one of the individuals may have a similar legal effect on another person. Two persons involved in a contract with a third person are said to be in privity with the other.

Probative value The tendency of an item of evidence to assist in proving what it was introduced to prove. Evidence is said to have probative value when it helps prove or disprove a fact that is at issue in a criminal case.

Proof (1) Establishing the truth of an allegation by evidence. (2) The evidence itself. The person claiming the affirmative of an allegation ordinarily has the necessity of proving it. (3) The affidavits made to support a claim or statement of fact, which is doubted or disputed or of which a person acting in a representative capacity requires evidence under oath.

Protective sweep A legal theory that permits police officers to make a quick and limited search of building, apartment, or room premises incident to an arrest and conducted with a few to protect the safety of police officers and others present who may be harmed. A protective sweep requires the presence of generally articulable facts that, taken together with rational inferences, would lead an officer to conclude that the area to be swept may harbor an individual who poses a danger to those on the arrest scene. See *Maryland v. Buie*, 494 U.S. 325, 110 S. Ct. 1093. 1990 U.S. LEXIS 1176 (1990).

RADAR Radio Detection and Ranging. A technology used by law enforcement to measure the distance and speed of motor vehicles by evaluating the frequency shift of radio waves that have bounced back from the target motor vehicle.

Real evidence Evidence that has physical essence; evidence provided by producing the physical items themselves in court as opposed to descriptions of the evidence.

Reasonable doubt "A reasonable doubt is an actual and substantial doubt arising from the evidence." *Victor v. Nebraska*, 511 U.S. 1, 5 (1994).

Rebuttal Proof that is given by one party in a lawsuit to explain or disprove evidence produced by the other party.

Recross-examination An examination of a witness by a cross-examiner subsequent to a redirect examination of the witness.

Redirect examination An examination of a witness by the direct examiner following the cross-examination by the opposing party.

Rejoinder The opportunity to introduce evidence contrary to the evidence introduced by the prosecution during the rebuttal.

Relevancy The connection between a fact tendered into evidence and the issue to be proved.

Relevant evidence Evidence having any tendency to make the existence of any fact that is of consequence to the determination of the action more probable or less probable than it would be without the evidence. FED. R. EVID. 401.

Reported testimony Testimony given by a witness at a prior hearing of the same or a different proceeding, or in a deposition taken in compliance with law in the course of the same or another proceeding. For this evidence to be admitted, the party against whom the testimony is now offered, or the predecessor in interest in a civil action or proceeding, must have had an opportunity and similar motive to develop that testimony by direct, cross, or redirect examination. Reported testimony is not excluded by the hearsay rule if the declarant is unavailable as a witness. FED. R. EVID. 804(b)(1).

Scientific evidence admissibility Admissibility of scientific evidence rests on several considerations: whether a scientific theory or technique can or has been tested; whether the theory or technique has been subjected to peer review and publication; the known or potential rate of error of the technique; the existence and maintenance of standards controlling the technique's operation; and whether the technique is generally accepted. A proponent of the scientific evidence has the burden of proving its relevancy, as well as the scientific reliability, by clear and convincing evidence.

Search incident to arrest Once a person has been arrested, police may search the person of the arrestee, his or her immediate effects, and the physical area within his or her immediate control. Probable cause to search is not required.

Secondary evidence Evidence that is inferior to primary or best evidence. It becomes admissible when the primary or best evidence of the fact in question has been lost or destroyed or is inaccessible through no fault of the offering party.

Self-authentication Documents that have within their contents proof of their genuine status and are what they are purported to be. For example, newspapers that have masthead logo and date and unique information contained within the paper are said to be self-authenticating.

Self-authenticating instrument or document Authenticity is taken as sufficiently established for purposes of admissibility without extrinsic evidence to that effect. Statutes frequently provide that certain classes of writings will be received in evidence "without further proof." Bank videotapes can be self-authenticating by their content and time and date stamp.

Self-defense The protection of one's person and property from injury. A person may defend himself when attacked, repel force by force, and even commit homicide in resisting an attempted felony involving a risk of death or serious injury. For example, a person may be justified in using deadly force to thwart an attempted murder, rape, robbery, or burglary.

Self-incrimination An act or declaration either as testimony at trial or prior to trial by which one implicates oneself in a crime.

Sequestration Separating or setting apart; excluding witnesses from the courtroom, except when testifying, to prevent one witness from being influenced deliberately or subconsciously by hearing what another witness says.

Spontaneous utterance A statement relating to a startling event or condition made while the declarant was under the stress of excitement caused by the event or condition. Such utterances are not excluded from evidence as hearsay, even though the declarant is available as a witness. FED. R. EVID. 803(2).

Stipulation An agreement; a bargain, proviso, or condition; for example, an agreement between opposing litigants that certain facts are true and are not in dispute. A stipulation is binding on the parties without consideration if it complies with an applicable statute, rule of court, or where the court has accepted the agreement. A jury is free to disregard the agreement, however.

Sufficiency of the evidence In a criminal case, whether the evidence is such that a jury could logically have found that a defendant was guilty beyond a reasonable doubt or that an affirmative defense was properly proven.

Summaries The contents of voluminous writings, recordings, computer-generated data, or photographs that cannot be conveniently examined in court may be presented in the form of a chart, summary, or calculation. The originals, or duplicates, shall be made available for examination or copying, or both, by other parties at a reasonable time and place. The court may order that they be produced in court. FED. R. EVID. 1006.

Ultimate issue The questions that must finally be answered, such as the defendant's guilt in a criminal action.

Unfair prejudice A prejudgment, or bias, that interferes with a person's impartiality and sense of justice.

Uniform Rules of Evidence Prepared by the National Conference of Commissioners on Uniform State Laws, these rules are patterned after the Federal Rules of Evidence and have numbering consistent with the Federal Rules. The Uniform Rules are designed for adoption by state legislatures.

Voiceprint identification Once promising technology, now in general disrepute, voiceprints were used in the trial of cases that required voice identification. An instrument known as a spectrograph produced "prints" of a person's voice for use in comparing such readings with the actual voice of the person involved. Such comparisons were intended to determine whether such person uttered the material words.

Waiver A positive act by which a known legal right is relinquished or abandoned.

Weight of evidence The balance or preponderance of evidence; the inclination of the greater amount of evidence, offered in trial, to support one side of the issue rather than the other.

Wiretapping A form of electronic eavesdropping in which, upon a court order, law enforcement officials surreptitiously listen to land and cell phone conversations, e-mail, text messages, and similar communications.

Index of Cases

A

B

C

D

E

F

G

H

I

M

N

O

Q

R

S

T

U

V

Y

Z

Index

Note: Page numbers followed by *b* indicate boxes.

I

J

S

U